MID-ATLANTIC

MACMILLAN • USA

Macmillan Travel
A Simon & Schuster Macmillan Company
15 Columbus Circle
New York, NY 10023

MACMILLAN is a registered trademark of Macmillan, Inc.

Manufactured in the United States of America

10 9 8 7 6 5 4 3 2 1

ISSN: 1079-3585
ISBN: 0-02-860143-2

SPECIAL SALES
Bulk purchases (10+ copies) of Frommer's travel guides are available to corporations at special discounts. The Special Sales Department can produce custom editions to be used as premiums and/or for sales promotion to suit individual needs. Existing editions can be produced with custom cover imprints such as corporate logos. For more information, write to Special Sales, Simon & Schuster, 1230 Avenue of the Americas, New York, NY 10020.

CONTENTS

MARYLAND

VIRGINIA

WEST VIRGINIA

INTRODUCTION

America on Wheels introduces a brand-new lodgings rating system—one that factors in the latest trends in travel preferences, technologies, and amenities and is based on thorough inspections by experienced travel professionals. We rate establishments from 1 to 5 flags, plus a unique rating we call Ultra, a special award reserved for only a handful of outstanding properties in each category. Our restaurant selections represent the ethnic diversity of today's dining scene and are categorized with symbols according to their special features, ambience, and services available. In addition, the series provides in-depth sightseeing information, including driving tours and best-of-the-state highlights.

STATE INTRODUCTIONS

Our coverage of each state in the *America on Wheels* series begins with background information that will help familiarize you with your destination. Included is a summary of the state's history and an overview of its geography, followed by practical tips that we hope you will find useful in planning your trip—what kind of weather to expect, what to pack, sources of information within the state, driving rules and regulations, and other essentials.

The "Best of the State" section provides you with a rundown of the top sights and attractions and the most popular festivals and special events around the state. It also includes infomation on spectator sports and an "A to Z" list of recreational activities available to you.

DRIVING TOURS

The scenic driving tours guide you along some of the most popular sightseeing routes. Every tour is keyed to a map and includes mileage information and precise directions, refreshment stops, and, for longer tours, recommended places to stay.

THE LISTINGS

The cities are organized alphabetically within each state. Below each city name, you'll find a map page number and map location. These refer to the color maps at the back of the book.

Types of Lodgings

Here's how we define the lodging categories used in *America on Wheels*.

Motel

A motel usually has 1 to 3 floors, and many of the guest rooms have doors facing the parking lot or outdoor corridors. A motel may only have a small, serviceable lobby and usually offers only limited services; the nearest restaurant may be down the street. A motel is most likely to be located alongside a highway or in a resort area.

Hotel

A hotel usually has 3 or more floors with elevators. It may or may not have parking, but if it does, entry to the guest rooms is likely to be through the lobby rather than directly from the parking lot. A range of lodgings is available (such as standard rooms, deluxe rooms, and suites), and a range of services is available (such as bellhops, room service, and a concierge). Many hotels have a restaurant or coffee shop open for breakfast, lunch, and dinner; they may have a cocktail lounge/bar. Recreational facilities may be available (such as a swimming pool, fitness center, and tennis courts).

Resort

A resort usually has more extensive facilities and recreational activities than a hotel, and offers 3 meals a day. The atmosphere is generally more informal than at comparable hotels.

Lodge

A lodge is essentially a small hotel in a rural, remote, or mountainous location. The atmosphere, service, and furniture may be more casual than you'd find in a regular hotel, and there may not be televisions or telephones in every guest room. The facilities usually include a coffee shop or restaurant, bar or cocktail lounge, game room, and indoor or outdoor swimming pool or hot tub. In ski areas, the lounge usually has a fireplace and facilities for storing ski gear.

Inn

An inn is a small-scale hotel or lodge, usually in an older building that may or may not have been designed for lodgings, and it is often located in interesting surroundings. An inn should have a warm, welcoming atmosphere, with a more homelike quality to its furnishings and facilities. The guest rooms may be individually decorated in a style appropriate to the inn's age and location, and the rooms may or may not have telephones, televisions, or private bathrooms. An inn usually has a lounge or sitting room for guests (with parlor games and perhaps a television) and a small dining room that may or may not be open to the public. Breakfast, however, is almost always served.

How the Lodgings Are Rated

Every hotel, motel, resort, inn, and lodge rated in this series has been subjected to a thorough hands-on inspection by our team of accomplished travel professionals. We ask the kinds of questions that readers would ask if they could inspect the rooms in advance for themselves (How good is the soundproofing? How firm is the bed? What condition are the room furnishings in?). Then all of the inspection reports are reviewed by regional editors who are experts on their territories. The top-rated properties are then rechecked by a special consultant who has been reviewing and critiquing luxury hotels around the world for almost 25 years. *Establishments are not charged to be included in our series.*

Our ratings are based on *average* guest rooms—not lavish suites or concierge floors—so they're not artificially high. Therefore, in some cases a hotel rated 4 flags may indeed have individual rooms or suites that might fall into the 5-flag category; conversely, a 4-flag hotel may have a few rooms in its lowest price range that might otherwise warrant 3 flags.

The detailed ratings vary by category of lodgings—for example, the criteria imposed on a hotel are more rigorous than those for a motel—and some features that are considered essential in, for example, a 4-flag city hotel are relaxed for a resort that offers alternative attractions, sporting facilities, and/or beautiful and spacious grounds. Likewise, amenities such as telephones and televisions—essential in hotels and motels—are not required in inns, often the destination for lovers of peace and quiet. Instead, the criteria take into account such features as individually decorated rooms and complimentary afternoon tea.

There are, of course, several basic attributes that apply to all lodgings across the board: the cleanliness and maintenance of the building as a whole; the housekeeping in individual rooms; safety, both indoors and out; the quality and practicality of the furnishings; the quality and availability of the amenities; the caliber of the facilities; the extent and/or condition of the grounds; the ambience and cleanliness in the dining rooms; and the caliber and professionalism of the service in relation to the rates and types of lodging. Since the *America on Wheels* rating system is highly rigorous, just because a property has garnered only 1 flag does not mean it is inadequate or substandard.

WHAT THE INDIVIDUAL RATINGS MEAN

⬛ 1 Flag

These properties have surpassed the minimum requirements of cleanliness, safety, convenience, and amenities; the staff may be limited, but guests can generally expect a friendly, hospitable greeting. They will have basic amenities, such as air conditioning or heating where appropriate, telephones, and televisions. The bathrooms may have only showers rather than tubs, and just 1 towel for each guest, but showers and towels must be clean. The 1-flag properties are by no means places to avoid, since they can represent exceptional value.

⬛⬛ 2 Flags

In addition to having all of the basic attributes of 1-flag lodgings, these properties will have some extra amenities, such as bellhops to help with the luggage, ice buckets in each room, and better quality furnishings. Some extra services may include availability of cribs and irons, and wake-up service.

☰☰☰ 3 Flags

These properties have all the basics noted above but also offer a more generous complement of amenities, such as firmer beds, larger desks, more drawer space, extra blankets and pillows, cable or satellite TV, alarm clock/radios, room service (although hours may be limited), and dry cleaning and/or laundry services.

☰☰☰☰ 4 Flags

This is the realm of luxury, with refinements in amenities, furnishings, and service—such as larger rooms, more dependable soundproofing, 2 telephones per room, in-room movies, in-room safes, thick towels, hair dryers, twice-daily maid service, turndown service, concierge service, and 24-hour room service.

☰☰☰☰☰ 5 Flags

These properties have everything the 4-flag properties have, plus a more personal level of service and more sumptuous amenities, among them bathrobes, superior linens, and blackout drapes for lightproofing. Facilities normally include a business center and fitness center. Generally speaking, guests pay handsomely to stay in these properties.

☸ Ultra

This crème-de-la-creme rating is reserved for those rare hotels and resorts, possibly also motels and inns, that are truly outstanding in every or almost every department—places with a "Grand Hotel" presence, an almost flawless level of service, and a standard of dining equal to that of the finest restaurants.

Unrated

In the few cases where an inspector was not able to make a detailed inspection, the property is listed as "Unrated." Also, in some cases where a property was in the process of changing owners or managers, or if the property was undergoing the kind of major renovations that made formal evaluation impossible, then, again, the inspectors have listed it as "Unrated."

Types of Dining

Restaurant

A restaurant serves complete meals.

Refreshment Stop

A refreshment stop serves drinks and/or snacks only (such as an ice cream parlor, bakery, or coffee bar).

How the Restaurants Were Evaluated

All of the restaurants reviewed in this series have been through the kind of thorough inspection described for accommodations, above. Our inspectors have evaluated everything from freshness of ingredients to noise level and spacing of tables.

Unique to the *America on Wheels* series are the easy-to-read symbols that identify for you a restaurant's special features, ambience, and services. With them you can determine at a glance whether a place is a local favorite, offers exceptional value, or is "worth a splurge."

How to Read the Listings

LODGINGS

Introductory Information

The rating is followed by the establishment's name, address, neighborhood (if located in a major city), telephone numbers, and fax number (if there is one). When appropriate, you'll also find the location of the establishment, highway information with exit number, and/or more specific directions. In the resort listings, the number of acres is indicated. Also included are our inspectors' comments, which provide some description and discuss any outstanding features or special information about the establishment. If the lodging is not rated, it will be noted at the end of this section.

Rooms

The number and type of accommodations available is followed by the information on check-in/check-out times. If there is anything worth noting about rooms, whether the size or decor or furnishings, inspectors' comments will follow.

Amenities

The amenities available in the majority of the guest rooms are indicated by symbols and then a list. Because travelers usually expect air conditioning, telephones, and televisions in their guest rooms, we specifically note when those amenities are not available. If the accommodations have minibars, terraces, fireplaces, or Jacuzzis, we indicate that here.

Services

The services available are indicated by symbols and then a list. There may be a fee for some of the services. "Babysitting available" means the establishment can put you in touch with local babysitters and/or agencies. An establishment that accepts pets may nevertheless place restrictions on the types or size of pets allowed.

Facilities

The facilities available are indicated by symbols followed by a list; all are on the premises, except for cross-country and downhill skiing, which are within 10 miles. The lifeguard listed refers to a beach lifeguard, not a pool lifeguard. Our "Accessible for People With Disabilities" symbol appears where establishments claim to have guest rooms with such accessibility.

Rates

If the establishment's rates vary throughout the year, then the rates given are for the high season. The rates listed are EP (no meals included), unless otherwise noted. We'll tell you if there is a charge for an extra person to stay in a room; if children stay free, and if so, up to what age; if there are minimum stay requirements; if the rates are ever higher for special events or holidays; if AP (3 meals) or MAP (breakfast and dinner) rates are also available; and/or if special packages are available. The parking rates (if the establishment has parking) are followed by the credit card information.

Always confirm the rates when you are making your reservations, and ask about taxes and other charges, which are not included in our rates.

RESTAURANTS

Introductory Information

If a restaurant is a local favorite, an exceptional value, or "worth a splurge," this will be noted by a special symbol at the beginning of the listing. Then the establishment's name, address, neighborhood (if located in a major city), and telephone number are listed. Next comes the location of the establishment, highway information with exit number, and/or more specific directions, as appropriate. The types of cuisine are followed by our inspectors' comments on everything from decor to menu highlights.

The "FYI" Heading

After the reservations policy, we tell you if there is live entertainment, a children's menu, a dress code, and a no-smoking policy for the entire restaurant. If the restaurant does not offer a full bar, we tell you what the liquor policy is.

Hours of Operation

Under the "Open" heading, "HS" indicates that the hours listed are for the high season only; otherwise, the hours listed are year-round. It's a good idea to call ahead to confirm the hours of operation, especially in the off-season.

Prices

Prices given are for the dinner main courses (unless otherwise noted). If a prix-fixe dinner is offered during all of the dinner hours, that price is listed here, too. This section ends with credit card information, followed by any appropriate symbol(s).

Accessibility for People With Disabilities

The accessibility symbol appears in listings where the restaurant has a level entrance or an access ramp, a doorway at least 36 inches wide, and restrooms that are on the same floor as the dining room, with doorways at least 32 inches wide and properly outfitted stalls.

ATTRACTIONS

Introductory Information

The name, street address, neighborhood (if located in a major city), and telephone number are followed by a brief rundown of the attraction's high points and key attributes—so you can quickly determine if it's worth a full day of exploration or just a brief detour.

Hours of Operation & Admission

Service information includes hours of operation and the cost of admission. The cost is indicated by 1 to 4 dollar signs ($, $$, $$$, or $$$$) or by "Free," if no fee is charged. It's a good idea to call ahead to confirm the hours.

DISABLED TRAVELER INFORMATION

The Americans with Disabilities Act (ADA) of 1990 required that all public facilities and commercial establishments be made accessible to disabled persons by January 26, 1992. Any property opened after January 26, 1993, must be built in accordance with the ADA Accessible Guidelines. Note, however, that not all establishments have completed their renovations to conform with the law; be sure to call ahead to determine if your specific needs can be met.

TAXES

State and city taxes vary widely and are not included in the prices in this book. Always ask about the taxes when you are making your reservations. State sales tax is given under "Essentials" in the introduction to each state.

A DISCLAIMER

Readers are advised that prices fluctuate in the course of time and travel information changes under the impact of the varied and volatile factors that affect the travel industry. The publisher cannot be held responsible for the experiences of readers while traveling. Readers are invited to send ideas, comments, and suggestions for future editions to: *America on Wheels*, Macmillan Travel, 15 Columbus Circle, New York, NY 10023.

ABBREVIATIONS

A/C	*air conditioning*
AP	*American Plan (rates include breakfast, lunch, and dinner)*
avail	*available*
BB	*Bed-and-Breakfast Plan (rates include full breakfast)*
bldg	*building*
CC	*credit cards*
CI	*check-in time*
CO	*check-out time*
CP	*Continental Plan (rates include continental breakfast)*
ctges	*cottages*
ctr	*center*
D	*double*
effic	*efficiencies*
evnts	*events*
HS	*high season*
info	*information*
int'l	*international*
ltd	*limited*
maj	*major*
MAP	*Modified American Plan (rates include breakfast and dinner)*
Mem Day	*Memorial Day*
mi	*miles*
min	*minimum*
MM	*mile marker*
PF	*prix fixe (a fixed-price meal)*
pking	*parking*
refrig	*refrigerator*
rms	*rooms*
rsts	*restaurants*
S	*single*
satel	*satellite*
spec	*special*
stes	*suites*
svce	*service*
tel	*telephone*
univ	*university*
w/	*with*
wknds	*weekends*

The following toll-free telephone numbers were accurate at press time; *America on Wheels* cannot be held responsible for any number that has changed. The "TDD" numbers are answered by a telecommunications service for the deaf and hard-of-hearing. Be sure to dial "1" before each number.

Lodgings

Best Western International, Inc
(800) 528-1234 Continental USA and Canada
(800) 528-2222 TDD

Budgetel Inns
(800) 4-BUDGET Continental USA and Canada

Budget Host
(800) BUD-HOST Continental USA

Clarion Hotels
(800) CLARION Continental USA and Canada
(800) 228-3323 TDD

Comfort Inns
(800) 228-5150 Continental USA and Canada
(800) 228-3323 TDD

Courtyard by Marriott
(800) 321-2211 Continental USA and Canada
(800) 228-7014 TDD

Days Inn
(800) 325-2525 Continental USA and Canada
(800) 325-3297 TDD

Doubletree Hotels
(800) 222-TREE Continental USA

Drury Inn
(800) 325-8300 Continental USA and Canada
(800) 325-0583 TDD

Econo Lodges
(800) 446-6900 Continental USA and Canada
(800) 228-3323 TDD

Embassy Suites
(800) 362-2779 Continental USA and Canada

Exel Inns of America
(800) 356-8013 Continental USA and Canada

Fairfield Inn by Marriott
(800) 228-2800 Continental USA and Canada
(800) 228-7014 TDD

Fairmont Hotels
(800) 527-4727 Continental USA

Forte Hotels
(800) 225-5843 Continental USA and Canada

Four Seasons Hotels
(800) 332-3442 Continental USA
(800) 268-6282 Canada

Friendship Inns
(800) 453-4511 Continental USA
(800) 228-3323 TDD

Guest Quarters Suites
(800) 424-2900 Continental USA

Hampton Inn
(800) HAMPTON Continental USA and Canada

Hilton Hotels Corporation
(800) HILTONS Continental USA and Canada
(800) 368-1133 TDD

Holiday Inn
(800) HOLIDAY Continental USA and Canada
(800) 238-5544 TDD

Howard Johnson
(800) 654-2000 Continental USA and Canada
(800) 654-8442 TDD

Hyatt Hotels and Resorts
(800) 228-9000 Continental USA and Canada
(800) 228-9548 TDD

Inns of America
(800) 826-0778 Continental USA and Canada

Intercontinental Hotels
(800) 327-0200 Continental USA and Canada

ITT Sheraton
(800) 325-3535 Continental USA and Canada
(800) 325-1717 TDD

La Quinta Motor Inns, Inc
(800) 531-5900 Continental USA and Canada
(800) 426-3101 TDD

Loews Hotels
(800) 223-0888 Continental USA and Canada

Marriott Hotels
(800) 228-9290 Continental USA and Canada
(800) 228-7014 TDD

Master Hosts Inns
(800) 251-1962 Continental USA and Canada

Meridien
(800) 543-4300 Continental USA and Canada

Omni Hotels
(800) 843-6664 Continental USA and Canada

Park Inns International
(800) 437-PARK Continental USA and Canada

Quality Inns
(800) 228-5151 Continental USA and Canada
(800) 228-3323 TDD

Radisson Hotels International
(800) 333-3333 Continental USA and Canada

Ramada
(800) 2-RAMADA Continental USA and Canada
(800) 228-3232 TDD

Red Carpet Inns
(800) 251-1962 Continental USA and Canada

Red Lion Hotels and Inns
(800) 547-8010 Continental USA and Canada

Red Roof Inns
(800) 843-7663 Continental USA and Canada
(800) 843-9999

Residence Inn by Marriott
(800) 331-3131 Continental USA and Canada
(800) 228-7014 TDD

Resinter
(800) 221-4542 Continental USA and Canada

Ritz-Carlton
(800) 241-3333 Continental USA and Canada

Rodeway Inns
(800) 228-2000 Continental USA and Canada
(800) 228-3323 TDD

Scottish Inns
(800) 251-1962 Continental USA and Canada

Shilo Inns
(800) 222-2244 Continental USA and Canada

Signature Inns
(800) 822-5252 Continental USA and Canada

Stouffer Renaissance Hotels International
(800) HOTELS-1 Continental USA and Canada
(800) 833-4747 TDD

Super 8 Motels
(800) 800-8000 Continental USA and Canada
(800) 533-6634 TDD

Susse Chalet Motor Lodges & Inns
(800) 258-1980 Continental USA and Canada

Travelodge
(800) 255-3050 Continental USA and Canada

Vagabond Hotels Inc.
(800) 522-1555 Continental USA and Canada

Westin Hotels and Resorts
(800) 228-3000 Continental USA and Canada
(800) 254-5440 TDD

Wyndham Hotels and Resorts
(800) 822-4200 Continental USA and Canada

Car Rental Agencies

Advantage Rent-A-Car
(800) 777-5500 Continental USA and Canada

Airways Rent A Car
(800) 952-9200 Continental USA

Alamo Rent A Car
(800) 327-9633 Continental USA and Canada

Allstate Car Rental
(800) 634-6186 Continental USA and Canada

Avis
(800) 331-1212 Continental USA and Canada

Budget Rent A Car
(800) 527-0700 Continental USA and Canada

Dollar Rent A Car
(800) 800-4000 Continental USA and Canada

Enterprise Rent-A-Car
(800) 325-8007 Continental USA and Canada

Hertz
(800) 654-3131 Continental USA

National Car Rental
(800) CAR-RENT Continental USA and Canada

Payless Car Rental
(800) PAYLESS Continental USA and Canada

Rent-A-Wreck
(800) 535-1391 Continental USA

Sears Rent A Car
(800) 527-0770 Continental USA and Canada

Thrifty Rent-A-Car
(800) 367-2277 Continental USA

U-Save Auto Rental of America
(800) 272-USAV Continental USA and Canada

Value Rent-A-Car
(800) 327-2501 Continental USA and Canada

Airlines

American Airlines
(800) 433-7300 Continental USA and Canada

Canadian Airlines International
(800) 426-7000 Continental USA
(800) 665-1177 Canada

Continental Airlines
(800) 525-0280 Continental USA
(800) 421-2456 Canada

Delta Air Lines
(800) 221-1212 Continental USA

Northwest Airlines
(800) 225-2525 Continental USA and Canada

Southwest Airlines
(800) 435-9792 Continental USA and Canada

Trans World Airlines
(800) 221-2000 Continental USA

United Airlines
(800) 241-6522 Continental USA and Canada

USAir
(800) 428-4322 Continental USA and Canada

Train

Amtrak
(800) USA-RAIL Continental USA

Bus

Greyhound
(800) 231-2222 Continental USA

THE TOP-RATED LODGINGS

Ultra

The Greenbrier, White Sulphur Springs, WV
Inn at Little Washington, Washington, VA
Inn at Perry Cabin, St Michaels, MD

5 Flags

Hotel Du Pont, Wilmington, DE

4 Flags

ANA Hotel, Washington, DC
Annapolis Marriott Waterfront, Annapolis, MD
Atlantic Hotel, Berlin, MD
Bavarian Inn and Lodge, Sheperdstown, WV
Belle Grae Inn, Staunton, VA
Bethesda Marriott Suites, Bethesda, MD
Boardwalk Plaza, Rehoboth Beach, DE
BWI Airport Marriott Hotel, Linthicum, MD
The Capital Hilton, Washington, DC
The Carlton, Washington DC
The Cavalier, Virginia Beach, VA
The Coconut Malorie, Ocean City, MD
Commonwealth Park Suites Hotel, Richmond, VA
Cross Keys Inn, Baltimore, MD
Doubletree Inn at the Colonnade, Baltimore, MD
Founders Inn and Conference Center, Virginia Beach, VA
Four Seasons Hotel, Washington, DC
Georgetown Inn, Washington, DC
The Grand Hotel, Washington, DC
Grand Hyatt Washington, Washington, DC
Harbor Court Hotel, Baltimore, MD
The Hay-Adams Hotel, Washington, DC
Historic Inns of Annapolis, Annapolis, MD
The Homestead, Hot Springs, VA
Hotel Sofitel, Washington, DC

Hyatt Regency Baltimore, Baltimore, MD
Hyatt Regency Bethesda, Bethesda, MD
Inn at Grist Mill Square, Warm Springs, VA
The Jefferson, Washington, DC
Jefferson Hotel, Richmond, VA
Keswick Inn, Keswick, VA
Lansdowne Conference Resort, Leesburg, VA
The Lighthouse Club, Ocean City, MD
Linden Row Inn, Richmond, VA
Loews Annapolis Hotel, Annapolis, MD
The Madison, Washington, DC
Martha Washington Inn, Abingdon, VA
McLean Hilton at Tysons Corner, McLean, VA
Morrison-Clark Inn, Washington, DC
Morrison House, Alexandria, VA
Norfolk Waterside Marriott, Norfolk, VA
Omni International Hotel, Norfolk, VA
Omni Shoreham Hotel, Washington, DC
Park Hyatt, Washington, DC
Radisson Patrick Henry Hotel, Roanoke, VA
Red Fox Inn, Middleburg, VA
Richard Johnston Inn, Fredericksburg, VA
The Ritz-Carlton Pentagon City, Arlington, VA
The Ritz-Carlton Tysons Corner, McLean, VA
The Ritz-Carlton Washington, Washington, DC
Roanoke Airport Marriott, Roanoke, VA
Sheraton Baltimore North Hotel, Towson, MD
Stouffer Harborplace Hotel, Baltimore, MD
Stouffer Mayflower Hotel, Washington, DC
The Tides Inn, Irvington, VA
The Tides Lodge, Irvington, VA
The Tidewater Inn, Easton, MD
Virginia Beach Resort Hotel and Conference Center, Virginia Beach, VA
Washington Hilton and Towers, Washington, DC
The Watergate Hotel, Washington, DC
Willard Inter-Continental Washington, Washington, DC
The Williamsburg Inn, Williamsburg, VA
Wintergreen Resort, Wintergreen, VA

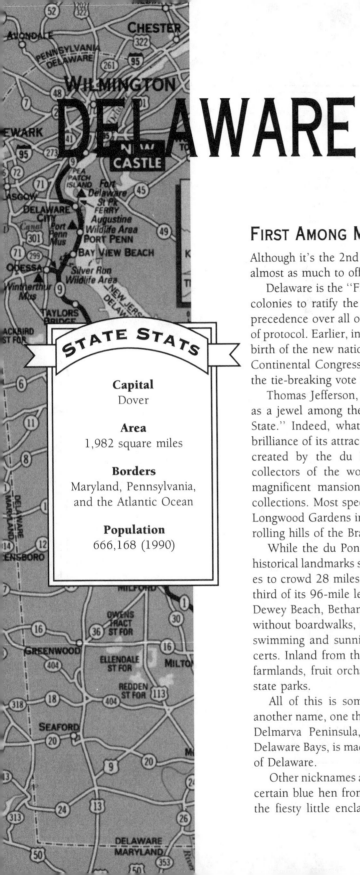

DELAWARE

FIRST AMONG MANY

Although it's the 2nd smallest state, behind Rhode Island, Delaware has almost as much to offer today's traveler as it has nicknames.

Delaware is the "First State," because it was the first of the original 13 colonies to ratify the US Constitution in 1787. Since then it has taken precedence over all other states at official functions and in other matters of protocol. Earlier, in 1776, Delaware had also played a crucial role in the birth of the new nation when Caesar Rodney, one of its delegates to the Continental Congress, rode all night from Dover to Philadelphia to cast the tie-breaking vote in favor of the Declaration of Independence.

Thomas Jefferson, author of that document, once described Delaware as a jewel among the states. That later was turned into the "Diamond State." Indeed, what is most gemlike about it is its size vis-à-vis the brilliance of its attractions. Above all, there are the estates and museums created by the du Pont family. Admirers of American culture and collectors of the work of its talented craftsmen, the du Ponts built magnificent mansions to house family members amid their extensive collections. Most spectacular of these are Winterthur and Nemours (and Longwood Gardens in Pennsylvania), which nestle around Hagley in the rolling hills of the Brandywine Valley.

While the du Pont legacy is the crowning glory of a rich heritage of historical landmarks scattered throughout the state, Delaware also manages to crowd 28 miles of Atlantic Coast into its small space—almost one third of its 96-mile length. The beach towns of Lewes, Rehoboth Beach, Dewey Beach, Bethany Beach, and Fenwick Island, some with and some without boardwalks, offer the full roster of summertime pleasures, from swimming and sunning to sandcastle contests and open-air band concerts. Inland from the beaches is the most rural part of the state, full of farmlands, fruit orchards, nature preserves, and some of Delaware's 11 state parks.

All of this is sometimes referred to as "Delmarvelous," a play on another name, one that applies to Delaware and two of its neighbors. The Delmarva Peninsula, a finger of land between the Chesapeake and Delaware Bays, is made up of part of Maryland and part of Virginia, but all of Delaware.

Other nicknames apply. During the Revolutionary War, roosters from a certain blue hen from Delaware won so many battlefield cockfights that the fiesty little enclave became known as the "Blue Hen State." (The nickname does *not* refer to the fact that poultry farming is big business in southern Delaware, which produces more than 180 million broiler chickens a year.) Of more recent derivation is the nickname, "Home of Tax-Free Shopping," which refers to the state's failure to impose a sales tax. That and beneficial tax treatment of corporations has made it a mecca for banks and large corporations. With more than half the Fortune 500 companies incorporated here, Delaware has earned another informal nickname: "Corporate Capital of the World."

From tax-free shopping to touring magnificent estates and museums to lying on its pristine Atlantic beaches, there is much to see and do in this delightful little state of many names.

A BRIEF HISTORY

GOING DUTCH   Delaware's written history goes back to 1609, when Henry Hudson, sailing under the Dutch flag, arrived at the broad bay between Cape Henlopen and Cape May. He and his contemporaries frequently plied these friendly waters, named later for an early Virginia governor, Lord De La Warr, who probably never saw his namesake.

Plentiful fish and a temperate climate attracted Dutch settlers as early as 1631, although this first colony, Zwaanendael (Valley of Swans), near Lewes, failed when the colonists were massacred by Native Americans in a misunderstanding over the theft of a piece of metal bearing a coat of arms.

Permanent settlement began in 1638 when Dutchman Peter Minuit, in the employ of Sweden, established a fort where Wilmington now stands. He named the fort and the nearby river Christina, in honor of the Swedish queen, and the settlers in New Sweden set about building log cabins, probably the New World's first.

In 1655, Peter Stuyvesant asserted Dutch control over the area and established a fort several miles to the south of the Swedish one. When the English took over in 1664, they named the Dutch stronghold New Castle. The area, in turn, became part of the land grant ceded to William Penn by the English king in 1681, and New Castle eventually became Delaware's colonial capital.

THE MASON-DIXON LINE   Until 1776, Delaware existed as the 3 lower counties of Pennsylvania. In fact, the state's unusually neat southern and western borders

are the handiwork of Charles Mason and Jeremiah Dixon, English surveyors hired from 1763 to 1768 to clear up a boundary dispute between Pennsylvania and Maryland. Not until much later did Mason and Dixon's Line come to delineate the boundary between slave and free states. (Delaware's northern border with Pennsylvania is also unique—a neat semicircle with a radius measuring 12 miles from the cupola of New Castle Court House.)

MIGRATION   Indentured servitude was the means by which many Presbyterian Scotch-Irish arrived in the 1700s. Irish Catholic immigrants increased rapidly during the potato famine of the 1840s. Many with skills sought jobs at the mills and factories springing up along the Brandywine River in northern Delaware.

Wilmington's ethnic populations were also growing. Italians, Poles, and other groups formed "little" areas of the city. In the 18th century, tobacco farmers of Anglo-Saxon heritage migrated with their slaves into

---

ᦰ *Fun Facts* ᦳ

• *The second-smallest state (only Rhode Island is smaller), Delaware is just 96 miles long and ranges from 9 to 35 miles wide.*

• *Delaware's average altitude—approximately 60 feet above sea level—is the lowest of any state. The state's highest point, Ebright Road in New Castle County, is only 442 feet above sea level.*

• *Three of America's oldest churches—Old Swedes (1698) in Wilmington, Old Welsh Tract (1703) near Newark, and Barratt's Chapel (1780) in Frederica—are still in use in Delaware.*

• *Coin Beach was so named because 18th-century coins, believed to have washed ashore from a passenger ship that sank off the Delaware coast in 1785, have been found there.*

• *The DuPont Company, based in Delaware, first developed and manufactured nylon at its plant in Seaford, known as the "nylon capital of the world."*

rural Kent and Sussex Counties from Maryland's Eastern Shore. Their Methodism flourished; Barratt's Chapel in Frederica is known as the "cradle of Methodism in America." Amish, Jewish, and Italian farm communities sprang up during the early 20th century.

THE AGE OF DU PONT   Among the immigrants was a Frenchman, Eleuthère Irenée du Pont de Nemours, who set up Hagley Mill, a black-powder (gun powder) factory along the fast-flowing waters of the Brandywine, in 1802. Du Pont and his family caught the wave of the approaching age of industrialism. Demand for cleared land created a wonderful market for quality explosives. So did timely wars.

By 1889 the company controlled more than 90 percent of the nation's gunpowder production. When Delaware passed easy laws of incorporation in 1899, E I du Pont de Nemours, Inc soon came into being. The company modernized, expanded, and diversified into the DuPont chemical company, which has given the world cellophane, acetate, rayon, Freon, Lucite, and its most famous manmade fiber, nylon.

THE CHESAPEAKE & DELAWARE CANAL   Already traversed by rivers, streams, and ponds, Delaware was cut in two in 1829 when the Chesapeake and Delaware Canal was built to join the Chesapeake Bay and the Delaware River and provided ocean-going vessels with a shortcut across the state. Many think the "Big Ditch" divided Delaware along philosophical as well as geographical lines. North of it are the urban and suburban workers and managers of New Castle County; downstate live the farmers of Kent and Sussex Counties. Historically, the 2 sections have opposed each other on virtually every issue—except Prohibition, which they both hated.

MODERN DELAWARE   Shipbuilding had been an important early industry, and today, ships from around the world still pass through the port of Wilmington, but since World War II, chemicals have been the state's largest industry. Down south, Sussex County chicken farmers have grown rich raising broilers to sell at home and abroad. Commercial development of the beach areas in recent years has made them the fastest growing part of the state.

Despite its friendliness to industry and traditional conservatism (Delaware was the last state to abandon slavery, it delayed giving women the vote as long as

possible, and in 1972 became the last state to abandon the whipping post as a form of punishment), the state does have a progressive streak. When Shell Oil tried to build a refinery in New Castle County in 1970, laws were passed prohibiting oil refiners and other types of industrial development along the shoreline. "To hell with Shell," said Governor Russell Peterson, a DuPont scientist and executive—and instant hero to ecologists across the nation.

A Closer Look
Geography

Delaware measures only 96 miles from north to south and varies from 9 to 35 miles from east to west. The hilly piedmont terrain around Wilmington in the north is in marked contrast to most of the state, which tends to be flat with a marshy, sandy shoreline. The fall line where these 2 geographic divisions meet supported a variety of water-powered industries in the Brandywine Valley in early times.

DISTANCES:

Wilmington

   13 miles NE of Newark
   29 miles SW of Philadelphia
   48 miles N of Dover
   70 miles NE of Baltimore
   88 miles NW of Rehoboth Beach
  108 miles NE of Washington

Dover

   43 miles SE of Newark
   43 miles NW of Rehoboth Beach
   48 miles S of Wilmington
   73 miles SE of Philadelphia
   98 miles NE of Washington
   99 miles E of Baltimore

Rehoboth Beach

   43 miles SE of Dover
   84 miles SE of Newark
   88 miles SE of Wilmington
  115 miles SE of Baltimore
  116 miles S of Philadelphia
  137 miles E of Washington

The state's 3 counties more or less delineate its geographic regions. The rolling piedmont begins north of the Chesapeake and Delaware Canal in **New Castle County,** home of Wilmington and the Brandywine Valley. Dover, the state capital, and the rest of central Delaware lie in **Kent County.** Occupying the southern third of the state, **Sussex County** has a split personality. While farms and quiet towns dot the flat countryside inland, along the Atlantic Ocean sits the busy summertime playground known as the **Delaware Beaches.**

Climate

Delaware enjoys a relatively mild climate, although temperatures along the coast can be 10°F cooler in summer and 10°F warmer in winter than inland. Wintertime visitors may find snow or brisk northwesterly winds. However, it seldom freezes until late fall, and the long Indian summers of autumn are everybody's favorite time of year.

What to Pack

Dress comfortably for the season, but bear in mind that the plenitude of palatial mansions open for touring encourages dressing up a little bit. Evenings can be cool and breezy, even at the beach, and summertime can feel damp. State parks and wildlife refuges are infamously buggy from early spring on, so bring lightweight socks, scarves, and plenty of insect repellent.

Tourist Information

Information, maps, and brochures are available at the Delaware Tourism Office, 99 Kings Hwy, PO Box 1401, Dover, DE 19903 (tel toll free 800/441-8846; fax 302/739-5749). In **Wilmington,** call the Greater Wilmington Convention and Visitors Bureau, 1300 N Market St, Suite 504, Wilmington, DE 19801 (tel 302/652-4088 from within the state or toll free 800/422-1181 from out of state). In **Dover,** call the Kent County Convention and Visitors Bureau (tel toll free 800/723-1736 or 800/233-KENT). For information on **southern Delaware,** contact the Sussex County Convention and Tourism Commission, PO Box 240, Georgetown, DE 19947 (tel 302/856-1818 or toll free 800/357-1818).

International visitors may call or write the Delaware Council for International Visitors, PO Box 831, Wilmington DE 19899 (tel 302/656-9928).

For current information on state parks, contact the State Recreation Office (tel 302/739-4413) or the Delaware Division of Parks and Recreation (tel 302/739-4702).

Delaware tourism literature normally includes information on nearby Pennsylvania attractions, such as Longwood Gardens and the Brandywine River Museum. For more information, contact the Brandywine Valley Tourist Information Center (tel toll free 800/228-9933) or the Delaware County Convention and Visitors Bureau (tel 215/565-3679).

AVERAGE MONTHLY TEMPERATURES (°F) & INCHES OF RAINFALL		
	Wilmington	**Lewes**
Jan	30/3.0	35/3.8
Feb	33/2.9	37/3.3
Mar	42/3.4	45/4.1
Apr	52/3.4	53/3.6
May	62/3.8	63/3.8
June	71/3.6	72/3.4
July	75/4.2	76/4.0
Aug	74/3.4	75/5.2
Sept	67/3.4	69/3.1
Oct	55/2.9	58/3.2
Nov	46/3.3	50/3.3
Dec	35/3.5	40/3.7

Driving Rules & Regulations

Speed limits are 55 mph on 4-lane, divided, and limited-access highways; 50 mph on 2-lane roads; 25 mph in business and residential districts; and 20 mph in school zones. Where posted limits differ from these, obey the signs. Seat belts are mandatory, and children under 4 must use approved child safety seats. Turning right on red is allowed after coming to a full stop.

You are legally drunk if your blood alcohol level is over .10. If you refuse to take a breathalyzer or sobriety test, you can be taken into custody.

Renting a Car

Check the yellow pages. The major companies present in Delaware include:

*   **Alamo** (tel toll free 800/327-9633)
*   **Avis** (tel 800/831-2847)
*   **Bayshore Leasing and Rental** (tel 800/882-4738)
*   **Budget** (tel 800/527-0700)
*   **Enterprise** (tel 800/325-8007)
*   **Hertz** (tel 800/654-3131)
*   **Payless** (tel 800/729-5377)
*   **Thrifty** (tel 800/367-2277)

Essentials

Area Code: The entire state is in the **302** area code.

Emergencies: Call **911** for the police, fire department, or an ambulance anywhere in the state. Many police departments monitor CB Emergency Channel 9.

Liquor Laws: Beer, wine, and liquor are sold in liquor stores only, which are closed Sundays. Provided a bar serves food (most do), it can also serve alcohol on Sunday. You must be 21 to purchase alcoholic beverages.

Smoking: All food-service establishments must maintain a nonsmoking section. Smoking is prohibited in libraries, theaters, auditoriums, and museums.

Taxes: There is no sales tax in Delaware, but there is an 8% hotel occupancy tax.

Time Zone: Delaware is in the Eastern time zone. Daylight saving time is in effect from the 1st Sunday in April through the last Sunday in October.

BEST OF THE STATE

What to See & Do

The proximity of historical and cultural activities in northern Delaware and the relaxing, casual lifestyle of the rural areas and beaches in southern Delaware could not be more convenient. Since nearly *everything* is above average, including the seafood and locally grown fruits and vegetables, travelers enjoy a "can't-go-far-wrong" comfort level.

BEACHES Rehoboth inspired the 1st beauty contest ever, which was held there in 1880. Delaware's 25-mile string of ocean beaches is just as beautiful today. Rehoboth and Bethany are biblical names, reminders of early religious camp meetings along the coast. Serenity survives, at least in spots. Historic **Lewes** and nearby Cape Henlopen are spacious and peaceful. **Rehoboth Beach** is the most popular and the largest coastal town. Narrow, sandy **Dewey Beach** attracts young people with its nightspots and ubiquitous water views. Southernmost **Bethany Beach** and **Fenwick Island** are "quiet resorts," thanks to strict building codes.

FAMILY FAVORITES The state publishes an annual *Calendar of Events* that conveniently marks events of interest to children with a "C" and is an invaluable aid when planning activities for the family (see "Tourist Information" above). Unique in Delaware is the **Children's Museum** in Wilmington, which gears interactive exhibits to ages 3 and up: "Experience the ripple of a wave; investigate a human ear. . . ." Children also adore the restored jail cells in the basement of Wilmington's **Old Town Hall Museum.**

CUISINE Look for steamed crabs and oysters on the halfshell along the coast; a variety of excellent ethnic foods around Wilmington; and Amish specialties such as fresh sausage and baked goods near Dover.

HISTORIC BUILDINGS & SITES Some buildings have been saved by moving them into historic enclaves;

architecturally rich **Willingtown Square** in Wilmington and the town of **Lewes** are examples of this preservation strategy. On the other hand, the historic structures of the 18th-century city of **New Castle** are architecturally diverse precisely because the town has not been "restored" (meaning all the way back to its beginnings as the colonial capital). Some entire towns, like the tiny sailing village of **Bethel,** are on the National Register. The Age of du Pont at its most gilded can be seen at **Nemours Mansion and Gardens,** near Wilmington, and at the elegantly restored **Hotel du Pont** in downtown Wilmington.

In addition to buildings, look for historic stone markers along the borders of the state. The **First Stone of the Transpeninsular Line,** on the grounds of the Fenwick Island Lighthouse, was the first stone marking the east-west boundary between Maryland and Pennsylvania's lower counties (which eventually became Delaware). Finished in 1751, the line was the forerunner of the Mason-Dixon Line.

MUSEUMS   If you only have time for two, see **Winterthur Museum and Gardens** and **Hagley Museum,** a short drive apart north of Wilmington. Winterthur's collection of 180-plus period rooms and the American antiques that decorate them is the best in the world. Hagley, an outdoor museum at the site of the 1st du Pont powder mill, offers a look at a 19th-century industrial village and at the first house inhabited by the du Ponts in America.

Delaware has many other fine museums large and small, with exhibits and special programs constantly bringing history to life. Shipbuilding, for instance, one of the state's most important early industries, is illustrated at the **Kalmar Nyckel Shipyard/Museum** and the **Maritime Center** in Wilmington, and at the **Zwaanendael Museum** in Lewes. Early shipbuilding tools and records can be seen at the **Lydia Ann B Cannon Museum** in Milton.

In a different vein, illustrators Howard Pyle and NC Wyeth, both native sons, are represented at the **Delaware Art Museum** in Wilmington. Other collections are in the **Delaware Center for the Contemporary Arts** in Wilmington and the **Sewell C Biggs Museum of American Art** in Dover.

PARKS & GARDENS   Chemists by trade, the du Ponts were closet botanists. Hundreds of beautifully landscaped acres at **Winterthur, Hagley,** and **Nemours** display splendid native and exotic plants, setting a high standard for other more modest but equally charming landscaped parks and gardens around the state.

SCENIC DRIVES   Miles of blue stone fences line the rolling country roads in the Brandywine Valley (along Del 100 and Del 52 from Wilmington to US 1 in Pennsylvania). Elsewhere, charming historic towns and waterside fishing villages offer fresh steamed crabs and oysters on the halfshell (Del 9 from New Castle to Dover and Del 8 from the Maryland border to Little Creek). In the South, antique shops and flea markets, quiet restaurants, and fabulous wildlife areas beckon beach goers to wander off the beaten path along Del 1 from Dewey Beach south to Fenwick Island, Del 5 from Oak Orchard to Del 24, and Del 24 from Millsboro to Laurel.

WILDLIFE REFUGES   The 15,000-acre **Bombay Hook National Wildlife Refuge** near Lewes offers auto tour routes, exploration via small boat or canoe, and nature trails leading to observation towers. The smaller **Prime Hook National Wildlife Refuge** near Milton has 2 trails, 4 boat ramps, 2 ponds, and 7 miles of canoe trails.

Events/Festivals

Delaware's 80-page *Calendar of Events* includes many seasonal activities and hundreds of annual events (see "Tourist Information," above).

Northern Delaware

- **St Patrick's Day Parade,** Wilmington. Sponsored by the Irish Culture Club of Delaware. Mid-March. Call 302/652-2970.
- **Wilmington Garden Day,** Wilmington. Guided bus tours of the top homes and gardens. May 1. Call 302/652-1966.
- **A Day in Old New Castle,** New Castle. The entire historic town opens to the public. 3rd Saturday in May. Call 302/322-5744.
- **Old Fashioned Ice Cream Festival,** Rockwood Museum, Wilmington. Bands, balloons, games, antiques, and crafts. 1st weekend after July 4. Call 302/761-4340.

- **Historic New Castle Antiques Show,** New Castle. See the best of the past. Last Sunday in August. Call 302/322-8411.
- **Hoots, Howls, and Haunts Halloween Carnival,** Wilmington. Ghosts and goblins at the Museum of Natural History. Late October. Call 302/658-9111.
- **Yuletide at Winterthur,** Winterthur. Tours and Victorian-style celebrations at Winterthur Museum and Gardens. Mid-November through December. Call 302/888-4600 or toll free 800/448-3883.

Central Delaware

- **Old Dover Days,** Dover. The capital's leading historic homes are open to the public, plus parades and maypole dancing. Late April. Call 302/734-1736.
- **Spring Tour of Historic Houses,** Odessa. Historic homes open for the season. Early May through July. Call 302/378-4069.
- **Tour DuPont,** Dover. The statewide bike race begins at Legislative Mall. Early May. Call 302/734-1736 or 302/773-0490.
- **Community Appreciation Days,** Dover Air Force Base. Historical Museum is focus for tours of the base. 3rd Saturdays, June through August. Call 302/677-3376.
- **Bluegrass Festival,** Harrington. Pickin' and fiddlin'. 3rd weekend in June. Call 302/492-1048.

Delaware Beaches

- **Great Delaware Kite Festival,** Lewes. Demonstrations and competitions at Cape Henlopen State Park. Early April. Call 302/645-8073.
- **Ocean to Bay Bike-a-Thon,** Fenwick Island. Bike racing along the beach. Late April. Call 302/539-2100 or toll free 800/962-7873.
- **World Champion Weakfish Tournament,** Slaughter Beach. Who can catch the biggest. Early June. Call 302/422-3344.
- **Quiet Resorts Golf Classic,** Fenwick Island. Early June. Call 302/539-2100 or toll free 800/962-SURF.
- **Zwaanendael Heritage Garden Tour,** Lewes. 1-day tour of historic houses and gardens. 4th Saturday in June. Call 302/645-8073.

- **Fourth of July Celebration,** Bethany Beach. Partying and fireworks. Call 302/539-8011.
- **Sandcastle Contest,** Rehoboth Beach. Adults and children compete at Delaware Seashore State Park. 2nd weekend in July. Call 302/739-4702.
- **Rehoboth Art League Annual Members' Fine Arts Show,** Rehoboth Beach. Mid-August. Call 302/227-8408.
- **Boardwalk Arts Festival,** Bethany Beach. Judged show attracts artists and artisans from far and wide. Last Saturday in August. Call 302/539-2100 or toll free 800/962-7873.
- **Coast Day,** Lewes. Open house at the University of Delaware's College of Marine Studies. 1st Sunday in October. Call 302/645-4346.

Southern Inland Delaware

- **Delmarva Hot-Air Balloon Festival,** Milton. Saturday of Memorial Day weekend. Call 302/684-1101.
- **Return Day,** Georgetown. The winners celebrate, the losers lament. Held biennially after Election Day. Call 302/856-1818 or toll free 800/357-1818.
- **The Laurel Watermelon Festival,** Laurel. Seed-spitting fun. August. Call 302/875-2277.
- **Nanticoke Indian Museum and Pow-Wow,** Millsboro. Celebration of Native American culture. 2nd weekend in September. Call 302/945-3400 or 302/945-7022.
- **Milton Holly Festival,** Milton. Red berries getting ready for Christmas. 2nd Saturday in December. Call 302/684-1101.
- **Farmer's Christmas,** Dover. Delaware Agricultural Museum and Village celebrates the season. Early December. Call 302/734-1618.

Spectator Sports

AUTO RACING Dover Downs International Speedway has NASCAR racing. Call 302/674-4600 for information, 302/734-RACE for tickets. **Delaware International Speedway,** on US 13 at Delmar, has NHRA drag racing. Call 302/846-3968.

BASEBALL For information and tickets to see Wilmington's minor-league **Blue Rocks,** call 302/888-BLUE.

COLLEGE ATHLETICS   For intercollegiate sports schedules, contact the **University of Delaware** (tel 302/UD1-HENS) and **Delaware State University** (tel 302/739-3553).

HORSE RACING   Delaware Park, southwest of Wilmington, at Stanton, has thoroughbred racing from mid-March to early November (tel 302/994-2521). Harness racing takes place at **Harrington Raceway,** one of the oldest pari-mutuel harness racing tracks in the United States, from September through November (tel 302/398-3551) and at **Dover Downs** (tel 302/674-4600 for information, 302/734-RACE for tickets) on winter weekends. Winterthur sponsors an amateur steeplechase in May (call 302/888-4600 or toll free 800/448-3883).

Activities A to Z

BICYCLING   Annual bike-a-thons and a bicycle rodeo, county bicycle touring clubs, and the state's excellent *Delaware Maps for Bicycle Users* series support this popular pastime. Commercial companies provide inn-to-inn biking tours. The Tour DuPont in May is among the world's top pro-cycling events.

BIRDWATCHING   Noting that the mud flats of the Delaware Bay at low tide are "a rich pudding stuffed with delicacies for birds with long, pointed bills," the Audubon Society recommends numerous Delaware locations. Waves of shorebirds traveling the **Atlantic Flyway** time their arrival in May to coincide with hordes of horseshoe crabs laying eggs; birdwatchers convene from far and wide to witness this special "crabfeast."

BOATING   So much water in Delaware, so little time to experience it all. The possibilities stretch from **dolphin- and whale-watching expeditions** and tall ship **schooner cruises** at Lewes to the **Cape May–Lewes Ferry** (a mini-cruise in itself) and the tiny **Woodland Ferry,** the state's last cable ferry, which began running across the Nanticoke River in 1793. Also consider windsurfing or sailing on the inland bays, or a sea kayak tour of the bays and wildlife areas. For information about boating laws and regulations contact the Delaware Recreation Office (tel 302/739-4413) or the Delaware Division of Parks and Recreation (tel 302/739-4702).

CAMPING   Some state parks offer camping facilities. See "Tourist Information," above. For information on several excellent private camping facilities write the Delaware Campground Association, PO Box 156, Rehoboth Beach, DE 19971.

FISHING   Accessible areas open for freshwater and non-tidal fishing provide trout and bass; crabbing and clamming in season. Saltwater fishing for weakfish, flounder, and blues is popular spring through early fall. Ocean-going charter boats at **Bowers Beach** offer a variety of services, while family-oriented head boats are reasonably priced.

For information on licensing, regulations, daily possession limits and locations of approved areas, contact the Division of Fish and Wildlife, 89 Kings Hwy, PO Box 1401, Dover, DE 19903 (tel 302/739-4431). The University of Delaware's Sea Grant Marine Advisory Service in Lewes provides information on how to use Delaware's marine resources (tel 302/645-4346).

GOLF   The **Delcastle Golf Club,** 801 McKennan's Church Rd (tel 302/995-1990), located southwest of Wilmington near Delaware Park racetrack, offers an 18-hole championship course, pro shop, driving range, and miniature golf course. A par-71 course is located at the **Old Landing Golf Course,** 300 Old Landing Rd, Rehoboth Beach (tel 302/227-3131).

HIKING   The Delaware Department of Natural Resources and Environmental Control, PO Box 1404, Dover, DE 19903 (tel 302/739-4403) publishes an excellent brochure called *Delaware Trails Guidebook: Hiking in the First State.*

HISTORIC TRAINS   Two lines, the **Queen Anne's** in Lewes (tel 302/644-1720) and the **Wilmington & Western** (tel 302/998-1930), offer train rides designed for tourists. Railroad artifacts are housed in a 1929 caboose museum by the Highball Signal near Delmar (tel 302/846-2645).

HUNTING   As a result of strict regulation, small game, deer, and waterfowl are plentiful in season. For information on licensing, regulations, daily possession limits, and locations of approved areas, write the Division of Fish and Wildlife, 89 Kings Hwy, PO Box 1401, Dover, DE 19903 (tel 302/739-4431).

SKATING Dover Skating Center (tel 302/697-3218), **Skate World II** in Rehoboth (tel 302/645-0463), and **Christiana Skating Center** (tel 302/366-0473) are all for rollerskaters.

TENNIS Indoor tennis courts are available at the **Dover Indoor Tennis Club** (tel 302/734-1404), which is open October–April and welcomes visitors.

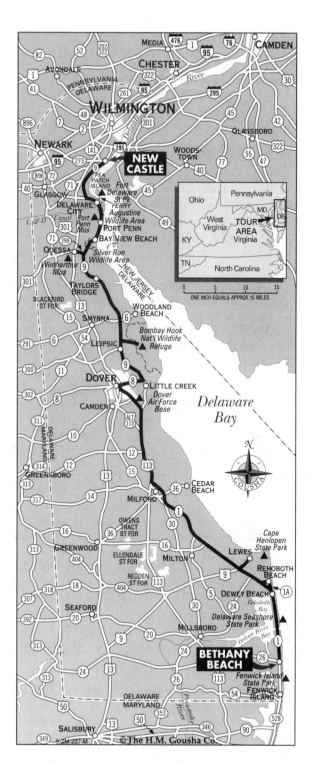

SCENIC DRIVING TOUR

COASTAL DELAWARE

Start: New Castle
Finish: Bethany Beach
Distance: 130 miles
Time: 1–3 days
Highlights: Historic towns and villages with restored 18th-century homes and other buildings; marshlands; wildlife preserves; Delaware's pleasant capital; splendid ocean beaches

This tour parallels the Delaware River through the southern two-thirds of the state. In the late 17th and early 18th centuries, this agricultural and fishing region was settled by colonists whose legacy endures in the many period homes still standing in quaint small towns, such as New Castle and Odessa. First, you'll follow Del 9, which skirts and sometimes crosses extensive marshlands; much of these wetlands are contained within wildlife preserves which give refuge to migrating birds. At Delaware's colonial-era capital in Dover, you'll pick up Del 1 and drive southeast to the oceanfront enclaves of Rehoboth Beach, Dewey Beach, Bethany Beach, and Fenwick Island, as well as to the dunes and unspoiled sands of Delaware Seashore State Park, which borders the Atlantic.

As you plan your trip, note that many of the key homes, museums, and buildings along this route are closed on Monday, and some are open only from April through October. For additional information on accommodations, restaurants, and attractions in the region covered by the tour, look under specific cities in the listings portion of this book.

Del 9, Del 141, and Del 273 converge 7 miles south of Wilmington, giving easy access to the first stop:

1. **New Castle,** a major seaport and Delaware's capital in English colonial times, and one of the country's best-preserved 18th-century villages. Indeed, New Castle seems suspended in time, for the town retains many of its early cobblestone streets, public buildings, and homes. It's the kind of place where you can still talk to a clerk through an open courthouse window. Maps for self-guided walking tours of the delightful historic district are available at the **New Castle Court House,** at 211

Delaware St (tel 302/323-4453), 2 blocks from the river. Built in 1722, this brick building's cupola marks the center of the 12-mile arc that forms Delaware's northern border with Pennsylvania. Other nearby attractions from the 1700s include **The Green,** between 2nd and 3rd Sts behind the Court House; the **Dutch House,** 32 E 3rd St facing The Green (tel 302/322-9168), now a museum with early-17th-century furnishings; the **Amstel House,** 4th and Delaware Sts (tel 302/322-2794), a fine example of Georgian architecture; and the federal-style **George Read II House and Gardens** (tel 302/222-8411) on The Strand (a 1-block cobblestone street near the river), the house has elaborately carved woodwork, relief plasterwork, and silver door hardware. The Court House and museums are all closed on Monday.

After taking a refreshment at the **David Finney Inn,** 216 Delaware St (tel 302/322-6367; assuming it has reopened after a 1994 fire), the **Cellar Gourmet Restaurant,** 208 Delaware (tel 302/323-0999), or the **Green Frog Tavern,** 114 Delaware (tel 302/322-1844)—all of them facing or near the Court House—proceed away from the river on Delaware St, go straight through the traffic signal at River Plaza Shopping Center, and turn left onto Del 9. Drive south 9½ miles to:

2. **Delaware City,** the terminus of the Chesapeake and Delaware Canal until the cross-peninsula waterway was moved south to Reedy Point in 1927. Until then, ships docked at locks here and at Chesapeake City near the canal's western end. The old lock stands at the foot of Clinton St (turn left at the stoplight) along what is now the Delaware City Branch Canal. Across the lock stands the headquarters for **Fort Delaware State Park** (tel 302/834-7941), from which a passenger ferry leaves for the fort out on Pea Patch Island. Completed in 1859, this massive granite structure was used as a prison camp during the Civil War. The ferry runs Wednesday–Saturday, June 15 through Labor Day. Fares are $4.50 for adults, $3 for children under age 15. Call 302/834-7941 for details.

South of town, Del 9 first crosses the narrow old canal and then climbs the high-rise span over the modern waterway, giving an expansive view of

---

🍺

REFRESHMENT STOP

You won't have another chance for refreshment for many miles, so walk across the park at the foot of Clinton St to the **Old Canal Restaurant and Inn** (tel 302/834-7472), which serves lunch Tuesday–Friday, 11:30am–2pm. If it's not open, try **Porto Pizza Place,** 88 Clinton St (tel 302/834-1261), for pizzas and deli sandwiches served in a simple, over-the-counter setting.

---

this massive engineering project, the Delaware River, and the surrounding countryside and marshes. Two miles past the bridge you'll come to **Port Penn,** a small fishing village on a narrow peninsula of high ground extending into the marshes. At the right of the stop sign is an interpretive museum which is open Wednesday–Sunday afternoons during the summer. After Port Penn, Del 9 runs through the marshes of Augustine Wildlife Area until reaching a T-intersection. Turn right at the intersection and follow Del 299 north 1½ miles to:

3. **Odessa,** a small village on the high ground just beyond Appoquinimink Creek. This was a major grain shipping port in the early 1800s, but it now seems almost like a ghost town of 18th- and 19th-century homes. The **Wintherthur Museum** (tel 302/378-4069) administers a collection of these lovely houses, which can be visited March–December, Tuesday–Saturday 10am–4pm, Sunday 1–4pm. Buy your tickets on 2nd St behind the Nature Tamed Better Furniture building, which houses America's largest collection of Victorian furniture. Tickets cost $7 for adults, $6 for seniors and students ages 12–16, $3 for children 5–11.

US 13 offers a shortcut from Odessa south to Dover, but this tour backtracks south on Del 299 until you pick up Del 9 again 1½ miles south of town. Continue south on Del 9 for 18 miles to Whitehall Neck Rd (Del 85), which goes to the left just south of the junction with Smyrna-Leipsic Rd.

Turn left on Whitehall Neck Rd and drive east 2½ miles to the visitors center of:

4. **Bombay Hook National Wildlife Refuge** (tel 302/653-9345), a 23-square-mile expanse of salt-marsh and freshwater pools and one of the most important migratory stops on the Great Atlantic Flyway. More than 250 species of birds nest here, including great bald eagles, between November and June. Land-based wildlife also abounds. You can walk the nature trails, take a 12-mile driving tour, and climb the 30-foot-tall observation towers. The visitors center is open Monday–Friday 8am–4pm year-round, weekends 9am–5pm during fall and spring. The refuge itself is open daily from sunrise to sunset all year. Fees are $4 per vehicle, $2 for pedestrians and bicyclists.

Return to Smyrna-Leipsic Rd (Del 9), turn left, and drive 1½ miles south to the little riverside village of Leipsic.

☕

REFRESHMENT STOP

Turn left on Market St in Leipsic to **Sambo's Tavern,** on Front St (tel 302/674-9724), overlooking the banks of the muddy Leipsic River. In true crab house fashion, you'll have newspapers for tablecloths and a roll of paper towels for napkins, which local residents consider absolutely necessary for cracking a mess of steamed crabs. Sambo's also serves sandwiches and fried seafood dishes, including terrific crab cakes. Platters cost $8–$18.

After lunch, continue south another 6½ miles, turn right on Del 8, and drive east 4 miles into the heart of:

5. **Dover,** chartered in 1683 by William Penn and Delaware's capital since state leaders moved inland to avoid British naval attacks on New Castle in 1777. Del 8 brings you into town along Division St, the boundary between the Colonial and Victorian sections of Dover. Turn left at the 2nd traffic signal after US 13 and follow State St south across

The Green at the center of old Dover. On its east end stands the 1792-vintage **Delaware State House,** S State St (tel 302/739-4266), now a museum. Turn left on Water St and left again on Federal St to the **Delaware State Visitors Center,** 406 Federal St (tel 302/739-4266), beside the State House at the corner of Duke of York St. It's the best place to get information and maps, and to begin a self-guided walking tour of the historic district. Upstairs is the **Sewell C Biggs Museum of American Art,** with a large collection of American decorative arts. Downtown highlights include the 1910 **Supreme Court** on The Green; the 1933 **Legislative Hall** on Legislative Ave between William Penn and Duke of York Sts; several 19th-century stores in the Loockerman St commercial area; and the **State Museum Complex,** 316 S Governors Ave (tel 302/739-2630), which includes a 1790 Presbyterian Church and the Johnson Victrola Museum.

Located in central Delaware, Dover is a good place for an overnight stop. Several modern motels (such as **Sheraton Inn–Dover, Comfort Inn of Dover,** and **Dover Budget Inn**) and numerous fast food and family-style restaurants sit along the Du Pont Hwy (US 13), the major commercial artery passing north-south through town.

From Dover, drive south on the combined US 113 and Del 1. **Dover Air Force Base** is 2 miles south of town; you can enter the main gate to visit its aviation museum (tel 302/677-3379). From there, keep going south and follow Del 1 when it branches off from US 113 at Milford. At 39 miles south of Dover Air Force Base, take Business US 9 to the left and drive north 2 miles into:

6. **Lewes,** northernmost of the Delaware beaches and an historic site in its own right. At the intersection of Business US 9 (Savannah Rd) and Kings Hwy stands the **Zaanendael Museum** (tel 302/645-9418), which commemorates the short-lived Dutch whaling colony established here in 1631. The **Chamber of Commerce Visitors Center** (302/645-8073) is located in the early 1700s Fisher-Martin House behind the museum, on Kings Hwy. (Open year-round Monday–Friday 10am–4pm; also open Saturday 10am–2pm in the summer). Here you can get a walking tour map

and explore the surrounding historic district and its more than 50 houses dating back to the 17th and 18th centuries (some have been moved here from other sites). The local historical society maintains the **Lewes Historical Complex,** a group of old homes and a country store at Shipcarpenter and Third Sts. The Lewes and Rehoboth Canal runs east-west through Lewes, which is a major center for recreational boating. The town has a number of sightseeing cruises, including whale- and dolphin-watching expeditions. The **Queen Anne's Railroad,** a steam train, departs from its station at 730 Kings Hwy (tel 302/644-1720) for rides into the surrounding countryside.

Turn right at the Lewes Beach end of Savannah Rd for the ferry to Cape May, NJ, and the Atlantic beaches of **Cape Henlopen State Park** (tel 302/645-8983), where trails lead through sand dunes to the cape and the 80-foot Great Dune, the highest sand dune between Cape Hatteras and Cape Cod.

🍺

REFRESHMENT STOP

Lewes has plenty of dining spots, including a number of fast-food emporia on Del 1 between here and Rehoboth Beach. Among the better restaurants in the historic district are **Gilligan's,** 134 Market St (tel 302/645-7866), with seafood specialties; **Jerry's American Cafe,** 115 2nd St (tel 302/645-9733), serving old-time favorites such as chicken pot pie and crab cakes; **Kupchick's Restaurant,** 3 E Bay Ave (tel 302/645-0420), with an international menu; and **La Rosa Negra,** 128 2nd St (tel 302/645-1980), featuring Italian entrees.

Backtrack to Del 1, turn left, drive south 4 miles, and take Del 1A to the left. This road dead-ends at the boardwalk of:

7. **Rehoboth Beach,** sometimes called the nation's Summer Capital because of its popularity with Washington, DC, residents who flock here to escape the real capital's summer heat and humidity. Two blocks from the beach, turn right on 2nd St, which becomes Bayard Ave (Del 1A), running south of Rehoboth's sister resort, **Dewey Beach.** This stretch of sand lacks Rehoboth's charm but has the advantage of fronting both the ocean and Rehoboth Bay, a mecca for watersports enthusiasts.

Del 1 passes through Dewey Beach as its main thoroughfare. A mile south of town it enters:

8. **Delaware Seashore State Park** (tel 302/227-8800), a narrow 7 miles of preserved beach and sand dunes separating the Atlantic from Rehoboth and Indian River Bays. The park has an ocean beach with a lifeguard, a bayside campground with RV hookups, and a full-service marina at Indian River Inlet, which lets fishing boats pass from the bay into the ocean for deep-sea fishing.

South of the park, Del 1 continues through a residential beach development until reaching the end of the tour at:

9. **Bethany Beach,** a quiet resort much favored by families who want to avoid the non-stop activity at Rehoboth and Dewey Beaches to the north and Ocean City, MD, to the south. Turn left at the stop light to reach Bethany's small commercial and boardwalk area.

South of town, the 2½-mile-long **Fenwick Island State Park** (tel 302/539-9060) separates Bethany from **Fenwick Island,** a beach resort extension of Ocean City just across the Maryland line. There you can see the 1859 **Fenwick Lighthouse,** which sits right on the state line. On its grounds is the First Stone of the Transpeninsular Line, which divides Maryland from Delaware.

From Ocean City, you can take the driving tour "Maryland's Eastern Shore" (see the Maryland chapter) in reverse.

BEAR

Map page M-3, B7

Attraction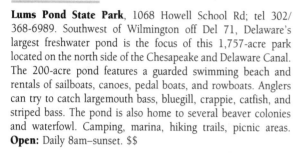

Lums Pond State Park, 1068 Howell School Rd; tel 302/ 368-6989. Southwest of Wilmington off Del 71, Delaware's largest freshwater pond is the focus of this 1,757-acre park located on the north side of the Chesapeake and Delaware Canal. The 200-acre pond features a guarded swimming beach and rentals of sailboats, canoes, pedal boats, and rowboats. Anglers can try to catch largemouth bass, bluegill, crappie, catfish, and striped bass. The pond is also home to several beaver colonies and waterfowl. Camping, marina, hiking trails, picnic areas. **Open:** Daily 8am–sunset. $$

BETHANY BEACH

Map page M-3, C8

Motels

≣ Bethany Arms Motel and Apartments, 5 Atlantic Ave, PO Box 1600, Bethany Beach, DE 19930; tel 302/539-9603. Exit Del 1 at Del 26; go 2 blocks to Atlantic Ave, then south to Hollywood St. Located at the south end of the Bethany Beach boardwalk, with direct access to the beach and nearby shops, this property comprises several buildings of varying ages and levels of renovation. **Rooms:** 52 rms and effic. CI 2pm/CO 11am. Middle-aged rooms are of several types, clean but not exciting. **Amenities:** A/C, cable TV, refrig. Some units w/terraces. **Services:** Beach equipment rental available. **Facilities:** 1 rst, 1 beach (ocean), lifeguard, board surfing. **Rates:** HS July 1–Labor Day $85–$95 S or D; from $110 effic. Extra person $5. Children under 3 stay free. Min stay HS and wknds. Lower rates off-season. Spec packages avail. Pking: Outdoor, free. Ltd CC.

≣≣ Harbor View Motel, Del 1, Box 102, Bethany Beach, DE 19930; tel 302/539-0500; fax 302/539-5170. 3 mi N of Bethany Beach. At edge of Delaware Seashore Park, 1 mi S of Indian River Inlet. Built in the mid-1980s on the site of a fishing camp, this bayfront motel still appeals to those who trailer their boats here to enjoy the outdoors. **Rooms:** 60 rms and effic. CI 2pm/CO 11am. Nonsmoking rms avail. **Amenities:** A/C, cable TV. All units w/terraces. King-bed rooms have refrigerators. **Services:** **Facilities:** 1 bar (w/entertainment), lifeguard. Picnic tables and barbecue grills in backyard. Excellent fishing in area. Crabbing off bulkhead. Ocean beaches across highway via

walkway. **Rates (CP):** HS July–Labor Day $80–$90 S or D; from $95 effic. Extra person $10. Children under 6 stay free. Min stay HS. Lower rates off-season. Higher rates for spec evnts/hols. Pking: Outdoor, free. Maj CC.

Restaurants

Dream Café, Pennsylvania Ave and Campbell Place, Bethany Beach; tel 302/539-1588. Located 1 block north of Garfield Pkwy and 1 block west of Boardwalk, next to Post Office. **Cafe/ Coffeehouse/Deli.** Works of local artists are hung gallery-style in this simple, uncrowded deli/cafe. Fare includes light, contemporary American selections, pasta, salads, quiche, brie, and fresh-baked breads. Espresso bar. Eat here or carry out an elegant alfresco lunch for the beach. Also at: 26 Baltimore Ave, Rehoboth Beach (tel 302/226-2233). **FYI:** Reservations not accepted. Children's menu. No liquor license. No smoking. **Open:** HS Mem Day–Labor Day daily 7am–10pm. Reduced hours off-season. Closed some hols; Thanksgiving–Easter. **Prices:** Lunch main courses $4–$7. Maj CC.

Harbor Lights Restaurant, Del 1, Bethany Beach; tel 302/ 539-3061. At the edge of Delaware Seashore Park. **American/ Seafood.** Simple rooms with wood-paneled walls, nautical prints, and hanging plants are decorated in blue and white. A large upstairs bar has windows overlooking the bay. This is fishing country, so seafood dishes, including crab, are the mainstays. The wine list is extensive for such a menu. Separate room for smoking. **FYI:** Reservations accepted. Band/blues/ dancing/jazz/rock. Children's menu. **Open:** HS Mem Day–Labor Day daily 5–10pm. Reduced hours off-season. Closed some hols; Nov–Mar. **Prices:** Main courses $11–$25. Maj CC.

Holiday House Seafood Restaurant, Garfield Pkwy and the Boardwalk, Bethany Beach; tel 302/539-7298. Follow Del 1 to Garfield Pkwy; go east. **Seafood/Buffet.** Red is the predominant color in this semicasual seashore establishment with inlaid tables in mirrored rooms. Large windows afford views of the boardwalk and ocean. Most people come for the seafood buffet, but also available are some beef, chicken, and pasta entrees. Carryout available. **FYI:** Reservations recommended. Children's menu. **Open:** HS Mem Day–Labor Day breakfast daily 8–11:30am; lunch daily 11:30am–2pm; dinner daily 5–9pm. Reduced hours off-season. Closed Jan–Mar. **Prices:** Main courses $9–$17. Maj CC.

CENTREVILLE

Map page M-3, B7 (NW of Wilmington)

Restaurant 🍴

Buckley's Tavern, 5812 Kennett Pike, Centreville; tel 302/656-9776. Exit I-95 at Delaware Ave. **American.** Colonial decor, with good-quality wood tables and chairs in a rustic setting. Traditional American entrees with some regional and low-fat selections. Same menu in dining room, lounge, and rooftop deck. Light menu served after dining room closes. Good choice of international and domestic microbrewery beers. **FYI:** Reservations accepted. Children's menu. Dress code. **Open:** Lunch Mon–Fri 11:30am–2:30pm, Sat 11:30am–3pm; dinner Mon–Wed 5:30–9:30pm, Thurs–Sat 5:30–10pm, Sun 5–9pm; brunch Sun 11am–3pm. Closed some hols. **Prices:** Main courses $13–$20. Maj CC. 🍺

DEWEY BEACH

Map page M-3, C8 (S of Rehoboth Beach)

Motels 🏨

≣≣ **Atlantic Oceanside**, 1700 Del 1, Dewey Beach, DE 19971; tel 302/227-8811 or toll free 800/422-0481. Standard highway motel that's clean, well maintained, and close to the ocean. **Rooms:** 60 rms and effic; 14 ctges/villas. CI 3pm/CO 11am. Nonsmoking rms avail. Recently refurbished units are neat and clean. **Amenities:** 🛏 ⬛ A/C, cable TV w/movies, refrig. **Services:** 🔲 ⬛ Babysitting. **Facilities:** 🔲 🔲 1 rst, lifeguard. Heated outdoor pool and sun deck are on the highway side of the premises. **Rates:** HS July–Sept $75–$99 S or D; from $85 effic; from $169 ctge/villa. Extra person $7. Children under 14 stay free. Min stay HS and wknds. Lower rates off-season. Higher rates for spec evnts/hols. Spec packages avail. Pking: Outdoor, free. Maj CC.

≣≣ **The Bay Resort**, 126 Bellevue St, on the bay, PO Box 461, Dewey Beach, DE 19971; or toll free 800/922-9240. Exit Del 1 at Bellevue St. Attractive and fresh, this simple motel has its own little bayfront lagoon and pier. **Rooms:** 68 rms and effic. CI 3pm/CO 11am. Standard motel rooms are cheerful. **Amenities:** 🛏 ⬛ A/C, cable TV w/movies. All units w/terraces. **Services:** 🔲 Social director, children's program, babysitting. **Facilities:** 🔲 🔲 1 beach (cove/inlet), lifeguard, washer/dryer. Nearby boat rentals on the bay. Swimming is not especially good from the motel's beach. Good crabbing from the pier in summer. **Rates (CP):** HS June 24–Sept 1 $79–$139 S or D; from $89 effic. Extra person

$10. Children under 12 stay free. Min stay HS and wknds. Lower rates off-season. Higher rates for spec evnts/hols. Spec packages avail. Pking: Outdoor, free. Ltd CC.

≣≣≣ **Best Western Gold Leaf**, 1400 Del 1, Dewey Beach, DE 19971; tel 302/226-1100 or toll free 800/422-8566; fax 302/226-9785. This modern, well-maintained motel is convenient to both ocean beaches and bay water sports. **Rooms:** 75 rms. CI 2pm/CO 11am. Express checkout avail. Nonsmoking rms avail. Units are scrupulously clean. **Amenities:** 🛏 A/C, cable TV w/movies, refrig, in-rm safe. All units w/terraces, 1 w/Jacuzzi. **Services:** 🚐 🔲 Many sports and social events can be arranged in conjunction with Ruddertowne, across the street. **Facilities:** 🔲 🔲 🔲 Lifeguard, washer/dryer. Rooftop pool has nice views. **Rates (CP):** HS Mem Day–Labor Day $98–$178 S or D. Extra person $10. Children under 12 stay free. Min stay HS. Lower rates off-season. Higher rates for spec evnts/hols. MAP rates avail. Spec packages avail. Pking: Indoor/outdoor, free. Maj CC.

DOVER

Map page M-3, B7

Motels 🏨

≣≣ **Best Western Galaxy Inn**, 1700 E Lebanon Rd, Dover, DE 19901; tel 302/735-4700 or toll free 800/528-1234; fax 302/735-1604. A well-maintained highway motel close to Dover Air Force Base. **Rooms:** 64 rms. CI 2pm/CO 11am. Nonsmoking rms avail. Neat and clean. **Amenities:** 🛏 A/C, cable TV w/movies. Some units w/Jacuzzis. **Services:** 🚐 🔲 Car-rental desk. **Facilities:** 🔲 🔲 Lifeguard. McDonald's restaurant next door. **Rates (CP):** $47–$60 S or D. Extra person $5. Children under 12 stay free. Min stay spec evnts. Higher rates for spec evnts/hols. Pking: Outdoor, free. Maj CC.

≣≣ **Comfort Inn of Dover**, 222 S du Pont Hwy, Dover, DE 19901; tel 302/674-3300 or toll free 800/221-2222; fax 302/674-3300. On US 13 at Loockerman St, N of jct US 13/113. This quiet property is set back from the main highway and is convenient to both historic downtown and Dover Air Force Base. **Rooms:** 94 rms and effic. CI 2pm/CO noon. Nonsmoking rms avail. **Amenities:** 🛏 A/C, cable TV w/movies. **Services:** 🔲 **Facilities:** 🔲 🔲 🔲 1 rst, 1 bar, lifeguard. Access to indoor pool, hot tub, and fitness center at Sheraton Inn and Conference Center Dover, about 2 miles north on US 13. TGI Fridays restaurant adjacent. **Rates (CP):** HS May–Labor Day $51–$61 S; $55–$67 D; from $67 effic. Extra person $5. Children under 18 stay free. Lower rates off-season. Higher rates for spec evnts/hols. Pking: Outdoor, free. Maj CC. Special rates for persons over 50.

≝ **Dover Budget Inn**, 1426 N du Pont Hwy, Dover, DE 19901; tel 302/734-4433; fax 302/734-4433. On US 13, ½ mi S of Del 1. As its name implies, this is a moderately priced highway motel, about 8 years old. **Rooms:** 69 rms and effic. CI 1pm/CO 11am. Nonsmoking rms avail. Standard rooms in good condition. **Amenities:** 🛗 A/C, satel TV w/movies. **Services:** ⇦ ⇨ **Facilities:** ⛱ Lifeguard, washer/dryer. **Rates:** HS June–Sept $42–$45 S; $47–$50 D; from $65 effic. Extra person $5. Children under 16 stay free. Lower rates off-season. Pking: Outdoor, free. Maj CC.

≝≝≝ **Sheraton Inn and Conference Center Dover**, 1570 N du Pont Hwy, Dover, DE 19901; tel 302/678-8500 or toll free 800/325-3535; fax 302/678-9073. Exit 104 off Del 1. On US 13 at Del 1. A large motel maintained to a high standard, near shopping malls and other stores in Dover's commercial and shopping area. Large public areas and extensive conference and meeting facilities. **Rooms:** 156 rms and stes. CI 2pm/CO noon. Express checkout avail. Nonsmoking rms avail. Attractive decor and good-quality furnishings. **Amenities:** 🛗 🐾 A/C, satel TV w/movies. 1 unit w/terrace, some w/Jacuzzis. **Services:** ✕ 🚗 🛋 ⇦ Car-rental desk, babysitting. **Facilities:** ⛱ 🏋 2K ⛳ 2 rsts, 2 bars (w/entertainment), lifeguard, spa, whirlpool. **Rates:** $75–$95 S; $80–$105 D; from $125 ste. Extra person $10. Children under 12 stay free. Min stay spec evnts. Higher rates for spec evnts/hols. MAP rates avail. Spec packages avail. Pking: Outdoor, free. Maj CC.

Restaurants 🍽

Captain John's Restaurant, 518 Bay Rd at jct US 13/113, Dover; tel 302/678-8166. **American.** Five cheerful, bright dining rooms in casual family restaurant. Traditional beef, chicken, and seafood entrees are reasonably priced. Large salad bar. **FYI:** Reservations accepted. Children's menu. No liquor license. **Open:** Daily 6am–10pm. Closed Dec 25. **Prices:** Main courses $5–$15; PF dinner $6–$11. Ltd CC. 🎫 ⛱

W T Smithers, 140 S State St, Dover; tel 302/674-8875. Exit US 13 at Lockerman St; turn right onto State St. **New American/Seafood.** The dining rooms in this early 19th-century house are done in green and white and have bare wood floors. Wide range of American entrees with strong international influences. Extensive salad menu. **FYI:** Reservations accepted. Band/rock. **Open:** Daily 11am–10pm. Closed Labor Day. **Prices:** Main courses $7–$20. Maj CC. ■

Attractions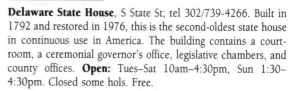

Delaware State House, S State St; tel 302/739-4266. Built in 1792 and restored in 1976, this is the second-oldest state house in continuous use in America. The building contains a courtroom, a ceremonial governor's office, legislative chambers, and county offices. **Open:** Tues–Sat 10am–4:30pm, Sun 1:30–4:30pm. Closed some hols. Free.

Delaware State Museum Complex, 316 S Governors Ave; tel 302/739-3260. Three museums are clustered here: the Meetinghouse Gallery I, formerly a Presbyterian church, built in 1790 and now the home of rotating exhibits highlighting life in Delaware; Meeting House Gallery II, a showcase for turn-of-the-century crafts; and the Johnson Victrola Museum, a tribute to Dover-born Eldridge Reeves Johnson, inventor and founder of the Victor Talking Machine Company, known today as RCA. The Johnson Museum is designed as a 1920s Victrola dealer's store, with an extensive collection of talking machines and early recordings. **Open:** Tues–Sat 10am–3:30pm. Free.

Delaware Agricultural Museum and Village, 866 N du Pont Hwy; tel 302/734-1618. Devoted to the preservation of 200 years of Delaware's agricultural heritage, this museum houses exhibitions on the poultry, dairy, and produce industries, plus harvesting and farm machinery. Other, smaller buildings in the adjacent prototype 1890s village include a 1-room schoolhouse, a gristmill, a sawmill, a blacksmith shop, and a farmhouse. **Open:** Jan–Mar, Mon–Fri 10am–4pm; Apr–Dec, Tues–Sat 10am–4pm, Sun 1–4pm. $

Sewell C Biggs Museum of American Art, 406 Federal St; tel 302/674-2111. Located in what was once the Kent County Building (circa 1858) on the 2nd and 3rd floors of what is now the Delaware State Visitors Center, this collection features paintings, silver, and furniture by American artists. **Open:** Wed–Sat 10am–4pm. Free.

John Dickinson Plantation, Kitts-Hummock Rd; tel 302/739-3277. This was the boyhood home of John Dickinson, one of Delaware's foremost statesmen of the Revolutionary period. The house is an example of Delaware plantation architecture, built around 1740 and furnished with period antiques. **Open:** Jan–Feb, Tues–Sat 10am–3:30pm; Mar–Dec, also Sun 1:30–4:30pm. Free.

Killens Pond State Park, County Rd 384; tel 302/284-4526 or 284-3412 (campgrounds). Located 13 miles south of Dover on County Rd 384, off US 13. The highlight of this park is a 66-acre scenic mill pond, a popular spot for anglers who are rewarded with largemouth bass, catfish, carp, perch, crappie, bluegills, and pickerel. Canoes, rowboats, and pedal boats can be rented during the summer months. Other recreational opportunities in the 1,040-acre park include a 25-meter outdoor pool, hiking trails, an 18-hole disc golf course, playgrounds, and picnic areas. Modern and primitive campgrounds and cabin rentals are available. **Open:** Daily 8am–sunset. $$

Dover Air Force Base, 201 18th St (Del 113); tel 302/677-3379 or 677-5938. Dover's second-largest industry and the biggest airport facility on the East Coast, this base is also the home of the 436th Air Lift Wing and the giant C-5 Galaxy airplane, one of world's largest operational aircraft. Visitors can tour the base museum, which houses a collection of vintage aircraft and artifacts that reflect the history and evolution of both the base and the USAF. **Open:** Mon–Sat 9am–3pm. Free.

FENWICK ISLAND

Map page M-3, C8 (S of Bethany Beach)

Motels 🛏

🏳 **Atlantic Budget Inn Mason-Dixon**, Ocean Hwy and Del 54, Fenwick Island, DE 19944; tel 302/539-7673 or toll free 800/432-8038. On Del 1 at Md–Del state line. Straddling the Mason-Dixon Line, this older motel has been well maintained and adheres to the standards of a small local chain. **Rooms:** 48 rms and effic. CI 3pm/CO 11am. Nonsmoking rms avail. Larger, nicer, and more expensive rooms are in the back section of the building. **Amenities:** 🛏 A/C, cable TV w/movies, refrig. Some units w/terraces. **Services:** 🍽 **Facilities:** 🔥 Lifeguard. Public beaches with lifeguards are 2 blocks away across the highway. **Rates:** HS July–Labor Day $68–$88 S or D; from $78 effic. Extra person $8. Children under 12 stay free. Min stay HS and wknds. Lower rates off-season. Higher rates for spec evnts/hols. Pking: Outdoor, free. Maj CC.

🏳🏳 **Fenwick Islander**, Del 1 and S Carolina Ave, Fenwick Island, DE 19944; tel 302/539-2333 or toll free 800/346-4520. 1 mi N of Md state line. The same families return each year to this simple, neatly kept motel. Adjacent to canal on the bay side of the island. **Rooms:** 62 rms. CI 2pm/CO 11am. Units are very basic, without cooking utensils or even coat hangers. **Amenities:** 🛏 A/C, cable TV. Some units w/terraces. Stoves and sinks. **Facilities:** 🔥 ⅙ Lifeguard, washer/dryer. Excellent ocean beach across the highway a block away. **Rates:** HS Apr–Oct $89–$104 S or D. Extra person $10. Children under 6 stay free. Min stay HS. Lower rates off-season. Higher rates for spec evnts/hols. Spec packages avail. Pking: Outdoor, free. Maj CC.

🏳🏳 **Fenwick Sea Charm**, Oceanfront and Lighthouse Rd, Fenwick Island, DE 19944; tel 302/539-9613. Turn toward beach onto Lighthouse Rd from Del 1; 1st block north of state line. A collection of simple cottages and rooms by the sea. Decor is out of the 1960s; neat and attractive. **Rooms:** 47 rms and effic. CI 2pm/CO 10am. Seven units are basic motel rooms. All others have full kitchens and dinette tables. **Amenities:** 🛏 A/C, cable TV w/movies, refrig. No phone. All units w/terraces. **Facilities:** 🔥 ⅙ 1 beach (ocean), lifeguard. Excellent beach with lifeguards in summer. Barbecue grills at each building. Adjacent to miniature golf. **Rates:** HS June 24–Aug 26 $80–$90 S or D; from $80 effic. Extra person $10. Children under 3 stay free. Min stay HS. Lower rates off-season. Pking: Outdoor, free. Ltd CC.

🏳 **Sands Motel**, Del 1 (Ocean Hwy), at Indian St, Fenwick Island, DE 19944; tel 302/539-7745. Families might otherwise pass this older motel by, but it is nicer inside than appearances from the highway would indicate. Renovation is needed, but the owner keeps the property clean. **Rooms:** 37 rms and effic. CI 2pm/CO 11am. Large rooms and apartments are decorated in 1960s browns with light wood-paneled walls. Neat, clean, and attractive, if not in the latest style. A variety of sizes from single rooms to 2-bedroom apartments. **Amenities:** 🛏 A/C, cable TV w/movies, refrig. No phone. **Services:** 🍽 🍷 **Facilities:** 🔥 Lifeguard. Excellent ocean beaches less than a block away, behind motel. **Rates:** HS June–Labor Day $62–$83 S or D; from $89 effic. Extra person $7. Children under 2 stay free. Min stay HS. Lower rates off-season. Spec packages avail. Pking: Outdoor, free. Maj CC.

Restaurants 🍽

Harpoon Hanna's, Del 54 on the Bay, Fenwick Island; tel 302/539-3095. 1 mi W of Del 1. **American/Seafood.** Dark wood and high ceilings hung with plants surround the dark blue dining room of this nice seafood house on the water. Large windows and an outdoor deck look out on the boat canal. Menu is primarily fish and shellfish, with some beef, poultry, and pasta. **FYI:** Reservations not accepted. Rock. Children's menu. **Open:** Lunch daily 11am–4pm; dinner daily 4–9pm; brunch Sun 10am–3pm. **Prices:** Main courses $8–$28. Maj CC. 🍴 🖼 🏞 ⅙

Libby's Restaurant, Ocean Hwy (Del 1) and Dagsboro St, Fenwick Island; tel 302/539-7379. **American.** Paneled walls with nautical prints characterize this family restaurant with booths in pink and gray. American family food is featured. Dinners include salad bar. Also at: Ocean Hwy, Bethany Beach (tel 302/539-4500). **FYI:** Reservations accepted. Children's menu. **Open:** HS Mem Day–Labor Day breakfast daily 7am–3pm; lunch daily 11:30am–3pm; dinner Mon–Sat 3–10pm, Sun 1pm–10. Reduced hours off-season. Closed Dec 1–mid-Feb. **Prices:** Main courses $7–$19. Ltd CC. 🍴 ♥

★ **Tom and Terry's Seafood Restaurant**, Del 54, Fenwick Island; tel 302/436-4161. 1½ mi W of Del 1. **Regional American/Seafood.** Guests can watch the sunset from large windows overlooking the bay and salt marshes at this very popular and often crowded seafood establishment. Tables have glass tops over lace cloths. The furniture is of light wood. The restaurant is an outgrowth of the adjacent seafood market, which still supplies the ingredients. Prime rib also available. **FYI:** Reservations not accepted. Children's menu. **Open:** HS May–Nov lunch daily 11:30am–4pm; dinner daily 5–10pm. Reduced hours off-season. Closed Dec 25. **Prices:** Main courses $16–$20. Ltd CC. ▲▲ ♥

Uncle Raymond's Ocean Grill Restaurant and Bar, Del 1 and Atlantic Ave, Fenwick Island; tel 302/539-1388. **American/Seafood.** This traditional, casual, and unpretentious Eastern Shore–style seafood house has colonial tables and chairs and wood-paneled walls with old beer posters. The basic American seafood menu includes steamed crabs, served at picnic tables outside on a large deck or inside in the small dining room. Some items for landlubbers available. **FYI:** Reservations accepted. Children's menu. **Open:** HS Mem Day–Labor Day daily 11am–1am. Reduced hours off-season. Closed Oct–Apr. **Prices:** Main courses $9–$17. Ltd CC. ⬛ &

Warren's Station, 1406 Ocean Hwy (Del 1), at Indian St, Fenwick Island; tel 302/539-7156. **American.** There's an informal, family atmosphere in this white-and-blue room accented with knotty pine and paintings of beach scenes. Straightforward American family fare is the order of the day. **FYI:** Reservations not accepted. Children's menu. No liquor license. **Open:** HS May–Sept breakfast daily 8am–noon; lunch daily 11am–4pm; dinner daily 4–9pm. Reduced hours off-season. Closed Oct–Apr. **Prices:** Main courses $6–$15. Ltd CC. ⬛ ♥

Attractions 💼

Fenwick Island Lighthouse, Del 54. Built in 1859 on the Transpeninsular Line and still in operation today, this is one of the Delaware shore's oldest landmarks. Its beams can be seen for 15 miles. **Open:** June–Aug, Wed 2–4pm. Free.

Nanticoke Indian Museum, intersection of Del 24 and Del 5; tel 302/945-7022. Five miles east of Millsboro, on the Indian River, this former Native American schoolhouse contains artifacts and various historical displays on the lifestyle of the Nanticoke tribe. Each September about 500 tribe members convene for 2 days of ceremonial dancing, storytelling, crafts, and food. Visitors are welcome. **Open:** May–Sept, Tues–Fri 9am–4pm, Sat 10am–4pm, Sun noon–4pm; Oct–Apr, Tues–Thurs 9am–4pm, Sat noon–4pm. $

Fenwick Island State Park, Del 1; tel 302/539-9060. Just south of Bethany Beach, the park features 3 miles of seacoast beaches and dunes as well as 344 acres of parkland and open bayfront that's ideal for fishing, crabbing, and boating. Facilities include a boardwalk, showers, changing rooms, and a snack area. Birdwatchers will find rare seabirds, such as tern, piping plover, and black skimmer, nesting in protected areas. **Open:** Daily sunrise–sunset. $$

FORT DELAWARE STATE PARK

Map page M-3, B7 (S of Wilmington)

Located on Pea Patch Island in the Delaware River; boats depart from Delaware City on the north side of the Chesapeake and Delaware Canal, off Del 9. Designated a National Historic Site, this Union fortress dates back to 1859, when it was built to protect the ports of Wilmington and Philadelphia. It also served as a prison for Confederate prisoners during the Civil War. A new living history program features costumed guides who conduct tours of the old fort and relate stories of Delaware's role in the Civil War. In addition, a 30-minute slide program details the fort's rich history, and 2 small museums feature artifacts and displays from the fort's past.

Pea Patch Island also features the largest wading bird nesting area on the east coast. Visitors can view 9 species of herons, egrets, and ibis from a scenic nature trail or an observation tower at the edge of the marsh area. Fort Delaware is open Apr–Sept, hours vary, call the park office at 302/834-7941 for more details.

FREDERICA

Map page M-3, B8

Attraction 💼

Barratt's Chapel and Museum, Del 113; tel 302/335-5544. Listed on the National Register of Historic Places and one of Delaware's most significant religious sites, the church is known as the "cradle of Methodism." An example of traditional Georgian architecture, it was erected in 1780. In 1784 Francis Asbury and Dr Thomas Coke, an emissary of John Wesley, met here and formulated plans for the organization of the Methodist Episcopal Church in America. A reconstructed 18th-century vestry has been added to the complex. **Open:** Sat–Sun 1:30–4:30pm. Free.

GEORGETOWN

Map page M-3, C8

Attraction 🖼

Treasures of the Sea Exhibit, Del 18; tel 302/856-5700. Located just west of the town and west of Del 113 at the Delaware Technical and Community College, this display presents a collection of gold, silver, and other artifacts recovered from the 1622 shipwreck of the Spanish galleon *Nuestra Señora de Atocha*. **Open:** Mon–Tues 10am–4pm, Fri noon–4pm, Sat 9am–1pm. $

GREENVILLE

Map page M-3, C7 (SW of Harrington)

Restaurant 🍴

Ashby's Clam Bar, in Greenville Center, 3801 Kennett Pike, Greenville; tel 302/655-8000. I-95 at Delaware Ave N. **American/Seafood.** High wooden ceilings and exposed beams, clerestory windows that brighten the room. Fish and shellfish prepared in a variety of regional ways. Also some steaks and burgers. Popular for lunch and dinner. **FYI:** Reservations recommended. **Open:** Daily 11:30am–1am. Closed some hols. **Prices:** Main courses $12–$20. Maj CC. 🖼 💟 ♿

Attractions 🖼

Delaware Museum of Natural History, Del 52; tel 302/658-9111. This museum houses over 100 exhibits and dioramas featuring birds, shells, and mammals as well as displays on the Great Barrier Reef, an African water hole, and Delaware's fauna. There is also a hands-on discovery room for young visitors, plus a continuous showing of nature films. **Open:** Mon–Sat 9:30am–4:30pm, Sun noon–5pm. Closed some hols. $$

Brandywine Creek State Park, Adams Dam Rd; tel 302/577-3534. Originally a dairy farm owned by the du Pont family, this 795-acre park is bisected by the Brandywine Creek and is home to a variety of flora and wildlife, including deer and an active bluebird population; hawks can be seen migrating over the valley from mid-September to mid-November. The park incorporates 12 miles of hiking trails and Delaware's first 2 nature preserves—Tulip Tree Woods, a stand of 190-year-old tulip poplar, and Freshwater Marsh, home to the elusive Muhlenberg bog turtle. **Open:** Daily 8am–sunset. $$

LEWES

Map page M-3, C8

Motels 🛏

🏨🏨 **The Beacon Motel**, 514 Savannah Rd, Lewes, DE 19958; tel 302/645-4888 or toll free 800/735-4888. Del Business 9 exit off Del 1. This bright, spacious motel enjoys a nice location between the town and the beach. **Rooms:** 66 rms. CI 3pm/CO 11am. Nonsmoking rms avail. Standard-size rooms. **Amenities:** 🛗 A/C, cable TV w/movies, refrig. All units w/terraces. **Services:** 🍽 **Facilities:** 🔲 🔳 Lifeguard. Nice rooftop pool and 2 sun decks. Adjacent deli serves breakfast and lunch. **Rates:** HS July 4–Labor Day $80–$115 S or D. Extra person $5. Children under 12 stay free. Lower rates off-season. Higher rates for spec evnts/hols. Pking: Outdoor, free. Maj CC.

🏨 **Cape Henlopen Motel**, Savannah and Anglers Rds, PO Box 243, Lewes, DE 19958; tel 302/645-2828 or toll free 800/447-3158. This roadside motel dates from 1960 but is a clean place to sleep. Anglers and outdoor-lovers should feel at home here, along with families on a tight budget. **Rooms:** 28 rms. CI 1pm/CO 11am. Rooms have shag carpet, corduroy bedspreads, deck chairs, concrete-block walls. **Amenities:** 🛗 A/C, cable TV. **Services:** 🍽 **Rates:** HS July–Aug $60–$75 S or D. Extra person $5. Min stay HS and spec evnts. Lower rates off-season. Higher rates for spec evnts/hols. Pking: Outdoor, free. Maj CC.

Inns

🏨🏨🏨 **The Inn at Canal Square**, 122 Market St, Lewes, DE 19958; tel 302/645-8499 or toll free 800/222-7902; fax 302/645-7083. Exit Del 1 at Savannah St, then left at 2nd St. Modern yet traditional hotel on the canal in town. Pleasant lobby. **Rooms:** 22 rms and stes; 1 ctge/villa. CI 3pm/CO 11am. Units are attractive, with good-quality mahogany-finished furniture, nice fabrics, and framed prints. Separate 2-story, 2-bedroom houseboat with sun deck is permanently moored in marina. **Amenities:** 🛗 🔲 🍽 A/C, cable TV w/movies. Some units w/terraces. **Services:** 🍽 Babysitting. **Facilities:** 🔳 Arrangement with nearby fitness/tennis center for reduced rates. **Rates (CP):** HS June 17–Sept 29 $75–$125 D; from $225 ctge/villa. Extra person $15. Min stay HS and wknds. Lower rates off-season. Spec packages avail. Pking: Outdoor, free. Ltd CC.

🏨🏨🏨 **The New Devon Inn**, 2nd and Market Sts, PO Box 516, Lewes, DE 19958; tel 302/645-6466 or toll free 800/824-8754; fax 302/645-7196. Exit Del 1 at Savannah Rd, then left on 2nd St. On the National Register of Historic Places, this 1926 hotel has been carefully updated with modern facilities while maintaining pedestal sinks and other historically accurate furnishings. Original pine floor throughout. Unsuitable for children under 12. **Rooms:** 26 rms and stes. CI 2pm/CO 11am. All rooms are individually decorated with period furniture. Sizes range from small to large, and there's 1 spacious suite. **Amenities:** 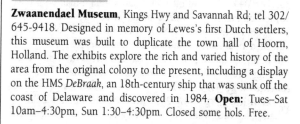 A/C. TVs on request. **Services:** Twice-daily maid svce. **Facilities:** 1 rst, 1 bar, guest lounge w/TV. An art gallery and 5 shops are downstairs. **Rates:** HS May 27–Oct 10 $95–$105 D; from $145 ste. Extra person $10. Min stay HS and wknds. Lower rates off-season. Spec packages avail. Pking: Outdoor, free. Ltd CC. Bicycle-tour packages in conjunction with other historic inns.

Restaurants

Gilligan's, 134 Market St, Lewes; tel 302/645-7866. Exit Del 1 at Savannah Ave; turn left on 2nd St, then right on Market St. **Caribbean.** A waterfront room with deck on the Lewes Canal enables guests to watch the boats go by. Caribbean-style entrees and pastas add to a mostly seafood menu. **FYI:** Reservations not accepted. Children's menu. Dress code. **Open:** Lunch daily 11am–3:30pm; dinner daily 5–10pm. Closed Nov–Mar. **Prices:** Main courses $13–$20. Maj CC.

Jerry's American Café, 115 2nd St, Lewes; tel 302/645-9733. Exit Del 1 at Lewes; turn left at 2nd St. **International/Seafood.** Informal but with refinement, the pleasant rooms here are decorated with interesting posters and local artwork. Several seafood specialties are augmented by meat and poultry prepared with an international flair. **FYI:** Reservations recommended. Dress code. **Open:** Breakfast Mon–Fri 7–10am, Sat 8–10:30am; lunch Mon–Sat 11am–4pm; dinner Mon–Thurs 4:30–9pm, Fri–Sat 4:30–10pm; brunch Sun 9am–2pm. Closed some hols. **Prices:** Main courses $9–$18. Maj CC.

Kupchick's Restaurant, 3 E Bay Ave, Lewes; tel 302/645-0420. Exit Del 1 at Savannah St. **American/Seafood.** An unpretentious building on the beach presents a simple, attractive formal dining room and an informal area by the bar. Both rooms serve traditional American cuisine with an emphasis on beef and seafood. Some more interesting preparations are on the dining room menu. Everything is cooked fresh, and breads and desserts are made on premises. **FYI:** Reservations recommended. Dress code. **Open:** HS Mem Day–Nov daily 4:30–9:30pm. Reduced hours off-season. Closed some hols; Jan–Feb 14. **Prices:** Main courses $6–$24. Maj CC.

★ **La Rosa Negra**, 128 2nd St, Lewes; tel 302/645-1980. Exit Del 1 at Savannah St; turn left at 2nd St. **Italian/Seafood.** Black and white with red accents and attractive table settings make a pleasant environment for Italian cuisine done in traditional and regionally specialized styles. Half-size portions available. Although it is not really accessible for the disabled, former presidential press secretary and anti-gun advocate Jim Brady dines here regularly. **FYI:** Reservations recommended. Dress code. **Open:** Lunch daily 11:30am–2:30pm; dinner daily 5–9:30pm. Closed some hols. **Prices:** Main courses $7–$16. Maj CC.

Attractions

Zwaanendael Museum, Kings Hwy and Savannah Rd; tel 302/645-9418. Designed in memory of Lewes's first Dutch settlers, this museum was built to duplicate the town hall of Hoorn, Holland. The exhibits explore the rich and varied history of the area from the original colony to the present, including a display on the HMS *DeBraak*, an 18th-century ship that was sunk off the coast of Delaware and discovered in 1984. **Open:** Tues–Sat 10am–4:30pm, Sun 1:30–4:30pm. Closed some hols. Free.

Lewes Historical Complex, 3rd and Shipcarpenter Sts; tel 302/645-7670. This cluster of buildings administered by the Lewes Historical Society includes an early plank house, a country store, and the Burton-Ingram House (circa 1789). This home, known for its fine collection of early American furniture, is constructed of hand-hewn timbers and cypress shingles; the cellar walls are made of stones and bricks once used as a ship's ballast. **Open:** July–Mar, Tues–Fri 10am–3pm, Sat 10am–12:30pm; Apr–June, Sat–Sun 1–3pm. $$

Cape Henlopen State Park, 42 Cape Henlopen Dr; tel 302/645-8983. A 2,500-acre park bordered on one side by the Atlantic and on another by Delaware Bay, popular for swimming, tennis, picnicking, hiking, bayshore crabbing, and pier fishing. A refurbished World War II observation tower (115 steps) offers some of the best coastal views for miles. **Open:** Daily 8am–sunset. $$

LITTLE CREEK

Map page M-3, B8 (E of Dover)

Restaurant

★ **Village Inn**, Del 9, Little Creek; tel 302/734-3245. 3 mi E of Dover. Exit US 13 at Del 9. **American/Seafood.** Large local clientele visits these rustic dining rooms with beamed ceilings and colonial-style furniture. Seafood, steaks, and prime rib. **FYI:** Reservations accepted. Children's menu. **Open:** Lunch Tues–Fri 11am–2pm, Sat 11am–3pm, Sun noon–3pm; dinner Tues–Fri 4:30–10pm, Sat 3–10pm, Sun noon–9:30pm. Closed some hols. **Prices:** Main courses $13–$17. Ltd CC.

NEWARK

Map page M-3, B7

Hotel 🛏

≣≣≣ **Christiana Hilton Inn**, 100 Continental Dr, Newark, DE 19713; tel 302/454-1500 or toll free 800/445-8667; fax 302/366-0448. Exit 4B off I-95. Follow Churchman's Rd (Del 58) to Continental Dr. Well equipped for business travelers and for meetings, the hotel has attractively decorated public areas furnished traditionally. **Rooms:** 266 rms and stes. Exec-level rms avail. CI 2pm/CO 11:30am. Express checkout avail. Non-smoking rms avail. Good-quality traditional furniture. **Amenities:** 🛎 💧 A/C, cable TV w/movies. **Services:** ✗ 🖙 🖾 🍸 **Facilities:** 🔟 🍽 🏊 👌 2 rsts (*see also* "Restaurants" below), 2 bars, lifeguard, whirlpool. Well-regarded restaurant, English pub-style lounge. Pool, whirlpool, and gazebo in central court-yard. **Rates:** $109 S; $119 D; from $185 ste. Children under 12 stay free. Higher rates for spec evnts/hols. MAP rates avail. Spec packages avail. Pking: Outdoor, free. Maj CC.

Motel

≣≣ **Fairfield Inn**, 65 Geoffrey Dr, Newark, DE 19713; tel 302/292-1500 or toll free 800/228-2800. Exit 4B off I-95. A Marriott-operated, budget-priced motel for business and high-way travelers, this one is a neat, clean, and friendly place to stay. **Rooms:** 135 rms. CI 3pm/CO noon. Express checkout avail. Nonsmoking rms avail. Exceptionally clean. Energy-saving lights, heating, and cooling. **Amenities:** 🛎 💧 A/C, cable TV w/movies. **Services:** 🚚 🖾 🍸 Babysitting. Fax and copying services. **Facilities:** 🔟 👌 Lifeguard. **Rates (CP):** HS May–Sept $41–$52 S; $47–$56 D. Extra person $3. Children under 16 stay free. Lower rates off-season. Pking: Outdoor, free. Maj CC. Seniors discounts and "membership" plans available.

Restaurant 🍴

Ashley's, in Christiana Hilton Inn, 100 Continental Dr, Newark; tel 302/454-1500. Exit 4B off I-95. Follow Del 58 (Churchman's Rd) to Continental Dr, turn left. **American/Seafood.** With a large chandelier in the center and comfortable, upholstered chairs at the tables, this blue-and-peach room is upscale but casual. Veal, lamb, fish, and chicken are served in appropriate sauces, both à la carte and in 3 fixed-priced specials. Very good local and regional reputation. **FYI:** Reservations recommended. **Open:** Tues–Sat 6–10pm. **Prices:** Main courses $16–$32; PF dinner $22–$28. Maj CC. 👌

Attraction 🏛

White Clay Creek State Park, 425 Wedgewood Rd; tel 302/731-1310. Formerly Walter S Carpenter Jr State Park, this 1,600-acre expanse comprises the Carpenter Recreation Area, the White Clay Creek Preserve, and Possum Hill. The park features 16 miles of hiking trails, including one path to the granite markers used to sketch the Delaware-Pennsylvania line. Anglers can fish for trout in White Clay Creek or for bass, bluegills, and crappie in Millstone and Cattail Ponds. Winter activies include cross-country skiing, ice skating, sledding, and shotgun deer hunting on a lottery system. Picnic area, disc golf, volleyball courts, primitive youth camping. **Open:** Daily 8am–sunset. $$

NEW CASTLE

Map page M-3, B7

Motels 🏨

≣≣≣ **Ramada Inn–New Castle**, I-295 and US 13, PO Box 647, New Castle, DE 19720; tel 302/658-8511 or toll free 800/272-6232; fax 302/658-3071. Exit I-295 at US 13 N. Hotel is 1 mi S of Delaware Memorial Bridge. Like many others of the chain, this motel offers nice public areas and pleasant, tradition-ally furnished rooms. **Rooms:** 131 rms and stes. CI 2pm/CO noon. Nonsmoking rms avail. **Amenities:** 🛎 💧 A/C, cable TV w/movies. Some units for long-term guests have refrigerators and coffeemakers available. **Services:** ✗ 🚚 🖾 🍸 🐾 Twice-daily maid svce, car-rental desk, babysitting. Can arrange tours to Brandywine Valley, New Castle, and 3 Little Bakers Dinner Theater. **Facilities:** 🔟 🏊 👌 1 rst, 1 bar (w/entertainment), lifeguard, games rm, lawn games, washer/dryer. Fitness center and golf courses nearby. **Rates:** $69 S; $75 D. Extra person $12. Children under 12 stay free. Min stay spec evnts. Higher rates for spec evnts/hols. Spec packages avail. Pking: Outdoor, free. Maj CC. AARP, corporate, and other discounts. Weekend packages.

≣ **Rodeway Inn**, 111 S du Pont Hwy, New Castle, DE 19720; tel 302/328-6246 or toll free 800/321-6246; fax 302/328-9493. On US 13 at Del 273, just S of Wilmington Airport. Same owner has maintained this older motel well since 1976. Several de-tached buildings are spread over a large lawn with mature trees. **Rooms:** 40 rms. CI 1pm/CO noon. Nonsmoking rms avail. **Amenities:** 🛎 A/C, cable TV w/movies. **Services:** 🚚 🍸 🐾 **Facilities:** 1 rst, 1 bar, lawn games. Adjacent restaurant owned by motel proprietor. **Rates:** HS May–Aug $45–$52 S; $49–$59 D. Extra person $5. Children under 18 stay free. Min stay spec evnts. Lower rates off-season. Higher rates for spec evnts/hols. Pking: Outdoor, free. Maj CC. AARP discount.

Restaurants 🍴

Air Transport Command, 143 N du Pont Hwy (US 13), New Castle; tel 302/328-3527. Exit Del 141E off I-95. **American.** Dine here among sandbagged walls and World War II bric-a-brac, including trucks and jeeps. Large windows look onto runway of the Wilmington airport (earphones at tables let guests listen to control tower). Music and photos from 1940s complete the mood. Hearty, simple fare with an emphasis on steak and prime rib. **FYI:** Reservations recommended. Band/dancing. Children's menu. Dress code. **Open:** Lunch Mon–Sat 11am–3pm; dinner Sun–Thurs 3–10pm, Fri–Sat 3–11pm; brunch Sun 9:30am–3pm. **Prices:** Main courses $14–$20. Maj CC. 🔟 ▵ ▾ ⅓

Lynnhaven Inn, 154 N du Pont Hwy, New Castle (New Castle County Airport); tel 302/328-2041. **American/Seafood.** Colonial furnishings in large dining rooms decorated in attractive, muted colors. Beef and seafood in traditional American style have been served here by the same owners for more than 40 years, attesting to consistent quality. Popular in area as a pleasant place to take families or friends. **FYI:** Reservations accepted. Children's menu. **Open:** Lunch Mon–Fri 11:30am–3:30pm; dinner Mon–Thurs 3:30–9:30pm, Fri 3:30–10pm, Sat 4–10pm, Sun 1–9pm. Closed Dec 25. **Prices:** Main courses $11–$25. Maj CC. ▾

Attractions 📷

Old Court House, 211 Delaware St; tel 302/323-4453. One of the oldest known surviving courthouses in the United States, it once served as Delaware's colonial capitol. Its cupola is the center of the "12-mile circle," which creates the northern boundary between Delaware and Pennsylvania. The building's contents include portraits of men important to Delaware's early history, the original speaker's chair, and excavated artifacts. **Open:** Tues–Sat 10am–3:30pm, Sun 1:30–4:30pm. Free.

George Read II House and Garden, 42 the Strand; tel 302/322-8411. Built between 1791 and 1804, the house is a fine example of federal architecture in a lovely garden setting. Features of the interior include elaborately carved woodwork, relief plasterwork, gilded fanlights, and silver door hardware. **Open:** Mar–Dec, Tues–Sat 10am–4pm, Sun noon–4pm; Jan–Feb, Sat 10am–4pm, Sun noon–4pm. $$

Amstel House, 4th and Delaware Sts; tel 302/322-2794. Dating back to the 1730s, this house is a model of 18th-century Georgian architecture. It was once the home of Nicholas Van Dyke, a state governor, and is furnished with antiques and decorative arts of the period. **Open:** Mar–Dec, Tues–Sat 11am–4pm, Sun 1–4pm; Jan–Feb, Sat 11am–4pm, Sun 1–4pm. $

Dutch House, the Green; tel 302/322-9168. One of the oldest brick houses in Delaware, it has remained almost unchanged since its construction circa 1700. The furnishings, including a hutch table, a 16th-century Dutch Bible, and a courting bench, reflect the lifestyle of New Castle's early Dutch settlers. During seasonal celebrations, the dining table is set with authentic foods and decorations. **Open:** Mar–Dec, Tues–Sat 11am–4pm, Sun 1–4pm; Jan–Feb, Sat 11am–4pm, Sun 1–4pm. $

Old Library Museum, 40 E 3rd St; tel 302/328-8215. Built in 1892, this unique hexagonal building is the home of the New Castle Historical Society and is used as a library and museum. A representative of fanciful Victorian architecture, the building is attributed to noted Philadelphia architect Frank Furness. **Open:** Mar–Dec, Thurs–Sun 1–4pm; Jan–Feb, Sat 11am–4pm, Sun 1–4pm. Free.

ODESSA

Map page M-3, B7

Attraction 📷

Historic Houses of Odessa, 2nd and Main Sts; tel 302/378-4069. In the 17th century, Odessa, north of Dover, prospered as a grain-shipping port and peach grower. Today the town is a good example of a rural American adaptation of urban Georgian architecture; its historic houses are the centerpiece of the town. Administered by the Winterthur Museum in Wilmington, the structures include the Corbit-Sharp House, a 3-story brick home dating back to 1774; the Wilson-Warner House, built in 1769; and the Brick Hotel Gallery, a Federal-style building from 1822. **Open:** Mar–Dec, Tues–Sat 10am–4pm, Sun 1–4pm. $$

REHOBOTH BEACH

Map page M-3, C8

Hotels 🏨

🏢🏢🏢 **Boardwalk Plaza**, 2 Olive Ave, at the Boardwalk, Rehoboth Beach, DE 19971; tel 302/227-7169 or toll free 800/332-3224; fax 302/227-0561. Exit 1A off Del 1. It's back to 1890s style and grace at this Victorian-inspired resort, the top place to stay at the Delaware ocean beaches. A touch of humor and appropriate lobby music help set a turn-of-the-century tone. **Rooms:** 84 rms, stes, and effic. Exec-level rms avail. CI 3pm/CO 11am. Express checkout avail. Nonsmoking rms avail. Authentic furnishings and decor throughout. **Amenities:** 🛏 🛁 📺 🍽 A/C, cable TV w/movies, refrig, bathrobes. Some units w/minibars, some w/terraces, some w/Jacuzzis. **Services:** 🍴 🛏 🚐 🖼 ⌛ Car-rental desk, social director, masseur, children's program, babysitting. The staff is exceptionally helpful. Uniformed maids keep facilities spotless and attractive. **Facilities:** 🛗 ⛳ 💯 ♿ 1 rst, 1 beach (ocean), lifeguard, whirlpool, washer/dryer. The pool, with whirlpool jets, is small for a swimming pool but large for a spa. Closed to children in evening. **Rates:** HS Mid-July to Labor Day $180–$210 S or D; from $210 ste; from $250 effic. Extra person $10. Children under 6 stay free. Min stay HS. Lower rates off-season. Higher rates for spec evnts/hols. MAP rates avail. Spec packages avail. Pking: Indoor/outdoor, free. Maj CC.

≣≣ Henlopen Hotel, 511 N Boardwalk, PO Box 16, Rehoboth Beach, DE 19971; tel 302/227-2551 or toll free 800/441-8450; fax 302/227-8147. Exit 1A off Del 1. Nicely renovated, this older hotel is directly on the boardwalk and convenient to the center of town. Views are better than at many properties in this area, and the building is quiet. **Rooms:** 93 rms. CI 3pm/CO 11am. Nonsmoking rms avail. Mini-suite units are large, with separate living and sleeping areas. **Amenities:** 🕿 ♨ 📺 A/C, cable TV. All units w/terraces. **Services:** ✗ ⌛ **Facilities:** 💯 ♿ 2 rsts, 2 bars, 1 beach (ocean), lifeguard, games rm, beauty salon. **Rates:** HS July–Labor Day $130–$185 S or D. Extra person $10. Children under 18 stay free. Min stay HS. Lower rates off-season. Higher rates for spec evnts/hols. Pking: Indoor, free. Maj CC.

Motels

≣≣ Admiral Motel, 2 Baltimore Ave, Rehoboth Beach, DE 19971; tel 302/227-2103 or toll free 800/428-2424; fax 302/227-3620. Exit 1A off Del 1. While not on the beach, this comfortable motel is very close to the breakers, a block from downtown, and 60 feet from the boardwalk. **Rooms:** 73 rms. CI 3pm/CO 11am. Nonsmoking rms avail. Upper-floor rooms have ocean views over rooftops. **Amenities:** 🕿 ♨ A/C, cable TV w/movies, refrig. Some units w/Jacuzzis. **Facilities:** 💯 Lifeguard. Nice outdoor pool with adjacent sun deck and outdoor spa. **Rates:** HS July 15–Labor Day $92–$113 S or D. Extra person $10. Children under 11 stay free. Min stay HS. Lower rates off-season. Higher rates for spec evnts/hols. Spec packages avail. Pking: Indoor/outdoor, free. Maj CC.

≣ Atlantic Sands Hotel, 101 N Boardwalk, Rehoboth Beach, DE 19971; tel 302/227-2511 or toll free 800/422-0600; fax 302/227-9476. Exit 1A off Del 1. An excellent location on the boardwalk is the attraction at this motel, whose lobby is more impressive than its rooms. Some maintenance and refurbishing was needed at time of inspection. **Rooms:** 114 rms and effic. CI 3pm/CO 11am. Nonsmoking rms avail. Deluxe rooms are just somewhat larger than standard units. Units are classified as oceanfront, ocean view, and side. **Amenities:** 🕿 A/C, cable TV w/movies, refrig. Some units w/terraces, some w/Jacuzzis. Deluxe rooms have hair dryers, coffeemakers, and sink. **Services:** 🖼 ⌛ **Facilities:** 💯 ⛳ 200 1 rst, 1 beach (ocean), lifeguard, games rm, whirlpool, playground. Welcoming pool and sun deck overlook the ocean. Also hot tub and gas grills. Rooftop has sun deck. **Rates:** HS July–Sept $119–$198 S or D; from $168 effic. Extra person $10. Children under 12 stay free. Min stay HS and wknds. Lower rates off-season. Higher rates for spec evnts/hols. Pking: Outdoor, free. Maj CC.

≣≣≣ Brighton Suites Hotel, 34 Wilmington Ave, Rehoboth Beach, DE 19971; tel 302/227-5780 or toll free 800/227-5788; fax 302/227-6815. Exit 1A off Del 1. A modern, attractive motel near the boardwalk and center of town, this establishment is well planned for families. Central hallways open to an attractive, multi-floor atrium. **Rooms:** 66 stes. CI 3pm/CO 11am. Non-smoking rms avail. All rooms are suite-size, with sleep sofas suitable for children. Suites for the disabled are equipped with Murphy beds. **Amenities:** 🕿 ♨ 🍷 A/C, cable TV w/movies, refrig, in-rm safe. All units w/terraces. 2 TVs, wet bars. **Services:** 🚐 ⌛ Children's program, babysitting. **Facilities:** 💯 ⛳ 250 ♿ 2 rsts, lifeguard. Attractive, small indoor pool and large sun deck, whose roof and walls open in warm weather. Very good facilities for the disabled, including ramp to pool. **Rates:** HS July 4–Aug 27 from $149 ste. Extra person $10. Children under 16 stay free. Min stay HS and wknds. Lower rates off-season. Higher rates for spec evnts/hols. MAP rates avail. Spec packages avail. Pking: Indoor, free. Maj CC.

≣≣ Oceanus Motel, 6 2nd St, PO Box 324, Rehoboth Beach, DE 19971; tel 302/227-9436 or toll free 800/852-5011. Exit 1A off Del 1. Turn right at 1st traffic light. This mid-rise motel is arranged around an L-shaped outdoor pool on the street side. **Rooms:** 38 rms. CI 3pm/CO noon. Nonsmoking rms avail. Attractive, bright rooms are decorated in pastels. Small, basic bathrooms. All king rooms have sleep sofas. **Amenities:** 🕿 A/C, cable TV w/movies, refrig. Microwaves in king rooms. **Services:** ⌛ **Facilities:** 💯 Lifeguard. **Rates (CP):** HS June 10–Sept 1 $69–$119 S or D. Extra person $7. Children under 11 stay free. Min stay HS. Lower rates off-season. Spec packages avail. Pking: Outdoor, free. Ltd CC.

≣≣ Sandcastle Motel, 123 2nd St, Rehoboth Beach, DE 19971; tel 302/227-0400 or toll free 800/372-2112. Exit 1A off Del 1. Turn left at first traffic light. This simple, well-kept motel, convenient to the center of town, has a monochromatic blue-gray color scheme. **Rooms:** 62 rms. CI 3pm/CO 11am. **Amenities:** 🕿 ♨ 🍷 A/C, cable TV w/movies, refrig, in-rm safe. All units w/terraces. Wet bar in each room. **Services:** ⌛

Facilities: 🏋 🎿 Lifeguard, sauna. Small indoor pool but large sun deck. Parking garage. **Rates:** HS July–Aug $59–$115 S or D. Extra person $7. Children under 11 stay free. Min stay HS and wknds. Lower rates off-season. Higher rates for spec evnts/hols. Spec packages avail. Pking: Indoor, free. Maj CC.

Restaurants 🍽

Ann Marie's Italian and Seafood Restaurant, 208 2nd St, at Wilmington Ave, Rehoboth Beach; tel 302/227-9902. Exit 1A off Del 1. Turn right at 2nd St. **Italian/Seafood.** Attractive, almost Victorian decor is found at this restaurant with both tables and booths. Formality varies from room to room; some have glass-covered tablecloths, others vinyl. Homemade Italian cuisine and American-style seafood are the mainstays. The Victorian-style Taylor's Seashore Restaurant adjacent is under the same management. **FYI:** Reservations recommended. Children's menu. **Open:** HS Late May–Sept daily 4–11pm. Reduced hours off-season. Closed Nov–Mar. **Prices:** Main courses $8–$16. Maj CC. 💟

Blue Moon, 35 Baltimore Ave, Rehoboth Beach; tel 302/227-6515. Exit 1A off Del 1. **New American.** Floral prints and colorful artwork by local and international artists are the highlight at this establishment. The floor of the outdoor patio is redesigned by local painters each year. Cuisine is "aggressively American" with international and ethnic influences. **FYI:** Reservations recommended. No smoking. **Open:** HS Apr–Oct dinner daily 6–11pm; brunch Sun 11am–2pm. Reduced hours off-season. Closed some hols; Dec–Jan. **Prices:** Main courses $16–$26. Maj CC. 💟 🍷 🎴 💟

Chez la Mer, 210 2nd St, Rehoboth Beach; tel 302/227-6494. Exit 1A off Del 1. **Continental/Seafood.** Diners can choose a country French room, an informal front porch, or a rooftop deck at this old house. *Wine Spectator* award–winning wine list complements a continental menu that stresses fresh seafood. All stocks, soups, salad dressings, and desserts are made on site. Chef will accommodate special dietary requirements. **FYI:** Reservations accepted. Dress code. **Open:** HS May–Sept Sun–Thurs 5:30–10pm, Fri–Sat 5:30–10:30pm. Reduced hours off-season. Closed Thanksgiving; Dec–Mar. **Prices:** Main courses $15–$28. Maj CC. 💟 🍷 🎴 💟

The Club Potpourri Restaurant and Lounge, 316 Rehoboth Ave, Rehoboth Beach; tel 302/227-4227. Exit 1A off Del 1. Located 1 block past State Rd. **Eclectic/Seafood.** Hanging lanterns, green plants, and wicker in the dining room, along with skylights and comfortable bar seating make this a pleasant, popular spot. An eclectic, international collection of seafood, beef, and fowl is supplemented by a half-dozen dinner specials

served 5–7pm and ranging from $10 to $14. **FYI:** Reservations recommended. Jazz. Children's menu. Dress code. **Open:** HS Mar–Oct daily 5–10pm. Reduced hours off-season. Closed some hols; Dec 10–26. **Prices:** Main courses $16–$22. Maj CC. 💟 💟

Dream Café, 26 Baltimore Ave, Rehoboth Beach; tel 302/226-2233. Located 1 block north of Rehoboth Ave and 1 block west of the Boardwalk. **Cafe/Coffeehouse/Deli.** Simple wooden tables and chairs and a fine old Steinway upright piano punctuate this concrete-block basement opened to the light with greenhouse windows. Quiche, pastas, salads, brie, and other light, contemporary fare are featured, along with fresh-baked breads, croissants, and bagels. Herbal teas, espresso available. **FYI:** Reservations not accepted. Children's menu. No liquor license. No smoking. **Open:** HS Mem Day–Labor Day daily 7am–11pm. Reduced hours off-season. Closed some hols. **Prices:** Lunch main courses $4–$7. Maj CC.

Grotto Pizza, 36 Rehoboth Ave, Rehoboth Beach; tel 302/227-4571. Exit 1A off Del 1. **Italian/Pizza.** Two floors of dining rooms done in bright red and white come with comfortably padded chairs and a friendly staff. The place is best known for its pies, which are hand-tossed in a display kitchen so customers can watch, but other Italian meals are also available. This original location has grown into a regional chain; additional locations in Delaware and Pennsylvania. **FYI:** Reservations not accepted. Children's menu. **Open:** HS May 1–Oct 15 daily 11am–2:30am. Reduced hours off-season. Closed some hols. **Prices:** Main courses $5–$6. Maj CC. 🅿 🚗 💟 ♿

La La Land, 22 Wilmington Ave, Rehoboth Beach; tel 302/227-3887. Exit Del 1 at Rehoboth Ave; turn right on 1st St, then left onto Wilmington Ave. **International.** New Age hits the beach here, with splashes of color and stars everywhere in a tasteful, playful combination. Bamboo surrounds an attractive patio. "International combinations" best describes the cuisine, such as Cajun-spiced mahimahi with corn salsa and guacamole. Excellent wine list. **FYI:** Reservations accepted. Dress code. **Open:** HS June–Aug lunch daily 11:30am–3pm; dinner daily 6–11:30pm. Reduced hours off-season. Closed some hols; Nov–Mar. **Prices:** Main courses $18–$24. Ltd CC. 💟 🍷

The Lamp Post Restaurant, Del 1 at Del 24, Rehoboth Beach; tel 302/645-9132. **American.** A split personality here: one dining room is set with tablecloths for dinner, while an informal room with hatch-cover tables is open for all meals. Menu features "take the family out to dinner" fare—meat, fish, and chicken in traditional American styles. **FYI:** Reservations not accepted. Children's menu. **Open:** HS Mem Day–Sept breakfast daily 7am–noon; lunch daily 11:30am–4pm; dinner Sun–Thurs 4–9:30pm, Fri–Sat 4–10pm. Reduced hours off-season. Closed Dec 25. **Prices:** Main courses $9–$17. Maj CC. 🎴 💟

Obie's by the Sea, on the Boardwalk at Olive Ave, Rehoboth Beach; tel 302/227-6261. Exit 1A off Del 1. **Barbecue/Burgers/Seafood.** An informal, youthful place with high beamed ceilings and roll-up windows opening to the outdoors. A deck is adjacent to the boardwalk. Burgers, barbecue, and light seafood meals are aimed at beachgoers on the go. Menu is on the place mat. Good spot for lunch or a quick supper. **FYI:** Reservations not accepted. Children's menu. **Open:** HS May–Columbus Day daily 11:30am–1am. Reduced hours off-season. Closed Columbus Day–Apr. **Prices:** Main courses $9–$14. Maj CC. 🍴 🏞 👪

Oscar's Seafood House, 247 Rehoboth Ave, at Christian St, Rehoboth Beach; tel 302/227-0789. Exit Del 1 at Rehoboth Ave. **American/Seafood.** Formerly known as Cafe on the Green but still under the same family's management, this seafood house is light and casual, thanks to pastels, mirrors, green plants, and varnished oak tables. Seafood is primary draw, but some meat, poultry, and pasta too. **FYI:** Reservations accepted. Children's menu. Dress code. **Open:** HS Mem Day–Labor Day breakfast daily 8–11am; lunch daily 11am–5pm; dinner daily 4–10:30pm. Reduced hours off-season. Closed some hols; Nov–Feb. **Prices:** Main courses $14–$18. Maj CC. 🍴 👪 💟

Pierre's Pantry, 1st St at Wilmington Ave, Rehoboth Beach; tel 302/227-7537. Exit 1A off Del 1. Turn right onto 1st St. **Cafe/Deli.** This bright, street-front gourmet deli/cafe with oak-and-glass tables offers a wide range of carryout snacks, including specialty sandwiches and soups, plus interesting light entrees featuring fresh ingredients. Also sells a variety of bagels and vegetarian items. **FYI:** Reservations not accepted. No liquor license. No smoking. **Open:** HS Mem Day–Labor Day daily 7am–9pm. Reduced hours off-season. Closed Dec 25. **Prices:** Main courses $6–$14. No CC. ♿

★ **Royal Treat**, 4 Wilmington Ave, Rehoboth Beach; tel 302/227-6277. Exit 1A off Del 1. **Ice cream/Breakfast.** This old house has a homey and friendly setting and is a popular place for breakfast, which, other than ice cream, is the only food served. Breakfast is along traditional American lines; the old-fashioned ice cream parlor dishes up real shakes and sundaes. **FYI:** Reservations not accepted. No liquor license. No smoking. **Open:** HS Mem Day–Labor Day daily 8am–11:30pm. Reduced hours off-season. Closed Labor Day–Mother's Day. **Prices:** Lunch main courses $4–$7. No CC. 👪

Sea Horse Restaurant, 330 Rehoboth Ave, at State Rd, Rehoboth Beach; tel 302/227-7451. Exit 1B off Del 1. **American/Seafood.** A saltwater aquarium at the entrance, a big fireplace, and subdued mauve color scheme are accompanied by classical background music. Known for seafood, with fresh items depending on the daily catch. Some nonseafood dishes available. Friday night seafood buffet all year, but no brunch buffet in July

and August. Dinner theater runs all year in a separate room (admission $23–$27). **FYI:** Reservations recommended. Children's menu. Dress code. **Open:** HS Mem Day–Labor Day lunch daily 11:30am–4pm; dinner daily 4–10pm; brunch Sun 10am–2pm. Reduced hours off-season. **Prices:** Main courses $13–$19. Maj CC. 🍴 💟 ♿

Sidney's Side Street—A Restaurant and Blues Place, 25 Christian St, Rehoboth Beach; tel 302/227-1339. Exit 1A off Del 1. Turn right at Christian St. **Cajun/Creole.** Pleasant, informal rooms in pastels with an impressive collection of glossy black-and-white movie stills. The specialty is Cajun and Creole cuisines, and a "grazing" menu permits sampling smaller portions of several dishes or satisfies small appetites. Even a "flight tasting" wine sampler is available. Blues and jazz musicians perform beginning at 9:30pm from Friday to Wednesday during summer, Friday and Saturday in the off season. **FYI:** Reservations recommended. Blues. **Open:** HS Mem Day–Labor Day dinner daily 5:30–10pm; brunch Sun 11am–2pm. Reduced hours off-season. Closed some hols. **Prices:** Main courses $14–$20; PF dinner $28.50. Maj CC. 🍴 💟

Summer House Restaurant and Saloon, 228 Rehoboth Ave, Rehoboth Beach; tel 302/227-3895. Exit 1A off Del 1. **American/Seafood.** Hanging ferns, green wallpaper, and bleached-oak tables give informality to this establishment offering a selection of beef and seafood in classic styles. **FYI:** Reservations accepted. Dancing/rock. Children's menu. Dress code. **Open:** HS Apr 15–Oct 1 daily 5–11pm. Reduced hours off-season. Closed some hols; Oct 1–Apr 15. **Prices:** Main courses $13–$22. Maj CC. 💟

Attractions 💼

Rehoboth Railroad Station Visitors Center, 501 Rehoboth Ave (Lighthouse Island Park); tel 302/227-2233. Erected in 1879 when there was regular train service to Rehoboth Beach, this station is an example of late Victorian style and ornamentation. Service came to an end in the late 1920s, and today this restored building serves as the visitors center for the chamber of commerce. **Open:** Mon–Fri 9am–5pm, Sat 10am–1pm; Mem Day–Labor Day also Sun 10am–1pm. Free.

Anna Hazzard Museum, 17 Christian St; tel 302/227-7819. Named for a former owner and civic leader, this house is one of the original "tent" buildings erected during Rehoboth's camp-meeting era. This is a good place to gain a perspective on Rehoboth and its early days. **Open:** Year-round, by appointment. Free.

Delaware Seashore State Park, Inlet 850, Del 1; tel 302/227-2800. Ten-mile-long beachland, located 2 miles south of

Rehoboth Beach, offers both the crashing surf of the Atlantic and the gentle waters of Rehoboth Bay. Facilities include lifeguard-supervised swimming, surfing, and fishing. Full-service boat marina, bayshore campground. **Open:** Daily 8am–sunset. $$

SEAFORD

Map page M-3, C7

Attraction 📼

Trapp Pond State Park, Del 13; tel 302/875-5153. Just over 10 miles southeast of Seaford is a 966-acre inland expanse rich in freshwater wetlands. This is also the northernmost natural stand of bald-cypress trees in the country. From a variety of hiking trails throughout the park, visitors can observe native animal species; flowering plants; and birds, including blue herons, owls, hummingbirds, warblers, bald eagles, and pileated woodpeckers. Guarded beach, water sports, picnic and camping sites. **Open:** Daily 8am–sunset. $$

SMYRNA

Map page M-3, B7

Restaurant 🍽️

Boon Docks Restaurant, Bayview Rd (Rd 82), Smyrna; tel 302/653-6962. Exit US 13 at Del 6 E, go 2½ miles to Bayview Rd, turn left; between Del 6 and Del 9. **Seafood/Steak.** Formerly a hunting lodge, this informal crab house is appropriately named, since it's off the beaten path. Rustic decor inside and a crab deck with picnic tables outside. Reasonably priced fish, shellfish, and beef in traditional Eastern Shore and Cajun styles. Bar offers drinks with names like Swampwater. **FYI:** Reservations not accepted. Country music/dancing. Children's menu. **Open:** HS Mar–Jan daily 11am–10pm. Reduced hours off-season. Closed some hols. **Prices:** Main courses $8–$14. Ltd CC. 🅿️ 💟 ♿

Attraction 📼

Bombay Hook National Wildlife Refuge, Del 9; tel 302/653-9345 or 653-6872. 8 miles NE of Dover. 15,000-acre haven for wildlife, including over 250 species of migrating and resident birds. Created in 1937, it is one of the state's most important environmental resources and an essential link in the Great Atlantic Flyway. The site includes acres of salt marsh, swamp, freshwater pools, croplands, and woods, attracting such species as Canadian and snow geese, great egrets, black-crowned night

herons, and the bald eagle, which nests here from early December to mid-May; also found here are white-tailed deer, foxes, otters, opossums, woodchucks, and muskrats. Features of the park include auto-tour routes, walking paths, nature trails, and 30-foot observation towers. **Open:** Mon–Fri 7:30am–4pm, Sat–Sun sunrise–sunset. $$

WILMINGTON

Map page M-3, B7

Hotels 🏨

🟰🟰🟰 **Guest Quarters Suite Hotel**, 707 King St, Wilmington, DE 19801; tel 302/656-9300 or toll free 800/424-2900; fax 302/656-2459. Delaware Ave exit off I-95 to 11th St, then right on King St. Downtown hotel is arranged around an atrium; tastefully furnished. **Rooms:** 49 stes. CI 3pm/CO noon. Express checkout avail. Nonsmoking rms avail. **Amenities:** 🛁 🔥 🖥️ 🍴 A/C, cable TV, refrig. Wet bars. **Services:** ✕ VP 🖼️ ↩️ 🐕 Van shuttle for local transportation. Full buffet breakfast. Very friendly and efficient staff. **Facilities:** 🏋️ 🔟0 ♿ 1 rst, 1 bar. Health spa available nearby. Restaurant and bar are pleasant. **Rates (BB):** From $89 ste. Extra person $10. Children under 16 stay free. MAP rates avail. Spec packages avail. Pking: Outdoor, $7.50. Maj CC.

🟰🟰🟰 **Holiday Inn–Downtown**, 700 King St, at Custom House Plaza, Wilmington, DE 19801; tel 302/655-0400 or toll free 800/465-4329; fax 302/655-5488. Delaware Ave exit off I-95 to 11th St, then right on King St. This downtown motel has large public areas and extensive meeting and convention facilities. Convenient to city businesses. **Rooms:** 217 rms and stes. CI 3pm/CO noon. Express checkout avail. Nonsmoking rms avail. Comfortable rooms are traditionally furnished. **Amenities:** 🛁 🔥 🖥️ 🍴 A/C, satel TV w/movies. **Services:** ✕ 🐕 🖼️ ↩️ 🐕 Babysitting. **Facilities:** 🔥 🏋️ 🔟K ♿ 1 rst, 1 bar, lifeguard, games rm, whirlpool, beauty salon, washer/dryer. Attractive indoor pool area. **Rates:** $69–$85 S or D; from $85 ste. Extra person $10. Children under 18 stay free. Min stay spec evnts. MAP rates avail. Spec packages avail. Pking: Indoor, $6. Maj CC.

🟰🟰🟰🟰🟰 **Hotel du Pont**, 11th and Market Sts, Wilmington, DE 19801 (Downtown); tel 302/594-3100 or toll free 800/441-9019; fax 302/656-2145. Exit 7 or 7A off I-95. Follow Del 52 south to hotel. An old-timer dating to 1913, now modernized and upgraded after recent 20-month shutdown and $40 million from owners EM Nemours du Pont Co, whose head offices share this 12-story Italian Renaissance–style structure. **Rooms:** 216 rms and stes. CI 3pm/CO 1pm. Express checkout avail. Nonsmoking rms avail. Newly enlarged rooms designed with input from frequent travelers; unusually efficient, in soothing colors of beige, peach, and mocha against mahogany cabinetry. His/her closets. Bathrooms of Spanish marble, with oversize tubs and separate showers. Sealed windows are a drawback for those desiring fresh air. **Amenities:** 🛏 ⚕ 🍴 A/C, cable TV w/movies, refrig, VCR, voice mail, in-rm safe, shoe polisher, bathrobes. All units w/minibars, some w/Jacuzzis. Lots of extras include bathroom slippers, dimmer switches, integrated TV/VCR in revolving cabinet for viewing from both bed and couch, voice mail in 3 languages. **Services:** 🍽 🔑 VP 🗚 ↵ Twice-daily maid svce, babysitting. Afternoon tea in elegant lounge. Laptops for rent. Town car for complimentary trips to banks and offices. **Facilities:** 🍴 400 ⅙ 4 rsts (*see also* "Restaurants" below), 2 bars (1 w/entertainment), sauna, beauty salon. Special privileges at Du Pont Country Club. New fitness center, with top-of-the-line equipment and complimentary overnight laundering of gym clothes. Two of the top restaurants in Wilmington. **Rates:** $119–$209 S or D; from $285 ste. Children under 18 stay free. Spec packages avail. Pking: Indoor/outdoor, $9. Maj CC.

📶 📶 📶 **Radisson Hotel Wilmington**, 4727 Concord Pike (US 202), Wilmington, DE 19803; tel 302/478-6000 or toll free 800/333-3333; fax 302/477-1492. Exit I-95 at US 202; hotel is 3 mi N. Formerly a Sheraton, this hotel offers very good conference facilities as well as comfortable guest rooms. Public areas are traditional, with mahogany furniture. **Rooms:** 154 rms and stes. CI 3pm/CO noon. Express checkout avail. Nonsmoking rms avail. Spacious and traditionally furnished. **Amenities:** 🛏 ⚕ A/C, cable TV w/movies. **Services:** ✕ 🚐 🗚 ↵ Babysitting. Shuttle van available for local destinations, including Amtrak station. Award-winning Sunday brunch. **Facilities:** 🍴 🍴 350 1 rst, 1 bar, washer/dryer. Pool has privacy fence. Day care nearby for small fee. **Rates:** $109–$119 S or D; from $150 ste. Children under 12 stay free. MAP rates avail. Spec packages avail. Pking: Outdoor, free. Maj CC. Many discounts available.

📶 📶 📶 **Sheraton Suites Wilmington**, 422 Delaware Ave, Wilmington, DE 19801; tel 302/654-8300 or toll free 800/325-3535; fax 302/654-6036. Exit I-95 at Delaware Ave; go south 3 blocks. This is a modern, classic hotel with marble floors at the entrance and subdued decor with an art-deco touch. **Rooms:** 230 stes. Exec-level rms avail. CI 3pm/CO noon. Express checkout avail. Nonsmoking rms avail. **Amenities:** 🛏 ⚕ 🍴 A/C, cable TV w/movies, refrig. Units have wet bars; irons and ironing boards; TVs in living room, bedroom, and bathroom. **Services:** ✕ 🚐 🗚 ↵ Babysitting. **Facilities:** 🍴 🍴 200 ⌨ ⅙ 1 rst, 1 bar (w/entertainment), lifeguard, spa, sauna, washer/dryer. Restaurant and bar in art-deco style. **Rates (MAP):** From $89 ste. Extra person $10. Children under 12 stay free. Spec packages avail. Pking: Indoor, $7. Maj CC. Weekend packages available.

📶 📶 📶 **Wilmington Hilton**, 630 Naamans Rd at I-95, Wilmington, DE 19703; tel 302/792-2700 or toll free 800/445-8667; fax 302/798-6182. A comfortable highway hotel with attractive public areas, dining room, and lounge. Friendly staff contributes to informal atmosphere. **Rooms:** 193 rms. Exec-level rms avail. CI 3pm/CO noon. Express checkout avail. Nonsmoking rms avail. Nicely furnished rooms are larger than average. **Amenities:** 🛏 ⚕ A/C, satel TV w/movies, voice mail. **Services:** ✕ 🔑 🚐 🗚 ↵ ↝ Car-rental desk, babysitting. **Facilities:** 🍴 🍴 800 ⅙ 1 rst, 1 bar (w/entertainment), lifeguard, games rm, lawn games. Pretty pool area with privacy fence and tables for light dining. **Rates:** $99–$132 S or D. Children under 18 stay free. Lower rates off-season. MAP rates avail. Spec packages avail. Pking: Outdoor, free. Maj CC.

Motels

📶 📶 📶 **Best Western Brandywine Valley Inn**, 1807 Concord Pike (US 202), Wilmington, DE 19803; tel 302/656-9436 or toll free 800/537-7772; fax 302/656-8564. Take exit for US 202 off I-95, drive north for 3 miles. An attractive property, built around a central courtyard. Well kept, with better-than-average furnishings and decor. Attractive lobby has piano, large windows, and high ceilings. **Rooms:** 95 rms, stes, and effic. CI 2pm/CO noon. Nonsmoking rms avail. Traditionally furnished. 10 have full cooking facilities. **Amenities:** 🛏 📺 A/C, refrig, voice mail. About half the units have microwaves and refrigerators. **Services:** ✕ 🗚 ↵ ↝ Courtesy van to local area. **Facilities:** 🍴 ⅙ Lifeguard. Howard Johnson restaurant adjacent. **Rates:** HS Apr–Oct $65–$79 S; $69–$85 D; from $85 ste; from $79 effic. Extra person $5. Children under 18 stay free. Min stay spec evnts. Lower rates off-season. Higher rates for spec evnts/hols. Spec packages avail. Pking: Outdoor, free. Maj CC. Many special getaway packages.

📶 📶 📶 **Courtyard by Marriott/Wilmington Downtown**, 1102 West St, Wilmington, DE 19801; tel 302/429-7600 or toll free 800/321-2211; fax 302/429-9167. Exit I-95 at Delaware Ave. A well-maintained downtown motel with pleasing traditional decor and furnishings. **Rooms:** 125 rms. CI 3pm/CO noon. Nonsmoking rms avail. Quiet, spacious rooms. **Amenities:** 🛏 ⚕ 📺 A/C, cable TV w/movies, refrig, VCR. Some units w/Jacuzzis. 18 rooms have microwaves. Iron and ironing board in each. **Services:** 🚐 🗚 ↵ **Facilities:** 🍴 30 1 rst, 1 bar. **Rates:** HS Sept–June $99 S; $109 D. Extra person $10. Lower rates off-season. Pking: Indoor, $7.50. Maj CC. AARP and government discounts.

📶 **Tally Ho Motor Lodge**, 5209 Concord Pike (US 202), Wilmington, DE 19803; tel 302/478-0300 or toll free 800/445-0852; fax 302/478-2401. Exit I-95 at US 202; motel is 4½ mi N. A standard motel in reasonably good condition. Several restaurants and shops nearby. **Rooms:** 100 rms. CI noon/CO noon. Nonsmoking rms avail. Average rooms with parking in front of each. **Amenities:** 🛏 A/C, cable TV w/movies. **Services:** 🚗 ⤵ ⟳ Car-rental desk. **Facilities:** 🗔 Washer/dryer. **Rates (CP):** HS Mar–Nov $38 S; $42 D. Extra person $5. Children under 12 stay free. Lower rates off-season. Higher rates for spec evnts/hols. Spec packages avail. Pking: Outdoor, free. Ltd CC.

Restaurants 🍴

⭐ **Brandywine Room**, in Hotel du Pont, 11th and Market Sts, Wilmington (Downtown); tel 302/594-3100. Exit 7A or 7 off I-95. Follow Del 52 south to hotel. **American.** More casual than the du Pont's Green Room, but just as serious about fresh ingredients and courteous service. The 3 connecting rooms date from the hotel's debut in 1913; 2 have high ceilings and wood paneling, one has cozy booths, and all are graced with Wyeth paintings. The menu features breaded oysters with black pepper and balsamic sauce; curried scallops; crab and shrimp with pineapple; and grilled porterhouse steak with garlic and wild mushroom sauce. **FYI:** Reservations recommended. Children's menu. Dress code. No smoking. **Open:** Sun–Thurs 6–11pm. **Prices:** Main courses $19.50–$26.50. Maj CC. 🍴 VP 🔥

⭐ **Columbus Inn**, 2216 Pennsylvania Ave, Wilmington; tel 302/571-1492. Exit I-95 at Del 52. **American.** The interior reflects the history of this building, which was the early 18th-century tollgate to the Kennet Pike. Decor includes a large collection of paintings by Frank Jefferies, noted local artist. Traditional and regional American cuisine is on tap, as is an award-winning wine list. **FYI:** Reservations recommended. Piano. Children's menu. Jacket required. **Open:** HS Sept–May lunch Mon–Fri 11:30am–3pm; dinner Mon–Sat 5pm–midnight; brunch Sun 11am–3pm. Reduced hours off-season. Closed some hols. **Prices:** Main courses $15–$22; PF dinner $14.92. Maj CC. 🍴🖼💟🔥

Constantinou's House of Beef and Seafood, 1616 Delaware Ave, Wilmington; tel 302/652-0655. Exit I-95 at Delaware Ave N; go 6 blocks. **Seafood/Steak.** Dark paneled rooms are furnished with antiques, including chandeliers, moldings, and mirrors from various old hotels, theaters, and homes. Variety of fish and shellfish dishes, and award-winning steaks are grilled in the dining room. **FYI:** Reservations recommended. Children's menu. Dress code. **Open:** Lunch Mon–Fri 11am–4pm; dinner daily 4–7pm. Closed some hols. **Prices:** Main courses $15–$40. Maj CC. 🍴💟

Feby's Fishery, 3701 Lancaster Pike, Wilmington; tel 302/998-9501. Exit I-95 at Del 141 N; turn right onto Del 48.

Seafood. In an informal, nautical room with varnished wood tables, a racing powerboat hangs on the wall. Good local reputation for fresh seafood, which is prepared broiled, fried, or Italian-style, plus steaks. **FYI:** Reservations recommended. Children's menu. Dress code. **Open:** Lunch Mon–Fri 11am–4pm; dinner Mon–Thurs 4–9pm, Fri–Sat 4–10pm. Closed some hols. **Prices:** Main courses $15–$20. Maj CC. 💟🔥

The Garden Restaurant and Tea Room, in the Henry du Pont Winterthur Museum, Del 52, Wilmington; tel 302/888-4826. 5 mi N of Wilmington. Delaware Ave exit off I-95. **American.** Set in the park-like Winterthur estate, this open and airy space looks out on great natural beauty at all times of the year. A variety of light American entrees and an Oriental stir-fry are offered. Limited wine selection but excellent champagne. Appealing desserts. Elegant afternoon tea is popular. **FYI:** Reservations recommended. Dress code. No smoking. **Open:** Lunch Tues–Fri 11:30am–4:30pm, Sun 3–4:30pm; brunch Sun 10am–1:30pm. Closed some hols. **Prices:** Lunch main courses $10–$13. Maj CC. 🏞 🔥

Govatos Restaurant and Homemade Candies, 800 Market Street Mall, Wilmington; tel 302/652-4082. Exit I-95 at Delaware Ave; turn right on King St, then right on 8th St. **American/Italian/Candies.** With both charm and history, this candy shop and restaurant celebrated its 100th anniversary in 1994. A variety of traditional American and Italian entrees is offered for lunch, plus an excellent assortment of candies, including nirvana-inducing chocolates. Adjacent Govatos Tavern has the same menu. **FYI:** Reservations not accepted. Beer and wine only. **Open:** Breakfast Mon–Sat 8–11am; lunch Mon–Sat 11am–3:30pm. Closed some hols. **Prices:** Lunch main courses $5–$7. No CC.

🌱 **Green Room**, in Hotel du Pont, 11th and Market Sts, Wilmington (Downtown); tel 302/594-3100. Exit 7A or 7 off I-95. Follow Del 52 S to hotel. **Continental/French.** Gracious old-time setting, polite and responsive service, first-rate cuisine. The handsome Edwardian room has a carved wood ceiling, a minstrel gallery, and wood-paneled walls hung with paintings by the Wyeth family. Specialties include lump crabmeat and shrimp mousse served with a champagne-mustard sauce; saddle of rabbit with sun-dried cherries; and grilled swordfish with a fennel sorrel sauce. **FYI:** Reservations recommended. Harp. Jacket required. No smoking. **Open:** Breakfast Mon–Fri 7–10:30am, Sat 7–11am, Sun 7–9am; lunch Mon–Sat 11:30am–2pm; dinner Fri–Sat 6–10pm; brunch Sun 10am–2pm. **Prices:** Main courses $18.75–$28.50. Maj CC. 🌱 🍴 💟 VP 🔥

Griglia Toscana, in the Rockford Shops, 1412 N Dupont St, Wilmington (West End); tel 302/654-8001. Exit 7 or 7B off I-95. Go west on Delaware Ave, bear right at fork, go 5 blocks to N

Dupont St, turn left. **Italian.** Unpretentious and casual, located in a small shopping center near Trolley Square. Tuscan and other northern Italian specialties, including a variety of pastas. Meat and fish prepared on a grill visible from dining room. Pizzas baked in wood-fired oven. Noted Italian wine list. Toscana to Go in same shopping center (302/655-8600). **FYI:** Reservations recommended. Dress code. **Open:** Lunch Mon–Fri 11:30am–2pm; dinner daily 5:30–10pm. Closed some hols. **Prices:** Main courses $10–$21. Maj CC. &

Kid Shelleen's, 1801 W 14th St, at Scott St, Wilmington; tel 302/658-4600. Exit I-95 at Del 52 N; turn right at Pennsylvania Ave, then right on Scott St. **Regional American.** Western-movie decor sets the scene at this restaurant named after the character played by Lee Marvin in *Cat Ballou*. Exceptional mural in banquet room. Pleasant patio for outdoor dining. American dishes with a flair, some with California influence, but this is Delaware-style, not a West Coast fern restaurant. A popular, busy place. **FYI:** Reservations accepted. Children's menu. Dress code. **Open:** Mon–Sat 11am–midnight, Sun 10am–3pm. Closed some hols. **Prices:** Main courses $5–$15. Maj CC. ▲

Ristorante Carucci, in Wawaset Plaza, 504–506 Greenhill Ave, Wilmington; tel 302/654-2333. Exit 7 or 7B off I-95. Turn right on Delaware Ave; bear left on Pennsylvania Ave; turn left on Greenhill Ave. **Italian.** A fun restaurant, this simple, black-and-white room has splashes of colorful art, but nothing that distracts from the music provided by the opera-singing wait staff (some of whom have won competitions). Seafood, beef, and lamb grilled in northern Italian style, plus pasta dishes. The trio wine tasting is a great value. **FYI:** Reservations recommended. Piano/singer. Dress code. No smoking. **Open:** Lunch Mon–Fri 11:30am–2:30pm; dinner Mon–Sat 5:30pm–midnight. Closed Dec 25. **Prices:** Main courses $14–$24. Maj CC. &

Sal's Petite Marmite, 603 N Lincoln St, Wilmington (Little Italy); tel 302/652-1200. Exit 7 or 7B off I-95. **French.** This French restaurant, incongruously located in Little Italy, is in an old building decorated in classic dark colors and furnished simply but comfortably. Winner of many awards for fine French cuisine. **FYI:** Reservations recommended. Dress code. **Open:** Lunch Mon–Fri 11:30am–2pm; dinner Mon–Sat 5–10pm. Closed some hols. **Prices:** Main courses $17–$28; PF dinner $35–$45. Maj CC. ♥ ▲

The Shipley Grill, 913 Shipley St, Wilmington; tel 302/652-7797. Exit I-95 at Delaware Ave; turn right on Shipley St. **American/Seafood.** Dark paneling and well-worn traditional booths and tables are set with good linen and china in a comfortable, casual fashion. American-style steak and seafood are offered. Bar area adjacent to dining room is popular after-theater spot. **FYI:** Reservations recommended. Dress code.

Open: HS Oct–Mar lunch Mon–Fri 11am–3pm; dinner daily 5:30–10pm. Reduced hours off-season. Closed some hols. **Prices:** Main courses $13–$22. Maj CC.

The Silk Purse and Sow's Ear, 1307 N Scott St, Wilmington; tel 302/654-7666. Exit 7 or 7B off I-95. Follow Delaware Ave west to Del 52, turn right on N Scott St. **New American.** The Silk Purse downstairs is more formal than the whimsical Sow's Ear upstairs, which has mirrored walls and a tasteful, attractive decor. Light, creative treatment of fresh seafood, beef, and lamb in a fusion of continental and American styles. It's very easy to miss this inconspicuous building. **FYI:** Reservations accepted. Dress code. **Open:** Tues–Thurs 5:30–9:30pm, Fri–Sat 5:30–10pm. Closed some hols. **Prices:** Main courses $14–$24. Maj CC. ♥ &

Temptations, in Trolley Sq Shopping Center, Delaware Ave and Dupont St, Wilmington; tel 302/429-9162. Exit I-95 at Delaware Ave N; go 6 blocks. **Cafe/Ice cream.** A simple, old-fashioned interior in subdued reds and pinks has tables and a large ice cream bar. Sandwiches, salads, and other light lunches. Sundaes and other ice cream specialties are impressive. Also at: 2900 Concord Pike, at Brandywine Square, Wilmington (tel 302/478-9094). **FYI:** Reservations accepted. No liquor license. **Open:** HS Apr–Sept Mon–Thurs 10am–10pm, Fri–Sat 10am–11pm, Sun noon–5pm. Reduced hours off-season. Closed some hols. **Prices:** Lunch main courses $3–$6. Maj CC. ▩

Terrace at Greenhill, at Ed Oliver Golf Course, 800 N Du Pont Rd, Wilmington (Greenville); tel 302/575-1990. Exit I-95 at Delaware Ave N. **Regional American.** Both the simple, green-and-pastel room and the outdoor terrace enjoy fine view of the golf course and of Wilmington, especially impressive at night. Emphasis on regional seafood, but other American entrees available. Good selection of beers from around the world. Exceptional Sunday brunch menu. **FYI:** Reservations recommended. Children's menu. Dress code. **Open:** Lunch Mon–Sat 11:30am–2:30; dinner Mon–Thurs 5–9pm, Fri–Sat 5–10pm, Sun 4–9pm; brunch Sun 10am–3pm. Closed Dec 25. **Prices:** Main courses $10–$14. Maj CC. ▲ ▧ ♥ &

Tiffin, 1210 N Market St, Wilmington; tel 302/571-1133. Exit I-95 at Delaware Ave; go east to N Market St. **New American/Californian.** Pastel shades and contemporary artworks, light wood and wicker furniture make for a casual dining room. Light treatment of fish, shellfish, poultry, and meat entrees uses sauces with an international influence, as in breast of duck with raspberry vinaigrette. Pretty central courtyard. **FYI:** Reservations recommended. Dress code. **Open:** Lunch Mon–Fri 11:30am–2:30pm; dinner Mon–Thurs 5:30–10pm, Fri–Sat 5:30–11pm. Closed some hols. **Prices:** Main courses $16–$22. Ltd CC.

Waterworks Café, 16th and French Sts, Wilmington; tel 302/ 652-6022. Exit I-95 at Delaware Ave S; turn left on French St. **American/Continental.** Large windows in this century-old waterworks building overlook the Brandywine River downtown. Pleasant outdoor deck. Mostly American seafood and beef with continental sauces. Discount with Taste of the Brandywine and Entertainment card. **FYI:** Reservations recommended. Dress code. **Open:** Lunch Tues–Fri 11:30am–2:30pm; dinner Tues– Sat 5:30–9pm. Closed some hols. **Prices:** Main courses $16– $25. Maj CC. 🍴 ⛰ ♿

Attractions 💼

Old Swedes Church, 606 Church St; tel 302/652-5629. Erected in 1698, this is one of the oldest houses of worship in the United States. The church remains in its original form and is still regularly used for religious services. The churchyard predates the church by 60 years and was used as a burying ground for early settlers of Fort Christina and its community. A nearby recon-structed farmhouse depicts the everyday life of early Swedish settlers. **Open:** Mon, Wed, Fri–Sat 1–4pm. Free.

Old Town Hall, 512 Market St; tel 302/655-7161. A museum operated by the Historical Society of Delaware, this landmark building features permanent and rotating exhibits of antique silver, furniture, and related objects. In addition, restored jail cells in the basement are open to the public. **Open:** Tues–Fri noon–4pm, Sat 10am–4pm. Free.

Willingtown Square, 505 Market St Mall; tel 302/655-7161. These 4 stately 18th-century houses were moved from other parts of the city to this site in 1975–76; they now enclose a beautiful brick courtyard. Owned by the Historical Society, the houses are not open to the public. **Open:** Daily 24 hours.

Delaware Art Museum, 2301 Kentmere Pkwy; tel 302/ 571-9590. Renowned for its collections of American art (from 1840 to the present), this museum is the home of the largest holding of works by Howard Pyle, the father of American illustration and founder of the Brandywine school of painting. Other outstanding examples of American sculpture, photogra-phy, and crafts—traditional and contemporary—are also on view, as is the largest display of English pre-Raphaelite art in the United States. **Open:** Tues–Sat 10am–5pm, Sun noon–5pm. Closed some hols. $$

Winterthur Museum and Gardens, Rt 52; tel 302/888-4600 or toll free 800/448-3883. Named after a town in Switzerland, this 9-story mansion and country estate 6 miles northwest of Wilmington was once the country home of Henry Francis du Pont. Today it is the Brandywine Valley's star attraction, ranked as one of the world's premier collections of American antiques

and decorative arts. Du Pont himself, a collector of furniture, made the initial acquisitions, and the collection grew over the years. The objects, which include Chippendale furniture, silver tankards by Paul Revere, and a dinner service made for George Washington, are displayed in over 180 period rooms.

The museum offers several types of guided tours, including a 1-hour general overview tour and a 2-hour in-depth decorative arts tour that requires reservations. Tours begin in a new pavilion known as the **Galleries,** featuring a 10-minute audiovisual program and a series of interactive exhibits that provide back-ground about the mansion.

The meticulously landscaped 980-acre grounds are planted with a variety of native and exotic plants. Access to the gardens, which can be toured via self-guided walk or tram ride (Apr–Oct), is included in the admission fee. Special seasonal events, museum store, bookshop, restaurant. **Open:** Tues–Sat 9am– 5pm, Sun noon–5pm. Closed some hols. $$$

Hagley Museum, Del 141; tel 302/658-2400. This peaceful woodland setting directly on the Brandywine River is the spot that drew French émigré Eleuthère Irénée du Pont de Nemours to establish a black powder mill here in 1802. The first of the du Pont family developments in America, this mill was the forerun-ner of the large chemical companies developed by subsequent generations. Today the 240-acre outdoor museum re-creates the lifestyle and atmosphere of the original 19th-century mill village through a series of restored buildings, displays, replicas, demon-strations, working machines, and gardens. The highlight is a building called **Eleutherian Mills,** the first (1803) du Pont home in America, a Georgian-style residence furnished to reflect 5 generations of the du Ponts. **Open:** Mar 15–Dec, daily 9:30am–4:30pm; Jan–Mar 14, Mon–Fri guided tour at 1:30pm, Sat–Sun 9:30am–4:30pm. Closed some hols. $$$

Nemours Mansion and Gardens, Rockland Rd; tel 302/ 651-6912. Another du Pont home in the Brandywine Valley is this 300-acre estate of Alfred I du Pont, a 102-room Louis XVI– style château with landscaped gardens. Built in 1909–10, Ne-mours was named after the du Pont ancestral home in north-central France. The house contains antique furnishings, Oriental rugs, tapestries, and paintings dating from the 15th century, as well as personal items—vintage automobiles, billiards equip-ment, and bowling alleys.

The gardens, which stretch almost ⅓ mile along the main promenade from the mansion, represent one of the finest examples of formal French-style gardens in America. Guided tours of the mansion and gardens take a minimum of 2 hours. Reservations are recommended; visitors must be over 16 years of age. **Open:** May–Nov, Tues–Sat tours at 9 and 11am, 1 and 3pm; Sun tours at 11am, 1 and 3pm. $$$

Rockwood Museum, 610 Shipley Rd; tel 302/761-4340 or 571-7776. Inspired by an English country house, the rural Gothic mansion was designed in 1851 for Joseph Shipley, one of the city's early merchant bankers. The house itself is furnished with a blend of 17th-, 18th-, and 19th-century decorative arts from the United States, Britain, and continental Europe; the elaborate conservatory features a brilliant array of Victorian flora. Outbuildings include a porter's lodge, gardener's cottage, carriage house, and barn. Six acres of exotic foliage and landscaping complete the grounds. **Open:** Tues–Sat 11am–4pm. Special seasonal hours; closed some hols. $$

Delaware History Museum, 504 Market St; tel 302/655-7161. This new museum, housed in a restored 1940s F W Woolworth building, focuses on the state's agriculture, water-based industries, and corporate life. Recent exhibits have included "Delaware Goes to War" and "Distinctly Delaware," exploring the multicultural background of the state. **Open:** Tues–Fri noon–4pm, Sat 10am–4pm. Closed some hols. Free.

Delaware Center for the Contemporary Arts, 103 E 16th St; tel 302/656-6466. Focuses on contemporary visual arts that reflect everyday life, including controversial and provocative issues. Exhibits include paintings, drawings, tapestries, photographs, and sculptures, by both national and local artists. Annual art auction in mid-April. **Open:** Tues–Fri 11am–5pm, Sat–Sun 1–5pm. Closed Aug and some hols. Free.

Kalmar Nyckel Foundation, 1124 E 7th St; tel 302/429-7447. Set on the shores of the Christina River, this project aims to re-create the story of the first permanent European settlement in the Delaware Valley in 1638. It comprises a museum, a working 17th-century shipyard, and a full-scale working replica of the *Kalmar Nyckel*, the ship that first sailed to this area from Sweden. **Open:** Mon–Fri 10am–4:30pm. Free.

Delaware State Arts Council, Carvel State Office Bldg, 820 N French St; tel 302/577-3540. The umbrella arts organization for Delaware has in its headquarters building 2 galleries that showcase local arts and crafts exhibits. **Open:** Mon–Fri 8am–4:30pm. Free.

Delaware Children's Museum, 601 Market St; tel 302/658-0797. Designs and presents exhibits, programs, and events that promote learning by providing children with hands-on explorations in nature, creativity, and the global community. **Open:** Tues–Sat 10am–4pm. $

Grand Opera House, 818 N Market St; tel 302/658-7897 (info) or 652-5577 (box office). Much of Wilmington's nightlife is centered around this impressive restored Victorian showplace. Built in 1871 as part of a Masonic temple, this 1,100-seat facility is one of the finest examples of cast-iron architecture in America and is listed on the National Register of Historic Places. Recognized as Delaware's Center for the Performing Arts, it is home to **OperaDelaware** and the **Delaware Symphony Orchestra**. It also offers a program of guest artists in ballet, jazz, chamber music, pop concerts, and theatrical productions. **Open:** Call for schedule. $$$$

Brandywine Zoo, 1001 N Park Dr (Brandywine Park); tel 302/571-7747. On view in Delaware's only zoo are such exotica as monkeys, llamas, a giant sloth, a Siberian tiger, and South American species of pythons, parrots, and boas. **Open:** Daily 10am–4pm. $

Bellevue State Park, 800 Carr Rd; tel 302/577-3390. Located on the northeast perimeter of the city, this 270-acre park was once the home of the William du Pont family. Recreational facilities include 2 indoor and 8 outdoor clay tennis courts; an equestrian facility with indoor and outdoor arenas; and a fishing pond stocked with bass, catfish, and sunfish. A bandshell hosts concerts and performances June–Aug. Picnic areas, garden paths, fitness trails. **Open:** Daily 8am–sunset. $$

DISTRICT OF COLUMBIA

THE SPIRIT OF AMERICA IN STONE

Washington, DC—the capital of the United States and the governmental seat of the premiere global power—is also every American's hometown. Its site was selected in 1791 by George Washington, first president of a new nation embodying revolutionary ideals of freedom and democracy— ideals based on the political principles outlined by Thomas Jefferson in the Declaration of Independence. Its monuments, memorials, and major offices of government have always evoked the spirit in which this nation was founded. The White House is one of the world's few residences of a head of state that has always welcomed visitors ("I never forget," said Franklin Delano Roosevelt, "that I live in a house owned by all the American people").

At the Capitol, topped by a 19½–foot statue of Freedom, the public can sit in on the House of Representatives or the Senate in session. And few visitors will fail to be inspired by the serene classical dignity of the Supreme Court, its pledge etched in a frieze over a Corinthian-columned entrance: "Equal Justice Under Law." Equally moving are the walls of the Lincoln Memorial, inscribed with the stirring words of the visionary president. It is fitting that another freedom-loving American, Dr Martin Luther King, Jr, chose the steps of Lincoln's shrine to proclaim "I have a dream." And the nation's most cherished documents—the Declaration of Independence, the Constitution, and the Bill of Rights—are on view in the National Archives. Washington is a federal showplace worthy of a great nation—a beautiful city of beaux-arts architecture, grand boulevards, grassy malls, monumental sculpture, and circular fountained plazas. But most importantly, it exemplifies what is finest about America.

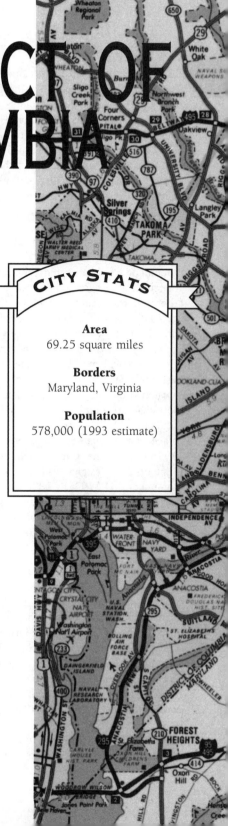

CITY STATS

Area
69.25 square miles

Borders
Maryland, Virginia

Population
578,000 (1993 estimate)

A Brief History

A CITY IS BORN   In 1783, Congress proposed that a federal city be built to house the government of the newly independent United States of America. After some wrangling about its location, New Yorker Alexander Hamilton and Virginian Thomas Jefferson worked out a compromise: The South would pay off the North's Revolutionary War debts in exchange for northern support of a southern capital. President George Washington, an experienced surveyor, selected the city's site and hired French military engineer Pierre Charles L'Enfant to lay it out.

L'Enfant's design was inspired by Paris, with broad avenues radiating from squares and circles centered on monumental fountains and sculptures. The Mall was conceived as a ceremonial avenue of embassies and other important buildings with Pennsylvania Avenue as the city's main thoroughfare. L'Enfant was a genius, and his plan (which can be seen in the Library of Congress) was magnificent, but his arrogance and impatience with politics alienated city building commissioners. In 1792 he was fired.

Though much of L'Enfant's plan would languish for more than a century, a city slowly began to rise along the Potomac. The cornerstone of the "presidential palace" (later renamed the White House) was laid in 1792, that of the Capitol building (on a hill that L'Enfant had designated "a pedestal waiting for a monument") in 1793. By 1800 Congress was installed in the Capitol (though only its first wing was completed), and President John Adams and his wife had taken up residency in the executive mansion. Then came the War of 1812.

A CITY IS BURNED   On August 24, 1814, the British fleet sailed into Chesapeake Bay, marched on the capital, and set fire to the fledgling city. Luckily, torrential rains that evening halted the flames, and a tornado, though causing some further damage the next day, daunted the British troops. Though many felt Washington was doomed (Congress came within 9 votes of abandoning it as the American capital), an editorial in the *National Intelligencer* rallied municipal pride with the admonition that moving the capital would be tantamount to "kissing the rod an enemy has wielded." Thomas Jefferson donated his own books to replace the destroyed contents of the Library of Congress, and, in 1817, the charred walls of the executive mansion were painted white—transforming it ever after into the White House.

The city got a boost in 1829, when Englishman James Smithson died, leaving a bequest of half a million dollars "to found at Washington, under the name of the Smithsonian Institution, an establishment for the increase and diffusion of knowledge." The first Smithsonian building (today the "castle" housing its information center) was erected in 1849.

THE UNION SHALL GO ON   The Civil War turned the capital into an armed camp. Churches were used as hospitals, parks became campgrounds, and attention

---

❧ *Fun Facts* ❧

- *In the early days of the federal government, ambassadors to Washington were provided with "hardship pay" in compensation for enduring the inconvenience of living there.*

- *Franklin Delano Roosevelt was the only president to be inaugurated in a ceremony held at the White House.*

- *Upon completion of his design for the city of Washington, French architect Pierre L'Enfant presented a $95,000 bill to the government for his services. Years later, Congress made a sole payment of $2,500 to him.*

- *No library in the world surpasses the Library of Congress in size. Its 2.85 million square feet of space and more than 575 miles of shelving house more than 101 million items.*

- *The presidential desk in the Oval Office, carved from the British ship* Resolute, *was presented by Queen Victoria to President Rutherford B Hayes.*

- *In 1835, President Andrew Jackson paid off the national debt. This would be the only time in the history of the United States that the federal books would be balanced.*

- *Herbert Hoover was the first US president to have a telephone on his desk.*

turned from constructing federal buildings to constructing forts. But Lincoln insisted that, in spite of everything, work on the Capitol must continue. "If people see the Capitol going on, it is a sign we intend the Union shall go on," he said. When its giant dome was completed in 1863, a 35-star flag flew overhead, and a 35-gun salute honored all the states in the Union. After the war, President Ulysses S Grant appointed the flamboyant Alexander "Boss" Shepherd to the Board of Public Works and gave him free reign to make the city a showplace. Under his administration, 100 miles of streets—among them Pennsylvania Avenue—were paved and lighted, sewers were installed, more than 50,000 trees were planted . . . and the city was saddled with over $20 million in debt.

THE CITY BEAUTIFUL   In 1900 Michigan Senator James McMillan, a retired railroad mogul with training in engineering and architecture, determined to realize L'Enfant's exalted vision for America's capital city. At his personal expense, he sent an illustrious committee —landscapist Frederick Law Olmsted, sculptor Augustus Saint-Gaudens, and noted architects Daniel Burnham and Charles McKim—to study the landscaping and architecture of Europe's great capitals. The famous words of Daniel Burnham best exemplify the committee's aims: "Make no little plans. They have no magic to stir men's blood, and probably themselves will not be realized. Make big plans, aim high in hope and work, remembering that a noble and logical diagram once recorded will never die, but long after we are gone will be a living thing, asserting itself with every growing consistency."

The committee's plans, all implemented along with L'Enfant's "noble and logical diagram," included the development of a complete park system, beautification of the Mall, the selection of sites for government buildings, and designs for the Lincoln and Jefferson Memorials, the Arlington Memorial Bridge, and a reflecting pool between the Lincoln Memorial and the Washington Monument. Several awe-inspiring buildings—the Library of Congress, the Corcoran Gallery, and Union Station (designed by Burnham)—were completed by the turn of the century. Under President William Howard Taft, the famous cherry trees (a gift from Japan) were planted in the Tidal Basin, and a National Commission of Fine Arts was created to advise on fountains, statues, and monuments. The city was

further beautified during the 1930s Depression under FDR's Works Progress Administration.

WASHINGTON TODAY   Washington in the 1990s is, architecturally and culturally, a city that all Americans can view with pride. It is a city that boasts the Smithsonian Institution, containing more than a dozen museums plus the National Zoo, and the John F Kennedy Center for the Performing Arts, a great cultural center; impressive governmental buildings and stirring monuments and memorials; and a host of delightful outdoor attractions. For the visitor, Washington offers an inimitable melange of big-city sophistication, natural beauty, political panache, and historical perspective.

A CLOSER LOOK
Geography

Situated on the northern bank of the Potomac River, Washington lies midway along the eastern seaboard of the United States, about 80 miles inland from the Atlantic Ocean. At its highest elevation, in northwest Washington, it rises 390 feet. Its lowest elevation is sea level, at the riverbank.

Climate

Lushly planted with trees, flower gardens, and verdant grounds (including many areas designed by America's foremost landscape architect, Frederick Law Olmsted),

DRIVING DISTANCES:
37 miles SW of Baltimore
106 miles NE of Richmond, VA
133 miles SW of Philadelphia
158 miles NW of Williamsburg, VA
221 miles SE of Pittsburgh
233 miles SW of New York
353 miles NE of Charleston, WV
381 miles NE of Charlotte, NC
429 miles SW of Boston
608 miles NE of Atlanta
671 miles SE of Chicago
1,057 miles NE of Miami
1,099 miles NE of New Orleans
2,825 miles NE of San Francisco

Washington enjoys a beautiful spring and fall. It's a delight to stroll the city's streets, the C&O Canal, rustic parks, monument grounds, and the Arboretum during cherry blossom season or when fall foliage is at its peak. Temperatures are moderate to cold November through March, making winter a good season for indoor museum visiting—and the same might be said of the city's humid and sultry summers.

What to Pack

Let comfort be your guide. Few cities have more museums and sightseeing attractions, and you're going to be spending entire days walking around them. If your feet hurt, those days will not be pleasant. Pack your most comfortable shoes and clothing, keeping your wardrobe especially light in summer. You might, however, carry a sweater even in hot weather; interior spaces are often frigidly air conditioned. In winter, you'll need a hat, coat (a down jacket is lightest and easiest to pack and carry), and boots. And any season, a fold-up umbrella is a good idea.

Though you can find casual restaurants and clubs, Washingtonians do dress for dinner and shows. If your travel plans include dinner at an upscale restaurant, the theater, or a concert, jackets and ties are essential for men, and women will want to have at least one dressy outfit.

You don't need to pack a travel iron. Almost all hotels can provide irons at the front desk. Hairdryers are also usually available.

Tourist Information

BEFORE LEAVING HOME   Contact the Washington, DC Convention and Visitors Association, 1212 New York Ave NW, Washington, DC 20005 (tel 202/789-7000), and request a free map, a calendar of events, and a booklet called *The Washington, DC Guide* that lists hotels, restaurants, shopping, sights, and more.

Your senator and/or congressional representative can provide special passes for tours of the White House, the Capitol, the Kennedy Center, the FBI, and the Bureau of Engraving and Printing. These tours may be more comprehensive than regular tours, and, since they're for specific times, they guarantee admission (not always a sure thing in busy tourist seasons) and spare you the necessity of standing in long lines.

Address requests to representatives to: US House of Representatives, Washington, DC 20515; and to senators to: US Senate, Washington, DC 20510. Write as far in advance as possible, since the ticket allotment for each site is limited, and be sure to include the exact dates of your trip. Note: Before writing, try calling your senator or congressperson's local office; in some states you can obtain passes by phone.

For a free copy of *Washington Weekends,* a brochure listing reduced weekend rates at dozens of Washington hotels, write or call the DC Committee to Promote Washington, PO Box 27489, Washington, DC 20038-7489 (tel 202/724-4091 or toll free 800/422-8644).

UPON ARRIVAL   Be sure to visit the Washington Visitor Information Center in the Willard Collection of Shops (next to but not in the Willard Inter-Continental Hotel) on Pennsylvania Avenue NW between 14th and 15th Streets (tel 202/789-7038). Just a block from the White House, this facility provides a wide array of free maps and brochures, and its staff can answer all your questions. Hours are Monday through Saturday from 9am to 5pm.

The Smithsonian Information Center, housed in the original 1849 Victorian red sandstone Smithsonian building at 1000 Jefferson Dr SW (tel 202/357-2700), provides an excellent overview of and orientation to the museum complex. It's open daily from 9am to 5:30pm.

Driving Rules & Regulations

In the District, the speed limit is 25 miles per hour, unless otherwise posted. The driver, all front-seat passengers, and rear-seat passengers under the age of 18 must wear seat belts. Children under 4 must ride in an approved child-restraint seat. Drunk-driving laws are strictly enforced, and the penalties are severe. Carrying open containers of alcohol in vehicles is unlawful. Read parking signs carefully; otherwise you may be ticketed and towed to one of the city's impoundment lots, where you will have to pay $75 to retrieve your vehicle.

Renting a Car

A car is absolutely unnecessary in Washington, DC, and because parking tends to be expensive (free street parking is almost nil), it's even something of an inconvenience (see "Public Transportation," below).

You may, however, wish to rent one for excursions to nearby places of interest in Virginia (such as Mount Vernon, Potomac plantations, and Fredericksburg) or Annapolis in Maryland. All of the major car-rental firms are represented here. Their toll-free phone numbers are:

- **Alamo** (tel 800/327-9633)
- **Avis** (tel 800/331-1212)
- **Budget** (tel 800/527-0700)
- **Hertz** (tel 800/654-3131)
- **National** (tel 800/227-7368)
- **Thrifty** (tel 800/367-2277)

Public Transportation

Washington's Metrorail (subway) system is extensive, clean, efficient, and easy to use, with stops at or near almost every sightseeing attraction. The first time you enter a Metro station, go to the kiosk and ask for a free Metro System Pocket Guide, which contains a map of the system, explains how it works, and lists the closest stops to major points of interest. There's also a comprehensive bus network with routes throughout the District and beyond. Call 202/637-7000 for Metrorail or bus routing information.

In addition, it's easy to hail a taxi, anywhere, any time. Taxis charge by the zone (no meters here), and drivers are allowed to pick up as many passengers as they can comfortably fit; expect to share.

Two sightseeing-tram companies—Tourmobile (tel 202/544-5100) and Old Town Trolley (tel 301/985-3020)—provide reasonably priced and comfortable transport to all major attractions. Call for details.

Essentials

Area Code: 202

Emergencies: Call **911** for police, the fire department, or an ambulance.

Liquor Laws: The minimum drinking age is 21. Establishments can serve alcoholic beverages Monday through Thursday from 8am to 2am, Friday and Saturday from 8am to 2:30am, and Sunday from 10am to 2am. Liquor stores are closed on Sunday.

Smoking: There are nonsmoking sections in all Washington restaurants with a seating capacity of 50 or more, bar area excluded. Almost all hotels have nonsmoking rooms. Smoking is not permitted in retail establishments (except for restaurants within retail establishments, such as department-store or Union Station eateries).

Taxes: Sales tax in the District is 11%. Keep in mind that it will be added to your hotel rate, along with a $1.50 per room, per night occupancy tax.

Time Zone: Washington is in the Eastern time zone. Daylight saving time (one hour ahead of Eastern Standard Time) is observed from the first Sunday in April until the last Sunday in October.

BEST OF THE CITY

What to See & Do

No city in the world offers as many museums, monuments, and tourist attractions. Highlights for the visitor include:

ARCHITECTURE Washington's architecture ranges from Georgetown's quaint Federal-style homes to gorgeous neoclassical museums and government buildings. There are so many of the latter that the city has been dubbed "Athens on the Potomac." The three major houses of government form a splendid architectural triumvirate—the **White House,** designed by Dubliner James Hoban after the country estate of an Irish duke; the magnificent white-domed **Capitol,** along with the **Lincoln Memorial** and the **Washington Monument,** one of the city's most famous landmarks; and Cass Gilbert's Corinthian-marble **Supreme Court.**

Other neoclassical masterpieces include the circular colonnaded **Jefferson Memorial,** the **National Archives,** and the West Wing of the **National Gallery** —all designed by John Russell Pope; the Italian Renaissance–style Thomas Jefferson Building of the **Library of Congress,** one of the most beautiful buildings in America; and **Union Station**—a monument to the great age of rail travel modeled after Rome's Baths of Diocletian and Arch of Constantine. Also notable: The Victorian red sandstone "castle"—first home of the **Smithsonian** museum complex—and the **Renwick**

Gallery, in the French Second Empire style. Both were designed by James Renwick.

CUISINE Washington is a great restaurant town. Many local chefs are in the vanguard of culinary trends, and in a city filled with foreign embassies there's plenty of good ethnic cuisine as well—everything from Spanish tapas to Indian tandoori. The city is especially known for its Ethiopian restaurants. In addition, fresh seafood comes in from Chesapeake Bay (look for crabcakes on many menus), and this being the south, cheese grits are also easy to come by.

FAMILY FAVORITES Popular children's sights include the **National Air and Space Museum** (IMAX films, missiles, rockets), the **National Museum of Natural History** (a discovery room and dinosaurs), the **FBI** (gangster memorabilia and a sharpshooting demonstration), the **Capital Children's Museum** (hands-on exhibits for kids), the **House Where Lincoln Died,** and the **National Zoological Park.** You'll want to take in all the historic government sites—the White House, the Supreme Court, the Capitol, and the major monuments and memorials. Also inquire about special children's activities at museum information desks, and call the **Kennedy Center** (tel 202/467-4600 or toll free 800/444-1324) and the **National Theatre** (tel 202/783-3370) for details about performances for kids.

MUSEUMS You won't see all of Washington's museums in one visit, and if you had several lifetimes, it wouldn't be long enough to view all of their contents. The **Smithsonian Institution** alone exhibits only 1% of its vast holdings at any given time, in more than 12 Washington museums. And that's not including the prestigious **National Gallery of Art,** equal in scope to New York's Metropolitan Museum or the Louvre in Paris; the exquisite **Phillips Collection,** conceived as "a museum of modern art and its sources"; the **National Geographic Society's Explorers Hall,** as fascinating as the magazine itself; collections of Pre-Columbian and Byzantine art at **Dumbarton Oaks;** the **United States Holocaust Memorial Museum,** and many more.

PARKS & GARDENS **West Potomac Park,** with 1,300 cherry trees ringing the Tidal Basin, is the site of the Vietnam Memorial, the Lincoln and Jefferson Memorials, and the Reflecting Pool. **East Potomac Park** contains 1,800 additional cherry trees. You can hike or bike along the towpath of the 184-mile **C&O Canal** or—from mid-April to mid-October—take a mule-drawn boat ride on it. **Rock Creek Park,** in the center of town, is a 1,750-acre greenbelt—one of the biggest and finest city parks in the nation. The highlight of the **US National Arboretum**—444 hilly acres of rhododendrons and azaleas, dogwoods and day lilies, boxwoods and cherry trees (and much more)—is the exquisite National Bonsai Collection. And you can observe abundant bird life, flora, and fauna on the foot trails of **Theodore Roosevelt Island,** an 88-acre wilderness preserve.

Beautiful gardens include **Dumbarton Oaks,** with 10 acres of formal gardens; the **United States Botanic Garden**—a lovely oasis at the east end of the Mall; the Victorian **Enid A Haupt Garden** on the Mall, with its central magnolia-lined parterre, floral swags, and ribbon beds; and the **Hirshhorn Museum's** delightful tree-shaded sunken sculpture garden.

Events/Festivals

Contact the Washington, DC Convention and Visitors Association (see "Tourist Information" above) for a calendar of events during the time of your visit. When in town, check the *Washington Post,* especially the Friday "Weekend" section, as well as the *City Paper,* a free weekly. Among the annual highlights:

- **Martin Luther King, Jr's Birthday.** Speeches, readings, concerts, prayer vigils, and a wreath laying at the Lincoln Memorial to honor the civil rights leader. 3rd Monday in January. Call 202/789-7000 for details.
- **Chinese New Year Celebration.** A 10-day festival with traditional firecrackers, dragon dancers, and colorful street parades in Washington's small Chinatown at 7th and H Sts, NW. Late January or early to mid-February. Call 202/789-7000 or 202/724-4093.
- **Abraham Lincoln's Birthday.** At the Lincoln Memorial, a wreath-laying ceremony and noon reading of the Gettysburg Address. February 12. Call 202/426-6895 for details.
- **George Washington's Birthday.** Celebratory events at the Washington Monument. February 22

(celebrated the 3rd Monday in February as Presidents Day). Call 202/426-6841 for details.

- **Smithsonian Kite Festival.** Throngs of kite enthusiasts fly their original creations on the Washington Monument grounds and compete for prizes. A Saturday in mid- or late March. Call 202/357-2700 for details.

- **Cherry Blossom Events.** The blossoming of the famous cherry trees is celebrated with a major parade, fireworks, fashion shows, concerts, a ball, and a marathon race. Late March or early April. Call 202/728-1135 for details.

- **White House Easter Egg Roll.** Hunting for eggs is the highlight for little kids (ages 3 to 6), but there's plenty for everyone else—Easter bunnies, egg-decorating exhibitions, magic shows, military drill teams, clog dancers, clowns, and more. Easter Monday between 10am and 2pm (arrive early) on the White House South Lawn and the Ellipse. Call 202/456-2200 for details.

- **Thomas Jefferson's Birthday.** A wreath-laying, speeches, and a military ceremony at the Jefferson Memorial. April 13. Call 202/462-6822 for details.

- **The Imagination Celebration.** A 2-week festival of performing arts for young people at the Kennedy Center for the Performing Arts. Events are free or moderately priced. Mid-April. Call 202/467-4600 for details.

- **White House Gardens.** Special free tours between 2 and 5pm of these beautifully landscaped creations. Four days per year only, 2 in mid-April and 2 in mid-October. Call 202/456-2200 for details.

- **Memorial Day.** Ceremonies at the Tomb of the Unknowns in Arlington National Cemetery (call 202/475-0856 for details) and the Vietnam Veterans Memorial (call 202/619-7222 for details). In the evening, the National Symphony Orchestra performs a free concert at 8pm on the Capitol's West Lawn (call 202/619-7222 for details). Last Monday in May.

- **Smithsonian Festival of American Folklife.** Dozens of events on the Mall including music (everything from Appalachian fiddling to Native American dance), food, concerts, games, and crafts demonstrations. 5 to 10 days surrounding July 4 weekend. Call 202/357-2700 for details.

- **Independence Day.** A massive daytime parade down Constitution Avenue, baseball games, concerts, crafts exhibitions, and a reading of the Declaration of Independence in front of the National Archives (a Revolutionary War encampment is set up for the occasion); at night, a National Symphony Orchestra concert on the Capitol steps and a fabulous fireworks display over the Washington Monument. July 4, all day. Call 202/789-7000 for details.

- **Tchaikovsky's 1812 Overture.** The US Army band performs this famous work, complete with roaring cannons, at the Sylvan Theatre on the Washington Monument grounds. August. Call 703/696-3718 for details.

- **National Frisbee Festival.** See world-class Frisbee champions and their disc-catching dogs on the Mall near the Air and Space Museum. 1st weekend in September. Call 301/645-5043 for details.

- **Washington National Cathedral Open House.** Stone carving, craft, carillon and organ demonstrations, as well as performances. Only time visitors can climb to the top of the central tower to see the carillon—a tremendous hike but a spectacular view. A Saturday in late September or early October. Call 202/537-6200 for details.

- **Marine Corps Marathon.** A 26-mile race that begins at the Iwo Jima Memorial in Washington and passes some of Washington's major monuments. 1st Sunday in November. Call 703/690-3431 for details.

- **Veterans Day.** Ceremonies to honor the nation's war dead at the Tomb of the Unknowns in Arlington National Cemetery (call 202/475-0856 for details) and at the Vietnam Veterans Memorial (call 202/619-7222 for details). November 11.

- **National Tree Lighting.** The President lights the national Christmas tree to the accompaniment of choral and orchestral music, kicking off a 2-week Pageant of Peace—a holiday celebration with seasonal music, caroling, state trees, and a Nativity scene. A Thursday in early December, between 5 and 6pm. Call 202/619-7222 for details.

- **White House Candlelight Tours.** The President's holiday decorations open to view on 3 selected December evenings between 6 and 8pm. Call 202/456-2200 for dates and details.

Spectator Sports

BASEBALL Pre-season major league exhibition games are held during the month of March at **Robert F Kennedy Memorial Stadium** (tel 202/547-9077 or 202/546-3337).

BASKETBALL The NBA's **Washington Bullets** play home games at the 19,000-seat USAir Arena in Landover, MD (tel 301/350-3400). College teams competing in the NCAA's Division I include the formidable **Georgetown University Hoyas,** who play at USAir Arena, and the **George Washington University Colonials,** who play at the Smith Center on the GW campus (tel 202/994-8584) and also host the Red Auerbach Colonial Classic tournament held December 2–3.

FOOTBALL Washington-area pro football fans are famously fanatic about their **Redskins,** who play their NFL home schedule at RFK Stadium (tel 202/547-9077 or 202/546-3337).

HOCKEY The NHL **Washington Capitals** play home games at USAir Arena in Landover, MD (tel 301/350-3400).

SOCCER Fans can catch the **Washington Warthogs** of the CISL (an indoor league) at USAir Arena (tel 301/350-3400) from June through August.

Activities A to Z

BICYCLING Both Fletcher's Boat House and Thompson's Boat Center (see "Boating" below) rent bikes, as does Big Wheel Bikes (tel 202/337-0254). The latter is right near the C&O Canal, a major cycling venue. Photo ID and a major credit card are required to rent bicycles. The *Washington Post's* Friday "Weekend" section lists cycling trips.

BOATING Fletcher's Boat House, Reservoir and Canal Roads (tel 202/244-0461), is about 3.2 miles from Georgetown right on the C&O Canal. Open March to mid-November, daily from 7:30am to dusk, it rents canoes and rowboats and sells fishing licenses, bait, and tackle. Thompson's Boat Center (tel 202/333-4861 or 202/333-9543) rents canoes, sailboats, rowing shells, and rowboats. It's open mid-April through early October, daily from 8am to 5pm.

CAMPING There are camping areas with picnic tables and fire grills along the C&O Canal every 5 miles or so from Fletcher's Boat House to Cumberland, Maryland. Use is on a first-come, first-served basis. Call 301/739-4200 for details.

FISHING The Potomac River provides good fishing from late February to November, but mid-March through June (spawning season) is peak. Perch and catfish are the most common catch, but during bass season a haul of 20 to 40 is not unusual. The Washington Channel offers good bass and carp fishing year-round. A fishing license is required. You can obtain one at Fletcher's Boat House (see above).

GOLF Within the District, there are public golf courses in Rock Creek Park (tel 202/882-7332 or 202/723-9832) and East Potomac Park (tel 202/863-9007).

HIKING A favorite place to hike is the C&O Canal, offering 184 miles of scenic towpath. There are also 15 miles of hiking trails in Rock Creek Park (maps are available at park headquarters). If you prefer group hikes, contact the Sierra Club (tel 202/547-2326 or 202/547-5551) or check hiking club listings in the Friday "Weekend" section of the *Washington Post.*

HORSEBACK RIDING The Rock Creek Park Horse Center on Glover Rd NW (tel 202/362-0117) offers rental horses, for trail rides and instruction, as well as 14 miles of wooded bridle paths.

ICE SKATING The C&O Canal, its banks dotted with cozy fires, is a delightful place to skate. Call 301/299-3613 for ice conditions.

JOGGING There's a 1.5-mile Perrier Parcourse with 18 calisthenics stations in Rock Creek Park, beginning near the intersection of Cathedral Ave and Rock Creek Pkwy. The Mall is another peaceful and popular area to jog among "Hill staffers" and many others.

TENNIS There are 144 outdoor public courts in the District at 45 locations. Court use is on a first-come, first-served basis. For a list of locations, call or write the DC Department of Recreation, 3149 16th St NW, Washington, DC 20010 (tel 202/673-7646). There are also courts in Rock Creek Park (tel 202/722-5949) and East Potomac Park (tel 202/554-5962).

WASHINGTON

Map page M-3, C6

In Maryland, see also Bethesda, Chevy Chase, Silver Spring;
In Virginia, see also Alexandria, Arlington, Fairfax, Falls
Church, McLean, Vienna

Hotels 🏨

≣ **Allen Lee Hotel**, 2224 F St NW, Washington, DC 20037
(Foggy Bottom); tel 202/331-1224 or toll free 800/462-0186.
Between 22nd and 23rd Sts. Looks more like an apartment
building than a hotel. This older property shows signs of wear
resulting from many guests. Located in the George Washington
University area. **Rooms:** 85 rms. CI noon/CO noon. 35 rooms
have private baths. **Amenities:** 🛗 A/C, TV. **Rates:** HS May–Sept
$33–$40 S; $42–$55 D. Extra person $6. Children under 12
stay free. Lower rates off-season. No CC.

≣≣≣≣ **ANA Hotel**, 2401 M St NW, Washington, DC
20037; tel 202/429-2400 or toll free 800/262-4683; fax 202/
457-5010. Minutes from Georgetown and the Kennedy Center,
this hotel has a tranquil setting, from the gracious lobby to the
loggia and garden courtyard. **Rooms:** 416 rms and stes. Exec-
level rms avail. CI 3pm/CO 1pm. Express checkout avail.
Nonsmoking rms avail. All rooms have sitting areas and an
oversize desk. **Amenities:** 🛗 A/C, TV, voice mail. All units
w/minibars, some w/terraces. Each room has 3 phones (2 are
speaker phones) with 2 lines and hold buttons. **Services:** VP 🖼
🛒 🍷 Car-rental desk. Currency exchange. Complimentary
shoe shine. **Facilities:** 🏋 🔥 Washer/dryer. Large fitness center
has aerobics classes, tanning booths, lap pool, exercise rooms,
health spa, juice bar, and lounge. **Rates:** HS Sept–Nov/Mar–May
$220–$255 S; $250–$285 D; from $600 ste. Extra person $30.
Children under 18 stay free. Lower rates off-season. AP rates
avail. Spec packages avail. Pking: Indoor, $15.75. Maj CC.
Weekend packages include breakfast, parking, use of health
club.

≣≣ **The Bellevue Hotel**, 15 E St NW, Washington, DC 20001
(Capitol Hill); tel 202/638-0900 or toll free 800/327-6667; fax
202/638-5132. Between New Jersey Ave and N Capitol St. An
extremely elegant lobby lighted by a huge brass-and-crystal
chandelier has Moorish touches throughout, including multiple
arches, small leaded windows, and red marble columns. Convenient to Union Station. **Rooms:** 137 rms and stes. CI 4pm/CO
noon. Nonsmoking rms avail. Unfortunately the lobby's promise
of elegance is not fulfilled in the rooms, which are functional and
large but lack attention to detail. **Amenities:** 🛗 A/C, cable TV

w/movies. **Services:** ✗ 🖼 🛒 Babysitting. Complimentary buffet
breakfast. Elevator is attended. **Facilities:** 🔳 💻 🔥 1 rst, 1 bar.
Rates (BB): HS Mar–May/Sept–Nov $79–$119 S; $89–$135 D;
from $250 ste. Extra person $50. Children under 18 stay free.
Lower rates off-season. Spec packages avail. Pking: Indoor, $8.
Maj CC. Rates are extremely low given the hotel's location and
free breakfast.

≣≣ **Best Western Downtown Capitol Hill**, 724 3rd St NW,
at G St, Washington, DC 20001 (Capitol Hill); tel 202/842-4466
or toll free 800/242-4831; fax 202/842-4831. Located near
Union Station, Chinatown, and the Convention Center, this red-
brick property offers guests a clean and comfortable place to
stay. **Rooms:** 59 rms. CI 2pm/CO noon. Nonsmoking rms avail.
Amenities: 🛗 A/C, TV. **Services:** 🖼 🛒 🍷 Complimentary
newspaper, continental breakfast, evening hors d'oeuvres.
Facilities: 🔳 🔥 1 rst, 2 bars (1 w/entertainment). **Rates (CP):**
HS Mar–July $79–$105 S or D. Extra person $10. Children
under 18 stay free. Lower rates off-season. Spec packages avail.
Pking: Outdoor, free. Maj CC.

≣≣ **Canterbury Hotel**, 1733 N St NW, Washington, DC
20036 (Dupont Circle); tel 202/393-3000 or toll free 800/
424-2950; fax 202/785-9581. Built as apartments in 1901, this
small European-style hotel offers intimacy and hospitality in the
heart of the Dupont Circle area. **Rooms:** 99 rms. CI 2pm/CO
noon. Nonsmoking rms avail. All units have kitchenettes.
Amenities: 🛗 🔥 🎷 A/C, cable TV, refrig, shoe polisher. All
units w/minibars. A few units have microwave ovens. **Services:**
✗ VP 🖼 **Facilities:** 🔳 1 rst, 1 bar. Complimentary privileges
at nearby health club. **Rates (CP):** HS Sept–Nov/Mar–June
$175 S; $195 D. Extra person $20. Children under 12 stay free.
Lower rates off-season. Spec packages avail. Pking: Indoor, $10.
Maj CC.

≣≣≣≣ **The Capital Hilton**, 1001 16th Street, at K St,
Washington, DC 20036; tel 202/393-1000 or toll free 800/
HILTONS; fax 202/393-7992. A club-like atmosphere prevails in
this cherrywood-paneled lobby with contemporary art and
furniture. Convenient location in the heart of Washington's
business district 2 blocks from the White House and 2 metro
stations. **Rooms:** 543 rms and stes. Exec-level rms avail. CI
3pm/CO noon. Express checkout avail. Nonsmoking rms avail.
The hotel originally had 800 rooms, but space was reallocated to
create bigger units. Large marble baths with small TVs and
phones. Deluxe tower rooms have extras, such as concierge
lounge with bar. **Amenities:** 🛗 🔥 🎷 A/C, cable TV, refrig, voice
mail, shoe polisher. All units w/minibars, some w/terraces. Irons
and boards. **Services:** 🍽 ☎ VP 🖼 🛒 Babysitting. **Facilities:**
🏋 🔳 💻 🔥 2 rsts, 1 bar (w/entertainment), sauna, steam rm,
beauty salon. Twigs dining room has garden-like ambience,

while Trader Vic's captures a South Seas mood. **Rates:** HS Sept–Nov/Mar–June $185–$230 S or D; from $300 ste. Children under 18 stay free. Lower rates off-season. Spec packages avail. Pking: Indoor, $22. Maj CC.

Capitol Hill Suites, 200 C St SE, at 2nd St, Washington, DC 20003 (Capitol Hill); tel 202/543-6000 or toll free 800/424-9165; fax 202/547-2608. One block to Library of Congress, US House of Representatives, Capitol South metro station, and shops and restaurants along Pennsylvania Ave SE. **Rooms:** 152 stes and effic. CI 3pm/CO noon. Nonsmoking rms avail. Spacious suites with living areas are suited for long-term stays. **Amenities:** A/C, cable TV, refrig, voice mail, shoe polisher. Kitchenettes have sink, small fridge, 2-burner stove. **Services:** Evening cocktails, morning newspaper and coffee. **Facilities:** Washer/dryer. Complimentary passes to nearby health club. **Rates:** HS Sept–Nov/Mar–June from $115 ste; from $115 effic. Extra person $15. Children under 18 stay free. Lower rates off-season. Higher rates for spec evnts/hols. Spec packages avail. Pking: Indoor, $12. Maj CC. Weekend and long-term rates available.

The Carlton, 923 16th St NW, at K St, Washington, DC 20006; tel 202/879-6911 or toll free 800/562-5661; fax 202/638-4321. Many Washington and world notables have been through this spacious lobby, which has exquisite furnishings and decor and is the site of afternoon tea accompanied by a harpist. A definite European air is manifest in the 1926 building's Italian Renaissance exterior. **Rooms:** 197 rms and stes. CI 3pm/CO 1pm. Express checkout avail. Nonsmoking rms avail. **Amenities:** A/C, cable TV, refrig, voice mail, in-rm safe, shoe polisher, bathrobes. All units w/minibars. Candies and bottled water. Fax machines in some rooms. **Services:** Twice-daily maid svce, children's program, babysitting. Complimentary cocktail-hour hors d'oeuvres in lounge bar. Free local calls. **Facilities:** 1 rst, 1 bar (w/entertainment), beauty salon. **Rates:** HS Sept–Nov/Mar–June $240–$280 S or D; from $500 ste. Extra person $25. Children under 18 stay free. Lower rates off-season. Pking: Indoor, $10–$20. Maj CC. Various weekend and romance packages available.

The Carlyle Suites, 1731 New Hampshire Ave NW, Washington, DC 20009 (Dupont Circle); tel 202/234-3200 or toll free 800/964-5377; fax 202/387-0085. Between R and S Sts. This older art-deco building has a small lobby with black and white tiles, chrome, mirrors, and neon lighting. Formerly an apartment complex, it specializes in long-term stays. **Rooms:** 176 stes. CI 3pm/CO 1pm. Nonsmoking rms avail. Interesting architectural features such as alcoves and parquet floors. Most units have fully equipped kitchenettes. **Amenities:** A/C, TV w/movies, refrig, voice mail. Some units have computer/fax

connections. **Services:** **Facilities:** 1 rst, 1 bar, washer/dryer. Free use of nearby health club. Restaurant serves both meals and snacks. **Rates:** HS Apr–Aug from $119 ste. Extra person $10. Children under 18 stay free. Lower rates off-season. Spec packages avail. Pking: Outdoor, free. Maj CC. Long-term rates available.

The Center City Hotel, 1202 13th St NW, at M St, Washington, DC 20005; tel 202/682-5300 or toll free 800/458-2817; fax 202/371-9624. Formerly a Best Western, this hotel now has new management, which has instituted cost-cutting measures such as eliminating cable TV from rooms. Nevertheless, premises remains well kept and in good order. Quality of the neighborhood might detract somewhat from a guest's visit. **Rooms:** 100 rms. CI 2pm/CO 11am. Nonsmoking rms avail. **Amenities:** A/C, refrig, in-rm safe, shoe polisher, bathrobes. 1 unit w/Jacuzzi. **Services:** Twice-daily maid svce, masseur. **Facilities:** 2 rsts, 2 bars (1 w/entertainment), lifeguard, racquetball, squash, spa, sauna, steam rm, whirlpool. **Rates (CP):** HS Mar–Oct $85 S; $95 D. Extra person $10. Children under 16 stay free. Lower rates off-season. Higher rates for spec evnts/hols. Spec packages avail. Pking: Outdoor, $9. Maj CC.

Comfort Inn Downtown, 500 H St NW, Washington, DC 20001 (Chinatown); tel 202/289-5959 or toll free 800/234-6423; fax 202/682-9152. Chain motel in heart of Chinatown and its restaurants and shops, 1 block to metro station. **Rooms:** 194 rms and stes. Exec-level rms avail. CI noon/CO noon. Nonsmoking rms avail. **Amenities:** A/C, cable TV w/movies, shoe polisher. Fortune cookies in rooms. **Services:** Car-rental desk. Complimentary manager's reception twice weekly. **Facilities:** 1 rst, 1 bar, washer/dryer. Discount coupons for nearby health club. **Rates:** HS June–July $89 S; $99 D; from $109 ste. Extra person $10. Children under 6 stay free. Lower rates off-season. Spec packages avail. Pking: Indoor, $11.20. Maj CC.

Connecticut Avenue Days Inn, 4400 Connecticut Ave NW, Washington, DC 20008; tel 202/244-5600 or toll free 800/966-3060; fax 202/244-6794. Between Yuma and Albermarle Sts. A chain property offering reasonable rates. Although removed from downtown, it has easy access to Washington attractions via nearby Van Ness metro station. **Rooms:** 155 rms and stes. CI 2pm/CO noon. Nonsmoking rms avail. **Amenities:** A/C, cable TV, in-rm safe. **Services:** Babysitting. **Facilities:** **Rates (CP):** HS Mar 15–Nov 15 $99 S; $109 D; from $129 ste. Extra person $10. Children under 18 stay free. Lower rates off-season. Spec packages avail. Pking: Indoor/outdoor, $5. Maj CC. Weekend rates available.

≣≣≣ **Courtyard by Marriott**, 1900 Connecticut Ave NW, at Leroy Place, Washington, DC 20009; tel 202/332-9300 or toll free 800/842-4211; fax 202/328-7039. Although this mid-rise hotel lacks the trademark courtyard of this business traveler-oriented chain, it does command a panoramic view of Washington from a hilltop perch. Intimate, club-like atmosphere prevails in lounge reserved for guests' use only. **Rooms:** 147 rms and stes. CI 3pm/CO noon. Express checkout avail. Nonsmoking rms avail. Rooms lack sofas and easy chairs found in other members of this chain. **Amenities:** 🛏 🕭 📺 A/C, cable TV w/movies, voice mail, in-rm safe. Some units w/minibars. Long phone cords. **Services:** ✕ 🖼 ⇄ ⟨⟩ Babysitting. Complimentary afternoon cookies and coffee. **Facilities:** 🔟 60 ⚫ 1 rst, 1 bar, lifeguard, washer/dryer. Restaurant serves breakfast and dinner only. Bar open 5–11pm. **Rates:** HS Apr–June/Sept–Oct $120 S; $135 D; from $155 ste. Extra person $15. Children under 18 stay free. Lower rates off-season. Higher rates for spec evnts/hols. Spec packages avail. Pking: Indoor, $10. Maj CC.

≣≣ **Days Inn Downtown**, 1201 K St NW, Washington, DC 20005; tel 202/842-1020 or toll free 800/562-3350; fax 202/289-0336. Convenient downtown location, 2 blocks from metro station. Caters to tourists and tour groups. **Rooms:** 220 rms and stes. CI 2pm/CO 1pm. Nonsmoking rms avail. Some rooms have kitchenettes. **Amenities:** 🛏 A/C, satel TV w/movies, refrig, voice mail, shoe polisher. **Services:** 🖼 ⇄ ⟨⟩ **Facilities:** 🔟 🍽 200 Lifeguard. **Rates:** HS Apr–Sept $75–$98 S; $75–$105 D; from $110 ste. Extra person $10. Children under 17 stay free. Lower rates off-season. Higher rates for spec evnts/hols. Spec packages avail. Pking: Indoor, $8.50. Maj CC. Kids under 12 eat free.

≣≣≣ **Doubletree Hotel Park Terrace**, 1515 Rhode Island Ave NW, Washington, DC 20005; tel 202/232-7000 or toll free 800/222-TREE; fax 202/332-7152. Between 15th and 16th Sts NW. A modern downtown hotel with a European flair. Located 6 blocks north of the White House between Thomas and Scott circles. **Rooms:** 219 rms and stes. CI 3pm/CO noon. Express checkout avail. Nonsmoking rms avail. **Amenities:** 🛏 🕭 📺 A/C, cable TV w/movies. All units w/minibars. Suites have kitchenettes with small refrigerators, microwaves, ice makers. **Services:** ◎ 📵 🖼 ⇄ Babysitting. **Facilities:** 🍽 🍴 🖥 ⚫ 1 rst, 1 bar, washer/dryer. Restaurant looks like large living room with chandelier, carved oak fireplace. **Rates:** $125–$155 S or D; from $195 ste. Extra person $10. Children under 18 stay free. Higher rates for spec evnts/hols. Spec packages avail. Pking: Indoor, $12.50. Maj CC.

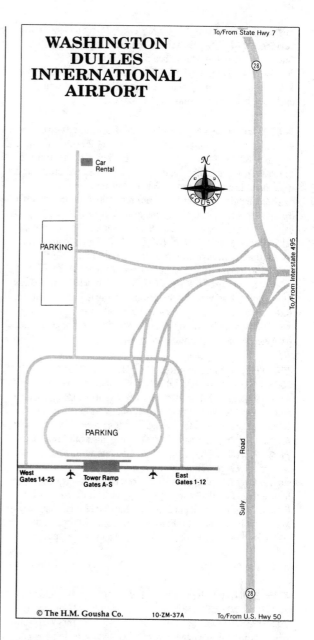

WASHINGTON DULLES INTERNATIONAL AIRPORT

To/From State Hwy 7

Car Rental

PARKING

PARKING

West Gates 14-25

Tower Ramp Gates A-S

East Gates 1-12

To/From Interstate 495

Sully Road

© The H.M. Gousha Co.   10-ZM-37A   To/From U.S. Hwy 50

≣≣ **Dupont Plaza Hotel**, 1500 New Hampshire Ave NW, Washington, DC 20036 (Dupont Circle); tel 202/483-6000 or toll free 800/421-6662; fax 202/328-3265. Large lounge has panoramic view of the park in center of Dupont Circle. Convenient to restaurants, exclusive shops, metro, Embassy Row. Caters to tour groups. **Rooms:** 314 rms and stes. Exec-level rms avail. CI 3pm/CO 1pm. Express checkout avail. Nonsmoking rms avail. **Amenities:** 🕿 🐧 A/C, cable TV w/movies, refrig. **Services:** ✗ VP 🖾 ↵ Babysitting. **Facilities:** 300 🐧 1 rst, 1 bar. Guests get passes to YMCA health club. **Rates:** HS Apr–June/Sept–Nov 15 $145–$165 S or D; from $185 ste. Extra person $20. Children under 13 stay free. Lower rates off-season. Spec packages avail. Pking: Indoor, $13. Maj CC.

≡≡≡ **Embassy Row Hotel**, 2015 Massachusetts Ave NW, Washington, DC 20036 (Dupont Circle); tel 202/265-1600 or toll free 800/424-2400; fax 202/328-7526. In the heart of Embassy Row, this hotel caters to corporate executives and diplomats. Lobby has wall murals of embassies, marble floors, recessed lighting, low ceilings. **Rooms:** 196 rms and stes. CI 3pm/CO noon. Nonsmoking rms avail. **Amenities:** 🕿 🐧 A/C, cable TV w/movies, in-rm safe, shoe polisher. Many rooms have refrigerators. **Services:** ✗ ➤ VP 🖾 ↵ Twice-daily maid svce, babysitting. Concierge will organize special tours and programs for children. On-site limousine service. **Facilities:** 🐧 200 🐧 1 rst, 1 bar, lifeguard. Free use of health club 4 blocks away. Access ramps for guests with disabilities are through parking garage. **Rates:** HS Apr–May/Sept–Oct $169–$189 S or D; from $220 ste. Children under 18 stay free. Lower rates off-season. Spec packages avail. Pking: Indoor, $12. Maj CC.

≡≡ **Embassy Square Suites**, 2000 N St NW, Washington, DC 20036 (Dupont Circle); tel 202/659-9000 or toll free 800/424-2999; fax 202/429-9546. Two blocks from Dupont Circle and its metro station, surrounded by shops and restaurants, this all-suites hotel is ideal for families and long-term stays. **Rooms:** 250 stes. CI 4pm/CO noon. Nonsmoking rms avail. **Amenities:** 🕿 🐧 A/C, cable TV, refrig, VCR. All units w/minibars, some w/terraces. Large, comfortable suites have full-size refrigerators, stoves, ovens, sinks, flatware. **Services:** ✗ ➤ 🖾 ↵ ⌁ Babysitting. **Facilities:** 🐧 ⌨ 100 🐧 Lifeguard, washer/dryer. Free privileges at nearby health club. **Rates (CP):** HS Sept–Nov/Mar–June from $119 ste. Extra person $20. Children under 18 stay free. Lower rates off-season. Higher rates for spec evnts/hols. Spec packages avail. Pking: Indoor, $10. Maj CC. Long-term rates available.

≡≡ **Embassy Suites**, 1250 22nd St NW, Washington, DC 20037; tel 202/857-3388 or toll free 800/362-2779; fax 202/293-3173. Between M and N Sts. Located in the West End neighborhood near Foggy Bottom, this 9-story building is constructed around an atrium with cascading waterfalls, lots of trees and plants, terra cotta tiles, wood benches, and wrought-iron tables and chairs. **Rooms:** 318 stes. CI 3pm/CO noon. Express checkout avail. Nonsmoking rms avail. All units have private bedroom and living room with fully equipped kitchen. **Amenities:** 🕿 🐧 🖭 ⌁ A/C, cable TV w/movies, refrig, voice mail. 1 unit w/Jacuzzi. TVs in both rooms, irons and boards.

Toiletries on request. **Services:** ✗ ➤ 🖾 ↵ Babysitting. Complimentary breakfast and evening reception. **Facilities:** 🐧 ⌨ 225 🖳 🐧 1 rst, 1 bar, lifeguard, games rm, spa, sauna, whirlpool, washer/dryer. Moderately priced Italian restaurant on premises. **Rates (BB):** From $204 ste. Extra person $20. Children under 18 stay free. Spec packages avail. Pking: Indoor, $14. Maj CC.

≡≡ **Embassy Suites Chevy Chase Pavilion**, 4300 Military Rd, Washington, DC 20015 (Friendship Heights); tel 202/362-9300 or toll free 800/EMBASSY; fax 202/686-3405. An all-suites hotel located in the Chevy Chase Pavilion, an upscale shopping and office complex at the Friendship Heights metro station. Hotel opens to large atrium in center of the mall. **Rooms:** 198 stes. CI 3pm/CO noon. Express checkout avail. Nonsmoking rms avail. Units have separate bedrooms and living rooms. **Amenities:** 🕿 🐧 🖭 A/C, cable TV, refrig, VCR, voice mail, shoe polisher. Some units w/minibars. Both rooms are equipped with TVs; VCRs are in bedrooms. Full kitchens contain microwaves. **Services:** ✗ 🖾 ↵ Babysitting. Complimentary made-to-order breakfast, manager's reception every evening. **Facilities:** 🐧 ⌨ 150 🖳 🐧 1 rst, 3 bars, lifeguard, spa, sauna, steam rm, whirlpool, beauty salon, washer/dryer. Full health club on top floor. **Rates (BB):** HS Mar–June/Sept–Nov $180 S; $195 D. Extra person $15. Children under 16 stay free. Lower rates off-season. Higher rates for spec evnts/hols. Spec packages avail. Pking: Indoor, $10. Maj CC.

≡≡≡≡ **Four Seasons Hotel**, 2800 Pennsylvania Ave NW, at M St, Washington, DC 20007 (Georgetown); tel 202/342-0444 or toll free 800/332-3442; fax 202/944-2076. Located 12 blocks away from the White House in a 5-story brick structure. Often attracts high-profile guests. **Rooms:** 196 rms and stes. CI 3pm/CO noon. Express checkout avail. Nonsmoking rms avail. Fairly small rooms, but smart and efficient. Some overlook the Chesapeake & Ohio (C&O) Canal, some face inner courtyard. **Amenities:** 🕿 🐧 ⌁ A/C, cable TV w/movies, refrig, voice mail, in-rm safe, shoe polisher, bathrobes. All units w/minibars. Phones have 2 lines. **Services:** ⎆ ➤ VP 🖾 ↵ ⌁ Twice-daily maid svce, masseur, children's program, babysitting. Complimentary early morning coffee in lobby. Free limo to downtown offices. Portable phones, faxes, PCs, and pagers for rent. Overnight laundry. **Facilities:** 🐧 ⌨ 800 🐧 2 rsts, 1 bar (w/entertainment), lifeguard, sauna, steam rm, whirlpool. Stunning 3-story fitness center with vaulted ceiling and skylight and indoor lap pool. Massage rooms (with speaker phones). Library of language tapes. Private nightclub. **Rates:** HS Sept–Nov/mid-Mar–May 31 $265–$310 S; $295–$340 D; from $575 ste. Extra person $30. Children under 18 stay free. Lower rates off-season. Spec packages avail. Pking: Indoor, $20. Maj CC. Rates depend on floor and view.

≣≣≣ **The Georgetown Dutch Inn**, 1075 Thomas Jefferson St NW, Washington, DC 20007 (Georgetown); tel 202/337-0900 or toll free 800/388-2410; fax 202/333-6526. Just below M St. A charming and elegant all-suites hotel ideally situated amid Georgetown shops and a plethora of fine restaurants, which more than makes up for lack of on-premises dining room. **Rooms:** 47 stes. Exec-level rms avail. CI 3pm/CO noon. Suites are elegantly decorated and furnished with federal-period reproductions. **Amenities:** 🛏 🐧 🎬 A/C, cable TV w/movies, refrig. 1 unit w/terrace. **Services:** ✗ 🧖 🐱 Babysitting. Complimentary continental breakfast. **Facilities:** 🏊 **Rates (CP):** HS Mar 15–June 15/Sept 15–Nov 15 from $110 ste. Extra person $20. Children under 17 stay free. Lower rates off-season. Spec packages avail. Pking: Indoor, free. Maj CC.

≣≣≣≣ **Georgetown Inn**, 1310 Wisconsin Ave NW, Washington, DC 20007 (Georgetown); tel 202/333-8900 or toll free 800/424-2979; fax 202/625-1744. A European-style hotel with definite American colonial-era accents. Lobby distinguished by a huge hemispheric chandelier composed of hundreds of crystals. **Rooms:** 95 rms and stes. CI 3pm/CO noon. Nonsmoking rms avail. Attractive rooms have dark-wood furniture, silk and brocade fabrics. **Amenities:** 🛏 🐧 A/C, cable TV, bathrobes. **Services:** ✗ 🆅🅿 🧖 🐱 Babysitting. Complimentary newspaper. **Facilities:** 🍽 🏊 🐧 1 rst, 1 bar (w/entertainment), games rm, washer/dryer. **Rates:** HS Aug–Nov $129–$149 S; $149–$169 D; from $209 ste. Extra person $20. Children under 13 stay free. Lower rates off-season. Higher rates for spec evnts/hols. Pking: Indoor, $15. Maj CC.

≣≣≣ **Georgetown Suites**, 1111 30th St NW, at M St, Washington, DC 20007 (Georgetown); tel 202/298-7800 or toll free 800/348-7203; fax 202/333-5792. Located near the C&O Canal in Georgetown, this establishment's accommodations range from studios to 2-bedroom town houses with separate entrance. **Rooms:** 133 stes and effic. CI 3pm/CO noon. All units have fully equipped kitchens and contemporary furnishings. **Amenities:** 🛏 🐧 🎬 🐧 A/C, cable TV, refrig, voice mail, shoe polisher. Dishwashers and microwaves, irons and boards. **Services:** 🧖 🐱 🐬 Complimentary continental breakfast. **Facilities:** 🍽 Washer/dryer. **Rates (CP):** From $125 ste; from $110 effic. Children under 18 stay free. Spec packages avail. Pking: Indoor, $10. Maj CC.

≣≣≣ **Georgetown University Conference Center and Guest House**, 3800 Reservoir Rd NW, Washington, DC 20057 (Georgetown); tel 202/687-3200 or toll free 800/228-9290; fax 202/687-3297. One of the city's largest conference facilities, this comfortable hotel managed by the Marriott Corporation is hidden away on campus behind Georgetown University Hospital. **Rooms:** 146 rms and stes. Exec-level rms avail. CI 3:30pm/

CO noon. Express checkout avail. Nonsmoking rms avail. **Amenities:** 🛏 🐧 🐧 A/C, cable TV w/movies, voice mail. **Services:** ✗ 🆅🅿 🚐 🧖 🐱 Twice-daily maid svce, social director, babysitting. **Facilities:** 🏋 🎿 🏊 🍽 🐧 🖥 💺 🐧 2 rsts, 1 bar, lifeguard, games rm, lawn games, racquetball, spa, sauna, steam rm, whirlpool, washer/dryer. Food service ranges from carryout pizza to formal dining room. University's bookstore on premises. Exercise privileges at GU's Yates Field House. **Rates (CP):** $140 S; $155 D; from $165 ste. Extra person $15. Spec packages avail. Pking: Indoor, $10. Maj CC.

≣≣≣ **The Governor's House Holiday Inn**, 1615 Rhode Island Ave, Washington, DC 20036; tel 202/296-2100 or toll free 800/821-4367; fax 202/331-0227. Intimate lobby, convenient downtown location. **Rooms:** 152 rms and stes. CI 3pm/CO noon. Express checkout avail. Nonsmoking rms avail. Rooms freshly redone. **Amenities:** 🛏 🐧 A/C, cable TV w/movies, shoe polisher. **Services:** ✗ 🍽 🆅🅿 🧖 🐱 🐬 Babysitting. **Facilities:** 🏋 🏊 🐧 1 rst, 1 bar, lifeguard. Pleasant restaurant has exposed brick walls, lots of photographs and posters. Free use of adjoining health club with Olympic-size pool, racquetball courts, exercise equipment. **Rates:** $125 S; $140 D; from $165 ste. Extra person $15. Children under 18 stay free. Higher rates for spec evnts/hols. Spec packages avail. Pking: Indoor, $14. Maj CC.

≣≣≣≣ **The Grand Hotel**, 2350 M St NW, Washington, DC 20037; tel 202/429-0100 or toll free 800/848-0016; fax 202/429-9759. Very understated elegance in lobby and rooms of this modern hotel convenient to Georgetown, Kennedy Center, downtown businesses, attractions. **Rooms:** 263 rms and stes. CI 3pm/CO 1pm. Nonsmoking rms avail. **Amenities:** 🛏 🐧 🐧 A/C, cable TV w/movies, refrig, shoe polisher, bathrobes. All units w/minibars, some w/terraces, some w/fireplaces, some w/Jacuzzis. Exquisite baths have sunken tubs, marble vanities, large mirrors. **Services:** 🍴 🍽 🆅🅿 🧖 🐱 Twice-daily maid svce, babysitting. Known for attentive, multilingual staff. High tea daily (reservations suggested). **Facilities:** 🏋 🍽 🏊 🐧 1 rst, 2 bars (1 w/entertainment). **Rates:** $175–$270 S; $195–$300 D; from $550 ste. Extra person $20. Spec packages avail. Pking: Indoor, $15–18. Maj CC.

≣≣≣≣ **Grand Hyatt Washington**, 1000 H St NW, Washington, DC 20001; tel 202/582-1234 or toll free 800/233-1234; fax 202/637-4797. A refreshing, 12-story atrium with fountains, cascading waterfall, and walkways across a sparkling lagoon characterizes this large, group-oriented hotel across the street from the Convention Center. **Rooms:** 907 rms and stes. Exec-level rms avail. CI 3pm/CO noon. Express checkout avail. Nonsmoking rms avail. Rooms have city or atrium views. **Amenities:** 🛏 🐧 A/C, cable TV w/movies, refrig, voice mail.

Some units w/minibars, some w/Jacuzzis. **Services:** ✗ ▣ 🚐 ▨ 🎧 Twice-daily maid svce, masseur, children's program, babysitting. **Facilities:** ⌂ 🏓 🎱 💻 ♿ 3 rsts, 3 bars (2 w/entertainment), spa, sauna, steam rm, whirlpool. Lounges range from quiet piano music to raucous sports bar. **Rates:** HS Apr–May/Sept–Oct $234 S; $259 D; from $475 ste. Extra person $25. Children under 12 stay free. Lower rates off-season. Spec packages avail. Pking: Indoor, $12. Maj CC.

▤▤ Guest Quarters Suite Hotel–New Hampshire Avenue, 801 New Hampshire Ave NW, Washington, DC 20037 (Foggy Bottom); tel 202/785-2000 or toll free 800/424-2900; fax 202/785-9485. Between H and I Sts. An all-suites hotel convenient to Kennedy Center, downtown businesses, shops, restaurants. **Rooms:** 101 stes. CI 3pm/CO noon. Express checkout avail. Nonsmoking rms avail. Units have fully equipped kitchens. All living rooms have sleep sofas. **Amenities:** 🛁 ⚏ ▣ 🍴 A/C, cable TV w/movies, refrig. All units w/minibars. Units have dishwashers; some have microwaves, which are available for others on request. Some business units have computers. TVs in both living rooms and bedrooms. **Services:** ✗ VP ▨ 🎧 Babysitting. **Facilities:** ⌂ ⓯ ♿ Lifeguard, washer/dryer. Free membership in nearby health club. **Rates:** From $180 ste. Extra person $15. Children under 18 stay free. Spec packages avail. Pking: Indoor, $15. Maj CC. Weekend packages include breakfast.

▤▤ Guest Quarters Suite Hotel–Pennsylvania Avenue, 2500 Pennsylvania Ave NW, Washington, DC 20037; tel 202/333-8060 or toll free 800/424-2900; fax 202/338-3818. An all-suites hotel convenient to Kennedy Center, downtown businesses, shops, restaurants. Outdoor landscaped patio has tables and chairs. **Rooms:** 123 stes. CI 3pm/CO noon. Nonsmoking rms avail. Units have fully equipped kitchens. All living rooms have sleep sofas. **Amenities:** 🛁 ⚏ ▣ 🍴 A/C, cable TV w/movies, refrig. All units w/minibars. Units have dishwashers; some have microwaves, which are available for others on request. Some business units have computers. TVs in both living rooms and bedrooms. **Services:** ✗ VP ▨ 🎧 Babysitting. **Facilities:** ⓯ ♿ Washer/dryer. Free membership in nearby health club. **Rates:** From $99 ste. Extra person $15. Children under 18 stay free. Higher rates for spec evnts/hols. Spec packages avail. Pking: Indoor, $13. Maj CC. Weekend packages include breakfast.

▤▤▤ Hampshire Hotel, 1310 New Hampshire Ave NW, at N St, Washington, DC 20036 (Dupont Circle); tel 202/296-7600 or toll free 800/296-7600; fax 202/293-2476. Behind an undistinguished glass-and-concrete facade, guests will discover 18th-century decor and numerous amenities in this former apartment building. **Rooms:** 82 rms and stes. CI 3pm/CO noon. Nonsmoking rms avail. Spacious units, most with kitchens. **Amenities:** 🛁 ⚏ ▣ 🍴 A/C, cable TV, refrig, voice mail. Some

units w/minibars, some w/terraces. On-line phone service for news, information, shopping, pizza delivery. **Services:** ✗ VP ▨ 🎧 ▨ Complimentary newspapers. **Facilities:** ⓾ 💻 ♿ 1 rst, 1 bar, washer/dryer. Passes to nearby health club. **Rates:** $139 S; $149 D; from $139 ste. Extra person $20. Children under 12 stay free. Higher rates for spec evnts/hols. Spec packages avail. Pking: Indoor/outdoor, $10. Maj CC.

▤ Harrington Hotel, 11th and E Sts NW, Washington, DC 20004; tel 202/628-8140 or toll free 800/424-8532; fax 202/347-3924. An older but well-maintained hotel with small, dated rooms. In the heart of downtown, near metro. **Rooms:** 265 rms and stes. CI 2pm/CO noon. Nonsmoking rms avail. Bare but clean rooms. **Amenities:** 🛁 A/C, TV. **Services:** 🎧 ▨ **Facilities:** ♿ 2 rsts, 1 bar, washer/dryer. Cafeteria serves home-style meals. Bar provides sandwiches and salads. **Rates:** HS June–Oct $65–$79 S; $69–$89 D; from $85 ste. Extra person $5. Children under 16 stay free. Lower rates off-season. Higher rates for spec evnts/hols. Spec packages avail. Pking: Indoor, $5. Maj CC.

▤▤▤▤ The Hay-Adams Hotel, 1 Lafayette Sq at 16th and H Sts NW, Washington, DC 20006; tel 202/638-6600 or toll free 800/424-5054; fax 202/638-2716. On Lafayette Square across from the White House, this exquisite Italian Renaissance hotel sits on the former site of homes belonging to John Hay and Henry Adams. Built in 1927, it has retained its original charm while offering all the amenities expected of a full-service luxury hotel. The lobby features fine English antiques, a 17th-century tapestry, and gilt moldings. **Rooms:** 143 rms and stes. CI 3pm/CO 1pm. Express checkout avail. Nonsmoking rms avail. Individually decorated rooms have high ceilings, carved moldings, and marble baths. **Amenities:** 🛁 ⚏ 🍴 A/C, cable TV, refrig, voice mail, in-rm safe, shoe polisher, bathrobes. All units w/minibars, some w/terraces. **Services:** 🍽 ▣ VP ▨ 🎧 Twice-daily maid svce, babysitting. **Facilities:** ⓾⓿ 2 rsts, 1 bar (w/entertainment), washer/dryer. **Rates:** $210–$360 S or D; from $280 ste. Extra person $30. Children under 16 stay free. Spec packages avail. Pking: Indoor, $18. Maj CC.

▤▤▤ Henley Park, 926 Massachusetts Ave NW, at K St, Washington, DC 20001; tel 202/638-5200 or toll free 800/222-8474; fax 202/638-6740. A stately, elegant, European-style hotel built in 1927 as apartments. Near Convention Center, metro. **Rooms:** 96 rms and stes. CI 3pm/CO noon. Nonsmoking rms avail. Distinctively decorated with antique furniture, silk grass cloth. **Amenities:** 🛁 ⚏ A/C, cable TV w/movies, refrig, shoe polisher, bathrobes. All units w/minibars. Selection of magazines in rooms. **Services:** 🍽 ▣ VP ▨ 🎧 Babysitting. High tea served 4–6pm daily. **Facilities:** ⓰⓿ 1 rst, 1 bar. **Rates:**

$165–$215 S; $185–$235 D; from $295 ste. Extra person $10. Children under 16 stay free. Spec packages avail. Pking: Indoor, $15. Maj CC.

≣≣≣ Holiday Inn Capitol, 550 C St SW, Washington, DC 20024; tel 202/479-4000 or toll free 800/HOLIDAY; fax 202/479-4353. South of the Mall, this hotel is convenient to the National Air and Space Museum and most other key capital sights. **Rooms:** 529 rms and stes. CI 3pm/CO noon. Express checkout avail. Nonsmoking rms avail. Modest rooms are comfortable and clean. **Amenities:** 🛋 🕭 A/C, cable TV, voice mail, shoe polisher. Some units w/minibars. **Services:** ✕ 🖾 🖵 ◁ Babysitting. **Facilities:** 🖀 🙌 🔲 🖳 🕭 2 rsts, 1 bar, lifeguard, spa, beauty salon, washer/dryer. Rooftop pool with landscaping, flowers. **Rates:** $149 S or D; from $189 ste. Children under 18 stay free. Higher rates for spec evnts/hols. Spec packages avail. Pking: Indoor, $9. Maj CC.

≣≣≣ Holiday Inn Central, 1501 Rhode Island Ave NW, at 15th St NW, Washington, DC 20005 (Dupont Circle); tel 202/483-2000 or toll free 800/248-0016; fax 202/797-1078. A modern hotel with convenient downtown location, comfortable lobby with overstuffed chairs. **Rooms:** 213 rms and stes. CI 3pm/CO noon. Express checkout avail. Nonsmoking rms avail. Pleasant and clean. **Amenities:** 🛋 🕭 🖿 🖣 A/C, cable TV w/movies, voice mail. Some units w/terraces. **Services:** ✕ 🖙 🖾 ◁ Complimentary coffee in lobby, hors d'oeuvres in evening. **Facilities:** 🖀 🙌 🔲 🕭 1 rst, 1 bar, lifeguard, games rm, washer/dryer. Rooftop pool, pleasingly quaint restaurant. **Rates:** $129 S; $142 D; from $150 ste. Extra person $13. Children under 18 stay free. Higher rates for spec evnts/hols. Spec packages avail. Pking: Indoor, $10. Maj CC. Seniors discounts, weekend rates available. Kids eat free with parents in summer.

≣ Holiday Inn Franklin Square, 1155 14th St NW, Washington, DC 20005; tel 202/737-1200 or toll free 800/HOLIDAY; fax 202/783-5733. An older property right on Thomas Circle. Shows wear and tear, need of renovation. **Rooms:** 208 rms and stes. Exec-level rms avail. CI 3pm/CO noon. Express checkout avail. Nonsmoking rms avail. **Amenities:** 🛋 🕭 🖣 A/C, cable TV w/movies. **Services:** 🖙 🖾 🖾 ◁ **Facilities:** 🖀 🔲 🕭 1 rst, 1 bar, lifeguard, washer/dryer. Restaurant serves breakfast only. **Rates:** HS May–Oct $100–$140 S or D; from $160 ste. Extra person $13. Children under 18 stay free. Lower rates off-season. Spec packages avail. Pking: Outdoor, $10. Maj CC.

≣≣ Hotel Anthony, 1823 L St NW, Washington, DC 20036; tel 202/223-4320 or toll free 800/424-2970; fax 202/223-8546. Small property in the heart of downtown, near restaurants and shops. **Rooms:** 98 rms and stes. CI noon/CO 11am. Express checkout avail. Although dated, rooms are spacious and comfortable, with sitting areas, kitchenettes or wet bars. Although called

suites, they are 1 large room. **Amenities:** 🛋 🖿 A/C, cable TV, refrig, shoe polisher. **Services:** ✕ 🖾 ◁ Babysitting. **Facilities:** 🖾 1 rst, 1 bar, beauty salon. Free use of nearby health club. **Rates:** HS Mar–June/Sept–Nov $135 S; $145 D; from $120 ste. Extra person $10. Children under 16 stay free. Lower rates off-season. Higher rates for spec evnts/hols. Spec packages avail. Pking: Indoor, $12. Maj CC. Weekend rates available.

≣≣ Hotel Lombardy, 2019 I St NW, Washington, DC 20006 (Foggy Bottom); tel 202/828-2600 or toll free 800/424-5486; fax 202/872-0503. Rich wood paneling greets guests in the lobby of this comfortable hotel, originally built as an apartment house. Old-fashioned, manually operated elevator and molding over room doors still remain. **Rooms:** 126 rms and stes. CI 3pm/CO noon. Express checkout avail. Nonsmoking rms avail. Most rooms and suites have kitchens. **Amenities:** 🛋 🕭 🖿 A/C, cable TV w/movies, refrig, shoe polisher, bathrobes. All units w/minibars. **Services:** ✕ 🖾 ◁ Twice-daily maid svce, babysitting. **Facilities:** 🖾 1 rst, washer/dryer. **Rates:** $115 S; $130 D; from $150 ste. Extra person $10. Children under 16 stay free. Higher rates for spec evnts/hols. Spec packages avail. Pking: Indoor, $11.20. Maj CC.

≣≣≣≣ Hotel Sofitel, 1914 Connecticut Ave NW, at Florida Ave, Washington, DC 20009; tel 202/797-2000 or toll free 800/424-2464; fax 202/462-0944. Built in 1906 as an elegant apartment building on Embassy Row, this European-style hotel caters to discriminating travelers. Intimate lobby has gilt-framed paintings, ornate molding. **Rooms:** 145 rms and stes. CI 3pm/CO 1pm. Express checkout avail. Nonsmoking rms avail. Spacious rooms show unique architectural details from apartment days. **Amenities:** 🛋 🕭 🖣 A/C, cable TV w/movies, refrig, voice mail, in-rm safe, bathrobes. All units w/minibars, 1 w/Jacuzzi. **Services:** 🍴 🖙 🖾 🖾 ◁ Twice-daily maid svce, babysitting. European-schooled concierge and rest of multilingual staff pay much attention to detail. **Facilities:** 🔲 🖳 1 rst, 1 bar. **Rates:** HS Jan–May/Sept–Nov $185–$205 S; $205–$225 D; from $280 ste. Extra person $25. Children under 12 stay free. Lower rates off-season. Spec packages avail. Pking: Indoor, $10. Maj CC.

≣≣≣ Hotel Washington, 15th St and Pennsylvania Ave NW, Washington, DC 20004; tel 202/638-5900 or toll free 800/424-9540; fax 202/638-1595. Recent improvements have added new appeal to this Washington institution within a block of the White House, the Mall, upscale shops, the National Theater, and the Willard and JW Marriott hotels. **Rooms:** 344 rms and stes. CI 1pm/CO 3pm. Express checkout avail. Nonsmoking rms avail. Rooms have traditional mahogany furniture, marble baths, historical prints. **Amenities:** 🛋 🕭 🖣 A/C, cable TV w/movies, refrig, voice mail, shoe polisher. Some units w/minibars.

Services: ⃞ ⃞ VP ⃞ ⃞ ⃞ Babysitting. **Facilities:** ⃞ ⃞ ⃞ ⃞ 2 rsts, 2 bars, spa, sauna. Rooftop Sky Terrace overlooking the White House and Mall is a favorite local spot for cocktails. **Rates:** $159–$205 S; $174–$219 D; from $410 ste. Extra person $18. Children under 14 stay free. Higher rates for spec evnts/hols. Spec packages avail. Pking: Indoor, $15.75. Maj CC.

≣≣≣ **Howard Johnson's Hotel & Suites**, 1430 Rhode Island Ave NW, Washington, DC 20005 (Downtown); tel 202/462-7777 or toll free 800/368-5690; fax 202/332-3519. Between 14th St NW and Scott Circle. A moderately priced hotel in close proximity to Convention Center and attractions. **Rooms:** 184 rms and stes. CI 1pm/CO noon. Nonsmoking rms avail. Suites have full kitchens. **Amenities:** ⃞ A/C, cable TV w/movies, refrig, in-rm safe. Hair dryers available on request. **Services:** ✕ VP ⃞ ⃞ **Facilities:** ⃞ ⃞ ⃞ 1 rst, 1 bar, lifeguard, games rm, washer/dryer. **Rates:** $82 S; $92 D; from $102 ste. Extra person $10. Children under 12 stay free. Higher rates for spec evnts/hols. Pking: Indoor, $7.84. Maj CC.

≣≣ **Howard Johnson's Lodge**, 2601 Virginia Ave NW, Washington, DC 20037 (Foggy Bottom); tel 202/965-2700 or toll free 800/654-2000; fax 202/965-2700 ext 7910. It was from this hotel that the Democratic National Committee offices in the Watergate building across the street were bugged in 1972, leading to the infamous scandal that brought down the Nixon presidency. It is still a moderately priced property within walking distance of the Kennedy Center and Potomac River. **Rooms:** 193 rms. CI 3pm/CO noon. Nonsmoking rms avail. Standard motel-style rooms. **Amenities:** ⃞ ⃞ A/C, TV, refrig, VCR, shoe polisher. Some units w/terraces. Movies for rent in lobby. **Services:** ⃞ ⃞ ⃞ **Facilities:** ⃞ ⃞ ⃞ 1 rst, lifeguard, games rm, washer/dryer. Family restaurant on premises. Use of Watergate Health Club across street for a fee. **Rates:** HS Apr–Aug $73–$91 S; $82–$99 D. Extra person $5. Children under 18 stay free. Lower rates off-season. Spec packages avail. Pking: Indoor, free. Maj CC.

≣≣≣≣ **The Jefferson**, 1200 16th St NW, at M St, Washington, DC 20036; tel 202/347-2200 or toll free 800/368-5966; fax 202/331-7982. An unassuming exterior gives way to an ornate lobby with marble floor, numerous Persian rugs, and chandeliers strung from arched ceilings—all a mere prelude to the rest of this fine hotel, which has been catering to famous journalists and literary figures since 1923. **Rooms:** 100 rms and stes. CI 3pm/CO 1pm. Nonsmoking rms avail. Each elegant room is individually decorated, many featuring fine European antiques. **Amenities:** ⃞ ⃞ ⃞ A/C, cable TV w/movies, VCR, stereo/tape player, shoe polisher, bathrobes. All units w/minibars, 1 w/fireplace, 1 w/Jacuzzi. **Services:** ⃞ ⃞ VP ⃞ ⃞ ⃞ Twice-daily maid svce, babysitting. Entire front office staff is trained in

concierge duties. **Facilities:** ⃞ ⃞ 1 rst (see also "Restaurants" below), 1 bar (w/entertainment). The dining room is one of Washington's finest places to eat. **Rates:** $220–$260 S; $235–$275 D; from $320 ste. Extra person $20. Children under 18 stay free. Spec packages avail. Pking: Indoor, $20. Maj CC.

≣≣≣ **JW Marriott Hotel**, 1331 Pennsylvania Ave NW, at E St, Washington, DC 20004 (Downtown); tel 202/393-2000 or toll free 800/228-9290; fax 202/626-6991. Flagship of the Marriott chain, this large convention hotel adjacent to the National Theater and 2 blocks from the Mall and the White House has an attractive 2-story lobby with marble floors, comfortable seating, and crystal chandeliers. The facility opens to an enclosed shopping mall with upscale shops and 2 food courts. **Rooms:** 772 rms and stes. Exec-level rms avail. CI 4pm/CO noon. Express checkout avail. Nonsmoking rms avail. Rooms are richly appointed with dark wood furniture. **Amenities:** ⃞ ⃞ A/C, cable TV w/movies, voice mail, shoe polisher. Some units w/terraces, 1 w/Jacuzzi. **Services:** ⃞ ⃞ VP ⃞ ⃞ ⃞ Car-rental desk, masseur, babysitting. **Facilities:** ⃞ ⃞ ⃞ ⃞ ⃞ 2 rsts, 2 bars (1 w/entertainment), lifeguard, games rm, spa, sauna, whirlpool. Food and beverage outlets range from casual to elegant. **Rates:** HS Sept–Nov/Mar–June $195–$205 S or D; from $575 ste. Children under 18 stay free. Lower rates off-season. Higher rates for spec evnts/hols. Spec packages avail. Pking: Indoor, $16–$25. Maj CC.

Loews L'Enfant Plaza Hotel, 480 L'Enfant Plaza SW, Washington, DC 20024; tel 202/484-1000 or toll free 800/243-1166; fax 202/646-4456. Located among government office buildings near the Mall and Smithsonian Institution museums, this hotel caters to both business travelers and families with children. Pets are definitely welcomed and pampered, and 70% of pet fees go to the Humane Society. Unrated. **Rooms:** 370 rms and stes. CI 3pm/CO 1pm. Express checkout avail. Nonsmoking rms avail. **Amenities:** ⃞ ⃞ ⃞ A/C, cable TV w/movies, refrig, VCR, voice mail, in-rm safe, shoe polisher. All units w/minibars, some w/terraces. **Services:** ✕ ⃞ VP ⃞ ⃞ ⃞ Twice-daily maid svce, social director, children's program, babysitting. **Facilities:** ⃞ ⃞ ⃞ ⃞ ⃞ 1 rst, 2 bars, lifeguard, games rm, spa, beauty salon, day-care ctr. Large health club. Attractive rooftop pool with snack bar, umbrella tables. **Rates:** $205–$225 S or D; from $475 ste. Extra person $20. Children under 16 stay free. Higher rates for spec evnts/hols. Spec packages avail. Pking: Indoor, $16. Maj CC.

≣≣≣ **The Madison**, 15th and M Sts NW, Washington, DC 20005; tel 202/862-1600 or toll free 800/424-8577; fax 202/785-1255. One of Washington's finest hotels is frequented by heads of state, royalty, and other very important guests. Modern yet ornate public areas are adorned with Louis XVI antiques. **Rooms:** 353 rms and stes. Exec-level rms avail. CI 3pm/CO 1pm. Nonsmoking rms avail. Every room has Oriental rugs. Some have works by well-known artists. Quality of all furnishings is exquisite. **Amenities:** 🔒 🅱 🍷 A/C, cable TV w/movies, refrig, VCR, shoe polisher, bathrobes. All units w/minibars, some w/terraces. Every guest provided fruit plate upon arrival. **Services:** 🍽️ 🗝️ VP 🛏️ 🖤 Twice-daily maid svce, masseur, babysitting. Multilingual concierge staff caters to international clientele. **Facilities:** 🏌️ 800 💻 ⚓ 4 rsts, 3 bars, spa. **Rates:** $235 S; $255 D; from $395 ste. Extra person $30. Higher rates for spec evnts/hols. Spec packages avail. Pking: Indoor, $7–$14. Maj CC.

≣≣≣ **Marriott at Metro Center**, 775 12th St NW, Washington, DC 20005; tel 202/737-2200 or toll free 800/992-5891; fax 202/347-0860. Formerly a Holiday Inn Crowne Plaza, this modern hotel recently switched to Marriott management. Convenient downtown location at Metro Center station, surrounded by shops, restaurants, businesses. **Rooms:** 456 rms and stes. Exec-level rms avail. CI 4pm/CO noon. Express checkout avail. Nonsmoking rms avail. **Amenities:** 🔒 🅱 🖵 🍷 A/C, cable TV, refrig, voice mail. All units w/minibars, 1 w/Jacuzzi. **Services:** ✗ 🗝️ VP 🛏️ 🖤 Twice-daily maid svce, car-rental desk. **Facilities:** 🏌️ 🏊 550 💻 ⚓ 1 rst, 1 bar, lifeguard, spa, sauna, steam rm, whirlpool. **Rates:** HS Sept–Thanksgiving $159–$174 S or D; from $500 ste. Children under 12 stay free. Lower rates off-season. Spec packages avail. Pking: Indoor, $12. Maj CC.

≣≣ **Marriott's Residence Inn**, 1000 29th St NW, at K St, Washington, DC 20007 (Georgetown); tel 202/298-1600 or toll free 800/331-3131; fax 202/333-2019. Hidden away in a convenient corner of Georgetown, this all-suites property is superbly equipped for the guest who prefers the feel of home rather than a room in a busier, more populous hotel. Patio provides opportunity to relax outside and meet fellow guests. **Rooms:** 78 stes. CI 3pm/CO noon. Express checkout avail. Nonsmoking rms avail. Spacious, comfortable units have full kitchens, separate dining area. **Amenities:** 🔒 🅱 🖵 🍷 A/C, cable TV w/movies, refrig. **Services:** 🛏️ 🖤 🌐 Complimentary newspaper. Continental breakfast. Grocery shopping. **Facilities:** 🏌️ 50 ⚓ Washer/dryer. Guests can swim at nearby Marriott. **Rates (CP):** HS Apr–June/Sept–Nov from $79 ste. Extra person $10. Lower rates off-season. Spec packages avail. Pking: Indoor, $13. Maj CC.

≣ **Master Host Inn–Walter Reed**, 6711 Georgia Ave NW, at Aspen St, Washington, DC 20012; tel 202/722-1600 or toll free 800/251-1962; fax 202/723-3979. A block from Walter Reed Army Hospital, this 4-story hotel has a small lobby, and public areas could stand some attention. **Rooms:** 72 rms and stes. CI 2pm/CO noon. Nonsmoking rms avail. Pleasantly large and well-decorated rooms. **Amenities:** 🔒 A/C, cable TV w/movies. Some units w/terraces. **Services:** ✗ 🛏️ 🖤 🌐 **Facilities:** 🏌️ 1 rst, 1 bar, lifeguard. Chinese restaurant on premises. **Rates (CP):** HS May–Sept $37–$45 S; $42–$49 D; from $54 ste. Extra person $4. Children under 17 stay free. Lower rates off-season. Spec packages avail. Pking: Outdoor, free. Maj CC. AARP and military discounts.

≣≣≣≣ **Omni Shoreham Hotel**, 2500 Calvert St NW, at Connecticut Ave, Washington, DC 20008 (Woodley Park); tel 202/234-0700 or toll free 800/843-6664; fax 202/332-1373. A landmark built in 1930 on the edge of Rock Creek Park, this gracious and charming hotel has hosted inaugural balls for every president from Franklin D Roosevelt to Bill Clinton. Memorabilia exhibit in main lobby captures much of hotel's links to nation's history. **Rooms:** 770 rms and stes. CI 3pm/CO noon. Express checkout avail. Nonsmoking rms avail. **Amenities:** 🔒 🅱 A/C, cable TV w/movies, shoe polisher. Some units w/terraces. **Services:** ✗ 🗝️ 🛏️ 🖤 Social director, children's program, babysitting. Kids Concierge looks after the tots. **Facilities:** 🏌️ 💦3 🏊 2.5K 💻 ⚓ 1 rst, 2 bars (1 w/entertainment), lifeguard, lawn games, spa, sauna. Marquis Lounge is a popular local venue for political comedy. Gourmet shop sells carryout picnic fare. **Rates:** HS Mar–Apr/Sept–Oct $195 S; $220 D; from $395 ste. Children under 18 stay free. Lower rates off-season. Spec packages avail. Pking: Indoor/outdoor, $12. Maj CC.

≣≣≣≣ **Park Hyatt**, 1201 24th St NW, at M St, Washington, DC 20037; tel 202/789-1234 or toll free 800/922-7275; fax 202/457-8823. A European-style hotel with an emphasis on service. Traditional furniture and museum-quality art in public areas lend old-time ambience to a modern structure with contemporary charm. Just 3 blocks from Georgetown. **Rooms:** 224 rms and stes. CI 3pm/CO noon. Express checkout avail. Nonsmoking rms avail. Large rooms all have sitting areas with sofas. **Amenities:** 🔒 🅱 🍷 A/C, cable TV w/movies, refrig, voice mail, shoe polisher, bathrobes. All units w/minibars, some w/terraces, 1 w/fireplace, some w/Jacuzzis. Marble baths have brass fixtures, TVs with radios, porcelain canisters for toiletries. **Services:** 🍽️ 🗝️ VP 🛏️ 🖤 🌐 Twice-daily maid svce, masseur, babysitting. **Facilities:** 🏌️ 🏊 400 💻 ⚓ 1 rst, 2 bars (1 w/entertainment), lifeguard, spa, sauna, steam rm, whirlpool, beauty salon. The lounge features dancing to big bands on Saturday nights. **Rates:** HS Sept–Oct/Mar–June $280–$305 S or

D; from $325 ste. Extra person $25. Children under 18 stay free. Lower rates off-season. Spec packages avail. Pking: Indoor, $18. Maj CC. Weekend rates available.

Quality Hotel Downtown, 1315 16th St NW, at N St, Washington, DC 20036; tel 202/232-8000 or toll free 800/228-5151; fax 202/667-9827. An all-suites hotel conveniently located in the heart of downtown near Scott Circle. Unrated. **Rooms:** 137 rms. CI 1pm/CO noon. Express checkout avail. Nonsmoking rms avail. **Amenities:** ⊞ ⊡ ⌑ A/C, cable TV w/movies, refrig, shoe polisher. Corporate-level units have robes, alarm clocks, computer/fax jacks. **Services:** ✗ ⊶ ⊠ ⌐ Car-rental desk, babysitting. **Facilities:** ⊡ ⌂ 60 ⌑ ⌙ 1 rst, 1 bar, lifeguard, games rm, spa, sauna, steam rm, whirlpool, washer/dryer. Free privileges at nearby health club. **Rates:** $89–$160 S; $180 D. Extra person $10. Children under 18 stay free. Spec packages avail. Pking: Indoor, $8.50. Maj CC.

☰☰☰☰ The Ritz-Carlton Washington, 2100 Massachusetts Ave NW, at Q St, Washington, DC 20008 (Dupont Circle); tel 202/293-2100 or toll free 800/241-3333; fax 202/293-0641. An understated exterior gives way to rich Ritz-Carlton elegance in this luxury hotel in the heart of Embassy Row, a block from Dupont Circle metro station. **Rooms:** 206 rms and stes. Exec-level rms avail. CI 2pm/CO noon. Express checkout avail. Nonsmoking rms avail. Club Level rooms and suites on top 2 floors have goose-down beds. **Amenities:** ⊞ ⌂ ⌑ A/C, cable TV, refrig, in-rm safe, shoe polisher, bathrobes. All units w/minibars, 1 w/Jacuzzi. Club Level units have VCRs with video library. **Services:** ⌾ ⊶ ⊻⊻ ⊠ ⌐ Twice-daily maid svce, babysitting. Those staying on Club Level can take advantage of own concierge lounge with 5 daily food presentations, get complimentary use of fitness center. **Facilities:** ⌂ 300 1 rst, 1 bar (w/entertainment), steam rm. Jockey Club Restaurant is famous locally. **Rates:** $195–$340 S or D; from $350 ste. Children under 18 stay free. Pking: Indoor, $20. Maj CC.

☰☰ Savoy Suites Georgetown, 2505 Wisconsin Ave NW, Washington, DC 20007; tel 202/337-9700 or toll free 800/944-5377; fax 202/337-3644. Just north of Calvert St. White brick building with mansard roof and imitation balconies, located north of Georgetown in a residential neighborhood with nearby shops and restaurants. **Rooms:** 150 stes. CI 3pm/CO 1pm. Nonsmoking rms avail. Suites actually are 1 large room. **Amenities:** ⊞ A/C, satel TV w/movies, voice mail. Some units

w/Jacuzzis. Rooms that don't have kitchenettes with microwaves have small refrigerators instead. **Services:** ✗ ⊠ ⌐ ⊲ Car-rental desk, babysitting. **Facilities:** 200 ⌑ ⌙ 1 rst, 1 bar, washer/dryer. **Rates:** From $119 ste. Extra person $10. Children under 18 stay free. Spec packages avail. Pking: Indoor, free. Maj CC.

☰☰☰ State Plaza Hotel, 2117 E St NW, Washington, DC 20037 (Foggy Bottom); tel 202/861-8200 or toll free 800/424-2859; fax 202/659-8601. Near the State Department, George Washington University, and the Kennedy Center. **Rooms:** 215 stes. CI 3pm/CO noon. Nonsmoking rms avail. Nicely appointed units range from studios to 1-bedroom models with living and dining areas. **Amenities:** ⊞ ⌂ ⊡ A/C, cable TV w/movies, refrig. All units w/minibars. **Services:** ✗ ⊶ ⊠ ⌐ Twice-daily maid svce. **Facilities:** ⌂ 100 ⌙ 1 rst, 1 bar, washer/dryer. **Rates:** From $125 ste. Extra person $20. Children under 16 stay free. Higher rates for spec evnts/hols. Spec packages avail. Pking: Indoor, $12. Maj CC. Weekend rates available.

☰☰☰☰ Stouffer Mayflower Hotel, 1127 Connecticut Ave NW, Washington, DC 20036; tel 202/347-3000 or toll free 800/HOTELS-1; fax 202/466-9082. Between L and M Sts. Home of presidential inaugural balls since the 1920s and regular lunch spot for the late FBI director J. Edgar Hoover, this downtown landmark underwent a thorough renovation in the 1980s, which restored its ornate lobby and striking block-long promenade and brought its rooms up to luxury standards. **Rooms:** 659 rms and stes. CI 3pm/CO noon. Express checkout avail. Nonsmoking rms avail. Guest rooms are individually decorated and furnished with period reproductions. **Amenities:** ⊞ ⌂ ⌑ A/C, cable TV w/movies, refrig, shoe polisher, bathrobes. Some units w/minibars, 1 w/terrace, some w/Jacuzzis. Baths have TVs. **Services:** ⌾ ⊶ ⊻⊻ ⊠ ⌐ ⊲ Twice-daily maid svce, babysitting. **Facilities:** ⌂ 1K ⌙ 2 rsts, 1 bar (w/entertainment), sauna, steam rm, beauty salon. **Rates:** $240 S or D; from $450 ste. Extra person $25. Children under 18 stay free. Higher rates for spec evnts/hols. Spec packages avail. Pking: Indoor, $11.50. Maj CC.

☰☰☰ Washington, DC, Renaissance Hotel, 999 9th St NW, at K St, Washington, DC 20001 (Downtown); tel 202/898-9000 or toll free 800/228-9898; fax 202/789-4213. A 2-story atrium lobby with bar highlights this modern establishment across the street from the Convention Center. Near Chinatown and numerous restaurants. **Rooms:** 800 rms and stes. Exec-level rms avail. CI 3pm/CO noon. Express checkout avail. Nonsmoking rms avail. **Amenities:** ⊞ ⌂ A/C, cable TV w/movies, refrig, voice mail. All units w/minibars, some w/terraces, some w/Jacuzzis. **Services:** 🍽️ ☎️ VP 🛄 🔄 🍷 Car-rental desk, babysitting. Club Tower-level rooms get continental breakfast, afternoon hors d'oeuvres, private lounge, turndown service. **Facilities:** 🎱 🏋️ 1.1K 💻 ♿ 2 rsts, 1 bar, spa, sauna, steam rm, whirlpool, beauty salon. Health club free to Club Tower guests, small charge for others. **Rates:** HS Mar–June/Sept–Nov $185 S; $205 D; from $400 ste. Extra person $20. Children under 16 stay free. Lower rates off-season. Higher rates for spec evnts/hols. Spec packages avail. Pking: Indoor, $14. Maj CC.

≣≣≣≣ **Washington Hilton and Towers**, 1919 Connecticut Ave NW, at T St, Washington, DC 20009 (Kalorama); tel 202/483-3000 or toll free 800/HILTONS; fax 202/265-8221. The largest hotel in Washington, this 10-story structure consists of 2 semicircles flaring from their meeting point at its public areas. Its perch atop a hill gives rooms at higher levels great views over the city. One of the city's biggest convention and banquet venues. President Ronald Reagan was shot and wounded while leaving here in 1981. **Rooms:** 1,123 rms and stes. Exec-level rms avail. CI 3pm/CO noon. Express checkout avail. Nonsmoking rms avail. Bright and cheerful. Cabana rooms have very high ceilings, garden views. **Amenities:** 📺 ⚙️ A/C, cable TV w/movies, refrig. All units w/minibars, some w/Jacuzzis. All rooms have irons and boards. Tower units have fax machines. Cabana rooms have wet bars, coffeemakers. **Services:** ✕ ☎️ 🛄 🔄 🍷 Car-rental desk, masseur, babysitting. **Facilities:** 🎱 🖼️ 🏋️ 3.5K 💻 ♿ 2 rsts, 2 bars (1 w/entertainment), lifeguard, steam rm. **Rates:** $190–$240 S or D; from $400 ste. Extra person $20. Children under 18 stay free. Spec packages avail. Pking: Indoor, $12. Maj CC.

≣≣≣ **Washington Vista**, 1400 M St NW, at T St, Washington, DC 20005; tel 202/429-1700 or toll free 800/VISTA-DC; fax 202/785-0786. A soaring, 14-story atrium lobby with many live plants and fresh flower arrangements sets the tone at this modern hotel in the center of downtown. A huge lobby clock visible to all keeps track of every passing minute. **Rooms:** 400 rms and stes. Exec-level rms avail. CI 3pm/CO noon. Express checkout avail. Nonsmoking rms avail. **Amenities:** 📺 ⚙️ 🍷 A/C, cable TV w/movies, refrig, voice mail, shoe polisher. All units w/minibars, some w/terraces, some w/Jacuzzis. Many rooms have balconies overlooking atrium. **Services:** 🍽️ ☎️ VP 🛄 🔄 Twice-daily maid svce, babysitting. Executive floors have private lounge serving breakfast, snacks, drinks, and hors d'oeuvres. **Facilities:** 🏋️ 🖼️ 400 ♿ 2 rsts, 2 bars. **Rates:** HS Mar–Jun/Sept–Nov $165–$240 S; $190–$265 D; from $310 ste. Extra person $25. Children under 18 stay free. Lower rates off-season. Higher rates for spec evnts/hols. Spec packages avail. Pking: Indoor, $15. Maj CC.

≣≣≣≣ **The Watergate Hotel**, 2650 Virginia Ave NW, Washington, DC 20037 (Foggy Bottom); tel 202/965-2300 or toll free 800/424-2736; fax 202/337-7915. An exquisite lobby with giant spotlighted flower arrangement, marble-tile floor, columns, and a grand piano is merely a prelude to one of Washington's finest hotels. Its location across Rock Creek Parkway from the Potomac River provides water views to many rooms and suites. The Watergate Office Building, site of the 1972 eavesdropping incident that led to President Richard Nixon's downfall, is next door. **Rooms:** 235 rms, stes. Exec-level rms avail. CI 3pm/CO noon. Express checkout avail. Nonsmoking rms avail. With decor by an interior designer, rooms have kitchenettes, 2 closets. **Amenities:** 📺 ⚙️ 🍷 A/C, cable TV w/movies, refrig, shoe polisher, bathrobes. All units w/minibars, some w/terraces. Lots of amenities, such as umbrellas. Kitchen starter kit available on request. Children's movies for rent at front desk. **Services:** 🍽️ ☎️ VP 🛄 🔄 🍷 Twice-daily maid svce, car-rental desk, social director, masseur, children's program, babysitting. Complimentary shoe shines, limousine transport within the District of Columbia. **Facilities:** 🎱 🚲 🏋️ 500 💻 ♿ 2 rsts (see also "Restaurants" below), 2 bars, lifeguard, games rm, spa, sauna, steam rm, whirlpool, beauty salon. **Rates:** HS April–June/Sept–Dec $260–$285 S; $285–$310 D; from $385 ste. Extra person $25. Children under 18 stay free. Lower rates off-season. Spec packages avail. Pking: Indoor, $15. Maj CC.

≣≣≣≣ **Willard Inter-Continental Washington**, 1401 Pennsylvania Ave NW, Washington, DC 20004 (Downtown); tel 202/628-9100 or toll free 800/327-0200; fax 202/637-7326. This beaux arts masterpiece has stood as a landmark at Pennsylvania Avenue and 14th St, 2 blocks from the White House and the Mall, since 1902. There has been a hotel on this corner since 1816 and a Willard Hotel since the 1850s. As such, it's steeped in national lore. The present building was closed from 1968 to 1986, when a complete renovation restored its grandeur. Today the Willard is an elegant luxury hotel worthy of the presidents and other famous notables who have graced its guest list. Hotel opens to shopping arcade with upscale shops. **Rooms:** 345 rms and stes. CI 3pm/CO noon. Express checkout avail. Nonsmoking rms avail. Gilt-framed French prints and Edwardian reproductions are part of the elegant luxury. **Amenities:** 📺 ⚙️ 🍷 A/C, cable TV w/movies, refrig, voice mail, shoe polisher, bathrobes. All units w/minibars. Suites have 2-line phones. **Services:** 🍽️ ☎️ VP 🛄 🔄 🍷 Twice-daily maid svce, babysitting. **Facilities:** 🏋️ 600 💻 ♿ 2 rsts (see also "Restaurants" below), 2 bars (1 w/entertainment). Excellent restaurants. **Rates:** HS Sept–July $260–$350 S; $290–$380 D; from $495 ste. Extra person $30. Children under 18 stay free. Lower rates off-season. Spec packages avail. Pking: Indoor, $15.75. Maj CC.

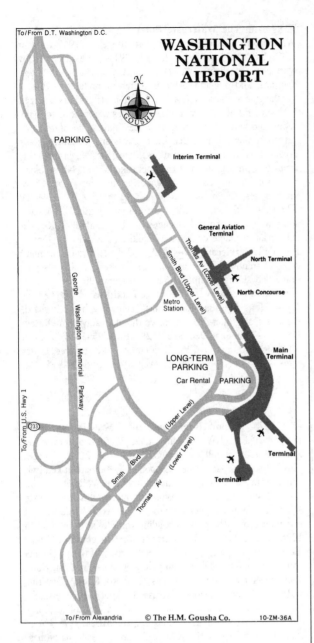

WASHINGTON NATIONAL AIRPORT

To/From D.T. Washington D.C.

PARKING

Interim Terminal

General Aviation Terminal

North Terminal

North Concourse

Smith Blvd (Upper Level)

Thomas Av (Lower Level)

Metro Station

Main Terminal

George Washington Memorial Parkway

LONG-TERM PARKING

Car Rental   PARKING

(Upper Level)

Smith Blvd

Thomas Av (Lower Level)

Terminal

Terminal

To/From U.S. Hwy 1

To/From Alexandria   © The H.M. Gousha Co.   10-ZM-36A

Motels

Channel Inn, 650 Water St SW, Washington, DC 20024 (Downtown); tel 202/554-2400 or toll free 800/368-5668; fax 202/368-1164. Between 7th St and Maine Ave. The city's only waterfront accommodations, convenient to metro and Maine Avenue seafood restaurants. Lobby wall hangings and ship models make guests feel like old salts. **Rooms:** 100 rms and stes. CI 1pm/CO noon. Rooms facing the Potomac River offer views of numerous yachts docked in Washington Channel. Units on top floors have cathedral ceilings. **Amenities:** A/C, cable TV w/movies, shoe polisher. All units w/terraces. **Services:** Twice-daily maid svce, car-rental desk, babysitting. Same-day laundry service except Sunday. **Facilities:** 1 rst, 1 bar, lifeguard. **Rates:** $80–$100 S; $80–$110 D; from $150 ste. Extra person $10. Children under 12 stay free. Spec packages avail. Pking: Indoor, free. Maj CC.

Days Inn Northeast, 2700 New York Ave NE (US 50), Washington, DC 20002; tel 202/832-5800 or toll free 800/329-7466; fax 202/269-4317. A clean, well-kept motel on the northeastern outskirts of the District of Columbia. **Rooms:** 195 rms. CI 2pm/CO noon. Nonsmoking rms avail. **Amenities:** A/C, TV. **Services:** **Facilities:** 1 rst, 1 bar (w/entertainment), lifeguard, washer/dryer. Restaurant off the lobby is well furnished. **Rates:** HS Apr–Sept $39–$56 S; $56–$72 D. Extra person $5. Children under 13 stay free. Lower rates off-season. Spec packages avail. Pking: Outdoor, free. Maj CC. Represents good value for the rates charged.

Inns

Adams Inn, 1744 Lanier Place NW, Washington, DC 20009 (Adams-Morgan); tel 202/745-3600 or toll free 800/578-6807; fax 202/332-5867. Between Calvert St and Ontario Rd. Lovely turn-of-the-century homes with period furnishings and appealing decor in one of Washington's most interesting and diverse residential neighborhoods. **Rooms:** 25 rms (13 w/shared bath). CI 3pm/CO noon. No smoking. Each room individually decorated. Those without baths have in-room sinks. **Amenities:** A/C. **Services:** Babysitting, afternoon tea served. **Facilities:** Washer/dryer, guest lounge w/TV. Public phone in foyer. **Rates (CP):** $45 S or D w/shared bath, $60 S or D w/private bath. Extra person $10. Children under 2 stay free. Spec packages avail. Pking: Indoor/outdoor, $7. Ltd CC.

Capitol Hill Guest House, 101 5th St NE, at A St, Washington, DC 20002 (Capitol Hill); tel 202/547-1050. Convenient to the US Capitol and Library of Congress, this is a well-kept Victorian-era row house. Neighborhood is exceptionally quiet with little traffic on nearby streets. Unsuitable for children under 8. **Rooms:** 10 rms (all w/shared bath). CI 2pm/CO 11am. No smoking. **Amenities:** A/C. No phone or TV. Rooms on top floor have ceiling fans. **Services:** Afternoon tea and wine/sherry served. **Facilities:** Guest lounge. **Rates (CP):** HS Mar–June/Sept–Nov $45–$75 S or D w/shared bath. Extra person $10. Lower rates off-season. Spec packages avail. Ltd CC.

≣≣ **Embassy Inn**, 1627 16th St NW, Washington, DC 20009 (Dupont Circle); tel 202/234-7800 or toll free 800/423-9111; fax 202/234-3309. Between Q and R Sts. Constructed in 1922, this federal-style building fits in among large town houses along 16th St, one of the capital's finest neighborhoods in the days before suburbs. Attractive lobby doubles as lounge for guests. No elevator in this 4-story building. **Rooms:** 38 rms. CI 3pm/CO noon. Comfortable rooms furnished in federal style. **Amenities:** 🛗 🕭 A/C, TV. **Services:** ⌴ ⌴ Twice-daily maid svce, babysitting, wine/sherry served. Complimentary newspapers, coffee, continental breakfast in lobby. **Facilities:** Guest lounge. **Rates (CP):** HS Feb–June $69–$110 S or D. Extra person $10. Children under 18 stay free. Lower rates off-season. Spec packages avail. Ltd CC.

≣≣ **Hotel Windsor Park**, 2116 Kalorama Rd NW, Washington, DC 20008; tel 202/483-7700 or toll free 800/247-3064; fax 202/332-4547. Located in a residential neighborhood dotted with embassies, and within walking distance of Dupont Circle and Adams Morgan restaurants and shops, this brick structure offers simple but comfortable accommodations. **Rooms:** 43 rms and stes. CI 2pm/CO 1pm. **Amenities:** 🛗 A/C, cable TV w/movies, refrig. **Services:** ⌴ **Facilities:** 🛆 **Rates (CP):** HS Apr–June/Oct–Nov $68–$78 S or D; from $89 ste. Extra person $10. Children under 18 stay free. Lower rates off-season. Spec packages avail. Ltd CC.

≣≣ **The Kalorama Guest House**, 1854 Mintwood Place NW, Washington, DC 20009; tel 202/667-6369; fax 202/319-1262. Between 19th St and Columbia Rd. Three late-19th-century row houses in quiet residential neighborhoods—Kalorama Heights and Woodley Park—have been converted into a modern inn while retaining the charms of yesteryear. **Rooms:** 31 rms and stes (19 w/shared bath). CI 2pm/CO 11am. Each room individually decorated with brass bed and comforter. **Amenities:** 🕭 A/C. No phone or TV. Some units w/terraces. **Services:** ⌴ Wine/sherry served. Continental breakfast, afternoon sherry served in the parlor. **Facilities:** ⌴ Washer/dryer, guest lounge. **Rates (CP):** HS Apr–June/Sept–Nov $40–$75 S or D w/shared bath, $55–$95 S or D w/private bath; from $90 ste. Extra person $5. Lower rates off-season. Spec packages avail. Pking: Indoor/outdoor, $7. Ltd CC.

≣≣≣ **Morrison-Clark Inn**, Massachusetts Ave, at 11th St NW, Washington, DC 20001 (Thomas Circle); tel 202/898-1200 or toll free 800/332-7898; fax 202/289-8576. From 1923 until 1980, these 2 Italianate houses, on the National Register of Historic Places, served as a hostel for the Soldiers, Sailors, Marines and Airmen Club. After extensive remodeling, they were reopened in 1988 as this very fine inn. Victorian decor predominates in the public parlors, capturing the era when the structures were probably built. **Rooms:** 54 rms and stes. CI 3pm/CO noon. Guest rooms have high ceilings and are individually decorated in various styles. **Amenities:** 🛗 🕭 A/C, cable TV w/movies, shoe polisher. Some units w/terraces. **Services:** ✕ 🆅🅿 ⌴ ⌴ Twice-daily maid svce, social director, masseur, children's program, afternoon tea and wine/sherry served. **Facilities:** 🛏 ⌴ 🛆 1 rst (see also "Restaurants" below), 1 bar, guest lounge. An elegant Victorian drawing room, the dining room is one of Washington's finest eateries. **Rates (CP):** HS Mar 15–June/Sept 15–Nov 25 $125–$185 S or D; from $145 ste. Extra person $20. Children under 12 stay free. Lower rates off-season. Higher rates for spec evnts/hols. Spec packages avail. Pking: Indoor, $10. Ltd CC.

≣≣≣ **Normandy Inn**, 2118 Wyoming Ave NW, Washington, DC 20008 (Kalorama); tel 202/483-1350 or toll free 800/424-3729; fax 202/387-8241. A rather plain modern facade reminiscent of an economy motel masks a warm and hospitable small hotel with many inn features. **Rooms:** 75 rms. CI noon/CO noon. Comfortable, attractive rooms. **Amenities:** 🛗 🕭 🖵 ⌴ A/C, satel TV w/movies, refrig, shoe polisher. **Services:** ✕ 🗝 🛆 ⌴ ⌴ Afternoon tea served. Continental breakfast available in parlor or room at reasonable price. Coffee and tea available all day in the parlor, with cookies set out at teatime. **Facilities:** 🛆 Guest lounge. **Rates:** HS Mar–June/Sept–Nov $94–$104 S or D. Children under 12 stay free. Lower rates off-season. Spec packages avail. Pking: Indoor, $10. Ltd CC. Weekend rates available.

≣≣ **The Tabard Inn**, 1739 N St NW, Washington, DC 20036 (Dupont Circle); tel 202/785-1277; fax 202/785-6173. Cozy and warm, unhurried and tranquil, this establishment is in the heart of the Dupont Circle restaurant area. **Rooms:** 40 rms (13 w/shared bath). CI 2pm/CO 11am. Finished wood floors with large Oriental carpets. **Amenities:** 🛗 A/C. Ceiling fans, inoperable but attractive fireplaces. **Services:** ⌴ ⌴ **Facilities:** ⌴ 1 rst, 1 bar, guest lounge. **Rates (CP):** $58–$91 S or D w/shared bath, $99–$142 S or D w/private bath. Ltd CC.

≣≣ **Windsor Inn**, 1842 16th St NW, at T St, Washington, DC 20009 (Dupont Circle); tel 202/667-0300 or toll free 800/423-9111; fax 202/234-3309. Operated in conjunction with the Embassy Inn, this brick building on a residential portion of busy 16th St was a boardinghouse and inn from the 1920s to 1962. The present owners reopened it in 1985. Art-deco touches recapture the Roaring '20s spirit. There is no elevator nor off-street parking. Unsuitable for children under 18. **Rooms:** 46 rms and stes. CI 3pm/CO noon. Clean and comfortable rooms sport mahogany reproductions. **Amenities:** 🛗 A/C, TV. **Services:** 🛆 ⌴ Twice-daily maid svce, babysitting, wine/sherry served. Continental breakfast is served in lobby or in guests' rooms.

Facilities: ⊡ Guest lounge. **Rates (CP):** HS Feb–June $69–$110 S or D; from $105 ste. Children under 18 stay free. Lower rates off-season. Spec packages avail. Ltd CC.

Restaurants ⑾

Ⓢ **Adams Morgan Spaghetti Garden**, 2317 18th St NW, Washington; tel 202/265-6665. Near Columbia Rd. **Italian.** An unpretentious, budget-priced eatery with red tile floor, small brick bar, and blue chairs and tables. Menu offers traditional Italian pastas and some meat and chicken dishes. **FYI:** Reservations accepted. **Open:** Mon–Sat noon–midnight, Sun noon–11pm. Closed some hols. **Prices:** Main courses $4.50–$10.95. Maj CC.

Aditi Indian Cuisine, 3299 M St NW, Washington (Georgetown); tel 202/625-6825. **Indian.** Contemporary decor with large mirror, plants, Indian wall hangings, and elegant stairwell to 2nd-floor dining room. Brass chandelier in entrance. Cuisine ranging from samosas to vegetable curries to meat and chicken from the tandoor oven. Most notable choice is the sampler Aditi Dinner. **FYI:** Reservations recommended. **Open:** Lunch Mon–Sat 11:30am–2:30pm, Sun noon–2:30pm; dinner Sun–Thurs 5:30–10:30pm, Fri–Sat 5:30–10pm. Closed Thanksgiving. **Prices:** Main courses $4.95–$13.95. Maj CC. ●

Alekos, 1732 Connecticut Ave NW, Washington (Dupont Circle); tel 202/667-6211. Between R and S Sts. **Greek.** Corinthian columns support arches over stucco walls, which along with green plants are reflected in mirrors. Ceiling fans turn overhead. Specialties change from time to time and could be stuffed spring lamb and vegetables, broiled flounder, calf's liver, or broiled sea scallops, all prepared in the Greek fashion. **FYI:** Reservations accepted. **Open:** Mon–Fri 11am–11pm, Sat–Sun noon–11pm. Closed Dec 25. **Prices:** Main courses $10–$16. Maj CC. ●

★ **America**, in Union Station, 50 Massachusetts Ave NE, Washington (Capitol Hill); tel 202/682-9555. **Regional American.** Using the magnificent arches and curves of Union Station, and with wall murals depicting events in US history, this 3-level restaurant lives up to its name. Solid wooden tables and chairs. A mix of cuisines is offered, from southwestern fajitas to New York Reuben sandwiches. Death by Chocolate cake is just that. **FYI:** Reservations recommended. **Open:** Daily 11:30am–midnight. Closed Dec 25. **Prices:** Main courses $8–$18. Maj CC. ⅕

★ **The American Cafe**, 227 Massachusetts Ave NE, Washington (Capitol Hill); tel 202/547-8500. **Eclectic.** Member of a successful local chain, this one near the US Senate office buildings has exposed-brick and plaster walls, lots of plants, light woods, and mirrors to create a garden-like setting. Menu features light fare and full meals from various American regional and international cuisines. Additional locations throughout the District of Columbia, Maryland, and northern Virginia. **FYI:** Reservations accepted. Children's menu. **Open:** Mon–Thurs 11am–11pm, Fri–Sat 11am–midnight, Sun 10am–10pm. Closed some hols. **Prices:** Main courses $5.50–$13. Maj CC. ⛴ ▦

The Art Gallery Grille, 1712 I St NW, Washington; tel 202/298-6658. **Eclectic.** Contemporary decor is highlighted by neon lights. Menu offers salads, burgers, and a variety of cuisines including Tex-Mex, deli, and Middle Eastern. Bar open until 2am. **FYI:** Reservations accepted. Dancing. **Open:** Breakfast Mon–Fri 6–10:30am; lunch Mon–Fri 11am–3pm; dinner Mon–Fri 4:30–11pm. Closed some hols. **Prices:** Main courses $5.95–$13.95. Maj CC. ⛴ 🚐 ⅕

★ **Au Pied de Cochon**, 1335 Wisconsin Ave NW, Washington (Georgetown); tel 202/333-5440. Just below O St. **French.** This long-standing French restaurant in an old corner building with high ceilings has copper pots and photos on its brick walls, small marble tables, and, as you might expect in a place called the Pig's Foot, plenty of pig accents. French menu has some items with Basque influence. Open all day, but daily special begins at 4pm. Glassed sidewalk patio area. Adjoining shop sells French bread and pastries to carry out. **FYI:** Reservations not accepted. **Open:** Daily 24 hrs. **Prices:** Main courses $6–$11. Maj CC. ● ▼

Aux Fruits de Mer, 1329 Wisconsin Ave NW, Washington (Georgetown); tel 202/333-2333. **French.** Sister to Au Pied de Cochon, next door, this French cafe, brasserie, and bar in the heart of Georgetown has low ceilings to help create an intimate atmosphere. Marble-top tables, Tiffany ceiling lamps accent red upholstered booths and dark wood chairs. French seafood selections feature lobster stuffed with crabmeat, bouillabaisse. **FYI:** Reservations accepted. **Open:** Dinner Sun–Wed 5–11:30pm, Thurs–Sat 5pm–4am; brunch Sun 10:30am–3:30pm. **Prices:** Main courses $6.95–$12.95. Maj CC. ● ▼

Bamiyan Afghan Restaurant, 3320 M St NW, Washington (Georgetown); tel 202/338-1896. **Afghani.** Oriental carpets, brass lanterns, and artwork from Afghanistan create an appropriate atmosphere to enjoy cuisine from that war-torn country. Menu offers vegetarian specialties as well as mint-and yogurt-flavored meat dishes. **FYI:** Reservations not accepted. **Open:** Lunch daily 11:30am–2pm; dinner daily 5:30–11pm. Closed some hols. **Prices:** Main courses $7.25–$14. Maj CC. ▦

★ **Bistro Français**, 3124–28 M St NW, Washington (Georgetown); tel 202/338-3830. **French.** French decorative touches and gold and dark wood walls and ceilings bring Parisian flair and elegance here. There's a wide range of traditional choices, from roast pigeon with truffle gravy to organic chicken with Dijon mustard sauce. Early-bird specials in effect 5–7pm and

10:30pm–1am. **FYI:** Reservations recommended. **Open:** Sun–Thurs 11am–3am, Fri–Sat 11am–4am. Closed Dec 25. **Prices:** Main courses $12.95–$17.95. Maj CC. 💟 ⬛ VP

The Bombay Club, 815 Connecticut Ave NW, Washington; tel 202/659-3727. **Indian.** One of the most refined and elegant Indian restaurants anywhere, this excellent establishment a block from the White House hearkens back to days of the Raj, with its slow-moving white ceiling fans, antiques, gold-framed pictures, cartoons, and magazine covers from the British Empire era. Gourmet Indian cuisine is nicely presented. Both vegetarian curries and tandoori meat dishes are all perfectly seasoned. **FYI:** Reservations recommended. Piano. **Open:** Lunch Mon–Fri 11:30am–2:30pm; dinner Mon–Thurs 6–10:30pm, Fri–Sat 6–11pm, Sun 5:30–9pm; brunch Sun 11:30am–2:30pm. Closed some hols. **Prices:** Main courses $7.95–$18. Maj CC. 💟 VP &

★ **Bombay Palace**, 2020 K St NW, Washington; tel 202/331-0111. **Indian.** Plush modern decor features recessed ceilings and lighting, upholstered chairs, and mirrors reflecting a collection of Indian art. Menu offers many meat and seafood dishes as well as vegetarian curries. Samplers are popular, as are weekend lunch buffets. **FYI:** Reservations recommended. Dress code. **Open:** Lunch Mon–Fri 11:30am–2:30pm, Sat–Sun noon–2:30pm; dinner Sun–Thurs 5:30–10pm, Fri–Sat 5:30–10:30pm. Closed some hols. **Prices:** Main courses $6.50–$16.95. Maj CC. 💟 VP &

Cafe at the Corcoran Gallery of Art, 17th St NW, Washington; tel 202/638-1590. Between E St and New York Ave. **Cafe.** Soaring atrium over potted palms surrounded by Greek columns, classical busts, and a reproduction of the frieze from the Parthenon. Among the various sandwiches made with hearth-baked breads are the vegetable, turkey, and salmon; also available are soups, desserts, and a selection of coffees. **FYI:** Reservations recommended. Beer and wine only. No smoking. **Open:** Wed 11am–8pm, Thurs–Mon 11am–4pm. Closed some hols. **Prices:** Lunch main courses $6–$10. Maj CC. 💟 ⬛

Cafe Petitto, 1724 Connecticut Ave NW, Washington (Dupont Circle); tel 202/462-8771. **Italian.** The uncomplicated wooden tables and chairs are overshadowed by walls filled with family mementos, patriotic hangings, maps of Sicily. Specialties on an extensive menu include tortellini filled with veal, Sicilian linguine with shrimp and sun-dried tomatoes, and Naples rigatoni with chicken. Owned by the same family, Capo's Bar adjoins the restaurant and serves it through a connecting door. **FYI:** Reservations not accepted. **Open:** Mon–Thurs 11:30am–midnight, Fri–Sat 11:30am–1am, Sun 11:30am–10:30pm. Closed Dec 25. **Prices:** Main courses $9–$13; PF dinner . Maj CC. 📷

Center Café and Union Station Oyster Bar, in Union Station, 50 Massachusetts Ave NE, Washington (Capitol Hill); tel 202/682-0143. **Pizza/Seafood/Tex-Mex.** Among the shops under the majestic arching roof of Union Station, this diner is guarded by Roman centurion sculptures, part of the rail station's original decoration. The granite bar inside is impressive. Varied cuisines are offered, with emphasis on Tex-Mex. Cafe Pizzettes are wafer-thin pizzas with choice of toppings. **FYI:** Reservations not accepted. **Open:** Breakfast Mon–Fri 8–11am; lunch Mon–Fri 11am–4pm, Sat–Sun 11:30am–4pm; dinner Sun–Thurs 4–10:30pm, Fri–Sat 4pm–midnight. Closed Dec 25. **Prices:** Main courses $8.95–$14.95. Maj CC. ⬛ 🖼 &

Charing Cross, 3027 M St NW, Washington (Georgetown); tel 202/338-2141. **Italian.** Subdued lights and tastefully configured dark, varnished wood provide a sense of calm appropriate for enjoyable dining. Menu features the Italian mainstays of spaghetti, linguine, rigatoni, and lasagna among others. Seafood and pasta dishes are in the upper price ranges. Poultry, veal, sausage are the principal meats served. **FYI:** Reservations accepted. **Open:** Mon–Fri 11am–2am, Sat 5pm–2am. **Prices:** Main courses $7–$14. Maj CC. 💟

★ **The Childe Harold**, 1610 20th St NW, Washington (Dupont Circle); tel 202/483-6702. Between Q and R Sts. **Eclectic.** The 3 dining areas of this restaurant have their own distinct character. The main room is highlighted by dark wood, mirrors, flower arrangements, sconces with round shades, and portions of this old town home's original 1890s wallpaper still intact. The pub area is dominated by bare brick and, with 2 TVs, seems almost a sports bar. Outside dining reveals views of busy Connecticut Ave near the Dupont metro station. Main courses feature seafood, chicken, veal, and steak prepared a variety of ways. The Guards, 2915 M St NW in Georgetown (tel 202/965-2350), is a related establishment. **FYI:** Reservations accepted. **Open:** Mon–Thurs 11:30am–2am, Fri–Sat 11:30am–3am, Sun 10:30am–2am. **Prices:** Main courses $11–$17. Maj CC. 🍰

★ **China Doll Gourmet**, 627 H St NW, Washington (Chinatown); tel 202/289-4755. **Chinese/Thai.** Walnut-finished walls and bar, with mirrors and sconces along one side of the dining room. The chef's recommendations begin with roast duck Cantonese and include hot, thin slices of lamb with vegetables. A large number of Cantonese seafood dishes and a generous menu of vegetables add substance to the offerings. **FYI:** Reservations accepted. **Open:** Sun–Thurs 11am–10pm, Fri–Sat 11am–midnight. **Prices:** Main courses $7–$25. Maj CC. 📷 &

Ⓢ **China Inn**, 629–31 H St NW, Washington (Chinatown); tel 202/842-0910. **Chinese.** Oldest establishment on Chinatown's H St restaurant row, this landmark offers red-carpet dining on 2 levels, the upper reached via a winding staircase. Quiet atmosphere enhanced by paper paintings and framed Chinese prints. Some unusual potions are served, such as fish dipped in boiling water with spices, but most items are standard Cantonese fare. Dim sum served daily 11am–3pm. A very good bargain. **FYI:** Reservations recommended. **Open:** Sun–Thurs 11am–1am, Fri–Sat 11am–2pm. **Prices:** Main courses $9.25–$28.50. Maj CC.

Churreria Madrid Restaurant, 2505 Champlain St NW at Columbia Rd, Washington (Adams-Morgan); tel 202/483-4441. **Spanish.** Downstairs dining room has brick floors and white stucco walls hung with memorabilia of Spain and of the proprietors' families. Upstairs is less personalized. Over 60 different ways to enjoy home-style Spanish cuisine, from paella to tripe. Churros, a pretzel- and funnel cake–like dessert, is a specialty. **FYI:** Reservations accepted. **Open:** Tues–Sat 11am–10:30pm, Sun 11am–10pm. Closed some hols; Aug–Sept. **Prices:** Main courses $5.10–$11.25. Maj CC. 📷

★ **Cities**, 2424 18th St NW, Washington (Adams-Morgan); tel 202/328-7194. **Eclectic.** Neon lights and a large dragon are parts of unusual and intriguing decor at this eclectic restaurant whose menu changes every year to reflect the cuisines of international cities. Hong Kong brought Asian fare in 1994. **FYI:** Reservations recommended. **Open:** Mon–Thurs 6–11pm, Fri–Sat 6–11:30pm, Sun 11am–9:30pm. **Prices:** Main courses $12–$19.50. Maj CC. ⚅

City Lights of China, 1731 Connecticut Ave NW, Washington (Dupont Circle); tel 202/265-6688. Between R and S Sts. **Chinese.** Sparse, minimal decorations here, where Chinese specialties include Peking duck, crispy fried shredded beef, and stir-fried tofu. Also on menu are cold and hot appetizers, soups, and numerous other pork, beef, lamb, chicken, duck, and seafood dishes. **FYI:** Reservations accepted. **Open:** Mon–Thurs 11:30am–10:30pm, Fri 11:30am–11pm, Sat noon–11pm, Sun noon–10:30pm. Closed Thanksgiving. **Prices:** Main courses $9–$22. Maj CC. 📷

★ **Clyde's**, 3236 M St NW, Washington (Georgetown); tel 202/333-9180. **Burgers/Seafood/Steak.** The original Clyde's, this Georgetown pub started a local chain back in 1963 and continues to be popular. Bar near entrance is more traditionally pub-like, with checked tablecloths and walls hung with historic prints. Rear bar and dining rooms are a mix of French and contemporary, and plants create a garden-like feel in some areas. Pub staples, pastas, and regional favorites, such as soft-shell crabs. **FYI:** Reservations accepted. Children's menu. **Open:** Mon–Fri 11:30am–1am, Sat 9am–1am, Sun 9am–1am. Closed Dec 25. **Prices:** Main courses $10–$15. Maj CC. ♥ 📷

Copperfield's, in the Brawner Building, 888 17th St, NW, at I St, Washington; tel 202/293-2217. **New American.** The feel of

an English country inn is fostered by copper tabletops, plaid wallpaper, antiques, and Tiffany lamps. Popular spot for breakfast. Lunch brings salads, burgers, sandwiches, and such full meals as Maryland crab cakes and chicken linguine. **FYI:** Reservations recommended. Dress code. **Open:** Breakfast Mon–Fri 7–10:30am; lunch Mon–Fri 11am–3:30pm. Closed some hols. **Prices:** Lunch main courses $4.95–$6.95. Maj CC. ♥ 📷

Dutch Mill Deli, 639 Indiana Ave NW, Washington; tel 202/347-3665. Between 6th and 7th Sts. **Deli.** Simple hardwood tables, black upholstered stack chairs, and a tile floor are what you find in this establishment devoting little time to aesthetics. Regular deli fare only, such as bagels and lox, sandwiches of beef brisket, kosher salami. **FYI:** Reservations not accepted. **Open:** Mon–Sat 7am–4pm. Closed some hols. **Prices:** Lunch main courses $4–$9. No CC. 📷 📷

Encore Café, in the Kennedy Center for the Performing Arts, New Hampshire Ave NW at Rock Creek Pkwy, Washington (Foggy Bottom); tel 202/416-8560. **New American/Cafeteria.** Grand views of the Potomac River make this cafeteria-style eatery atop the Kennedy Center a popular pre-theater stop. Contemporary furnishings add class, as do prime rib, crab cakes, lasagna, baked swordfish, and other entrees worthy of many restaurant menus. Shares chef and kitchen with the Roof Terrace Restaurant. **FYI:** Reservations not accepted. Children's menu. Beer and wine only. No smoking. **Open:** Daily 11am–8pm. **Prices:** Main courses $4.75–$12. Maj CC. 📷 📷 ⚅

★ **Famous Luigi's**, 1132 19th St NW, Washington; tel 202/331-7574. Between L and M Sts. **Italian.** White paint, ceiling tiles and fans, checked tablecloths, and comfortable straw-bottom chairs produce a decidedly Italian environment in this upscale eatery. Diverse menu emphasizing pizza ranges from stuffed mushrooms to fettuccine and shrimp. **FYI:** Reservations not accepted. **Open:** Mon–Sat 11am–2am, Sun noon–midnight. Closed Dec 25. **Prices:** Main courses $6.50–$20. Maj CC. 🚗

Food and Co, 1200 New Hampshire Ave, at M St, Washington (Dupont Circle); tel 202/223-8070. **Cafe/Deli.** Colorfully packaged coffee beans and international deli goods add pizzazz to the varnished wood and red brick floor. Specializing in a variety of sandwiches, patés, quiches, and vegetarian dishes. **FYI:** Reservations not accepted. Beer and wine only. **Open:** Mon–Fri 8am–9pm, Sat 10am–7pm, Sun 10am–5pm. Closed Dec 25. **Prices:** Main courses $3–$8.50. Ltd CC. 📷

Food for Thought, 1738 Connecticut Ave NW, Washington (Dupont Circle); tel 202/797-1095. Near S St. **Eclectic/Vegetarian.** The decor is modest, with minimal aesthetic emphasis. The long, hall-like room is oriented toward a stage. Of 8 entrees offered, 5 are vegetarian: enchiladas, vegetables and brown rice, lasagna, grilled tofu, and sandwiches made with bean and sunflower patties. For those otherwise inclined, there are organically raised trout, charcoal-grilled beef with vegetables, and chicken wings. **FYI:** Reservations not accepted. Blues/country music/guitar/jazz/piano/singer. **Open:** Mon–Thurs 11:30am–12:30am, Fri 11:30am–2am, Sat noon–2am, Sun 4pm–12:30am. Closed some hols. **Prices:** Main courses $7–$10. Maj CC.

The Gangplank on the Potomac, 600 Water St SW, Washington; tel 202/554-5000. **American/Seafood.** The riverfront establishment actually is 3 restaurants in 1, each with a different theme and menu. The dining room offers an upscale, pleasing decor and such daily specials as swordfish kabob. The bar provides a relaxed social atmosphere, sandwiches, and moderately priced specials, such as a vegetarian garden burger. A seasonal concrete patio serves salads, sandwiches, and limited entrees to be eaten in wide-open spaces over the river. Patio open only 4pm–1:30am during warm months. **FYI:** Reservations recommended. Jacket required. **Open:** Lunch Mon–Thurs 11:30am–2pm, Fri–Sat 11am–3pm; dinner Sun–Thurs 5:30–10pm, Fri–Sat 5:30–11pm; brunch Sun 11am–3pm. Closed some hols. **Prices:** Main courses $4–$27. Maj CC. ♥ ≜ ▲ ♥

★ **Garrett's Restaurant and Railroad Bar**, 3003 M St NW, Washington (Georgetown); tel 202/333-1033. **Eclectic.** The highlight is an upstairs atrium with glass ceiling above 2 brick walls. A trompe l'oeil mural forms a perfect reflection of the dining area, making it seem twice as large. Menu is topped by a 16-ounce char-grilled New York strip steak served with baked potato and vegetable. Other offerings include grilled salmon filet with butter sauce and baby-back ribs. **FYI:** Reservations recommended. Children's menu. **Open:** Sun–Thurs 11:30am–2am, Fri–Sat 12pm–3am. **Prices:** Main courses $6–$18. Maj CC. ▣ ▲ ♥

⑤ **Greek Port Restaurant**, 1736 Wisconsin Ave NW, Washington (Georgetown); tel 202/333-0111. Between R and S Sts. **Greek.** Home-like atmosphere is enhanced by family photos on the walls, while home-style cooking features stuffed grape leaves and cabbage, moussaka, roast lamb, and other traditional Greek dishes. **FYI:** Reservations accepted. **Open:** Lunch Mon–Sat 11:30am–2:30pm; dinner Mon–Sat 5:30–11pm. Closed some hols. **Prices:** Main courses $7–$12.50. Ltd CC.

HI Ribster's, 800 Water St SW, Washington; tel 202/479-6857. **Regional American/Barbecue.** Uncomplicated decor in this riverfront restaurant uses plain tables and booths, pictures, tapestries, and cacti to create a southwestern flavor. Favorites on the place-mat menu are barbecued baby-back ribs, beef ribs, wet or dry Memphis-style spare ribs, and chicken. **FYI:** Reservations

not accepted. Children's menu. **Open:** Mon–Fri 11am–10pm, Sat noon–11pm, Sun noon–10pm. Closed some hols. **Prices:** Main courses $8–$16. Maj CC. ≜ ▲ ▦ ♥

Hogate's, 800 Water St SW, Washington; tel 202/484-6300. **Seafood/Steak.** The large restaurant has successfully carried off the nautical motif dictated by its riverfront location. Highly varnished wooden tables with substantial upholstered captain's chairs are surrounded by maritime relics. In addition to hot and chilled appetizers like steamed clams and shucked oysters, menu emphasizes fried, broiled, and sautéed seafood platters. Lobster, shrimp, crab legs and cakes, clams, mussels, and fish all appear. **FYI:** Reservations recommended. Children's menu. **Open:** Mon–Thurs 11am–10pm, Fri 11am–11pm, Sat noon–11pm, Sun 10:30am–10pm. Closed Dec 25. **Prices:** Main courses $12–$29. Maj CC. ♥ ▮ ≜ ▲ ᵹ

★ **Houston's**, 1065 Wisconsin Ave NW, Washington (Georgetown); tel 202/338-7760. Located just below M St. **Burgers/Seafood/Steak.** Pleasing and unusual decor of finished dark wood, unfinished exposed beams, and ducts highlight this spot popular with the younger set. There are burgers with a variety of toppings, but fish, chicken, and beef dishes make this more than a burger palace. Wide selection of salads, including an eggless Caesar. **FYI:** Reservations not accepted. **Open:** Sun–Thurs 11:15am–11pm, Fri–Sat 11:15am–1am. Closed Dec 25. **Prices:** Main courses $6.75–$18. Maj CC. ▦ ᵹ

★ **Hunan Chinatown**, 624 H St NW, Washington (Chinatown); tel 202/783-5858. **Chinese.** Subdued wall coverings and ceramic-tile floor emphasize the cubicle-like arrangement of half of this restaurant, while a prismatic mirror reflects the diners and bar across the room. Peking duck leads the list of recommended dishes, with additional specialties including orange beef, giant shrimp sautéed with vegetables, prawns with walnuts, and whole Hunan-style fish. **FYI:** Reservations accepted. **Open:** Sun–Thurs 11am–11pm, Fri–Sat 11am–midnight. Closed some hols. **Prices:** Main courses $10–$25. Maj CC. ▦

★ **Iron Gate Restaurant**, 1734 N St NW, Washington (Dupont Circle); tel 202/737-1370. Between 17th and 18th Sts. **Mediterranean.** An extraordinary update of this 1890s stable has turned some of the old stalls into booths. Subdued lighting, dark woods, and a brick fireplace add to romantic atmosphere, with pleasant garden dining in good weather. From Greece and Turkey to Morocco and Italy come the dishes on this varied, gourmet-quality menu. **FYI:** Reservations recommended. No smoking. **Open:** Mon–Fri 11:30am–10pm, Sat 5–10pm, Sun 10:30am–9pm. Closed some hols. **Prices:** Main courses $14.50–$19. Maj CC. ♥ ▮ ≜ ▣

Jean-Louis at the Watergate, in the Watergate Hotel, 2650 Virginia Ave NW, Washington (Foggy Bottom); tel 202/298-4488. **French.** Mirrors on ceilings and behind lighted curtains plus an abundance of fresh flowers create an exclusive and tasteful environment in one of Washington's finest restaurants. Changing daily depending on availability of fresh produce, menu features the owner/chef's renowned experimental French cuisine. **FYI:** Reservations recommended. Jacket required. **Open:** Tues–Sat 5:30–10pm. Closed some hols; Aug–Labor Day. **Prices:** PF dinner $85–$95. Maj CC. ❤ ✉ &

The Jefferson Restaurant, in the Jefferson Hotel, 1200 16th St NW at M St, Washington (Downtown); tel 202/347-2200. **Regional American.** Leather walls offset by indirect lighting and off-white moldings are strikingly done and supplemented by finished wood floors. Chef creates smoked lamb chops with lamb sausage, fresh corn griddle cakes and watermelon pickles, blueberry barbecued venison with sweet potato salad, and confetti of vegetables and grilled tuna. **FYI:** Reservations recommended. Jazz. Children's menu. Dress code. **Open:** Breakfast Mon–Sat 7–10:30am; lunch Mon–Sat 11:30am–2:30pm; dinner daily 6–10:30pm; brunch Sun 7am–2:30pm. **Prices:** Main courses $19–$24; PF dinner $55. Maj CC. ❤ **VP** &

Katmandu, 2100 Connecticut Ave NW, at S St and Florida Ave, Washington (Kalorama); tel 202/483-6470. **Nepali/Kashmiri.** Decor fails to develop the potential Nepalese and Kashmiri themes that permeate the cuisine. Specialties are boneless chicken marinated in herbs and grilled on charcoal, filet of mutton with Himalayan herbs. **FYI:** Reservations recommended. **Open:** Lunch daily 11:30am–2:30pm; dinner daily 5:30–10pm. **Prices:** Main courses $5–$8. Ltd CC.

Kelly's The Irish Times, 14 F St NW, Washington (Capitol Hill); tel 202/543-5433. **American/Irish.** Well-used bar is indicative of many toasts offered at this quintessential Irish pub, bedecked with appropriate memorabilia, flags, escutcheons, and photos of the old country. Standard pub fare, including half-pound burgers, is supplemented by the chef's apple and blueberry pies. Live Irish music Wednesday to Sunday evenings. The Dubliner Restaurant and Pub, 520 N Capitol St (202/737-3773), with an entrance next door on F St NW, is a more upscale version of an Irish drinking and eating establishment. **FYI:** Reservations accepted. Guitar. **Open:** Daily 11am–2am. Closed Dec 25. **Prices:** Main courses $4.50–$12. Maj CC. &

Kolbeh, 1645 Wisconsin Ave NW, Washington (Georgetown); tel 202/342-2000. Between Reservoir Rd and Q St. **Middle Eastern/Iranian.** Mirrored walls and ceiling and light woods provide a feeling of spaciousness in which to enjoy Middle Eastern cuisine with an Iranian flair. Variety of lamb dishes

offered. **FYI:** Reservations accepted. **Open:** Mon–Thurs 11:30am–10pm, Fri–Sun 11:30am–11pm. **Prices:** Main courses $8–$14. Maj CC.

Kozy Korner Restaurant, 1253 20th St NW, at N St, Washington (Dupont Circle); tel 202/785-4314. **American/Greek/Italian.** Well-coordinated colors supplemented with Tiffany lamps, ceiling fans, and brass wall hangings seem incongruous alongside the budget-minded prices in this popular eatery. Noted for Italian and Greek specialties, including gyro and souvlaki sandwiches. **FYI:** Reservations not accepted. **Open:** Mon–Sat 7am–10pm, Sun 8am–2:30pm. Closed some hols. **Prices:** Main courses $4.55–$8.50. Ltd CC. 👥

★ **Kramerbooks & Afterwords Cafe**, 1517 Connecticut Ave NW, Washington; tel 202/387-1462. Between Q St and Dupont Circle. **Eclectic.** The first combination bookstore/restaurant in Washington and still the most popular. The cafe portion has grown and now includes a solarium on the 19th St sidewalk behind the original bookstore. Menu offers a mix of international and American regional cuisine with some of the chef's own combinations, such as Thai jambalaya over fettuccine. **FYI:** Reservations not accepted. Blues/jazz. **Open:** Sun–Thurs 7:30am–1am, Fri–Sat 24 hrs. **Prices:** Main courses $8–$11.75. Maj CC. ⛴

Le Lion d'Or, 1150 Connecticut Ave NW, at M St, Washington (Dupont Circle); tel 202/296-7972. **French.** To step across the threshold of this fine establishment is to save the cost of traveling to Paris. An elegantly appointed dining room features huge chandeliers beneath cloth canopies, potted plants, copper cookware, and a variety of artistic paintings, lending an ambience suitable to one of America's finest restaurants. The talented owner/chef cooks such treats as Dover sole sautéed in artichokes, veal filet with shiitake mushrooms, and roast pigeon with mushrooms. Menu is in French with no translation. **FYI:** Reservations recommended. Jacket required. **Open:** Lunch Mon–Fri noon–2pm; dinner Mon–Sat 6–10pm. Closed some hols; Aug. **Prices:** Main courses $20–$29. Maj CC. ❤ &

The Lunch Garden, 1015 18th St NW, Washington; tel 202/331-0860. Between K and L Sts. **Eclectic.** Bright, cheerful, clean establishment accented by green plants and gray and white tile floors. Sandwich menu includes hand-carved turkey, beef, and ham along with subs and platters served with bread and vegetables. **FYI:** Reservations not accepted. No liquor license. **Open:** Mon–Fri 7am–5pm. Closed some hols. **Prices:** Lunch main courses $3.95–$4.95. No CC. 👥

Marché Café and Bar, 1810 K St NW, Washington; tel 202/293-3000. **Cafe/French.** A modern French bistro with mirrors, which add significantly to sense of spaciousness. Menu changes daily, includes French dishes with some Spanish and other cuisines. **FYI:** Reservations accepted. Children's menu. **Open:** Lunch Mon–Fri 11am–3:30pm; dinner Mon–Fri 5–9pm. Closed some hols. **Prices:** Main courses $8–$11; PF dinner $10.95. Maj CC. 🔲 🔻

Mixtec, 1792 Columbia Rd, at 18th St, Washington (Adams-Morgan); tel 202/332-1011. **Mexican.** Mexican cantina setting for authentic ethnic cuisine in one of Washington's most ethnically diverse and lively neighborhoods. Hand-painted wicker chairs, colorful hanging paper lanterns add festive air. Gaily painted tin ornaments hang on wall of larger dining room. Mexican fare uses corn tortillas made on premises. **FYI:** Reservations not accepted. Beer and wine only. **Open:** Mon–Thurs 11am–10pm, Fri–Sun 11am–midnight. Closed Dec 25. **Prices:** Main courses $4.75–$9.95. Ltd CC.

Morrison-Clark Inn, Massachusetts Ave NW, at 11th St, Washington (Downtown); tel 202/289-8580. **New American.** Elegantly detailed Victorian decor in the dining room of this historic inn. Award-winning chef "does her own thing" in the kitchen. Examples are grilled halibut with roasted red-pepper aioli and eggplant flan, and smoked pork loin with honey mustard-herb sauce served with a grits soufflé. **FYI:** Reservations recommended. Jacket required. No smoking. **Open:** Lunch Mon–Fri 11am–2pm; dinner Sun–Thurs 6–9:30pm, Fri–Sat 6–10:30pm; brunch Sun 11am–2pm. Closed some hols. **Prices:** Main courses $18–$22. Maj CC. ❤ 🔲 ⬛ 🔲 ⚞VP⚟

Morton's of Chicago, 3251 Prospect St NW, Washington (Georgetown); tel 202/342-6258. **Seafood/Steak.** White stucco walls with carefully chosen hangings, Oriental runners, light wood floors, a varnished oak bar, and etched glass give class to this upscale steak house, a member of the Chicago-based chain. A 3-pound porterhouse tops the offerings, which range from aged filet mignon, prime rib, and chops to Maine lobsters and fresh fish. **FYI:** Reservations recommended. Dress code. **Open:** Mon–Sat 5:30–11pm, Sun 5–10pm. Closed some hols. **Prices:** Main courses $16–$59. Maj CC. ⚞VP⚟ ᕲ

National Gallery of Art Cafes, 6th and Constitution Aves NW, Washington (Capitol Hill); tel 202/347-9401. **American/Cafe/International.** Three eateries grace the National Gallery. Stunning on all counts, the cafeteria-style Concourse Cafe, in the tunnel connecting the gallery's 2 wings, features a 2-story waterfall, atrium with chrome ceiling, and marble-top tables. The Garden Cafe, in the West Wing, sports much greenery and blooming flowers as well as an 11th-century bronze statute of Venus. The Terrace, in the East Wing, has light, contemporary wall decorations and outstanding views of greenery outside. Menus often are created based on the theme of current exhibits. **FYI:** Reservations not accepted. Children's menu. Beer and wine

only. No smoking. **Open:** HS Apr–Nov Mon–Sat 11:30am–3pm, Sun noon–6:30pm. Reduced hours off-season. Closed some hols. **Prices:** Lunch main courses $6–$11. Maj CC. ❤ 🔲 🔲 🔲 ᕲ

Nora: An Organic Restaurant, 2132 Florida Ave NW at R St, Washington (Dupont Circle); tel 202/462-5143. **International/Organic.** A sense of quiet elegance and clubbiness pervades. Though quite diverse, the offerings have 1 thing in common: They are produced from additive-free meat and organically grown produce. Recent examples have included veal and cashew curry with brown rice and apricot chutney; Chesapeake Bay softshell crabs with charred tomato sauce, corn pudding, and grilled squash; and veal scaloppine with tomatoes, thyme, roasted new potatoes, and French beans. **FYI:** Reservations recommended. No smoking. **Open:** Mon–Thurs 6–10pm, Fri–Sat 6–10:30pm. Closed some hols. **Prices:** Main courses $19–$25. Ltd CC. ❤ 🔲

✹ **Old Ebbitt Grill**, 675 15th St NW, Washington (Downtown); tel 202/347-4801. Between F and G Sts. **American.** Although this mid-19th-century pub was moved here in the 1980s from its original quarters, glazed glass panels, burgundy velvet upholstery, wooden booths, real gas lights, sconces, and stuffed boar and antelope heads help maintain its historical ambience. Main courses vary frequently, but menu always offers a variety of soups, salads, burgers, and sandwiches. **FYI:** Reservations recommended. **Open:** Mon–Fri 7:30am–1am, Sat 8am–1am, Sun 9:30am–1am. Closed Dec 25. **Prices:** Main courses $9–$15. Maj CC. 🔲 ᕲ

♥✹ **Palm Restaurant**, 1225 19th St NW, Washington (Adams Morgan); tel 202/293-9091. **American/Italian.** Known locally as the Palm. Walls here are covered with caricatures of longtime patrons, many of them famous politicians and news media personalities who hang out here for ample portions of seafood, poultry, steaks, chops, and pasta. Popular items are jumbo Maine lobster and thin, crispy fried potatoes and onion rings. **FYI:** Reservations recommended. Dress code. **Open:** Lunch Mon–Fri 11:45am–3pm; dinner Mon–Fri 3–10:30pm, Sat 6–10:30pm, Sun 5:30–9:30pm. Closed some hols. **Prices:** Main courses $12.50–$27. Maj CC. ⚞VP⚟

✹ **Paolo's Ristorante**, 1303 Wisconsin Ave NW, at N St, Washington (Georgetown); tel 202/333-7353. **Italian.** Mirrored walls and subdued lighting contribute to a sense of good times and fellowship. Menu includes pizza, pasta, and other traditional Italian favorites. Pizza served at the bar until last call. **FYI:** Reservations not accepted. **Open:** Mon–Thurs 11:30am–12:30am, Fri 11:30am–2am, Sat 11:30am–12:30am, Sun 11am–midnight. **Prices:** Main courses $7.25–$17. Maj CC.

Paru's, 2010 S St NW, Washington; tel 202/483-5133. Located just east of Connecticut Ave. **Indian.** This storefront eatery with a carryout counter and only 8 tables might as well be in Madras, so authentic are its south Indian vegetarian selections, such as masala dosai, a rolled pancake filled with spicy potato curry. Paper plates and cups are de rigueur at this clean, bargain establishment. **FYI:** Reservations not accepted. No liquor license. **Open:** Mon–Sat 11:30am–8:30pm. Closed some hols. **Prices:** Main courses $2.50–$8. No CC.

Patisserie Café Didier, 3206 Grace St NW, Washington (Georgetown); tel 202/342-9083. Off Wisconsin Ave just below M St. **Cafe/Continental.** Pastels, white straw-back chairs, straw lamp shades, and a copse of real plants and flower arrangements are most restful and pleasing to the eye. In addition to a full range of pastries, daily specials include various croissants, Danish, and scones. Other featured items include quiche, sandwiches, and salads. **FYI:** Reservations accepted. No liquor license. **Open:** Tues–Sun 8am–7pm. Closed some hols. **Prices:** Lunch main courses $7–$9. Ltd CC. ♥ 📷

The Peasant Restaurant and Bar, 801 Pennsylvania Ave NW, Washington; tel 202/638-2140. **Eclectic.** Off-white walls and green ceilings, carpet, and curtains are set off by numerous gilded chandeliers, all creating a fine club-like atmosphere. The menu, presented on a small chalkboard, has inventive daily specials such as herb-crusted filet, Tuscan lamb, sun-dried cherry pork, and grilled salmon with juniper berries. **FYI:** Reservations accepted. **Open:** Mon 11am–10pm, Tues–Fri 11am–11pm, Sat 5:30–11pm, Sun 5–9pm. Closed some hols. **Prices:** Main courses $12–$23. Maj CC. ♥ 🍴 ☑ 🆅🅿 &

★ **Peyote Café**, 2319 18th St NW, Washington (Adams-Morgan); tel 202/462-8330. Between Belmont and Kalorama Rds. **Southwestern/Tex-Mex.** Southwestern decor highlighted by neon signs, a jukebox, and a wood bar surrounded by highback stools. Sharing space with Roxanne/On the Rox (see listing below), this is primarily a bar, although numerous interesting salads, sandwiches, and such Tex-Mex specialties as Peco Phil's pizza with a grilled cornmeal crust are served. **FYI:** Reservations accepted. **Open:** Dinner Sun–Thurs 5pm–1am, Fri–Sat 5pm–3:30am; brunch Sat–Sun 10am–3pm. **Prices:** Main courses $6–$14. Maj CC.

Prime Rib, 2020 K St NW, Washington (Foggy Bottom); tel 202/466-8811. **American/Seafood/Steak.** Art-deco touches, black pillars, abundant mirrors, and striking art on the walls set an appropriate ambience for the Washington businesspeople and power brokers who frequent this meat-and-potatoes establishment. Aged prime rib roasted in its own juice is the main attraction, but steaks, lamb, pork, and lobster are also listed. Indulgent desserts. **FYI:** Reservations recommended. Piano.

Jacket required. **Open:** Lunch Mon–Fri 11:30am–3pm; dinner Mon–Thurs 5–11pm, Fri–Sat 5–11:30pm. Closed some hols. **Prices:** Main courses $15–$24. Maj CC. ♥ 🆅🅿

★ **Red Sage**, 605 14th St NW, at F St, Washington (Downtown); tel 202/638-4444. **New Southwestern.** An overall southwestern theme prevails in these 3 adjoining, architecturally creative restaurants, each with its own nuances. Adobe predominates in ceilings and walls, although the Chili Bar has a painted sky complete with clouds and lightning. The main dining room's largest area has a horse theme, with massive timbers supporting the ceiling above lighted, flower-filled alcoves. The Library provides more intimate dining, thanks to finished wood, high-quality table linens, and ash-colored chairs. Menu is fittingly southwestern, with cowboy rib-eye steaks and barbecued black beans heading the list. Also glazed quail, grilled swordfish, 3 varieties of chili. **FYI:** Reservations recommended. **Open:** Mon–Sat 11:30am–11:30pm, Sun 4:30–11:30pm. Closed Dec 25. **Prices:** Main courses $16–$29. Maj CC. 📷 &

Red Sea, 2463 18th St NW, Washington (Adams-Morgan); tel 202/483-5000. Located near Columbia Rd. **Ethiopian.** Red table linen and vinyl-upholstered chairs. Many posters of Ethiopia complement the Ethiopian dishes, including lyb, a spicy cheese, and some red-hot meat selections. Meals are served in traditional fashion on a round piece of steamed Ethiopian bread. Fingers are used to pick up food with pieces of bread resembling wet napkins. **FYI:** Reservations accepted. **Open:** Daily noon–2am. Closed July 4. **Prices:** Main courses $6.15–$10.15. Maj CC.

Reeve's Restaurant and Bakery, 1306 G St NW, Washington (Downtown); tel 202/628-6350. Between 13th and 14th Sts. **American.** Light woods, marble tile, and judicious use of mirrors provide a very pleasing atmosphere enhanced by rust-tone upholstered booths. Although regular restaurant fare such as burgers, pasta dishes, and salads are on the menu, the specialties here are desserts, like strawberry-rhubarb pie and a rich German chocolate cake. **FYI:** Reservations not accepted. No liquor license. **Open:** Mon–Sat 7am–6pm. Closed some hols. **Prices:** Lunch main courses $4–$6.50. Ltd CC. &

Refectory, Room S-112, 1st floor of US Capitol, Washington; tel 202/224-4870. **Diner.** There's nothing fancy about this fast-food diner under the US Senate chamber in the Capitol. Famous Senate bean soup is the only notable offering among a variety of sandwiches and simple main courses. Closing times depend on when the Senate adjourns for the day. **FYI:** Reservations not accepted. No liquor license. **Open:** Mon–Fri 8am–9pm. Closed some hols. **Prices:** Main courses $4–$8. Maj CC. 📷 &

Ristorante Tiberio, 1915 K St NW, Washington; tel 202/ 452-1915. **Italian.** Many stucco arches and walls hung with contemporary art create a simple but elegant ambience in which to indulge in gourmet Italian cuisine. In addition to choosing from a variety of meat, fish, fowl, and pasta options, you are invited to ask for your favorite unlisted dish. **FYI:** Reservations recommended. Jacket required. **Open:** Lunch Mon–Fri 11:45am–2:30pm; dinner Mon–Sat 6–10:30pm. Closed some hols. **Prices:** Main courses $17–$33. Maj CC. ♥ VP

Roof Terrace Restaurant, in the Kennedy Center for the Performing Arts, New Hampshire Ave NW at Rock Creek Pkwy, Washington (Foggy Bottom); tel 202/416-8555. **Regional American.** Elegant chairs and linen beneath 18-foot ceilings are complemented by views of many Washington monuments from this restaurant atop the Kennedy Center. Adjoining Hors d'Oeuvres Lounge has marble-top tables for pre-theater drinks and snacks. Menu features a regional variety, including mesquite-grilled salmon, smoked duck, crab cakes with herbs. Brunch served all year, but for dinner the restaurant is open only on performance nights. **FYI:** Reservations recommended. Children's menu. Jacket required. No smoking. **Open:** Lunch daily 11am–3pm; dinner daily 5:30–9pm; brunch Sun 11:30am–3pm. **Prices:** Main courses $22–$24; PF dinner $33. Maj CC. ♥ 🍴 ▲▲ ♿

Roxanne/On the Rox, 2319 18th St NW, Washington (Adams-Morgan); tel 202/462-8330. Between Belmont and Kalorama Rds. **Southwestern.** Sharing space with the Peyote Cafe, the main dining room's walls are hung with western paintings and southwestern mementos, including a longhorn skull. Upstairs, the Starlit Rooftop Terrace offers outdoor dining with a view. Southwestern cuisine is taken seriously. **FYI:** Reservations accepted. **Open:** Mon–Fri 5–11pm, Sat 11:30am–midnight, Sun 11:30am–11pm. **Prices:** Main courses $8.95–$14.95. Maj CC. ♥ ⚓

✱ **Ruth's Chris Steak House**, 1811 Connecticut Ave NW, Washington; tel 202/797-0033. **Regional American/Steak.** Brick walls, dark exposed beams, low stucco ceilings, and lantern light bring rustic elegance to this Washington favorite. Cozy alcoves offer intimate seating, and a separate room has a brick fireplace and hearth. Corn-fed, carefully aged steaks are the mainstays, with lamb and veal chops, chicken, lobster, salmon, and tuna also put to the coals. **FYI:** Reservations recommended. **Open:** Daily 5–10:30pm. Closed some hols. **Prices:** Main courses $15.95–$29.95. Maj CC. ♥ ⚓ VP

Sea Catch Restaurant and Raw Bar, 1054 31st St NW, Washington (Georgetown); tel 202/337-8855. Located just below M St. **Seafood/Steak.** Two-centuries-old bricks and beams combine with contemporary light wood in this seafood emporium that cooks up live Maine lobsters, crab cakes, swordfish steak, and other morsels from the sea's harvest. **FYI:** Reservations recommended. Children's menu. **Open:** Lunch Mon–Sat noon–3pm; dinner Mon–Sat 5:30–10pm. Closed some hols. **Prices:** Main courses $16–$26. Maj CC. ♥ 🍴 ⚓ 📷 ▲▲ ♥ VP

Seasons, in Four Seasons Hotel, 2800 Pennsylvania Ave at M St, Washington (Georgetown); tel 202/342-0810. **New American/ Seafood.** Plush decor features prints of antique birds lining lacquered walls, leather banquettes, and stone floors. Specialties include smoked haddock in cream sauce flavored with malt whisky; loin of venison with root vegetables and bramble sauce; crispy oriental sea bass with ginger sauce; and sugar-crusted baked rice pudding. **FYI:** Reservations recommended. Children's menu. Dress code. **Open:** Breakfast Mon–Fri 7–11am, Sat–Sun 8–10am; lunch Mon–Fri noon–2:30pm; dinner daily 6:30–10:30pm; brunch Sat–Sun 10am–2:30pm. **Prices:** Main courses $16–$29. Maj CC. VP ♿

1789, 1226 36th St NW at Prospect St, Washington (Georgetown); tel 202/965-1789. **American.** Extra-dark woods and thematic wall hangings create an elegant country-inn ambience in this federal-period town house named for the year Georgetown was incorporated. Offerings are pure Americana, from pan-fried soft-shell crabs to barbecued Carolina quail. Some dishes have an unusual flair, such as veal scaloppine with okra. **FYI:** Reservations recommended. Jacket required. **Open:** Daily 6–10:30pm. Closed Dec 25. **Prices:** Main courses $16–$25. Maj CC. ♥ 🍴 ♥ VP

Sfuzzi, in Union Station, 50 Massachusetts Ave NE, Washington (Capitol Hill); tel 202/842-4141. **Italian.** Realistic frescoes and additional Italianate touches make it easy to imagine a Venetian canal beyond the soaring ceiling of Union Station, which itself suggests classical Italian architecture. Plain black tables and cane-back chairs add to appealing scene. Changing menu features Italian fare of pasta, seafood, and meat. Two-hour validated parking in Union Station garage. **FYI:** Reservations accepted. Children's menu. **Open:** Lunch Mon–Fri 11:30am–2pm, Sat 11:30am–3pm; dinner Mon–Thurs 6–10pm, Fri 6–11pm, Sat 5–11pm, Sun 5–9pm; brunch Sun 11:30am–3pm. Closed some hols. **Prices:** Main courses $14.50–$22; PF dinner $14.50. Maj CC. ♥ 🍴 ▲▲

✱ **Sherill's Bakery**, 233 Pennsylvania Ave SE, Washington (Capitol Hill); tel 202/544-2480. **American/Cafe.** A landmark on Capitol Hill, this 1940s-vintage eatery was immortalized in the Emmy-winning and Oscar-nominated documentary *Fine Food, Fine Pastries,* which spotlighted this family-owned and -operated enterprise. Pastries are made on premises. Other selections are plain American fare, such as home-style meatloaf and crab cakes. Popular for breakfast. **FYI:** Reservations not accepted. No liquor license. **Open:** Mon–Fri 6am–7pm, Sat–Sun 7am–7pm. Closed Dec 25. **Prices:** Main courses $4.95–$9.95. No CC.

★ **Sholl's Colonial Cafeteria**, in Esplanade Mall, 1990 K St NW, Washington; tel 202/296-3065. **American/Cafeteria.** Washington's most popular and least expensive cafeteria is plain, with few decorative touches except plastic plants. A variety of fresh, plainly prepared foods are offered along the line. Roast beef and fried chicken are mainstays. **FYI:** Reservations not accepted. No liquor license. No smoking. **Open:** Breakfast daily 7–10:30am; lunch daily 11am–2:30pm; dinner daily 4–8pm. Closed some hols. **Prices:** Main courses $1.65–$5. No CC. 👥

Sichuan Pavillion, in Int'l Sq Bldg, 1820 K St NW, Washington; tel 202/466-7790. **Chinese.** Pleasingly subdued wall colors are enhanced by Chinese art and decorative objects in this upscale restaurant. Wall-size screens separate private dining rooms from public areas. Spicy Szechuan cuisine is the prime offering, with crispy whole fish a house specialty. **FYI:** Reservations recommended. **Open:** Mon–Fri 11am–10pm, Sat–Sun noon–10pm. Closed Thanksgiving. **Prices:** Main courses $7–$20. Maj CC. ♥

South Buffet, in Dirksen Senate Office Building, 1st and C Sts NE, Washington (Capitol Hill); tel 202/224-4249. **Cafeteria.** Cloth tablecloths, historical photos of the Capitol area, and drinks delivered to the table add extra touches to this otherwise self-serve facility operated by the US Senate. Menu, consisting of basic choices, changes weekly. **FYI:** Reservations not accepted. Children's menu. No liquor license. **Open:** Mon–Fri 11:30am–2:30pm. Closed some hols. **Prices:** Lunch main courses $5.25–$7.75. Maj CC. 👥 &

Station Grill, in Union Station, 50 Massachusetts Ave NE, Washington (Capitol Hill); tel 202/898-4745. **American.** Dark colors from ceiling to the wooden chairs and subdued lighting seem to help quiet the multitude of sounds coming from the busy marble hallway outside. Good choices are roasted half chicken with spices, a crab-cake platter, char-grilled rib-eye in teriyaki sauce, open-face omelet with vegetables and cheese, London broil, and linguine. Various appetizers, soups, salads, burgers, and sandwiches round out the options. Two-hour validated parking in adjoining parking garage. **FYI:** Reservations not accepted. Children's menu. **Open:** Mon–Fri 8am–10pm, Sat 9am–10pm, Sun 9am–9pm. Closed Dec 25. **Prices:** Main courses $5–$18. Maj CC. 👥

Szechuan Gallery Restaurant, 617 H St NW, Washington (Chinatown); tel 202/898-1180. **Chinese.** Tufted leatherette booths, wood tables thickly laminated with clear plastic, nicely

framed Oriental prints, and an attractive oak bar work together to give this establishment a bit more elegance than is sometimes found in Chinese restaurants. A mix of Szechuan and Taiwanese cuisines makes for spicy selections. Good value. **FYI:** Reservations recommended. **Open:** Sun–Thurs 11am–3am, Fri–Sat 11am–4am. **Prices:** Main courses $8–$25. Maj CC.

Tandoor Restaurant, 3316 M St NW, Washington (Georgetown); tel 202/333-3376. **Indian.** Indian-style brass lights, teak, paintings, and tapestries set the tone for this ethnic restaurant featuring meat dishes from the tandoor oven and a selection of curries. Dining room in rear, known separately as Madurai, offers interesting vegetarian twists on traditional Indian cuisine. Vegetarian weekend buffet offers good sampling. **FYI:** Reservations recommended. No smoking. **Open:** Lunch daily 11:30am–2:30pm; dinner Mon–Sat 5:30–10:30pm, Sun 5:30–10pm. **Prices:** Main courses $6–$10. Maj CC. ♥ &

★ **Thai Taste**, 2606 Connecticut Ave NW, Washington (Woodley Park); tel 202/387-8876. Located just off Calvert St. **Thai.** Uncomplicated decor consists of a combination of tables and black booths lighted by antique art-deco electric sconces, but little in the way of ethnic identity. Fried beef or chicken in spicy red curry and coconut milk, soft-shell crabs sautéed with chili paste, and other Thai delights. **FYI:** Reservations recommended. **Open:** Sun–Thurs 11:30am–10:30pm, Fri–Sat 11:30am–11pm. Closed some hols. **Prices:** Main courses $5–$11. Maj CC. 🚗

Timberlake's, 1726 Connecticut Ave NW, Washington (Dupont Circle); tel 202/483-2266. Between R and S Sts. **Burgers/Seafood/Steak.** A varnished bar, overhead fans, and especially 2 TVs foster the sports-bar ambience in the front room of this restaurant. The back dining room with overhead skylights, growing plants, and modest wall hangings should make daytime dining pleasant. Menu changes every week, with a lobster special on Mondays and prime rib on Tuesday. Regular entrees include spinach fettuccine; trout sautéed with tomatoes, onions, olives, and lemon butter; steak au poivre; and a crab-cake platter. Sandwiches too. **FYI:** Reservations accepted. **Open:** Sun–Thurs 10:30am–midnight, Fri 11:30am–1am, Sat 10:30am–1am. Closed some hols. **Prices:** Main courses $6–$13. Maj CC.

★ **The Tombs**, 1226 36th St NW, at Prospect St, Washington (Georgetown); tel 202/337-6668. **Burgers/Pizza/Pub.** College memorabilia and a rathskeller atmosphere hint as to the clientele at this friendly institution near Georgetown University. A balanced choice of several types of salads, burgers, and sandwiches plus daily specials—2 or 3 regular meals to keep Hoya students going between exams or basketball games. **FYI:** Reservations not accepted. **Open:** Mon–Fri 11:30am–1:30am, Sat 11am–2:30am, Sun 9:30am–1:30am. Closed some hols. **Prices:** Main courses $4.75–$7.25. Maj CC. ◉

Trio Restaurant, 1537 17th St NW at Q St, Washington (Dupont Circle); tel 202/232-6305. **Burgers/Seafood/Steak.** One of the last 1950s-style restaurants left in Washington, with red vinyl booths and modernistic chandeliers dangling from a ceiling of rose and 2 shades of green. The regular menu is plain American fare—roast turkey with dressing, combination seafood platter, hot roast-beef sandwiches—but more interesting daily specials might include fresh Buffala mozzarella cheese as an appetizer, grilled tuna with fresh field greens vinaigrette as main course. **FYI:** Reservations not accepted. **Open:** Daily 7:30am–midnight. Closed Dec 25. **Prices:** Main courses $5–$11. Maj CC. ♨ ⚹

★ **Uptown Bakers**, 3313 Connecticut Ave NW, Washington (Cleveland Park); tel 202/362-6262. Located just north of Macomb St. **Gourmet bakery.** Simple white plastic tables and chairs, and blue and white tile floors in this bakery specializing in a variety of breads, cakes, pies, pastries. A limited number of sandwiches at lunch. Bakeries are not required by DC law to have public rest rooms, and this one doesn't. Also at: 3471 N Washington Blvd, Arlington, VA (tel 703/527-6262), at Virginia Square metro station. **FYI:** Reservations not accepted. No liquor license. No smoking. **Open:** Daily 7am–9pm. **Prices:** No CC. 👪

Vidalia, 1990 M St NW, Washington (Dupont Circle); tel 202/659-1990. **Regional American.** Cozy, country-inn ambience is enhanced by smooth white stucco walls and brass chandeliers. Inventive chef is well known for blending southern ingredients, such as country ham, kale, and Vidalia onions, with Yankee fare to concoct adventurous dishes. Crab cakes with bell pepper, jicama slaw, and spicy Chesapeake Bay seasoned mayonnaise is a regular favorite. **FYI:** Reservations recommended. **Open:** Lunch Mon–Fri 11:30am–2:30pm; dinner Mon–Sat 5:30–10:30pm. Closed some hols. **Prices:** Main courses $17–$19.75. Maj CC. ◉ VP ⚹

Vie de France, in the Capitol Gallery Bldg, 600 Maryland Ave SW, Washington (L'Enfant Plaza); tel 202/554-7870. Off Independence Ave SW. **French.** An outgrowth of a fine local bakery of the same name, this cafe with sturdy oak tables (some with umbrellas), wicker-back chairs, and some booths has photos of France to set the mood for fine French soups, salads, and pastries, and sandwiches made with fresh croissants and crispy baguettes. Entertainment Wednesday–Friday nights. Also at: 2nd floor of Esplanade Mall, 1990 K St NW (tel 202/659-0055).

FYI: Reservations recommended. **Open:** Mon–Tues 7am–8pm, Wed–Fri 7am–9pm, Sat 7am–3pm. Closed some hols. **Prices:** Main courses $7–$11. Maj CC.

★ **Vietnam Georgetown Restaurant**, 2934 M St NW, at 29th St, Washington; tel 202/337-4536. **Vietnamese.** Mirrors and white walls and tablecloths brighten up this small, 20-table restaurant. Still, it's an intimate room, and Vietnamese paintings add a sense of place. Outdoor dining on brick patio under huge shade tree is pleasant during warm weather. A pioneer Vietnamese restaurant in this area, which now has many, but still a fine bargain eatery. **FYI:** Reservations accepted. No smoking. **Open:** Sun–Thurs 11am–11pm, Fri–Sat noon–midnight. **Prices:** Main courses $6.25–$8.50. Ltd CC. ♨

The Willard Room, in the Willard Inter-Continental Hotel, 1401 Pennsylvania Ave NW, Washington (Downtown); tel 202/637-7440. **New American/French.** This elegant dining room possesses a sense of grandeur. Some brass and crystal chandeliers hang from its ornate ceiling, and others are affixed to varnished wood bases. Double rows of massive green faux-marble columns support the enormous finished oak beams that cross the dining room. Beneath are near-baronial chairs of brocaded tapestry-like design surrounding superbly decorated tables. Unique renditions of new American and French entrees include sautéed filet of cod with a cauliflower mousseline and Pernod-saffron-tomato sauce; roasted veal with ragout of fresh octopus and brie, served with a vanilla lobster velouté; and sautéed medallions of venison with caramelized turned apples and juniper-berry coriander pastry leaves. **FYI:** Reservations recommended. Piano. Jacket required. **Open:** Breakfast Mon–Fri 7:30–10am; lunch Mon–Fri 11:30am–2pm; dinner daily 6–10pm; brunch Sun 11am–2pm. Closed some hols. **Prices:** Main courses $18–$32. Maj CC. ◉ ▣ VP

The Wright Place, in the Nat'l Air and Space Museum, Independence Ave at 4th St SW, Washington; tel 202/371-8777. **Burgers/Cafe/Salads.** Contemporary light-wood chairs and granite-look tabletops surrounded by glass walls and ceilings supported by a modernistic arrangement of different size pipes. A view of Washington skies and the nearby Capitol could distract a diner from such specials as charbroiled beef cutlet, Brunswick stew, and vegetarian tamale pie, supplemented by a variety of sandwiches, soups, and vegetables. **FYI:** Reservations accepted. **Open:** Daily 11:30am–3pm. Closed Dec 25. **Prices:** Lunch main courses $7–$10. Maj CC. ▣ ⛰ 👪

Zed's Ethiopian Cuisine, 3318 M St NW, Washington (Georgetown); tel 202/333-4710. **Ethiopian.** Mirrors reflect minimal decorations hinting at Ethiopia, but this friendly establishment is known not for its decor but as one of Washington's best and least expensive ethnic restaurants. House specialties include beef in a spicy sauce. Meals are served traditionally on large pieces of Ethiopian bread. **FYI:** Reservations not accepted. **Open:** Daily 11am–11pm. Closed some hols. **Prices:** Main courses $6.50–$12.75. Maj CC.

Zorba's Café, 1612 20th St NW at Connecticut Ave, Washington (Dupont Circle); tel 202/387-8555. **Greek.** With simple decor, clean and uncluttered, this Greek fast-food restaurant offers high-quality food at low prices. Greek standards, such as moussaka and souvlaki, abound. A variety of daily specials includes potatoes marinated with oregano and other herbs, then baked and served with dolmades and pita. **FYI:** Reservations not accepted. Dress code. Beer and wine only. **Open:** Mon–Sat 11am–11:30pm, Sun noon–10:30pm. Closed Dec 25. **Prices:** Main courses $4–$14. No CC. 🍰

Attractions 💼

MONUMENTS

Jefferson Memorial; tel 202/426-6822. South of the Washington Monument, on Ohio Drive. A beautiful columned rotunda in the style of the Pantheon in Rome, the memorial was built on land reclaimed from the Potomac River now known as the Tidal Basin. Work began in 1939, and the memorial was opened to visitors in 1943.

Within the memorial is a 19-foot bronze statue of Jefferson standing on a 6-foot pedestal of black Minnesota granite. The sculpture is the work of Rudulph Evans, who was chosen from more than 100 artists in a nationwide competition. The interior walls bear engraved excerpts from Jefferson's many writings. The quotation inscribed on the rotunda's circular frieze reads: "I have sworn upon the altar of God eternal hostility against every form of tyranny over the mind of man."

Park rangers give short talks to visitors on request. **Open:** Daily 24 hours; park staff on duty 8am–midnight. Free.

Washington Monument, 15th St and Constitution Ave NW (the Mall); tel 202/426-6839. Directly south of the White House, at 15th St and Constitution Ave NW, this stark 555-foot marble obelisk is the city's most visible landmark. The cornerstone was laid on July 4, 1848, but the breakout of the Civil War and funding problems brought construction to a halt until 1876, when President Grant approved federal monies to complete the project. Dedicated in 1885, the monument opened to the public in 1888.

A large elevator takes visitors to the top for a spectacular, 360° view. Guided "Down the Steps" tours are given, subject to

staff availability, on weekends at 10am and 2pm (varies in summer), relating much about the monument's construction and about the 193 carved stones, including a piece of stone from the Parthenon, inserted into the interior walls. There is a snack bar near the entrance to the monument on 15th St. **Open:** First Sun Apr–Labor Day, daily 8am–midnight; rest of the year, daily 9am–5pm. Free.

Lincoln Memorial, 23rd St NW between Constitution and Independence Aves (the Mall); tel 202/426-6895. Located directly west of the Mall, in Potomac Park, this memorial attracts more than 6 million visitors each year. Designed by Henry Bacon in 1912 and dedicated in 1922, the temple-like memorial has 36 fluted Doric columns representing the states of the union at the time of Lincoln's death, plus 2 at the entrance. To the west, the Arlington Memorial Bridge over the Potomac recalls the reunion of North and South.

The memorial chamber, under 60-foot ceilings, has limestone walls inscribed with the Gettysburg Address and Lincoln's Second Inaugural Address. Two 60-foot murals by Jules Guerin on the north and south walls depict, allegorically, Lincoln's principles and achievements. Most powerful is Daniel Chester French's 19-foot-high seated statue of Lincoln in deep contemplation in the central chamber.

Information center and bookstore on lower lobby level. Ranger talks are given on request. **Open:** Daily 24 hours; park staff on duty 8am–midnight. Free.

Vietnam Veterans Memorial (the Mall); tel 202/634-1568. The memorial is located across from the Lincoln Memorial, east of Henry Bacon Dr between 21st and 22nd Sts NW, within Constitution Gardens. It consists of 2 walls of polished black granite inscribed with the names of almost 60,000 Americans killed or missing in action between 1959 and 1975. The names are listed in chronological order, with the walls rising in height toward their midpoint at the height of the conflict, then receding again as the war drew to a close; directories at either end of the memorial help visitors to locate names.

In 1984 a life-size sculpture of 3 American soldiers in Vietnam by Frederick Hart was installed at the entrance plaza. Another sculpture, the **Vietnam Veterans Women's Memorial,** was added on Veterans Day in 1993. **Open:** Daily 24 hours; rangers on duty 8am–midnight. Free.

United States Navy Memorial, 701 Pennsylvania Ave NW (Federal Triangle); tel 202/737-2300 or toll free 800/821-8892. Authorized by Congress in 1980 to honor the men and women of the US Navy, this memorial is centered around a 100-foot-diameter circular plaza bearing a granite world map flanked by fountains and waterfalls salted with waters from the 7 seas. Exhibits include interactive video kiosks that provide a wealth of information about navy ships, aircraft, and history; the Navy Memorial Log Room, with computerized record of past and present navy personnel; and the Presidents Room, honoring 6 US presidents who served in the navy and 2 who were secretaries of the navy. The 30-minute film plays hourly throughout the day (additional fee charged). Guided tours are available from the front desk, subject to availability. **Open:** Mon–Sat 9:30am–5pm, Sun noon–5pm. Closed Dec 25. Free.

PUBLIC & GOVERNMENT BUILDINGS

The White House, 1600 Pennsylvania Ave NW (visitor entrance gate on East Executive Ave) (the Mall); tel 202/456-7041. Since the cornerstone was laid in 1792, the Executive Mansion has gone through considerable changes. Its numerous occupants often left their mark on it during their residence. Repairs and refurnishing were supervised by the Madison administration after the building was burned by the British in the War of 1812; the North and South porticoes were added in the 1820s (terms of James Monroe and John Quincy Adams); electricity was installed in 1891, during Benjamin Harrison's presidency; the West Wing, which includes the Oval Office, was added during Theodore Roosevelt's tenure; and in 1948 the interior of the building was completely gutted and replaced with a new framework of concrete and steel (the Truman family resided for 4 years at Blair House during the project).

Highlights of the tour include the East Room, scene of great gala receptions and other dazzling events; the Green Room (named in the 19th century for its green upholstery) which was Thomas Jefferson's dining room and is today used as a sitting room; the oval Blue Room (where presidents and first ladies have officially received guests since the Jefferson administration) decorated in the French Empire style chosen by James Monroe in 1817; the Red Room, used as a reception room, usually for small dinners; and the State Dining Room, a superb setting for state dinners and luncheons.

More than a million people line up annually to see the White House. Tickets are *required* Memorial Day–Labor Day; they are distributed at one of the kiosks on the Ellipse (at 15th St and Constitution Ave NW) beginning at 8am for that day only. Tickets are time stamped, so waiting in line is not necessary.

Free tickets for a more intensive—and guided—'VIP' tour may be requested 6–8 weeks in advance from your congressperson or senator. These tours last 35–50 minutes and begin at 8:15, 8:30, and 8:45am; they are conducted by guides who provide explanatory commentary throughout the visit. **Open:** Tues–Sat 10am–noon. Free.

United States Capitol, entrance on E Capitol St and 1st St NW (Capitol Hill); tel 202/225-6827. As our most tangible national symbol since its first wing was completed in 1800, and the place where all our laws are debated, the Capitol is perhaps the most

important edifice in the United States. For 34 years it housed not only both houses of Congress but also the Supreme Court and, for 97 years, the Library of Congress.

The Rotunda, 97 feet across under a 180-foot dome, is the hub of the Capitol; on its curved walls are 8 immense oil paintings depicting events in American history, such as the reading of the Declaration of Independence and the surrender of Cornwallis at Yorktown. A trompe l'oeil frieze overhead illustrates events from Columbus's landing through the Wright brothers' flight at Kitty Hawk. There is also a life-size marble statue of Abraham Lincoln.

National Statuary Hall was originally the chamber of the House of Representatives, but was abandoned for that purpose because of its acoustics—guides demonstrate that a whisper can be heard clearly from across the room. In 1864 it became Statuary Hall, and each state was invited to donate 2 statues of native sons to the collection. Individuals represented here include Henry Clay, Ethan Allen, and Daniel Webster.

The **House and Senate chambers** can be viewed only during the congressional VIP tour (see below). The House of Representatives chamber, the largest legislative chamber in the world, is where Congress assembles to hear the president's annual State of the Union address.

Guided tours of the Capitol depart every 15 minutes between 9am and 3:45pm and last about 30 minutes. The congressional VIP tour begins at 8am. This tour is longer and includes a visit to either the House or Senate chamber, but it requires an advance ticket, obtained from your congressperson or senator. Passes to House and Senate sessions are also available from legislators, and some congressional committee meetings are open to the public. **Open:** Daily 9am–4:30pm. Rotunda open to 8pm from Easter–Labor Day most years (determined annually). Free.

Supreme Court of the United States, 1 1st St NE (Capitol Hill); tel 202/479-3000. Located east of the Capitol between E Capitol St and Maryland Ave. Until 1935 the Supreme Court convened in the Capitol Building. The neoclassical marble building that houses the court today was considered rather grandiose by many when the design was first unveiled, but it does serve to reflect the power and dignity represented by the nation's highest tribunal.

The court is in session Monday–Wednesday from 10am–3pm (with a lunch-hour recess from noon–1pm) from the 1st Monday in October through late April, alternating (in approximately 2-week intervals) between "sittings" to hear cases and deliver opinions and "recesses" for consideration of business before the court. From mid-May through early July, the public can attend brief sessions (about 15 minutes) at 10am on Monday, during which time the justices release orders and opinions. About 150 gallery seats are set aside each day for the general public—arrive at least an hour early.

When court is not in session, free lectures are given in the courtroom that discuss court procedure and the building's architecture. Lectures are given 9:30am–3:30pm every hour on the half hour. Afterward, visitors can explore the **Great Hall** and view a 20-minute film on the workings of the court. **Open:** Mon–Fri 9am–4:30pm. Closed federal hols. Free.

Library of Congress, 101 Independence Ave SE (Capitol Hill); tel 202/707-5000 or 707-5458. (*Note: Due to a restoration project that is scheduled to continue through early 1995, tours currently leave from the James Madison Memorial Building, 101 Independence Ave SE. Call in advance for up-to-the-minute information.*)

This is the nation's library, established in 1800 "for the purchase of such books as may be necessary for the use of Congress," but over the years it has been expanded to serve all Americans. Today the collection includes more than 101 million items, ranging from books, audiotapes, and motion-picture reels to Stradivari violins, and it grows at the rate of 10 items per *minute*. The ornate Italian Renaissance–style **Thomas Jefferson Building,** erected between 1888 and 1897, was designed to house the burgeoning collection in a setting that would rival the finest cultural institutions of Europe. There are elegant floor mosaics from Italy, over 100 murals, and allegorical paintings. Upon completion of an extensive restoration project, the building will reopen to the public. The James Madison Memorial Building provides additional exhibit and research space, while the John Adams Building contains a book depository and several reading rooms.

Tours leave Monday through Friday at 10am, and 1 and 3pm from the James Madison Building. A 22-minute video about the library is shown every half hour beginning at 8:35am. **Open:** Mon–Fri 8:30am–9pm, Sat 8:30am–6pm. Closed some hols. Free.

National Archives, Constitution Ave (between 7th and 9th Sts NW) (Federal Triangle); tel 202/501-5000. Keeper of America's documentary heritage, the National Archives displays the nation's most cherished treasures in appropriately awe-inspiring surroundings. Housed in the Rotunda of the Exhibition Hall are the nation's 3 charter documents—the Declaration of Independence, the US Constitution, and the Bill of Rights—along with a 1297 version of the Magna Carta. All are on view daily to the public.

Most famous as a center of genealogical research—Alex Haley began his work on *Roots* here—the archives are sometimes called "the nation's memory." The vast accumulation of information spans 2 centuries of census figures, military records,

maps, charts, motion-picture films, and much more. Anyone age 16 or over may apply for a research card by presenting a photo ID at Room 207.

The Circular Gallery houses major traveling exhibitions covering a variety of topics. Guided tours are given weekdays at 10:15am and 1:15pm by appointment only (phone 501-5205 for details). **Open:** Daily 10am–9pm. Free.

Folger Shakespeare Library, 201 E Capitol St SE (Capitol Hill); tel 202/544-7077. By 1930, when Henry Clay Folger and his wife, Emily, laid the cornerstone of a building designed to house their collection of printed Shakespearean works, they had amassed 93,000 books, 50,000 prints and engravings, and thousands of manuscripts. The facility today contains some 250,000 books and is an important research center not only for Shakespearean scholars but also for those studying the English and continental Renaissance. On display in the Great Hall are rotating exhibits from the permanent collection—costumes, playbills, musical instruments, and more.

The building's Georgian marble facade is decorated with 9 bas-relief scenes from Shakespeare's plays. A statue of Puck stands in the west garden, and quotations from the Bard and from contemporaries like Ben Jonson adorn the exterior walls.

Free walk-in tours are given at 11am. The Elizabethan Theater, located at the end of the Great Hall, hosts concerts, readings, and Shakespeare-related events. **Open:** Mon–Sat 10am–4pm. Closed some hols. Free.

Department of the Treasury, Pennsylvania Ave at 15th St NW (the Mall); tel 202/622-0896. A magnificent granite structure in the Greek revival style, it was built over a period of 33 years (1836–69). The impressive east front colonnade contains 30 columns that are 36 feet tall and carved from a single block of granite.

A 90-minute guided tour focuses on the history of the Treasury Department and on the architectural history of the building, including its recent restoration. The offices of Samuel P Chase, secretary of the treasury during the Civil War, and the suite of offices used by President Andrew Johnson following the assassination of Abraham Lincoln have been restored to their 1860s appearance. Portraits of former treasury secretaries are hung in gilded frames throughout various corridors. Also on the tour are the 1864 vault and the marble Cash Room, site of Ulysses S Grant's inaugural reception in 1869.

Tours are by reservation only. Visitors must arrive 10 minutes before the scheduled tour time to check in and receive a building pass; visitors over the age of 16 must bring a form of photographic identification. **Open:** Tours Sat at 10, 10:20, 10:40, and 11am. Closed some hols. Free.

Bureau of Engraving and Printing, 14th and C Sts SW (the Mall); tel 202/874-3188. A staff of about 2,000 works here around the clock, producing bills at the rate of 22.5 million a day. In addition to printing currency, the bureau is responsible for manufacturing postage stamps (more than 30 billion per year), treasury bonds, and even specialty items like White House invitations.

The 25-minute **self-guided tour** (with audiovisual aids and staff on hand to answer questions) begins with a short introductory film. Large windows allow visitors to view the various processes involved in making money. Exhibits include money no longer in use, counterfeit money, and an enlarged photo of a $100,000 bill designed for official transactions (since 1969, the largest denomination printed for general use has been $100). After the tour, you can visit the **Visitor Center,** which houses informative exhibits, videos, money-related electronic games, and a display of $1 million. Unique gifts, such as bags of shredded money, may be purchased here as well. **Open:** Mon–Fri 9am–2pm. Closed some hols. Free.

Federal Reserve Building, 20th and C Sts (the Mall); tel 202/452-3149. Completed in 1937 and designed by noted Philadelphia architect Paul-Philippe Cret. Visitors may take a 45-minute guided tour through the building, during which they tour the halls of the Federal Reserve and its boardroom (when it is not in use), and are shown a film detailing the functions of the Federal Reserve. Also within the building is a permanent collection of 19th- and 20th-century American and European art, which may be viewed only by advance reservation. **Open:** Tours, Thurs at 2:30pm; art exhibits, Mon–Fri 11:30am–2pm or by reservation. Free.

Federal Bureau of Investigation, J Edgar Hoover FBI Building, E St NW (Federal Triangle); tel 202/324-3447. Over half a million annual visitors learn why crime doesn't pay by touring the headquarters of the FBI. The attraction is especially popular with kids. Displays include weapons used by big-time gangsters, plus more than 400 photographs of the felons who made the bureau's 10 Most Wanted list since its inception in 1950. Visitors can also see the DNA Lab; Firearms Unit; Metal Analysis Unit; and the Forfeiture and Seizure Unit, where there is a display of jewelry, furs, and other valuables confiscated from illegal narcotics operations. The 1-hour tour ends with a sharpshooting demonstration given by an agent. To beat the crowds, arrive for the tour before 8:45am or write to a senator or congressperson for a scheduled reservation as far in advance as possible. **Open:** Mon–Fri 8:45am–4:15pm. Closed some hols. Free.

Department of State Building, 2201 C St NW; tel 202/647-3241. Even though the introductory lecture and tour discuss the functions performed by the State Department, this is primarily a fine arts tour of the department's Diplomatic Reception Rooms. These rooms, replete with 18th-century American furniture, paintings, and decorative art, are used by the secretary of state and other high government officials for formal, official government entertaining. Highlights of the tour are the desk at which the Treaty of Paris was signed in London, and an architectural tabletop desk believed to have belonged to Thomas Jefferson.

Reservations are required for this free tour and may be made up to 90 days in advance. It is wise to call 3–6 weeks prior to their preferred tour date. Visitors must arrive 20 minutes prior to the scheduled tour time, and adults must submit a valid photo ID. **Open:** Tours, Mon–Fri at 9:30 and 10:30am and 2:45pm. Closed some hols. Free.

Martin Luther King Memorial Library, 901 G St NW; tel 202/727-1111 or 727-0321. Dedicated in 1972, the new main library for the District of Columbia was designed by noted architect Mies van der Rohe. Among its special areas are the Library for the Blind and Physically Handicapped, a Black Studies Division, an AP Wire Service machine in the front lobby, art exhibits in 3 galleries on the A level and in the G Street window, and a local history section with a vast collection of photographs, clippings, and archives from the now-defunct Washington *Star* newspaper. **Open:** Mid-June–Labor Day, Mon and Thurs 9am–9pm, Tues–Wed and Fri–Sat 9am–5:30pm; rest of the year, Mon–Thurs 9am–9pm, Fri–Sat 9am–5:30pm, Sun 1–5pm. Closed some hols. Free.

National Academy of Sciences, 2101 Constitution Ave; tel 202/334-2436. Located between 21st and 22nd Sts, directly across from the Vietnam Veterans Memorial; a 12-foot-tall statue of Albert Einstein stands on the front lawn. The National Academy of Sciences is a private organization that acts as an advisor to the federal government. The facility houses both art and science exhibits, which change every 3 months; open for self-guided tours. Regular chamber music series (call for schedule). **Open:** Mon–Fri 9am–5pm. Closed some hols. Free.

Organization of American States, 17th St NW and Constitution Ave; tel 202/458-3000. Founded on Pan American Day, April 14, 1890, the OAS comprises 35 American republics of the western hemisphere, including the United States. One of Washington's most beautiful buildings, the headquarters features many Mediterranean touches, such as terra-cotta-tiled roof, wrought-iron balconies, and arched doorways. The skylit garden patio contains palm trees and tropical plants surrounding a rose-colored fountain, as well as the Peace Tree planted by President Taft when the building was dedicated.

Flags of all member nations hang in the **Hall of Heroes,** and busts on marble pedestals of such heroes of the Americas as José Martí, Simón Bolívar, and George Washington line the walls. High-ranking dignitaries are received in the **Hall of the Americas,** adorned with glittering Tiffany chandeliers and 24 Corinthian columns supporting a 45-foot vaulted ceiling. Adjoining is the old **Council Room,** with bronze relief panels depicting the exploits of Cortés, Bolívar, Balboa, and others. Guided tours by appointment only, subject to staff availability. **Open:** Mon–Fri 9:30am–5pm. Closed some hols. Free.

Voice of America, 330 Independence Ave NW (the Mall); tel 202/619-3919. Tour entrance on C Street, between 3rd and 4th Sts NW. On February 24, 1942, just 79 days after the United States' entry into World War II, the Voice of America began its first broadcast with the words "Here speaks a voice from America." Today, VOA radio broadcasts in 46 different languages and is heard by tens of millions of listeners around the world.

Tours of the facility last about 45 minutes and include a broadcast studio, the master control room, and the newsroom. Visitors may listen in on a live broadcast (if in progress) in whatever language VOA is broadcasting at the time. **Open:** Tours, Mon–Fri 8:40, 9:40, and 10:40am and 1:40 and 2:40pm. Closed some hols. Free.

Union Station, 50 Massachusetts Ave NE, between 1st and 2nd Sts (Capitol Hill); tel 202/371-9441. Union Station, a monument to the great age of rail travel, was built between 1903 and 1907 and painstakingly restored in the late 1980s to its original grandeur at a cost of $180 million. When it opened in 1907, this was the largest train station in the world, elaborately finished with acres of white marble flooring, a half-million-dollars' worth of 22-karat gold leaf, rich Honduran mahogany, hand-stenciled ceilings, and stunning murals.

Today, Union Station is a transportation center augmented by shopping, dining, and entertainment opportunities: 3 levels of retail shops, a 9-screen cinema complex, and a food court have been installed, along with an elliptical mahogany kiosk in the center of the Main Hall that houses a café and a visitor information center. **Open:** Daily 24 hours; shops Mon–Sat 10am–9pm, Sun noon–6pm. Free.

Pavilion at the Old Post Office, 1100 Pennsylvania Ave (Federal Triangle); tel 202/289-4224. One of the capital's most popular spots, the Pavilion is located in the former headquarters of the US Postal Service, built in 1899. The facility now houses dozens of specialty shops and eateries, daily live entertainment, and an indoor miniature golf course. The Bell Clock Tower stands 315 tall and is the 2nd-highest structure in DC. The tower's open-air observation deck offers unrivaled views of the

city. **Open:** Mem Day–Labor Day, daily 10am–8pm; early Sept–late May, Mon–Sat 10am–6pm, Sun noon–6pm. Observation Deck, daily 8am–10pm, weather permitting. Free.

MUSEUMS

United States Holocaust Memorial Museum, 100 Raoul Wallenberg Place SW (15th St SW) (the Mall); tel 202/488-0400. This museum, mandated by an act of Congress in 1980 and opened in 1993, serves the dual purpose of commemorating the dead and educating the living about the dangers of prejudice and the fragility of personal freedom. The museum building itself was designed to be deliberately bleak and disturbing, with somber spaces and towers on the structure that recall the guard towers of Auschwitz.

Upon entering the museum's permanent exhibition, each visitor receives an ID card bearing the likeness of an actual person who experienced the Holocaust, then learns of that person's fate while retracing the chronology of more than a decade of Nazi persecution. Most of the people whose lives are documented on these cards were dead by 1945.

Exhibits include a railroad freight car of the type used to transport Polish Jews from Warsaw to the Treblinka death camp, a segment of an actual Auschwitz barracks, concentration camp uniforms, photographs, diaries, documentary films, and mementos. The 2nd floor includes accounts of the many non-Jews throughout Europe who helped protect Jews or assisted their escape.

Also in the museum are interactive videos, temporary exhibits, films, and lectures. Tickets may be obtained for a fee in advance through Ticketmaster; same day tickets are available from the museum box office, which opens at 9am daily in the summer, at 10am the rest of the year. **Open:** Daily 10am–5:30pm. Closed some hols. Free.

National Gallery of Art, north side of the Mall between 3rd and 7th Sts NW (the Mall); tel 202/737-4215. The museum was a gift to the nation from Andrew W Mellon, who also contributed the nucleus of the collection, including 21 masterpieces from the Hermitage. It now houses one of the world's foremost collections of Western painting, sculpture, and graphic arts from the Middle Ages through the 20th century.

The original **West Building,** a neoclassic pink-marble structure designed by John Russell Pope, showcases works from the permanent collection. Galleries are devoted to Italians of the Renaissance and 17th and 18th centuries, including the only Da Vinci outside Europe, *Ginevra De' Benci*; late 19th-century Americans, including Homer and Sargent; and Spaniards El Greco, Goya, and Velázquez. There are also 17th- and 18th-century prints, Chinese porcelains, small Renaissance bronzes, 16th-century Flemish tapestries, and 18th-century decorative arts.

The **East Building** is an asymmetrical trapezoid with glass walls and lofty tetrahedron skylights designed by I M Pei. It houses important traveling exhibitions but also contains a massive aluminum Alexander Calder mobile suspended from the skylight and an immense bronze sculpture by Henry Moore.

Audio tours and free guided highlight tours (phone for details) are highly recommended. Three restaurants, several shops. **Open:** Mon–Sat 10am–5pm, Sun 11am–6pm. Closed some hols. Free.

Phillips Collection, 1600 21st St NW, at Q St (Dupont Circle); tel 202/387-2151 or 387-0961. Conceived as a "museum of modern art and its sources," this intimate establishment is the oldest museum of modern art in the country.

The fully refurbished museum contains over 2,500 works of 19th- and 20th-century European and American painting and sculpture. Paintings include 5 van Goghs, 7 Cézannes, and 6 Georgia O'Keeffes (although not all can be displayed at once). Modernists are represented by Klee, Rothko, Whistler, Ryder, and Matisse. An ongoing series of temporary shows is presented as well. Free tours are given on Wednesday and Saturday at 2pm. On Thursday from September through July the museum remains open until 8:30pm, and a $5 admission charge takes effect at 5pm. **Open:** Tues–Wed and Fri–Sat 10am–5pm, Thurs 10am–8:30pm, Sun noon–7pm. Closed some hols. $$$

Corcoran Gallery of Art, 500 17th St NW, between E St and New York Ave (the Mall); tel 202/638-3211 or 638-1439 (recorded info). The first art museum in Washington, and one of the first in the country, the Corcoran Gallery was housed from 1874 to 1896 in the red-brick and brownstone building that is now the Renwick Gallery (see below). When the collection outgrew its quarters it was transferred in 1897 to its present Beaux Arts building, designed by Ernest Flagg.

The collection itself—shown in rotating exhibits—focuses chiefly on American art, from 18th-century portraiture to 20th-century modernism. Non-American works include a room of exquisite Corot landscapes; another of medieval and Renaissance tapestries; and a wing housing an eclectic grouping of European paintings, Delft porcelains, a Louis XVI salon doré, and more.

Free 30-minute guided tours are given at 12:30pm (and at 7:30pm on Thurs). Museum shop; restaurant. **Open:** Mon, Wed, and Fri–Sun 10am–5pm, Thurs 10am–9pm. Closed some hols. $

National Geographic Society's Explorers Hall, 17th and M Sts NW; tel 202/857-7588. The National Geographic Society was formed in 1888 to further "the increase and diffusion of geographic knowledge." At Explorers Hall, the Society's headquarters, a 7-minute video introduces visitors to the worldwide activities of the National Geographic Society.

There are dozens of fascinating displays—most in the form of interactive video exhibits. In **Geographica,** on the north side of the hall, guests can touch a "tornado," learn how caves are formed, and study the origins of humankind. **Earth Station One** is an interactive amphitheater that simulates an orbital flight.

Among the numerous artifacts on display are pieces of equipment from Adm Robert E Perry's 1909 expedition to the North Pole; a scale model of the diving saucer in which Jacques Cousteau descended to 25,000 feet; and an egg from Madagascar's extinct 1,000-pound flightless species known as the "elephant bird." A 3.9-billion-year-old moon rock is displayed in the small planetarium, and excerpts of National Geographic TV specials are screened in the Television Room. On-premises shop sells all National Geographic publications, plus maps, games, and videos. **Open:** Mon–Sat 9am–5pm, Sun 10am–5pm. Closed Dec 25. Free.

National Building Museum, 401 F St NW; tel 202/272-2448. Mandated by an act of Congress in 1980, this museum explores the "act, process, art, and business of building." The permanent exhibit "Washington: Symbol and City" examines the forces that molded the nation's capital. A hands-on, interactive exhibit, it is designed to be experienced by the blind. Other museum collections include artifacts and records of the built environment, such as drawings, photographs, and documents.

A guided tour explores the NBM's home—the landmark **Pension Building** (1881–1887). The building's Great Hall, scene of gala inaugural balls, contains 8 of the largest Corinthian columns in the world. A permanent exhibit on the construction of the building and its subsequent history is located on the 2nd floor. Educational programs, special events. Museum shop. **Open:** Mon–Sat 10am–4pm, Sun noon–4pm; guided tours at 12:30 and 1:30pm Sat and Sun. Closed Dec 25. Free.

Capital Children's Museum, 800 3rd St NE (at H Street) (Capitol Hill); tel 202/543-8600. Hands-on exhibits allow children to explore, play games, and learn about a variety of subjects, from communications and history to physical science and anthropology. Included are a replica of a 30,000-year-old cave, an interactive TV studio, a maze with optical illusions, and a talking (in 22 languages) Tower of Language staircase. Inquire about ongoing workshops, demonstrations, and theater presentations for children. **Open:** Daily 10am–5pm. Closed some hols. $$$

National Portrait Gallery, 8th and F Sts NW; tel 202/357-2700. Persons who have made "significant contributions to the history, development, and culture of the United States" are represented here, in paintings, sculpture, photographs, and other forms of portraiture.

In addition to the **Hall of Presidents** (on the 2nd floor), notable exhibits include Gilbert Stuart's famed "Lansdowne" portrait of George Washington, a portrait of Mary Cassatt by Degas, 19th-century silhouettes by French-born artist August Edouart, Jo Davidson's sculpture portraits, and a self-portrait by John Singleton Copley. On the mezzanine, the Civil War is documented in portraiture. The magnificent **Great Hall** on the 3rd floor is open to the public. It served as a Civil War hospital and was used by Abraham and Mary Lincoln to receive guests at his second inaugural ball.

Tours are given daily, usually 10am–3pm (call 357-2920 for tour information). **Open:** Daily 10am–5:30pm. Closed Dec 25. Free.

DAR Museum, 1776 D St NW (the Mall); tel 202/879-3241. Memorial Continental Hall is the national headquarters of the Daughters of the American Revolution and a museum of American decorative arts from the 17th to the mid-19th century. Preserved here and on rotating display is a collection of early American art and artifacts that includes Chinese export porcelain, English pottery, needlework samplers, pewterware, period furnishings, glassware, and silver. Among the many notable paintings is a Rembrandt Peale portrait of George Washington.

Four floors are occupied by 33 rooms furnished as if they were in 18th- and 19th-century homes. Exhibits from the Americana Collection of documents, wills, correspondence, and other period papers are displayed on the 2nd floor. The "Children's Attic" is filled with 19th-century toys, dolls, and children's furnishings; "Touch of Independence" has hands-on exhibits of everyday colonial items. Also on the premises is the **Children's American Revolution Museum,** featuring items and exhibits illustrating the Revolutionary era.

Free guided tours are offered 10am–2:30pm on weekdays or 1–5pm on Sunday; period rooms and "Touch of Independence" are accessible only by tour. The DAR's extensive library has thousands of books, pamphlets, and manuscripts dealing mainly with genealogy (call 879-3229 for details). **Open:** Mon–Fri 8:30am–4pm, Sun 1–5pm. Closed some hols. Free.

B'nai B'rith Klutznick National Jewish Museum, 1640 Rhode Island Ave NW (Dupont Circle); tel 202/857-6583. On the premises of the international headquarters of B'nai B'rith, this museum documents 20 centuries of Jewish history, much of it in displays of ceremonial and folk-art objects. Among the permanent exhibits are a worldwide collection of ancient and modern Torahs, menorahs, prayer shawls, Passover plates, religious books, marriage contracts, and coins. A sports hall of fame honors such athletes and sports personalities as Sandy Koufax, Hank Greenberg, Red Auerbach, and Mel Allen. A small sculpture garden of Biblical bronzes by American sculptor Phillip

Ratner is on the premises; a museum shop/bookstore offers Jewish antiquities and modern crafts. Guided tours are given daily. **Open:** Sun–Fri 10am–5pm. Closed some hols. Free.

Department of the Interior Museum, 1849 C St NW (the Mall); tel 202/208-4743. Once nicknamed "the Department of Everything Else," the Interior Department originally had a mix of many executive branch responsibilities. Today, it includes the Bureau of Land Management, Bureau of Indian Affairs, National Park Service, US Geological Survey, Bureau of Reclamation, Bureau of Mines, US Fish and Wildlife Service, and Territorial and International Affairs. Exhibits include documents, geological samples, Indian pottery and basketry, and a diorama of Hoover Dam, as well as a diorama of a mine explosion that led to the creation of the Bureau of Mines in 1910. The building itself is architecturally significant, and contains numerous murals and sculptures, mostly added during the New Deal era of President Franklin D Roosevelt. (These may be viewed via guided tour; advance reservation only.) **Open:** Mon–Fri 8am–5pm. Closed some hols. Free.

Washington Navy Yard, 9th and M Sts SE; tel 202/433-4882 or 433-3534. Encompasses 3 military museums and a US Navy destroyer. Exhibits in the **Navy Museum** include 14-foot-long model ships, undersea vehicles *Alvin* and *Triste,* working sub periscopes, a space capsule that kids can climb in, and, at the dock, a decommissioned destroyer to tour. The **Marine Corps Historical Museum** is less hands-on, featuring exhibit cases and Marine Corps mementos. The **Navy Art Gallery** is a small museum with paintings of naval actions created by combat artists. **Open:** Mon–Fri 9am–4pm, Sat–Sun 10am–5pm. Free.

National Museum of Women in the Arts, 1250 New York Ave NW (at 13th St); tel 202/783-5000. A relatively new museum (opened 1987) celebrating "the contribution of women to the history of art." Founders Wilhelmina and Wallace Holladay donated the core of the permanent collection—more than 1,500 works by 500 women spanning the 16th through the 20th centuries. Housed in a landmark 1907 building designed as a Masonic temple, the collection includes works by Barbara Hepworth, Georgia O'Keeffe, Nancy Graves, and many others. The museum's library contains more than 8,000 volumes. **Open:** Mon–Sat 10am–5pm, Sun noon–5pm. Closed some hols. $

Hillwood Museum, 4155 Linnean Ave NW; tel 202/688-8500. Hillwood was the Washington residence of cereal heiress, art collector, and philanthropist Marjorie Merriweather Post (1887–1973). The mansion and auxiliary exhibition buildings contain her collection of fine and decorative arts. Included are dinner plates commissioned by Catherine the Great, Easter eggs by Carl Fabergé, 18th-century French tapestries, and chalices and icons from imperial Russia. The Russian collection is considered to be the most representative outside Russia. Guided tours of the 20-room house last 2 hours. The gardens and auxiliary buildings are visited without a guide.

The **Dacha,** a one-room adaptation of a Russian country house, displays Russian objects. The **Native American Building** (1983) features a part of Mrs Post's collection of Native American objects. The **C W Post Wing** houses paintings, sculpture, and furnishings assembled at the turn of the century by Post's father, Charles W Post.

The **Hillwood Gardens** include a formal French parterre surrounding a pool with charming statuary. The Japanese garden features enchanting quiet pools and a stream. Also here are a rose garden, a greenhouse, and a cutting garden. Museum shop; cafe. **Open:** Grounds, Tues–Sat 11am–4:30pm (must enter grounds by 3pm); tours of main house, Tues–Sat by reservation only. Closed some hols. $$$$

National Museum of Health and Medicine, Bldg 54, Walter Reed Army Medical Center; tel 202/576-2348. Located at Walter Reed Army Medical Center, Alaska Ave at 16th St NW. Established more than a century ago as the Army Medical Museum, it contains diverse collections that illustrate the critical connection between history and medical technology. Exhibits include one of the largest microscope exhibits anywhere in the world, a hands-on computerized "cadaver" used by medical students to practice surgical techniques, medicinal leeches, the bullet that killed Abraham Lincoln, actual human pathological and anatomical specimens preserved by silicone, and an exhibit dealing with AIDS. Guided tours are available. **Open:** Daily 10am–5:30pm. Closed some hols. Free.

Textile Museum, 2320 S St NW; tel 202/667-0441. In 1896 George Hewitt Myers made the first acquisition in what would become one of the world's greatest collections of rugs and textiles. His wide-ranging collection, specializing in handwoven pieces, includes Islamic, Tibetan, Chinese, Caucasian, Turkish, and Navajo rugs. Among the textiles are Peruvian tunics, Chinese silks, Mexican serapes, Navajo blankets, and Egyptian tapestries. The collection totals roughly 14,000 textiles and 1,400 rugs and spans a period from 3500 BC to the present. The **Arthur D Jenkins Library,** located on the 3rd floor of the gallery, offers literature and visual resources that reflect and interpret the museum's collections.

Guided tours are given September–May, every Wednesday, Saturday, and Sunday at 2pm. The gift shop offers an extensive collection of books on carpets and textiles, as well as such items as pillows, scarves, and ties. **Open:** Mon–Sat 10am–5pm, Sun 1–5pm. Library: Wed–Sat 10am–2pm. Closed some hols. Free.

National Aquarium, 14th St and Constitution Ave NW; tel 202/482-2825 (recorded info) or 482-2826. Located in the Department of Commerce Building. The oldest aquarium in the United States, this facility was established in 1873 by the Federal Fish Commission for "the artificial propagation of desirable fishes." Today some 1,700 specimens, representing over 200 varieties of fish, amphibians, and reptiles, are on public view. A touch tank allows visitors to examine such marine creatures as sea urchins, starfish, and snails. Cafeteria on premises. **Open:** Daily 9am–5pm. Closed Dec 25. $

National Museum of American Jewish Military History, 1811 R Street NW; tel 202/265-6280. Operating under the auspices of the Jewish War Veterans of the USA, this museum documents and preserves the contributions of Jewish Americans who served in the armed forces. Featured are changing exhibits covering various topics relating to Jewish American soldiers from World War I through the Gulf War. Guided tours by appointment. **Open:** Mon–Fri 9am–5pm, Sun 1–5pm. Closed some hols. Free.

SMITHSONIAN INSTITUTION

Smithsonian Information Center, 1000 Jefferson Dr SW (the Mall); tel 202/357-2700. The Smithsonian Institution evolved out of an endowment by James Smithson, an English scientist who had never been to America. In 1829 he bequeathed his entire fortune to the US government. Congress created a corporate entity to carry out Smithson's will in 1846, and the Smithsonian Institution became a reality. The collection now amounts to more than 140 million objects from all over the world.

The Smithsonian is composed of 14 museums; 9 buildings are located between the Washington Monument and the Capitol on the Mall. Other buildings devoted to specialized exhibits are within walking distance of the Mall, and farther out, the National Zoological Park and the Anacostia Museum are also Smithsonian responsibilities.

The Smithsonian's orientation center is appropriately housed in the **"Castle,"** the original Victorian red-sandstone Smithsonian building—James Smithson's crypt is located here. The main information area is the Great Hall, where a 20-minute video overview of the Institution runs throughout the day in 2 theaters. Interactive videos offer comprehensive information about the Smithsonian and all other capital attractions and transportation; brochures and parking maps are available here. A stop at the center is highly recommended, especially for first-time visitors to the Smithsonian. Most of the museums are within easy walking distance of the facility.

Dial-a-Museum (tel 357-2020) provides recorded information about daily goings-on at all Smithsonian museums. **Open:** Most Smithsonian buildings: daily 9am–5:30pm; museums with other hours are noted. Closed Dec 25. Free.

National Air and Space Museum, 4th and 7th Sts SW (the Mall); tel 202/357-2700 or 357-1686 for IMAX ticket info. The National Air and Space Museum preserves artifacts from every era in the development of manned flight, from Kitty Hawk to Tranquility Base. There are 23 galleries, each filled with fascinating exhibits and enhanced by interactive computers and slide and video shows.

Highlights of the **1st floor** include famous airplanes (like the *Spirit of St Louis*) and spacecraft (such as the *Apollo 11* command module); a moon rock that people can actually touch; numerous historical exhibits; and rockets, spacecraft, and lunar exploration vehicles. A major exhibit on the *Enola Gay,* the plane that dropped the atomic bomb on Hiroshima, will open here in spring 1995.

Occupying the **2nd floor** are a walk-through mock-up of the *Skylab* orbital workshop, plus galleries focusing on such topics as the solar system, US manned space flight, and military aviation during the 2 world wars. Seven exhibit areas are taken up by "Beyond the Limits: Flight Enters the Computer Age," illustrating applications of computer technology to air and space travel. Another major exhibit, "Where Next, Columbus?" looks at some possibilities for the next 500 years of exploration, featuring a fiber optic scale model of the solar system, a simulated Martian terrain, a small theater showing 3 short films, and much more.

Not to be missed are the IMAX films, shown in the **Samuel P Langley Theater** on a screen 5 stories high and 7 stories wide. Arrive early to purchase tickets for any of the 11 daily showings; the theater is on the first floor. Tickets for the museum's state-of-the-art **Albert Einstein Planetarium** should also be purchased in advance; the planetarium is on the second floor.

Free 1½-hour highlight tours are given daily at 10:15am and 1pm. Recorded tours, narrated by astronauts, are also available for rental. A cafeteria and restaurant are available to the public, and the museum shop sells everything from model kits to freeze-dried astronaut ice cream. **Open:** Daily 10am–5:30pm; hours may be extended in summer. Closed Dec 25. Free.

Hirshhorn Museum and Sculpture Garden, Independence Ave and 7th St SW (the Mall); tel 202/357-2700. Set on massive sculptured piers 14 feet above the ground, the museum's contemporary cylindrical concrete-and-granite building shelters a plaza courtyard where 75 sculptures are displayed. Inside the museum, the permanent collection is displayed on the 2nd and 3rd floors; sculpture is exhibited in the inner galleries, which have floor-to-ceiling windows, and paintings and drawings are installed in the outer galleries. Across the street is a tree-shaded sunken sculpture garden providing additional exhibit space.

Among the best-known pieces in the collection are Rodin's *The Burghers of Calais* and 4 bas-reliefs by Matisse known as *The Backs*. Free guided tours are given several times a day. A guided "touch tour" for the visually impaired covers 35 sculptures

within the museum. For details, inquire at the information desk on the plaza level. **Open:** Daily 10am–5:30pm. Closed Dec 25. Free.

Arthur M Sackler Gallery, 1050 Independence Ave SW (the Mall); tel 202/357-2700. Opened in 1987, this museum of Asian art showcases major traveling exhibitions from around the world. Exhibition areas are entirely underground, with entrance provided through an above-ground pavilion in the garden behind the "Castle. The permanent collection includes Chinese bronzes from the Shang (1700–1028 BC) through the Han (206 BC–AD 220) dynasties; Chinese jade figures spanning the millennia from 3000 BC to the 20th century; Chinese paintings and lacquerware (from the 10th to the 20th centuries); 20th-century Japanese ceramics and works on paper; ancient Near Eastern works in silver, gold, bronze, and clay; and stone and bronze sculptures from South and Southeast Asia. The museum also contains the important Vever collection of Islamic art from the 11th to the 19th centuries, featuring manuscripts, paintings, and calligraphy.

The gallery shop offers a wide array of books on Asian art, reproductions, and gifts. Inquire at the information desk about temporary exhibits, highlight tours, and special programs. **Open:** Daily 10am–5:30pm. Closed Dec 25. Free.

National Museum of African Art, 950 Independence Ave SW (the Mall); tel 202/357-2700 or 357-4600. This is the only national art museum in the United States devoted to research in, and the collection and exhibition of, African art. Founded in 1964 and part of the Smithsonian since 1979, the museum was moved to its present location on the Mall in 1987.

The permanent collection of over 7,000 objects (shown in rotating exhibits) predominantly features the art of the vast sub-Saharan regions, along with many pieces from the 19th and 20th centuries, with works from the western part of Sudan and the Guinea Coast particularly well represented. Highlights of the permanent collection include a display of Royal Benin art from Nigeria and the Eliot Elisofon Photographic Archives, with more than 300,000 photographic prints and transparencies on African arts and culture. (The archives and the Warren M Robbins Library are open to the public only by appointment.)

Special programs include events, children's programs, films, lectures, storytelling, guided tours, and demonstrations; inquire at the information desk. **Open:** Daily 10am–5:30pm. Closed Dec 25. Free.

Enid A Haupt Garden, 10th St and Independence Ave SW (the Mall); tel 202/357-2700. Tranquil oasis with central parterre and 1870s cast-iron furnishings, elaborate flower beds and borders, plant-filled turn-of-the-century urns, and lush baskets hung from

19th-century–style lampposts. **Open:** Mem Day–Labor Day, daily 7am–8pm; early Sept–late May, daily 7am–5:45pm. Closed Dec 25. Free.

Freer Gallery of Art, Jefferson Dr and 12th St SW (the Mall); tel 202/357-2700. Opened in 1923, the gallery contains Asian art and American works from the 19th and early 20th centuries. The Asian collection includes Chinese and Japanese sculpture, painting, lacquerware, metalwork, and ceramics; early Christian illuminated manuscripts; Japanese screens and woodblock prints; Chinese jades and bronzes; Korean ceramics; Near Eastern manuscripts, metalwork, and miniatures; ancient Near East metalware; and Indian sculpture, manuscripts, and paintings.

Among the American works are over 1,200 pieces by Whistler, including the famous **Peacock Room** permanently installed in Gallery XII. Originally a dining room designed for a London mansion, the room features a painting by Whistler, who also adorned the walls with paintings of golden peacocks.

An underground exhibition space connects the Freer to the neighboring Sackler Gallery (see above). The **Meyer Auditorium** presents free chamber music concerts, dance performances, and other programs. Museum shop. **Open:** Daily 10am–5:30pm. Closed Dec 25. Free.

Arts and Industries Building, 900 Jefferson Dr SW (the Mall); tel 202/357-2700. Completed in 1881 as the first National Museum, this red-brick and sandstone structure was the scene of President Garfield's inaugural ball. Since 1976 it has housed exhibits from the 1876 United States International Exposition in Philadelphia—a celebration of the nation's 100th birthday that featured the latest advances in technology. The Exposition was re-created here in 1976 for the Bicentennial.

The entrance floor is like a turn-of-the-century mall with displays of Victorian furnishings, fashions, clocks, tools, photographic equipment, and medicines. Areas off the central rotunda contain such machinery as steam and gas engines and printing presses, plus a display of weaponry and vehicles, including a steam locomotive.

An area called the Experimental Gallery, in the building's south hall, features interactive exhibits covering topics from race relations to the history of graphic arts. The Discovery Theater hosts a variety of programs (call 202/357-1500 for details and ticket info). A Victorian-themed shop sells books, jams and jellies, china, reproduction antique dolls, and more. **Open:** Daily 10am–5:30pm. Closed Dec 25. Free.

National Museum of American Art, 8th and G Sts NW; tel 202/357-2700. The NMAA owns more than 35,000 works representing 2 centuries of our national art history. A rotating sampling of about 1,000 of these works are on display at any given time. The museum is housed in the palatial 19th-century Old Patent Office Building, which it shares with the National Portrait Gallery (see above).

Twentieth-century art occupies the most exalted setting: the 3rd-floor **Lincoln Gallery,** with vaulted ceilings and marble columns. Mid- to late 19th-century artists are on the 2nd floor, as is the **Hiram Powers Gallery,** housing the contents of the 19th-century neoclassic sculptor's Florence studio. The 1st floor features 19th- and 20th-century folk art and the **Art of the West Gallery**. A unique work of folk art on the first floor is James Hampton's visionary religious piece, *Throne on the Third Heaven of the Nation's Millennium General Assembly,* completely covered in aluminum and gold foil.

Special exhibitions are presented throughout the year. Free tours are given at noon on weekdays and at 2pm on Sat and Sun. There is a courtyard cafeteria on the premises. **Open:** Daily 10am–5:30pm. Closed Dec 25. Free.

Renwick Gallery of the National Museum of American Art, Pennsylvania Ave and 17th St NW; tel 202/357-2700. A department of the National Museum of American Art, the Renwick is housed in a historic mid-1800s landmark building of the French Second Empire style. It is a national showcase for American creativity in crafts. The rich and diverse display of objects here includes both changing exhibitions of contemporary works and pieces dating from the 19th and 20th centuries that are part of the museum's permanent collection. The museum shop offers books on crafts and decorative arts, as well as crafts items, many for children. **Open:** Daily 10am–5:30pm. Closed Dec 25. Free.

National Museum of American History, 12th and 14th Sts NW (the Mall); tel 202/357-2700. Dealing with "everyday life in the American past," this museum preserves bits and pieces from each stage of America's transformation from upstart colony to global superpower.

Exhibits on the 1st floor (enter on Constitution Avenue) explore the development of farm machines, power machinery, transportation, timekeeping, phonographs, and typewriters. Here, too, is the Palm Court, with re-creations of turn-of-the-century buildings, including an entire post office that was brought here from Headsville, West Virginia.

Entering from the Mall, visitors find themselves on the 2nd floor facing the original Star-Spangled Banner, 30 by 42 feet, that inspired Francis Scott Key to write the US national anthem in 1814. Also here is a fascinating demonstration of a Foucault pendulum, a copy of the original model exhibited in Paris in 1851.

A vast collection of ship models, uniforms, weapons, and other things military is found on the 3rd floor. Major exhibits focus on the experiences of GIs in World War II and the postwar world as well as the internment of Japanese-Americans during that war. Other areas include money and medals, textiles, printing and graphic arts, and ceramics.

Inquire at the information desk about highlight tours. Hands-on activities for children are featured at the Demonstration Center. Shops, bookstore; cafeteria. **Open:** Daily 10am–5:30pm. Closed Dec 25. Free.

National Museum of Natural History, 9th and 12th Sts NW (the Mall); tel 202/357-2700. (*Note: Due to renovation projects currently underway at the museum, certain exhibit areas may be relocated within the building or temporarily closed.*)

Within the museum are more than 120 million artifacts and specimens, ranging from one of the largest African elephants ever bagged by a hunter in our time to the legendary Hope Diamond, the single most popular display in the museum.

On the **Mall level** are exhibits illustrating 3.5 billion years of evolution, with fossils ranging from stromatolites to dinosaur bones, including many ancient land and sea creatures. The World of Mammals and Life in the Sea are also here, the latter featuring a living coral reef in a 3,000-gallon tank.

The **2nd floor** features the Hall of Gems, with the Hope Diamond, the 182-carat Star of Bombay sapphire once owned by Mary Pickford, a rare red diamond (one of 5 in the world), and a pair of Marie Antoinette's earrings. Also here are the **O Orkin Insect Zoo,** an exhibit with living insects; and the **Naturalist Center,** a resource center for the study of the natural sciences. On display are skeletons that range from the tiny to the gigantic, plus exhibits illustrating the origins of Western cultures.

Free highlight tours are given daily at 10:30am and 1:30pm, but a self-guided audio tour provides the most comprehensive commentary on exhibits (available in the Rotunda for a nominal fee). A **Discovery Room,** filled with creative hands-on activities and games for children, is on the first floor, as is a popular exhibit dealing with Native American cultures. Changing exhibits are featured throughout the year. Cafeteria, several shops. **Open:** Daily 10am–5:30pm; hours may be extended in summer. Closed Dec 25. Free.

National Postal Museum, 2 Massachusetts Ave NE, at 1st St; tel 202/357-2700. This newest addition to the Smithsonian complex appropriately occupies the palatial Beaux Arts quarters of the City Post Office Building designed by architect Daniel Burnham. Created to house and display the Smithsonian's national philatelic and postal history collection of more than 16 million objects, the museum also documents America's postal history from 1673 (about 170 years before the advent of stamps, envelopes, and mailboxes) to the present.

In the central gallery 3 planes that carried mail in the early 20th century are suspended from a 90-foot atrium ceiling. The exhibit also contains a railway mail car, a 1851 mail/passenger

coach, and a Ford Model-A mail truck. Another exhibit illustrates how mail served to bind families together in the developing nation. It includes correspondence from a Revolutionary War soldier to his wife, from immigrants to their families back home, and from pioneers during America's westward expansion. The Civil War section includes the story of Henry "Box" Brown, a Southern slave who had himself mailed to a Pennsylvania abolitionist in 1856.

There is a vast philatelic research library on the premises; also a stamp store and museum shop. **Open:** Daily 10am–5:30pm. Closed Dec 25. Free.

Anacostia Museum, 1901 Fort Place SE; tel 202/287-3382 or 357-2700. This unique Smithsonian establishment was created in 1967 as a neighborhood museum. Its major focus is the history and cultural interests of the predominantly black Anacostia community. Over the years it has expanded to include every aspect of black history, art, and culture, both American and worldwide. The collection includes more than 5,000 items, ranging from videotapes and sheet music to historical documents and works of art. The museum also produces a varying number of shows each year, and offers a comprehensive schedule of free educational programs. Call for an events calendar (which always includes children's activities) or pick one up at the museum. **Open:** Daily 10am–5pm. Closed Dec 25. Free.

HISTORIC HOMES

Frederick Douglass National Historic Site (Cedar Hill), 1411 W Street SE; tel 202/426-5961. Born a slave in 1818, Frederick Douglass fled north in 1838 and became a leading national force in the struggle for abolition and equal rights. An orator, diplomat, and essayist, he lectured widely, founded and published his own newspaper, met with Abraham Lincoln to protest treatment of black soldiers during the Civil War, and eventually held government posts as US marshal of the District of Columbia and consul general to Haiti, among others.

In 1877, Douglas bought Cedar Hill, the handsome Victorian house high on a hill overlooking the Anacostia River, where he lived and worked until his death in 1895. The 21-room house, whitewashed brick with green shutters and Doric columns supporting the front porch, contains many of the original furnishings and personal memorabilia of the Douglass family. Among them are photographs (in the entrance foyer) of abolitionist John Brown, a close friend. In the library are more than 1,000 books belonging to Douglass. An original piano is displayed in the family room. **Open:** Mid-Apr to mid-Oct, daily 9am–5pm; mid-Oct to mid-Apr, daily 8am–4pm. Closed some hols. Free.

The House Where Lincoln Died (Petersen House), 516 10th St NW; tel 202/426-6830 or 426-6924 (tour info). Furnished in period style, the house looks much as it did on the night the president was carried here after the shooting at Ford's Theatre, across the street. The room where Lincoln died on the morning of April 15, 1865, contains a bed of the same design as the original, complete with the original bloodstained pillowcase on which his head rested. From this room Secretary of War Stanton announced, "Now he belongs to the ages." **Open:** Daily 9am–5pm. Closed Dec 25. Free.

Woodrow Wilson House, 2340 S Street NW; tel 202/387-4062. Washington's only presidential museum, this fashionable Georgian revival townhouse, located just off Embassy Row, is where President Wilson retired after leaving office in 1921. After Wilson's death in 1924, his wife, Edith, continued to live in the house, carefully preserving its mementos and furnishings. On her death in 1961, she bequeathed the house and its contents to the National Trust for Historic Preservation. Each room today offers a glimpse into the life—personal and public—of the 28th president. The museum contains a 7,000-item collection of the Wilsons' personal artifacts. Guided tours are available. **Open:** Tues–Sun 10am–4pm. Closed some hols. $$

Christian Heurich Mansion, 1307 New Hampshire Ave NW (Dupont Circle); tel 202/785-2068. A 5-story, 31-room late Victorian built around 1900 by well-known German brewer Christian Heurich. It is furnished with elaborate Victorian pieces, 80%–90% of which are original to the Heurich family. A garden of the late Victorian style was created by the Smithsonian Horticultural Society.

The mansion now houses the Historical Society of Washington, DC, as well as the society's Library of Washington History, a research library filled with unique sources focusing on Washington's social history. The library's collection includes some 70,000 photographs, dating back more than 120 years. Changing historical displays highlight various aspects of Washington society. The entire mansion may be viewed only on a guided tour; the garden and library are open to the public during business hours. **Open:** Tours, Wed–Sat, phone for times. Closed some hols. $

Decatur House, 748 Jackson Place; tel 202/842-0920. This 3-story federal-style brick townhouse (1818–19) was designed by noted architect Benjamin Latrobe. His client was Commodore Stephen Decatur, the naval hero famous for his victories in the War of 1812. The 1st floor is furnished in the style of Decatur's occupancy, with period furnishings and mementos of his life and naval exploits. The 2nd floor is Victorian in decor, reflecting the period of residence by Gen Edward Fitzgerald Beale. The house's architecture and design are explained on 30-minute guided tours given daily on the hour and half hour. Period Christmas decora-

tions are featured in December, and the house hosts an annual craft fair in November. **Open:** Tues–Fri 10am–3pm, Sat–Sun and hols noon–4pm. Closed some hols. $

The Octagon, 1799 New York Ave NW, at 18th St between E and F Sts; tel 202/638-3221. One of the first townhouses built in Washington, the Octagon was designed in 1798 for Col John Tayloe III, a Virginia planter, breeder of racehorses, and friend of George Washington. Steeped in history, the building was a prominent social center in the early 1800s. When the White House was burned in 1812, James and Dolley Madison moved into the Octagon; it was here that Madison signed the Treaty of Ghent in 1815, establishing peace with Great Britain.

In an ongoing project, the house is being returned as nearly as possible to its original state. On the 2nd floor is the circular Treaty Room (Madison's study), containing the table on which Madison signed the Treaty of Ghent and the box in which the treaty arrived from Britain. Below the magnificent oval staircase, an ongoing archeological dig is underway. Tours of the house are available daily. **Open:** Tues–Fri 10am–4pm, Sat–Sun noon–4pm. Closed some hols. $

Tudor Place, 1644 31st St NW (Georgetown); tel 202/965-0400. The builder of Tudor Place, Thomas Peter, was the son of a successful Scottish tobacco merchant. His wife, Martha Parke Custis, was a granddaughter of Martha Washington. The large neoclassical house, surrounded by extensive gardens, was designed by William Thornton, architect of the US Capitol; it was completed in 1816. Intended as a shrine to the Washingtons' memory, it still contains many relics from Mount Vernon. The house is filled with original furniture, silver, porcelain and glass, portraits and photographs, textiles, books, and manuscripts, giving visitors a rare insight into American cultural history.

The **gardens** of Tudor Place retain the expanse of green lawns, parterres, and woodland developed by the Peters in the federal period. Guided tours of the house are given by reservation only. Special tours of the garden are conducted during the summer (phone for details). **Open:** Gardens: Tues–Sat 10am–4pm. Closed some hols. $$

Dumbarton Oaks, 1703 32nd St NW (Georgetown); tel 202/338-8278 or 342-3200. This 19th-century Georgetown mansion was the residence of Robert Wood Bliss and his wife, Mildred. In 1940 the Blisses turned over the estate, their extensive Byzantine collection, a library of works on Byzantine civilization, and 16 acres (including 10 acres of formal gardens) to Harvard University. Twenty years later they also donated their collection of pre-Columbian art and Mrs Bliss's library of rare books on landscape gardening.

Today the 16-acre estate is a research center for studies in Byzantine and pre-Columbian art and archeology, as well as landscape architecture. The Byzantine collection is one of the world's finest, with illuminated manuscripts, a 4th-century sarcophagus, and a 13th-century icon of St Peter. The collection of pre-columbian art features jade and serpentine figures from the Olmec civilization (an ancient Mexican culture dating back some 3,000 years), Mayan relief panels, and textiles from 900 BC to the Spanish Conquest.

The historic **Music Room,** furnished in French, Italian, and Spanish antiques, was the setting for the 1944 Dumbarton Oaks Conferences that led to the founding of the United Nations. On display are pieces of sculpture, paintings, and tapestries, including El Greco's *The Visitation*. The formal gardens contain an orangery, a rose garden and groves of cherry trees. **Open:** Garden (weather permitting), Nov–Mar, daily 2–5pm; Apr–Oct, daily 2–6pm. Collections, Tues–Sun 2–5pm. Closed some hols. $

Meridian International Center, 1624 and 1630 Crescent Place NW; tel 202/939-5552. The Meridian International Center is a nonprofit institution dedicated to the promotion of international understanding through the exchange of people, ideas, and arts. Founded in 1960, the center hosts cultural programs, rotating art exhibitions, concerts, lectures, and other events. Meridian's 3-acre site takes up an entire city block, and comprises 2 historic mansions designed by John Russell Pope: the White-Meyer Mansion (1912), a red-brick Georgian-style home; and the Meridian House (1921), executed in the 18th-century French renaissance style. **Meridian Hill Park,** located across from the center, encompasses just over 1 city block. Begun in 1914 and completed in 1936, the park recently underwent an award-winning restoration. **Open:** Hours vary; phone for schedule. $

Anderson House, 2118 Massachusetts Ave NW; tel 202/785-2040. This historic house/museum is located in a preserved turn-of-the-century Embassy Row beaux arts mansion. It features rotating exhibits from a permanent collection that includes portraiture by early American artists; 18th-century paintings; 17th-century tapestries; Asian and European decorative arts; and collections of books, medals, and swords, as well as silver, glass, and china. A free concert series is offered to the public one Saturday each month at 1:30pm; from Apr–Oct, the US Air Force Chamber Players also offer free concerts, twice a month from Oct–May (phone for schedule and further details). **Open:** Tues–Sat 1–4pm. Closed some hols. Free.

CHURCHES

Washington National Cathedral, Mount St Alban, Massachusetts and Wisconsin Aves; tel 202/537-6200. Pierre L'Enfant's 1791 plan for the capital city included "a great church for national purposes," but possibly because of early America's fear of mingling church and state, more than a century elapsed before the foundation for the National Cathedral was laid. The 6th-largest cathedral in the world, it was completed with the placement of a final stone atop a pinnacle on the west front towers on September 29, 1990—83 years from the day of its inception.

English gothic in style, complete with flying buttresses and 101 gargoyles, the cathedral is built in the shape of a cross, its nave 10 stories high from its marble floor to the vaulting. Its 20th-century origins are evident in such details as the Space Window, a stained-glass window containing a moon rock brought back by the crew of *Apollo 11*. The landscaped grounds contain 2 gardens, 5 schools (including the College of Preachers), and a greenhouse. President Woodrow Wilson and his wife are buried here, as are Helen Keller and her companion, Anne Sullivan.

Tours leave continually from the west end of the nave Mon–Sat from 10am–3:15pm and Sun from 12:30–2:45pm. Allow time to visit the observation gallery, where 70 windows provide panoramic views. There is a large gift shop on the premises. **Open:** Daily 10am–4:30pm. Free.

St John's Church, 16th and H Streets; tel 202/347-8766. Every president of the United States since James Madison has worshiped at the Episcopal church across Lafayette Square from the White House. The Greek revival building, with a dome and colonnaded portico entrance, was designed by Benjamin Latrobe. The **Parish House** next door is also open to the public. It served as the residence of British Minister Lord Ashburton during US-British negotiations in 1842 to settle the Canadian boundary dispute. Guided tours of the church are offered every Sunday after the 11am service. Organ recitals are given Wednesday at 12:10pm, except July–Sept and during Lent. **Open:** Daily 8am–4pm; services or organ recitals Mon–Fri 12:10pm, Sun 8,9, and 11am. Free.

Basilica of the National Shrine of the Immaculate Conception, 4th St and Michigan Ave NE; tel 202/526-8300. The National Shrine is the largest Roman Catholic church in the United States and among the largest churches in the world. Construction of the basilica dates to 1920, when the cornerstone was laid. The **Crypt Church,** which recalls the catacombs of ancient Rome, has been in continuous use since 1926. The Great Upper Church was dedicated in 1959, but additional chapels are still being added, each reflecting the religious heritage brought to America by generations of immigrants.

Guided tours last 1 hour and require no reservation. The basilica also offers a summer recital series (phone for details).

Open: Apr–Oct, daily 7am–7pm; Nov–Mar, daily 7am–6pm. Guided tours Mon–Sat 9–11am and 1–3pm on the hour, and Sun 1:30–4pm. Free.

Franciscan Monastery, 1400 Quincy St NE; tel 202-526-8300. Located within the church and on the grounds is what is known as "'the Holy land of America"—a collection of replicas of the principal shrines and chapels found in the Holy Land. The main shrine is a replica of the Holy Sepulcher, the tomb of Jesus Christ. Other replicas include the Grotto of Lourdes in southern France, the Grotto of Gethsemane, the Chapel of the Ascension on Mt Olivet, and the Nativity Grotto in Bethlehem. The crypt of the church contains replicas of the Catacombs of Rome and has fine copies of early Christian art and inscriptions. Guided tours conducted by the friars. **Open:** Tours (on the hour), Mon–Sat 9–11am and 1–4pm, Sun 1–4pm. Closed some hols. Free.

PARKS & GARDENS

National Zoological Park, 3000 block of Connecticut Ave NW (Woodley Park); tel 202/673-4800 or 673-4717. Established in 1889, the National Zoo is home to more than 4,000 animals of some 500 species, many rare and/or endangered. Animals live in large, open enclosures designed to simulate their natural habitats. The zoo's star resident is Hsing-Hsing, a giant panda donated by the People's Republic of China. He is most regularly seen at feeding time, 11am and 3pm.

Special exhibits include **ZOOlab,** a learning lab where visitors can handle and examine such objects as hummingbird eggs, read zoology texts, and peer at specimens through a microscope (ticket required); the **Invertebrate Exhibit,** the only one of its kind in the country, which teaches about starfish, sponges, giant crabs, anemones, insects, and other spineless creatures; the **Reptile Discovery Center,** which offers a closer look at reptiles and amphibians; and **Amazonia,** an immense glass-domed building housing plants, fish, and animals of the Amazon River region. (Special exhibit hours and days of operation vary; phone ahead.)

An audiotape tour is available. Snack bars, restaurant; picnicking permitted. Gift shops; stroller rentals. **Open:** Summer, daily: grounds, 8am–8pm; animal buildings, 9am–6pm. Rest of year, daily: grounds 8am–6pm; animal buildings, 9am–4:30pm. Closed Dec 25. Free.

United States National Arboretum, 3501 New York Ave NE; tel 202/475-4815. A research and educational center focusing on trees and shrubs, the National Arboretum's 9½ miles of paved roads meander through 444 hilly acres of rhododendrons, azaleas, magnolias, hollies, peonies, and a great deal more. A different species of plant life is in bloom at almost every time of year; in autumn the arboretum is ablaze with the reds and oranges of changing leaves.

The **National Bonsai and Penjing Museum,** a Bicentennial gift from Japan, is a collection of 53 miniature trees, some more than 3 centuries old. The area also includes a Japanese garden. The arboretum's **acropolis** was created with 22 of the original columns from the US Capitol, which were removed a few decades ago when they were deemed too fragile to support the building's new marble construction. The **National Bird Garden** features berrying shrubs that attract a variety of species of birds. The **New American Garden,** opened in 1990, is a collection of ornamental grasses and perennials along brick walkways with carefully placed teak benches. The **American Friendship Garden** also features an extensive array of perennials and bulb plants.

Frequent tours, lectures, and workshops are offered. A guidebook is available in the gift shop. **Open:** Mon–Fri 8am–5pm, Sat–Sun and hols 10am–5pm; Bonsai Collection, daily 10am–3:30pm. Closed Dec 25. Free.

United States Botanic Garden, 100 Maryland Ave SW (east end of the Mall) (the Mall); tel 202/225-8333. Originally conceived by Washington, Jefferson, and Madison and opened in 1820, the Botanic Garden is a lovely oasis—a series of connected glass-and-stone buildings and greenhouses that has been described as a "living museum under glass." The park contains a rose garden, a large year-round collection of orchids, and other themed areas, with tropical, subtropical, and desert plants, and featuring a Dinosaur Garden of cycods, mosses, and liverworts that existed in the Jurassic era. The complex also includes **Bartholdi Park,** which centers on a splendid cast-iron fountain created by Frédéric-Auguste Bartholdi, designer of the Statue of Liberty. Special shows, lectures, and classes (phone ahead). **Open:** Daily 9am–5pm. Free.

Kenilworth Aquatic Gardens, Anacostia Ave and Douglas St NE; tel 202/426-6905. Located directly across the Anacostia River from the National Arboretum. This 12-acre haven is the only national park site devoted to water plants. The gardens today are a showcase for wetland plants, as well as such animals as turtles, snakes, and frogs and 40 different species of migratory birds. Water lilies, lotuses, and other water plants bloom from mid-May until the first frost. A mile-long river trail may be followed through the gardens' 77-acre marshland to the Potomac River. Visits to the gardens should begin at the visitors center. Guided tours available on weekends in the summer. **Open:** Mem Day–Labor Day, daily 7am–5pm (visitor center 9am–4:30pm); rest of the year, daily 7am–4pm (visitor center 8am–4pm). Free.

Rock Creek Park, 5000 Glover Rd NW; tel 202/282-1063 or 426-6829 (Nature Center). A 1,750-acre valley, it's one of the biggest and finest city parks in the nation. Parts of it are still wild, and it is not unusual to spot deer scurrying through some remote wooded sections. The park's facilities include the Carter Barron Amphitheatre, playgrounds, an extensive system of beautiful wooded hiking trails, old forts to explore, and sports facilities, including an 18-hole golf course. An 11-mile bike path runs from the Lincoln Memorial through the park into Maryland, all of it paved. On weekends and holidays a large part of the park is closed to vehicular traffic.

For full information on park programs and facilities, visit the **Rock Creek Nature Center.** The center also presents weekend planetarium shows for kids (minimum age 4 years) and adults, nature films, crafts demonstrations, and guided nature walks, plus lectures, shows, concerts, and other events. Self-guided nature trails begin here.

Pierce Mill, an original 19th-century gristmill on Rock Creek, is open to visitors (Wed–Sat 8am–4:30pm). The old carriage house now houses the **Art Barn,** exhibiting the work of local artists (Wed–Sun 10am–5pm. Located near the Nature Center is the **Rock Creek Park Horse Center,** offering trail rides Tues–Thurs 1:30–3pm and Sat–Sun noon–3:15pm. **Open:** Park, daily; headquarters Mon–Fri 7:45am–4:15pm; Nature Center Wed–Sun 9am–5pm. Closed some hols. Free.

THEATERS, CONCERT HALLS & OTHER VENUES

John F Kennedy Center for the Performing Arts, New Hampshire Ave NW at Rock Creek Pkwy (Foggy Bottom); tel 202/467-4600 or toll free 800/444-1324. Opened in 1971, the Kennedy Center is both a national performing arts center and a memorial to John F Kennedy. Set on 17 acres overlooking the Potomac, the striking $73 million facility contains an opera house, a concert hall, 2 stage theaters, and a film theater. The best way to see the Kennedy Center—including areas not available to the public—is on a free 50-minute guided tour, given daily between 10am and 1pm. Tours depart from a small waiting area on Level A, one level below the main floor.

The tour first visits the **Hall of Nations,** where flags of all countries recognized by the United States are displayed. Throughout the center are numerous gifts from more than 40 nations, including all the marble used in the building (3,700 tons), donated by Italy. Gifts of other nations inlcude 18 crystal chandeliers from Sweden, tapestries by Henri Matisse from France, an alabaster vase dating from 2600 BC from Egypt, and a Barbara Hepworth sculpture from England. Stops on the tour include the Grand Foyer, Israeli Lounge, African Room, Opera House, Hall of States, and Performing Arts Library. **Open:** Daily 10am–midnight. Closed some hols. Free.

Ford's Theatre, 511 10th St NW, between E and F Sts; tel 202/347-4833 or 426-6924 (tour info). On April 14, 1865, President Lincoln was part of the audience at Ford's Theater, one of Washington's most popular playhouses, for a performance of the comedy *Our American Cousin.* Everyone was laughing at a line of dialogue when Lincoln was shot by actor John Wilkes Booth. The president was carried across the street, to the home of William Petersen, where he died the next morning. Ordered closed by Secretary of War Edwin Stanton, the theater was used for many years afterward by the War Department. In 1893, 22 clerks were killed when 3 floors of the building collapsed. The building remained in disuse until the 1960s, when it was remodeled and restored to its appearance on the night of the tragedy. Today it is once again the setting for theatrical performances.

Except during rehearsals or matinee performances (phone ahead), visitors can see the theater and retrace Booth's movements on the night of the shooting. Free 15-minute talks are given throughout the day on the assassination and the history of the theater. Located in the basement, the **Lincoln Museum** contains, among other items, the Derringer pistol used by Booth, the clothes worn by Lincoln the night he was shot, and the killer's diary outlining his rationalization for the deed. **Open:** Daily 9am–5pm. Closed some hols. Free.

National Theatre, 1321 Pennsylvania Ave NW (Federal Triangle); tel 202/628-6161 or toll free 800/447-7400. The luxurious, federal-style National Theatre (circa 1835), elegantly renovated in 1983 for $6.5 million, is the oldest continuously operating theater in Washington and the 3rd-oldest in the nation. The National is also the closest thing Washington has to a Broadway-style playhouse. Managed by New York's Shubert Organization, the National presents star-studded hits—often pre- or post-Broadway—all year round. A recent season included productions of *Annie Get Your Gun, My Fair Lady* starring Richard Chamberlain, *A Chorus Line, Six Degrees of Separation* starring Marlo Thomas, and *Grease* with Rosie O'Donnell. Call for schedule information. $$$$

Arena Stage, 6th St and Maine Ave SW; tel 202/488-3300. Now in its 5th decade, the Arena Stage is the home of one the longest-standing acting ensembles in the nation. Several works nurtured here have moved to Broadway, and many graduates—among them *LA Law*'s Jill Eikenberry and Michael Tucker, Ned Beatty, James Earl Jones, and Jane Alexander—have gone on to commercial stardom.

The Arena's subscription-season productions (there are 8 annually) are presented on 2 stages—the Fichandler (a theater-in-the-round), and the smaller, fan-shaped Kreeger. In addition, the Arena houses the Old Vat, a space used for new play readings and productions. Call for schedule information. $$$$

Warner Theatre, 1299 Pennsylvania Ave NW (Federal Triangle); tel 202/783-4000. Opened in 1924 as the Earle Theatre (a movie/vaudeville palace) and restored to its original appearance in 1992 at a cost of $10 million, this stunning neoclassical-style theater features a gold-leafed grand lobby and auditorium.

Everything is plush and magnificent, from the glittering crystal chandeliers to the gold-tasseled swagged-velvet draperies. The Warner offers year-round entertainment, alternating dance performances and Broadway shows with entertainment by such headliners as Liza Minnelli, Frank Sinatra, and Tony Bennett. Call for schedule information. $$$$

Source Theatre Company, 1835 14th St NW; tel 202/462-1073. Washington's major producer of new plays, the Source also mounts works of established playwrights. It presents top local artists in a year-round schedule of dramatic and comedy plays; each July a 4-week showcase of new plays, the Washington Theatre Festival, presents 50 new works to Washington audiences. Call for schedule information. $$$$

Shakespeare Theatre, 450 7th St NW; tel 202/393-2700. This internationally renowned classical ensemble company, which for 2 decades performed at the Folger Shakespeare Library, moved to larger quarters at the above address in 1992. Under the direction of Michael Kahn, it offers 3 Shakespearean productions and one other classical work each September-to-June season. Call for schedule information. $$$$

Robert F Kennedy Memorial Stadium/DC Armory, E Capitol St between 19th and 20th Sts NE; tel 202/547-9077 or 546-3337. The 55,000-seat stadium is the home of the NFL's Washington Redskins. Events at RFK (and at the 10,000-seat DC Armory complex) include wrestling, nationally televised boxing, roller derby, the circus, soccer games, concerts, and rodeos. $$$$

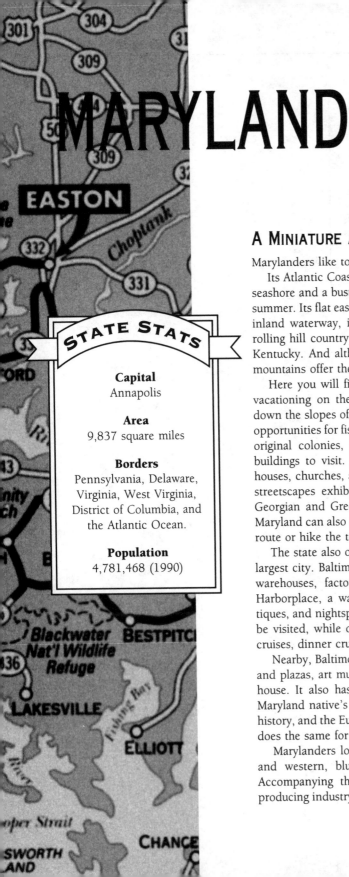

MARYLAND

A MINIATURE AMERICA

Marylanders like to boast that their state is "America in miniature."

Its Atlantic Coast has long beaches shared by both a pristine national seashore and a bustling resort, making it seem a little like Florida during summer. Its flat eastern farmlands are as rich as any of the Midwest. As an inland waterway, its great Chesapeake Bay rivals the Great Lakes. Its rolling hill country has more thoroughbred horses per square mile than Kentucky. And although not nearly as high as the Rockies, its western mountains offer their own scenic beauty.

Here you will find something to do all year long, from summertime vacationing on the 10-mile beach at Ocean City to wintertime skiing down the slopes of the Alleghenies. The Chesapeake Bay offers countless opportunities for fishing, boating, and other water sports. As one of the 13 original colonies, the state has historic sites to explore and historic buildings to visit. Annapolis alone has more than 1,500 18th-century houses, churches, and public buildings, and elsewhere are towns whose streetscapes exhibit a medley of architectural styles from federal and Georgian and Greek revival to Queen Anne and Victorian. Visitors to Maryland can also catch a vintage steam train traveling a scenic mountain route or hike the towpath of a vintage canal.

The state also offers more up-to-date and urban entertainments in its largest city. Baltimore's Inner Harbor, once a ramshackle assemblage of warehouses, factories, and urban neglect, has been revitalized with Harborplace, a waterfront complex of restaurants, food markets, boutiques, and nightspots. Here also is the spectacular National Aquarium to be visited, while out on the water is every type of craft, offering lunch cruises, dinner cruises, and moonlight sails.

Nearby, Baltimore has a revitalized business district, modern buildings and plazas, art museums, theaters, a symphony orchestra, and an opera house. It also has the Cab Calloway Jazz Institute, which houses the Maryland native's memorabilia as part of its collection of Maryland jazz history, and the Eubie Blake National Museum and Cultural Center, which does the same for the ragtime great.

Marylanders love their music, and festivals are dedicated to country and western, bluegrass, rock 'n' roll, Irish folk, blues, and more. Accompanying these are festivals celebrating the Delmarva chicken-producing industry, Maryland wine, and Maryland seafood—fishing tournaments, oyster-shucking contests, crab races, crab-picking competitions, and crab cook-offs.

Luckily for motorists, all this bounty comes in a relatively compact package—just 200 miles from end to end. So that wherever you are when the mood strikes, you'll get there while the food's still hot and the music is still playing.

A BRIEF HISTORY

IN SEARCH OF FREEDOM   The Algonquins and other Native American tribes had been living along the Chesapeake Bay and the inland rivers feeding it long before the tiny ships *Ark* and *Dove* brought Maryland's first colonists in 1634. Having been granted land by Lord Baltimore, whose Calvert family owned the colony, that band of 140 mostly Catholic settlers came in search of religious tolerance they had not enjoyed in Protestant England. They founded a town named St Mary's City and quickly enacted laws guaranteeing religious freedom. Their colony became known as Maryland, which after independence took an appropriate nickname, the "Free State."

A group of Puritans arrived in 1649 and established Annapolis, which grew into a center of commerce, trade, and learning. It became the colonial capital in 1649 and still is Maryland's seat of government. In 1722, other settlers named their new town Baltimore, which would come to dwarf Annapolis in size and importance.

AFTER INDEPENDENCE   From November 1783 to August 1784, Annapolis served as the first peacetime capital of the United States and was the scene of meetings of the Continental Congress. Maryland ratified the new US Constitution in April 1788, and became a hub of transportation during the country's early years. The major seaport at Baltimore was linked to the frontier at Cumberland, in the state's western panhandle, by the first National Pike; the nation's first passenger railroad was opened between Baltimore and Ellicott City; and the Chesapeake & Ohio Canal along the Maryland side of the Potomac River was completed as far west as Cumberland.

OH, SAY CAN YOU SEE   Maryland was a major battleground during the War of 1812, as British troops followed the Potomac River to Washington, where they burned the Capitol and White House. In 1814, they laid siege to Fort McHenry in Baltimore Harbor. It was during the rockets' red glare of that bombardment that Marylander Francis Scott Key composed the words to "The Star-Spangled Banner."

CIVIL WAR   Despite its "Free State" nickname, Maryland was a slave state at the outbreak of the Civil War, and President Abraham Lincoln sent Union troops to put down a riot and virtually occupy Baltimore early in that conflict. The state saw its only major action on September 17, 1862, at the Battle of Antietam, the bloodiest single day of the war.

MODERN MARYLAND   Transportation and industry grew after the Civil War, and they continue to make Maryland a prosperous state strategically located between North and South. In 1952, the 4.3-mile-long William Preston Lane Jr. Bridge spanning the Chesapeake Bay was built at Annapolis, joining the eastern counties to the rest of the state by road and making possible resort development at Ocean City. Once down on its heels, Baltimore has made a remarkable comeback in the past 2 decades, with its Inner Harbor and

---

✦ *Fun Facts* ✦

• *Maryland became known as the "Old Line State" after George Washington praised the colony's "troops of the line," who led the way in many Revolutionary War encounters.*

• *The British colony of Maryland was named for Queen Henrietta Maria, the wife of King Charles I.*

• *The majestic Chesapeake Bay, Maryland's most prominent feature, provides the state with more than 3,000 miles of coastline.*

• *In southern Maryland, tobacco was once so prized it was used as legal tender.*

• *Although a southern state, Maryland remained loyal to the Union throughout the Civil War.*

• *The official state dog is the Chesapeake Bay retriever, a breed that originated in Maryland in the early 19th century.*

the surrounding area a showplace of urban revitalization.

A Closer Look

Geography

Situated midway along the Atlantic seaboard, Maryland is a mix of flat coastal plain, rolling hills, and mountains reaching as high as 3,300 feet above sea level. The state's geometrically perfect eastern and northern borders with Delaware and Pennsylvania are the results of a survey by Charles Mason and Jeremiah Dixon between 1763 and 1768; hence, the Mason-Dixon Line. The Potomac River forms most of its twisting southern border.

Maryland's most distinguishing geographical feature is the **Chesapeake Bay,** which it shares with Virginia to the south. The world's largest estuary, this magnificent body of inland water and its winding tributaries give the state some 4,000 miles of waterfront property and provide a home to some 3,000 species of plants and animals, including Canada geese, bald eagles, whistling swans, and ospreys. It also is a treasure trove of seafood, harvested by a hearty gang known as watermen.

Maryland's **Eastern Shore** lies on the Delmarva Peninsula between the Chesapeake and the Atlantic Ocean. This relatively flat land was settled in the early 1600s, and historic towns like Oxford, St Michaels, Princess Anne, and Chestertown still boast homes dating from the colonial period. Most people derive their livings from the bay and the land, including those employed by Perdue, Inc of Salisbury, one of the nation's largest poultry producers. On the Atlantic coast—or "down the ocean"—sits the lively beach resort of Ocean City, frequented in summertime by droves of inland residents. South of Ocean City beckons the enchanting, undeveloped paradise of Assateague Island National Seashore. And on the Bay side is Crisfield, so-called "Seafood Capital of the World."

Southern Maryland consists of the state's other peninsula, formed by the Chesapeake Bay and Potomac River. It was here at St Mary's that Maryland was founded in 1634. The area still is Maryland's prime tobacco-growing region, although it is increasingly a bedroom community for the huge Washington, DC, metropolitan area to its northwest.

The rolling hills of **Central Maryland** make up the heart of the state and are home to Baltimore, one of the nation's major seaports. The 45-mile strip between Baltimore and Washington has become one large met-

DRIVING DISTANCES:

Annapolis

30 miles SE of Baltimore
31 miles E of Washington, DC
77 miles SE of Frederick
117 miles NW of Ocean City
145 miles NE of Richmond, VA
171 miles SE of Cumberland
225 miles SW of New York, NY
416 miles NE of Charleston, WV

Baltimore

30 miles N of Annapolis
39 miles NE of Washington, DC
47 miles SE of Frederick
147 miles SE of Cumberland
147 miles SE of Ocean City
153 miles NE of Richmond, VA
211 miles SW of New York, NY
386 miles NE of Charleston, WV

Cumberland

94 miles NW of Frederick
141 miles NW of Baltimore
141 miles NW of Washington, DC
169 miles NW of Annapolis
245 miles NE of Charleston, WV
263 miles SW of Philadelphia, PA
286 miles NW of Ocean City
332 miles SW of New York, NY

Ocean City

117 miles SE of Annapolis
144 miles S of Philadelphia, PA
147 miles SE of Baltimore
148 miles SE of Washington, DC
194 miles SE of Frederick
250 miles SW of New York, NY
262 miles NE of Richmond, VA
286 miles SE of Cumberland

ropolitan area, swallowing in-between towns like Laurel. Such Maryland suburbs as Bethesda, Chevy Chase, Silver Spring, College Park, Rockville, and Gaithersburg are very much under the spell of Washington. North and west of Baltimore, however, are the pastures of horse and dairy farms. And Annapolis, the state capital on the Chesapeake, still retains the historical ambience of its colonial beginnings.

From Frederick to Frostburg, **Western Maryland** consists of foothills rising to the ridges of the Allegheny Mountains. An old Native American footpath through this region became the National Pike, America's first official highway. Known today as US 40, it still follows the old trail through the mountains. In the far western panhandle sits Deep Creek Lake, a year-round resort area.

Climate

The best times to visit are during the warm days and cool evenings of spring and autumn. Summers can be uncomfortably hot and humid. Unpredictable winters can be bitterly cold or relatively moderate, with freezing weather and snow more common in the mountains than in the rest of the state.

What to Pack

Outdoor summertime activities will require shorts and lightweight shirts, blouses, and dresses. Bring a jacket or wrap for cool spring and autumn evenings, and even summer ones in the mountains. Winter requires moderately heavy coats, hats, boots, and gloves. A few restaurants require men to wear jackets and ties; others insist on "smart casual" attire—no cut-off jeans, tank tops, skimpy halters, or bare feet. Pack at least one respectable outfit for evening wear.

Comfortable walking shoes, a hat, sunglasses, and a folding umbrella will always come in handy. Bring sunscreen and insect repellent during the summer months, especially for visits to the Eastern Shore.

Tourist Information

The **Maryland Office of Tourism Development,** 9th Floor, 217 E Redwood St, Baltimore, MD 21202 (tel 410/333-6611, or toll free 800/543-1036), provides free copies of its annual *Destination Maryland,* which contains a complete list of attractions, activities, accommodations, state parks, and campgrounds throughout the state. Ask for separate booklets describing family travel opportunities and listing fairs, festivals, and special events.

Most cities and towns have visitor information offices or chambers of commerce that provide details about their locales. Largest is the **Baltimore Area Visitors Center,** 300 W Pratt St, Baltimore, MD 21202 (tel 410/837-4636, or toll free 800/282-6632).

Maryland operates visitors centers near its borders on all interstate highways leading into the state, and on US 15 south of Pennsylvania, US 13 north of Virginia, and US 301 north of the Potomac River. Centrally

AVERAGE MONTHLY TEMPERATURES (°F) & INCHES OF RAINFALL			
	Cumberland	**Baltimore**	**Salisbury**
Jan	30/2.4	35/3.1	34/3.6
Feb	33/2.3	37/3.2	37/3.5
Mar	43/3.1	47/3.6	45/4.2
Apr	54/3.2	57/3.2	54/3.2
May	63/3.7	67/4.1	63/3.6
June	71/3.3	76/3.3	72/3.6
July	75/3.8	80/3.7	78/4.3
Aug	74/3.3	79/4.3	75/5.3
Sept	67/3.1	72/3.5	69/3.7
Oct	55/2.8	60/3.0	58/3.4
Nov	45/2.8	50/3.6	49/3.2
Dec	35/2.6	39/3.8	39/3.7

located welcome centers are on I-95 at Laurel between Baltimore and Washington, and in the State House, on State Circle in Annapolis.

Driving Rules & Regulations

Although you would never guess it by the way Marylanders drive, the speed limit is 55 mph (*not* 65 mph) on all interstate highways. Many other rural highways have a 50 mph limit. In-town speed limits vary.

Drivers and all front-seat passengers must wear seat belts. Children under 4 or less than 40 pounds must ride in an approved safety seat; those under 10 or more than 40 pounds must wear seat belts or ride in an approved safety seat. Police strictly enforce drunk-driving laws.

Renting a Car

Rental cars are widely available in Maryland's metropolitan areas. It pays to shop around, since promotional deals, weekend rates, age requirements, and group discounts vary. The major companies in Maryland include:

* **Alamo** (tel toll free 800/327-9633)
* **Avis** (tel 800/831-2847)
* **Budget** (tel 800/527-0700)
* **Hertz** (tel 800/654-3131)
* **National** (tel 800/227-7368)
* **Thrifty** (tel 800/367-2277)

Essentials

Area Code: The area code for Baltimore, Annapolis, and the Eastern Shore is **410**; for southern and western Maryland and the suburbs of Washington, DC, **301.**

Emergencies: Call **911** for the police, fire department, or an ambulance from anywhere within Maryland.

Liquor Laws: Privately owned package stores sell beer, wine, and liquors, which are not available at grocery and convenience stores in Maryland. The legal drinking age is 21.

Smoking: The state of Maryland has announced plans to prohibit smoking in all workplaces. The regulation was being challenged as we went to press, but don't be surprised to find that smoking is banned in all bars, restaurants, and other public areas.

Taxes: The state sales tax is 5%. Many localities also impose hotel taxes.

Time Zone: All of Maryland is in the Eastern time zone. Daylight saving time (one hour ahead of Eastern Standard Time) is observed from the 1st Sunday in April until the last Sunday in October.

BEST OF THE STATE
What to See & Do

BATTLEFIELDS   With one exception, Maryland escaped most of the heavy fighting during both the American Revolution and the Civil War. That one exception was the Battle of Antietam, near Sharpsburg, when Union troops met the advancing Confederates on September 17, 1862. It was the single bloodiest day of the war, with a combined casualty list of 23,110 men killed or wounded. The battlefield is now the **Antietam National Battlefield.**

HISTORIC BUILDINGS & SITES   It seems that the streets of every Maryland town are lined with historic homes and commercial buildings. But **Annapolis** excels in this respect, with the largest concentration of 18th-century buildings in America, including the oldest US state capitol in continuous use. Architecture buffs will also find the Eastern Shore rich in towns with historic districts, including **Easton,** which has some 40 18th- and 19th-century buildings, **Salisbury,** and **Chestertown.** In Western Maryland, **Frederick** has a 33-block district of well-preserved 18th- and 19th-century mansions and town houses.

The state also has a number of historic sites of national importance, beginning with **Antietam National Battlefield,** at Sharpsburg, near Frederick. Two more frequently visited sites are the 1797-vintage **USS Frigate *Constellation*,** the oldest warship of the US Navy, and **Fort McHenry National Monument and Historic Shrine,** where Francis Scott Key wrote "The Star-Spangled Banner" during the War of 1812. Both are in Baltimore Harbor.

HISTORIC TRAINS Railroad buffs will find plenty of interest in Maryland, home of the nation's first passenger train. Old engines and other equipment are displayed in the **Baltimore and Ohio (B&O) Railroad Museum** in Baltimore and the **B&O Railroad Station Museum** in Ellicott City. The **Western Maryland Scenic Railroad** operates a vintage steam train through the lovely mountain valley between Cumberland and Frostburg.

MUSEUMS In addition to those dedicated to railroads, Maryland has many other museums devoted to a wide variety of subjects. Baltimore leads the way with **Babe Ruth's Birthplace**, the **Baltimore Maritime Museum, Streetcar Museum, Baltimore Museum of Art,** the **Great Blacks in Wax Museum, American Indian Cultural Center and Museum, Edgar Allen Poe House,** and **H L Mencken House.** At Ocean City, the **Delmarva Shipwreck and Historical Museum** houses relics of shipwrecks and a collection of Native American artifacts.

BEACHES Ocean City's 10-mile-long beach is bordered by boardwalk, hotels, resorts, condominiums, restaurants, and amusement parks. A few miles south, the preserved expanse of **Assateague Island National Seashore** offers 30 miles of undisturbed sand and surf.

CUISINE H L Mencken once described the Chesapeake Bay as a "great protein factory." He meant the enormous amount of crabs, oysters, clams, and fish harvested from the Bay each year, which in turn means great seafood eating in Maryland. Tops on the list is the **blue crab,** served steamed and sprinkled with spice. Most local residents will gladly demonstrate how to "crack" these hard-shelled morsels. You also can order the soft-shell version or enjoy the meat in **crab cakes,** one of Maryland's characteristic dishes. And with all that poultry on the Eastern Shore, try some southern-style fried chicken.

FAMILY FAVORITES A water-oriented recreational facility with land-based carnival rides, **Adventure World** at Largo is the state's only theme park. Nevertheless, families will find much to keep them occupied in Maryland. Children usually enjoy the **Baltimore Zoo,** the **Catoctin Mountain Zoological Park** in Thurmont, and **Plumpton Park Zoo** in Rising Sun. The National Aquarium in Baltimore's Inner Harbor offers 5,000 sea mammals, fish, birds, and reptiles, plus a jungle display with exotic tropical birds and animals. The **Maryland Science Center** in Baltimore has hands-on educational exhibits for everyone. Other suggestions include traditional family vacations at places such as **Ocean City** and **Deep Creek Lake,** or looking for wild ponies on **Assateague Island.**

Events/Festivals

Maryland has hundreds of special events and festivals each year, all of them listed in the *Maryland Celebrates!* booklet published by the Maryland Department of Tourism Development (see "Tourist Information," above). Following are some of the most popular.

The Eastern Shore

- **North American Wildlife Craft Show,** Ocean City. Leading artists and carvers offer their works for sale. Mid-January. Call toll free 800/OC-OCEAN.
- **Chestertown Tea Party Festival,** Chestertown. Re-enacts local 1774 protest against British tea tax. Parade, art show, music, entertainment. 3rd weekend in May. Call 410/778-0416.
- **Queen Anne's County Waterman's Festival,** Kent Narrows. Celebrates seafood gatherers' unique way of life with food, entertainment, workboat contests. Wells Cove Public Landing. 1st weekend in June. Call 410/827-4810.
- **Bay Country Music Festival,** Centreville. Outdoor bluegrass, country, rock 'n' roll in 4-H Park. 2nd Saturday in June. Call 410/827-4810.
- **Canal Day,** Chesapeake City. Carriage and boat rides, music, artisans, crab feast celebrate the Chesapeake and Delaware Canal. Last Saturday in June. Call 410/392-7922 or 410/885-3112.
- **National Hard Crab Derby and Fair,** Crisfield. Crab picking, cooking, and racing, plus pageants and parades. Annual event since 1947. Somers Cove Marina. Labor Day weekend. Call 410/968-2682.
- **Olde Princess Anne Days,** Princess Anne. Only chance to tour 18th- and 19th-century homes, with costumed guides. Start at Teackle Mansion. 1st weekend in October. Call 410/651-2986, or toll free 800/521-9189.

- **Waterfowl Festival,** Easton. Major show of wildlife paintings and carvings, including antique decoys. Food and crafts for sale. 2nd weekend in November. Call 410/822-4567.

Southern Maryland

- **Maryland Day Weekend,** St Mary's. Historic town opens to celebrate founding of Maryland there in 1634. Weekend nearest March 25. Call 301/862-0990, or toll free 800/762-1634.
- **Governor's Cup Yacht Race,** St Mary's. Largest overnight yacht race on East Coast leaves waterfront at St Mary's College. 1st weekend in August. Call 301/862-0380.
- **Historic Pageant and Blessing of the Fleet,** St Clement's Island. Boat ride from Colton's Point to historic island, hayride to festivities, food, blessing of workboats. 1st weekend in October. Call 301/769-2222.
- **St Mary's County Oyster Festival,** Leonardtown. National oyster-shucking and cooking contests, seafood, entertainment, and children's games. 3rd weekend in October. Call 301/863-5015.

Central Maryland

- **Annapolis Heritage Antiques Show,** Annapolis. Dealers offer 18th- and 19th-century furnishings, works of art. National Guard Armory. Mid- to late January. Call 410/222-1919.
- **Babe Ruth's Birthday Party,** Baltimore. Celebrate the anniversary of The Bambino's birth in 1895. Babe Ruth Museum. February 6. Call 410/727-1539.
- **St Patrick's Day,** Baltimore. City's large Irish community celebrates with parade, 3-mile marathon, lots of green. Call 410/837-4636, or toll free 800/282-6632.
- **Annapolis Spring Boat Show,** Annapolis. Region's largest features sailboats and powerboats. City Dock. 3rd weekend in April. Call 410/268-8828.
- **Annapolis Waterfront Festival,** Annapolis. Arts and crafts, flotillas of tall ships, boat races, music. City Dock. Last weekend in April. Call 410/269-0661 or 410/268-8890.

- **Preakness Festival,** Baltimore. Week-long celebrations culminate in the Preakness Stakes, 2nd jewel of thoroughbred racing's Triple Crown. Pimlico Race Course. Week before 3rd Saturday in May. Call 410/837-3030 for festivities, 410/542-9400 for Preakness tickets.
- **Maryland Seafood Festival,** Annapolis. Sample the bounty of the Bay at Sandy Point State Park. 2nd weekend in September. Call 410/268-7682.
- **New Market Days,** New Market. Maryland's antique capital goes all out, with food, crafts, entertainment, and all 30 shops open. Last weekend in September. Call 301/865-3926.
- **United States Sailboat Show,** Annapolis. Hundreds of "rag haulers" and their accessories displayed in tents at City Dock. 1st weekend in October. Call 410/268-8828.
- **United States Power Boat Show,** Annapolis. "Stink pots" and their accessories move into same City Dock tents used by sailboat show. 2nd weekend in October. Call 410/268-8828.
- **State House by Candlelight,** Annapolis. Maryland's historic capitol is decorated for Christmas. 1st weekend in December. Call 410/974-3400.

Western Maryland

- **Winterfest Weekend,** Deep Creek Lake. Wisp Ski Resort hosts ski races, parties, frigid golf tournament. 1st weekend in March. Call 301/387-4911.
- **National Pike Festival,** Washington County. Conestoga wagon train travels US 40, the original National Pike, accompanied by arts and crafts, old-fashioned entertainment. 3rd weekend in May. Call 301/791-3130, or toll free 800/228-STAY.
- **Fort Frederick Rendezvous,** Big Pool. Re-enactment of life during the French and Indian Wars of the 1750s. Fort Frederick State Park. Last weekend in May. Call 301/842-2155.
- **McHenry Highland Festival,** McHenry. Traditional gathering of the clans, with bagpipes, dances, sheep dogs. Garret County Fairgrounds. 1st Saturday in June. Call 301/334-1948.
- **Heritage Days Festival,** Cumberland. Tours of historic homes and buildings, arts and crafts, entertainment, children's program. Call 301/759-4400, or toll free 800/872-4650.

- **Chesapeake and Ohio Canal Boat Festival,** Cumberland. Canal boats on display, Civil War re-enactments, music, food, arts and crafts. North Branch of C&O National Historical Park. 2nd weekend in July. Call 301/777-5905, or toll free 800/508-4748.
- **Rocky Gap Country/Bluegrass Music Festival,** Cumberland. Nationally-known entertainers, Baltimore Symphony Orchestra, local musicians, workshops, arts and crafts. Rocky Gap State Park. 1st weekend in August. Call 301/724-2511, or toll free 800/424-2511.
- **Maryland Railfest,** Cumberland. 3-day festival of railroad history, rides on Western Maryland Scenic Railroad. Late October. Call 301/759-4400, or toll free 800/TRAIN-50.
- **Antietam National Battlefield Memorial Illumination,** Sharpsburg. Lighting of 23,110 luminaries provides haunting memorial to dead and wounded of the Civil War battle. 1st Saturday in December. Call 301/842-2722.

Spectator Sports

BASEBALL The American League **Baltimore Orioles** play in the modern yet classic Oriole Park at Camden Yards, 333 W Camden St, Baltimore (tel 410/685-8900). Inquire early, since the "O's" usually pack this beautiful, Inner Harbor ballpark. Old-time fans will enjoy visiting Babe Ruth's Birthplace, now a baseball museum within walking distance of Camden Yards at 216 Emory St.

Popular minor league teams include the **Bowie Baysox** (tel 301/805-6000), the **Frederick Keys** (tel 301/662-0013), and the **Hagerstown Suns** (tel 301/791-6266).

BASKETBALL The NBA **Washington Bullets** play most of their games at USAir Arena in Landover, on Central Avenue just off I-95 east of Washington, DC, but they appear a few times each season at the Baltimore Arena. Call 301/350-3400 for schedules and tickets.

COLLEGE ATHLETICS The University of Maryland **Terrapins** play their Atlantic Coast Conference games at Cole Field House in College Park. For information call 301/314-7070.

FOOTBALL Baltimore's entry into the Canadian Football League, **Baltimore CFL,** plays its home games at Memorial Stadium, on 33rd Street at Ellerslie Ave. Call 410/554-1040 for schedules and tickets.

GOLF The world's top PGA pros tee off during the first week of June in the **Kemper Open** at the Tournament Player's Club at Avenel, near I-495 in Potomac. Call 301/469-3737 for dates and tickets.

HORSE RACING **Pimlico Race Course** at Hayward and Winner Aves in Baltimore (tel 410/542-9400) has daily racing and hosts the Preakness Stakes on the 3rd Saturday in May. **Laurel Race Course,** at Md 98 and Race Track Rd in Laurel, is another thoroughbred racing venue (tel 301/725-0400, or toll free 800/638-1859). **Rosecroft Raceway** in Fort Washington (tel 301/567-4000) features harness racing.

ICE HOCKEY The NHL **Washington Capitals** face off at USAir Arena in Landover (tel 410/350-3400). The minor league **Baltimore Skipjacks** play in the Baltimore Arena, 201 W Baltimore St (tel 410/347-2010).

Activities A to Z

BICYCLING Maryland has several areas ideal for bike riding, beginning with the 184-mile towpath of the **C&O Canal National Historical Park,** which follows the Potomac River from Washington, DC, to Cumberland. The 13-mile **Baltimore-Annapolis Trail** runs north from US 50 and Md 2 just outside Annapolis. Several flat rural roads on the Eastern Shore have wide paved shoulders to accommodate bikes, such as Md 20 between Chestertown and Rock Hall, and Md 333 between Easton and Oxford.

For information about trails throughout the state, call the Maryland State Highway Administration's bicycling hotline, Monday–Friday 8:15am–4:15pm (tel 410/333-1663). The Geography Department of the University of Maryland-Baltimore County (tel 410/455-2002) publishes a guide to biking and hiking trails in the Baltimore-Annapolis area. Commercial companies offer inn-to-inn touring and camping.

Spectators can watch the pros race through Maryland on the annual **Tour DuPont** in early May. Downtown Hagerstown is the finish line for the Maryland portion of this 1,000-mile race that begins in Wilmington, Delaware. For information call 301/791-3080.

BIRDWATCHING   The Eastern Shore is a prime area for watching birds, especially in **Blackwater National Wildlife Refuge** south of Cambridge and in **Assateague Island National Seashore,** which adjoins the Chincoteague National Wildlife Refuge just below the Virginia line. For information, contact the Audubon Naturalist Society for the Middle Atlantic States, 8940 Jones Mill Rd, Chevy Chase, MD (tel 301/652-9188).

BOATING   The Chesapeake Bay and its many tributaries are a draw for pleasure craft of all types. Every waterfront town and village has at least one marina, many of which rent or charter power boats and sailboats. The Maryland Office of Tourism Development's *Destination Maryland* has a complete town-by-town list (see "Tourist Information," above). Annapolis, one of the world's major sailing centers, has 3 excellent schools where both children and adults can learn to sail.

The state's slow-moving coastal rivers and creeks offer gentle going for canoeists and kayakers, and its swift-flowing mountain streams pose challenges. A number of outfitters provide boats and guides, especially in the towns along the Potomac River.

Several scenic cruises operate in Baltimore, Annapolis, and Ocean City. Water taxis, useful for sightseeing, scoot around Baltimore's Inner Harbor, and day cruises leave Crisfield for Virginia's unusual Tangier Island.

CAMPING   The state is well equipped for campers, whether they pitch a tent along the Appalachian Trail or hook up the RV near a big city. Twenty-two of Maryland's 44 state parks have camping facilities, and there are more than 30 private campgrounds. For a complete list, request a copy of the Maryland Office of Tourism Development's *Destination Maryland* (see "Tourist Information," above).

FISHING   With the deep sea off its Atlantic Ocean beaches, the saltwater expanse of the Chesapeake Bay, and hundreds of freshwater streams and lakes, it's difficult to go anywhere in the state that isn't a few minutes drive from someone's favorite fishing hole. The Maryland Office of Tourism Development's *Destination Maryland* has a chart showing when and where to try your luck (see "Tourism Information," above). Separate freshwater and Chesapeake Bay **licenses** are required of both Marylanders and visitors alike, including a special stamp for striped bass (or "rockfish"). For information, contact the Fish, Heritage and Wildlife Service, E-1, Maryland Department of Natural Resources, 580 Taylor Ave, Annapolis, MD 21401 (tel 410/974-3211).

GOLF   Duffers can play almost year-round on Maryland's numerous public and private golf courses. Most famous is Potomac's Tournament Player's Club at Avenel, home of the annual Kemper Open. Most hotels and resorts can arrange a tee time at a local course. The Maryland Office of Tourism Development's *Destination Maryland* lists all courses county-by-county.

GUIDED EXCURSIONS   Several guided tours are available in Baltimore and Annapolis, but one unusual excursion is the **John Wilkes Booth Escape Route Bus Tour,** which retraces the steps of Abraham Lincoln's assassin into southern Maryland. The bus leaves the Surratt House Museum in Clinton several times a year. Reservations are essential (tel 301/868-1121).

HIKING   Numerous trails include the state's 37 miles of the **Appalachian Trail** and the 184-mile-long towpath of the C&O Canal National Historic Park along the Potomac River. The 29-mile **Catoctin Trail** links 3 state parks and Cunningham Falls. For the Baltimore-Annapolis area, ask for a copy of the University of Maryland-Baltimore County Geography Department's guide to local hiking and biking trails (tel 410/455-2002).

HORSEBACK RIDING   Maryland has a plethora of stables, especially in the horse country that runs from north of Baltimore through the rolling hills of central Maryland. Hotels and local tourist offices can help arrange riding.

HUNTING   In addition to its famous ducks and Canada geese in the Atlantic Flyway on the Eastern Shore, Maryland offers grouse, whitetail deer, and even wild turkeys to be hunted. The state has thousands of acres of public hunting lands, state forests, and parks. For information about licenses, seasons, and bag limits, contact the Wildlife Division, Maryland Department of Natural Resources, 580 Taylor Ave, Annapolis, MD 21401 (tel 410/974-3195).

SHOPPING   Most Maryland towns have at least one antiques shop, and **Baltimore's Antique Row** has more than 75 shops along the 700 and 800 blocks of Howard Street just northwest of the Inner Harbor. Another antiquer's paradise is New Market, on US 40 east of Frederick.

A number of outlet malls dot the state, with major shopping along US 50 near both ends of the Chesapeake Bay Bridge.

SKIING   Maryland's one downhill ski facility is **Wisp Resort** in Deep Creek Lake (tel 301/387-5581), which has 4 miles of slopes and trails, a 610-foot drop, and snowmaking equipment. Many state parks, especially those in western Maryland, have cross-country trails.

TENNIS   The temperate climate makes tennis a popular outdoor sport most of the year in Maryland, which has a host of public and private courts. Some of the larger hotels and resorts have their own facilities for guests, and most others can point you to nearby courts.

WATER SPORTS   Fronted by the Atlantic Ocean and backed by Assawoman and Isle of Wight Bays, the narrow but long resort town of Ocean City offers a host of water sports, especially windsurfing and parasailing.

SCENIC DRIVING TOUR #1

MARYLAND'S EASTERN SHORE

Start: Easton
Finish: Ocean City
Distance: 170 miles
Time: 2–3 days
Highlights: 17th- and 18th-century towns and villages; scenic expanses of forests, farmland, and marshes; winding waterways; wildlife refuges; a ferry ride; fabulous seafood; pounding surf at a major beach resort

This tour follows US 50 (the so-called Ocean Gateway) across the low, waterway-laced Delmarva Peninsula, which Marylanders call their Eastern Shore. You'll detour from this major highway to visit lovely water-front towns like St Michaels and Oxford, 2 of the state's oldest municipalities, and wildlife refuges set aside for the waterfowl that make this area famous among birdwatchers, photographers, woodcarvers, and hunters. You'll also have many opportunities to sample the succulent Chesapeake seafood harvested by the area's hearty Watermen. While most stops are in colonial-era towns and villages, you'll end up in a far different world: The high-rise condominiums of Ocean City, a bustling and very modern summertime beach resort.

For additional information on accommodations, restaurants, and attractions in the region covered by the tour, look under specific cities in the listings portion of this book.

US 50 can be congested with weekend beach traffic from Memorial Day to Labor Day. The worst driving times are Friday nights and Saturday mornings eastbound, Sunday evenings westbound. Plan accordingly.

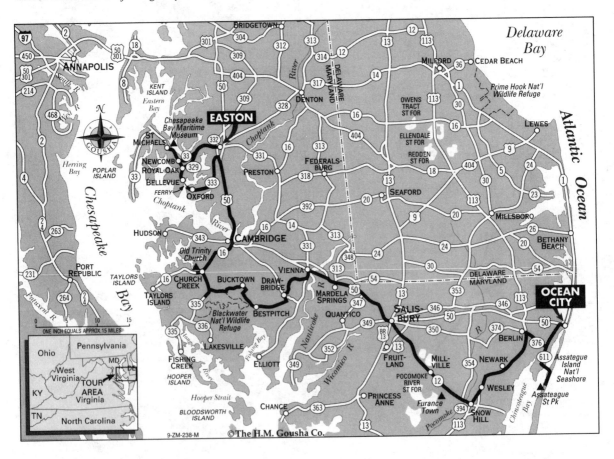

ONE INCH EQUALS APPROX. 15 MILES

9-ZM-238-M   ©The H.M. Gousha Co.

US 50 crosses the Chesapeake Bay east of Annapolis. From the Bay Bridge, it's 26 miles to:

1. **Easton,** a peaceful little community (pop 8,500) facing the center of the bay yet sheltered by the coves of the Miles and Red Avon Rivers. William Penn once preached at the **Third Haven Meeting House,** built in 1692 at 405 S Washington St (tel 410/822-0293), ½ mile south of the **Talbot County Court House.** There has been a court house at this Washington St site between Dover and Federal Sts since 1711 (the present one was finished in 1974). Many other Easton homes and commercial buildings are also from the Federal period. The **Historical Society Museum,** 25 S Washington St (tel 410/822-0773), and the nearby James and Joseph Neall Houses (both restored residences of Quaker cabinetmaker brothers), focus on Easton's past. They are open Tuesday–Saturday from 10am–4pm, Sunday 1–4pm. A host of upscale shops around the Court House attest to Talbot's being one of the wealthiest counties on the Eastern Shore.

Consider spending at least 1 night in this area. In Easton, the charming **Tidewater Inn** may be found at Dover and Harrison Sts, and there are comfortable chain motels, such as **Comfort Inn** and **Days Inn,** on the US 50 commercial strip east of town. You can also bunk down in St Michaels or Oxford, the next stops on this tour. This area is a very popular weekend retreat, so advance reservations are strongly advised. For refreshment, nearly every fast food chain has an outlet along US 50 in Easton, and there are fine seafood restaurants in both St Michaels and Oxford.

From downtown Easton, take Bay St (Md 33) west for 6½ miles to a delightful view of the Miles River from atop the Oak Creek Bridge. From there it's 2½ miles to the trendy shops along Talbot St, the main thoroughfare of charming:

2. **St Michaels,** an important Miles River shipbuilding port from the late 1600s until the 1830s, when its shipwrights worked on the small Chesapeake Bay bugeye and skipjack sailboats. Turn right on Mill St to visit the excellent **Chesapeake Bay Maritime Museum** (tel 410/745-2916), where examples of these and other local vessels are on display. From there, you can take a self-guided walking tour around the harbor and have lunch at the rustic **Crab Claw** (tel 410/745-2900) seafood restaurant or another waterside eatery. Other sights include the **Cannonball House** on Mulberry St, which received its name during the War of 1812, when St Michaels's residents blacked out the town and hung lanterns in the trees to fool an attacking British fleet into overshooting their houses. Their ruse worked, except for one shot which hit the chimney on Cannonball House.

From St Michaels, backtrack 3 miles east on Md 33, turn right on Md 329, and follow the signs south 4½ miles to the 9-car **Oxford-Bellevue Ferry** (tel 410/745-9023), which shuttles across the Tred Avon River until 9pm from June through Labor Day, until sunset from March to May and from September to mid-December. Fares are $4.50 for car and driver, 50¢ for each passenger. (The ferry doesn't operate from mid-December until March 1st, so during that time return to Easton on Md 33, turn right on the Easton Pkwy (Md 322), and right again on Md 333 to reach the next stop.) While riding the ferry for 20 minutes, grab a free brochure with a map of:

3. **Oxford,** a serene little town on a narrow peninsula formed by the Tred Avon River and Town Creek. There was a Colonial settlement here as early as 1673. The historic 1710 **Robert Morris Inn** stands opposite the ferry landing at the corner of Morris St and The Strand, which skirts the river. Find a place to park, explore this gem of a town on foot, and enjoy the seafood at one of the restaurants on Town Creek.

REFRESHMENT STOP

The **Trappe Station Country Store,** at the junction of Md 333 and Almshouse Rd (tel 410/822-9338), isn't a country store any more but a fine little deli where you can chow down on country-style breakfasts, sandwiches, burgers, and fresh salads, which are priced $3–$4.50.

Take Morris St (Md 333) out of town and drive 4 miles east to Trappe Station.

From behind the store, follow Almshouse Rd east 2½ miles through the countryside to the second stop sign. Turn right there on US 50 (it isn't marked) and drive 8 miles east to the broad Choptank River. On the other side lies:

4. **Cambridge.** The 2nd largest town on Maryland's Eastern Shore, it lacks the charm of St Michaels and Oxford. Turn right on Maryland Ave to reach Cambridge Creek, the town's harbor; beyond that are the **Dorchester County Courthouse** and **Christ Church,** opposite each other on High St. Turn right on High St to observe a number of nearby 17th- and 18th-century homes. There's a riverside park and marina at the end of High St. The small **Brannock Maritime Museum** is at Talbot Ave and Tubman St (tel 410/228-1245), 8 blocks west of the court house, but it's open only Saturday 10am–4pm and Sunday 1–4pm. East of US 50, on Greenway Dr via Maryland Ave, you will find the Dorchester County Historical Society's **Meredith House** (built circa 1760) and adjacent **Neild Museum,** which feature maritime, industrial, and farming exhibits in a Georgian-style residence. They are open Tuesday–Saturday 9am–5pm (tel 410/228-7953).

From Maryland Ave, go 1 mile east on US 50, turn right on Md 16, and drive 7 miles west to the whitewashed community of Church Creek. Keep going through the Md 335 intersection for exactly 1 mile for a look at **Old Trinity Church.** Built in the 1670s, this is one of America's oldest Episcopal churches. Backtrack to Md 335, turn right, and follow the signs 5 miles south to:

5. **Blackwater National Wildlife Refuge** (tel 410/228-2677), on the edge of south Dorchester County's Everglades-like marshlands. This former muskrat fur farm is a major stop for Canada geese and other migratory birds along the Atlantic Flyway. The visitor center on Key Wallace Dr has interpretive displays, maps of the refuge, and restrooms. The sanctuary has a driving loop, a tower overlook, and hiking trails, which are open year-round daily from dawn to dusk. Admission is $3 per vehicle or motorbike, $1 for pedestrians and bicyclists.

At this point, you could backtrack to Cambridge and US 50. Instead, take the scenic route along unnumbered county roads for 25 miles to Vienna. (Drive carefully through these marshes, forests, and farmlands, and watch out for right-angle curves.) From the refuge, turn right and go about 2½ miles east on Key Wallace Dr to a T-intersection. Turn left on Maple Dam Rd (which returns to Cambridge), and drive only 3/10 of a mile north then bear right onto Greenbriar Rd. Follow it east about 2½ miles to a T-intersection with Bestpitch Ferry Rd, turn right, and continue east about 13 miles (crossing a 1-lane wooden bridge along the way) to another T-intersection at Drawbridge. Turn right on narrow but paved Steele's Neck Rd and drive east 4.8 miles to its T-intersection with Vienna-Henry's Crossroads Rd. Turn left and drive 2 miles north to the town of Vienna, known primarily for its electric power plant on the Nanticoke River. To reach US 50, turn left on Race St, then right on Gay St (Md 331), where you will find one of those combination gasoline station–food marts, our first chance at refreshment since Cambridge.

Get on US 50 east and drive 17 miles for an overnight stop.

On the upper reaches of the Wicomico River, **Salisbury** is the Eastern Shore's largest city, chief commercial center, and home of the Perdue chicken empire, one of whose processing plants you'll pass on your way into town. Although Ocean City is only 30 miles east, Salisbury is a centrally located place to spend a night before your last sidetrip off US 50. Several modern and comfortable chain motels (such as **Sheraton Salisbury Inn, Comfort Inn,** and **Hampton Inn),** as well as most of the town's shopping centers and restaurants, are 3 miles north of US 50 on Salisbury Blvd (US 13).

While you're here, you can visit the 12-acre open-air **Salisbury Zoo,** 755 S Park Dr (tel 410/548-3188), and the **Ward Museum of Wildfowl Art,** 909 Schumaker Dr (tel 410/860-BIRD), the largest of its kind in the world, featuring antique decoys, contemporary carvings, and paintings. Both attractions are on the east side of town.

From Salisbury, take Md 12 south. If you are traveling between April and the end of October, then turn right 13½ miles south of Salisbury onto Furnace Rd. Drive 1 mile west, where in a forest on the left you will find:

6. **Furnace Town** (tel 410/632-2032), a restored early 19th-century company town built around the ruins of the Nassawango Iron Works' 45-foot-tall chimney. Exhibits explain how the furnace extracted iron from limonite deposits (known as bog ore) from the surrounding swamps. The Nature Conservancy maintains a 1-mile nature trail through the cypress swamp behind the chimney. The town is open April–October, daily 11am–5pm. Admission is $3 adults, $1.50 children under 18.

Back at Md 12, continue south 4 miles to:

7. **Snow Hill,** once an important port on the Pocomoke River and today an attractive waterfront town with more than 100 buildings dating back a century or more. You will want to see the small but impressive collection of historic clothes and artifacts at the **Julia A Purnell Museum** on Market St (tel 410/632-0515). Open April–October, Monday–Friday 10am–4pm, weekends 1–4pm. **All Hallows Episcopal Church,** at Market and Church Sts, was built around 1750. The **Mt Zion One-Room School Museum,** at Church and Ironside Sts, looks exactly as it did in 1900 (open Thursday–Sunday 1–4pm). The winding, jungle-

---

☕

REFRESHMENT STOP

The **Snow Hill Inn Restaurant,** 104 E Market St (tel 410/632-2102), a bed-and-breakfast in a restored 1790s vintage house, offers a charming setting for dining in this colonial-era town. Specialties are fresh seafood and lamb chops. Lunch items run $3–$8; main courses at dinner are priced $10–$15. The inn has 3 guest rooms upstairs.

---

like Pocomoke River is a favorite spot for canoeing, especially between Snow Hill and Shad Landing, in the swamps of Pocomoke State Forest downstream. **Pocomoke River Canoe Company** (tel 410/632-3971), near the bridge, rents boats and equipment from April through November. During the summer *Tillie the Tug* makes 1-hour-long excursions on the river from its dock at Strugis Park on River St. Fares are $6.

From downtown, take Market St (Md 394) east to US 113, then follow it north 14 miles to Berlin. Turn right there on Md 376, go 4 miles east to Md 611, turn right and drive 5 miles south to:

8. **Assateague Island National Seashore** (tel 410/641-2120), Maryland's share of this unspoiled, 37-mile-long barrier island. Here you can see the wild ponies made famous at Chincoteague, across the border in Virginia, and enjoy what seems like endless miles of undeveloped surf beach. The seashore and adjoining state park have camping, visitor centers, hiking trails, and public beach facilities. Both are open from 8am to dusk and charge admission fees.

From Assateague, backtrack north on Md 611 for 8 miles, turn east on US 50, and cross Isle of Wight Bay into:

9. **Ocean City,** whose high-rise condominiums and hotels stand in stark contrast to the pristine beach we just left behind. A small fishing village was established in 1875 on this skinny barrier island, with the Atlantic on one side and Assawoman and Isle of Wight Bays on the other. Now Ocean City is a major summertime vacation destination with a multitude of amusements, excellent fishing and water sports (everything from jet skiing and parasailing to sailboating and windsurfing), a host of fine seafood restaurants, and accommodations ranging from small motels to large convention resorts.

From Ocean City, you can drive north across the state line to Bethany Beach and take the driving tour "Coastal Delaware" (see the Delaware chapter) in reverse.

SCENIC DRIVING TOUR #2

WESTERN MARYLAND VIA THE NATIONAL PIKE

Start: Frederick
Finish: Deep Creek Lake
Distance: 175 miles
Time: 2–4 days
Highlights: Valleys dotted with horse and dairy farms; mountain panoramas; historic towns and villages; a restored fort; a major Civil War battlefield; the C&O Canal National Historical Park; a cavern with unusual stalagmites and stalactites; year-round fun at a mountain lake

This tour follows the routes of the National Pike and the National Road, both built soon after the founding of the United States to further the young nation's westward expansion. Today this drive is known as US 40, although stretches of it now merge with I-70 and I-68. These modern highways still follow ancient Native American footpaths through Western Maryland's rolling valleys and across the region's heavily forested mountain ridges. Near Hancock, the tour skirts the Potomac River and its adjacent C&O Canal. These 2 famous waterways run a parallel course a few miles to the south. With a centuries-old route and bountiful natural beauty surrounding you, your drive will be both a historic and scenic tour de force.

For additional information on accommodations, restaurants, and attractions in the region covered by the tour, look under specific cities in the listings portion of this book.

I-70 and US 15 intersect in the Middletown Valley at the first stop:

1. **Frederick,** whose photogenic historic district is studded with well-preserved 18th- and early 19th-century buildings which recall its founding in 1745 by German and English settlers. Among them are the **Roger Brooke Taney House** and **Francis Scott Key Museum,** both located at 123 S Bentz St (tel 301/663-8687). Taney was the US Supreme Court Justice who swore in Abraham Lincoln and 5 other US presidents. His law partner, Francis Scott Key, wrote the words to "The Star Spangled Banner" during the War of 1812. The museum is open April–October, Saturday–Sunday 10am–4pm. The flag also was the focus of events in 1862 at the **Barbara Fritchie House and Museum,** 154 W Patrick St (tel 301/698-0630), where the Unionist Mrs Fritchie, then in her 90s, refused Confederate General Stonewall Jackson's order to lower her Stars and Stripes. That inspired John Greenleaf Whittier to pen his famous line: "Shoot if you must this old grey head, but spare your country's flag." Information and organized tours of these and other attractions in the area are available at the **Frederick Tourism Council,** 19 E Church St (tel 301/663-8687), just south of Patrick St.

   Follow W Patrick St (Alternate US 40) west out of Frederick. This is the Old National Pike, which

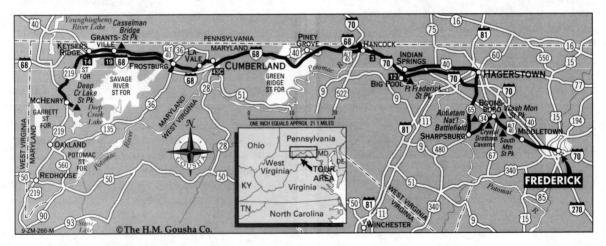

after Middletown Valley begins to climb South Mountain. At the top of Turner's Gap, turn right and drive 1 mile to:

2. **Washington Monument State Park** (tel 301/791-4767), where a stone tower was constructed in 1827 as the country's first memorial to George Washington. On a clear day, you can see parts of Maryland, Virginia, and West Virginia from the tower. The Appalachian Trail winds through the park, which has picnic and camping facilities. It's open Fri–Mon, 8am–dusk.

♨ REFRESHMENT STOP

Atop Turner's Gap, opposite the Washington Monument State Park turn-off, stands the **Old South Mountain Inn** (tel 301/371-5400 from the Frederick side of the mountain, or 301/431-6155 from the Hagerstown side). Built in 1799 during stagecoach days, this charming inn offers early American ambience and a variety of cuisines, all excellently prepared. Portraits of early US presidents in the cozy lounge are balanced at the entrance by photos of many modern politicos who have dined here. Dinner main courses cost $15–$25. Closed Monday.

From South Mountain, you should descend into Hagerstown Valley, which is known as the Shenandoah Valley down in Virginia. After 3 miles you'll arrive in **Boonsboro,** a small town founded in 1744 not by Daniel Boone but by his reputed relatives, brothers George and William Boone. There take a left on Potomac St and follow Md 34 south 2 miles to:

3. **Crystal Grottoes Caverns** (tel 301/432-6336), which were discovered in 1920 during excavation of a rock quarry. Unusual stalactites and stalagmites can be seen during 30-minute guided tours. Open April–October, daily 9am–6pm; November–March, weekends 11am–4pm. Admission is $7 adults, $3.50 children 11 and under.

From the caverns, keep going south 4 miles through the rolling fields along Md 34 to the little village of:

4. **Sharpsburg,** where the road actually goes through **Antietam National Cemetery.** Here lie some of the more than 23,000 men who were killed and wounded on September 17, 1862, the single bloodiest day of the Civil War. Turn right on Md 65 and follow the signs to **Antietam National Battlefield** (tel 301/432-5124), where Union troops stopped General Robert E Lee's first attempt to invade the North (his next try ended at Gettysburg a year later). Lee's failure at Antietam caused Great Britain to delay recognizing the Confederate government, thereby changing the course of the war. President Abraham Lincoln issued his preliminary Emancipation Proclamation a few days later. The battlefield is open daily from dawn to dusk. The visitors center has historical exhibits and shows an audiovisual program every half-hour; it is open Memorial Day–Labor Day 8:30am–6pm; the rest of the year 8:30am–5pm. Admission to the visitors center is $2 per person, $4 per family.

From the battlefield, drive 12 miles north on Md 65 into downtown:

5. **Hagerstown,** noted for its Early American stone buildings. Worth seeing is the **Jonathan Hager House and Museum** (tel 301/739-8393), on Key St in the City Park (from Md 65, turn left on Wilson Blvd, right on Virginia Ave, and follow the signs). The house was the fort-like home of Jonathan Hager, a German who settled here in 1739 and later founded the village which took his name. Today, period furnishings and artifacts are on display. **Zion Reformed Church,** at Potomac and Church Sts, dates back to 1744 and is the city's oldest building. The **Miller House,** 135 W Washington St (tel 301/797-8782), a federal-period townhouse, is home to the **Valley Store Museum** (which displays period furnishings and Civil War memorabilia) as well as the Washington County Historical Society. The **Maryland Theater,** near the Public Square, has been restored to its 1915 neoclassical grandeur. For maps and more information, drop by the **Washington County Con-**

vention and Visitors Bureau, 1826 Dual Hwy (tel 301/791-3130, or 797-8800 for recorded information).

Hagerstown is the last sizable city we will visit in western Maryland and, although it lacks the charm of Frederick, its motels and restaurants offer a good place to stay and dine before we head into the mountains.

From Hagerstown, US 40 follows W Franklin St and resumes its westward trek along the Old National Pike. If you take this scenic route, go 15 miles west to **Indian Springs.** If you opt for the faster I-70, drive 20 miles to exit 12 for **Big Pool.** In either case, turn left on Md 56 at Indian Springs or at exit 12, and drive 1 mile east to:

6. **Fort Frederick State Park** (tel 301/842-2155), home of an impressive fort built in 1756 during the French and Indian Wars. Settlers huddled inside its thick stone walls during a Native American uprising in 1763, British prisoners of war lived here during the American Revolution, and it was a Union outpost during a brief Civil War skirmish. Costumed guides are on hand from May through October to explain the fort and its interior buildings, which have been restored to their 1758 appearance. The park is open daily 8am–dusk. The visitors center is open Memorial Day–Labor Day 8am–4pm; September–October, open weekends only. The C&O Canal runs through the park, which has picnicking and primitive camping facilities.

From the fort, backtrack on Md 56 and take I-70 west at Big Pool. The Interstate, the C&O Canal, and the CSX Railroad all run along the Potomac River for the next 10 miles to exit 3 and:

7. **Hancock,** an important early 19th-century waystation on both the National Pike and the C&O Canal. Stop at the **C&O Canal National Historical Park visitor center** (tel 301/722-8226), on the right as you drive into town on Main St (Alternate US 40); the center has exhibits on the canal's history. Then drive along the canal by turning left on Pennsylvania Ave. There are remnants of lock, dams, and lock houses along the way. The area also has a towpath, a nearly level trail for walkers and bicyclists.

🍵

REFRESHMENT STOP

Hancock is still an important transportation center, for this is where I-70 turns north into Pennsylvania, and I-68 begins. We will take I-68, a relatively new highway with scant service facilities, for the next 38 miles, so gas up and take a refreshment break in Hancock. Main St has a **Hardees,** a **Pizza Hut,** and several local restaurants.

Since 1946, Hancock residents have been eating at the **Park-N-Dine** (tel 301/678-5242), where they can overlook the C&O Canal while waiting for American and Italian fare. Main courses cost $4–$7.

The Old National Pike (known as both Alternate US 40 and Md 144) laboriously climbs 4 Allegheny mountains west of Hancock. Take this much slower route if you have plenty of time. If not, get on I-68 at Hancock and drive west 38 miles to exit 43C in downtown:

8. **Cumberland,** which in the 1800s was the "Gateway to the American West." The C&O Canal reached Cumberland in 1850, and the town was the beginning point of the National Rd. Cumberland later was an important stop on the Chesapeake and Ohio Railroad, which also followed the Potomac River westward. From exit 43C, turn left on Harrison St and drive straight into the parking lot of the **Allegany County Visitor Center** (tel 301/777-5905) in the old railroad station, which also houses a small **C&O Canal museum** and the ticket office of the **Western Maryland Scenic Railroad** (tel 301/759-4400). If you can stay overnight, be sure to take this 34-mile round-trip vintage steam train ride between Cumberland and Frostburg. The scenic mountain valley route includes the Cumberland Narrows, Helmstetter's Horseshoe Curve, various tunnels, and panoramic vistas.

In Cumberland, you will want to stroll around the Washington St **Historic District** on the western side of town, with the 1851 **Emmanuel**

Episcopal Church at 16 Washington St, as well as many 18th-century homes featuring elaborate stained-glass windows, graceful cupolas, and sloping mansard roofs. You can also view the exterior of **George Washington's Headquarters** during the French and Indian War; this log cabin is located in Riverside Park on Greene St at the junction of Wills Creek and the Potomac River.

As the primary commercial center of far western Maryland, Cumberland has good motels, such as **Holiday Inn,** and the charming **Inn at Walnut Bottom.**

From downtown Cumberland, follow Henderson Ave and Alternate US 40 for 5 miles west through the Narrows, an appropriately named gorge through Wills Mountain. On the other side, you'll drive into:

9. **LaVale,** where on the left next to Cooper Tires you will see Maryland's last **Toll Gate House** left from the National Rd. Although federal money was used to build the road, the US Government ceded it to the states, which immediately levied tolls. Built about 1833, the small brick building charged 12 cents for each horse and rider, 6 cents for each score of sheep or hogs. It's open weekends 1:30–4:30pm, but you can look in the windows anytime.

Keep going west on Alternate US 40 for 5 more miles to:

10. **Frostburg,** where Mesach Frost built a log cabin for his bride when they got married in 1812. When stagecoaches began running along the new National Rd, the Frosts turned their home into an inn named Highland Hall. Later it became the Frost Mansion, a summer retreat for the rich and famous. Get your bearings and information at the **Allegany County Visitor Center** (tel 301/777-5905) in the old Palace Theater on Main St (Alternate US 40). The refurbished railroad depot contains a casual restaurant, and the **Thrasher Carriage Collection,** 19 Depot St (tel 301/689-3380), is next door (turn right at the Exxon Station at the beginning of the hilltop business district). The collection, stored in a renovated warehouse, features late 19th- and early 20th-century horse-drawn carriages, formal closed vehicles, milk wagons, open sleighs, funeral wagons,

dogcarts, and more. **Failinger's Gunther Hotel,** on Main St in the center of town, is a grand 1897 4-story landmark offering rooms individually furnished in the Victorian style.

From Frostburg, continue west 17 miles on I-68 or Alternate US 40 to:

11. **Grantsville,** an Amish and Mennonite town which became another stagecoach stop on the National Rd. A mile before the village is **Casselman Bridge State Park,** where you can still see the single-span structure that carried the National Rd and US 40 over the Casselman River from 1812 until 1933. In a setting more like medieval England than western Maryland, this old stone bridge provides an excellent photo opportunity.

🍺 REFRESHMENT STOP

Adjoining Casselman Bridge State Park is **Penn Alps,** US 40 (tel 301/895-5985), originally a stagecoach stop built in 1818 and now a nonprofit restaurant and crafts shop marketing the works of more than 2,000 regional artisans (watch some of them at work in Spruce Forest Artisan Village, on the Penn Alps grounds). You will have to ask to see the original log cabin, which now is a private dining room in the center of the complex. The restaurant offers standard American fare and Pennsylvania Dutch–style meals. Main courses cost $8–$11.

If you don't dine at Penn Alps, drive a mile into Grantsville to the **Casselman Restaurant and Motel** (tel 301/895-5266), a federal-style house built in 1824 as another stagecoach waystation. From the front porch, the central hallway leads past living rooms furnished with antiques. The dining room's bill of fare includes grilled ham, fried chicken, baked fish, and that local delicacy, breaded beef brains. Main courses cost $6.50–$9.

From Grantsville, continue west 6 miles on I-68 or Alternate US 40 to Keyser's Ridge (exit 14). Here you'll leave the National Rd, turn left on US 219, and drive 15 miles south to:

12. **Deep Creek Lake,** a man-made body of water surrounded by a major resort area offering a multitude of sporting activities year-round, including wintertime skiing at **Wisp Resort** on Marsh Hill Rd. Turn left before the bridge for **Deep Creek Lake State Park,** or keep going across the bridge and get your bearings at a lakeside information office (tel 301/387-6171), which is open mid-May to mid-October, Sunday–Thursday, 10am–6pm; Friday–Saturday until 8pm. You can easily spend a week in the area exploring the lake and the mountains, which include Backbone Ridge, the highest point in Maryland at 3,360 feet. Several other state parks and lakes are within short drives. The town of Oakland, 10 miles south on US 219, was a favorite summer retreat of US presidents and other notables in Victorian times.

From Deep Creek Lake, you can take US 219 south 34 miles into Canaan Valley and follow the driving tour "New River Gorge to the Highlands" (see the West Virginia chapter) in reverse.

ABERDEEN

Map page M-3, B7

Hotels

≣≣ **Holiday Inn Chesapeake House**, 1007 Beards Hill Rd, Aberdeen, MD 21001; tel 410/272-8100 or toll free 800/HOLIDAY; fax 410/272-1714. Exit 85 off I-95. Acceptable, basic accommodations suitable for family or business travel. **Rooms:** 122 rms, stes, and effic. Exec-level rms avail. CI 2pm/CO noon. Express checkout avail. Nonsmoking rms avail. **Amenities:** ☎ 🕭 A/C, cable TV w/movies. Some units w/terraces. **Services:** ✗ 🖃 ⊂⊅ ⊲⊳ Children's program. **Facilities:** 🛱 🔲 & 1 rst, 1 bar, whirlpool, washer/dryer. Indoor pool has pleasant garden and sunning area adjacent. **Rates:** HS May–Sept $79–$84 S; $89–$94 D; from $125 ste; from $84 effic. Extra person $10. Children under 18 stay free. Lower rates off-season. Higher rates for spec evnts/hols. Pking: Outdoor, free. Maj CC.

≣≣≣ **Sheraton Inn Aberdeen**, 980 Beards Hill Rd, Aberdeen, MD 21001; tel 410/273-6300 or toll free 800/346-3612; fax 410/575-7195. 30 mi N of Baltimore. Exit 85 off I-95. A clean, pleasant place to stay. Convenient to Aberdeen and Havre de Grace. **Rooms:** 131 rms and stes. Exec-level rms avail. CI 2pm/CO 11am. Express checkout avail. Nonsmoking rms avail. **Amenities:** ☎ 🕭 A/C, cable TV w/movies, refrig. Some units w/minibars. **Services:** ✗ 🖃 ⊂⊅ ⊲⊳ Secretarial services include fax, photocopying, overnight mail. **Facilities:** 🛱 🔧 🔲 ⬛ & 1 rst, 2 bars (1 w/entertainment), racquetball, sauna, whirlpool, washer/dryer. Free use of adjacent health club. **Rates:** HS May–Aug $74–$84 S; $79–$89 D; from $109 ste. Extra person $10. Children under 18 stay free. Lower rates off-season. Spec packages avail. Pking: Outdoor, free. Maj CC.

ANNAPOLIS

Map page M-3, B7

Hotels

≣≣≣≣ **Annapolis Marriott Waterfront**, 80 Compromise St, Annapolis, MD 21401; tel 410/268-7555 or toll free 800/336-0072; fax 410/269-5864. Exit US 50 at Rowe Blvd; turn right on College Ave, then right on Church Circle, right on Duke of Gloucester, and left on St Mary's St. Follow to Compromise St. Within easy walking distance of the historic district and marinas, this full-service waterfront hotel has outstanding views of Annapolis harbor and the Severn River. **Rooms:** 150 rms and stes. CI 4pm/CO 11am. Express checkout avail. Nonsmoking rms avail. **Amenities:** ☎ 🕭 🖣 A/C, cable TV w/movies, refrig, bathrobes. Some units w/terraces, some w/Jacuzzis. **Services:** ✗ 🖃 VP 🚌 🖾 ⊂⊅ Car-rental desk, babysitting. **Facilities:** 🔧 🔲 & 1 rst, 1 bar (w/entertainment). **Rates:** HS Apr–Oct $145–$225 S or D; from $325 ste. Min stay spec evnts. Lower rates off-season. Higher rates for spec evnts/hols. MAP rates avail. Spec packages avail. Pking: Indoor/outdoor, $10. Maj CC.

≣≣≣ **Courtyard by Marriott**, 2559 Riva Rd, Annapolis, MD 21401 (Parole); tel 410/266-1555 or toll free 800/321-2211; fax 410/266-6376. Exit 22 off US 50. Turn right on Riva Road, go ½ mile. A nicely landscaped, attractive hotel arranged around a central courtyard. **Rooms:** 149 rms and stes. CI 3pm/CO noon. Express checkout avail. Nonsmoking rms avail. **Amenities:** ☎ 🕭 ⬛ A/C, cable TV w/movies, refrig. All units w/minibars, all w/terraces. Hot water dispenser. **Services:** 🚌 🖾 ⊂⊅ Car-rental desk, babysitting. **Facilities:** 🛱 🔧 🔲 & 1 rst, 1 bar, lifeguard, spa, whirlpool, washer/dryer. Restaurant serves breakfast and lunch only. Very nice pool area with solarium. **Rates:** HS May–Oct $69–$87 S; $69–$97 D; from $119 ste. Children under 16 stay free. Min stay spec evnts. Lower rates off-season. Higher rates for spec evnts/hols. Pking: Outdoor, free. Maj CC. Rates vary with advance reservation.

≣≣≣≣ **Loews Annapolis Hotel**, 126 West St, Annapolis, MD 21401 (West Annapolis); tel 410/263-7777 or toll free 800/526-2593; fax 410/268-7777. Exit US 50/301 at Rowe Blvd; turn right on College Ave, go around Church Circle, turn right on West St and go 3 blocks. This modern, full-service hotel is a few blocks from the center of historic Annapolis. **Rooms:** 217 rms and stes. Exec-level rms avail. CI 3pm/CO noon. Express checkout avail. Nonsmoking rms avail. Top 2 floors have luxury rooms, with higher level of services and concierge-directed lounge. **Amenities:** ☎ 🕭 ⬛ A/C, cable TV w/movies, refrig. All units w/minibars, some w/terraces. **Services:** ✗ 🖃 VP 🚌 🖾 ⊂⊅ ⊲⊳ Car-rental desk, children's program, babysitting. Van service to areas within the city. **Facilities:** 🔧 🔲 & 1 rst (see also "Restaurants" below), 1 bar (w/entertainment), beauty salon. Extensive meeting facilities include a lovely atrium area. Aerobics, racquetball, tanning salon, masseurs, swimming at nearby facilities for an additional fee. **Rates:** $120–$135 S; $135–$155 D; from $175 ste. Extra person $15. Children under 17 stay free. Min stay spec evnts. MAP rates avail. Spec packages avail. Pking: Indoor/outdoor, $6–$9. Maj CC. Children under 5 dine free.

≣≣≣ **Wyndham Garden Hotel**, 173 Jennifer Rd, Annapolis, MD 21401 (Parole); tel 410/266-3131 or toll free 800/351-9209. Exit 23 off US 50. Across from Annapolis Mall. An attractive, comfortable hotel conveniently located adjacent to a shopping mall and restaurants. **Rooms:** 197 rms and stes. CI 4pm/CO noon. Express checkout avail. Nonsmoking rms avail. **Amenities:** ▥ ▨ A/C, satel TV w/movies, shoe polisher. **Services:** ✕ ▣ ▦ ▧ ↻ Babysitting. **Facilities:** ▥ ▨ ▨ ▯ ▨ 1 rst, 1 bar (w/entertainment), lifeguard, spa, sauna, whirlpool. Extensive meeting-room space in several areas, totaling 8,500 square feet, has flexible floor plan for groups of various sizes. Business center is well equipped. **Rates:** HS Apr–Nov $69–$129 S; $79–$149 D; from $125 ste. Extra person $10. Children under 16 stay free. Lower rates off-season. Higher rates for spec evnts/hols. AP rates avail. Spec packages avail. Pking: Outdoor, free. Maj CC.

Motels

▦▦▦ **Annapolis Holiday Inn Hotel and Conference Center**, 210 Holiday Court, Annapolis, MD 21401 (Parole); tel 410/224-3150 or toll free 800/465-4329; fax 410/224-3413. Exit 22 off US 50. Turn left onto Riva Rd, then left onto Holiday Court. The largest hotel in Annapolis enjoys a suburban location near shopping centers and restaurants. **Rooms:** 220 rms and stes. CI 4pm/CO noon. Express checkout avail. Nonsmoking rms avail. Half have king beds, half have 2 doubles. A bridal suite is available. **Amenities:** ▥ ▨ A/C, satel TV w/movies. **Services:** ✕ ▦ ▧ ↻ ↻ Car-rental desk. **Facilities:** ▥ ▨ ▨ 1 rst, 1 bar, lifeguard, games rm, playground, washer/dryer. Golf, swimming, and tennis are nearby. **Rates:** HS Apr–Oct $69–$119 S; $79–$129 D; from $139 ste. Extra person $10. Children under 19 stay free. Min stay spec evnts. Lower rates off-season. MAP rates avail. Spec packages avail. Pking: Outdoor, free. Maj CC.

▦▦ **Comfort Inn**, 76 Old Mill Bottom Rd N, Annapolis, MD 21401; tel 410/757-8500 or toll free 800/221-2222; fax 410/757-4409. 3 mi E of Annapolis. exit 28 off US 50/301. Follow Bay Dale Dr to Old Mill Bottom Rd N. A well-maintained chain motel convenient to downtown Annapolis and the US Naval Academy, although other nearby establishments have more extensive facilities. **Rooms:** 60 rms. CI 2pm/CO 11am. Nonsmoking rms avail. Rooms are attractively decorated and very clean. **Amenities:** ▥ ▨ A/C, cable TV w/movies. Some units w/Jacuzzis. Some rooms have large mirrors. **Services:** ↻ **Facilities:** ▥ ▨ Lifeguard, washer/dryer. **Rates (CP):** HS Apr–mid Nov $50–$90 S; $60–$100 D. Extra person $8. Children under 18 stay free. Min stay spec evnts. Lower rates off-season. Higher rates for spec evnts/hols. Spec packages avail. Pking: Outdoor, free. Maj CC.

Inns

▦▦▦ **Gibson's Lodgings**, 110 Prince George St, Annapolis, MD 21401; tel 410/268-5555; fax 410/268-2775. Exit US 50 at

Rowe Blvd. These 3 historic houses adjacent to the US Naval Academy have a central courtyard. Public rooms are exceptionally attractive. **Rooms:** 21 rms and stes (14 w/shared bath). CI 2pm/CO 11am. No smoking. Professionally decorated and comfortable rooms come in a variety of sizes. **Amenities:** ▨ A/C. No phone or TV. 1 unit w/terrace. **Services:** ▦ Wine/sherry served. Large breakfasts, served in the pleasant courtyard, feature home-baked breads. **Facilities:** ▨ ▨ Guest lounge w/TV. **Rates (BB):** $58–$85 S or D w/shared bath; $88–$120 S or D w/private bath; from $110 ste. Extra person $10. Min stay spec evnts. Pking: Outdoor, free. Ltd CC.

▦▦▦▦ **Historic Inns of Annapolis**, 16 Church Circle, Annapolis, MD 21401; tel 410/263-2641 or toll free 800/847-8882; fax 410/268-3813. Exit US 50 at Rowe Blvd. These 4 historic properties—the Maryland Inn, Governor Calvert House, State House Inn, and Robert Johnson House—combine great historic charm with modern amenities. All are centrally located in the historic district and close to the waterfront. **Rooms:** 137 rms and stes. CI 3pm/CO noon. Each comfortable room is different, but all have antique furnishings. **Amenities:** ▥ A/C, cable TV. 1 unit w/terrace, some w/Jacuzzis. **Services:** ✕ ▣ ▦ ▧ ↻ Twice-daily maid svce, car-rental desk, babysitting. Management is especially helpful with information and arrangements in Annapolis. **Facilities:** ▨ ▨ 1 rst, 2 bars (1 w/entertainment). Guests use nearby Marriott Athletic Club free. **Rates:** HS Apr–Oct $115–$185 S or D; from $225 ste. Children under 18 stay free. Lower rates off-season. Spec packages avail. Pking: Indoor, $10. Ltd CC.

▦▦ **Scotlaur Inn**, 165 Main St, Annapolis, MD 21401; tel 410/268-5665. Exit US 50/301 at Rowe Blvd; turn right on Calvert St, then right on Duke of Gloucester, left on Green St, and left on Main St. A separate entrance leads to these quiet rooms above Chick and Ruth's Delly. Unsuitable for children under 10. **Rooms:** 10 rms. CI 2pm/CO 11am. No smoking. Although not sumptuous, these "real Annapolis" rooms are comfortable and were tastefully decorated by the same person who did several historic buildings in town. **Amenities:** ▥ A/C, TV. **Services:** ↻ **Facilities:** 1 rst (see also "Restaurants" below). A municipal parking garage is behind the building. The deli downstairs serves full meals 24 hours a day. **Rates (BB):** $55–$75 S or D. Extra person $5. Min stay spec evnts. Higher rates for spec evnts/hols. Spec packages avail. Pking: Indoor/outdoor, $8. Ltd CC.

Restaurants ▦

Armadillo's, 132 Dock St, Annapolis; tel 410/268-6680. Exit US 50/301 at Rowe Blvd; turn right at Calvert St, go around Church Circle, turn right on Duke of Gloucester and left on

Green St; proceed to City Dock. **American/Southwestern.** California meets Maryland in this pleasant, relaxed establishment, whose colonial brick and timber interior is decorated with southwestern art. In keeping with the theme, a variety of fajitas, quesadillas, and other Mexican-American favorites are complemented by a few traditional American beef and seafood dishes. Sunday brunch also has a southwestern orientation. Popular with regular local clientele and tourists alike. **FYI:** Reservations not accepted. Band/blues/rock. **Open:** Lunch daily 11am–5pm; dinner daily 5–11pm; brunch Sun 11am–3pm. Closed Dec 25. **Prices:** Main courses $10–$17. Maj CC. 🔲 🔲

Buddy's Crabs and Ribs, 100 Main St, Annapolis; tel 410/626-1100. Exit US 50/301 at Rowe Blvd; turn left on Calvert St, go around Church Circle, turn right on Duke of Gloucester and left on Green St; proceed to City Dock. **Regional American/ Barbecue/Seafood.** With a bright, airy dining room and windows overlooking City Dock, this large establishment is more elegant than most traditional Chesapeake Bay crab houses but is still informal. Steamed blue crabs and barbecued ribs are featured, but other traditional main courses, sandwiches, and light fare are also available. Buffet specials at lunch and dinner. Priority seating. Validated parking. Much of dining area is converted to dance floor at night, when a DJ spins tunes. **FYI:** Reservations not accepted. Dancing. Children's menu. **Open:** Breakfast Sun 8:30am–1pm; lunch Mon–Thurs 11am–11pm, Fri–Sat 11am–midnight, Sun 11am–10pm; dinner Mon–Thurs 11am–11pm, Fri–Sat 11am–midnight, Sun 11am–10pm. **Prices:** Main courses $9–$16. Maj CC. 🔲 🔲 🚗 🔲 ⅋

Cafe Normandie, 185 Main St, Annapolis; tel 410/263-3382. Exit US 50/301 at Rowe Blvd; turn left on Calvert St, go around Church Circle, turn right on Duke of Gloucester, left on Conduit St, and left on Main St. **French.** Stucco and oak walls with simple, comfortable seating in booths and small areas that make for easy conversation. Enjoys area reputation as a very good country-French restaurant with a wide selection of wines and interesting daily specials. Competent, Parisian-born owner/chef and friendly staff make French cuisine "user friendly." **FYI:** Reservations recommended. Children's menu. No smoking. **Open:** Breakfast daily 8am–noon; lunch daily 11am–4:45pm; dinner Sun–Thurs 5–10pm, Fri–Sat 5–10:30pm. Closed Dec 25. **Prices:** Main courses $6–$20. Maj CC. 🔲 🔲

♦ **Carrol's Creek Restaurant**, 410 Severn Ave, Annapolis (Eastport); tel 410/263-8102. Exit US 50/301 at Rowe Blvd; turn right on College Ave, go around Church Circle, turn right on Duke of Gloucester, go across bridge to Severn Ave, turn left, then left into Annapolis City Marina. **American/Seafood.** Set among the yachts at a pier in Eastport, the restaurant has big windows with splendid views of Annapolis harbor and the US Naval Academy. On Wednesday night you can watch sailboats departing Annapolis Yacht Club to race. Varnished-wood interior complements the scene. Fresh seafood predominates in specialty dishes. Meat, fowl, and pasta also offered. Gourmet carryout shop on premises. **FYI:** Reservations recommended. No smoking. **Open:** Lunch Mon–Sat 11:30am–4pm; dinner Mon–Sat 5–10pm, Sun 3–9pm; brunch Sun 10am–2pm. **Prices:** Main courses $13–$24; PF dinner $22. Maj CC. 🔲 🔲 🔲 ⅋

★ **Chick and Ruth's Delly**, in the Scotlaur Inn, 165 Main St, Annapolis; tel 410/269-6737. Exit US 50/301 at Rowe Blvd; turn right on Calvert St, go around Church Circle, turn right on Duke of Gloucester, left on Green St and left on Main St. **Deli/Jewish.** A New York deli in the heart of Maryland, this bustling, friendly place is one of the last remnants of what Annapolis was like before gentrification began 2 decades ago. The walls are covered with interesting political and historic photos accumulated over years by owners of this popular meeting spot near the state capitol. Sandwiches are named for local and state politicos. Breakfast available 24 hours. Dinner specials vary. **FYI:** Reservations not accepted. Children's menu. Beer and wine only. **Open:** Daily 24 hrs. Closed Dec 25–Jan 2. **Prices:** Main courses $5–$8; PF dinner $6. No CC. 🔲 🔲

The Corinthian, in Loews Annapolis Hotel, 126 West St, Annapolis; tel 410/263-7777. Exit US 50/301 at Rowe Blvd; turn right on Calvert St, then right on West St; go 2 blocks. **New American.** Traditionally furnished with comfortable upholstered chairs, this light and elegant hotel dining room is one of the finest restaurants in town. American seafood, beef, lamb, pork, and fowl are given a continental/contemporary touch. Very attractive bar has pianist. **FYI:** Reservations recommended. Piano. Children's menu. Dress code. **Open:** Breakfast Mon–Sat 6:30–11am, Sun 6:30am–2pm; lunch Mon–Sat 11am–2pm; dinner daily 5–10pm; brunch Sun 11am–2pm. **Prices:** Main courses $17–$22; PF dinner $23. Maj CC. ♥ 🆅🅿 ⅋

The Harbour House, 87 Prince George St, Annapolis; tel 410/268-0771. Exit US 50/301 at Rowe Blvd; turn right on Calvert St, go around Church Circle, turn right on Duke of Gloucester and left on Green St; proceed to City Dock. **American/Seafood.** The bright main dining room has fine views of the harbor, enhanced by a quiet, green-and-white decor. The informal terrace outdoors is popular in summer. Traditional beef, chicken, crab, and shrimp dishes predominate, with combination platters available. Opened in 1960 as Annapolis's original fine-dining place, it's been busy ever since. **FYI:** Reservations recommended. Children's menu. Dress code. **Open:** Breakfast Sun 8:30am–1pm; lunch Mon–Fri 11:30am–2:30pm, Sat–Sun 11:30am–3pm; dinner Mon–Fri 5–10pm, Sat–Sun 3–10pm. Closed some hols. **Prices:** Main courses $14–$18. Maj CC. 🔲 ⅋

Harry Browne's, 66 State Circle, Annapolis (State Circle); tel 410/263-4332. Exit US 50/301 at Rowe Blvd; turn right on College Ave, go around Church Circle, turn right on School St to State Circle. **Continental.** Opposite the Maryland statehouse, this tasteful, elegant establishment features custom serving plates and wine-colored, upholstered chairs. Classical background music. Menu small but interesting, with nice treatment of beef, lamb, seafood, and pasta. Wine list is extensive and the staff knowledgeable. **FYI:** Reservations recommended. Guitar/piano. No smoking. **Open:** Lunch Mon–Sat 11am–3pm; dinner Sun 3:30–9pm, Mon–Thurs 5:30–10pm, Fri–Sat 5:30–11pm; brunch Sun 10am–3pm. Closed Dec 25. **Prices:** Main courses $16–$18. Ltd CC. 🍷 ⚓ VP ♿

★ **Little Campus Inn**, 61–63 Maryland Ave, Annapolis; tel 410/263-9250. Exit US 50/301 at Rowe Blvd; turn left on College Ave, right on Prince George St, and right on Maryland Ave. **American.** Operated by the same family since 1924 and a traditional gathering place for legislators, students, and neighborhood residents. Photos accent brick and wood walls. Moderately priced entrees are traditional American fare with an occasional excursion into regional foods. **FYI:** Reservations accepted. Children's menu. **Open:** Lunch Mon–Sat 11am–3pm; dinner Mon–Sat 5–10:30pm. Closed some hols. **Prices:** Main courses $8–$13; PF dinner $12. Maj CC. 📠 ♿

Middleton Tavern, 2 Market Space and Randall St, Annapolis (City Dock); tel 410/263-3323. Exit US 50/301 at Rowe Blvd; turn right at Calvert St, go around Church Circle, then right on Duke of Gloucester and left on Green St; proceed to City Dock. **American/Italian/Southwestern.** A historic tavern in use since Revolutionary times, the brick and wood rooms are decorated with nautical and outdoor items and attract the sailing crowd as well as landlubber locals and tourists. A varied American menu covers southwestern, seafood, and beef. No guaranteed reservations, but call ahead for preferred seating. Very busy in summer and autumn. **FYI:** Reservations not accepted. Blues/guitar/rock. Children's menu. Dress code. **Open:** Daily 11:30am–midnight. **Prices:** Main courses $14–$18. Maj CC. 🍴 🍹

♣ **Northwoods Restaurant**, 609 Melvin Ave, Annapolis (West Annapolis); tel 410/268-2609. Exit US 50/301 at Rowe Blvd; turn left onto Melvin Ave, go 1 block. **Continental.** Considered by many to be the finest continental restaurant in the Annapolis area. Dining room is tasteful and quiet, decorated in pastels. An attractive, fenced deck offers outdoor dining in spring and fall. Fresh ingredients and skillful preparation of seafood, beef, fowl, and pasta. Excellent appetizers. **FYI:** Reservations recommended. Dress code. **Open:** Mon–Sat 5:30–10pm, Sun 5–9pm. Closed some hols. **Prices:** Main courses $16–$20; PF dinner $23. Maj CC. 🍷 ⚓

O'Leary's Seafood Restaurant, 310 3rd St, Annapolis (Eastport); tel 410/263-0884. Exit US 50/301 at Rowe Blvd; go around Church Circle, turn right on Duke of Gloucester, go across bridge, turn left on Severn Ave, follow to 3rd St. **Seafood.** Light wood beams in an open, bright room with large windows looking out on marinas but not the water. A changing selection of fresh fish, posted daily on a chalkboard. May be mesquite grilled, sautéed, poached, baked, blackened, or served in a sautéed medley. **FYI:** Reservations recommended. Children's menu. Dress code. No smoking. **Open:** Mon–Thurs 5:30–10pm, Fri–Sat 5–11pm, Sun 5–10pm. Closed some hols. **Prices:** Main courses $14–$22. Maj CC.

Reynolds Tavern, 7 Church Circle at Franklin St, Annapolis; tel 410/626-0380. Exit US 50/301 at Rowe Blvd; turn right at College Ave, then proceed to Church Circle. **Regional American.** The National Trust for Historic Preservation owns this faithfully restored 18th-century inn furnished with antiques. American entrées have creative sauces enhanced by fresh herbs grown on the premises. **FYI:** Reservations recommended. Guitar. Dress code. **Open:** HS Mem Day–Oct lunch Mon–Fri 11:30am–2pm, Sat 11:30am–4pm; dinner Mon–Thurs 6–9pm, Fri–Sat 6–10pm, Sun 5:30–8:30pm; brunch Sun 11am–2pm. Reduced hours off-season. Closed Dec 25. **Prices:** Main courses $13–$24; PF dinner $20. Maj CC. 🍴 ⚓ 🖼 ♿

Riordan's Saloon and Restaurant, 26 Market Space, Annapolis; tel 410/263-5449. Exit US 50/301 at Rowe Blvd; turn right on Calvert St, go around Church Circle, turn right on Duke of Gloucester, and left on Green St; proceed to City Dock. **American/Seafood.** Owned by former NBA basketball star Mike Riordan, this pub is adorned with dark wood, brass and antique wall mirrors, and Tiffany-style lamps. Upstairs windows overlook the harbor. A variety of fresh seafood and beef main courses are supplemented by moderately priced lunch and dinner specials. Classic saloon fare. **FYI:** Reservations recommended. Children's menu. Dress code. **Open:** Daily 11am–2am. Closed Dec 25. **Prices:** Main courses $11–$17. Maj CC.

Rustic Inn, 1803 West St, Annapolis; tel 410/263-2626. Exit US 50/301 at Crownsville. **American/French.** Country French rooms, each slightly different from the others, are built from timbers of a century-old barn. Soft, classical background music adds to ambience. Swiss-trained owner cooks up American seafood and beef and a variety of daily French choices. Freshness results from buying from the market each day. Affordable wine specials. Off the beaten tourist trail but popular with locals, who often spend hours dining here. Closed on Sunday except Easter, Mother's Day, and other special events. **FYI:** Reservations recommended. Children's menu. Dress code. **Open:** Mon–Thurs 5–10pm, Fri–Sat 5–11pm. Closed Labor Day. **Prices:** Main courses $12–$16. Maj CC. 🌐 🖼 ♿

Treaty of Paris Restaurant, 16 Church Circle, at Duke of Gloucester St, Annapolis; tel 410/263-2641. Exit US 50/301 at Rowe Blvd; turn right at College Ave, proceed to Church Circle. **New American.** Situated downstairs in an 18th-century building, this dining room is authentic and comfortable. Fresh preparation and style of American foods stressed. Meals can be made from extensive appetizer listings. Light fare offered in tavern. Desserts are made in-house. Free valet parking at night. Jazz offered in the King of France Tavern 5 nights a week. **FYI:** Reservations recommended. Jazz. Jacket required. **Open:** Breakfast Mon–Fri 6:30–11:30am, Sat 7:30–11:30am, Sun 8–9am; lunch daily 11:30am–3pm; dinner Mon–Thurs 6–10pm, Fri–Sat 6–11pm, Sun 5:30–9:30pm; brunch Sun 10am–2pm. **Prices:** Main courses $12–$22; PF dinner $20–$25. Maj CC. 🖥 🖼 💟 ⱽᴾ

Attractions 💼

Maryland State House, State Circle; tel 410/974-3400. Built in 1772, this is the oldest US state capitol in continuous legislative use and was the setting for the ratification of the Treaty of Paris, which ended the Revolutionary War. The building's dome, the largest of its kind constructed entirely of wood, is made of cypress beams and is held together by wooden pegs. Exhibits in the State House depict life in Annapolis during colonial times. **Open:** Daily 9am–5pm. Closed some hols. Free.

US Naval Academy, King George and Randall Sts; tel 410/263-6933. Founded in 1845, the US Navy's undergraduate professional college—and a National Historic Site—is spread over 30 acres along the Severn River. Visitors can explore the grounds and tour the chapel and crypt of John Paul Jones as well as the Preble Hall Museum, which exhibits nautical relics, paintings, ship models, and other historic items relating to the navy's role in wars, global exploration, and space. **Open:** Daily 9am–5pm. Closed some hols. Free.

Maritime Museum, 77 Main St; tel 410/268-5576. This historical diorama is housed in the old Victualling Warehouse. Exhibits show visitors what the waterfront looked like in 1751–91, when the port of Annapolis was in its heyday. **Open:** Daily 9am–5pm. Closed some hols. Free.

William Paca House and Garden, 186 Prince George St; tel 410/263-5553. Built in 1763, this was the home of William Paca, a signer of the Declaration of Independence and a governor of Maryland during the Revolutionary period. It is a 5-part structure, with a stalwart central block, and a total of 37 rooms.

The adjacent 2-acre pleasure garden includes 5 elegant terraces, a fish-shaped pond, a Chinese Chippendale bridge, a domed pavilion, and a wilderness garden. **Open:** Mar–Dec, Mon–Sat 10am–4pm, Sun noon–4pm; Jan–Feb, Fri–Sun 10am–4pm. $$

Hammond-Harwood House, 19 Maryland Ave; tel 410/269-1714. This 1774 house is one of the finest examples of Georgian architecture in the United States, famous for its center doorway of tall Ionic columns. The interior is a showcase of decorative ornamentation and wood carvings. **Open:** Mon–Sat 10am–4pm, Sun noon–4pm. Closed some hols. $$

Banneker-Douglass Museum, 84 Franklin St; tel 410/974-2893. Named after two former local residents, Benjamin Banneker and Frederick Douglass, the museum presents arts and crafts, exhibits, lectures, and films, all designed to portray the historical life and cultural experiences of African-Americans in Maryland. **Open:** Tues–Fri 10am–3pm, Sat noon–4pm. Closed some hols. Free.

Charles Carroll House, 107 Duke of Gloucester St; tel 410/269-1737. Built in 1721 and enlarged in 1770, it is the birthplace and dwelling of Charles Carroll of Carrollton, the only Roman Catholic to sign the Declaration of Independence. Visitors can tour the house, the 18th-century terraced boxwood gardens, and the 19th-century wine cellar. **Open:** Fri 10am–4pm, Sat 10am–2pm, Sun noon–4pm. $$

BALTIMORE

Map page M-3, B7

See also **Pikesville, Towson**

TOURIST INFORMATION

Baltimore Area Convention and Visitors Centers Main office at 300 W Pratt St, ground floor (tel 410/837-4636 or 800/282-6632). Open Mon–Sat 9am–5:30pm. Booths at Baltimore–Washington International Airport, Pier C (main entrance) and Pier D (international terminal), and next to Light Street Pavilion, Harborplace. Kiosk in main lobby at Pennsylvania Railroad Station, 1525 N Charles St.

PUBLIC TRANSPORTATION

Light Rail Operates Mon–Fri 6am–11pm, Sat 8am–11pm, Sun 11am–7pm. Trains run every 15 minutes. Travels north-south, from Timonium to Glen Burnie; within the downtown area, rail runs along Howard St. Minimum fare $1.25. For information call 410/333-3434.

Mass Transit Administration (MTA) Subway and Buses
Connects downtown area with many local suburbs. New above-ground rail lines are modern versions of old trolley cars, attached to overhead wires; 35 stops available along 27 miles of new lines. Minimum fare $1.25. For information call 410/333-3434.

Buses connect all sections of the city. Base fare $1.25. For schedules and information call 410/333-3434.

Baltimore Trolley Motorized trolley-style bus that is a replica of Baltimore's original cable cars. Fully narrated tour stops at all major hotels and attractions. Operates continuously 10am–4pm, with reduced hours Nov–Mar. One-day fare $9 adults, $4.50 children 5–12, under 5 free; allows unlimited use all day.

Hotels 🛏

Baltimore Marriott Inner Harbor, 110 S Eutaw St, at Lombard St, Baltimore, MD 21202 (Inner Harbor); tel 410/962-0202 or toll free 800/228-9290. Exit I-95 at I-395 S, turn left on Lombard St. Across street from Orioles Park at Camden Yards and 1 block from the Convention Center, this well-kept hotel has attractive rooms and public spaces. **Rooms:** 525 rms and stes. Exec-level rms avail. CI 4pm/CO noon. Express checkout avail. Nonsmoking rms avail. **Amenities:** 🛁 ₾ 🖥 A/C, cable TV w/movies. Some units w/minibars. **Services:** ✕ 🗝 🚗 ⬛ ₾ 🛎 Car-rental desk, babysitting. Friendly, accommodating staff. Concierge level has lounge, continental breakfast, and other services. **Facilities:** 🏠 🏋 🎱 ₺ 1 rst, 1 bar, lifeguard, spa, sauna, washer/dryer. **Rates:** HS Apr–Oct $179–$215 S or D; from $195 ste. Extra person $15. Children under 18 stay free. Lower rates off-season. MAP rates avail. Spec packages avail. Pking: Indoor, $8. Maj CC.

Brookshire Inner Harbor Suite Hotel, 120 E Lombard St, Baltimore, MD 21202; tel 410/647-0013 or toll free 800/647-0013; fax 410/625-0912. An all-suites hotel conveniently located 1 block from Inner Harbor attractions. **Rooms:** 90 stes. CI 3pm/CO noon. Express checkout avail. Nonsmoking rms avail. Two-room suites are sizable, with kitchenettes and snack bars. Units facing Lombard St have water views but get more street noise than others. **Amenities:** 🛁 ₾ 🖥 A/C, cable TV w/movies, refrig. All units w/minibars. **Services:** ✕ 🆅🅿 🚗 ⬛ ₾ **Facilities:** ₺ 1 rst, 1 bar. Rooftop restaurant. Guests can use complete health club 5 blocks away. **Rates:** From $165 ste. Extra person $20. Children under 18 stay free. Pking: Indoor, $15. Maj CC. AARP discounts.

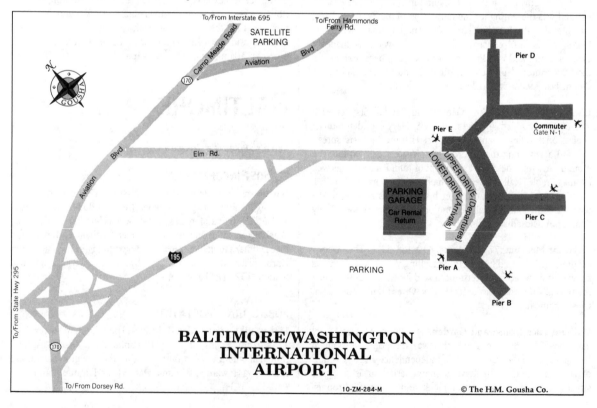

BALTIMORE/WASHINGTON INTERNATIONAL AIRPORT

10-ZM-284-M © The H.M. Gousha Co.

≡≡≡≡ **Cross Keys Inn**, 5100 Falls Rd, Baltimore, MD 21210 (Village of Cross Keys); tel 410/532-6900 or toll free 800/532-KEYS; fax 410/532-2403. Exit 10A off I-83. Go east on Northern Pkwy, then south on Falls Rd for ½ mi. Wonderful, resort-like accommodations and facilities in a huge complex, including a large shopping court and garden plaza. **Rooms:** 148 rms and stes. CI 3pm/CO 11am. Express checkout avail. Nonsmoking rms avail. Lovely, elegant, and spacious rooms. Top-floor units have cathedral ceilings. **Amenities:** 📶 🅰 📺 A/C, cable TV w/movies, shoe polisher. Some units w/terraces. **Services:** ✕ ⬛ 🖉 Shuttle bus, newspapers, business services including typing. **Facilities:** 🏋 🚤 📶 🖥 🕭 3 rsts, 1 bar, lifeguard, sauna, whirlpool. Gorgeous pool surrounded by an intimate garden. The restaurant prices are surprisingly reasonable. **Rates:** $109–$119 S or D; from $140 ste. Extra person $10. Children under 16 stay free. Min stay spec evnts. Higher rates for spec evnts/hols. MAP rates avail. Spec packages avail. Pking: Indoor/outdoor, free. Maj CC.

≡≡≡ **Days Inn Inner Harbor**, 100 Hopkins Place at Lombard St, Baltimore, MD 21202; tel 410/576-1000 or toll free 800/329-7466; fax 410/576-9437. Exit I-95 at I-395; turn right on Pratt St, then left on Hanover St, then left on Lombard St. One of the better hotels in this chain, this one is convenient to Orioles Park at Camden Yards and the Convention Center. **Rooms:** 250 rms and stes. CI 3pm/CO noon. Nonsmoking rms avail. Suites are actually large rooms with alcoves. **Amenities:** 📶 🅰 A/C, cable TV w/movies, in-rm safe. Some rooms and all suites have refrigerators. **Services:** ✕ 🖙 🚤 ⬛ 🖉 Car-rental desk, babysitting. **Facilities:** 🏋 📶 🕭 1 rst, 1 bar, lifeguard, washer/dryer. Nice pool courtyard with adjacent terrace restaurant. Arrangement with nearby health club for sports and fitness. Parking in adjacent garage. **Rates:** HS Apr–Sept $105–$115 S; $115–$125 D; from $125 ste. Extra person $10. Children under 16 stay free. Lower rates off-season. Higher rates for spec evnts/hols. Spec packages avail. Pking: Indoor, $7. Maj CC.

≡≡≡≡ **Doubletree Inn at the Colonnade**, 4 W University Pkwy, Baltimore, MD 21218; tel 410/235-5400 or toll free 800/222-TREE; fax 410/235-5572. Just west of Charles St. Entry to rotunda-like lobby is actually through a colonnade at this very elegant, European-style hotel with classical Roman decor. Adjacent to Johns Hopkins University's Homewood Campus. **Rooms:** 125 rms and stes. CI 3pm/CO noon. Express checkout avail. Nonsmoking rms avail. Spacious and comfortable. **Amenities:** 📶 🅰 A/C, cable TV, voice mail, bathrobes. Some units w/terraces, some w/Jacuzzis. **Services:** ✕ 🆅🅿 ⬛ 🖉 ⬗ Masseur. **Facilities:** 🏋 🚤 📶 🕭 1 rst, 1 bar, lifeguard, whirlpool, beauty salon. Pool has domed glass roof, Italian marble, Tivoli lights. Polo Grill is award-winning restaurant. **Rates:** HS Apr–June/Sept–Nov $119–$159 S or D; from $225

ste. Extra person $15. Children under 18 stay free. Min stay spec evnts. Lower rates off-season. Spec packages avail. Pking: Indoor, $6–$8. Maj CC.

≡≡≡≡ **Harbor Court Hotel**, 550 Light St, Baltimore, MD 21202 (Inner Harbor); tel 410/234-0550 or toll free 800/824-0076; fax 410/659-5925. Exit 53 off I-95. Turn right on Conway St, then right on Light St; go 1½ blocks. A modern rendition of a classic hotel. Public spaces are quietly refined, with oil paintings, Oriental carpets, and marble floors. Well maintained and attractively decorated. **Rooms:** 203 rms and stes. CI 3pm/CO noon. Express checkout avail. Nonsmoking rms avail. **Amenities:** 📶 🅰 🍴 A/C, satel TV w/movies, refrig, shoe polisher, bathrobes. All units w/minibars. **Services:** 🍽 🖙 🆅🅿 🚤 ⬛ 🖉 Twice-daily maid svce, car-rental desk, masseur, babysitting. Friendly, helpful staff. **Facilities:** 🏋 🏊 ⬔ 🚤 📶 🖥 🕭 2 rsts (see also "Restaurants" below), 1 bar (w/entertainment), racquetball, spa, sauna, whirlpool, beauty salon. Exceptional fitness center, with tanning, massage, and many machines. Lovely rooftop gardens and tennis court. **Rates:** $140–$205 S or D; from $350 ste. Extra person $10. Children under 18 stay free. MAP rates avail. Spec packages avail. Pking: Indoor, $10–$12. Maj CC. Weekend family rates available.

≡≡≡ **Holiday Inn Inner Harbor**, 301 W Lombard St, Baltimore, MD 21201; tel 410/685-3500 or toll free 800/465-4329; fax 410/727-6169. Exit I-95 at I-395; turn left onto Lombard St. A $6.5 million renovation in 1993 made this downtown hotel attractive. Located between the Bromo-Seltzer Tower and Orioles Park at Camden Yards, it is convenient to the major Baltimore attractions. **Rooms:** 375 rms and stes. CI 3pm/CO noon. Express checkout avail. Nonsmoking rms avail. Rooms are attractive and in good condition. **Amenities:** 📶 🅰 📺 A/C, cable TV w/movies. Some units w/terraces, some w/Jacuzzis. **Services:** ✕ 🖙 🚤 ⬛ 🖉 ⬗ Car-rental desk, babysitting. **Facilities:** 🏋 🚤 📶 🕭 1 rst, 1 bar, lifeguard, sauna. **Rates:** $109–$119 S or D; from $225 ste. Extra person $10. Children under 18 stay free. Min stay spec evnts. Spec packages avail. Pking: Outdoor, $5. Maj CC. Kids eat free.

≡≡≡≡ **Hyatt Regency Baltimore**, 300 Light St, Baltimore, MD 21202 (Inner Harbor); tel 410/528-1234 or toll free 800/233-1234; fax 410/685-3362. Exit I-95 at I-395; turn right at Conway St, then left at Charles St. Hotel garage off Charles. A large hotel catering to conventioneers and other business travelers as well as families and tourists, this building has expansive glass areas and skylights making for dramatic public spaces. **Rooms:** 489 rms and stes. Exec-level rms avail. CI 3pm/CO noon. Express checkout avail. Nonsmoking rms avail. Standard, pleasant rooms. Views from most, either of city or harbor. **Amenities:** 📶 🅰 📺 🍴 A/C, cable TV w/movies, refrig, voice mail. All units w/minibars, 1 w/Jacuzzi. **Services:** 🍽️ 🔑 VP 🚐 🔒 🛎️ Car-rental desk, social director, babysitting. **Facilities:** 🏋️ 🏊 ● 3 ⛳ 🎾 💻 🦽 2 rsts (*see also* "Restaurants" below), 3 bars (2 w/entertainment), lifeguard, spa, sauna, whirlpool. Rooftop restaurant has excellent harbor view, as does nicely landscaped rooftop pool. Large fitness center opens onto rooftop tennis courts. **Rates:** HS Apr–Sept $175–$200 S; $200–$225 D; from $300 ste. Extra person $25. Children under 18 stay free. Min stay spec evnts. Lower rates off-season. MAP rates avail. Spec packages avail. Pking: Indoor, $8–$12. Maj CC.

🏛️🏛️🏛️ **The Latham Hotel**, 612 Cathedral St, Baltimore, MD 21202 (Mt Vernon Square); tel 410/727-7101 or toll free 800/528-4261; fax 410/789-3312. Exit I-95 at I-395; follow Howard St to Monument St, turn right, then right on Cathedral St. A classic, European-style hotel with marble staircase from the lobby and Baccarat crystal chandelier. Quiet and elegant. **Rooms:** 104 rms and stes. CI 3pm/CO noon. Nonsmoking rms avail. **Amenities:** 🔒🏊🖥️ 🍷 A/C, cable TV w/movies, refrig. All units w/minibars, some w/Jacuzzis. Private Reserve rooms have bathrobes, irons, and boards. Some have wet bars. **Services:** ✗ 🔑 VP 🚐 🔒 🛎️ Twice-daily maid svce, car-rental desk, babysitting. Van to local attractions. Complimentary shoe shine, newspaper, turndown in all rooms. **Facilities:** 🏛️ 💻 🦽 2 rsts, 2 bars (1 w/entertainment). Reading room. Well-regarded rooftop restaurant has splendid views of city. Use of local health club. **Rates:** $135–$155 S; $150–$170 D. Extra person $20. Children under 18 stay free. MAP rates avail. Spec packages avail. Pking: Indoor, $10. Maj CC.

🏛️🏛️🏛️ **Omni Inner Harbor Hotel**, 101 W Fayette St, at Baltimore St, Baltimore, MD 21201; tel 410/752-1100 or toll free 800/843-6664; fax 410/625-3805. Exit I-95 at I-395. This large, modern, high-rise hotel in the heart of the business district was refurbished in 1994. Popular for conventions. **Rooms:** 703 rms, stes, and effic. Exec-level rms avail. CI 3pm/CO noon. Express checkout avail. Nonsmoking rms avail. **Amenities:** 🔒🏊 🖥️ 🍷 A/C, cable TV w/movies, refrig. Some units w/minibars, some w/Jacuzzis. Club floor rooms have bathrobes. **Services:** ✗ 🔑 VP 🚐 🔒 🛎️ Car-rental desk, babysitting. Attentive, helpful staff. **Facilities:** 🏛️ ⛳ 🎱 💻 🦽 2 rsts, 1 bar (w/entertainment), lifeguard, games rm. Health club across street has racquetball, sauna, aerobics, lap pool. **Rates:** HS Mar 15–June 14/July 15–Nov 15 $145 S; $165 D; from $250 ste; from $300 effic. Extra person $20. Children under 18 stay free. Min stay spec evnts. Lower rates off-season. MAP rates avail. Spec packages avail. Pking: Indoor, $9–$14. Maj CC.

🏛️🏛️🏛️ **Radisson Plaza Lord Baltimore**, 20 W Baltimore St, Baltimore, MD 21202 (Inner Harbor); tel 410/539-8400 or toll free 800/333-3333; fax 410/625-1060. Exit I-95 at I-395; go 3

blocks to Baltimore St; turn right. The Lord Baltimore is a grand old hotel built in 1928, with high, decorated ceilings in the lobby, massive stairway rails, brass trim. Public areas were renovated in 1993. Pianist often performs in main lobby. **Rooms:** 440 rms, stes, and effic. Exec-level rms avail. CI 3pm/CO noon. Express checkout avail. Nonsmoking rms avail. Rooms vary in size. Some are rather small. All were renovated in 1994. **Amenities:** 🔒🏊 A/C, cable TV w/movies. Some units w/Jacuzzis. **Services:** ✗ 🔑 VP 🚐 🔒 🛎️ 🐕 Car-rental desk, masseur, babysitting. Active, helpful concierge, bellhops, and valet-parking attendants. Good service. **Facilities:** ⛳ 800 💻 🦽 1 rst, 1 bar (w/entertainment), spa, sauna, whirlpool, washer/dryer. The lounge has jazz. Deli, gift shop under construction at time of inspection. **Rates:** HS Apr–Thanksgiving $114 S; $129 D; from $199 ste; from $600 effic. Extra person $15. Children under 18 stay free. Min stay spec evnts. Lower rates off-season. MAP rates avail. Spec packages avail. Pking: Indoor, $12. Maj CC.

🏛️🏛️ **Ramada Inn Inner Harbor**, 8 N Howard St, Baltimore, MD 21201; tel 410/539-1188 or toll free 800/272-6232; fax 410/539-6411. Exit 53 off I-95. Neither a typical Ramada nor an ultra-quaint inn, this 1888 downtown hotel is in good condition and has an air of quiet comfort. Pleasant lobby decorated nicely in period style. **Rooms:** 90 rms and stes. CI 2pm/CO noon. Nonsmoking rms avail. Some rooms are small, while a few are fairly large. All offer basic comfort under high ceilings. **Amenities:** 🔒 A/C, cable TV. 1 unit w/Jacuzzi. **Services:** ✗ 🚐 🔒 🛎️ 🐕 Car-rental desk, babysitting. **Facilities:** 70 🦽 1 rst, 1 bar, games rm. Fitness center 2 blocks away. **Rates:** HS Apr–Oct $78 S or D; from $98 ste. Extra person $5. Children under 18 stay free. Lower rates off-season. MAP rates avail. Spec packages avail. Pking: Indoor, $7. Maj CC.

🏛️🏛️🏛️ **Sheraton Inner Harbor**, 300 S Charles St, Baltimore, MD 21202; tel 410/962-8300 or toll free 800/325-3535; fax 410/962-8211. Exit 53 off I-95. This large hotel is the official Baltimore Orioles headquarters. Central to Baltimore attractions, including Camden Yards ballpark. Enclosed walkways lead to Inner Harbor, Convention Center. **Rooms:** 337 rms and stes. Exec-level rms avail. CI 3pm/CO noon. Express checkout avail. Nonsmoking rms avail. **Amenities:** 🔒🏊🖥️ 🍷 A/C, cable TV w/movies, refrig. All units w/minibars. Nintendo games, irons and boards. **Services:** ✗ 🔑 🚐 🔒 🛎️ 🐕 Car-rental desk, babysitting. **Facilities:** 🏛️ ⛳ 2K 💻 🦽 1 rst, 2 bars (1 w/entertainment), lifeguard, games rm, sauna. **Rates:** HS Apr–June/Sept–Nov $155–$185 S or D; from $325 ste. Extra person $15. Children under 18 stay free. Min stay spec evnts. Lower rates off-season. Spec packages avail. Pking: Indoor, $9. Maj CC.

🏛️🏛️🏛️ **Sheraton International Hotel at BWI Airport**, 7032 Elm Rd, Baltimore, MD 21240; tel 410/859-3300 or toll free

800/638-5858; fax 410/859-0565. Exit 1A off I-95. Turn left at Elm Rd. Closest hotel to BWI Airport terminal; well-situated for either business or pleasure travelers. No elevator. **Rooms:** 196 rms and stes. Exec-level rms avail. CI 3pm/CO noon. Express checkout avail. Nonsmoking rms avail. **Amenities:** 🛏 🔥 📺 A/C, cable TV w/movies, voice mail. Shaving mirrors and hair dryers in executive rooms. **Services:** 🍽 🚐 🖂 ⌥ ⌤ Car-rental desk, babysitting. Airport arrivals and departures displayed on video screens in lobby. Executive rooms receive turndown service. **Facilities:** 🎣 ⛳ 🏊 ⌘ 1 rst, 2 bars (1 w/entertainment), lifeguard. Large pool set in a well-kept courtyard. Well-regarded restaurant. **Rates (CP):** $117 S; $127 D; from $130 ste. Extra person $10. Children under 18 stay free. MAP rates avail. Spec packages avail. Pking: Outdoor, free. Maj CC.

≣≣≣≣ **Stouffer Harborplace Hotel**, 202 E Pratt St, Baltimore, MD 21202 (Inner Harbor); tel 410/547-1200 or toll free 800/468-3571; fax 410/783-9676. Exit 53 off I-95. Follow I-95 to Pratt St, turn right, then left on South St. The largest hotel on Baltimore's scenic Inner Harbor, this is a comfortable, modern hotel with traditional charm and service. **Rooms:** 622 rms and stes. Exec-level rms avail. CI 3pm/CO noon. Express checkout avail. Nonsmoking rms avail. Some rooms have harbor views. Executive-level rooms are same size as standard units but offer extra services. **Amenities:** 🛏 🔥 A/C, cable TV w/movies, refrig. All units w/minibars, some w/Jacuzzis. **Services:** 🍽 🗝 VP 🚐 🖂 ⌥ ⌤ Babysitting. Wake up includes newspaper and coffee or tea. Club level includes continental breakfast and hors d'oeuvres. USAir ticket office in hotel. **Facilities:** 🎣 ⛳ 🏊 ⌘ 1 rst, 2 bars (1 w/entertainment), lifeguard, spa, sauna, whirlpool. Pretty rooftop courtyard adjacent to pool and fitness center. Gallery shopping arcade within building has wide variety of shops and dining. Arrangement with nearby athletic club for racquetball, squash, etc. **Rates:** $165–$245 S; $185–$265 D; from $450 ste. Extra person $20. Children under 18 stay free. MAP rates avail. Spec packages avail. Pking: Indoor, $8–$11. Maj CC.

≣≣≣≣ **The Tremont Hotel**, 8 E Pleasant St, Baltimore, MD 21202 (Mount Vernon); tel 410/576-1200 or toll free 800/873-6668; fax 410/244-1154. Off I-95, follow I-395 to Conway St, turn right, then left on Charles St and right on Pleasant St. Lots of repeat business, the result of comfortable accommodations, helpful staff, and a quiet location. **Rooms:** 60 effic. CI 3pm/CO noon. Nonsmoking rms avail. Spacious, quiet units are converted apartments with full kitchens. **Amenities:** 🛏 🔥 📺 A/C, cable TV w/movies, refrig. TV in both living room and bedroom. **Services:** 🗙 VP 🚐 🖂 ⌥ ⌤ Car-rental desk, babysitting. Messages delivered to rooms. Highly personalized service. **Facilities:** 🏊 1 rst, 1 bar. Access to pool, fitness center at both Tremont Plaza Hotel and, for a fee, major fitness center

nearby. **Rates:** HS Apr–June/Sept–Nov $129 S or D; from $99 effic. Extra person $20. Children under 16 stay free. Lower rates off-season. Higher rates for spec evnts/hols. Spec packages avail. Pking: Outdoor, $8.50. Maj CC.

≣≣≣ **Tremont Plaza Hotel**, 222 St Paul Place, at Saratoga St, Baltimore, MD 21202; tel 410/727-2222 or toll free 800/873-6668; fax 410/244-1154. Exit I-95 at I-395 N; turn right on Conway St, left on Charles St, right on Pleasant St, then right on St Paul Place. Formerly an apartment building, this hotel is narrow but quite tall, so upper floors are very quiet. **Rooms:** 230 effic. CI 3pm/CO noon. Nonsmoking rms avail. Rooms, all suites with full kitchens, are very spacious, quiet, and comfortable for extended stays. **Amenities:** 🛏 🔥 📺 A/C, cable TV w/movies, refrig. **Services:** 🗙 VP 🚐 🖂 ⌥ ⌤ Car-rental desk, babysitting. High standard of service. **Facilities:** 🎣 ⛳ 🏊 ⌘ 1 rst, 1 bar, lifeguard, games rm, sauna, washer/dryer. Popular deli in hotel. Lounge decorated with photos of celebrities who have stayed here. Access to fitness center 1 block away for a fee. **Rates:** HS Apr–June/Sept–Nov from $109 effic. Extra person $20. Children under 16 stay free. Lower rates off-season. Higher rates for spec evnts/hols. Spec packages avail. Pking: Indoor, $8.50. Maj CC.

Motels

≣≣≣ **Best Western Baltimore East**, 5625 O'Donnell St, Baltimore, MD 21224; tel 410/633-9500 or toll free 800/528-1234; fax 410/633-4314. Exit 57 off I-95. Completely renovated in 1994. Attractive motel, convenient to East Baltimore. Adjacent to Peter Pan/Trailways bus terminal. **Rooms:** 173 rms and stes. Exec-level rms avail. CI 3pm/CO noon. Nonsmoking rms avail. Pleasant, bright, spacious. **Amenities:** 🛏 🔥 A/C, cable TV w/movies. Some units w/Jacuzzis. **Services:** 🗙 🚐 🖂 ⌥ Babysitting. **Facilities:** 🎣 ⛳ 🏊 🖥 ⌘ 1 rst, 2 bars (1 w/entertainment), lifeguard, games rm, spa, sauna, whirlpool, washer/dryer. Indoor pool. Dinner theater with Hawaiian show. Country-and-western lounge with line dancing and band. **Rates:** $69–$84 S; $79–$94 D; from $94 ste. Extra person $10. Children under 18 stay free. MAP rates avail. Spec packages avail. Pking: Outdoor, free. Maj CC.

≣≣≣ **Clarion Hotel–Harrison's Pier 5**, 711 Eastern Ave, Baltimore, MD 21202; tel 410/783-5553 or toll free 800/252-7466; fax 410/783-1469. Exit I-95 at I-395; turn right on Pratt St, then right on President St, then right on Eastern Ave; go 2 blocks. An exceptionally pretty central courtyard with a full-size sailing skipjack replica sets the Chesapeake theme of this waterfront property. **Rooms:** 71 rms and stes. CI 3pm/CO noon. Express checkout avail. Nonsmoking rms avail. A bit larger than average, 2nd-floor rooms have cathedral ceilings and sliding door facing the harbor or the city. **Amenities:** 🔒 👥 📺 A/C, cable TV w/movies, refrig. All units w/minibars, some w/terraces, some w/Jacuzzis. **Services:** ✗ VP 🚐 🖼 👕 🐾 Car-rental desk, babysitting. **Facilities:** 🛳 400 👥 1 rst, 1 bar (w/entertainment). Marina. Floating crab feast aboard bay boats moored at the restaurant, which has good reputation for seafood. **Rates:** HS Apr–Nov $139–$169 S; $149–$179 D; from $199 ste. Extra person $10. Children under 17 stay free. Min stay spec evnts. Lower rates off-season. Spec packages avail. Pking: Outdoor, $8. Maj CC.

≣≣≣ Comfort Inn Airport, 6921 Baltimore-Annapolis Blvd, Baltimore, MD 21225 (Baltimore-Washington Int'l Airport); tel 410/789-9100 or toll free 800/221-2222; fax 410/355-2854. Exit 6A off I-695. Follow Md 170 for ¼ mile. A convenient, modern motel near the Baltimore Beltway and within walking distance of local light-rail system for trips into downtown Baltimore. **Rooms:** 200 rms and stes. CI 3pm/CO 11am. Express checkout avail. Nonsmoking rms avail. Standard motel rooms. **Amenities:** 🔒 👥 A/C, cable TV w/movies. 1 unit w/Jacuzzi. Closed captioning for TVs. **Services:** 🚐 🖼 👕 🐾 Babysitting. Shuttle to Amtrak station. **Facilities:** 🛳 👕 400 👥 1 rst, 1 bar, games rm, spa, sauna, whirlpool, washer/dryer. **Rates (CP):** HS Apr–June/Sept–Nov $68–$72 S; $74–$80 D; from $125 ste. Extra person $8. Children under 17 stay free. Lower rates off-season. Spec packages avail. Pking: Outdoor, free. Maj CC.

≣≣ Holiday Inn Security/Belmont, 1800 Belmont Ave, Baltimore, MD 21244; tel 410/265-1400 or toll free 800/465-4329; fax 410/281-9569. 12 mi W of Inner Harbor. Exit 17 off I-695. An older, well-maintained motel convenient to the Baltimore Beltway and a large shopping mall. Popular for family reunions. **Rooms:** 136 rms. CI 2pm/CO noon. Express checkout avail. Nonsmoking rms avail. **Amenities:** 🔒 👥 A/C, satel TV w/movies. **Services:** ✗ 🖼 👕 🐾 **Facilities:** 🔲 200 👥 1 rst, 1 bar, lifeguard, washer/dryer. **Rates:** $67–$77 S or D. Children under 12 stay free. MAP rates avail. Pking: Outdoor, free. Maj CC. Group rates.

≣≣≣ Ramada Hotel, 1701 Belmont Ave, Baltimore, MD 21207; tel 410/265-1100 or toll free 800/272-6232; fax 410/944-2326. 12 mi W of Inner Harbor. A chain motel, convenient to interstate highways, US Social Security Administration headquarters, large shopping mall. **Rooms:** 205 rms and stes. Exec-level rms avail. CI 3pm/CO 11am. Nonsmoking rms avail. Standard rooms in good but not outstanding condition. **Amenities:** 🔒 A/C, satel TV w/movies, voice mail. Some units w/terraces. **Services:** ✗ 🚐 🖼 👕 🐾 Car-rental desk. Courtesy van to Amtrak station. **Facilities:** 🔲 200 👥 1 rst, 1 bar, lifeguard, games rm. Olympic-size indoor pool. Guests can use nearby athletic club for a fee. **Rates (CP):** HS Apr–Sept $64 S; $69 D; from $125 ste. Extra person $5. Children under 18 stay free. Min stay wknds and spec evnts. Lower rates off-season. Higher rates for spec evnts/hols. Pking: Outdoor, free. Maj CC.

≣≣≣ The Shirley-Madison Inn/Biltmore Suites, 205 W Madison St, Baltimore, MD 21201 (Mt Vernon); tel 410/728-6550 or toll free 800/868-5064; fax 410/728-5829. Between Park and Howard Sts. This lovely brick hotel on a quiet, tree-lined side street has provided comfortable accommodations since 1890. Separating the 2 main buildings, a charming courtyard sports willow trees, small bubbling pond, wrought-iron tables and chairs. Common areas and rooms are sprinkled with antiques and decorated in rose and cream. Overlooking Madison St through double-hung windows, lobby displays etched-glass doors and intricate woodwork on stairway. **Rooms:** 23 rms and stes. CI 2pm/CO 11am. Nonsmoking rms avail. Most sizable units are apartment-like, with sitting rooms and kitchenettes. Wooden armoires double as TV cabinets and closets. **Amenities:** 🔒 👥 📻 A/C, cable TV, refrig. Some units w/minibars, some w/terraces. **Services:** ✗ 🍴 🚐 🖼 👕 🐾 Continental breakfast and evening wine-and-cheese receptions in lobby. Staff members are extremely warm and helpful. **Facilities:** 13 🖥 👥 Main building is not readily accessible to disabled guests, but other facilities are available to them. **Rates (CP):** HS Mar–Sept $85–$95 S or D; from $95 ste. Extra person $10. Children under 18 stay free. Min stay. Lower rates off-season. Higher rates for spec evnts/hols. Pking: Indoor, $2.50. Maj CC.

Inns

≣≣≣ Admiral Fell Inn, 888 S Broadway, Baltimore, MD 21202 (Fells Point); tel 410/522-7377 or toll free 800/292-4667; fax 410/522-0707. Exit 59 off I-95. Follow Eastern Ave west for 2 miles, turn left on Broadway, go 4 blocks. With completion of its 1994 restoration, this lovely inn in historic Fells Point district should be more popular than ever. It has a quiet, comfortable, friendly atmosphere and Queen Anne reproduction furnishings. Neighborhood shops provide beauty salon and other services. **Rooms:** 50 rms and stes. CI 3pm/CO noon. Rooms vary in shape and size, but all have period furnishings and modern conveniences. Most have canopy beds. **Amenities:** 🔒 A/C, cable TV. 1 unit w/fireplace, some w/Jacuzzis. **Services:** VP 🖼 👕 🐾 Car-rental desk, afternoon tea served. Pets only within guidelines. Ice available through front desk. Van service to athletic club. **Facilities:** 40 👥 3 rsts, 2 bars, guest lounge. **Rates (CP):** $135–$195 S or D; from $225 ste. Extra person $15. Children under 16 stay free. MAP rates avail. Spec packages avail. Pking: Outdoor, free. Ltd CC.

The Inn at Henderson's Wharf, 1000 Fell St, Baltimore, MD 23231 (Fells Point); tel 410/522-7777 or toll free 800/522-2088; fax 410/522-7087. Exit I-95 at Eastern Ave, go west; turn left on Wolfe, follow to Fell St. Only the exterior walls are old, but this traditionally furnished, modern, comfortable inn is faithful to its heritage in mood. Outstanding decor in public areas. Fells Point shops and restaurants nearby. **Rooms:** 38 rms and effic. CI 3pm/CO noon. No smoking. Bright and spacious rooms, with nice views of the marina or beautiful, well-tended central courtyard. **Amenities:** A/C, satel TV w/movies. **Services:** Car-rental desk, masseur, babysitting, afternoon tea served. Very accommodating staff will provide concierge-level services. **Facilities:** Washer/dryer, guest lounge. Marina with slips available for guests. **Rates (BB):** HS Apr–Nov $110–$135 S or D. Extra person $15. Children under 18 stay free. Min stay spec evnts. Lower rates off-season. Higher rates for spec evnts/hols. MAP rates avail. Spec packages avail. Pking: Outdoor, free. Ltd CC.

Restaurants

Berry and Eliott's, in Hyatt Regency Baltimore, 300 Light St, Baltimore (Inner Harbor); tel 410/528-1234. Across from Light St Pavilion. **Regional American/Seafood.** All tables enjoy views of the Inner Harbor from windows running the entire length of this restaurant atop the high-rise Hyatt Regency Baltimore. Award-winning cuisine features crabmeat and crab cakes, oysters, red snapper, and other seafood, with Black Angus sirloin for landlubbers. Very popular because of the view. **FYI:** Reservations recommended. **Open:** Lunch Mon–Fri 11:30am–2pm; dinner daily 5–10pm; brunch. **Prices:** Main courses $18–$25. Maj CC.

Bertha's, 734 S Broadway, Baltimore (Fells Point); tel 410/327-5795. **British/Seafood.** Name comes from an antique stained-glass window, now hanging on the wall, which was discovered in this old building. Wooden decor has rustic look. Fun place to eat. Well known in Baltimore for mussels. Afternoon high tea, served Monday to Saturday, requires reservations. **FYI:** Reservations accepted. Jazz. **Open:** Sun–Thurs 11:30am–11pm, Fri–Sat 11:30am–midnight. Closed some hols. **Prices:** Main courses $11–$19. Ltd CC.

The Brass Elephant, 924 N Charles St, Baltimore (Mt Vernon); tel 410/547-8480. Between Reed and Eager Sts. **Regional American/Italian.** Tables are scattered throughout the front parlor and dining room of this grand 1861 row house. Fireplaces no longer work, but mantels were carved by Rhinehardt and Meislehm. Historic ambience enhanced by leaded-glass windows, wooden staircase leading to 2nd-floor lounge. Specializes in fine northern Italian cuisine, all freshly prepared. Excellent wine list. Smoking permitted only in rear room offering light fare. **FYI:** Reservations recommended. **Open:** Lunch Mon–Fri 11:30am–2pm; dinner Mon–Thurs 5:30–9:30pm, Fri–Sat 5:30–11pm, Sun 5–9pm. Closed some hols. **Prices:** Main courses $10.50–$22; PF dinner $16. Maj CC.

Burke's Café, 36 Light St, at Lombard St, Baltimore (Inner Harbor); tel 410/752-4189. **Eclectic.** Rustic atmosphere is enhanced by wood and brick walls in both dining room and large bar of this establishment famous for large, scrumptious onion rings. Also daily specials, wide range of sandwiches, seafood, and German dishes. Food service available at bar. **FYI:** Reservations accepted. Children's menu. **Open:** Daily 7am–2am. Closed some hols. **Prices:** Main courses $7.50–$17. Maj CC.

The Chart House, 601 E Pratt St, Baltimore (Inner Harbor); tel 410/539-6616. Next to aquarium. **Seafood/Steak.** Next to the National Aquarium. Though wooden decor creates comfortable atmosphere, multiple dining areas may get noisy. Menu offers other favorites, but seafood is house specialty. **FYI:** Reservations recommended. Jazz. Children's menu. Dress code. **Open:** Lunch daily 11:30am–2:30pm; dinner Mon–Thurs 5–10pm, Fri 5–10:30pm, Sat 4–11pm, Sun 4–9:30pm; brunch Sun 11:30am–2:30pm. Closed some hols. **Prices:** Main courses $15.50–$23.95. Maj CC.

Chiapparelli's, 237 S High St, Baltimore (Little Italy); tel 410/837-0309. **Italian.** One of Baltimore's most popular Little Italy eateries for half a century, it has an appropriate red brick interior hung with pictures of Italian street scenes. Large menu has nearly 50 main courses, mostly traditional Italian. Large house salad is famous in town. Daily specials and a fixed-price lunch offered. **FYI:** Reservations recommended. Children's menu. **Open:** Mon–Thurs 11am–11:30pm, Fri–Sat 11am–1am, Sun 11am–11:30pm. Closed some hols. **Prices:** Main courses $8.95–$22. Maj CC.

Da Mimmo, 217 S High St, Baltimore (Little Italy); tel 410/727-6876. **Italian.** One of the city's finest restaurants has a red floral motif with good-quality china, silver, and stemware. Rather large bar on main floor features many pictures of famous patrons, including President Clinton. Italian fare ranges from popular pastas to some truly extraordinary dishes. **FYI:** Reservations recommended. Piano. **Open:** Mon–Thurs 11:30am–11:30pm, Fri 11:30am–1am, Sat 5pm–1am, Sun 2–11:30pm. Closed some hols. **Prices:** Main courses $10–$25. Maj CC.

Foster's Oyster Bar-Restaurant, 606 S Broadway, Baltimore (Fells Point); tel 410/558-3600. **Seafood.** Part of this high-quality establishment is casual and features an oyster raw bar. Other dining area is more romantic, with fancier table settings.

Italian and southwestern seafood dishes are produced, but kitchen is best known for local delicacies, such as rock fish (striped bass) and Maryland-style crab cakes. **FYI:** Reservations recommended. Dress code. **Open:** Mon–Thurs 11:30am–10pm, Fri–Sat 11:30am–midnight, Sun 11am–10pm. Closed Dec 25. **Prices:** Main courses $11–$19. Maj CC. ♥ ▣

♥ **Hampton's**, in Harbor Court Hotel, 550 Light St, Baltimore (Inner Harbor); tel 410/234-0550. Across from Science Center. **Seafood/Southwestern.** Victorian flair characterizes one of Baltimore's finest restaurants, in one of its very best hotels. Gourmet cuisine ranges from Dover sole and rack of lamb to blackened buffalo steak and other exotic fare. Service lives up to the restaurant's fine reputation. **FYI:** Reservations recommended. Jacket required. **Open:** Dinner Tues–Thurs 5:30–10pm, Fri–Sat 5:30–11pm, Sun 5:30–10pm; brunch Sun 10:30am–2:30pm. **Prices:** Main courses $25–$32. Maj CC. ♥ ▦ VP &

Harrison's Pier 5, in Harrison's Pier 5 Clarion Inn, 711 Eastern Ave, Baltimore (Inner Harbor); tel 410/783-5553. **Regional American/Seafood.** An Eastern Shore theme prevails in this modern structure built to resemble a traditional Chesapeake Bay lighthouse. Menu carries out the theme with regional dishes, such as crab cakes and fried oysters, plus prime rib and other meat selections. Chef's weekly specials often wander in other directions, from Jamaican jerked chicken to Tennessee-style barbecued pork. Outdoor dining when weather permits. **FYI:** Reservations recommended. Blues/country music/jazz. Children's menu. Dress code. **Open:** Daily 7am–11pm. Closed Dec 25. **Prices:** Main courses $16.95–$21.95. Maj CC. ♥ ▱ ▦ &

Haussner's, 3244 Eastern Ave, Baltimore (Highlandtown); tel 410/327-8365. Exit 59 off I-95. Go 2 miles west. **German/Seafood.** Just about every square inch of this restaurant is covered with art, providing a feast for the eyes. For the palate, the food is always excellent, with a focus on hearty German cuisine including seafood items. The bakery products alone make this worth a visit. **FYI:** Reservations not accepted. Dress code. **Open:** Tues–Sat 11am–10pm. Closed Dec 25. **Prices:** Main courses $7.20–$29.95. Maj CC. &

★ **Louie's Bookstore Café**, 518 N Charles St, Baltimore (Mt Vernon); tel 410/962-1224. Between Centre and Franklin Sts. **Regional American/Vegetarian.** The front of this establishment really is a bookstore, but in the rear are a long bar and ice cream–parlor tables and chairs. Seating is on main floor, in a loft, and, in good weather, outside in a small garden. Highlights here, however, are musicians from the Peabody Conservatory and artists from the Maryland Institute of Art; both schools also supply waiters, bartenders, and much of the clientele, bestowing bohemian flair. A friendly, laid-back, comfortable place that prides itself on providing a showcase for young talent. **FYI:**

Reservations recommended. Guitar/harp/jazz/piano. **Open:** HS Sept–Nov Mon 11:30am–midnight, Tues–Thurs 11:30am–1am, Fri–Sat 11:30am–2am, Sun 10:30am–midnight. Reduced hours off-season. Closed some hols. **Prices:** Main courses $8–$14. Ltd CC. ▱ &

Obrycki's, 1727 E Pratt St, Baltimore (Fells Point); tel 410/732-6399. **Seafood.** Brick arches, wood beams, brass chandeliers, wall sconces, and Shaker chairs exude Baltimore history. Highlight is seafood, especially steamed crabs. A city institution for more than 50 years. **FYI:** Reservations not accepted. Children's menu. **Open:** Mon–Sat noon–11pm, Sun noon–9:30pm. Closed some hols; Nov 15–Apr 1. **Prices:** Main courses $13.25–$24.95. Maj CC. ▮ VP &

The Orchid, 419 N Charles St, Baltimore (Mt Vernon); tel 410/837-0080. Between Centre and Mulberry Sts. **French/Asian.** In the 1st floor of a row house, this intimate restaurant has an Oriental flair, with screens and drawings scattered throughout the dining rooms. Food reflects the theme—lamb chops under Thai curry sauce, Malaysian-style chicken breast, and Singapore shrimp and scallops—but French influence is also felt. Co-owners/chefs use only fresh ingredients. After-theater menu available Friday and Saturday 10am–11:30pm. **FYI:** Reservations recommended. **Open:** Lunch Tues–Fri 11:30am–2:30pm; dinner Tues–Thurs 5–10:30pm, Fri–Sat 5–11:30pm, Sun 4–9:30pm. Closed some hols. **Prices:** Main courses $11–$21; PF dinner $18. Maj CC. ♥

Paolo's Ristorante, in Harborplace Light St Pavilion, 301 Light St, Baltimore (Inner Harbor); tel 410/539-7060. **Italian.** An open kitchen with wood-burning oven is a big draw at this modernly decorated restaurant in the Harbor Place shopping complex. Best known for pizza. **FYI:** Reservations not accepted. Children's menu. **Open:** Mon–Fri 11am–1am, Sat–Sun 10:30am–1am. Closed some hols. **Prices:** Main courses $7.95–$15.95. Maj CC. ♥ ▦ &

The Pavilion at the Walters, 600 N Charles St, Baltimore (Mt Vernon); tel 410/727-2233. Between Centre and Monument Sts. **Regional American.** At the site of the original garden of the Hackerman House, an 1850s mansion and now the Walters Art Gallery's Museum of Asian Art. Descend a grand, curving double staircase, within which sits a fountain with bronze *Boy and Panther Cub* by noted American sculptor Malvina Hoffmann, to the pristine classicism of a white-walled dining room. Seating is scattered among towering pillars and skylights, which flood the room in daylight, create dramatic shadows at night. Salads, sandwiches, pastas, and light main courses. **FYI:** Reservations recommended. No smoking. **Open:** Lunch Tues–Fri 11:30am–3:30pm, Sat–Sun 11am–4pm; dinner Thurs–Fri 5:30–9pm. Closed some hols. **Prices:** Main courses $6–$12. Maj CC. ♥ &

Phillips Harborplace, in Harborplace Light St Pavilion, 301 Light St, Baltimore (Inner Harbor); tel 410/685-6600. **Regional American/Seafood.** Hanging Tiffany-style lamps and lots of wood and brass at this seafood emporium well known in Baltimore as a tourist attraction. Patio open in good weather features decorative metal chairs and umbrella tables. Maryland crab is the specialty, but raw bar is popular. Piano bar is a local favorite. Food also available at raw bar and carryout counter in the mall area. **FYI:** Reservations not accepted. Piano/sing along. Children's menu. **Open:** Sun–Thurs 11am–11pm, Fri–Sat 11am–midnight. Closed some hols. **Prices:** Main courses $12.95–$27.90. Maj CC. 🍴 🎦 ♿

Prime Rib, 1101 N Calvert St, at E Chase St, Baltimore (Mt Vernon); tel 410/539-1804. **American.** In a row house on a steep side street behind a high-rise apartment building, this New York–style restaurant has had consistently excellent food and service for more than 25 years. Unassuming entrance leads to rather dark, quietly elegant room where fresh flower arrangements, ebony piano, mirrors, and small table lights set a mellow, romantic ambience. Naturally, main offerings are prime cuts of aged beef only lightly seasoned to enhance the natural flavors. **FYI:** Reservations recommended. Piano. Jacket required. **Open:** Mon–Sat 5pm–midnight, Sun 4–11pm. Closed some hols. **Prices:** Main courses $15–$25. Maj CC. ♥ ♿

★ **Restaurante Tio Pepe**, 10 E Franklin St, Baltimore (Downtown); tel 410/539-4675. Between St Paul and Charles Sts. **Spanish.** Several steps lead from street level to this large restaurant with 6 dining rooms, 3 of them small and private. Decor, music, and staff uniforms are strictly Spanish, and specialties hail from Alhambra, Madrid, Seville, and other parts of Iberia. Entire preparation and presentation are authentic. **FYI:** Reservations recommended. Jacket required. **Open:** Lunch Mon–Fri 11:30am–2:30pm; dinner Mon–Fri 5–10:30pm, Sat 4–11:30pm, Sun 4–10:30pm. Closed some hols. **Prices:** Main courses $13–$21. Maj CC. ♥ ♿

★ **Sabatino's**, 901 Fawn St, at High St, Baltimore (Little Italy); tel 410/727-9414. **Italian.** Wonderful Italian aromas greet patrons at the small entry, which opens to several dining rooms on 3 levels, making this large establishment seem smaller. Red brick walls and low ceilings make basement area feel grotto-like, while upstairs rooms are lighter, airier. Extensive traditional Italian menu; all sauces, pastas, salad dressings, and breads prepared on premises. Minimum $7.50 per person. Disabled patrons should call ahead to reserve tables on the main level. **FYI:** Reservations recommended. Dress code. **Open:** Daily noon–3am. Closed some hols. **Prices:** Main courses $8.95–$23.95. Maj CC.

★ **Tony Cheng's Szechuan Restaurant**, 801 N Charles St, at Madison St, Baltimore (Mt Vernon); tel 410/539-6666. **Chinese.** In a large brick row house in the Mount Vernon Historical District, the 2 main dining rooms retain their original plasterwork, although walls are painted dark burgundy with light rose and gray trim. Double-hung, floor-to-ceiling windows add light for lunch, historic touch at night. Large selection of spicy Szechuan dishes is augmented by mild Cantonese fare. **FYI:** Reservations recommended. Dress code. **Open:** Mon–Thurs 11am–10:15pm, Fri–Sat 11am–11:30pm, Sun 11am–10pm. Closed Thanksgiving. **Prices:** Main courses $8.95–$31.50. Maj CC. 🚗

Water Street Exchange, 110 Water St, Baltimore (Inner Harbor); tel 410/332-4060. Just off Light St. **Burgers/Cajun/Tex-Mex.** High ceilings, exposed brick, wall sconces, mirrors, and highly polished oak wainscoting set a formal tone for this pub's main dining room, which is 1 flight below a large, casual bar. In addition to pub-style burgers, sandwiches, and salads, there's a mix of Cajun, Tex-Mex, pasta, and seafood. Bar is popular spot on weekend evenings, when crowds of young people often spill out onto a front brick patio. **FYI:** Reservations accepted. **Open:** Mon–Wed 11:30am–9pm, Thurs 11:30am–midnight, Fri–Sat 11:30am–2am. Closed some hols. **Prices:** Main courses $5.25–$16. Maj CC. 🍴 ♿

Women's Industrial Exchange, 333 N Charles St, at E Pleasant St, Baltimore (Downtown); tel 410/685-4388. **Cafe/Tearoom.** Located in an early 19th-century row house, this plain but very clean tearoom harkens back to 1881, when it opened as a means for needy to women to earn money. Historic atmosphere is enhanced by wainscoting, soft colors, ceiling fans, and 2 original fireplaces. Elderly doorman ushers guests into front parlor filled with handmade quilts, crocheted work, and baked goods for sale. Tearoom in rear offers home-style breakfasts and unpretentious lunch platters served by friendly, veteran waitresses. Basement room has "quick lunch" counter (only place where smoking's allowed) for sandwiches. A scene in the movie *Sleepless in Seattle* was filmed here. **FYI:** Reservations not accepted. No liquor license. No smoking. **Open:** Mon–Fri 7am–2pm. Closed some hols. **Prices:** Lunch main courses $3.25–$7. No CC. 🍴 🎦

Attractions 💼

National Aquarium, 501 E Pratt St (Inner Harbor); tel 410/576-3800. This spectacular 5-level glass-and-steel structure stretches over Piers 3 and 4 of the Inner Harbor. It contains more than 5,000 specimens of mammals, fish, rare birds, reptiles, and amphibians. All the creatures are on view in settings that re-create their natural habitats, which include a South American rain forest, an Atlantic coral reef, and an open-ocean tank. The **Marine Mammal Pavilion** houses Atlantic bottlenose dolphins in a 1.2-million-gallon complex of 4 pools surrounded by the world's largest acrylic windows and a 1,300-seat amphitheater. In addition, there are nature films, an aquatic education resource center, and an animal care and research complex. **Open:** Mid-Sept–mid-May, Sat–Thurs 10am–5pm, Fri 10am–8pm; mid-May–mid-Sept, Mon–Thurs 9am–5pm, Fri–Sat 9am–8pm. $$$$

US Frigate *Constellation*, Constellation Dock, Pier 1, Pratt St (Inner Harbor); tel 410/539-1797. Continuously afloat longer than any other ship in the world, the *Constellation* was launched from Baltimore in 1797. It was the first boat the US Navy put to sea and the first to defeat an enemy man-of-war. **Open:** June 15–Labor Day, daily 10am–8pm; Labor Day–Oct 14, May 15–June 14, daily 10am–6pm; Oct 15–May 14, daily 10am–4pm. $$

Harborplace, Light and Pratt Sts (Inner Harbor); tel 410/332-4191. This historic area, positioned right on the waterfront, has been designed to duplicate the look of an early steamship pier headquarters. It is made up of 2 pavilions named after the streets they occupy—the Light Street Pavilion and the Pratt Street Pavilion. The contemporary, bright, and airy complex of restaurants, food markets, curiosity shops, and trendy boutiques has made this the centerpiece of Baltimore's revitalization. **Open:** Stores, Mon–Sat 10am–10pm, Sun noon–6pm. Closed some hols.

Maryland Science Center, 601 Light St (Inner Harbor); tel 410/685-5225. Situated on the edge of the Inner Harbor, the science center features hundreds of hands-on activities, live demonstrations, and displays ranging from a simulated space station control center to experiments revealing the properties of sight, sound, magnetism, light, and mechanics. In addition, visitors can attend a show at the 5-story IMAX movie theater or the Davis Planetarium. **Open:** Mon–Fri 10am–5pm, Sat–Sun 10am–6pm. Closed some hols. $$$

Top of the World, 401 E Pratt St (Inner Harbor); tel 410/837-4515. This observatory on the 27th floor of the World Trade Center, the world's tallest pentagonal building, offers a sweeping overview of the whole harbor and the city. In addition, hands-on displays, exhibits, and multimedia presentations explore Baltimore's history. **Open:** Mon–Sat 10am–4:30pm, Sun noon–4:30pm. $

Baltimore Maritime Museum, Pier 3 (Pratt St) (Inner Harbor); tel 410/396-5528. This outdoor complex is the home of the USCG cutter *Taney*, the last ship still afloat that fought in Pearl Harbor; the submarine USS *Torsk*, which sank the last enemy ship in World War II; and the lightship *Chesapeake*, a floating lighthouse built in 1930. The vessels are moored to the dock and are open to visitors. **Open:** Mon–Fri 9am–5pm, Sat–Sun 9:30am–7pm. $$

Fort McHenry National Monument and Historic Shrine, E Fort Ave (Inner Harbor); tel 410/962-4299. The birthplace of the American national anthem, written by Francis Scott Key during the 1814 Battle of Baltimore. Fort McHenry was an active military base until 1925, when it was designated a national park. To assist visitors in touring the fort, there are historical and military exhibits, explanatory maps, and a 15-minute film shown every half-hour. **Open:** Mid-June–Labor Day, daily 8am–8pm; Sept–early June, daily 8am–5pm. Closed some hols. $

Star-Spangled Banner Flag House and 1812 Museum, 844 E Pratt St (Inner Harbor); tel 410/837-1793. The restored home of Mary Pickersgill, the seamstress who created the 30-by-42-foot red, white, and blue Fort McHenry flag that inspired Francis Scott Key to compose "The Star-Spangled Banner." The federal-style house (1793) is full of period furnishings and a collection of early American art. **Open:** Mon–Sat 10am–4pm. Closed some hols. $

The Shot Tower, 801 E Fayette St (Inner Harbor); tel 410/396-5894. A local landmark, this 215-foot-tall brick structure was built in 1828 for the production of lead shot ammunition. Exhibits illustrate how shot was produced by pouring molten lead through perforated pans from "dropping stations" high up in the tower. **Open:** Daily 10am–4pm. Free.

Holocaust Memorial, corner of Water, Gay, and Lombard Sts; tel 410/752-2630. This open-air memorial center and sculpture stand as a stark reminder of the 6 million Jews murdered by the Nazis in Europe between 1933 and 1945. **Open:** Daily 24 hours. Free.

Baltimore and Ohio (B&O) Railroad Museum, 901 W Pratt St; tel 410/752-2490. Often called a railroad university, this museum has hundreds of exhibits—from double-decker stagecoaches on iron wheels and early diesels to steam locomotives and the 1830 Mount Clare Station, the nation's first passenger and freight station. Also on display is the 1844 roundhouse with the original B&O tracks and turntable. **Open:** Daily 10am–5pm. Closed some hols. $$

Babe Ruth Birthplace & Museum/Maryland Baseball Hall of Fame, 216 Emory St (Inner Harbor); tel 410/727-1539. The restored house and adjoining museum contain personal mementos of George Herman "Babe" Ruth, otherwise known as the "Sultan of Swat." The exhibits, which focus on the Baltimore Orioles and Maryland baseball as well as the great Babe, include such touchable items as hats, bats, and gloves; there's also an audiovisual presentation on the Babe and World Series film highlights. **Open:** Daily 10am–4pm. Closed some hols. $$

Baltimore Museum of Industry, 1415 Key Hwy; tel 410/727-4808. Housed in the 1865 Baltimore oyster cannery, this museum illustrates the industrial history of the city through a series of 19th-century workshop settings—from a machine shop and a print shop to a clothing factory and cannery works. **Open:** Wed 7–9pm, Thurs–Fri and Sun noon–5pm, Sat 10am–5pm. $$

Christopher Columbus Center of Marine Research and Exploration, Piers 5 and 6 (Pratt St) (Inner Harbor); tel 410/547-8727. Slated to open in the fall of 1995, this $160 million attraction will be a world center for marine research. It will include 4 major units—marine biotechnology, nautical archeology, a training and development center, and a public exhibition center with hands-on exhibits.

Walters Art Gallery, 600 N Charles St (Charles St/Mt Vernon); tel 410/547-9000. Designed in an Italianate palazzo style, the museum has more than 30,000 works of art spanning 5,000 years. The collection includes Asian, Egyptian, Greek, Roman, Byzantine, medieval, renaissance, baroque, romantic, impressionist, and art nouveau works. **Open:** Tues–Sun 11am–5pm. Closed some hols. $$

Baltimore City Life Museums, 800 E Lombard St (Inner Harbor); tel 410/396-3524 or 396-4545. A collection of museums and historic sites, four of which are clustered together on "museum row." The following attractions can be visited individually or together for one all-inclusive price. The **Carroll Mansion**, the home of the patriot Charles Carroll and his family, explores the lifestyle of a wealthy 19th-century Baltimore family with period furnishings and decorative arts. The **Center for Urban Archaeology** is a life-size excavation pit that shows archeologists at work. The **1820 House**, a reconstructed 19th-century row house, was once the home of a middle-class wheelwright and his family. And the **Courtyard Exhibition Center** displays exhibits illustrating the city's history. **Open:** Apr–Oct, Tues–Sat 10am–5pm, Sun noon–5pm; Nov–Mar, Tues–Sat 10am–4pm, Sun noon–4pm. $

Peale Museum, 225 Holliday St (Charles St/Mt Vernon); tel 410/396-1149. Built in 1814 by American portrait painter Rembrandt Peale, the oldest museum building in the United States was also Baltimore's first city hall. A member of the City Life Museums, it houses a collection of historical photographs, prints, and paintings of Baltimore and the Peale family. **Open:** Apr–Oct, Sat 10am–5pm, Sun noon–5pm; Nov–Mar, Sat 10am–4pm, Sun noon–4pm. $

H L Mencken House, 1524 Hollins St (Charles St/Mt Vernon); tel 410/396-7997. One of the City Life museums, this stately 19th-century row house was the home of the influential and caustic writer and editor Henry Louis Mencken, the "Sage of Baltimore." The house has been restored to include many of Mencken's original furnishings and belongings. **Open:** Apr–Oct, Sat 10am–5pm, Sun noon–5pm; Nov–Mar, Sat 10am–4pm, Sun noon–4pm. $

Baltimore Museum of Art, 10 Art Museum Dr (Charles St/Mt Vernon); tel 410/396-7100. The largest museum in Maryland, with over 120,000 artworks, most notably the Cone Collection of 20th-century art with works by Matisse, Picasso, and Cézanne. Also featured are the arts of Africa, Asia, and Oceania, plus 2 outdoor sculpture gardens. **Open:** Wed–Fri 10am–4pm, Sat–Sun 11am-6pm. Closed some hols. $$$

Edgar Allan Poe House, 203 N Amity St (Charles St/Mt Vernon); tel 410/396-7932. This tiny house where the great poet and short-story writer Edgar Allan Poe lived from 1832 to 1835 contains Poe memorabilia plus period furniture, changing exhibits, and a video presentation of leading Poe works. **Open:** Apr–July, Oct–mid-Dec, Wed–Sat noon–3:45pm; Aug–Sept, Sat noon–4pm. $

Maryland Historical Society, 201 W Monument St (Charles St/Mt Vernon); tel 410/685-3750. Houses many of the city's great treasures, such as the original "Star-Spangled Banner" manuscript; silver tureens from America's largest 19th-century silver collection; and maps, prints, relics, and artifacts, all depicting Maryland long ago. **Open:** Tues–Fri 10am–5pm, Sat 9am–5pm, Sun 1–5pm. $$

Great Blacks in Wax Museum, 1601–3 E North Ave; tel 410/563-3404. The nation's first and only wax museum dedicated to famous African-American heroes and historical legends. The people portrayed include inventors, pilots, religious and education leaders, and scientists. **Open:** Jan 15–Oct 15, Tues–Sat 9am–6pm, Sun noon–6pm; Oct 16–Jan 14, Tues–Sat 9am–5pm, Sun noon–5pm. $$$

Eubie Blake National Museum & Cultural Center, 34 Market Place; tel 410/625-3113. Located in the heart of the city, this center, dedicated to Baltimore-born ragtime great James Hubert "Eubie" Blake, displays items from his life such as his piano and original sheet music. There is also a gallery with changing exhibits of current interest by local artists. **Open:** Mon–Fri 8:30am–4:30pm. Closed some hols. Free.

Basilica of the Assumption of the Blessed Virgin Mary, 408 N Charles St (Charles St/Mt Vernon); tel 410/727-3564. Dating from 1806, this was the first metropolitan cathedral in the

United States. Designed by Benjamin Henry Latrobe, the same architect who designed the nation's capitol, the neoclassical church features a grand organ, stained-glass windows, and paintings that were gifts from European kings. Guided tours are conducted on the 2nd and 4th Sunday of each month at 11:30am. **Open:** Mon–Fri 7am–3:45pm, Sat–Sun 7am–6:30pm. Free.

Old St Paul's Church, Charles and Saratoga Sts (Charles St/Mt Vernon); tel 410/685-3404. Opened in 1856, this church is part of a parish dating back to 1692 and is the mother church for the Episcopal diocese of Baltimore. Designed by Richard Upjohn in basilica style, it is noted for its Tiffany windows and inlaid mosaic work. **Open:** Mon–Fri 8:15am–5:30pm, Sun 8:30am–12:30pm. Free.

Lacrosse Hall of Fame Museum, 113 W University Pkwy; tel 410/235-6882. This unique museum presents 350 years in the history of lacrosse, America's oldest sport, and a particular favorite in Maryland. The displays include rare photographs and photomurals of men and women at play, art, vintage equipment and uniforms, sculptures, trophies, and memorabilia. **Open:** June–Feb, Mon–Fri 9am–5pm; Mar–May, Mon–Fri 9am–5pm, Sat 10am–3pm. Closed some hols. $

Baltimore Zoo, Greenspring Ave, Druid Hill Park; tel 410/396-7102. This natural expanse comprises 150 acres of grassy slopes, tree-topped hills, and mountain caves providing an agreeable habitat to more than 1,200 animals, birds, and reptiles from 7 continents, including rhinos, zebras, gazelles, bears, and black-footed penguins. There is also an 8-acre interactive children's zoo. **Open:** Daily 10am–4pm. Closed Dec 25. $$$

Oriole Park at Camden Yards, 333 W Camden St (Inner Harbor); tel 410/685-9800. Situated between two 19th-century landmarks—the Baltimore & Ohio Railroad Warehouse and Camden Station—this is the Baltimore Orioles new "old-fashioned ballpark," fashioned after big-league parks from the early 1900s such as Ebbets Field in Brooklyn, Fenway Park in Boston, and Wrigley Field in Chicago. The style is obtained through the use of steel, rather than concrete trusses, an arched brick facade, a sun roof over the upper deck, an asymmetrical playing field, and natural grass turf. Go to a game or take a behind-the-scenes tour given weekdays when the Orioles are not playing. **Open:** Call for schedule. $$$$

Pimlico Race Course, Park Heights and Belvedere Aves; tel 410/542-9400. Located about 5 miles from the Inner Harbor on the city's northwest side, this is Maryland's oldest thoroughbred track and the site of the annual Preakness Stakes. Also on the grounds is the **National Jockey's Hall of Fame**, open 9–11am during the racing season, free of charge. **Open:** Mid-Mar–late May, early Aug–early Oct. Call for schedule. $

Pier Six Concert Pavilion, Pier 6, off Pratt St (Inner Harbor); tel 410/625-1400. A 4,300-seat concert pavilion in the format of a 6-point open-air aluminum tent. It presents the top names of the music industry in live concerts from May through September. **Open:** Call for schedule. $$$$

Peabody Conservatory of Music, 1 E Mt Vernon Place (Charles St/Mt Vernon); tel 410/659-8124. A division of Johns Hopkins University, it is America's oldest school of music, dating back to 1866. From September through May there are more than 60 events open to the public, featuring the Peabody Symphony Orchestra and student performers. **Open:** Call for schedule. $$$

Lyric Opera House, 1404 W Mt Royal Ave; tel 410/685-0692. A replica of Germany's Leipzig music hall, this impressive facility is home to the Baltimore Opera Company, which performs classic operas during an October-to-May season. **Open:** Call for schedule. $$$$

Joseph Meyerhoff Symphony Hall, 1212 Cathedral St; tel 410/783-8000. Famed for its acoustics, this 2,450-seat hall is the home of the Baltimore Symphony Orchestra and Baltimore Chorale Arts Society; it also presents visiting classical and pops artists. **Open:** Call for schedule. $$$$

Baltimore Arena, 201 W Baltimore St; tel 410/962-8000. This facility, with a seating capacity of 16,000, plays host to a changing program of entertainment and sports events. Featured on the schedule are concerts, plays, circuses, ice shows, and soccer and hockey matches. **Open:** Call for schedule. $$$$

BALTIMORE-WASHINGTON INTERNATIONAL AIRPORT

See Baltimore, Glen Burnie, Hanover, Linthicum

BERLIN
Map page M-3, C8

Inn 🏨

≡≡≡≡ Atlantic Hotel, 2 N Main St, Berlin, MD 21811; tel 410/641-3589; fax 410/641-4928. Exit US 50 at Main St. A beautiful Victorian-era hotel, carefully restored and furnished throughout with high-quality antiques. Enclosed and open porches for sitting. **Rooms:** 16 rms. CI 3pm/CO 11am. No smoking. Accurate in period style, very lovely rooms range from large to quite small. **Amenities:** 🏨 🛁 A/C. **Facilities:** 2 rsts (*see also* "Restaurants" below), 1 bar (w/entertainment), guest lounge. **Rates (CP):** HS June–Oct $65–$135 D. Extra person $20. Children under 12 stay free. Min stay HS and wknds. Lower rates off-season. Spec packages avail. Pking: Outdoor, free. Ltd CC.

Restaurant 🍴

Atlantic Hotel Restaurant, in Atlantic Hotel, 2 N Main St, Berlin; tel 410/641-3589. Exit US 50 at Main St. **Regional American.** In the beautifully restored Atlantic Hotel (1895), a Victorian landmark that evokes *Age of Innocence* luxury, with period antiques throughout. A short but varied menu is marked by interesting sauces, while the extensive wine list reflects the manager's interest in American vintages. **FYI:** Reservations recommended. Piano. Dress code. No smoking. **Open:** Lunch Mon–Thurs noon–9pm, Fri–Sat noon–10pm, Sun 3–9pm; dinner Mon–Thurs 6–9pm, Fri–Sat 6–10pm, Sun 5–9pm; brunch Sun 11am–2pm. Closed Dec 25. **Prices:** Main courses $19–$26. Ltd CC. ♥ 🍴 ♿

BETHESDA
Map page M-3, C6 (N of Washington, DC)

Hotels 🏨

≡≡ American Inn of Bethesda, 8130 Wisconsin Ave (Md 355), Bethesda, MD 20814; tel 301/656-9300 or toll free 800/323-7081; fax 301/656-2907. Exit 34 off I-495. Go south on Wisconsin Ave. A clean and comfortable, if not esthetically appealing, hotel. Convenient to shops, restaurants, and metro. Property has considerably more potential than has been realized. **Rooms:** 76 rms and stes. CI 3pm/CO 12:30pm. Nonsmoking rms avail. **Amenities:** 🏨 A/C, cable TV. **Services:** 🍴 **Facilities:** 🔧 📶 2 rsts, 1 bar, washer/dryer. Reasonably priced Latin American restaurant on premises. **Rates (CP):** $80 S; $90 D; from $90 ste. Extra person $10. Children under 18 stay free. Spec packages avail. Pking: Outdoor, free. Maj CC. Weekend rates available.

≡≡≡ Bethesda Marriott Hotel, 5151 Pooks Hill Rd, Bethesda, MD 20814; tel 301/897-9400 or toll free 800/228-9290; fax 301/897-0192. Exit 34 off I-495. Follow Md 355 to Pooks Hill Rd, turn right. A fine suburban hotel in a private residential setting yet adjacent to the Capital Beltway (I-495). Frequented by groups, tourists, and business travelers. **Rooms:** 407 rms and stes. Exec-level rms avail. CI 4pm/CO noon. Express checkout avail. Nonsmoking rms avail. **Amenities:** 🏨 🛁 A/C, cable TV w/movies, voice mail. Some units w/terraces, 1 w/fireplace. Iron and board in all rooms. **Services:** ✕ 🔑 🚗 🛎 🍴 Twice-daily maid svce, car-rental desk, babysitting. Morning newspaper delivered to rooms. Morning coffee available in lobby. Activities desk arranges local tours. **Facilities:** 🔧 🏋 🏊 🖥 ♿ 3 rsts, 1 bar, lifeguard, games rm, spa, sauna, steam rm, whirlpool, washer/dryer. **Rates:** $160 S; $180 D; from $275 ste. Children under 18 stay free. Spec packages avail. Pking: Outdoor, free. Maj CC.

≡≡≡ Bethesda Marriott Suites, 6711 Democracy Blvd, at Fernwood Rd, Bethesda, MD 20817; tel 301/897-5600 or toll free 800/228-9290; fax 301/530-1427. Follow I-495 to I-270 exit I-270 at Democracy Blvd E. A modern, all-suites hotel in a nicely landscaped office park containing the corporate headquarters of Marriott Hotels; 2-story lobby has large windows, skylights, ficus trees, bar. **Rooms:** 274 stes. CI 4pm/CO 1pm. Express checkout avail. Nonsmoking rms avail. Most units have sofa beds. All have desk, sinks, dressing area in bath. Attractively furnished. **Amenities:** 🏨 🛁 📺 🍴 A/C, cable TV w/movies, refrig. Some units w/terraces. Large TVs, iron and boards. **Services:** ✕ 🚗 🛎 🍴 🐕 Twice-daily maid svce, babysitting. Complimentary barbecue 1 night a week in summer. Complimentary morning newspaper and grocery delivery. **Facilities:** 🔧 🏋 🖥 ♿ 1 rst, 1 bar, lifeguard, whirlpool, washer/dryer. **Rates (CP):** From $130 ste. Children under 18 stay free. Higher rates for spec evnts/hols. Spec packages avail. Pking: Indoor, free. Maj CC.

≡≡≡ The Bethesda Ramada Hotel and Conference Center, 8400 Wisconsin Ave, Bethesda, MD 20814; tel 301/654-1000 or toll free 800/331-5252; fax 301/654-0751. This contemporary hotel exhibits considerable exterior appeal; however, neither services, room decor, nor amenities realize the full potential of the building or its location 2 blocks from National Institutes of Health and its metro station. **Rooms:** 160 rms and stes. CI 3pm/CO 1pm. Nonsmoking rms avail. **Amenities:** 🏨 🛁 A/C, cable TV w/movies. Some units w/terraces. **Services:** ✕ 🛎 🐕 Car-rental desk. **Facilities:** 🔧 🖥 ♿ 1 rst, 1 bar (w/entertainment), lifeguard, washer/dryer. Olympic-size pool. **Rates:** HS Feb–Apr/Sept–Oct $79 S; $79 D; from $150 ste. Extra person $10. Children under 10 stay free. Lower rates off-season. Higher rates for spec evnts/hols. Spec packages avail. Pking: Indoor/outdoor, free. Maj CC.

≣≣≣ Holiday Inn, 8120 Wisconsin Ave (Md 355), Bethesda, MD 20814; tel 301/652-2000 or toll free 800/631-5954. Exit 34 off I-495. Go south on Wisconsin Ave. A moderately priced hotel in downtown Bethesda, surrounded by numerous restaurants, night spots, and exclusive shops. **Rooms:** 270 rms and stes. CI 4pm/CO noon. Express checkout avail. Nonsmoking rms avail. **Amenities:** 🛎 🛋 A/C, cable TV w/movies. Some units w/minibars, some w/terraces. **Services:** ✗ 🚗 🖼 🍴 🍸 Complimentary shuttle service to Bethesda Naval Medical Center/National Institutes of Health metro station. Pets allowed but cannot be left unattended in rooms. **Facilities:** 🏊 🍴 🔭 🖥 ⚓ 1 rst, 1 bar (w/entertainment), lifeguard, games rm, washer/dryer. Headlines Cafe specializes in low-cholesterol, healthy selections. Comedy Club entertainment Wednesday to Saturday evenings. **Rates:** $126 S or D; from $149 ste. Children under 19 stay free. Spec packages avail. Pking: Indoor, free. Maj CC.

≣≣≣≣ Hyatt Regency Bethesda, 1 Bethesda Metro Ctr, Bethesda, MD 20814; tel 301/657-1234 or toll free 800/233-1234; fax 301/657-6453. On Wisconsin Ave at Old Georgetown Rd. A contemporary hotel in downtown Bethesda at metro station plaza, which hosts festivals, concerts, and entertainment in summer months. Atrium lobby. **Rooms:** 381 rms and stes. Exec-level rms avail. CI 4pm/CO noon. Express checkout avail. Nonsmoking rms avail. Attractive and comfortable rooms have luxurious marble baths with attractive floral wallpaper and well-lighted 3-way mirrors. **Amenities:** 🛎 🛋 🍷 A/C, cable TV w/movies, refrig, VCR, voice mail. Some units w/minibars, some w/terraces. **Services:** ✗ 🔌 🆅🅿 🖼 🍴 Twice-daily maid svce, babysitting. Complimentary newspaper. **Facilities:** 🏊 🍴 🔭 🖥 ⚓ 1 rst, 1 bar, lifeguard, spa, sauna, whirlpool, playground. Health club is at rooftop level. **Rates:** $135–$165 S; $160–$190 D; from $175 ste. Extra person $25. Children under 16 stay free. Spec packages avail. Pking: Indoor, $9–$11. Maj CC.

≣≣≣ Marriott Residence Inn, 7335 Wisconsin Ave, Bethesda, MD 20814; tel 301/718-0200 or toll free 800/331-3131; fax 301/718-0679. A home away from home attractive for long-term stays. **Rooms:** 187 stes. CI 3pm/CO noon. Express checkout avail. Nonsmoking rms avail. All units have 2 rooms, fully equipped kitchens. **Amenities:** 🛎 🛋 📺 🍷 A/C, cable TV w/movies, refrig, voice mail. Some units w/terraces. Microwaves. First-nighters kit includes coffee and popcorn. **Services:** 🔌 🆅🅿 🚐 🖼 🍴 🍸 Babysitting. Specializing in personal services, with social hours for guests and barbecues in

summer. Complimentary continental breakfast. **Facilities:** 🏋 🍴 📮 ⚓ Lifeguard, games rm, sauna, washer/dryer. **Rates (CP):** From $154 ste. Extra person $10. Children under 18 stay free. Spec packages avail. Pking: Indoor, $10. Maj CC. Charge for extra persons applies only when additional beds are required.

Restaurants 🍴

Armadilla Grill, 8011 Woodmont Ave at Cordell Ave, Bethesda; tel 301/907-9637. **Southwestern.** Native American spirit dolls grace the entry to this "casual restaurant in the Santa Fe tradition." Desert colors and Native American accents, such as Navajo and Hopi rugs, add proper ambience for eating southwestern fare. **FYI:** Reservations accepted. Children's menu. No smoking. **Open:** Sun–Thurs 5–10pm, Fri–Sat 5–11pm. Closed some hols. **Prices:** Main courses $8–$16.75. Maj CC. ♥

The Athenian Plaka, 7833 Woodmont Ave, Bethesda; tel 301/986-1337. **Greek.** Gold trim, white archways, and murals of Greece adorn the walls, while Greek music adds to the Mediterranean atmosphere. Favorites from the old country such as roast lamb, kabobs, and Greek-style seafood. Outdoor tables available in fair weather. **FYI:** Reservations accepted. **Open:** Sun–Thurs 11am–10pm, Fri–Sat 11am–11pm. **Prices:** Main courses $8.50–$14.95. Maj CC. ♥ 🆅🅿 ⚓

Bacchus, 7945 Norfolk Ave, Bethesda; tel 301/657-1722. Between St Elmo and Fairmont Aves. **Greek.** Middle Eastern atmosphere begins at entry, continues through stone courtyard with tables and into dining room with magnificent chandelier and regional decor. Extensive appetizers include hummus, baba ghanouj, kibbeh, and other Lebanese favorites. Main courses continue the theme: kabobs, rice dishes with lamb, beef, chicken. **FYI:** Reservations recommended. **Open:** Lunch Mon–Fri noon–2pm; dinner Sun–Thurs 6–10pm, Fri–Sat 6–10:30pm; brunch. Closed some hols. **Prices:** Main courses $13.25–$14.75. Maj CC. ♥ 🆅🅿

Bangkok Garden, 4906 St Elmo Ave, Bethesda; tel 301/951-0670. Between Old Georgetown Rd and Norfolk Ave. **Thai.** A multitude of Siamese artifacts and souvenirs sets tone for Thai cuisine ranging from mild shrimp curry with coconut milk and peanut sauce to spicy soft-shell crabs or whole fish in chili and garlic. An intriguing specialty is whole pineapple stuffed with fried rice. **FYI:** Reservations recommended. Dress code. **Open:** Mon–Thurs 11am–10:30pm, Fri–Sat 11am–11pm, Sun 4–10pm. Closed some hols. **Prices:** Main courses $6.25–$17.50. Maj CC.

Café Bethesda, 5027 Wilson Lane, Bethesda; tel 301/657-3383. **New American/French.** Intimate dining is enhanced by stark white tablecloths, wicker chairs, and French paintings gracing the walls of this small, bright restaurant. **FYI:** Reservations recommended. Dress code. Beer and wine only. No smoking. **Open:** Lunch Mon–Fri 11:30am–2pm; dinner daily 5pm–close; brunch Sun 10am–2pm. Closed some hols; Jan 1–Jan 15. **Prices:** Main courses $14–$21; PF dinner $12. Maj CC. ♥ ☑

Cottonwood Cafe, 4844 Cordell Ave, Bethesda; tel 301/656-4844. Between Norfolk and Woodmont Aves. **Southwestern.** Warm desert colors, adobe-like walls, Navajo zigzag rugs give a sense of region and an artistic touch to this 2-level restaurant that cooks up mesquite-grilled chicken, steak, fresh fish, and other southwestern favorites. **FYI:** Reservations recommended. **Open:** Lunch Mon–Sat 11:30am–2:30pm; dinner daily 5:30–10pm. Closed some hols. **Prices:** Main courses $12.65–$19.75. Maj CC. ♥ VP &

Fabs' Bistro, 4870 Cordell Ave, at Norfolk Ave, Bethesda; tel 301/913-0071. **French/Italian.** A bright white Mediterranean look prevails at this restaurant, where brick walls separate 2-tiered dining area. Green plants and a few art-deco paintings add accents to simple decor. Most menu items are grilled, served with light sauces of southern France. **FYI:** Reservations accepted. **Open:** Lunch Mon–Fri 11:30am–2:30pm; dinner daily 5–10:30pm. **Prices:** Main courses $7.95–$13.95; PF dinner $12.95. Maj CC. ♥ ☑ VP

Foong Lin Restaurant, 7710 Norfolk Ave, at Fairmont Ave, Bethesda; tel 301/656-3427. **Chinese.** A family-style Chinese restaurant in a corner storefront, accented by hanging baskets and Oriental paintings and screens. A mix of Cantonese, Szechuan, Hunan, and Mongolian cuisines. Low-fat items offered. **FYI:** Reservations accepted. **Open:** Mon–Thurs 11am–10:30pm, Fri–Sat 11am–11pm, Sun noon–10pm. **Prices:** Main courses $7.50–$14. Maj CC. &

La Miche, 7905 Norfolk Ave, at St Elmo Ave, Bethesda; tel 301/986-0707. **French.** Baskets hanging from exposed beams contribute to a warm ambience that matches the country-style French cuisine, ranging from veal kidneys in mustard sauce to roast rack of lamb. A fixed-price, 4-course dinner offers a taste of seafood and lamb. Only women's rest room is equipped for guests with disabilities. **FYI:** Reservations recommended. Dress code. **Open:** Lunch Mon–Fri 11:30am–2:30pm; dinner daily 6–10pm. Closed some hols. **Prices:** Main courses $14–$23; PF dinner $44. Maj CC. VP

Parioli, 4800 Elm St, Bethesda; tel 301/951-8600. Just off Wisconsin Ave. **Italian.** Winding black iron stairs lead to bright dining area with wine rack; gold-framed Italian paintings on textured, reddish stone walls; black chairs contrasting with white tablecloths. Italian fare such as *bucatine* (thick pasta with bacon

in a red chili–tomato sauce). **FYI:** Reservations recommended. No smoking. **Open:** Lunch Mon–Fri 11:30am–2:30pm; dinner Sun–Thurs 5:30–10pm, Fri–Sat 5:30–11pm. **Prices:** Main courses $11–$13. Maj CC. ♥ VP

★ **Rio Grande Cafe**, 4919 Fairmont Ave, Bethesda; tel 301/656-2981. Between Old Georgetown Rd and Norfolk Ave. **Tex-Mex.** One of George Bush's favorite taco haunts when he lived at 1600 Pennsylvania Ave, this popular eatery looks like a southwestern roadhouse, with billboard-style advertisements painted on adobe-like walls, straightback wooden chairs, and exposed metal rafters. Strictly Tex-Mex menu: tacos, enchiladas, burritos, fajitas, and other regular fare augmented with mesquite-grilled frogs' legs, quail, chicken, or beef. **FYI:** Reservations not accepted. Dress code. **Open:** Mon–Thurs 11:30am–11pm, Fri–Sat 11:30am–11:30pm, Sun 11:30am–10:30pm. **Prices:** Main courses $6.50–$14. Maj CC. &

St Elmo's Café, 7820 Norfolk Ave, at St Elmo Ave, Bethesda; tel 301/657-1607. **New American/French.** Large windows slide open to a sidewalk dining area at this cafe-style eatery, making it a pleasant spot for lunch. New owners took over in 1994 and were promising to take this establishment more upscale and to add a bar upstairs with live jazz on weekends. **FYI:** Reservations accepted. Jazz. Dress code. **Open:** Lunch daily 11:30am–3pm; dinner Mon–Thurs 5–10pm, Fri–Sat 5–11pm, Sun 11:30am–9:30pm; brunch Sun 11:30–2:30pm. Closed some hols. **Prices:** Main courses $8–$13.50. Maj CC. ☑ VP

★ **Tako Grill**, 7756 Wisconsin Ave, Bethesda; tel 301/652-7030. Exit I-495 at Wisconsin Ave. **Japanese.** There's a small Japanese inn feel to this downtown restaurant with peaked, blond wood ceiling. Each black enamel table has an Oriental painting, sake vase with orchid. Sushi bar serves traditional Japanese selections, while menu offers cooked items including soft-shell crabs. An excellent bargain. **FYI:** Reservations not accepted. Beer and wine only. **Open:** Lunch Mon–Fri 11:30am–2pm; dinner Mon–Thurs 5:30–9:45pm, Fri–Sat 5:30–10:15pm. Closed some hols; Jan 1–3. **Prices:** Main courses $8.95–$16. Maj CC.

Terramar, 7800 Wisconsin Ave, Bethesda; tel 301/654-0888. Exit I-495 at Wisconsin Ave, go south. **South American/Latin American.** A sunny Latin American–style dining room with whitewashed walls, archways, fountain. Bar has red-tile roof-like canopy. Indoor courtyard. Nicaraguan fare includes seafood and beef dishes on seasonal menu. Nicaraguan entertainment Friday and Saturday. Smoking in bar only. **FYI:** Reservations recommended. Children's menu. No smoking. **Open:** Lunch Tues–Fri 11:30am–2:30pm; dinner Tues–Thurs 5–10pm, Fri–Sat 5–11pm, Sun 5–9pm. Closed some hols. **Prices:** Main courses $11–$20. Maj CC. ♥

★ **Tragara**, 4935 Cordell Ave, Bethesda; tel 301/951-4935. Between Old Georgetown Rd and Norfolk Ave. **Italian.** Art-deco curves and a burgundy-and-pink color scheme set off this elegantly simple establishment, one of the area's most popular upscale Italian restaurants. Dark red window lets guests glimpse talented chef at work in kitchen. Gourmet northern Italian dishes are headed by swordfish with currants, pine nuts, and basil. Specials offered on seasonal basis. **FYI:** Reservations recommended. Dress code. **Open:** Lunch Mon–Fri noon–2pm; dinner daily 6–10pm. Closed some hols. **Prices:** Main courses $21–$25. Maj CC. 🆅🅿 &

Volare Ristorante Italiano, 4926 St Elmo Ave, Bethesda; tel 301/907-7503. Between Old Georgetown Rd and Norfolk Ave. **Italian.** Two small dining rooms are festooned with potted and hanging plants, creating a garden-like atmosphere in a narrow storefront setting. Italian opera on sound system complements the traditional Italian menu augmented by nightly specials. **FYI:** Reservations recommended. Dress code. **Open:** Lunch Mon–Fri 11am–2pm; dinner Sun–Fri 5–9:30pm, Sat 5–10:30pm. Closed some hols. **Prices:** Main courses $10–$16. Maj CC. &

Attraction 📼

Clara Barton National Historic Site, 5801 Oxford Rd; tel 301/492-6245. Once the headquarters for the American Red Cross, today it displays furniture and other possessions once belonging to the woman who founded the organization. Visitors must take one of the guided tours that are offered hourly on the half-hour. **Open:** Daily 10am–5pm. Closed some hols. Free.

CAMBRIDGE

Map page M-3, C7

Attractions 📼

Old Trinity Church, Md 16; tel 410/228-2940. Eight miles southwest of Cambridge is this landmark church built circa 1685 and meticulouly restored in recent years. It is one of the oldest Episcopal churches in active use in the United States. **Open:** Mar–Dec, Wed–Sat 9am–5pm, Sun noon–5pm; Jan–Feb, Sun 11am–4pm. Free.

Dorchester Heritage Museum, 1904 Horn Point Rd; tel 410/228-1899. Highlights local history and heritage with exhibits in aviation, archeology, and maritime industries. **Open:** Apr–Oct, Sat–Sun 1–4:30pm. Free.

Meredith House, 902 Greenway Dr; tel 410/228-7953. The Georgian-style residence, circa 1760, includes the Governor's Room honoring past leaders of Maryland who are associated with Dorchester county, plus an antique doll collection. The adjacent Neild Museum contains exhibits on local maritime and industrial development and on farm life, as well as an original 1831 McCormick reaper. Other attractions on the property are an herb garden, a meat house, and an 18th-century stable. **Open:** Thurs–Sat 10am–4pm. Free.

Blackwater National Wildlife Refuge, Key Wallace Dr; tel 410/228-2677. A 17,000-acre site of rich tidal marsh, freshwater ponds, and woodlands, located 12 miles southeast of Cambridge. The refuge serves as a resting and feeding area for migrant and wintering wildfowl, including huge flocks of Canadian geese and ducks. The grounds are also the home of 3 endangered species: the bald eagle, the Delmarva fox squirrel, and the migrant peregrine falcon. Visitors center, wildlife trail, 5-mile wildlife drive, hiking and biking paths. **Open:** Daily sunrise–sunset. $

CHESAPEAKE CITY

Map page M-3, B7 (S of Elkton)

Restaurants 🍴

Bayard House Restaurant, 11 Bohemia Ave, Chesapeake City; tel 410/885-5040. 6 mi S of Elkton. On Md 213, at C&D Canal. **New American.** This historic building dating to the late 18th century is furnished authentically with Hitchcock and spindle-back chairs and fine needlepoint hangings. Lower level and outdoor deck overlook Chesapeake and Delaware Canal; interesting canal museum is nearby. Menu features light, creative treatment of American dishes, with an emphasis on seafood. **FYI:** Reservations recommended. Dress code. No smoking. **Open:** Lunch Mon–Sat 11:30am–3pm, Sun noon–2:30pm; dinner Mon–Thurs 5–9pm, Fri–Sat 5–10pm, Sun 4–9pm. Closed some hols. **Prices:** Main courses $16–$19. Maj CC. 🍷 ⛴ 🏖 &

Schaefer's Canal House, 208 Bank St, Chesapeake City; tel 410/885-2200. 5 mi S of Elkton. On Md 213, at C&D Canal. **Regional American/Seafood.** Spacious wood-beamed rooms with cathedral ceilings overlook busy Chesapeake and Delaware Canal. Chesapeake Bay pilots board passing ships here; home ports and destinations are announced to guests. Traditional and regional American entrées feature such Eastern Shore favorites as crab cakes and oysters. This special-occasion restaurant accepts no reservations on Saturday during summer months, when a reggae band plays on outdoor patio. **FYI:** Reservations accepted. Island music. Dress code. **Open:** Breakfast daily 8–11am; lunch Mon–Sat 11am–4pm, Sun 11am–4pm; dinner Mon–Sat 4–10pm, Sun noon–9pm. Closed Dec 25. **Prices:** Main courses $18–$28. Maj CC. ⛴ 🏖 &

Attraction 🛍

C&D Canal Museum, 815 Bethel Rd; tel 410/885-5622. Located on the waterfront at 2nd St. A series of exhibits depicts the history and operation of the 160-year-old canal that connects the Chesapeake and Delaware Bays. **Open:** Mon–Sat 8:15am–4:15pm; also Apr–Oct, Sun 10am–6pm. Free.

CHESTERTOWN

Map page M-3, B7

Motel 🛏

≣≣≣ **Great Oak Lodge**, 22170 Great Oak Landing Rd, Chestertown, MD 21620; tel 410/778-2100 or toll free 800/526-3464; fax 410/778-3977. 70 acres. This older but adequately maintained waterfront motel is on an extensive marina and golf-course complex next to a popular pleasure-boating harbor. **Rooms:** 28 rms. CI 2pm/CO 11am. Standard motel rooms, some with excellent views of Fairlee Creek. **Amenities:** 🛁 🜨 A/C, satel TV w/movies. **Services:** ✗ ⟲ Twice-daily maid svce, babysitting. Yacht brokerage, ship's store, boat repairs. **Facilities:** 🛗 🚴 ⚠ ▶₉ ⚓₁ 🎱₁₂₀ 1 rst, 4 bars (2 w/entertainment), 1 beach (cove/inlet), lifeguard, games rm, lawn games, whirlpool, washer/dryer. Large restaurant is on the water, has nice view. Marina. Beach suitable for small boats, not swimming. **Rates:** HS Apr–Jan $50–$75 S; $65–$90 D. Extra person $15. Children under 12 stay free. Min stay wknds and spec evnts. Lower rates off-season. MAP rates avail. Spec packages avail. Pking: Outdoor, free. Maj CC.

Inn

≣≣≣ **Imperial Hotel**, 208 High St, Chestertown, MD 21620; tel 410/778-5000; fax 410/778-9662. Take exit for Cross St off Md 213; turn left onto High St and go 1 block. This beautiful turn-of-the-century hotel is like a time capsule in the center of this historic and picturesque riverfront town. **Rooms:** 13 rms, stes, and effic. CI 3pm/CO 11am. No smoking. Faithfully furnished with antiques in excellent condition. **Amenities:** 🛁 📺 A/C, cable TV w/movies. 1 unit w/terrace. **Services:** ✗ ⟲ Masseur, babysitting. **Facilities:** 🛗 ⚓ 1 rst (*see also* "Restaurants" below), 1 bar (w/entertainment), washer/dryer, guest lounge w/TV. Fine restaurant done in same late-Victorian decor. Swimming available at nearby Washington College. **Rates (CP):** $95–$125 D; from $150 ste; from $175 effic. Extra person $35. Children under 8 stay free. Min stay spec evnts. Pking: Outdoor, free. Ltd CC.

Restaurant 🍴

Imperial Hotel Restaurant, in Imperial Hotel, 208 High St, Chestertown; tel 410/778-5000. Exit Md 213 at Cross St; turn left at High St and go 1 block. **Regional American/Seafood.** The authentic late-Victorian dining room in the restored 1903 hotel offers award-winning wine list and cuisine oriented toward American seafood and regional dishes. Extensive list of aperitifs, brandies, and cognacs, plus a variety of coffees. **FYI:** Reservations recommended. Jazz. Dress code. No smoking. **Open:** Lunch Tues–Sat 11:45am–2pm; dinner Tues–Sat 5:30–9pm. Closed Dec 25. **Prices:** Main courses $15–$20. Ltd CC. 🍷 ✉ ⚒

Attraction 🛍

St Paul's Church, 7579 Sandy Bottom Rd; tel 410/778-3180. Erected in 1713, this is one of the oldest continually used churches in Maryland. Among the notables buried in the church's oak tree–shaded graveyard is actress Tallulah Bankhead. **Open:** Daily 9am–5pm. Free.

CHEVY CHASE

Map page M-3, C6 (NW of Washington, DC)

Restaurant 🍴

La Ferme, 7101 Brookville Rd, Chevy Chase (Brookville); tel 301/986-5255. From Chevy Chase Circle, go east on Western Ave, turn left onto Brookville Rd; ½ mile to restaurant. **French.** Tucked away in an affluent residential neighborhood, this former barn has been expertly decorated in a French country style. High peaked ceiling adds spaciousness. Patio for outdoor dining when weather permits. Traditional French cuisine includes variety of fish selections plus various meats, all excellently prepared by co-owner/chef. **FYI:** Reservations recommended. Dress code. **Open:** Lunch Tues–Fri noon–2pm; dinner Tues–Sat 6–10pm, Sun 5–9pm. Closed Dec 25. **Prices:** Main courses $18–$22. Maj CC. ✉ ⚒

COCKEYSVILLE

Map page M-3, B7 (N of Baltimore)

Restaurant 🍴

★ **Gibby's**, in Padonia Plaza, 22 W Padonia Rd, Cockeysville; tel 410/560-0703. Exit 17 off I-83. **Seafood.** Whimsical pictures of fish and Chesapeake Bay scenes give this place a cheerful, comfortable atmosphere. Seafood is flown in from the restaurant's own processing plant in Florida. Be prepared to wait in line. **FYI:** Reservations recommended. Children's menu. **Open:** Mon–Sat 11am–2am, Sun noon–2am. Closed some hols. **Prices:** Main courses $11.95–$24.95. Maj CC. ▪▪ &

COLLEGE PARK

Map page M-3, C6 (NE of Washington, DC)

Motels ☐

≣≣≣ **Best Western Maryland Inn & Fundome**, 8601 Baltimore Blvd, College Park, MD 20740; tel 301/474-2800 or toll free 800/528-1234; fax 301/474-0714. Exit 25B off I-495. Follow US 1 S for ¾ mile. A well-kept older property, this motel is convenient to the University of Maryland. Outdoor courtyard off enclosed atrium. Lovely, large trees. **Rooms:** 121 rms and stes. CI 2pm/CO noon. Nonsmoking rms avail. Standard rooms, some on pool atrium and some exterior. New furniture and carpeting installed in 1994. **Amenities:** ☎ ⚎ A/C, cable TV w/movies. **Services:** ⟐ ⟑ Car-rental desk. Free shuttle to Metro station. **Facilities:** ⟐ ⟑ ⟐ 1 rst, 1 bar, lifeguard, games rm, spa, sauna, whirlpool. Putting green, shuffleboard, billiard table, very attractive pool and whirlpool in atrium. **Rates (BB):** $70 S or D; from $120 ste. Extra person $5. Children under 12 stay free. Higher rates for spec evnts/hols. Pking: Outdoor, free. Maj CC.

≣≣ **Days Inn College Park**, 9137 Baltimore Ave, College Park, MD 20740; tel 301/345-5000 or toll free 800/329-7466; fax 301/345-4577. Exit 25 off I-495. Follow US 1 S for ½ mile. A middle-aged motel in average condition, kept clean and neat. **Rooms:** 68 rms. CI 1pm/CO noon. Nonsmoking rms avail. Standard motel-type rooms. **Amenities:** ☎ A/C, cable TV w/movies. **Services:** ⟐ ⟐ ⟑ Car-rental desk. **Facilities:** ⟐ 1 rst (see also "Restaurants" below), 1 bar, lifeguard. Well-regarded Korean restaurant on premises. Large pool. **Rates:** $48–$60 S; $53–$65 D. Extra person $5. Children under 18 stay free. Pking: Outdoor, free. Maj CC.

≣≣≣ **Holiday Inn**, 10000 Baltimore Blvd, College Park, MD 20740; tel 301/345-6700 or toll free 800/872-5564; fax 301/441-4923. 5 mi N of Washington DC. exit 25 off I-495. Follow US 1 N to motel. Newly renovated and attractively decorated, this motel has been significantly enlarged. **Rooms:** 222 rms and stes. CI 3pm/CO noon. Nonsmoking rms avail. All units recently redecorated. **Amenities:** ☎ ⚎ ⟐ A/C, cable TV w/movies. Some units w/minibars. **Services:** ✕ ⟐ ⟐ ⟑ Car-rental desk, babysitting. Courtesy van to metro station. **Facilities:** ⟐ ⟐ ⟐ & 1 rst, 1 bar, lifeguard, games rm, spa, sauna, whirlpool, washer/dryer. Family-style steak restaurant on premises. Nice

indoor pool and exercise room. **Rates:** $84 S; $90 D; from $150 ste. Extra person $6. Children under 18 stay free. Spec packages avail. Pking: Outdoor, free. Maj CC.

≣≣ **Quality Inn**, 7200 Baltimore Blvd, College Park, MD 20740; tel 310/864-5820 or toll free 800/221-2222; fax 301/927-8634. 2 mi N of Washington DC. exit 25B off I-495. Left on US 1; follow US 1 S for 3 miles. Convenient to the University of Maryland and just 3 blocks from College Park metro station, this motel is good for events at the college and for long-term stays. **Rooms:** 154 rms and effic. CI 3pm/CO noon. Nonsmoking rms avail. Recently refurnished and in good condition. **Amenities:** ☎ ⚎ A/C, cable TV. Some units w/terraces. **Services:** ⟐ ⟑ Car-rental desk, babysitting. **Facilities:** ⟐ & 1 rst, lifeguard, washer/dryer. Laundry. **Rates (CP):** HS Sept–Nov/Mar–June $49–$54 S; $54–$59 D; from $59 effic. Extra person $5. Children under 18 stay free. Lower rates off-season. Higher rates for spec evnts/hols. MAP rates avail. Spec packages avail. Pking: Outdoor, free. Maj CC. Long-term rates available.

≣ **Royal Pine Inn**, 9113 Baltimore Blvd, College Park, MD 20740; tel 301/345-4900 or toll free 800/660-5162; fax 301/345-3017. 3 mi N of Washington, DC. exit 25 off I-495. Follow US 1 S for ½ mile. This older motel has seen regular maintenance but could use some sprucing up with new carpets and paint. Still it is an adequate, basic facility in a convenient location. **Rooms:** 114 rms and effic. CI noon/CO noon. Nonsmoking rms avail. Larger than average rooms; some are family-size. **Amenities:** ☎ A/C, cable TV w/movies. **Services:** ⟐ ⟐ ⟑ Car-rental desk. Tours of Washington, DC, pick up at lobby. **Facilities:** ⟐ & Lifeguard. **Rates (CP):** HS May–Sept $53 S; $58 D; from $60 effic. Extra person $5. Children under 18 stay free. Lower rates off-season. Higher rates for spec evnts/hols. Pking: Outdoor, free. Maj CC.

Restaurant ⍨

Yijo, in Days Inn College Park, 9137 Baltimore Ave, College Park; tel 301/345-6500. 4 mi N of Washington DC, exit 25 off I-495. Go south on US 1 for ½ mile. **Korean.** Two simple rooms off the lobby of a motel. Neat but unpretentious. Extensive Korean menu, authentic and reasonably priced. Friendly, accommodating service. **FYI:** Reservations recommended. **Open:** Lunch daily 11:30am–2pm; dinner daily 2–10:30pm. **Prices:** Main courses $8–$14. Maj CC.

COLUMBIA

Map page M-3, B6 (S of Ellicott City)

Hotel 🛏

≣≣≣ **The Columbia Inn Hotel and Conference Center**, 10207 Wincopin Circle, Columbia, MD 21044; tel 410/730-3900 or toll free 800/638-2817; fax 410/730-1290. 18 mi SW of Baltimore. Follow I-95 to Md 175 W; turn left onto Wincopin Circle. Beautifully set on the lake in Columbia, this hotel caters to corporate travelers on weekdays and offers many special packages to pleasure travelers on weekends. Located across street from major shopping mall. **Rooms:** 289 rms and stes. CI 3pm/CO noon. Express checkout avail. Nonsmoking rms avail. Many rooms provide excellent views. **Amenities:** 🛏 🕸 A/C, satel TV w/movies. **Services:** ✗ 🚐 🖼 🛎 🕙 Car-rental desk, babysitting. Tours of Washington, Baltimore, other nearby sights arranged. **Facilities:** 🗗 ⚠ 🖿 🖾 🎱 🕸 1 rst, 1 bar, lifeguard, washer/dryer. Restaurant has very nice lake view, well-regarded Sunday brunch. Guest passes to 7 nearby swim, golf, and fitness clubs. **Rates (CP):** HS Mar–Nov $114 S or D; from $225 ste. Extra person $15. Children under 18 stay free. Lower rates off-season. Spec packages avail. Pking: Indoor/outdoor, free. Maj CC.

Motel 🛏

≣≣≣ **Columbia Hilton Inn**, 5485 Twin Knolls Rd, Columbia, MD 21045; tel 410/997-1060 or toll free 800/235-0653; fax 410/997-0169. 18 mi SW of Baltimore. exit 41 off I-95. Follow Md 175 W for 6 miles; turn left on Thunder Hill Hill Rd then right on Twin Knolls Rd. Modern motel with a dramatic atrium and attractive public areas. **Rooms:** 152 rms and stes. CI 3pm/CO noon. Express checkout avail. Nonsmoking rms avail. **Amenities:** 🛏 🕸 A/C, satel TV w/movies. Some units w/mini-bars. Wet bars, microwaves in suites. **Services:** ✗ 🖼 🛎 Car-rental desk, babysitting. Van to Columbia businesses and shopping. **Facilities:** 🗗 🎱 🎱 🕸 1 rst, 1 bar, spa, sauna, whirlpool. Very nice indoor pool in a bright, airy space. **Rates:** $117 S; $127 D; from $225 ste. Extra person $10. Children under 18 stay free. Spec packages avail. Pking: Outdoor, free. Maj CC.

Restaurants 🍴

⑤ **Cover to Cover Café**, in Owen Brown Village Center, 7284 Cradlerock Way, Columbia; tel 410/381-9200. 18 mi SW of Baltimore. Exit I-95 at Md 32 W; turn right on Broken Land Pkwy, right on Cradlerock Way, then left into Owen Brown Center. **New American/Cafe.** Unique, inexpensive, appealing, and informal. The room, in a bookstore, has simple decor and bentwood furniture. A sidewalk cafe is open during fine weather. French-American cafe-style dishes with some southwestern influence. Entertainment is folk or light rock, including guitar, piano, or dulcimer. **FYI:** Reservations accepted. Children's menu. No smoking. **Open:** Mon–Thurs 11am–9pm, Fri–Sat 11am–10pm, Sun 3–8pm. Closed some hols. **Prices:** Main courses $6–$14. Maj CC. 🚐 🗹 🕸

The King's Contrivance Restaurant, 10150 Shaker Dr, Columbia; tel 410/995-0500. 18 mi SW of Baltimore. Exit I-95 at Md 32 W; follow Shaker Dr ½ mile north. **French/International/Italian.** In a 19th-century house, quiet and distinctive dining rooms are decorated and furnished in federal style. French and Italian entrees feature meat, fish, and pasta selections. **FYI:** Reservations recommended. Dress code. **Open:** Lunch Mon–Fri 11:30am–2pm; dinner Mon–Sat 5:30–9pm, Sun 4–8pm. Closed some hols. **Prices:** Main courses $14–$23; PF dinner $16. Maj CC. 🍽

CRISFIELD

Map page M-3, D7

Motels 🛏

≣ **Pines Motel**, N Somerset Ave, PO Box 106, Crisfield, MD 21817; tel 410/968-0900. Exit US 13 at Md 143; follow Md 143 to Somerset Ave, turn left; go 4 blocks. This simple, basic motel with clean, neat rooms is located in a residential neighborhood. **Rooms:** 40 rms and effic. CI noon/CO 11am. Nonsmoking rms avail. Efficiency units are in a newer section. **Amenities:** A/C, cable TV, refrig. No phone. Most units do not have phones. **Facilities:** 🗗 Picnic tables and barbecue grill. **Rates:** HS July–Aug $50–$70 S or D; from $65 effic. Extra person $5. Min stay spec evnts. Lower rates off-season. Higher rates for spec evnts/hols. Pking: Outdoor, free. No CC.

≣≣ **Somers Cove Motel**, 707 RR Norris Dr, PO Box 387, Crisfield, MD 21817; tel 410/968-1900 or toll free 800/827-6637. Take exit for Md 413 off US 13; turn left at 4th St, then right onto RR Norris Dr. A basic but good place to stay, this motel next to the municipal marina attracts boating and fishing enthusiasts. The exterior is ready for some refinishing. **Rooms:** 40 rms and effic. CI 11am/CO 11am. Rooms are standard and adequate, recently repainted. No pictures on the walls. **Amenities:** 🛏 A/C, cable TV w/movies. Some units w/terraces. Private balconies have some views of the marina. **Services:** 🚐 🛎 Car-rental desk. **Facilities:** 🗗 🚲 🖿 **Rates:** HS Mem Day–

Labor Day $65–$70 S or D; from $70 effic. Extra person $5. Min stay spec evnts. Lower rates off-season. MAP rates avail. Spec packages avail. Pking: Outdoor, free. Ltd CC.

Restaurants ⍩

Captain's Galley, 1021 W Main St, Crisfield; tel 410/968-1636. Exit US 13 at Md 413. **Seafood.** Large windows look onto the water from this paneled room with nautical bric-a-brac and wood-grained formica tables. Crabmeat, and especially some of the best crab cakes available anywhere, built this restaurant's reputation. The delicate seasoning is sold to take home. Discounts for seniors over 60. **FYI:** Reservations recommended. Children's menu. **Open:** HS Mem Day–Sept breakfast daily 8am–noon; lunch Sun–Thurs 11am–9pm, Fri–Sat 11am–10pm; dinner Sun–Thurs 11am–9pm, Fri–Sat 11am–10pm. Reduced hours off-season. Closed some hols. **Prices:** Main courses $6–$17. Ltd CC. 🖼 ♿

Watermen's Inn, 9th and Main Sts, Crisfield (Town Center); tel 410/968-2119. Exit US 13 at Md 413. **American/Seafood.** Works by local artists are displayed in this informal, country-style establishment. Noise from adjacent local bar does not intrude on dining room. Known for crab and shellfish, but beef and fish are featured, many in creative sauces. **FYI:** Reservations recommended. Children's menu. **Open:** HS Mem Day–Sept breakfast Tues–Sat 8–11am, Sun 8am–noon; lunch Tues–Sat 11:30am–10pm, Sun 11:30am–9pm; dinner Tues–Sat 5–10pm, Sun 5–9pm. Reduced hours off-season. Closed some hols. **Prices:** Main courses $8–$15. Maj CC. 💟

Attractions 🏛

J Millard Tawes Museum, 39th St on the Somers Cove Marina; tel 410/968-2501. Founded in 1982 to honor a Crisfield-born former governor of Maryland, this museum features exhibits that provide background about the history of the town and the development of the city's seafood industry. **Open:** May–Sept, daily 10am–4pm; Oct–Apr, Mon–Fri 10am–4pm. Closed some hols. $

Teackle Mansion, Mansion St; tel 410/651-3020. Built in 1801–1803 and patterned after a Scottish manor house, this was the residence of Littleton Dennis Teackle, an associate of Thomas Jefferson and one of the principal transoceanic shipping magnates of the 18th century. With 2 entrances, one fronting the Manokin River and one facing the town, the grand house measures nearly 200 feet in length and is symmetrically balanced throughout. The interior includes elaborate plaster ceilings, mirrored windows, a 7-foot fireplace and beehive oven, American Chippendale furniture, Della Robbia (fruit-designed) ceilings, a Tudor-Gothic pipe organ, an 1806 silk world map, and a 1712 family Bible. **Open:** Wed 1–3pm, Sat 11am–3pm, Sun 2–4pm. $

Smith Island, Tangier Sound; tel 410/968-2500. Visitors come to Smith Island, Maryland's only inhabited offshore island, to exerience another era. Smith Islanders are the direct descendants of British colonists who first settled the island in the early 1700s. Because of their isolation from the mainland, they speak to this day with a distinct accent, said to be a holdover of the Elizabethan-Cornwall accent. Today the island is a world apart—there are no sidewalks, beaches, convenience stores, boat rentals, movie theaters, liquor stores, bars, fast-food chains, boutiques, laundromats, or taxi cabs. Passenger ferries to the island depart year-round from Crisfield's city dock daily at noon. The ferry fee includes round-trip transportation, sightseeing on the island, and a family-style lunch at one of the local homes or guesthouses. $$$$

CUMBERLAND
Map page M-3, B5

Hotel 🛏

≣≣ Holiday Inn, 100 S George St, Cumberland, MD 21502; tel 301/724-8800 or toll free 800/HOLIDAY; fax 301/724-4001. Exit 43C off I-68. Convenient downtown location for this nicely maintained facility, 25 miles from skiing. **Rooms:** 130 rms and stes. CI 2pm/CO noon. Nonsmoking rms avail. Integrated decor. King or 2-bedded rooms, some with pull-out sofas; 1 room for the disabled available. **Amenities:** 🗄 ♨ A/C, cable TV, voice mail. **Services:** ✗ 🚗 🖂 🍴 🍷 Twice-daily maid svce. Friendly staff. Safe-deposit boxes available. **Facilities:** 🖿 🏊 ♿ 1 rst (*see also* "Restaurants" below), 1 bar (w/entertainment), lifeguard. Use of facilities at local YMCA. **Rates:** HS May–Sept $69 S or D; from $129 ste. Children under 18 stay free. Lower rates off-season. Higher rates for spec evnts/hols. Spec packages avail. Pking: Outdoor, free. Maj CC. Children eat free. Ski, golf, and bike packages. Weekly and monthly rates available.

Inn

≣≣≣ Inn at Walnut Bottom, 120 Greene St, Cumberland, MD 21502; tel 301/777-0003 or toll free 800/926-9718; fax 301/777-1629. Exit 43A off I-68. A gracious 19th-century inn in 2 small buildings near historic area of Cumberland and the Chesapeake and Ohio Canal towpath. Complete with oak bannister and floors, antiques, chandeliers, and comfy wicker-furniture parlor with games and parakeets. Nonsmoking throughout. **Rooms:** 12 rms and stes (4 w/shared bath). CI 3pm/ CO 11am. 4 rooms share bath. All uniquely decorated in antique and period reproduction furniture. Rooms accommodate 2 people in twin beds, a queen bed, or a full bed, and some have a day bed for a 3rd person, for extra charge; 2-family suites available. **Amenities:** ☎ ⏷ A/C, cable TV, stereo/tape player, bathrobes. **Services:** ✕ ⤵ Babysitting. Parlor offers tea and coffee. Full country-inn breakfast. Trays delivered for breakfast if guest is checking out before restaurant opens. Lunches packed on request. Dinners brought to room if necessary. **Facilities:** ⎄ 1 rst (*see also* "Restaurants" below), 1 bar, guest lounge. Communal refrigerator. Small gift shop sells local wares. **Rates (CP):** $65 S w/shared bath, $75 S or D w/private bath; from $95 ste. Extra person $10. Children under 5 stay free. Min stay wknds. Spec packages avail. Pking: Outdoor, free. Ltd CC. MAP available for groups. Special packages available for horseback riding, canoeing, bicycling, theater, golf.

Restaurants ⑪

Harrigan's, in Cumberland Holiday Inn, 100 S George St, Cumberland; tel 301/724-8800. Exit 43C off I-68. **American.** Quiet dining in low-ceilinged room decorated with framed paintings of the area and impressionist murals. Floor-to-ceiling windows along one side and white-banistered area add lightness to the solid mahogany chairs and tables. Steaks a specialty, and all-you-can-eat dinners available some nights. **FYI:** Reservations recommended. Band/comedy/piano/singer. Children's menu. **Open:** Daily 6am–10pm. **Prices:** Main courses $6.50–$16.95. Maj CC. 👫 ▽ ⅙

★ **Mason's Barn**, I-86 at exit 46, Cumberland; tel 301/ 722-6155. **American.** This family-operated restaurant is in an antiques-adorned barn with loft. A favorite of locals and travelers for 40 years, it serves up down-home country cooking the likes of burgers and sandwiches, "bread bowl" soups, and slow-roasted prime rib. **FYI:** Reservations recommended. Children's menu. **Open:** Breakfast Mon–Fri 7–11am, Sat–Sun 7am–1pm; lunch daily 11am–4pm; dinner Mon–Sat 4–10pm, Sun 1–10pm. Closed Dec 25. **Prices:** Main courses $7.95–$14.95. Maj CC. 👫

★ **Oxford House**, in the Inn at Walnut Bottom, 118 Greene St, Cumberland; tel 301/777-7101. Exit 43A off I-68. **New American/Continental/Seafood.** Located in a 19th-century inn, this dining room presents traditional country-inn food in an intimate low-ceilinged room with oak chairs and large tables. Specialties are fresh filleted salmon, crab, and homemade desserts. **FYI:** Reservations accepted. Children's menu. No smoking. **Open:**

Lunch daily 11am–3pm; dinner Mon–Sat 5–9:30pm. Closed some hols. **Prices:** Main courses $8.95–$16.95; PF dinner $19.95. Maj CC. ▮ ▽

★ **Pennywhistle's**, 25 N Centre St, Cumberland; tel 301/ 724-6626. Exit 43C off I-68. **Cafe.** Sparkling bright, this fresh American-style downtown cafe, with overhead grape arbor, has placed plexiglass between the tables, fostering privacy. Flowered vinyl tablecloths and cut flowers add to attractive atmosphere. Specialties include chicken salad and the "Pennywhistle" vegetable soup and salad. Vegetarian fare available. **FYI:** Reservations not accepted. Beer and wine only. **Open:** Mon–Sat 8am–5pm. Closed some hols. **Prices:** Lunch main courses $5–$6. Ltd CC. ⛴ ⅙

Attractions ▥

George Washington's Headquarters, Riverside Park, Greene St; tel 301/777-5905. The log cabin, believed to be the only remaining section of the original Fort Cumberland, was used by Washington as his official quarters during the French and Indian War. The cabin interior is not accessible, but there is a viewing window and a tape-recorded description activated by a push button. **Open:** Daily 24 hours. Free.

History House, 218 Washington St; tel 301/777-8678. This restored 18-room dwelling contains such antique furnishings as a Victorian courting couch and an 1840 square grand piano. Other features include an early 19th-century brick-walled garden and a basement kitchen with authentic cooking utensils, a fireplace, a coal stove, dishes, and pottery. **Open:** May–Oct, Tues–Sat 11am–4pm, Sun 1:30–4pm; Nov–Apr, Tues–Sat 11am–4pm. $

Emmanuel Episcopal Church, 16 Washington St; tel 410/ 777-3364. Built on the foundations of Fort Cumberland, where George Washington began his military career, this parish dates back to 1803. The church, which contains original Tiffany stained-glass windows and a scale model of Fort Cumberland, is open to the public only during services: Thursday at 10:30am and Sunday at 8 and 10am. Free.

Thrasher Carriage Museum, 19 Depot St; tel 301/689-3380. The museum displays an extensive collection of late 19th- and early 20th-century horse-drawn carriages: formal closed vehicles, milk wagons, open sleighs, funeral wagons, dogcarts, phaetons, and runabouts. **Open:** May–Sept, daily 11am–4pm; Oct–Apr, Sat–Sun noon–4pm. $

Toll Gate House, La Vale exit off Md 40A; tel 301/777-5905. Built in 1836, this historic toll gate house is the last of its kind in Maryland. When the country's first national road was built, federal funds were used to finance it; ownership was then turned over to the states, which built toll gate houses to collect tolls from travelers. **Open:** May, Sept–Oct, Sun 1:30–4:30pm; June–Aug, Fri–Sun 1:30–4:30pm. Free.

Western Maryland Scenic Railroad, 13 Canal St; tel 301/759-4400. A vintage steam train that makes a 34-mile round-trip excursion between Cumberland and Frostburg. The trip follows a scenic mountain valley route through the Cumberland Narrows, Helmstetter's Horseshoe Curve, various tunnels, many panoramic vistas, and a 1,300-foot elevation change between the two destinations. The trip takes 3 hours, including a 1½-hour layover in Frostburg for local sightseeing. **Open:** Call for schedule. $$$$

C&O Canal Boat, North Branch exit off Md 51; tel 301/729-3136. A full-scale boat modeled after the ones that used to move along the 184-mile canal between Georgetown and Cumberland. It features a captain's cabin with furnishings from the 1828–1924 canal era, a hay house where feed was stored for the mules, and an on-board mule stable. A restored log-cabin lock house is located nearby. **Open:** June–Aug, Sat–Sun 1–5pm. Free.

C&O Canal National Historical Park, Canal St; tel 301/722-8226. The C&O Canal came to this area in 1850, after 184 miles of ditch and towpath had been contructed. Today it is maintained by the National Park Service, and the canal has evolved as Cumberland's tourism focal point. Start a visit at the Canal Visitor Center, in the Western Maryland Station Center at track level, to see the background exhibits on the canal's history. There are remnants here of locks, dams, and lock houses. **Open:** Visitor center, Wed–Sat 10am–5pm, Tues and Sun 1–4pm. Free.

Rocky Gap State Park, Md 1; tel 301/777-2138. This park features a 243-acre lake with 3 full-service beaches. Popular activities include fishing, swimming, hiking, and biking. There's also a 278-unit campsite. **Open:** Daily sunrise–sunset. $

DEEP CREEK LAKE

Map page M-2, B4

See also McHenry, Oakland

Attractions

Wisp Four Seasons Resort, Marsh Hill Rd; tel 301/387-4911. Maryland's largest ski area features an elevation of 3,080 feet and a vertical rise of 610 feet. The 23 major ski runs on 80 acres of terrain offer night skiing as well as daytime runs. In summer, the resort welcomes visitors to its 18-hole championship golf course. **Open:** Daily year round; call for hours. $$$$

Deep Creek Lake State Park, State Park Rd; tel 301/387-5563. This recreation area features a 700-foot sandy beach on the shore of Maryland's largest freshwater lake. Guarded swimming area, boating, picnicking, and camping. **Open:** Apr–Oct, daily sunrise to sunset. $

EASTON

Map page M-3, C7

Hotel 🏨

📗📗📗📗 **The Tidewater Inn**, 101 E Dover St, at Harrison St, Easton, MD 21601; tel 410/822-1300 or toll free 800/237-8775; fax 410/820-8847. Exit US 50 at Dover St. This lovely historic building has been meticulously renovated and furnished with antique reproductions. It is beautifully maintained. One-year advance reservations necessary for Waterfowl Festival. **Rooms:** 114 rms and stes. CI 3pm/CO noon. Express checkout avail. Nonsmoking rms avail. Rooms are spacious and charming, with fine furnishings. Since building is historic, bathrooms are small. **Amenities:** 🛁 🔅 🎙 A/C, cable TV w/movies, shoe polisher. **Services:** ✕ 🆅🅿 🚗 🛎 🖐 🥂 Babysitting. Complimentary van to golf, boating, and nearby towns of Oxford and St Michaels. Staff is very accommodating. **Facilities:** 🛋 🌳 🖳 ⅙ 2 rsts, 1 bar (w/entertainment), washer/dryer. Attractive courtyard pool. Kennel in basement. Nearby fitness club. **Rates:** HS Apr–July/Sept–Nov $94–$150 S; $104–$160 D; from $150 ctge/villa. Extra person $10. Children under 16 stay free. Min stay spec evnts. Lower rates off-season. Higher rates for spec evnts/hols. AP and MAP rates avail. Spec packages avail. Pking: Outdoor, free. Maj CC.

Motel

📗📗 **Days Inn**, 7018 Ocean Gateway (US 50), PO Box 968, Easton, MD 21601; tel 410/822-4600 or toll free 800/329-7466; fax 410/820-9723. This older motel has been reasonably well maintained and is neat and clean inside and out. Reserve a year in advance for fall Waterfowl Festival. **Rooms:** 80 rms and stes. CI 3pm/CO 11am. Express checkout avail. Nonsmoking rms avail. **Amenities:** 🛁 🎙 A/C, cable TV. 2 suites have refrigerators. Plans to install modem lines in 1995. **Services:** 🛎 🖐 🥂 **Facilities:** 🛋 🌳 ⅙ Games rm. **Rates (CP):** HS Apr–Oct $45–$73 S; $53–$77 D; from $73 ste. Extra person $4–$5. Children under 16 stay free. Min stay spec evnts. Lower rates off-season. Higher rates for spec evnts/hols. Pking: Outdoor, free. Maj CC.

Restaurants ▯❙▯

Legal Spirits, 42 E Dover St, at Harrison St, Easton; tel 410/820-0033. Exit US 50 at Dover St. **New American/Seafood.** Situated in a historic building adjacent to the restored Avalon Theater, an art deco landmark, this tasteful, comfortable, and popular restaurant is attractively done in appropriate style, with 1930s gangster memorabilia on the walls of 1 room and a stained-glass window in the other. A wide range of American dishes are done with a light touch. **FYI:** Reservations recommended. Children's menu. **Open:** Lunch Mon–Sat 11:30am–5pm; dinner Mon–Thurs 5–10pm, Fri–Sat 5–11pm. Closed some hols. **Prices:** Main courses $9–$19. Maj CC. ▮ ▯ �.

Peach Blossoms, 14 N Washington St, Easton; tel 410/822-5220. Exit US 50 at Dover St; turn right onto Washington St. Across from courthouse. **New American.** Contemporary art and mirrors give an appearance of space to this long and narrow but bright modern dining room. Seafood and meats in the new American style with interesting sauces dominate a menu that varies throughout the year. **FYI:** Reservations recommended. Children's menu. No smoking. **Open:** Breakfast Sun 8–11am; lunch Wed–Sat 11:30am–2pm; dinner Wed–Sat 6–9pm; brunch Sun 11am–1:30pm. Closed some hols. **Prices:** Main courses $16–$20. Ltd CC. ♥ ᵴ.

Attractions ▣

Historical Society of Talbot County, 25 S Washington St; tel 410/822-0773. This society maintains 8 historic buildings, 5 of which are open to the public. A focal point of the historic district, the buildings include an 1850s commercial building, the headquarters of the society and site of a modern museum with changing exhibits; the 1795 Joseph Neall House and the 1810 James Neall House, both restored homes of Quaker cabinetmaker brothers; the partially restored 1670 Wenlocke Christison House, known locally as "The Ending of Controversie" House; and the 1810 Tharpe House, which now serves as a museum shop and library. The buildings surround a federal-style garden, also open to visitors. **Open:** Tues–Sat 10am–4pm, Sun 1–4pm. $

Third Haven Friends Meeting House, 405 S Washington St; tel 410/822-0293. Believed to be the oldest frame building dedicated to religious meetings in the United States and the oldest known building in Maryland, the pine-and-oak structure has been used continuously since the late 17th century. **Open:** Daily 9am–5pm. Free.

Academy of the Arts, 106 South St; tel 410/822-0455 or 822-ARTS (recorded info). A regional arts center with changing exhibits about the area and the entire Eastern Shore. Concerts are also periodically staged here. **Open:** Mon–Sat 10am–4pm, Wed 10am–9pm. Free.

Orrell's Biscuits, 14124 Old Wye Mill Rd; tel 410/822-2065. A family enterprise producing a unique biscuit that has been a tradition for over 300 years. In their kitchen-turned-bakery, the Orrell family produces hundreds of biscuits every day using an original recipe that lacks baking powder or soda. The Orrells and their staff literally "beat" these doughy treats, and then shape each one by hand into the size of a walnut, producing a crusty biscuit with a soft center. Visitors are welcome to watch the baking process, sample the results, and purchase at the source. **Open:** Call ahead for times. Free.

Wye Mill, Md 662 off Md 50; tel 410/827-6909. This mill, dating from the 17th century, is the earliest industrial-commercial building in continuous use in the state. Visitors today can see the mill in operation and sample some of the flour, whole wheat, or cornmeal.

Nearby is the **Wye Oak**, the largest white oak in the United States and Maryland's official state tree. It is 37 feet in circumference, 95 feet high, and over 400 years old. **Open:** Apr–Dec, Sat–Sun 11am–4pm, and by appointment. $

ELLICOTT CITY

Map page M-3, B6

Hotel ▣

≣≣≣ **Turf Valley Hotel & Country Club**, 2700 Turf Valley Rd, Ellicott City, MD 21042; tel 410/465-1500 or toll free 800/666-TURF; fax 410/465-8280. 15 mi W of Baltimore. exit 83 off I-70. Said to be one of the finest golf resorts on the East Coast, this modern hotel is set on a lovely course. In fine condition, the property is continually being improved and enlarged. Lovely landscaping throughout. **Rooms:** 173 rms and stes. CI 3pm/CO noon. Nonsmoking rms avail. Pretty decor and large sliding doors give nice views of rolling hills. **Amenities:** ▯ ᵴ A/C, cable TV w/movies. All units w/terraces. **Services:** ✕ ▯ ▤ ▨ ↵ Car-rental desk, babysitting. Informal but courteous staff. **Facilities:** ▯ ▸₅₄ ▨₂ ▨₂ ▯ ▯ ▯ ᵴ 2 rsts, 3 bars (2 w/entertainment), lifeguard, lawn games. Lighted driving range and putting green. Large pool and lounging area. Softball, volleyball, basketball. **Rates:** HS Apr–Nov $85–$95 S or D; from $105 ste. Extra person $10. Children under 12 stay free. Lower rates off-season. MAP rates avail. Spec packages avail. Pkng: Outdoor, free. Maj CC.

Restaurants 🍴

★ **Crab Shanty**, 3410 Plumtree Dr, Ellicott City; tel 410/465-9660. Exit I-70 at US 29 S; go 1 mile to US 40, turn right. **Regional American/Seafood.** Mixed in with a Chesapeake Bay motif in this elegant but casual crab house are antique leaded-glass windows, wooden spindles, and carved brackets from Victorian homes; solid oak beams from an old barn; and the sled in which Bing Crosby rode in the movie *White Christmas*. Seafood specialties are cooked to order using fresh ingredients, in both traditional Maryland and French styles. Pianist plays Wednesday to Saturday evenings. Carryout available. **FYI:** Reservations not accepted. Piano. Children's menu. Dress code. **Open:** Lunch Mon–Fri 11:30am–2:30pm; dinner Mon–Thurs 5–10pm, Fri–Sat 5–11pm, Sun 2–9pm. Closed some hols. **Prices:** Main courses $8.75–$23.50. Maj CC. 🍷 💑 &

Il Giardino Ristorante, in Golden Triangle Shopping Center, 8809 Baltimore Nat'l Pike, Ellicott City; tel 410/461-1122. Follow I-70 to US 29 S to US 40 E. **Italian.** Large greenhouse window on one end sets the tone for this dining room decorated in pale greens with white wainscoting. Aroma greets guests, announces traditional and reasonably priced Italian fare, with extensive selection of salads. Pizzas available to carry out. **FYI:** Reservations recommended. Children's menu. Dress code. **Open:** Mon–Thurs 5–10pm, Fri–Sat 5–11pm, Sun 4–9pm. Closed some hols. **Prices:** Main courses $7.50–$18. Maj CC. 💑

Tersiguel's French-Country Restaurant, 8293 Main St, Ellicott City; tel 410/464-4004. Follow US 29 to US 40 E; turn right at light, then left onto Main St. **French.** A historic house in a historic town. Dining rooms in this highly regarded establishment are furnished simply and with photos and mementos of Brittany. A wide range of fish, shellfish, grilled meats, and French specialties. Extensive wine list includes interesting regional country choices. Prix-fixe specials for both lunch and dinner. **FYI:** Reservations recommended. Dress code. **Open:** Lunch daily 11:30am–2:30pm; dinner Sun–Thurs 5–9pm, Fri–Sat 5–10pm. Closed some hols. **Prices:** Main courses $15–$26; PF dinner $28. Maj CC. ♥ 🍴

Attraction 🏛

B&O Railroad Museum, 2711 Maryland Ave; tel 410/461-1944. This is where the first terminus of the first railroad in the United States was located. Today it is a registered National Historic Landmark and houses a full-size B&O caboose, railroad displays, and other memorabilia. **Open:** Mon and Wed–Sat 11am–4pm, Sun noon–5pm. $

FREDERICK
Map page M-3, B6

Hotels 🏨

🏨🏨🏨 **Hampton Inn**, 5311 Buckeystown Pike, Frederick, MD 21701; tel 301/698-2500 or toll free 800/426-7866; fax 301/695-8735. Exit 31B off I-270. A step up from the usual chain-hotel look. Large lobby with nice touches: aquarium, free popcorn, tables with chairs. An outdoor pavilion with a small pond and arched bridge. **Rooms:** 160 rms, stes, and effic. CI 3pm/CO noon. Nonsmoking rms avail. Hospitality suites available. **Amenities:** 📺 🛁 A/C, cable TV w/movies. Some units w/Jacuzzis. 4 rooms have phones in bathroom. **Services:** 🛎 🍽 🐾 Children's program. Free local calls. **Facilities:** 🏋 🍸 🏊 & 1 rst, 1 bar, lifeguard. Catch-and-release fishing in pond. Bar just off lobby is separately owned and operated. Fitness center has stair-stepper, Universal weights. **Rates (CP):** $57–$65 S or D; from $100 ste; from $75 effic. Children under 18 stay free. Pking: Outdoor, free. Maj CC.

🏨🏨🏨 **Holiday Inn**, 5400 Holiday Drive, Frederick, MD 21701; tel 301/694-7500 or toll free 800/HOLIDAY; fax 301/694-0589. Exit 31A off I-70. A nicely decorated facility near shopping mall and restaurants. **Rooms:** 155 rms and stes. CI 3pm/CO 11am. Express checkout avail. Nonsmoking rms avail. Most rooms recently redone. They have rich wood furnishings, which set them apart from the standard hotel room. Four suites plus 13 King Executives with sitting areas; 6 rooms for the disabled. **Amenities:** 📺 🛁 A/C, cable TV w/movies. Some units w/terraces. 40 rooms have refrigerators; 40 have microwaves. King Executives have VCRs, coffeemakers. **Services:** ✕ 🚗 🛎 🍽 🐾 Children's program, babysitting. **Facilities:** 🏋 🎾 🏊 🍸 🏊 & 1 rst, 1 bar (w/entertainment), lifeguard, lawn games, spa, sauna, whirlpool, playground, washer/dryer. Holidome has pool with skylight and umbrella tables, greenery, and sauna. Miniature golf. Courtyard restaurant and entertainment in lounge/bar 4 nights a week. **Rates:** HS Apr–Nov 1 $75 S; $85 D; from $215 ste. Extra person $10. Children under 19 stay free. Lower rates off-season. Higher rates for spec evnts/hols. Spec packages avail. Pking: Outdoor, free. Maj CC. $15 extra for King Executives. Special weekend rates.

Motel

🏨🏨 **Comfort Inn**, 420 Prospect Blvd, Frederick, MD 21701; tel 301/695-6200 or toll free 800/221-2222; fax 301/695-7895. Jefferson St exit off US 15 N or off I-270. Clean and attractive, with added practical touches. It's far enough off the highway to feel suburban while still being convenient to the interstate.

Within walking distance of shopping centers, and a few miles from the main square of Frederick and restaurants. **Rooms:** 117 rms. CI 3pm/CO noon. Nonsmoking rms avail. **Amenities:** 🛏 A/C, cable TV w/movies. Some units w/terraces. **Services:** ✗ 🖭 🕹 ⬦ 24-hour coffee in lobby. Passes for Charles Town, West Virginia, racetrack (25 miles). **Facilities:** 🔓 ⊌ ⊡ ⬜ & 1 rst, washer/dryer. Room with exercise equipment. Laundry room. **Rates (CP):** $49 S; $58 D. Extra person $5. Children under 18 stay free. Pking: Outdoor, free. Maj CC.

Restaurants 🍴

Ⓢ ✳ **Brown Pelican**, 5 E Church St, Frederick (Historic District); tel 301/695-5833. Exit I-70 at exit 54, or I-270 at exit 31A. **Continental/Seafood.** Just off the main square in the historic district, the Brown Pelican is in the basement of a 1700s-era building. Dark-beamed ceiling, comfortably wide bar, and waterfowl paintings. Voted best restaurant in Frederick 3 years running by local newspaper and magazine. Best picks are catch of the day, veal dishes. **FYI:** Reservations recommended. **Open:** Lunch Mon–Fri 11:30am–3pm; dinner Mon–Thurs 5–9:30pm, Fri–Sun 5–10pm. Closed some hols. **Prices:** Main courses $12–$17. Maj CC. ❤ 🏛

✳ **The Province Restaurant**, 129 N Market St, Frederick (Historic District); tel 301/663-1441. Exit 31 off I-270. **American.** This local favorite in the historic district has a distinctive personality. Handmade cane chairs from New England, antique pieces, brick walls decorated with locally stitched quilts, and a view of the herb garden out back create an atmosphere that is both historic and folksy. Try the desserts. The prix-fixe menu is available only Tuesday to Thursday. **FYI:** Reservations recommended. **Open:** Lunch Mon–Fri 11:30am–3pm, Sat 11:30am–3pm, Sun 11am–2:30pm; dinner Tues–Thurs 5:30–9pm, Fri–Sat 5:30–10pm, Sun 4–8pm; brunch Sat 11:30am–3pm, Sun 11am–2:30pm. Closed some hols. **Prices:** Main courses $13–$18; PF dinner $15–$16. Maj CC. ❤ 🏛

The Province Too, 12 E Patrick St, Frederick (Historic District); tel 301/663-3315. **Deli/Vegetarian.** Squeaky wood floors, round oak table with soda fountain chairs, and pastry chefs creating before guests' eyes all make for a fun little spot for specialty desserts, homemade soups, and some 20 sandwiches, including vegetarian versions. One of the few downtown restaurants open for breakfast on Sundays. **FYI:** Reservations not accepted. No liquor license. **Open:** Mon–Fri 7am–5pm, Sat 9am–4pm, Sun 8am–3pm. Closed some hols. **Prices:** Lunch main courses $3.50–$5. Ltd CC. 🖭 &

✳ **Red Horse Restaurant**, 966 W Patrick St, Frederick; tel 301/663-3030. Located at jct US 40/15. **Seafood/Steak.** Busy

and crowded, this popular restaurant presents a western theme, with wagon-wheel lights, fireplace, beamed barn ceilings, and large-portion steaks. Nightly entertainment in downstairs bar, including dance area. **FYI:** Reservations recommended. Country music/dancing. Children's menu. Dress code. **Open:** Lunch Mon–Fri 11:30am–3pm; dinner Mon–Sat 4:30–10:30pm, Sun 4–9pm. Closed some hols. **Prices:** Main courses $13.95–$28.95. Maj CC. ❤ 🖾 ⬇ &

♟ **Tauraso's**, in Everdy Square, 6 E St, Frederick; tel 301/663-6600. Exit I-270 at Patrick St. **Regional American/Italian/Seafood.** Located in the artistic area of Frederick in what was once called Shab Row, the restaurant boasts a unique decor that includes open ceilings with exposed steam pipes painted bright red and a large brick-walled, 2-level bar area sporting the same red pipes above. The dining room itself grows elegant, thanks to black marble tables, chandelier lighting, and a view of the patio dining area. Local reputation for fine food, especially seafood. **FYI:** Reservations recommended. **Open:** Sun–Thurs 11am–10pm, Fri–Sat 11am–11pm. Closed some hols. **Prices:** Main courses $12.95–$23.95. Maj CC. ❤ 🍽 &

Attractions 💼

Antietam Battlefield, Md 65; tel 410/447-5124. The site of the single bloodiest day of the Civil War. More than 23,000 men were killed or wounded here when Union forces met and stopped the first southern invasion of the North on September 17, 1862. A visitor center at the battlefield has historical exhibits and shows an 18-minute audiovisual program every half-hour. **Open:** Daily 8:30am–5pm. Closed some hols. $

Frederick County Historical Society Museum, 24 E Church St; tel 302/663-1188. Exhibits here focus on local historical figures, such as Roger B Taney, chief justice of the US Supreme Court and author of the infamous *Dred Scott* decision, and Francis Scott Key, author of "The Star-Spangled Banner." There is also a genealogical library and a formal garden on the premises. **Open:** Mon–Sat 10am–4pm, Sun 1–4pm. $

Schifferstadt, 1110 Rosemont Ave; tel 301/663-3885. Built in 1756, this is the oldest standing house in Frederick as well as one of America's finest examples of German colonial architecture. Unusual original features include an enclosed staircase, a vaulted cellar and chimney, and a 5-plate cast-iron stove. **Open:** Tues–Sat 10am–4pm, Sun noon–4pm. Closed some hols. $

National Shrine of St Elizabeth Ann Seton, 333 S Seton Ave; tel 301/447-6606. The home of the United States' first canonized saint. The complex includes the Stone House, where Mother Seton established her religious community in 1809, and the

White House, where she began the first parochial school in America. **Open:** Daily 10am–5pm. Closed Mon Nov–Apr; some hols. Free.

Lily Pons Water Garden, 6800 Lilypons Rd; tel 301/874-5133. Named after famed opera singer Lily Pons, who visited here in 1936, the site is one of the largest suppliers of ornamental fish and aquatic plants in the world and houses acres of water lilies and goldfish ponds. The lilies are at their blooming peak in July. **Open:** Mar–Oct, daily 10am–5pm; Nov–Feb, Mon–Sat 10am–4:30pm. Closed Easter. Free.

Rose Hill Manor Children's Museum, 1611 N Market St; tel 301/694-1646. This "living history" museum, in a 1790s Georgian mansion that was the home of Maryland's first governor, is designed to let children experience a little early American life: combing unspun wool, throwing a shuttle on the loom, and adding a few stitches to a quilt. Other activities include soap making, candle dipping, quilting bees, barn raising, and apple-butter boiling. Costumed guides conduct walking tours. **Open:** Apr–Oct, Mon–Sat 10am–4pm, Sun 1–4pm; Mar, Nov, Dec, weekends only. $

Crystal Grottoes Caverns, Md 34; tel 301/432-6336. Located 15 miles northwest of Frederick near Boonsboro. Maryland's only commercial underground caverns, these formations were created by millions of years of chemical and mineral action beneath the earth's surface. Today, nature's work can be seen in the corridors of limestone lined with jeweled stalactites and stalagmites. Guided tours are given. **Open:** Mar–Nov, daily 9am–6pm; Dec–Feb, Sat–Sun 11am–5pm. $$$

Barbara Fritchie House and Museum, 154 W Patrick St; tel 301/698-0630. At the age of 95, Barbara Fritchie bravely waved the Stars and Stripes in the path of Confederate soldiers and was immortalized in a poem by John Greenleaf Whittier as the "bravest of all in Frederick-town." A visit to the house includes a video presentation of her life and times; a collection of mementos including quilts and linens; and period clothing and furniture. **Open:** Apr–Sept, Mon and Thurs–Sat 10am–4pm, Sun 1–4pm; Oct–Nov, Sat 10am–4pm, Sun 1–4pm. $

FROSTBURG

Map page M-3, B5

Hotels 🛏

■≡ **Comfort Inn**, Md 36 N at Frostburg Industrial Park, Frostburg, MD 21532; tel 301/689-2050 or toll free 800/221-2222; fax 301/689-2050. Exit 34 off I-68. A skylight and small atrium area in lobby add to the mood at this sparkling-clean facility. **Rooms:** 100 rms and stes. CI 4pm/CO 11am. Nonsmoking rms avail. Integrated decor. 8 king rooms, 2 honeymoon suites, 2 family suites. **Amenities:** 🛏 A/C, cable TV. Some units w/terraces, some w/Jacuzzis. Microwaves available. **Services:** 🍴 🛎 Coffee/tea bar area in lobby 24 hours. Continental breakfast in upper-level lobby area with tables and chairs. **Facilities:** 🧍 🖥 🏊 ⚐ Landscaped outdoor seating area with stone picnic tables. Cooperative arrangement with nearby country club for use of pool, golf course. **Rates (CP):** HS May–Oct $61 S or D; from $73 ste. Extra person $5. Children under 18 stay free. Lower rates off-season. Higher rates for spec evnts/hols. Pking: Outdoor, free. Maj CC.

■≡ **Failinger's Hotel Gunter**, 11 W Main St, Frostburg, MD 21532; tel 301/689-6511. Exit 34 off I-68. Aptly described as offering turn-of-the-century charm, this fine old downtown hotel (circa 1896) has been lovingly restored. A massive oak stairway greets guests, hallways display old gilt-framed photos and lantern wall sconces, and the huge lobby with ornate candelabra is comfortable for residents of the facility as well as guests. Family-owned and -operated. **Rooms:** 17 rms. CI 1pm/CO 11am. Charming, individually decorated rooms have nice touches, such as canopy beds, antique vanity sitting table, claw-foot tub. Floral splashes on curtains and bedspreads, or lighter feel courtesy of filmy white curtains and canopies. **Amenities:** 🛏 A/C, cable TV w/movies. Refrigerator and microwave available. **Services:** 🍴 🛎 **Facilities:** 🧍 🖥 2 bars (1 w/entertainment). Museum in basement includes replica of an underground coal mine, the original jail where prisoners were once kept when being transported over the Old Trail Rd. **Rates (CP):** $45 S; $50–$55 D. Extra person $5. Children under 15 stay free. Pking: Outdoor, free. Maj CC. Long-term rates available.

Restaurants 🍴

♦ **Au Petit Paris Restaurant Français**, 86 E Main St, Frostburg; tel 301/689-8946. Exit 34 off I-68. **French.** The rich and colorful ambience of Paris prevails, starting with a Montmartre-style alleyway leading to the restaurant. Of 3 dining areas, 1 is 100 years old. Throughout are unique and interesting accents, such as the wall-size terra-cotta wine rack, kiosk replica, chandeliers, and old lace curtains. Lounge area has plush chairs and working fireplace. This family-owned and -operated restaurant offers a variety of fine French dishes, with specialties of seafood, beef, and veal. **FYI:** Reservations recommended. Dress code. **Open:** Daily 6–9:30pm. Closed some hols. **Prices:** Main courses $10.50–$27.95. Maj CC. ♥ ⚐

★ **Giuseppe's**, 11 Bowery St, Frostburg; tel 301/689-2220. Exit 34 off I-68. **Italian/Seafood/Steak.** This intimate Italian restaurant in a restored 1890s building offers casual dining on 2 levels, with a bar on each floor. Favorites include veal dishes and cappellini with a hearty marinara sauce. **FYI:** Reservations accepted. Children's menu. **Open:** Sun 3–9pm, Mon–Thurs 4:30–11pm, Fri–Sat 3–11pm. Closed some hols. **Prices:** Main courses $6.95–$15.95. Maj CC. ▣

GAITHERSBURG

Map page M-3, B6 (N of Rockville)

Hotels ▣

▤▤ **Comfort Inn at Shady Grove**, 16216 Frederick Rd, Gaithersburg, MD 20877; tel 301/330-0023 or toll free 800/228-5150; fax 301/258-1950. Exit 8 off I-270. A modern, clean hotel convenient to restaurants, shops, and metro station. **Rooms:** 127 rms. Exec-level rms avail. CI 2:30pm/CO 11am. Nonsmoking rms avail. Simple hotel-style rooms have neutral decor. **Amenities:** ▣ ▣ ▣ A/C, cable TV, shoe polisher. **Services:** ▣ ▣ ▣ ▣ Complimentary shuttle to metro station and nearby businesses, shops. Some local restaurants will deliver to hotel. Manager's reception weekly. **Facilities:** ▣ ▣ ▣ ▣ Lifeguard, washer/dryer. Two restaurants within walking distance give discounts. **Rates (CP):** HS spring–fall $59 S; $65 D. Extra person $6. Children under 18 stay free. Lower rates off-season. Higher rates for spec evnts/hols. Spec packages avail. Pking: Outdoor, free. Maj CC.

▤▤▤ **Courtyard by Marriott**, 805 Russell Ave, Gaithersburg, MD 20879; tel 301/670-0008 or toll free 800/336-6880; fax 301/948-4538. Exit I-270 at Md 124 E; follow Montgomery Village Ave to Russell Ave, turn left. Member of a chain of comfortable hotels catering to business travelers. Surrounded by landscaped office park. **Rooms:** 203 rms and stes. CI 3pm/CO 1pm. Express checkout avail. Nonsmoking rms avail. Decorated in pastels. King-bed rooms have sofas. **Amenities:** ▣ ▣ ▣ A/C, cable TV w/movies. 1 unit w/minibar. All rooms have hot-water taps for tea and instant coffee. Phones have on-line service with information about tourist attractions, items of local interest, stock quotes, business news, reservations service. **Services:** ▣ ▣ ▣ **Facilities:** ▣ ▣ ▣ ▣ 1 rst, 1 bar, lifeguard, sauna, whirlpool, washer/dryer. Nicely landscaped outdoor pool. Restaurant serves breakfast and dinner only. **Rates:** $59–$87 S or D; from $250 ste. Extra person $5–$10. Children under 12 stay free. Higher rates for spec evnts/hols. Spec packages avail. Pking: Outdoor, free. Maj CC.

▤▤▤ **Gaithersburg Hilton**, 620 Perry Pkwy, Gaithersburg, MD 20877; tel 301/977-8900 or toll free 800/599-5111; fax 301/869-8597. Exit I-270 at MD 124 E; turn right on Md 355, then right onto Perry Pkwy. This modern hotel has an attractive lobby with marble floors, indirect lighting, comfortable hunter-green furniture, and large floral arrangements. **Rooms:** 301 rms and stes. Exec-level rms avail. CI 3pm/CO noon. Express checkout avail. Nonsmoking rms avail. Handsome decor includes colorful spreads, nice artwork. Furniture a bit worn. **Amenities:** ▣ ▣ A/C, cable TV w/movies. Some units w/terraces. Iron and board in all rooms. **Services:** ▣ ▣ ▣ ▣ ▣ Car-rental desk, babysitting. **Facilities:** ▣ ▣ ▣ ▣ 1 rst, 1 bar, lifeguard, games rm, spa, sauna, steam rm, whirlpool, washer/dryer. Quiet, cozy restaurant with polo theme has attractive green-burgundy-navy blue color scheme, wing chairs, booths, fireplace. Attractive indoor-outdoor pool. **Rates:** $55–$105 S or D; from $250 ste. Children under 18 stay free. Higher rates for spec evnts/hols. Spec packages avail. Pking: Outdoor, free. Maj CC.

▤▤ **Holiday Inn**, 2 Montgomery Village Ave, Gaithersburg, MD 20879; tel 301/948-8900 or toll free 800/465-4329; fax 301/258-1940. Exit 11 off I-270. Quiet suburban hotel convenient to shopping mall. **Rooms:** 304 rms and stes. CI 3pm/CO 1pm. Nonsmoking rms avail. All rooms recently refurbished. **Amenities:** ▣ ▣ ▣ A/C, cable TV w/movies. Some units w/minibars, some w/terraces. **Services:** ▣ ▣ ▣ ▣ Car-rental desk. **Facilities:** ▣ ▣ ▣ ▣ 1 rst, 1 bar (w/entertainment), lifeguard, games rm, spa, whirlpool, washer/dryer. Nicely done indoor pool opens to outdoor table area with restaurant and bar service. **Rates:** HS Mar–June/Sept–Nov 15 $65–$85 S or D; from $175 ste. Children under 19 stay free. Lower rates off-season. Higher rates for spec evnts/hols. Spec packages avail. Pking: Indoor/outdoor, free. Maj CC.

Motel

▤ **Econo Lodge**, 18715 N Frederick Ave, Gaithersburg, MD 20879; tel 301/963-3840 or toll free 800/424-4777; fax 301/948-7443. Exit 11A off I-270 S. Set at the crest of a high hill, this chalet-style hotel has dark peaked wooden eaves and shutters, beamed lobby with attractive sitting area. A few miles from metro station. **Rooms:** 400 rms. CI 3pm/CO noon. Nonsmoking rms avail. Blond wood furniture, pastel paintings and spreads brighten basic rooms. Some minor housekeeping problems, but rooms are clean. **Amenities:** ▣ A/C, cable TV w/movies. Some rooms have clock radios. **Services:** ▣ ▣ ▣ Free local calls. Games available at front desk. **Facilities:** ▣ ▣ Washer/dryer. Snack bar with 24-hour coffee and tea. **Rates:** HS May–Sept $45–$51 S or D. Extra person $6. Children under 12 stay free. Lower rates off-season. Higher rates for spec evnts/hols. Pking: Outdoor, free. Maj CC.

Restaurants 🍴

Hunan Palace, 9011 Gaither Rd, Gaithersburg; tel 301/977-8600. Exit 8 off I-270. Follow Shady Grove Rd east to Gaither Rd, turn left. **Chinese.** Blond wood tables and booths, Oriental paintings make for simple but pleasing decor. More than 100 main courses feature Taiwanese cooking, a bit spicier than Cantonese. One of the best bargains in area. **FYI:** Reservations not accepted. **Open:** Daily 11:30am–10pm. **Prices:** Main courses $8.95–$20. Maj CC.

Ichiban, 637 N Frederick Ave, Gaithersburg; tel 301/670-0560. Exit 11 off I-270N. Go north on Frederick Ave. **Japanese/Korean.** Small rock-garden entry with bonsai trees, lattice-work windows, wood booths and tables, and subdued lighting from paper lanterns provide Oriental setting for a mix of Japanese and Korean cuisines. Some dishes cooked at table. Separate sushi bar. Karaoke entertainment. **FYI:** Reservations accepted. **Open:** Mon–Thurs 11:30am–10pm, Fri–Sat 11:30am–11pm, Sun 12:30–10pm. **Prices:** Main courses $8.95–$16. Maj CC. ⑤

Thai Sa-Mai, 8369 Snouffer School Rd, Gaithersburg; tel 301/963-1800. Exit 8 off I-270. **Thai.** Only 12 tables in this intimate dining room done in gray and mauve. Fresh rose on each formica-top table with soda fountain–style chairs. Paintings of Thailand, carved temple peaks in bar area set tone for noodle dishes and southern Thai curries. Each dish prepared individually. Extensive menu features many vegetarian dishes. **FYI:** Reservations accepted. Beer and wine only. **Open:** Tues–Thurs 11am–9:30pm, Fri 11am–10:30pm, Sat 4–10:30pm, Sun 5–9pm. **Prices:** Main courses $6.75–$8.25. Ltd CC.

GLEN BURNIE

Map page M-3, B7 (S of Baltimore)

Motel 🏨

≣≣ **Holiday Inn Glen Burnie South**, 6600 Ritchie Hwy, Glen Burnie, MD 21061 (Baltimore-Washington Int'l Airport); tel 410/761-8300 or toll free 800/465-4329; fax 410/760-4966. 6 mi S of Baltimore. exit 3B off I-695. Go south on Ritchie Hwy. An older motel, this property has been maintained well. Sits across street from Maryland Motor Vehicles Administration headquarters. Close to several shopping malls. **Rooms:** 100 rms. CI 3pm/CO noon. Nonsmoking rms avail. **Amenities:** 🎧 ❄ A/C, cable TV w/movies. **Services:** ✕ ⊠ ⇦ ⇦ **Facilities:** 🛁 🖾₅₀ ⑤ 1 rst, 1 bar, lifeguard. Free access to Bally's Health Spa nearby. **Rates:** HS Apr–Oct $69 S or D. Extra person $10. Children

under 18 stay free. Lower rates off-season. Higher rates for spec evnts/hols. MAP rates avail. Spec packages avail. Pking: Outdoor, free. Maj CC. Children eat free.

GRANTSVILLE

Map page M-2, B4 (W of Cumberland)

Restaurant 🍴

★ **Penn Alps Restaurant and Craft Shop**, US Alt 40, Grantsville; tel 301/895-5985. Exit 22 off I-68W. **Regional American.** Housed in the last remaining log tavern on the first National Rd, this restaurant is part of the Spruce Forest Artisan Village. Some buildings date to the Revolutionary War era, and festivals and special events are dedicated to showcasing the work of some 2,000 artisans. The restaurant offers a gift shop in its open-beamed lobby, complete with rocking chairs and old lantern lights. Oak tables and floor, country curtains add to the sense of place. Alpine Room has floor-to-ceiling windows and plank walls. Another small dining area is in the 1813 Old Stagecoach Building. Specialties: unique breads, Pennsylvania Dutch fries, Mennonite sausage, and dried corn. **FYI:** Reservations accepted. Children's menu. No liquor license. No smoking. **Open:** HS Mem Day–Oct Mon–Sat 7am–8pm, Sun 7am–3pm. Reduced hours off-season. Closed some hols. **Prices:** Main courses $8–$14. Ltd CC. 🍴 ⑤

Attraction 📷

Yoder's Country Market, Md 669; tel 301/895-5148. Started as a Mennonite family farm enterprise in 1932, this has grown from a 1-room butcher shop to an extensive specialty market offering Amish, Mennonite, and Pennsylvania Dutch food and craft items. **Open:** Mon–Sat 8am–6pm. Free.

GRASONVILLE

Map page M-3, B7 (E of Annapolis)

See also **Stevensville**

Motels 🏨

≣≣≣ **Comfort Inn Kent Narrows**, 3101 Main St, Grasonville, MD 21638; tel 410/827-6767 or toll free 800/828-3361; fax 410/827-8626. Exit 42 off US 50/301. This handsome new motel sits at Kent Narrows, a popular and growing boating center, where work and pleasure craft seem to be everywhere. Outlet shopping nearby. **Rooms:** 87 rms, stes, and effic. CI 3pm/CO 11am. Nonsmoking rms avail. Some rooms have water views; others face the highway. **Amenities:** 🛏 📞 🎢 A/C, cable TV w/movies, refrig. Some units w/Jacuzzis. Microwaves in each unit. **Services:** 🧺 🍽 Large continental breakfast. **Facilities:** 🏋 🍴 🎿 ♿ Lawn games, sauna, whirlpool, washer/dryer. Restaurants and bars are adjacent. Nearby fishing, bike and boat rentals, parasailing. **Rates (CP):** HS May–Nov $83–$112 S; $93–$122 D; from $145 ste; from $155 effic. Extra person $8. Children under 18 stay free. Lower rates off-season. Spec packages avail. Pking: Outdoor, free. Maj CC. Senior discounts.

🏨🏨 **Grasonville/Kent Island Sleep Inn**, 101 VFW Ave, Grasonville, MD 21638; tel 410/827-5555 or toll free 800/627-5337; fax 410/827-8801. 1 mi E of Kent Narrows, exit 43B or 44A off US 50/301. A nearly new building with much more attractive rooms and lobby than one expects from a standard-looking highway motel. Near Kent Narrows boating center and outlet malls. **Rooms:** 51 rms and stes. CI 3pm/CO 11am. Nonsmoking rms avail. **Amenities:** 🛏 📞 A/C, cable TV w/movies. Some units w/Jacuzzis. Deluxe rooms have refrigerators, VCRs, and attractive Jacuzzi-tub combinations. **Services:** 🍽 Car-rental desk. **Facilities:** 🏋 🎿 ♿ **Rates (CP):** HS June–Oct $46–$75 S; $50–$80 D; from $85 ste. Extra person $6. Children under 18 stay free. Min stay spec evnts. Lower rates off-season. Spec packages avail. Pking: Outdoor, free. Maj CC. Many special plans, including golf packages.

Restaurants 🍴

⑤ Anglers, 3015 Kent Narrows Way S, Grasonville (Kent Narrows); tel 410/827-6717. Exit 41 or 42 off US 50/301. Follow Md 18 past Kent Narrows Bridge. **American/Seafood.** A friendly mix of local watermen and the well-to-do makes this simple, clapboard building a legend in the area. The late entertainer Jackie Gleason used to stop in to shoot pool. Apparently a charmed place, too, since one owner won $10 million in the lottery. Basic American fare is offered at low prices. Popular for breakfast and daily dinner specials ($4 to $6 for complete meals). **FYI:** Reservations not accepted. **Open:** Sun–Thurs 7am–midnight, Fri–Sat 7am–2am. Closed some hols. **Prices:** Main courses $4–$10. Ltd CC. ♿

Annie's Paramount Steak House, 500 Kent Narrows Way N, Grasonville; tel 410/827-7103. Exit 42 off US 50/301. **American/Seafood/Steak.** Attractive woods and ceiling fans highlight this comfortable establishment overlooking Kent Narrows and its marinas. Although known primarily for steaks and prime rib, it's also strong on seafood. **FYI:** Reservations accepted. Piano. Children's menu. Dress code. **Open:** Lunch Mon–Sat 11am–

4pm; dinner Mon–Thurs noon–10:30pm, Fri–Sat noon–11:30pm; brunch Sun 9am–2pm. Closed Dec 25. **Prices:** Main courses $9–$22. Maj CC. 🖼 ♿

★ **Fisherman's Inn**, Main St, Grasonville; tel 410/827-8807. Exit 42 off US 50/301. **American/Seafood.** This large room with big windows on its water side is decorated with ship models, duck-stamp prints, and antique oyster plates. Traditional Eastern Shore seafood is the mainstay. Directly on Kent Narrows, the Crab Deck cooks up steamed crabs and other Chesapeake fare. Bands perform on weekends. **FYI:** Reservations not accepted. Band/country music/dancing/rock. Children's menu. Dress code. **Open:** Daily 11am–9:30pm. Closed Dec 25. **Prices:** Main courses $10–$19. Maj CC. 🚢 🖼 🅿 ♿

Harris Crab House, in Kent Narrows, 433 N Kent Narrows Way, Grasonville; tel 410/827-9500. Exit 42 off US 50/301. Turn right at stop sign, then right into restaurant. **Seafood.** This classic waterfront crab house has a large, simple room with long tables covered with brown wrapping paper. Both expansive windows and a large rooftop deck overlook Kent Narrows. Since the place is an outgrowth of a seafood-packing house, its primary business is shellfish. **FYI:** Reservations not accepted. Dress code. **Open:** HS May–Oct daily 11am–11pm. Reduced hours off-season. Closed Dec 25. **Prices:** Main courses $9–$15. Ltd CC. 🚢 🖼 ♿

The Narrows Restaurant, 3023 Kent Narrows Way S, Grasonville; tel 410/827-8113. Exit 42 off US 50/301. **New American/Seafood.** A fair-weather sun room and open deck augment this bright, waterfront dining room with skylights and windows looking out on Kent Narrows. Seafood, beef, and chicken are prepared in a light style and served with interesting sauces. **FYI:** Reservations accepted. Children's menu. Dress code. **Open:** Lunch Mon–Sat 11am–4pm; dinner Mon–Sat 4–9pm, Sun 11am–9pm; brunch Sun 11am–2pm. Closed Dec 25. **Prices:** Main courses $12–$25. Ltd CC. 🍷 🚢 🖼 ♿

GREENBELT

Map page M-3, B7 (W of Aberdeen)

Attraction 🖼

NASA/Goddard Space Flight Visitor Center, exit 22A to Greenbelt off I-95; tel 301/286-8981. Established in 1959, this was NASA's first major scientific laboratory devoted entirely to the exploration of space. Visitor center tours include special working areas that show satellite control, spacecraft construction, and communication operations. Exhibits housed inside the center offer such interactive experiences as piloting a personal manned maneuvering unit to retrieve a satellite in space and controlling a spacecraft by steering a gyro-chair. Picnic area, gift shop. **Open:** Daily 10am–4pm. Closed some hols. Free.

HAGERSTOWN

Map page M-3, B6

Hotels 🏨

≝≝≝ **Best Western Venice Inn**, 431 Dual Hwy, Hagerstown, MD 21740; tel 301/733-0830 or toll free 800/2-VENICE; fax 301/733-4978. Exit 6A off I-81, or exit 32B off I-70. A full-service hotel with luxurious 2-tiered lobby. Convenient to major thoroughfare but set back from traffic on huge lot. A motel building is also on the property. **Rooms:** 210 rms, stes, and effic. CI 2pm/CO noon. Express checkout avail. Nonsmoking rms avail. Efficiencies have full kitchens. Rooms for disabled guests on each floor. **Amenities:** 🛎 👤 A/C, cable TV w/movies. Some units w/minibars, some w/terraces, some w/Jacuzzis. 1 executive suite with bar. **Services:** ✕ 🚗 🖨 🖕 🏧 Twice-daily maid svce, babysitting. Turndown service on request. **Facilities:** 🏋 🍴 600 🖥 👤 1 rst, 1 bar (w/entertainment), lifeguard, games rm, beauty salon. Liquor store with wine cellar. 6-lane, Olympic-size pool. Golf course across the street and skiing within 16 miles. **Rates:** $55–$66 S; $58–$70 D; from $125 ste; from $85 effic. Children under 18 stay free. Pking: Outdoor, free. Maj CC. Special weekend packages, with meals, start at $200.

≝≝ **Holiday Inn**, 900 Dual Hwy, Hagerstown, MD 21740; tel 301/739-9050 or toll free 800/422-2SKI; fax 301/739-8347. Exit 32B off I-70, or exit 6A off I-81. Pleasant facility with small but attractive lobby and courteous staff. Skiing 16 miles away. **Rooms:** 140 rms and stes. CI 3pm/CO noon. Express checkout avail. Nonsmoking rms avail. 1 bridal suite, 2 conference suites with Murphy bed. Rooms classified as singles or kings; 2 rooms for disabled guests available. **Amenities:** 🛎 👤 A/C, cable TV w/movies. Some units w/terraces. Conference suites have computer jacks. **Services:** ✕ 🚗 🖨 🖕 🏧 Children's program. **Facilities:** 🏋 150 👤 1 rst, 1 bar (w/entertainment), playground, washer/dryer. Free use of fitness center ½ mile away. **Rates:** $55 S; $60 D; from $68 ste. Extra person $8. Children under 18 stay free. Spec packages avail. Pking: Outdoor, free. Maj CC. Ski packages available. Kids 12 and under eat free.

≝ **Ramada Inn Convention Center**, 901 Dual Hwy, Hagerstown, MD 21740; tel 301/733-5100 or toll free 800/272-6232; fax 301/733-9192. Exit 6B off I-81, or exit 32B off I-70. Lobby, which has elegant touches like old marble fireplaces and Japanese screens, is nevertheless a bit frayed in areas. Mud in entryway and venetian blinds in front windows also detract.

Rooms: 212 rms, stes, and effic. CI 2pm/CO noon. Express checkout avail. Nonsmoking rms avail. Rooms, some poolside, acceptable. **Amenities:** 🛎 👤 A/C, cable TV w/movies, voice mail. Some units w/minibars, some w/fireplaces, some w/Jacuzzis. Some rooms have sun decks. **Services:** ✕ 🚗 🖨 🖕 🏧 **Facilities:** 🏋 🍴 2K 👤 1 rst, 1 bar (w/entertainment), spa, sauna, steam rm, whirlpool, washer/dryer. Volleyball court. Swimming pool area is inviting atrium, including running track. Restaurant offers hearty lunch buffet, healthy light fare, extensive menu. **Rates (CP):** $59–$64 S; $64–$69 D; from $95 ste; from $150 effic. Extra person $5. Children under 18 stay free. Pking: Outdoor, free. Maj CC.

≝≝ **Sheraton Inn Hagerstown Conference Center**, 1910 Dual Hwy, Hagerstown, MD 21740; tel 301/790-3010 or toll free 800/325-3535; fax 301/733-4559. Exit 6B off I-81, or exit 32B off I-70. Spacious lobby, including palace-size gilt-framed mirror, lends air of elegance to this property. **Rooms:** 108 rms and stes. CI 2pm/CO noon. Nonsmoking rms avail. 2 honeymoon rooms, 2 executive suites. **Amenities:** 🛎 👤 A/C, cable TV w/movies, stereo/tape player. Some units w/minibars, some w/Jacuzzis. Executive suites have computer/fax jack. **Services:** ✕ 🚗 🖨 🖕 🏧 Babysitting. Professional staff is informed and courteous. **Facilities:** 🏋 🍴 700 👤 1 rst, 1 bar (w/entertainment), spa, sauna, steam rm, whirlpool, beauty salon. **Rates (CP):** HS May–Oct $56–$60 S or D; from $75 ste. Extra person $4. Children under 12 stay free. Lower rates off-season. Spec packages avail. Pking: Outdoor, free. Maj CC.

≝ **Wellesley Inn**, 1101 Dual Hwy, Hagerstown, MD 21740; tel 301/733-2700 or toll free 800/444-8888; fax 301/791-2106. Exit 6A off I-81, or exit 32B off I-70. This small, intimate, and charming hotel has a cozy lobby with bricked fireplace sitting area. **Rooms:** 84 rms and stes. CI 2pm/CO 11am. Nonsmoking rms avail. Rooms are on the small side but attractively decorated and inviting. **Amenities:** 🛎 📺 A/C, cable TV w/movies. Some rooms have refrigerators. **Services:** ✕ 🖨 🖕 🏧 **Facilities:** 👤 Cooperative arrangement with restaurant across the street for room service until 10pm. **Rates (CP):** HS May–Nov $42–$50 S; $49–$56 D; from $66 ste. Extra person $5. Children under 18 stay free. Lower rates off-season. Spec packages avail. Pking: Outdoor, free. Maj CC. Ski package for White Tail, 16 miles away.

Attractions 🏛

Washington County Museum of Fine Arts, 91 Key St; tel 301/739-5727. The galleries here offer changing exhibits of 19th- and 20th-century American art. On Sunday the museum offers diverse musical programs in its concert hall. **Open:** Tues–Sat 10am–5pm, Sun 1–6pm. Closed some hols. Free.

Jonathon Hager House and Museum, 110 Key St; tel 301/739-8393. The home of the city's founder is situated on the northern edge of City Park. The 3½-story structure was built in 1739 by Hager himself and is styled in the German tradition, with a large chimney at its center and 22-inch-thick walls. It has been completely restored and outfitted with authentic period furnishings. Next door is the Hager Museum, a collection of hundreds of farm implements, coins, household items, clothing, and other artifacts from the Hagerstown area. **Open:** Apr–Dec, Tues–Sat 10am–4pm, Sun 2–5pm. $

Mansion House Art Center, 135 W Washington St; tel 301/797-8782. Built in 1818, this museum features a collection of dolls, clocks, and furniture from the federal period. There are exhibits on the C&O Canal and the Civil War, as well as a re-creation of a turn-of-the-century general store. **Open:** Wed–Fri 1–4pm, Sat 2–5pm. $

Hagerstown Roundhouse Museum, 300 S Burhans Blvd; tel 301/739-4665. Depicts the history of the 7 railroads that passed through the city, including the Western Maryland Railroad, making Hagerstown the "Hub City." **Open:** Fri–Sun 1–5pm. $

Ziem Vineyards, Md 63; tel 301/223-8352. This 8-acre winery is set in a farmland complex that includes a 200-year-old stone house, a spring house, and a bank barn. It produces all of its wines (5 whites and 10 reds) from grape to bottle. Visitors are welcome to tour the facilities, taste the wines, and buy the product at the source. **Open:** Thurs–Sun 1–6pm. Free.

Hagerstown City Park, Virginia Ave; tel 301/739-4673. Among the nation's most beautiful natural city parks is this 50-acre oasis centered around an artificial lake that is home to hundreds of ducks, swans, and geese. Among the facilities are tennis courts, softball fields, wooded picnic areas, flower gardens, and an open-air band shell. **Open:** Daily sunrise to sunset. Free.

Fort Frederick State Park, 11100 Fort Frederick Rd; tel 301/842-2155. Built in 1756, the fort served as Maryland's frontier defense during the French and Indian War. Today the stone wall and 2 barracks have been restored to their original appearance and house exhibits on the history of the fort. Activities in the park include hiking, picnicking, fishing, boating, and camping. **Open:** Daily sunrise–sunset. Free.

HANOVER
Map page M-3, B6

Motel 🏨

≣≣≣ **Ramada Hotel BWI Airport**, 7253 Parkway Dr, Hanover, MD 21076 (Baltimore-Washington Int'l Airport); tel 410/712-4300 or toll free 800/272-6232; fax 410/712-0921. 15 mi S of Baltimore. exit 43E off I-95. Follow Md 100 to US 1; follow US 1 to Dorsey Rd, turn left, then left onto Parkway Dr. Formerly part of the Howard Johnson chain, this motel has been completely renovated. Convenient to Amtrak as well as the airport. **Rooms:** 132 rms. CI 3pm/CO noon. Express checkout avail. Nonsmoking rms avail. Standard room recently furnished and decorated in pastels. Suites are to be added in 1995. **Amenities:** 🛏 ⓓ A/C, satel TV w/movies. All units w/terraces. Balconies are small. TVs have closed captioning. **Services:** ✕ 🚐 ⌧ ⌨ Babysitting. **Facilities:** 🗍 🔲 🏋 🏊 ⅒ 1 rst, 1 bar (w/entertainment), lifeguard, games rm, washer/dryer. Game room has billiard table. Free access to nearby health club with Olympic-size pool. **Rates:** HS Apr–Aug $98 S; $108 D. Extra person $5. Children under 16 stay free. Lower rates off-season. MAP rates avail. Spec packages avail. Pking: Outdoor, free. Maj CC. Extensive discounts.

HAVRE DE GRACE
Map page M-3, B7

Attractions 💼

Havre de Grace Maritime Museum, 100 Lafayette St; tel 410/939-4800. This museum displays artifacts, memorabilia, and photographs representing the time when Havre de Grace was a major hub for water-related commerce and recreational activities on the Upper Chesapeake Bay. In addition, there are educational programs and displays on local maritime history, as well as an annual classic boat show every June. **Open:** May–Sept, Sat–Sun 1–5pm. Free.

Steppingstone Museum, 461 Quaker Bottom Rd; tel 410/939-2299. Located on what was once a working Harford County farm, this living history museum is dedicated to preserving and demonstrating the rural arts and crafts of the late 1800s and early 1900s. The main farmhouse is furnished with turn-of-the-century pieces, including a kitchen with a woodburning stove and an ice box. Other historic buildings include a blacksmith shop, woodworking shop, dairy, potter's shed, canning house, and carriage barn. There are 26 sites in all. **Open:** May–Oct, Sat–Sun 1–5pm. $

Concord Point Lighthouse, Lafayette St; tel 410/939-9040. Built in 1827, it is the oldest continually operated lighthouse in the state of Maryland. Its construction coincided with the opening of the Chesapeake and Delaware Canal linking the Chesapeake and Delaware Bays. Today the lighthouse the most photographed and painted structure in the city and is the starting point of the self-guided tour of Havre de Grace available at the visitors center. **Open:** May–Oct, Sat–Sun 1–5pm. Free.

KENT ISLAND

See Grasonville, Stevensville

LA PLATA

Map page M-3, C6

Motel 🛏

≣≣ Best Western La Plata Inn, 6900 Crain Hwy (US 301), La Plata, MD 20646; tel 301/934-4900 or toll free 800/528-1234; fax 301/934-5389. An attractive, modern roadside motel of brick and stucco, it appears more like a low-rise office building or apartment complex. Clean and comfortable throughout. Short drive to shops and restaurants. **Rooms:** 74 rms and stes. CI 2pm/CO 11am. Nonsmoking rms avail. All units pleasant mauve-and-blue color scheme. L-shaped suites have living area with bay windows, sofas. **Amenities:** 🛏 ⚲ A/C, cable TV w/movies, refrig. Microwaves. Wet bars, 2 TVs in suites. **Services:** 🕹 🐕 Continental breakfast served in light alcove off lobby. **Facilities:** 🔼 🏊 ⚿ Washer/dryer. Small pool in rear surrounded by wooden fence. **Rates (CP):** $48 S; $53 D; from $65 ste. Extra person $5. Children under 16 stay free. Pking: Outdoor, free. Maj CC. Pet fee.

Attraction 🚩

Smallwood State Park, Md 225; tel 301/743-7613. This 630-acre recreational area includes the restored home of Revolutionary War hero Gen William Smallwood. Also located on the grounds are Sweden Point Marina and Mattawoman Natural Area. Picnicking, hiking, and boat rentals. **Open:** Daily sunrise–sunset. $

LAUREL

Map page M-3, B6

Motels 🛏

≣≣≣ Best Western Maryland Inn, 15101 Sweitzer Lane, Laurel, MD 20707; tel 301/776-5300 or toll free 800/200-0333; fax 301/604-3667. Exit I-95 at Md 198 W. A better-than-average chain motel with excellent entertainment facilities for families with children as well as an executive level on the top floor. **Rooms:** 205 rms and stes. Exec-level rms avail. CI 3pm/CO noon. Express checkout avail. Nonsmoking rms avail. Executive-level units have king beds. Some 1st-floor rooms have both exterior and atrium access. **Amenities:** 🛏 ⚲ A/C, satel TV w/movies, voice mail. Executive-level units have hair dryers, coffeemakers. **Services:** ✗ 🖨 🕹 Babysitting. Complimentary full breakfast. Van service to rental car agencies and local businesses. **Facilities:** 🔼 🛢 300 ⚿ 1 rst, 1 bar, lifeguard, games rm, spa, sauna, whirlpool, washer/dryer. Putting green, pool, shuffleboard, billiard table, and video games in atrium. **Rates (BB):** $65 S; $71 D; from $105 ste. Extra person $6. Children under 18 stay free. Higher rates for spec evnts/hols. Pking: Outdoor, free. Maj CC.

≣≣ Comfort Suites, 14402 Laurel Place, Laurel, MD 20707; tel 301/206-2600 or toll free 800/628-7760; fax 301/725-0056. Exit 33A off I-95. Follow Md 198 E to US 1 S, turn left; go 1 mile to Mulberry St, turn right. A recent, attractive motel adjacent to several shopping centers and near Fort Meade and a pretty park with lake. **Rooms:** 119 rms and stes. CI 2pm/CO noon. Nonsmoking rms avail. Most are large hotel rooms with a sitting area and not true suites, but all are attractively decorated and comfortable. **Amenities:** 🛏 ⚲ 🖥 A/C, cable TV w/movies, refrig. Microwaves in most rooms. **Services:** 🚐 🖨 🕹 🐕 Car-rental desk. Van transportation. Very accommodating and competent staff. **Facilities:** 🔼 🛢 🎾 🛢 120 ⚿ Lifeguard, games rm, lawn games, spa, whirlpool, playground, washer/dryer. Golf course ¾ mile away. Jogging trail adjacent to motel. Some local restaurants give 20% discount. **Rates (CP):** $78–$125 S or D; from $59 ste. Extra person $10. Children under 18 stay free. Higher rates for spec evnts/hols. Pking: Outdoor, free. Maj CC.

≣≣ Holiday Inn, 3400 Ft Meade Rd, Laurel, MD 20724; tel 301/498-0900 or toll free 800/HOLIDAY. Exit Md 295 at Md 198; drive west for ½ mi. An older but well-kept highway motel convenient to Laurel Race Track and the Baltimore-Washington Pkwy (Md 295). **Rooms:** 120 rms. CI 1pm/CO 11am. Nonsmoking rms avail. Standard rooms recently got new carpets and wallpaper. **Amenities:** 🛏 ⚲ A/C, satel TV w/movies. **Services:** ✗ 🖨 🕹 🐕 Car-rental desk. Complimentary full breakfast.

Facilities: ⛽ 🛒 📟 ⟨ 1 rst, 1 bar, lifeguard, games rm, washer/dryer. Pleasant pool and sun-deck area, small fitness room; 18-hole golf course and driving range within 2 miles. **Rates (BB):** $69 S; $75 D. Extra person $6. Children under 18 stay free. MAP rates avail. Pking: Outdoor, free. Maj CC.

LA VALE

Map page M-3, B5 (W of Cumberland)

Hotel 🖼

≣≣≣ **Best Western Braddock Motor Inn**, 1268 National Hwy, La Vale, MD 21502; tel 301/729-3300 or toll free 800/296-6006; fax 301/729-3300 ext 602. Exit 39 off I-68. Wrap-around sun deck adjoining glassed-in pool form 1 entrance to this attractive facility. Landscaping and walkway corridors with large floor-to-ceiling windows lend an air of quality to this sparkling-clean facility. **Rooms:** 108 rms and stes. CI 2pm/CO 11am. Nonsmoking rms avail. Rooms have the standard integrated decor of a chain, but some offer a larger area for sitting and oak furnishings in fine shape, including large desks. 11 suites with pull-out sofas. **Amenities:** 🛅 A/C, cable TV, shoe polisher. Some units w/Jacuzzis. Some suites have 2 phones. Refrigerators, microwaves, and VCRs for rent. **Services:** ✗ 🚐 🖼 ↻ Babysitting. **Facilities:** ⛽ 🛒 📟 ⟨ 1 rst, 1 bar, games rm, spa, sauna, whirlpool. Miniature golf and bowling across the highway. **Rates:** $44–$52 S; $50–$58 D; from $75 ste. Extra person $6. Children under 18 stay free. Higher rates for spec evnts/hols. Spec packages avail. Pking: Outdoor, free. Maj CC. Anniversary, Getaway packages offered.

LEONARDTOWN

Map page M-3, C7

Attractions 🖼

Calvert Marine Museum, Md 2; tel 410/326-2042. Nestled on the shore of the Patuxent River near the Chesapeake Bay, this museum focuses on life above, below, and on Maryland's waters. In the Fossils of the Calvert Cliffs exhibit, visitors view fossil shark teeth, crocodile jaws, and whale skulls collected from the Calvert Cliffs, and stand beneath the open jaws of the extinct giant great white shark. Also, the museum has created a living salt marsh with blue crabs, fiddler crabs, and green-backed heron.

Outdoor attractions include cruises around Salomons Harbor on the **Wm B Tennison,** the oldest Coast Guard–licensed passenger vessel on the Chesapeake. On the shore is the **Drum**

Point Lighthouse, circa 1883, one of only 3 remaining screwpile lights on the Chesapeake Bay. South of the main museum is the **J C Lore Oyster House,** which displays tools and gear used by local watermen to harvest fish, crabs, oysters, and eels. **Open:** Daily 10am–5pm. Closed some hols. $

Sotterley Plantation, Md 245; tel 301/373-2280. Set on a working colonial plantation along the Patuxent River, the mansion contains period furnishings, a Chinese Chippendale staircase, and other handcarved woodwork. On the grounds are a formal garden, a smoke house, a spinning cottage, a custom house, slave quarters, an 18th-century necessary house, and a tobacco farming museum. **Open:** June–Oct, Tues–Sat 11am–4pm. $$

Potomac River Museum, Bayview Rd; tel 301/769-2222. This museum traces the history of the area and life along the Potomac River through archeological exhibits. The building also houses an 1890 country store and an 1840 little red school house. **Open:** Mon–Fri 9am–5pm, Sat–Sun noon–4pm. Closed some hols. $

LINTHICUM

Map page M-3, B6 (S of Baltimore)

Hotel 🖼

≣≣≣≣ **BWI Airport Marriott Hotel**, 1743 W Nursery Rd, Linthicum, MD 21240 (Baltimore-Washington Int'l Airport); tel 410/859-8300 or toll free 800/228-9290; fax 410/859-3369. 10 mi S of Baltimore. Exit I-95 at Md 295. Modern design and spacious, bright public areas in pastels make this a very attractive hotel. Convenient to BWI Airport. **Rooms:** 310 rms and stes. Exec-level rms avail. CI 3pm/CO 1pm. Express checkout avail. Nonsmoking rms avail. **Amenities:** 🛅 ⚡ A/C, cable TV w/movies, voice mail. Some units w/Jacuzzis. Concierge-level units have shoe polishers, bathrobes, scales, hair dryers. Irons and boards in all rooms. **Services:** ✗ ⊷ 🚐 🖼 ↻ ⇲ Car-rental desk, masseur, babysitting. Friendly, accommodating staff. **Facilities:** ⛽ 🛒 📺 ⟨ 1 rst, 2 bars, lifeguard, spa, whirlpool, washer/dryer. Dramatic, lovely pool with waterfall and high windows. Excellent fitness, games, massage facilities. **Rates:** $69–$135 S or D; from $250 ste. Children under 12 stay free. MAP rates avail. Spec packages avail. Pking: Outdoor, free. Maj CC. Weekend rates include breakfast.

Motel 🖼

≣≣≣ **Holiday Inn BWI**, 890 Elkridge Landing Rd, Linthicum, MD 21090 (Baltimore-Washington Int'l Airport); tel 410/859-8400 or toll free 800/465-4329; fax 410/684-6778. 10 mi S of Baltimore. Busy chain motel with good services. **Rooms:** 255 rms and stes. CI 3pm/CO noon. Express checkout avail. Non-smoking rms avail. King rooms are substantially larger than standard. **Amenities:** 🛏 🅿 📺 A/C, cable TV w/movies. **Services:** ✗ 🚙 🖼 🍴 🐾 Car-rental desk, babysitting. **Facilities:** 🛗 🏊 ⛳ 🏖 💻 🛗 1 rst, 1 bar, lifeguard, washer/dryer. Large pool and separate children's pool. **Rates:** $99 S or D; from $191 ste. Extra person $10. Children under 12 stay free. Higher rates for spec evnts/hols. MAP rates avail. Spec packages avail. Pking: Outdoor, free. Maj CC. Children eat free during summer. Priority Club rates include continental breakfast.

MCHENRY

Map page M-2, B4 (N of Oakland)

See also Deep Creek Lake, Oakland

Hotel 🏨

▆▆ **Royal Oaks Inn**, Deep Creek Dr, RD 2, PO Box 11, McHenry, MD 21541; tel 301/387-4200; fax 301/387-4204. Exit 14A off I-68. Travel 14 miles south on US 219. An architecturally pleasing, white stucco, multilevel facility ¼ mile from Deep Creek Lake. Inviting lobby has high ceiling, mirrors, special seating area. **Rooms:** 77 rms and stes. CI 3pm/CO 11am. Nonsmoking rms avail. Spacious rooms with Italian-marble bathrooms; 22 king-bedded and 23 queen-bedded units have pull-out sofas. Two family rooms feature small adjoining room. Honeymoon suite has kitchenette, 2 baths; business suite is the same minus a bath. **Amenities:** 🛏 A/C, cable TV. Some units w/Jacuzzis. **Services:** 🍴 🐾 Continental breakfast in lobby. **Facilities:** 🏊 🖼 🛗 Skiing nearby. **Rates (CP):** $40–$70 S or D; from $200 ste. Extra person $5. Children under 12 stay free. Spec packages avail. Pking: Outdoor, free. Maj CC. Special-occasion, sports packages available.

Motels

▆▆ **Innlet Motor Lodge**, Deep Creek Dr, PO Box 178, McHenry, MD 21541; tel 301/387-5596. Exit 14A off I-68. Follow US 219 south to McHenry. This small and friendly motel offers sparkling rooms that open onto a rail porch and a rolling green lawn with ducks. Deep Creek Lake just beyond. **Rooms:** 20 rms. CI 2pm/CO 11am. All rooms overlook Deep Creek Lake and Wisp Ski Resort; 1 room for the disabled available. Rooms offer integrated decor, excellent mattresses. Sink separate from bathroom area. **Amenities:** 🛏 A/C, cable TV w/movies. All units w/terraces, some w/fireplaces. **Services:** 🍴 🐾 Well-behaved pets allowed. Logs and duck food for sale at desk. **Facilities:** 🏊 🖼 🛗 1 beach (lake shore). Boat dock, picnic tables. **Rates:** HS

June 29–Oct 31/Dec 24–Mar 15 $65–$75 S or D. Extra person $5. Children under 12 stay free. Min stay wknds. Lower rates off-season. Pking: Outdoor, free. Maj CC.

▆ **Point View Inn**, US 219, PO Box 100, McHenry, MD 21541; tel 301/387-5555. Exit 14A off I-68. Drive 16 miles south on US 219. Rustic building, largely stone, set by Deep Creek Lake. Public porch. **Rooms:** 24 rms and stes. CI 2pm/CO 11am. Nonsmoking rms avail. Country theme throughout, including such special touches as rocking chairs. All individually decorated with antique reproductions and country furnishings, and all afford view of Deep Creek Lake. Rooms could be fresher. **Amenities:** 🛏 Cable TV w/movies. No A/C. All units w/terraces, some w/fireplaces. Some rooms have clock radios, VCRs. **Services:** 🍴 Masseur. **Facilities:** 🏊 🖼 🛗 1 rst, 2 bars (1 w/entertainment), 1 beach (lake shore), beauty salon. Outdoor dining available at adjoining restaurant. **Rates:** $46–$58 S; $56–$68 D; from $75 ste. Extra person $10. Children under 12 stay free. Pking: Outdoor, free. Maj CC.

Resort

▆▆▆ **Wisp Resort Hotel**, Marsh Hill Rd, Star Rte 2, PO Box 35, McHenry, MD 21541; tel 301/387-5581 or toll free 800/462-9477; fax 301/387-4127. Exit 14A off I-68. Go 13 miles on 219 to Deep Creek Lake. Travel 13 miles south on US 219. 90 acres. This ski and golf resort set by Deep Creek Lake has a hospitable staff and nice views of a duck pond and Deep Creek in front, mountain trails in rear. **Rooms:** 168 rms and stes. CI 5pm/CO 11am. Nonsmoking rms avail. Comfortable rooms; 2 VIP suites consist of 2 rooms and full kitchen, dining room; 100 minisuites, some with queen-size beds and separate master bedroom, some with 2 doubles; 3 rooms for the disabled. All standard rooms have a pull-out sofa. **Amenities:** 🛏 A/C, cable TV w/movies, refrig. Some units w/fireplaces. **Services:** 🍴 **Facilities:** 🛗 🚲 ⛳ 🏊 🖼 🏌 💻 🛗 2 rsts (see also "Restaurants" below), 1 bar, games rm, lawn games, whirlpool. Olympic-size pool with adjoining hot tub. Miniature golf, ice skating, 30 miles of trails. Mountain bikes for rent. Pizza snack bar. **Rates:** HS Dec 26–Mar 7 $75–$145 S or D; from $135 ste. Children under 6 stay free. Lower rates off-season. Spec packages avail. Pking: Outdoor, free. Maj CC. In high season, more expensive on weekends than midweek. Ski and golf packages available.

Restaurant 🍴

Bavarian Room, in the Wisp Resort Hotel, Marsh Hill Rd, McHenry; tel 301/387-4911. Exit 14A off I-68. **Seafood/Steak.** Located on the lower level of the McHenry House at this ski resort, the Bavarian offers rathskeller decor, including red-checked tablecloths, half-timbered walls, and huge stone fireplace. Soup and salad bar. Intimate dining on seafood, pasta, and signature steaks, such as 20-ounce porterhouse. **FYI:** Reservations not accepted. **Open:** Sun–Thurs 5–10pm, Fri–Sat 5–10:30pm. **Prices:** Main courses $11–$18. Maj CC. ♥ 🔼

OAKLAND

Map page M-2, B4

See also Deep Creek Lake, McHenry

Motel 🛏

▤▤ **Alpine Village Inn**, Glendale Rd (Rte 4), PO Box 5200, Oakland, MD 21550; tel 301/387-5534 or toll free 800/343-5253; fax 301/387-4119. Exit 14A off I-68. Chalet-style lodge and cabins offering lakefront view, bubbling spring in wooded setting, and rustic decor. Extended lobby area has intimate sections (1 with fireplace) with stone walls, games, large tables. **Rooms:** 29 rms; 14 ctges/villas. CI 4pm/CO 11am. Open-beam ceilings and brick-and-wood walls create a warm mood. Of 29 lodge rooms, 9 have kitchenette. Some studio apartments off main lobby and some rooms on sun-deck level. **Amenities:** 🛁 A/C, cable TV w/movies. All units w/terraces, some w/fireplaces. **Services:** 🛎 **Facilities:** 🔲 ⅄ 🔲 ♿ 1 beach (lake shore), playground, washer/dryer. Picnic tables and grill overlook lake. Free boat docking. **Rates (CP):** HS Mem Day–Labor Day $50–$75 S or D. Extra person $5. Min stay HS and wknds. Lower rates off-season. Pking: Outdoor, free. Maj CC. High-season rates prevail on all weekends, holidays, festivals, deer season, and Christmas and New Year's weeks; 2- and 3-bedroom chalets have minimum-stay requirements.

Restaurants 🍴

The Four Seasons, in Will of the Wisp, US 219, Oakland; tel 301/387-5503. Exit 14A off I-68. **Continental/Seafood/Steak.** This elegant stone and wood dining area, complete with a chandelier hanging from the high ceiling, overlooks Deep Creek Lake. All dinners include soup or salad, vegetable or starch, and dessert. One of few restaurants in area to welcome reservations. Specialties include tortellini soup with andouille sausage, flounder 4 seasons. **FYI:** Reservations accepted. Children's menu. Dress code. **Open:** Breakfast daily 7:30–11:30am; lunch daily 11:30am–2pm; dinner daily 5–9:30pm. Closed Dec 25. **Prices:** Main courses $9.95–$18.50. Maj CC. 🔼

⑤ **Pizzeria Uno Restaurant**, US 219, Oakland; tel 301/387-4866. Exit 14A off I-68. From I-68, 20 miles to restaurant on US 219. **New American/Burgers/Pizza.** A classy step up

from a pizzeria, it offers a range of foods and a view of Deep Creek Lake from many tables and booths. Open-beamed ceilings, massive stone fireplace in center, funky neon-light accents, and framed movie posters add to the fun. Best are pastas, Chicago-style deep-dish pizza, orange roughy, Delmonico steaks. **FYI:** Reservations not accepted. Children's menu. **Open:** Mon–Thurs 11am–midnight, Fri–Sat 11am–1am, Sun 11am–11pm. **Prices:** Main courses $4.75–$10.95. Maj CC. 👥 ♿

⑤ ✭ **Silver Tree Inn Restaurant**, Glendale Rd, Oakland; tel 301/387-4040. Exit 14A off I-68. Follow US 219 to Glendale Rd. **Italian/Seafood/Steak.** Set in the woods adjacent to Deep Creek Lake and the Alpine Inn. The 1890s decor is dominated by 2 huge stone-hearth fireplaces and log walls providing a warm and rustic dining atmosphere. A separate windowed section overlooks the lake. Adjacent building on the water, accessible by boat, has raw bar and entertainment. Favorites include lasagna, crab imperial, and prime rib. **FYI:** Reservations not accepted. **Open:** Sun 4–10pm, Mon–Thurs 5–10pm, Fri–Sat 5–11pm. **Prices:** Main courses $5–$35. Maj CC.

OCEAN CITY

Map page M-3, C8

Hotels 🛏

▤▤▤ **Carousel Hotel and Resort**, 11700 Coastal Hwy, at 118th St, Ocean City, MD 21842; tel 410/524-1000 or toll free 800/641-0011; fax 410/524-7766. Exit US 50 at Md 90; turn left on Coastal Hwy and proceed to 118th St. Once the showplace in this part of Ocean City, this large resort hotel is beginning to show its age. Nevertheless, it's right on an excellent stretch of beach, and sports an exceptional atrium. Popular with groups year-round. **Rooms:** 265 stes and effic. CI 4pm/CO 11am. Nonsmoking rms avail. Rooms are either oceanfront, ocean view, street side, or facing an ice-skating rink. Those on street and rink sides are noisier than others. **Amenities:** 🛁 A/C, cable TV w/movies, refrig. Some units w/minibars, some w/terraces. **Services:** ✕ 🔑 🆅🅿 🚐 🖂 🛎 Social director, children's program, babysitting. Bellhops, concierge, and social director during high season only. **Facilities:** 🔲 🛥 🎱 ♿ 2 rsts, 3 bars (w/entertainment), 1 beach (ocean), lifeguard, games rm, spa, sauna, steam rm, whirlpool. Indoor ice-skating rink. Attractive indoor pool. **Rates:** HS June 1–Sept 5 from $179 ste; from $99 effic. Extra person $10. Children under 17 stay free. Min stay HS. Lower rates off-season. MAP rates avail. Spec packages avail. Pking: Indoor/outdoor, free. Maj CC.

▤▤▤▤ **The Coconut Malorie**, 201 60th St, in the Bay, Ocean City, MD 21842; tel 410/723-6100 or toll free 800/

767-6060; fax 410/524-9327. Exit US 50 at Md 90; follow to Coastal Hwy. This luxury hotel on the bay side of Ocean City has an entrance of white marble. **Rooms:** 85 stes. Exec-level rms avail. CI 4pm/CO noon. Nonsmoking rms avail. Bright and airy rooms are decorated in elegant island style—off-whites, dark or light wood, high-quality Haitian art, tile floors. **Amenities:** 📺 🛁 🖨 ☎ A/C, cable TV w/movies, refrig, VCR, bathrobes. All units w/terraces, all w/Jacuzzis. Luxury rooms have tables set with linen, good grade of china, and stainless cutlery. **Services:** ✗ 🗝 VP 🚐 🧺 ⌂ Twice-daily maid svce, car-rental desk, masseur, babysitting. Arrangements for van transportation to and use of a health club, beach, and other facilities are made through hotel. **Facilities:** 🍴 175 ⅙ 1 rst (see also "Restaurants" below), 1 bar, lifeguard. All water sports are nearby. Beautiful library and gallery of Haitian art are in the Tower Room. **Rates:** HS June 15–Sept 15 from $159 ste. Extra person $15. Children under 6 stay free. Min stay HS and wknds. Lower rates off-season. Spec packages avail. Pking: Outdoor, free. Maj CC.

≣≣≣ **Dunes Manor Hotel**, 28th St at Oceanfront, Ocean City, MD 21842; tel 410/289-1100 or toll free 800/523-2888; fax 410/289-4905. Exit US 50 at Baltimore Ave and go north; turn right at 28th St. A Victorian-style resort hotel with reproduction furniture and attractive balconies overlooking the ocean. Very pretty lobby and public rooms. **Rooms:** 170 rms and stes. CI 3pm/CO 11am. Nonsmoking rms avail. **Amenities:** 📺 🛁 A/C, cable TV w/movies, refrig. All units w/terraces. Microwave. **Services:** ✗ 🚐 ⌂ Babysitting. Complimentary afternoon tea daily. **Facilities:** 🍴 🛎 180 ⅙ 1 rst, 1 bar (w/entertainment), 1 beach (ocean), lifeguard, spa, whirlpool. Nearby golf, fishing, and water sports. **Rates:** HS June 24–Sept 25 $119–$189 S or D; from $230 ste. Extra person $10. Children under 17 stay free. Min stay HS. Lower rates off-season. Spec packages avail. Pking: Indoor/outdoor, free. Maj CC.

≣≣≣ **Princess Royale Oceanfront Hotel and Conference Center**, Oceanfront at 91st St, Ocean City, MD 21842; tel 410/524-7777 or toll free 800/476-9253; fax 410/524-7787. Exit US 50 at Md 90; turn left at Coastal Hwy and proceed to 91st St. A dramatic, modern, oceanfront resort hotel with extensive facilities. **Rooms:** 327 stes and effic. CI 4pm/CO 11am. Express checkout avail. Nonsmoking rms avail. All units have fully equipped kitchens, separate sitting rooms. Atrium rooms overlook a dramatic pool area and have ocean view through a high glass wall. **Amenities:** 📺 🖨 ☎ A/C, cable TV w/movies, refrig, in-rm safe. All units w/terraces, some w/Jacuzzis. All have 2 TVs. "Green" timers automatically shut off lights after guests leave units. **Services:** ✗ VP 🚐 🧺 ⌂ Car-rental desk, masseur, children's program, babysitting. **Facilities:** 🍴 🚲 🖥 🛎 800 ⅙ 1 rst, 4 bars (2 w/entertainment), 1 beach (ocean), lifeguard, games rm, lawn games, spa, sauna, whirlpool, beauty salon,

washer/dryer. Miniature golf. **Rates:** HS July–Aug from $139 ste. Extra person $15. Children under 12 stay free. Min stay spec evnts. Lower rates off-season. AP and MAP rates avail. Spec packages avail. Pking: Indoor, free. Maj CC. Efficiencies rent by week only ($1,855–$2,410/wk).

≣≣≣ **Sheraton Fontainebleau Hotel**, 10100 Ocean Hwy, at 101st St, Ocean City, MD 21842; tel 410/524-3535 or toll free 800/638-2100; fax 410/524-3834. Exit US 50 at Md 90, turn left at Coastal Hwy and proceed to 101st St. This large oceanfront hotel is conveniently located on the Gold Coast near shopping. It is self-contained and enjoyable year-round. **Rooms:** 287 rms, stes, and effic. CI 3pm/CO 11am. Express checkout avail. Nonsmoking rms avail. **Amenities:** 📺 🛁 A/C, cable TV w/movies, refrig. All units w/terraces. **Services:** ✗ VP 🚐 🧺 ⌂ 🐾 Masseur, babysitting. **Facilities:** 🍴 🛎 1.5K ⅙ 2 rsts, 5 bars (2 w/entertainment), 1 beach (ocean), lifeguard, games rm, spa, sauna, whirlpool, beauty salon. **Rates:** HS July–Sept $150–$285 S or D; from $150 ste. Extra person $14. Children under 18 stay free. Min stay HS and wknds. Lower rates off-season. MAP rates avail. Spec packages avail. Pking: Outdoor, free. Maj CC. Efficiencies rent by week only ($1,300–$1,500/wk).

Motels

≣≣≣ **Best Western Flagship Oceanfront**, 2600 Baltimore Ave, at 26th St, Ocean City, MD 21842; tel 410/289-3384 or toll free 800/638-2106, 800/429-3147 in MD. Exit US 50 at Baltimore Ave and go north to 26th St. A good, well-kept oceanfront motel, with better-than-average facilities for this area. **Rooms:** 93 rms and effic. CI 3pm/CO 11am. Nonsmoking rms avail. All rooms have an ocean view, though some are limited; 6 are directly on the oceanfront. All rooms have 2 double beds. Attractive decor. **Amenities:** 📺 🛁 🖨 ☎ A/C, cable TV w/movies, refrig, VCR. All units w/terraces. **Services:** ⌂ Children's program, babysitting. **Facilities:** 🍴 🚲 🖥 🛎 1 rst, 1 bar (w/entertainment), 1 beach (ocean), lifeguard, games rm, spa, sauna, whirlpool, playground, washer/dryer. Restaurant offers all-you-can-eat buffets. **Rates:** HS June 24–Aug 27 $144 S or D; from $154 effic. Extra person $7. Children under 4 stay free. Min stay. Lower rates off-season. Higher rates for spec evnts/hols. MAP rates avail. Spec packages avail. Pking: Outdoor, free. Maj CC.

≣≣ **Brighton Suites**, 12500 Coastal Hwy, at 125th St, Ocean City, MD 21842; tel 410/250-7600 or toll free 800/225-5788; fax 410/250-7603. Exit US 50 at Md 90; turn left on Coastal Hwy and proceed to 125th St. On the highway 1 block from the ocean, this stucco motel lacks views but has good, clean accommodations and is well maintained. Shopping malls across Ocean Hwy. **Rooms:** 57 stes. CI 3pm/CO 11am. Nonsmoking rms avail. Rooms for the disabled have Murphy beds to give more open floor space during the day. **Amenities:** 🛗 ⚙ 🗟 A/C, cable TV w/movies, refrig, in-rm safe. All units w/terraces. **Services:** 🛎 Twice-daily maid svce, babysitting. **Facilities:** 🖼 ⚓ 📶 ⛴ ⅃ Lifeguard, washer/dryer. Bike rentals and other sports available nearby. **Rates:** HS July 4–Aug 27 from $119 ste. Extra person $10. Children under 16 stay free. Min stay HS. Lower rates off-season. Higher rates for spec evnts/hols. MAP rates avail. Spec packages avail. Pking: Indoor/outdoor, free. Maj CC.

≣≣≣ **Castle in the Sand Hotel**, Oceanfront at 37th St, PO Box 190, Ocean City, MD 21842; tel 410/289-6846 or toll free 800/552-7263; fax 410/289-9446. Exit US 50 at Baltimore Ave; turn right on Coastal Hwy; then right on 37th St. Spread over an entire block, several buildings include detached cottages, oceanfront and street-side rooms and suites. Friendly management. **Rooms:** 176 rms, stes, and effic; 33 ctges/villas. CI 3pm/CO 11am. Nonsmoking rms avail. Some units are oceanside; others are bayside. Most have cooking facilities. Pleasant decor. **Amenities:** 🛗 🗟 A/C, cable TV w/movies, refrig. Some units w/terraces. **Services:** ✗ 🚐 🛎 Social director, children's program, babysitting. Beach-equipped wheelchair available. **Facilities:** 🖼 📶 ⅃ 1 rst, 2 bars (w/entertainment), 1 beach (ocean), lifeguard, games rm, lawn games, washer/dryer. Large sun deck. Very large pool with diving board. **Rates:** HS June 4–Labor Day $123–$169 S or D; from $139 ste; from $139 effic. Extra person $7. Children under 11 stay free. Min stay HS. Lower rates off-season. Higher rates for spec evnts/hols. MAP rates avail. Spec packages avail. Pking: Outdoor, free. Maj CC. Cottages/villas rent by week only ($605–$1,035/wk).

≣≣ **Comfort Inn Boardwalk**, 5th St and Oceanfront, Ocean City, MD 21842; tel 410/289-5155 or toll free 800/282-5155. Exit US 50 at Baltimore Ave and go north to 5th St. An oceanfront chain motel with nicely decorated rooms and hallways and a convenient location near the south end of the boardwalk. **Rooms:** 84 effic. CI 3pm/CO 11am. Nonsmoking rms avail. Attractively decorated efficiencies. Some are oceanfront; others overlook parking lot or have partial ocean views. **Amenities:** 🛗 🗟 A/C, cable TV w/movies, refrig. All units w/terraces. **Services:** 🛎 Babysitting. **Facilities:** 🖼 ⅃ 1 beach (ocean), lifeguard. An attractive, kidney-shaped indoor pool. **Rates (CP):** HS June 24–Aug 21 from $119 effic. Extra person $10. Children under 12 stay free. Min stay HS. Lower rates off-season. Spec packages avail. Pking: Outdoor, free. Maj CC.

≣≣ **Comfort Inn Gold Coast**, 11201 Coastal Hwy, at 112th St, Ocean City, MD 21842; tel 410/524-3000 or toll free 800/221-2222; fax 410/524-8255. Exit US 50 at Md 90; turn left on Coastal Hwy, then left on 112th St. A well-kept, better-than-average motel on Sinepuxent Bay, 2 blocks from ocean, and next

to a shopping center. **Rooms:** 202 rms and stes. CI 3pm/CO 11am. Nonsmoking rms avail. **Amenities:** 🛗 A/C, cable TV w/movies, refrig. Some units w/Jacuzzis. Each room has sink and microwave. **Services:** 🛎 Very hospitable, competent staff. **Facilities:** 🖼 📶 ⅃ 1 rst, lifeguard, whirlpool, playground, washer/dryer. Adjacent to 24-hour restaurant. **Rates:** HS Mem Day–Labor Day $85–$165 S or D; from $345 ste. Extra person $10. Children under 18 stay free. Min stay HS and wknds. Lower rates off-season. MAP rates avail. Spec packages avail. Pking: Outdoor, free. Maj CC. Golf packages available.

≣≣≣ **Days Inn Bayside**, 4201 Coastal Hwy, Ocean City, MD 21842; tel 410/289-6488 or toll free 800/329-7466; fax 410/289-1617. Exit US 50 at Md 90; follow to Coastal Hwy and 42nd St. This facility is set up especially well for conventioneers, rather than for beach-goers, although the oceanfront is not far away. Adjacent to convention center, restaurants, and stores. **Rooms:** 162 rms and stes. CI 4pm/CO 11am. Nonsmoking rms avail. Wide variety of room views: some of the bay, some of the distant ocean. **Amenities:** 🛗 ⚙ A/C, cable TV w/movies. All units w/terraces. **Services:** 🛎 🚐 Car-rental desk, children's program. **Facilities:** 🖼 📶 ⅃ Games rm, washer/dryer. Public tennis and basketball courts as well as public beach nearby. Miniature golf next door. **Rates (CP):** HS June–Aug $60–$200 S or D; from $90 ste. Extra person $10. Children under 18 stay free. Min stay HS and wknds. Lower rates off-season. MAP rates avail. Spec packages avail. Pking: Outdoor, free. Maj CC.

≣≣ **Econo Lodge/Sea Bay Inn**, 6007 Coastal Hwy, Ocean City, MD 21842; tel 410/524-6100 or toll free 800/888-2229; fax 410/524-6100. Exit US 50 at Md 90; turn right on Coastal Hwy. A chain motel on the bay side of Ocean City, with easy access to sports facilities and the ocean. **Rooms:** 92 rms. CI 3pm/CO 11am. Nonsmoking rms avail. **Amenities:** 🛗 A/C, cable TV w/movies, refrig. All units w/terraces. Some have coffeemakers. All have wet bar, microwave. **Services:** 🚐 🗾 🛎 Babysitting. **Facilities:** 🖼 📶 ⅃ 1 rst, washer/dryer. Adjacent to lighted public tennis courts. Guests get 50% discount at nearby fitness center. **Rates:** HS June 10–Sept 4 $84–$114 S or D. Extra person $10. Children under 18 stay free. Min stay HS and wknds. Lower rates off-season. Spec packages avail. Pking: Outdoor, free. Maj CC. Golf packages available.

≣≣ **Fenwick Inn**, 13801 Coastal Hwy, at 138th St, Ocean City, MD 21842; tel 410/250-1100 or toll free 800/492-1873; fax 410/250-0087. Exit US 50 at Md 90; turn left on Coastal Hwy. A modern, glass-and-concrete motel on the bay side of the highway, near the northern end of Ocean City. **Rooms:** 201 rms, stes, and effic. CI 3pm/CO 11am. Express checkout avail. Nonsmoking rms avail. Suites are better furnished and equipped with 2 baths, walk-in closets. **Amenities:** 🛗 ⚙ A/C, cable TV w/movies, refrig. Suites have stoves. **Services:** ✗ 🛒 🍽 **Facilities:** 🗄 🏊 🚺 1 rst, 1 bar (w/entertainment), games rm, whirlpool. Rooftop restaurant with view. **Rates:** HS July 1–Labor Day $99–$159 S or D; from $250 ste; from $139 effic. Extra person $10. Children under 18 stay free. Min stay wknds. Lower rates off-season. MAP rates avail. Spec packages avail. Pking: Outdoor, free. Maj CC. Golf packages available.

≣≣ **Georgia Belle Hotel**, 12004 Coastal Hwy, at 120th St, Ocean City, MD 21842; tel 410/250-4000 or toll free 800/542-4444; fax 410/250-9014. Exit US 50 at Md 90; turn left on Coastal Hwy and proceed to 120th St. A stucco-and-concrete motel close to the beach. Clean and basic. **Rooms:** 98 rms and stes; 1 ctge/villa. CI 2pm/CO 11am. Nonsmoking rms avail. Large, simple rooms. Some have ocean view across parking lot; some can see ocean from side. **Amenities:** 🛁 A/C, cable TV w/movies, refrig. All units w/terraces. Microwaves and refrigerators available for a fee. **Services:** 🍽 🚐 🛒 🍽 Babysitting. **Facilities:** 🗄 🏊 🚺 1 rst. Passes available to nearby fitness and health center. **Rates:** HS June–Aug $99–$175 S or D; from $119 ste. Extra person $6. Children under 12 stay free. Min stay HS. Lower rates off-season. Higher rates for spec evnts/hols. AP and MAP rates avail. Spec packages avail. Pking: Outdoor, free. Ltd CC. Efficiencies rent by week only ($1,200/wk). Golf and other packages available.

≣≣≣ **Holiday Inn Oceanfront**, 6600 Coastal Hwy, at 67th St, Ocean City, MD 21842; tel 410/524-1600 or toll free 800/638-2106; fax 410/524-1135. Exit US 50 at Md 90; turn left on Coastal Hwy. A large resort motel with extensive indoor facilities. **Rooms:** 216 effic. CI 3pm/CO 11am. Nonsmoking rms avail. Fairly large rooms. Separate sitting area with its own sofa bed can be partitioned off. **Amenities:** 🛁 🚻 📺 🍷 A/C, cable TV w/movies, refrig. All units w/terraces. **Services:** ✗ 🎨 🛒 **Facilities:** 🗄 🏊 🎳 🏊 🚺 1 rst (*see also* "Restaurants" below), 2 bars, 1 beach (ocean), lifeguard, games rm, lawn games, spa, sauna, whirlpool, washer/dryer. Attractive outdoor pool/bar/tennis court area. Tanning rooms. Very large game room with pool table and video games. **Rates:** HS July 1–Aug 28 from $159 effic. Extra person $9. Children under 19 stay free. Min stay HS. Lower rates off-season. Higher rates for spec evnts/hols. AP and MAP rates avail. Spec packages avail. Pking: Outdoor, free. Maj CC. Golf packages available for nearby courses.

≣≣≣ **Howard Johnson Hotel on the Boardwalk**, 1109 Atlantic Ave, Ocean City, MD 21842; tel 410/289-7251 or toll free 800/926-1122; fax 410/289-3435. Exit US 50 at Baltimore Ave. Right on the boardwalk and beach, this motel has all the facilities of a standard oceanfront resort. **Rooms:** 90 rms. CI 3pm/CO 11am. Nonsmoking rms avail. Rooms range in size but are furnished similarly. **Amenities:** 🛁 A/C, cable TV w/movies,

refrig, in-rm safe. All units w/terraces. Amenities vary somewhat from room to room. Some have hair dryers and refrigerators. **Services:** ✗ 🛒 **Facilities:** 🗄 🚲 🎿 🚺 1 rst, 1 bar, 1 beach (ocean), lifeguard, board surfing. **Rates (CP):** HS June 10–Sept 4 $109–$169 S or D. Extra person $5. Children under 12 stay free. Min stay HS and wknds. Lower rates off-season. Higher rates for spec evnts/hols. Spec packages avail. Pking: Indoor, free. Maj CC. Premium for oceanfront rooms.

≣≣≣ **Quality Inn Beachfront**, Oceanfront at 33rd St, PO Box 910, Ocean City, MD 21842; tel 410/289-1234 or toll free 800/221-2222. Exit US 50 at Baltimore Ave N; turn right at 33rd St. A nearly new chain motel with attractive decor throughout. **Rooms:** 75 rms and effic. CI 3pm/CO 11am. Nonsmoking rms avail. All are oceanfront or ocean view. Most are efficiencies. **Amenities:** 🛁 🚻 A/C, cable TV w/movies, refrig, VCR. All units w/terraces. **Services:** ✗ 🛒 **Facilities:** 🗄 🏊 🚺 1 rst, 1 beach (ocean), lifeguard, games rm, sauna, steam rm, whirlpool, washer/dryer. A very attractive indoor pool and spa in an atrium. Restaurant serves breakfast only. **Rates:** HS July 15–Aug 28 $158–$234 S or D; from $158 effic. Extra person $10. Min stay HS. Lower rates off-season. Higher rates for spec evnts/hols. Pking: Indoor, free. Maj CC.

≣≣≣ **Quality Inn Boardwalk**, 1601 Boardwalk, at 17th St, Ocean City, MD 21842; tel 410/289-4401 or toll free 800/638-2106; fax 410/289-8620. Exit US 50 at Baltimore Ave; go north to 17th St. A well-maintained, middle-aged oceanfront hotel with an excellent location on the boardwalk. Good choice for families. **Rooms:** 179 rms and effic. Exec-level rms avail. CI 3pm/CO 11am. Nonsmoking rms avail. Furnishings are better than average. All but 20 rooms are oceanfront. **Amenities:** 🛁 🚻 🍷 A/C, satel TV w/movies, refrig. Some units w/terraces. Most units have stove, microwave, and refrigerator. **Services:** 🛒 Video cameras available for a fee. **Facilities:** 🗄 🎳 🚺 1 rst, 1 beach (ocean), lifeguard, games rm, spa, sauna, steam rm, whirlpool, washer/dryer. Tanning room. **Rates:** HS June 26–Labor Day $114–$134 S or D; from $144 effic. Extra person $7. Children under 6 stay free. Min stay HS. Lower rates off-season. Spec packages avail. Pking: Outdoor, free. Maj CC. Attractive packages for those over 50.

≣≣≣ **Quality Inn Oceanfront**, 5400 Coastal Hwy, at 54th St, Ocean City, MD 21842; tel 410/524-7200 or toll free 800/638-2106; fax 410/723-0018. Exit US 50 at Md 90; turn right at Coastal Hwy and proceed to 54th St. North of the boardwalk, this oceanfront resort motel is built around an attractive atrium with pools, ponds, spas, tropical plants, and, especially interesting for children, parrots and other birds. **Rooms:** 130 effic. CI 3pm/CO 11am. Nonsmoking rms avail. All units are attractively decorated efficiencies done in beach-theme pastels. **Amenities:**

🛅 ♨ ☜ A/C, cable TV w/movies, refrig. All units w/terraces. Microwaves. **Services:** ✗ ♫ **Facilities:** 🎱 ♬¹ ⚑ ⚓ 1 rst, 1 bar, 1 beach (ocean), lifeguard, games rm, spa, sauna, whirlpool, playground, washer/dryer. Pool is outdoors. **Rates:** HS July–Aug 28 from $154 effic. Extra person $5. Children under 6 stay free. Min stay wknds. Lower rates off-season. Higher rates for spec evnts/hols. MAP rates avail. Spec packages avail. Pking: Outdoor, free. Maj CC.

≣≣ Ramada Limited Oceanfront, Oceanfront at 32nd St, PO Box 160, Ocean City, MD 21842; tel 410/289-6444 or toll free 800/638-2106; fax 410/289-0108. Exit US 50 at Baltimore Ave; go north, then right at 32nd St. Formerly the Stardust Oceanfront, this well-kept but basic motel should be upgraded in 1995 to Ramada standards. Located on the ocean in a pleasant area behind the dunes. **Rooms:** 76 effic. CI 3pm/CO 11am. All units are efficiencies. Some are oceanfront; others have ocean views. **Amenities:** 🛅 ♨ ☐ ☜ A/C, cable TV w/movies, refrig. Some units w/terraces. **Services:** ♫ Maid replaces towels each afternoon after swimming time. **Facilities:** 🎱 ⚙ 1 beach (ocean), lifeguard, lawn games, washer/dryer. Volleyball on private beach area. **Rates (CP):** HS July 1–Aug 27 from $152 effic. Extra person $7. Children under 3 stay free. Min stay HS. Lower rates off-season. Higher rates for spec evnts/hols. Spec packages avail. Pking: Outdoor, free. Maj CC. Favorable weekly rates.

≣≣ Talbot Inn, 311 Talbot St, PO Box 548, Ocean City, MD 21842; tel 410/289-9125 or toll free 800/659-7703; fax 410/289-6792. Take US 50 to Ocean City; turn right on Philadelphia Ave, then right on Talbot St. A basic but exceptionally well-maintained property with efficiency units. Located near fishing and watersports center of Ocean City. **Rooms:** 34 effic. CI 2pm/CO 11am. Very clean and neat. **Amenities:** 🛅 A/C, cable TV, refrig. Microwaves. **Facilities:** ☐ ⚓ 1 rst, 1 bar (w/entertainment). Parasailing available. Well-known MR Ducks Cafe with bar is a popular gathering place on the waterfront. **Rates:** HS June 10–Sept 5 from $75 effic. Extra person $4. Children under 2 stay free. Min stay HS and wknds. Lower rates off-season. Pking: Outdoor, free. Ltd CC.

Inn

≣≣≣≣ The Lighthouse Club, 56th St, in the Bay, Ocean City, MD 21842; tel 410/524-5400 or toll free 800/767-6060; fax 410/524-9327. Exit US 50 at Md 90; turn right on Coastal Hwy, then right on 56th St. Styled as a large lighthouse, this building is situated among the natural marshes of Sinepuxent Bay. Hallways are adorned with nautical prints. Unsuitable for children under 18. **Rooms:** 23 stes. CI 4pm/CO noon. Large rooms are very light and airy, outfitted with elegant island-style furniture including 4-poster beds. Some closets have doors; some

do not. **Amenities:** 🛅 ☐ ☜ A/C, cable TV w/movies, refrig, VCR, bathrobes. All units w/terraces, some w/fireplaces, all w/Jacuzzis. China and good-quality glassware in rooms. **Services:** ✗ ☞ VP ⚗ ☒ ♫ Car-rental desk. **Facilities:** 🎱 1 rst, 1 bar, lifeguard. Guests enjoy all facilities at Coconut Malorie hotel and at nearby health club. **Rates (CP):** HS June 15–Sept 15 from $129 ste. Extra person $15. Min stay HS. Lower rates off-season. MAP rates avail. Spec packages avail. Pking: Outdoor, free. Ltd CC.

Restaurants 🍴

The Bayside Skillet/The Crepe and Omelette Place, 77th St and Coastal Hwy, Ocean City; tel 410/524-7950. Exit US 50 at Md 90; turn left on Coastal Hwy and proceed to 77th St. **Seafood/Crepes & omelettes.** A pretty dining room, done in light wood, pink, and white, with large windows and a central skylight. Also has outdoor dining on the deck overlooking the bay. Crepes and omelettes are specialties, with a few soups and other light dishes. Dinner (in season only) is primarily seafood. A favorite place for light fare. **FYI:** Reservations not accepted. Beer and wine only. **Open:** HS June–Sept daily 24 hrs. Reduced hours off-season. Closed Dec 25. **Prices:** Main courses $10–$18. Ltd CC. ♥ ⚓ ⚙

Bonfire, 71st and Coastal Hwy, Ocean City; tel 410/524-7171. Exit US 50 at Md 90. **American/Chinese/Seafood.** A large establishment with several warm, semiformal dining rooms. The very large oval bar is comfortable. American and Chinese fare are offered; all-you-can-eat seafood and prime rib buffet is popular. **FYI:** Reservations recommended. Band/dancing. Children's menu. **Open:** HS May–Oct 1 daily 4–10pm. Reduced hours off-season. Closed Christmas week. **Prices:** Main courses $10–$25. Maj CC. 🎬 ▼

Capital Bill Bunting's Angler, 312 Talbot St, Ocean City; tel 410/289-7424. Follow US 50 to Philadelphia Ave, turn right, go 1 block to Talbot St, turn right. **American/Seafood.** An outdoor deck and excellent views of the boat harbor more than make up for the simple decor of this traditional seafood restaurant, family-owned since 1938. Fresh seafood predominates, but other American fare is offered. Each dinner includes complimentary cruise aboard a party boat. **FYI:** Reservations recommended. Rock. Children's menu. **Open:** HS May–Sept breakfast daily 5am–noon; lunch daily 11am–5pm; dinner daily 3:30–10pm. Reduced hours off-season. Closed Oct–Apr. **Prices:** Main courses $10–$20. Ltd CC. ⚓ 🖼 ▼ VP ⚙

Dumser's Dairyland Restaurant, 12305 Coastal Hwy, at 123rd St, Ocean City; tel 410/250-5543. Exit US 50 at Md 90; turn left on Coastal Hwy and proceed to 123rd St. **American/**

Cafe. A bright, traditional cafe/ice cream parlor with old-fashioned ceiling fans and drop lights, white wooden booths, and pastel walls. Standard American breakfast and lunch plus *real* ice cream shakes, sodas, and floats. Ice cream and baked goods made on premises; 1940s musical memorabilia on walls. **FYI:** Reservations not accepted. Children's menu. Dress code. No liquor license. **Open:** HS June–Labor Day breakfast daily 7am–4pm; lunch daily 11am–11pm; dinner daily 4–11pm. Reduced hours off-season. Closed Dec 25. **Prices:** Main courses $7–$16. Ltd CC. ⬛ &

Fager's Island, in the Coconut Malorie, 60th St on the bay, Ocean City; tel 410/524-5500. Exit US 50 at Md 90. **American/Seafood.** Attractive rooms in blue with large windows on Sinepuxent Bay. Nice sunset views. Bar is less formal than dining room, which has dark woods, green linen, and wood chairs. Mostly seafood with various specialty sauces for dinner. Seafood raw bar. Fresh breads. Won award for best wine selection in Maryland. Wine list contains regional descriptions and maps. **FYI:** Reservations recommended. Dancing/rock. Children's menu. **Open:** Lunch daily 11am–10pm; dinner daily 5–10:30pm; brunch Sun 11am–3pm. **Prices:** Main courses $17–$25. Maj CC. ⬛ ⬛ VP &

Hanna's Marina Deck, 306 Dorchester St, Ocean City; tel 410/289-4411. **American/Seafood.** Fresh seafood, breads, and muffins are signatures of this simple restaurant with wooden deck floor and large windows looking out on the boat harbor. Some beef, veal, and poultry are offered. **FYI:** Reservations accepted. Children's menu. Dress code. **Open:** HS Apr–Oct lunch Mon–Sat 11:30am–4pm; dinner Mon–Sat 4–11pm, Sun 3–11pm; brunch Sun 10am–3pm. Reduced hours off-season. Closed some hols; Mid Oct–Mar. **Prices:** Main courses $8–$20. Maj CC. ⬛ ⬛ ⬛ VP

Harrison's Harbor Watch, Boardwalk S overlooking inlet, Ocean City; tel 410/289-5121. Exit US 50 at Baltimore Ave. **Seafood.** Casual, with booths and tile-topped tables overlooking Ocean City Inlet. Fresh seafood is kept refrigerated throughout shipping, storage, and preparation. Some pasta, meat, and fowl dishes. Access for the disabled on 1st floor only. Efficient, computerized order system. **FYI:** Reservations recommended. Children's menu. **Open:** HS Mid-May–mid-Oct lunch daily 11:30am–10pm; dinner daily 4:30–10pm. Reduced hours off-season. Closed Dec 25. **Prices:** Main courses $10–$20. Maj CC. ⬛ ⬛ &

Higgins' Crab House, 31st St and Coastal Hwy, Ocean City; tel 410/289-2581. Exit US 50 at Baltimore Ave; go north to 31st St. **Seafood.** A classic Maryland crab house with wood paneling and tables covered with rolls of brown paper. The bar is for service, not lingering. Fresh steamed hard crabs are the specialty, but other seafood dishes are available, plus barbecued ribs and a few other meat and chicken offerings. Also at: Md 33 and Pea Neck Rd, St Michaels (tel 410/745-5056). **FYI:** Reservations accepted. Children's menu. **Open:** HS May–Sept daily 2:30–10pm. Reduced hours off-season. Closed some hols; Dec–Jan. **Prices:** Main courses $11–$20. Maj CC. ⬛

The Hobbit Restaurant and Bar, 81st St and the Bay, Ocean City; tel 410/524-8100. Exit US 50 at Md 90; turn left at Coastal Hwy and proceed to 81st St; turn left. **Cafe/Continental.** Attractive dining rooms in mauve and gray, with large windows overlooking a saltwater marsh and Sinepuxent Bay. Café menu with excellent selection of salads and other light fare in addition to dinner menu. **FYI:** Reservations accepted. Children's menu. **Open:** Lunch daily 11am–midnight; dinner daily 5–10pm. Closed Dec 25. **Prices:** Main courses $15–$21. Maj CC. ⬛ ⬛ &

⑤ **Paul Revere Smorgasbord**, 2nd St and Boardwalk, Ocean City; tel 410/524-1776. Exit US 50 at Baltimore Ave. **American/Seafood.** Brick and rough-hewn wood walls, bare wood tables, and colonial decor in this large restaurant that often serves 2,000 diners a day in peak summer season. Straightforward, American-style food. Price (reduced for children) covers all-you-can-eat meal, with large salad and dessert bars. **FYI:** Reservations not accepted. Children's menu. Beer and wine only. **Open:** HS June–Sept daily 3:30–9pm. Reduced hours off-season. Closed Oct–Mar. **Prices:** PF dinner $7.99. Ltd CC. ⬛ ⬛ &

★ **Phillips Crab House**, 2004 Philadelphia Ave, at 20th St, Ocean City; tel 410/289-6821. Exit US 50 at Baltimore Ave; go north to 20th St. **Seafood.** Dark wood paneling and inlaid tables covered with white butcher paper. Tiffany-style lamps in most dining rooms, along with stained-glass windows. Downstairs has an à la carte menu, while upstairs is an all-you-can-eat buffet. Crab and seafood dominate in both. The 13 dining rooms and 6 kitchens, including 2 display-cooking areas upstairs, make this one of the largest restaurants in Maryland. **FYI:** Reservations not accepted. Children's menu. **Open:** HS June–Sept lunch daily noon–4pm; dinner daily 4–10pm. Reduced hours off-season. Closed some hols; Nov–Easter. **Prices:** Main courses $8–$22. Maj CC. ⬛ &

♣ **Reflections**, in Holiday Inn Oceanfront, 6600 Coastal Hwy, Ocean City; tel 410/524-5252. MD 90 exit off US 50. **New American/French.** Not your average hotel restaurant. Brick walls, statuary, and attractive furnishings make for a classical setting at this award-winning establishment with reputation for fine dining. Affiliated with the *Chaine des Rotisseurs,* chef is highly qualified and well recognized. Menu changes daily, according to availability of fresh items. Specialty is tableside cooking. Exceptional wine list. **FYI:** Reservations recommended. Dress code.

No smoking. **Open:** Breakfast daily 6:30–11:30am; lunch daily 11:30am–1pm; dinner daily 4–10pm. **Prices:** Main courses $15–$26. Maj CC. ⊙ ☑ ⚹

Windows on the Bay, in Ocean City Health Club, 6103 Sea Bay Dr, Ocean City; tel 410/723-DINE. Exit US 50 at Md 90; turn right on Coastal Hwy, then right on 61st St; follow to Sea Bay Dr. **International.** A very attractive 2nd-floor dining room decorated simply and in excellent taste. Comfortable seating and fine views of Sinepuxent Bay. A wide range of American, French, Italian, and German dishes prepared by chef with very good reputation. Breads baked on premises. **FYI:** Reservations recommended. Piano. Children's menu. Dress code. **Open:** Daily 5–9:30pm. Closed some hols; Christmas week. **Prices:** Main courses $9–$18. Maj CC. ⊙ ⛰ ☑

Attractions 🖼

Ocean City Life-Saving Station Museum, 813 S Atlantic Ave; tel 410/289-4991. Perched on the southern tip of the boardwalk, this small museum is housed in a building that dates from 1891. Displays include rare artifacts of the region; dollhouse models depicting Ocean City in its early years; a pictorial history of the significant hurricanes and storms that have hit the mid-Atlantic coast; saltwater aquariums with indigenous sea life; and a unique collection of sand from around the world. **Open:** June–Sept, daily 11am–10pm; May, Oct, daily 11am–4pm; Nov–Apr, Sat–Sun noon–4pm. $

Ocean City Wax Museum, Boardwalk at Wicomico St; tel 410/289-7766. Some of the over 150 lifelike figures here are in settings enhanced by animation, high-tech lighting, and sound effects. The cast of characters ranges from such Hollywood greats as Charlie Chaplin and Marilyn Monroe to such music stars as Elvis Presley, Michael Jackson, and Dolly Parton. In addition, there are scenes from classic movies and fairy tales, as well as great moments of history from the California gold rush to man's first walk on the moon. **Open:** Daily, call to confirm times. $$

Trimper's Park, Boardwalk between S Division and S 1st Sts; tel 410/289-8617. This amusement park, established in 1887, has over 100 rides and attractions including a water flume and a 1902 merry-go-round with hand-carved animals. **Open:** May–Sept, daily 1pm–midnight; Feb–Apr and Oct–Nov, Sat–Sun only. $

Jolly Roger, 30th St and Coastal Hwy; tel 410/289-3477. Home to Ocean City's largest roller coaster, as well as miniature golf courses, a petting zoo, water slides, and magic shows. Each attraction is priced individually. **Open:** May–Sept, daily 2pm–midnight.

Frontier Town and Rodeo, Md 1; tel 410/289-7877. Set on 38 acres of woodland, this park features an 1860s replica of a western town, rodeos, cowboy and dance-hall shows, stagecoach rides, riverboats, a steam train, and a giant water slide. Children can also ride the trails, pan for gold, or visit a petting zoo. Free shuttle bus between park and downtown Ocean City. **Open:** Mid-June–Labor Day, daily 10am–6pm. $$$

Assateague State Park, Md 611; tel 410/641-2120. Situated on an island 10 miles south of Ocean City, the park is famous for the bands of wild ponies that roam the land. Although they are a thrill to see, visitors are warned to keep a safe distance; these animals can kick and bite, and it is illegal to feed or touch them. The park has 2 miles of ocean frontage, with a white-sand beach and dunes up to 14 feet high. Visitors can swim, surf, fish, and picnic, and there are over 300 campsites. **Open:** Daily sunrise to sunset. $

OXFORD

Map page M-3, C7 (S of Easton)

Inns 🛏

≣≣ **Oxford Inn**, 510 S Morris St, PO Box 627, Oxford, MD 21654; tel 410/226-5220. Exit US 50 at Md 333; follow Oxford Rd to Morris St. This handsome old clapboard building is at the edge of town, within walking distance of the harbor and historic district. The wide front porch is used for outdoor dining and watching the boats and cars pass by. **Rooms:** 11 rms and stes (4 w/shared bath). CI 2pm/CO 11am. No smoking. No TVs in rooms, but sitting room has cable TV. Armoires substitute for closets. **Amenities:** A/C. No phone or TV. **Services:** ✗ 🚗 Babysitting, wine/sherry served. **Facilities:** 🅿️ 1 rst, 1 bar, playground, guest lounge w/TV. Public tennis courts across street. Public beach nearby. Bicycle rentals available in town. **Rates (CP):** HS May–Nov $70–$100 S or D w/shared bath, $95–$135 S or D w/private bath; from $150 ste. Extra person $10. Children under 10 stay free. Min stay wknds. Lower rates off-season. Spec packages avail. Pking: Outdoor, free. Ltd CC.

≣≣≣ **Robert Morris Inn**, N Morris St and the Strand, PO Box 709, Oxford, MD 21654; tel 410/226-5111; fax 410/226-5744. Take Md 333 off US 50. Beautiful historic inn was originally the home of Robert Morris, "financier of the Revolution." Decorated and furnished in an authentic manner. When the restaurant is closed (mid-January to mid-March), rooms are available only on weekends. **Rooms:** 34 rms, stes, and effic. CI 3pm/CO noon. No smoking. Decor varies, but all rooms are furnished with antiques and reproductions. **Amenities:** A/C. No phone or TV. Some units w/terraces. Rooms in the Sandaway

House (1875) have private porches overlooking the Tred Avon River. **Services:** 🚐 Car-rental desk. **Facilities:** 🔟 ⅏ 1 rst (*see also "Restaurants" below*), 1 bar, 1 beach (cove/inlet), guest lounge w/TV. Nice beach for swimming except during late-summer jellyfish season. **Rates:** HS Apr–Thanksgiving $70–$180 D; from $100 ste; from $120 effic. Children under 10 stay free. Min stay HS and wknds. Lower rates off-season. Spec packages avail. Pking: Outdoor, free. Ltd CC. Closed: mid Jan–Mar.

Restaurants 🍴

★ **Pier St Restaurant**, 104 W Pier St, Oxford; tel 410/226-5171. From US 50, follow Md 333 W to Oxford; turn left at Morris St, then right on Pier St. **Regional American/Seafood.** A traditional Maryland crab house and still part of a seafood-packing business, this pleasant, windowed dining room opens to a deck beside the Tred Avon River. Locals come here for spectacular river views and seafood, especially crab cakes made from fresh local crabmeat. Prime rib, chicken, and steak are available. **FYI:** Reservations recommended. Children's menu. **Open:** Lunch daily 11:30am–4:30pm; dinner Mon–Sat 4:30–9:30pm, Sun 11:30am–9:30pm. Closed some hols; Dec–Mar. **Prices:** Main courses $10–$17. Ltd CC. 🍱 🏞️

Robert Morris Inn, N Morris St and the Strand, Oxford; tel 410/226-5111. From US 50, follow Oxford Rd (Md 333) to Morris St; adjacent to ferry dock. **Regional American/Seafood.** Located in the family home of Robert Morris, a financier of the American Revolution, this historic inn and tavern has old wood paneling in some rooms, wallpaper in others, reproduction period chairs in all. Famous for crab cakes but has a good variety of other seafood and meat entrees. **FYI:** Reservations not accepted. Children's menu. Jacket required. **Open:** HS Apr–Nov breakfast Wed–Mon 8–11am; lunch Wed–Mon noon–3pm; dinner Wed–Mon 6–9pm. Reduced hours off-season. Closed Dec 25; mid-Jan–Mar. **Prices:** Main courses $13–$27. Ltd CC. ♥ 🍱 ⅏

PIKESVILLE

Map page M-3, B7 (N of Baltimore)

Hotels 🏨

≡≡≡ Comfort Inn Northwest, 10 Wooded Way, Pikesville, MD 21208; tel 410/484-7700 or toll free 800/732-2458; fax 410/653-1516. Exit 20 off I-695. This is a very acceptable, comfortable place to stay, convenient to the Baltimore Beltway (I-695). **Rooms:** 179 rms, stes, and effic. CI 3pm/CO 11am. Nonsmoking rms avail. Clean rooms have simple but coordinat-ed decor. **Amenities:** 📺 ⅏ A/C, cable TV w/movies, shoe polisher. Some units w/terraces. **Services:** 🗑️ 🔧 🥂 **Facilities:** 🔧 🔟 ⅏ 1 rst, lifeguard, playground, washer/dryer. **Rates (CP):** HS May–Aug $49–$55 S; $52–$59 D; from $89 ste; from $89 effic. Lower rates off-season. Higher rates for spec evnts/hols. Pking: Outdoor, free. Maj CC.

≡≡≡ Pikesville Hilton Inn, 1726 Reisterstown Rd, Pikesville, MD 21208; tel 410/653-1100 or toll free 800/445-8667; fax 410/484-4138. Exit 20 off I-695. A polished, elegant hotel with resort-like facilities and ambience, beautiful lobby. **Rooms:** 171 rms and stes. Exec-level rms avail. CI 3pm/CO noon. Express checkout avail. Nonsmoking rms avail. Nice, well-furnished rooms. **Amenities:** 📺 ⅏ 🥂 A/C, cable TV w/movies, shoe polisher. Some units w/terraces. **Services:** ✕ 🚐 🗑️ 🔧 Car-rental desk, masseur. **Facilities:** 🔧 🔘 🎾 🚣 📦 🖥️ ⅏ 1 rst, 1 bar (w/entertainment), lifeguard, spa, sauna, whirlpool, beauty salon. Lovely pool surrounded by flowers, trees, good patio furniture. **Rates (CP):** HS May–Oct $88–$118 S; $98–$128 D; from $300 ste. Extra person $10. Children under 12 stay free. Lower rates off-season. Spec packages avail. Pking: Indoor/outdoor, free. Maj CC.

Restaurant 🍴

Puffin's, 1000 Reisterstown Rd, Pikesville; tel 410/486-8811. Exit 20 off I-695. **Californian.** The atmosphere is a cross between a simple local restaurant and an art gallery, with paintings, sculpture, textiles, jewelry, and other artworks on display and for sale virtually everywhere. Color scheme is black and white. Healthy food here, with no red meat and no dairy products used in preparation. Vegetarians and those with dietary restrictions will feel right at home. **FYI:** Reservations recommended. No smoking. **Open:** Lunch Mon–Sat noon–2:30pm; dinner Mon–Thurs 5:30–9:30pm, Fri–Sat 5:30–10:30pm, Sun 5–8:30pm. Closed some hols. **Prices:** Main courses $8–$20. Maj CC. 🖼️ ⅏

POCOMOKE CITY

Map page M-3, D8

Motels 🏨

≡≡ Days Inn Pocomoke, 15 Ocean Hwy (US 13), Pocomoke City, MD 21851; tel 410/957-3000 or toll free 800/325-2525; fax 410/957-3147. This standard chain motel is in average condition. **Rooms:** 87 rms. CI 1pm/CO 11am. Nonsmoking rms avail. **Amenities:** 📺 A/C, cable TV. All rooms have steam baths. **Services:** ✕ 🗑️ 🔧 🥂 Car-rental desk, babysitting. **Facilities:**

⛫ 150 ♿ 1 rst, 1 bar. **Rates:** HS June–Sept $61–$73 S or D. Extra person $6. Children under 18 stay free. Lower rates off-season. Higher rates for spec evnts/hols. Pking: Outdoor, free. Maj CC. Senior and other discounts.

▤▤ **Quality Inn**, 825 Ocean Hwy (US 13), PO Box 480, Pocomoke City, MD 21851; tel 410/957-1300 or toll free 800/221-2222; fax 410/957-9329. This middle-aged motel is in good if not superior condition. **Rooms:** 64 rms. CI 1pm/CO 11am. Nonsmoking rms avail. **Amenities:** ⛫ A/C, cable TV. Some units w/Jacuzzis. Deluxe rooms have refrigerators. **Services:** ▨ ⌂ ⚲ Car-rental desk, babysitting. Complimentary newspapers. **Facilities:** ⛫ 20 1 rst, 1 bar. Picnic tables and grills on a wooded lawn. **Rates (CP):** HS June 15–Labor Day $73–$84 S or D. Extra person $5. Children under 18 stay free. Lower rates off-season. Pking: Outdoor, free. Maj CC. Senior discounts.

POTOMAC

Map page M-3, B6 (S of Rockville)

Restaurant ⛏

♦ **Old Angler's Inn**, 10801 MacArthur Blvd, Potomac; tel 301/365-2425. Exit 41 off I-495. 2 mi W of I-495. **New American.** This 1860s structure on 10 acres near the C&O Canal has an elegant country decor, with lace curtains, floral wallpaper, wooden floors. Cozy lounge/bar area has upholstered sofas around a fireplace. Calling on a variety of cuisines, chef is known for creative daily specials using fresh and sometimes exotic ingredients. Berries are picked on the grounds, seafood is smoked in-house. Jackets are requested for men in the dining room; more casual dress appropriate for stone patio under huge trees. Dining room is nonsmoking on Friday and Saturday. **FYI:** Reservations recommended. Dress code. **Open:** Lunch Tues–Sat noon–2:30pm; dinner Tues–Sat 6–10:30pm, Sun 5:30–9:30pm; brunch Sun noon–2:30pm. **Prices:** Main courses $21–$29; PF dinner $55. Maj CC. ♥ ▮ ☰ ▣

ROCKVILLE

Map page M-3, B6

Hotels ▤

▤▤ **Clarion Hotel**, 1251 W Montgomery Ave, Rockville, MD 20850; tel 301/424-4940 or toll free 800/366-1251; fax 301/424-1047. Exit 6B off I-270. Popular with business travelers. **Rooms:** 162 rms and stes. CI 3pm/CO noon. Express checkout avail. Nonsmoking rms avail. **Amenities:** ⛫ A/C, cable

TV w/movies, voice mail. **Services:** ✕ ⌇ 🖥 ▨ ⌂ ⚲ Car-rental desk. Complimentary van service to metro, local businesses. **Facilities:** ⛫ ◻ 100 ◻ ♿ 1 rst, 1 bar, lifeguard, games rm. 24-hour business center. **Rates:** $74 S; $78 D; from $89 ste. Extra person $10. Children under 18 stay free. Spec packages avail. Pking: Outdoor, free. Maj CC. Weekend rates.

▤▤▤ **Courtyard by Marriott**, 2500 Research Blvd, Rockville, MD 20850; tel 301/670-6700 or toll free 800/321-2211; fax 301/670-9023. Exit 8 off I-270. Drive west on Shady Grove Rd, turn left on Research Blvd. Attractive lobby with skylights, pastel colors, lots of brass and plants, fireplace. Beautiful landscaped gardens and gazebo in center courtyard. **Rooms:** 157 stes. CI 3pm/CO 1pm. Express checkout avail. Nonsmoking rms avail. All units have desks. **Amenities:** ⛫ ◻ ▦ A/C, cable TV w/movies. Some units w/minibars, some w/terraces. Long phone cords, hot-water tap for tea and instant coffee. Some units have patio or balcony overlooking courtyard. Special phone with on-line information, reservations service, shopping. **Services:** ✕ ▨ ⌂ **Facilities:** ⛫ ◻ 50 ♿ 1 rst, 1 bar, lifeguard, whirlpool, washer/dryer. Restaurant serves breakfast and dinner buffets only. **Rates:** $49–$89 S; $55–$99 D; from $88 ste. Children under 18 stay free. Spec packages avail. Pking: Outdoor, free. Maj CC.

▤▤▤ **Holiday Inn Crowne Plaza**, 1750 Rockville Pike (Va 355), Rockville, MD 20852; tel 301/468-1100 or toll free 800/638-5963; fax 301/468-0308. Exit I-270 at Montrose Rd; go east 1¾ mile to Rockville Pike, turn left; go ¾ mile. A 7-story atrium lobby with putting green, gazebo restaurant, and bar highlights this suburban hotel. **Rooms:** 315 rms and stes. Exec-level rms avail. CI 3pm/CO noon. Express checkout avail. Nonsmoking rms avail. **Amenities:** ⛫ ◻ ▦ A/C, cable TV w/movies, voice mail. Some units w/terraces, some w/Jacuzzis. **Services:** ✕ ⌇ VP 🖥 ▨ ⌂ Car-rental desk, masseur, children's program. **Facilities:** ⛫ ◻ 800 ◻ ♿ 2 rsts, 2 bars (1 w/entertainment), lifeguard, games rm, spa, sauna, whirlpool, beauty salon. Free use of extensive health club with 6 racquetball courts, Nautilus, weights, aerobics classes. Studebaker's nightclub popular with local singles. **Rates:** $115–$155 S or D; from $225 ste. Extra person $10. Children under 19 stay free. Higher rates for spec evnts/hols. Spec packages avail. Pking: Indoor/outdoor, free. Maj CC.

▤▤▤ **Ramada Inn at Congressional Park**, 1775 Rockville Pike (Va 355), Rockville, MD 20852; tel 301/881-2300 or toll free 800/255-1775; fax 301/881-9047. Exit I-270 at Montrose Rd; go east to Rockville Pike, turn left. Special emphasis on business travelers at this suburban hotel directly across from metro station. **Rooms:** 160 rms and stes. Exec-level rms avail. CI 2pm/CO noon. Nonsmoking rms avail. Executive level has oversize recliners, large desks. **Amenities:** 🖥️♨️📺A/C, cable TV w/movies, refrig. Some units w/minibars. Small refrigerators in executive-level rooms. **Services:** ✕ 🚐 📠 🍽️ 🛎️ Those on executive level get complimentary morning newspapers, business services. **Facilities:** 🏊 ⅙ 1 rst. **Rates:** $69–$105 S or D; from $150 ste. Extra person $8. Children under 18 stay free. Spec packages avail. Pking: Outdoor, free. Maj CC.

≣≣≣ **Woodfin Suites**, 1380 Piccard Dr, Rockville, MD 20850; tel 301/590-9880 or toll free 800/237-8811; fax 301/590-9614. Exit 8 off I-270. 1 mi W of Va 355. Elegant, all-suites facility in landscaped office park. The 3-tiered lobby features grand piano, ornate fireplace with hearth, floor-to-roof windows. **Rooms:** 203 stes. CI 4pm/CO noon. Nonsmoking rms avail. All units have completely stocked kitchens and open to courtyards, 1 with pool. Most units have sitting area and separate bedroom; some have 2 bedrooms. **Amenities:** 🖥️♨️📺 A/C, cable TV w/movies, refrig, VCR, stereo/tape player, in-rm safe. Some units w/fireplaces. Irons and boards in all units. **Services:** 📠 🍽️ 🛎️ Free van service within 5-mile radius includes Metro station. Complimentary newspapers. Daily coffee service. Full 24-hour business center with computers, printers, typewriters, fax, copier. **Facilities:** 🏋️ 🚴 🎱 🖥️ ⅙ 1 rst, 1 bar, lifeguard, whirlpool, washer/dryer. **Rates (CP):** From $127 ste. Extra person $15. Children under 12 stay free. Spec packages avail. Pking: Outdoor, free. Maj CC. Pet fee $2 daily plus $100 deposit.

Restaurants 🍴

Andalucia, 12300 Wilkins Ave, Rockville; tel 301/770-1880. **Spanish.** Unpretentious brick building on a side street in an industrial office park houses this small Spanish restaurant. Dining area accented with Iberian paintings, shawls, and fans on the walls, white lace curtains. Paella and other Spanish-style fresh seafood dishes are the specialties. Reservations recommended on weekends. **FYI:** Reservations accepted. **Open:** Lunch Tues–Fri 11:30am–2:30pm; dinner Tues–Thurs 5:30–10pm, Fri–Sat 5:30–10:30pm, Sun 4:30–9:30pm. Closed some hols. **Prices:** Main courses $11.50–$16.95. Maj CC.

Benjarong, in Wintergreen Plaza, 855-C Rockville Pike, Rockville; tel 301/424-5533. Exit 6 off I-270. Follow Montgomery Ave east to Rockville Pike; turn right. **Thai.** Peaceful Oriental decor: Thai ceramic pieces, vases, huge carved elephant, and Buddha. Window display of brass works, mirrors also add sense of place. Excellent selection of Thai dishes, including curries and hot-pepper selections. Large portions. **FYI:** Reservations recommended. **Open:** Mon–Thurs 11:30am–9:30pm, Fri–Sat 11:30am–10:30pm, Sun 5–9:30pm. Closed some hols. **Prices:** Main courses $7–$11. Maj CC. ⅙

Bombay Bistro, 98 W Montgomery Ave, Rockville; tel 301/762-8798. Exit 6A off I-270. Follow Md 28 to Rockville Pike (Md 355) west; turn right on Washington St, then left on W Montgomery Ave. **Indian.** Outside it's a 1-story brick business building tucked away on a side street, but it's a bit of India inside, thanks to slow-turning ceiling fans, hanging plants, Indian fabrics on wall, bamboo curtains and chairs. A blend of south Indian vegetarian curry dishes, such as *masala dosai*, and meat and chicken kabobs from a tandoor oven. **FYI:** Reservations not accepted. Beer and wine only. **Open:** Lunch Mon–Fri 11am–2:30pm, Sat–Sun noon–3pm; dinner Sun–Thurs 5–9:30pm, Fri–Sat 5–10pm. Closed Labor Day. **Prices:** Main courses $5.95–$9.95. Ltd CC.

Four Rivers, 184 Rollins Ave, at Jefferson St, Rockville; tel 301/230-2900. Exit 4A off I-270. Follow Montrose Rd to Jefferson St, turn left. **Chinese.** Shares unpretentious 1-story brick building with a dry cleaner, but inside are simply but pleasantly decorated dining areas with red booths, pink tablecloths, Oriental paintings, fish and lobster tanks. Chinese menu features whole fish and other spicy Szechuan selections. A good bargain. **FYI:** Reservations accepted. **Open:** Mon–Fri 11:30am–10:30pm, Sat–Sun 11:30am–11pm. Closed Thanksgiving. **Prices:** Main courses $7.25–$24.95. Maj CC.

Ⓢ **Il Pizzico**, 15209 Frederick Rd, Rockville; tel 301/309-0610. Exit 6A off I-270. **Italian.** An intimate restaurant with simple tile floor, stucco-like walls, salmon-colored tablecloths, fresh-cut flowers, murals of Italy on the walls. Chef has been cited for fine Italian cuisine at modest prices. **FYI:** Reservations not accepted. **Open:** Lunch Mon–Fri 11am–2:30pm; dinner Mon–Thurs 5–9:30pm, Fri–Sat 5–10pm. Closed some hols; last week of Aug. **Prices:** Main courses $6.95–$12.95. Maj CC. ❤️⅙

Kashmir Palace, 855-A Rockville Pike (MD 355), Rockville; tel 301/251-1152. Exit 6 off I-270. Follow Montgomery Ave (Md 28) east to Rockville Pike, turn right. **Indian.** Richly and elegantly decorated with Indian folk art, gold, and brass; quiet Indian music is a soothing background. Choose from a wide selection of northern Indian and Pakistani dishes. Meats are grilled in a traditional tandoor oven. Popular Sunday buffet noon–3pm. **FYI:** Reservations accepted. **Open:** Lunch daily 11:30am–2:30pm; dinner daily 5:30–10:30pm. Closed Dec 25. **Prices:** Main courses $6.95–$11.95. Maj CC. ⅙

Ⓢ **Sam Woo Restaurant**, in Edmonton Shopping Center, 1054 Rockville Pike (Md 355) at Edmonton Dr, Rockville; tel 301/424-0495. Exit 6 off I-270. Follow Montgomery Ave (Md 28) to Rockville Pike; turn right. **Japanese/Korean.** Some of the blond-wood tables in this Orientally adorned restaurant have grills in the middle for barbecuing Korean-style meat dishes. Also Japanese selections. "Samoo Special" is broiled short ribs, special whole fish in house chili sauce. All-you-can-eat luncheon buffet. **FYI:** Reservations recommended. **Open:** Mon–Fri 11:30am–11pm, Sat–Sun noon–11pm. Closed some hols. **Prices:** Main courses $7.50–$16. Maj CC.

ST MARY'S CITY

Map page M-3, D7 (NW of Point Lookout)

Attractions

Historic St Mary's City, Md 5; tel 301/862-0990. Maryland's first capital has been transformed into an 800-acre outdoor history museum. Attractions include a replica of the square-rigged *Maryland Dove,* one of the two ships that brought the first settlers and supplies from England; the reconstructed 1676 State House; the Godiah Spary Tobacco Plantation; and a visitor center that houses an archeology exhibit. **Open:** Mar–Nov, Wed–Sun 10am–5pm.

Point Lookout State Park, Md 5; tel 301/872-5688. This 580-acre peninsula at the confluence of the Chesapeake Bay and the Potomac River is the location of Fort Lincoln, an earthen building constructed by Confederate prisoners, as well as 2 monuments honoring the 3,364 Confederate soldiers that died in prison camps here. The visitor's center contains a civil war museum, open weekends May–Sept. The park has an extensive beach, swimming, fishing, picnicking, hiking trails, and play-grounds. **Open:** Daily sunrise–sunset.

ST MICHAELS

Map page M-3, C7 (W of Easton)

Hotel

St Michaels Harbour Inn and Marina, 101 N Harbor Rd, St Michaels, MD 21663; tel 410/745-9150 or toll free 800/955-9001; fax 410/745-9001. This modern waterfront hotel has splendid views of St Michaels harbor and the Maritime Museum docks. **Rooms:** 46 rms and stes. CI 4pm/CO noon. All rooms have queen or king beds. **Amenities:** A/C, cable TV w/movies, refrig. Some units w/terraces. Most rooms are suites with sink, refrigerator, and counter but no cooking facilities. **Services:** Car-rental desk, babysitting. **Facilities:** 1 rst, 2 bars (1 w/entertainment), whirlpool, washer/dryer. This is one of the few establishments in the area with water sports. **Rates:** HS May 27–Oct 9 $139–$199 S or D; from $189 ste. Extra person $12. Children under 18 stay free.

Min stay HS and wknds. Lower rates off-season. Spec packages avail. Pking: Outdoor, free. Maj CC. Special theme weekends, such as wine tasting, during off-season.

Motel

Best Western St Michaels Motor Inn, 1228 S Talbot St, St Michaels, MD 21663; tel 410/745-3333 or toll free 800/528-1234; fax 410/745-2906. Take exit for Md 322 off US 50; drive west on Md 33 for 9 mi. Highway motel. A modern alternative to the historic accommodations in the center of St Michaels. **Rooms:** 93 rms. CI 3pm/CO 11am. Nonsmoking rms avail. Pleasant, standard motel rooms. **Amenities:** A/C, TV. Some units w/terraces. **Services:** **Facilities:** Large lawn area. **Rates (CP):** HS Apr–Nov $62–$73 S; $68–$88 D. Extra person $8. Children under 18 stay free. Lower rates off-season. Higher rates for spec evnts/hols. Pking: Outdoor, free. Maj CC. Less expensive than most in the area.

Inns

Inn at Perry Cabin, 308 Watkins Lane, St Michaels, MD 21663; tel 410/745-2200 or toll free 800/722-2949; fax 410/745-3348. 20 mi W of Easton. From Easton, take US 322 to Md 33 to St Michaels. 25 acres. An imposing 2-story white clapboard manor, owned by British industrialist Sir Bernard Ashley, with several additions, on Maryland's Eastern Shore, surrounded by extensive lawns and endless miles of river. Unsuitable for children under 10. **Rooms:** 41 rms and stes. CI 3pm/CO noon. All different rooms, some new and shipshape, some old and tilty as an old inn should be. Filled with antiques and period objects; decorated stem to stern with Laura Ashley fabrics and stocked with Laura Ashley toiletries. **Amenities:** A/C, cable TV, bathrobes. Some units w/terraces, some w/Jacuzzis. Mineral water and fresh fruit in every room. **Services:** Twice-daily maid svce, babysitting, afternoon tea served. Coffee and tea at any time. Pampering, butler-style service. **Facilities:** 1 rst (see also "Restaurants" below), 1 bar (w/entertainment), games rm, lawn games, sauna, steam rm, guest lounge. More recreational facilities than usual in an inn of this size, including classic launches for trips on the river, indoor pool, billiard room. Double wooden deck chairs on the lawns. Delightful restaurant with fireplaces and view of river. **Rates (BB):** $175–$325 D; from $325 ste. Extra person $50. Spec packages avail. Pking: Outdoor, free. Ltd CC. Rates are the highest in the area but not out of sight given the setting, amenities, and service. Guest are advised to make dinner reservations when they reserve rooms, especially on weekends.

Wades Point Inn on the Bay, Wades Point Rd, PO Box 7, St Michaels, MD 21663; tel 410/745-2500. Exit 322 off

US 50. 120 acres. A stay at this Victorian inn is like a visit to grandmother's. Many wide porches beckon for reading, conversing, or relaxing. A new adjacent building has more modern comforts. Unsuitable for children under 1. **Rooms:** 23 rms and effic (7 w/shared bath). CI 2pm/CO 11am. No smoking. Rooms vary from small, 1890s-style with shared bath, to large, air-conditioned rooms on the bay. **Amenities:** No A/C, phone, or TV. Some units w/terraces. **Services:** ⤸ Babysitting, afternoon tea served. **Facilities:** 🏠 🖾 🔟 ᚼ Lawn games, guest lounge w/TV. Large bayfront grounds are suitable for fishing, crabbing, or launching a small boat. Beach frontage is along a bulkhead. **Rates (CP):** $74–$85 D w/shared bath, $74–$165 D w/private bath; from $165 effic. Extra person $10. Children under 12 stay free. Min stay wknds. Spec packages avail. Pking: Outdoor, free. Ltd CC. Closed: Jan–Feb.

Resort

≡≡≡ **Harbourtowne Golf Resort and Conference Center**, Md 33 and Martingham Dr, St Michaels, MD 21663; tel 410/745-9066 or toll free 800/446-9066; fax 410/820-9142. Take exit for Md 332 off US 50; drive west on Md 33 through St Michaels; turn right onto Martingham Dr. 153 acres. This attractive waterfront golf resort adjacent to the historic town of St Michaels has outstanding public areas. **Rooms:** 111 rms and stes. CI 3pm/CO 11am. Nonsmoking rms avail. All rooms have water views. **Amenities:** 🖥 🕿 🖭 A/C, cable TV w/movies. All units w/terraces, some w/fireplaces. **Services:** 🚗 🖾 ⤸ 🐾 Babysitting. **Facilities:** 🖾 🚵 ⚠ 🗔 ▶18 🖾 🖳 🛶 🚐 350 ᚼ 2 rsts, 2 bars (1 w/entertainment), 1 beach (cove/inlet), lifeguard, games rm, lawn games. Pete Dye–designed golf course is in excellent condition. Beach is protected, on shallow water. Horseback riding and other activities can be arranged nearby. **Rates (CP):** HS May–Sept $145–$175 S or D; from $250 ste. Extra person $10. Children under 18 stay free. Min stay wknds. Lower rates off-season. Higher rates for spec evnts/hols. AP and MAP rates avail. Spec packages avail. Pking: Outdoor, free. Maj CC. Golf packages available.

Restaurants 🍴

Crab Claw, Navy Point, by Maritime Museum, St Michaels; tel 410/745-2900. From US 50, follow Md 33 W to St Michaels, turn right on Mill St. **Seafood.** A St Michaels tradition, this 2-story, large-windowed building on the harbor has casual dining on the dock during good weather, or inside, where exposed dark wood beams, red-checked tablecloths, and captain's chairs add to the nautical ambience. Seafood here is famous, especially steamed hard crabs and crab cakes. Said to be St Michaels's only restaurant still under original ownership. **FYI:** Reservations

recommended. Children's menu. **Open:** Daily 11am–10pm. Closed some hols; Dec–Mar. **Prices:** Main courses $11–$16. No CC. 🍴 🏔 ᚼ

Higgins' Crab House, 1218 S Talbot St, St Michaels; tel 410/745-5151. From US 50, follow Md 33 W for 9 mi. **American/Seafood.** Nautical decor creates an Eastern Shore feeling at this restaurant that grew out of a still-active seafood-packing business. Reasonably priced seafood is cooked in traditional style. Some nonseafood dishes offered. **FYI:** Reservations recommended. Dress code. **Open:** HS Apr–Dec Sun–Thurs 11am–9pm, Fri–Sat 11am–10pm. Reduced hours off-season. Closed some hols. **Prices:** Main courses $10–$16. Maj CC. 🖾 🖳 💟 ᚼ

♣ **Inn at Perry Cabin**, in the Inn at Perry Cabin, 308 Watkins Lane, St Michaels; tel 410/745-2200. 20 mi W of Easton via US 322 to Md 33 into St Michaels. **Continental.** The refined setting, excellent cuisine, and good value justify the lengthy drive to get here. The country inn decor features floor-to-ceiling mullioned windows that overlook lawns and private docks. A terrace is used for cocktails and after-dinner coffee. Specialties include duck spring roll with plum chutney; noisettes of lamb with gâteau of eggplant and potato puree; medallions of swordfish, red snapper, and salmon on spinach pasta; and white chocolate crème brûlée with kirsch-flavored cherries. Guests can finish their evening with a game of billiards. **FYI:** Reservations recommended. Piano. Jacket required. No smoking. **Open:** Breakfast daily 8–10:30am; lunch daily 12:30–2:30pm; dinner daily 6–9:30pm; brunch Sun 12:30–2:30pm. **Prices:** PF dinner $55. Maj CC. 💟 🖳 🖾 🖾 🏔 ᚼ

Morsels, 205 N Talbot St, St Michaels; tel 410/745-2911. From US 50, follow Md 33 W. **New American/Californian.** Small and informal, this eclectic place has photos and mementos of the owners' sailboat cruises to the Caribbean. Fresh and innovative preparations with a touch of French and California influence. Renovation and expansion are planned during 1995. **FYI:** Reservations accepted. Children's menu. Beer and wine only. **Open:** HS May–Dec breakfast Sun 8:30am–noon; lunch daily 11am–4pm; dinner Sun–Thurs 5:30–9pm, Fri–Sat 5:30–10pm. Reduced hours off-season. Closed Dec 25. **Prices:** Main courses $12–$16. Ltd CC. 🍴

St Michaels Crab House, 305 Mulberry St, St Michaels; tel 410/745-3737. From US 50, follow Md 33 W to St Michaels, turn right on Mulberry St. **Regional American/Seafood.** The bricks and exposed beams of this converted packing house add authenticity to a lovely location and view. Primarily a crab house, it serves up many other traditional Maryland-style seafood choices and a few beef and chicken selections. **FYI:** Reservations recommended. Children's menu. **Open:** HS Apr–Oct Sun–Thurs

11am–10pm, Fri–Sat 11am–11pm. Reduced hours off-season. Closed some hols; Jan–Feb. **Prices:** Main courses $10–$18. Ltd CC. 🚤 🏞️ 👥

Town Dock Restaurant, 125 Mulberry St, St Michaels; tel 410/745-5577. From US 50, follow Md 33 W to St Michaels, turn right on Mulberry St. **Regional American/International/Seafood.** Attractive pastels, large windows, and ceiling fans augment some of the finest harbor views of any St Michaels restaurant. Diners enjoy the panoramas from an inside dining room, enclosed porch, or deck. Known for seafood with an international touch. **FYI:** Reservations recommended. Children's menu. **Open:** HS Apr–Dec lunch daily 11am–4pm; dinner daily 11am–10pm; brunch Sun 11am–2pm. Reduced hours off-season. Closed Dec 25. **Prices:** Main courses $13–$22. Maj CC. 🚤 🏞️ 🅅

208 Talbot, 208 N Talbot St, St Michaels; tel 410/745-3838. From US 50, follow Md 33 W for 9 miles. **New American.** Country, colonial, and wicker furnishings enhance the brick walls and beamed ceilings of this old favorite among St Michaels seafood houses. Entrees are innovative and attractively presented. Excellent local and regional reputation for fine dining. **FYI:** Reservations recommended. Children's menu. Dress code. No smoking. **Open:** HS Mar–Dec lunch Tues–Fri noon–2pm; dinner Tues–Sat 5–10pm, Sun 5–9pm; brunch Sun 11am–2pm. Reduced hours off-season. Closed Dec 25; Presidents' Day–mid Mar. **Prices:** Main courses $19–$24. Ltd CC.

Attractions 🎒

Chesapeake Bay Maritime Museum, Mill St (Navy Point); tel 410/745-2916. Dedicated to the preservation of maritime history, this waterside museum consists of 18 buildings on 6 acres of land. Some of the highlights are an authentic 110-year-old Chesapeake Bay lighthouse, a comprehensive bay-craft collection, a boat restoration shop, an extensive waterfowl decoy collection, and an aquarium featuring life from local waters. **Open:** Hours vary according to season. Closed some hols. $$$

St Mary's Square Museum, 409 St Mary's Square; tel 410/745-9561. Located in the historic St Mary's Square in the center of town, the main building (1800) was originally part of a steam and grist mill. The adjacent "Teetotum" building displays exhibits significant to local history and culture. **Open:** May–Oct, Sat–Sun 10am–4pm. Free.

SALISBURY

Map page M-3, C8

Hotel 🛎️

≡≡≡ **Sheraton Inn Salisbury**, 300 S Salisbury Blvd, Salisbury, MD 21801; tel 410/546-4400 or toll free 800/325-3535; fax 410/546-2528. On US 13 Business, ¾ mi S of US 50. A downtown motel adjacent to municipal Riverwalk Park. Underwent some renovation and upgrading in 1994. **Rooms:** 156 rms. CI 3pm/CO noon. Express checkout avail. Nonsmoking rms avail. Spacious rooms, all the same size, but some have king beds. **Amenities:** 📷 ☕ A/C, cable TV w/movies. 1 unit w/terrace. Wet bars in some rooms. **Services:** ✕ 🚗 🖇️ 🔔 **Facilities:** 🏋️ 🏊 🎱 ♿ 1 rst, 1 bar, games rm. **Rates:** HS May–Sept $72–$140 S or D. Extra person $20. Children under 18 stay free. Min stay spec evnts. Lower rates off-season. Higher rates for spec evnts/hols. MAP rates avail. Spec packages avail. Pking: Outdoor, free. Maj CC.

Motels

≡≡ **Comfort Inn Salisbury**, 2701 N Salisbury Blvd, Salisbury, MD 21801; tel 410/543-4666 or toll free 800/221-2222; fax 410/749-2639. On US 13, 3 mi N of US 50. An attractive, well-maintained motel of recent vintage. **Rooms:** 96 rms. CI 3pm/CO 11am. Nonsmoking rms avail. Large and nicely furnished rooms. **Amenities:** 📷 A/C, cable TV w/movies, refrig. Some units w/Jacuzzis. **Services:** 🖇️ 🔔 🧹 **Facilities:** 🎱 ♿ Lawn games. Guests may use pool at Holiday Inn next door. **Rates (CP):** HS Mem Day–Labor Day $54–$62 S; $62–$67 D. Extra person $6. Children under 18 stay free. Lower rates off-season. Spec packages avail. Pking: Outdoor, free. Maj CC. Special rates for persons over 50.

≡≡≡ **Hampton Inn**, 1735 N Salisbury Blvd, Salisbury, MD 21801; tel 410/546-1300 or toll free 800/426-7866; fax 410/546-0370. On Business US 13, 1½ mi N of US 50. This chain motel with good accommodations is conveniently located near shopping centers and Salisbury State University. **Rooms:** 102 rms. CI 3pm/CO noon. Express checkout avail. Nonsmoking rms avail. **Amenities:** 📷 ☕ 📺 A/C, cable TV w/movies. **Services:** 🖇️ 🔔 🧹 **Facilities:** 🏋️ 🎱 ♿ 1 rst, 1 bar (w/entertainment). Well-regarded restaurant next door. **Rates (CP):** HS May–Sept $56–$67 S; $61–$72 D. Children under 18 stay free. Min stay spec evnts. Lower rates off-season. Higher rates for spec evnts/hols. Spec packages avail. Pking: Outdoor, free. Maj CC. Discounts for those over 50.

≣≣≣ **Holiday Inn–Salisbury**, 2125 N Salisbury Blvd, Salisbury, MD 21801; tel 410/742-7142 or toll free 800/465-4329; fax 410/742-5194. On US 13, 3 mi N of US 50. A large motel typical of this chain, it's well maintained and has full facilities. **Rooms:** 123 rms. CI 3pm/CO 11am. Express checkout avail. Nonsmoking rms avail. **Amenities:** 🛏 ⚂ 🖀 A/C, cable TV w/movies. Closed-captioned TV. **Services:** ✕ ⬧ ⤿ ⬥ Babysitting. Games, coloring books available. **Facilities:** ⚄ 🌊 ⚄ 1 rst, 1 bar, washer/dryer. Large, attractive pool in courtyard. **Rates:** HS Apr–Sept $63–$73 S; $71–$81 D. Extra person $8. Children under 18 stay free. Lower rates off-season. Higher rates for spec evnts/hols. MAP rates avail. Spec packages avail. Pking: Outdoor, free. Maj CC. Children under 13 eat free.

Restaurants 🍽

English's Family Restaurant, 735 S Salisbury Blvd, Salisbury; tel 410/742-8182. On Business US 13, 1 mi S of US 50. **Regional American/Seafood.** A classic railroad car–style diner front is reminiscent of the 1930s. Dining room adjoins. Basic American family fare with regional items, such as crab cakes. The English's Family Restaurant chain began here in 1933. **FYI:** Reservations accepted. Children's menu. **Open:** Sun–Thurs 6am–9pm, Fri–Sat 6am–10pm. Closed Dec 25. **Prices:** Main courses $6–$12. Ltd CC. ⬛ ⚄

Webster's 1801, 1801 N Salisbury Blvd, Salisbury; tel 410/742-8000. On Business US 13, 1 mi S of shopping mall. **American/Steak.** An informal but attractive steak house with an especially nice lounge and outdoor deck. Beef predominates, plus a short selection of other traditional American entrees. **FYI:** Reservations accepted. Band/dancing. Children's menu. **Open:** Mon–Thurs 4–9pm, Fri–Sat 4–10pm. Closed some hols. **Prices:** Main courses $9–$22. Maj CC. ⬛ ⬥ ⚄

Attractions 📷

Ward Museum of Wildfowl Art, 909 S Schumaker Dr; tel 410/742-4988. In this area known for its waterfowl population, this museum is a key attraction, the largest of its kind in the world. It is a prime showcase for displays of antique decoys and contemporary carvings, as well as paintings and works on paper. Interpretive galleries help visitors trace the development of the art form from hunters' tools to sculpture. **Open:** Mon–Sat 10am–5pm, Sun noon–5pm. Closed Dec 25. $$

Poplar Hill Mansion, 117 Elizabeth St (Newton Historic District); tel 410/749-1776. The mansion was constructed in the Georgian/federal style and features 2nd-story Palladian windows, several bull's-eye windows, cornice moldings, and a fanlight over the fluted-pilaster front doorway. Also on display are collections of period furniture and original fireplaces and mantels. **Open:** Sun 1–4pm and by appointment. Free.

Pemberton Hall, Pemberton Dr off Md 349; tel 410/742-1741. Listed on the National Register of Historic Places, this 1741 gambrel-roofed brick house is one of Maryland's oldest, located 2 miles southwest of downtown. It is surrounded by a park with nature trails, a picnic area, and a pond. **Open:** May–Oct, Sun 2–4pm and by appointment. Closed some hols. Free.

Salisbury Zoological Park, 755 S Park Dr (City Park); tel 410/548-3188. A 12-acre open-air zoo in the heart of City Park. It houses more than 200 mammals, birds, and reptiles in naturalistic habitats among shade trees and exotic plants. Major exhibits include spectacled bears, monkeys, jaguars, bison, bald eagles, and waterfowl, all native to North, Central, and South America. **Open:** June–Aug, daily 8am–7:30pm; Sept–May, daily 8am–4:30pm. Closed some hols. Free.

Maryland Lady, 505B W Main St; tel 410/543-2466. An 85-foot Victorian-style riverboat offering narrated cruises. The route takes in a variety of sights—from the Salisbury skyline and historic river homes to tugboats, barges, and wildlife and waterfowl in natural habitats. Four types of cruises are offered; reservations are required at least 48 hours in advance. **Open:** Times vary, call for schedule. $$$

SILVER SPRING

Map page M-3, C6 (N of Washington, DC)

Hotels 🏨

≣≣≣ **Courtyard by Marriott–Silver Spring**, 12521 Prosperity Dr, at Cherry Hill Rd, Silver Spring, MD 20904 (White Oak); tel 301/680-8500 or toll free 800/321-2211; fax 301/680-9232. 4½ mi N of I-495 via US 29. A typical member of this comfortable chain, with a landscaped courtyard with gazebo for sitting. Attractive lobby has fireplace set among glass panels looking to courtyard. Located in office park. **Rooms:** 146 rms and stes. CI 3pm/CO noon. Express checkout avail. Nonsmoking rms avail. Dark wood furniture and bright floral spreads. Framed prints carry out color scheme. King rooms have sofas. All have large desks. **Amenities:** 🛏 ⚂ 🖀 A/C, cable TV w/movies. All units w/terraces. Hot-water tap for tea and coffee, long phone cords. **Services:** ✕ ⬧ ⤿ Morning newspapers at door. **Facilities:** ⚄ 🏊 🌊 ⚄ 1 rst, lifeguard, whirlpool, washer/dryer. Lobby restaurant serve all meals but dinner on Saturday and Sunday. **Rates:** $84 S; $94 D; from $107 ste. Extra person $10. Children under 12 stay free. Spec packages avail. Pking: Outdoor, free. Maj CC.

≣≣≣ **Quality Hotel**, 8727 Colesville Rd, Silver Spring, MD 20910 (Downtown); tel 301/589-5200 or toll free 800/376-7666; fax 301/588-1841. Exit 30B off I-495. Go south on Colesville Rd for ½ mile; between Fenton and Spring Sts. A 14-story downtown hotel within walking distance of metro station, shopping mall, restaurants, movies. Marble-floored lobby is attractive but not easily accessible for guests with disabilities. **Rooms:** 254 rms and stes. CI 3pm/CO noon. Express checkout avail. Nonsmoking rms avail. Above-average dark wood furniture lends touch of elegance. King-bed rooms have easy chairs. **Amenities:** 🛢 👌 A/C, satel TV w/movies. Some units w/terraces. **Services:** ✗ 🖼 ↵ **Facilities:** 🔓 🗐 👌 2 rsts, 1 bar, lifeguard, games rm, sauna. Indoor pool on 9th floor open weekday evenings, all day on weekends. Cafe-style restaurant open for breakfast and lunch; Italian eatery serves dinner. **Rates (CP):** $94–$97 S; $104–$107 D; from $105 ste. Extra person $10. Children under 18 stay free. Min stay spec evnts. Spec packages avail. Pking: Indoor, free. Maj CC.

Restaurant 🍴

Crisfield Seafood Restaurant, in Lee Plaza, 8606 Colesville Rd at Georgia Ave, Silver Spring (Downtown); tel 301/588-1572. Exit 30B off I-495. Follow Colesville Rd south for ½ mile. **Seafood.** Named for the Maryland Eastern Shore town known as the "Seafood Capital of the World," this long-time family establishment moved to these modern quarters a few years ago, when urban redevelopment caused its funky, industrial-area home of many decades to be torn down. Adorned with tile floors and wall accents, plain white tables and booths, Chesapeake-area paintings. Popular with locals in search of fresh Maryland-style seafood. Free parking in rear after 4pm. **FYI:** Reservations accepted. Children's menu. Dress code. **Open:** Sun 4–10pm, Mon–Thurs 11:30am–10pm, Fri 11:30am–11pm, Sat 4–11pm. Closed some hols. **Prices:** Main courses $13–$22; PF dinner $20. Maj CC. 👌

STEVENSVILLE

Map page M-3, B7 (E of Annapolis)

See also **Grasonville**

Inn 📷

≣≣≣ **Kent Manor Inn**, 500 Kent Manor Dr, PO Box 291, Stevensville, MD 21666; tel 410/643-5757; fax 410/643-8315.

Exit 37 off US 50/301. Follow Md 8 S to Kent Manor Dr, turn left. 226 acres. A truly beautiful country inn that sits on what originally was a private estate on Thompson Creek. The building dates from the early 19th century and has been carefully restored. Unsuitable for children under 8. **Rooms:** 24 rms and stes. CI 3pm/CO 11am. Rooms are in excellent condition and furnished in period style. **Amenities:** 🛢 👌 A/C, TV. All units w/terraces, some w/fireplaces. **Services:** 🚗 ↵ Babysitting. **Facilities:** 🔓 ⚠ 🗐 🎣 ▣ 👌 1 rst, 1 bar, lawn games, guest lounge w/TV. A well-regarded restaurant downstairs specializes in seafood, beef, and veal. A pier and waterfront along the creek permit fishing, crabbing, and small-boat recreation. **Rates (BB):** $109–$149 D; from $139 ste. Extra person $8. Children under 18 stay free. Spec packages avail. Pking: Outdoor, free. Ltd CC.

Restaurant 🍴

Café Sophie, 401 Love Point Rd, Stevensville (Old Stevensville); tel 410/643-8811. Exit US 50/301 at Md 18. **French.** This former country store with blue, white, and a touch of red recalls the small-town restaurants of France. The owner/chef, a former opera singer and weaver for Coco Chanel, made Jackie Kennedy's inaugural gown. Menu varies according to her preferences, but all selections prepared in provincial French style from fresh ingredients. **FYI:** Reservations recommended. Dress code. Beer and wine only. No smoking. **Open:** Lunch Wed–Fri 11am–3pm, Sat–Sun noon–3pm; dinner Fri–Sat 6:30–9:30pm. Closed some hols. **Prices:** PF dinner $14.95. No CC. ◉

TANEYTOWN

Map page M-3, B6

Inn

≣≣≣ **Antrim 1844**, 30 Trevanion Rd, Taneytown, MD 21787; tel 410/756-6812 or toll free 800/858-1844; fax 410/756-2744. ½ mi E of town square. 24 acres. Lovely and charming, this 1844 inn offers a sense of tranquil elegance. While ordinary in some respects—the porch is nondescript, the grounds not grand—it does feature impressive antique furnishings and unusual decorating themes. Unsuitable for children under 6. **Rooms:** 9 rms and stes; 5 ctges/villas. CI 3pm/CO noon. Each room is unique; 9 are in the main house; 5 are in separate cottages. A converted barn, icehouse, and plantation overseer's house serve as suites. The icehouse has an 18th-century vanity with original hand-painted sink in bath area. Featherbeds, antiques are highlights. **Amenities:** A/C. No phone or TV. Some units w/minibars, some w/terraces, some w/fireplaces, some w/Jacuzzis. **Services:** ✗ VP 🖼 ↵ Babysitting, afternoon tea and wine/sherry served. Country buffet tray outside the door each morning, hors d'oeuvres in living room in evening, gourmet picnic baskets fixed for lunch on request. **Facilities:** 🎰 ⬚ 🚲 ⬚ 🏊 ⬚ 🖵 ⬚ 1 rst, 1 bar (w/entertainment), lawn games, guest lounge. Outdoor pavilion. Pool is painted black and retains heat. Outdoor area, including croquet and garden, popular for private parties. **Rates (CP):** $150–$300 D; from $200 ctge/villa. Extra person $50. Min stay wknds. Spec packages avail. Pking: Outdoor, free. Ltd CC.

THURMONT
Map page M-3, B6 (E of Hagerstown)

Motel 🏨

≣≣≣ **Cozy Country Inn**, 103 Frederick Rd, Thurmont, MD 21788; tel 301/271-4301; fax 301/271-4301. This fun inn set among the mountains has a character all its own. Behind the pale pink exterior is decor with a Camp David/presidential emphasis. The inn is set right on highway but does have cozy, intimate feel. You're surrounded by a collectibles shop, handmade jewelry, craft classes, more. **Rooms:** 16 rms, stes, and effic; 5 ctges/villas. CI 2pm/CO noon. Express checkout avail. Executive, Premium, and Traditional rooms, some with waterbed. The newly remodeled rooms are styled to recall presidents, political dignitaries, or newspeople who've visited Camp David or Cozy Inn. For example, the Roosevelt Room has hangings from Hyde Park, a model of FDR's bed, oversize bath. **Amenities:** 🛏 📞 ⬚ 🍷 A/C, cable TV w/movies, refrig, VCR. Some units w/minibars, some w/terraces, some w/fireplaces, some w/Jacuzzis. Many have refrigerators; some have towel warmers, pants pressers, wet bars, VCRs. **Services:** ✗ ⬚ ⬚ **Facilities:** 🏊 ⬚ ⬚ 🖵 ⬚ 1 rst (*see also* "Restaurants" below), 1 bar. Golf course nearby. Restaurant next door. **Rates (CP):** $36 S; $42–$46 D; from $75 ste; from $43 effic; from $75 ctge/villa. Extra person $4. Children under 12 stay free. Min stay spec evnts. Pking: Outdoor, free. Maj CC.

Restaurant 🍴

★ **Cozy Restaurant**, in the Cozy Country Inn, 103 Frederick Rd, Thurmont; tel 301/271-7373. **American.** One of a kind, funky, eclectic, and fun, this old touched-by-history restaurant features treadle sewing tables and a huge buffet area sporting its own neon sign and canopy, in addition to picture windows and a wall mural. Dark-timbered hallway displays everything from Camp David memorabilia and corral fencing to an old theater ticket booth and arcade games. Meat-and-potatoes fare is served simply and inexpensively; desserts are unique. **FYI:** Reservations recommended. Children's menu. Dress code. **Open:** HS Apr 11–

Jan 9 Mon–Thurs 11am–8:45pm, Fri 11am–9:15pm, Sat 8am–9:15pm, Sun 8am–8:45pm. Reduced hours off-season. Closed Dec 25. **Prices:** Main courses $8–$12. Maj CC. 🛑 🚢 ⬚ ⬚ ⬚

Attractions 🎦

Catoctin Zoo Park, 13019 Catoctin Furnace Rd; tel 301/271-7488. This is a wildlife, breeding, and petting zoo in a 30-acre woodland setting. It is home to more than 500 animals, including big cats, monkeys, bears, and farmyard pets. **Open:** Summer, daily 9am–6pm; rest of year, daily 9am–5pm. $$$

Catoctin Mountain Park, Md 77 off Md 15; tel 301/663-9388. Located 3 miles west of Thurmont and about 15 miles north of downtown Frederick. Adjacent to Camp David, the presidential retreat, lies this 5,769-acre park administered by the National Park Service. Facilities include hiking trails, fishing, cross-country skiing, camping, and cabin rentals. **Open:** Information center, daily 10am–4:30pm. Closed some hols. Free.

TILGHMAN
Map page M-3, C7 (SW of Easton)

Restaurants 🍴

Bay Hundred Restaurant, Md 33, at Knapps Narrows, Tilghman; tel 410/886-2622. 15 mi W of St Michaels; exit 322 off US 50. **International/Seafood.** Guests watch the workboats in Knapps Narrows from this open, airy eatery whose porch dining area is decorated in quiet good taste. Regional seafood dishes are interspersed with southwestern, Cajun, Japanese, and Thai entrees. **FYI:** Reservations recommended. **Open:** HS Mar–Dec lunch daily 11:30am–4:30pm; dinner daily 5:30–9:30pm. Reduced hours off-season. Closed some hols. **Prices:** Main courses $13–$19. Maj CC. 🖼

★ **Harrison's Chesapeake House**, Md 33, Tilghman; tel 410/886-2121. 15 mi W of St Michaels. Follow Md 33 W through St Michaels to Tilghman Island; about 1 mile past Knapps Narrows. **American/Seafood.** One of the oldest restaurants on the Chesapeake, this old building with paneled walls looks out over the water. The waiting room and porch are Eastern Shore friendly and comfortable. Family-style service from a menu emphasizing seafood but with a selection of landlubber entrees. **FYI:** Reservations accepted. Country music. Children's menu. **Open:** Breakfast daily 6–11am; lunch daily 11am–5pm; dinner daily noon–10pm. Closed Dec 25. **Prices:** Main courses $10–$18. Ltd CC.

TOWSON
Map page M-3, B7

Hotel 🏨

≣ ≣ ≣ **Sheraton Baltimore North Hotel**, 903 Dulaney Valley Rd, Towson, MD 21204; tel 410/321-7400 or toll free 800/433-7619; fax 410/296-9534. Exit 27A off I-695. A great place for business conferences, with facilities geared to the business traveler. Well-kept grounds. Skywalk leads to region's largest shopping mall. **Rooms:** 282 rms and stes. Exec-level rms avail. CI 3pm/CO noon. Express checkout avail. Nonsmoking rms avail. Quiet rooms have good desk space. **Amenities:** 🛎 🛢 🖵 A/C, cable TV w/movies, refrig, stereo/tape player, shoe polisher. Some units w/minibars. **Services:** ✕ 🖾 VP 🚗 🖾 🗘 Car-rental desk, babysitting. **Facilities:** 🛗 🛢 800 🖵 ⅙ 2 rsts, 2 bars (1 w/entertainment), lifeguard, spa, sauna, whirlpool, washer/dryer. Nice restaurant and bar facilities. Ballroom. **Rates:** HS Feb–Oct $126 S; $138 D; from $146 ste. Extra person $12. Children under 12 stay free. Min stay spec evnts. Lower rates off-season. Pking: Indoor/outdoor, free. Maj CC.

Motel

≣ **Ramada Inn–Towson/Baltimore**, 8712 Loch Raven Blvd, Towson, MD 21286; tel 410/823-8750 or toll free 800/2-RAMADA; fax 410/823-8644. Exit 29B off I-695. Very low-end but clean property in need of renovation. **Rooms:** 122 rms. CI 3pm/CO noon. Nonsmoking rms avail. Rooms can be noisy, as they are near busy intersection. **Amenities:** 🛎 🛢 A/C, cable TV w/movies. **Services:** ✕ 🚗 🖾 🗘 🖣 **Facilities:** 🛗 120 ⅙ 1 rst, 1 bar, lifeguard, washer/dryer. Independent seafood restaurant in the building. **Rates (CP):** HS Mar–Aug $49–$59 S; $59–$69 D. Extra person $5. Children under 18 stay free. Lower rates off-season. Higher rates for spec evnts/hols. Pking: Outdoor, free. Maj CC.

Restaurants 🍴

Café Troia, in the Penthouse Condominiums, 28 W Allegheny Ave, Towson (business district); tel 410/337-0133. Exit 27A off I-695. **Italian.** Elegant pastels, high ceilings, and attractive print fabrics create a pleasant atmosphere in both dining areas and bar of this informal establishment offering good, authentic Italian fare and fine wines. Bar serves appetizers from main menu, excellent breads, and Belgian chocolates. **FYI:** Reservations recommended. Dress code. No smoking. **Open:** Lunch Tues–Fri 11am–3pm; dinner Sun 5–10pm, Mon–Sat 5–11pm. **Prices:** Main courses $10–$20. Maj CC. 💗

Hersh's Orchard Inn, 1528 E Joppa Rd, Towson; tel 410/823-0384. Exit 29B off I-695. **American/Continental/Seafood.** Formal but cozy, with tapestry-like patterned fabric and dark woods. Entrance has photos of famous patrons from worlds of sports and entertainment. Emphasis on seafood and other fine American selections. Extensive wine list. Service from uniformed staff is very good. **FYI:** Reservations recommended. Piano. Dress code. **Open:** Mon–Thurs 11:30am–10pm, Fri–Sat 11:30am–11pm, Sun noon–9pm. Closed some hols. **Prices:** Main courses $10.95–$25.95. Maj CC. 💗 VP

WALDORF
Map page M-3, C6

Hotel 🏨

≣ ≣ ≣ **Holiday Inn Waldorf**, 1 St Patrick's Dr, at Crain Hwy (US 301), Waldorf, MD 20603; tel 301/645-8200 or toll free 800/HOLIDAY; fax 301/843-7945. A pleasant, 3-story brick building set off from busy US 301 by a lawn dotted with pine trees. Grounds are well landscaped, including trees to break up parking lot. Attractive lobby has polished brick floor, early American furnishings. Convenient to shopping centers, mall, restaurants. **Rooms:** 192 rms, stes, and effic. CI 3pm/CO 11am. Express checkout avail. Nonsmoking rms avail. Units on front have view of lawn. Some suites have cooking facilities. **Amenities:** 🛎 🛢 🖵 A/C, cable TV w/movies. 1 unit w/minibar. **Services:** ✕ 🖾 🗘 🖣 **Facilities:** 🛗 🛢 250 ⅙ 1 rst, 1 bar (w/entertainment), lifeguard, beauty salon, washer/dryer. Large pool with ample concrete deck for sunning. **Rates (CP):** $58 S; $64 D; from $70 ste; from $70 effic. Extra person $6. Children under 18 stay free. Pking: Outdoor, free. Maj CC.

Motels

≣ ≣ **Econo Lodge Waldorf**, US 301 at Acton Lane, Waldorf, MD 20601; tel 301/645-0022 or toll free 800/55-ECONO; fax 301/645-0058. A clean and comfortable chain motel. Brick building located among shopping centers, discount stores, restaurants. **Rooms:** 89 rms and stes. CI noon/CO 11am. Nonsmoking rms avail. **Amenities:** 🛎 🛢 A/C, cable TV w/movies, refrig. Some units w/Jacuzzis. Half of rooms have refrigerators and microwaves. 2 large suites have Jacuzzi in living room. **Services:** 🗘 🖣 **Facilities:** 15 Games rm, washer/dryer. **Rates (CP):** HS Apr–Oct $41–$46 S; $46–$51 D; from $130 ste. Extra person $5. Children under 12 stay free. Lower rates off-season. Higher rates for spec evnts/hols. Pking: Outdoor, free. Maj CC. $15 pet fee.

≣≣ **HoJo Inn by Howard Johnson**, 3125 Crain Hwy (US 301), at Md 228, Waldorf, MD 20602; tel 301/645-8200 or toll free 800/826-4504; fax 301/932-5090. Entrance behind Po' Folks Restaurant. This older, low-slung motel has been immaculately maintained and improved over the years. Spotlessly clean throughout. Convenient to shopping centers, malls, restaurants. **Rooms:** 110 rms and effic. Exec-level rms avail. CI 3pm/CO 11am. Express checkout avail. Nonsmoking rms avail. Standard rooms have bright wood furniture, light color schemes. Some have been turned into executive rooms with sofas, better-quality dark furniture, desks. **Amenities:** 📶 A/C, cable TV w/movies, refrig, in-rm safe. Executive rooms have coffeemakers. **Services:** ✕ ⬜ ⤴ ⬤ Babysitting. Limited room service. **Facilities:** � ⬜ ♿ Restaurant does not serve breakfast. Small pool surrounded by concrete deck and wooden fence to screen from parking lot. Free use of nearby fitness center. **Rates (CP):** HS Mar–Oct $42–$44 S; $43–$45 D; from $48 effic. Extra person $2. Children under 18 stay free. Lower rates off-season. Higher rates for spec evnts/hols. Spec packages avail. Pking: Outdoor, free. Maj CC. Weekend rates, romantic getaway packages. Fee for pets.

Attraction 💼

Dr Samuel A Mudd House; tel 301/645-6870 or 934-8464. US 301 to Md 5, then left on Md 205; after 4 miles, turn right onto Poplar Hill Rd, then right onto Dr Samuel Mudd Rd; the house is ⁴⁄₁₀ mile from there. Situated on 10 acres of family farmland. John Wilkes Booth went to Dr Mudd to have his broken leg set after he fatally shot President Lincoln in 1865. Tours of the home and its period furnishings are often conducted by members of the Mudd family. **Open:** Apr–Nov, Wed 11am–3pm, Sat–Sun noon–4pm. $

WHITEHAVEN

Map page M-3, C7 (SW of Salisbury)

Restaurant 🍴

The Red Roost, Clara Rd, Whitehaven; tel 410/546-5443. Exit US 50 at Md 349; go 6½ miles to Md 352, then 8 miles to Clara Rd; turn left. **Regional American/Seafood.** The name is appropriate, since this unusual eatery is in a converted chicken house, with rustic bare wood walls and ceilings, plain wooden furniture, and tables covered with brown paper. Known for massive all-you-can-eat seafood, fried chicken, and rib specials. Popular with bus tours drawn by a sing-along, party atmosphere. **FYI:** Reservations not accepted. Piano/sing along/singer. Children's menu. **Open:** HS May–Labor Day Mon–Fri 5:30–10pm, Sat 4:30–10pm, Sun 4–9pm. Reduced hours off-season. Closed some hols; Nov–mid-Mar. **Prices:** Main courses $7–$22. Maj CC. 📷

VIRGINIA

A STATE OF LOVE

They knew what they were doing back in 1969 when they decided that "Virginia is for lovers." Long ocean beaches beckon for hand-in-hand strolls. Mountain vistas entice arms to be slipped softly around shoulders. Fireplaces in comfortable resorts invite cuddling on cold winter nights.

For nature lovers, Virginia is a beauty—from the Eastern Shore, where wild ponies live on Assateague Island and where peregrine falcons, snow geese, snowy egrets, and great blue herons have all been spotted, to the Blue Ridge Mountains and the Shenandoah Valley, dappled with wildflowers, dogwood, and azaleas in spring, fiery with foliage in fall. The Skyline Drive and the Blue Ridge Parkway are two of the most scenic drives in America.

But those whose love is most rewarded in Virginia are lovers of American history. The country was born here when the first permanent English settlement in the New World took root on the banks of the James River in 1607. And the colonial past lives on in 18th-century Williamsburg, a gem of restoration and reconstruction where wigs are still powdered, the minuet is still taught, and the militia still drilled. The American Revolution was won at Yorktown, and 7 of the first 12 presidents were born and lived in Virginia. Some of their homes—such as Mount Vernon and Monticello—provide a crash course in 18th- and 19th-century art, architecture, agriculture, domestic economics, and political thought. Preserved here, too, are the battlefields where tens of thousands of men died during the bloody Civil War. And African American history has markers embedded in Virginia's soil. Slaves' quarters are still visible at numerous plantations, such as Carter's Grove near Williamsburg, in this state where slavery first took hold. The Booker T Washington National Monument preserves the plantation cabin—dirt floor, glassless windows—that was this great American's boyhood home.

Virginia has much more to offer besides history—a spa resort in the town of Hot Springs that has hosted presidents from Jefferson through Reagan, horse farms in green rolling Hunt Country, and a growing wine industry. But when it comes to the number, significance, and evocative power of its historical treasures, no state in the Union can rival the Old Dominion.

STATE STATS

Capital
Richmond

Area
39,704 square miles

Borders
District of Columbia,
Maryland, West Virginia,
Tennessee, Kentucky,
North Carolina,
the Atlantic Ocean

Population
6,491,000 (1993 estimate)

A BRIEF HISTORY

JAMESTOWN When the *Susan Constant, Godspeed,* and *Discovery* dropped anchor off Cape Charles on April 26, 1607, it was the end of a long and cramped voyage for 105 colonists who had left England seeking gold and fortune in the New World. The difficult journey was only a prelude to things to come, beginning with an attack by Native Americans on that first day. Abandoning Cape Charles, the colonists explored the wide rivers on the western shore of the Chesapeake Bay before settling on a small island 60 miles upstream. They named the river James, for their King James I, and their new home Jamestown.

Nearly half their lot died the first year, victims of starvation, Native American raids, and typhoid fever. Only the heroics of a mercenary braggart named Captain John Smith held the colony together. Smith is remembered, however, for having been saved from execution by Pocahontas, daughter of the powerful chief Powhatan.

The colonists never found gold, but in 1613 John Rolfe, who later married Pocahontas, introduced a mild version of tobacco, which quickly found favor in most of Europe. Profits and more colonists flowed into Jamestown and other new settlements along the rivers. In 1619, the settlers chose the members of America's first legislative body, the House of Burgesses. That same year, a Dutch ship unloaded 20 Africans to work as indentured servants. For the English colonists, it was the first step down a long road to freedom. For African Americans, it was the beginning of slavery.

WILLIAMSBURG In 1699, the colonists moved their capital from cramped Jamestown to nearby Williamsburg, which soon became a center of agitation for an independent America. While the Burgesses debated, English settlers were advancing westward into the hills of central Virginia joined by Scotch-Irish and German settlers moving in from Pennsylvania. Out on the frontier, the pioneers ran into both hostile Native Americans and the French, who were encroaching onto British-claimed land from the west. When the French and Indian War broke out in the 1750s, the colonial government turned to a young surveyor to lead the Virginia militia: George Washington.

The British won that war, but when King George III increased colonial taxes to pay for it, protests against "taxation without representation" erupted up and down the Atlantic seaboard. In Williamsburg, the infamous Stamp Act of 1765 caused the House of Burgesses to pass the Virginia Resolves, calling for colonial rights based on a constitution. The Stamp Act was repealed in 1766, but a hated tax on tea remained. After the Boston Tea Party in 1773, Richard Henry Lee led the House of Burgesses in creating a standing committee to communicate with the other colonies to discuss grievances against Britain. In turn, that led to the first Continental Congress, which met in Philadelphia the following year.

LIBERTY OR DEATH In 1775, fiery orator Patrick Henry delivered one of the most famous speeches in American history. Urging that the Virginia militia be

✤ *Fun Facts* ✤

• *Over 60% of Civil War battles were fought in Virginia.*

• *Memorial Day, which originated in Petersburg, VA, is actually of Confederate origin. National observance of the holiday began after the Civil War, when Petersburg schoolgirls decorated the graves of soldiers who died fighting for the Confederacy.*

• *In Richmond, adventurers can take a white-water rafting trip through the center of the metropolis.*

• *The College of William and Mary, in Williamsburg, is the second-oldest college in the United States (only Harvard University is older). It opened its doors in 1694.*

• *Mount Vernon, the estate of George Washington, is the second-most visited historic home in the United States, with over 1 million visitors a year. Only the White House has more visitors.*

• *Virginia has more miles of trout streams than roads.*

• *Virginia's Natural Bridge, which spans Cedar Creek, stands 215 feet tall and is one of the Seven Natural Wonders of the World.*

armed, he stood in Richmond's St John's Church and shouted: "Is life so dear or peace so sweet as to be purchased at the price of chains and slavery? Forbid it, Almighty God! I know not what course others may take, but as for me, give me liberty, or give me death!"

Hostilities already had broken out at Lexington and Concord by the time the Second Continental Congress met in 1775 and declared war on Great Britain. To lead its Continental Army, the Congress chose George Washington.

At this point the colonists were fighting to defend their rights as British subjects. However, meeting in Williamsburg during June 1776, the Virginia Convention urged its congressional delegates to vote for independence, and it passed a Bill of Rights drafted by George Mason. A month later in Philadelphia, 33-year-old Virginian Thomas Jefferson based the Declaration of Independence on Mason's bill. Issued on July 4, 1776, Jefferson's document turned the 13 colonies into a new nation.

YORKTOWN   The American Revolution raged for 5 more years. Virginia saw little fighting until 1781, when a British army under Lord Cornwallis was encamped at Yorktown. Washington quickly marched his army south from New York and trapped Cornwallis between his forces and the French navy offshore. Cornwallis's surrender on October 19, 1781, led directly to American independence.

BIRTHPLACE OF PRESIDENTS   The new nation relied heavily on Virginians in its early years, giving the Old Dominion a new nickname, "Birthplace of Presidents."

After the Articles of Confederation, which had set up a loose league of 13 states in 1781, proved unworkable, a Constitutional Convention met in Philadelphia in 1787 to devise a new national government. Jefferson was in France, but the delegates chose Washington as their president. Another Virginian, James Madison, fought for a Bill of Rights and crafted the bicameral Virginia Compromise, under which members of the House of Representatives are elected proportionally by population, while each state has 2 Senators.

Taking office in 1789 as the 1st president, Washington selected Jefferson as his secretary of state and carved the District of Columbia out of Maryland and Virginia, including all of what is now Arlington and

most of Alexandria (they were later returned to Virginia).

As the 3rd president, Jefferson almost doubled the size of the United States by adding the Louisiana Purchase. Madison followed Jefferson to the White House in 1809 and led the nation into the War of 1812, during which he and wife Dolley narrowly escaped before the British burned the Capitol and White House. The 5th president, Virginian James Monroe, author of the Monroe Doctrine, continued the nation's westward push.

In all, Virginia provided 7 of America's first 12 presidents. The others were Charles City County neighbors William Henry Harrison and John Tyler, and Zachary Taylor. Woodrow Wilson was born in Staunton, although he was living in New Jersey when he was elected in 1912.

THE CIVIL WAR   While its native sons were busy governing on the Potomac, Virginia reverted to its agricultural ways. The quiet times were short-lived, however, for slavery soon became the cause of much national tension. In 1859, abolitionist John Brown staged a raid on Harper's Ferry, a federal arsenal now in West Virginia but then in Virginia. When abolitionist Abraham Lincoln was elected president in 1860, the cotton-growing states of the Deep South seceded from the Union and formed the Confederacy. When they fired on Fort Sumter in South Carolina in April 1861, the war had begun. Virginia quickly seceded, Richmond became the capital of the Confederacy, and within a year a Virginian named Robert E Lee became commander of its Army of Northern Virginia.

Virginia was the main battleground of 6 major Union campaigns to capture Richmond. The first was stopped in July of 1861 at the First Battle of Manassas. The second campaign advanced up the peninsula between the York and James Rivers in 1862 but bogged down just 9 miles from Richmond. Lee stopped the third campaign at the Second Battle of Manassas later that same year. The fourth came through Fredericksburg in December 1862 and nearly reached Richmond before Lee turned it back. The fifth, early in 1863, was stopped at Chancellorsville, where Lee suffered the loss of General Stonewall Jackson, accidentally shot by his own men.

Tired of indecisive generals, Lincoln in 1864 picked the unrelenting Ulysses S Grant to head all Union armies. Grant soon launched a sixth and final campaign against the Confederate capital. His first battle with Lee came during the Wilderness Campaign west of Fredericksburg. Lee technically won, but instead of retreating as his predecessors had, Grant skirted Lee's forces until June 1864, when he laid siege to Petersburg, a key railroad junction 23 miles south of Richmond. The ensuing 9-month standoff took its toll on the rebels, and on April 1, 1865, Grant's forces broke through the Confederate line.

With Richmond lost, Lee retreated westward toward Danville, last capital of the Confederacy. He got as far as Appomattox Court House, where Grant's forces blocked his way. On April 8, 1865, the two great generals met in the living room of Wilbur McLean's farmhouse. Lee's surrender that day ended Virginia's 4-year ordeal.

RECOVERY   Like the rest of the South, Virginia lay devastated. Its farms were ruined, one-seventh of its white men were either dead or disabled, its slaves were free but unemployed, its few industries lay in shambles, and one third of its land was now named West Virginia. But the survivors slowly began to recover. Eastern plantation owners turned to sharecropping to make their large holdings productive. New railroads opened up coal mining in the west and turned Hampton Roads into a major port. And thanks to its popularity during the Civil War, tobacco became even more lucrative.

Prosperity didn't come to all, however, for the sharecropping system effectively replaced slavery, and so-called Jim Crow laws at the turn of the century legalized segregation, making second-class citizens of all Virginians of African descent. Then the Great Depression aggravated the poverty that was still prevalent in many parts of the state. Things finally turned upward for good during World War II, when federal military spending brought prosperity to northern Virginia, Hampton Roads, and the coal fields of the west.

MODERN VIRGINIA   Once the domain of large plantations, today's Virginia is a mix of farms and factories, small towns, and cities, its economy dependent on agriculture, manufacturing, service industries, tourism, and government. A prosperous commercial crescent has developed along an urban corridor that begins in northern Virginia and follows I-95 south to Richmond and I-64 east to Hampton Roads.

A CLOSER LOOK
Geography

Shaped like a triangle, Virginia stretches more than 400 miles from the beaches and marshes along the Atlantic Ocean westward to the ridges and peaks of the Allegheny Mountains.

Tidewater is what Virginians call the eastern quarter of their state, a flat coastal plain flanking the mighty Chesapeake Bay and split into 3 long peninsulas (or "necks" in local parlance) by the Potomac, Rappahannock, York, and James Rivers. Antebellum plantations still occupy the heavily wooded banks of these broad rivers. However, where tobacco and cotton were once kings, Norfolk, Portsmouth, Newport News, Hampton, and Virginia Beach, have grown to form a sprawling metropolis on the shores of Hampton Roads, the world's largest natural harbor and home to America's biggest naval base. Just to the south of these vibrant cities lies the forbidding wilderness of the Great Dismal Swamp, a national wildlife refuge.

The **Eastern Shore**, Virginia's share of the Delmarva Peninsula, is barely visible across Hampton Roads. The southern tip of the peninsula, it is tied to the mainland by the thin thread of the 17.6-mile Chesapeake Bay Bridge-Tunnel, which reaches from Norfolk to Cape Charles and is the longest such structure in the world. Countless waterways and islands slice through the ocean and bay coasts of this sparsely populated rural area, whose economic mainstays are farming and raising millions of chickens. Chincoteague National Wildlife Refuge and Assateague Island National Seashore, both near the quaint village of Chincoteague, are havens for wild ponies and birds. Out in the Chesapeake, residents of remote Tangier Island still speak with the Elizabethan lilt of their ancestors.

Central Virginia lies to the west of the coastal plain, its rolling hill country often called the Piedmont, the state's industrial and intellectual heartland. Here are such exciting small cities as Richmond, Virginia's vibrant capital; Charlottesville, home of Thomas Jefferson's Monticello and the University of Virginia; Petersburg, whose fall meant the end of the Confederacy; and Lynchburg, proud of historic homes that tobacco built.

Northern Virginia, at the top of the Piedmont, is now the wealthiest part of the Old Dominion. Once no more than Washington, DC's sleepy bedroom suburbs,

Charlottesville

64 miles NE of Lynchburg

69 miles NW of Richmond

115 miles NE of Roanoke

120 miles SW of Washington, DC

163 miles NW of Norfolk

242 miles SE of Charleston, WV

Lynchburg

51 miles NE of Roanoke

64 miles SW of Charlottesville

113 miles SW of Richmond

184 miles SW of Washington, DC

207 miles NW of Norfolk

233 miles SE of Charleston, WV

Norfolk

94 miles SE of Richmond

163 miles SE of Charlottesville

200 miles SE of Washington, DC

207 miles SE of Lynchburg

259 miles SE of Roanoke

405 miles SE of Charleston, WV

Richmond

69 miles SE of Charlottesville

94 miles NW of Norfolk

109 miles SW of Washington, DC

113 miles NE of Lynchburg

164 miles NE of Roanoke

311 miles SE of Charleston, WV

Roanoke

51 miles SW of Lynchburg

115 miles SW of Charlottesville

164 miles SW of Richmond

182 miles SE of Charleston, WV

223 miles SE of Washington, DC

259 miles NW of Norfolk

Arlington, Alexandria, Falls Church, and Fairfax County have exploded with high-tech firms and now have the state's largest and most diverse urban population, highest per-capita income, and worst traffic jams. But history lives, with Old Town Alexandria, the Arlington National Cemetery, and George Washington's Mount Vernon attracting millions of visitors every year. To the south are historic Fredericksburg and its Civil War battlefields. To the west are the undulating hills, fashionable small towns, manicured estates, and well-groomed horses of the Virginia Hunt Country.

Moving westward across the state, the Piedmont rises until it meets the **Blue Ridge,** first of the seemingly endless ridges that form the Appalachian Mountains. Along its spine run the breathtaking Skyline Drive and, continuing where it leaves off, the Blue Ridge Parkway, two of America's most scenic roadways.

The **Shenandoah Valley,** beyond the Blue Ridge, was the breadbasket of the Confederacy and saw its share of Civil War battles. Here are picturesque, historic towns such as Winchester, New Market, Harrisonburg, Staunton, and Lexington. Here, too, is Mother Nature's work—above ground at Natural Bridge and Hot Springs and underneath at Luray Caverns.

The **Southwest Blue Ridge Highlands** to the south of the Shenandoah grow ever higher and more spectacular as you drive into Virginia's western tail from busy Roanoke. This mountainous region sports Mt Rogers, Virginia's highest peak and home of its own national recreation area; quaint towns such as Abingdon and Big Stone Gap; the 850-foot Natural Tunnel; the largest canyon east of the Mississippi at Breaks Interstate Park; and Cumberland Gap, Daniel Boone's doorway to Kentucky.

Climate

Of Virginia's 4 temperate seasons, the warm days and cool evenings of spring and autumn are unquestionably the best times to sightsee, especially when the leaves change color in early autumn. Summers can be uncomfortably hot and humid. Winters can range unpredictably from bitterly cold to relatively moderate. Wintertime snow is common in the mountains, less so in northern and central Virginia, and infrequent on the Eastern Shore and in Tidewater.

During most of the year, rain tends to fall in cloudy, damp periods, with a wet day or two followed by brilliant sunshine. Summer features intense thunderstorms, which are usually brief but should be taken seriously; seek shelter.

What to Pack

Outdoor summer activities demand shorts and lightweight shirts, blouses, and dresses—but remember

AVERAGE MONTHLY TEMPERATURES (°F) & INCHES OF RAINFALL			
	Arlington	**Norfolk**	**Richmond**	**Hot Springs**
Jan	35/2.7	39/3.8	36/3.2	29/3.0
Feb	38/2.7	42/3.5	39/3.2	32/2.9
Mar	47/3.2	49/3.7	48/3.6	41/3.7
Apr	57/2.7	57/3.0	56/3.3	50/3.4
May	66/3.7	66/3.8	66/3.8	60/4.2
June	76/3.4	74/3.8	74/3.6	67/3.4
July	80/3.8	78/5.1	78/5.0	71/4.5
Aug	79/3.9	77/4.4	77/4.8	70/3.7
Sept	71/3.3	72/3.9	70/3.3	63/3.4
Oct	60/3.0	61/3.2	59/3.5	53/3.8
Nov	50/3.1	52/2.9	50/3.2	43/3.5
Dec	39/3.1	44/3.2	40/3.3	33/2.8

that air conditioning can make restaurants, shops, and indoor attractions seem like Alaska. Spring and autumn evenings—and even summer ones in the mountains—can be nippy enough for a jacket or wrap. Winter requires moderately heavy coats, hats, boots, and gloves. Some restaurants require men to wear jackets and ties, but smart casual attire usually will fit in.

A few items will be useful anytime, including comfortable walking shoes, a hat, sunglasses, and a folding umbrella. Bring sunscreen and insect repellent during the summer months.

Tourist Information

The **Virginia Division of Tourism,** 901 E Byrd St, Richmond, VA 23219 (tel 804/786-2051, fax 804/786-1919), provides free copies of its annual *Virginia Travel Guide,* which is full of information about attractions, activities, accommodations, and special events throughout the state. The guide also lists local visitors bureaus maintained by most cities and towns.

If you're in Richmond, the central **Welcome Center** is in the Bell Tower, Capitol Square (tel 804/786-4484). Other Virginia welcome centers are located near the borders on the interstate highways leading into the state and on US 13 south of the Maryland line.

Driving Rules & Regulations

The speed limit is 65 mph on rural interstate highways, 55 mph in built-up areas and on state highways. In-town speed limits vary. Driver and all front-seat passengers must wear seat belts, and children under age 4 or less than 40 pounds must ride in an approved safety seat. Drunk-driving laws are strictly enforced, and the penalties are severe. Carrying open containers of alcohol in vehicles is unlawful.

Renting a Car

Traveling by car is the best way to see the Old Dominion, and rentals are widely available in the metropolitan areas. Some shopping around is in order, since promotional deals, weekend rates, age requirements, and group discounts can vary. Your travel agent can provide advice.

Here are the major companies with offices in Virginia, along with their toll-free numbers:

- **Alamo** (tel 800/327-9633)
- **Avis** (tel 800/831-2847)
- **Budget** (tel 800/527-0700)
- **Dollar Rent-A-Car** (tel 800/800-4000)
- **Hertz** (tel 800/654-3131)
- **National** (tel 800/227-7368)
- **Thrifty** (tel 800/367-2277)

Essentials

Area Code: As of July 15, 1995, Virginia will have 3 area codes. Until then, the area code for Northern Virginia and all of the Shenandoah Valley and the southwestern Blue Ridge Highlands will be **703.** After then, the area code for most of northern Virginia will remain 703, but the code for the area from Leesburg south through the Shenandoah Valley and the southwestern Blue Ridge Highlands will become **540.** For central Virginia, Tidewater, and the Eastern Shore, the code will remain **804.** Consult the front white pages of any local telephone directory for an area code map, or dial 411 for information.

Emergencies: Call **911** for police, the fire department, or an ambulance from anywhere within Virginia.

Liquor Laws: Many grocery and convenience stores sell beer and wine. A few localities now have privately owned ''package stores,'' but in most places other types of liquor can be purchased only from government-operated Alcohol Beverage Control (ABC) stores. Licensed restaurants and bars can dispense alcoholic beverages by the glass (known as ''liquor by the drink'' in Virginia). The statewide legal drinking age is 21, and proof of age including a photo may be required.

Taxes: The sales tax is 4½% in most of Virginia. Some localities add another half a percent to this statewide levy, and many jurisdictions also impose additional taxes on hotel rooms.

Time Zone: All of Virginia is in the Eastern time zone. Daylight saving time (1 hour ahead of Eastern Standard Time) is observed from the first Sunday in April until the last Sunday in October.

BEST OF THE STATE
What to See & Do

BATTLEFIELDS Virginians are justly proud of their role in winning the American Revolution and, although it was in a lost cause, of the blood their young men spilled during the Civil War. That pride shows in numerous preserved battlefields such as **Yorktown,** where Cornwallis' surrender ended the Revolutionary War; **Manassas National Battlefield Park,** scene of 2 early Confederate successes; and the **Fredericksburg and Spotsylvania National Military Park,** which also embraces sites related to the battles of **Chancellorsville** and the **Wilderness. Richmond National Battlefield Park** includes the bloody **Cold Harbor** battlefield, where 7,000 Union troops were killed or wounded in a mere 30 minutes in 1864; and **Petersburg National Battlefield** was the scene of the 9-month siege that clinched the final Union victory. The farmhouse where Lee surrendered is today the **Appomattox Court House National Historic Park.**

BEACHES Sand and sun reign supreme along Virginia's Atlantic coast: The 27 miles of **Virginia Beach** constitute the world's longest resort beach. Those who object to hotels and cottages will find the 45 totally undeveloped miles of **Assateague Island National Seashore** a more congenial paradise.

CUISINE Like their Maryland neighbors to the north, Virginians enjoy the bounty of the Chesapeake Bay, which means seafood lovers can get their fill from one end of the state to the other. Another local delicacy is strong Virginia country ham from the smokehouses of Smithfield. And in the fall, don't miss those wonderfully fresh Shenandoah Valley apples and the sweet cider made from them.

FAMILY FAVORITES Two major theme parks attract local families and visitors alike. Kids of any age enjoy the wild rides, water park, ice show, and *Star Trek* characters at **Paramount's King's Dominion,** 20 miles north of Richmond. At **Busch Gardens Williamsburg,** they learn about the Old World at 9 re-created 17th-century European villages, then get their thrills on rides like the Loch Ness Monster. For a less exciting, but equally interesting and more educational outing, the entire family can take a history lesson at **Colonial Williamsburg,** then detour several miles southwest to **Jamestown** or northeast to **Yorktown.** All three are now part of the Colonial National Historical Park.

MUSEUMS Beyond the multitude of fine institutions dedicated to preserving its illustrious past, Virginia has museums for those interested in everything from outer space to the briny deep. Two particularly renowned fine-arts museums are the **Chrysler Museum of Art,** in Norfolk, especially noted for its 8,000-piece glass collection, including much Tiffany glass, and Richmond's **Virginia Museum of Fine Arts,** noted not only for paintings but also for the largest collection of Fabergé objets d'art outside Russia.

HISTORIC BUILDINGS & SITES   For visitors, Virginians' reverence for the past means well-preserved historic sites in almost every nook and cranny of the state, beginning with **Colonial Williamsburg,** the granddaddy of all restored towns, where 88 buildings surviving from the 18th century have been supplemented with some 500 buildings reconstructed on their original sites. Nearby are **Jamestown,** remnant of the first permanent English settlement in the New World, and **Yorktown,** a Revolutionary War battlefield and old colonial town.

Other key sights include George Washington's **Mount Vernon,** one of the most-loved and most-visited sites in America, and George Mason's nearby **Gunston Hall.** In the Charlottesville area is the hilltop **Monticello** that Thomas Jefferson designed for himself in 16th-century Italian style; the homes of the 4th and 5th presidents, James Madison's **Montpelier** and James Monroe's **Ash Lawn-Highland,** are nearby. In Richmond is the **Virginia State Capitol,** also designed by Thomas Jefferson. Other estates belonging to the nation's forefathers, their relatives, and contemporaries include **Scotchtown,** near Richmond, Patrick Henry's plantation home; **Kenmore,** in Fredericksburg, built for George Washington's sister, Betty; and several 18th-century tobacco planters' plantations on the James River.

NATURAL WONDERS   From the uninhabited **Atlantic barrier islands** and the **Great Dismal Swamp** to the impressive limestone formation known as the **Natural Bridge,** at Lexington, and the limestone caves of the Shenandoah Valley—Virginia boasts many natural attractions worth a visit. Some have been turned into commercial enterprises, but most are in their God-given state. The **Blue Ridge Mountains** are themselves a natural wonder.

PARKS   Virginia literally is dotted with national and state parks, wildlife reserves, and recreation areas, beginning with **Shenandoah National Park.** Sandwiched between the Alleghenies and the Blue Ridge Mountains, it extends from Front Royal, 90 miles west of Washington, DC, to Rockfish Gap, about 90 miles

west of Richmond. In addition, many of the mountain ridges flanking the Shenandoah Valley are managed as national forests, offering a wide range of outdoor activities, from picnicking to rock climbing.

SCENIC DRIVES   Many of Virginia's major highways —I-81, which runs north-south in the western part of the state, and I-64, which cuts east-west across the center, for example—are scenic drives in their own right, but it's difficult to top the glorious views from the **Skyline Drive** and **Blue Ridge Parkway.** Actually one road, these two drives snake northward along the Blue Ridge some 400 miles from North Carolina's Great Smoky Mountains to Front Royal. Other scenic roads include the **Colonial Parkway** through Jamestown, Williamsburg, and Yorktown; the **George Washington Memorial Parkway** along the Potomac River from Arlington to Mount Vernon; and the **Chesapeake Bridge-Tunnel** across the mouth of Hampton Roads.

WINERIES   Wine has been made in Virginia since Jamestown days, and the Piedmont—especially around **Charlottesville** and **Middleburg**—is now home to about 40 commercial wineries. Many are open to the public and offer tastes of their produce.

Events/Festivals

For a complete list of events, ask for a copy of the annual *Virginia Travel Guide* published by the Virginia Division of Tourism (see "Tourist Information," above).

Statewide

- **Historic Garden Week.** Gardens and grounds of more than 200 landmarks are open only during the last week in April. Contact Garden Club of Virginia, 112 E Franklin St, Richmond, VA 23219 (tel 804/644-7776).

Tidewater

- **International Azalea Festival,** Norfolk. Parades, ceremonies, crowning of queen, military displays in honor of NATO. 2nd and 3rd weeks in April. Call 804/622-2312.
- **Seafood Festival,** Chincoteague. All-you-can-eat feast at Tom's Cove. 1st weekend in May. Advance tickets necessary from Eastern Shore Chamber of Commerce, Drawer R, Melfa, VA 23410 (tel 804/336-6161).

- **Harborfest,** Norfolk. Boat races, tall ships, military demonstrations, fireworks, partying at Town Point Park. 1st weekend in June. Call 804/627-5329.
- **Pony Swim and Auction,** Chincoteague. Famous roundup when local cowpokes herd wild ponies across Assateague Channel to Memorial Park. Last Wednesday in July. Call 804/336-6161.
- **Yorktown Day,** Yorktown. Celebrates Cornwallis' surrender in 1781, at Yorktown Battlefield. October 19. Call 804/898-3400.

Northern Virginia

- **Robert E Lee Birthday Celebration,** Alexandria and Arlington. Music, food, open houses at Lee's Boyhood Home, Alexandria, and at Arlington House, Arlington National Cemetery. January 19. Call 703/557-0613.
- **George Washington's Birthday,** Alexandria. Three days of Old Town parades, open house at Mount Vernon, banquet and costume ball at Gadsby's Tavern. Weekend preceding the 3rd Monday in February. Call 703/838-4200. Other celebrations in Fredericksburg (tel 703/373-1776); George Washington's Birthplace National Monument (tel 804/224-1732); Mary Washington House (tel 703/373-1569); and Winchester (tel 703/662-6550).
- **Vintage Virginia Wine Festival,** Great Meadow Steeplechase Course, The Plains. Chance to taste the state's best vintages. 1st weekend in May. Call toll free 800/277-CORK.
- **Virginia Hunt Country Stable Tour,** Upperville. One of the few times private estates and horse farms are open to the public. Memorial Day weekend. Call 703/592-3711.
- **Memorial Day Service,** Arlington. The President lays a wreath on the Tomb of the Unknowns, Arlington National Cemetery. Last Monday in May. Call 202/475-0856.
- **Virginia Scottish Games,** Alexandria. Bagpipes and fiddles, Highland dancing and games, Scottish foods. Late July. Call 703/838-5005.

Central Virginia

- **James Madison's Birthday,** Montpelier, Orange County. Ceremony and reception at Madison's home. March 16. Call 703/672-2728.

- **Patrick Henry Speech Reenactment,** Richmond. Hear "Give me liberty or give me death" at St John's Church, site of the Second Virginia Convention (1775). Sunday closest to March 23. Call 804/648-5015.
- **Thomas Jefferson's Birthday,** Charlottesville. Wreath laying, fife-and-drum corps, speeches at Monticello. April 13. Call 804/984-9822.
- **Dogwood Festival,** Charlottesville. Parade, queen's coronation, fireworks, fashion show, other events while the dogwoods bloom. Mid-April. Call 804/295-3141.
- **James River Bateau Festival,** Lynchburg to Richmond. A moving 8-day festival follows a boat race down the James River. Mid-June. Call 804/847-1811.
- **Ashlawn-Highland Summer Festival,** Charlottesville. President James Monroe's home hosts opera, concerts, traditional bonfire. End of June to mid-August. Tickets at box office (tel 804/293-4500).
- **Virginia State Fair,** State Fairgrounds, Richmond. Agriculture exhibits and judging, carnival rides. Last week in September. Call 804/228-3200.

Shenandoah Valley

- **Highland Maple Festival,** Monterey. Celebrates rising of the sap with demonstrations, crafts, antique sale. 2nd and 3rd weekends in March. Call 703/468-2550.
- **Virginia Horse Festival,** Lexington. Equestrian events, competitions, auctions, and art shows. Mid-April. Call 703/463-4300.
- **Shenandoah Apple Blossom Festival,** Winchester. Five days of celebrations kick off the valley's number one crop. Parade, beauty pageant, marathon, arts and craft shows. 1st week in May. Call 703/662-3863.
- **Shenandoah Valley Music Festival,** Orkney Springs. Jazz under the stars. Saturdays in July and August, Labor Day weekend. Call 703/459-3396.

Southwest Blue Ridge Highlands

- **Barter Theater Opens,** Abingdon. Nation's oldest repertory company begins annual season. Mid-April. Tickets at box office (tel toll free 800/368-3240).

- **Chautauqua Festival in the Park,** Wytheville. A week's worth of antiques, arts and crafts shows, music, and ballet. Mid-June. Call 703/223-3365.
- **Virginia Highlands Festival,** Abingdon. Appalachian Mountain culture on display, featuring musicians, artists, antiques, handcrafts. Late July. Call 703/676-2282 or toll free 800/435-3440.
- **Old Time Fiddlers' Convention,** Galax. Oldest and largest annual gathering of country musicians. Mid-August. Call 703/236-0668.

Spectator Sports

AUTO RACING   Stock-car and drag racing are big-time sports in Virginia, which has more than 25 race tracks and speedways. **Richmond International Raceway** (tel 804/345-7223) and **Martinsville Speedway** (tel 703/956-3151) host Winston Cup and Busch Grand National Series races. Hampton's **Langley Raceway** (tel 804/865-1992) holds NASCAR or Winston Cup races. **Bristol International Raceway** (tel 615/764-1161), on the Tennessee side of Bristol, has the world's fastest half-mile NASCAR track.

BASEBALL   Virginia doesn't have major league baseball, but 2 Class AAA teams vie for fans' affections: the **Norfolk Tides** (tel 804/622-2222) and the **Richmond Braves** (tel 804/359-4444 or toll free 800/849-4627). Three teams avidly compete in Class A: the **Salem Buccaneers** (tel 703/389-3333), the **Lynchburg Red Sox** (tel 804/528-1144), and the **Prince William Cannons,** who play near Woodbridge (tel 703/590-2311).

COLLEGE ATHLETICS   Several universities play intercollegiate football, basketball, and baseball schedules during the respective seasons. Leaders of the pack are the **University of Virginia Cavaliers** (or "Wahoos") in Charlottesville (for schedules and ticket information, call 804/924-8821, or toll free 800/542-8821 from within Virginia), and the **Virginia Tech Hokies** in Blacksburg (tel 703/231-6731, or toll free 800/828-3244).

HORSE RACING   Steeplechase racing is the sport of kings in the Old Dominion. The biggest of these is the **Virginia Gold Cup,** at The Plains in early May (tel 703/347-2612 or toll free 800/69-RACES). Not far behind are the **Strawberry Hill Races,** at Richmond's Strawberry Hill Exposition & Convention Center in mid-April (tel 804/228-3200).

ICE HOCKEY   The minor league **Hampton Roads Admirals** play from October through March at the Norfolk Scope (tel 804/640-1212).

Activities A to Z

BICYCLING   Scenic roads beckon bicyclists throughout Virginia, including all 214 miles of the **Blue Ridge Parkway** from Waynesboro south to the North Carolina line. The beautiful **Mount Vernon Trail,** 17 miles along the Potomac River from Arlington to the first president's home, is connected to the 184-mile towpath trail of the C&O Canal National Historical Park in Maryland and Washington, DC. The Boston-to-Florida East Coast Bicycle Trail continues another 253 miles south to the John H Kerr Reservoir on the North Carolina line. Other favorites are the 13-mile Colonial Parkway between Yorktown and Jamestown, 16 miles in Chincoteague National Wildlife Refuge, and the 57 miles in New River Trail State Park between Galax and Pulaski. Most main towns along the routes have bike rental shops.

BIRDWATCHING   Both the Eastern Shore and Blue Ridge Mountains are major flyways for migratory birds. Hundreds of resident species can be found in several national parks and wildlife refuges, including the world-class Chincoteague National Wildlife Refuge.

BOATING   The Atlantic Ocean, Chesapeake Bay, 15 major lakes, and rivers galore make boating a major activity. Marinas are numerous and hundreds of boat launching sites are available. For information about boating laws and regulations, contact the Virginia Department of Game and Inland Fisheries, 4010 W Broad St, Richmond, VA 23230 (tel 804/367-0939).

CAMPING   Campgrounds abound in Virginia's 21 national and 35 state parks, and the state has more than 150 private campgrounds and RV parks. For a list of state parks, contact the Virginia Department of Conservation and Recreation, 203 Governor St, Suite 302, Richmond, VA 23219 (tel 804/786-1712). For information about private facilities, write or call the Virginia Campground Association, 2101 Libbie Ave, Richmond, VA 23230 (tel 804/288-3065).

CANOEING Rivers like the **Shenandoah, James, Maury,** and **New** offer slow-moving waters as well as Class IV mountain rapids. Several outfitters rent canoes (and inner tubes) and provide guides in Bentonville, Luray, Front Royal, and other towns along the South Fork of the Shenandoah. Other popular put-in spots are at Lexington and Scottsville on the James, and in Pembroke on the gorgeous New River, which cuts its way through the famous New River Gorge into West Virginia.

CRUISING Visitors can see Virginia from the water by taking a sightseeing cruise of Norfolk and Hampton harbors; by cruising down the Potomac from Alexandria to Mount Vernon; or down the James River from Richmond and Hopewell to the plantations lining the riverbank. Full-day cruises to unique Tangier Island leave from Reedville on the mainland side of the Chesapeake and from Onancock on the Eastern Shore.

FISHING The state has rich saltwater fishing grounds, more than 250 species of freshwater fish, and 185 streams stocked with 850,000 trout annually. Licenses are required for both saltwater and freshwater fishing. For details contact the Virginia Department of Game and Inland Fisheries, 4010 W Broad St, Richmond, VA 23230 (tel 804/367-9369).

GOLF Duffers will find more than 130 golf courses, including courses that are considered among the best in America at 4 resorts—Williamsburg Inn and Kingsmill in Williamsburg, The Homestead in Hot Springs, and Wintergreen. For information about private courses, call the Golf Line of the Virginia Resorts Association (tel toll free 800/932-2259).

HIKING Virginia has hundreds of miles of trails through its thousands of acres of parks, national forests, and recreation areas. Leading the list are the state's 450-plus miles of the winding, 2,100-mile-long **Appalachian Trail,** which follows the scenic ridges above the Blue Ridge Parkway and Skyline Drive. Entry points are at every road crossing.

HORSEBACK RIDING Stables are especially numerous around Leesburg and Middleburg in the Hunt Country west of Washington, DC, and up and down the Shenandoah Valley, where Lexington's **Virginia Horse Center** hosts horse-related functions all year. Riding is easily arranged throughout these areas.

HUNTING Wild game includes squirrel, grouse, bear, deer, bobcat, fox, duck, goose, rabbit, pheasant, and quail. For information about licenses, seasons, and bag limits, contact the Virginia Department of Game and Inland Fisheries, 4010 W Broad St, Richmond, VA 23230 (tel 804/367-9369).

SHOPPING As would be expected in a state so deeply rooted in American history, almost every town and village in the Old Dominion has boutiques filled with colonial and Victorian-era antiques. Local handicrafts can be found in the Shenandoah Valley and in the southwest highlands, especially exquisite pottery. Discount shoppers will find a number of outlet centers throughout Virginia, all of them dwarfed by the 240 stores in Dale City's **Potomac Mills Mall,** the world's largest outlet center.

SKIING Virginia has 4 downhill skiing resorts: **Bryce Mountain** (tel 703/856-2122) in Bayse, **The Homestead** (tel 703/839-5500), **Massanutten** (tel 703/289-9441) near Harrisonburg, and **Wintergreen** (tel 804/325-2200).

TENNIS Many hotels and resorts have courts for their guests' use, and most cities and towns maintain courts open to the public.

WATER SPORTS Virginia Beach offers a wide range of water sports, from jet skiing and powerboat racing to snorkeling and scuba diving. Most resorts and hotels can help make arrangements.

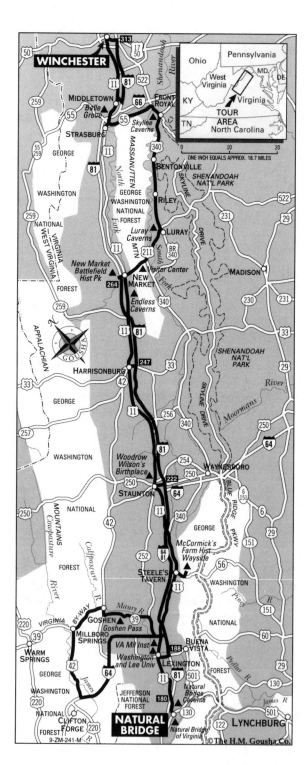

SCENIC DRIVING TOUR #1

THE SHENANDOAH VALLEY

Start:	Winchester
Finish:	Natural Bridge
Distance:	175 miles
Time:	2–4 days
Highlights:	Rolling hills dotted with farms and apple orchards; magnificent underground caverns and a 215-foot-high natural bridge; historic small towns; Civil War battlefields and museums; graves of Robert E Lee and Stonewall Jackson; birthplace of Woodrow Wilson

Following the route of I-81 (one of America's most scenic interstate highways) and US 11 (the historic Valley Pike), this tour takes you the length of Virginia's lovely Shenandoah Valley, whose Shawnee name means "Daughter of the Stars." The 2 highways go up and down over hill and dale through some of the Mid-Atlantic's most beautiful countryside. As a backdrop, the gentle folds of the Blue Ridge Mountains rise to the east of the Valley; to the west begin the rugged Allegheny Mountains. At the end of the tour, US 11 actually crosses the awesome Natural Bridge, where George Washington carved his initials. In addition to this wonder, you'll visit several underground caverns, and detour into the primordial woodlands of Shenandoah National Park and the George Washington National Forest. As the "Breadbasket of the Confederacy," the Valley was fought over throughout the Civil War, and several battlefields and museums still remind the traveler of that bloody conflict.

Atop the Blue Ridge Mountains to the east run 2 of America's premier scenic roads: The **Skyline Drive** and the **Blue Ridge Parkway.** A multitude of sharp curves and a strictly enforced 45-mph speed limit translate into slow-going traffic, but the mountain vistas make a detour on either road worth the extra time.

For additional information on accommodations, restaurants, and attractions in the region covered by the tour, look under specific cities in the listings portion of this book.

I-81, US 11, US 50, US 340, US 522, and Va 7 all give easy access to the first stop:

1. **Winchester,** the Valley's oldest town and its unofficial "Apple Capital." Settled in 1732 by Quakers and Germans, Winchester was twice George Washington's headquarters, first when he surveyed the area and later when he commanded Virginia's militia during the French and Indian Wars. You'll want to visit the small stone building where Washington had his office, at W Cork and S Braddock Sts (tel 703/662-4412). Winchester changed hands 70 times during the Civil War. When Confederate General Thomas J "Stonewall" Jackson was in town, he made his headquarters 5 blocks north of Washington's at 415 N Braddock St (tel 703/667-3242).

Begin your tour of these and other historic attractions by taking exit 313 off I-81 and following the signs to the **Winchester-Frederick County Visitor Center,** 1360 S Pleasant Valley Rd (tel 703/662-4135). It's on the grounds of **Abram's Delight,** Winchester's oldest home, built of native limestone in 1754 on an attractive site by a lake. Or you can go straight to the **Old Town Welcome Center,** N Cameron and Boscawen Sts (tel 703/722-6367), in the heart of the historic district. Both centers have walking-tour brochures and are open daily 9am–5pm. (One walking tour visits youthful haunts of country music legend Patsy Cline, a Winchester native whose grave is south of town on Va 644 just west of US 522.)

From Winchester, both I-81 and US 11 go 12 miles "up" the Valley (that is, south) to:

2. **Middletown,** a small roadside village noted for its antique shops; the **Wayside Theater,** Main St (tel 703/869-1776), which presents excellent theatrical productions from the end of May to mid-October; and **Belle Grove Plantation** (tel 703/869-2028), a late 18th-century graystone manor house 2 miles south of town off US 11. Now a National Trust museum, Belle Grove was built between 1794 and 1797 by Major Issac Hite, who relied on his brother-in-law, Thomas Jefferson, for architectural advice. The building has Palladian-style front windows and columns, and the interior is furnished with period antiques.

During the Civil War, Union General Philip Sheridan's troops were camped on the open fields around the house when Confederate forces under General Jubal Early staged a surprise attack. The Rebels initially won the Battle of Cedar Creek, but Sheridan rallied his troops and turned defeat into victory. There's a small battlefield visitors center on the road to the plantation.

📭

REFRESHMENT STOP

You can sample more Colonial charm at the **Wayside Inn** (tel 703/869-1797), on US 11 in the heart of Middletown. Travelers have been taking meals and renting rooms at this establishment since 1797. Today, the beautifully restored dining room serves fine traditional Virginian cuisine, some from recipes handed down since Jeffersonian times. Lunch entrees cost $6–$11; dinner main courses cost $14–$23.

From Belle Grove, drive 3 miles south on US 11 until you reach:

3. **Strasburg,** where children will enjoy the hands-on Civil War museum at **Hupps Hill Battlefield Park** (tel 703/465-5884), at the north end of town. The number of antique shops around Strasburg's stoplight demonstrate why this little town is known as the "Antique Capital of Virginia." Turn left at the light and drive a block east on Va 55 to the **Strasburg Museum** (tel 703/465-3175) in the old railroad station, where Stonewall Jackson brought his stolen Union locomotives after the Great Train Raid on Martinsburg, West Virginia.

Head east from Strasburg on Va 55. Ahead of you looms **Massanutten Mountain,** a long ridge which cuts the Shenandoah Valley into 2 parts. I-81 and US 11 run down the west side. You'll drive around the north end for 11 miles to US 340. Turn right here and drive south along a commercial strip full of restaurants into:

4. **Front Royal,** where the notorious Confederate spy Belle Boyd pried secrets from her Union

lovers. Turn left on Main St at the **Warren County Court House** and drive 3 blocks east to the local **Visitors Center** (tel 703/635-3185) in the old railroad station. Get a walking-tour map here and explore the **Belle Boyd Cottage,** 101 Chester St (tel 703/636-1446). Other attractions include the **Warren Rifles Confederate Museum,** 95 Chester St (tel 703/636-6982), featuring memorabilia from the War Between the States. Trolley tours operate from the visitors center during warm weather.

The northern entrance to the Skyline Drive and **Shenandoah National Park** is on US 340, just south of town. One mile beyond the entrance are **Skyline Caverns** (tel 703/635-4545 or toll free 800/296-4545), where an underground waterfall plummets 37 feet into a trout stream. The cave also is noted for rare, flower-like anthodite formations.

From the caverns, drive south on US 340 (Stonewall Jackson Memorial Hwy), which parallels the winding South Fork of the Shenandoah River and runs through the villages of **Bentonville, Compton,** and **Riley.** Private companies in each of these villages rent canoes and inner tubes for river excursions. Follow this scenic road 24 miles south to:

5. **Luray,** best known for **Luray Caverns** (tel 703/743-6551), Virginia's largest underground wonderland. Tourists have been visiting the caverns since they were discovered in 1878, making Luray one of the state's most popular attractions. Paved walkways lead down to such cavernous wonders as the **Great Stalactite Pipe Organ,** which can actually play music. Outside the cavern stands a carillon and the **Car and Carriage Caravan,** a fine collection of antique automobiles and carriages.

The caverns are 2 miles west of Luray on the US 211 Bypass, upon which you'll continue up and over Massanutten Mountain for 15 miles. This is the most scenic part of the tour, so stop at the overlooks for views back across the Valley. At the top of New Market Pass sits the **visitors center** (tel 703/564-8300) of **George Washington National Forest.** From here, proceed on down the mountain's west side to:

6. **New Market,** where the entire student body of Virginia Military Institute (VMI) marched up from Lexington to help defeat a larger Union force on May 15, 1864. Turn right just west of I-81 and drive to the end of the service road to the **New Market Battlefield Historical Park** (tel 703/740-3101). Maintained by VMI, the battlefield and its Hall of Valor Civil War Museum are dedicated to the Civil War students and all other young men who have served their country. (On the way to the park, you'll pass a cavalry museum and the New Market Battlefield Military Museum; neither is part of the VMI operation.) The Shenandoah Valley Travel Association has a **tourist information office** (tel 703/740/3132) opposite the Battlefield Park turnoff; it has a free reservations phone, in case you decide to stay overnight in the area.

🍷

REFRESHMENT STOP

New Market has the usual collection of fast food restaurants at its I-81 interchange, but for good home cooking, visit the **Southern Kitchen** (tel 703/740-3514), on US 11 less than ½ mile south of the stoplight. Since 1955, Ruby Newland and family have been serving lightly breaded fried chicken and other local fare. Her establishment has a 1950s small-town ambience, including a soda fountain in 1 dining room. Main courses cost $6–$12.

For another look underground, proceed 3 miles south on US 11 to **Endless Caverns** (tel 703/740-3993, or 800/544-CAVE). As far as anyone knows, this cave really is endless; you'll see stalactites, stalagmites, giant columns, and limestone pendants. From here, keep driving 18 miles south on either I-81 or US 11 to **Harrisonburg,** an agricultural center, home of James Madison University, and a good stopping place for a meal or an overnight stay. If you choose not to rest here, push on south another 25 miles to:

7. **Staunton,** pronounced "STAN-ton" by the locals, where President Woodrow Wilson was born in 1856 in the Presbyterian Manse. His minister-father soon moved to a church in Georgia, but Staunton still claims the World War I leader as its own. **Woodrow Wilson's Birthplace,** Coalter and Frederick Sts (tel 703/885-0897), a handsome Greek revival building, is now a national shrine and the local welcome center. A next-door museum has exhibits on Wilson's life.

Across the street is **Mary Baldwin College,** a noted "finishing" school for girls. Walking-tour maps for Staunton's Victorian downtown are available at Wilson's Birthplace and at the **Staunton/Augusta County Travel Information Office** (tel 703/332-3972), near exit 222 off I-81 (follow US 250 west and the tourist information signs).

Also worth a visit is the nearby **Museum of American Frontier Culture,** also off US 250 west of exit 222 (tel 703/332-7850). This living museum contains working 19th-century farms, one local and one each from England, Northern Ireland, and Germany. Staff members in period costumes plant fields and tend livestock.

The country-singing Statler Brothers, also Staunton natives, have built their own **Mini-Museum** at 501 Thornrose Ave (tel 703/805-7297), off Churchville Ave (US 250) west of downtown. Tours are given Monday–Friday at 2pm. The Statlers throw a July 4th bash each year in Gypsy Hill Park across the street.

Staunton offers a good place for an overnight rest. The town has good chain motels near exit 222 off I-81 (near the tourist information office and the Museum of American Frontier Culture). Two properties in town have their own special ambiance: The **Belle Grae Inn** (515 W Frederick St), with rooms in a well-restored Victorian house; and the European-style **Frederick House** at 28 N New St.

From Staunton, continue south on I-81 or US 11 for 16 miles to Steele's Tavern. Turn left there on Va 606 and drive a mile east to:

8. **McCormick's Farm Historic Wayside** (tel 703/377-2255), where Cyrus McCormick revolutionized farming by building the first effective grain reaper in 1831. The farm's log blacksmith shop and grist mill are now a museum where you can see one of Cyrus' first machines. The farm is open daily April–December, 9am–5pm; January–March, Monday–Friday 9am–5pm.

Return to US 11 or I-81 and head south 16 miles to:

9. **Lexington,** among the most historic and photogenic towns in the Valley, with a lovingly restored downtown, Washington and Lee (W&L) University, and the Virginia Military Institute (VMI). You'll have much to see in this resting place of generals Stonewall Jackson, Robert E Lee, and George C Marshall—and Jackson's and Lee's horses. Begin at the **Lexington Visitors Center,** 102 E Washington St (tel 703/463-3777), which provides an excellent brochure with walking and driving tour maps. Be sure to visit the **Stonewall Jackson House,** 8 E Washington St (tel 703/463-2552), where the Confederate hero lived while teaching philosophy at VMI. The home features many of his possessions and has photographs and a slide show about Jackson's residency here. The **Virginia Military Institute Museum** in Jackson Memorial Hall, VMI Campus (tel 703/464-7232), facing VMI's fabled Parade Ground, contains Jackson's stuffed horse and the bullet-pierced raincoat he was wearing the night his own men accidentally shot him at Chancellorsville. The VMI campus also is home to the **George C Marshall Museum and Library** (tel 703/463-2552), named in honor of the 1906 alumnus who became the Army's Chief of Staff during World War II and who, as Secretary of State, won the Nobel Peace Prize for creating the Marshall Plan.

From the end of the Civil War until his death in 1870, General Robert E Lee served as president of Washington and Lee University, which adjoins VMI (the brick sidewalks belong to VMI; the concrete ones to Washington and Lee). Lee designed the president's house on campus and supervised the building of the Victorian-Gothic **Lee Chapel** (tel 703/463-8768), his burial place and shrine. The chapel, which today is used for concerts and other events, contains both Edward Valentine's white marble statue of Lee and Charles Wilson Peale's portrait of George Washington.

Lee's office in the lower level of the building has been preserved as a museum, and his famous horse Traveller is buried in a plot outside.

From Lexington, a gorgeous 60-mile side trip follows the Virginia By-Way (Va 39) northwest from Lexington through the Goshen Pass, where the Maury River cuts an 1,800-foot-deep gorge through the Allegheny Mountains. Return via Va 42 and I-64, certainly one of the most beautiful interstate highways anywhere.

From Lexington, drive 12 miles south on US 11, where the highway actually crosses:

10. **Natural Bridge** (tel 703/291-2121 or toll free 800/533-1410), a 215-foot-tall limestone arch over Cedar Creek. Some people consider this 90-foot-long structure to be one of the world's greatest natural wonders. George Washington surveyed the property in the mid-1700s and carved his initials on the arch, and Thomas Jefferson bought it in 1774. Even though the bridge is a major commercial tourist attraction today, it is still fascinating to walk along the creek under the soaring bridge and see Washington's initials.

Also here are the **Natural Bridge Zoo** and the **Natural Bridge Wax Museum,** which has more than 100 life-size figures of leading characters in the area's history and folklore. And you can make a final foray underground into **Natural Bridge Caverns.** The Natural Bridge area has a restaurant and lodging facilities on the premises.

From Natural Bridge, both I-81 and US 11 go 39 miles south to Roanoke, the largest city in western Virginia and the gateway to the state's ruggedly beautiful Southwest Highlands. Or you can backtrack to Lexington and take I-64 east to Charlottesville and Richmond, or west to Beckley and the beginning of the driving tour "New River Gorge to the Highlands" (see the West Virginia chapter).

SCENIC DRIVING TOUR #2

COLONIAL VIRGINIA

Start: Richmond
Finish: Yorktown
Distance: 100 miles
Time: 1–5 days
Highlights: Civil War battlefields; antebellum plantations along the scenic James River; tributes to early American history at Jamestown, Williamsburg, and Yorktown; amusement parks

Following the so-called Plantation Route (Va 5) and the aptly named Colonial Parkway, this tour explores the peninsula between the James and York Rivers where the history of English-speaking America began (at Jamestown) and later flourished (in Williamsburg). Wealthy colonial landowners used their tobacco profits to build grand manor houses on the James River.

George Washington won the American Revolution by trapping Lord Cornwallis at Yorktown in 1781. And during the Civil War, Union General George McClellan led a bloody but unsuccessful campaign up this peninsula.

The major plantations between Richmond and Jamestown can be seen in one day. Some plantations and farms have small bed-and-breakfast operations, but most travelers stay in Richmond or Williamsburg, each of which demands at least a day's visit.

For additional information on accommodations, restaurants, and attractions in the region covered by the tour, look under specific cities in the listings portion of this book.

I-95, I-64, US 1, and US 301 all converge at:

1. **Richmond,** Virginia's state capital since 1780, capital of the Confederacy from 1861-1865, and today a blend of historic neighborhoods, modern downtown high-rises, and sprawling suburban industrial complexes. Begin your visit at the **Metro**

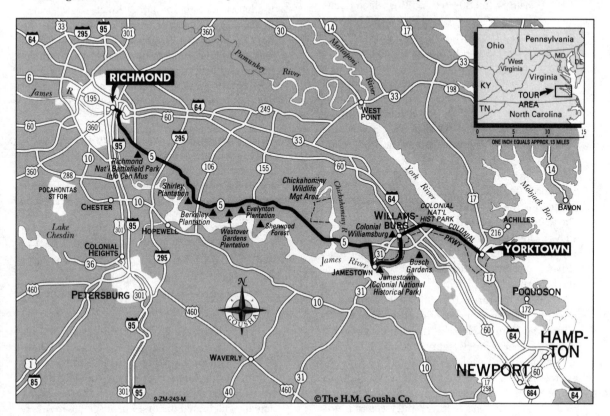

Richmond Visitors Center, 1710 Robin Hood Rd (tel 804/782-2777), in an old railway station opposite The Diamond baseball stadium (near exit 78 off I-95). Children can climb aboard a steam engine and red caboose while adults gather a wealth of information about the city.

From the visitors center, proceed to such sights as the **State Capitol,** 9th and Grace Sts (tel 804/358-4901), designed in the Classical Revival style by Thomas Jefferson; the 1741 **St John's Church,** 2401 E Broad St (tel 804/648-5015); **John Marshall House,** 818 E Marshall St (tel 804/648-7998), the restored home of a notable American patriot and US chief justice from 1801–1835; the **Museum of the Confederacy,** 1201 E Clay St (tel 804/649-1861), with the largest Confederate collection in the country, most of it contributed by veterans; the lovely **Monument Avenue** and its median-strip statues to Civil War heroes; the **Edgar Allen Poe Museum,** 1914–1916 E Main St (tel 804/648-5523), which documents the poet's life; and the **Virginia Museum of Fine Arts,** The Boulevard and Grove Ave (tel 804/367-0844), with impressive collections of art nouveau, art deco, 19th- and 20th-century French paintings, contemporary American art, and works from India, Tibet, and Nepal.

Begin your driving tour at **Chimborazo Park,** 3315 E Broad St, in the historic Church Hill residential neighborhood. During the Civil War, the now-vacant fields in the park were the site of a hospital that treated some 76,000 Confederate wounded. The red brick building is the visitors center for the **Richmond Battlefield National Park** (tel 804/226-1981). Inside you'll find displays dealing with the Civil War fighting that raged around Richmond, and maps plotting a 60-mile driving tour through the scattered battlefields on the eastern side of the city.

From the visitors center, turn left on Broad St and proceed west to 25th St, observing on the corner **St John's Church,** the white clapboard structure where Patrick Henry gave his "Liberty or Death" speech. Turn left on 25th St, go 3 blocks south, and turn left (east) on Main St (Va 5). Keep going east on Va 5, bearing right at the fork leading under the railroad trestle (this Y-intersection is not

well marked). You may be surprised at how quickly this heavily industrial part of town ends and beautiful rural countryside begins.

Continue east 6 miles to Battlefield Park Rd. If you aren't a Civil War buff, keep going straight on Va 5 to the 3rd stop. But if you are, turn right into:

2. **Fort Harrison,** the largest single section of the Richmond Battlefield National Park. The crape myrtle–fringed road runs 6½ miles past the remains of Forts Gilmer, Gregg, Johnson, Harrison, and Hoke—earthwork structures that were built as part of the city's Confederate defense. Union forces captured Fort Harrison in September 1864, but the armies then settled down into trench warfare until the war ended 6 months later. Fort Harrison has its own small visitors center, which is open daily during the summer 9am–5pm, weekends only during spring and fall. From here, continue south to Fort Hoke, where Hoke-Brady Rd forks to the left and ends at Union-built Fort Brady overlooking the James River.

From Fort Brady, backtrack 1 mile and turn right on Kingsland Rd (ignoring the signs for Va 5 and Richmond) and drive 5 miles east through forests and fields until it dead-ends at Va 5, known here as New Market Rd. There is no road sign, but turn right and head east 8½ miles to Rte 608. Turn right there and follow the signs to:

3. **Shirley Plantation,** Charles City (tel 804/829-5121), founded in 1613 as Virginia's first plantation and home of the Carter-Lee family since its square brick manor house was built on a riverside knoll in 1724. Noted for its hanging staircase, the mansion is where Anne Hill Carter married Revolutionary War hero Henry "Lighthorse Harry" Lee. (As a youth, their son Robert E Lee used to play here while visiting his grandfather.) Open daily, except Christmas, from 9am–5pm.

From Shirley, backtrack to Va 5, turn right, and drive 3 miles east to the signs for:

4. **Berkeley Plantation,** Charles City (tel 804/829-6018), where a small party of settlers came ashore in 1619 and promptly gave thanks for their safe journey from England. Despite the Pilgrims of Massachusetts getting all the credit, this group actually celebrated the first Thanksgiving in Amer-

ica, and the event is duly commemorated annually on the first Sunday in November. The Harrison family bought the Berkeley land in 1691 and in 1726 built the Georgian-style mansion, which belonged to Benjamin Harrison V, who signed the Declaration of Independence and whose son and grandson, William Henry Harrison and Benjamin Harrison, both served as president of the United States. Benedict Arnold's British troops sacked the plantation during the American Revolution, and General George McClellan made it one of his headquarters during the Peninsula Campaign of 1862. Open daily, except Christmas Day, 8am–5pm.

After you leave Berkeley, turn right on the narrow dirt road and drive 2 miles south to **Westover Plantation** (tel 804/829-2882), whose Georgian manor house was built in the 1730s by William Byrd II. His many descendants have gone on to make names for themselves as governors, senators, and explorers. Of all the James River plantations, Westover makes best use of its water-front location and enjoys a great river view. The house is open only during Historic Garden Week in late April, but you can tour the classical gardens daily, except Christmas, 9am–6pm. Leave your $2 admission in an honor box by the brick gate next to the river.

REFRESHMENT STOP

Westover's owners have turned one of their outbuildings into the **Coach House Tavern** (tel 804/829-6003), a colonial-style eatery with panel windows looking out to the manor house gardens. In keeping with tradition, the menu offers such Virginia fare as pork barbecue, country ham, and crab cakes. Lunch main courses cost $5–$11. Open daily for lunch only, except Christmas, 11:30am–3pm.

Now drive back to Va 5, turn right and continue east 1½ miles to **Westover Church,** where Captain William Perry, who died in 1637, is buried within the riverside grounds. His tombstone is America's 3rd-oldest grave marker. The church itself was constructed in the 1730s. Another ½ mile east on Va 5 brings us to:

5. **Evelynton Plantation** (tel 804/829-5075), which William Byrd II gave as a dowry for his daughter Evelyn, who is believed to have died of a broken heart when he refused permission for her to marry the man she loved. She is buried at Westover Church, but some say her ghost still roams this adjacent property. The plantation was bought in 1847 by Edward Ruffin, Jr, son of the man who fired the first shot on Fort Sumter, SC, to begin the Civil War. The original mansion was burned during a Civil War skirmish. The present colonial revival structure dates back to 1935, but it looks as if it were built 2 centuries earlier. The house and boxwood gardens are open daily (except Christmas, Thanksgiving, and New Year's Day), 9am–5pm.

REFRESHMENT STOP

Other than the Coach House Tavern at Berkeley Plantation, your best bet for a meal in these parts is the pleasant **Indian Fields Tavern** (tel 804/829-5004), in a restored Victorian-era farmhouse 2½ miles east of Evelynton on Va 5. Emphasis is on local ham, pork sausage, and crab cakes, with scrumptious sandwiches offered at lunch. Lunch entrees cost $5.50–$12; dinner main courses, $15–$22.

From Indian Fields Tavern, drive 5½ miles east on Va 5 to the last of our plantation stops:

6. **Sherwood Forest** (tel 804/829-5377), home of President John Tyler, the nation's 10th vice-president who succeeded to the White House in 1841 upon the death of his neighbor, President William Henry Harrison. The original part of this long, clapboard house was built in 1660, but it was expanded over the years until reaching the length

of a football field. Although not on the water, it is the only James River plantation with its own ballroom, and it contains a remarkable collection of Tyler family memorabilia. The grounds are open daily 9am–5pm; house tours are by appointment only.

From Sherwood Forest, continue 14½ miles east on Va 5, crossing the Chickahominy River to Va 614 (Grennsprings Rd). Turn right and make your way south 2 miles to a traffic light at Va 31. Go straight through the light into the major tourist attraction of:

7. **Jamestown,** which today consists of 2 historical parks commemorating North America's first permanent English-speaking settlement, established here in 1607. The first park is **Jamestown Settlement** (tel 804/253-4838), where you will see recreations of **Powhatan Indian Village,** with many exhibits dealing with Native American culture and technology in 17th-century coastal Virginia; **James Fort,** built by Captain John Smith and his colonists in 1607; and the 3 cramped ships that transported the colonists from England. A pavilion contains actual artifacts from that era. Costumed staff members provide information about the village, fort, and ships. The settlement is open daily, except Christmas and New Year's Day, 9am–5pm.

The other place to visit here is the Jamestown portion of **Colonial National Historical Park** (tel 804/229-1773). This national park is on the actual 17th-century "James Cittie" settlement location. Although little is left other than some excavated foundations and part of a brick church tower, there is a 1907 reconstruction of **Memorial Church,** site of America's first elected assembly, the House of Burgesses. Don't miss the **Glasshouse,** where costumed staff members make glass just as the colonists did. Walking trails wander through the old settlement site, and a 5-mile drive loops through the pitch and tar swamp whose mosquitoes made life miserable for the colonists. The park is open daily during the summer 8:30am–5:30pm; during spring and fall, until 5pm; and during the winter; until 4:30pm. Admission is $8 per vehicle, $2 per biker or pedestrian.

From Jamestown, take the Colonial Pkwy for 9 miles, first along the James River's scenic banks and then north until you go through a tunnel. On the north side, take a left around the traffic circle to the visitors center of:

8. **Colonial Williamsburg,** the beautifully restored old capital with 88 original buildings and more than 500 structures that have been painstakingly rebuilt on their 18th-century foundations. Here you can visit the **Capitol** building, the **Governor's Palace,** taverns, houses, a hospital, and galleries. A number of 18th-century craft demonstrations are offered in the historic area, including cabinetmaking, silversmithing, printing, wigmaking, and candlemaking. Staff members in period costumes actually reenact life as it was during the 1700s, and they even speak the English of that day. Cars aren't allowed in the historic area, but shuttle buses leave every few minutes from the **visitor center** (tel 804/220-7645), where you can get booklets and maps, watch an introductory film, and buy tickets to see the historic area.

A few attractions near Williamsburg are worth a visit, starting with **Busch Gardens,** off US 60 about 3 miles east of the historic district (tel 804/253-3350). This 360-acre amusement park has rides and shows amid reproductions of 17th-century hamlets. **Water Country USA,** off Va 199 northeast of town (tel 804/229-9300), is a water-oriented theme park with 40 acres of man-made attractions such as a wave pool, rapids, and an Olympic-size swimming pool. And if you're "born to shop," you can head for **Williamsburg Pottery Factory** (tel 804/564-3326) or the huge collection of outlet shops 5 miles west of town on Richmond Rd (US 60).

When you've had a thorough look around Williamsburg, get back on the Colonial Pkwy and drive 11½ miles north to:

9. **Yorktown,** where George Washington defeated Lord Cornwallis in 1781 and for all practical purposes won the American Revolution. Follow the signs to the **Yorktown Victory Center** (tel 804/887-1776), where you can learn about the siege that led to Cornwallis's surrender. An excellent 28-minute film follows the American and

French armies' routes to Yorktown, and costumed guides explain what 18th-century life was like on a farm and in the Continental Army camp outside. Open daily, except Christmas and New Year's Day, 9am–5pm.

From the Victory Center, turn right and drive downhill along Water St, enjoying the view of the York River. Turn right on Read St and drive uphill to a left on Ballard St, then a left at the sign for the National Park. That will take you to the National Park Service's **visitor center** (tel 804/898-3400), the starting point for touring the battlefields, which is open daily 8:30am–sunset. A museum displays Washington's actual sleeping tent and many other artifacts from the time of his victory. Get a visitor's guide with maps and set out on the 7-mile Battlefield Route and the 10-mile Encampment Route. Be prepared to stop along these gorgeous drives to explore particular points of interest, such as the **Grand French Battery,** the early 18th-century **Moore House,** and **Surrender Field.**

Other sights may be viewed in town, including several historic homes; the restored **Swan Tavern,** Main and Ballard Sts (tel 804/898-3033), with an antiques shop; and the 98-foot marble **Victory Monument,** authorized by Congress in 1781 but not actually built until a century later.

From Yorktown, US 17 leads south to Newport News, where it intersects with I-64. Go east to Norfolk and Virginia Beach, or west to return to Richmond.

ABINGDON

Map page M-2, E2

Hotel 🛏

≝ ≝ ≝ ≝ **Martha Washington Inn**, 150 W Main St, Abingdon, VA 24210; tel 703/628-3161 or toll free 800/ 533-1014; fax 703/628-8885. Exit 17 off I-81. A mid-1980s restoration turned this 1832 southern mansion and former college into a magnificent hotel with elegant antique furnishings. Many parlors on the lobby floor, which opens to verandas with rocking chairs. Each floor also has a veranda. The inn is a short walk to the Barter Theater and minutes from museums and shops. **Rooms:** 61 rms and stes. Exec-level rms avail. CI 2pm/ CO noon. Nonsmoking rms avail. Individually furnished units. **Amenities:** 🛏 ⓣ A/C, cable TV w/movies, shoe polisher. Some units w/minibars, some w/fireplaces, some w/Jacuzzis. Free sparkling water in rooms. **Services:** ✕ ▣ 𝗩𝗣 🐾 ◩ ⌣ Twice-daily maid svce, babysitting. Southern hospitality prevails. Bellhop brings complimentary afternoon tea to rooms. **Facilities:** ▣ ⓛ 2 rsts, 2 bars (1 w/entertainment). **Rates:** $85–$130 S or D; from $150 ste. Extra person $10. Children under 12 stay free. Higher rates for spec evnts/hols. Spec packages avail. Pking: Outdoor, free. Maj CC. Offers plan including dinner.

Motels

≝ ≝ **Alpine Motel**, 882 E Main St, PO Box 658, Abingdon, VA 24210; tel 703/628-3178. Exit 19 off I-81. Large, well-kept grounds on a hill with views of the highlands combine with numerous nearby restaurants and a short 2-mile drive to the Barter Theater to make this a desirable spot for Abingdon visitors. **Rooms:** 19 rms. CI noon/CO 11am. Nonsmoking rms avail. **Amenities:** 🛏 ⓣ A/C, cable TV. **Services:** ◩ **Facilities:** Playground. **Rates:** HS Apr–Nov 15 $36–$45 S or D. Extra person $4. Lower rates off-season. Pking: Outdoor, free. Maj CC.

≝ ≝ **Comfort Inn Abingdon**, VA 140, PO Box 2223, Abingdon, VA 24210; tel 703/676-2222 or toll free 800/ 228-5150; fax 703/676-2222 ext 307. Exit 14 off I-81. A modern, well-furnished chain motel just 5 minutes from Abingdon's historic district. **Rooms:** 80 rms. CI 2pm/CO noon. Nonsmoking rms avail. Traditional decor is well suited to this historic area. **Amenities:** 🛏 A/C, cable TV w/movies. **Services:** ◩ ⌣ **Facilities:** ⓕ ⓛ **Rates (CP):** HS Apr–Oct $45–$70 S; $50–$80 D. Extra person $10. Children under 18 stay free. Min stay spec evnts. Lower rates off-season. Higher rates for spec evnts/hols. Pking: Outdoor, free. Maj CC.

≝ ≝ **Holiday Inn Express**, 940 E Main St, Abingdon, VA 24210; tel 703/676-2829 or toll free 800/465-4329; fax 703/ 676-2605. Exit 19 off I-81. One of the top representatives of its chain, this modern facility is close to historic district and numerous restaurants. Large lobby has TV and comfortable seating. **Rooms:** 80 rms and stes. Exec-level rms avail. CI 2pm/ CO 11am. Express checkout avail. Nonsmoking rms avail. Exceptionally well-kept rooms are done in soothing pastels. **Amenities:** 🛏 ⓣ A/C, cable TV w/movies. Some units w/Jacuzzis. **Services:** ◩ ⌣ **Facilities:** ⓕ ⓛ ⓛ Washer/dryer. **Rates (CP):** HS Apr–Nov $45–$55 S; $50–$60 D; from $75 ste. Extra person $5. Children under 19 stay free. Lower rates off-season. Higher rates for spec evnts/hols. Pking: Outdoor, free. Maj CC.

Restaurants 🍴

★ **Starving Artist Cafe**, in Depot Sq, 134 Wall St, Abingdon; tel 703/628-8445. Exit 17 off I-81. Turn left on Main St, then left onto Wall St. **Eclectic.** As befits the name, rotating art exhibits adorn the walls of this informal cafe. Traditional fare includes house-specialty Maryland-style crab cakes, plus Cajun prime rib and vegetarian entrees. Lunch features sandwiches named for artists and authors. A favorite of Barter Theater goers. **FYI:** Reservations not accepted. Children's menu. Beer and wine only. **Open:** Lunch Mon 11am–2pm, Tues–Sat 11am–3pm; dinner Tues–Sat 5–9pm. Closed some hols; 1st week in September. **Prices:** Main courses $15–$18. Maj CC. 🍽

Ⓢ **The Tavern**, 222 E Main St, Abingdon; tel 703/628-1118. Exit 17 off I-81. Turn right at Main St. **International/Vegetarian.** Built in 1779, this faithfully restored tavern with exposed beams, wooden tables, and plank floors provides an intimate ambience as well as a sense of community. Patio and 2nd-floor porch have outside seating overlooking gardens. Chef prepares many traditional meals in untraditional manner and is willing to depart from menu on request. Aroma of smoking meat lures Saturday lunch clientele back for dinner. After-dinner drinks sipped by fire. Reservations taken in 2-hour slots. **FYI:** Reservations recommended. Children's menu. **Open:** Daily 11am–10pm. Closed Dec 25. **Prices:** Main courses $10–$17. Maj CC. 🍴 🍽 📷 ⓛ

ALEXANDRIA

Map page M-3, C6

Hotels 🛏

≝ ≝ ≝ **Best Western Old Colony**, 625 1st St, at N Washington St, Alexandria, VA 22314 (Old Town); tel 703/548-6300 or toll free 800/528-1234; fax 703/684-7782. Exit 1 off I-95. Follow US 1 north. An attractive, pleasant hotel on 7 acres at the north end of Old Town Alexandria. Began life as a motel in 1958 but has been expanded and greatly improved. The brick main building has a colonial-accented lobby and, upstairs, 3 floors of modern rooms. **Rooms:** 332 rms and stes. CI 3pm/CO noon. Express checkout avail. Nonsmoking rms avail. Comfortable, nicely decorated and furnished rooms have basically the same features, but the old motel wings have smaller baths. **Amenities:** 🛁 ⚱ A/C, cable TV w/movies, shoe polisher. Some units w/terraces, some w/Jacuzzis. Refrigerators available for a fee. Some rooms have computers/fax ports. **Services:** ✗ 🚐 ⊠ ⌂ Complimentary hors d'oeuvres in lounge Monday to Friday 5–7pm. **Facilities:** 🛗 📞 [750] ⚿ 1 rst, 1 bar (w/entertainment), lifeguard, games rm, spa, sauna, whirlpool. Nicely appointed, dark-wood bar and restaurant off lobby. Gazebo on rooftop for meetings, lounging. Conference center to rear has more extensive meeting facilities. **Rates:** HS Mar–Apr/Sept–Oct $89–$125 S; $99–$135 D; from $125 ste. Extra person $10. Children under 17 stay free. Lower rates off-season. Spec packages avail. Pking: Indoor/outdoor, free. Maj CC.

≡≡ **Comfort Inn Landmark**, 6254 Duke St, Alexandria, VA 22312; tel 703/642-3422 or toll free 800/435-6868; fax 703/642-3422. Exit 3B off I-395. This well-maintained hotel is located near several large shopping centers. **Rooms:** 148 rms. CI 2pm/CO noon. Nonsmoking rms avail. Some king-bed rooms have easy chairs. **Amenities:** 🛁 📞 A/C, cable TV w/movies. Some units w/Jacuzzis. **Services:** ⊠ ⌂ Car-rental desk. Free van to Van Dorn metro station. **Facilities:** 🛗 [90] ⚿ 1 rst, 1 bar, lifeguard. Restaurant serves breakfast and dinner Monday to Saturday, breakfast only Sunday. Fast-food outlet is adjacent. **Rates (CP):** HS Apr–June $60 S; $66 D. Extra person $6. Children under 12 stay free. Lower rates off-season. Pking: Outdoor, free. Maj CC.

≡≡≡ **Courtyard by Marriott**, 2700 Eisenhower Ave, Alexandria, VA 22314; tel 703/329-2323 or toll free 800/428-1105; fax 703/329-2323. Exit 2 off I-95. The courtyard is missing at this mid-rise hotel, but clubby public rooms with bright wood paneling lend a nice ambience. Essentially a business travelers' establishment. Located near a metro station in an area of industrial warehouses. **Rooms:** 176 rms and stes. CI 3pm/CO 1pm. Express checkout avail. Nonsmoking rms avail. Bright, attractively decorated rooms have large desks. **Amenities:** 🛁 ⚱ 📞 A/C, satel TV w/movies. Some units w/terraces, 1 w/Jacuzzi. **Services:** ✗ ⊠ ⌂ Babysitting. Free shuttle to Eisenhower Avenue metro station. **Facilities:** 📞 [60] ⚿ 1 rst, 1 bar, whirlpool. Lobby restaurant serves breakfast buffet, express lunch, and à la carte dinners. **Rates:** HS mid-Feb to June/Sept–

Nov $109 S; $119 D; from $250 ste. Extra person $10. Children under 12 stay free. Lower rates off-season. Higher rates for spec evnts/hols. Pking: Indoor/outdoor, free. Maj CC.

≡≡≡ **Embassy Suites**, 1900 Diagonal Rd, Alexandria, VA 22314; tel 703/684-5900 or toll free 800/EMBASSY; fax 703/684-1403. Exit 1 off I-95. Between Duke and King Sts. This all-suites hotel with a stunning, garden-like atrium enjoys a convenient location opposite King Street metro and Alexandria Amtrak stations. Shops and restaurants adjacent. **Rooms:** 268 stes. CI 3pm/CO noon. Express checkout avail. Nonsmoking rms avail. All units except Presidential suites have sleep sofas. Homey, richly furnished living rooms have round tables, while large armoires conceal closet space, TVs, and desks. Entry to suites is from walkways overlooking atrium. **Amenities:** 🛁 ⚱ 📞 ⚑ A/C, cable TV w/movies, refrig, voice mail. Some units w/terraces. Wet bars, microwaves, and 2 TVs in each unit. **Services:** ✗ ⊠ ⌂ Babysitting. Full breakfasts and complimentary evening cocktails served in atrium. Free shuttle to heart of Old Town. **Facilities:** 🛗 📞 [325] 🖥 ⚿ 1 rst, 2 bars (1 w/entertainment), lifeguard, games rm, sauna, whirlpool, washer/dryer. Indoor pool opens to sun deck. **Rates (CP):** HS Apr–May/Sept–Oct from $139 ste. Extra person $15. Children under 12 stay free. Lower rates off-season. Spec packages avail. Pking: Indoor, $5–$10. Maj CC. Weekend rates by suite type, not number of occupants.

≡≡ **Executive Club Suites**, 610 Bashford Lane at N Washington St, Alexandria, VA 22314 (Old Town); tel 703/739-2582 or toll free 800/535-2582; fax 703/548-0266. Exit 1 off I-95. Formerly an apartment building, this comfortable all-suites hotel is conveniently located on the northern end of Old Town Alexandria, near National Airport. Ideal for stays of a week or longer. **Rooms:** 78 stes. CI noon/CO 11am. All units are attractively decorated with dark wood furniture and plaid chairs and spreads and are equipped with kitchens and sleep sofas. Floor plans vary. **Amenities:** 🛁 ⚱ 📞 ⚑ A/C, cable TV w/movies, refrig, voice mail. Rooms have irons and boards and 2 TVs. **Services:** 🚐 ⊠ ⌂ 🔔 Dinner provided once a week, outside in good weather. Complimentary wine, beer, and soda at evening sessions. Free shuttle to metro station. **Facilities:** 📞 [30] 🖥 ⚿ Lifeguard, sauna, washer/dryer. Club Room downstairs hosts breakfasts and evening sessions. **Rates (CP):** HS Mar–Oct from $139 ste. Lower rates off-season. Spec packages avail. Pking: Outdoor, free. Maj CC. Rates vary by length of stay.

≡≡ **Guest Quarters Suite Hotel**, 100 S Reynolds St at Duke St, Alexandria, VA 22304; tel 703/370-9600 or toll free 800/424-2900; fax 703/370-0467. Exit 3A off I-395. Families will find comfortable temporary homes at this converted apartment building with spacious, well-equipped 1-, 2-, and 3-bedroom apartments. Within walking distance of restaurants and shops.

Rooms: 225 effic. CI 3pm/CO noon. Express checkout avail. Nonsmoking rms avail. Nicely furnished and decorated in earth tones, all units have sleep sofas, full kitchens, and dining areas. **Amenities:** 🛅 🛆 🖭 🍴 A/C, cable TV w/movies, refrig. Some units w/terraces. All apartments except junior models are equipped with dishwashers and 2 TVs. **Services:** ✕ 🖼 🗘 ⟳ Extensive breakfast included in rates. Free shuttle to Van Dorn metro station. **Facilities:** 🖪 🖳 🔲₈₀ 🖦 1 rst, 1 bar, lifeguard, games rm, washer/dryer. Restaurant open for breakfast and dinner. **Rates (CP):** HS Apr–Oct from $150 effic. Extra person $20. Children under 18 stay free. Lower rates off-season. Spec packages avail. Pking: Outdoor, free. Maj CC.

≣≣≣ **Holiday Inn Old Town**, 480 King St, Alexandria, VA 22314 (Old Town); tel 703/549-6080 or toll free 800/368-5047. Exit 1 off I-95. Go north on US 1; at Pitt St. Few Holiday Inns can match the charm of this federal-style brick structure, built around a courtyard, in the heart of Old Town Alexandria. Period reproductions abound, in both the elegant lobby and the rooms. **Rooms:** 227 rms and stes. CI 3pm/CO noon. Express checkout avail. Nonsmoking rms avail. Relatively spacious rooms are furnished and decorated with the federal period in mind. King-bed units have sleep sofas and tables rather than desks. **Amenities:** 🛅 🛆 🖭 🍴 A/C, cable TV w/movies, in-rm safe. All units w/minibars, some w/terraces. Suites have balconies overlooking the courtyard. **Services:** ⦿ ⊷ 🚐 🖼 🗘 ⟳ Twice-daily maid svce, children's program, babysitting. Free shuttle to metro station. Morning coffee and danish, afternoon coffee and cookies, evening snacks in lobby. Manager's reception every Wednesday. **Facilities:** 🖪 🖳 🔲₂₅₀ 🖦 2 rsts, 1 bar, lifeguard, sauna, beauty salon, washer/dryer. **Rates:** HS Mar 15–June/Sept–Nov 15 $125 S; $140 D; from $195 ste. Extra person $15. Children under 19 stay free. Lower rates off-season. Spec packages avail. Pking: Indoor, $6. Maj CC. Weekend packages available.

≣≣≣ **Sheraton Suites**, 801 N St Asaph St at N Madison St, Alexandria, VA 22314 (Old Town); tel 703/836-4700 or toll free 800/235-3535; fax 703/548-4514. Exit 1 off I-95. Near the northern end of Old Town, this brick building contains comfortable suites plus many amenities offered by full-service hotels. Formerly the Marriott Suites. **Rooms:** 249 stes. Exec-level rms avail. CI 3pm/CO 1pm. Express checkout avail. Nonsmoking rms avail. Most units are identical except for bed arrangement. About half have sleep sofas. **Amenities:** 🛅 🛆 🖭 🍴 A/C, cable TV w/movies, refrig. Some units w/terraces. All units are equipped with wet bars, irons, and ironing boards. Microwaves available at no charge. **Services:** ✕ 🚐 🖼 🗘 ⟳ Babysitting. Full breakfast included in rates. **Facilities:** 🖪 🖳 🔲₉₀ 🖦 1 rst, 1 bar, lifeguard, spa, whirlpool, washer/dryer. Pool in health club opens to brick sun deck. **Rates (CP):** HS Mar–mid-June/Sept 7–Nov 30 from

$149 ste. Extra person $15. Children under 17 stay free. Min stay wknds. Lower rates off-season. Higher rates for spec evnts/hols. Spec packages avail. Pking: Indoor, $7. Maj CC. Weekend packages available.

Motels

≣ **Econo Lodge Old Town**, 700 N Washington St at Wythe St, Alexandria, VA 22314 (Old Town); tel 703/836-5100 or toll free 800/237-2243; fax 703/519-7015. Exit 1 off I-95. Go north on US 1. A very basic but clean motel convenient to Old Town sights, shops, and restaurants. L-shaped brick building faces parking lot. **Rooms:** 39 rms. CI 2pm/CO 11am. Nonsmoking rms avail. Spacious rooms have bright wood-grained furniture, large dressing areas outside bath. Upstairs rooms have entries off interior corridors; downstairs units open to parking lot or balcony walkway. **Amenities:** 🛅 A/C, cable TV. **Services:** 🚚 🗘 ⟳ Babysitting. **Rates:** HS Mem Day–Labor Day $60 S; $70 D. Extra person $5. Children under 18 stay free. Lower rates off-season. Higher rates for spec evnts/hols. Pking: Outdoor, free. Maj CC. Pet deposit. AARP, over-50 discounts.

≣≣ **Hampton Inn**, 4800 Leesburg Pike, Alexandria, VA 22302; tel 703/671-4800 or toll free 800/HAMPTON; fax 703/671-2442. Exit 5 off I-395. 1 mi W on Va 7. A modern, well-managed motel with a lovely atrium lobby. Numerous restaurants, shopping centers, and discount clothing stores are within walking distance. **Rooms:** 130 rms. CI 3pm/CO noon. Nonsmoking rms avail. Rooms with king-size beds have work areas. **Amenities:** 🛅 🛆 🍴 A/C, cable TV w/movies. **Services:** 🖼 🗘 Babysitting. Free local calls. **Facilities:** 🖪 🖳 🔲₁₈ 🖦 Lifeguard. Pool is surrounded by concrete deck without landscaping. **Rates (CP):** $76–$79 S; $83–$86 D. Children under 18 stay free. Pking: Outdoor, free. Maj CC. Weekend rates available.

Inn

≣≣≣≣ **Morrison House**, 116 S Alfred St, Alexandria, VA 22314 (Old Town); tel 703/838-8000 or toll free 800/367-0800; fax 703/684-6283. Exit 1 off I-95. Take US 1 N; between King and Prince Sts. Although built in 1985, this comfortable, federal-style brick inn has the feel of 18th-century Alexandria, with period reproductions throughout its elegant lounge, library, and dining room. The lounge also has a working fireplace and period music. **Rooms:** 45 rms and stes. CI 3pm/CO noon. All rooms have large mahogany armoires containing closet space and TVs. Beds are tall federal-style models, and 2 deluxe units have canopy beds. **Amenities:** 🛅 🛆 🍴 A/C, cable TV w/movies, bathrobes. **Services:** ⦿ ⊷ 🆅🅿 🖼 🗘 Twice-daily maid svce, car-rental desk, babysitting. Big chocolate chip cookies as welcoming gifts. Complimentary morning coffee and afternoon tea.

Facilities: 🚗 ♿ 1 rst, 1 bar (w/entertainment), guest lounge. Health club facilities available nearby. **Rates:** $175–$210 S or D; from $295 ste. Extra person $20. Children under 18 stay free. Spec packages avail. Pking: Indoor, $10. Ltd CC.

Restaurants 🍴

Bilbo Baggins Wine Café and Restaurant, 208 Queen St, Alexandria (Old Town); tel 703/683-0300. Between Lee and Fairfax Sts. **New American/Italian.** A huge oak wine chest graces one of the 5 dining rooms in this cozy establishment noted for its cellar. Varnished wood, some exposed brick, and varying ceiling heights in these old residences add informal charm. Creative pasta dishes are the specialty, along with grilled beef, veal, and seafood served with unusual sauces. Daily specials can include grilled salmon topped with a puree of Maine fiddlehead greens. Salads and sandwiches offered at all meals. Breads and desserts made on premises. Discounted evening parking in garage across street. **FYI:** Reservations not accepted. **Open:** Lunch Mon–Fri 11:30am–2:30pm; dinner Mon–Sat 5:30–10:30pm, Sun 4:30–9:30pm; brunch Sun 11am–2:30pm. Closed some hols. **Prices:** Main courses $12–$16. Maj CC. 🍽️ ♿

Bread and Chocolate, 611 King St, Alexandria (Old Town); tel 703/548-0992. Between Washington and St Asaph Sts. **New American/Californian/Pastries.** Entering this small but pleasant bakery, you pass a display case brimming with European pastries. In fact, fresh pastries for breakfast and healthful California-style salads and sandwiches are the highlights here. Varnished-wood diner-style counter, tables, and trim provide a modern touch. Also at: 5189 Leesburg Pike, in Skyline Mall, Falls Church (tel 703/379-8005). **FYI:** Reservations not accepted. No liquor license. No smoking. **Open:** Mon–Sat 7am–7pm, Sun 8am–7pm. Closed Dec 25. **Prices:** Lunch main courses $6–$8. Ltd CC.

Cajun Bangkok, 907 King St, Alexandria (Old Town); tel 703/836-0038. Between Patricia and Alfred Sts. **Cajun/Thai.** Tastefully decorated with plants, inlaid tile tables, and paintings of Thailand on lavender walls. Owner/chef is known locally for blending of spicy Thai and Cajun cuisines—from red curry beef Penang to New Orleans shrimp casserole. **FYI:** Reservations accepted. **Open:** Sun–Thurs 5–10pm, Fri–Sat 5–11pm. Closed some hols. **Prices:** Main courses $9.95–$13.95. Maj CC. ♿

The Chart House, 1 Cameron St, Alexandria (Old Town); tel 703/684-5080. **Seafood/Steak.** One of the few waterfront eateries in the Washington, DC, metropolitan area, this tropical-style restaurant under a high peaked roof furnishes fine river views through its window-paneled walls and from an outside dining area. Potted plants, cane furniture, and staff dressed in aloha shirts set a relaxed, islandy tone. Steaks and seafood are the highlights of a limited menu augmented by daily specials featuring catches from far-off places like Hawaii and Nova Scotia. Large salad bar, included with main courses, sits beside open kitchen with grills going. **FYI:** Reservations recommended. Dress code. **Open:** Dinner Mon–Thurs 5–10pm, Fri–Sat 5–11pm, Sun 4–10pm; brunch Sun 11am–2:30pm. **Prices:** Main courses $15.50–$30. Maj CC. 🍽️ 🏞️ ♿

East Wind, 809 King St, Alexandria (Old Town); tel 703/836-1515. Between Columbus and Alfred Sts. **Vietnamese.** Rose carpets, tablecloths, and wall panels balance nicely with knotty pine room dividers supporting rows of tropical plants. This upscale Vietnamese restaurant is known for consistently fine cuisine, especially seafood and pork dishes. **FYI:** Reservations recommended. **Open:** Lunch Mon–Fri 11:30am–2:30pm; dinner daily 5:30–10:30pm. Closed some hols. **Prices:** Main courses $10–$16. Maj CC. 🚗

⭐ **Fish Market**, 105 King St at Union St, Alexandria (Old Town); tel 703/836-5676. **Seafood.** Several dining rooms and bars on 2 levels carry nautical themes at this large, popular, pub-like establishment. Traditional Chesapeake-style seafood main courses and salads are offered, plus burgers and sandwiches for both lunch and dinner. **FYI:** Reservations not accepted. Guitar/piano/singer. Dress code. **Open:** Mon–Sat 11:15am–2am, Sun 11:30am–midnight. Closed some hols. **Prices:** Main courses $7.50–$15. Maj CC.

⭐ **Gadsby's Tavern**, 138 N Royal St, at Cameron St, Alexandria (Old Town); tel 703/548-1288. **American.** Even the staff looks the part at this popular stop on walking tours of historic Old Town. Their 18th-century costumes complement the period furniture and decor of what was the dining rooms of the City Hotel (1792), a registered national landmark. (The original tavern is now a museum next door.) The menu offers contemporary regional favorites as well as dishes from Alexandria's pre-Revolutionary days. During summer, steamed blue crabs are served in the rear courtyard, where a full bar is set up. **FYI:** Reservations recommended. Singer. Children's menu. **Open:** Lunch Mon–Sat 11:30am–3pm; dinner daily 5:30–10pm; brunch Sun 11am–3pm. Closed some hols. **Prices:** Main courses $14–$23. Ltd CC. ▮

Geranio, 722 King St, Alexandria (Old Town); tel 703/548-0088. Between Washington and Columbus Sts. **Italian.** Archways join the 2 dining rooms of this building, which dates to the 1860s. Whitewashed brick walls adorned with paintings of Italian scenes and flowers brighten this place, a local favorite since 1976. Northern Italian seafood is featured, along with predominantly homemade pastas. Lobster with light tomato sauce over linguine is served all year. Entry for persons with disabilities in rear. **FYI:** Reservations recommended. Dress code. **Open:** Lunch Mon–Fri 11:30am–2:30pm; dinner Mon–Sat 6:30–10:30pm, Sun 5:30–9:30pm. Closed some hols. **Prices:** Main courses $11–$15. Maj CC. 🖼 &

Hard Times Café, 1404 King St, Alexandria (Old Town); tel 703/683-5340. Between West and Peyton Sts. **Pub/Southwestern.** A bar at the rear lends a pub-like atmosphere to this small establishment. Oak booths are designed to resemble a Texas-style cafe. Texas- and Cincinnati-style chilies are served plain or with spaghetti or beans. Disabled entry to side. Also at: 3028 Wilson Blvd, Arlington (703/528-2233). **FYI:** Reservations not accepted. Children's menu. Beer and wine only. **Open:** Sun–Thurs 11am–10pm, Fri–Sat 11am–11pm. Closed Dec 25. **Prices:** Main courses $4.50–$6. Maj CC. &

La Bergerie Restaurant Français, in the Shops at Crilleg, 218 N Lee St, Alexandria (Old Town); tel 703/683-1007. Between Cameron and Queen Sts. **French.** Exposed antique brick and individually lit paintings lend elegant charm to this fine French restaurant. Round booths provide privacy and a romantic atmosphere. Owner/chef adds his own Basque specialties to a traditional French menu. **FYI:** Reservations recommended. Dress code. **Open:** Lunch Mon–Sat 11:30am–2:30pm; dinner Mon–Thurs 6–10:30pm, Fri–Sat 6–11pm. Closed some hols. **Prices:** Main courses $15–$24; PF dinner $25. Maj CC. ♥

Landini Brothers, 115 King St, Alexandria (Old Town); tel 703/836-8404. Between Lee and Union Sts. **Italian.** Stone walls and rough-hewn beams from this building's days as a colonial warehouse give this Italian restaurant lots of rustic but romantic charm. Cuisine from northern Italy is usual, but daily Tuscan-style specials stand out. **FYI:** Reservations recommended. Dress code. **Open:** Mon–Sat 11:30am–11pm, Sun 3–10pm. Closed some hols. **Prices:** Main courses $11.50–$21. Maj CC. ♥

Ⓢ ★ **Le Gaulois Café Restaurant**, 1106 King St, Alexandria (Old Town); tel 703/739-9494. Between Henry and Fayette Sts. **French.** This comfortable spot is decorated like a country French living room, with working fireplace, grandfather clock, china cupboard, memento plates, and paintings. Seasonal menus feature excellent home-style French fare, emphasizing seafood in traditional sauces. A long-established local favorite. **FYI:** Reservations recommended. **Open:** Lunch Mon–Sat 11:30am–5pm; dinner Mon–Thurs 5:30–10:30pm, Fri–Sat 5:30–11pm. Closed some hols. **Prices:** Main courses $7–$16. Maj CC. 🖼 &

Le Refuge, 127 N Washington St, Alexandria (Old Town); tel 703/548-4661. Between King and Cameron Sts. **French.** Exposed wooden beams and walls adorned with paintings and knickknacks from France set an appropriate ambience at this small establishment specializing in country-style French cuisine,

including homemade pâtés. **FYI:** Reservations recommended. Dress code. **Open:** Lunch Mon–Sat 11:30am–2:30pm; dinner Mon–Sat 5:30–10pm. Closed some hols. **Prices:** Main courses $14–$16. Maj CC. ♥

Murphy's, 713 King St, Alexandria (Old Town); tel 703/548-1717. Between Washington and Columbus Sts. **Cajun/Irish/Pub.** A long bar dominates this typical dark-wood Irish pub. Stew from the old country and corned beef and cabbage appear, but most of the menu here is charbroiled and Cajun-style main courses and pub-style burgers and sandwiches. Irish bands entertain from 9pm daily. **FYI:** Reservations not accepted. Band. **Open:** Mon–Thurs 11am–midnight, Fri–Sat 11am–1:30am, Sun 10am–midnight. Closed Dec 25. **Prices:** Main courses $6–$11. Maj CC.

Ⓢ **Radio Free Italy**, in Torpedo Factory Food Pavillion, 5 Cameron St at the Potomac River, Alexandria (Old Town); tel 703/683-0361. **Italian.** A black-and-white, tile-floored mezzanine dining area distinguishes this eatery from other fast-food operations on the Potomac River side of the Torpedo Factory. Order carryout items downstairs or à la carte on the mezzanine. Pasta and wood-fired pizzas are the chief offerings, along with Italian-style meat and chicken dishes. Take-out items can be carried to brick patio overlooking the river. Access to the mezzanine is by steps only. **FYI:** Reservations not accepted. Children's menu. **Open:** Daily 11:30am–11pm. Closed some hols. **Prices:** Main courses $7–$14. Maj CC.

★ **RT's Restaurant**, 3804 Mt Vernon Ave, Alexandria; tel 703/684-6010. Near Commonwealth Ave. **Cajun/Seafood.** Among the 3-dimensional modern art lining the walls of this varnished-oak pub/eatery is a work containing the unwashed plate used by President Clinton, who with Vice President Gore and their wives came to partake of spicy Cajun-style seafood and such regional favorites as Maryland fried oysters. **FYI:** Reservations recommended. Children's menu. **Open:** Mon–Thurs 11am–10:30pm, Fri–Sat 11am–11pm, Sun 4–9pm. Closed some hols. **Prices:** Main courses $12–$19. Maj CC.

Santa Fe East, 110 S Pitt St, Alexandria (Old Town); tel 703/548-6900. Between King and Prince Sts. **Southwestern.** Several cozy dining rooms tastefully decorated in New Mexico styles run the gamut from formal to outdoor. There are 2 working fireplaces. A limited menu features southwestern-influenced cuisine, such as blue corn tortillas layered with smoked chicken and cheese. **FYI:** Reservations recommended. Dress code. **Open:** Mon–Thurs 11:30am–10pm, Fri–Sat 11:30am–11pm, Sun 11am–10pm. Closed some hols. **Prices:** Main courses $10–$18. Maj CC. 🚢 🖼 &

✿ **Taverna Cretekou**, 818 King St, Alexandria (Old Town); tel 703/548-8688. Between Columbus and N Alfred Sts. **Greek.** Arches and white stucco create a Mediterranean island atmosphere, appropriate for one of the most popular Greek restaurants in the region. A cross-section of traditional dishes is offered, 5 of which can be sampled as part of the house special. Live Greek entertainment Tuesday, Wednesday, and Thursday evenings. A lamb roasts in the courtyard dining area in fine weather. **FYI:** Reservations recommended. Band. Dress code. **Open:** Lunch Tues–Fri 11:30am–2:30pm, Sat noon–4pm, Sun 11am–3pm; dinner Tues–Fri 5–10:30pm, Sat 4–11pm, Sun 5–9:30pm. Closed some hols. **Prices:** Main courses $10.50–$16. Maj CC. ☲

Tavola, 710 King St, Alexandria (Old Town); tel 703/683-9070. Between Washington and Columbus Sts. **Italian.** A very bright dining room features white walls and tablecloths, blond wood chairs, bright tile floors, and a ficus tree standing under a skylight. Lights hung from rods spotlight each table. Some Italian-style seafood specialties are grilled over charcoal. Shares kitchen with Terrazza at same address. **FYI:** Reservations accepted. Dress code. **Open:** Lunch Mon–Fri 11:30am–2:30pm; dinner daily 5:30–10:30pm. Closed some hols. **Prices:** Main courses $10–$16. Maj CC.

The Tea Cosy, 119 S Royal St, Alexandria (Old Town); tel 703/836-8181. Between King and Prince Sts. **British.** Framed antique advertisements for English products grace this bright, cheerful tearoom annex to a shop purveying British goods. Authentic Cornish pasty, shepherd's pie, and sausage rolls lead the list of country-style offerings. **FYI:** Reservations not accepted. Beer and wine only. **Open:** Sat–Thurs 10am–6pm, Fri 10am–9pm. Closed some hols. **Prices:** Lunch main courses $3–$7. Ltd CC. ♿

✿ **Tempo**, 4231 Duke St at N Gordon St, Alexandria; tel 703/370-7900. Exit 3A off I-395. **Californian/French/Italian.** Bright white walls hung with large seascapes have completely transformed this former service station into a pleasant small dining room, whose steel rafters and ventilator tubes now add to the charm. A blend of Italian, French, and California cuisines include some creative pasta offerings and reflect the origins of the proprietors, a French-born chef and his California-bred wife. Off the beaten path in a predominantly suburban residential area, this find is a local favorite for quality and value. **FYI:** Reservations recommended. **Open:** Lunch Sun–Fri 11:30am–2:30pm; dinner Mon–Sat 5:30–10pm, Sun 5:30–9pm. Closed some hols. **Prices:** Main courses $11–$16. Maj CC.

Terrazza, 710 King St, Alexandria (Old Town); tel 703/683-6900. Between Washington and Columbus Sts. **Italian.** The more formal sibling of Tavola, which shares the same address,

this dining room has spotlights over each table, plush carpeting, and impressionist paintings on the walls, setting a romantic atmosphere. Limited selection of fine Italian pastas, meat, and fish; Maine lobster in tomato sauce is the house specialty. **FYI:** Reservations recommended. Jacket required. **Open:** Lunch Mon–Fri 11:30am–2:30pm; dinner daily 5:30–10:30pm. Closed some hols. **Prices:** Main courses $14–$23. Maj CC. ♥♿

Two Nineteen Restaurant, 219 King St, Alexandria (Old Town); tel 703/549-1141. Between Fairfax and Lee Sts. **Creole.** The main dining rooms are elegant re-creations of Victorian-era New Orleans mansions, while the bars and outdoor dining area are casual and relaxed. French-accented Creole cuisine is the chef's specialty, along with grilled meats and traditional Chesapeake seafood. **FYI:** Reservations recommended. Jazz. Children's menu. Dress code. **Open:** Mon–Thurs 11am–10:30pm, Fri–Sat 11am–1am, Sun 10am–10pm. Closed some hols. **Prices:** Main courses $14–$24; PF dinner $30. Maj CC. ♥☲

Union Street Public House, 121 S Union St, Alexandria (Old Town); tel 703/548-1785. Between King and Prince Sts. **New American/Seafood.** Exposed brick, dark wood, and tin ceilings give this lively pub/restaurant lots of historical ambience befitting its location in the heart of the historic district. In addition to salads and pub-style sandwiches, the menu offers grilled beef, chicken, and seafood plus a selection of pasta dishes. Raw bar in its own room serves up oysters and clams on the half shell. **FYI:** Reservations not accepted. Children's menu. **Open:** Mon–Sat 11:30am–1:15am, Sun 11am–1:15am. Closed Dec 25. **Prices:** Main courses $9–$17. Maj CC. ▉ ♿

The Warehouse Bar and Grill, 214 King St, Alexandria (Old Town); tel 703/683-6868. Between Fairfax and Lee Sts. **Seafood/Steak.** Cartoons of numerous local and national celebrities line the walls of this pleasantly decorated steak and seafood emporium. Upstairs, the other dining room sits under a skylight. Meat and fish served with a variety of sauces are the chief offerings, though a limited sandwich menu is available. **FYI:** Reservations recommended. Children's menu. Dress code. **Open:** Breakfast Sat 8:30–10:30am; lunch Mon–Sat 11am–4pm; dinner Mon–Thurs 5–10:30pm, Fri–Sat 5–11pm, Sun 4–9:30pm; brunch Sun 10am–4pm. Closed some hols. **Prices:** Main courses $13–$19. Maj CC. ♿

Refreshment Stop ☕

★ **The Deli on the Strand**, 211 the Strand, Alexandria (Old Town); tel 703/548-7222. Entrance on S Union St, between Duke and Prince Sts. **Deli.** An attractive wood interior brightens this modern deli, a favorite with locals and bicyclists passing through Old Town. The only seating is outside on a narrow deck.

Sandwiches and fresh salads are made behind the display case. **Open:** Mon–Fri 7:30am–7pm, Sat–Sun 7:30am–8pm. Closed some hols. Maj CC.

Attractions 💼

Christ Church, 118 N Washington St; tel 703/549-1450. This sturdy Georgian-style red-brick church would be an important national landmark even without its two most distinguished members, Washington and Lee. It has been in continuous use since 1773. Traditionally, the president of the United States attends a service here on a Sunday close to Washington's birthday and sits in his pew. The bell tower, galleries, and organ were added in the early 1800s, the "wineglass" pulpit in 1891; however, much of the church has been restored to its original appearance. The Parish Hall contains an exhibit on the history of the church. The graveyard was Alexandria's first and only burial ground until 1805; the remains of 36 Confederate soldiers are interred here. **Open:** Mon–Fri 9am–4pm, Sat 9am–noon, Sun 2–4:30pm. Free.

Lyceum, 201 S Washington St; tel 703/838-4994. This Greek revival building houses a museum focusing on Alexandria's history from colonial times through the 20th century. Traveling exhibits are featured, mainly dealing with architecture and the decorative arts. Built in 1839, the Lyceum served as a lecture, meeting, and concert hall, a hospital during the Civil War, and a private residence. Tourist information about Alexandria and all of Virginia is also available here. **Open:** Mon–Sat 10am–5pm, Sun 1–5pm. Closed some hols. Free.

Fort Ward Museum and Park, 4301 W Braddock Rd; tel 703/838-4848. A 45-acre museum, park, and historic site, the area centers on an actual Union fort, erected in the early 1860s as part of a system of forts designed to protect Washington, DC. Self-guided tours begin at the Fort Ward ceremonial gate; visitors can explore the replica of an officer's hut and the restored Northwest Bastion. The museum has Civil War weaponry, armor, correspondence, and other artifacts, and also features changing exhibits. Concerts are given on selected evenings in summer; living history programs on certain weekends (call for details). Picnic areas with grills are near the fort. **Open:** Park, daily 9am–sunset; museum, Tues–Sat 9am–5pm, Sun noon–5pm. Closed some hols. Free.

Gadsby's Tavern Museum, 134 N Royal St; tel 703/838-4242. Alexandria was at the crossroads of colonial America, and Alexandria's center was Gadsby's Tavern. It consists of 2 buildings (one Georgian, one federal) dating from 1770 and

1792, respectively. The rooms have been restored to their 18th-century appearance using colonial inventories that include such minutiae as lemon squeezers.

Guided tours (30 minutes) offered throughout the day illustrate the important role of taverns in 18th-century American social life; special living history tours are offered the last Sunday of every month. A colonial-style restaurant occupies 3 restored tavern rooms. **Open:** Apr–Sept, Tues–Sat 10am–5pm, Sun 1–5pm; Oct–Mar, Tues–Sat 11am–4pm, Sun 1–4pm. Closed some hols. $

Alexandria Black History Resource Center, 638 N Alfred St; tel 703/838-4356. Housed in a 1940s building that originally housed the black community's first public library, the center exhibits historical objects, photographs, documents, and memorabilia relating to African-American Alexandrians from the 18th century forward. The permanent collection is supplemented by twice-yearly rotating exhibits, and walking tours and other activities are offered. **Open:** Tues–Sat 10am–4pm. Closed some hols. Free.

Boyhood Home of Robert E Lee, 607 Oronoco St; tel 703/548-8454. Revolutionary War cavalry hero Henry "Light Horse Harry" Lee brought his wife, Ann Hill Carter, and their 5 children to this early federal-style mansion in 1812, when Robert E Lee was 5 years old. A tour of the house, which was built in 1795, provides a glimpse into the gracious lifestyle of Alexandria's gentry. The tour covers the entire house, including the nursery, Mrs Lee's room, the parlor, the winter and summer kitchens, and the back garden, which features a boxwood garden and a magnolia tree planted in 1812. **Open:** Mon–Fri 10am–3:30pm, Sat 10am–4pm, Sun 1–4pm. Closed some hols and Dec 15–Jan 31 (open on the Sun nearest Jan 19, Robert E Lee's birthday). $

Ramsay House, 221 King St; tel 703/838-4200 or 838-5005 (24-hr events recording). Built in the mid-1720s, Ramsay House in one of the oldest remaining structures in Alexandria. Today it serves as a visitor information center and houses the Convention and Visitors Bureau. Here visitors can pick up a self-guided walking tour map and brochures about the area, find out about special events that might be taking place, and purchase discounted tickets for 4 historic Alexandria properties. A 13-minute video gives an overview of Alexandria's rich past. Guided walking tours depart from the house. **Open:** Daily 9am–5pm and, frequently, on Thursday night to 9pm. Closed some hols. Free.

Lee-Fendall House, 614 Oronoco St; tel 703/548-1789. Frequent visitor "Light Horse Harry" Lee never actually lived here, but he did sell the land to Philip Richard Fendall (himself a Lee on his mother's side), who built the house in 1785. Thirty-seven

Lees occupied the house over the next 118 years. Guided tours of the house provide insight into family life in the 1850s and include the colonial garden, with its magnolia and chestnut trees, roses, and boxwood-lined paths. A permanent collection of doll houses and miniature architecture is supplemented by changing special exhibits. Tours last about 30 minutes and depart continually throughout the day. **Open:** Tues–Sat 10am–4pm, Sun noon–4pm. Closed some hols. $

Carlyle House, 121 N Fairfax St; tel 703/549-2997. Built in 1753, Carlyle House was an important social and political center in colonial Alexandria. Maj Gen Edward Braddock, commander-in-chief of British forces in North America, made the house his headquarters during the French and Indian Wars. Tours of the house (40 minutes) include the parlor and study where Braddock met with 5 colonial governors to ask them to raise taxes to finance his campaign. Rooms are furnished in period style; one room contains an exhibit explaining 18th-century construction methods. **Open:** Tues–Sat 10am–4:30pm, Sun noon–4:30pm. $

Friendship Firehouse, 107 S Alfred St; tel 703/838-3891. The Friendship Fire Company was Alexandria's first firefighting organization, established in 1774. Local tradition names George Washington as one of the founding members. In 1855 the original building burned down and the fashionable Italianate structure that stands today was erected on the same spot. It houses a museum with exhibits on the history of firefighting and the Friendship Company. **Open:** Thurs–Sat 10am–4pm, Sun 1–4pm. Free.

Stabler-Leadbetter Apothecary, 105 S Fairfax St; tel 703/836-3713. When it closed its doors in 1933, this landmark drugstore was the second-oldest in continuous operation in America (it opened in 1792). Forced to close by the Depression, its doors were simply locked, with most of the herbs, potions, and patent medicines remaining in their drawers. The apothecary today looks much as it did when it was in operation, its shelves lined with antique hand-blown medicinal bottles and patent medicines, mortars and pestles, pill rollers, and scales stamped with the royal crown. The shop's comprehensive records include an 1802 order for castor oil from Martha Washington at Mount Vernon. **Open:** Mon–Sat 10am–4pm, Sun noon–5pm (sometimes closed for lunch); sometimes closed in winter. Closed some hols. $

Old Presbyterian Meeting House, 321 S Fairfax St; tel 703/549-6670. This brick church was built by Scottish pioneers in 1775. Though it wasn't George Washington's church, the Meeting House bell tolled continuously for 4 days after his death in December 1799, and memorial services were preached from the pulpit here by Presbyterian, Episcopalian, and Methodist ministers. The original Meeting House was gutted by a lightning fire in

1835, but it was restored around the old walls in the style of the day a few years later. In 1949 the buidling was reopened by the Presbyterian Church (USA) and looks today much as it did after the restoration after the fire. Interred in the church graveyard are many notable Alexandrians. **Open:** Tues–Fri 9am–3pm; Sun services at 8:30 and 11am. Free.

Schooner *Alexandria*, Jones Point Park; tel 703/549-7078. A Baltic trader vessel built in 1929, this Swedish three-masted, gaff-rigged topsail schooner was remodeled for passenger use in the 1970s. Tours of the ship explore above and below deck, and visit one stateroom (the others are used by the crew) and the rather elegant Main Salon downstairs. **Open:** When in port (usually in winter; call ahead), Sat–Sun noon–5pm. Free.

APPOMATTOX

Map page M-3, D5

Attractions 💼

Appomattox Court House National Historic Park; tel 804/352-8987. Located approximately 20 miles east of Appomattox on US 460. Here, on April 9, 1865, in the parlor of Wilmar McLean's farmhouse, Robert E Lee's surrender of the Army of Northern Virginia to Ulysses S Grant signaled the end of a bitter conflict. The 20 or so houses, stores, courthouse, and tavern that comprised the little village called Appomattox Court House have been restored, and visitors today can walk the country lanes in rural stillness where these events took place. Maps of the park are available at the Visitors Center, which also features slide presentations and exhibits. Several buildings are open to the public. **Surrender Triangle,** where the Confederates were ordered to lay down their arms, is outside Kelly House. **Open:** Sept–May, daily 8:30am–5pm; June–Aug, daily 9am–5:30pm. $

Holliday Lake State Park; tel 804/248-6308. Holliday Lake is a 250-acre state park located 8 miles from Appomattox Court House National Historical Park (see above). The lake is a popular swimming site Memorial Day–Labor Day; guided canoe trips are offered during the summer season. In addition, Holliday Lake offers superior fishing all year round (a Virginia state fishing license is required). Boat rentals are also available.

Other park activities and facilities include camping, hiking, a playground, a horseshoe pit, and beach volleyball. **Open:** Park, daily dawn–dusk; office, Mon–Fri 8am–4:30pm, Sat–Sun hours vary. $

ARLINGTON

Map page M-3, C6

Hotels 🏨

≡≡≡ Arlington Renaissance Hotel, 950 N Stafford St, Arlington, VA 22203 (Ballston); tel 703/528-6000 or toll free 800/228-9898; fax 703/528-4386. Exit 71 off I-66. With excellent location above Ballston metro station, this comfortable hotel occupies lower 3 levels of high-rise condominium building. Elevated walkways lead from lobby to shopping mall. Easily the best hotel in the Ballston area. Stays busy on weekdays. **Rooms:** 209 rms and stes. Exec-level rms avail. CI 3pm/CO noon. Express checkout avail. Nonsmoking rms avail. Nicely appointed rooms have colonial-style furniture, including armoires to hide TVs. **Amenities:** 🛎️🗝️📺 ⚓ A/C, satel TV w/movies, refrig, voice mail, bathrobes. Some units w/minibars. Shoe polishers on each floor. **Services:** ✕ ⚐ ↵ ⚘ Masseur, babysitting. Club Level has daily newspapers, book swap, complimentary breakfast. **Facilities:** 🛍️ 🏋️ 🅿400 🖥️ ⚹ 1 rst, 1 bar (w/entertainment), lifeguard, spa, sauna, whirlpool, washer/dryer. Deli and cafe on premises. **Rates:** HS Jan 15–July 1/Sept–Dec 15 $130–$160 S or D; from $195 ste. Extra person $15. Children under 16 stay free. Lower rates off-season. Spec packages avail. Pking: Indoor, free. Maj CC. Weekend rates available.

≡≡ Best Western Arlington Inn and Tower, 2480 S Glebe Rd at I-395, Arlington, VA 22206 (South Arlington); tel 703/979-4400 or toll free 800/426-6886; fax 703/685-0051. Exit 7B off I-395. Some rooms in this clean hotel are in the original 2-story motel block, which dates from the 1960s, while others are in a modern 8-story tower built in the 1980s. **Rooms:** 325 rms. CI 3pm/CO noon. Nonsmoking rms avail. Opening directly to parking lot, old-wing rooms are slightly larger whereas tower rooms are somewhat better equipped. All have 2 vanities, and some have sofas. **Amenities:** 🛎️🗝️ A/C, satel TV w/movies. Some units w/Jacuzzis. **Services:** 🚐 ⚐ ↵ Free shuttle to metro stations. **Facilities:** 🛍️ 🏋️ 🅿200 ⚹ 1 rst, 1 bar, lifeguard, games rm, washer/dryer. **Rates:** HS Mar 15–Labor Day $50–$90 S or D. Extra person $4. Lower rates off-season. Higher rates for spec evnts/hols. Spec packages avail. Pking: Outdoor, free. Maj CC. Weekend packages.

≡≡≡ Comfort Inn–Enterprise Square, 1211 N Glebe Rd at Washington Blvd, Arlington, VA 22201 (Ballston); tel 703/247-3399 or toll free 800/228-5150; fax 703/524-8739. Exit 71 off I-66. A clean and comfortable chain hotel occupying part of a modern office building with a brick facade. Within walking distance of Ballston Commons shopping mall, several restaurants, and metro station. **Rooms:** 126 rms and stes. CI noon/CO 11am. Nonsmoking rms avail. In addition to a standard hotel room, junior suites have a separate sitting room and can be joined with a 3rd room to make a large suite. **Amenities:** 🛎️ A/C, cable TV w/movies. **Services:** ✕ ⚐ ↵ Twice-daily maid svce. **Facilities:** 🅿30 ⚹ 1 rst, 1 bar, playground. Guests have access to nearby health club with pool for a fee. Coffee shop–style restaurant with separate bar. **Rates (CP):** HS Mar–Nov 15 $79 S; $84 D; from $89 ste. Extra person $5. Children under 18 stay free. Lower rates off-season. Higher rates for spec evnts/hols. Spec packages avail. Pking: Indoor, free. Maj CC. Weekend rates available.

≡≡≡ Courtyard by Marriott Crystal City/Nat'l Airport, 2899 Jefferson Davis Hwy at 27th St S, Arlington, VA 22202; tel 703/549-3434 or toll free 800/847-4775; fax 703/549-0320. Exit 9 off I-395. Take US 1 to 27th St S; head east. Unlike most of this chain, this high-rise hotel lacks a courtyard. Large mahogany-paneled lounge and dining area has a club-like elegance. **Rooms:** 272 rms and stes. CI 3pm/CO 1pm. Express checkout avail. Nonsmoking rms avail. King rooms have love seats, some convertible. **Amenities:** 🛎️🗝️📺 ⚓ A/C, cable TV w/movies, voice mail. **Services:** ✕ 🚐 ⚐ ↵ Babysitting. **Facilities:** 🛍️ 🏋️ 🅿100 ⚹ 1 rst, 1 bar, lifeguard, whirlpool, washer/dryer. **Rates:** HS Mar 20–June 10 $99–$139 S; $109–$149 D; from $179 ste. Extra person $15. Children under 16 stay free. Lower rates off-season. Higher rates for spec evnts/hols. Spec packages avail. Pking: Indoor, $8. Maj CC. Weekend packages.

≡≡≡ Crystal Gateway Marriott, 1700 Jefferson Davis Hwy, Arlington, VA 22202 (Crystal City); tel 703/920-3230 or toll free 800/228-9290; fax 703/979-6332. Exit 9 off I-395. An attractive, full-service high-rise hotel convenient to National Airport. Underground passage leads to Crystal City shopping mall and metro station. Some public areas are under an angled skylight, creating an open and airy feeling. Does considerable group business. Recently renovated. Entry is on S Eads St. **Rooms:** 694 rms and stes. Exec-level rms avail. CI 4pm/CO noon. Express checkout avail. Nonsmoking rms avail. Rooms are tastefully decorated with dark wood furniture and elegant armoires, which hold TVs. **Amenities:** 🛎️🗝️ A/C, cable TV w/movies, voice mail. **Services:** ✕ 🖨️ 🚐 ⚐ ↵ ⚘ **Facilities:** 🛍️ 🏋️ 🅿2K 🖥️ ⚹ 3 rsts, 2 bars, lifeguard, spa, sauna, whirlpool, washer/dryer. Atrium Cafe, off lobby, serves snacks and light fare. Tuscany's Restaurant offers Italian cuisine. **Rates:** $149–$172 S; $149–$192 D; from $275 ste. Children under 12 stay free. Spec packages avail. Pking: Indoor, $10. Maj CC. Weekend rates available.

≡≡≡ Doubletree Hotel Nat'l Airport–Pentagon City, 300 Army-Navy Dr, Arlington, VA 22202; tel 703/416-4100 or toll free 800/222-TREE; fax 703/521-0286. Exit 9 off I-395. This unusual hotel sports 2 towers with a skylighted lobby in between. **Rooms:** 632 rms and stes. Exec-level rms avail. CI 3pm/CO noon. Express checkout avail. Nonsmoking rms avail. Standard hotel rooms, some with fine views over the Potomac River to Washington, DC, are in the older north tower. Best views are from odd-numbered rooms. The newer tower has executive rooms, with sofas, and suites, which have a sitting parlor with couch. **Amenities:** 🛋 ☖ A/C, cable TV w/movies, refrig, stereo/tape player, voice mail. Some units w/terraces, some w/Jacuzzis. **Services:** ✗ ☎ 🚗 🏖 ⌂ 🍷 Masseur, babysitting. Free shuttle to Pentagon, Pentagon City mall, and metro station. Potomac Club provides newspapers, continental breakfasts, and evening cocktails for extra fee. **Facilities:** 🏊 🍴 600 🖥 ⟓ 2 rsts, 2 bars (1 w/entertainment), lifeguard, racquetball, spa, sauna. On the top floor, the Penthouse Restaurant and revolving Skydome Lounge take advantage of the views. Pleasant, garden-like cafe at lobby level. Basketball court in fitness center. **Rates:** $135–$155 S; $155–$175 D; from $250 ste. Extra person $20. Children under 18 stay free. Spec packages avail. Pking: Indoor, $9. Maj CC.

The Executive Club, 108 S Courtyard Rd, Arlington, VA 22204 (Fort Myer); tel 703/522-2582 or toll free 800/535-2582; fax 703/486-2694. Exit 8 off I-395. Take Va 27 north to 52nd St exit, then go 1 block to Courtyard Rd, turn right. This converted brick apartment complex consists of 2-story buildings around an attractive courtyard with pool and a patio with umbrella tables. Convenient to Fort Myer. Excellent for long-term stays. **Rooms:** 74 stes. CI noon/CO noon. Express checkout avail. Nonsmoking rms avail. All units are fully equipped apartments with either a bedroom or a bedroom with den. Comfortably furnished with color-coordinated decor. **Amenities:** 🛋 ☖ 📺 A/C, cable TV w/movies, refrig, voice mail. **Services:** 🚗 🏖 ⌂ 🍷 Babysitting. Evening happy hour daily. Continental breakfast served in lobby. **Facilities:** 🏊 🍴 🖥 Lifeguard, spa, sauna, whirlpool, washer/dryer. **Rates (CP):** From $139 ste. Higher rates for spec evnts/hols. Pking: Outdoor, free. Maj CC. Long-term rates available.

Howard Johnson National Airport Hotel, 2650 Jefferson Davis Hwy, Arlington, VA 22202 (Crystal City); tel 703/684-7200 or toll free 800/278-2243; fax 703/684-3217. Exit 9 off I-395. A well-maintained high-rise hotel on southern end of Crystal City. Convenient to National Airport. **Rooms:** 279 rms and stes. CI 4pm/CO noon. Nonsmoking rms avail. All rooms tastefully decorated, though standard units are small. Executive-level rooms are larger, equipped with 2 vanities and love seats. **Amenities:** 🛋 ☖ 📺 A/C, cable TV w/movies. **Services:** ✗ 🚗 🏖 ⌂ 🍷 Car-rental desk, babysitting. **Facilities:** 🏊 🍴 300 ☖ 1 rst, 1 bar, lifeguard, washer/dryer. Moderately priced chain restaurant on premises is good for families. **Rates:** $115–$125 S;

$125–$135 D; from $200 ste. Extra person $10. Children under 10 stay free. Spec packages avail. Pking: Indoor, $5. Maj CC. Weekend packages available.

Hyatt Arlington at Key Bridge, 1325 Wilson Blvd, at N Nash St, Arlington, VA 22209 (Rosslyn); tel 703/525-1234 or toll free 800/233-1234; fax 703/875-3393. Exit 73 off I-66. Follow either US 29 or Lee Hwy to Fort Myer Dr to Wilson Blvd. A concrete-and-glass structure amid surrounding high-rise office buildings. Convenient to shops, restaurants, Rosslyn metro station. Recent renovations spiffed up rooms. **Rooms:** 302 rms and stes. Exec-level rms avail. CI 3pm/CO noon. Express checkout avail. Nonsmoking rms avail. Business Plan rooms have large desks. **Amenities:** 🛋 ☖ 🍷 A/C, cable TV w/movies, voice mail. Business Plan rooms have fax machines, coffeemakers, makeup mirrors. All units have irons and boards. **Services:** ✗ ☎ VP 🏖 ⌂ 🍷 Car-rental desk, children's program, babysitting. Business Plan rooms receive continental breakfast in own lounge and free outside dialing. **Facilities:** 🍴 300 🖥 ☖ 1 rst, 2 bars, washer/dryer. 1 of 2 lounges serves as sports bar. **Rates:** $165 S; $190 D; from $300 ste. Extra person $25. Children under 18 stay free. Higher rates for spec evnts/hols. Spec packages avail. Pking: Indoor, $6. Maj CC. Weekend rates include free parking.

Hyatt Regency Crystal City, 2799 Jefferson Davis Hwy (US 1), at S 27th St, Arlington, VA 22202 (Crystal City); tel 703/418-1234 or toll free 800/233-1234; fax 703/418-1289. Exit 9 off I-395. At this V-shaped high-rise hotel, glass-enclosed elevators ascend from a skylighted, 3-story atrium with bar, lounge, and trees. The well-used but reasonably well-maintained property caters to groups and business travelers. **Rooms:** 685 rms and stes. Exec-level rms avail. CI 3pm/CO noon. Express checkout avail. Nonsmoking rms avail. Rooms with king-size beds have love seats; those with 2 beds do not. **Amenities:** 🛋 ☖ 🍷 A/C, cable TV w/movies, shoe polisher. Some units w/terraces. Business Plan rooms have fax machines, coffeemakers, irons and boards, and hair dryers. Suites have wet bars. **Services:** ✗ ☎ 🚗 🏖 ⌂ Babysitting. Complimentary morning newspaper delivered to room weekdays. Complimentary coffee in restaurant 6–7am. Those in Business Plan rooms get free local calls and continental breakfast. Gold Passport rooms come with concierge service, complimentary breakfast, turndown service. Concierge arranges discounts for tennis and golf at local clubs. Free shuttle around Crystal City: to and from metro station, shops, and restaurants. **Facilities:** 🏊 🍴 1.6K 🖥 ☖ 2 rsts, 2 bars, lifeguard, spa, sauna, whirlpool. Rooftop seafood restaurant has good views. Rather small outdoor pool on 2nd floor. **Rates:** $170 S; $195 D; from $225 ste. Extra person $25. Children under 18 stay free. Spec packages avail. Pking: Indoor, $9. Maj CC.

≣≣≣**Key Bridge Marriott Hotel**, 1401 Lee Hwy (US 29), at Fort Myer Dr, Arlington, VA 22209 (Rosslyn); tel 703/524-6400 or toll free 800/228-9290; fax 703/542-8964. Exit 73 off I-66. Recent renovation has brought rooms in this 2nd-oldest Marriott property up to same level as elegant dark-wood lobby and excellent location. Within walking distance of Georgetown (across Key Bridge) and within blocks of Rosslyn metro station. **Rooms:** 584 rms and stes. Exec-level rms avail. CI 3pm/CO 1pm. Express checkout avail. Nonsmoking rms avail. Rooms from 5th floor up have great views. Those in front look to Washington, DC; those in rear to Georgetown and Potomac River. Dark wood furniture has rich appearance. **Amenities:** 📞 🐕 A/C, cable TV w/movies, voice mail. Some units w/terraces. All units have irons and boards. Windows can be opened in about half the rooms. **Services:** ✕ 🍽 🛅 ↺ ◁ Car-rental desk, babysitting. Free shuttle to Rosslyn metro station. **Facilities:** 🛋 ▬ 700 🖥 ᕦ 2 rsts, 2 bars (1 w/entertainment), lifeguard, spa, sauna, whirlpool, beauty salon, washer/dryer. Top-floor restaurant enjoys views of Washington, DC. Adjacent bar is popular spot for weekend dancing. Attractive indoor-outdoor pool area. **Rates:** $169 S; $189 D; from $199 ste. Extra person $20. Children under 18 stay free. AP rates avail. Spec packages avail. Pking: Indoor/outdoor, $6. Maj CC. Weekend packages include free parking.

≣≣**Quality Hotel Arlington**, 1200 N Courthouse Rd at Arlington Blvd, Arlington, VA 22201; tel 703/524-4000 or toll free 800/228-5151; fax 703/524-1046. Exit 8 off I-395. Follow Va 27 W to US 50 E. A once-small motel, this well-managed and constantly improving property has expanded to include 2 former apartment buildings and a large meeting facility. Hosts groups and small conventions. **Rooms:** 400 rms, stes, and effic. Exec-level rms avail. CI 3pm/CO noon. Nonsmoking rms avail. Units are of various sizes and shapes. A few still have kitchens. Club Royale rooms and Quality Suites have sleeper sofas. Comfort Tower has standard rooms with 1 queen or double bed. Original motel rooms are equipped with 2 beds. **Amenities:** 📞 A/C, cable TV w/movies, refrig. Some units w/terraces, some w/Jacuzzis. Club Royale rooms and Quality Suites have wet bars, hair dryers, coffeemakers. **Services:** ✕ 🛅 ↺ Those staying in Club Royale–level rooms receive continental breakfast and evening cordials in attended lounge. **Facilities:** 🛋 ▬ 275 ᕦ 1 rst, 1 bar, lifeguard, spa, sauna, washer/dryer. Resort-size pool surrounded by extensive concrete deck, largest in Arlington County. Restaurant has pleasant dining room with picture windows on 3 sides. **Rates:** HS Mar 20–Sept 10 $73–$79 S; $79–$85 D; from $101 ste; from $101 effic. Extra person $6–14. Children under 18 stay free. Lower rates off-season. Pking: Outdoor, free. Maj CC. Weekend rates available.

≣≣≣≣**The Ritz-Carlton Pentagon City**, 1250 S Hayes St, Arlington, VA 22202; tel 703/415-5000 or toll free 800/241-3333; fax 703/415-5061. Exit 9 off I-395. Rich wood paneling, Oriental rugs, and European tapestries adorn the elegant public areas of this full-service, luxury hotel. Adjoins the Fashion Center shopping mall and Pentagon City metro station. **Rooms:** 345 rms and stes. Exec-level rms avail. CI 3pm/CO noon. Express checkout avail. Nonsmoking rms avail. All rooms are plushly appointed with cherrywood furniture, fabric wallpaper, paintings, and comfortable easy chairs. The Ritz-Carlton suite has 2 bedrooms and a full kitchen. Club level units enjoy partial view of Washington. **Amenities:** 📞 🐕 🍴 A/C, cable TV w/movies, refrig, VCR, in-rm safe, bathrobes. All units w/minibars, 1 w/Jacuzzi. **Services:** 🍽 🍽 VP 🚗 🛅 ↺ Twice-daily maid svce, car-rental desk, masseur, children's program, babysitting. Club level units have concierge service, 5 food presentations daily, including continental breakfast. **Facilities:** 🛋 ▬ 800 ᕦ 1 rst, 1 bar (w/entertainment), spa, sauna, steam rm, whirlpool. Lobby Lounge serves continental breakfast, buffet lunch, afternoon tea, and light evening fare. The Grill is a highly rated dining room. Lap pool in fitness center. **Rates:** $160–$200 S; $180–$220 D; from $300 ste. Extra person $20. Children under 18 stay free. Spec packages avail. Pking: Indoor, $7–$15. Maj CC. Weekend packages.

≣≣≣**Sheraton National Hotel**, 900 S Orme St, Arlington, VA 22204 (Navy Annex); tel 703/521-1900 or toll free 800/468-9090; fax 703/521-0332. Exit 8 off I-395. Follow Washington Blvd W to Columbia Pike. Convenient to the Pentagon and Navy Annex, this comfortable high-rise hotel has great views over Washington, DC, and surrounding area. Youth tour groups are segregated in lower-level wing. **Rooms:** 424 rms and stes. Exec-level rms avail. CI 3pm/CO 1pm. Express checkout avail. Nonsmoking rms avail. Front rooms have best views. All units have 2 vanities. King rooms have sofa beds and easy chair. **Amenities:** 📞 🐕 🛗 A/C, cable TV w/movies. Some units w/minibars. **Services:** ✕ 🚗 🛅 ↺ Free shuttle to metro, shopping mall. **Facilities:** 🛋 ▬ 2K 🖥 ᕦ 2 rsts, 2 bars, lifeguard, spa, sauna, washer/dryer. Lobby-level Café Brasserie has tropical ambience. On the top level, formal Stars Restaurant and indoor pool with sun deck share the views. **Rates:** $116 S; $118 D; from $145 ste. Extra person $15. Children under 16 stay free. Spec packages avail. Pking: Indoor, $3. Maj CC. Weekend packages.

Motels

≣≣**The Americana Hotel**, 1400 Jefferson Davis Hwy, Arlington, VA 22202 (Crystal City); tel 703/979-3772 or toll free 800/548-6261; fax 703/979-0547. Exit 9 off I-395. The last family-owned and -operated motel near National Airport, this exceptionally clean and well-maintained establishment is now dwarfed by the surrounding high-rise towers of Crystal City. Early 1960s-era building and attentive owners create an atmosphere that harkens back to a less-hurried time. Some corridors are outside. Entrance is on S Eads St. **Rooms:** 100 rms. CI noon/CO 11am. Nonsmoking rms avail. Rooms in front subject to highway noise. Decor is tasteful; dark wood furniture adds touch of class. **Amenities:** 🕭 A/C, cable TV w/movies. All units w/terraces. Air conditioning units mounted through walls. **Services:** 🚗 🖂 ⌂ Car-rental desk. **Facilities:** Washer/dryer. **Rates (CP):** $60 S; $65 D. Children under 18 stay free. Pking: Outdoor, free. Maj CC.

☰☰ Days Inn Arlington, 2201 Arlington Blvd (US 50) at Pershing Dr, Arlington, VA 22201 (Fort Myer); tel 703/525-0300 or toll free 800/329-7466; fax 703/525-5671. Exit 8 off I-395. Follow Va 27 N to US 50 E. This clean but dated 1960s motel has been reasonably well maintained; 2-story U-shaped structures are built around parking lot and small pool. Walking distance to Fort Myer, shops. **Rooms:** 128 rms. CI 2pm/CO noon. Nonsmoking rms avail. Bright modern furniture and spreads make rooms attractive. Some units on ends of buildings are larger than most others. **Amenities:** 🕭 ♨ A/C, cable TV w/movies. All units w/terraces. **Services:** 🖂 ⌂ Car-rental desk, babysitting. Coffee in lobby. Free van to metro station. **Facilities:** 🔐 🎱 1 rst, 1 bar, lifeguard. Family-style restaurant off lobby. **Rates:** HS Apr–Sept $58–$73 S or D. Extra person $6. Children under 17 stay free. Lower rates off-season. Higher rates for spec evnts/hols. Pking: Outdoor, free. Maj CC.

☰☰ Washington/Arlington Cherry Blossom Travelodge, 3030 Columbia Pike, Arlington, VA 22204 (South Arlington); tel 703/521-5570 or toll free 800/578-7878; fax 703/271-0081. Exit 7B off I-395. Go north on Glebe Rd, turn right on Columbia Pike. A clean, well-maintained older motel; recently underwent renovations. Location is convenient to shops, restaurants, and the Pentagon. Pentagon City Mall and metro station less than 2 miles away. **Rooms:** 76 rms and effic. CI 3pm/CO noon. Nonsmoking rms avail. Efficiency units have kitchenettes and dining tables. **Amenities:** 🕭 ♨ 🖥 A/C, cable TV w/movies, refrig, shoe polisher. **Services:** ✗ ⌂ Limited room service from adjacent Thai restaurant. Free local calls. **Facilities:** 🏊 🎱 ᗒ Washer/dryer. Guests have free access to pool 2 blocks away. **Rates (CP):** HS Mar 14–Nov 13 $59–$69 S or D; from $69 effic. Extra person $7. Children under 18 stay free. Lower rates off-season. Higher rates for spec evnts/hols. Spec packages avail. Pking: Outdoor, free. Maj CC. AAA and AARP discounts.

Restaurants 🍽

The American Café, in Ballston Commons Mall, Wilson Blvd at S Glebe Rd, Arlington (Ballston); tel 703/522-2236. **Regional American/International.** On ground level of mall, this pleasant, cafe-style dining room has brick walls and windows looking out to Wilson Blvd and sidewalk patio area for outdoor dining during good weather. Convenient location 2 blocks from Ballston metro station. Menu offers an eclectic mix of regional American fare, such as local crab cakes and Chattanooga chicken pot pie, and international dishes with a Thai influence. Member of local chain with other locations in region. **FYI:** Reservations not accepted. Children's menu. **Open:** Mon–Sat 11am–9:30pm, Sun 11am–6pm. Closed some hols. **Prices:** Main courses $7–$13. Maj CC. 🍴 ᗒ

Atami, 3155 Wilson Blvd, Arlington (Clarendon); tel 703/522-4787. **Japanese.** Very large traditional Japanese prints and paper lanterns lend an appropriate air to this cozy establishment noted for sushi and sashimi, which are prepared at a bar at the rear of the dining room. (All-you-can-eat sushi for $25.) Cooked meals such as teriyaki, tempura, and yosenabe also available. **FYI:** Reservations recommended. **Open:** Mon–Thurs 11am–10pm, Fri–Sat 11am–10:30pm, Sun 5–10pm. Closed some hols. **Prices:** Main courses $7–$13. Ltd CC.

Atlacatl, 2716 Washington Blvd, Arlington; tel 703/524-9032. Near Pershing Dr. **Mexican/Salvadoran.** The front of this small building looks like a carryout place, but a narrow corridor leads to a somewhat cramped dining room decorated with a few wood carvings and other Salvadoran memorabilia. Steaks and chicken and fish dishes from the old country dominate, but Mexican-style chimichangas, burritos, and tacos are also offered. It was once Arlington's most popular Central American restaurant, but its other location, at 2602 Columbia Pike, at N Barton St (703/920-3680), is now busier. **FYI:** Reservations not accepted. **Open:** Daily 11am–10pm. Closed Dec 25. **Prices:** Main courses $6–$10. Maj CC.

Bangkok Gourmet, 523 S 23rd St at S Eads St, Arlington (Crystal City); tel 703/521-1305. **Thai.** Mirrors along one wall and bright white paint elsewhere make this narrow storefront establishment seem bigger than it is. Linen and flowers add elegance. Young chef prepares variety of gourmet Thai selections; menu changes quarterly. Small sidewalk dining area is enclosed during cool months. On Crystal City's Restaurant Row. **FYI:** Reservations accepted. No smoking. **Open:** Lunch Tues–Fri 11am–3pm; dinner daily 5:30–10pm. Closed some hols. **Prices:** Main courses $11–$15; PF dinner $27. Ltd CC. 🍴

⑤ Cafe Dalat, 3143 Wilson Blvd, Arlington (Clarendon); tel 703/276-0935. **Vietnamese.** Behind a plain storefront is one of the better bargains in Little Saigon (the area around Clarendon metro station), if not one of its most elegant restaurants. It has small dark wood tables, stucco walls adorned with maps and paintings of Vietnam, and the original pressed-tin ceiling of the building's mercantile days. A wide range of family-style Vietnamese dishes, with emphasis on grilled seafood and crepes stuffed with shrimp, chicken, and vegetables. **FYI:** Reservations not accepted. **Open:** Sun–Thurs 11am–9:30pm, Fri–Sat 11:45am–10:30pm. Closed some hols. **Prices:** Main courses $6–$8. Ltd CC.

Carlyle Grand Café, in Shirlington Village, 4000 S 28th St, at I-395, Arlington (Shirlington); tel 703/931-0777. **New American/Californian.** Black-and-white tile floors, lots of plants, and art deco touches highlight this large, 2-story establishment. Downstairs is pub-like, while upstairs dining room under a huge skylight is somewhat more formal. Wicker and rattan chairs lend a California air. Menu offers a mix of Cajun, West Coast, and other regional selections, most light and healthful. Call ahead for priority on waiting list. Outdoor dining on sidewalk. **FYI:** Reservations not accepted. No smoking. **Open:** Mon–Tues 11:30am–11pm, Wed–Thurs 11:30am–midnight, Fri–Sat 11:30am–1am, Sun 10am–11pm. Closed some hols. **Prices:** Main courses $11–$14.50. Maj CC. 🏛 💟 ♿

⑤ **Chez Froggy**, 509 S 23rd St, at S Eads St, Arlington (Crystal City); tel 703/979-7676. US 1 exit off I-395. **French.** A narrow storefront establishment with a row of tables down each side and walls hung with French impressionist reproductions. Known for frogs' legs sautéed in butter and garlic, plus fish prepared with traditional French sauces. Daily specials depend on availability of produce. Excellent value for quality. A neighborhood favorite. Small sidewalk dining area open in good weather. **FYI:** Reservations accepted. Dress code. **Open:** Lunch Mon–Fri 11am–2pm; dinner Mon–Sat 5:30–10pm. Closed some hols; 2 weeks in Aug. **Prices:** Main courses $11–$20. Ltd CC. 🏛

Delhi Dhaba Indian Café and Carry Out, 2424 Wilson Blvd, Arlington (Courthouse); tel 703/524-0008. **Indian.** Guests order cafeteria-style in the front of this very clean establishment and take their meals, on Styrofoam trays and plates, to a simple but attractive dining room at the rear. TVs playing Indian music videos provide ethnic atmosphere. Local young professionals and families who have emigrated from India flock here for authentic but inexpensive northern Indian cuisine, such as chicken and lamb kabobs prepared in tandoori ovens, plus spicy meat, seafood, and vegetable curries. Located 2 blocks west of Courthouse metro. **FYI:** Reservations not accepted. Beer and wine only. No smoking. **Open:** Sun–Thurs 11am–10pm, Fri–Sat 11am–11pm. **Prices:** Main courses $4–$6. Maj CC. ♿

Food Factory, 4221 N Fairfax Dr, Arlington (Ballston); tel 703/527-2279. **Indian/Middle Eastern/Afghan.** Arches and plastic flowers add a slight bit of charm to this carryout restaurant with cafeteria-style display case. Formica tables arranged in long rows in dining room. Char-grilled beef, lamb, and chicken kabobs, wrapped in large pieces of fresh Afghan-style bread, are the specialty. Meat and vegetable curries served too. All meat slaughtered by Islamic ritual. Very popular among local South Asian immigrants and as a good-value lunch spot for nearby office workers. Entrance is from parking lot at rear of building. **FYI:** Reservations not accepted. No liquor license. **Open:** Mon–Fri 11am–10pm, Sat–Sun noon–10pm. **Prices:** Main courses $5–$6. No CC.

★ **Hard Times Café**, 3028 Wilson Blvd, Arlington (Clarendon); tel 703/528-2233. **Regional American.** Subdued lighting from lamps hung over wooden booths, state flags, college banners, and historical photos give this chili parlor a pub-like atmosphere. Larger of 2 dining rooms looks like small-town eatery with bar in 1 corner. Specialties are spicy Texas- and Cincinnati-style chilies served with beans or spaghetti, plus pub-style chicken wings, burgers, and sandwiches. Popular with young professionals. Also at: 1404 King St, Old Town Alexandria (tel 703/683-5340). **FYI:** Reservations not accepted. Children's menu. Beer and wine only. **Open:** Sun–Thurs 11am–10pm, Fri–Sat 11am–11pm. Closed some hols. **Prices:** Main courses $4–$6. Maj CC. ♿

Hunan Number 1, 3033 Wilson Blvd at N Garfield St, Arlington (Clarendon); tel 703/528-1177. **Chinese.** Bas-relief scenes on walls and porcelain statues transmit elegance at one of the more upscale Chinese restaurants in Arlington. Chef specializes in live Maine lobsters, kept in dining room tank, as well as shrimp, scallops, and whole fish in spicy Hunan-style sauces. Entrance on N Garfield St. **FYI:** Reservations recommended. **Open:** Daily 11am–2am. Closed Thanksgiving. **Prices:** Main courses $9–$22. Maj CC. 🍴 ♿

⑤ **La Cantinita's Havana Café**, 3100 Clarendon Blvd, Arlington (Clarendon); tel 703/524-3611. **Cuban.** Coral and lagoon colors evoke Miami's South Beach at this family-owned, Cuban-style cafe with widely spaced tables. Picture windows and recessed photo of tropical beach give feeling of even more space. Such Havana favorites as shredded beef, marinated roast pork, and pressed sandwiches at lunchtime. Outdoor dining in plaza of office building in good weather. **FYI:** Reservations not accepted. **Open:** Mon–Fri 11am–11pm, Sat 4–11pm, Sun 4–10pm. **Prices:** Main courses $7–$15. Ltd CC. 🏛 ♿

Little Viet Garden, 3012 Wilson Blvd, Arlington (Clarendon); tel 703/522-9686. **Vietnamese.** A small but pleasing bistro-style establishment whose lush garden-like decor sets it off from other

Little Saigon restaurants. Outdoor dining at umbrella tables in fine weather. House specialties are crispy Vietnamese spring rolls and such main courses as grilled beef wrapped in vine leaves. Dinner specials daily. Jazz plays on speakers, and live jazz bands perform outdoors in July. **FYI:** Reservations not accepted. **Open:** Lunch Mon–Fri 11am–2:30pm, Sat–Sun 11am–5pm; dinner daily 5–10pm. Closed some hols. **Prices:** Main courses $5.50–$11. Maj CC. 🍰

Ⓢ ✹ **Matuba**, 2915 Columbia Pike, at Walter Reed Dr, Arlington (South Arlington); tel 703/521-2811. **Japanese.** Dining room a bit cramped but pleasantly trimmed and furnished with bright varnished wood. Sushi is prepared at a bar in the rear, but cooked Japanese meals are also available. This popular spot provides excellent quality for the price. **FYI:** Reservations recommended. Beer and wine only. **Open:** Lunch Mon–Fri 11:30am–2pm; dinner Sun–Thurs 5:30–10pm, Fri–Sat 5:30–10:30pm. Closed some hols. **Prices:** Main courses $6.50–$12; PF dinner $9. Maj CC.

Nam Viet, 1127 N Hudson St, at Wilson Blvd, Arlington (Clarendon); tel 703/522-7110. **Vietnamese.** Subdued lighting, blood-red chairs, and pink tablecloths give this narrow restaurant a touch of class. Walls are adorned with smoked mirror panels and paintings of Vietnamese landscapes. Chef specializes in marinated chicken, beef, pork, and shrimp char-grilled on skewers and served over noodles and vegetables. Outdoor dining on wooden deck. **FYI:** Reservations recommended. **Open:** Sun–Thurs 10am–10pm, Fri–Sat 10am–11pm. Closed some hols. **Prices:** Main courses $7–$11. Maj CC. 🍰

Pho Cali/The Quality Seafood Place, 1621 S Walter Reed Dr, at S Glebe Rd, Arlington (South Arlington); tel 703/920-3800. **Vietnamese.** A rose-and-pink color scheme accented with potted plants, hanging baskets, and year-round strips of holly belie the storefront appearance of this pleasant establishment known for its Vietnamese-style Dungeness crabs and other seafood, as well as Chesapeake Bay renditions of spiced blue crabs. Northern Vietnam hot pots are a specialty. Outdoor dining in good weather. **FYI:** Reservations accepted. **Open:** Sun–Thurs 9am–10pm, Fri–Sat 9am–11pm. **Prices:** Main courses $5–$16. Maj CC. 🍰

Ⓢ **Pho 75**, in Colonial Village Shopping Center, 1711 Wilson Blvd at N Quinn St, Arlington (Rosslyn); tel 703/525-7355. **Vietnamese.** A very plain and simple establishment with Formica-top tables in long rows and a few Vietnamese photos to lend a bit of atmosphere. Noted not for decor but for budget prices for the only item offered: excellent noodle soups with a variety of meats and vegetable toppings. Also at: 3103 Graham Rd, at

Arlington Blvd, Falls Church (tel 703/204-1490). **FYI:** Reservations not accepted. No liquor license. **Open:** Daily 9am–8pm. Closed Dec 25. **Prices:** Main courses $4.25–$5. No CC.

Ⓢ ✹ **Queen Bee Restaurant**, 3181 Wilson Blvd, Arlington (Clarendon); tel 703/527-3444. **Vietnamese.** Prepare to wait for a table on weekends at this place, long a favorite with locals. Mirrored panels along 1 wall give a feeling of space while reflecting large Vietnamese photos and paintings on the other. Lighting is subdued. Vietnamese dishes are very well prepared, making this one of the area's best bargains. **FYI:** Reservations not accepted. Beer and wine only. No smoking. **Open:** Daily 11am–10pm. Closed some hols. **Prices:** Main courses $5.50–$7.50. Ltd CC.

✹ **Red Hot and Blue**, 1600 Wilson Blvd at N Pierce St, Arlington (Rosslyn); tel 703/276-7430. **Barbecue.** Photos of famous politicians and blues musicians create a pub-like aura at this Memphis-style barbecue house, one of whose founding partners was the late Lee Atwater, advisor to President George Bush and an amateur blues guitarist. Smoked pork ribs, either "dry" or "wet" in the Memphis tradition, are the main offering, plus barbecued chicken, burgers, and sandwiches. Occasional live entertainment when blues artists are in town. Carryout available here and at 3014 Wilson Blvd, in Clarendon (703/243-1510). **FYI:** Reservations not accepted. Children's menu. **Open:** Mon–Thurs 11am–10pm, Fri–Sat 11am–11pm, Sun noon–9pm. Closed some hols. **Prices:** Main courses $4.50–$16.50. Maj CC. ♿

✹ **Ristorante Portofino**, 526 S 23rd St, at S Eads St, Arlington (Crystal City); tel 703/929-8200. **Italian.** What was once the living room of a former residence is now an elegant dining room with nonworking fireplace and drawn shutters. A 2nd eating area is like an enclosed garden with multitude of tropical plants and white cafe tables and chairs. Northern Italian-style chicken, veal, and fish dishes predominate. Family-owned establishment is one of area's most popular Italian spots. **FYI:** Reservations recommended. Dress code. **Open:** Lunch Mon–Fri 11am–2pm; dinner daily 5–10pm. Closed some hols. **Prices:** Main courses $14–$19. Maj CC. ♥

Tom Sarris' Orleans House, 1213 Wilson Blvd, at N Lynn St, Arlington (Rosslyn); tel 703/524-2929. **New American.** A Louisiana atmosphere prevails here. The main dining room is designed like a New Orleans courtyard; dining is on the main level and on balconies set off by wrought-iron railings. Famous for reasonably priced cuts of prime rib. Also offers steaks and seafood items. Popular with tourists and meat-and-potato locals. **FYI:** Reservations not accepted. Children's menu. **Open:** Mon–Fri 11am–11pm, Sat 4–11pm, Sun 4–10pm. Closed some hols. **Prices:** Main courses $8–$14. Maj CC.

Attractions ⯐

Arlington National Cemetery, Arlington National Bridge at Jefferson Davis Hwy; tel 703/692-0931. One of America's most famous national shrines, this cemetery honors many national heros and more than 230,000 war dead, veterans, and dependents. Five-star Gen John J Pershing is buried here, as are President William Howard Taft and Supreme Court Justice Thurgood Marshall.

The **gravesite of John Fitzgerald Kennedy,** 35th US president, has a low crescent wall embracing a marble terrace inscribed with some of the most famous JFK quotations. Senator Robert Kennedy's gravesite is nearby, marked by a simple white cross. Nearby is the well-known **Marine Corps Memorial,** depicting the raising of the American flag on Iwo Jima. A tribute to marines who died in all wars, this is one of the largest statues ever cast in bronze. The 49-bell **Netherlands Carillon,** a gift from the people of the Netherlands, is located close to the Iwo Jima statue. Concerts are given on Saturdays from April through September (phone 285-2598 for schedule).

The **Tomb of the Unknowns,** containing the unidentified remains of soldiers from both World Wars through the Vietnam War, is located here. Soldiers stand guard at the tomb 24 hours a day; changing of the guard is performed every 30 minutes from April–September (hourly the rest of the year).

Arlington House (tel 703/557-0613), located within the cemetery grounds, was for 30 years the residence of Gen Robert E Lee and his family. Hosts in costume give an orientation talk and answer questions; visitors may take self-guided tours of the house and the small museum next door. (Apr–Sept, daily 9:30am–6pm; Oct–Mar, daily 9:30am–4:30pm; closed some hols).

Near Arlington House is the **grave of Pierre Charles L'Enfant,** overlooking a fine view of Washington, DC, the city he designed. Free.

Theodore Roosevelt Island, George Washington Memorial Parkway; tel 703/285-2598. A serene 88-acre wilderness preserve, Theodore Roosevelt Island is a memorial to the 26th president, in recognition of his contributions to conservation. In the northern center of the island, overlooking an oval terrace encircled by a water-filled moat, stands a 17-foot bronze statue of Roosevelt. From the terrace rise four 21-foot granite tablets inscribed with the tenets of his philosophy.

The island was inhabited as far back as the 1600s by Native Americans. Today the complex ecosystem incorporates swamp, marsh, and upland forest, creating a habitat for abundant bird life as well as rabbits, chipmunks, great owls, fox, muskrat, turtles, and groundhogs. There are 2½ miles of foot trails winding throughout the preserve. Picnicking is permitted on the grounds near the memorial.

To get to the island, take the George Washington Memorial Parkway exit north from the Theodore Roosevelt Bridge. The parking area is accessible only from the northbound lane; from there, a pedestrian bridge connects the island with the Virginia shore. **Open:** Daily 8am–dusk. Free.

The Pentagon, Boundary Channel Dr N; tel 703/695-1776. This immense, 5-sided building, the headquarters of the American military establishment, was built during the early years of World War II. It is the world's largest office building, with 6 million square feet of floor space accommodating 24,000 employees in a self-contained world that has its own bank and post office. Tours of the facility take about 60 minutes (no reservation necessary) and begin with an introductory film about the development of the Pentagon. Highlights include the **Commander-in-Chief's Corridor,** lined with portraits of past presidents, and the **Flag Corridor,** where historical and modern state and territorial flags are displayed.

The best way to get to the Pentagon is via Metrorail's Blue or Yellow line. By car, take I-395 to Boundary Channel Drive North Parking Exit. *Note:* A photo ID (a license or passport) must be presented upon admission, and all bags are searched. **Open:** June–Aug, Mon–Fri 9:30am–3:30pm; Sept–May, Mon–Fri 9am–3pm. Closed some hols. Free.

ASHLAND

Map page M-3, D6

See also **Doswell**

Motels ⯐

≣≣ Best Western Hanover House, Va 6, PO Box 1215, Ashland, VA 23005; tel 804/550-2805 or toll free 800/528-1234; fax 804/550-3843. Exit 86 off I-95. A clean and comfortable if not overly attractive motel within easy drive of Paramount's King's Dominion amusement park. **Rooms:** 93 rms. CI 3pm/CO noon. Nonsmoking rms avail. **Amenities:** ⯐ ⯐ A/C, satel TV w/movies. All units w/terraces. **Services:** ⯐ **Facilities:** ⯐ ⯐ ⯐ 1 rst, 1 bar (w/entertainment), washer/dryer. Country Kitchen Restaurant on premises. Suzanne's Lounge has ongoing entertainment, including country-and-western line dancing. **Rates:** HS May–Sept $65–$75 S or D. Extra person $5. Children under 12 stay free. Lower rates off-season. Higher rates for spec evnts/hols. Spec packages avail. Pking: Outdoor, free. Maj CC.

≣≣≣ Holiday Inn Ashland–Richmond, 810 England St (Va 54 at I-95), Ashland, VA 23005; tel 804/798-4231 or toll free 800/922-4231; fax 804/798-9074. Exit 92 off I-95. Convenient to Paramount's King's Dominion amusement park, this comfortable motel has well-landscaped grounds. On a strip with fast-food restaurants, service stations. **Rooms:** 167 rms and stes. CI 3pm/CO 11am. Express checkout avail. Nonsmoking rms avail. **Amenities:** 🛗 ⛱ 📺 A/C, cable TV. Some units w/terraces. **Services:** ✗ 🛍 ⌂ Complimentary coffee and newspapers. **Facilities:** 🔥 🍴 175 ⛱ 1 rst, 1 bar (w/entertainment), washer/dryer. With fun decor, Fender's Lounge has entertainment Friday and Saturday evenings. **Rates:** HS June–Sept $66–$96 S or D; from $76 ste. Children under 16 stay free. Lower rates off-season. Higher rates for spec evnts/hols. Spec packages avail. Pking: Outdoor, free. Maj CC.

▆▆ **Ramada Inn Ashland**, 806 England St, Ashland, VA 23005; tel 804/798-4262; fax 804/798-7009. Exit 92 off I-95. A clean, comfortable chain motel convenient to Paramount's King's Dominion amusement park. On a strip with fast-food restaurants, service stations. **Rooms:** 90 rms and stes. CI 2pm/CO noon. Nonsmoking rms avail. **Amenities:** 🛗 A/C, cable TV. Free coffee and newspapers. **Services:** ⌂ **Facilities:** 🔥 12 ⛱ 1 rst. Aunt Sarah's Pancake House on premises. **Rates:** HS May 30–Sept 7 $43 D; from $43 ste. Extra person $5. Children under 18 stay free. Lower rates off-season. Spec packages avail. Pking: Outdoor, free. Maj CC.

Inn

▆▆▆ **The Henry Clay Inn**, 114 N Railroad Ave, PO Box 135, Ashland, VA 23005; tel 804/798-3100 or toll free 800/343-4565. 15 mi N of Richmond. exit 92 off I-95. The perfect place for those who prefer the comfort, hospitality, and charm of a country inn. Beautifully and elegantly furnished. Front porch is lined with rocking chairs. Large parlor has fireplace. The 2nd-floor balcony adds to appeal. Convenient to Paramount's King's Dominion amusement park. **Rooms:** 15 rms and stes. CI 2pm/CO 11am. No smoking. Each room individually decorated, yet all provide high-quality accommodations and simple luxury. **Amenities:** 🛗 ⛱ A/C, cable TV. 1 unit w/Jacuzzi. **Services:** Homemade breads and muffins served at breakfast. **Facilities:** 40 ⛱ 1 rst, guest lounge. Small restaurant, art gallery, gift shop. **Rates (CP):** $65–$80 D; from $125 ste. Extra person $15. Children under 16 stay free. Spec packages avail. Pking: Outdoor, free. Ltd CC.

Restaurants 🍴

Homemades by Suzanne, 102 N Railroad Ave, Ashland; tel 804/798-8331. Exit 92 off I-95. Follow England St west to Railroad Ave, turn right. **Deli.** Wonderful aromas come from goodies baking in this restaurant near Ashland's historic railroad. Emphasis is on fresh, homemade edibles rather than decor: a hodgepodge of bare wood tables, baskets, wall murals, and prints. Best are sandwiches, salads, and desserts. **FYI:** Reservations not accepted. No liquor license. No smoking. **Open:** Mon–Fri 9am–6pm, Sat 10am–3pm. Closed some hols. **Prices:** Main courses $3.85–$12.25. Ltd CC. 🍴

The Smokey Pig, US 1, Ashland; tel 804/798-4590. Exit 92B off I-95. S of Va 54. **Barbecue/Burgers/Seafood.** This southern-style barbecue house is festooned with ceiling fans, Tiffany lamps, checked tablecloths under glass tops, plants, and lots of pig prints, collectibles, and crafts. Specialty is pit-cooked pork, including ribs, although menu also offers a variety of beef and seafood dishes. **FYI:** Reservations accepted. **Open:** Tues–Sat 11am–9pm, Sun 12–9pm. Closed some hols. **Prices:** Main courses $2.25–$18.95. Ltd CC. ⛱

BASYE

Map page M-3, C5 (NW of New Market)

Lodge 🛏

▆▆ **Sky Chalet Country Inn**, Va 263 W, PO Box 300, Basye, VA 22810; tel 703/856-2147; fax 703/856-2436. Exit 273 off I-81. Take Va 263 W 12 miles. Quaint mountaintop lodges have spectacular views. Orkney Springs, home of Shenandoah Music Festival in summer, is 3 miles away. Skiing, golf, hiking, swimming, fishing, and canoeing are minutes away. **Rooms:** 5 rms; 5 ctges/villas. CI 3pm/CO 11am. Cozy cabins are rustic and simple but clean and heated. **Amenities:** No A/C, phone, or TV. Some units w/terraces, some w/fireplaces. Rocking chairs and hammocks. **Services:** 🚗 ⌂ Ice provided from front desk. **Facilities:** 🍴 15 2 rsts (see also "Restaurants" below), 1 bar. **Rates (CP):** HS May–Nov $49–$55 S or D; from $65 ste. Extra person $10. Children under 5 stay free. Min stay spec evnts. Lower rates off-season. Higher rates for spec evnts/hols. Spec packages avail. Pking: Outdoor, free. Ltd CC.

Restaurant 🍴

★ **Sky Chalet Country Restaurant**, in Sky Chalet Country Inn, Va 263, Basye; tel 703/856-2147. Exit 273 off I-81. Follow Va 11 S to Va 263 W; go 12 miles. **American/Continental.** Great views and a genuinely rustic mountain atmosphere, thanks to wooden chairs and tables, large stone fireplace, and a stuffed moose head. Relaxed and casual but fine dining. Although regular menu is traditional, weekends see European specials. Veranda overlooks valley. **FYI:** Reservations recommended. Children's menu. **Open:** HS May–Sept Fri–Sun 6–9pm. Reduced hours off-season. Closed Dec 25. **Prices:** Main courses $8–$18. Ltd CC. ⛰

BEAVERDAM

Map page M-3, D6 (N of Ashland)

Attraction

Scotchtown; tel 804/227-3500. Follow Va 671 to Va 685 north to Scotchtown. One of Virginia's oldest plantation houses, Scotchtown is a charming white clapboard home built by Charles Chiswell of Williamsburg, probably around 1719. Patrick Henry bought the house in 1770, and a year later came to live here with his wife and 6 children. The house has been beautifully restored and furnished with 18th-century antiques, some of them associated with the Henry family. In the study, Henry's mahogany desk-table remains, and bookshelves still hold his law books. Special events include the Scottish Festival Games in late May and Christmas Candlelight Tours the first weekend in December. **Open:** Apr, weekends only, May–Oct, Tues–Sat 10am–4:30pm, Sun 1:30–4:30pm. $$

BEDFORD

Map page M-2, D4

Lodge 🏨

▬▬▬ **Peaks of Otter Lodge**, MM 86 Blue Ridge Pkwy, PO Box 489, Bedford, VA 24523; tel 703/586-1081; fax 703/586-4420. Located on the Blue Ridge Pkwy at the base of Sharp Top Mountain, this lodge is very popular at leaf-changing time, when it provides spectacular views of an array of colors. Accessible to many attractions, which complement hiking, fishing, and generally quiet nature of property. **Rooms:** 62 rms and stes. CI 3pm/CO noon. Nonsmoking rms avail. Rooms furnished in pale-blue country rustic style. Glass walls, which open to individual patios, provide lake and mountain views. **Amenities:** 🛋 🅐 A/C. All units w/terraces. Ranger station across road gives interpretive nature talks. Restored pioneer farm within short hike. **Services:** 🍴 **Facilities:** 🅿 🎿 🛎 🔥 2 rsts, 1 bar. **Rates:** HS Oct $68–$73 S or D; from $90 ste. Extra person $6.25. Children under 16 stay free. Lower rates off-season. Higher rates for spec evnts/hols. MAP rates avail. Pking: Outdoor, free. Ltd CC.

BIG STONE GAP

Map page M-2, E1

Motel 🏨

▬ **Country Inn**, 627 Gilley Ave, PO Box 142, Big Stone Gap, VA 24219; tel 703/523-0374; fax 703/523-5043. Hidden in the highlands close to the Kentucky border, this rural motel offers a night's sleep and little more. Apparent dinginess comes from age, not lack of cleanliness. Saving grace is proximity to the *Lonesome Pine* outdoor drama. **Rooms:** 44 rms. CI noon/CO noon. Nonsmoking rms avail. Clean rooms are sparse and basic, with old furniture. **Amenities:** 🛋 🅐 A/C, cable TV w/movies. **Services:** 🍴 🛎 Babysitting. **Facilities:** RV park is adjacent to motel. **Rates:** $28–$33 S or D. Extra person $3. Children under 12 stay free. Pking: Outdoor, free. Maj CC.

Attractions 💼

Southwest Virginia Museum, 10 W 1st St; tel 703/523-1322. This 4-story Victorian mansion contains exhibits detailing the human history of this region. Topics include Native Americans, settlers, and workers in the coal industry, which prospered here around the turn of the century. Two of the 2nd-floor galleries chronicle the life and times of prominent local citizens and 8-term US Congressman C Bascom Slemp. The museum shop features ornate reproduction jewelry, books, toys, and porcelain dolls. **Open:** Mon–Thurs 10am–4pm, Fri 9am–4pm, Sat 10am–5pm, Sun 1–5pm. Closed Mon Jan–Feb, and some hols. $

June Tolliver House, Jerome St at Clinton Ave; tel 703/523-4707 or 523-1235. The June Tolliver House is where the heroine of John Fox, Jr's novel *The Trail of the Lonesome Pine* lived while attending school. A bestseller in the early 1900s, the novel tells the story of a romance between a beautiful young mountain woman and a handsome mining engineer from the Northeast against the backdrop of the great coal and iron boom in southwestern Virginia that brought so many drastic changes to the mountain people's way of life. Free guided tours include 19th-century parlor furnishings, June Tolliver's bedroom, and the John Fox, Jr Memorial Room.

In the adjoining **June Tolliver Playhouse**, a 2½-hour musical stage adaptation of the *Trail of the Lonesome Pine* by Earl Hobson Smith is performed for an 11-week season, ending Labor Day weekend. Visitors may call ahead to make reservations for the show. **Open:** Mid-May to mid-Dec, Tues–Wed 10am–5pm, Thurs–Sat 10am–8pm, Sun 2–6pm. Drama presentation: late June–Labor Day weekend, Thurs–Sat 8pm. $$$

John Fox, Jr, House and Museum, 117 Shawnee Ave; tel 703/523-2747 or 523-1235. This National and Virginia Historic Landmark serves both as a museum and a memorial to the Fox family. Built in 1888, the house is filled with beautiful furnishings and mementos of John Fox and his family. While living here, Fox wrote *The Trail of the Lonesome Pine, The Little Shepherd of Kingdom Come,* and other full-length novels in addition to more than 500 short stories. **Open:** Mid-May–mid-Dec, Tues–Wed 2–5pm, Thurs–Sun 2–6pm (days and hours may vary, phone ahead). $

BLACKSBURG

Map page M-2, E3

Hotel ▥

▤▤▤ **Blacksburg Marriott**, 900 Prices Fork Rd, Blacksburg, VA 24060; tel 703/552-7001 or toll free 800/228-9290; fax 703/552-0827. Exit 118 off I-81. Follow US 460 W for 9 miles to Prices Fork Rd. A large stone fireplace, balcony, and tall ceilings in the public areas provide a warm welcome to this hotel just minutes from Virginia Tech and shopping centers. **Rooms:** 148 rms and stes. Exec-level rms avail. CI 3pm/CO 1pm. Express checkout avail. Nonsmoking rms avail. Very spacious rooms are elegantly appointed with dark furniture and floral decor. **Amenities:** 🛀 ⚱ ▤ 🍶 A/C, cable TV w/movies, bathrobes. Some units w/terraces. Patios with tables and chairs face an interior courtyard with swimming pool. **Services:** ✗ ⚐ ⌂ ⬗ Babysitting. **Facilities:** ⬗ ⬗1 ⬗ ⬗ 2 rsts, 1 bar (w/entertainment), games rm, whirlpool, playground. **Rates:** $89–$99 S or D; from $150 ste. Extra person $10. Children under 18 stay free. Min stay spec evnts. Higher rates for spec evnts/hols. Spec packages avail. Pking: Outdoor, free. Maj CC. Attractive weekend packages.

Motels

▤▤▤ **Best Western Red Lion Inn**, 900 Plantation Rd, Blacksburg, VA 24060; tel 703/552-7770; fax 703/552-6346. Exit 118 off I-81. Follow US 460 W for 10 miles, to Prices Fork Rd. Attractive English tudor-style inn is located on 13 acres, making the nearby highway seem far away. Stone walls and fireplace in lobby are inviting; outside gazebo is romantic. Near Virginia Tech, Radford University, and good fishing. **Rooms:** 104 rms and stes. CI noon/CO 11am. Nonsmoking rms avail. **Amenities:** 🛀 ⚱ A/C, cable TV w/movies. **Services:** ✗ ⚐ ⌂ ⬗ Babysitting. **Facilities:** ⬗ ⬗3 ⬗ 1 rst, 1 bar, playground. Restaurant serves on patio, weather permitting. **Rates:** $45–$48

S; $62–$64 D; from $125 ste. Extra person $6. Children under 17 stay free. Min stay spec evnts. Higher rates for spec evnts/hols. Pking: Outdoor, free. Maj CC.

▤▤ **Comfort Inn**, 3705 S Main St, Blacksburg, VA 24060; tel 703/951-1500 or toll free 800/228-5150; fax 703/951-1530. Exit 118 off I-81. Follow 460 W for 6 miles. Convenient to the center of town, this modern facility is favored by those attending Virginia Tech functions. Shopping centers and restaurants are within a mile. **Rooms:** 80 rms and stes. Exec-level rms avail. CI 3pm/CO 11am. Nonsmoking rms avail. Rooms are exceptionally well furnished with dark woods and subdued floral upholstery. **Amenities:** 🛀 ⚱ A/C, cable TV w/movies. 1 unit w/minibar. **Services:** ⚐ ⌂ **Facilities:** ⬗ ⬗10 ⬗ Pool enjoys a spectacular panoramic view of the Blue Ridge Mountains. **Rates (CP):** $53–$58 S or D; from $85 ste. Extra person $5. Children under 18 stay free. Min stay spec evnts. Higher rates for spec evnts/hols. Spec packages avail. Pking: Outdoor, free. Maj CC.

▤▤ **Holiday Inn Blacksburg**, 3503 Holiday Lane, Blacksburg, VA 24060; tel 703/951-1330 or toll free 800/465-4329; fax 703/951-4847. Exit 118 off I-81. Go west on US 460 for 6 miles. Close to Virginia Tech, Smithfield Plantation, and downtown Blacksburg. **Rooms:** 98 rms and stes. Exec-level rms avail. CI 3pm/CO noon. Express checkout avail. Nonsmoking rms avail. **Amenities:** 🛀 ⚱ ▤ A/C, cable TV w/movies. 1 unit w/Jacuzzi. Some units have coffeemakers, refrigerators. **Services:** ✗ ⚐ ⌂ ⬗ **Facilities:** ⬗ ⬗200 ⬗ 1 rst, 1 bar (w/entertainment), washer/dryer. **Rates:** $48–$55 S or D; from $100 ste. Extra person $5. Children under 19 stay free. Min stay spec evnts. Higher rates for spec evnts/hols. Spec packages avail. Pking: Outdoor, free. Maj CC.

BREAKS INTERSTATE PARK

Map page M-2, E2

Visitor center located 7 miles north of Haysi, just off Va 80. Established by a joint action of the Kentucky and Virginia legislatures in 1954, Breaks Interstate Park covers more than 4,500 acres of woodland and striking mountain scenery that span the border between the 2 states. Within the park, the Russell Fork River has carved the largest canyon east of the Mississippi. More than 5 miles long and 1,600 feet deep, the canyon surrounds the river with sheer vertical walls throughout most of the park. The river winds around the **Towers,** an imposing pyramid of rocks over ½ mile long and ⅓ mile wide. Overlooks along the way provide spectacular views.

The park has 13 hiking trails, ranging from easy to extremely steep. Wooded areas are ideal for birdwatching. Other facilities include a swimming pool, boat dock and rentals, lake and pond fishing, horseback riding, and camping. The **visitor center** (tel 703/865-4413 or 865-4414) features natural and historical exhibits, as well as an exhibit on the local coal industry. Occasional shows are held in the amphitheater.

BRISTOL

Map page M-2, E2

Motels 🛏

≣≣ **Comfort Inn**, 2368 Lee Hwy, Bristol, VA 24201; tel 703/466-3881 or toll free 800/4-CHOICE; fax 703/466-6544. Exit 5 off I-81. A quiet, small motel tucked into a hillside yet offering convenient access to the interstate. Proximity to Bristol International Raceway makes this a popular spot for NASCAR fans. **Rooms:** 60 rms and stes. CI noon/CO 11am. Nonsmoking rms avail. **Amenities:** 🛋 🔥 A/C, cable TV w/movies. Some units w/Jacuzzis. **Services:** ⬛ 🛁 **Facilities:** 🔶 🔟 🔥 **Rates (CP):** HS May–Oct $49–$95 S; $54–$95 D; from $65 ste. Extra person $7. Children under 18 stay free. Min stay spec evnts. Lower rates off-season. Higher rates for spec evnts/hols. Pking: Outdoor, free. Maj CC.

≣≣ **Days Inn**, 1014 Old Airport Rd, PO Box 1746, Bristol, VA 24203; tel 703/669-9353 or toll free 800/329-7466; fax 703/669-6974. Exit 7 off I-81. Sitting atop a hill overlooking I-81, this motel is both accessible and unusually quiet. Bristol International Raceway is 15 minutes away. **Rooms:** 122 rms and stes. Exec-level rms avail. CI 2pm/CO noon. Nonsmoking rms avail. **Amenities:** 🛋 A/C, cable TV w/movies. **Services:** ✕ 🛏 🛁 🛁 🗔 **Facilities:** 🔶 🔟 🔥 1 rst, 1 bar, playground. Guests get discount to use Bristol Wellness Center. **Rates (CP):** HS Apr–Sept $40–$55 S; $45–$60 D; from $40 ste. Extra person $5. Children under 12 stay free. Lower rates off-season. Higher rates for spec evnts/hols. Spec packages avail. Pking: Outdoor, free. Maj CC.

≣≣ **HoJo Inn**, 15589 Lee Hwy, Bristol, VA 24202; tel 703/669-1151 or toll free 800/446-4656; fax 703/669-1153. Exit 10 off I-81. Proximity to the interstate and Dixie Pottery make this a convenient location. **Rooms:** 60 rms. CI 9am/CO noon. Nonsmoking rms avail. **Amenities:** 🛋 A/C, cable TV w/movies, refrig. All units w/terraces. **Services:** ✕ 🗔 🗔 **Facilities:** 🔶 1 rst. **Rates:** $38–$46 S; $42–$52 D. Extra person $8. Children under 18 stay free. Min stay spec evnts. Higher rates for spec evnts/hols. Pking: Outdoor, free. Maj CC.

≣≣ **Holiday Inn West**, W State St and Euclid Ave, Bristol, VA 24203; tel 703/669-7171 or toll free 800/465-4329; fax 703/669-7171. Exit 3 off I-81. This large and sprawling property is in the city, yet the units face a large hillside, giving a woodsy feel. Close to Bristol International Raceway, Dixie Pottery, and restaurants. **Rooms:** 123 rms. CI noon/CO noon. Express checkout avail. Nonsmoking rms avail. **Amenities:** 🛋 🔥 A/C, cable TV w/movies. Some units w/terraces. **Services:** ✕ 🛁 🗔 🗔 Security officer patrols this spread-out establishment at night. **Facilities:** 🔶 📖 🔥 1 rst, 1 bar. **Rates:** $42–$46 S; $44–$48 D. Children under 18 stay free. Min stay spec evnts. Higher rates for spec evnts/hols. Pking: Outdoor, free. Maj CC.

Attraction 💼

Rocky Mount Museum; tel 615/538-7396. Located 11 miles southwest on US 11 E. Rocky Mount is a 2-story log cabin built between 1770 and 1772 by William Cobb. From 1790 through 1792 it served as the capitol of the Territory of the United States South of the River Ohio under Governor William Blount. It is the oldest original territorial capitol in the country.

A living history program, with interpreters in period costume, re-creates a typical day in the lives of the William Cobb family, their servants, and neighbors in the year 1791. Lambing and planting are demonstrated in the spring, shearing in the summer, and harvesting in the fall. The kitchen shed, blacksmith shop, barn, weaving cabin, and smokehouse have all been restored. A museum of regional history contains such artifacts as a genuine 18th-century mountain wagon, and also a large collection of works by noted Tennessee portraitist Samuel Shaver. **Open:** Mar–Dec, Mon–Sat 10am–5pm, Sun 2–6pm; Jan–Feb, Mon–Fri 10am–5pm. Closed some hols and Dec 20–Jan 6. $$

BROOKNEAL

Map page M-3, E5

Attraction 💼

Red Hill, Patrick Henry National Memorial; tel 804/376-2044. Located at Va 40 and County Routes 600 and 619; follow signs. The fiery orator's last home, Red Hill is a modest frame farmhouse, authentically reconstructed on the original foundation after fire destroyed it in 1919. The overseer's cottage that Patrick Henry used as a law office is an original structure. Henry retired to Red Hill in 1794 after serving 5 terms as governor of Virginia. Failing health forced him to refuse numerous posts, including those of chief justice of the Supreme Court and secretary of state.

The Visitors Center presents a 15-minute video on Henry's life at Red Hill and exhibits a large collection of Henry memorabilia, including Peter Rothermel's painting depicting Patrick Henry's famous speech before the Virginia House of Burgesses ("If this be treason, make the most of it"). The site's most striking feature, the osage orange tree, standing 64 feet tall and spanning 96 feet, is listed in the American Forestry Hall of Fame. **Open:** Apr–Oct, daily 9am–5pm; Nov–Mar, daily 9am–4pm. Closed some hols. $

BUENA VISTA

Map page M-2, D4

Motel 🛏

≣≣ Buena Vista Motel, 447 E 29th St (US 60), Buena Vista, VA 24416; tel 703/261-2138. Exit 188A off I-81. Go 3 miles on US 60 E. An older motel close to town, conveniently located minutes from historic Lexington, Blue Ridge Pkwy, Virginia Horse Center. **Rooms:** 19 rms. CI 11am/CO 11am. Express checkout avail. Nonsmoking rms avail. Exceptionally spacious rooms. **Amenities:** 🛏 A/C, cable TV. **Services:** ✕ ⌂ ◁ **Facilities:** 📇 1 rst. Adjoining restaurant. **Rates:** HS July–Oct $44–$54 S or D. Extra person $4. Lower rates off-season. Pking: Outdoor, free. Maj CC.

CARMEL CHURCH

Map page M-3, D6 (N of Richmond)

See also Doswell

Motels 🛏

≣≣ Comfort Inn, I-95 and Va 207, Carmel Church, VA 22546; tel 804/448-2828 or toll free 800/228-5150; fax 804/448-4441. Exit 104 off I-95. About halfway between Richmond and Fredericksburg, this comfortable property is 6 miles from Paramount's King's Dominion, making it one of the closest motels to that popular amusement park. **Rooms:** 140 rms and stes. CI 2pm/CO noon. Nonsmoking rms avail. **Amenities:** 🛏 A/C, cable TV. **Services:** ⌂ ◁ **Facilities:** 📇 📇 🖥 ㄽ 1 rst, games rm, washer/dryer. Aunt Sarah's Pancake House on premises. **Rates:** HS May–Sept $56–$62 S or D; from $70 ste. Lower rates off-season. Spec packages avail. Pking: Outdoor, free. Maj CC.

≣≣ Days Inn, I-95 and Va 207, PO Box 70, Carmel Church, VA 22546; tel 804/448-2011 or toll free 800/325-2525. Exit

104 off I-95. A clean, comfortable, and well-landscaped facility convenient to Paramount's King's Dominion amusement park. **Rooms:** 122 rms. CI 2pm/CO noon. Nonsmoking rms avail. **Amenities:** 🛏 A/C, cable TV. **Services:** ⌂ ◁ Free coffee in lobby. **Facilities:** 📇 1 rst, playground. **Rates:** HS May–Sept $62–$63 S or D. Children under 18 stay free. Lower rates off-season. Spec packages avail. Pking: Outdoor, free. Maj CC.

CHANTILLY

Map page M-3, C6 (NW of Falls Church)

Hotels 🛏

≣≣ Comfort Inn Dulles Int'l Airport, 4050 Westfax Dr, Chantilly, VA 22021 (Dulles Airport); tel 703/818-8200 or toll free 800/325-7760; fax 703/968-6871. 7 mi S of Dulles Airport. Exit 53 off I-66, then follow Va 28 N to US 50 W. This modern, 7-story brick hotel in a near-rural setting has a friendly staff and more amenities than usual for members of this motel chain. **Rooms:** 140 rms. CI 3pm/CO 11am. Nonsmoking rms avail. All rooms are clean and comfortable. L-shaped king units. **Amenities:** 🛏 ㄽ 🖥 A/C, cable TV w/movies. Refrigerators and microwaves available. King units have fax jacks. **Services:** 🚐 ㄽ ⌂ ◁ Babysitting. **Facilities:** 📇 📇 📇 ㄽ 1 rst, lifeguard, games rm, whirlpool, washer/dryer. Indoor pool opens to fenced patio for sunning. Pool open weekday mornings and evenings, all day Saturday and Sunday. Deluxe continental breakfast served in attractive cafe off lobby. **Rates (CP):** HS Apr–May/Sept–Oct $65–$75 S; $75–$85 D. Extra person $10. Children under 18 stay free. Lower rates off-season. Spec packages avail. Pking: Outdoor, free. Maj CC. Weekend and long-term rates available.

≣≣≣ Washington Dulles Airport Marriott, 333 W Service Rd, Chantilly, VA 22021; tel 703/471-9500 or toll free 800/228-9290; fax 703/661-6785. In Dulles Airport complex; follow Service Rd west to hotel. The only hotel actually on the Dulles Airport grounds, this sprawling 1972 building underwent a complete renovation in 1994, which brought it back to Marriott standards of cleanliness and comfort. Hotel sits on 22 acres beside a man-made lake. **Rooms:** 370 rms and stes. Exec-level rms avail. CI 4pm/CO noon. Express checkout avail. Nonsmoking rms avail. Spacious rooms furnished with dark, colonial-style furniture and bright spreads and drapes. Lots of light from floor-to-ceiling windows. **Amenities:** 🛏 ㄽ 🖥 A/C, satel TV w/movies, voice mail. Some units w/terraces. Concierge Level units have robes, coffeemakers, valet stands, concierge lounge. **Services:** ✕ 🚐 🚐 ㄽ ⌂ Car-rental desk, babysitting. **Facilities:** 📇 📇 📇 🖥 ㄽ 1 rst, 1 bar, lifeguard, lawn games, spa, sauna, whirlpool, washer/dryer. Large picnic area with basketball and volleyball courts, horseshoe and softball areas. Indoor pool opens to outdoor pool in landscaped courtyard with extensive, resort-like area for sunning. **Rates:** HS Labor Day–July 4 $119 S; $134 D; from $250 ste. Extra person $15. Children under 18 stay free. Lower rates off-season. Spec packages avail. Pking: Outdoor, free. Maj CC.

Attraction 💼

Sully Plantation, 3701 Pender Dr; tel 703/437-1794. Built in 1793 by Richard Bland Lee (''Light Horse Harry'' Lee's brother), the original plantation was situated on more than 3,000 acres and consisted of a main house, dairy, smokehouse, kitchen building, and slave quarters. Today the house is furnished with period antiques approximating the style in which the Lees lived. **Open:** Mar–Dec, Wed–Mon 11am–5pm; Jan–Feb, Sat–Sun 11am–3:30pm. Closed some hols. $$

CHARLES CITY

Map page M-3, D6

Attractions 💼

Berkeley, 12602 Harrison Landing Rd; tel 804/829-6018. In 1691 Berkeley was acquired by the Harrison family, members in good standing of Virginia's aristocratic ruling class. Following a 10-minute slide presentation, 20-minute guided tours of the house are given through the day by guides in colonial dress. Allow at least another half hour to explore the magnificent grounds and gardens. **Open:** Daily 9am–5pm. Closed Dec 25. $$$

Shirley Plantation, 501 Shirley Plantation Rd; tel 804/829-5121. Another historic James River plantation, Shirley was founded in 1613 and has been in the same family since 1660. The present mansion dates from 1723. The house survived the Revolution, the Civil War, and Reconstruction, as did the dependencies, which include an 18th-century laundry (later used as a schoolhouse, where Robert E Lee had lessons as a boy). Several 35-minute tours are given throughout the day. **Open:** Daily 9am–5pm (last tour 4:30pm). Closed Dec 25. $$$

CHARLOTTESVILLE

Map page M-3, D5

Hotels 💼

≡≡≡ **Courtyard by Marriott**, 638 Hillsdale Dr, Charlottesville, VA 22901; tel 804/973-7100 or toll free 800/321-2211; fax 804/973-7128. Exit 124 off I-64. Take US 29 N 2 miles. Very attractive hotel close to the highway and a major shopping mall but far enough removed to be quiet. Immaculate grounds have well-tended flowers and shrubs. University of Virginia and historic sights are 3 miles away. **Rooms:** 150 rms and stes. CI 3pm/CO noon. Express checkout avail. Nonsmoking rms avail. Attractive and clean. Convenient for business travelers, rooms have desk, ample seating on sofa. **Amenities:** 🛏 ⚷ A/C, cable TV w/movies, refrig. Some units w/minibars, some w/terraces. **Services:** ✗ 🚗 ⌷ 🛎 Complimentary coffee and tea in lobby. **Facilities:** 🏋 🛁 🔟 ⚷ 1 rst, 1 bar, whirlpool, washer/dryer. Lobby lounge with TV. Well-equipped exercise room. Guests can use health club 1½ miles away. Dining area serves breakfast, lunch, and dinner for guests. **Rates:** $54–$85 S or D; from $72 ste. Children under 18 stay free. Min stay spec evnts. Higher rates for spec evnts/hols. Spec packages avail. Pking: Outdoor, free. Maj CC.

≡≡ **English Inn of Charlottesville**, 2000 Morton Dr, Charlottesville, VA 22901; tel 804/971-9900 or toll free 800/786-5400; fax 804/977-8008. Well-kept grounds surround this Tudor-style hotel with an attractive lobby. Near the University of Virginia, major shopping malls. Friendly and helpful staff. **Rooms:** 88 rms and stes. CI 2pm/CO noon. Nonsmoking rms avail. Recent major renovation. **Amenities:** 🛏 ⚷ A/C, cable TV, refrig. Some units w/minibars. VCRs and movies can be rented. **Services:** 🚗 🛁 🛎 Babysitting. Complimentary tea and coffee available 24 hours in conservatory. **Facilities:** 🏋 🛁 🔟 ⚷ Sauna. **Rates (CP):** $58 S; $63 D; from $63 ste. Extra person $7. Children under 18 stay free. Higher rates for spec evnts/hols. Pking: Outdoor, free. Maj CC.

≡≡ **Holiday Inn Monticello**, 1200 Fifth St, Charlottesville, VA 22901; tel 804/977-5100 or toll free 800/465-4329; fax 804/293-5228. Exit 120 off I-64. This typical Holiday Inn is well maintained and has small but neatly landscaped and attractive grounds. Major renovation begun in 1994 should bring improvements. Easy to find and convenient to interstate and university. **Rooms:** 135 rms and stes. Exec-level rms avail. CI noon/CO noon. Express checkout avail. Nonsmoking rms avail. **Amenities:** 🛏 ⚷ 🍴 A/C, cable TV w/movies. **Services:** ✗ 🛁 🛎 Social director. **Facilities:** 🏋 🔟 ⚷ 1 rst, 1 bar, washer/dryer.

Rates: $68–$78 S or D; from $110 ste. Children under 18 stay free. Min stay spec evnts. Higher rates for spec evnts/hols. Spec packages avail. Pking: Outdoor, free. Maj CC.

Motels

≣ **Econo Lodge South**, 400 Emmet Street (US 29), Charlottes-ville, VA 22903; tel 804/296-2104 or toll free 800/424-4777; fax 804/296-2104. Exit 118B off I-64. A very basic but clean facility directly across a major highway from the University of Virginia athletic center. Reservations are necessary due to close proximity to university. **Rooms:** 60 rms. CI 1pm/CO 11am. Nonsmoking rms avail. Management has promised new spreads, drapes, and carpets, which were needed at inspection. **Amenities:** ☎ A/C, cable TV. Several rooms have small refriger-ators and microwaves. **Services:** ⌂ Free morning coffee. **Facilities:** ⌂ Restaurant next door. **Rates:** HS May–Oct $41–$51 S; $45–$55 D. Extra person $5. Children under 18 stay free. Lower rates off-season. Higher rates for spec evnts/hols. Pking: Outdoor, free. Maj CC.

≣ **Hampton Inn**, 2035 India Rd, Charlottesville, VA 22906; tel 804/978-7888 or toll free 800/426-7866; fax 804/973-0436. A basic, functional, and clean hotel devoid of most extras. Located in an attractive shopping center, easily seen from US 29. Convenient to several restaurants, University of Virginia. **Rooms:** 130 rms and stes. Exec-level rms avail. CI 2pm/CO noon. Express checkout avail. Nonsmoking rms avail. Small, clean, adequate rooms with no frills. Worn bedspreads were slated for replacement. **Amenities:** ☎ ☖ A/C, cable TV w/movies. **Services:** ⌂ ☒ ⌂ Babysitting. Complimentary morning newspapers. Continental breakfast served in the lobby. All-day coffee. **Facilities:** ⌂ ☒ ☖ **Rates (CP):** $51–$53 S; $60–$62 D; from $100 ste. Children under 18 stay free. Min stay spec evnts. Lower rates off-season. Higher rates for spec evnts/hols. Pking: Outdoor, free. Maj CC.

Resort

Boar's Head Inn and Sports Club, US 250 W, PO Box 5307, Charlottesville, VA 22903; tel 804/296-2181 or toll free 800/476-1988; fax 804/977-1306. Exit 118B off I-64. Follow US 250 W for 1½ miles. 53 acres. An attractive resort from the outside, with well-groomed grounds containing trees, benches, flowers, and a lake with tame geese for guests to feed. Lobby a bit dark and worn. Convenient to University of Virginia and historic sites. Unrated. **Rooms:** 173 rms, stes, and effic. Exec-level rms avail. CI 4pm/CO noon. Express checkout avail. Nonsmoking rms avail. **Amenities:** ☎ ☖ ☒ A/C, cable TV w/movies. Some units w/minibars, some w/terraces, some w/fireplaces. **Services:** ✗ ☒ ☒ ☒ ⌂ Social director, masseur, children's program,

babysitting. **Facilities:** ⌂ ⌀ ☒ ▶18 ☒ ☒20 ☒ 400 ☖ 3 rsts, 1 bar (w/entertainment), lifeguard, racquetball, squash, sauna, playground. **Rates:** $124–$220 S; $134–$230 D; from $210 ste; from $210 effic. Extra person $10. Children under 16 stay free. Min stay spec evnts. Spec packages avail. Pking: Outdoor, free. Maj CC.

Restaurants ᵮᵮᵮ

C&O Restaurant, 515 E Water St, Charlottesville; tel 804/971-7044. **Regional American/French.** Brick walls and ex-posed beams hint at history and romance at this small restaurant in an early-20th-century house in historic downtown area. Though jackets are required in the formal upstairs dining room, downstairs bistro is more casual. Reservations recommended upstairs, not accepted in bistro. Menu features international styles of seafood and meat dishes. **FYI:** Dress code. **Open:** Lunch Mon–Fri 11:30am–3:00pm; dinner Sun–Thurs 5:30–10:00pm, Fri–Sat 5:30–11:00pm. Closed some hols; Jan 1–14. **Prices:** Main courses $8–$17. Ltd CC. ▮ ☑

The Coffee Exchange, in the Downtown Mall, 120 E Main St, Charlottesville; tel 804/295-0975. **Coffeehouse.** A small but clean and attractive coffeehouse full of aromas from roasted beans and fresh-baked muffins, breads, and desserts. Sandwich-es, salads, and light, inexpensive meals also featured. Coffees can be ordered by mail. A favorite of downtown workers. **FYI:** Reservations not accepted. Beer and wine only. No smoking. **Open:** Mon–Thurs 8am–5pm, Fri–Sat 8am–8pm, Sun 9am–5pm. Closed some hols. **Prices:** Main courses $3.95–$5.50. Ltd CC.

Eastern Standard, in the Downtown Mall, 102 Old Preston Ave, Charlottesville; tel 804/295-8668. **New American/Californi-an.** Small restaurant in an older building at the end of the Downtown Mall. Decor is eastern, while food is American. Not a place for a special meal or fancy night out, but a pleasant place to grab a quick bite while shopping or sight-seeing. Healthful sandwiches include a vegetarian broccoli burger. **FYI:** Reserva-tions accepted. Blues/guitar/jazz. **Open:** Lunch Tues–Fri 11am–2:30pm; dinner Tues–Sun 5–10pm. Closed some hols; Aug 1–14. **Prices:** Main courses $8.95–$18.95. Maj CC.

The Hardware Store Restaurant, in the Downtown Mall, 316 E Main St, Charlottesville; tel 804/977-1518. **Eclectic.** An old brick-walled commercial building converted to an eatery that caters to the college crowd. Subdued lighting softens the noisy, crowded yet fun place to eat. Circular stairs lead to upstairs area. A wide variety of items includes sandwich combinations, delicious desserts, old-fashioned sodas. **FYI:** Reservations recommended. **Open:** Mon–Thurs 11am–9pm, Fri–Sat 11am–10pm. Closed some hols. **Prices:** Main courses $4.75–$5. Ltd CC. ◾

Miller's, in the Downtown Mall, 109 W Main St, Charlottesville; tel 804/971-8511. **American.** This small bar/restaurant in a historic building has a long bar backed by a huge mirror. Small, close tables and stage at one end hint at evening entertainment aimed at college students. In daylight, cleanliness leaves much to be desired. Pub-style sandwiches and grilled steak, chicken, and fish. **FYI:** Reservations not accepted. Blues/jazz. **Open:** Mon–Fri 11:30am–1:30am, Sat 5pm–1:30am. Closed some hols. **Prices:** Main courses $6–$10. Maj CC.

Attractions 🏛

Monticello, Va 53; tel 804/984-9822 or 984-9800. Monticello was the home of Thomas Jefferson, who designed the house and oversaw its construction. The estate, considered an architectural masterpiece, was the first Virginia plantation to sit atop a mountain (great houses were usually built close to rivers). The house was originally Palladian in design, but Jefferson later incorporated features of Parisian architecture, having been inspired by the homes of French noblemen during his tenure as minister to France. Construction first began in 1769, but over a 40-year period Jefferson continued to expand, remodel, and rebuild parts of his home.

The house is restored as closely as possible to its appearance during Jefferson's retirement years. Nearly all of the furniture and household items were owned by Jefferson or his family. The garden has been extended to its original 1,000-foot length, and the Mulberry Row dependencies—including the smokehouse, blacksmith shop, nailery, servants' quarters—have been excavated. (The name comes from the mulberries Jefferson had planted there.)

In the entrance hall, which was a museum in Jefferson's day, is a 7-day calendar clock, one of Jefferson's inventions, which still works. Just off the entrance hall are Jefferson's high-ceilinged bedroom, where he died at age 83, and the library, which contained 6,000 books that Jefferson later gave to the Library of Congress. The tour also includes Jefferson's study, which contains one of his telescopes; the parlor, a semi-octagonal room with a Jefferson-designed parquet cherry floor; the dining room; and the orchard and gardens.

Jefferson's grave in the family burial ground (still in use) is inscribed with his own words: "Here was buried Thomas Jefferson / Author of the Declaration of American Independence / of the Statute of Virginia for Religious Freedom / and Father of the University of Virginia." After visiting the graveyard, visitors may take a shuttle bus back to the parking area or follow a path through the woods. **Open:** Mar–Oct, daily 8am–5pm; Nov–Feb, daily 9am–4:30pm. Closed Dec 25. $$$

Ash Lawn–Highland, James Monroe Pkwy (County Rd 795); tel 804/293-9539. Located 2½ miles past Monticello (see above) on County Rd 795. James Monroe's influence on early American history goes beyond his accomplishments as the nation's 5th president. Monroe fought in the Revolution, was wounded at Trenton, recovered, and went on to hold more offices than any other president, including several foreign ministries.

In 1793 he purchased 1,000 acres adjacent to Monticello, where he built an estate he called Highland (the name Ash Lawn dates to 1838). Monroe served as ambassador to Britain and Spain; was 4 times governor of Virginia; served as Jefferson's ambassador to France, where he negotiated the Louisiana Purchase; held various cabinet posts; and was elected president in 1816. When Monroe retired from office in 1825, he was deeply in debt and was forced to sell the beloved farm where he'd hoped to spend his last days.

Today the 535-acre estate is owned and maintained as a working farm by the College of William and Mary (Monroe's alma mater). Guided tours (40 minutes) include the 5 remaining original rooms, along with the basement kitchen, the overseer's cottage, restored slave quarters, and the smokehouse. Some of the Monroes' furnishings and other belongings are still here. Livestock, vegetable and herb gardens, and colonial craft demonstrations recall elements of daily life on the Monroe's plantation. Horses, cattle, and sheep graze in the fields and peacocks roam the boxwood gardens. Many special events throughout the year (phone ahead). **Open:** Mar–Oct, daily 9am–6pm; Nov–Feb, daily 10am–5pm. Closed some hols. $$$

Virginia Discovery Museum; tel 804/977-1025. Located at the east end of the Downtown Mall, this facility offers numerous hands-on exhibits and programs for young people. The Colonial Log House, an authentic structure that once stood on a site in New Bedford, Virginia, is outfitted with 19th-century furnishings. A series of exhibits deals with the senses and the Fun and Games exhibit has an array of games, including bowling and giant checkers. Changing exhibits, arts and crafts studio. Free admission first Sunday of every month. **Open:** Tues–Sat 10am–5pm, Sun 1–5pm. $

Historic Michie Tavern, Va 20; tel 804/977-1234. Built in 1784 by William Michie to capitalize on the well-traveled stagecoach route that ran through his property. The Michies also farmed and operated a general store, and their descendants owned the property until 1910. It was moved to its present location near Monticello (see above) and painstakingly restored. Behind the tavern are reproductions of the old log kitchen, dairy, somkehouse, ice house, and root cellar. The general store has been re-created, along with a crafts shop; the Virginia Wine Museum is also on the premises. Behind the store is a gristmill that has operated continuously since 1797.

A tribute to early preservationists, the tavern still plays host to travelers in much the same style as it did 2 centuries ago. In the "Ordinary," a converted log cabin with original hand-hewn walls and beamed ceilings, a lunch of southern cuisine is served on pewter plates at rustic oak tavern tables (daily 11:30am–3pm). **Open:** Daily 9am–5pm. Closed some hols. $$

University of Virginia, University Ave; tel 804/924-7969. Jefferson's "academical village," the University of Virginia is graced with spacious lawns, serpentine-walled gardens, colonnaded pavilions, and a classical rotunda inspired by the Pantheon in Rome. Rightly called the father of this institution, Jefferson conceived it, wrote the charter, raised the money for its construction, selected the site, drew the plans, laid the cornerstone in 1817, supervised construction, served as the first rector, selected the faculty, and created the curriculum.

The focal point of the university and starting point of tours is the **Rotunda** (at Rugby Road), restored according to Jefferson's original design. The tour includes the oval chemistry room; the Rotunda bell, once used to wake students at dawn; classrooms; the library; and the magnificent colonnaded **Dome Room**. The room occupied by Edgar Allan Poe when he was a student here is furnished as it would have been in 1826 and is open to visitors.

The Alexander Galt statue of Jefferson on the 2nd floor of the Rotunda (originally the main entry level) is said to be an excellent likeness; another statue, by Sir Moses Ezekiel, is on the esplanade north of the Rotunda. **Open:** Daily. Closed for 2 weeks around Dec 25. Free.

The Mall; tel 804/296-8548. Located on Main St, between 2nd St W and 6th St E. Stroll into the 20th century along a charming pedestrian brick mall extending for about 8 blocks of downtown. Free.

McGuffey Art Center, 201 2nd St NW; tel 804/295-7973. In the center, just a few blocks off the Mall, local artists and craftspeople have studio exhibits and sell their creations. The **Second Street Gallery,** showing contemporary art from all over the United States, is also located here. **Open:** Tues–Sat 10am–5pm, Sun noon–5pm. Closed some hols. Free.

Oakencroft Vineyard, Barracks Rd; tel 804/296-4188. There have been vineyards here since the 18th century, and Thomas Jefferson hoped one day to produce quality wines in Virginia. This vineyard, set on 17 acres of rolling farmland, has a tasting room housed in a red barn, and offers rustic tables for picnicking. A self-guided tour takes about 20 minutes. **Open:** Apr–Dec, daily 11am–5pm; Jan–Mar, by appointment. Free.

CHESAPEAKE
Map page M-3, E7

Motels 🏨

≣≣ **Comfort Suites**, 1550 Crossways Blvd, Chesapeake, VA 23320; tel 804/420-1600 or toll free 800/428-0562; fax 804/420-0099. Exit 289B off I-64. Follow Greenbrier Pkwy S to Crossways Center; go north on Crossways Blvd. This modern motel close to industrial parks has amenities to appeal to business travelers. Nice lobby has high-quality furnishings; adjacent area with TV, comfortable seating. Lots of nearby shopping, including a major mall. **Rooms:** 124 stes. CI 11am/CO 11am. Express checkout avail. Nonsmoking rms avail. All units are large suites, very well furnished and appointed. Brass lamps, sofa beds, arched walls give a homey feel. **Amenities:** 🛗 🍸 A/C, cable TV w/movies, refrig. Some units w/terraces. Microwaves in all units. **Services:** 🛅 🍽 Free continental breakfast served in room with tables and comfortable chairs. **Facilities:** 🛗 🍱 🔲 🕭 Games rm, spa, sauna, steam rm, whirlpool, washer/dryer. Nice pool area. Whirlpool is within a wooden gazebo. **Rates (CP):** HS May 15–Sept 15 from $65 ste. Extra person $7. Children under 18 stay free. Lower rates off-season. Spec packages avail. Pking: Outdoor, free. Maj CC. Government rates available.

≣≣ **Days Inn**, 1433 N Battlefield Blvd, Chesapeake, VA 23320; tel 804/547-9262 or toll free 800/258-5353; fax 804/547-4334. Exit 290B off I-64. Follow Va 168 S for 1 block. This budget motel is close to shopping, hospital, and office parks. **Rooms:** 88 rms and effic. CI 2pm/CO noon. Nonsmoking rms avail. **Amenities:** 🛗 A/C, cable TV w/movies, refrig. Some units w/terraces. **Services:** 🛅 🍽 Free continental breakfast. **Facilities:** 🛗 🍱 🕭 Washer/dryer. **Rates (CP):** HS Mem Day–Labor Day $55–$60 S; $60–$65 D; from $55 effic. Extra person $5. Children under 18 stay free. Lower rates off-season. Higher rates for spec evnts/hols. Pking: Outdoor, free. Maj CC.

≣≣ **Hampton Inn**, 701A Woodlake Dr, Chesapeake, VA 23320; tel 804/420-1550 or toll free 800/HAMPTON; fax 804/424-7414. Exit 289A off I-64. Go north on Greebrier Pkwy ⅛ mile; turn right on Woodlake Dr. Located in light industrial park, this clean chain motel is popular with business travelers. Tourism business increases in summer. Lobby has microwave, TV, and ample seating. **Rooms:** 119 rms. CI 2pm/CO noon. Nonsmoking rms avail. Cheerful rooms with mauve rugs, blue floral bedspreads, pretty framed prints on walls. **Amenities:** 🛗 🍸 A/C, cable TV w/movies. **Services:** 🛅 🍽 Twice-daily maid svce. **Facilities:** 🛗 🍱 🕭 **Rates (CP):** HS May 1–Sept 5 $47–$49 S;

$54–$56 D. Children under 18 stay free. Min stay spec evnts. Lower rates off-season. Higher rates for spec evnts/hols. Pking: Outdoor, free. Maj CC.

≝≝≝ **Holiday Inn Chesapeake**, 725 Woodlake Dr, Chesapeake, VA 23320; tel 804/523-1500 or toll free 800/HOLIDAY; fax 804/523-0683. Exit 289A off I-64. Go north on Greenbrier Pkwy for ⅛ mile; turn right on Woodlake Dr. This comfortable chain motel is popular with business travelers. **Rooms:** 190 rms and stes. CI 2pm/CO noon. Express checkout avail. Nonsmoking rms avail. Attractively decorated with teal accents. **Amenities:** 🛢 🔥 A/C, cable TV w/movies, refrig. Some units w/minibars. Spacious suites have wet bars, microwaves, and refrigerators. **Services:** ✕ 🚐 ⊠ ♫ Twice-daily maid svce. **Facilities:** 🔆 🏌️ 🏊 ⅙ 1 rst (*see also* ''Restaurants'' below), 1 bar, spa, whirlpool. Attractive indoor pool area has vaulted ceiling, skylight. Exercise room adjacent. Restaurant has 3 affordable entrees nightly. **Rates:** $68–$72 S; $76–$80 D; from $90 ste. Extra person $8. Children under 18 stay free. Min stay spec evnts. Spec packages avail. Pking: Outdoor, free. Maj CC. Sweetheart packages.

Restaurants 🍴

Key West, in Holiday Inn Chesapeake, 725 Woodlake Dr, Chesapeake; tel 804/523-1500. Exit 289A off I-64. Follow Greenbrier Pkwy N to Woodlake Dr, turn right. **Regional American/Seafood/Steak.** Walls of windows with view of outdoor fountains give this motel restaurant a light and cheerful ambience. Accents include rattan chairs, tables partitioned by drapes, teal and burgundy scheme. Value-priced nightly specials ($9–$11) include such offerings as pork tenderloin with orange pecan sauce and backfin crab cake, and come with vegetables, salad, rolls, dessert. Regular menu has seafood, steak, chicken, pork selections. **FYI:** Reservations accepted. Children's menu. **Open:** HS Mar–Nov daily 6:30am–10:30pm. Reduced hours off-season. Closed Dec 25. **Prices:** Main courses $7–$16. Maj CC. ♥ ⅙

The Locks Pointe at Great Bridge, 136 Battlefield Blvd N, Chesapeake; tel 804/547-9618. Exit 290B off I-64. Go 4¼ mi on Va 168S. Located just north of Great Bridge Locks. **Seafood/Steak.** White tablecloths with green toppers set a dressy but casual atmosphere for this popular restaurant overlooking the Intracoastal Waterway. Solarium room used for Sunday brunch. Fresh seafood imaginatively prepared with spices and sauces is the highlight. Soft-shell crab seasonally; chicken, filet mignon round out the menu. Hodad's bar has patio seating, indoor dining area, and menu that includes raw bar, sandwiches, pasta. Live entertainment on summer weekends. Hodad's open daily 4pm–2am. **FYI:** Reservations recommended. Children's menu.

Open: Lunch Tues–Fri 11am–3pm; dinner Tues–Sat 5–10pm, Sun 3–9pm; brunch Sun 11am–3pm. Closed Dec 25. **Prices:** Main courses $14–$23. Maj CC. 🍴 🏔 ⅙

CHESTERFIELD
Map page M-3, D6

Attraction 💼

Pocahontas State Park, 10301 State Park Rd; tel 804/796-4255. Comprising more than 7,000 acres, this park offers fishing and boating on Beaver Lake, as well as hiking, biking, and picnicking. Many facilities are accessible to people with disabilities, including the swimming pool. Individual and group campsites; interpretive programs in summer. **Open:** Park, daily; visitor center, Mem Day–Labor Day, Sat–Sun 10am–6pm. $

CHINCOTEAGUE
Map page M-3, D8

Motels 🏨

≝≝ **Assateague Inn**, 6570 Chicken City Rd, Chincoteague, VA 23336; tel 804/336-3738; fax 804/336-1179. Exit US 13 at Va 175 E. This condominium complex enjoys a quiet spot among pine trees at the edge of an attractive marsh. **Rooms:** 26 rms and effic. CI 3pm/CO 11am. **Amenities:** 🛢 🔥 🖥 A/C, cable TV w/movies, refrig. All units w/terraces. Efficiencies have microwaves and cook-tops. **Services:** ♫ Babysitting. **Facilities:** 🔆 🏌️ 🏊 Lawn games, spa, whirlpool, playground. Picnic tables and grills. Pier into creek for crabbing. Restaurant nearby. **Rates:** HS July–Aug $62 S or D; from $92 effic. Extra person $5. Children under 13 stay free. Min stay wknds. Lower rates off-season. Pking: Outdoor, free. Maj CC.

≝ **Beach Road Motel**, 6151 Maddox Blvd, Chincoteague, VA 23336; tel 804/336-6562. Exit US 13 at Va 175 E, turn left. Drive 7 blocks to Maddox Rd, turn right. Although this very simple motel has few amenities, it's absolutely clean and neat and is maintained to a high standard. Nicely landscaped grounds. **Rooms:** 20 rms; 3 ctges/villas. CI 2pm/CO 11am. Some of the basic rooms were remodeled recently and have a lighter, more modern feel. **Amenities:** 🛢 🖥 A/C, cable TV, refrig. 1 unit w/terrace. **Services:** ♫ **Facilities:** 🔆 Picnic tables and outdoor grills. **Rates:** HS June 17–Sept 4 $58–$79 S or D. Extra person $5. Children under 10 stay free. Min stay HS. Lower rates off-season. Pking: Outdoor, free. Ltd CC. Cottages/villas rent by week only ($470/wk).

≣≣ Birchwood Motel, 3650 Main St, Chincoteague, VA 23336; tel 804/336-6133 or toll free 800/445-5147; fax 804/336-6535. Exit US 13 at Va 175 E; turn right at light, then go ½ mi. This older motel is in exceptionally fine condition. Large lawn. **Rooms:** 41 rms. CI 2pm/CO 11am. Nonsmoking rms avail. Standard motel-style rooms except for 2 large, family-size units. **Amenities:** 🛁 📺 A/C, cable TV, refrig. **Services:** ⟲ **Facilities:** 🛐 🚴 Lawn games, playground. Shuffleboard. **Rates:** HS June 17–Sept 5 $61 S; $66–$80 D. Extra person $5. Children under 10 stay free. Min stay spec evnts. Lower rates off-season. Pking: Outdoor, free. Maj CC. Cottages rent by week only (from $475/wk).

≣≣ Driftwood Motor Lodge, 7105 Maddox Blvd, PO Box 575, Chincoteague, VA 23336; tel 804/336-6557 or toll free 800/553-6117; fax 804/336-6558. Exit US 13 at Va 175; turn left at light, then right on Maddox Blvd; drive 2 mi. The closest motel to the national wildlife refuge, this is an attractive, well-kept, and comfortable base for exploration and trips to the beach. **Rooms:** 52 rms. CI 3pm/CO 11am. Nonsmoking rms avail. All rooms are spacious and attractive. Some have views across street to the marshlands. **Amenities:** 🛁 A/C, cable TV w/movies, refrig. All units w/terraces. **Services:** ⟲ Babysitting. **Facilities:** 🛐🚴 Fast-food outlet across street. **Rates:** HS July 1–Sept 7 $82 S or D. Extra person $6. Children under 12 stay free. Min stay wknds. Lower rates off-season. Higher rates for spec evnts/hols. Pking: Outdoor, free. Maj CC.

≣≣≣ Island Motor Inn, 711 N Main St, Chincoteague, VA 23336; tel 804/336-3141 or toll free 800/832-2925; fax 804/336-1483. Exit US 13 at Va 175 E, turn left and go 3 blocks. This very pretty motel enjoys a spectacular waterfront setting on the Intracoastal Waterway. Renovations will add hotel-type indoor corridors in 1995. **Rooms:** 48 rms. CI 3pm/CO 11am. Nonsmoking rms avail. All rooms have views of Chincoteague Bay. **Amenities:** 🛁 💧 A/C, cable TV w/movies, refrig. All units w/terraces. **Services:** ⟲ Babysitting. Very accommodating staff. Land safari tours of Assateague National Wildlife Refuge. **Facilities:** 🛐 🛁 🏊 🚴 Spa, whirlpool, washer/dryer. Pier on the bay. Indoor pool planned for 1995. **Rates:** HS June 10–Sept 6 $78–$125 S or D. Extra person $10. Children under 15 stay free. Min stay HS. Lower rates off-season. Pking: Outdoor, free. Maj CC.

≣ Lighthouse Motel, 4218 N Main St, Chincoteague, VA 23336; tel 804/336-5091. Va 175 E exit off US 13. This neat, clean, and simple older motel is on the main street of town. Owners continually upgrade the facility. **Rooms:** 25 rms and effic. CI 2pm/CO 11am. Nonsmoking rms avail. Basic but clean rooms are of various sizes in 3 separate buildings. **Amenities:** 🛁 📺 A/C, cable TV, refrig. 1 unit w/terrace. **Services:** ⟲

Facilities: 🛐 🚴 Whirlpool. Screened pavilion for picnics. **Rates:** HS June 18–Sept 17 $45–$65 S or D; from $58 effic. Extra person $5. Min stay HS and wknds. Lower rates off-season. Higher rates for spec evnts/hols. Spec packages avail. Pking: Outdoor, free. Maj CC.

≣≣≣ The Refuge Motor Inn, 7058 Maddox Blvd, PO Box 378, Chincoteague, VA 23336; tel 804/336-5511 or toll free 800/544-8469; fax 804/336-6134. Va 175 E exit off US 13. Built of gray wood and appearing more like a residential condominium complex than a motel, this attractive establishment is well situated near the national wildlife refuge. Horses on property are for viewing, not riding. **Rooms:** 72 rms and effic. CI 3pm/CO 11am. Nonsmoking rms avail. All units are attractive. Suites are lovely and large and have skylights and full kitchens. **Amenities:** 🛁💧 A/C, cable TV, refrig. All units w/terraces, some w/Jacuzzis. **Services:** ⟲ Masseur, babysitting. Narrated boat cruises on Chincoteague Channel are of particular interest to bird-watchers. **Facilities:** 🛐 🚴 🛁 🏊 🚴 Lawn games, sauna, whirlpool, playground, washer/dryer. Excellent year-round pool area. Fast-food outlet next door. **Rates:** HS June 10–Sept 4 $80–$95 S or D; from $160 effic. Extra person $8. Children under 12 stay free. Min stay wknds. Lower rates off-season. Higher rates for spec evnts/hols. Pking: Outdoor, free. Maj CC.

≣ Sea Hawk Motel, 6250 Maddox Blvd, Chincoteague, VA 23336; tel 804/336-6527. Exit US 13 at Va 175 E. Although the decor is dated, this roadside motel is clean and well maintained. **Rooms:** 28 rms and effic; 3 ctges/villas. CI 2pm/CO 11am. Basic motel units and very large efficiencies are decorated in 1960s earth tones and adorned with bright paintings and prints. **Amenities:** 🛁 📺 A/C, satel TV, refrig. **Services:** ⟲ Babysitting. **Facilities:** 🛐 🚴 Playground. **Rates:** HS June 10–Sept 8 $60 S or D; from $62 effic. Extra person $5. Min stay wknds and spec evnts. Lower rates off-season. Pking: Outdoor, free. Maj CC. Cottages/villas rent by week only ($475/wk).

≣≣ Sea Shell Motel, 3720 Willow St, Chincoteague, VA 23336; tel 804/336-6589. Va 175 E exit off US 13. Although older, this is a comfortable, neat, and clean motel. **Rooms:** 40 rms and effic; 6 ctges/villas. CI 1pm/CO 11am. Nonsmoking rms avail. Units were recently redecorated. Efficiencies are home-like and spacious, with large eat-in kitchens. **Amenities:** 🛁 📺 A/C, cable TV, refrig. **Services:** ⟲ Babysitting. **Facilities:** 🛐 🚴 Picnic tables sit on a deck under trees. **Rates:** HS June 17–Sept 6 $58–$62 S or D. Extra person $4. Children under 1 stay free. Min stay wknds and spec evnts. Lower rates off-season. Pking: Outdoor, free. Maj CC. Cottages/villas and efficiencies rent by week only (from $425/wk).

≣≣ Sunrise Motor Inn, 4491 Chicken City Rd, PO Box 185, Chincoteague, VA 23336; tel 804/336-6671; fax 804/336-1226.

Exit US 13 at Va 175 E. This simple, attractive motel is exceptionally clean and neat. **Rooms:** 24 rms and effic. CI 2pm/CO 11am. **Amenities:** ⛉ A/C, cable TV, refrig. **Services:** 🛎 **Facilities:** 🏊 Pool has a slide for kids. Screened pavilion, grills, and picnic tables on the lawn. **Rates:** HS June 12–Sept 8 $62 S or D. Extra person $6. Children under 12 stay free. Min stay wknds. Lower rates off-season. Pking: Outdoor, free. Maj CC. Efficiencies rent by week only (from $500/wk).

≣≣≣ **Waterside Motor Inn**, 3761 S Main St, PO Box 347, Chincoteague, VA 23336; tel 804/336-3434; fax 804/336-1878. Exit US 13 at Va 175 E. Located on the waterway. **Rooms:** 45 rms and effic. CI 2:30pm/CO 11am. Nonsmoking rms avail. All rooms have nice views of boats and sunsets; the higher the floor, the better the view. **Amenities:** ⛉💆📺 A/C, cable TV w/movies, refrig. All units w/terraces. Deluxe rooms have VCRs. **Services:** 🛎 Babysitting. **Facilities:** 🏊🚤⚓🛥️🎾♿ Spa, whirlpool. Pool located beside the waterway. Pier with boat slips available for boating and windsurfing. Very pretty solarium with Jacuzzi and exercise equipment has water view. Picnic tables by the water. **Rates:** HS June 10–Oct 11 $85–$135 S or D. Extra person $5. Children under 12 stay free. Min stay HS. Lower rates off-season. Pking: Outdoor, free. Maj CC. Efficiencies rent by week only (from $500/wk).

Inn

≣≣≣ **Channel Bass Inn**, 6228 Church St, Chincoteague, VA 23336; tel 804/336-6148 or toll free 800/249-0818. Exit US 13 at Va 175 E; turn left at light, then right on Church St. This Victorian house has been carefully restored inside, with beautiful public areas. Innkeeper is a noted master chef whose dining room is widely known for fine cuisine. Unsuitable for children under 10. **Rooms:** 5 rms and stes. CI 3pm/CO noon. No smoking. Very attractive rooms have high-quality furnishings and period decor. **Amenities:** 💆 A/C, bathrobes. No phone or TV. **Services:** ✗ Babysitting. Cooking classes offered. **Facilities:** 1 rst (*see also* "Restaurants" below), guest lounge. **Rates:** HS May–Nov $85 S or D; from $185 ste. Min stay wknds and spec evnts. Lower rates off-season. MAP rates avail. Spec packages avail. Pking: Outdoor, free. Ltd CC.

Restaurants 🍴

♟ **Channel Bass Inn**, 6228 Church St, Chincoteague; tel 804/336-6148. Exit US 13 at Va 175 E; turn left at light, then right on Church St. **International.** A master chef serves up fine food in the dining room of this Victorian-era house, now an inn with period furniture and especially attractive public areas. Reservations are essential, since no more than 18 diners are served each evening. Prices are high, but the experience is exceptional. The

chef blends Spanish and other cuisines in unique combinations and teaches a cooking school, whose participants stay in the inn. **FYI:** Reservations recommended. Dress code. Beer and wine only. No smoking. **Open:** Daily 6:30–8:30pm. Closed some hols. **Prices:** Main courses $30–$42. Ltd CC. ♥

⑤ **Etta's Family Restaurant**, East Side Dr at Assateague Channel, Chincoteague; tel 804/336-5644. Exit US 13 at Va 175 E. **American/Seafood.** A friendly staff and pretty view of passing boats make this simple, bright waterfront room a nice family dining choice. Traditional dishes, plus small-appetite selections for children and adults 60 and over. **FYI:** Reservations accepted. Children's menu. No liquor license. **Open:** HS July–Aug lunch daily 11am–5pm; dinner daily 5–9pm; brunch Sun 11am–2pm. Reduced hours off-season. Closed Columbus Day–Apr 1. **Prices:** Main courses $9–$16. Ltd CC. 🍽🏔🍴💳♿

Landmark Crab House, in Landmark Plaza, N Main St, Chincoteague; tel 804/336-5552. Exit US 13 at Va 175 E. **Seafood/Steak.** Hatch-cover tables and red accents adorn this room with large windows overlooking the bay. Outdoor deck perfect for great sunsets. Seafood, especially crab, shrimp, and clams, are the big deals here, with a few beef and chicken selections. Beef is said to be of very good quality. Large salad bar. Breads are baked on premises. Adjacent Shucking House Cafe serves breakfast and lunch in an attractive pierside setting. **FYI:** Reservations recommended. Piano. Children's menu. Dress code. **Open:** HS May–Sept breakfast daily 8–11:30am; lunch daily 11:30am–3pm; dinner daily 5–10pm. Reduced hours off-season. Closed Nov–Mar. **Prices:** Main courses $11–$17. Maj CC. 🍽🏔🍴💳♿

The Village Restaurant, 6576 Maddox Blvd, Chincoteague; tel 804/336-5120. Exit US 13 at Va 175 E; turn left at light, then right onto Maddox Blvd. **American/Seafood.** Light, attractive, simple decor and traditional American entrees, with an emphasis on fresh seafood. **FYI:** Reservations accepted. Children's menu. **Open:** Daily 5–10pm. Closed Dec 25. **Prices:** Main courses $11–$16. Maj CC. ♿

Attractions 🏛

Oyster and Maritime Museum, 7125 Maddox Rd; tel 804/336-6117. On display here is a large collection of fossils, exhibits, and dioramas documenting the history of Chincoteague and the surrounding region. Also live marine specimens, films; research library. **Open:** May–Labor Day, Mon–Sat 10am–5pm, Sun noon–4pm; spring and fall, open weekends (phone for schedule). $

Assateague Island; tel 804/336-6122. A barrier island protecting Chincoteague Island from the Atlantic Ocean, Assateague Island boasts over 37 miles of primitive beaches on its east coast, the northern part of which is in Maryland. At the Virginia end, lifeguard-protected beaches at Toms Cove have bathhouses and toilet facilities. Chincoteague Island is connected to the larger barrier island by a small bridge, and to the mainland by causeways and bridges (US 13 and Va 175).

Chincoteague National Wildlife Refuge is owned and managed by the US Fish and Wildlife Service. In spring or fall, when visitors are few, the refuge offers miles of undisturbed marsh, lake, and ocean vistas with shorebirds, ponies, and other wildlife. The refuge visitor center is open all year, but hours vary seasonally. Another visitor center, at Toms Cove, is managed by the National Park Service (tel 804/336-6577).

Marguerite Henry's children's book, and later, the film, *Misty of Chincoteague,* aroused wide interest in the annual **Pony Penning and swim.** Every July, Chincoteague's wild ponies (actually stunted horses) are rounded up on the island and swim the inlet to Chincoteague. Foals are sold at auction, and the rest swim back to the island.

Birdwatchers know Assateague Island as a prime Atlantic Flyway habitat known for sightings of peregrine falcons, snow geese, great blue herons, and snowy egrets. The annual Water-fowl Week is generally held around Thanksgiving.

Outdoor activities on Assateague also include shell collecting (most productive at the tip of Toms Cove), and hiking and biking. Also on Assateague Island is the **Assateague Island National Seashore.** For more information contact Refuge Manager, Chincoteague Wildlife Refuge, PO Box 62, Chincoteague, VA 23336 (tel 804/336-5593). **Open:** Daily, year-round; hours vary, phone ahead. $$

CLIFTON
Map page M-3, C6 (NE of Manassas)

Restaurant 🍽️

The Hermitage Inn, 7134 Main St, Clifton; tel 703/266-1623. Exit 53 off I-66. Follow Va 28 S to US 29 N to Clifton Rd; turn right, then go 4½ miles south (bear right at T intersection). **Californian/French/Mediterranean.** The 2-story clapboard building dates from the mid-19th century, when this small picturesque village 5 miles south of Centreville was frequented by US presidents and other notables, who came for its warm mineral springs. Like the quaint village, the restaurant retains lots of historical ambience. New managers took over in 1994 with plans to convert 2 downstairs rooms with fireplaces into bar and lounge. Flagstone patio provides al fresco dining in fine weather. **FYI:** Reservations recommended. Dress code. **Open:**

Lunch Tues–Sat 11:30am–2:30pm; dinner Tues–Sat 6–10pm, Sun 5–9pm; brunch Sun 11:30am–3pm. **Prices:** Main courses $12.50–$23. Maj CC. 🍴 🛎️ 🔥

CLIFTON FORGE
Map page M-2, D4

Restaurant 🍽️

⑤★ **Michel Café and French Restaurant**, 424 E Ridgeway St, Clifton Forge; tel 703/862-4119. Exit 24 off I-64. **French/Seafood/Steak.** Hidden away in an old railroad town nestled in the Virginia highlands, this authentic country French cafe is outfitted with wood paneling, stucco walls, a collection of French artifacts, and window boxes full of flowers. Regular menu features backfin crab cakes, pepper steak, and Allegheny Mountains trout, but daily specials depend on fresh seasonal ingredients. Well worth a very short side trip off I-64. **FYI:** Reservations accepted. **Open:** Mon–Sat 5–9pm. Closed Dec 25. **Prices:** Main courses $8–$19. Maj CC.

Attraction 💼

Douthat State Park; tel 703/862-7200. Located 8 miles north of town; exit 27 off I-64, then go 7 miles north on Va 629. Some of Virginia's most outstanding mountain scenery can be found in this park. A 50-acre lake, stocked with trout, has a sandy swimming beach, camping, cabins, and picnic areas. A restaurant overlooks the lake. **Open:** Daily 8am–10pm. $

COLLINSVILLE
Map page M-2, E4 (S of Roanoke)

Motel 🛏️

☰☰☰ **Dutch Inn**, 633 Virginia Ave, Collinsville, VA 24078; tel 703/647-3721; fax 703/647-4857. Exit US 220 Business at Martinsville. A towering windmill stands at entrance to this motel. Close to a NASCAR speedway and the Blue Ridge Mountains, this is a popular location. Shopping nearby. **Rooms:** 150 rms, stes. Exec-level rms avail. CI 3pm/CO noon. Non-smoking rms avail. Rooms are spacious and well kept. **Amenities:** 📺 🍽️ A/C, cable TV w/movies, refrig, bathrobes. Some rooms have refrigerators. **Services:** ✗ 🛎️ 🔔 Babysitting. 24-hour coffee in lobby. **Facilities:** 🏋️ 🍴 🏊 ⛱️ 1 rst, 1 bar, sauna, whirlpool. Restaurant is a local favorite. Pool surrounded by trees. **Rates:** $48–$56 S or D; from $85 ste. Extra person $8. Children under 16 stay free. Min stay. Higher rates for spec evnts/hols. Spec packages avail. Pking: Outdoor, free. Maj CC.

COVINGTON

Map page M-2, D4

Motels 🛏

≡≡≡ Comfort Inn, 203 Interstate Dr, Covington, VA 24426; tel 703/962-2141 or toll free 800/221-2222; fax 982/965-0964. Exit 16 off I-64. Near the George Washington National Forest and Douthat State Park, both with fishing, hunting, hiking, and camping. **Rooms:** 99 rms and stes. Exec-level rms avail. CI 3pm/CO 11am. Nonsmoking rms avail. Standard rooms are in a traditional motel building. Suites in newer Executive Annex have sitting rooms. **Amenities:** 🛏 📷 🖥 A/C, cable TV w/movies, VCR. Suites have 2 TVs. **Services:** 🛏 🍴 🐾 **Facilities:** 🔥 ♨ 120 🚶 2 rsts, 1 bar (w/entertainment), whirlpool. **Rates (CP):** $54–$60 S; $62–$68 D; from $60 ste. Extra person $8. Children under 18 stay free. Spec packages avail. Pking: Outdoor, free. Maj CC.

≡≡≡ Holiday Inn Covington, I-64 and US 60, PO Box 920, Covington, VA 24426; tel 703/962-4951 or toll free 800/465-4329; fax 703/962-4951. Exit 16 off I-64. On a hillside above the interstate with a nice view of surrounding mountains. Proximity to restaurants and shopping center. **Rooms:** 79 rms. CI 2pm/CO noon. Express checkout avail. Nonsmoking rms avail. **Amenities:** 🛏 🐾 🖥 A/C, cable TV w/movies. **Services:** ✗ 🛏 🍴 🐾 **Facilities:** 🔥 225 🚶 1 rst, 1 bar. **Rates:** $52–$70 S or D. Extra person $4. Children under 18 stay free. Min stay spec evnts. Higher rates for spec evnts/hols. Spec packages avail. Pking: Outdoor, free. Maj CC.

CULPEPER

Map page M-3, C6

Motels 🛏

≡≡ Culpeper Comfort Inn, 890 Willis Lane, Culpeper, VA 22701; tel 703/825-4900; fax 703/825-4900. Intersection of US 29 and US 29 Business. An exceptionally clean and neat motel with very attractive grounds sporting pretty flowers. **Rooms:** 49 rms. CI 2pm/CO 11am. Nonsmoking rms avail. Attractive, neat, and very clean. **Amenities:** 🛏 🐾 🖥 A/C, cable TV w/movies. **Services:** 🛏 🍴 🐾 Children's program. Continental breakfast more elaborate than most. **Facilities:** 🔥 🚶 Small pool is nicely

landscaped. Walking distance to family restaurant. **Rates (CP):** $55–$62 D. Extra person $8. Higher rates for spec evnts/hols. Spec packages avail. Pking: Outdoor, free. Maj CC. $10 pet fee. AARP discounts.

≡≡ Holiday Inn, US 29 S at US 29 Bypass, PO Box 1206, Culpeper, VA 22701; tel 703/825-1253 or toll free 800/HOLIDAY; fax 703/825-7134. An older but clean and well-managed motel convenient to highway. Attractive for families on the road. Convenient to Commonwealth Park, historic Culpeper, Civil War battlefields. **Rooms:** 159 rms and stes. CI noon/CO noon. Express checkout avail. Nonsmoking rms avail. Clean, adequate-size rooms. **Amenities:** 🛏 🐾 A/C, satel TV w/movies. **Services:** ✗ 🛏 🍴 🐾 Babysitting. Visual smoke detectors available. **Facilities:** 🔥 300 🚶 1 rst, 1 bar (w/entertainment), washer/dryer. **Rates:** HS June–Oct $49–$59 S; $53–$60 D. Extra person $4. Children under 18 stay free. Lower rates off-season. Spec packages avail. Pking: Outdoor, free. Maj CC.

DANVILLE

Map page M-2, E4

Motels 🛏

≡≡ Best Western of Danville, 2121 Riverside Dr, Danville, VA 24541; tel 804/793-4000 or toll free 800/528-1234; fax 804/799-5516. Exit 58E off US 29. Built on the river, close to a major city route with restaurants, shopping malls. **Rooms:** 99 rms. Exec-level rms avail. CI noon/CO 11am. Nonsmoking rms avail. Some rooms have river views. Dark mahogany furnishings give air of solidity and repose. **Amenities:** 🛏 🐾 A/C, cable TV w/movies. Some units w/Jacuzzis. **Services:** 🍴 🐾 **Facilities:** 🔥 65 🚶 Free golf at local club. Picnic tables and a small dock on river for guests' use. **Rates (CP):** $69–$79 S or D. Extra person $5. Children under 16 stay free. Higher rates for spec evnts/hols. Spec packages avail. Pking: Outdoor, free. Maj CC.

≡≡≡ Howard Johnson Hotel, 100 Tower Dr, Danville, VA 24540; tel 804/793-2000 or toll free 800/654-2000; fax 804/792-4621. Exit 58W off US 29. Only 5 minutes from downtown and adjacent to a large shopping mall, motel sits high atop a hill overlooking highway. **Rooms:** 118 rms. Exec-level rms avail. CI 2pm/CO noon. Nonsmoking rms avail. Well-furnished and spacious rooms. **Amenities:** 🛏 🐾 A/C, cable TV w/movies. Some units w/terraces. **Services:** 🛏 🍴 **Facilities:** 🔥 150 🚶 1 rst, 1 bar, washer/dryer. **Rates:** $52–$66 S; $60–$74 D. Extra person $6. Children under 18 stay free. Min stay spec evnts. Higher rates for spec evnts/hols. Spec packages avail. Pking: Outdoor, free. Maj CC.

≣≣ **Stratford Inn**, 2500 Riverside Dr, Danville, VA 24540; tel 804/793-2500 or toll free 800/326-8455; fax 804/793-6960. This older motel in the city boasts an excellent restaurant. Easy access to downtown. **Rooms:** 160 rms and stes. CI noon/CO noon. Nonsmoking rms avail. **Amenities:** 🛏 📺 🍴 A/C, cable TV. Some units w/Jacuzzis. **Services:** ✗ 🖐 🚗 🐾 Car windshields cleaned gratis each morning, weather permitting. **Facilities:** 🏋 ⛳ 🎱 ♿ 1 rst, 1 bar (w/entertainment), whirlpool, washer/dryer. Attractive area with heated pool. Passes available to local health club. **Rates (BB):** $48–$58 S or D; from $81 ste. Extra person $5. Children under 19 stay free. Min stay spec evnts. Higher rates for spec evnts/hols. Spec packages avail. Pking: Outdoor, free. Maj CC.

Restaurant 🍴

★ **Bogies**, 927 S Main St, Danville; tel 804/793-6797. On US 86S, 1½ mi S of jct US 29/58. **American/Steak.** Bogart movies provide the theme, and dark furnishings and judicious use of reds and lighting lend an intimate cafe atmosphere. Moderate prices make this a local favorite close to downtown and hospital. Steaks featured at dinner, lighter fare at lunch. **FYI:** Reservations accepted. Piano. Children's menu. **Open:** Mon–Thurs 11am–10pm, Fri 11am–11:30pm, Sat 5–11:30pm, Sun 5–10pm. Closed Dec 25. **Prices:** Main courses $7–$14. Maj CC. 📠 ♿

Attraction 💼

Danville Museum of Fine Arts and History (Last Capitol of the Confederacy), 975 Main St; tel 804/793-5644. Notified that General Lee's forces would be unable to prevent the fall of Richmond, President Davis and the Confederate government fled to Danville. For a few weeks in the spring of 1865 this restored Victorian mansion (1857), home of Maj W T Sutherlin, served as the Confederate capitol. Part of the mansion, including the library, parlor, and the bedroom used by Davis, has been restored. The remainder of the house serves as a historical and fine arts museum, with a permanent collection that includes furniture, decorative arts, silver, textiles, and historical costumes. **Open:** Tues–Fri 10am–5pm, Sat–Sun 2–5pm. Closed some hols. Free.

DELAPLANE

Map page M-3, C6 (N of Marshall)

Attraction 💼

Sky Meadows State Park, 11012 Edmonds Lane; tel 703/592-3556. Rich in history, this peaceful 1,800-acre park on the eastern side of the Blue Ridge Mountains has rolling pastures, woodlands, and scenic vistas. The park offers only primitive hike-in campsites; hiking trails include access to the Appalachian Trail. Visitor center, nature and history programs spring–fall. **Open:** Daily 8am–dusk. $

DOSWELL

Map page M-3, D6 (N of Richmond)

For lodgings and dining, see Ashland, Carmel Church, Hanover

Attraction 💼

Paramount's Kings Dominion, Va 30 exit off I-95; tel 804/876-5000. This 400-acre family amusement park offers 44 rides and attractions and 10 live shows throughout the day. The park's star attraction is **Sky Pilot,** a flight trainer–style ride that simulates aerobatic flight maneuvers. Wild Water Canyon is a wet-and-wild ride simulating white-water rafting with all the thrills and excitement, but without the danger. Other highlights include the Shock Wave, a stand-up, looping rollercoaster; Wayne's World theme area, based on the hit movie; and Hurricane Reef, with water-based rides. Shops, restaurants. **Open:** June–Labor Day, daily (hours vary); late Mar–May and Sept–early Oct, weekends only (hours vary). $$$$

DUFFIELD

Map page M-2, E1 (E of Pennington Gap)

Attraction 💼

Natural Tunnel State Park; tel 703/940-2674. Follow signs along US 23 S and Va 871 E. An 850-foot-long tunnel, 100 feet in diameter, that was cut through a limestone ridge by Stock Creek, is accessible to the public. Other scenic features include a wide chasm between steep stone walls, surrounded by several pinnacles or "chimneys." Facilities include a visitor center, campsite, picnic grounds, an amphitheater, swimming pool, and chairlift. **Open:** Daily sunrise–sunset. $

Dulles International Airport

See Chantilly, Herndon, Reston, Sterling

Emporia

Map page M-3, E6

Motels ▤

≣≣ Hampton Inn, 1207 W Atlantic St, Emporia, VA 23847; tel 804/634-9200 or toll free 800/HAMPTON; fax 804/634-9200 ext 100. Exit 11B off I-95. Follow US 58 W for ½ mile. A clean, modern chain motel just off I-95. **Rooms:** 115 rms and stes. CI 2pm/CO 11am. Nonsmoking rms avail. Attractive deep-green carpet, floral bedspreads. **Amenities:** ☎ A/C, cable TV w/movies. **Services:** ⇨ ⇦ **Facilities:** ⅙ ₺ Restaurant adjacent. **Rates (CP):** HS June–Sept $45–$51 S or D. Children under 18 stay free. Min stay wknds. Lower rates off-season. Pking: Outdoor, free. Maj CC.

≣≣≣ Holiday Inn, 311 Florida Ave, at jct I-94 and US 58E, Emporia, VA 23847; tel 804/634-4191 or toll free 800/HOLIDAY; fax 804/634-4191. Exit 11A off I-95. A well-kept chain motel just off I-95. **Rooms:** 144 rms. CI 2pm/CO noon. Express checkout avail. Nonsmoking rms avail. Nicely appointed with teal-and-burgundy color scheme. **Amenities:** ☎ ₫ A/C, cable TV w/movies. Some units w/terraces. **Services:** ✗ ⊠ ⇨ ⇦ Babysitting. **Facilities:** ⅙ ⁊₅ ₺ 1 rst, 1 bar, playground, washer/dryer. Spacious pool area. Picnic under shade trees on grounds. **Rates:** $49–$51 S; $55–$57 D. Extra person $6. Children under 19 stay free. Spec packages avail. Pking: Outdoor, free. Maj CC.

Fairfax

Map page M-3, C6 (W of Falls Church)

Hotels ▤

≣≣ Comfort Inn University Center, 11180 Main St, at Jermantown Rd, Fairfax, VA 22030 (Fair Lakes); tel 703/591-5900 or toll free 800/221-2222; fax 703/591-5900. Exit 57A off I-66. Go 1 mile on US 50 E to Jermantown Rd.

Convenient to Fair Oaks Mall and the Patriot Center, this clean, well-managed chain motel has more than the usual facilities for such establishments. **Rooms:** 212 rms and effic. CI 3pm/CO 11am. Express checkout avail. Nonsmoking rms avail. Majority of units have full kitchens hidden by louvered walls. **Amenities:** ☎ ₫ ¶ A/C, cable TV w/movies, refrig. Some units w/Jacuzzis. Some units have Jacuzzis in bedroom area, with sliding glass window to bath. **Services:** ✗ ⊠ ⇨ ⇦ Car-rental desk, masseur, babysitting. **Facilities:** ⅙ ⁊₸ ₅₀₀ 🖥 ₺ 1 rst, 1 bar, lifeguard, games rm, beauty salon, playground, washer/dryer. Chinese restaurant on premises. Public park with tennis courts next door. **Rates (CP):** HS Mar 15–Nov 1 $65–$95 S or D; from $75 effic. Extra person $10. Children under 18 stay free. Lower rates off-season. Higher rates for spec evnts/hols. Spec packages avail. Pking: Outdoor, free. Maj CC. Weekend packages.

≣≣ Fair Oaks Courtyard by Marriott, 11220 Lee Jackson Hwy (US 50), at Jermantown Rd, Fairfax, VA 22030 (Fair Lakes); tel 703/273-6161 or toll free 800/321-2211; fax 703/273-3505. Exit 57A off I-66. Located at Fair Oaks Corporate Park. Convenient to Fair Oaks Mall and the Patriot Center, this comfortable motor hotel is built around a landscaped courtyard. Attractive lobby area has fireplace. **Rooms:** 144 rms and stes. CI 3pm/CO 1pm. Express checkout avail. Nonsmoking rms avail. Designed with business travelers in mind, rooms have large desks. 1-bed rooms have comfy easy chairs. **Amenities:** ☎ ₫ ₫ A/C, satel TV w/movies. Some units w/terraces. Long phone cords and hot-water dispensers for coffee and tea. **Services:** ⊠ ⇨ **Facilities:** ⅙ ⁊₸ ₉₀ ₺ 1 rst, 1 bar, lifeguard, whirlpool, washer/dryer. Lobby restaurant serves breakfast only. **Rates:** $76 S; $81 D; from $89 ste. Children under 18 stay free. Spec packages avail. Pking: Outdoor, free. Maj CC. Weekend packages.

≣≣ Hampton Inn, 10860 Lee Hwy, at Fairchester Dr, Fairfax, VA 22030; tel 703/385-2600 or toll free 800/HAMPTON; fax 703/385-2742. Exit 60 off I-66. Follow Va 123 S to US 29/50 W. This modern motor hotel, near Fair Oaks Mall and the Patriot Center, is within walking distance of shops and restaurants. **Rooms:** 86 rms and stes. CI 3pm/CO noon. Nonsmoking rms avail. All units are pleasantly decorated with blond wood furniture and bright fabrics. **Amenities:** ☎ ₫ ¶ A/C, satel TV w/movies. **Services:** ⊠ ⇨ **Facilities:** ⁊₸ ₃₀ ₺ **Rates (CP):** $66–$68 S; $71–$73 D; from $76 ste. Children under 18 stay free. Spec packages avail. Pking: Outdoor, free. Maj CC. Weekend packages.

≣≣≣ Hyatt Fair Lakes, 12777 Fair Lakes Circle, Fairfax, VA 22033; tel 703/818-1234 or toll free 800/233-1234; fax 703/818-3140. Exit 55 off I-66. Take Fairfax County Pkwy; N to Fair Lakes Pkwy; go east to Fair Lakes Circle. Close to Fair Oaks Mall and county government offices, this attractive modern high-rise sits in a 620-acre office park. A spacious lobby under skylights has an outdoor ambience. **Rooms:** 316 rms and stes. Exec-level rms avail. CI 3pm/CO noon. Express checkout avail. Nonsmoking rms avail. All rooms are suite-size, with dividers between sitting and sleeping areas. End units are semicircular and have floor-to-ceiling windows. All rooms have separate vanities outside shower/toilet. **Amenities:** 🛅 ⚱ 🎇 A/C, satel TV w/movies, shoe polisher. 1 unit w/Jacuzzi. Business Plan units have business center. **Services:** ✗ 🚐 🖼 ↵ ⬧ Twice-daily maid svce, children's program, babysitting. Complimentary shuttle to Fair Oaks Mall. **Facilities:** 🖻 ⚙️ 🖳 450 🖵 🕭 1 rst, 1 bar, lifeguard, spa, sauna, whirlpool. Restaurant and bars are off the lobby. Golf arranged at local courses. **Rates:** $95–$115 S; $115–$140 D; from $375 ste. Extra person $25. Children under 18 stay free. Spec packages avail. Pking: Outdoor, free. Maj CC.

🏨 **Wellesley Inn**, 10327 Lee Hwy, Fairfax, VA 22030 (Fairfax City); tel 703/359-2888 or toll free 800/444-8888; fax 703/385-9186. Exit 60 off I-66. An attractive, antique-brick building adjacent to shops and restaurants, this basic chain hotel offers clean rooms but few other facilities or services. **Rooms:** 83 rms and stes. CI 2pm/CO 11am. Express checkout avail. Nonsmoking rms avail. Pleasantly decorated with light-tone fabrics, rooms have separate vanities. All have dinette tables with 2 chairs. **Amenities:** 🛅 ⚱ 🎇 A/C, cable TV w/movies. **Services:** ✗ 🖼 ↵ ⬧ Babysitting. **Facilities:** 🕭 Adjacent Red Lobster restaurant provides limited room service. **Rates (CP):** HS Mar–Nov 1 $55–$70 S or D; from $85 ste. Children under 12 stay free. Lower rates off-season. Higher rates for spec evnts/hols. Spec packages avail. Pking: Outdoor, free. Maj CC. Weekend rates.

Motel

🏨🏨 **Holiday Inn Fairfax City**, 3535 Chain Bridge Rd, at I-66, Fairfax, VA 22030 (Fairfax City); tel 703/591-5500 or toll free 800/HOLIDAY; fax 703/591-7483. Exit 60 off I-66. Built in 1967, this brick-and-stone motel enjoys a park-like setting among shade trees and landscaped grounds. Attractive public areas with large picture windows were recently refurbished. **Rooms:** 127 rms. CI 3pm/CO noon. Nonsmoking rms avail. Furniture, carpets, and walls show age and wear, but owners plan to redecorate in 1995. King-bed rooms have full-size sofa beds. **Amenities:** 🛅 ⚱ A/C, cable TV w/movies. **Services:** ✗ 🖼 ↵ ⬧ Babysitting. Complimentary morning coffee and newspapers in lobby. Guests get discount at nearby gym. **Facilities:** 🖻 200 🕭 1 rst, 1 bar (w/entertainment), lifeguard, washer/dryer. Beautifully landscaped pool area is the highlight here. Popular with local Dallas Cowboys fans, downstairs lounge bar has billiard tables, dancing on weekends. **Rates:** $79 S or D. Extra

person $6. Children under 12 stay free. Higher rates for spec evnts/hols. Spec packages avail. Pking: Outdoor, free. Maj CC. Weekend packages.

Restaurants 🍽

Artie's, in Fairfax Circle Center, 3260 Old Lee Hwy, Fairfax (Fairfax City); tel 703/273-7600. Exit 62 off I-66. Go south on Nutley St to US 29; drive west to Fairfax Circle. **New American/Pub.** Lots of bright brass, varnished oak, and a pressed-tin ceiling make for Victorian charm, while tropical plants growing under skylights add a California touch to this neighborhood pub/restaurant. Specialties are light pasta dishes, but pub fare and grilled items also are offered. **FYI:** Reservations not accepted. Dress code. **Open:** Sun 10:30am–10pm, Mon–Thurs 11:30am–11pm, Fri–Sat 11:30am–midnight. **Prices:** Main courses $10–$16. Maj CC. 💟 🕭

Fish Stories, in the Mosby Building, 10560 Main St, Fairfax (Fairfax City); tel 703/273-1999. Exit 60 off I-66. Follow Va 123 S to North St W (becomes Main St). **Seafood.** Works by local artists are displayed on a rotating basis in this bright restaurant on the ground floor of an office building. Large picture windows look out on residential neighborhood. Fireplace in bar adds warmth in winter. Owner/chef specializes in fresh seafood, brought from as far as Alaska, in traditional sauces. Noted for chocolate desserts. Entry for people with disabilities on parking lot side of building. **FYI:** Reservations recommended. Children's menu. Dress code. **Open:** Lunch Mon–Fri 11:30am–3pm; dinner Mon–Sat 5–10pm, Sun 5–9pm; brunch Sun 11am–3pm. Closed some hols. **Prices:** Main courses $8–$16. Maj CC. 🕭

FALLS CHURCH

Map page M-3, C6

Hotel 🏨

🏨🏨🏨 **Fairview Park Marriott**, 3111 Fairview Park Dr, Falls Church, VA 22042; tel 703/849-9400. Exit 8 off I-495. Follow US 50 E to Fairview Park Dr S. This relatively new hotel, set on attractive grounds in an office park near the Capital Beltway, has impressive public areas that combine traditional furnishings with modern architectural touches. Building wraps around a multi-tiered courtyard with fountain pools. **Rooms:** 430 rms and stes. Exec-level rms avail. CI 4pm/CO noon. Express checkout avail. Nonsmoking rms avail. Comfortably furnished with business travelers in mind, each unit has large desks and comfortable easy chairs. **Amenities:** 🛅 ⚱ A/C, satel TV w/movies, voice mail. Some units w/minibars, some w/terraces. **Services:** ✗ 🖭 VP

🚐 ⛄ 🍴 ◈ Babysitting. Free shuttle to Dunn Loring metro station. Concierge level units on 2 floors enjoy attended lounge, complimentary breakfast, evening snacks. **Facilities:** 🛗 🛎 1.3K ⛓ 1 rst, 2 bars (1 w/entertainment), lifeguard, games rm, spa, sauna, whirlpool, washer/dryer. **Rates:** $125 S; $145 D; from $250 ste. Min stay wknds. Spec packages avail. Pking: Indoor, free. Maj CC. Weekend packages.

Motel

▤▤ **Best Western Falls Church Inn**, 6633 Arlington Blvd, at Annandale Rd, Falls Church, VA 22042; tel 703/532-9000 or toll free 800/336-3723; fax 703/237-0730. Exit 8 off I-495. An older but very-well-maintained motel convenient to downtown Falls Church and to discount stores at Seven Corners Shopping Center. Other shops and restaurants are within walking distance. Popular with groups. **Rooms:** 106 rms and effic. CI 1pm/CO noon. Nonsmoking rms avail. King rooms in front of building are spacious by motel standards. All units have 2 vanities. **Amenities:** 🛗 ❄ 📺 A/C, cable TV w/movies, shoe polisher. **Services:** ✗ ⛄ 🍴 Babysitting. **Facilities:** 🛗 300 1 rst, 1 bar. Mexican restaurant serves American-style breakfasts. **Rates (CP):** HS Mar 15–Sept $65–$76 S; $71–$82 D; from $76 effic. Extra person $5. Children under 18 stay free. Lower rates off-season. Spec packages avail. Pking: Outdoor, free. Maj CC.

Restaurants 🍴

Duangrat's Thai Restaurant, 5878 Leesburg Pike, Falls Church (Bailey's Cross Roads); tel 703/820-5775. W of jct Va 7/244. **Thai.** Storefront location on a busy highway belies the quiet elegance of this fine ethnic eatery offering near-gourmet cuisine at affordable prices. Specialties are whole crispy fish, delicately sweet ginger chicken, and Panang beef prepared with coconut milk. Lunch sampler plates, offered Monday to Thursday 11:30am–2:30pm, are excellent value. **FYI:** Reservations recommended. Dress code. **Open:** Sun–Thurs 11:30am–10:30pm, Fri–Sat 11:30am–11pm. Closed Thanksgiving. **Prices:** Main courses $6–$20. Maj CC.

Fortune Chinese Seafood Restaurant, in Greenforest Shopping Center, 5900 Leesburg Pike, Falls Church (Bailey's Cross Roads); tel 703/998-8888. W of jct Va 7/244. **Chinese.** A storefront restaurant with large dining room attractively decorated with Chinese paintings and furniture. Tanks hold live lobsters and crabs for seafood specialties, which draw crowds, as does dim sum served from a cart daily 11am–3pm. Often hosts large groups, such as wedding parties. **FYI:** Reservations not accepted. Dress code. **Open:** Sun–Thurs 11am–10pm, Fri–Sat 11am–11:30pm. **Prices:** Main courses $7.50–$36. Maj CC. ⛓

Haandi, in Falls Plaza Shopping Ctr, 1222 W Broad St, Falls Church (West Falls Church); tel 703/533-3501. Exit 66 off I-66. Go ½ mile on Va 7 S. **Indian.** Recessed stylized landscapes create impression of looking out onto the subcontinent's passing scene, while chandeliers add elegance to this shopping center eatery with surprisingly fine northern Indian cuisine. Booths line each wall, with well-spaced tables down the middle. Specialties are chicken and lamb kabobs. Curries are delicate and well seasoned. Reservations accepted Sunday to Thursday only. Smoking allowed at lunch. **FYI:** Reservations not accepted. Dress code. No smoking. **Open:** Lunch daily 11:30am–2:30pm; dinner Sun–Thurs 5–10pm, Fri–Sat 5–10:30pm. Closed some hols. **Prices:** Main courses $8–$14. Maj CC.

Lan's Vietnamese Restaurant, 7236 Arlington Blvd at Graham Rd, Falls Church; tel 703/204-2882. Exit 8 off I-495. Go 1 mile east on Arlington Blvd (US 50) to Graham Rd; opposite Loehmann's Plaza Shopping Center. **Vietnamese.** A small, cozy family-owned restaurant with booths on 1 side and a long row of tables on the other. Mirrors make narrow space seem larger. Home-style Vietnamese specialties include crispy noodles and seafood, grilled pork vermicelli, and low-fat chicken grilled with lemon sauce. **FYI:** Reservations recommended. **Open:** Sun–Thurs 11am–10pm, Fri–Sat 11am–11pm. **Prices:** Main courses $5–$8. Ltd CC.

Mountain Jack's, 127 E Broad St, Falls Church; tel 703/532-6500. Exit 66 off I-66. Follow Va 7 S for 1½ miles. **Seafood/Steak.** Lots of dark paneling gives a cozy feeling to this popular steak house. Booths in 1 of 3 dining areas are spacious but can be subject to noise coming from nearby bar. Regular tables are spaced closer together but are in quieter areas. Best known for prime rib and char-grilled steaks and seafood, either plain or with a variety of French-accented sauces. **FYI:** Reservations recommended. Comedy/country music/guitar. Dress code. **Open:** Lunch Mon–Fri 11:30am–2pm; dinner Mon–Thurs 5–10pm, Fri–Sat 5–11pm, Sun noon–9pm. **Prices:** Main courses $13–$19. Maj CC. ⛓

Panjshir, 924 W Broad St, Falls Church; tel 703/536-4566. Exit 66 off I-66. Go 1 mile on Va 7 S. **Afghan.** Subdued lighting, dark paneling, booths, and widely spaced tables set the mood at this small but pleasant restaurant. Very popular with local residents for its excellently prepared Afghan selections, including several kabobs and mint-accented dumplings with meat and yogurt sauce. Also at: 224 W Maple Ave, Vienna (tel 703/281-4183). **FYI:** Reservations not accepted. **Open:** Lunch Mon–Sat 11am–2pm; dinner daily 5–10pm. Closed some hols. **Prices:** Main courses $10–$13. Maj CC.

♣ �֍ **Peking Gourmet Inn**, in Culmore Shopping Center, 6029 Leesburg Pike, Falls Church (Bailey's Cross Roads); tel 703/

671-8088. ½ mi W of jct Va 7/244. **Chinese.** Photos of famous politicians, media personalities, and entertainers overwhelm the Chinese lanterns and paintings at one of the area's most popular Asian restaurants. Attracted by gourmet-quality Peking duck and other northern Chinese specialties, President Bush dined here several times while in the White House. The establishment is easily overlooked in the nondescript Culmore Shopping Center. **FYI:** Reservations recommended. Dress code. **Open:** Sun–Thurs 11am–10:30pm, Fri–Sat 11am–midnight. Closed Thanksgiving. **Prices:** Main courses $7.50–$24; PF dinner $22–$30. Maj CC.

Attraction 📷

The Falls Church, 115 E Fairfax St; tel 703/532-7600. This church was reconstructed in 1959 according to the original plans of the 1732 church building. The original building was used as a recruiting center during the Revolution and as a hospital during the Civil War. **Open:** Sun–Fri; call for hours. Closed some hols. Free.

FARMVILLE

Map page M-3, D5

Motel 🛏

≣≣ **Days Inn**, US 15 and US 460 Bypass, Farmville, VA 23901; tel 804/392-6611 or toll free 800/DAYS-INN; fax 804/392-9774. Built of brick in 1990, this clean, efficiently run motel is convenient to Longwood College and within walking distance of restaurants and shops. **Rooms:** 60 rms. CI 2pm/CO 11am. Nonsmoking rms avail. Standard motel rooms spiffed up with bright floral spreads. **Amenities:** 📞 ⌁ A/C, cable TV w/movies. **Services:** ⌁ 🍴 **Facilities:** 🛗 🏊 ⚘ **Rates (CP):** $46 S; $51 D. Extra person $5. Children under 18 stay free. Higher rates for spec evnts/hols. Pking: Outdoor, free. Maj CC.

FOREST

Map page M-2, D4 (W of Lynchburg)

Attraction 📷

Poplar Forest, Country Rd 661; tel 804/525-1806. Called "Thomas Jefferson's other home," Poplar Forest was at one time the seat of a 4,800-acre plantation that was a main source of Jefferson's income. In 1806, while he was president, Jefferson assisted the masons in laying the foundation for the dwelling, which he had also designed.

Opened to the public in 1985, the octagonal Poplar Forest is currently the subject of an archeological and architectural research project. Visitors are able to see relics from the building and grounds as they are discovered and exhibited. **Open:** Apr–Nov, Wed–Sun 10am–4pm. Closed Dec–Mar. $$

FREDERICKSBURG

Map page M-3, C6

See also Spotsylvania

Hotel 🛏

≣≣ **Comfort Inn Southpoint**, 5422 Jefferson Davis Hwy, Fredericksburg, VA 22407; tel 703/898-5550 or toll free 800/221-2222; fax 703/891-2861. Exit 126 off I-95 S, or exit 126B off I-95 N. A modern motel in the Massaponax Outlet Shopping Center. Within walking distance of shops and restaurants. **Rooms:** 125 rms. CI 3pm/CO noon. Nonsmoking rms avail. Rooms have light, attractive walls and carpets, coordinated spreads and drapes. Colonial-style furniture and pictures of Fredericksburg historic buildings add atmosphere. **Amenities:** 📞 A/C, cable TV w/movies. **Services:** ⌁ 🍴 Guests receive discounts at outlet shops. **Facilities:** 🛗 ⚿ 🏊 ⚘ Sauna, steam rm, whirlpool. **Rates (CP):** HS June–Aug $37–$60 S; $42–$86 D. Extra person $6. Children under 18 stay free. Lower rates off-season. Pking: Outdoor, free. Maj CC.

Motels

≣≣ **Best Western Johnny Appleseed Inn**, 543 Warrenton Rd (US 17 N), Fredericksburg, VA 22406; tel 703/373-0000 or toll free 800/633-6443; fax 703/377-5676. Exit 133B off I-95. Although area around motel is paved, property has 15 acres and backs on woods. Convenient to historic district. Lobby is uninspired but clean. **Rooms:** 88 rms. CI 2pm/CO noon. Nonsmoking rms avail. Clean, with motel-style furniture. **Amenities:** 📞 A/C, cable TV w/movies, VCR. **Services:** ⌁ 🍴 ⌁ Coffee and tea in lobby. **Facilities:** 🛗 🏊 1 rst, playground, washer/dryer. Tent for gatherings. **Rates:** HS May–Sept $36 S; $42 D. Extra person $8. Children under 18 stay free. Lower rates off-season. Spec packages avail. Pking: Outdoor, free. Maj CC. AARP discount.

≣≣ **Econo Lodge**, I-95 and Va 3 W, Fredericksburg, VA 22404; tel 703/786-8374 or toll free 800/424-4777; fax 703/786-8811. Exit 130B off I-95. Drive west on Va 3 to 1st light. A small, inexpensive, and friendly motel with old and new buildings. Quiet location away from the highway, which can be difficult to find (it's next to a Ramada Inn). Aunt Sarah's Pancake

House is next door. Other restaurants and large mall with movie theater are nearby. **Rooms:** 96 rms. CI 11am/CO 11am. Nonsmoking rms avail. Rooms in new wing have bright new furniture; those in original building are nondescript. **Amenities:** 🛁 A/C, cable TV. **Services:** 🛎 Babysitting. **Facilities:** 🔥 **Rates (CP):** HS June–Aug $32–$37 S; $36–$43 D. Extra person $5. Children under 18 stay free. Lower rates off-season. Pking: Outdoor, free. Maj CC.

≣≣ Hampton Inn, 2310 William St, at I-95, Fredericksburg, VA 22401; tel 703/371-0330 or toll free 800/426-7866; fax 703/371-1753. Exit 130A off I-95. Located in commercial area with many nearby shops, restaurants, beauty salon. Convenient to historic district and large mall. Central courtyard has minimal shrubs and other plants. **Rooms:** 166 rms. CI 3pm/CO noon. Nonsmoking rms avail. Clean, with soft color schemes. **Amenities:** 🛁 A/C, cable TV w/movies. Some units w/minibars. **Services:** 🛎 🛎 **Facilities:** 🔥 🏊 🔥 Washer/dryer. Fenced, well-landscaped pool area. **Rates (CP):** HS Apr–Oct $43–$47 S; $48–$54 D. Children under 19 stay free. Lower rates off-season. Higher rates for spec evnts/hols. Spec packages avail. Pking: Outdoor, free. Maj CC.

≣≣≣ Holiday Inn North, 564 Warrenton Rd (US 17 N), Fredericksburg, VA 22405; tel 703/371-5550 or toll free 800/HOLIDAY; fax 703/373-3641. Exit 133B off I-95 N, or exit 133 off I-95 S. Attractive, well-maintained motel surrounded by extensive plantings. Lobby furnished with colonial reproductions. Convenient to historic district. **Rooms:** 148 rms. CI 2pm/CO noon. Express checkout avail. Nonsmoking rms avail. Clean, fresh rooms have pleasingly soft color scheme. **Amenities:** 🛁 🏊 A/C, satel TV w/movies, refrig, VCR. Some units w/terraces, some w/Jacuzzis. Refrigerators and microwaves available. **Services:** ✗ 🛄 🛎 🛎 Babysitting. Will help arrange airport transfers. **Facilities:** 🔥 🏊 🔥 1 rst, 1 bar (w/entertainment), washer/dryer. Attractive pool area surrounded by motel units. Bar can be noisy. **Rates:** HS Apr–Oct $50–$62 S; $47–$67 D. Extra person $7. Children under 12 stay free. Lower rates off-season. Higher rates for spec evnts/hols. Spec packages avail. Pking: Outdoor, free. Maj CC.

≣≣ Holiday Inn South, 5324 Jefferson Davis Hwy, Fredericksburg, VA 22408; tel 703/898-1102 or toll free 800/465-4239; fax 703/898-2017. Exit 126 off I-95. Flower beds help brighten entrance to this motel near Massaponax Outlet Shopping Center. Convenient to historic district, Mary Washington College, and nearby restaurants and shops. **Rooms:** 198 rms. CI 3pm/CO noon. Express checkout avail. Nonsmoking rms avail. Although somewhat dark, rooms are fairly well decorated, with color-coordinated curtains and spreads. **Amenities:** 🛁 🏊 A/C, cable TV w/movies. **Services:** ✗ 🛄 🛎

🛎 Babysitting. **Facilities:** 🔥 🛺 🏊 🖥 🔥 1 rst, 1 bar (w/entertainment), games rm, spa, sauna, steam rm, whirlpool, washer/dryer. **Rates:** HS June–Aug $40–$65 S; $60–$65 D. Extra person $6. Children under 18 stay free. Lower rates off-season. Spec packages avail. Pking: Outdoor, free. Maj CC.

Inns

≣≣ Fredericksburg Colonial Inn, 1707 Princess Anne St, Fredericksburg, VA 22401; tel 703/371-5666. White picket fence and blue awning and shutters give this curved, 2-story white structure a Civil War–era appearance. The mood continues inside, where there are mid-19th-century furnishings and a wide staircase that leads from the lobby to a landing with 2 grandfather clocks and then on to the 2nd floor. **Rooms:** 30 rms, stes, and effic. CI 2pm/CO 11am. Each unit is differently decorated: mostly Victorian furniture among some Empire and Early American. Civil War pictures adorn walls. **Amenities:** 🛁 🏊 A/C, cable TV, refrig. **Services:** 🛎 🛎 Babysitting. **Facilities:** 🏊 🔥 Guest lounge w/TV. **Rates (CP):** $55 S or D; from $65 ste; from $70 effic. Children under 13 stay free. Spec packages avail. Pking: Outdoor, free. Ltd CC.

≣≣≣ Kenmore Inn, 1200 Princess Anne St, Fredericksburg, VA 22401 (Old Town); tel 703/371-7622 or toll free 800/437-7622; fax 703/371-5480. Exit 130B off I-95. Take William St (Va 3) E to Charles St, turn left, go 2 blocks to Lewis St, turn right. Local residents like to relax on white wicker furniture on the long front porch of this 1796 house, located on a tree-lined street in the historic district. Unsuitable for children under 18. **Rooms:** 12 rms and stes. CI 2pm/CO noon. All rooms are large, and each is individually decorated in colonial style. Cozy corner sitting area has table with 2 glasses and decanter of sherry. **Amenities:** 🛁 🏊 A/C. Some units w/fireplaces. **Services:** ✗ 🚐 🛄 🛎 Babysitting, afternoon tea and wine/sherry served. Masseur on call. **Facilities:** 🏊 🔥 3 rsts, 2 bars (1 w/entertainment), washer/dryer, guest lounge w/TV. Dining room is one of finest places to eat in Fredericksburg, with outdoor seating in good weather. Small bar in lounge, pub on lower level. **Rates:** $85–$150 S or D; from $125 ste. Extra person $10. Min stay. AP and MAP rates avail. Spec packages avail. Ltd CC.

≣≣≣≣ Richard Johnston Inn, 711 Caroline St, Fredericksburg, VA 22401 (Old Town); tel 703/899-7606. Exit 130B off I-95. Go east on William St (Va 3) to downtown; follow signs to Fredericksburg Visitors Center. Near the Rappahannock River in the heart of Old Town Fredericksburg opposite the visitor center, this antique-laden 18th-century house is a convenient place to stay for those in search of a quiet, restful retreat. The Old Town trolley stops in front and can take you to historical buildings, antique and other shops, and interesting restaurants. Unsuitable for children under 12. **Rooms:** 9 rms and stes. CI 2pm/CO 11am. No smoking. Clean, comfortable rooms furnished with period furniture, including upholstered chairs and sofas, lovely canopy beds; 2 suites on lower level open to terrace. **Amenities:** A/C. No phone or TV. Some units w/minibars, some w/terraces. **Services:** Afternoon tea served. Continental breakfast served in beautiful dining room. **Facilities:** Guest lounge w/TV. **Rates:** $90–$115 S or D; from $130 ste. Extra person $10. Min stay spec evnts. Pking: Outdoor, free. Ltd CC.

Resort

Sheraton Inn Fredericksburg Conference Center, 2801 Plank Rd, PO Box 618, Fredericksburg, VA 22404; tel 703/786-8321 or toll free 800/682-1049; fax 703/786-3957. Exit 130A off I-95. Go west on Va 3 to first light. 310 acres. Extensive plantings throughout the grounds are a pleasing touch at this resort convenient to historic district, Mary Washington College. **Rooms:** 196 rms and stes. CI 2pm/CO noon. Express checkout avail. Nonsmoking rms avail. Nicely appointed, well-coordinated rooms have colonial-style furniture. **Amenities:** A/C, cable TV w/movies. All units w/terraces, 1 w/Jacuzzi. Some rooms have patios with table and chairs. **Services:** Twice-daily maid svce, car-rental desk, babysitting. Rental cars delivered to hotel. Food can be ordered from pool area. Masseur planned. **Facilities:** 18 1 2K 1 rst, 2 bars (1 w/entertainment), lifeguard, games rm, playground. Restaurant has large informal patio for outdoor dining in good weather. Planned additions include health club, beauty salon, day-care center. **Rates:** HS Apr–Nov $80–$105 S; $90–$115 D; from $150 ste. Extra person $10. Children under 18 stay free. Lower rates off-season. Spec packages avail. Pking: Outdoor, free. Maj CC.

Restaurants

La Petite Auberge, 311 William St (Va 3), Fredericksburg; tel 703/371-2727. Exit 130B off I-95. Between Charles and Princess Anne Sts. **French/European.** An attractive garden-like setting with cushioned metal chairs, brick walls, and many oil paintings, including some by local artists. Chef is very innovative. Curried chicken salad is especially good. Crabmeat selections and smoked trout with local sweet-red-pepper jelly lead dinner list. **FYI:** Reservations recommended. **Open:** Lunch Mon–Sat 11:30am–2:30pm; dinner Mon–Sat 5:30–10pm. Closed some hols. **Prices:** Main courses $7.95–$19.95. Maj CC.

Le Lafayette, 623 Caroline St, Fredericksburg; tel 703/373-6895. Exit 130B off I-95. Follow Va 3 (William St) east into downtown. **Regional American/French.** Lovely old house with colonial touches, including wide moldings, chair rails, Windsor-style chairs, large windows, plank floors, and period colors and wallpaper. Limited menu of traditional French fare is augmented by daily specials announced by wait staff. **FYI:** Reservations recommended. Dress code. **Open:** Lunch Tues–Sun 11:30am–3pm; dinner Tues–Sun 5:30–10:30pm; brunch Sun 11:30am–3pm. Closed some hols. **Prices:** Main courses $12–$22; PF dinner $13. Maj CC.

Sammy T's, 801 Caroline St at Hanover St, Fredericksburg; tel 703/371-2008. Exit 130B off I-95. Follow Va 3 (William St) east into downtown. **American/Middle Eastern/Vegetarian.** Tavern decor prevails, with mirror-backed bar running the length of wall. Seating is all high wooden booths. Wood walls painted white sport travel posters. Ceiling is old-fashioned metal. Soups, sandwiches, salads, and other light food, plus some entrees. A friendly neighborhood-style pub with regular local clientele. **FYI:** Reservations not accepted. Dress code. Beer and wine only. **Open:** Mon–Sat 7:30am–midnight, Sun 7:30am–9pm. Closed some hols. **Prices:** Main courses $4.50–$8. Ltd CC.

Santa Fe Grill and Saloon, 216 William St, Fredericksburg; tel 703/371-0500. Exit 130B off I-95. Follow Va 3 (William St) east into downtown. **Southwestern/Tex-Mex.** An eye-catching, red-and-black storefront establishment with western decor suits its southwestern and Tex-Mex entrees, all prepared fresh on premises. Good choice for families or anyone young at heart. **FYI:** Reservations accepted. Dress code. **Open:** HS Easter–Thanksgiving Mon–Thurs 11:30am–10pm, Fri–Sat 11:30am–11pm, Sun noon–8:30pm. Reduced hours off-season. Closed Dec 25. **Prices:** Main courses $7–$14. Maj CC.

Shoney's Family Restaurant, 2203 William St (Va 3), Fredericksburg; tel 703/371-5400. Exit 130A off I-95. Follow Va 3 W. **American.** Real and plastic plants and a tan-brown-green color scheme are the decor at this chain restaurant, featuring a well-lit buffet area. Large selection of items aimed at satisfying a family's tastes. **FYI:** Reservations not accepted. Children's menu. No liquor license. **Open:** Sun–Thurs 6am–midnight, Fri–Sat 6am–3am. Closed Dec 25. **Prices:** Main courses $6–$8. Maj CC.

The Smythe's Cottage and Tavern, 303 Fauquier St, Fredericksburg; tel 703/373-1645. Exit 130B off I-95. Follow Va 3 (William St) east into downtown. **Regional American/Continental/Southern Colonial.** A white picket fence surrounds this small white cottage with blue trim, which sits under large trees. Colonial decor inside is accompanied by traditional southern-style fare, such as fresh crab cakes, biscuits served with country ham. Friendly staff adds to warm tavern-like feeling. **FYI:** Reservations recommended. Children's menu. **Open:** Mon–

Thurs 11am–9pm, Fri–Sat 11am–10pm, Sun noon–9pm. Closed some hols. **Prices:** Main courses $9.95–$15. Ltd CC. ● ▮ ⬙ ▣

Sophia Street Station, 503 Sophia St, Fredericksburg; tel 703/371-3355. **Continental.** Lots of railroad memorabilia in one small dining area and lounge of this old riverfront station. Trains are etched into mirror over bar. A club car room hosts more formal dining, while main dining room, with dark flowered vinyl tablecloths and plastic floral arrangements, has less ambience. House special is prime rib, but menu contains range of entrees, burgers, sandwiches, and salads. **FYI:** Reservations recommended. Guitar. Children's menu. Dress code. **Open:** Mon–Tues 11:30am–midnight, Wed–Sat 11:30am–2am, Sun 10am–11pm. **Prices:** Main courses $8–$15. Maj CC. ▦ ♥ ⅊

Attractions ▦

Fredericksburg Area Museum and Cultural Center, 907 Princess Anne St; tel 703/371-5668. The museum occupies the 1816 Town Hall, located in Market Square. The 1st floor houses temporary exhibits relating to regional and cultural history; permanent exhibits on the 2nd floor cover Native American history all the way through the modern era, along with audiovisual presentations and crafts demonstrations. Symposiums are also held. On the 3rd floor, the hall's 19th-century council chamber is another area used for changing exhibits. **Open:** Mar–Nov, Mon–Sat 9am–5pm, Sun 1–5 pm; Dec–Feb, Mon–Sat 10am–4pm, Sun 1–4pm. Closed some hols. $

James Monroe Museum and Memorial Library, 908 Charles St; tel 703/889-4559. This low brick building commemorates Monroe's life and times. He came to Fredericksburg in 1786 to practice law and went on to hold a number of public offices before becoming 5th president of the United States. His shingle hangs outside the building, which is furnished with pieces from the Monroes' White House years or their retirement home.

The museum contains 2 Rembrandt Peale portraits of Monroe and such personal items as the formal attire he wore as US ambassador to the court of Napoleon, his dueling pistols, and his wife's wedding slippers. Monroe was the only US president besides Washington who fought in the Revolution, and he shared the grim winter at Valley Forge. Among the items on display are the gun and canteen he carried into battle. The library of some 10,000 books is a reconstruction of Monroe's own personal collection. Guided tours are given throughout the day and informative videos are available. **Open:** Mar–Nov, daily 9am–5pm; Dec–Feb, daily 10am–4pm. Closed some hols. $

Hugh Mercer Apothecary Shop, 1020 Caroline St; tel 703/373-3362. Dr Hugh Mercer practiced medicine and operated this shop from 1761 to 1776, before giving his life as a Revolutionary War brigadier general. Presented in a living history format, tours are conducted by Mercer's "house wench," a guide in period costume, who discusses colonial medicinal practices and surgical techniques. Medical implements of the era are introduced, which include bleeding devices, a tooth key, and amputation instruments. The downstairs apothecary displays medicinal herbs and other potions commonly dispensed in the 18th century. The herbs are grown on site in the physic garden, which is open to the public; signs describe the plants and explain their uses. **Open:** Mar–Nov, daily 9am–5pm; Dec–Feb, daily 10am–4pm. Closed some hols. $

Rising Sun Tavern, 1304 Caroline St; tel 703/371-1494. This was originally a residence, built in 1760 by Charles Washington, George's youngest brother. From the 1790s it served as a tavern for 30 years. The building has been restored, not reconstructed, although the 17th-and 18th-century furnishings are not all originals. The 30-minute tour provides many insights into colonial life, and includes the Great Room, the ladies' retiring room, the taproom, and the bedrooms, including a room where Lafayette once stayed. The tavern's original license is displayed in the downstairs hall. **Open:** Mar–Nov, daily 9am–5pm; Dec–Feb, daily 10am–4pm. Closed some hols. $

St George's Episcopal Church, 905 Princess Anne St; tel 703/373-4133. Martha Washington's father and John Paul Jones's brother are buried in the graveyard of this church. Members of the first parish congregation included Mary Washington and Revolutionary War generals Hugh Mercer and George Weedon. The original church was built in 1732; the current Romanesque structure (which boasts 3 signed Tiffany windows) was completed in 1849. During the Battle of Fredericksburg the church was hit at least 25 times, and in 1863 it was used by General Lee's troops for religious revival meetings. In 1864, when wounded Union soldiers filled every available building in town, it was used as a hospital. **Open:** Mon–Sat 9am–5pm (subject to availability); Sun services at 8 and 10:30am. Free.

The Presbyterian Church, 810 Princess Anne St; tel 703/373-7057. This Presbyterian church dates to the early 1800s, though the present Greek revival building was completed in 1855. Like St George's, it served as a hospital during the Civil War. Cannonballs in the front left pillar and scars on the walls of the loft and belfry remain to this day. The present church bell replaced one that was given to the Confederacy to be melted down for making cannons. **Open:** Mon–Sat 8:30am–4pm, Sun service at 11am (summer, 10am). Free.

Masonic Lodge Number 4, Princess Anne and Hanover Sts; tel 703/373-5885. Not only is this the mother lodge of the father of our country, it's also one of the oldest Masonic lodges in

America, established, it is believed, around 1735. Although the original building was down the street, the Masons have been meeting at this address since 1812. On display are a silver punchbowl used to serve Lafayette, a Gilbert Stuart portrait of Washington in its original gilt federalist frame, and the 1668 Bible on which Washington took his Masonic obligation (oath). Tours are given throughout the day. **Open:** Mon–Sat 9am–4pm, Sun 1–4pm. Closed some hols. $

Fredericksburg and Spotsylvania National Military Park, 1013 Lafayette Blvd; tel 703/373-6122. This national park preserves the memory of the tragic engagements that took place in 1863–64, when the Union armies attempted to break through the stalwart fortifications at Fredericksburg and reach the capital of the Confederacy at Richmond.

A self-guided driving tour of the park begins at the **Fredericksburg Battlefield Visitor Center.** The tour includes 16 sites relating to 4 major battles that were fought in the vicinity. The center offers tour brochures, museum displays, and a 12-minute slide show orientation. Tapes and tape players are available for rent that give audio tours describing each battle in detail.

In the Battle of Fredericksburg (Dec 11–15, 1862) Union Gen Ambrose E Burnside's invading force of 110,000 troops engaged the smaller, but better-situated army of Gen Robert E Lee and was crushed by Lee's entrenched Confederates.

At the Battle of Chancellorsville (May 1–4, 1863) Lee was again victorious, this time defeating Gen Joseph Hooker. The Confederate victory was costly; among the many casualties was Gen "Stonewall" Jackson who died several days later at a nearby plantation house at Guinea Station. A recording and signs at the house tell of Jackson's final days (get further info at the Visitor Center).

The first encounter between Lee and Gen Ulysses S Grant was the Battle of the Wilderness (May 5–6, 1864). When the 2 armies had battled to a stalemate, Grant ordered his troops to circle around Lee's firmly dug-in defenses, and move on toward Richmond.

Lee and Grant met again 2 days later, at the Battle of Spotsylvania Court House (May 8–21, 1864). Once again Grant charged around Lee's flank and raced on toward Richmond. Grant's successful flanking campaign proved to be the first in a series of battles that eventually crippled Lee's formidable Army of Northern Virginia.

Further information requests can be directed to Fredericksburg and Spotsylvania National Military Park, 120 Chatham Lane, Fredericksburg, VA 22405 (tel 703/371-0802). **Open:** Visitor Center, daily 9am–5pm; extended hours in summer. Closed some hols. Free.

The Courthouse, Princess Anne and George Sts; tel 703/372-1066. Fans of architecture will appreciate a short visit to this building. Designed by James Renwick, who also designed New York's St Patrick's Cathedral as well as the Renwick Gallery and the original Smithsonian "Castle" in Washington, DC, this Gothic revival courthouse was built 1853 and is still used for that purpose. **Open:** Mon–Fri 8am–4pm. Free.

Mary Washington House, 1200 Charles St; tel 703/373-1569. George Washington purchased this house for his mother, Mary Ball Washington, in 1772. She was 62 years old and had been living at nearby Ferry Farm since 1739. Lafayette paid his respects to Mary Washington here during the Revolution. In 1789 Washington received his mother's blessing before going to New York to be inaugurated as president. He did not see her again; she died later that year. Hostesses in colonial garb give 30-minute tours throughout the day. **Open:** Mar–Nov, daily 9am–5pm; Dec–Feb, daily 10am–4pm. $$

Belmont, 224 Washington St; tel 703/899-4860. Situated on 27 hillside acres overlooking the falls of the Rappahannock River, Belmont began as an 18th-century farmhouse (the central 6 rooms of the house date to the 1790s) and was enlarged to a 22-room mansion by a later owner. Tours (about 1 hour) are given throughout the day. The house is furnished with art treasures, family heirlooms, and European antiques of American artist Gari Melchers, who lived here from 1916 until his death in 1932. There are many wonderful paintings in the house, including works by Brueghel, Rodin, and Melchers himself. **Open:** Apr–Sept, Mon–Sat 10am–5pm, Sun 1–5pm; Oct–Mar, Mon–Sat 10am–4pm, Sun 1–4pm. Closed some hols. $

Chatham, 120 Chatham Lane; tel 703/373-4461. This pre-Revolutionary mansion, built between 1768 and 1771 by wealthy planter William Fitzhugh, has figured prominently in American history. A fourth-generation American, Fitzhugh was an important supporter and financier of the Revolution. During the Civil War, the house, then belonging to J Horace Lacy, served as headquarters for Federal commanders and as a Union field hospital. Lincoln visited the house twice, and Walt Whitman and Clara Barton cared for the wounded here. Self-guided tours include 5 rooms of the house, and plaques on the grounds that identify battle landmarks. **Open:** Daily 9am–5pm. Closed some hols. Free.

Kenmore, 1201 Washington Ave; tel 703/373-3381. This mid-18th-century Georgian mansion was built for Betty Washington (George's sister) by her husband, Fielding Lewis, one of the wealthiest planters in Fredericksburg. The original plantation covered nearly 1,300 acres and produced tobacco, grains, and flax. Today the house is meticulously restored to its colonial appearance. All of the woodwork and paneling are original, as are the molded plaster ceilings and cornices. The authentic period furnishings include several Lewis family pieces. The tour winds up in the kitchen, where spiced tea and gingerbread (Mary Washington's recipe, the same she served to Lafayette in 1784) are served. **Open:** Mar–Nov, daily 9am–5pm; Dec–Feb, daily 10am–4pm. $$

FRONT ROYAL

Map page M-3, C5

Hotel 🛏

≡≡≡ **Quality Inn Skyline Drive**, 10 Commerce Ave, Front Royal, VA 22630; tel 703/635-3161. Exit 6 off I-66 W, or exit 13 off I-66 E. A nicely turned-out hotel with interesting decorating touches in rooms and efficient and inviting facilities, from the gift shop to the bar. **Rooms:** 107 rms. CI 1pm/CO 11am. Nonsmoking rms avail. All king rooms have pull-out sofas. Some rooms have wood trim, a half-timbered look, and mahogany furnishings, a distinctive touch. **Amenities:** 🛎 ☊ A/C, cable TV w/movies. Microwaves and refrigerators in 25% of rooms. **Services:** ✕ ⊠ ⊋ Turndown service on request. **Facilities:** 🛠 🦞 📺 1 rst, 1 bar (w/entertainment). Nice restaurant, with entertainment at piano bar. **Rates (CP):** HS Sept–Oct $55–$75 S or D. Extra person $9. Children under 18 stay free. Lower rates off-season. Spec packages avail. Pking: Outdoor, free. Maj CC. Special golf and ski packages available.

Motels

≡ **Scottish Inn**, 533 S Royal Ave, Front Royal, VA 22630; tel 703/636-6168 or toll free 800/251-1962; fax 703/636-3120. Exit 13 off I-66. A basic, clean, no-frills facility offering a modest rate. Reserve early during October. **Rooms:** 20 rms. CI open/CO 11am. Nonsmoking rms avail. **Amenities:** 🛎 A/C, cable TV w/movies. Irons available at desk. Roll-away beds for $4. **Services:** ⊋ ⊲ **Facilities:** Copy machine in lobby. **Rates:** HS July–Oct $40–$48 S or D. Extra person $4. Children under 12 stay free. Lower rates off-season. Pking: Outdoor, free. Maj CC. Weekly rates available except in high season.

≡≡ **Twin Rivers Motel**, 1801 Shenandoah Ave, Front Royal, VA 22630; tel 703/635-4101. 1¾ mi S of I-66. This modest facility is well kept and, mindful of families, has some helpful facilities. Located at northern entrance to Skyline Dr. **Rooms:** 20 rms. CI noon/CO 11am. Nonsmoking rms avail. Basic clean rooms. 1 room with king-size bed. **Amenities:** 🛎 A/C, cable TV w/movies. **Services:** ⊋ Roll-aways available. Pets are sometimes allowed with a deposit. **Facilities:** 🛠 Outdoor grill area, swing set. **Rates:** HS Apr–Oct $38 S; $42 D. Extra person $5. Lower rates off-season. Pking: Outdoor, free. Maj CC.

Restaurant 🍴

Royal Oak Restaurant, in Quality Inn Skyline Drive, 10 Commerce Ave, Front Royal; tel 703/635-3161. Exit 6 off I-66 W, or exit 13 off I-66 E. **New American.** Quiet dining by candlelight amid dark oak furnishings, country knickknacks, and antique pieces. A wooden bar area and piano add to the enjoyment. Prime rib the specialty. **FYI:** Reservations recommended. Piano. Children's menu. **Open:** Sun–Thurs 4–10pm, Fri–Sat 4–11pm. Closed Dec 25. **Prices:** Main courses $6.95–$9.95. Maj CC. 🍷 &

Attractions 🏛

Warren Rifles Confederate Museum, 95 Chester St; tel 703/636-6982. Preserved here are numerous pieces of Confederate memorabilia from the Civil War. Included are battle flags, weapons, uniforms, letters, diaries, and other personal effects. **Open:** Mid-Apr through Oct, Mon–Sat 9am–5pm, Sun noon–5pm. Closed Nov to mid-Apr and some hols. $

Belle Boyd Cottage, 101 Chester St; tel 703/636-1446. Moved in 1982 from its original location, this restored cottage was the home of Confederate spy Belle Boyd. For 2 years Boyd supplied the Confederacy with valuable intelligence obtained by her close contact with Union forces occupying Front Royal, information that resulted in a decisive victory for the South at the Battle of Front Royal (May 21, 1862). Guided tours (30 min); an 1862 formal garden surrounds the house. A reenactment of the Battle of Front Royal is staged the second weekend in May. **Open:** Apr–Oct, Mon–Fri 11am–4pm, Sat–Sun by appointment. Closed some hols. $

GALAX

Map page M-3, E3

See also Hillsville

Attraction 🏛

New River Trail State Park; tel 703/699-6778. One of Virginia's newest and most unusual parks, New River Trail State Park is laid out as a linear park or "greenway," a relatively recent trend in public parks. Still under development, New River Trail is a 57-mile-long state park that follows an abandoned railroad right-of-way from Galax, Va, northeast to Pulaski, Va. Much of the area fronts the historic and scenic New River. **Shot Tower Historical State Park** (see below) is now located within the boundaries of this new park.

The park is ideal for hiking, bicycling, and horseback riding, with opportunities for fishing and picnicking as well. Camping facilities are planned for the future. The trail includes 2 tunnels and 3 major bridges, with nearly 30 smaller bridges and trestles. The park also serves as a link to numerous other outdoor recreation areas, including Mount Rogers National Recreation Area.

Shot Tower Historical State Park, the headquarters area for New River Trail State Park, is located roughly at the midpoint of the trail, about 27 miles northeast of Galax (just off US 52, near where the highway crosses the New River). Built around 1807, the Shot Tower stands 75 feet high and is 20 feet square at its base; its stone walls are 2½ feet thick, possibly to maintain a constant temperature for the cooling shot. A pouring kettle in the top of the tower was used to pour molten lead through sieves equipped with meshes of varying sizes to produce varying types of shot. The globules of lead became round as they fell 150 feet down the shaft and into a large kettle of water.

The tower was declared a National Historic Mechanical Engineering Landmark by the American Society of Mechanical Engineers in 1981. The park offers picnicking sites and a visitor center. **Open:** Daily, dawn–dusk. Shot Tower: Sat–Sun and hols only, 10am–6pm. $

GEORGE WASHINGTON BIRTHPLACE NATIONAL MONUMENT

Map page M-3, C6

Located 40 miles east of Fredericksburg, off Va 3 and Va 204. Encompassing some 500 acres along Pope's Creek (a tributary of the Potomac), this park contains a charming re-creation of Washington's first home. He was born here on February 22, 1732, the first child of Augustine and Mary Ball Washington. When George was 3½ the family moved to the Mount Vernon estate.

The original house burned to the ground in 1779, and there were no records to indicate what it looked like. The present house, known as **Memorial House,** is representative of a typical plantation house of the 1700s, and has been furnished with pieces appropriate to the period.

The **visitor center** (tel 804/224-1732) screens a 14-minute film. Tours include the house, the herb garden, and a separate building that contains the kitchen and a weaving room. Graves of some Washington family members, including George's father, are in a small burial ground on the property. Children will

particularly enjoy the small-scale farm, with horses, chickens, and cows; picnic area. The monument is open daily 9am–5pm. Closed some hols.

GREAT FALLS

Map page M-3, C6 (W of Washington, DC)

Restaurants ⑪

⑤ **Falls Landing Restaurant**, in Village Center, 774 Walker Rd at Georgetown Pike, Great Falls; tel 703/759-4650. **Continental/Seafood.** Dark beams, colonial-style furniture, and exposed brick set an elegant and romantic tone. Fireplaces in both dining rooms, and patio dining in good weather. Continental preparation of fresh lobster (always on the menu), fish, and local seasonal items such as soft-shell crab are the main attractions. Salads and vegetables included in price of main courses. **FYI:** Reservations recommended. Children's menu. Dress code. **Open:** Lunch Mon–Fri 11:30am–2:30pm; dinner Mon–Thurs 5:30–10pm, Fri–Sat 5:30–10:30pm, Sun 4–9pm. Closed some hols. **Prices:** Main courses $16–$22. Maj CC. ♥ ⚓ 🎴 ᕱ

La Bonne Auberge, in Great Falls Center, 9835 Georgetown Pike at Walker Rd, Great Falls; tel 703/759-3877. **French.** A small, traditional dining room greets guests, but choice seating here is in a garden-like, plant-festooned, and skylighted area that opens on a patio with outdoor tables in good weather. Owner/chef learned traditional French cooking at home in Hong Kong and now applies his skills to fish and meat selections. Daily specials stress fresh seafood. **FYI:** Reservations recommended. Dress code. **Open:** Lunch Mon–Fri 11:30am–2:30pm; dinner Mon–Sat 6–10pm, Sun 5–8:30pm. Closed some hols. **Prices:** Main courses $15–$25. Maj CC. ♥ ⚓ ᕱ

♥ ✦ **L'Auberge Chez François**, 332 Springvale Rd at Beach Mill Rd, Great Falls; tel 703/759-3800. From Georgetown Pike, follow Springvale Rd north to Beach Mill Rd. **French.** A well-dressed but relaxed crowd usually packs this charming country French chalet in a near-rural setting. It's long been one of this area's most popular spots to celebrate such special occasions as birthdays, anniversaries, and marriage proposals—so popular, in fact, that reservations are taken up to 4 months in advance. Classical French cooking is on order, with some country-style selections mixed with creative dishes that have inspired a cookbook by the chef/owner. **FYI:** Reservations recommended. Children's menu. Jacket required. **Open:** Tues–Sat 5:30–9:30pm, Sun 2–8:30pm. Closed some hols. **Prices:** Main courses $30–$37.50. Maj CC. ᕱ

★ **Serbian Crown Restaurant**, in Old Mill Market Sq, 1141 Walker Rd at Colvin Mill Rd, Great Falls; tel 703/759-4150. **French/Russian/Serbian.** Dark, intimate dining rooms and a section with picture windows and flower baskets are hung with large paintings of Eastern European personages and landscapes. Chicken Kiev, Serbian stuffed cabbage, and Dover sole meunière can be found on this ethnically diverse menu. An excellent value at $22, the early-bird 4-course dinner is popular prior to shows at nearby Wolftrap Farm Park for the Performing Arts. Nightly entertainment by pianist or Gypsy musicians. **FYI:** Reservations recommended. Piano. Dress code. **Open:** Daily 5:30–9:30pm. Closed some hols. **Prices:** Main courses $16–$26. Maj CC. 💖 💟 ⑤

HAMPTON

Map page M-3, E7

Motels 🏨

≣≣≣ **Courtyard by Marriott**, 1917 Coliseum Dr, Hampton, VA 23666; tel 804/838-3300 or toll free 800/321-2211; fax 804/838-6387. Exit 263B off I-64. Like its counterparts, this Courtyard hotel is geared for business travelers. Courtyard itself has pool, gazebo, winding paved walkways with nice landscaping. Located a half-block from Hampton Coliseum. Restaurants, shopping nearby. Attractive public areas. **Rooms:** 146 rms and stes. CI 3pm/CO noon. Express checkout avail. Nonsmoking rms avail. Rooms have extra-long desks, tasteful and comfortable furniture. **Amenities:** 🛗 ⑤ A/C, cable TV w/movies. Some units w/terraces. Some suites have 2 TVs. Honeymoon suite has chocolate, champagne. **Services:** 🖼 🗇 **Facilities:** 🔓 🖤 🔟 🖳 ⑤ 1 rst, whirlpool, washer/dryer. Whirlpool room plays new-age music. Restaurant serves only full and continental breakfasts. **Rates:** HS Apr–Sept $59 S or D; from $69 ste. Children under 12 stay free. Min stay spec evnts. Lower rates off-season. Higher rates for spec evnts/hols. Spec packages avail. Pking: Outdoor, free. Maj CC. Rates include up to 5 persons per room.

≣≣ **Fairfield Inn**, 1905 Coliseum Dr, Hampton, VA 23666; tel 804/827-7400 or toll free 800/228-2800; fax 804/827-7400. Exit 263B off I-64. A budget, no-frills Marriott motel within walking distance of Hampton Coliseum. Shopping, restaurants nearby. Lobby has microwave. **Rooms:** 134 rms. CI 3pm/CO noon. Express checkout avail. Nonsmoking rms avail. Some rooms overlook pool. Card-key security system. Renovation scheduled for late 1995. **Amenities:** 🛗 A/C, cable TV w/movies. **Services:** 🖼 🗇 **Facilities:** 🔓 🔟 ⑤ **Rates (CP):** HS May–Aug $40–$55 S or D. Children under 18 stay free. Lower rates off-season. Pking: Outdoor, free. Maj CC. Military rates available.

≣≣ **Hampton Inn**, 1813 W Mercury Blvd, Hampton, VA 23666; tel 804/838-8484 or toll free 800/HAMPTON; fax 804/838-8484 ext 777. Exit 263B off I-64. A budget chain motel close to Hampton Coliseum, shopping, restaurants, and movie theaters. Attracts business travelers. **Rooms:** 132 rms and stes. CI 3pm/CO noon. Nonsmoking rms avail. **Amenities:** 🛗 ⑤ A/C, cable TV w/movies. **Services:** ✗ 🚐 🖼 🗇 🐾 Babysitting. Continental breakfast served in area off lobby. Adjacent Holiday Inn provides room service during restaurant hours. **Facilities:** 🖼 🔟 ⑤ Guests may use pool, fitness center, game room at adjacent Holiday Inn. **Rates (CP):** HS May 28–Sept 4 $48–$55 S; $52–$61 D; from $75 ste. Extra person $6. Children under 18 stay free. Min stay spec evnts. Lower rates off-season. Higher rates for spec evnts/hols. Pking: Outdoor, free. Maj CC.

≣≣≣ **Holiday Inn Coliseum**, 1815 W Mercury Blvd, Hampton, VA 23666; tel 804/838-0200 or toll free 800/842-9370; fax 804/838-0200 ext 7700. Exit 263B off I-64. A large motel close to Hampton Coliseum, shopping, movie theaters, restaurants. Spacious, airy public areas includes atrium with restaurant, bar, pool, fitness center, game room. **Rooms:** 324 rms and stes. CI 3pm/CO noon. Express checkout avail. Nonsmoking rms avail. Newer rooms have indoor corridors; some overlook atrium. Mauve accents, dark-finished art deco–style furniture. **Amenities:** 🛗 ⑤ 🖭 A/C, cable TV w/movies. Some units w/terraces, some w/Jacuzzis. **Services:** ✗ 🗝 🚐 🖼 🗇 Children's program. **Facilities:** 🔓 🖼 🖤 🔟 🖳 ⑤ 1 rst, 1 bar, games rm, spa, sauna, whirlpool, washer/dryer. Fitness trail begins on premises, ends at Hampton Coliseum. **Rates:** HS June–Aug $82–$89 S; $89–$96 D; from $180 ste. Extra person $7. Children under 18 stay free. Min stay spec evnts. Lower rates off-season. Higher rates for spec evnts/hols. Spec packages avail. Pking: Outdoor, free. Maj CC.

Restaurants 🍴

Captain George's Seafood Restaurant, 2710 W Mercury Blvd, Hampton; tel 804/826-1435. Exit 263B off I-64. **Seafood/Steak.** Resin-coated tables with recessed rope and seashells, ceiling fans, and stained-glass murals with sea scenes set nautical tone. Separate, larger room has wooden tables, captain-style chairs, blue cloth napkins. Seafood buffet with wide selection or traditional seafood dishes à la carte. Also at: 1956 Laskin Rd, Virginia Beach (804/428-3494); 2272 Old Pungo Ferry Rd, Virginia Beach (804/721-3463); 5363 Richmond Rd, Williamsburg (804/565-2323); 4700 W Broad St, Richmond (804/359-0222). **FYI:** Reservations not accepted. Children's menu. **Open:** Mon–Fri 4:30–10pm, Sat 4–10pm, Sun noon–10pm. Closed Dec 25. **Prices:** Main courses $15–$23; PF dinner $18. Maj CC. 👥 ⑤

Fisherman's Wharf, 14 Ivy Home Rd, Hampton; tel 804/723-3113. Exit 265A off I-64. Follow LaSalle Ave south to Kecoughtan Rd (US 60) east; turn right on Ivy Home Rd. **Seafood.** Many windows offer an expansive water view of Hampton Roads harbor, while nautical decor includes wooden, resin-coated tables; leather, padded captain's chairs; paintings of ships; brass ship lanterns. Huge wooden ship's hull supports grand seafood buffet, with more than 75 items. Popular choices include baked shrimp stuffed with backfin crab meat and Australian rock-lobster tail. Group seating in main dining room. Also at: 1571 Bayville St, Norfolk (804/480-3133). **FYI:** Reservations accepted. Children's menu. **Open:** Mon–Fri 5–10pm, Sat 4–10:30pm, Sun noon–10pm. Closed Dec 25. **Prices:** Main courses $10–$28; PF dinner $18.95. Maj CC. 🔺

The Smokehouse, in Sheraton Inn-Coliseum, 1215 W Mercury Blvd, Hampton; tel 804/838-5011. Exit 263B off I-64. Go ¼ mile on W Mercury Blvd. **Barbecue/Steak.** Bright red tablecloths, wooden floor, rich wood accents, and tasteful framed paintings give this hotel restaurant a cozy feel. Smoked meats, including baby-back ribs, chicken, turkey, and shrimp kabobs, are specialties. Fresh catches and pasta also offered. **FYI:** Reservations accepted. Children's menu. **Open:** Breakfast daily 6:30–11am; lunch daily 11am–2pm; dinner daily 5–10pm; brunch–Sun 11am–2pm. **Prices:** Main courses $7–$11. Maj CC. 🔳

Attractions 💼

Virginia Air and Space Center/Hampton Roads History Center, 600 Settlers Landing Rd; tel 804/727-0900. The official visitor center for NASA Langley Research Center, this museum is located in downtown Hampton. Interactive exhibits let visitors launch a rocket, visit the planet Mars, or view themselves as an astronaut working in space. Ten air and space craft are suspended from the center's 94-foot ceiling, including the *Apollo 12* command module. Large-screen IMAX films are shown daily (additional fee charged).

The **Hampton Roads History Center** tells the 400-year history of Hampton. Settled around 1610, it is one of the oldest towns in the United States. Exhibits include an 18th-century custom house and tavern. **Open:** Summer, Mon–Wed 10am–5pm, Thurs–Sat 10am–7pm, Sun noon–7pm; rest of the year, Mon–Sat 10am–5pm, Sun noon–5pm. Closed some hols. $$$$

Casemate Museum, exit 268 off I-64; tel 804/727-3391. Located on the active army base of Fort Monroe, where Jefferson Davis was imprisoned in 1865 after the Civil War. Visitors can view displays of military memorabilia and enter the sparsely furnished room where Davis was held prisoner. **Open:** Daily 10:30am–4:30pm. Closed some hols. Free.

Hampton University Museum, Hampton University; tel 804/727-5308. Hampton University was founded in 1868 to provide an education for newly freed African-Americans. The museum is housed in Academy Building, an 1881 red-brick landmark on the waterfront in the historic section of the campus. Notable holdings include an African collection comprising more then 2,700 art objects and artifacts representing 887 ethnic groups and cultures; also works by Harlem Renaissance artists and extensive Oceanic and Asian objects. **Open:** Mon–Fri 8am–5pm, Sat–Sun noon–4pm. Free.

HANOVER

Map page M-3, D6 (E of Ashland)

See also **Ashland, Carmel Church**

Restaurant 🍽️

Houndstooth Café, US 301 at Va 54, Hanover; tel 804/537-5404. 6 mi E of Ashland; exit 92B off I-95. Follow Va 54 E for 6 mi. **Barbecue/Seafood.** Although decor is simple, with checked flooring, a fox-hunting theme is carried through this pleasant local eatery emphasizing homemade sandwiches, salads, and desserts; barbecue and seafood dominate the main courses. Convenient to Paramount's King's Dominion amusement park. **FYI:** Reservations not accepted. Beer and wine only. **Open:** Tues–Thurs 11am–8pm, Fri–Sat 11am–9pm. Closed some hols. **Prices:** Main courses $2.50–$16.95. Ltd CC.

HARDY

Map page M-2, E4 (E of Roanoke)

Attraction 💼

Booker T Washington National Monument, Va 122 S; tel 703/721-2094. Although Booker T Washington called his boyhood home a plantation, the Burroughs farm was small—207 acres—with never more than 11 slaves. The cabin where Washington was born was also the plantation kitchen. He and his brother and sister slept on a dirt floor and there was no glass in the windows. Overcoming the obstacles of poverty and prejudice, he achieved national prominence as an author, educator, founder of the Tuskegee Institute in Alabama, and adviser to presidents.

At this memorial to one of America's great African-American leaders, several farm buildings have been reconstructed and demonstrations are given that illustrate farm life in the pre–Civil War Virginia of Washington's childhood. The visitor center offers a slide show and distributes a self-guided plantation tour map of the original Burroughs property. **Open:** Daily 8:30am–5pm. Closed some hols. Free.

HARRISONBURG

Map page M-3, C5

Hotel 🖭

≝≝≝ Sheraton Inn, 1400 E Market St, Harrisonburg, VA 22801; tel 703/433-2521 or toll free 800/325-3535; fax 703/434-0253. Exit 247 off I-81. A modern hotel boasting a large lobby fireplace. Close to ski area and tours of Civil War battlefields. **Rooms:** 138 rms and stes. Exec-level rms avail. CI 3pm/CO noon. Express checkout avail. Nonsmoking rms avail. **Amenities:** 🛅 🕹 🖭 A/C, cable TV w/movies. Some units w/terraces. **Services:** ✕ 🖾 🖑 Babysitting. **Facilities:** 🖪 🏌 🐟 🏊 ⭤ 1 rst, 1 bar (w/entertainment), sauna, whirlpool. Cafe. Exceptionally large indoor pool area surrounded by patio tables. Guests have free use of nearby fitness club. **Rates:** HS May–Nov $88–$96 S; $98–$106 D; from $115 ste. Extra person $10. Min stay spec evnts. Lower rates off-season. Spec packages avail. Pking: Outdoor, free. Maj CC.

Motels

≝≝ Comfort Inn, 1440 E Market St, Harrisonburg, VA 22801; tel 703/433-6066 or toll free 800/221-2222; fax 703/434-0253. Exit 247 off I-81. A city motel near restaurants, malls, and James Madison University. Massanutten ski resort is 10 miles away. **Rooms:** 60 rms. CI 3pm/CO noon. Nonsmoking rms avail. Light and airy rooms decorated in soft pastels. **Amenities:** 🛅 A/C, cable TV w/movies. **Services:** 🖾 🖑 **Facilities:** 🖪 🏌 🐟 ⭤ Small poolside cafe. **Rates (CP):** HS May–Oct $50–$61 S or D. Extra person $5. Children under 18 stay free. Lower rates off-season. Higher rates for spec evnts/hols. Pking: Outdoor, free. Maj CC.

≝≝ Econo Lodge, 1703 E Market St, PO Box 1311, Harrisonburg, VA 22802; tel 703/433-2576 or toll free 800/424-4777; fax 703/433-2576 ext 198. Exit 247 off I-81. Drive east for ½ mile on US 33. In the heart of the Shenandoah Valley, this chain motel is near James Madison University, Skyline Dr, Civil War battlefields, museums, and outdoor activities. Restaurants nearby. **Rooms:** 88 rms and stes. Exec-level rms avail. CI 2pm/CO 11am. Express checkout avail. Nonsmoking rms avail. All units recently refurbished. **Amenities:** 🛅 A/C, cable TV w/movies, voice mail. Some units w/Jacuzzis. **Services:** 🖾 🖑 🐟 Babysitting. **Facilities:** 🖪 🏌 🐟 🐾 ⭤ Pretty view from pool area.

Rates (CP): HS Apr–Dec $40–$56 S; $45–$61 D; from $75 ste. Extra person $5. Children under 18 stay free. Min stay spec evnts. Lower rates off-season. Higher rates for spec evnts/hols. Spec packages avail. Pking: Outdoor, free. Maj CC.

≝≝ HoJo Inn, 605 Port Republic Rd, PO Box 68, Harrisonburg, VA 22801 (James Madison University); tel 703/434-6771 or toll free 800/446-4656. Exit 245 off I-81. A well-maintained older property directly opposite James Madison University. **Rooms:** 134 rms. CI 2pm/CO noon. Nonsmoking rms avail. Rooms are extremely large by today's motel standards. **Amenities:** 🛅 A/C, cable TV. All units w/terraces. **Services:** 🖾 🖑 🐟 **Facilities:** 🖪 🟦 ⭤ 1 rst. **Rates:** $40–$45 S; $45–$50 D. Extra person $5. Children under 18 stay free. Min stay spec evnts. Higher rates for spec evnts/hols. Spec packages avail. Pking: Outdoor, free. Maj CC.

≝≝≝ Ramada Inn, 1 Pleasant Valley Rd, Harrisonburg, VA 22801; tel 703/434-9981 or toll free 800/434-7456; fax 703/434-7088. Exit 243 off I-81. A quiet location with wonderful view of the surrounding hills. Near James Madison University, Bridgwater College, and Eastern Mennonite College. **Rooms:** 130 rms. CI 2pm/CO noon. Express checkout avail. Nonsmoking rms avail. Basic motel-style rooms. **Amenities:** 🛅 🕹 🖭 A/C, cable TV w/movies. **Services:** ✕ 🖑 **Facilities:** 🖪 🟦 ⭤ 1 rst, 1 bar. Tennis and golf nearby. **Rates:** HS July–Oct $45–$51 S or D. Extra person $6. Children under 18 stay free. Lower rates off-season. Higher rates for spec evnts/hols. Spec packages avail. Pking: Outdoor, free. Maj CC.

Restaurant 🍽

✸ Texas Steakhouse and Saloon, 1688 E Market St, Harrisonburg; tel 703/433-3650. Exit 247 off I-81. **Steak.** Large fireplace, stuffed animals, and western flair make this an all-around favorite with college students, families, and businesspeople. Mesquite-grilled steaks are the main attraction, but menu also offers ribs, "Texas pheasant" (chicken), and sandwiches. **FYI:** Reservations not accepted. Children's menu. **Open:** Mon–Thurs 11am–10pm, Fri–Sat 11am–11pm, Sun 11am–9pm. Closed Dec 25. **Prices:** Main courses $8–$18. Maj CC. 🍴 🖼 ⭤

Attraction 🖼

George Washington National Forest, I-81; tel 703/564-8300. Deerfield Ranger District accessible 10 miles west on US 250. The George Washington National Forest covers more than a million acres of mountains and valleys in northwestern Virginia and West Virginia. Steeped in American tradition, it has served as a westward passage for Native Americans and pioneers and as a battleground in the Revolutionary and Civil Wars. In addition to a wide variety of wildflowers and other flora, there is abundant wildlife. Species include bear, deer, turkey, grouse, and 160 species of songbird.

Numerous old woods roads and hiking trails offer the best access to the various areas of the forest, including part of the famous **Appalachian Trail**. Among the other activities enjoyed in the forest are picnicking, camping, sightseeing, hunting, fishing, swimming, and boating. For detailed information contact the Forest Supervisor, George Washington National Forest, Harrison Plaza, Harrisonburg, VA 22801. **Open:** Daily sunrise–sunset. Free.

HERNDON

Map page M-3, B6 (NW of Arlington)

Hotels 🏨

🏨🏨 **Comfort Inn Herndon**, 200 Elden St, Herndon, VA 22070 (Dulles Airport); tel 703/437-7555 or toll free 800/221-2222; fax 703/437-7572. 4 mi E of Dulles Airport. exit 3 off Dulles Toll Rd. A comfortable chain hotel with attractive lobby. Convenient to Dulles Airport, shops, restaurants. **Rooms:** 103 rms and stes. CI 2pm/CO noon. Nonsmoking rms avail. King rooms have sofas. **Amenities:** 🏠 🛁 📺 A/C, cable TV w/movies, refrig. **Services:** 🚐 🛄 ↩ **Facilities:** 🏋 ⛳ ♿ Guests get discounts at nearby restaurants. **Rates (CP):** $67 S; $73 D; from $85 ste. Extra person $6. Children under 18 stay free. Higher rates for spec evnts/hols. Spec packages avail. Pking: Outdoor, free. Maj CC. Weekend rates available.

🏨🏨🏨 **Courtyard by Marriott–Herndon**, 533 Herndon Pkwy, Herndon, VA 22070 (Dulles Airport); tel 703/478-9400 or toll free 800/321-2211. 2½ mi E of Dulles Airport. exit 2 off Dulles Toll Rd. A typical example of this comfortable chain. Attractive lobby with fireplace and walls of windows looking out to landscaped courtyard. Convenient to shops, restaurants. **Rooms:** 146 rms and stes. CI 3pm/CO 1pm. Express checkout avail. Nonsmoking rms avail. King rooms have sofas. **Amenities:** 🏠 🛁 📺 A/C, satel TV w/movies, voice mail. All units w/terraces. Suites have refrigerators, 2 TVs. All have hot-water tap for coffee/tea. **Services:** 🚐 🛄 ↩ Babysitting. **Facilities:** 🏋 🏋 💯 ♿ 1 bar, lifeguard, whirlpool, washer/dryer. Lobby dining area serves breakfast only. Bar open evenings. **Rates:** $89 S; $99 D; from $103 ste. Children under 12 stay free. Spec packages avail. Pking: Outdoor, free. Maj CC. Weekend rates available.

🏨🏨🏨 **Hyatt Dulles**, 2300 Dulles Corner Blvd, Herndon, VA 22071 (Dulles Airport); tel 703/713-1234 or toll free 800/233-1234; fax 703/713-3406. Exit 1 off Dulles Access Rd. Follow Va 28 S to Frying Pan Rd, turn left, then left on Horse Pen Rd. Attractive, lush lobby with skylights and fountain distinguishes this modern hotel in an office-park setting near Dulles Airport. **Rooms:** 317 stes. Exec-level rms avail. CI 3pm/CO noon. Express checkout avail. Nonsmoking rms avail. Counters divide living and sleeping areas. **Amenities:** 🏠 🛁 🍽 A/C, cable TV w/movies, voice mail, shoe polisher. TVs on counter swivel between living and sleeping areas. Many suites have irons and boards. Refrigerators available. **Services:** ✕ 🚐 🛄 ↩ Children's program, babysitting. Will arrange tennis and golf. **Facilities:** 🏠 🏋 💯 🖥 ♿ 1 rst, 1 bar, lifeguard, spa, sauna, whirlpool. Pool opens to attractive courtyard, has weekday morning and evening hours only. Restaurant and bar partially share lobby skylights. **Rates:** $139 S; $164 D; from $250 ste. Extra person $25. Children under 18 stay free. Spec packages avail. Pking: Outdoor, free. Maj CC. Weekend packages available.

🏨🏨🏨 **Washington Dulles Marriott Suites**, 13101 Worldgate Dr, Herndon, VA 22070 (Dulles Airport); tel 703/709-0400 or toll free 800/228-9290; fax 703/709-0426. 2 mi E of Dulles Airport. exit 2 off Dulles Toll Rd. Worldgate Dr, turn right. This attractive all-suites hotel just off Dulles Toll Road stands at end of modern shopping center with restaurants, movie theaters, copy center with computer rentals. **Rooms:** 256 stes. CI 3pm/CO 1pm. Express checkout avail. Nonsmoking rms avail. French doors separate sitting area from bedroom. Floral-print spreads fit into green-and-mauve color scheme. Large baths have doors to both sleeping and sitting areas. **Amenities:** 🏠 🛁 📺 🍽 A/C, cable TV w/movies, refrig. Some units w/terraces. All units have wet bars, irons and boards, 2 TVs. Phones have call-waiting. **Services:** ✕ 🚐 🛄 ↩ Twice-daily maid svce, car-rental desk, babysitting. Morning coffee and pastries in lobby. **Facilities:** 🏠 🏋 💯 ♿ 1 rst, 1 bar, lifeguard, sauna, whirlpool, washer/dryer. Attractive indoor-outdoor pool area has large sun deck off 3rd floor. Guests have free use of adjoining health club. **Rates:** HS Mar–June/Sept–Dec from $140 ste. Children under 16 stay free. Lower rates off-season. Spec packages avail. Pking: Indoor/outdoor, free. Maj CC. Weekend packages available.

🏨🏨🏨 **Washington Dulles Renaissance Hotel**, 13869 Park Center Rd, Herndon, VA 22071 (Dulles Airport); tel 703/478-2900 or toll free 800/228-9898; fax 703/478-9286. Exit 1 off Dulles Access Rd. Follow Va 28 S to McLearen Rd, turn left, then left into hotel. A modern semicircular building connected to an office complex with shops and restaurants, this comfortable hotel has an attractive lobby. **Rooms:** 301 rms. Exec-level rms avail. CI 3pm/CO 1pm. Express checkout avail. Nonsmoking rms avail. Spacious rooms have bright modern furniture and light drapes and spreads. Baths have separate dressing areas. **Amenities:** 🏠 🛁 A/C, satel TV w/movies. Some units w/minibars. **Services:** ✕ 🚐 🛄 ↩ 🍽 Car-rental desk. **Facilities:** 🏠

🔲 📺 🔲 👤 1 rst, 3 bars (2 w/entertainment), lifeguard, racquetball, spa, sauna, steam rm, whirlpool, beauty salon. Indoor-outdoor pool is part of state-of-the-art health club. Zodiac lounge has sports bar ambience. **Rates:** $99–$129 S; $109–$139 D. Extra person $10. Children under 18 stay free. Pking: Outdoor, free. Maj CC.

Motel

≣≣ **Marriott Residence Inn**, 315 Elden St, at Herndon Pkwy, Herndon, VA 22070 (Dulles Airport); tel 703/435-0044 or toll free 800/331-3131; fax 703/437-4007. 4 mi E of Dulles Airport. exit 3 off Dulles Toll Rd. Essentially an apartment complex built around a central courtyard with outdoor pool. Attractive lobby has fireplace, coffeepot, tables and chairs for meals and guest get-togethers. Family restaurants and shopping centers nearby. Most guests stay weeks or more. **Rooms:** 168 effic. CI 3pm/CO noon. Nonsmoking rms avail. Attractive and comfortably furnished units vary from studios to 2-bedroom apartments. All have full kitchens. **Amenities:** 📺🐾📺 A/C, cable TV w/movies, refrig, voice mail. All units w/terraces, some w/fireplaces. All units have ironing boards; irons, VCRs, videos, and hair dryers are available. **Services:** 📺🐾🔲 Breakfast served in lobby, as are full dinner on Wednesday and light snacks Monday, Tuesday, Thursday. **Facilities:** 📺🔲👤 Lifeguard, whirlpool, playground, washer/dryer. All-purpose sports court for tennis, volleyball, basketball. Guests have free use of nearby health club. **Rates (CP):** HS Mar–Oct from $110 effic. Children under 18 stay free. Lower rates off-season. Spec packages avail. Pking: Outdoor, free. Maj CC. Weekend packages available.

Restaurant 🍽

The Ice House Café and Oyster Bar, 760 Elden St, Herndon; tel 703/471-4256. 4 mi E of Dulles Airport. exit 2 off Dulles Toll Rd. **Regional American/Continental/Thai.** Mounted moose, walrus, and deer heads give hunting-lodge charm to this storefront with varnished tongue-in-groove pine walls adorned with turn-of-the-century photos of Herndon, then a small rural town. Limited menu offers a mix of American, continental, and Thai cuisines. Live jazz Friday and Saturday 8pm–midnight. Park next door in former service station lot. **FYI:** Reservations recommended. Jazz. Dress code. **Open:** Lunch Mon–Fri 11:30am–2:30pm; dinner Mon–Sat 6–10:30pm, Sun 5:30–8:30pm. Closed some hols. **Prices:** Main courses $12–$19. Maj CC. 🍴👤

HILLSVILLE
Map page M-2, E3

Motel 🛏

≣≣ **Knob Hill Motor Lodge**, 305 E Stuart Dr, Hillsville, VA 24343; tel 703/728-2131. Exit 14 off I-77. Drive east on US 221 and 58 for 2.7 miles. Convenient to the interstate and the Blue Ridge Pkwy, this homey older establishment is popular with those attending the annual Galax Fiddler's Convention. **Rooms:** 19 rms. CI 2pm/CO 11am. **Amenities:** 📺 🍴 A/C, cable TV w/movies. **Services:** 🔲 📺 🔲 Babysitting. **Rates:** HS Mar–Oct $32–$35 S; $35–$37 D. Extra person $5. Lower rates off-season. Higher rates for spec evnts/hols. Pking: Outdoor, free. Maj CC.

HOPEWELL
Map page M-3, D6

Motel 🛏

≣≣ **Days Inn**, 4911 Oaklawn Blvd, Hopewell, VA 23860; tel 804/458-1500 or toll free 800/458-3297; fax 804/458-9159. Exit 4 off I-95. An attractive brick structure with tile roof and pretty courtyard pool. Convenient to restaurants, some offering discounts to guests. Good location for touring James River Plantations. **Rooms:** 115 rms. CI noon/CO 11am. Nonsmoking rms avail. Pleasant and comfortable. **Amenities:** 📺 A/C, cable TV, refrig. Some units w/Jacuzzis. **Services:** 🔲 Shuttle to nearby locations. Coffee in lobby. Complimentary barbecue on Wednesday. **Facilities:** 📺 📺 👤 Games rm, washer/dryer. **Rates (CP):** $40–$70 S; $45–$85 D. Children under 12 stay free. Pking: Outdoor, free. Maj CC.

HOT SPRINGS
Map page M-2, D4

Motel 🛏

≣≣ **Roseloe Motel**, US 220 N, PO Box 590, Hot Springs, VA 24445; tel 703/839-5373. A small, quiet motel just minutes from the Homestead resort and such activities as skiing, golfing, canoeing, horseback riding, and soaking in mineral springs. **Rooms:** 14 rms and effic. CI 3pm/CO noon. Nonsmoking rms avail. Units with kitchens ideal for families. **Amenities:** 📺 A/C, cable TV w/movies. **Services:** 🖼 🧺 ⚓ **Facilities:** 🛝 🎿 **Rates:** $34–$44 S or D; from $37 effic. Extra person $4. Children under 18 stay free. Pking: Outdoor, free. Ltd CC.

Resort

⟮⟮⟮⟮ **The Homestead**, US 220 N, PO Box 2000, Hot Springs, VA 24445; tel 703/839-5500 or toll free 800/336-5771; fax 703/839-7782. Exit 151B off I-18. Follow US 220 N to Hot Springs. 15,000 acres. Combining rich historical ambience with present-day elegance, this deluxe resort is nestled in the Allegheny Mountains. Travelers have come for rejuvenating benefits of natural hot springs since the 18th century. **Rooms:** 521 rms and stes. Exec-level rms avail. CI 4pm/CO noon. Express checkout avail. Nonsmoking rms avail. Recently renovated, choice west wing rooms have paintings and photographs reflecting history of area and resort's construction. **Amenities:** 🔐 🍷 🍽 🖥 A/C, cable TV w/movies, refrig, bathrobes. Some units w/minibars, some w/terraces, some w/fireplaces. **Services:** ✕ 🔑 VP 🚗 🖼 🧺 Twice-daily maid svce, social director, masseur, children's program, babysitting. Attentive staff fulfills most guest requests. Instruction in skiing, ice skating, golf, and fly fishing. **Facilities:** 🔥 🚴 🎱 ▶54 ⛳ 🎿 🎣11 🏊 1.5K 🖥 ♿ 7 rsts, 2 bars (1 w/entertainment), lifeguard, games rm, lawn games, spa, sauna, steam rm, whirlpool, beauty salon, playground. Olympic-size ice-skating rink, 3 golf courses with practice facilities, bowling lanes, carriage rides, shooting club, cinema. **Rates:** HS Mid-Apr–mid-Nov $185–$275 S; $215–$295 D; from $350 ste. Extra person $25. Children under 18 stay free. Min stay spec evnts. Lower rates off-season. Higher rates for spec evnts/hols. AP and MAP rates avail. Spec packages avail. Pking: Outdoor, free. Maj CC.

IRVINGTON

Map page M-3, D7

Resorts 🎱

⟮⟮⟮⟮ **The Tides Inn**, King Carter Dr, PO Box 480, Irvington, VA 22480 (Carter's Creek); tel 804/438-5000 or toll free 800/843-3746; fax 804/438-5222. 90 mi E of Fredericksburg. exit 130B off I-95. Follow Va 3 to Irvington. 50 acres. Venerable riverside retreat enjoys beautiful water and forest views wherever you look. Lovely, well-kept buildings and grounds plus friendly staff create relaxed, well-mannered atmosphere. Attractive public areas have plentiful seating inside and out. **Rooms:** 110 rms and stes. CI 3:30pm/CO 2pm. Nonsmoking rms avail. Superb units are homey, with well-coordinated drapes, spreads, and wallpaper. Baseboards and crown molding

give a historic air. **Amenities:** 🔐 🍷 🍽 🖥 A/C, cable TV, refrig, VCR. Some units w/terraces, 1 w/Jacuzzi. **Services:** ✕ 🔑 🚗 🖼 🧺 ⚓ Twice-daily maid svce, social director, children's program, babysitting. **Facilities:** 🔥 🚴 ⛳ 🎱 ▶27 🎣4 🏊 50 ♿ 3 rsts, 1 bar (w/entertainment), 1 beach (cove/inlet), lifeguard, games rm, washer/dryer. The 9-hole, par-3 golf course is free to guests. Lovely restaurants on premises. Guests use local fitness center for small fee. Yacht available for river rides. **Rates (MAP):** HS May 6–Oct $186–$206 S; $244–$688 D; from $456 ste. Extra person $53. Children under 12 stay free. Lower rates off-season. AP rates avail. Spec packages avail. Pking: Outdoor, free. Maj CC.

⟮⟮⟮⟮ **The Tides Lodge**, 1 St Andrews Lane, PO Box 309, Irvington, VA 22480 (Carter's Creek); tel 804/438-6000 or toll free 800/248-4337; fax 804/438-5950. 90 mi E of Fredericksburg. exit 130B off I-95. Follow Va 3 to Irvington. 175 acres. Well-kept grounds leading to this rustic-looking lodge are part of golf course shared with Tides Inn. Very attractive Scottish motif to large lobby with long reception desk. **Rooms:** 60 rms; 1 ctge/villa. Exec-level rms avail. CI 3:30pm/CO 1pm. Express checkout avail. Nonsmoking rms avail. Attractive rooms have pictures of hunting scenes and carry on Scottish motif of public areas. Good-quality furniture with comfortable seating arrangements. **Amenities:** 🔐 🍷 🍽 🖥 A/C, cable TV, refrig. All units w/terraces, 1 w/fireplace. **Services:** ✕ VP 🚗 🖼 🧺 ⚓ Twice-daily maid svce, children's program, babysitting. Golf clinics, yacht cruises, morning newspapers. Will arrange car rental, appointments at beauty salon in town. Van or gondola rides to Tides Inn. **Facilities:** 🔥 🚴 ⛳ ▶18 🎿 🎣3 🏊 100 ♿ 2 rsts, 1 bar (w/entertainment), lifeguard, games rm, lawn games, spa, sauna, playground, washer/dryer. **Rates:** HS Apr–May/Sept–Oct $158–$170 S; $178–$203 D; from $290 ctge/villa. Extra person $25. Children under 18 stay free. Min stay wknds. Lower rates off-season. Higher rates for spec evnts/hols. AP and MAP rates avail. Spec packages avail. Pking: Outdoor, free. Maj CC.

Attraction 🏛

Historic Christ Church, Va 3; tel 804/438-6855. Elegant in its simplicity and virtually unchanged since it was completed in 1732, Christ Church was a gift to the community from one man, Robert "King" Carter. Among Carter's descendants are 8 governors of Virginia, 2 US presidents (the 2 Harrisons), Gen Robert E Lee, and Chief Justice of the US Supreme Court Edward D White.

Inside the church, the pulpit and all 26 original pews remain. Heating and lighting systems were never added, so the church is now only used for services during the summer. Robert Carter's tomb and the graves of several relatives are on the grounds.

Open: Church, daily 9am–5pm; Carter Reception Center and Museum, Apr–Thanksgiving Day, Mon–Fri 10am–4pm, Sat 1–4pm, Sun 2–5pm. Free.

JAMESTOWN

Map page M-3, E7 (S of Williamsburg)

For lodgings and dining, see Williamsburg

Attractions

Jamestown Settlement, Va 31S; tel 804/898-3400. Located on the Virginia Peninsula, between the James and York Rivers. The story of Jamestown, the first English settlement in the New World, is documented here in museum exhibits and living-history demonstrations. The exploits of Capt John Smith, leader of the colony; his legendary rescue from execution by the Powhatan princess Pocahontas; and a vivid picture of life in 17th-century Virginia are all re-created near the original site of the first colony. Archeologists have excavated more than 100 building frames, evidences of manufacturing ventures (pottery, winemaking, brickmaking, and glassblowing), early wells, and old roads, as well as millions of artifacts of everyday life.

The **indoor/outdoor museum,** operated by the Commonwealth of Virginia, is open all year, although outdoor exhibit areas are closed January–February. After purchasing tickets, visit the changing exhibit gallery just off the lobby and then the orientation theater to view a 20-minute film that provides an introduction to Jamestown.

Beyond the theater, 3 large permanent museum galleries feature artifacts, documents, decorative objects, dioramas, and graphics relating to the Jamestown period. The English Gallery focuses on Jamestown's beginnings in the Old World. The Powhatan Indian Gallery explores the origins and culture of the Native Americans who lived near Jamestown. The Jamestown Gallery deals with the history of the colony during its first century of existence.

Leaving the museum complex, visitors come directly into the **Powhatan Indian Village,** representing the culture and technology of a highly organized chiefdom of 32 tribes that inhabited coastal Virginia in the early 17th century. There are several mat-covered longhouses as well as a garden and a ceremonial dance circle. Historical interpreters tend gardens, tan animal hides, and make bone and antler tools, flint-knap projectile points, and pottery.

Triangular **James Fort** is a re-creation of the one constructed by the Jamestown colonists on their arrival in the spring of 1607. Inside are 18 primitive wattle-and-daub structures representing Jamestown's earliest buildings. Interpreters are engaged in activities typical of early 17th-century life.

A short walk from James Fort are reproductions of the 3 **ships** that transported the 104 colonists to Virginia. Visitors can board and explore the largest ship, the 110-foot *Susan Constant,* and talk with an interpreter about the 4½-month voyage from England. The *Godspeed* retraced the 1607 voyage from England to Virginia in 1985. The smallest ship, *Discovery,* is often open to visitors in the summer and is used for demonstrations of 17th-century sailing techniques.

Jamestown is a unit of **Colonial National Historical Park,** and is located on the western end of the 23-mile Colonial Parkway. At the eastern end of the parkway is Yorktown Battlefield (*see* "Yorktown"). Along the way, the parkway passes under and by Colonial Williamsburg (*see* "Williamsburg"). **Open:** Daily 9am–5pm. Closed some hols. Free.

Jamestown Island, Va 31S; tel 804/229-1733. Exploration of the actual site of the first permanent English settlement in America begins at the **visitor center,** where a 12-minute orientation film is shown every 30 minutes.

Exhibits at the center document the 92 years when Jamestown was the capital of Virginia. From the visitor center, a footpath leads to the actual site of **"James Cittie,"** where reconstructed brick foundations of 17th-century homes, taverns, shops, and the statehouse are enhanced by artists' renderings and recorded narratives. Spring through fall there are frequent half-hour guided tours of the site, and in summer there are living-history programs. Directly behind the remains of the tower of one of Virginia's first brick churches (1639) is the **Memorial Church,** a 1907 gift of the Colonial Dames of America. It houses remnants of early Jamestown churches.

The footpath continues to the seawall, believed to be the site of the original James Fort and the May 13, 1607 landing site. There are many monuments and memorials throughout James Cittie; a memorial cross marks some 300 shallow graves of colonists who died during the "Starving Time," the winter of 1609–10.

A fascinating **5-mile loop drive** (beginning at the Visitor Center parking lot) winds through 1,500 wilderness acres of woodland and marsh that have been allowed to return to a natural state to approximate the landscape as 17th-century settlers found it. Markers and large paintings interpret aspects of the daily activities of the colonists—tobacco growing, lumbering, silk production, pottery making, farming, etc. Audio tours for rent in the bookstore.

By the time of the Revolution, Jamestown was all but abandoned. A shifting of the James River sometime in the late 1700s cut the site off from the mainland and made an island of the Jamestown site. **Open:** Daily 9am–5pm; extended hours in summer. Closed Dec 25. $$$

KESWICK

Map page M-3, D5 (W of Charlottesville)

Resort

≡≡≡≡ **Keswick Inn**, 701 Country Club Drive, Keswick, VA 22947; tel 804/979-3440 or toll free 800/274-5391; fax 804/979-3457. Exit I-64 at Shadwell (US 250). 600 acres. An elegant English country house with beautifully landscaped grounds overlooking a golf course and lake. Very quiet. Everything is designed for guests' comfort. The resort, decorated in Laura Ashley fabrics and wall coverings, is owned by the late designer's former husband. **Rooms:** 48 rms and stes. CI noon/CO noon. Express checkout avail. Nonsmoking rms avail. Beautiful rooms are individually decorated in luxurious styles. **Amenities:** A/C, cable TV w/movies, bathrobes. Some units w/terraces. **Services:** Twice-daily maid svce, social director, masseur, babysitting. Guests enjoy full country breakfast, traditional English afternoon tea, and gourmet 5-course dinners. **Facilities:** 2 rsts, 1 bar, games rm, lawn games, spa, sauna, steam rm, whirlpool, beauty salon. **Rates (MAP):** $265–$465 S or D; from $545 ste. Extra person $80. Children under 18 stay free. Min stay spec evnts. Spec packages avail. Pking: Outdoor, free. Maj CC.

KEYSVILLE

Map page M-3, E5

Motel

≡ **Sheldons Motel**, Va 2, PO Box 189, Keysville, VA 23947; tel 804/736-8434; fax 804/736-9402. ¼ mi S of jct US 15/360. An older motel with an attractive colonial style. Rough-hewn exterior of adjacent restaurant helps compensate for the plain rooms fronting the parking lot. **Rooms:** 39 rms. CI noon/CO noon. Nonsmoking rms avail. Surprisingly clean, comfortable, and spacious rooms considering nondescript brick motel-style buildings. Some have pleasing view of rolling hills of dairy farm across road. **Amenities:** A/C, cable TV w/movies, refrig. **Services:** **Facilities:** 1 rst. Adjacent restaurant is a local favorite, specializing in fresh pork dishes and other country fare. **Rates:** HS Mem Day–Labor Day $32–$46 S; $38–$46 D. Extra person $6. Children under 11 stay free. Lower rates off-season. Pking: Outdoor, free. Maj CC. Rates highest on weekends.

KING GEORGE

Map page M-3, C6 (SE of Fredericksburg)

Attraction

Caledon Natural Area, 11617 Caledon Rd; tel 703/663-3861. Caledon, while overseen by the Virginia Division of State Parks, is actually a natural area, not a park. Only 800 of its 2,579 acres are available for public use, and only for passive recreational use such as picnicking, hiking, and bird-watching. No overnight camping facilities are available.

Four miles of **hiking trails** travel through Caledon's hardwood forest, one of the few remaining hardwood forest preserves in this region. The rest of the natural area is restricted to provide a protected habitat for American bald eagles. In the summer, Caledon shelters one of the largest concentrations of bald eagles in this part of the country, as well as more than 200 other species of birds. The area is one of the most popular bird-watching spots in Virginia. **Open:** Daily, 8am–sunset; visitor center Mem Day–Labor Day, Wed–Sun 9am–5pm (schedule varies; phone ahead). Free.

LEESBURG

Map page M-3, B6

Hotel

≡≡ **Carradoc Hall Hotel**, 1500 E Market St, Leesburg, VA 22075; tel 703/771-9200 or toll free 800/552-6702; fax 703/771-1575. Unique in its architecture and perched on a green knoll, this hotel comprises both an old mansion dating back to the 1700s and a separate low-slung red-plank building with a white porch railing, hanging plants, and an air of country living about it. A bit frayed and worn in areas but an interesting property. **Rooms:** 120 rms and stes. CI noon/CO 10am. Express checkout avail. Nonsmoking rms avail. All rooms redone recently. Interesting old furniture, including 2-poster beds, but some furnishings chipped. **Amenities:** A/C, cable TV. Some units w/terraces, some w/fireplaces. **Services:** X Babysitting. **Facilities:** 1 rst, 2 bars (1 w/entertainment), lifeguard, washer/dryer. Adjoining the Pub, a working brick fireplace and cozy sitting area. Free golfing across the highway. **Rates (CP):** $55–$59 S or D; from $105 ste. Children under 5 stay free. Spec packages avail. Pking: Outdoor, free. Maj CC.

Resort

≣≣≣≣**Lansdowne Conference Resort**, 44050 Woodridge Pkwy, Leesburg, VA 22075; tel 703/729-8400 or toll free 800/541-4801; fax 703/729-4096. 20.5 acres. An elegant hotel set apart from the world on rolling green hills, but only a short distance from highway. Emphasis here is on staff professionalism, tasteful decor, and first-rate facilities for travelers. A diversity of restaurants and recreational opportunities add to sense of full-service, luxury resort. **Rooms:** 305 rms and stes. CI 4pm/CO 11am. Express checkout avail. Nonsmoking rms avail. Half of the rooms have king beds, the other half double beds. **Amenities:** 🛏️🛋️ A/C, cable TV w/movies, voice mail, bathrobes. Some units w/minibars, some w/terraces, 1 w/Jacuzzi. VCRs and refrigerators available free. **Services:** ✗☞ VP 🚗 🗻 ♫ Twice-daily maid svce, car-rental desk, social director, masseur, children's program, babysitting. In-room dining. Two concierges: one for business groups, one for individual travelers. TV message centers throughout the lobby. **Facilities:** 🛋️ 🚴 ▢ ▶18 ✖️ ◉ 🛳️ 📺 💻 ♿ 2 rsts (*see also* "Restaurants" below), 3 bars (1 w/entertainment), lifeguard, games rm, lawn games, racquetball, spa, sauna, steam rm, whirlpool, beauty salon. Fully supervised playroom for children 3–12. Stone tavern offers darts, billiards, shuffleboard. A 5,000-square-foot health club includes combination locks on wood lockers, towels, trainer, shop. Spa offers full complement of services, including facials, massages. Cafe adjoining pool. Horseback riding arranged. Fishing and recreation field ¼ mile away at Potomac River. **Rates:** $99–$169 S or D; from $250 ste. Extra person $20. Children under 18 stay free. Spec packages avail. Pking: Outdoor, free. Maj CC.

Restaurants 🍽️

The Green Tree, 15 S King St, at Queen St, Leesburg; tel 703/771-9300. **Seafood/Steak.** From the Williamsburg stemware to the ladder-back chairs, this restaurant honors its historic 18th-century building just up the block from Leesburg's main square. Rich wood, brick floor, 2 working fireplaces, and servers in period costume add to flavor. Recipes of the 1700s were researched at the Library of Congress for accuracy. Special period dinners served throughout the day on Thanksgiving and Christmas, feast on New Year's Eve. An all-you-can-eat Sunday brunch is available. **FYI:** Reservations recommended. Children's menu. **Open:** Mon–Sat 11am–10pm, Sun 11am–10pm. **Prices:** Main courses $11–$17; PF dinner $12.95–$15.95. Maj CC. ▮ ♿

The Potomac Grill, in Lansdowne Resort, 44050 Woodridge Pkwy, Leesburg; tel 703/729-9300. Exit Va 7 at Ashburn. **Regional American.** At this intimate restaurant in the luxurious Lansdowne Resort, large windows look onto open land and mountains, while inside mahogany tables and sturdy chairs make for a clubby atmosphere. The simple decor, with understated elegance, matches the menu of hearty food at a good price. Specialty is rib-eye steaks. **FYI:** Reservations recommended. Piano/singer. Children's menu. **Open:** Lunch Tues–Fri 2–5:30pm, Sat–Sun 11am–5:30pm; dinner Tues–Sat 5:30–11pm. **Prices:** Main courses $15–$22. Maj CC. ▲ VP ♿

Tuscarora Mill Restaurant, in Market Station Complex, 203 Harrison St SE, Leesburg; tel 703/771-9300. Located 1 block S of Va 7. **New American/Cafe.** This 1899 mill, with massive timber construction and original grain bins, is artfully utilized as a restaurant. The cafe in front is a rustic setting for lighter fare. A spacious rear area with fireplace is available for groups. Known for its wine list—one of the most extensive in the area—Tuscarora Mill has been written up in wine magazines and offers a wine tasting every 2 months. Specialty is fresh seafood. Offers "small plate" entrees. **FYI:** Reservations recommended. **Open:** HS Oct–Dec lunch Mon–Fri 11:30am–2:30pm, Sat–Sun Noon–3pm; dinner Mon–Thurs 5:30–9:30pm, Fri–Sat 5:30–10pm, Sun 5–9pm. Reduced hours off-season. Closed some hols. **Prices:** Main courses $9.50–$20. Maj CC. ▮ 🖼️ ♿

Attractions 💼

Loudon Museum, 14–16 Loudon St SW; tel 703/777-7427. Chronicles the history of Loudon County from the colonial era to the present. Exhibits feature Native American artifacts, Civil War memorabilia, audiovisual presentations, and more. Some hands-on and changing exhibits; lectures and workshops; gift shop. The museum also presents tours of historic homes and gardens of Leesburg (by reservation). **Open:** Mon–Sat 10am–5pm, Sun 1–5pm. Closed some hols and 3 weeks mid-Jan to mid-Feb. Free.

Ball's Bluff Battlefield; tel 703/352-5900 or 729-0596. Located just off US 15, north of the Va 7 junction. Ball's Bluff Battlefield was the site of the third major engagement of the Civil War (Oct 21, 1861). A total of 3,400 troops were involved, with Union forces under the command of Edward Dickinson Baker, US senator from Oregon. Surrounded by Confederate forces, fully half of Baker's force was either killed, wounded, or captured. Baker himself was killed, the only senator ever killed in battle. His death brought about the first major congressional investigation into war conduct. At this battle, Oliver Wendell Holmes, Jr, later to become Chief Justice of the Supreme Court, was wounded.

A ¾-mile walking trail circles the 170-acre battlefield; interpretive exhibits along the way are planned for the near future. There are 3 exhibits currently at the battlefield's national cemetery, which is one of the smallest in the United States.

Guided tours may be arranged in advance. A living history re-enactment takes place on the weekend day nearest the October 21 anniversary of the battle. **Open:** Daily dawn–dusk. Free.

LEON

Map page M-3, C6 (SW of Culpeper)

Restaurant 🍴

Prince Michel Restaurant, in Prince Michel de Virginia Winery, US 29 S, Box 77, Leon; tel 703/547-9720. Between Culpepper and Madison, Va. **French.** Fresh flowers, pastel colors, and floor-to-ceiling trompe l'oeil murals make this restaurant on the lower level of the winery seem like a small European cafe. Patio facing display vineyard and Blue Ridge Mountains offers pleasant outdoor dining when weather permits. Well-known chef cooks in French style using fresh herbs, fruit, and vegetables. Menu changes daily. **FYI:** Reservations recommended. Combo/jazz. Jacket required. **Open:** Lunch Thurs–Sat noon–2pm, Sun 11:30am–2:30pm; dinner Thurs–Sat 6–9pm. **Prices:** PF dinner $50. Maj CC. 🍷 📹 ♿

LEXINGTON

Map page M-2, D4

Motels 🏨

≡≡ Comfort Inn, US 11 S, PO Box 905, Lexington, VA 24450; tel 703/463-7311 or toll free 800/628-1956; fax 703/463-4590. Exit 188B off I-81, follow US 11 N 3 mi; or exit 55 off I-64. Proximity to major interstates and the Virginia Horse Center make this a convenient location. Although it's close to the city, large grounds give a country-like feeling. **Rooms:** 80 rms. CI 2pm/CO 11am. Nonsmoking rms avail. Exceptionally clean. **Amenities:** 🛏 🔥 📺 A/C, cable TV w/movies. **Services:** ✗ 🛎 🔧 🍽 Lobby offers 24-hour coffee, decks of cards, and board games, adding touch of hospitality. **Facilities:** 🏊 ♿ Heated indoor pool is especially appreciated in winter. **Rates:** HS June–Aug $60–$65 S; $65–$70 D. Extra person $5. Children under 18 stay free. Lower rates off-season. Higher rates for spec evnts/hols. Spec packages avail. Pking: Outdoor, free. Maj CC.

≡≡≡ Holiday Inn, US 11 at I-64, PO Box 11088, Lexington, VA 24450; tel 703/463-7351 or toll free 800/465-4329. Exit 55 off I-64; or exit 188B off I-81, then 3 mi on US 11 N. Extensive grounds give a country flavor to this motel, located near restaurants, historic district, Virginia Horse Center, and 2 colleges. Usually is booked heavily on special college weekends.

Rooms: 72 rms. CI 3pm/CO noon. Nonsmoking rms avail. Recent recarpeting gives bright and fresh look. **Amenities:** 🛏 🔥 A/C, cable TV w/movies. **Services:** ✗ 🛎 🔧 🍽 Babysitting. **Facilities:** 🏊 ♿ 1 rst, 1 bar, washer/dryer. Spacious and cheery restaurant on premises. **Rates:** HS May–Sept $64–$70 S or D. Extra person $5. Children under 13 stay free. Lower rates off-season. Higher rates for spec evnts/hols. Spec packages avail. Pking: Outdoor, free. Maj CC.

Inn

≡≡≡ Alexander-Witherow House and Campbell Inn, 11 N Main St, Lexington, VA 24450; tel 703/463-2044. Exit 188B off I-81. These circa-1790 city inns are across Main St from each other in the heart of Lexington's historic district and minutes from Virginia Military Institute. **Rooms:** 23 rms and stes. CI 2pm/CO noon. Faithfully restored rooms are furnished with antiques. Each unit has its own ambience, but all are spacious. **Amenities:** 🛏 🔥 📺 A/C, cable TV w/movies, refrig. Some units w/minibars. **Services:** 🛎 🔧 Babysitting, wine/sherry served. **Facilities:** ♿ Pool and tennis courts at nearby Maple Hall available to guests. **Rates:** HS Apr–June/Sept–Oct $80–$120 S; from $135 ste. Extra person $15. Lower rates off-season. Spec packages avail. Pking: Outdoor, free. Ltd CC.

Restaurants 🍴

★ **Harbs'**, 19 W Washington St, Lexington; tel 703/464-1900. Exit 188B off I-81. Follow US 60 (Nelson St) west; turn right at Jefferson St, and right onto Washington St. **Cafe/Vegetarian.** Lively cafe and outdoor patio in historic downtown, with art exhibitions monthly. Candlelight dinners. Freshly baked breakfast and sandwich breads, pasta, salads, and gourmet soups are regular features. Dinner menu varies weekly but always includes a vegetarian pasta. Picnic baskets prepared for theater outings. **FYI:** Reservations accepted. Children's menu. **Open:** Sun–Mon 9am–8pm, Tues–Thurs 8am–9pm, Fri–Sat 8am–10pm. Closed some hols. **Prices:** Main courses $7–$13. Ltd CC. 🍷

★ **The Palms**, 101 W Nelson St, Lexington; tel 703/463-7911. Exit 188B off I-81. **American/Cafe/Eclectic.** Wooden tables and chairs combine with bright green booths to make this a favorite with local residents and the college crowd, who come for an eclectic mix of freshly prepared foods. Good eats, friendly people, and the energy of a college town together with historic ambience. **FYI:** Reservations not accepted. Children's menu. **Open:** Daily 11:30am–11pm. Closed Dec 25. **Prices:** Main courses $10–$15. Ltd CC. 🍺

The Willson-Walker House Restaurant, 30 N Main St, Lexington; tel 703/463-3020. Exit 188B off I-81. Follow US 60

(Nelson St) west, turn right on Main St. **New American.** An 1820s classical revival home decorated with period antiques, located in Lexington's downtown historic district. Gourmet American cuisine, especially seafood. Afternoon tea Wednesdays 3–5pm November to March. **FYI:** Reservations recommended. Children's menu. Dress code. No smoking. **Open:** Lunch Tues–Sat 11:30am–2:30pm; dinner Tues–Sat 5:30–9pm. Closed some hols. **Prices:** Main courses $14–$19. Maj CC. ▮ ⛴ 🖼 ⚹

Attractions 🎒

Lee Chapel and Museum, Washington and Lee University, Lechter Ave and Washington St; tel 703/463-8768. Robert E Lee served as president of Washington College from 1865 until his death in 1870. Soon thereafter, the school's name was changed to Washington and Lee University. The magnificent Victorian-Gothic brick and native limestone chapel was built in 1867 at Lee's request. A white marble sculpture of Lee by Edward Valentine portrays the general recumbent. Lee's remains are in a crypt below the chapel along with those of other family members. Among the museum's most important holdings are Charles Wilson Peale's portrait of George Washington wearing the uniform of a colonel in the British army and the painting of General Lee in Confederate uniform by Theodore Pine. The portraits hang in the chapel auditorium. **Open:** Mid-Oct to mid-Apr, Mon–Sat 9am–4pm, Sun 2–5pm; mid-Apr to mid-Oct, Mon–Sat 9am–5pm, Sun 2–5pm. Free.

Stonewall Jackson House, 8 E Washington St; tel 703/463-2552. Maj Thomas Jackson came to Lexington in 1851 to take a post as teacher of physics and artillery tactics at VMI. In 1858 Jackson purchased this house, 5 blocks from the institute. He lived here with his wife until 1861, when he left to answer Gen Lee's summons. Two years later, Jackson's body was returned to Lexington for burial at the Presbyterian church cemetery on South Main Street.

The house has been restored and contains many of Jackson's personal possessions. Appropriate period furnishings duplicate items on the inventory of Jackson's estate made shortly after his death at Chancellorsville in 1863. Photographs, text, and a slide show tell the story of the Jacksons' stay here. **Open:** Sept–May, Mon–Sat 9am–5pm, Sun 1–5pm; June–Aug, daily 9am–6pm. Closed some hols. $$

Virginia Military Institute Museum, Jackson Memorial Hall, VMI campus; tel 703/464-7232. The VMI Museum displays uniforms, weapons, and memorabilia from cadets who attended the college and fought in numerous wars. Of special note are the VMI coatee (tunic) that belonged to Gen George S Patton, Jr (VMI, 1907), and Stonewall Jackson's VMI uniform coat and the

bullet-pierced raincoat he wore at the Battle of Chancellorsville. The George C Marshall Museum is also on the VMI campus (see below).

Sometimes called the West Point of the South, VMI opened in 1839. The most dramatic episode in the school's history took place during the Civil War Battle of New Market (May 15, 1864). More than 200 teenage VMI cadets, called upon to reinforce Confederate defenses, played a major role in blocking a Union advance. A month later, Union Gen David Hunter retaliated, burning VMI to the ground. **Open:** Mon–Sat 9am–5pm, Sun 2–5pm. Closed some hols. Free.

George C Marshall Museum, VMI Campus; tel 703/463-7103. This impressive white building houses the archives and research library of Gen of the Army George Catlett Marshall, a 1901 graduate of VMI. Marshall's illustrious military career included service in World War I as Gen Pershing's aide-de-camp, and in World War II, as army chief of staff and secretary of defense under President Truman. But he is probably best known for the Marshall Plan, which fostered the postwar economic recovery of Europe. He became the first career soldier to receive the Nobel Prize for Peace (1953). Marshall's Nobel medallion is among the personal items on display at the museum. **Open:** Daily 9am–5pm. Closed some hols. $

Virginia Horse Center; tel 703/463-7060. Located on Va 39W, near the intersection of I-64 and I-81. Sprawling across nearly 400 acres just outside Lexington, the center offers horse shows, seminars, and sales of fine horses. Annual events include an Arabian Horse Show, US Ponies of America Association events, American Saddlebred Horse Association shows, Miniature Horse Classic, and qualifying competitions for the Pan American Games. Also on the schedule are English and Western riding demonstrations, equine art and photography shows, wagon rides, fox-hunting demonstrations, and tack equipment displays. For a full program of events and associated fees, contact the center at PO Box 1051, Lexington, VA 24450. **Open:** Daily, schedule varies.

LORTON

Map page M-3, C6 (S of Alexandria)

For lodgings and dining, see Alexandria

Attractions 🎒

Gunston Hall, 10709 Gunston Rd; tel 703/550-9220. This was the magnificent estate of George Mason (1725–92), the statesman and political thinker who drafted the Virginia Declaration of Rights (after which the US Bill of Rights was modeled) and whose ideas formed the basis of the Declaration of Independence. A member of the committee that drafted the US Constitution, Mason refused to sign the ratified version because it didn't abolish slavery or, initially, contain a Bill of Rights.

An 11-minute film introduces visitors to the estate, and there is a small museum of Mason family memorabilia. In Mason's library and study is the writing table on which he penned the Virginia Declaration of Rights. The tour also includes several outbuildings, including the kitchen, dairy, laundry, and school-house (Mason had 9 children). Also on the grounds is the family graveyard where Mason himself is buried. **Open:** Daily 9:30am–5pm. Closed some hols. $$

Pohick Church, 9301 Richmond Hwy; tel 703/339-6572. Built in the 1770s from plans drawn up by George Washington, this church has been restored to its original appearance and has an active Episcopal congregation. The interior was designed by George Mason, owner of Gunston Hall, with box pews like those common in England at the time. During the Civil War Union troops stabled their horses in the church and stripped the interior—the east wall was used for target practice. **Open:** Daily 9am–4:30pm. Free.

Pohick Bay Regional Park, 6501 Pohick Bay Dr; tel 703/339-6104. Located near Gunston Hall (see above) on Va 242, this is a 1,000-acre park focusing on water-oriented recreation, occupying a spectacular bayside setting on the historic Mason Neck peninsula. It has one of the largest swimming pools on the East Coast, and offers boat access to the Potomac (sailboat and paddleboat rentals are available), 150 campsites, a 4-mile bridle path, scenic nature trails, and 18-hole golf course and pro shop, miniature golf, and sheltered picnic areas with grills. **Open:** Daily 8am–dusk. $$

Mason Neck State Park, 7301 High Point Rd; tel 703/550-0960. An 1,800-acre area of marsh and uplands, this park is a primary nesting site for the American bald eagle. Weekend guided canoe trips (Apr–Oct; reservation necessary) offer the best chance of viewing bald eagles in their natural habitat, but some are occasionally spotted closer to developed areas. Best viewing in winter, and in the morning and evening. Visitor center with exhibits, information (summer only); hiking, picnicking. **Open:** Daily 8am–dusk. $

LURAY

Map page M-3, C5

See also **Shenandoah National Park**

Motels 🛏

🍴 **Intown Motel**, 410 W Main St, Luray, VA 22835; tel 703/743-6511; fax 703/743-6511. Convenient to downtown and the caverns, this motel is basic but clean. It's owned and operated by a family, who all work to help guests. **Rooms:** 40 rms. CI open/CO noon. Nonsmoking rms avail. Rooms have nicely integrated decor. Honeymoon room is larger and has better furnishings. **Amenities:** 🛏 A/C, cable TV w/movies. **Services:** ✗ ⊡ ⊲ **Facilities:** ⊡ 1 rst, lawn games, playground. **Rates:** HS Apr–Nov $55–$68 S or D. Extra person $5. Children under 18 stay free. Lower rates off-season. Higher rates for spec evnts/hols. Pking: Outdoor, free. Maj CC.

🍴🍴 **Luray Caverns Motel**, US 211, PO Box 748, Luray, VA 22835; tel 703/743-6551. This white colonial-style motel in the Blue Ridge Mountains has a beautiful view and sparkling-clean accommodations. While modest in decor, it's a change from larger motels. Located opposite Luray Caverns. **Rooms:** 19 rms and effic. CI 11am/CO 11am. All are ground-level rooms, all have view of mountains; 1 apartment with screened-in porch available. **Amenities:** 🛏 A/C, cable TV. Some units w/terraces. **Services:** ⊡ ⊲ **Facilities:** ⊡ **Rates:** HS Apr–Nov $52–$56 S or D. Extra person $7. Children under 16 stay free. Lower rates off-season. Higher rates for spec evnts/hols. Spec packages avail. Pking: Outdoor, free. Maj CC. Golf and tennis packages available.

🍴🍴 **Luray Caverns Motel East**, US 211, PO Box 748, Luray, VA 22835; tel 703/743-4531. Across from the entrance to Luray Caverns, with view in back of mountain greenery. **Rooms:** 25 rms and effic; 18 ctges/villas. CI 11am/CO 11am. Larger-than-average, sparkling-clean rooms with pleasant decor. Cottages, some with two rooms, are not as bright but are good for families and modestly priced. Mattresses could be better. **Amenities:** 🛏 A/C, cable TV w/movies. Some units w/terraces. Stove and fridge in apartment. **Services:** ⊡ ⊲ **Facilities:** ⊡ ⧖ Picnic table by pond. **Rates:** HS Apr–Nov $52–$56 S or D; from $109 effic; from $42 ctge/villa. Children under 16 stay free. Lower rates off-season. Higher rates for spec evnts/hols. Spec packages avail. Pking: Outdoor, free. Maj CC. Golf and tennis packages available.

🍴🍴🍴 **Ramada Inn**, US 211 E Bypass, Luray, VA 22835; tel 703/743-4521 or toll free 800/2-RAMADA; fax 703/743-6863.

Set at the base of Blue Ridge Mountains, this hotel offers acres of green space, a lobby with antique furnishings, and a museum of presidential memorabilia, including items from John Adams's desk. Not your usual chain operation, the hotel is owned by an aficionado of antiques and presidents. It shows—from antique wooden horses in the hallway to old campaign posters in the dining room. **Rooms:** 99 rms and stes. CI 3pm/CO noon. Nonsmoking rms avail. Stunning "Antique Luxury" rooms, with period furnishings and wallpaper; 2 presidential suites. **Amenities:** 🛁 🍴 A/C, cable TV w/movies. Some units w/Jacuzzis. VCRs, microwaves, and refrigerators free upon request. Computer/fax jack at front desk. **Services:** ✗ 🖼 🍴 🚲 Turndown service available upon request. **Facilities:** 🔒 🍴 150 🖥 🚿 1 rst, 1 bar, lawn games, playground, washer/dryer. Small area offering souvenirs, small fitness room, bar with super TV, miniature golf. **Rates:** HS June–Nov $65–$75 S or D; from $95 ste. Extra person $7. Children under 18 stay free. Lower rates off-season. Spec packages avail. Pking: Outdoor, free. Maj CC. Special ski and golf packages available.

Lodges

≣≣≣ **Big Meadows Lodge**, Skyline Drive MM 51.2, PO Box 727, Luray, VA 22835; tel 703/999-2221 or toll free 800/999-4714; fax 703/743-7883. A rustic lodge offering many nature activities and splendid mountain views from main lounge and dining room. National Park Service visitor center and interpretive area nearby. Open mid-March through November only. **Rooms:** 83 rms and stes; 10 ctges/villas. CI 3pm/CO noon. Nonsmoking rms avail. Rustic rooms have wormy chestnut wall paneling. **Amenities:** No A/C, phone, or TV. Some units w/terraces, some w/fireplaces. **Services:** 🍴 Car-rental desk. **Facilities:** 🏇 🚿 1 rst, 1 bar (w/entertainment), playground. Horseback riding available nearby. Many nature and hiking trails. **Rates:** $60–$86 S or D; from $85 ste; from $63 ctge/villa. Extra person $5. Children under 16 stay free. Higher rates for spec evnts/hols. MAP rates avail. Spec packages avail. Pking: Outdoor, free. Maj CC.

≣≣≣ **Skyland Lodge**, Skyline Drive MM 41.8, PO Box 727, Luray, VA 22835; tel 703/999-2211 or toll free 800/999-4714; fax 703/743-7883. Exit 264 off I-81. Set high in the mountains on Skyline Dr in Shenandoah National Park, this lodge has spectacular views of the valley below. Open mid-March through November only. **Rooms:** 177 rms and stes; 19 ctges/villas. CI 2pm/CO noon. Nonsmoking rms avail. A mix of accommodations, from quaint rustic cabins to spacious new suites. **Amenities:** Cable TV. No A/C or phone. All units w/terraces, some w/fireplaces. **Services:** 🍴 Children's program. **Facilities:** 30 🚿 1 rst, 1 bar, playground. Hiking trails, horseback and pony riding nearby. **Rates:** $72–$92 S or D; from $105 ste; from $43 effic.

Extra person $5. Children under 16 stay free. Higher rates for spec evnts/hols. MAP rates avail. Spec packages avail. Pking: Outdoor, free. Maj CC.

Restaurants 🍴

★ **Brookside Restaurant**, US 211, Luray; tel 703/743-5698. **American.** There's nothing fancy here, but this basic family-owned restaurant is a favorite with locals. The old stone structure with wagon-wheel lights and fans spinning overhead is filled with knickknacks and framed country scenes. The decor matches the country cooking, featuring an all-you-can-eat buffet. Lighter, healthier fare also offered. The specialties here are the desserts, especially the peach cobbler. **FYI:** Reservations accepted. Children's menu. Beer and wine only. **Open:** HS June–Oct daily 7am–9pm. Reduced hours off-season. Closed some hols; mid-Dec–mid-Jan. **Prices:** Main courses $6–$14. Maj CC. 🖼 🎲

Parkhurst Restaurant, US 211, Luray; tel 703/743-6009. 2 mi W of Luray Caverns. **International.** Featuring international cuisine, this onetime country inn set high above the highway offers elegant dining in a front dining area with a chandelier and dark wood and in 2 larger, modern rooms. The large paneled bar area also has tables. Restaurant is one of 300 *Wine Spectator* Award winners in the country. The specialty is colonial-style steak. **FYI:** Reservations recommended. Children's menu. **Open:** Sun–Thurs 4–10pm, Fri–Sat 4–11pm. Closed some hols. **Prices:** Main courses $10–$20. Maj CC. ♥ 🖼

Attraction 🏛

Luray Caverns, US 211; tel 703/743-6551. The formation of these caverns, an extensive series of limestone caves and streams, began over 400 million years ago, as water from the surface penetrated the limestone through cracks resulting from shifting of the earth's crust. As water filled the gaps, it dissolved more and more rock, gradually carving out the underground labyrinth of rooms and passageways. Stalactites, formed by water dripping from the ceilings, and stalagmites, formed from the ground up, meet and form columns. In an active case such as Luray, these formations "grow" 1 cubic inch every 120 years.

The caverns are noted for the beautiful cascades of natural colors found on interior walls. Also of note is the "stalacpipe" organ, which combines the work of man and nature. It produces music when stalactites are tapped by rubber-tipped plungers triggered by an electronic keyboard. Guided tours (1 hour) depart every 20 minutes and follow a system of brick and concrete walkways. **Open:** June 15–Labor Day, daily 9am–7pm;

Mar 15–June 14, daily 9am-6pm; day after Labor Day through Oct 31, daily 9am-6pm; Nov 1– Mar 14, Mon–Fri 9am-4pm, Sat–Sun 9am–5pm. $$$$

LYNCHBURG

Map page M-2, D4

Hotels ▣

≣≣≣ Holiday Inn, US 29 and Odd Fellows Rd, PO Box 10729, Lynchburg, VA 24506; tel 804/847-4424 or toll free 800/465-4329; fax 804/846-4965. 2 mi S of downtown. Detached units surround a large grassy lawn with pool, creating a safe area for children. **Rooms:** 256 rms and stes. Exec-level rms avail. CI 3pm/CO noon. Express checkout avail. Nonsmoking rms avail. **Amenities:** ☎ ⓐ A/C, cable TV w/movies. **Services:** ✕ ♨ △ ↵ Babysitting. **Facilities:** ⑤ ▨ 👶 1 rst, 1 bar, washer/dryer. **Rates:** $58–$68 S or D; from $94 ste. Higher rates for spec evnts/hols. Spec packages avail. Pking: Outdoor, free. Maj CC.

≣≣≣ Holiday Inn Crowne Plaza, 601 Main St, Lynchburg, VA 24504 (Downtown); tel 804/528-2500 or toll free 800/HOLIDAY; fax 804/528-0062. Exit US 29 at Main St. A nicely appointed, very clean hotel in the heart of Lynchburg. **Rooms:** 238 rms. Exec-level rms avail. CI 3pm/CO noon. Express checkout avail. Nonsmoking rms avail. **Amenities:** ☎ ⓐ ☎ A/C, cable TV w/movies. Some units w/minibars, some w/Jacuzzis. **Services:** ✕ ☎ VP ♨ △ ↵ Babysitting. **Facilities:** ⑤ ☎ ▨ 👶 1 rst, 1 bar, whirlpool. **Rates:** HS May–Nov $55–$89 S; $55–$89 D. Extra person $15. Children under 18 stay free. Lower rates off-season. Spec packages avail. Pking: Indoor/outdoor, free. Maj CC.

≣≣ Howard Johnson Lodge, US 29 N, PO Box 10729, Lynchburg, VA 24506; tel 804/845-7041 or toll free 800/446-4656; fax 804/845-0222. 2 mi N of downtown. Located opposite a shopping mall. **Rooms:** 70 rms. CI 2pm/CO noon. Nonsmoking rms avail. The front rooms enjoy views of the Blue Ridge Mountains from their private patios. **Amenities:** ☎ A/C, cable TV w/movies. All units w/terraces. **Services:** ✕ △ ↵ ☎ **Facilities:** ⑤ 👶 1 rst, washer/dryer. **Rates:** HS May–Oct $62–$69 S; $69–$75 D. Extra person $7. Children under 18 stay free. Lower rates off-season. Higher rates for spec evnts/hols. Pking: Outdoor, free. Maj CC.

≣≣ Lynchburg Comfort Inn, US 29 and Odd Fellows Rd, PO Box 10729, Lynchburg, VA 24506; tel 804/847-9041 or toll free 800/221-2222; fax 804/847-8513. 2 mi S of downtown. Attractively set in a semiwooded area, yet close to the city. The pool is good for children since it is well protected from roads. **Rooms:** 123 rms. Exec-level rms avail. CI 3pm/CO noon. Express checkout avail. Nonsmoking rms avail. **Amenities:** ☎ A/C, cable TV w/movies. Some units w/terraces. **Services:** ✕ ☎ ♨ △ ↵ ☎ **Facilities:** ⑤ ▨ 👶 **Rates (CP):** $39–$89 S; $39–$94 D. Extra person $5. Children under 18 stay free. Higher rates for spec evnts/hols. Spec packages avail. Pking: Outdoor, free. Maj CC.

≣≣≣ Lynchburg Hilton, 2900 Candler's Mountain Rd, Lynchburg, VA 24502; tel 804/237-6333 or toll free 800/445-8667; fax 804/237-4277. 3½ mi S of downtown. Take exit 128W off US 29; or exit US 460 at Candler's Mountain Rd. Exceptional decor accents this fine hotel. Great attention paid to lighting in rooms and lobby. **Rooms:** 167 rms and stes. Exec-level rms avail. CI 2pm/CO 11am. Express checkout avail. Nonsmoking rms avail. **Amenities:** ☎ ⓐ ☎ A/C, cable TV w/movies. Rooms for those with handicaps equipped with visual signal for telephone rings. **Services:** ✕ ♨ △ ↵ Babysitting. **Facilities:** ⑤ ☎ ▨ 🖥 👶 1 rst, 1 bar (w/entertainment), spa, whirlpool, beauty salon, washer/dryer. **Rates:** $75–$110 S; $95–$130 D; from $186 ste. Extra person $20. Children under 18 stay free. Higher rates for spec evnts/hols. Spec packages avail. Pking: Outdoor, free. Maj CC.

Motels

≣≣ Best Western Lynchburg, 2815 Candlers Mountain Rd, Lynchburg, VA 24502; tel 804/237-2986 or toll free 800/528-1234; fax 804/237-2987. 3½ mi S of downtown. Exit Candlers Mountain Road N off US 460; or exit 128W off US 29. A very clean motel with a friendly, efficient staff. Located near shopping mall and restaurants. **Rooms:** 87 rms. Exec-level rms avail. CI 2pm/CO 11am. Nonsmoking rms avail. **Amenities:** ☎ A/C, cable TV. **Services:** △ ↵ **Facilities:** ⑤ ▨ 👶 **Rates (CP):** HS Apr–Oct $40–$49 S; $43–$59 D. Extra person $4. Lower rates off-season. Higher rates for spec evnts/hols. Pking: Outdoor, free. Maj CC.

≣≣≣ Days Inn Lynchburg, 3220 Candler's Mountain Rd, Lynchburg, VA 24502; tel 804/847-8655 or toll free 800/787-DAYS; fax 804/846-DAYS. 3½ mi S of downtown. Take exit 128E off US 29; or exit US 460 at Candler's Mountain Rd. An exceptionally attractive and well-managed chain motel with congenial staff. Conveniently located near shopping mall and restaurants. **Rooms:** 131 rms. Exec-level rms avail. CI 2pm/CO noon. Nonsmoking rms avail. **Amenities:** ☎ ⓐ A/C, cable TV w/movies. All units w/terraces. **Services:** ✕ ♨ △ ↵ **Facilities:** ⑤ ▨ 👶 1 rst, playground. Guests bowl free at neighboring lanes. **Rates (BB):** HS May–Oct $54–$79 S; $59–

$84 D. Extra person $5. Children under 18 stay free. Lower rates off-season. Higher rates for spec evnts/hols. Spec packages avail. Pking: Outdoor, free. Maj CC.

≣ **Timberlake Motel**, 11222 Timberlake Rd, Lynchburg, VA 24502; tel 804/525-2160; fax 804/525-5104. On US 460, 2 mi W of US 29. A small, basic roadside motel operated by a family. Close to many restaurants, easy access to Lynchburg attractions. **Rooms:** 41 rms and effic. CI 2pm/CO 11am. Nonsmoking rms avail. Comfortable rooms are clean, quiet. **Amenities:** 🛁 📞 A/C, cable TV w/movies, refrig. 1 unit w/Jacuzzi. **Services:** 🖾 ↻ **Facilities:** 🔲 Whirlpool, washer/dryer. **Rates:** $38–$43 S or D; from $57 effic. Extra person $3. Children under 12 stay free. Pking: Outdoor, free. Maj CC. Weekly rates available.

Restaurants 🍽️

Café France, in Forest Plaza West Shopping Center, 3225 Old Forest Rd, Lynchburg; tel 804/385-8989. Exit US 29 at US 501 N. **New American/Continental/Eclectic.** A tasteful and quiet eatery with a pastel color scheme featuring prints of flowers and posters. Many daily specials prepared with fresh seafood, veal, lamb, and vegetables plus the house specialty: pastas. Carryout available Tuesday to Saturday 11am–10pm. Small gourmet shop has wide selection of wines. **FYI:** Reservations recommended. Children's menu. **Open:** Lunch Mon 10am–3pm, Tues–Sat 11:30am–3pm; dinner Tues–Sat 5:30–10pm. Closed some hols. **Prices:** Main courses $6–$22. Maj CC. &

★ **Crown Sterling**, 6120 Fort Ave, Lynchburg; tel 804/239-7744. Exit US 501 S at Fort Ave. **Seafood/Steak.** Wood panels, 2 fireplaces, and candles give an understated elegance to this steak house, which has served a loyal local following for more than 20 years. **FYI:** Reservations accepted. Children's menu. Beer and wine only. **Open:** Mon–Sat 5–10pm. Closed some hols. **Prices:** Main courses $10–$20. Maj CC. ♥ 📧 &

★ **Emil's**, in Boonsboro Shopping Center, US 501 N, Lynchburg; tel 804/384-3311. Exit US 29 or US 460 at US 501 N. **French/Swiss.** Candlelight and dark wood paneling give a solid, comfortable feel to this popular restaurant known for its tableside flambés and French flair. An in-house bakery prepares many French and Swiss pastries. **FYI:** Reservations accepted. Children's menu. Beer and wine only. **Open:** Mon–Sat 10am–10pm. Closed some hols. **Prices:** Main courses $6–$17. Maj CC. ♥ &

The Farm Basket, 2008 Langhorne Rd, Lynchburg; tel 804/528-1107. Exit US 460 or US 29 at US 501 Business N. **Regional American.** Part of a small, delightful complex featuring a fresh-fruit-and-vegetable stand, gourmet food and kitchen shop, and a crafts gallery, this lunchtime eatery has country-style

decor and spacious windows overlooking a large deck and creek. Light lunches feature freshly made seasonal specialties. **FYI:** Reservations accepted. No liquor license. **Open:** Mon–Sat 10am–5pm. Closed some hols. **Prices:** Lunch main courses $3–$5.95. Ltd CC.

Attraction 🏛️

South River Meeting House, 5810 Fort Ave; tel 804/239-2548. Pioneer Quakers settled in this area in the middle of the 18th century. They established the South River Meeting House in 1754, and completed the present stone building in 1798. Due to economic hardship, their opposition to slavery, and the expectation of civil unrest, the Quakers had left the area by the 1940s; most went to Ohio and other free states.

In 1899 the Presbyterians purchased the ruins of the abandoned Meeting House, restored the building as a church, and held their first service in 1901. The restored church was named the Quaker Memorial Presbyterian Church in honor of its heritage.

Several early Quaker leaders are buried in the adjacent cemetery, and today the church is a Virginia Historic Landmark, listed on the National Register of Historic Places. An authentic restoration was completed in 1990. Guided tours of the site can be arranged by calling in advance. **Open:** Sept–May, Mon–Fri 9am–3pm; June–Aug, Mon–Fri 9am–12:30pm. Closed some hols. Free.

MANASSAS

Map page M-3, C6

Hotels 🏨

≣≣ **Best Western**, 8640 Mathis Ave, Manassas, VA 22110; tel 703/368-7070 or toll free 800/258-7177; fax 703/368-7292. Exit 53 off I-66. An acceptable facility with clean appearance and decor, spacious lobby, cordial staff. Closer to downtown Manassas than to battlefield and interstate area, making it a bit quieter than those busy places. **Rooms:** 60 rms. CI 3pm/CO 11am. Nonsmoking rms avail. Appearance is pleasing, though some furniture is scarred. **Amenities:** 🛁 📷 A/C, cable TV w/movies. Some units w/Jacuzzis. Refrigerators and microwaves available. Coffeemakers in some rooms. **Services:** 🖾 ↻ ↺ Babysitting. **Facilities:** 🏋️ 📷 & 1 rst, 1 bar, sauna, steam rm, whirlpool, washer/dryer. Small area for exercise has stationary bike, sauna, Jacuzzi. **Rates:** $53–$58 S; $48–$68 D. Extra person $5. Children under 12 stay free. Min stay spec evnts. Pking: Outdoor, free. Maj CC.

☰☰☰ **Courtyard by Marriott**, 10701 Battleview Pkwy, Manassas, VA 22110; tel 703/335-1300 or toll free 800/321-2211; fax 703/335-9442. Exit 47B off I-66. A touch of elegance and luxury, from the nicely decorated sitting areas in the lobby to the landscaped courtyard. **Rooms:** 149 rms and stes. CI 3pm/CO 1pm. Express checkout avail. Nonsmoking rms avail. **Amenities:** 🔒 ⚱ 🖵 A/C, cable TV w/movies, refrig. All units w/terraces. Shower massage. Instant hot-water tap for coffee/tea in each bathroom. King suites include refrigerator, TV in bedroom and parlor. **Services:** 🖨 ⊋ **Facilities:** 🗼 🍴 ⛱ ⚹ 1 rst, 1 bar, whirlpool, washer/dryer. **Rates:** HS Mar–Oct $53–$64 S; $53–$69 D; from $59 ste. Extra person $5. Children under 18 stay free. Lower rates off-season. Pking: Outdoor, free. Maj CC. Weekend packages available. Rates based on room, not occupancy. Discounts for 7 consecutive nights.

☰☰ **Hampton Inn**, 7295 Williamson Blvd, Manassas, VA 22110; tel 703/369-1100 or toll free 800/HAMPTON; fax 703/369-1100 ext 101. Exit I-66 at Va 234; inn ahead at 2nd light. An inviting facility with cordial staff, pleasant decor, and lobby seating area with tables and hanging plants. Full renovation expected by 1996. Near Manassas battlefield. **Rooms:** 125 rms and stes. CI 3pm/CO 11am. Nonsmoking rms avail. 5 suites have king-size bed and sitting room. **Amenities:** 🔒 ⚱ A/C, cable TV w/movies. Some units w/Jacuzzis. Refrigerators available free. Hair dryers available at desk. Suites have 2 phones. **Services:** 🆚🅿 🖨 ⊋ Coffee is available and extensive continental breakfast served in lobby seating area. Roll-away beds available free. **Facilities:** 🗼 🍴 🍽 ⚹ Washer/dryer. TGI Friday's restaurant just across parking lot. Guest laundry on premises. Stair-stepper, exercise bike, and Nautilus system in fitness center. **Rates (CP):** $51–$89 S; $49–$53 D; from $99 ste. Children under 18 stay free. Min stay spec evnts. Higher rates for spec evnts/hols. Pking: Outdoor, free. Maj CC.

☰☰☰ **Holiday Inn Manassas Battlefield**, 10800 Vandor Lane, Manassas, VA 22110; tel 703/335-0000 or toll free 800/HOLIDAY; fax 703/361-8440. Exit 47B off I-66. A chain motel that underwent total renovation in 1994. **Rooms:** 160 rms. CI 2pm/CO noon. Nonsmoking rms avail. Rooms have blended decor, pleasant sitting areas. **Amenities:** 🔒 ⚱ A/C, cable TV w/movies. Some units w/terraces. VCRs available. **Services:** ✗ 🖨 ⊋ ⟳ Children's program. **Facilities:** 🗼 🍴 🍽 ⚹ 1 rst, 1 bar (w/entertainment), lifeguard, washer/dryer. A small fitness area includes Nautilus equipment. **Rates:** HS Apr–Oct $53–$59 S or D. Extra person $6. Children under 18 stay free. Lower rates off-season. Spec packages avail. Pking: Outdoor, free. Maj CC. May 5 to September 10, children eat free (up to 4 children per family). Special packages for Civil War tours, golf.

☰☰ **Ramada Inn**, 10820 Balls Ford Rd, Manassas, VA 22110; tel 703/361-8000 or toll free 800/292-6232; fax 703/361-8000 ext 310. Exit 47B off I-66. Modest but inviting facility with pleasant lobby sitting area and nicely groomed pool area in center of courtyard. Outdoor corridors a bit cracked here and there, but rooms are clean. **Rooms:** 121 rms. CI 2pm/CO noon. Nonsmoking rms avail. **Amenities:** 🔒 ⚱ A/C, cable TV w/movies. Refrigerators and microwaves available. **Services:** ✗ 🖨 ⊋ ⟳ **Facilities:** 🗼 🍽 ⚹ 1 rst, 1 bar (w/entertainment). Bar features live country-and-western music on weekends. **Rates:** HS Apr–Oct $40–$60 S; $45–$65 D. Extra person $5. Children under 18 stay free. Lower rates off-season. Pking: Outdoor, free. Maj CC.

Motel

☰ **Days Inn**, 10653 Balls Ford Rd, Manassas, VA 22110; tel 703/368-2800 or toll free 800/DAYS-INN; fax 703/368-0083. Exit 47B off I-66. No frills but all the basics, plus a pleasant decor. Convenient to interstate, battlefield, restaurant. **Rooms:** 120 rms. CI 2pm/CO 11am. Nonsmoking rms avail. Rooms are clean, but some small upkeep problems (need for new carpet, upholstery) noted in 1 room. **Amenities:** 🔒 ⚱ A/C, cable TV w/movies, VCR. **Services:** 🖨 ⊋ **Facilities:** 🗼 ⚹ Washer/dryer. **Rates:** HS Apr–Aug $37–$46 S; $37–$53 D. Extra person $6. Children under 18 stay free. Lower rates off-season. Higher rates for spec evnts/hols. Pking: Outdoor, free. Maj CC. Battlefield Package includes room and admission to battlefield.

Restaurants 🍴

★ **Mike's Diner**, 8401 Digges Rd, Manassas; tel 703/361-5248. **American.** With its huge windows and wall panels sporting impressionist murals, Mike's is a bright and fun place for travelers looking for large servings, solid American fare, and old-fashioned booths. This local favorite with a friendly staff provides seating up front if you have to wait for the good food. Specials include "ribs night" and a basic meat-and-veggies plate. No bar but drinks available. Breakfast served 24 hours a day. **FYI:** Reservations not accepted. Children's menu. **Open:** Daily 24 hrs. Closed Dec 25. **Prices:** Main courses $4.50–$7.95. Maj CC. 🖼 🍴 ⚹

Pargo's, 10651 Balls Ford Rd, Manassas; tel 703/369-5800. Exit 47 off I-66. **Regional American.** This trendy restaurant filled with hanging plants creates a colorful atmosphere with picture windows, balloons, multilevel floors, brick walls, and chrome-framed pop art. Salads and pastas are favorites, and food is served with flair. Some booths and some tables with lamps or candles offer more intimate dining. **FYI:** Reservations not accepted. Children's menu. **Open:** Mon–Thurs 11am–midnight, Fri–Sat 11am–2am, Sun 10:30am–midnight. Closed Dec 25. **Prices:** Main courses $6.95–$16.95. Maj CC. ⊚ &

Attractions 🖼

Manassas Museum, 9101 Prince William St; tel 703/368-1873. Established in 1974, the Manassas Museum interprets the history and culture of the northern Virginia Piedmont region. The museum's collection includes prehistoric tools, Civil War weapons and uniforms, Victorian costumes, quilts, and many other items from the past. There is an extensive collection of photographs, and 2 video programs describe the settlement of the area and the legacy of the Civil War. The museum also provides architectural and walking/driving tour brochures covering the Old Town district. **Open:** Tues–Sun 10am–5pm; open Mon hols. Closed some hols. $

Manassas National Battlefield Park, 6511 Sudley Rd (Va 234); tel 703/361-1339. The first massive clash of the Civil War took place here on July 21, 1861, when a force of 35,000 well-equipped but poorly trained Union troops commanded by Gen Irvin McDowell were met by Gen P G T Beauregard's Confederate army, which was deployed along a stream known as Bull Run. The 10 hours of heavy fighting that ensued shocked both sides and shattered hopes for a quick end to the war. It was here that Col (later Gen) Thomas Jackson earned the nickname "Stonewall."

North and South met again on the fields of Manassas in August 1862. The 2nd Battle of Manassas secured Gen Robert E Lee's place in history—his 55,000 men soundly defeated the Union army under Gen John Pope.

The 2 battles are commemorated at the 5,000-acre battlefield park. The visitors center has a museum, a 13-minute slide show, and a battle map program that tell the story of the battles. There are a number of self-guided walking tours that highlight Henry Hill, Stone Bridge, and the other critical areas of the 1st Manassas battlefield. A 12-mile driving tour covers the sites of 2nd Manassas, which raged over a much larger area. **Open:** Summer, daily 8:30am–6pm; winter, daily 8:30am–5pm. $

MARION

Map page M-2, E2

Motel 🏨

≣≣ **Holiday Inn**, 1424 N Main St, Marion, VA 24354; tel 703/783-3193 or toll free 800/465-4329; fax 703/783-3193. Exit 47 off I-81. This older city motel offers easy access to Hungry Mother State Park and Mt Rogers National Recreation Area. **Rooms:** 119 rms. CI 2pm/CO noon. Express checkout avail. Nonsmoking rms avail. Rooms are exceptionally large by today's standards. **Amenities:** 🛗 & A/C, cable TV. Refrigerators and microwaves on request. **Services:** ✕ 🖾 ⇦ ⇦ **Facilities:** 🛐 🎱 & 1 rst, 1 bar, washer/dryer. Complimentary golf privileges at local course. **Rates:** HS Apr–Labor Day $45–$51 S or D. Extra person $4. Children under 19 stay free. Min stay spec evnts. Lower rates off-season. Higher rates for spec evnts/hols. Spec packages avail. Pking: Outdoor, free. Maj CC. Children under 12 eat free in restaurant during summer.

Attractions 🖼

Grayson Highlands State Park; tel 703/579-7092 or 579-7142 (visitor center). This 5,000-acre park is located near Virginia's highest point, Mt Rogers; 25 miles south on Va 16, then 9 miles west on Va 58. Grayson Highlands State Park offers 9 scenic hiking trails, one leading to the 5,729-ft summit of Mt Rogers. Bordering the park on the north, the Mt Rogers National Recreation Area (see below) includes a section of the Appalachian Trail that also leads to the summit. In addition to day-use hours, the park offers overnight camping at 73 sites; reservations are suggested on weekends and holidays. There are also 3 picnic areas, bridle paths and stables for visiting horses, and a special camping area for visitors bringing horses and trailers.

The visitor center houses a craft shop, a book store, and a museum of local history. In one of the picnic areas is a model homestead, with authentically reconstructed pioneer log cabins and a barn. An array of special events held at the park include weekend entertainment programs for campers, planned hikes throughout the summer, and the Grayson Highlands Fall Festival, an annual event offered in late September. **Open:** Park, May–Oct, daily 8am–10pm. Visitor center, Mem Day–Labor Day, daily 10am–6pm. $

Hungry Mother State Park; tel 703/783-3422. Located 4 miles north on Va 16. Comprising beautiful woodlands and a 108-acre lake in the heart of the mountains, Hungry Mother has long been a regional favorite. The park features a sandy beach and bathhouse, boat launch, hiking trails, and a handicapped-accessible fishing pier. Campsites and cabins are available. Restaurant, visitor center. **Open:** Park, daily. Visitor center, Mem Day–Labor Day, Sat–Sun 10am–6pm. $

Mt Rogers National Recreation Area, Va 16; tel 703/783-5196. Encompassing some 115,000 acres in the central Appalachians, Mt Rogers National Recreation Area includes some of the most varied topography in the eastern United States, from dense forests to large, open grasslands. The highest point in the state, Mt Rogers (5,729 feet) is located here. Hiking is extremely popular; 60 miles of the Appalachian Trail run through the area, along with numerous other trails.

Campgrounds with improved facilities are located throughout the area. The two largest, **Beartree** and **Grindstone,** feature hard-surfaced campsites, drinking water, and bathhouses with flush toilets and warm showers. In addition, Beartree Campground, 7 miles east of Damascus on Va 58, has a sandy swimming beach and a stocked 14-acre lake for fishing. Grindstone Campground, on Va 603 between Konnarock and Troutdale, offers easy access to hiking trails and to several challenging mountain bike trails.

For further information, write to Area Ranger, Mt Rogers National Recreation Area, Rte 1, Box 303, Marion, VA 24354. **Open:** Daily 24 hours. Free.

MARTINSVILLE

Map page M-2, E4

Motel 🏨

Best Western Inn, US 220 Business N, PO Box 1183, Martinsville, VA 24114; tel 703/632-5611 or toll free 800/528-1234; fax 703/632-1168. A city motel adjacent to a shopping center. Center of town is less than 5 minutes away. **Rooms:** 97 rms. CI 3pm/CO noon. Nonsmoking rms avail. **Amenities:** 📺 🍷 🖥 A/C, cable TV w/movies. **Services:** ✕ 🍴 🐾 **Facilities:** 🏊 🍸 👥 ⑂ 1 rst, 1 bar (w/entertainment), washer/dryer. Pool backs to a wooded hill, giving sense of seclusion. **Rates:** $38–$50 S or D. Extra person $8. Children under 11 stay free. Min stay spec evnts. Pking: Outdoor, free. Maj CC.

Restaurant 🍽

★ **Mountain Top Deli**, in Holiday Shopping Center, 1208 Virginia Ave (US 220 Business), Martinsville; tel 703/666-2235. **American/Deli.** Adjoining a health food store, this small cafe-style deli has movie posters on wall and black-and-white checkerboard ceiling. Table and counter seating. Fresh daily specials. Variety of deli sandwiches and salads always available. Reduced fat and low sodium emphasized. **FYI:** Reservations not accepted. No liquor license. No smoking. **Open:** Mon–Tues 9am–6pm, Wed 9am–3pm, Thurs 9am–6pm, Fri 9am–5pm, Sat 9am–3pm. Closed some hols; July 4th week. **Prices:** Main courses $3.50–$5. No CC.

MCLEAN

Map page M-3, C6 (NW of Washington, DC)

Hotels 🏨

Best Western Tysons Westpark, 8401 Westpark Dr, McLean, VA 22102 (Tysons Corner); tel 703/734-2800 or toll free 800/533-3301; fax 703/821-8872. Exit 10 off I-495. Follow Va 7 W ½ mile to Westpark Dr, turn right. Convenient to both Tysons Corner malls and numerous other shopping centers, this unpretentious but full-service hotel offers comfortable rooms and facilities attractive to families. **Rooms:** 301 rms and stes. Exec-level rms avail. CI 2pm/CO noon. Nonsmoking rms avail. Attractively decorated units have mauve-and-green scheme, dark wood furniture, 2 vanities. **Amenities:** 📺 🍷 A/C, cable TV w/movies, voice mail. Refrigerators available. **Services:** ✕ 🔑 📠 🍴 🐾 Babysitting. Executive-level units enjoy attended lounge with complimentary breakfast, evening cocktails. **Facilities:** 🏊 🍸 👥 ⑂ 1 rst, 1 bar (w/entertainment), lifeguard, games rm, spa, sauna, whirlpool, washer/dryer. Although indoors, restaurant has patio-like ambience with exposed-brick walls, wrought-iron railing, lots of plants. **Rates:** $69–$95 S or D; from $125 ste. Extra person $14. Children under 18 stay free. Spec packages avail. Pking: Outdoor, free. Maj CC. Extra-person rates apply only when cot required. Weekend packages available.

Holiday Inn Tysons Corner, 1950 Chain Bridge Rd, McLean, VA 22102 (Tysons Corner); tel 703/893-2100 or toll free 800/HOLIDAY; fax 703/893-2100 ext 2227. Exit 11B off I-495. The buildings of this mid-rise hotel wrap around a lovely landscaped courtyard. Recent renovations make this better than most Holiday Inns. Both Tysons Corner malls are within walking distance. **Rooms:** 314 rms and effic. Exec-level rms avail. CI 3pm/CO 1pm. Express checkout avail. Nonsmoking rms avail. King-bed rooms have recliners with reading lamp. Dark colonial-style furniture adds class. **Amenities:** 📺 🍷 📠 🍴 A/C, cable TV w/movies. Some units w/terraces. **Services:** ✕ 🔑 🍴 Free van transfers to nearby office buildings. **Facilities:** 🏊 🍸 👥 ⑂ 1 rst, 1 bar (w/entertainment), lifeguard, games rm, spa, whirlpool. Restaurant has attractive garden-like setting. Bar features golden-oldie hits for dancing. Junior Olympic-size indoor pool opens to courtyard. **Rates:** HS Mar–June/Sept–Oct $132 S or D. Children under 18 stay free. Lower rates off-season. Spec packages avail. Pking: Outdoor, free. Maj CC. Weekend rates available.

McLean Hilton at Tysons Corner, 7920 Jones Branch Dr, McLean, VA 22102; tel 703/847-5000 or toll free 800/HILTONS; fax 703/761-5207. Exit 10B off I-495. Follow Va 123 S to Tysons Blvd; turn right, then right on Westpark Dr;

proceed to Jones Branch Dr. A triangular building wrapped around a stunning atrium, this full-service hotel hosts entertainers appearing at Wolf Trap Farm National Park for the Performing Arts. Fountains lend a cool, relaxing ambience to atrium bar and lounge. Manicured office-park setting is near Tysons Corner shopping malls. **Rooms:** 458 rms and stes. Exec-level rms avail. CI 3pm/CO noon. Express checkout avail. Nonsmoking rms avail. Entry to most units is off atrium walkways. Attractive bright, modern furniture and coordinated color schemes. Door numbers in braille. **Amenities:** ▨ ☖ ▣ ◀ A/C, cable TV w/movies, refrig, voice mail, shoe polisher. All units w/minibars. Deluxe rooms have irons and boards. Club-level rooms have VCRs, robes, makeup mirrors, valet stands. **Services:** ✕ ☞ ☒ ♫ For those in club-level rooms, breakfast and evening snacks served in concierge lounge. **Facilities:** ☐ ❢ ▨ ☐ ☖ 1 rst, 2 bars (w/entertainment), lifeguard, spa, sauna, washer/dryer. Pool has doors opening to sun deck. Restaurant is off atrium. Flamingo's has sports bar/nightclub atmosphere. **Rates:** $120–$195 S; $140–$215 D; from $250 ste. Children under 18 stay free. Spec packages avail. Pking: Outdoor, free. Maj CC.

▤▤▤▤ **The Ritz-Carlton Tysons Corner**, 1700 Tysons Blvd, McLean, VA 22102; tel 703/506-4300 or toll free 800/241-3333; fax 703/506-4305. Exit 11B off I-495. Follow Va 123 S to Tysons Blvd, turn right. Rich wood paneling, paintings hung on fabric walls, and Oriental rugs on marble floors complete an elegant scene at this luxury hotel attached to the upscale Galleria at Tysons II shopping mall. Arrival lobby is at street level, whereas main lobby, along with mall entrance, is an elevator ride up on 4th floor. **Rooms:** 399 rms and stes. Exec-level rms avail. CI 3pm/CO noon. Express checkout avail. Nonsmoking rms avail. Dark woods, fabric wall coverings, and marble baths grace every room. The 2-bed rooms contain oversize twins instead of doubles. Spacious executive suites have French doors separating parlor from bedroom. **Amenities:** ▨ ☖ ◀ A/C, satel TV w/movies, in-rm safe, bathrobes. All units w/minibars, some w/fireplaces, some w/Jacuzzis. Luxury-level rooms have VCRs and fax machines. **Services:** ◎ ☞ ▥ ☒ ♫ Twice-daily maid svce, car-rental desk, masseur, children's program, babysitting. Those on luxury level can take advantage of concierge lounge with 5 food presentations daily. Front desk converts foreign currency. Complimentary shoe shines. **Facilities:** ☐ ❢ ▨ ☐ ☖ 2 rsts (see also "Restaurants" below), 1 bar (w/entertainment), lifeguard, spa, sauna, steam rm, whirlpool. Coffee shop in addition to The Restaurant. Tennis and golf arranged at local clubs. **Rates:** $139–$179 S or D; from $325 ste. Children under 16 stay free. Spec packages avail. Pking: Indoor, free. Maj CC.

Restaurants ⑾

Café Taj, in Marketplace Shops, 1379 Beverly Rd at Old Dominion Dr, McLean (Downtown); tel 703/827-0444. **Indian.** Marble floors and a small fountain make this small, cafe-style dining room furnished with stark ebony tables and chairs feel a bit like the Taj Mahal. Chicken, beef, and lamb from the tandoori oven are specialties, with a few vegetarian curries too. **FYI:** Reservations not accepted. **Open:** Lunch daily 11:30am–2:30pm; dinner Sun–Thurs 5:30–10pm, Fri–Sat 5:30–10:30pm. **Prices:** Main courses $8–$13. Maj CC. ☖

★ **Da Domenico's**, 1992 Chain Bridge Rd at Leesburg Pike (Va 7), McLean (Tysons Corner); tel 703/790-9000. Exit 10 off I-495. Go west on Va 7 to service road after Va 123 interchange, turn right. **Italian.** This unusual dining room is designed like a Victorian Virginia home. Fretwork sets off a fake front porch, and smaller dining areas inside are furnished to evoke that era. Emphasis is on traditional Italian pasta, veal, beef, and seafood, plus daily specials determined by availability of local produce. Very popular. Friendly host sometimes sings opera at tableside. **FYI:** Reservations recommended. Dress code. **Open:** Mon–Fri 11:30am–11pm, Sat 5–11pm. Closed some hols. **Prices:** Main courses $10–$26. Maj CC. ☖

★ **Evans Farm Inn**, 1696 Chain Bridge Rd, McLean; tel 703/356-8000. Exit 11 off I-495. Go north on Va 123 to entrance on Dolly Madison Blvd. **American.** This farmhouse is on a 28-acre estate complete with barnyard animals and vegetable garden supplying fresh produce. Colonial America is the theme, including serving staff attired in period costume. Exposed beams, 18th-century furniture, and 5 working fireplaces add to the charm. Traditional American fare predominates, including Virginia country ham. Breads, cakes, and pies are baked on premises. Romantic Sitting Duck Pub on lower level serves lunch and dinner daily, brunch Sunday 11am–2pm. Entrances on both Chain Bridge Rd and Dolly Madison Blvd (Va 123). **FYI:** Reservations recommended. Piano. Children's menu. Dress code. **Open:** Lunch Sun–Fri 11:30am–2:30pm, Sat 11:30am–3pm; dinner Sun–Thurs 5–9pm, Fri–Sat 5–10pm. Closed Dec 25. **Prices:** Main courses $14–$24. Maj CC. ♥ ▮ ▣

Hunan Lion II, in the Galleria at Tysons II, 2001 International Dr, McLean (Tysons Corner); tel 703/883-1938. Exit 11 off I-495. Follow Va 123 S to International Dr, turn right and proceed to mall entrance. **Chinese.** There is no Chinese decor here, but bright wood chairs go nicely with beige walls and rose seat backs to create a modern, cheerful eatery on the 2nd level of the Galleria shopping mall. Menu offers a wide variety of Cantonese dishes, highlighted by daily specials derived from fresh local produce. **FYI:** Reservations not accepted. **Open:** Mon–Sat 11:30am–10pm, Sun 11:30am–9pm. Closed some hols. **Prices:** Main courses $5.50–$17. Maj CC. &

J R's Stockyards Inn, 8130 Watson St, at Int'l Dr, McLean; tel 703/893-3390. Exit 11 off I-495. Follow Va 123 S to Int'l Dr, turn left, then right on Watson St. **Seafood/Steak.** Built to resemble an Old West ranch house, this steak house, with rough-hewn walls and exposed beams, seems almost barn-like. Smoky aroma of thick steaks over a wood fire fills the place. Also prime rib and some seafood selections. **FYI:** Reservations recommended. Dress code. **Open:** Lunch Mon–Fri 11:30am–2pm; dinner Mon–Thurs 5:30–10pm, Fri–Sat 5:30–11pm, Sun 5–9:30pm. Closed some hols. **Prices:** Main courses $13–$26. Maj CC.

Kazan Restaurant, in McLean Shopping Center, 6813 Redmond Dr, at Old Chain Bridge Rd, McLean; tel 703/734-1960. Exit 11 off I-495. Follow Va 123 N to Old Dominion Dr, turn right; at Center Dr, turn right into shopping center. **Middle Eastern/Turkish.** A Turkish motif reigns in this relatively small dining room with tent-like drapes hanging Middle East–fashion from its ceiling. Deep-blue wall tiles and brass pitchers from the old country add to the romance. Authentic Turkish cuisine includes kabobs and several meat and seafood dishes with exotic spices. A few continental dishes placate the less adventurous. **FYI:** Reservations recommended. Children's menu. Dress code. **Open:** Lunch Mon–Fri 11am–3pm; dinner Mon–Thurs 5–10pm, Fri–Sat 5–11pm. **Prices:** Main courses $12–$17. Maj CC. ♥ &

La Mirabelle, in McLean Square Shopping Center, 6645 Old Dominion Dr, McLean; tel 703/893-8484. Exit 11 off I-495. Follow Va 123 N to Old Dominion Dr, turn right; near Whittier Ave. **French.** European country ambience prevails in this heavy-beamed dining room with a fireplace in 1 corner and tufted booths along walls hung with mirrored panels and impressionist paintings. Ceiling spotlights set off the tables. Traditional French menu is about equally divided between meat and seafood. Popular piano bar sits in front, away from dining room. **FYI:** Reservations accepted. Piano. **Open:** Lunch Mon–Fri 11:30am–2pm; dinner Mon–Sat 5–9pm, Sun 5–8pm. Closed some hols. **Prices:** Main courses $14–$24. Maj CC. ♥ ⊡

The Restaurant, in the Ritz-Carlton Tysons Corner, 1700 Tysons Blvd, McLean; tel 703/506-4300. Exit 11B off I-495. Follow Va 123 S to Tysons Blvd, turn right. **American/Continental.** Plushly upholstered chairs and antique furnishings highlight the elegant, continental-style dining room of this luxury hotel attached to the Galleria at Tysons II shopping mall. A limited dinner menu comprises gourmet American and continental cuisine, with an emphasis on healthful ingredients. Dinners are either 2, 3, or 4 courses only. Luncheon buffets are popular. **FYI:** Reservations recommended. Children's menu. Dress code. **Open:** Daily 6:30–10pm. **Prices:** PF dinner $32–$43. Maj CC. ♥ VP &

MEADOWS OF DAN

Map page M-2, E3 (NW of Stuart)

Restaurants ▥

Le Chien Noir, in Chateau Morrisette Winery, Winery Rd, PO Box 766, Meadows of Dan; tel 703/593-2865. 7 mi N of Meadows of Dan. Near MM 172 of the Blue Ridge Pkwy, at jct US 221/58. **Eclectic/International.** Unpretentious French country decor amid exposed beams, stucco walls, fireplaces, and hardwood floors. Several dining rooms, each with its own character. An outdoor patio overlooks the vineyard. Seasonal menus contain freshly prepared lamb and fish. Calling ahead is strongly recommended since hours may change and inclement weather can close Blue Ridge Parkway. Jazz concert and festival 2nd Saturday of each month June to October. Winery open daily. **FYI:** Reservations recommended. Jazz. Beer and wine only. **Open:** Lunch Wed–Sat 11am–2pm, Sun 11am–3pm; dinner Fri–Sat 6–9pm. Closed some hols; Christmas week. **Prices:** Main courses $15–$19. Maj CC. ♥ ⊜ ⊡ ⊠ &

Mabry Mill, MM 176, Blue Ridge Pkwy, Meadows of Dan; tel 703/952-2947. Between US 58 and US 221. **Regional American.** Casual dining in a rustic, home-like atmosphere at the site of a gristmill, sawmill, and blacksmith shop on the Blue Ridge Parkway. A self-guided tour of the premises illustrates these pioneer industries. Specialties are cornmeal and buckwheat pancakes made from grains stone-ground in the adjacent gristmill. Hiking, camping, and picnicking nearby. **FYI:** Reservations not accepted. Children's menu. No liquor license. **Open:** HS June–Aug daily 8am–7pm. Reduced hours off-season. Closed some hols; Nov–May. **Prices:** Lunch main courses $2–$4.50. Maj CC. &

MIDDLEBURG

Map page M-3, C6 (SW of Aldie)

Inn ▦

▤▤▤▤ **Red Fox Inn**, 2 E Washington St, Middleburg, VA 22117; tel 703/687-6301 or toll free 800/223-1728; fax 703/687-3338. 45 mi W of Washington DC. exit 57B off I-66W. Dating back to 1728, this impressive and elegant inn consists of 5 historic structures within a city block. It captures the flavor of colonial living while at the same time providing modern touches. Hospitable innkeepers. Fresh flowers throughout. **Rooms:** 24 rms and stes. CI 3pm/CO noon. Individually decorated rooms and suites have antiques or reproductions. Some suites large enough for grand piano, with view of backyard. **Amenities:** 🛏 🕭 A/C, cable TV, stereo/tape player, bathrobes. Some units w/terraces, some w/fireplaces. Some rooms have 2 phones, refrigerators. **Services:** ✗ ⇦ Petit fours and the morning paper in each room add to the sense of pampering. Can make arrangements for area activities, such as horseback riding and balloon rides. Business services at desk. Night watchman on duty. **Facilities:** 🔲 2 rsts, 2 bars (1 w/entertainment). Noted restaurants on premises. **Rates (CP):** HS Mar–June/Sept–Dec $135–$145 D; from $145 ste. Extra person $25. Children under 12 stay free. Lower rates off-season. Pking: Outdoor, free. Ltd CC.

Restaurants 🍴

★ **Coach Stop Restaurant**, 9 E Washington St (US 50), Middleburg; tel 703/687-5515. Exit 57B off I-66 W. **American.** In the charming, upscale town of Middleburg, noted for horse farms, this cozy restaurant captures the flavor of its community with hunt-country photos and paintings and a dark-paneled bar the length of a wall. Winner of the Wine *Spectator* Award. A local favorite, the family-run facility offers such specialties as homemade onion rings, fresh seafood, and calf's liver. **FYI:** Reservations recommended. Children's menu. **Open:** Mon–Sat 7am–9:30pm, Sun 8am–9pm. Closed some hols. **Prices:** Main courses $11–$17. Maj CC. 🅿️

★ **Red Fox Inn and Mosby's Tavern**, 2 E Washington St (US 50), Middleburg; tel 703/687-6301. Exit 57B off I-66 W. **Regional American/Continental.** Old pine floors, Windsor chairs, pewter mugs, and low-beamed ceiling transport you back to 1728, when the inn first opened. Fine dining by a fireplace or in Mosby's Tavern, an oak-paneled pub, also with a fireplace, where more casual fare is served. The focus is continental and regional cuisine, including Old Virginia classics such as peanut soup and crab cakes. **FYI:** Reservations recommended. Children's menu. **Open:** Breakfast Sat–Sun 8–10am; lunch Mon–Fri 11am–5pm, Sat 11am–4pm; dinner Mon–Fri 5–9pm, Sat 5–9:30pm, Sun 4–8pm; brunch Sat 11am–4pm, Sun noon–4pm. **Prices:** Main courses $18.95–$22.95; PF dinner $37–$45. Maj CC. ♥ 🍴 🔥

MIDDLETOWN
Map page M-3, B5 (S of Stephens City)

Attraction 🏛

Belle Grove Plantation, US 11; tel 703/869-2028. One of the finest homes in the Shenandoah Valley, this beautiful stone mansion was built in the late 1700s by Maj Isaac Hite, whose grandfather, Joist Hite, first settled in the valley in 1732. Thomas Jefferson was actively involved in Belle Grove's design; the Palladian-style front windows and columns are an example of his influence. The interior is furnished with period antiques.

During the Civil War the house suffered considerable damage during the Battle of Cedar Creek. Union Gen Philip Sheridan's army, which occupied the plantation, was attacked by Confederate forces led by Gen Jubal Early on October 19, 1864. The result was a decisive victory for the Confederacy, but Sheridan was still able to sweep through the valley, laying waste to the rich farmlands that were the breadbasket of the South. **Open:** Mid-Mar to mid-Nov, Mon–Sat 10am–4pm, Sun 1–5pm. $$

MIDLOTHIAN
Map page M-3, D6 (W of Richmond)

Motel 🛏

🟰🟰🟰 **Days Inn Chesterfield**, 1301 Huguenot Rd, at US 60 and Va 147, Midlothian, VA 23113; tel 804/794-4999 or toll free 800/325-2525; fax 804/794-1022. 6 mi W of Richmond. Adjacent to Chesterfield Towne Center Mall. This property makes you feel very comfortable, almost pampered, as compared with other chain motels. Shopping mall and numerous restaurants, shops, and activities are nearby. **Rooms:** 120 rms and stes. CI 3pm/CO noon. Nonsmoking rms avail. Decor is simple and tasteful. Each spacious unit has a desk. **Amenities:** 🛏 🕭 📺 A/C, cable TV. **Services:** ⇦ Continental breakfast served in lobby. **Facilities:** 🔲 ⅙ 1 rst, washer/dryer. **Rates (CP):** $45–$48 D; from $59 ste. Children under 18 stay free. Spec packages avail. Pking: Outdoor, free. Maj CC.

MONTEREY

Map page M-2, C4

Inn 🏨

☰☰☰ **Highland Inn**, 450 Main St at jct US 250/220, PO Box 40, Monterey, VA 24465; tel 703/468-2143. 46 mi NW of Staunton. On the National Register of Historic Places, this large, quaint country home built in 1904 has not been gentrified by innkeepers. George Washington National Forest surrounds property. Excellent choice during Highland Maple Festival in March. **Rooms:** 17 rms and stes. CI 2pm/CO 11am. Mix of nicely kept furniture and antiques. **Amenities:** ⚱ Cable TV. No A/C or phone. Ceiling fans. **Services:** ⬭ ⤵ Babysitting. **Facilities:** 1 bar, guest lounge. Tavern open during dining room hours (Wed–Sat 6–8pm, Sun 11am–2pm). **Rates (CP):** $49–$69 S; from $49 ste. Pking: Outdoor, free. Ltd CC.

MOUNTAIN LAKE

Map page M-2, E3 (NW of Blacksburg)

Resort 🏨

☰☰☰ **Mountain Lake**, Va 700, Mountain Lake, VA 24136; tel 703/626-7121 or toll free 800/346-3334; fax 703/626-7172. Exit US 460 at Va 700 N, or take exit 118 off I-81. Beautiful mountaintop resort hotel, 50 miles southwest of Roanoke, overlooks 1 of only 2 natural freshwater lakes in Virginia. Two TV lounges with VCRs. The movie *Dirty Dancing* was filmed here. Some 2,500 acres protected by Mountain Lake Wilderness Conservancy. Hotel open to individual guests only on weekends from November 1 through April 30. **Rooms:** 66 rms and stes; 15 ctges/villas. Exec-level rms avail. CI 5pm/CO 11am. Nonsmoking rms avail. **Amenities:** 🕿 No A/C or TV. Some units w/terraces, some w/fireplaces, some w/Jacuzzis. Window and ceiling fans make up for lack of air conditioning. **Services:** ✗ ⓥⓟ 🚐 ⤵ Social director, masseur, children's program, babysitting. **Facilities:** 🚴 ⛵ 🏊 🧖 🎣 ⛳ ⛳ 📺 1 rst, 1 bar, 1 beach (lake shore), lifeguard, games rm, lawn games, sauna, whirlpool, playground, washer/dryer. Hiking trails. Indoor recreational facility with billiards, table tennis, shuffleboard, and ice skating. Fishing tours, wine-and-cheese lake cruises, horse-drawn carriage and sleigh rides. **Rates (MAP):** HS May–Oct $95–$200 S; $145–$245 D; from $110 ste; from $85 ctge/villa. Extra person $20–$35. Children under 4 stay free. Min stay spec evnts. Lower rates off-season. AP and MAP rates avail. Spec packages avail. Pking: Outdoor, free. Maj CC.

MOUNT VERNON

Map page M-3, C6

Attractions 🏛

Mount Vernon; tel 703/780-2000. Access via George Washington Memorial Parkway (Va 400), which ends at Mount Vernon. The Mount Vernon estate was purchased in 1858 by the Mount Vernon Ladies' Association from John Augustine Washington, great-grandnephew of the first president.

There is no formal guided tour, but attendants stationed throughout the house and grounds answer questions and a map is provided. The house is an outstanding example of colonial architecture. Many of the furnishings are original pieces acquired by Washington, and the rooms have been repainted in the original colors favored by George and Martha. There are a number of family portraits, and the rooms are appointed as if actually in day-to-day use. A 4-acre exhibit called "George Washington, Pioneer Farmer" includes a replica of Washington's 16-sided barn and fields of crops he grew. A museum on the property contains memorabilia and explains details of the restoration project.

After leaving the house, visitors can tour the outbuildings—the kitchen, slave quarters, storeroom, smokehouse, overseer's quarters, coach house, and stables (allow about 2 hours to see everything). George and Martha are both buried on the estate, as are 24 other family members. Public memorial services are held every year on the third Monday in February, the date commemorating Washington's birthday; admission is free that day. Other special events throughout the year. **Open:** Apr–Aug, daily 8am–5pm; Mar and Sept–Oct, daily 9am–5pm; Nov–Feb, daily 9am–4pm. $$$

Woodlawn Plantation; tel 703/780-4000. Located 3 miles west of Mount Vernon on US 1, Woodlawn was originally a 2,000-acre section of Washington's Mount Vernon estate (today some 130 acres remain). He gave it as a wedding gift to his adopted daughter (and Martha's actual granddaughter) Eleanor Parke Custis and her fiancé, Major Lawrence Lewis (who was Washington's nephew). The restored mansion and formal gardens reflect many periods of its history. Tours, given on the half hour, last 30 minutes.

Also on the grounds are **Grand View**, a house built 100 yards from the mansion in 1858 (not open to the public); and Frank Lloyd Wright's **Pope–Leighy House**, built in Falls Church in 1940 and moved here in 1964 after it was slated for demolition. It was a prototype of Wright's "Usonian" style of architecture, which aspired to well-designed housing for middle-income people. **Open:** Feb–Dec, daily 9:30am–4:30pm; Jan, Sat–Sun 9:30am–4:30pm (Pope-Leighy House remains closed weekdays in Feb). Closed some hols. $$

George Washington's Grist Mill Historic State Park, 5514 Mt Vernon Memorial Hwy; tel 703/550-0960 or 780-3383 (weekends). Located 3 miles west of Mount Vernon on Va 225. The Woodlawn part of Mount Vernon contained a gristmill that neighboring farmers used for grinding corn and wheat. In 1932 the Virginia Conservation Commission purchased part of the property known as Dogue Run Farm, on which the mill and other buildings had been located. The site was excavated, and part of the original wheel, part of the trundlehead, complete with wheel buckets, and other articles were found. Guided tours of the mill (45 min) are given throughout the day. Picnicking. **Open:** Mem Day–Labor Day, Sat–Sun and hols only, 10am–6pm. $

NATURAL BRIDGE

Map page M-2, D4 (SW of Lexington)

Resort 🛏

≡≡≡ Natural Bridge of Virginia Resort and Conference Center, US 11, PO Box 57, Natural Bridge, VA 24578; tel 703/291-2121 or toll free 800/533-1410; fax 703/291-1896. Exit 175 off I-81. 1,600 acres. A full-service resort nestled in the Shenandoah Valley and surrounded by mountains and streams. Older section to be completely renovated in 1995. The same owners operate the Stonewall Inn next door. **Rooms:** 180 rms and stes. CI 3pm/CO noon. Nonsmoking rms avail. **Amenities:** 🛏 A/C, cable TV w/movies. Some units w/terraces. **Services:** ✗ ⟵ ⟨ Babysitting. Pets allowed in older part of hotel at present. **Facilities:** 🛠 ⚠ 🛏 🎿 🏊² ⛳ 🗄 ⌂ 3 rsts, 1 bar (w/entertainment), games rm, playground. Indoor miniature golf. **Rates:** HS Apr–Oct $75–$95 S or D; from $95 ste. Children under 18 stay free. Lower rates off-season. MAP rates avail. Spec packages avail. Pking: Outdoor, free. Maj CC.

Attraction 📷

Natural Bridge, I-81; tel 703/291-2121 or toll free 800/533-1410. Thomas Jefferson called this bridge of limestone "the most sublime of nature's works . . . so beautiful an arch, so elevated, so light and springing, as it were, up to heaven." The bridge was part of a 157-acre estate Jefferson acquired in 1774 from King George III. It was included in the survey of western Virginia carried out by George Washington, who carved his initials into the face of the stone. The bridge rises 215 feet above cedar creek; its span is 90 feet long and spreads at its widest to

150 feet. It is believed that the Monocan Indian tribes used the bridge as a passageway and fortress, and it was worshiped by them as "the bridge of God."

A 45-minute sound-and-light show, *The Drama of Creation*, is conducted nightly beneath the bridge. Across the parking lot from the upper bridge entrance is the Natural Bridge Wax Museum. Restaurant, lodging facilities. **Open:** Bridge daily 8am–dusk; drama presented after dark. $$$

NEW MARKET

Map page M-3, C5

Hotel 🛏

≡≡ Quality Inn Shenandoah Valley, I-81 and Va 211, New Market, VA 22844; tel 703/740-3141 or toll free 800/221-2222. Despite its highway location, this property offers a lovely view of mountains. **Rooms:** 101 rms. CI noon/CO 2pm. Nonsmoking rms avail. Rooms feature 2-poster beds and nice fixtures. Bridal suite and conference suite available. **Amenities:** 🛏 A/C, cable TV w/movies. VCR and movie can be rented for $7; unlimited movies, $10. **Services:** ✗ ⟵ Room service available from restaurant (separate from hotel, but within the facility). Safe deposit boxes available at desk. **Facilities:** 🛠 🗄 🛏 ⚿ 1 rst, games rm, playground, washer/dryer. Miniature golf. Adjoining restaurant, Johnny Appleseed, is popular in area. **Rates:** HS May–Sept $49–$55 S; $56–$65 D. Extra person $6. Children under 18 stay free. Lower rates off-season. Spec packages avail. Pking: Outdoor, free. Maj CC.

Motel

≡≡ The Shenvalee, 9660 Fairway Dr, New Market, VA 22844; tel 703/740-3181; fax 703/740-8931. Off Congress St. This 1920s brick mansion with white columns, built on a knoll above its golf course, has separate motel unit adjoining. **Rooms:** 42 rms. CI 3pm/CO 1pm. All rooms afford a view of either mountains or golf course. **Amenities:** 🛏 A/C, cable TV, refrig. Some units w/terraces. VCRs on request. **Services:** ✗ 🚐 ⟵ ⟨ Turndown service on request. Accommodating staff. Fax machine available in office. **Facilities:** 🛠 ⛳²⁷ 🏊² 🗄 1 rst, 1 bar, beauty salon. Outside snack bar area near pool and golf course. **Rates:** HS Apr–Nov $50–$60 S or D. Extra person $7.50. Children under 12 stay free. Lower rates off-season. Spec packages avail. Pking: Outdoor, free. Maj CC. Golf packages available.

Attraction

New Market Battlefield Historical Park; tel 703/740-3101. From I-81 exit 67 take US 211W, then an immediate right onto County Road 305 (George Collins Pkwy); the battlefield is 1¾ miles away, at the end of the road.

The park commemorates the heroism of 250 cadets from the Virginia Military Institute, who participated in a Civil War battle on May 15, 1864. Faced with an attack by superior numbers, Gen John C Breckenridge was forced to call upon VMI for reinforcements. The cadets joined the battle, which resulted in the defeat of the Union force commanded by Maj Gen Franz Sigel.

The **Visitor Center** presents a film about the battle, and another about Stonewall Jackson's Shenandoah campaign. The final Confederate assault on the Union line is covered in a self-guided tour of the grassy field. In the center of the line of battle was the **Bushong Farmhouse,** today a museum of 19th-century valley life. Located at the actual battlefield site is the **New Market Battlefield Military Museum** (tel 703/740-8065), with over 2,000 military artifacts and personal items of American soldiers dating back to the time of the Revolution. Markers on the grounds indicate Union and Confederate troop positions. **Open:** Mar 15–June 14, daily 9am–5pm; June 15–Labor Day, daily 9am–7pm; day after Labor Day through Nov 14, daily 9am–5pm; Nov 15–Mar 14, daily 9am–4pm. $$$

NEWPORT NEWS

Map page M-3, E7

Hotels

The Inn at Kiln Creek, 1003 Brick Kiln Blvd, Newport News, VA 23602; tel 804/874-2600; fax 804/988-3237. Exit 255B off I-64. Go north on Jefferson Ave, turn right on Brick Kiln Blvd. Lodging on beautiful grounds of a country club, so naturally it feels more like a golf club than a resort. Excellent facilities. **Rooms:** 16 rms. CI 2pm/CO noon. Express checkout avail. Tasteful furnishings. Sliding glass doors open to patio overlooking golf course. **Amenities:** A/C, cable TV w/movies, refrig, in-rm safe. All units w/terraces. **Services:** X Children's program. **Facilities:** 2 rsts, 2 bars, lawn games, spa, sauna, steam rm, whirlpool. Indoor/outdoor pools. **Rates:** $80 S; $100 D. Children under 18 stay free. Higher rates for spec evnts/hols. Spec packages avail. Pking: Outdoor, free. Maj CC. Corporate and member rates available.

Omni Newport News Hotel, 1000 Batten Bay Blvd, Newport News, VA 23606; tel 804/873-6664 or toll free 800/THE-OMNI; fax 804/873-1732. Exit 258A off I-64. Follow Va 17 S for ¼ mi, turn right on Diligence Dr, right on Omni Way, then left on Batten Bay Blvd. The best digs in Newport News, upscale property in wooded office park caters to business travelers and conferences. Great attention to detail in public areas. Modern-style lobby overlooking pool has vaulted ceilings, beautiful lighting fixtures, fireplace. **Rooms:** 183 rms and stes. CI 3pm/CO noon. Express checkout avail. Nonsmoking rms avail. Mauve color scheme, including pleated shades. Parlor rooms have 2 full sofas, dining tables for 6, wet bars with brass stools. Motion detectors activate climate-control system when guests enter units. **Amenities:** A/C, cable TV w/movies, stereo/tape player. Some units w/minibars, some w/fireplaces, some w/Jacuzzis. **Services:** X Twice-daily maid svce, babysitting. **Facilities:** 1 rst, 2 bars (w/entertainment), lawn games, spa, sauna, whirlpool. Indoor pool with adjacent fitness room. Restaurant features regional Italian cuisine; attractive fireplace used to bake pizza. Patio bar has eclectic, islandy feel, with barrel halves built into bar, tables with rope edging, and vintage Coca-Cola refrigerator box. Nightclub has regular entertainment. **Rates:** $99–$129 S or D; from $275 ste. Extra person $10. Children under 17 stay free. Min stay spec evnts. AP and MAP rates avail. Spec packages avail. Pking: Outdoor, free. Maj CC.

Motel

Ramada Inn and Conference Center, 950 J Clyde Morris Blvd (Va 17 N), Newport News, VA 23601; tel 804/599-4460 or toll free 800/841-1112; fax 804/599-4336. Exit 258B off I-64. Newly renovated motel has a range of accommodations to appeal to both families and business travelers. **Rooms:** 220 rms and stes. Exec-level rms avail. CI 2pm/CO noon. Express checkout avail. Nonsmoking rms avail. Cheerful, tasteful decor includes bright floral bedspreads, blue carpet, whitewashed furniture. Suites have dark-finished Queen Anne furniture, beige accents. **Amenities:** A/C, cable TV w/movies. Some units w/Jacuzzis. Suites available with coffee-makers, refrigerators. **Services:** X Morning coffee available in lobby. Ramada Business Club members have access to business services, complimentary newspaper, drink coupon. **Facilities:** 1 rst, 1 bar, games rm. **Rates:** HS Mem Day–Labor Day $54–$69 S or D; from $135 ste. Extra person $5. Children under 18 stay free. Min stay spec evnts. Lower rates off-season. Higher rates for spec evnts/hols. Spec packages avail. Pking: Outdoor, free. Maj CC.

Attraction

Mariners' Museum, 100 Museum Dr; tel 804/595-0368. In a pleasant, 550-acre park setting, with a lake, picnic areas, and walking trails, the Mariners' Museum is dedicated to preserving the culture of the sea and its tributaries. Handcrafted ship models, scrimshaw, maritime paintings, decorative arts, working steam engines, and more are displayed in spacious galleries. An 18-minute film tells about worldwide maritime activity. Occasional demonstrations by costumed historical interpreters. **Open:** Daily 10am–5pm. Closed some hols. $$$

NORFOLK

Map page M-3, E7

TOURIST INFORMATION

Convention and Visitors Bureau At end of 4th View St (tel 804/441-1852 or 800/368-3097). Open daily 9am–7pm.

PUBLIC TRANSPORTATION

Tidewater Regional Transit System (TRT) Buses Operate 4:30am–1:30am. Base fare $1.10; additional 55¢ per zone. Exact change required. For information call 804/640-6300.

Norfolk Trolley Tour Operates May–Sept daily 11am–4pm. 7 stops at attractions downtown and in nearby neighborhoods. Purchase tickets at TRT kiosk at the Waterside. One-day fare $3.50 adults, $1.75 seniors and children under 12; allows unlimited use all day.

Hotels 🏨

≣≣≣ **Howard Johnson Hotel and Conference Center**, 700 Monticello Ave, Norfolk, VA 23510; tel 804/627-5555 or toll free 800/682-7678; fax 804/533-9651. In downtown Norfolk on US 460, 1 block S of jct US 58. Large downtown chain motel adjacent to Norfolk Scope and Chrysler Hall complex, 6 blocks from Waterside Festival Marketplace and Nauticus National Maritime Center. **Rooms:** 344 rms and stes. CI 3pm/CO noon. Nonsmoking rms avail. Attractively furnished. One suite is very large and has a kitchen equipped with full-size appliances. **Amenities:** 🛏 A/C, cable TV w/movies. Some units w/minibars. **Services:** ✕ 🚗 🖼 ↩ 🔧 Complimentary shuttle to downtown attractions. **Facilities:** 🔂 🛣 🎱 🍴 1 rst, 1 bar (w/entertainment), games rm, washer/dryer. Large swimming pool. Comedy club on premises operates Thursday to Saturday evenings. **Rates:** HS Mem Day–Labor Day $65–$69 S; $69–$79 D; from $150 ste. Extra person $10. Children under 12 stay free. Min stay spec evnts. Lower rates off-season. Higher rates for spec evnts/hols. Spec packages avail. Pking: Outdoor, free. Maj CC.

≣≣≣ **Norfolk Airport Hilton**, 1500 N Military Hwy, Norfolk, VA 23502 (Norfolk Int'l Airport); tel 804/466-8000 or toll free 800/422-7474; fax 804/466-8000. Exit 281 off I-64. Follow signs to Military Hwy, turn left, go ¾ mile to hotel. Location is central to naval bases and downtown Norfolk. **Rooms:** 250 rms and stes. CI 3pm/CO 1pm. Express checkout avail. Nonsmoking rms avail. **Amenities:** 🛏 🍴 🖼 🔧 A/C, cable TV w/movies, refrig, shoe polisher, bathrobes. Some units w/minibars, 1 w/terrace. Rooms have refreshment centers. **Services:** ✕ 🚗 🖼 🚗 ↩ 🔧 Complimentary snacks and entertainment in lounge Monday to Friday. **Facilities:** 🔂 🛣 🎱 🖥 ᵴ 3 rsts, 1 bar (w/entertainment), spa, sauna, steam rm, whirlpool. Pool has patio and seating area. **Rates:** HS May–Aug $69–$99 S or D; from $119 ste. Extra person $10. Children under 12 stay free. Lower rates off-season. Spec packages avail. Pking: Outdoor, free. Maj CC.

≣≣≣≣ **Norfolk Waterside Marriott**, 235 Main St, Norfolk, VA 23510 (Downtown); tel 804/627-4200 or toll free 800/228-9290; fax 804/628-6452. Opened in 1991 just 1 block from the downtown waterfront, Norfolk's best digs have an elegant lobby with crystal lamps, vases, chandeliers, antiques, marble floors, and overstuffed furniture. **Rooms:** 404 rms and stes. Exec-level rms avail. CI 4pm/CO noon. Express checkout avail. Nonsmoking rms avail. Spacious rooms are very well appointed and decorated. **Amenities:** 🛏 🍴 A/C, cable TV w/movies, voice mail. Some units w/minibars, 1 w/fireplace, 1 w/Jacuzzi. **Services:** ✕ 🚗 🖼 🚗 🖨 ↩ 🔧 Babysitting. **Facilities:** 🔂 🛣 🖥 ᵴ 2 rsts, 2 bars (w/entertainment), lifeguard, games rm, spa, sauna, whirlpool, washer/dryer. Indoor pool opens to outdoor sunning area. **Rates:** HS May 26–Sept 9 $80–$119 S or D; from $250 ste. Children under 17 stay free. Lower rates off-season. Pking: Indoor, $8–$10. Maj CC.

≣≣≣≣ **Omni International Hotel**, 777 Waterside Dr, Norfolk, VA 23510 (Downtown); tel 804/622-6664 or toll free 800/THE-OMNI; fax 804/625-8271. Conveniently located on the downtown waterfront adjacent to the Waterside shops, this modern hotel has a large marble entrance and lobby with excellent furnishings and seating. **Rooms:** 442 rms and stes. Exec-level rms avail. CI 3pm/CO noon. Express checkout avail. Nonsmoking rms avail. Well-appointed rooms range from standard to large suites. **Amenities:** 🛏 🍴 🔧 A/C, cable TV w/movies, voice mail, shoe polisher. Some units w/terraces, 1 w/Jacuzzi. Wet bars in suites. **Services:** ✕ 🚗 🖼 🚗 🖨 ↩ 🔧 Car-rental desk, babysitting. **Facilities:** 🔂 🛣 🖥 ᵴ 1 rst, 1 bar (w/entertainment). **Rates:** $108–$128 S; $118–$138 D; from $175 ste. Extra person $15. Children under 17 stay free. Min stay spec evnts. Higher rates for spec evnts/hols. Spec packages avail. Pking: Indoor/outdoor, $3–$8. Maj CC.

≣≣ **Ramada Norfolk**, 345 Granby St, Norfolk, VA 23510; tel 804/622-6682 or toll free 800/2-RAMADA; fax 804/623-5949. Exit I-64 at I-264. Dating to 1906, this downtown hotel is within walking distance of Waterside Festival Marketplace and Nauticus

National Maritime Center. Old-style lobby has lots of wooden columns. **Rooms:** 124 rms and stes. Exec-level rms avail. CI 3pm/CO noon. Express checkout avail. Nonsmoking rms avail. Tasteful, traditionally furnished rooms have 2 small baths. **Amenities:** 🛁 ♨ A/C, cable TV w/movies. Some units w/minibars. Refrigerators and microwaves available. **Services:** ✗ 🖼 🕾 ♨ Golf arranged. **Facilities:** 🎱 ♿ 1 rst, 1 bar (w/entertainment). Guests have use of Downtown Athletic Club and YMCA for fee. **Rates:** HS Mem Day–Labor Day $59–$80 S or D; from $80 ste. Extra person $10. Children under 18 stay free. Min stay spec evnts. Lower rates off-season. Higher rates for spec evnts/hols. Spec packages avail. Pking: Indoor/outdoor, free. Maj CC.

Motels

🏨🏨🏨 **Best Western Center Inn**, 1 Best Sq, Norfolk, VA 23502; tel 804/461-6600 or toll free 800/237-5517; fax 804/466-9093. Exit 284A off I-64. Almost hidden behind the Best Products store, this gray wooden structure surrounds a central area with clubhouse and indoor and outdoor pools, offering a relaxed atmosphere. **Rooms:** 152 rms and stes. CI 3pm/CO noon. Nonsmoking rms avail. **Amenities:** 🛁 A/C, cable TV w/movies, refrig, voice mail. **Services:** ✗ 🚗 🖼 🕾 Babysitting. **Facilities:** 🎱 🛢 ♿ 1 rst, 1 bar, sauna, whirlpool, washer/dryer.

Steak house is adjacent. **Rates (CP):** HS May 15–Sept 15 $58–$73 S; $66–$79 D; from $116 ste. Extra person $6. Children under 12 stay free. Min stay spec evnts. Lower rates off-season. Spec packages avail. Pking: Outdoor, free. Maj CC.

🏨🏨 **Econo Lodge Ocean View Beach–West**, 9601 4th View St at US 60, Norfolk, VA 23503; tel 804/480-9611 or toll free 800/768-5425; fax 804/480-1307. Exit 273 off I-64. A clean and modern chain motel across street from Ocean View Beach. **Rooms:** 71 rms, stes, and effic. CI 2pm/CO 11am. Nonsmoking rms avail. Small room for guests with disabilities lacks adequate turn space. **Amenities:** 🛁 ♨ A/C, cable TV w/movies, refrig. 1 unit w/terrace. Efficiencies have sink, stove, small refrigerator, dining table for 2. **Services:** 🕾 ♨ **Facilities:** 🎱 ♿ Spa, sauna, whirlpool, washer/dryer. Hot tub. **Rates (CP):** HS May 20–Sept 10 $51–$63 S; $56–$60 D; from $75 ste; from $65 effic. Extra person $5. Children under 18 stay free. Min stay spec evnts. Lower rates off-season. Higher rates for spec evnts/hols. Pking: Outdoor, free. Maj CC.

🏨🏨 **Hampton Inn Norfolk Naval Base**, 8501 Hampton Blvd, Norfolk, VA 23505; tel 804/489-1000 or toll free 800/HAMPTON; fax 804/489-4509. Exit I-64 at I-564 then go east on Terminal Blvd for 2½ miles, then north on Hampton Blvd for ½

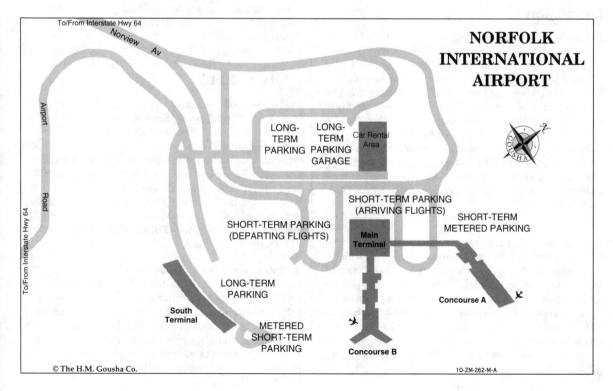

NORFOLK INTERNATIONAL AIRPORT

© The H.M. Gousha Co.

10-ZM-262-M-A

mile. Clean, modern chain motel adjacent to Norfolk Naval Base and many fast-food restaurants. **Rooms:** 119 rms and effic. CI 2pm/CO 11am. Nonsmoking rms avail. Bright and clean. 28 have kitchenettes. **Amenities:** 🛏 A/C, cable TV w/movies. Some units w/Jacuzzis. **Services:** 🔼 🍸 Children's program, babysitting. Continental breakfast served in attractive lobby area. Children's program, from Memorial Day to Labor Day, consists of videos shown in lobby. **Facilities:** 🗑 & Whirlpool. **Rates (CP):** $58 S; $64 D; from $60 effic. Children under 18 stay free. Pking: Outdoor, free. Maj CC.

〰〰 **Norfolk Hampton Inn–Airport**, 1450 Military Hwy, Norfolk, VA 23502 (Norfolk Int'l Airport); tel 804/466-7474 or toll free 800/426-7866; fax 804/466-7474 ext 309. Exit 281 off I-64. Modern chain motel. **Rooms:** 130 rms. CI 3pm/CO noon. Nonsmoking rms avail. **Amenities:** 🛏 💧 A/C, cable TV w/movies. **Services:** 🚗 🔼 🍸 Accommodating staff renders high-quality service for such an establishment. Free local calls. **Facilities:** 🗑 🏋 & Guests have free use of local health club. **Rates (CP):** HS Mem Day–Labor Day $49–$51 S; $55–$59 D. Children under 18 stay free. Lower rates off-season. Pking: Outdoor, free. Maj CC.

Restaurants 🍴

Doumar's, 1900 Monticello Ave, Norfolk; tel 804/627-4163. Exit I-264 at City Hall Ave; turn right on St Paul's Blvd, go 1 mile to Monticello Ave. **Barbecue/Burgers.** Interesting today for the historical perspective if not the culinary experience, this was Virginia's first drive-in and the state's first restaurant to have a soda fountain. In fact, service still comes right to your car. Inside seating is old-fashioned booths and counter. Other than ice cream, only sandwiches offered, with barbecue the house specialty. Cones have been homemade here since 1904 (original machine is on display). **FYI:** Reservations not accepted. No liquor license. **Open:** Mon–Thurs 8am–11pm, Fri–Sat 8am–midnight. Closed some hols. **Prices:** Main courses $1.30–$2.45. No CC. 🍽

★ **Elliot's**, 1421 Colley Ave, Norfolk (Ghent); tel 804/625-0259. **Regional American/Burgers.** Walls lined with old signs and memorabilia going back to the 1930s adorn this casual local favorite. Children's menu is a coloring book, and kids have used crayons to cover an entire wall with their creations. Favorites are chicken Alexander, seafood dishes, and burgers. **FYI:** Reservations accepted. Children's menu. Dress code. **Open:** Sun–Thurs 11am–10pm, Fri–Sat 11am–midnight. Closed some hols. **Prices:** Main courses $10.95–$14.95. Maj CC. 🍽 👪 &

Fisherman's Wharf Seafood Restaurant, in Willoughby Bay Marina, 1571 Bayville St, Norfolk; tel 804/480-3113. Exit 272 off I-64 E. **Seafood/Steak.** Overlooking Willoughby Bay, the open, airy dining room is accented with brass railings, nautical pictures, tables with inlaid shells, hanging plants, Tiffany-style lamps, and oak columns. Seafood buffet offers wide variety of seafood and fresh vegetables. **FYI:** Reservations accepted. Comedy. Children's menu. **Open:** Daily 11am–10pm. **Prices:** Main courses $14–$28; PF dinner $19. Maj CC. 🍽 👪 &

Il Porto Ristorante, in Waterside, 333 Waterside Dr, Norfolk; tel 804/627-4400. **Italian.** Checked tablecloths highlight tasteful decor at this Italian restaurant. Excellent view of Norfolk harbor from dining room and outside eating area. A variety of traditional meat, seafood, poultry, and pasta dishes from the old country. Pianist in the bar every evening. **FYI:** Reservations accepted. Piano. Children's menu. Dress code. **Open:** Daily 11am–11:30pm. Closed some hols. **Prices:** Main courses $9–$15. Maj CC. 🍽 🍽 &

Magnolia Steak, 749 W Princess Anne Rd, at Colley Ave, Norfolk (Ghent); tel 804/625-0400. **Italian/Seafood/Steak.** Lighted sailing pictures adorn the walls of this family-oriented restaurant with adjacent games room with billiard tables and sports on TV. Burgundy color scheme and overstuffed upholstered chairs at mahogany tables. An outside area seating 30 is used most of the year. Certified Angus beef is popular. Seafood dishes, pastas, and chicken also offered. Vegetables are fresh; desserts, homemade. **FYI:** Reservations accepted. **Open:** Daily 11:30am–1:30am. Closed some hols. **Prices:** Main courses $8–$19. Maj CC. 🍽 👪 &

Phillips Seafood Restaurant, in Waterside, 333 Warterside Dr, Norfolk; tel 804/627-6600. **Seafood.** Excellent view of the downtown waterfront from booths raised a step above floor level in this seafood emporium, part of a regional chain. Checked tablecloths and wrought-iron tables. Menu features traditional Chesapeake Bay seafood, with specials changing daily to reflect fresh catch. Outdoor dining and drinking area in good weather. Band plays in bar Friday and Saturday evenings. **FYI:** Reservations accepted. Combo/piano. Children's menu. Dress code. **Open:** Daily 11am–10pm. **Prices:** Main courses $13.95–$21.95. Maj CC. 🍽 🍽 &

★ **Ship's Cabin Seafood Restaurant**, 4110 E Ocean View Ave, Norfolk; tel 804/362-4659. Exit 278 off I-64. Turn right at Little Creek Rd (Va 165S), go 2½ miles to Shore Dr, turn left, go 1 mile. **New American/Seafood.** Sporting great views from perch on the Chesapeake Bay, and with a nautical theme augmented by large plants under high cathedral ceilings, this popular restaurant is top-notch. Low brick walls with mahogany caps divide dining room into sections. Attractive fireplace in bar is open to all sides.

Daily specials feature fresh, mostly local seafood. Also known for seafood kabobs and lamb shank. Sauces as well as desserts, ice creams, and sorbets made on premises. **FYI:** Reservations recommended. Children's menu. Dress code. **Open:** Mon–Thurs 5:30–10pm, Fri–Sat 5:30–10:30pm, Sun 5–10pm. Closed some hols. **Prices:** Main courses $11–$18. Maj CC. 🚻 🏞 🚗 ♿

★ **Surf Rider West**, 723 Newtown Rd, Norfolk; tel 804/461-6488. Exit 284B off I-64. 2 blocks beyond Virginia Beach Blvd. **Regional American/Seafood.** Wooden booths and tables and local beach decor lend a casual family atmosphere to this member of a small seafood restaurant chain. All seafood is fresh daily, including all–lump meat crab cakes. **FYI:** Reservations not accepted. Dress code. **Open:** Mon–Sat 11am–10pm. Closed some hols. **Prices:** Main courses $11.95–$15.95. Maj CC. 🚗

★ **Uncle Louie's**, in Wards Corner Shopping Center, 132 E Little Creek Rd, Norfolk; tel 804/480-1225. Exit 276 off I-64. Turn left at 2nd light. **Regional American/Seafood/Steak.** A storefront deli is only part of this fine, multifaceted class establishment. Behind the deli, wall hangings, murals, and a coordinated color scheme create an upbeat, casual atmosphere in a nicely decorated restaurant divided into sections by waist-high walls adorned with brass and glass fixtures. Etched-glass doors lead to bar and grill sections. Coffee shop specializes in freshly ground coffees and serves tea daily 2–5pm. Fresh seafood and Angus beef steaks are specialties. Bakery on premises provides fresh bread and desserts. **FYI:** Reservations recommended. Jazz. Children's menu. **Open:** Daily 8am–2am. Closed some hols. **Prices:** Main courses $11–$16. Maj CC. 🚻 🚗 ♿

Attractions 💼

Nauticus, the National Maritime Center, 1 Waterside Dr; tel 804/664-1000 or toll free 800/664-1080. Located in the heart of downtown Norfolk's Waterside complex, Nauticus is a high-tech, interactive museum concept combining educational content with the entertainment level of an amusement park. The 160,000-square-foot facility features nautical themes including shipbuilding, the US Navy, world commerce, and the marine environment.

Major exhibits include **Virtual Adventure,** a submarine ride where participants must cooperate in order to complete their assigned mission; **Aegis Theater,** a multimedia naval battle simulation; the **Nauticus Theater,** with a screen that rolls back to reveal a huge picture window overlooking one of America's largest and busiest natural harbors; the **Maritime Theater,** with a video presentation on the past and future of the shipbuilding industry; and the **Marine Exploratorium,** a roomful of large, colorful interactives for children, including a real ship's bridge, periscopes, and a giant wave tank.

A large area is devoted to marine biology and environmental science, where visitors can study all kinds of sea creatures in constantly changing aquaria, and observe scientists working in marine biology and oceanographic labs right on the exhibit floor. Exhibits in this area include Touchpool, Shark Encounter, Underwater Archeology, Charting, and Earth Monitoring.

The 2nd level of the facility houses the **Hampton Roads Naval Museum.** The collection is especially strong in naval artwork, ship models, and underwater artifacts. Guided tours are given by staff volunteers, many of whom are retired US Navy personnel.

Nauticus also includes a 600-foot pier where US Navy, foreign, and commerical vessels are made available for tours by visitors. The pier is also the location for spectacular laser shows with music and fireworks (nightly in summer). Restaurant; gift shop. **Open:** June–Labor Day, daily 9am–9pm; early Sept to mid-Dec, Sat–Sun 9am–9pm; late Dec, daily 9am–9pm. Closed Dec 25 and Jan–Feb. $$$$

Norfolk Naval Base Tour, 9079 Hampton Blvd; tel 804/444-7955. Norfolk has the world's largest naval installation, and visitors can take a guided bus tour of the base, enhanced by informed commentary by navy personnel. Sights include aircraft and aircraft carriers, submarines, and training centers. The bus passes Admiral's Row, a strip of Colonial Revival houses built at the turn of the century for the Jamestown Exposition. On weekends from 1 to 4:30pm there may be visits to selected ships in port, admission free. Tickets may be purchased at the TKT kiosk at Waterside or at the Naval Tour Office on Hampton Blvd. **Open:** Apr–Oct, daily 9am–2:30pm every half-hour. $$

Chrysler Museum of Art, 245 W Olney Rd; tel 804/664-6200. Walter P Chrysler, Jr, began to collect art at the age of 13, with the purchase of a small landscape by Renoir. Today, his magnificent collection spans artistic periods from ancient Egypt to the present. A 1,500-print photography collection includes works by Ansel Adams, W Eugene Smith, and others. The 8,000-piece glass collection, one of the finest and most comprehensive in the world, includes 200 Tiffany pieces. Adjoining is an outstanding collection of art nouveau furniture. Other 1st-floor galleries exhibit ancient Indian, Islamic, Oriental, African, and pre-Columbian art. Most 2nd-floor galleries are devoted to painting and sculpture. **Open:** Tues–Sat 10am–4pm, Sun 1–5pm. Closed some hols. Free.

Douglas MacArthur Memorial, MacArthur Sq, between City Hall Ave and Plume St, at Bank St; tel 804/441-2965. Located on MacArthur Square, between City Hall Ave and Plume St, at Bank St. The memorial is housed in Norfolk's recently renovated old city hall, an imposing domed structure with a columned front portico. Visitors view a film that uses news footage to document the major events of MacArthur's life. Eleven galleries are filled with memorabilia ranging from historic World War II surrender documents to the general's famous corncob pipe. **Open:** Mon–Sat 10am–5pm, Sun 11am–5pm. Closed some hols. Free.

Hunter House Victorian Museum, 240 W Freemason St; tel 804/623-9814. Built in 1894 in the Richardsonian Romanesque style, this was the home of prominent Norfolk merchant and banker James Wilson Hunter and his family. Rich in architectural details, the house displays an extensive collection of Victorian furnishings and decorative art, including a Renaissance Revival bedchamber suite, a period children's nursery, and several stained-glass windows. An exhibit of early 20th-century medical equipment, including an electrocardiograph machine, belonged to the late Dr. James Wilson Hunter, Jr. Guided tours are offered every half-hour. **Open:** Apr–Dec, Wed–Sat 10am–3:30 pm, Sun noon–3:30pm. Closed some hols. $

Moses Myers House, 331 Bank St; tel 804/664-6200. This handsome, early Federal brick town house set in a pretty garden was home to 5 generations of the Myerses from 1792 to 1930. The furnishings within are 70% original, and provide a unique glimpse into the lives of Jewish immigrants in 18th-century America. **Open:** Apr–Dec, Tues–Sat 10am–5pm, Sun noon–5pm. Closed some hols. $

Norfolk Botanical Gardens, Azalea Garden Rd; tel 804/640-6879. Immediately adjacent to Norfolk International Airport, this botanical garden encompasses 155 acres and features 12 miles of pathways. From early Apr to mid-June the grounds are brilliantly abloom with azaleas. The Statuary Vista is a beautiful setting for Moses Ezekiel's heroic-size statues (originally intended for the Corcoran Gallery in Washington) of great painters and sculptors—Rembrandt, Reubens, Dürer, and da Vinci, among others. Notable, too, are the rose garden, fragrance garden, and Italian Renaissance Garden. Guided trackless train and canal boat tours are available during the summer (additional fee charged). Educational programs, gift shop, garden tea house. **Open:** Daily 8:30am–sunset. $

Carrie B, the Waterside; tel 804/393-47355. The *Carrie B*, a reproduction of a 19th-century Mississippi riverboat, offers daytime and sunset cruises of Norfolk's harbor from the Waterside. Depending on the tour, visitors can see the shipyard, with nuclear subs and aircraft carriers, the naval base, or the site of the Civil War battle between the *Monitor* and the *Merrimac*. A 2½-hour sunset cruise is offered in the summer. **Open:** June–Labor Day, daily noon, 2pm, and 6pm; Apr–May and early Sept–Oct, daily noon and 2pm. $$$$

ONLEY

Map page M-3, D7 (SW of Accomac)

Motel 🛏

≡≡ **Comfort Inn**, 25297 Lankford Hwy, PO Box 205, Onley, VA 23418; tel 804/787-7787 or toll free 800/221-2222; fax 804/787-4641. This new, well-kept, hospitable establishment is a good place to stop between the Chesapeake Bay Bridge Tunnel and the turnoff to Chincoteague. In a rural area with few motels. Onancock and the Tangier Island ferry are 1½ miles away. **Rooms:** 80 rms and stes. CI 2pm/CO noon. Nonsmoking rms avail. All rooms have very attractive furnishings. **Amenities:** 🖥 🏊 A/C, cable TV, refrig. Deluxe models have microwaves and VCRs. **Services:** 🍽 **Facilities:** 🖼 🛎 🚶 Several fast-food and family restaurants are adjacent. **Rates (CP):** HS June 1–Sept 18 $56 S; $62 D; from $62 ste. Extra person $5. Children under 18 stay free. Lower rates off-season. Pking: Outdoor, free. Maj CC.

ORANGE

Map page M-3, C5

Inn 🛏

≡≡ **The Hidden Inn**, 249 Caroline St at jct US 15/Va 20, Orange, VA 22960; tel 703/672-3625 or toll free 800/841-1253; fax 703/672-5029. 7 acres. This attractive restored Victorian home surrounded by huge trees is now a bed-and-breakfast. Close to a major intersection for easy accessibility, and a short drive to restaurants and historic sites. Children are not encouraged in the main house, but an adjacent building accommodates families. Unsuitable for children under 12. **Rooms:** 10 rms; 2 ctges/villas. CI 3pm/CO noon. No smoking. Each room individually decorated. Some have old-fashioned wardrobes in lieu of closets. Separate honeymoon cottage with Jacuzzi. **Amenities:** 🏊 A/C, cable TV. No phone. Some units w/terraces, some w/fireplaces, some w/Jacuzzis. **Services:** Afternoon tea served. Full country breakfast. Afternoon tea. Candlelight picnic for 2 served in room on a large outside porch. **Facilities:** Guest lounge w/TV. **Rates (BB):** $59–$129 S or D; from $159 ctge/villa. Extra person $20. Min stay wknds. Pking: Outdoor, free. Ltd CC. Closed: Dec 24–25.

Attractions 🧳

Montpelier, Va 20; tel 703/672-2728. Located in Montpelier Station, 4 miles SW of Orange on Va 20 S. The home of James

Madison, Montpelier was opened to the public in 1987. From 1723 to 1844, the 2,700-acre estate overlooking the Blue Ridge Mountains was home to 3 generations of the Madison family.

Born in 1751, James Madison rose to prominence early in life. At the 1776 Constitutional Convention in Williamsburg, he made sure that the guarantee of religious freedom was included in the Virginia Declaration of Rights. Later, as a member of the federal Constitutional Convention, he worked for passage of the Bill of Rights and for the creation of the executive departments, efforts that earned him the title "Father of the Constitution." After 4 terms in Congress, Madison became secretary of state under Jefferson and in 1809 succeeded Jefferson as president, leading the new nation during the War of 1812. Madison's final years were taken up with the University of Virginia, where he served as rector.

The estate changed hands many times between 1844 and 1901, when it was acquired by William du Pont, Sr. His daughter added the steeplechase course and initiated the **Montpelier Hunt Races,** which are still held here every November. The National Trust acquired the property after her death in 1984.

Restoration efforts seek to compromise between the Madison and du Pont eras; the Madison rooms will be presented as they were in the 18th century, while the du Pont rooms will reflect their 20th-century appearance. As work progresses on the sparsely furnished 55-room house, exhibits document its transformation. While it is already an interesting tour, much more research and restoration work will be needed before Montpelier takes its place alongside similar Virginia attractions. **Open:** Daily 10am–4pm. Closed some hols. $$$

James Madison Museum, 129 Caroline St; tel 703/672-1776. Dedicated to the 4th president of the United States, called the "Father of the Constitution," this museum contains 4 permanent exhibits dealing with Madison's life and times. Madison artifacts in the main exhibit include presidential correspondence, fashions associated with his wife, Dolley, books from his personal library, and other personal items. Special exhibits are presented on a regular basis. Tours may be arranged by calling in advance. **Open:** Mar–Nov, Mon–Fri 9am–4pm, Sat–Sun 1–4pm; Dec–Feb, Mon–Fri 9am–4pm. Closed some hols. $

PETERSBURG

Map page M-3, E6

Hotel 🛏

≣≣≣ Petersburg Ramada, 380 E Washington St, Petersburg, VA 23803; tel 804/733-0000 or toll free 800/473-0005; fax 804/733-3927. Exit 50D off I-95 N; exit 52 off I-95 S.

Conscientiously staffed hotel with nicely decorated lobby equipped with small kitchen, including microwave, dining tables, refreshments. Convenient to attractions, sights, golf course. **Rooms:** 200 rms and stes. Exec-level rms avail. CI 3pm/CO noon. Nonsmoking rms avail. Although simple and not new, rooms are clean and comfortable. Doors secured with access cards instead of keys. **Amenities:** 🛆 A/C, satel TV w/movies, refrig. Not all rooms have remote-controlled TVs. **Services:** ✕ 🚐 🍴 🛎 **Facilities:** 🛅 🌅 ᾱ 1 rst, 1 bar (w/entertainment), washer/dryer. Outdoor pool is on 2nd floor. Green Door Restaurant on premises. Lounge has dancing on weekends. **Rates (CP):** $41–$45 S or D; from $75 ste. Extra person $5. Children under 18 stay free. Higher rates for spec evnts/hols. Spec packages avail. Pking: Indoor/outdoor, free. Maj CC. $10 pet fee.

Motels

≣≣≣ Best Western Petersburg, 405 E Washington St, Petersburg, VA 23803; tel 804/733-1776 or toll free 800/528-1234; fax 804/733-1776 ext 172. Exit 50D off I-95 N; exit 52 off I-95 S. A clean, comfortable motel near such historic attractions as plantations, Civil War battlefields, small towns. **Rooms:** 124 rms and stes. CI 2pm/CO noon. Nonsmoking rms avail. **Amenities:** 🛆 A/C, cable TV w/movies, refrig. Some units w/Jacuzzis. **Services:** ✕ 🚐 🖄 🍴 🛎 Complimentary coffee and newspapers. **Facilities:** 🛅 🌅 ᾱ 2 rsts, games rm, washer/dryer. 1 of 2 restaurants is next door. Guests can use YMCA. **Rates (CP):** $49–$57 D; from $95 ste. Extra person $5. Children under 12 stay free. Spec packages avail. Pking: Outdoor, free. Maj CC.

≣≣ Days Inn, 12208 S Crater Rd, Petersburg, VA 23805; tel 804/733-4400 or toll free 800/325-2525; fax 804/861-9559. 6 mi S of Petersburg. exit 13 off I-95. A comfortable motel conveniently located near historic sites, plantations. **Rooms:** 154 rms. CI 2pm/CO 11am. Nonsmoking rms avail. Attractive and comfortable rooms. **Amenities:** 🛆 ᾱ A/C, cable TV, refrig. **Services:** 🍴 🛎 Complimentary coffee in lobby. Free transportation to Fort Lee. **Facilities:** 🛅 🍽 🌅 ᾱ 1 rst, whirlpool, playground, washer/dryer. Pleasantly landscaped and well-maintained pool area. **Rates:** HS June–Sept $41–$59 D. Children under 18 stay free. Lower rates off-season. Higher rates for spec evnts/hols. Pking: Outdoor, free. Maj CC.

Restaurant 🍽

King's Barbeque, 3221 W Washington Rd, Petersburg; tel 804/732-5861. **Barbecue/Seafood.** A traditional southern-style barbecue house, this simply decorated establishment with booths and tables is widely known in these parts for its big brick fireplace in which pork and beef constantly smoke to perfection over hickory coals. Carvers stand at end of long counter and wield cleavers to slice or mince the barbecue to patrons' desires. Crispy fried chicken and homemade apple pie are other pleasers. A local favorite since 1946. Carryout available. **FYI:** Reservations accepted. Children's menu. No liquor license. **Open:** Tues–Sun 7am–9pm. Closed some hols. **Prices:** Main courses $4.25–$13.95. Ltd CC.

Attractions 💼

OLD TOWNE PETERSBURG

Petersburg Visitor's Center, 15 Bank St; tel 804/733-2400 or toll free 800/368-3595. Most often associated with the closing days of the Civil War, Petersburg has played an important role as a strategic center of commerce, trade, and transportation since before the Revolution. Residents—including one of the largest free black populations of any American city—enjoyed a comfortable lifestyle here typical of any industrialized city in the South. After a devastating fire destroyed the old town in the summer of 1815, a brick commercial district rose in its place. It quickly became a major crossroads for boats trading ships on the Appomattox River, and a major railroad center.

Explorations of Old Towne should begin at the **Visitor's Center (McIlwaine House)**, built in 1815 by Mayor George Jones. Tour guides are on hand to provide information, help plan itineraries, and secure reservations. A "Petersburg Pass" is available here that provides admission to the Siege Museum, Old Blandford Church, the Farmers Bank, Trapezium House, and Centre Hill Mansion (see below). **Open:** Daily 9am–5pm.

Old Blandford Church, 321 S Crater Rd; tel 804/733-2396. Built in 1735, this church has become a memorial to southern soldiers who perished in the Civil War. There are 15 magnificent stained-glass windows desgined by Louis Comfort Tiffany, each contibuted by a southern state. About 30,000 Confederate soldiers are buried in Blandford Cemetery, where the first Memorial Day was observed in June 1866. **Open:** Daily, 10am–5pm. Closed some hols. $

Farmers Bank; tel 804/733-2400. Tours of this building begin at the Visitor's Center. Built in 1817, the Petersburg Branch of the Farmers Bank of Virginia included living space on the upper floors for the cashier and his family. The original safe and vault are still here, and there is an authentic printing press of the type used when Confederate banks were allowed to print their own currency on site. **Open:** Daily; tours hourly on the half hour (inquire at Visitor's Center). $$

Siege Museum, 15 W Bank St; tel 804/733-2404. The story of how the citizens of Petersburg endured the 10-month siege of their town is preserved in this museum. Lavish lifestyles in the years preceding the Civil War gave way to a bitter struggle for survival in the last days of the Confederacy. The museum is located in the Exchange Building, built in 1839 as a commodities market. **Open:** Daily 10am–5pm. Closed some hols. $

Trapezium House, 244 N Market St; tel 804/733-2402. Tours begin at the Siege Museum (see above). Built by Charles O'Hara in 1817, this house was built without parallel walls or right angles because, as legend has it, O'Hara's West Indian slave told him that such a house could not harbor evil spirits. **Open:** Apr–Oct, daily; tours hourly on the half-hour (inquire at Siege Museum). $

Centre Hill Mansion, Center Hill Court; tel 804/733-2401. A showcase of Southern living and style, Centre Hill Mansion was built in 1823 in the federal style by the prominent Bolling family. The interior was later remodeled in the Greek Revival style of the 1840s. Ornate woodwork and plaster motifs accent a collection of period furnishings, including an 1886 rosewood Knabe Art grand piano. **Open:** Daily 10am–5pm. Closed some hols. $

OTHER ATTRACTIONS

Petersburg National Battlefield Park, Va 36; tel 804/732-3531. The last decisive engagement of the Civil War took place in this quiet town along the Appomattox River. The visitors center offers a museum as well as a multimedia presentation relating the story of the 10-month siege of Petersburg, which lasted from mid-June 1864 to early April 1865.

The battlefield park encompasses some 1,500 acres. The 4-mile battlefield driving tour has wayside exhibits and audio stations; some stops have short walking tours. Most fascinating is the site of the **Crater,** a huge depression in the ground. It was made when a group of Pennsylvania militia, including many miners, dug a passage beneath Confederate lines and exploded 4 tons of powder, creating the 170-by-60-foot crater. An extended driving tour follows the entire 16-mile siege line.

Grant relentlessly kept up his attempts to capture the city, although the cost in men was brutal. Finally, on April 2, 1865, Grant's all-out assault smashed through Lee's right flank, and that night Lee evacuated Petersburg. One week later came the surrender at Appomattox Court House. The **Five Forks Unit,** located about 6 miles southwest, preserves the site where Union forces finally broke the Confederate line. **Open:** Park, daily 7am–dusk; visitors center, daily 8am–5pm. Closed some hols. $$

PORTSMOUTH

Map page M-3, E7

Motel 🛏

≣≣≣ **Holiday Inn Waterfront**, 8 Crawford Pkwy, at Green St, Portsmouth, VA 23704 (Waterfront); tel 804/393-2573 or toll free 800/HOLIDAY; fax 804/399-1248. Located on the Elizabeth River, motel is popular with military and tour guests. **Rooms:** 232 rms and stes. CI 4pm/CO noon. Express checkout avail. Nonsmoking rms avail. Rooms with water views face either the adjacent marina or the river, which bustles with tugboats, military vessels, yachts. **Amenities:** 🛅 📺 A/C, cable TV w/movies. Water-view rooms have refrigerators. **Services:** ✕ ☒ 🖐 Public fax in lobby. **Facilities:** 🏋 🚣 🎱 ♨ ⚓ 1 rst, 1 bar (w/entertainment), washer/dryer. Guests can use tennis courts at adjacent apartment complex. **Rates:** $75–$81 S; $82–$88 D; from $170 ste. Extra person $6. Children under 19 stay free. Min stay spec evnts. Higher rates for spec evnts/hols. Spec packages avail. Pking: Indoor/outdoor, free. Maj CC. Discounts for patrons of adjacent marina.

Restaurant 🍴

The Max, 425 Water St, Portsmouth; tel 804/397-0176. Located downtown, on Portsmouth Waterfront. **New American/Seafood/Steak.** On the downtown Portsmouth waterfront, this large restaurant looks across harbor to Norfolk. Open and cheerful atmosphere created by colorful vinyl tablecloths, pastel napkins, deep-rose woodwork, and contemporary gray chairs. A favorite: chunks of shrimp and scallops in lobster sauce served over rice. Fresh daily catch can be ordered several ways. Beef and pasta dishes also available. **FYI:** Reservations recommended. Children's menu. Dress code. **Open:** Mon–Thurs 11:30am–10pm, Fri–Sat 11:30am–11pm, Sun 11:30am–9pm. Closed some hols. **Prices:** Main courses $11–$17. Maj CC. ⛰ ⚓

Attractions 🏛

THE PORTSMOUTH MUSEUMS

Naval Shipyard Museum, 2 High St; tel 804/393-8591. Established in 1949, this museum contains many artifacts, ship models, and other items relating to the seafaring history of this area from the time of its first settlement. Highlights include scale models of the Confederate ironclad CSS *Virginia* and other historic vessels associated with the port at Hampton Roads. **Open:** Tues–Sat 10am–5pm, Sun 1–5pm. Closed some hols.

Lightship Museum, London Slip; tel 804/393-8591 or 393-8741. Lighted beacons that helped mariners avoid dangerous shoals and enter safely into harbors at night were not all atop lighthouses. Years ago, lights were fixed to the tall masts of ships that anchored for months at a time in strategic locations off the coastline. Commissioned in 1916, *Lightship 101,* after 48 years of service in the Coast Guard, was donated to the city of Portsmouth in 1964 and permanently moored at the foot of Loudon Blvd. Now restored to its original condition, the ship serves as a floating museum illustrating the living and working conditions of those who served aboard the lightships during their many months at sea. **Open:** Tues–Sat 10am–5pm, Sun 1–5pm. Closed some hols.

1846 Courthouse, 420 High St; tel 804/393-8983. The Fine Arts Gallery, which houses changing art exhibitions, is undergoing an expansion that will involve all 3 levels of the building. The Children's Museum, formerly on the first floor, is being moved to a new building ½ block away in the Middle Street Mall. The adjoining **Community Arts Center** houses classrooms and laboratories, as well as galleries with permanent and changing exhibits. **Open:** Tues–Sat 10am–5pm, Sun 1–5pm. Closed some hols.

Children's Museum, 421 High St; tel 804/393-8983. Recently reopened in a new dedicated museum space, this hands-on museum especially for children features 14 exhibit galleries and a planetarium. **Open:** Daily 10am–5pm, Fri until 9pm.

OTHER ATTRACTIONS

Hill House, 221 North St; tel 804/393-0241. Built in the early 1800s, this 4-story English dwelling now serves as the headquarters of the Portsmouth Historical Association. The house contains the original furnishings collected by generations of the Hill family over 150 years. It remains in original condition after only limited renovation over the years. **Open:** Wed 12:30–5pm, Sat–Sun 1–5pm. Closed some hols. $

RADFORD

Map page M-2, E3

Motels 🛏

≣≣≣ **Best Western Radford Inn**, 1501 Tyler Ave, PO Box 1008, Radford, VA 24141; tel 703/639-3000 or toll free 800/628-1955; fax 639-3000. Exit 109 off I-81. Although it's in town, this large property in Williamsburg architectural style is in a rural setting. Large stone fireplace in lobby. Close to the university and downtown. Comfort Inn next door has same owners. **Rooms:** 72 rms. CI 3pm/CO noon. Express checkout avail. Nonsmoking rms avail. Very clean and spacious rooms, many with a view of pool and countryside. **Amenities:** 🛅 🖳 A/C, cable TV w/movies. **Services:** ✗ 🖾 🖵 🖫 **Facilities:** 🖫 🖳 🖭 ⚘ 1 rst, 1 bar (w/entertainment), games rm, sauna, whirlpool. **Rates:** $57–$62 S; $62–$67 D. Extra person $6. Children under 12 stay free. Min stay spec evnts. Higher rates for spec evnts/hols. Pking: Outdoor, free. Maj CC.

📰📰 **Comfort Inn**, 1501 Tyler Ave, PO Box 1008, Radford, VA 24141; tel 703/639-4800 or toll free 800/221-2222. Exit 109 off I-81. Although in town, this property sits well enough back on rural land to give a country feel. A totally nonsmoking motel. **Rooms:** 32 rms and stes. CI 3pm/CO noon. Exceptionally well-furnished rooms. **Amenities:** 🛅 ⚇ 🖭 🖳 A/C, cable TV w/movies. 1 unit w/Jacuzzi. **Services:** ✗ 🖾 🖵 🖫 **Facilities:** ⚘ Games rm. Guests have pool privileges at Best Western Radford Inn next door. **Rates:** $53–$58 S; $58–$63 D; from $135 ste. Extra person $5. Children under 18 stay free. Min stay spec evnts. Higher rates for spec evnts/hols. Pking: Outdoor, free. Maj CC.

📰📰 **Dogwood Lodge**, 7073 Lee Hwy, Radford, VA 24141; tel 703/639-9338. 2½ mi SW of Radford. Take exit 109 off I-81 and follow US 11 S; or take exit 98 off I-81 and follow US 11 N for 9 miles. Quiet, grassy setting high on a hill, back from the highway, and almost out of town. **Rooms:** 15 rms. CI noon/CO 11am. Nonsmoking rms avail. Each unit is individually decorated. **Amenities:** 🛅 A/C, cable TV. All units w/terraces. **Services:** 🖾 🖵 🖫 **Facilities:** Picnic tables on lawn. **Rates:** $25–$35 S or D. Extra person $3. Children under 12 stay free. Min stay spec evnts. Higher rates for spec evnts/hols. Pking: Outdoor, free. Ltd CC.

Attraction 🧳

Claytor Lake State Park; tel 703/674-5492. Located on Va 660, just off I-81 exit 101. Wooded hills and a 4,500-acre lake provide the setting for fishing, swimming, boating, camping, and hiking. Sport fishing is especially popular. The historic Howe House features exhibits on the life of early settlers in the region. **Open:** Daily. $

REEDVILLE

Map page M-3, D7

Attraction 🧳

Fisherman's Museum, Main St; tel 804/453-6529. The small village of Reedville, located on Cockrell's Creek, an inlet of Chesapeake Bay, provides a living image of the past with its Victorian mansions and seafaring atmosphere. Housed in the 1875 William Walker House, the Fishermen's Museum commemorates the industry around which the town was built. **Open:** May–Oct, Mon–Fri 3–5pm, Sat–Sun 1–3pm; Apr and Nov, Mon–Fri 3–5pm, Sat–Sun 1–3pm; Dec–Mar, Sat–Sun 3–5pm. Free.

RESTON

Map page M-3, B6 (NW of Arlington)

Hotel 🏨

📰📰📰 **Sheraton Reston Hotel**, 11810 Sunrise Valley Dr, Reston, VA 22091; tel 703/620-9000 or toll free 800/392-7666; fax 703/860-1594. Exit 3 off Dulles Toll Rd. Follow Reston Pkwy (Va 602) south to Sunrise Valley Dr, turn left. Situated in an attractive office-park setting on the outskirts of the planned community of Reston, this modern hotel wraps around a landscaped, resort-like courtyard with kidney-shaped swimming pool and large sun deck. **Rooms:** 312 rms and stes. Exec-level rms avail. CI 3pm/CO 1pm. Express checkout avail. Nonsmoking rms avail. Comfortable rooms are decorated in light color schemes. Some are in a tower, others in low-rise building forming semicircle around courtyard. **Amenities:** 🛅 ⚇ 🖭 A/C, cable TV w/movies, refrig, shoe polisher. Some units w/minibars. **Services:** 🍽 🖨 🖾 🖵 Children's program, babysitting. Free shuttle to shopping and restaurants. **Facilities:** 🖫 🖳 🖭 🖳 ⚘ 1 rst, 1 bar (w/entertainment), lifeguard, spa, sauna, whirlpool, playground. Reston Golf Course across the street. **Rates (CP):** HS Mar–June/Sept–Nov $99–$102 S; $109–$112 D; from $150 ste. Extra person $15. Children under 18 stay free. Lower rates off-season. Spec packages avail. Pking: Outdoor, free. Maj CC. Weekend packages.

RICHMOND

Map page M-3, D6

See also Midlothian, Sandston

TOURIST INFORMATION

Metro Richmond Convention and Visitors Bureau 550 E Marshall St, on 2nd floor of the 6th Street Marketplace (tel 804/782-2777 or 800/365-7272). Open Mon–Fri 8:30am–5pm.

Metro Richmond Visitors Center 1710 Robin Hood Rd, near the Boulevard at exit 78 (tel 804/358-5511). Open Sept–May daily 9am–5pm, June–August daily 9am–7pm. Same-day hotel reservations available, often at discounted rates.

Richmond International Airport Visitors Center Open daily, usually 9am–5pm (hours may vary). Same-day hotel reservations available, often at discounted rates. Call 804/236-3260.

PUBLIC TRANSPORTATION

Greater Richmond Transit Co Public Buses Service on most routes 5am–midnight. Fare $1.25. For information call 804/358-GRTC.

Greater Richmond Transit Co Trackless Trolley Cars Operate Mon–Sat 9am–midnight from Broad St to Shockoe Slip. Also operate Mon–Sat 10am–midnight from 6th Street Marketplace to Riverfront; Mon–Fri after 5pm service expands to Shockoe Bottom. Fare 25¢. For information call 804/358-GRTC.

Hotels 🖼

≣≣≣ The Berkeley Hotel, 1200 E Cary St, Richmond, VA 23219 (Shockoe Slip); tel 804/780-1300; fax 804/343-1885. Exit 74A off I-95 N, or exit 79 off I-95 S. In the historic Shockoe Slip district and surrounded by restaurants, shops, and attractions, this fine hotel boasts superior-quality furnishings and an inviting and elegant ambience. Most guests are repeat business travelers. **Rooms:** 55 rms. CI 2pm/CO noon. Nonsmoking rms avail. Standard rooms have 2 double beds. Executive units have king bed. **Amenities:** 🛁 ⚬ 🖥. A/C, cable TV. Some units w/terraces, 1 w/Jacuzzi. Executive units equipped with bottled water. **Services:** ✕ 🗝 🆅🅿 🖥 ↩ Twice-daily maid svce, masseur. Downtown shuttle van. European-style turndown service. **Facilities:** 🔳 💻 ⚓ 1 rst. Restaurant is acclaimed. Free use of major private health club nearby. **Rates:** $92–$164 S or D. Extra person $15. Children under 16 stay free. Spec packages avail. Pking: Indoor, free. Maj CC.

≣≣≣≣ Commonwealth Park Suites Hotel, 9th and Bank Sts, PO Box 455, Richmond, VA 23203; tel 804/343-7300; fax 804/343-1025. A European-style luxury hotel across from the state capitol. Within walking distance of downtown shops and restaurants. **Rooms:** 59 stes. CI 3pm/CO noon. Nonsmoking rms avail. All units are highly luxurious suites, with dark wood furniture, lovely sitting rooms, marble baths. Some have 2 bedrooms. **Amenities:** 🛁 ⚬ A/C, cable TV w/movies, refrig, stereo/tape player, bathrobes. All units w/minibars. **Services:** 🍽 🗝 🆅🅿 🚐 🖥 ↩ ◁ Twice-daily maid svce, masseur, babysitting. Complimentary transportation within downtown

area. Emphasis on high-quality service. **Facilities:** 🔳 ⚓ 2 rsts, 1 bar (w/entertainment), spa. Restaurants consist of casual breakfast/lunch facility and formal dining room serving dinner. **Rates:** HS Sept–May from $125 ste. Children under 18 stay free. Lower rates off-season. Higher rates for spec evnts/hols. Spec packages avail. Pking: Indoor, $9.75. Maj CC.

Courtyard by Marriott, 6400 W Broad St, Richmond, VA 23229; tel 804/282-1881 or toll free 800/321-2211; fax 804/288-2934. Exit 183B off I-64. Follow Broad St for ¼ mi. A beige complex built around a landscaped courtyard with outdoor swimming pool, this is one of the fine chain of hotels that primarily cater to businesspeople but are perfectly adequate for families and other travelers. Unrated. **Rooms:** 145 rms and stes. CI 3pm/CO noon. Express checkout avail. Nonsmoking rms avail. Rooms have pluses for business travelers, such as desks. **Amenities:** 🛁 ⚬ 🖥 A/C, satel TV. Some units w/terraces. Long phone cords, hot-water taps for tea and coffee. **Services:** ↩ Dinner delivery from nearby restaurants. **Facilities:** 🔳 🏓 ⚓ 1 rst, whirlpool, washer/dryer. Restaurant serves breakfast only. Honor bar in lobby during evenings. **Rates:** $69–$79 S or D; from $89 ste. Children under 18 stay free. Higher rates for spec evnts/hols. Pking: Outdoor, free. Maj CC.

≣≣≣≣ The Jefferson Hotel, Franklin and Adams Sts, Richmond, VA 23220 (Downtown); tel 804/788-8000 or toll free 800/424-8014; fax 804/344-5162. Exit 76B off I-95. Go south on US 1/301 to Franklin St, turn left. Originally built in 1895 and completely renovated during the 1980s at a cost of $34 million, the Jefferson is Richmond's premier hotel. A downtown landmark, the beaux arts brick building is a stunning blend of Renaissance and other architectural styles popular at the turn of the century. Inside, a statue of Thomas Jefferson stands under the Palm Court's circular, 70-foot-wide skylight. The colonnaded lobby sports a magnificent polished marble staircase strongly reminiscent of the one Rhett Butler carried Scarlett O'Hara up in *Gone with the Wind*. **Rooms:** 274 rms and stes. Exec-level rms avail. CI 3pm/CO noon. Express checkout avail. Nonsmoking rms avail. Rooms are decorated in 57 different luxurious styles. **Amenities:** 🛁 ⚬ 🍷 A/C, cable TV w/movies, bathrobes. All units w/minibars, some w/terraces, some w/Jacuzzis. **Services:** 🍽 🗝 🆅🅿 🖥 ↩ Twice-daily maid svce, babysitting. President's Club level has concierge lounge, continental breakfast, evening cocktails. **Facilities:** 🔳 2 rsts, 1 bar (w/entertainment), beauty salon. Lemaire, a full-service gourmet restaurant, is named for Jefferson's White House maitre d'hotel. TJ's Grill and Bar offers casual dining. The private library has a solid African mahogany fireplace and some of the hotel's original book collection. **Rates:** HS Mar–June/Sept–Nov $140–$175 S;

$155–$190 D; from $235 ste. Children under 12 stay free. Lower rates off-season. Spec packages avail. Pking: Outdoor, $7.50–$9. Maj CC. Romance and other packages available.

≣≣≣ **Omni Richmond Hotel**, 100 S 12th St, at Cary St, Richmond, VA 23219 (Shockoe Slip); tel 804/344-7000 or toll free 800/THE-OMNI; fax 804/648-1029. Exit 75A off I-95. Although showing some wear and tear, this busy hotel enjoys a convenient downtown location. **Rooms:** 363 rms, stes, and effic. Exec-level rms avail. CI 3pm/CO 1pm. Express checkout avail. Nonsmoking rms avail. **Amenities:** 📷 🐶 🍷 A/C, cable TV w/movies, stereo/tape player, voice mail, bathrobes. All units w/minibars. **Services:** ✕ ☞ 🆅🅿 🖼 🐶 Twice-daily maid svce, car-rental desk, babysitting. **Facilities:** 🔥 🔟 🖥 2 rsts (*see also* "Restaurants" below), 2 bars, day-care ctr. **Rates:** $119–$149 S; $134–$164 D; from $199 ste. Extra person $15. Children under 18 stay free. Higher rates for spec evnts/hols. Spec packages avail. Pking: Indoor, $8. Maj CC.

≣≣≣ **Radisson Hotel Richmond**, 555 E Canal St, Richmond, VA 23219; tel 804/788-0900 or toll free 800/333-3333; fax 804/788-0791. Exit 74A off I-95. Exit the Downtown Expwy at Canal St. Conveniently located among historical sights and shops, this comfortable hotel underwent a complete remodeling in 1994. **Rooms:** 297 rms and stes. Exec-level rms avail. CI 3pm/CO noon. Express checkout avail. Nonsmoking rms avail. Even the more basic rooms are very attractive, well equipped, and large enough to accommodate 4 persons. Many contain sleep sofas. **Amenities:** 📷 🍷 A/C, cable TV. Some units w/minibars. Many rooms have microwaves, wet bars. **Services:** ✕ ☞ 🖼 🐶 Concierge-level suites include continental breakfast. **Facilities:** 🔥 🐴 🔟 🐶 1 rst, spa, sauna, whirlpool. **Rates:** $94–$119 D; from $350 ste. Spec packages avail. Pking: Indoor, $5. Maj CC. No charge for parking on weekends.

≣≣≣ **Richmond Marriott**, 500 E Broad St, Richmond, VA 23219 (Downtown); tel 804/643-3400 or toll free 800/228-9290; fax 804/649-3725. Exit 74C off I-95. Go straight 9½ blocks on Broad St to hotel. One of Richmond's largest hotels, with many facilities and amenities and located downtown near many attractions. Popular with families and conventioneers. **Rooms:** 401 rms and stes. Exec-level rms avail. CI 4pm/CO noon. Express checkout avail. Nonsmoking rms avail. **Amenities:** 📷 🐶 A/C, cable TV w/movies, refrig, voice mail. Executive suites have bathrobes. Phones in club-level rooms have view screens. **Services:** ✕ ☞ 🆅🅿 🖼 🐶 🐶 Twice-daily maid svce, babysitting. Club level has well-appointed concierge lounge. **Facilities:** 🔥 🐴 🔟 🖥 🐶 3 rsts, 1 bar (w/entertainment), lifeguard, games rm, spa, sauna, steam rm, whirlpool, washer/dryer. Pool is small but extremely well kept and lovely.

Rates: $85–$114 S; $95–$124 D; from $85 ste. Children under 15 stay free. Higher rates for spec evnts/hols. Spec packages avail. Pking: Indoor, $5. Pking: Outdoor, $5. Maj CC.

Motels

≣ **Alpine Motel**, 7009 Brook Rd (US 1), Richmond, VA 23227; tel 804/262-4798. Exit 81 off I-95. Drive north on US 1 for 1½ miles. A well-kept, no-frills motel. **Rooms:** 20 rms. CI noon/CO 11am. Rooms are simple, clean, and comfortable. A few have waterbeds. Door security could be better. **Amenities:** 📷 A/C, cable TV, refrig, VCR. Ceiling fans. **Services:** 🐶 **Facilities:** 🔥 **Rates:** HS May–Oct $48–$60 D. Extra person $5. Children under 12 stay free. Lower rates off-season. Pking: Outdoor, free. Maj CC.

≣≣≣ **Best Western Governor's Inn**, 9848 Midlothian Tpk, Richmond, VA 23235; tel 804/323-0007 or toll free 800/528-1234; fax 804/272-0759. Exit I-95 at Midlothian Tpk W. Resembling a palace or castle, this motel is adjacent to shopping, restaurants, businesses. **Rooms:** 49 rms and stes. Exec-level rms avail. CI 3pm/CO noon. Nonsmoking rms avail. Spacious rooms. **Amenities:** 📷 🐶 A/C, cable TV, in-rm safe. Some units w/Jacuzzis. 25-inch TVs. **Services:** ✕ 🐶 Continental breakfast. **Facilities:** 🔥 1 rst, 1 bar. **Rates (CP):** HS June–Sept $58–$63 S or D; from $85 ste. Extra person $5. Children under 16 stay free. Lower rates off-season. Higher rates for spec evnts/hols. Pking: Outdoor, free. Maj CC.

≣≣≣ **Best Western James River Inn**, 8008 W Broad St, Richmond, VA 23229; tel 804/346-0000 or toll free 800/528-1234; fax 804/346-4547. Exit 83B off I-95. Follow Parham Rd to Broad St; turn left. Close to downtown yet far enough away to avoid the city congestion, this motel recently underwent remodeling. Attractive surrounding grounds with flowers and benches. **Rooms:** 177 rms. CI 11am/CO 3pm. Nonsmoking rms avail. Simple but pleasant decor. **Amenities:** 📷 A/C, cable TV. **Services:** ✕ 🚐 🐶 🐶 Complimentary morning coffee and newspaper. Continental breakfast. Limited room service provided by nearby Bennigan's restaurant. Free local calls. **Facilities:** 🔥 🐴 🔟 🐶 Games rm. **Rates (CP):** HS Apr–Oct $43–$50 S; $48–$55 D. Extra person $5. Children under 16 stay free. Lower rates off-season. Pking: Outdoor, free. Maj CC.

≣≣ **Comfort Inn Executive Center**, 7201 W Broad St, Richmond, VA 23294; tel 804/672-1108 or toll free 800/228-5150; fax 804/755-1625. Exit 183C off I-64. Just outside downtown Richmond, this establishment consists of 3 buildings with elegant, warmly decorated lobby. **Rooms:** 123 rms. CI 2pm/CO 11am. Nonsmoking rms avail. Furnishings are attractive, of better quality than at some Comfort Inns. **Amenities:** 📷

A/C, cable TV. **Services:** ⌨ ⌂ Complimentary newspaper. Deluxe continental breakfast and refreshments, including fresh fruits, in lobby. **Facilities:** 🔦 🔟 & Sauna, whirlpool, washer/dryer. **Rates (CP):** $53–$59 S or D. Extra person $6. Children under 18 stay free. Higher rates for spec evnts/hols. Pking: Outdoor, free. Maj CC.

🏨🏨 **Comfort Inn Midtown Conference Center**, 3200 W Broad St, Richmond, VA 23230; tel 804/359-4061 or toll free 800/228-5150; fax 804/359-3189. Exit 78 off I-95. Recent renovation spiffed up this comfortable hotel west of downtown Richmond, convenient to sights and attractions. **Rooms:** 160 rms and stes. CI 2pm/CO noon. Nonsmoking rms avail. Attractively furnished. **Amenities:** 📺 ⌂ A/C, cable TV w/movies. Suites have microwaves, wet bars, refrigerators. **Services:** ✗ 🚗 ⌂ 🔔 Complimentary newspapers. Continental breakfast served in lobby. Free local calls. **Facilities:** 🔦 🍽 🔢 ⛱ & Lifeguard, washer/dryer. **Rates (CP):** $49–$54 S or D; from $125 ste. Extra person $5. Children under 12 stay free. Pking: Indoor, free. Maj CC.

🏨🏨 **Days Inn North**, 1600 Robin Hood Rd, Richmond, VA 23220 (Northside); tel 804/353-1287 or toll free 800/325-2525; fax 804/355-2659. Exit 78 off I-95. Conveniently located near the metro tourist information office and the Diamond baseball stadium. **Rooms:** 99 rms. CI 3pm/CO noon. Nonsmoking rms avail. Units are not impressively decorated. **Amenities:** 📺 A/C, cable TV, in-rm safe. **Services:** 🔔 ⌂ **Facilities:** 🔦 🔢 1 rst. Restaurant serves breakfast, lunch, and dinner. **Rates:** $51–$55 S or D. Extra person $5. Children under 14 stay free. Pking: Outdoor, free. Maj CC.

🏨🏨🏨 **Holiday Inn Koger Center South**, 1021 Koger Center Blvd, Richmond, VA 23235; tel 804/379-3800 or toll free 800/465-4329; fax 804/379-2763. Exit I-95 at Midlothian Turnpike; drive west 2 miles, turn right onto Koger Center Blvd. Surrounded by businesses, shops, restaurants. Attractive lobby has marble floors, fountains, landscaped atrium. **Rooms:** 200 rms and stes. CI 3pm/CO 11am. Nonsmoking rms avail. Spacious rooms and baths. **Amenities:** 📺 🖥 A/C, cable TV. Some units w/minibars, 1 w/Jacuzzi. **Services:** ✗ 🚗 ⌂ 🔔 Children's program. Outstanding staff takes care of guests. **Facilities:** 🔦 🍽 🔢 & 1 rst, 1 bar (w/entertainment), washer/dryer. Mystery Cafe dinner theater on premises. Large pool and pretty restaurant. **Rates:** $74–$79 S or D; from $275 ste. Extra person $7. Children under 18 stay free. Spec packages avail. Pking: Outdoor, free. Maj CC.

Inn

🏨🏨🏨🏨 **Linden Row Inn**, 101 N 1st St, Richmond, VA 23219 (The Fan); tel 804/783-7000 or toll free 800/348-7424;

fax 804/648-7504. Exit 74A off I-95 N, or exit 79 off I-95 S. Built in 1847, this inn has charm and character in abundance, plus a location convenient to historic landmarks, museums, and other attractions. The brick-walled garden is said to be Edgar Allen Poe's inspiration for his "Enchanted Garden." **Rooms:** 71 rms and stes. CI 3pm/CO noon. Each room has authentic Victorian furnishings. Those facing the garden have more of a country flair than other units. **Amenities:** 📺 ⌂ A/C, cable TV. Some units w/fireplaces. **Services:** ✗ 🆅🅿 ⌂ Twice-daily maid svce, afternoon tea and wine/sherry served. Free downtown transportation. Complimentary continental breakfast and evening wine-and-cheese reception. Free use of nearby YMCA health club. **Facilities:** 🔢 & 1 rst, 1 bar, guest lounge. **Rates (CP):** $74–$137 D; from $137 ste. Children under 18 stay free. Higher rates for spec evnts/hols. Spec packages avail. Pking: Indoor, $3. Ltd CC.

Restaurants 🍴

Bill's Barbecue, 3100 North Blvd, Richmond; tel 804/358-8634. Exit 78 off I-95. **Barbecue.** Very plain, simple decor with a few live plants in this popular barbecue house with booths and cafe-style counter with stools. Minced smoked pork is the house specialty. Drive-through window serves carryout orders. Good place for country-style breakfasts. **FYI:** Reservations not accepted. No liquor license. **Open:** HS Apr–Nov Mon–Sat 7am–11pm, Sun 10am–11pm. Reduced hours off-season. Closed some hols. **Prices:** Main courses $4.49–$6.69. No CC. &

★ **Commercial Tap House**, 111 N Robinson St, Richmond (Upper Fan); tel 804/359-6544. Between Floyd and Grove Aves. **New American/Barbecue/Eclectic.** Pub-like atmosphere draws lots of customers to casual downstairs, while upstairs dining room is more formal, with wood walls and floors and huge iron lamps designed by local artist. Known for a large and unusual beer selection, including suds from small, lesser-known breweries. Tap room is famous for hot-sauce collection, especially Dave's Insanity Sauce. Menu is varied, from ribs to fish-and-chips. **FYI:** Reservations accepted. **Open:** Mon–Sat 5pm–2am, Sun 11am–2am. Closed some hols. **Prices:** Main courses $6–$19. Maj CC.

Coppola's Delicatessen, 2900 W Cary St, at Colonial St, Richmond (Carytown); tel 804/359-NYNY. **Deli/Italian.** Decor includes mirrors, Italian food products, prints, and maps of regions of Italy. Spaghetti's the specialty on an extensive menu of Italian deli fare. Located on a street brimming with shops. **FYI:** Reservations not accepted. Beer and wine only. No smoking. **Open:** Mon–Wed 10am–8pm, Thurs–Sat 10am–9pm. Closed some hols. **Prices:** Main courses $1–$7. No CC. 🍴

Gallego's, in Omni Richmond Hotel, 100 S 12th St, Richmond; tel 804/344-7000. Exit 75A off I-95. **Seafood/Steak.** Atmosphere of old-fashioned men's club prevails at this premium steak house, thanks to lots of dark wood and overstuffed chairs. Dim lighting adds a romantic touch. New York strips and porterhouses head the list, plus veal, lamb, pork chops, grilled chicken, salmon, and swordfish. **FYI:** Reservations accepted. Dress code. **Open:** Daily 5pm–2am. **Prices:** Main courses $15.95–$25.95. Maj CC. ♥ VP &

Grace Place Natural Food Restaurant and Store, 826 W Grace St, Richmond (The Fan); tel 804/353-3680. Between Schaeffer and Laurel Sts. **Vegetarian.** In keeping with a healthy approach, the decor is simple yet appealing and comfortable: antique wood tables, framed prints, wildflowers as table decorations. Vegetarian fare is offered, including a variety of salads, homemade soups, and freshly baked desserts. Outdoor dining is encouraged when weather permits. **FYI:** Reservations accepted. Beer and wine only. No smoking. **Open:** Sun–Thurs 11am–9:30pm, Fri–Sat 11am–10pm. Closed some hols. **Prices:** Main courses $8.50–$8.95. Ltd CC. ♠

James River Wine Bistro, 1520 W Main St, at Lombardy St, Richmond (The Fan); tel 804/358-4562. **Californian/International.** Ceiling fans, paintings, statues, fountains, sideboards, plants, and mirrors create simple elegance throughout the 3 dining rooms, bar, and outdoor patio. Listed on National Register of Historic Places, building was built soon after the Civil War and was used as a high school from 1870 to 1970. Menu offers a mix of cuisines, from Italian to Thai to southwestern, with accent on items from the mesquite grill. **FYI:** Reservations recommended. **Open:** Tues–Sun 11:30am–12:30am. Closed some hols. **Prices:** Main courses $1.95–$18.95. Maj CC. ♥ ▮

★ **Joe's Inn**, 205 N Shields Ave, Richmond (The Fan); tel 804/355-2282. Between Grove and Hanover Sts. **Diner.** Casual bar/restaurant hangout, with pictures of Miami Dolphins (owner's favorite NFL team) on walls, jukebox, wooden booths, ceiling fans. Famous for huge portions of pasta served with a variety of sauces. A local institution. **FYI:** Reservations not accepted. Children's menu. **Open:** Daily 8am–midnight. **Prices:** Main courses $4–$10. Ltd CC. ▦

Peking Pavillion, 1302 E Cary St, Richmond; tel 304/649-8888. **Chinese.** Ornate wood dividers provide privacy in one of the few Shockoe Slip restaurants in existence for more than 10 years, making it a Richmond staple. Traditional, expertly prepared Peking duck. Champagne brunch is very popular. **FYI:** Reservations accepted. Dress code. **Open:** Lunch Mon–Fri 11:30am–2:15pm; dinner Sun–Thurs 5–9:30pm, Sat 5–10:30pm; brunch Sun 11:30am–2pm. Closed Thanksgiving. **Prices:** Main courses $8.50–$22.50. Maj CC.

Sam Miller's Warehouse, 1210 E Cary St, Richmond; tel 804/644-5465. Exit 74A off I-95. **New American/Seafood/Steak.** Large, open dining area conveys the feel of the Shockoe Slip area when it was a market and warehouse district. Whole Maine lobster, an unusual find on Richmond menus, is a favorite; prime rib's another. An easygoing, fun place. **FYI:** Reservations recommended. Blues/combo/guitar/jazz/sing along. Children's menu. **Open:** HS Sept–Dec/Apr–May Mon–Sat 11am–2am, Sun 10am–2am. Reduced hours off-season. Closed Dec 25. **Prices:** Main courses $14.95–$24.95. Maj CC. ♥ ▮ ▦ &

★ **Strawberry Street Café**, 421 N Strawberry St, Richmond (The Fan); tel 804/353-6860. Between Park and Stuart Aves. **New American/Cafe.** Stained-glass windows and an art-deco flair highlight this neighborhood hangout. An antique bathtub serves as a well-stocked salad bar. Homemade chicken pot pie, gourmet burgers, shrimp quesadillas, eggs Benedict with lump crabmeat, and fantastic artichoke dip lead the menu. Located near Strawberry Street Vineyard, restaurant sports extensive wine list. Sunday brunch is very popular. **FYI:** Reservations accepted. **Open:** Lunch daily 11am–2:30pm; dinner daily 5pm–midnight; brunch–Sun 10am–5pm. Closed some hols. **Prices:** Main courses $5–$12. Maj CC.

Texas-Wisconsin Border Café, 1501 W Main St, at Plum St, Richmond (The Fan); tel 804/355-2907. **German/Southwestern/Tex-Mex.** A small cafe casually adorned with ceiling fans, prints, license plates from the Southwest, mirrors, and hunting trophies. As name implies, menu offers an unusual mix from Texas (chili is well regarded) and Wisconsin (bratwurst, potato pancakes, kielbasa, and other German and Polish selections). **FYI:** Reservations not accepted. Children's menu. **Open:** Daily 11am–2am. Closed some hols. **Prices:** Main courses $3.75–$7.95. Ltd CC. &

★ **The Tobacco Company Restaurant**, 12th and Cary Sts, Richmond; tel 804/782-9431. Exit 74A off I-95. **Seafood/Steak.** Downtown professionals are attracted to this restaurant in an 1860s-vintage tobacco warehouse next to the Omni Richmond Hotel. Enormous brass-fixture bar, lots of well-groomed plants, overstuffed Victorian sofas, and Tiffany lamps. Skylights make it light and airy in daytime. Exposed antique elevator overlooks large atrium while accessing various levels with 2 dining rooms, bar, nightclub. Extensive selection of salads; otherwise, mostly beef and seafood. Bar open 11:30am–2am daily. **FYI:** Reservations accepted. Band/piano. Dress code. **Open:** Lunch Mon–Sat 11:30am–2:30pm; dinner Mon–Fri 5:30–10:30pm, Sat 5–11pm, Sun 5:30–10pm; brunch Sun 11am–2:30pm. Closed some hols. **Prices:** Main courses $12.95–$26.95. Maj CC. &

Attractions 🧳

Virginia State Capitol, 9th and Grace Sts; tel 804/786-4344. The first of many public buildings created in the classical revival style, the Virginia State Capitol was designed by Thomas Jefferson. It is the 2nd-oldest working capitol in the United States, in continuous use since 1788.

The capitol's **rotunda** has a domed skylight ornamented in renaissance style. The room's dramatic focal point is Houdon's life-size statue of George Washington, said to be a perfect likeness. Busts of the 7 other US presidents from Virginia—Jefferson, Madison, Monroe, William Henry Harrison, Tyler, Taylor, and Wilson—are also in the rotunda.

The old **Hall of the House of Delegates** is now a museum. The former senate chamber, still used for occasional committee meetings, is where Stonewall Jackson's body lay in state after his death in 1863.

Free 30-minute tours of the capitol are given throughout the day. On the capitol grounds are the **Executive Mansion,** official residence of governors of Virginia since 1813; and the the old **Bell Tower,** built in 1824, which houses the official Virginia Division of Tourism's Welcome Center. **Open:** Tours given Apr–Nov, daily 9am–5pm; Dec–Mar, Mon–Sat 9am–5pm, Sun 1–5pm. Closed some hols. Free.

Governor's Mansion, Capitol Square; tel 804/371-2642. The oldest governor's residence in continuous use in the United States, this 2-story federal-style landmark was completed in 1813 and has been the official residence of Virginia's chief executives ever since. Guided tours (by appointment only) visit the 1st floor of the mansion, as well as the gardens and guest house. **Open:** June–early Sept, Tues and Fri; mid-Sept through May, Tues–Fri; by appointment only. Closed Dec and some hols. Free.

Museum and White House of the Confederacy, 1201 E Clay St; tel 804/649-1861. The Museum of the Confederacy houses the largest and most comprehensive collection of Confederate Civil War memorabilia in the country, much of it contributed by veterans, who often served as guides in the early days. All of the war's major events and campaigns are documented, and exhibits include a replica of Lee's headquarters, period clothing, uniforms, weapons, memorabilia, and art. Highlights of the more than 3 floors of exhibits include a chronology of Civil War history, an exhibit on antebellum African-American life entitled "From Sun-Up to Sun-Up," and "Embattled Emblem," an exhibit concerning the controversy surrounding the continued use of the Confederate battle flag. Research library (open by appointment only); gift shop. Living history programs scheduled in summer.

Next door to the museum is the mansion known as the **White House of the Confederacy.** This classical revival house was the official residence of Confederate President Jefferson Davis from 1861 to 1865, when Richmond served as the capital of the Confederacy. There are 11 period rooms of original furnishings, all decorated in the high Victorian style. Guided tours begin with a short history of the mansion, and take in all areas of the house. **Open:** White House and museum, Mon–Sat 10am–5pm, Sun noon–5pm. Closed some hols. $$$

Science Museum of Virginia/Ethyl UNIVERSE Theater, 2500 W Broad St; tel 804/367-1080. There are few "do not touch" signs in this museum's galleries, but hands-on exhibits are the norm, making it an ideal attraction for youngsters. Galleries house more than 250 exhibits on crystals, electricity, aerospace, chemistry, physics, and much more. The museum also features a Foucault pendulum and one of the world's largest analemmic sundials. Not to be missed are the shows at the 300-seat Ethyl UNIVERSE Planetarium/Space Theater, which include Omnimax films as well as sophisticated multimedia shows. The Science Museum is housed in the former Broad Street Station, designed in 1919 by John Russell Pope.

The museum also operates the **Virginia Aviation Museum,** located near the Richmond International Airport. A "shrine to the golden age of aviation," this facility boasts an extensive collection of vintage flying machines. **Open:** Mem Day–Labor Day, Mon–Thurs 9:30am–5pm, Sun noon–5pm; early Sept–late May, Mon–Thurs 9:30am–5pm, Fri–Sat 9:30am–9pm, Sun noon–5pm. Closed some hols. $$$

Virginia Museum of Fine Arts, the Boulevard and Grove Ave; tel 804/367-0844. Impressive collections housed here include art nouveau, art deco, 19th- and 20th-century French paintings, contemporary American art, and art from India, Nepal, and Tibet. The largest public Fabergé collection outside Russia—more than 300 objets d'art created for Czars Alexander III and Nicholas II—is also on display here. Other highlights include the Goya portrait *General Nicholas Guye,* a rare life-size marble statue of the Roman emperor Caligula, Monet's *Iris by the Pond,* and 6 magnificent Gobelins Don Quixote tapestries.

The **West Wing** houses the Mellon Collection of 20th-century British, French, and American paintings, drawings, prints, and sculpture; also the Sydney and Frances Lewis Collection of contemporary American painting and sculpture. A decorative art collection includes works by Tiffany and furnishings by Frank Lloyd Wright.

The museum also contains the 500-seat Theatre Virginia. Traveling exhibits; cafeteria. **Open:** Tues–Wed and Fri–Sun 11am–5pm, Thurs 11am–8pm. Closed some hols. $

Richmond Children's Museum, 740 Navy Hill Dr; tel 804/643-5436. This unusual museum seeks to introduce children to the arts, nature, and the world around them with participatory exhibits, classes, and workshops. Amateur spelunkers can investigate stalagmites and stalactites in the Cave. Playworks invites children to dress up and see what it feels like to be a police officer, a banker, or a shopkeeper. **Open:** Mon–Sat 10am–5pm, Sun 1–5pm. Closed some hols. $$

Valentine Museum, 1015 E Clay St; tel 804/649-0711. Documents the history of Richmond from the 17th through the 20th century. It includes the elegant federal-style Wickham-Valentine House, built in 1812 by attorney John Wickham. Highlights of the house include spectacular decorative wall paintings, perhaps the rarest and most complete set in the nation; the Oval Parlor; and the circular Palette Staircase.

The museum opened in 1898 with a concentration on general history, later developing to its current focus on Richmond. Exhibits cover social and urban history, decorative and fine arts, textiles, architecture, and more. The **Children's Gallery** has a replica of a 1-room schoolhouse and exhibits on historic dolls, toys, games, and photographs.

Guided house tours, included in the price of admission to the museum, are given hourly. **Open:** Mon–Sat 10am–5pm, Sun noon–5pm (extended hours in summer). $$

Richmond National Battlefield Park, 3215 E Broad St; tel 804/226-1981. A prime military objective throughout the Civil War, Richmond experienced 7 major Union assaults in the course of the conflict; in April 1865, when the city finally fell into federal hands, its fall heralded the end of the Confederacy.

A 60-mile tour of battlefields begins at the **Chimborazo Visitor Center** at the park entrance on East Broad Street. A 12-minute slide show about the Civil War is shown throughout the day, and a 3-hour auto-tape tour can be rented that describes the Seven Days Campaign of 1862. *Richmond Remembers,* is a 25-minute film documenting the socioeconomic impact of the Civil War on the Confederate capital. Park rangers are on hand to answer questions.

There are smaller visitor centers at **Fort Harrison,** about 8 miles southeast, and at **Cold Harbor,** about 10 miles northeast. The latter was the scene of a particularly bloody 1864 engagement in which 7,000 of Gen U S Grant's men were killed or injured in just 30 minutes. Living military history reenactments take place during the summer; inquire at Chimborazo. The Cold Harbor center is staffed in summer only; there are brochures, a bulletin board, electric map, and interpretive exhibits. Fort Harrison is staffed spring through fall. **Open:** Daily 9am–5pm. Closed some hols. Free.

Maggie L Walker National Historic Site, 110½ E Leigh St; tel 804/780-1380. Daughter of a former slave, Maggie L Walker was an especially gifted woman who achieved success in the world of finance and business and rose to become the first woman bank president in the country. She also became owner and editor of a newspaper. The bank she headed continues today as the Consolidated Bank and Trust, the oldest African-American–operated bank in the United States.

This red-brick house was Walker's residence from 1904 until her death in 1934, and remained in the Walker family until 1979. It has been restored to its 1930s appearance. **Open:** Wed–Sun 9am–5pm. Closed some hols. Free.

St Paul's Episcopal Church, 815 E Grace St; tel 804/643-3589. Consecrated in November 1845, St Paul's was designed in Greek revival style by Philadelphia architect Thomas S Stewart. The steeple was originally surmounted by an 11-foot octagonal spire, which was removed (as were other church spires in town) following a hurricane in 1900. The striking plaster work of the ceiling interweaves Greek, Hebrew, and Christian motifs radiating from the symbol of the Trinity. Stained-glass windows were added, beginning in 1890. They include 8 windows from the Tiffany studios and 2 windows designed as memorials to Robert E Lee. The reredos, a mosaic rendering of da Vinci's *The Last Supper,* is also by Tiffany. Guided tours are offered daily at 11am or by appointment. **Open:** Daily 10am–4:30pm; Sun services at 7:45, 9, and 11am. Free.

St John's Episcopal Church, 2401 E Broad St; tel 804/648-5015. Originally known as the "church on Richmond Hill," St John's dates back to 1741. Edgar Allan Poe's mother and signer of the Declaration of Independence George Wythe are buried in the graveyard. The congregation actually predates the church; it was established in 1611, and Alexander Whitaker, the first rector, ministered to the local tribes, instructed Pocahontas in Christianity, and baptized her.

The Second Virginia Convention met here in 1775 to discuss the rights of American subjects of the English king. In attendance were Thomas Jefferson, George Wythe, George Washington, and Patrick Henry, who gave his now-famous "liberty or death" speech here.

The 20-minute tour includes the original 1741 entrance and pulpit, the exquisite stained-glass windows, and the pew where Patrick Henry sat during the convention. From the last Sunday in May through the first Sunday in September, a living history program is staged, re-creating the convention, complete with actors in period garb and Patrick Henry's speech. **Open:** Mon–Sat 10am–3:30pm, Sun 1–3:30pm. Closed some hols. $

Agecroft Hall, 4305 Sulgrave Rd; tel 804/353-4241. This Tudor manor house once stood outside Manchester, England. Dating from the late 1400s, it was continuously occupied and added onto for centuries. In the 1920s, when the house was threatened with destruction, Mr and Mrs T C Williams, Jr, bought it, had it carefully taken down (every beam and stone numbered), and shipped it to Richmond for reconstruction in an elegant neighborhood overlooking the James.

Inside the house is a collection of tapestries, armor, pewter, paintings, and furnishings from the Tudor and Stewart periods. Guided tours (40 min) begin with a 12-minute slide presentation. Outside are a formal sunken English garden and 3 recreated 17th-century gardens (separate admission available). **Open:** Tues–Sat 10am–4pm, Sun 12:30–5pm. Closed some hols. $$

Edgar Allan Poe Museum, 1914–1916 E Main St; tel 804/648-5523. The Poe Museum consists of 4 buildings (enclosing an "Enchanted Garden") wherein the poet's life is documented. The complex is centered around the Old Stone House (ca 1736), which contains a shop and where a video presentation initiates guided tours of the museum. The other 3 buildings were added to house the growing collection of Poe artifacts and publications, now the largest in existence.

Among the items on display are photographs, portraits, documents, and other personal memorabilia. The Raven Room includes artist James Carling's evocative illustrations of "The Raven"; there is also an exhibition gallery featuring rotating exhibits. Tours are given throughout the day. **Open:** Sun–Mon 1–4pm, Tues–Sat 10am–4pm. Closed Dec 25. $$

John Marshall House, 818 E Marshall St; tel 804/648-7998. From 1801 to 1835, John Marshall served as Chief Justice of the Supreme Court, where he helped establish the American system of constitutional law and judicial review. The house he built between 1788 and 1790, still largely intact, is remarkable for many original architectural features. Original furnishings and personal items have been supplemented by period anitques and reproductions. The gracious dining room features the family's mahogany banquet table, set with porcelain, silver, glassware, and a Waterford crystal épergne. Guided tours take about 20 minutes. **Open:** Apr–Sept, Tues–Sat 10am–5pm, Sun 1–5pm; Oct–Mar, Tues–Sat 10am–4:30pm, Sun 1–4:30pm. Closed some hols. $

Wilton House, 215 S Wilton Rd; tel 804/282-5936. Originally built some 10 miles down the James River in 1753, this stately Georgian mansion was painstakingly disassembled and moved to its present site in 1933. Floors, mantels, brasses, paneling, and window panes were all preserved; fine period furnishings. Visitors enter via the central hall, whose back door gives onto the river. **Open:** Tues–Sat 10am–4:30pm, Sun 1:30–4:30pm. Closed Feb and some hols. $$

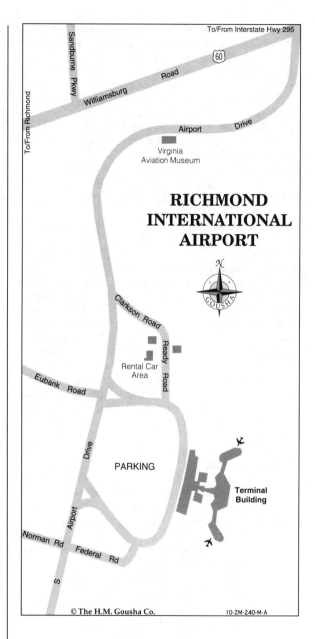

Hollywood Cemetery, 412 S Cherry St; tel 804/648-8501. Established in 1847, this is the burial place of 2 presidents of the United States (Monroe and Tyler), 6 Virginia governors, Confederate President Jefferson Davis, and Confederate generals J E B Stuart and George Pickett. Pickett's grave is alongside those of his men who fell at the Battle of Gettysburg. Maps are for sale in the office on weekdays only. **Open:** Daily 8am–5pm. Free.

Lewis Ginter Botanical Garden at Bloemendal, 1800 Lakeside Ave; tel 804/262-9887. In the 1880s, self-made Richmond millionaire, philanthropist, and amateur horticulturist Lewis Ginter built the Lakeside Wheel Club as a summer playground for the city's elite. His niece, Grace Arents, converted the property into a hospice for sick children and initiated extensive horticultural projects. Rare trees and shrubs were imported and planted in large beds on the front lawn, greenhouses were constructed, and a white gazebo and trellised seating areas were covered in rambling roses and clematis.

An ambitious expansion project is being undertaken at present that will greatly expand the facilities of the garden. **Open:** Daily 9:30am–4:30pm. Closed some hols. $

Maymont House and Park, 1700 Hampton St; tel 804/358-7166. Located just north of the James River, between the Boulevard (Va 161) and Meadow St. In 1886, Maj James Henry Dooley purchased a 100-acre dairy farm in Richmond, on which he built an opulent, 33-room mansion surrounded by beautifully landscaped grounds, including extensive Italian and Japanese gardens. The hay barn is today the **Parsons Nature Center,** with outdoor habitats for bison, elk, and bears. At the **Children's Farm,** youngsters can feed chickens, piglets, goats, cows, and sheep. A collection of horse-drawn carriages is on display at the **Carriage House,** and carriage rides are offered on weekends, Apr through mid-Dec. A tram operates on the grounds daily, Apr–Oct. Guided tours of the house are given continuously, noon–4:30pm Tuesday through Sunday. **Open:** Apr–Oct, daily 10am–7pm; Nov–Mar, daily 10am–5pm. Closed some hols. Free.

Meadow Farm Museum; tel 804/672-5106. Located 12 miles north of Richmond, at Martin and Courtney Rds in Glen Allen. In 1840 a country physician, Dr John Mosby Sheppard, inherited this farmhouse and 150 acres of pasture and woodlands. There he raised his family, practiced medicine, and ran a farm where he raised wheat, corn, tobacco, and other crops. Tour guides dressed in period clothing interpret the history of 2 centuries of rural middle-class life. Exhibits trace the family through several generations, and include a tobacco barn, a farrier's shop, and a facsimile of Dr Sheppard's medical office. **Open:** Museum, Tues–Sun noon–4pm; grounds, daily dawn–dusk. Closed mid-Dec to mid-Mar. $

6th Street Marketplace; tel 804/648-6600. Located along 6th St across Marshall, Broad, and Grace Sts. Part of a major urban-renewal effort in downtown Richmond, the Marketplace is concentrated on a glass-enclosed, elevated pedestrian bridge spanning Broad Street. It houses about 35 retail stores, a food court (in the historic Blues Armory, used to house Confederate troops during the Civil War), and several restaurants. Every Friday from May through September there's a street party with live bands and refreshments between 5 and 9pm. **Open:** Mon–Sat 10am–6pm, Sun 12:30–5:30pm. Free.

ROANOKE

Map page M-2, E4

Hotels 🏨

🏨🏨🏨 **Holiday Inn Tanglewood**, 4468 Starkey Rd SW, Roanoke, VA 24014; tel 703/774-4400 or toll free 800/465-4329; fax 703/774-1195. Exit US 220 or I-581 at Va 419 N; turn right onto Starkey Rd. Located in southwest Roanoke and close to most attractions, this is a surprisingly quiet yet fun place to stay. **Rooms:** 196 rms and stes. Exec-level rms avail. CI 3pm/CO noon. Express checkout avail. Nonsmoking rms avail. All are in 1 area away from meeting rooms, restaurant, and lounge. **Amenities:** 🛁 🔥 A/C, cable TV w/movies. **Services:** ✗ 🖛 🚐 🖾 🍴 🐾 Car-rental desk. Staff is energetic and helpful. Shoe shines available. **Facilities:** 🔥 900 🔥 1 rst, 1 bar (w/entertainment). Very lively Elephant Walk lounge is a local favorite, with disc jockey and dance floor. Guests pay $5 to use Roanoke Athletic Club, which has tennis, pool, racquetball, full fitness center. **Rates:** $88 S or D; from $128 ste. Children under 17 stay free. Spec packages avail. Pking: Outdoor, free. Maj CC.

🏨🏨🏨🏨 **Radisson Patrick Henry Hotel**, 617 S Jefferson St, Roanoke, VA 24011 (downtown); tel 703/345-8811 or toll free 800/833-4567; fax 703/342-9908. Exit 143 off I-81. Turn right onto Jefferson St, go 1 block. In downtown Roanoke, this 1925 Virginia historic landmark is on the National Register of Historic Places. Beautifully decorated large lobby invites guests to play chess, chat, write letters, or read. Within blocks of the market area and central to everything in Roanoke. **Rooms:** 125 rms, stes, and effic. CI 3pm/CO noon. Nonsmoking rms avail. Nicely furnished with poster beds, wallpaper, hunting and flower prints, cabinet-held TVs, large closet space. Most have kitchens. **Amenities:** 🛁 🔥 📺 A/C, cable TV w/movies, refrig. Some units w/minibars. **Services:** ✗ 🖛 VP 🚐 🖾 🍴 🐾 Social director, babysitting. **Facilities:** 🖵 🔥 1 rst, 1 bar, games rm, beauty salon, washer/dryer. Guest passes to YMCA and YWCA nearby. **Rates:** $109–$119 S or D; from $150 ste. Extra person $10. Children under 17 stay free. Spec packages avail. Pking: Outdoor, $3. Maj CC.

🏨🏨🏨🏨 **Roanoke Airport Marriott**, 2801 Hershberger Rd NW, Roanoke, VA 24017 (Roanoke Regional Airport); tel 703/563-9300 or toll free 800/228-9290; fax 703/563-9300 ext 7910. 5 mi N of downtown. exit 3W off I-581. Although located in a commercial area, this is a quiet hotel with enough property and landscaping to feel insulated. The 1st floor is spacious, with many sitting areas in addition to the lobby, restaurants, and lounges. Close to a large enclosed shopping mall featuring life-size dinosaurs modeled after the ones in *Jurassic Park*. **Rooms:** 320 rms and stes. Exec-level rms avail. CI 3pm/CO noon. Express checkout avail. Nonsmoking rms avail. **Amenities:** 🛁 🍸 A/C, cable TV w/movies, VCR. Some units w/terraces. Magazines. **Services:** 🍽️ 🚐 🛄 🧺 🐕 Car-rental desk, babysitting. Coffee and newspapers in lobby during morning. **Facilities:** 🏋️ 🏊 🛶 🎾 ♿ (*see also* "Restaurants" below), 2 bars, lifeguard, sauna, whirlpool. Indoor and outdoor pools. **Rates:** $99–$119 S; $119–$129 D; from $199 ste. Extra person $10. Children under 18 stay free. Higher rates for spec evnts/hols. Spec packages avail. Pking: Outdoor, free. Maj CC.

Motels

▮▮ **Days Inn Civic Center**, 535 Orange Ave, Roanoke, VA 24016; tel 703/342-4551 or toll free 800/329-7466; fax 703/343-3547. Exit 4E off I-581 S. A chain motel favored by families and business travelers because of its close proximity to downtown Roanoke and the historic City Market. **Rooms:** 257 rms. CI 2pm/CO 11am. Nonsmoking rms avail. **Amenities:** 🛁 A/C, cable TV w/movies. **Services:** 🛄 🧺 🐕 Babysitting. **Facilities:** 🏋️ 🏊 **Rates:** HS June–July $40–$50 S; $45–$50 D. Extra person $6. Children under 18 stay free. Lower rates off-season. Higher rates for spec evnts/hols. Pking: Outdoor, free. Maj CC.

▮▮ **Days Inn Interstate**, 8118 Plantation Rd, Roanoke, VA 24019 (Hollins); tel 703/366-0341 or toll free 800/952-4200; fax 703/366-3935. Exit 146 off I-81. Near Hollins College and less than a 10-minute drive to downtown Roanoke and Salem, this chain motel has plenty of parking for RVs and trucks. **Rooms:** 123 rms and stes. CI noon/CO noon. Nonsmoking rms avail. Some units open to interior corridors, others to outside of building. Some are close to I-81 and can be noisy. **Amenities:** 🛁 A/C, cable TV w/movies. 1 unit w/minibar. **Services:** 🚐 🛄 🧺 **Facilities:** 🏋️ 🏊 ♿ 1 rst, 1 bar. Basketball court. **Rates:** $38–$52 S; $48–$60 D; from $80 ste. Extra person $6. Children under 12 stay free. Higher rates for spec evnts/hols. Spec packages avail. Pking: Indoor, free. Maj CC.

▮▮▮ **Holiday Inn Airport**, 6626 Thirlane Rd, Roanoke, VA 24019; tel 703/366-8861 or toll free 800/HOLIDAY; fax 703/366-8861. Exit 143 off I-81. Conveniently located minutes from downtown Roanoke and Salem, regional airport, and Valley View Mall, the largest shopping complex in the area. **Rooms:** 163 rms and stes. Exec-level rms avail. CI 3pm/CO noon. Express checkout avail. Nonsmoking rms avail. Eight family rooms have 2 double beds, couch, and 2 bathrooms. **Amenities:** 🛁 🍸 📺 A/C, satel TV w/movies. **Services:** ✕ 🚐 🛄 🧺 🐕 Car-

rental desk. **Facilities:** 🏋️ 🏊 ♿ 1 rst, 1 bar (w/entertainment), washer/dryer. Free use of nearby fitness club and 2 golf courses. **Rates:** $55–$80 S or D. Extra person $4. Children under 19 stay free. Higher rates for spec evnts/hols. Spec packages avail. Pking: Outdoor, free. Maj CC.

▮▮ **Holiday Inn Civic Center**, 501 Orange Ave, Roanoke, VA 24016; tel 703/342-8961 or toll free 800/HOLIDAY. Exit 4E off I-581 S. A convenient motel to downtown Roanoke and the Civic Center, both an easy 5 minutes away. **Rooms:** 153 rms and stes. CI 2pm/CO 11am. Nonsmoking rms avail. **Amenities:** 🛁 🍸 A/C, satel TV w/movies. **Services:** ✕ 🛄 🧺 🐕 **Facilities:** 🏋️ 🏊 🖥️ 1 rst. Restaurant is a local favorite for Sunday brunch. **Rates:** $46–$52 S; $58–$64 D; from $62 ste. Extra person $4. Children under 12 stay free. Pking: Outdoor, free. Maj CC.

▮▮▮ **Ramada Inn–Roanoke**, 1927 Franklin Rd SW, Roanoke, VA 24014; tel 703/343-0121 or toll free 800/272-6232 in the US, 800/854-7854 in Canada; fax 703/343-0121 ext 599. Exit I-581 at Wonju St; turn left at Franklin Rd, go 3 blocks. A stream winds through this motel's grounds, across the street from a beautiful park. Close to shopping and Roanoke's attractions. **Rooms:** 125 rms and stes. CI 3pm/CO noon. Express checkout avail. Nonsmoking rms avail. Newly furnished, rooms have paintings with rural themes in pastels. **Amenities:** 🛁 🍸 A/C, cable TV w/movies. Computer/fax jacks available on request. Suites have refrigerators. **Services:** ✕ 🛄 🧺 🐕 Babysitting. **Facilities:** 🏋️ 🏊 ♿ 1 rst, 1 bar (w/entertainment), washer/dryer. Free use of nearby Gold's Gym. Tennis courts in park across street. **Rates:** HS Apr–Oct $48–$52 S; $55–$60 D; from $98 ste. Extra person $7. Children under 18 stay free. Lower rates off-season. Higher rates for spec evnts/hols. Pking: Outdoor, free. Maj CC.

Restaurants 🍽️

★ **Buck Mountain Grille**, US 220 S at Blue Ridge Pkwy, Roanoke; tel 703/776-1830. 2 mi S of Roanoke. **New American/Vegetarian.** Slip off the Blue Ridge Parkway or out of Roanoke to this restaurant with pleasing white walls accented with plants and monthly art shows. Booth and table seating. Eclectic and varied menu offers something for everyone, from pasta with crab and pesto to filet mignon. Unpretentious but professional service. **FYI:** Reservations accepted. Children's menu. No smoking. **Open:** Lunch Tues–Sun 11am–3pm; dinner Tues–Thurs 5–9pm, Fri–Sat 5–10pm, Sun 5–9pm. **Prices:** Main courses $10–$16. Maj CC. 🅿️

La Maison, 5732 Airport Rd, Roanoke; tel 703/366-2444. Exit 2N off I-581. **Continental.** Each room of this 1929 Georgian-style mansion is decorated with an abundance of impressionist art, antiques, and paintings. Even the closets are part of the decor. Known for Virginia seafood sausage appetizer (their own recipe) and baked Alaska. Prime rib special and lunch buffets offered. One small room available for intimate dinners. Outside dining in fine weather or by request. **FYI:** Reservations recommended. Jazz/piano. Children's menu. **Open:** Lunch Mon–Fri 11am–2pm; dinner Sun–Thurs 5–9pm, Fri–Sat 5–9:30pm. Closed some hols. **Prices:** Main courses $10–$33. Maj CC. ♥ ▮ 🍴 �&

♥ **The Library**, in Picadilly Sq, 3117 Franklin Rd SW, Roanoke; tel 703/985-0811. Exit I-581 at Wonju St; turn right at Franklin St (US 220 business S), go ½ mile. **Continental/French.** Roanoke's longtime favorite for special occasions, this elegant, quiet establishment is appointed with gold-framed paintings, shelves of books, and a huge brass espresso/cappuccino machine. Traditional French dishes, rack of lamb, Dover sole, and tableside preparation of cherries jubilee. Great attention to all details, from food preparation and service to exquisite table settings featuring Italian china. **FYI:** Reservations recommended. Jacket required. No smoking. **Open:** Tues–Sat 6–10pm. Closed some hols. **Prices:** Main courses $19–$25. Maj CC. ♥ 🚗

Macado's, 120 Church St, Roanoke; tel 703/342-7231. Exit I-581 at downtown; turn right on Church St, go 3 blocks. **Deli/ Eclectic.** The decor is eclectic: bicycles hanging from the ceiling, vintage car paintings and parts, but this fun establishment makes guests of all ages feel comfortable in its many informal dining areas. A sandwich-lover's delight, menu also offers quiches, pastas, and many sweets. Mesquite-grilled chicken and turkey are popular. Front of restaurant has deli, wine and cheese shop. **FYI:** Reservations not accepted. Children's menu. Dress code. **Open:** Mon–Thurs 10am–midnight, Fri–Sat 10am–1:30am, Sun 10am–10pm. Closed some hols. **Prices:** Main courses $5–$7. Maj CC. 🎮 &

Remington's, in Roanoke Airport Mariott, 2801 Hershberger Rd NW, Roanoke (Roanoke Regional Airport); tel 703/563-9300. 6 mi N of downtown Roanoke; exit 3W off I-581. **Regional American/Continental.** Decoratively folded napkins, tasteful table settings, old pieces of china, hunting prints, and low-hanging lights lend intimacy to this hotel restaurant. Menu changes several times a year to accommodate seasonal items as well as variety. **FYI:** Reservations recommended. **Open:** Tues–Sun 5–10pm. **Prices:** Main courses $18–$25. Maj CC. &

Attractions 📺

CENTER IN THE SQUARE

Science Museum of Western Virginia and Hopkins Planetarium; tel 703/343-7876 (recorded info) or 372-5710. Five floors

of exhibits in this facility illustrate various principles of science. Topics include energy, weather, and health; Chesapeake Bay Touch Tank, animal area. **Hopkins Planetarium** presents a variety of star shows (phone for schedule). **Open:** Mon–Sat 10am–5pm, Sun 1–5pm. Closed some hols. $$

Art Museum of Western Virginia; tel 703/342-5760. On Levels 1 and 2. On display here are works that range from tribal African to contemporary American. Features ArtVenture, an interactive children's art center with hands-on materials, texture wall, and rotating exhibits. **Open:** Tues–Sun 10am–5pm. Closed some hols. Free.

Roanoke Valley History Museum; tel 703/342-5770. Located on Level 3. Contains documents, tools, costumes, and weapons that tell the story of Roanoke from pioneer days to the 1990s. Rotating exhibits. **Open:** Tues–Fri 10am–4pm, Sat 10am–5pm, Sun 1–5pm. Closed some hols. $

Mill Mountain Theater, 1 Market Square SE; tel 703/342-5740 (box office). Box office located on Level 1. This theater company offers children's productions, lunchtime readings, and year-round matinee and evening performances. Phone for schedule and ticket information. $$$$

OTHER ATTRACTIONS

Star on the Mountain. Erected in 1949, this red neon sculpture stands 88 feet tall and uses 2,000 feet of neon tubing. It is visible from many parts of the city, but to see it up close (and for a panoramic view of the city), take Walnut Ave to the Mill Mountain Parkway Spur Road.

SALEM

Map page M-2, E4

Motels 🏨

≣≣ **Budget Host Blue Jay Motel**, 5399 W Main St, Salem, VA 24153 (Dixie Caverns); tel 703/380-2080 or toll free 800/283-4678. Exit 132 off I-81. Older, homey motel nestled in the mountains. Owners live on premises. A half-mile from Dixie Caverns and 6 miles to Salem. **Rooms:** 14 rms and effic. CI 2pm/CO 11am. **Amenities:** 🛏 🛁 A/C, cable TV. **Services:** 🔧 🐾 Babysitting. **Facilities:** 🍴 1 rst. Jägerheim Restaurant, on premises, is a pleasant surprise, with a wonderfully diverse menu and half-priced children's portions. **Rates:** HS May 27–Nov $34–$38 S or D; from $39 effic. Extra person $5. Children under 18 stay free. Lower rates off-season. Higher rates for spec evnts/hols. Spec packages avail. Pking: Outdoor, free. Maj CC.

⊨ **Knights Inn**, 301 Wildwood Rd, Salem, VA 24153; tel 703/389-0280 or toll free 800/843-5644; fax 703/387-1553. Exit 137 off I-81. A good location: within walking distance of many restaurants and minutes' drive to Dixie Caverns, Roanoke College, downtown Salem, and shopping mall. **Rooms:** 66 rms and effic. CI 3pm/CO noon. Nonsmoking rms avail. Simple but very clean rooms. Some have refrigerators. **Amenities:** 🛏 ⚱ A/C, cable TV w/movies. **Services:** ⌓ ⊲ **Facilities:** 🅿 ⅙ **Rates:** HS Apr–Nov $36–$40 S; $43–$55 D; from $45 effic. Extra person $4. Children under 18 stay free. Lower rates off-season. Spec packages avail. Pking: Outdoor, free. Maj CC. No discounts during special events.

⊨⊨⊨ **Quality Inn Roanoke/Salem**, 179 Sheraton Dr, PO Box 460, Salem, VA 24153; tel 703/562-1912 or toll free 800/228-5151; fax 703/562-0507. Exit 141 off I-81. Extremely quiet, nicely decorated motel with beautiful mountain views; 5 miles to Moyers Sport Complex and 3 miles to Salem Civic Center. **Rooms:** 120 rms and stes. CI 3pm/CO 11am. Nonsmoking rms avail. **Amenities:** 🛏 ⚱ A/C. Refrigerators, hair dryers, and computer/fax jacks provided upon request. **Services:** ✕ ⟐ ⊠ ⌓ ⊲ Car-rental desk, babysitting. **Facilities:** 🔒 ⟐ 🅿 ⅙ 1 rst, 1 bar, playground, washer/dryer. Putting green, badminton and volleyball court, basketball hoop, picnic tables, barbecue. **Rates:** HS Apr–Oct $48–$52 S; $53–$58 D; from $90 ste. Extra person $6. Children under 18 stay free. Lower rates off-season. Spec packages avail. Pking: Outdoor, free. Maj CC.

SANDSTON

Map page M-3, D6 (SW of Richmond)

Motel 🛏

⊨⊨ **Motel 6**, 5704 Williamsburg Rd, Sandston, VA 23150 (Richmond Int'l Airport); tel 804/222-7600; fax 804/222-4153. Exit 197A off I-64. A basic motel across street from Virginia Aviation Museum, near Richmond International Raceway. **Rooms:** 121 rms. CI noon/CO noon. Express checkout avail. Nonsmoking rms avail. Rooms are clean and comfortable. **Amenities:** 🛏 A/C, cable TV. **Services:** ⌓ ⊲ Free coffee in lobby. **Facilities:** 🔒 ⅙ Several nearby restaurants offer discounts to guests. **Rates:** $28 S. Extra person $4. Children under 17 stay free. Pking: Outdoor, free. Maj CC.

SHENANDOAH NATIONAL PARK

Map page M-3, C5

For lodgings and dining, see **Luray**

Encompassing 190,000 acres of mountains and forest, Shenandoah National Park was developed to rescue the slowly disappearing forest and declining animal population caused by decades of human settlement. The Civilian Conservation Corps (CCC) built recreational facilities in the 1930s, and, in 1939, the Skyline Drive was completed. Today over two-fifths of the park is considered wilderness, with more than 100 species of trees. Animals have returned, and sightings of smaller animals are frequent. Many of the park's natural wonders are visible from 75 designated overlooks along the **Skyline Drive**. The 105.4-mile drive runs the length of the park; access is sometimes limited November–March.

In spring, the green of leafing trees moves up the ridge at the rate of about 100 feet per day. Wildflowers begin to bloom in April; by late May the azaleas are in bloom, and the dogwood is at its height. Rhododendrons are in bloom in early June. Fall foliage, at its peak between October 10 and 25, attracts the most visitors to the park.

The northern park entrance is near the junction of I-81 and I-66, a mile south of Front Royal. The southern entrance is at Rockfish Gap, near the junction of US 250 and I-64, 18 miles east of Staunton. Park headquarters is about 3½ miles from the northern entrance, 4 miles west of Thornton Gap and 4 miles east of Luray on US 211. There are 2 **visitor centers** in the park that provide information, interpretive exhibits, films, slide shows, and nature walks. They can be reached at 703/999-2246, 999-3483, or 999-2266 (recorded information). The Dickey Ridge Visitor Center (milepost 4.6) is open April–November. Byrd Visitor Center (milepost 51) at Big Meadows is open daily, April–November and intermittently January–March.

SOUTH HILL

Map page M-3, E5

Motels 🛏

⊨ **Comfort Inn**, US 58 at I-85, South Hill, VA 23970; tel 804/447-2600 or toll free 800/221-2222; fax 804/447-2590. Exit 12 off I-85. Go west on US 58; make a U-turn at 2nd light. A basic but clean motel located among a bevy of restaurants, shops, and discount stores. Convenient to Lake Gaston. **Rooms:** 50 rms. CI

11am/CO 11am. Nonsmoking rms avail. **Amenities:** 📺 🖥️ A/C, cable TV w/movies. Most units have refrigerators and microwaves. **Services:** 🛅 🍽️ **Facilities:** ♿ Whirlpool. Holiday Inn with 24-hour Denny's restaurant is directly across street. Guests can use facilities at nearby health club. **Rates (CP):** HS Mem Day–Labor Day $40–$63 S or D. Extra person $6. Children under 12 stay free. Lower rates off-season. Pking: Outdoor, free. Maj CC. Highest on weekends.

≣≣ **Holiday Inn South Hill**, US 58 at I-85, South Hill, VA 23970; tel 804/447-3123 or toll free 800/HOLIDAY; fax 804/447-4237. Exit 12 off I-85. Follow US 58 W to motel. Convenient to Lake Gaston, this older but very well-maintained motel is built around a courtyard with swimming pool and sunning area. Located among shops and restaurants. **Rooms:** 152 rms. CI 1pm/CO noon. Express checkout avail. Nonsmoking rms avail. Standard motel rooms have vanity outside toilet/shower room. **Amenities:** 📺 🖥️ A/C, cable TV w/movies. Refrigerators and microwaves on request. **Services:** 🍽️ 🛅 🍽️ 🐕 Babysitting. **Facilities:** 🎱 🏊 🎰 ♿ 1 rst, 1 bar, games rm, washer/dryer. Denny's restaurant on premises open 24 hours. Guests have free use of health club in town. **Rates:** HS Mem Day–Labor Day $55–$58 S; $61–$69 D. Extra person $6. Children under 12 stay free. Lower rates off-season. Pking: Outdoor, free. Maj CC. Highest on weekends.

SPOTSYLVANIA

Map page M-3, C6 (SW of Fredericksburg)

Attraction 💼

Lake Anna State Park, 6800 Lawyers Rd; tel 703/854-5503. A 2,000-acre park bordering a 13,000-acre man-made lake, Lake Anna State Park is adjacent to Va 601 off Va 208. The lake was created in 1971 to provide coolant water for a Virginia Power nuclear plant. The state park was officially opened in 1983. The visitor center is a modern facility housing exhibits of local wildlife and history, as well as interpretive displays on gold mining. (The Goodwin Gold Mine was established nearby in the 1830s; gold mining in this area reached its peak in the 1840s.)

Boating and fishing on the lake are the most popular activities here, but the park also offers 8 nature trails, lakefront picnic areas, and a new swimming complex. Interpretive programs on nature and history are offered during the summer, which include children's programs, gold panning, and pontoon boat tours of the lake. **Open:** Park, daily 8am–dusk; visitor center, Mem Day–Labor Day, Wed–Sun 1–6pm. $

SPRINGFIELD

Map page M-3, C6 (W of Alexandria)

Hotel 🏨

≣≣≣ **Springfield Hilton**, 6650 Loisdale Rd, Springfield, VA 22150; tel 703/971-8900 or toll free 800/HILTONS; fax 703/971-8527. Exit 169A off I-95. Follow Va 644 E to Loisdale Rd, turn right. Located opposite a large shopping mall, this comfortable establishment offers the best accommodations in the Springfield area, highlighted by an attractive greenhouse lounge and indoor pool area. **Rooms:** 245 rms and stes. Exec-level rms avail. CI 3pm/CO 1pm. Express checkout avail. Nonsmoking rms avail. All rooms are decorated in light tones and bright wood furniture. Kings have sleep sofas. Parlor suites have 1 or 2 interconnecting bedrooms and are outfitted with reproduction antiques. Executive-level units have lounge. **Amenities:** 📺 🖥️ A/C, satel TV w/movies. Executive-level units have increased amenities, including robes. **Services:** ✕ 🛅 🍽️ 🐕 Executive-level guests receive breakfast. **Facilities:** 🎱 🎰 ♿ 1 rst, 1 bar (w/entertainment), lifeguard, games rm. Guests have free use of nearby health club. **Rates:** $98–$112 S; $108–$122 D; from $135 ste. Extra person $10. Children under 16 stay free. Spec packages avail. Pking: Outdoor, free. Maj CC.

STANLEY

Map page M-3, C5 (SE of New Market)

Inn 🛏️

≣≣≣ **Jordan Hollow Farm Inn**, Va 2, Stanley, VA 22851; tel 703/778-2285; fax 703/778-1759. 6 mi S of Luray. Off US 340. 144 acres. This colonial horse farm set on 144 acres in a secluded hollow offers homey but elegant country lodging and a 1790 farmhouse for dining. Views at the inn are of the duck pond, grazing horses and goats, porch-sleeping cats, and rolling hills, meadows, and forests beyond. **Rooms:** 20 rms. CI 3pm/CO noon. The vine-covered lodge building, Arbor View, is surrounded by a sun deck, and houses 16 individually decorated units with private bath and handmade furniture; each suitable for up to 4 people. In Mare Meadow, a hand-hewn log lodge, are 4 rooms, some with porches, nice for couples but not suitable for young children. All rooms open to outside. **Amenities:** 📺 🖥️ A/C, TV. All units w/terraces, some w/fireplaces, some w/Jacuzzis. Cable TV in 9 rooms. **Services:** 🐎 🛅 🍽️ Full breakfast and 4-course dinner included in rates. Room service during dining hours if guests want to remain in room. Fax machine, computer, and rollaways available. Many services, such as bellhop, on request.

Daily newspaper. **Facilities:** 🚴 🏊 🎿 📶 1 rst (*see also* "Restaurants" below), 2 bars, games rm, lawn games, washer/dryer, guest lounge. Small gift-purchase area. Stable with horses, for beginners or advanced riders, provides trail rides, some riding instruction, and picnic rides and carriage drives by prior arrangement. Guests can use public pool and recreation area across road for a small fee. Golf and tennis nearby. **Rates (MAP):** HS June–Oct $115–$180 S or D. Extra person $35. Children under 16 stay free. Lower rates off-season. Pking: Outdoor, free. Ltd CC. Service charge of 10% but no gratuities. Children 5–16 pay only for food.

Restaurant 🍽️

Jordan Hollow Farm Inn, Va 2, Stanley; tel 703/778-2285. 6 mi S of Luray. **American/Continental/French.** This 1790 farmhouse on 144 acres contains 200-year-old log cabin rooms and 100-year-old rooms with fox-country and West African decor. Fireplaces, antique furnishings, country curtains, and wallpaper add to sense of place. Front-yard tables sit under shade trees. Cuisine is "country continental with a French touch"; quail, pasta, and home-baked bread are favorites. **FYI:** Reservations recommended. Children's menu. **Open:** HS Apr–Nov daily 6am–9pm. Reduced hours off-season. **Prices:** PF dinner $20. Ltd CC. ❤️ 🍴

STAUNTON

Map page M-2, D4

Hotel 🏨

≡≡ Comfort Inn, 1302 Richmond Ave, at jct US 250/I-81, Staunton, VA 24401; tel 703/886-5000 or toll free 800/221-2222; fax 703/886-6643. Exit 222 off I-81. Adjacent to the Museum of American Frontier Culture and numerous restaurants, including a 24-hour waffle house, this highway hotel also is convenient to the Blue Ridge Mountains. **Rooms:** 97 rms and stes. Exec-level rms avail. CI 3pm/CO 11am. Nonsmoking rms avail. **Amenities:** 🛎️ ♨️ 📺 A/C, cable TV w/movies. Some units w/Jacuzzis. **Services:** 🛏️ 🍽️ Complimentary continental breakfast and newspaper daily. **Facilities:** 🏊 ♿ **Rates (CP):** $48–$69 S; $56–$77 D; from $64 ste. Extra person $8. Children under 18 stay free. Higher rates for spec evnts/hols. Spec packages avail. Pking: Outdoor, free. Maj CC.

Motels

≡≡ Best Western Staunton Inn, 260 Rowe Rd, Staunton, VA 24401; tel 703/885-1112 or toll free 800/752-9471; fax 703/

885-1112. Exit 222 off I-81. A chain motel adjacent to a family restaurant. Mary Baldwin College and outlet/antique shopping are nearby. **Rooms:** 80 rms. CI 3pm/CO 11am. Nonsmoking rms avail. **Amenities:** 🛎️ 📺 A/C, cable TV w/movies. **Services:** 🛏️ 🍽️ **Facilities:** 🏊 ♿ **Rates:** HS May–Oct $53–$100 S; $63–$100 D. Extra person $5. Children under 12 stay free. Lower rates off-season. Higher rates for spec evnts/hols. Spec packages avail. Pking: Outdoor, free. Maj CC.

≡≡≡ Holiday Inn Staunton, I-81 and Woodrow Wilson Pkwy, PO Box 3209, Staunton, VA 24402; tel 703/248-6020 or toll free 800/932-9061; fax 703/248-2902. Exit 225 off I-81. Conveniently located near American Museum of Frontier Culture, Woodrow Wilson Birthplace, wineries, and other attractions. **Rooms:** 112 rms. CI 3pm/CO noon. Express checkout avail. Nonsmoking rms avail. **Amenities:** 🛎️ ♨️ A/C, cable TV w/movies. Some units w/terraces. **Services:** ✕ 🍴 🛏️ 🍽️ Babysitting. **Facilities:** 🏊 ⬜350 ♿ 1 rst, 1 bar. Guests have golf and tennis privileges at adjacent Country Club of Staunton. **Rates:** $56–$95 S or D; from $111 ste. Extra person $6. Children under 18 stay free. Spec packages avail. Pking: Outdoor, free. Maj CC.

≡≡≡ Innkeeper, I-81 and Woodrow Wilson Pkwy, PO Box 2526, Staunton, VA 24402; tel 703/248-5111 or toll free 800/822-9899; fax 703/248-5111. Exit 225 off I-81. A former Sheraton, this motel enjoys a quiet location with pastoral views yet is just minutes from historic downtown Staunton. Central courtyard is spacious and well landscaped. **Rooms:** 100 rms. CI 3pm/CO 11am. Nonsmoking rms avail. Many rooms have a view of the countryside. **Amenities:** 🛎️ ♨️ A/C, cable TV. **Services:** ✕ 🛏️ 🍽️ 🍷 **Facilities:** 🏊 ⬜350 ♿ 1 rst, washer/dryer. **Rates (CP):** HS May–Oct $56–$65 S or D. Extra person $5. Children under 16 stay free. Lower rates off-season. Higher rates for spec evnts/hols. Spec packages avail. Pking: Outdoor, free. Maj CC.

Inns

≡≡≡≡ Belle Grae Inn, 515 W Frederick St, Staunton, VA 24401; tel 703/886-5151; fax 703/886-6641. Exit 222 off I-81. Follow US 250 W; turn right on Coalter St, then left on Frederick St. This city inn boasts a number of separate houses as well as the historic main house. Azaleas bloom in lovely grounds. Very close to a number of restored Victorian historic sites. Unsuitable for children under 6. **Rooms:** 12 rms and stes; 7 ctges/villas. CI 3pm/CO 11am. No smoking. Extremely private rooms with varied antiques and reproductions. **Amenities:** 🛎️ 📺 A/C, cable TV, bathrobes. Some units w/terraces, some w/fireplaces. **Services:** Afternoon tea and wine/sherry served. Truly gracious hospitality. Guests greeted with tea and cookies. Full breakfast and afternoon tea. Pre-dinner drinks served during parlor conversation. Ice brought to rooms. **Facilities:** ⌐70⌐ 𝒸 2 rsts (*see also* "Restaurants" below), guest lounge. Live entertainment in the Bistro. **Rates (BB):** $59–$115 D; from $109 ste; from $125 ctge/villa. Extra person $25. Min stay HS. MAP rates avail. Spec packages avail. Pking: Outdoor, free. Ltd CC.

≣≣≣ **Frederick House**, 28 N New St, at Frederick St, PO Box 1387, Staunton, VA 24401; tel 703/885-4220 or toll free 800/334-5575. Exit 222 off I-81. Follow US 250 (Richmond Rd) to Coalter St, turn right, then left on Frederick St. A European-style hotel in the center of town, with many fine old buildings and restaurants nearby. It comprises 5 connected town houses and has a pleasant herb and flower garden in rear. Furnishings are antiques or reproductions, and atmosphere is very homey. Smoking is not permitted on premises. **Rooms:** 14 rms and stes. CI 3pm/CO 11am. No smoking. Rooms vary in decor and size. **Amenities:** 🛏 A/C, cable TV w/movies, bathrobes. Some units w/terraces, some w/fireplaces. **Services:** 🖎 Babysitting, afternoon tea served. **Facilities:** ⌐20⌐ 1 rst, guest lounge w/TV. Guests can use health club next door. **Rates (AP):** $55–$95 S or D; from $85 ste. Extra person $20. Spec packages avail. Pking: Outdoor, free. Maj CC.

Resort

≣≣≣ **Ingleside Resort**, 1410 Commerce Rd, PO Box 1018, Staunton, VA 24402; tel 703/248-1201 or toll free 800/251-1962; fax 703/248-1003. Exit 225 off I-81. Go west on Woodrow Wilson Parkway 1 mile; turn right at US 11 N. 80 acres. Affiliated with Red Carpet Inns, this older resort contains spacious rooms with views of the Shenandoah Valley from beside an 18-hole golf course. **Rooms:** 210 rms and stes. CI 3pm/CO noon. Nonsmoking rms avail. Rooms are in 2- and 3-story blocks with valley views. Varying decor, but furniture is geared to comfort. **Amenities:** 🛏 🕭 A/C, satel TV, refrig. Some units w/terraces. **Services:** ✕ 🖎 ⟲ Babysitting. **Facilities:** 🔓 ▶18 🏊2 ⌐600⌐ 𝒸 3 rsts, 3 bars, lawn games, playground. **Rates:** HS Mar–Oct $42–$50 S; $50–$60 D; from $100 ste. Extra person $12.50. Children under 12 stay free. Min stay spec evnts. Lower rates off-season. Higher rates for spec evnts/hols. AP and MAP rates avail. Spec packages avail. Pking: Outdoor, free. Maj CC. Rates are exceptionally reasonable for a resort of this size and scope.

Restaurants 🍴

♠ **The Belle Grae Inn and Bistro**, in the Belle Grae Inn, 515 W Frederick St, Staunton; tel 703/886-5150. Exit 222 off I-81. Follow US 250 to Coalter St, turn right on Frederick St. **American.** The inn's dining room is furnished in Victorian fashion, with dark wooden tables and chairs and starched white

tablecloths, a fitting place to enjoy superbly prepared and presented meals. The Bistro, in another building, offers lighter food. A favorite of both locals and visitors. **FYI:** Reservations recommended. Piano. No smoking. **Open:** Dinner daily 6–9pm; brunch Sun 7:30am–2pm. Closed some hols. **Prices:** Main courses $14–$20. Maj CC. ♥ 🍽 𝒸

★ **The Beverly Restaurant**, 12 E Beverley St, Staunton; tel 703/886-4317. Exit 222 off I-81. Follow US 250 W to Frederick, turn left, left at Central, and left at Beverley St. **Diner.** The small diner/restaurant in the center of historic Staunton has country-style decor and friendly, casual atmosphere. Sandwiches and lighter meals provide alternative to fast-food restaurants. Known for teatime Wednesday and Friday afternoons. **FYI:** Reservations not accepted. No liquor license. **Open:** Mon–Thurs 6:30am–7pm, Fri 6:30am–7:30pm, Sat 6:30am–5pm. Closed some hols. **Prices:** Main courses $4–$6.50. Ltd CC.

The Depot Grille, in Staunton Station, 42 Middlebrook Ave, Staunton; tel 703/885-7332. Exit 222 off I-81. Follow US 250 into Staunton; turn left on Greenville Rd, then left at Augusta St. **Seafood/Steak.** Railroad memorabilia is appropriate decor in this casual restaurant in an old rail depot, now a shopping center with antique and gift shops. Long wooden bar is reminiscent of the 1920s. Steaks and seafood with a good variety of lighter fare. Braille menus available. **FYI:** Reservations accepted. Children's menu. No smoking. **Open:** Sun–Thurs 11am–10:30pm, Fri–Sat 11am–11:30pm. Closed Dec 25. **Prices:** Main courses $8–$20. Maj CC. 🍽 𝒸

Attractions 🖼

Woodrow Wilson Birthplace, 24 N Coalter St; tel 703/885-0897. This handsome Greek revival building, built in 1846 by a Presbyterian congregation as a manse for their ministers, stands next to an excellent museum detailing Wilson's life. As a minister, Wilson's father moved often, so the family left here when the future president was only 2 years old.

The museum's galleries trace Wilson's Scottish-Irish roots, his academic career as a professor and president of Princeton University, and his 2 terms as president of the United States (1913–21). In the carriage house is Wilson's presidential limousine, a Pierce-Arrow. **Open:** Mar–Nov, daily 9am–5pm; Dec, daily 10am–4pm; Jan–Feb, Mon–Sat 10am–4pm. Closed some hols. $$$

Museum of American Frontier Culture; tel 703/332-7850. Located west of I-81 near exit 22, the living history museum consists of 4 farmsteads from the 18th and 19th centuries. Staff members in period costume plant fields, tend livestock, and do domestic chores. **Open:** Mid-Mar–Nov, daily 9am–5pm; Dec–mid-Mar, daily 10am–4pm. Closed some hols. $$$

STERLING
Map page M-3, C6

Hotel 🛏

≣≣≣ **Holiday Inn Dulles**, 1000 Sully Rd (Va 28) at Holiday Dr, Sterling, VA 20166; tel 703/471-7411 or toll free 800/HOLIDAY; fax 703/471-7411 ext 515. 1½ mi N of Dulles Airport. exit 2 off Dulles Toll Rd. Go north on Sully Rd to Holiday Dr. Pleasant hotel with full facilities near Dulles Airport. Extensive 1994 renovation spiffed up everything from lobby to rooms. **Rooms:** 300 rms. Exec-level rms avail. CI 3pm/CO noon. Express checkout avail. Nonsmoking rms avail. Dark wood furniture adds elegance to rooms, which have desks and other features attractive to business travelers. King-bed units have reclining easy chairs. **Amenities:** 🛅 ⌘ ⌘ A/C, cable TV w/movies, voice mail. Long telephone cords. Some rooms have coffeemakers and microwaves. **Services:** ✕ 🚗 ⌘ ⌘ ⌘ Car-rental desk, babysitting. Guests on executive level have use of lounge with library, tea and coffee, continental breakfast. Free shuttle to nearby malls. **Facilities:** 🏋 🛎 🎱 💻 ⌘ 1 rst, 1 bar (w/entertainment), lifeguard, games rm, sauna, whirlpool, washer/dryer. Attractive indoor pool area. Lively Scrooples Bar is popular local hangout, with billiard room, Friday-night barbecues, DJ spinning dance tunes every evening. **Rates:** HS Mar–June $95–$105 S or D. Children under 18 stay free. Lower rates off-season. Spec packages avail. Pking: Outdoor, free. Maj CC. Rates include up to 4 people per room. Seniors discounts, weekend rates available. Children under 13 eat free in hotel restaurant.

Motel

≣≣ **Hampton Inn Dulles**, 45440 Holiday Dr, Sterling, VA 22170 (Dulles Airport); tel 703/471-8300 or toll free 800/HAMPTON; fax 703/471-8300 ext 408. 1½ mi N of Dulles Airport. exit 2 off Dulles Toll Rd. Follow Sully Rd (Va 28) to Holiday Dr, turn right. A comfortable motel convenient to Washington's Dulles International Airport. **Rooms:** 126 rms. CI noon/CO noon. Nonsmoking rms avail. Standard king-bed rooms have recliners and desks. Armoire-like cabinets serve as closets. **Amenities:** 🛅 ⌘ ⌘ A/C, satel TV w/movies, refrig. Some rooms have refrigerators. **Services:** 🚗 ⌘ ⌘ ⌘ Children's program. Coffee available all day in lobby. Free morning newspapers. Children's program on Friday and Saturday evenings.

Free local calls. **Facilities:** ⌘ Washer/dryer. Volleyball and basketball courts. Picnic area. Adjacent Holiday Inn Dulles has restaurant and popular bar. Guests get discounts at nearby restaurants, use of nearby sports complex. **Rates (CP):** HS Apr–June/Sept–Oct $70–$75 S; $75–$80 D. Children under 18 stay free. Lower rates off-season. Spec packages avail. Pking: Outdoor, free. Maj CC.

STRASBURG
Map page M-3, C5

Hotel 🛏

≣≣≣ **Hotel Strasburg**, 201 Holliday St, Strasburg, VA 22657; tel 703/465-9191 or toll free 800/348-8327; fax 703/465-4788. 90 mi W of Washington DC. Exit 298 off I-81. Step back in time to an authentic 1890s home, with squeaky wood floors, brass beds, lace-curtained windows, overstuffed armchairs, and marble-top tables. This 3-story Victorian was converted from a hospital to an inn in 1915 and offers an eclectic mix of old furnishings and modern touches. The friendly staff adds a sense of down-home hospitality. Items and furnishings on consignment from local antique dealers, so patrons can shop without leaving the inn. **Rooms:** 25 rms and stes. CI 2pm/CO 11am. Nonsmoking rms avail. All units are unique, and some offer separate sitting area. **Amenities:** 🛅 A/C, cable TV. Some units w/terraces, some w/Jacuzzis. **Services:** ⌘ ⌘ Continental breakfast Monday to Friday. **Facilities:** 🍽 1 rst (see also "Restaurants" below), 1 bar. Small beach a mile away. The Victorian dining room offers a country-fare buffet on its old sideboard. Light fare available in Depot Lounge, decorated with railroad memorabilia. **Rates (CP):** HS Apr–May/Oct–Nov $69 S or D; from $79 ste. Extra person $15. Children under 16 stay free. Lower rates off-season. MAP rates avail. Spec packages avail. Maj CC.

Restaurant 🍴

★ **Strasburg Hotel Restaurant**, in Strasburg Hotel, 201 Holliday St, Strasburg; tel 703/465-9191. Exit 298 off I-81. **American.** Country dining amid Victorian-age elegance. Period antiques and lace-curtained windows complement southern hospitality, service, and food. Choices range from light salads to filets, and favorites are chicken Shenandoah, pot pies, and pecan pie. Depot Lounge, with railroad memorabilia, offers lighter fare. **FYI:** Reservations recommended. Children's menu. **Open:** Lunch daily 11:30am–2:30pm; dinner Mon–Thurs 5–9pm, Fri–Sat 5–10pm, Sun 3–9pm; brunch Sun 11:30am–2:30pm. **Prices:** Main courses $7.95–$18.95. Maj CC. 🍴 🅿 ⌘

Attraction 💼

Strasburg Museum, E King St (Va 55); tel 703/465-3175. Housed in a 100-year-old landmark building that was originally an earthenware and pottery factory, this museum displays exhibits of local history. Artifacts from Native American, colonial, and Civil War eras are included. **Open:** Apr–Oct, daily 10am–4pm. $

STRATFORD

Map page M-3, C6

Attraction 💼

Stratford Hall Plantation, Va 214; tel 804/493-8038. This house, magnificently set on 1,600 acres above the Potomac, is renowned not only for its distinctive architectural style but for the illustrious family who lived here. Thomas Lee (1690-1750), who served as governor of the Virginia colony, built Stratford in the late 1730s. The Lees of Virginia played major roles in the formation of the United States: Richard Henry Lee, the delegate who made the motion for independence in the Continental Congress; his brother, Francis Lightfoot Lee, a signer of the Declaration of Independence; Henry "Light Horse Harry" Lee, a hero of the Revolutionary War; and his son, General Robert E Lee, the legendary Confederate military leader.

Guided tours of the restored house include the paneled Great Hall, which runs the depth of the house; the winter kitchen and estate offices; and the nursery, which contains Robert E Lee's crib. After the tour, guests can stroll the meadows and gardens of the 1,600-acre estate, which is still operated as a working farm. **Open:** Daily 9am–5pm. Closed Dec 25. $$$

TANGIER ISLAND

Map page M-3, D7

Cruises to tiny Tangier Island, a picturesque village of 750 souls, depart from the Hopkins General Store, 2 Market Square (tel 804/787-8220), near the town wharf in Onancock, located about 12 miles south on US 13 from the Chincoteague turnoff at Va 175. Departures June–September, Monday–Saturday at 10am.

There are no cars on the narrow streets of this unspoiled island, whose residents are mostly engaged in oystering, crabbing, and clamming. It was discovered by Capt John Smith in 1608, and the local accent is said to hark back to Elizabethan England.

The island offers an opportunity to enjoy the local culture, the serenity, and fresh sea air. The **Chesapeake House** serves sumptuous, family-style meals at reasonable prices from mid-April to late October, daily 11:30am–5pm. Overnight stays (including dinner and breakfast) are also available. For further details phone 804/891-2331.

TAPPAHANNOCK

Map page M-3, D6

Motel 🏨

≡≡ Days Inn, PO Box 1356, PO Box 1356, Tappahannock, VA 22560; tel 804/443-9200 or toll free 800/325-2525; fax 804/443-2663. On US 17, S of Tappahannock Center. A fairly attractive, 2-story red-brick building with a few shrubs in front. **Rooms:** 60 rms. CI 2pm/CO 11am. Nonsmoking rms avail. Walls in plain but clean rooms have watercolors of beach scenes. **Amenities:** 📞 A/C, satel TV, shoe polisher. **Services:** 🛎 **Facilities:** 👤 **Rates (CP):** HS Apr–Sept $44 S; $49 D. Extra person $6. Children under 12 stay free. Lower rates off-season. Spec packages avail. Pking: Outdoor, free. Maj CC. AARP discounts.

TROUTVILLE

Map page M-2, E4 (NE of Roanoke)

Motels 🏨

≡≡ Comfort Inn Troutville, 2654 Lee Hwy S, Troutville, VA 24175; tel 703/992-5600 or toll free 800/628-1957; fax 703/992-5600. 14 mi NE of Roanoke. exit 150A off I-81. Just minutes from Hollins College and the Blue Ridge Pkwy, surrounded by many restaurants, and close to a full-service truck stop. **Rooms:** 72 rms. Exec-level rms avail. CI 3pm/CO 11am. Nonsmoking rms avail. **Amenities:** 📞 🛁 📺 A/C, cable TV w/movies. **Services:** 🛏 🛎 **Facilities:** 🏋 👤 **Rates (CP):** HS May–Oct $56–$62 S or D. Extra person $5. Children under 18 stay free. Lower rates off-season. Higher rates for spec evnts/hols. Spec packages avail. Pking: Outdoor, free. Maj CC.

≡≡ Howard Johnson Motor Lodge, US 220, PO Box 100, Troutville, VA 24175; tel 703/992-3000 or toll free 800/446-4656; fax 703/992-4000. 14 mi NE of Roanoke. exit 150B off I-81. A very quiet motel located in a wooded area. Numerous restaurants and services nearby. **Rooms:** 70 rms. Exec-level rms avail. CI 1pm/CO noon. Nonsmoking rms avail. Exceptional attention paid to rooms. **Amenities:** 📞 A/C, cable TV w/movies.

Some units w/terraces. **Services:** 🛎 **Facilities:** 🗄 20 Playground, washer/dryer. **Rates:** HS Apr–Oct $48–$70 S; $54–$70 D. Extra person $6. Children under 18 stay free. Lower rates off-season. Spec packages avail. Pking: Outdoor, free. Maj CC.

TYSONS CORNER

See **McLean, Vienna**

VIENNA

Map page M-3, C6 (W of Washington, DC)

Hotels 🏨

≡≡≡ Embassy Suites Tysons Corner, 8517 Leesburg Pike, Vienna, VA 22182; tel 703/883-0707 or toll free 800/EMBASSY; fax 703/883-0694. Exit 10B off I-495. Follow Va 7 W for 1½ miles. Glass elevators and all corridors overlook an attractive atrium at this comfortable, all-suites hotel convenient to Tysons Corner shopping and restaurants. **Rooms:** 232 stes. CI 3pm/CO noon. Express checkout avail. Nonsmoking rms avail. Suites have separate parlor with sleep sofa, 1 king bed (no doubles or twins), fabric wallpaper, and upholstered furniture. **Amenities:** 🛗 🛁 📺 A/C, satel TV w/movies, refrig. Wet bars. **Services:** ✗ 🛄 🍴 Full breakfast, included in rates, served in atrium. Manager's reception each evening with complimentary cocktails. **Facilities:** 🗄 🏋 70 🛗 1 rst, 1 bar, lifeguard, spa, sauna, whirlpool. Deli-style restaurant opens to atrium at lobby level. Lavender-and-green lounge bar in center of atrium is accented with brass rails. **Rates (CP):** From $164 ste. Extra person $10. Children under 12 stay free. Higher rates for spec evnts/hols. Spec packages avail. Pking: Outdoor, free. Maj CC.

≡≡≡ Sheraton Premiere at Tysons Corner, 8661 Leesburg Pike, Vienna, VA 22182; tel 703/448-1234 or toll free 800/572-ROOM; fax 703/893-8193. Exit 10B off I-495. A stunning highrise tower whose surrounding public areas have lots of marble, columns, and skylights to create an outdoorsy yet elegant mood. **Rooms:** 455 rms and stes. Exec-level rms avail. CI 3pm/CO 1pm. Express checkout avail. Nonsmoking rms avail. All rooms being refurbished, which should make this otherwise fine hotel even more appealing. King rooms have angled windows and views from tower. **Amenities:** 🛗 🛁 A/C, cable TV w/movies, refrig. All units w/minibars, all w/terraces, some w/fireplaces, 1 w/Jacuzzi. Club-level units contain irons and boards, coffeemakers, hair dryers, robes, TVs in dressing area. King rooms also have bathrobes. **Services:** 🍽 🔑 VP 🛒 🛄 🍴 Twice-daily maid svce, masseur, babysitting. Free local calls on club level.

Facilities: 🗄 🏊 🏋 12k 🖥 🛗 2 rsts, 3 bars (1 w/entertainment), lifeguard, racquetball, squash, spa, sauna, steam rm, whirlpool, beauty salon. Extensive meeting areas, including grand ballroom, are well designed and attractive. Indoor pool under steel beams and glass has waterfall sliding down a wall, while outdoor pool sits in a resort-like courtyard. **Rates:** HS Sept–Nov/Mar–June $135–$155 S; $145–$165 D; from $250 ste. Extra person $10. Children under 18 stay free. Lower rates off-season. Higher rates for spec evnts/hols. MAP rates avail. Spec packages avail. Pking: Indoor/outdoor, free. Maj CC. Weekend packages available.

≡≡≡ Tysons Corner Marriott, 8028 Leesburg Pike, at Towers Crescent Dr, Vienna, VA 22182 (Tysons Corner); tel 703/734-3200 or toll free 800/228-9290; fax 703/734-5763. Exit 10 off I-495. Follow Va 7 W to hotel. This highrise hotel enjoys a convenient location immediately adjacent to Tysons Corner Center shopping mall. **Rooms:** 390 rms and stes. Exec-level rms avail. CI 4pm/CO noon. Express checkout avail. Nonsmoking rms avail. All rooms have rich wood furniture and earth-tone decor. King-bed rooms have easy chairs. Concierge level has private lounge. **Amenities:** 🛗 🛁 📺 A/C, cable TV w/movies, voice mail. **Services:** ✗ 🛄 🍴 Babysitting. Free shuttle to Dunn Loring metro station. **Facilities:** 🗄 🏋 750 🛗 1 rst, 2 bars (1 w/entertainment), lifeguard, sauna, steam rm, whirlpool, washer/dryer. Attractive indoor pool under skylights on 2nd floor. Popular Studebaker's bar and disco is on ground level. **Rates:** HS Mar 15–June 30/Sept 5–Nov 15 $134 S; $154 D; from $250 ste. Extra person $10. Children under 3 stay free. Lower rates off-season. Spec packages avail. Pking: Indoor/outdoor, free. Maj CC. Weekend packages available.

Motels

≡≡ Comfort Inn Tysons Corner, 1587 Spring Hill Rd, Vienna, VA 22182; tel 703/448-8020 or toll free 800/4-CHOICE; fax 703/448-0343. Exit 10 off I-495. Go west on Va 7 for 1½ miles, then left on Spring Hill Rd. This clean and comfortable motel is an exceptional value for the Tysons Corner area. Three motel blocks with standard rooms flank a central courtyard. Separate reception and restaurant buildings. **Rooms:** 250 rms and stes. CI 3pm/CO noon. Nonsmoking rms avail. King-bed rooms have easy chairs; otherwise, all units are identical except for bed arrangements. Vanities are outside toilet/shower. **Amenities:** 🛗 🛁 📺 A/C, cable TV w/movies. Phones have call-waiting. **Services:** 🚐 🛄 🍴 🔧 Car-rental desk. Deluxe continental breakfast included in rates. Free van to Dunn Loring metro station and shops in Tysons area. Free local calls. **Facilities:** 🗄 100 🛗 1 rst, lifeguard. Fuddrucker's restaurant on premises. Guests get discount at nearby health club. **Rates (CP):** HS Mar–May/Oct $59–$69 S; $64–$74 D; from

$80 ste. Extra person $5. Children under 17 stay free. Lower rates off-season. Spec packages avail. Pking: Outdoor, free. Maj CC.

≣≣ Marriott Residence Inn Tysons Corner, 8616 Westwood Center Dr, Vienna, VA 22182; tel 703/893-0120 or toll free 800/331-3131; fax 703/790-8896. Exit 10 off I-495. Follow Va 7 W 1 mile to Westwood Center Dr, turn left. Located near other hotels and the Tysons Corner shopping malls, this modern, California-style complex offers fully equipped apartments of varying sizes built around a landscaped pool area. **Rooms:** 96 effic. CI 3pm/CO noon. Nonsmoking rms avail. All units have fully equipped kitchens. Penthouse models have sleeping lofts overlooking spacious living area. **Amenities:** 🛏 🅰 🎦 A/C, cable TV w/movies, refrig. Some units w/terraces, some w/fireplaces. VCRs, tape library, hair dryers available. **Services:** 🖐 🍴 🍽 Grocery shopping. Evening cookouts or group meals provided for a fee. Maid service and linen changed every 2 days during long-term stays. **Facilities:** 🔥 🚲 🏋 🍴 🍽 🔥 🕤 Lifeguard, whirlpool, washer/dryer. Modern lobby lounge has TV and fireplace and serves breakfast and weeknight dinners. **Rates (CP):** From $129 effic. Extra person $10. Children under 18 stay free. Spec packages avail. Pking: Outdoor, free. Maj CC. Nonrefundable $85 deposit required for pets.

Restaurants 🍴

✸ Clyde's of Tysons Corner, 8332 Leesburg Pike at Chain Bridge Rd, Vienna (Tysons Corner); tel 703/734-1901. Exit 10B off I-495. Follow Va 7 W to 2d light past Va 123; turn right onto service road, and proceed to Chain Bridge Rd. **Regional American/Pub.** One of the largest restaurants in northern Virginia, this version of the Clyde's chain is noted for its Palm Terrace, which has a soaring skylight and wall-size murals with frolicking satyrs. So stunning it's been used as a movie set. Noted artists and artisans have contributed to decor in the several other dining areas. Pub-style sandwiches and burgers are augmented by regional seafood selections and grilled steaks. DJ spins tunes for dancing Friday and Saturday evenings. One of the area's most popular spots, it's often packed on weekends. **FYI:** Reservations recommended. Children's menu. **Open:** Mon–Sat 11am–2am, Sun 10am–2am. Closed some hols. **Prices:** Main courses $9–$15. Maj CC. 💟 🕤

Fedora Café, 8521 Leesburg Pike, Vienna (Tysons Corner); tel 703/556-0100. Exit I-495 at Va 7 W. **Eclectic.** Wall coverings to match a rose marble bar set the theme at this spacious cafe-style eatery with open kitchen and deli case at the entrance. Tiffany lighting and dark woods add to upscale ambience. Many char-grilled items are complemented by unusual offerings, such as pheasant ravioli. **FYI:** Reservations accepted. Children's

menu. Dress code. **Open:** Lunch Mon–Fri 11:30am–3pm, Sat noon–3pm; dinner Mon–Thurs 5:30–10:30pm, Fri–Sat 5:30–11pm, Sun 4:30–9:30pm; brunch Sun 10:30am–2:30pm. Closed some hols. **Prices:** Main courses $9–$19. Maj CC. 💟 🕤

Marco Polo Restaurant, 245 W Maple Ave at Pleasant St, Vienna; tel 703/281-3922. Exit 62 off I-66. Go north on Nutley St to W Maple Ave; head east. **Italian.** A number of small nooks with subdued lighting and dark wood trim add a feeling of intimacy to this otherwise large restaurant. Northern Italian seafood and pasta dishes have been the specialties since 1973. Italian buffet offered Thursday evenings. Luncheon buffet Tuesday to Friday. **FYI:** Reservations recommended. Children's menu. Dress code. **Open:** Mon–Thurs 11:15am–10:30pm, Fri–Sat 11:15am–11pm. Closed some hols. **Prices:** Main courses $11–$18. Maj CC. 🕤

♦ Morton's of Chicago, 8075 Leesburg Pike at Aline Ave, Vienna (Tysons Corner); tel 703/883-0800. Exit 10 off I-495. Follow Va 7 W to Aline Ave; go south. **Steak.** A lively but elegant dining room trimmed in rich mahogany, a wall full of photos of regulars and celebrities, and various displays of fresh food highlight this member of the Chicago steak house chain noted for top-quality steaks, veal, lamb, and fish, all displayed as a "living menu," which allows guests to choose their own cuts. **FYI:** Reservations recommended. Dress code. **Open:** Lunch Mon–Fri 11:30am–2:30pm; dinner Mon–Sat 5:30–11pm, Sun 5–10pm. Closed some hols. **Prices:** Main courses $17.50–$30. Maj CC. 💟 🆅🅿 🕤

Nizam's Restaurant, in Village Green Shopping Center, 523 W Maple Ave at Nutley St, Vienna; tel 703/938-8948. Exit 62 off I-66. Go north on Nutley St. **Middle Eastern/Turkish.** Various plates and Turkish knickknacks give this blond-wood dining room an ethnic flavor to match the thinly sliced doner kabobs and other traditional Turkish specialties of a noted owner/chef. A popular local eatery since 1974. **FYI:** Reservations recommended. Children's menu. Dress code. **Open:** Lunch Tues–Thurs 11am–3pm, Fri 11am–2:30pm; dinner Tues–Thurs 5:10–10pm, Fri–Sat 5–11pm, Sun 4–10pm. Closed Thanksgiving. **Prices:** Main courses $12.50–$17.50. Maj CC.

Phillips Seafood Grill, 8300 Boone Blvd, Vienna (Tysons Corner); tel 703/442-0400. Exit 10 off I-495. Follow Va 7 W to Gallows Rd, turn left, then right on Boone Blvd. **Seafood.** Dark wood, brass rails, and discreet lighting lend casual elegance to this upscale spot sandwiched between two high-rise office buildings. Dining rooms are divided to include space for some private tables; 1 room is under a lovely stained-glass dome. Specialties are char-grilled fish and lobster, plus traditional Chesapeake-style crab cakes and spiced shrimp. No fried food except potatoes. Small outside dining area open in fine weather.

FYI: Reservations not accepted. Children's menu. **Open:** Sun–Thurs 11am–10pm, Fri 11am–11pm, Sat 5–11pm. Closed Dec 25. **Prices:** Main courses $10–$25. Maj CC. ♥ VP

Primi Piatti, 8045 Leesburg Pike, at Aline Ave, Vienna; tel 703/893-0300. Exit 10 off I-495. Follow Va 7 W for ½ mile; restaurant opposite Tysons Corner Center mall. **Italian.** Potted tropical plants divide this open, cafe-style dining room accented by varnished wood chairs and moldings. Each table boasts a basket of fresh bread sticks. A wide variety of pastas, pizzas, and meat dishes are offered, all prepared in traditional styles from throughout Italy. **FYI:** Reservations recommended. Dress code. **Open:** Lunch Mon–Fri 11:30am–2:30pm; dinner Mon–Thurs 5:30–10pm, Fri–Sat 5:30–10:30pm. Closed some hols. **Prices:** Main courses $11–$18. Maj CC. VP &

Ristorante Bonaroti, in Wolftrap Shops, 428 E Maple Ave, Vienna; tel 703/281-7550. Exit 62 off I-66. Go north on Nutley St to W Maple Ave; go east 1 mile. **Italian.** Reproductions of the Italian masters, especially Michelangelo, set an appropriate theme in this pleasant, living room–like restaurant noted for northern Italian cuisine, especially homemade pastas. Extensive wine list. **FYI:** Reservations recommended. Children's menu. Dress code. **Open:** Mon–Fri 11:30am–10:30pm, Sat 5–11pm. Closed some hols. **Prices:** Main courses $12–$19. Maj CC. &

VIRGINIA BEACH

Map page M-3, E7

Hotels 🏨

The Atrium Resort Hotel, 21st St and Artic Ave, Virginia Beach, VA 23451; tel 804/491-1400 or toll free 800/967-8483; fax 804/491-7901. Exit I-64 at Virginia Beach; 2 blocks from oceanfront. Attractive 6-story atrium lobby outshines some units at this time-share operation 2 blocks from the beach. **Rooms:** 96 stes. CI 3pm/CO 11am. Nonsmoking rms avail. All units are 2-room suites with 2 double beds, full kitchens. **Amenities:** 🛏 🌢 A/C, cable TV w/movies, refrig. **Services:** 🖾 ⤵ Babysitting. **Facilities:** 🔋 ᴵ㎡ & Spa, whirlpool, washer/dryer. **Rates:** HS Mem Day–Labor Day from $109 ste. Extra person $10. Children under 18 stay free. Min stay wknds. Lower rates off-season. Higher rates for spec evnts/hols. Pking: Indoor/outdoor, free. Maj CC. Weekly rates and discounts available.

Barclay Towers Resort Hotel, 809 Atlantic Ave, Virginia Beach, VA 23451 (Oceanfront); tel 804/491-2700 or toll free 800/344-4473; fax 804/428-3790. Between 8th and 9th Sts. This hotel offers fabulous views from its oceanfront, boardwalk location. **Rooms:** 84 stes. CI 3pm/CO 11am. Nonsmoking

rms avail. All units are 2-bedroom suites equipped with kitchens, sleep sofas. **Amenities:** 🛏 🖳 A/C, cable TV w/movies, refrig. All units w/terraces. Irons and boards. **Services:** ✗ VP 🖾 ⤵ Babysitting. **Facilities:** 🔋 ᴵ㎡ 🔟 & 1 rst, 1 bar, 1 beach (ocean), lifeguard, games rm, spa, sauna, steam rm, whirlpool, washer/dryer. Restaurant, bar, and nightclub face ocean. **Rates:** HS June 17–Sept 4 from $189 ste. Extra person $10. Children under 18 stay free. Lower rates off-season. Spec packages avail. Pking: Outdoor, free. Maj CC. Weekly rates available.

Best Western Oceanfront, 1101 Atlantic Ave, Virginia Beach, VA 23451; tel 804/422-5000 or toll free 800/631-5000; fax 804/422-5000. Between 11th and 12th Sts. This hotel right on the oceanfront and boardwalk offers great views from all rooms and pool. **Rooms:** 110 rms and stes. CI 3pm/CO 11am. Nonsmoking rms avail. King-bed suites have sleep sofas. Honeymoon suite has waterbed. **Amenities:** 🛏 🌢 🖳 A/C, cable TV w/movies. All units w/terraces, 1 w/Jacuzzi. Suites have wet bars, refrigerators, and microwaves. **Services:** ✗ 🖭 🖾 ⤵ Babysitting. Services for guests with disabilities include a "suitcase" with special items. **Facilities:** 🔋 🚲 & 1 rst, 1 bar (w/entertainment), 1 beach (ocean), lifeguard, games rm, washer/dryer. Nightly entertainment and dancing on premises. **Rates:** HS June 15–Sept 15 $69–$95 S or D; from $110 ste. Extra person $10. Children under 12 stay free. Min stay wknds. Lower rates off-season. Higher rates for spec evnts/hols. Spec packages avail. Pking: Outdoor, free. Maj CC. Weekly rates available.

The Breakers Resort Inn, 16th St at the Oceanfront, Virginia Beach, VA 23451; tel 804/428-1821 or toll free 800/237-7532; fax 804/422-9602. A grassy lawn separates this 8-story building from the ocean beach in heart of resort area. **Rooms:** 56 rms and stes. CI 3pm/CO noon. Murphy beds in living room of king suites. **Amenities:** 🛏 🖳 A/C, cable TV w/movies, refrig. All units w/terraces, some w/Jacuzzis. King suites have Jacuzzis in bedroom. **Services:** ⤵ Babysitting. **Facilities:** 🔋 🚲 & 1 rst, 1 beach (ocean), lifeguard, washer/dryer. Free bicycles. Coffee shop with poolside dining serves morning breakfast, evening wine. **Rates:** HS June 24–Labor Day $106–$110 S or D; from $150 ste. Extra person $8. Children under 12 stay free. Min stay HS. Lower rates off-season. Higher rates for spec evnts/hols. Spec packages avail. Pking: Indoor/outdoor, free. Maj CC. Golf, honeymoon, anniversary packages available.

The Cavalier, 42nd St and Oceanfront, Virginia Beach, VA 23451; tel 804/425-8555 or toll free 800/980-5555; fax 804/428-7957. Actually 2 hotels operated as 1, the landmark Cavalier on the Hill was built in 1927 and still is a very traditional and elegant beach resort. Beautifully landscaped, partially treed grounds; Cavalier is spelled out in sculptured bushes on a bed of white rocks. Furnished with antiques, public areas are steeped in historic ambience. Ceiling fans cool large sitting rooms. Original 3 wings are being completely renovated. Opened in 1987, the high-rise Cavalier on the Ocean presents modern elegance while upholding the property's reputation for luxury and service. **Rooms:** 400 rms and stes. Exec-level rms avail. CI 3pm/CO 11am. Nonsmoking rms avail. Rooms in the older building are large, traditionally and exceptionally outfitted with antiques, crown molding, mahogany wardrobe closets with beveled glass to hide TVs, large baths with black and white tile and separate sinks. Units in newer oceanfront building are equally spacious and elegantly appointed, have modern baths. **Amenities:** 🛏 A/C, cable TV w/movies, refrig, voice mail. Some units w/terraces, some w/Jacuzzis. Some bathrooms have bidets. **Services:** ✗ ☛ 🆅🅿 △ ⌇ Social director, children's program, babysitting. Shuttle between the buildings. Extensive children's program includes feeding the kids. **Facilities:** 🛥 🚲 🎿 🏊2 🏊 🎾 🏊 🏊 □ ㊉ 3 rsts, 3 bars (1 w/entertainment), 1 beach (ocean), lifeguard, board surfing, games rm, lawn games, sauna, playground. Putting green. **Rates:** HS Mem Day–Labor Day $89–$125 S or D; from $189 ste. Extra person $20. Children under 18 stay free. Min stay spec evnts. Lower rates off-season. Spec packages avail. Pking: Indoor/outdoor, $5. Maj CC.

🏨🏨🏨 Clarion Resort and Conference Center, 501 Atlantic Ave, Virginia Beach, VA 23451 (Oceanfront); tel 804/422-3186 or toll free 800/345-3186; fax 804/491-3379. Between 5th and 6th Sts. Located on the oceanfront and boardwalk. **Rooms:** 168 rms, stes, and effic. CI 3pm/CO 11am. Nonsmoking rms avail. Suites have small kitchens. **Amenities:** 🛏 ⊘ 🔲 A/C, cable TV w/movies, refrig, VCR. All units w/terraces, some w/Jacuzzis. Suites have TVs in both sitting and sleeping rooms. **Services:** ✗ ☛ 🆅🅿 △ ⌇ Social director, masseur, children's program, babysitting. Full-time social director supervises activities from daily aerobic classes to board games. **Facilities:** 🛥 🚲 🏊1 🏊 🏊 ㊉ 1 rst, 2 bars (1 w/entertainment), 1 beach (ocean), lifeguard, games rm, spa, sauna, steam rm, whirlpool, washer/dryer. The pool here is on the rooftop, with view of the ocean. Award-winning restaurant. Coin-operated laundry. **Rates:** HS June 20–Aug 20 $125–$160 S or D; from $135 ste; from $90 effic. Extra person $10. Children under 12 stay free. Min stay HS and wknds. Lower rates off-season. Higher rates for spec evnts/hols. Spec packages avail. Pking: Indoor, free. Maj CC. Weekly rates and special golf, fishing, tennis packages available.

🏨🏨 Comfort Inn, 2800 Pacific Ave, at 28th St, Virginia Beach, VA 23451; tel 804/428-2203 or toll free 800/441-0684; fax 804/422-6043. A nice, clean place to stay, 1 block from the oceanfront in the resort area. **Rooms:** 135 rms. CI 2pm/CO 11am. Nonsmoking rms avail. Efficiency with small kitchen available. **Amenities:** 🛏 A/C, cable TV w/movies. **Services:** △

⌇ Babysitting. Free local calls. **Facilities:** 🛥 🚲 🏊 🏊 ㊉ Games rm, whirlpool, washer/dryer. **Rates (CP):** HS July–Aug $99–$149 S or D. Extra person $8. Children under 18 stay free. Min stay HS and spec evnts. Lower rates off-season. Higher rates for spec evnts/hols. Spec packages avail. Pking: Outdoor, free. Maj CC. Family and golf packages available.

🏨🏨 Comfort Inn Oceanfront, 2015 Atlantic Ave, Virginia Beach, VA 23451; tel 804/425-8200 or toll free 800/443-4733; fax 804/425-6521. Between 20th and 21st Sts. An all-suites hotel right on the ocean and overlooking the boardwalk in the heart of the resort district. Attractive lobby with large plants and flowers, good seating with view of ocean. **Rooms:** 83 stes. CI 3pm/CO 11am. Nonsmoking rms avail. All units have sleep sofas and kitchenettes. **Amenities:** 🛏 A/C, cable TV w/movies, refrig. All units w/terraces, 1 w/Jacuzzi. **Services:** ☛ △ ⌇ Babysitting. **Facilities:** 🛥 🚲 🏊 🏊 □ ㊉ 1 beach (ocean), lifeguard. Indoor pool overlooks ocean. Covered high-rise parking on same level as some rooms. **Rates (CP):** HS June 11–Labor Day from $165 ste. Extra person $10. Children under 12 stay free. Min stay HS. Lower rates off-season. Spec packages avail. Pking: Indoor/outdoor, free. Maj CC. Weekly rates, AARP discounts available.

🏨🏨🏨 Courtyard by Marriott, 5700 Greenwich Rd, Virginia Beach, VA 23462; tel 804/490-2002 or toll free 800/321-2211; fax 804/490-0169. Exit 284B off I-64. Like most others of this chain, which is oriented toward business travelers, this hotel with tastefully decorated lobby is built around a central, land-scaped courtyard. Quiet location. **Rooms:** 146 rms and stes. CI 3pm/CO noon. Express checkout avail. Nonsmoking rms avail. **Amenities:** 🛏 ⊘ 🔲 A/C, satel TV w/movies. Some units w/minibars, some w/terraces. Hot-water dispenser for coffee and tea in all units. Suites have refrigerators. **Services:** △ ⌇ Babysitting. Coffee in lobby. **Facilities:** 🛥 🏊 🏊 ㊉ 1 rst, 1 bar, whirlpool, washer/dryer. Lobby dining area serves breakfast only. **Rates:** HS Mem Day–Sept $79 S; $84 D; from $89 ste. Children under 18 stay free. Min stay HS. Lower rates off-season. Pking: Outdoor, free. Maj CC.

🏨🏨 The Dolphin Inn, 1705 Atlantic Ave, Virginia Beach, VA 23451 (Oceanfront); tel 804/491-1420 or toll free 800/365-3467; fax 804/425-8390. Between 17th and 18th Sts. An all-suites hotel on the oceanfront and boardwalk, providing great views. **Rooms:** 54 stes. CI 3pm/CO 11am. Nonsmoking rms avail. King suite contains sleep sofa. **Amenities:** 🛏 ⊘ 🔲 A/C, cable TV w/movies, refrig. All units w/terraces, all w/Jacuzzis. King suite has VCR, 2 TVs, 2 balconies, whirlpool in each room. Mirror permits ocean views from whirlpool. **Services:** △ ⌇ Babysitting. **Facilities:** 🛥 🚲 ㊉ 1 beach (ocean), lifeguard, washer/dryer. Rooftop deck and heated greenhouse. **Rates:** HS

Mem Day–Labor Day from $155 ste. Extra person $10. Children under 12 stay free. Min stay wknds. Lower rates off-season. Spec packages avail. Pking: Indoor, free. Maj CC. Weekly rates, AARP discounts available.

≣≣≣≣ **The Founders Inn and Conference Center**, 5641 Indian River Rd, Virginia Beach, VA 23464; tel 804/424-5511 or toll free 800/926-4466; fax 804/366-0613. Exit 286B off I-64. Go east on Indian River Rd for ¼ mile. A high-quality, no-smoking, no-alcohol facility operated by and adjacent to the Christian Broadcasting Network. Spacious grounds include pond with waterfowl. Beautiful public areas have colonial-style appointments and architecture. **Rooms:** 248 rms and stes. Exec-level rms avail. CI 4pm/CO noon. Express checkout avail. Very tasteful furnishings range from formal mahogany to country-style light woods and plaid bedspreads. **Amenities:** 🛏 👤 A/C, cable TV w/movies, voice mail, bathrobes. 1 unit w/terrace, some w/fireplaces. **Services:** ✕ 🖻 🖻 🖻 🖻 🖻 Social director, children's program, babysitting. Camp Founders Club has children's camp, whose activities include organized sports, storytelling. **Facilities:** 🖻 🚲 🖻 🖻 🖻 🖻 🖻 2 rsts (see also "Restaurants" below), lawn games, racquetball, spa, sauna, playground, washer/dryer. 120-seat dinner theater. Guests can watch taping of the "700 Club" cable TV show. Bookstore. Excellent fitness center with instructors. Guests can play at 2 nearby golf courses. **Rates (CP):** HS Mid-Mar–mid-Nov $79–$94 S or D; from $200 ste. Extra person $15. Children under 18 stay free. Lower rates off-season. Spec packages avail. Pking: Outdoor, free. Maj CC. Many packages available featuring trips to Virginia Beach, Colonial Williamsburg.

≣≣≣ **Four Sails Resort**, 3301 Atlantic Ave, Virginia Beach, VA 23451 (Oceanfront); tel 804/491-8100 or toll free 800/227-4213; fax 804/491-0573. Between 33rd and 34th Sts. On the ocean and boardwalk, this 13-story time-share building is family oriented. **Rooms:** 57 stes. CI 3pm/CO 11am. Units are 1- and 2-bedroom apartments, all with ocean views, full kitchens, queen-size sleep sofas. **Amenities:** 🛏 👤 🖻 A/C, cable TV w/movies, refrig, VCR, stereo/tape player. All units w/terraces, all w/Jacuzzis. TVs in sitting and sleeping areas, microwaves. Video rentals at front desk. **Services:** ✕ 🖻 🖻 Children's program, babysitting. **Facilities:** 🖻 🚲 🖻 🖻 1 rst, 1 bar, 1 beach (ocean), lifeguard, spa, sauna, washer/dryer. **Rates:** HS May 30–Oct 15 from $160 ste. Extra person $5. Children under 17 stay free. Min stay wknds. Lower rates off-season. Pking: Indoor/outdoor, free. Maj CC.

≣≣ **New Castle Motel**, Oceanfront at 12th St, Virginia Beach, VA 23451; tel 804/428-3981 or toll free 800/346-3176; fax 804/491-4394. On the beach and boardwalk. **Rooms:** 83 rms, stes, and effic. CI 2pm/CO 11am. All rooms have ocean views.

Amenities: 🛏 🖻 A/C, cable TV w/movies, refrig, bathrobes. Some units w/minibars, all w/terraces, some w/fireplaces, some w/Jacuzzis. Bedroom Jacuzzis, brass bath fixtures in all units. **Services:** ✕ 🖻 Babysitting. **Facilities:** 🖻 🚲 🖻 🖻 1 beach (ocean), lifeguard, whirlpool, washer/dryer. Sun deck on 5th floor has hot tub. Free bicycles. Snack shop on premises. Some parking in a high-rise deck on same floors as rooms. **Rates:** HS June 24–Aug $125 S or D; from $165 ste; from $125 effic. Extra person $8. Children under 17 stay free. Min stay spec evnts. Lower rates off-season. Higher rates for spec evnts/hols. Pking: Indoor/outdoor, free. Maj CC.

≣≣ **Princess Anne Inn**, 25th St at Oceanfront, Virginia Beach, VA 23451; tel 804/428-5611 or toll free 800/468-1111; fax 804/425-5815. Enjoys excellent views from location in middle of Virginia Beach oceanfront. **Rooms:** 60 rms. CI 3pm/CO 11am. Nonsmoking rms avail. Large rooms all have ocean views. **Amenities:** 🛏 A/C, cable TV w/movies, refrig. All units w/terraces. Microwaves available. **Services:** ✕ 🖻 🖻 **Facilities:** 🖻 🚲 🖻 🖻 1 rst, 1 bar, 1 beach (ocean), lifeguard, sauna, whirlpool. Pool area has tanning booth. **Rates:** HS July–Aug $120–$135 S or D. Extra person $5. Children under 12 stay free. Min stay wknds. Lower rates off-season. Pking: Outdoor, free. Maj CC. AARP discounts.

≣≣≣ **Station One Hotel**, 2321 Atlantic Ave, Virginia Beach, VA 23451 (Oceanfront); tel 804/491-2400 or toll free 800/435-2424; fax 804/491-8204. Between 23rd and 24th Sts. Located on the boardwalk next to the Life Saving Museum and an outdoor stage with daily entertainment during summer. **Rooms:** 104 stes. CI 3pm/CO 11am. Nonsmoking rms avail. **Amenities:** 🛏 🖻 A/C, cable TV w/movies, refrig. All units w/terraces. **Services:** ✕ 🖻 🖻 Babysitting. **Facilities:** 🖻 🚲 🖻 🖻 1 rst, 1 bar, 1 beach (ocean), lifeguard, sauna, whirlpool, washer/dryer. Restaurant on 4th floor has ocean view. Pool area has hot tub, extensive sun deck. Parking in adjacent high-rise garage at room levels. **Rates:** HS Mem Day–Labor Day from $99 ste. Extra person $7. Children under 17 stay free. Min stay HS and wknds. Lower rates off-season. Higher rates for spec evnts/hols. Pking: Indoor, free. Maj CC. Weekly rates and AARP discounts available.

≣≣≣≣ **Virginia Beach Resort Hotel and Conference Center**, 2800 Shore Drive (US 60), at Great Neck Rd, Virginia Beach, VA 23451; tel 804/481-9000 or toll free 800/468-2722, 800/422-4747 in VA; fax 804/496-7429. Enjoys a great location on Chesapeake Bay with private beach and beautiful sunsets. **Rooms:** 295 stes. Exec-level rms avail. CI 4pm/CO 11am. Express checkout avail. Nonsmoking rms avail. All units are suites with bay views, separate sleeping and sitting areas. **Amenities:** 🛏 A/C, cable TV w/movies, refrig, shoe polisher. All units w/terraces, some w/Jacuzzis. Microwaves, wet bars. **Services:** ✗ 🚗 🖎 ↺ Car-rental desk, masseur, children's program, babysitting. **Facilities:** 🖍 🚲 ⚠ 🖻 🛎 500 ⅋ 2 rsts (*see also* "Restaurants" below), 1 bar (w/entertainment), 1 beach (bay), spa, sauna, whirlpool, washer/dryer. Overlooking bay, large sun deck surrounds outdoor portion of pool. Water sports equipment rental on premises. Guests can play at nearby Virginia Beach Tennis Club. **Rates:** HS Mem Day–Labor Day from $136 ste. Extra person $10. Children under 18 stay free. Min stay spec evnts. Lower rates off-season. Spec packages avail. Pking: Indoor/outdoor, free. Maj CC.

Motels

🏊 Days Inn–Airport, 5708 Northampton Blvd, Virginia Beach, VA 23455 (Norfolk Int'l Airport); tel 804/460-2205 or toll free 800/325-2525; fax 804/363-8089. Exit 282 off I-64. This chain motel is close to Chesapeake Bay Bridge-Tunnel, naval bases. **Rooms:** 148 rms. CI 3pm/CO noon. Nonsmoking rms avail. **Amenities:** 🛆 A/C, cable TV w/movies, refrig. Some units w/terraces. **Services:** ✗ 🖎 ↺ Babysitting. Free coffee in lobby. **Facilities:** 🖍 🛎 250 ⅋ Sauna, washer/dryer. **Rates:** HS Apr–Sept $50–$60 S; $55–$65 D. Extra person $5. Children under 12 stay free. Lower rates off-season. Spec packages avail. Pking: Outdoor, free. Maj CC.

🏊 Econo Lodge Chesapeake Beach, 2968 Shore Dr (US 60), Virginia Beach, VA 23451; tel 804/481-0666 or toll free 800/424-4777; fax 804/481-4756. Chain motel 1 block from Chesapeake Bay beaches. **Rooms:** 41 rms and stes. CI 3pm/CO 11am. Nonsmoking rms avail. **Amenities:** 🛆 A/C, cable TV, refrig. Microwaves. **Services:** ↺ **Facilities:** 🖍 ⅋ **Rates:** HS Mem Day–Labor Day $70 S; $75 D; from $85 ste. Children under 12 stay free. Lower rates off-season. Pking: Outdoor, free. Maj CC.

🏊 The Executive Inn, 717 S Military Hwy, Virginia Beach, VA 23464; tel 804/420-2120 or toll free 800/678-3466; fax 804/523-2516. Located ¼ mi N of Indian River Rd. Older, independent motel close to shopping and restaurants. **Rooms:** 101 rms. CI 4pm/CO 11am. Nonsmoking rms avail. Rooms show some wear and tear but are clean. **Amenities:** 🛆 A/C, cable TV w/movies. Some rooms have refrigerators. **Services:** ✗ 🖎 ↺ 🖎 **Facilities:** 🖍 150 ⅋ 1 rst, 2 bars (1 w/entertainment), games rm, washer/dryer. **Rates:** HS Mem Day–Labor Day $69–$75 S or D. Extra person $5. Children under 12 stay free. Lower rates off-season. Higher rates for spec evnts/hols. Spec packages avail. Pking: Outdoor, free. Maj CC.

🏊 Fairfield Inn by Marriott, 4760 Euclid Rd, Virginia Beach, VA 23462; tel 804/499-1935 or toll free 800/228-2800; fax 804/499-1935. Exit I-64 at Va 44, then take exit 3B (Independence/Pembroke); turn left on Euclid Rd. Adjacent to a wooded area off the Virginia Beach Expressway, this L-shaped motel flanking a pool is centrally located to shopping, the beach, Oceana Naval Air Station, and Little Creek Amphibious Base. **Rooms:** 134 rms. CI 3pm/CO noon. Nonsmoking rms avail. All rooms are essentially the same except for bed configuration. **Amenities:** 🛆 🖎 A/C, cable TV w/movies. **Services:** 🖎 ↺ **Facilities:** 🖍 12 ⅋ Free guest use of Gold's Gym, 4 miles away. **Rates:** HS May–Labor Day $50–$64 S or D. Children under 18 stay free. Lower rates off-season. Higher rates for spec evnts/hols. Pking: Outdoor, free. Maj CC.

Restaurants 🍴

★ **Alexander's on the Bay**, 4536 Ocean View Ave, Virginia Beach; tel 804/464-4999. **Continental/Seafood.** Great view over Chesapeake Bay and the requisite nautical theme. Menu offers beef, veal, and seafood in continental preparations, plus such chef's creations as tuna Norfolk (sautéed yellowfin tuna capped with artichoke hearts, backfin crab meat, and hollandaise sauce). Outside dining area near bar has limited menu. **FYI:** Reservations recommended. Children's menu. Dress code. **Open:** Daily 5:30–10:30pm. Closed some hols. **Prices:** Main courses $11.95–$26.95. Maj CC. 🍽 🏔 VP ⅋

★ **Blue Pete's**, 1400 N Muddy Creek Rd, Virginia Beach; tel 804/426-2005. **Seafood/Steak/Pasta.** Lovely natural setting makes this well worth the drive to Tabernacle Creek in Back Bay National Wildlife Refuge. Dine inside or on creekside decks nearly surrounding building. Trees in creek are lighted at night. Inside are old furniture, plants, and great views. Menus feature original watercolor paintings of the restaurant, and among the best items are prime rib, broiled seafood. Vegetables are fresh, and desserts are homemade. Casual attire appropriate. Capt Dave Kelly's 45-minute wildlife refuge cruises depart restaurant's dock. **FYI:** Reservations accepted. Children's menu. Dress code. **Open:** Daily 6–10pm. Closed some hols; Nov–Feb. **Prices:** Main courses $17–$29. Maj CC. 🍽 🏔 💟 ⅋

Captain George's Seafood Restaurant, 1956 Laskin Rd, Virginia Beach; tel 804/428-3494. **Seafood.** Famous for its all-you-can-eat seafood buffet, this restaurant looks like the bow of an old ship, while inside sports nautical decor. Crowds seem smaller because main dining room is divided into sections. Also at: 2272 Old Pungo Ferry Rd, Virginia Beach (804/721-3463). **FYI:** Reservations not accepted. Children's menu. Dress code. **Open:** Mon–Thurs 4:30–10:30pm, Fri–Sun 4–10:30pm. **Prices:** Main courses $17.95–$28.95; PF dinner $17.95. Maj CC. 🍽 ⅋

★ **Gus' Mariner Restaurant**, in Ramada Inn, 57th St and Oceanfront, Virginia Beach; tel 804/425-5699. **Burgers/Seafood.** A well-appointed, casual hotel eatery with some of the area's best ocean views from giant windows right on the boardwalk. Excellent seafood makes this a favorite with locals as well as visitors. **FYI:** Reservations accepted. Children's menu. Dress code. **Open:** Tues–Sat 7am–10pm, Sun–Mon 7am–9pm. **Prices:** Main courses $15–$27. Maj CC. 🏦 🖼️ 📠 💟 �&

★ **Henry's at Lynnhaven Inlet**, 3319 Shore Dr, Virginia Beach; tel 804/481-7300. Located 5 miles from oceanfront, just before Lynnhaven Bridge. **Seafood/Steak.** Families are attracted to this open, airy seafood restaurant with fish swimming in saltwater tanks throughout it. Regional seafood dishes include crab soup and soft-shell crabs. Outside porch extends over Lynnhaven Inlet, giving close views of passing pleasure craft. **FYI:** Reservations recommended. Band. Children's menu. Dress code. **Open:** HS Mem Day–Labor Day Mon–Sat 11:30am–11pm, Sun 10am–11pm. Reduced hours off-season. **Prices:** Main courses $12.95–$22.95. Maj CC. 🏦 🖼️ 💟 VP �&

Le Chambord, 324 N Great Neck Rd, at Laskin Rd, Virginia Beach; tel 804/498-1234. **Continental/French.** One of the area's class acts, this elegant establishment with cobblestone, gas-lit entrance has overstuffed, semicircular booths and monogrammed china. Fine French cuisine and a few chef's creations like poached Carolina shrimp and sautéed chicken served over lemon pasta. Even the marble bathrooms are classy. **FYI:** Reservations recommended. Piano. Children's menu. Dress code. **Open:** Lunch daily 11:30am–3pm; dinner daily 6–11pm. Closed some hols. **Prices:** Main courses $15.95–$18.95. Maj CC. 💟 📠 🚗 �&

$ **The Lighthouse**, 1st St and Atlantic Ave, at Rudee Inlet, Virginia Beach; tel 804/428-7974. **Seafood/Steak.** Situated on both the ocean beach and Rudee Inlet, this seafood emporium enjoys incredible water views from all dining areas, including a covered one outside. Fresh local seafood dishes are the specialty, with a buffet during summer. Chef's nightly specials are less expensive than items from regular menu. Early birds and seniors get 10% discount. **FYI:** Reservations recommended. Children's menu. Dress code. **Open:** HS Mem Day–Labor Day Mon–Fri noon–11pm, Sat–Sun 10:30am–11pm. Reduced hours off-season. **Prices:** Main courses $13–$26; PF dinner $17.95. Maj CC. 🏦 🖼️ 💟 �&

Lynnhaven Fish House Restaurant, 22350 Starfish Rd, Virginia Beach; tel 804/481-0003. On Shore Dr, approximately 4 miles from the oceanfront, next to Lynnhaven Fishing Pier. **Seafood/Steak.** Bay and beach decor accents this seafood restaurant right on the Chesapeake Bay. Menu offers a wide range of regional seafood favorites and more-diverse items, such as scallops

Lynnhaven and casserole Prince, a medley of seafood baked in a special sauce. **FYI:** Reservations not accepted. Children's menu. Dress code. **Open:** Daily 11:30am–10:30pm. Closed some hols. **Prices:** Main courses $10.95–$18.95. Maj CC. 🖼️ �&

Morrison's Cafeteria, in Hilltop North Shopping Center, 981 Laskin Rd, Virginia Beach; tel 804/422-4755. **American/Home Cooking.** Like its sibling cafeterias found in shopping centers throughout the region, families and seniors come here for simple meat selections and southern-style vegetables at reasonable prices. Nothing fancy here, although the wait staff will bus your table. **FYI:** Reservations not accepted. Children's menu. Dress code. No liquor license. **Open:** HS Mem Day–Labor Day daily 11am–9pm. Reduced hours off-season. Closed Dec 25. **Prices:** Main courses $4.99–$7.28. Maj CC. 📠 �&

$ **Piccadilly Cafeteria**, in Lynnhaven Mall, 701 Lynnhaven Pkwy, Virginia Beach; tel 804/340-8788. Exit 284A off I-64. **Cafeteria.** There's nothing fancy about the Piccadilly Cafeterias, but there is something very fresh, as in everything being made from scratch, with no frozen or canned meats or vegetables. Even the mashed potatoes are real. For cafeterias, it's home-style cooking at its best. **FYI:** Reservations not accepted. Children's menu. No liquor license. **Open:** Daily 11am–8:30pm. Closed Dec 25. **Prices:** Main courses $3–$8. Maj CC. 📠 ᐸ

★ **Steinhilber's Thalia Acres Inn**, 653 Thalia Rd, Virginia Beach; tel 804/340-1156. Exit 284A off I-64. Follow Va 44 to exit 38 (Independence Blvd), turn right at Virginia Beach Blvd, and left at Thalia Rd. **Seafood/Steak.** This old home was converted into a restaurant in 1939 and has been a local favorite ever since. Shrimp fried in a special sauce are famous. Other original sauces add flavors to various seafood entrees. **FYI:** Reservations accepted. Children's menu. Dress code. **Open:** Mon–Sat 5–10pm. Closed some hols. **Prices:** Main courses $14.95–$31.95. Ltd CC. 💟 🏦 📠

Surf Rider North, in Haygood Shopping Center, 4501 Haygood Rd, Virginia Beach; tel 804/464-5992. Exit 284A off I-64. Take Va 44 to exit 3B; follow Independence Blvd to Haygood Rd. **Regional American/Burgers/Seafood.** Padded booths, wooden tables, and a nautical theme mark this family-oriented establishment known for its flounder, soft-shell crabs, scallops, and other seafood. Desserts are homemade. Also at: 605 Virginia Beach Blvd, Virginia Beach (804/422-3568); 700 Newtown Rd, Norfolk (804/461-6488). **FYI:** Reservations not accepted. Dress code. **Open:** Mon–Sat 11am–10pm. Closed some hols. **Prices:** Main courses $7.95–$14.95. Ltd CC. 📠 ᐸ

Swan Terrace, in Founders Inn and Conference Center, 5641 Indian River Rd, Virginia Beach; tel 804/366-5777. Exit 286B off I-64. Follow Indian River Rd east for ¼ mile. **American.** A very large and open floor plan, light-colored wood accents, and cream walls make this a very airy hotel dining room. Tasteful, traditional-style furnishings, a brass candelabra, fireplace, and plants add to pleasant environment. American heritage cuisine features filet mignon Jamestown, Kansas City rib-eye, and Maryland crab cakes. Buffet at lunch. **FYI:** Reservations recommended. Harp/piano. Children's menu. No liquor license. No smoking. **Open:** HS Apr–Dec breakfast daily 7–11am; lunch daily 11am–3pm; dinner daily 5:30–9pm. Reduced hours off-season. **Prices:** Main courses $13–$20. Maj CC. 🏧 🖼 📧 ⚓

★ **Tandom's Pine Tree Inn**, 2932 Virginia Beach Blvd, Virginia Beach (Lynnhaven); tel 804/340-3661. **Regional American/Continental/Seafood.** Opened as the Pine Tree Inn in 1927, this extremely well-appointed restaurant with chair rails, wallpaper, lanterns, a chandelier, and candlelight exudes a comfortable feeling. Fresh fish, shellfish, beef, veal, and chicken selections served with continental sauces, all complemented by an excellent salad bar graced with fresh oysters and clams. Friendly and efficient staff adds a casual feeling. **FYI:** Reservations recommended. Piano. Children's menu. Dress code. **Open:** Closed some hols. **Prices:** Main courses $14.95–$19.95. Maj CC. 🌐 🚗 📧 ⚓

Tradewinds, in Virginia Beach Resort and Conference Center, 2800 Shore Dr at Great Neck Rd, Virginia Beach; tel 804/481-9000. Exit 284A off I-64. Turn left at end of Va 44 (Virginia Beach Expwy), go north on 83rd St (turns into Shore Dr). **Continental/Seafood.** Right on the Chesapeake Bay, this place has great views (especially at sunset) and appropriate nautical decor. Center island has shrimp and oyster bar. Specialties are seafood, steaks, and Italian dishes. Fish du jour is freshly caught. Outside area near bar offers drinks and light dining from shrimp and oyster bar. **FYI:** Reservations recommended. Piano. Children's menu. Dress code. **Open:** HS Apr–Oct breakfast Mon–Sat 7–11am, Sun 7–10am; lunch Mon–Sat noon–3pm; dinner daily 5–11pm; brunch Sun 10am–3pm. Reduced hours off-season. **Prices:** Main courses $17–$24. Maj CC. 🌐 ⚓ 🏔 ⚓

Attractions 💼

Virginia Marine Science Museum, 717 General Booth Blvd; tel 804/425-FISH. This entertaining and educational museum, located on Owls Creek Salt Marsh, across Rudee Inlet from the resort area, focuses on Virginia's marine environment. Many of the exhibits are interactive, and visitors can view live sea animals in their natural living conditions. There is even a boardwalk that makes the marsh, its waterfowl, and other animals part of the experience. A 50,000-gallon aquarium is a model of the area from the Chesapeake Bay beach to the first island of the Bay Bridge-Tunnel. The touch-tank simulates the shallow waters of

the bay, and visitors may pick up and handle horseshoe crabs and other bay animals. Daily programs include fish feedings, guided tours, and special presentations. **Open:** Mon–Sat 9am–9pm, Sun 9am–5pm. Closed some hols. $$

Ocean Breeze Park, 849 General Booth Blvd; tel 804/425-1241 (recorded info) or 800/628-WILD. Located off Virginia Beach Expwy (I-264) exit 8 (S Birdneck Rd). An amusement park with attractions for all ages, Ocean Breeze offers Wildwater Rapids, a water park with flumes, slides, tube rides, and activity pools; Shipwreck Golf, a 36-hole miniature golf course with a nautical theme; Motorwork go-cart racing for all ages; and Strike Zone batting cage area. Adjoining is "Over-the-Edge" bungee jump tower. Pay-per-play charges apply at all except Wildwater Rapids. **Open:** Water park, Mem Day–Labor Day, daily (hours vary). Other areas, Mem Day–Labor Day, daily 3pm–midnight; May and Sept–Oct, Sat–Sun noon–7pm. $$$$

Seashore State Park and Natural Area, 2500 Shore Dr; tel 804/481-2131. Located 5 miles north on US 60, at Cape Henry. One of Virginia's most popular parks, Seashore offers recreational activities along with an opportunity to to explore a unique habitat featuring lagoons, large cypress trees, and rare plants. The visitor center has exhibits explaining this coastal environment. Recreational facilities include boat ramps, hiking and bicycle trails, campsites and cabins, and picnicking. **Open:** Daily 8am–sunset. $

WARM SPRINGS

Map page M-2, D4

Inn 🛏

🏨 🏨 🏨 **Inn at Gristmill Square**, Va 645, Warm Springs, VA 24484; tel 703/839-2231. A beautiful country inn composed of 4 buildings plus a restaurant/pub is located in a rural area within walking distance of historic Warm Springs pools. Many outdoor activities in area. **Rooms:** 16 rms and effic. CI 2pm/CO noon. No smoking. Large, comfortable rooms are individually decorated with antiques and reproductions. **Amenities:** 🛁 🛎 🗝 A/C, cable TV, refrig. Some units w/terraces, some w/fireplaces, 1 w/Jacuzzi. **Services:** 🛎 Babysitting. **Facilities:** 🍴 🍹 🏊 1 rst (see also "Restaurants" below), 1 bar, sauna, playground, guest lounge. Two golf courses within 20-minute drive. **Rates:** $65–$95 S or D; from $95 ste; from $125 effic. Extra person $10. Children under 12 stay free. MAP rates avail. Pking: Outdoor, free. Ltd CC.

Restaurant 🍽

♥ **Waterwheel Restaurant**, in the Inn at Gristmill Sq, Va 645, Warm Springs; tel 703/839-2231. **American/Continental.** In a rural highlands retreat, much of the old gristmill remains (grain sometimes seeps from the hoppers), creating a charmingly rustic yet peaceful, intimate atmosphere for fine dining. Fresh trout and daily pastas are the specialties. Wine cellar open for guests to make own selections. **FYI:** Reservations accepted. No smoking. **Open:** Sun–Thurs 6–9pm, Fri–Sat 6–10pm. Closed Dec 25. **Prices:** Main courses $18–$22. Ltd CC. ♥ 🎖

WARRENTON

Map page M-3, C6

Motels 🏨

≣≣ **Hampton Inn**, 501 Blackwell Rd, Warrenton, VA 22186; tel 703/349-4200 or toll free 800/426-7866; fax 703/349-4200. 40 mi SW of Washington, DC. exit 52 off US 29 S. Set back from the road in a peaceful country setting, surrounded by the sound of singing birds. Lobby area with antiques is a pleasant place to read. **Rooms:** 100 rms and stes. CI 2pm/CO noon. Nonsmoking rms avail. Old wardrobes rather than closets give otherwise standard room a bit of personality. **Amenities:** 🛏 ⌀ A/C, cable TV w/movies. Hair dryers available. 1 suite with fridge and microwave. **Services:** 🛎 ↵ 24-hour fax. Turndown service on request. Full breakfast buffet in lobby area. **Facilities:** 🎱 ⛳ 🏊 ⅄ Washer/dryer. Picnic area under trees, with tables and barbecue. **Rates (CP):** HS Mar 31–Oct $59–$69 S or D; from $87 ste. Extra person $5. Children under 18 stay free. Lower rates off-season. Higher rates for spec evnts/hols. Pking: Outdoor, free. Maj CC. Special rates for 7-day stay.

≣ **HoJo Inn**, 6 Broadview Ave, Warrenton, VA 22186; tel 703/347-4141 or toll free 800/IGO-HOJO; fax 703/347-5632. Exit US 17 or US 211 at Broadview Ave. Perky little place with average furnishings and decor but some nice touches, such as sitting area with tables overlooking the pool. **Rooms:** 79 rms. CI 11am/CO 11am. Nonsmoking rms avail. King-bedded units are spacious. Furniture a bit tired, but rooms are clean. **Amenities:** 🛏 A/C, cable TV w/movies. All units w/terraces. Some rooms have refrigerators. **Services:** ↵ 🍴 Free coffee in lobby. Turndown service available on request. **Facilities:** 🎱 🏊 ⅄ Big Boy restaurant within walking distance. **Rates:** $35–$46 S or D. Extra person $5. Children under 12 stay free. Pking: Outdoor, free. Maj CC.

Restaurant 🍽

Napoleon's, 67 Waterloo St, Warrenton; tel 703/347-1200. **American/Cafe.** Located in an 1830s-era house, this restaurant offers seating in the original section, on the terrace, or in the newer addition. All provide a nice atmosphere in which to eat such specialties as fettuccine and filet mignon. **FYI:** Reservations recommended. Singer. **Open:** HS Mar–Oct Sun–Thurs 11am–midnight, Fri–Sat 11am–1am. Reduced hours off-season. Closed Dec 25. **Prices:** Main courses $10–$15. Ltd CC. 🎖

WASHINGTON

Map page M-3, C5 (SE of Front Royal)

Inn 🏨

♨ **The Inn at Little Washington**, Middle and Main Sts, PO Box 300, Washington, VA 22747; tel 703/675-3800; fax 703/675-3100. 23 mi W of Warrenton. Off US 211. Turn-of-the-century house with double verandas, deftly restored and enlarged around a garden courtyard. Located in a village laid out by George Washington in 1769. **Rooms:** 12 rms and stes. CI 3pm/CO noon. Rooms furnished with antiques and lots of whimsy (like reproduction 1940s-style radios), but lots of comforts too (heated towel racks, half canopies above the beds, reading lamps beside beds and armchairs). **Amenities:** 🛏 ⌀ 🍷 A/C, bathrobes. Some units w/terraces, some w/Jacuzzis. Complimentary mineral water; fresh flowers. **Services:** 🍴 🅥🅟 ⅄ Twice-daily maid svce. Complimentary afternoon tea with scones. Cordial and efficient staff. **Facilities:** 🍽 1 rst (see also "Restaurants" below), 1 bar, guest lounge. Small lounge/library on 2nd floor. **Rates (CP):** $240–$495 S; from $390 ste. Extra person $40. Higher rates for spec evnts/hols. Pking: Outdoor, free. Ltd CC. Rates vary by day of week, month, and holidays. Guests are strongly advised to make reservations for room and restaurant at same time, as far ahead as possible.

Restaurant 🍽

♥ **The Inn at Little Washington**, Middle and Main Sts, Washington; tel 703/675-3800. 23 mi W of Warrenton. Off US 211. **American/French.** Vaguely Victorian decor, with tasseled lamps hanging low over the tables, and peach-and-cream drapes; there's also a tented pavilion. The chef emphasizes local produce in the imaginative, meticulously prepared and presented dishes, which may include rabbit sausage with sauerkraut braised in Virginia Riesling; grilled poussin (young chicken) marinated in blackberry vinegar; native rockfish roasted with forest mushrooms, pinenuts, and ruby grapes; and warm rhubarb pizza with ginger ice cream. The outstanding wine list features 3 pages of half-bottles ($13–$95) and a page of Virginia wines ($21–$42 per bottle). Reservations should be made weeks in advance. **FYI:** Reservations recommended. No smoking. **Open:** Wed–Fri 6–9:30pm, Sat 5:30–9:30pm, Sun 4–8:30pm. Closed Dec 25. **Prices:** PF dinner $78–$98. Ltd CC. ❤ 🍴 ♿

WATERFORD
Map page M-3, B6 (NW of Leesburg)

Attraction 🎒

Waterford Village, Country Rd 662 off Va 9; tel 703/882-3018. The enchanting hamlet of Waterford, with numerous 18th- and 19th-century buidings, is a National Historic Landmark. A Quaker from Pennsylvania named Amos Janney built a mill here in the 1740s. Other Quakers followed, and by 1840 most of the buildings now on Main Street were in place. In 1870 the railroad bypassed Waterford, slowing the pace of change so that much of the town remains preserved today. **Open:** Daily 24 hours. Free.

WAYNESBORO
Map page M-3, D5

Motels 🏨

≡≡ Comfort Inn, 640 W Broad St, Waynesboro, VA 22980; tel 703/942-1171 or toll free 800/221-2222. Exit 96 off I-64. Close to downtown and within minutes of Skyline Dr and Blue Ridge Pkwy, motel sits on a hill. **Rooms:** 75 rms. CI noon/CO noon. Nonsmoking rms avail. Very attractive. **Amenities:** 🛋 A/C, cable TV. Some units w/terraces. **Services:** 🗚 ↩ ⇄ Babysitting. **Facilities:** 🔥 ♿ Very nice pool area and patio with tables and chairs. Guests have free use of YMCA health club. **Rates (CP):** HS May–Oct $45–$55 S; $55–$65 D. Extra person $5. Children under 18 stay free. Lower rates off-season. Higher rates for spec evnts/hols. Spec packages avail. Pking: Outdoor, free. Maj CC.

≡≡≡ Holiday Inn Waynesboro-Afton, jct I-64, US 250, Skyline Dr, and Blue Ridge Pkwy, PO Box 849, Waynesboro, VA 22980 (Afton Mountain); tel 703/942-5201 or toll free 800/465-4329; fax 703/943-8746. Exit 99 off I-64. Scenic is the operative word at this motel high atop Afton Mountain at the entrance to both Skyline Dr and Blue Ridge Pkwy. Convenient location and great views make it popular in season. **Rooms:** 118 rms. Exec-level rms avail. CI 3pm/CO noon. Nonsmoking rms avail. All rooms are spacious; some have mountain views.

Amenities: 🛋 A/C, satel TV. **Services:** 🗚 🖼 ↩ ⇄ **Facilities:** 🔥 🏊 ♿ 1 rst, 1 bar (w/entertainment), washer/dryer. Restaurant and lounge overlook mountains and valleys. **Rates:** HS Aug–Oct $55–$66 S or D. Extra person $6. Children under 18 stay free. Min stay spec evnts. Lower rates off-season. Higher rates for spec evnts/hols. Spec packages avail. Pking: Outdoor, free. Maj CC.

WILLIAMSBURG
Map page M-3, B5

Hotels 🏨

≡≡≡ Fort Magruder Inn, US 60 E, PO Box KE, Williamsburg, VA 23187; tel 804/220-2250 or toll free 800/582-1010; fax 804/220-3215. Exit 242A off I-64. Exit 242A off I-64. Follow Va 199 W to US 60 W. Built on a Civil War battle site, this hotel is popular for conventions; its many amenities make it an enjoyable place to stay. **Rooms:** 303 rms and stes. Exec-level rms avail. CI 3pm/CO noon. Express checkout avail. Nonsmoking rms avail. Tastefully decorated and appointed. Spacious suites have exquisite furnishings. **Amenities:** 🛋 🔥 🖥 ⚏ A/C, cable TV, refrig. Some units w/minibars, some w/terraces. Several suites have wet bars, refrigerators. **Services:** 🗚 🖼 🚗 🖼 ↩ Twice-daily maid svce, babysitting. This hotel prides itself on service and hospitality. Free shuttle to Merchants Square in historic area. **Facilities:** 🔥 🚲 🏊 🍽 🏓 ♿ 1 rst, 1 bar (w/entertainment), games rm, spa, sauna, whirlpool, washer/dryer. Indoor and outdoor pools, exercise room. Golfing arranged at Kingsmill Resort. **Rates:** HS May–Labor Day $78–$108 S; $88–$118 D; from $200 ste. Children under 18 stay free. Lower rates off-season. Higher rates for spec evnts/hols. Spec packages avail. Pking: Outdoor, free. Maj CC. Package available including tickets to Busch Gardens or colonial Williamsburg.

≡≡≡ The Williamsburg Hospitality House, 415 Richmond Rd, Williamsburg, VA 23185; tel 804/229-4020 or toll free 800/932-9192; fax 804/220-1560. Exit 238 off I-64. Follow Va 143 E for ¼ mile to Va 132 S; turn right on Scotland St and follow to Richmond Rd. Across the street from the College of William and Mary, this hotel has large, beautiful, traditionally decorated public areas. Pleasant flagstone courtyard has umbrella tables, flowering trees, and fountain. **Rooms:** 296 rms and stes. CI 3pm/CO noon. Nonsmoking rms avail. Rooms are tastefully furnished with 18th-century reproductions. Suites are individually decorated in styles ranging from colonial to art deco. **Amenities:** 🛋 ⚏ A/C, cable TV w/movies, shoe polisher. **Services:** 🗚 🖼 🖼 ↩ Social director, babysitting. Business services include notary and 24-hour fax. Concierge arranges golf at 5 area courses. **Facilities:** 🔥 🏊 ♿ 2 rsts, 1 bar. Papillon restaurant is newly renovated. **Rates:** HS Mar 15–Dec 15 $123 S; $133 D; from $350 ste. Extra person $10. Children under 18 stay free. Min stay spec evnts. Lower rates off-season. Higher rates for spec evnts/hols. Spec packages avail. Pking: Indoor/outdoor, free. Maj CC.

Motels

Best Western Colonial Capitol Inn, 111 Penniman Rd, PO Box FA, Williamsburg, VA 23187; tel 804/253-1222 or toll free 800/446-9228; fax 804/229-9264. Exit 238 off I-64. Follow Va 143 E to Capital Landing Rd; merge onto US 60 W (Page St). Go ¼ mile to Penniman Rd. This family-oriented motel is 2 blocks from the historic area and 5 minutes from Busch Gardens. **Rooms:** 86 rms. CI 2pm/CO noon. Nonsmoking rms avail. **Amenities:** 🔥 🛁 A/C, cable TV. **Services:** ⌁ 🍽 **Facilities:** 🔥 ♿ Playground. Grassy area. **Rates:** HS June 17–Sept 4 $79–$89 S or D. Extra person $5. Children under 12 stay free. Min stay spec evnts. Lower rates off-season. Higher rates for spec evnts/hols. Spec packages avail. Pking: Outdoor, free. Maj CC. Colonial Capital package covers 2 nights and ticket to either colonial Williamsburg or Busch Gardens.

Capitol Motel, 924 Capitol Landing Rd, Williamsburg, VA 23185; tel 804/229-5215 or toll free 800/368-8383; fax 804/220-3810. Exit 238 off I-64. Follow Va 143 E to Capital Landing Rd. This pleasant, family-oriented, older budget motel is under new management. Large trees on and around premises. **Rooms:** 58 rms and stes. CI noon/CO 11am. Nonsmoking rms avail. Recent update of room furnishings. Some units have renovated bathrooms with pretty blue accents. New bedspreads and door locks throughout. Suites are roomy, with vanity area outside bathroom. **Amenities:** 🔥 A/C, cable TV. Some units w/terraces. **Services:** ⌁ Twice-daily maid svce. **Facilities:** 🔥 ♿ Pleasant pool area with 4 matching gazebos, good-quality lounge chairs. **Rates:** HS June 10–Sept 4 $50–$60 S or D; from $70 ste. Extra person $5. Children under 12 stay free. Lower rates off-season. Pking: Outdoor, free. Maj CC. AARP discount.

Captain John Smith Motor Lodge, 2225 Richmond Rd, Williamsburg, VA 23185; tel 804/220-0710 or toll free 800/933-6788. Exit 234 off I-64. Take Va 646 S to US 60 E; go 3 miles. Clean, budget-priced motel, close to Williamsburg Pottery. **Rooms:** 67 rms. CI 3pm/CO 11am. Nonsmoking rms avail. All rooms are decorated with mint-green and beige accents. **Amenities:** 🔥 🖵 A/C, cable TV w/movies, refrig. Some rooms have microwaves and refrigerators. **Services:** ⌁ **Facilities:** 🔥 Games rm. **Rates:** HS June–Sept $60 S; $64 D. Extra person $5. Children under 11 stay free. Lower rates off-season. Higher rates for spec evnts/hols. Pking: Outdoor, free. Maj CC. Senior discounts.

Comfort Inn Historic Area, 120 Bypass Rd, Williamsburg, VA 23185; tel 804/229-2000 or toll free 800/544-7774; fax 804/220-2826. Exit 238 off I-64. Drive ¼ mile east on Va 143, then south on Va 132, then east on US 60 (Bypass Rd). Budget motel a mile from historic area. Attractive lobby has decorative tile floor, large fireplace. **Rooms:** 152 rms. CI 2pm/CO 11am. Express checkout avail. Nonsmoking rms avail. Room furnishings are being updated. Some units have Queen Anne furniture, framed prints by local artist. **Amenities:** 🔥 A/C, cable TV. Some units w/terraces. **Services:** 🔑 🛁 ⌁ 🍽 Babysitting. Free continental breakfast in room adjacent to lobby, equipped with tables and chairs. **Facilities:** 🔥 ♿ Games rm, washer/dryer. Pool with wood deck and 4 matching gazebos is popular with families. **Rates (CP):** HS Mid-June–Labor Day $79–$89 S or D. Extra person $5. Children under 18 stay free. Min stay spec evnts. Lower rates off-season. Spec packages avail. Pking: Outdoor, free. Maj CC. Senior discount by advance reservation, depending on availability.

Courtyard by Marriott, 470 McLaws Circle, Williamsburg, VA 23185; tel 804/221-0700 or toll free 800/321-2211; fax 804/221-0741. Exit 242A off I-64. Go west on Va 199 to US 60, then east ¼ mile to Busch Corporate Center at McLaws Circle. Like all Marriott Courtyards, this motel is geared to business travelers, but it's close to Busch Gardens, making it attractive to families as well. **Rooms:** 151 rms and stes. CI 4pm/CO noon. Express checkout avail. Nonsmoking rms avail. Comfortable rooms have large desks. Some open to courtyard, including some poolside units. **Amenities:** 🔥 🛁 🖵 A/C, cable TV w/movies. Some units w/terraces. Long phone cords, hot-water dispenser for coffee and tea. Refrigerators available. **Services:** 🔑 🛁 ⌁ Social director. **Facilities:** 🔥 🏋 🍽 ♿ 1 rst, 1 bar, games rm, whirlpool, washer/dryer. Indoor/outdoor pool. **Rates:** HS June–mid-Sept $92 S or D; from $110 ste. Children under 18 stay free. Lower rates off-season. Higher rates for spec evnts/hols. Spec packages avail. Pking: Outdoor, free. Maj CC. Government and military rates available.

Days Inn Busch Gardens Area, 90 Old York Rd, Williamsburg, VA 23185; tel 804/253-6444 or toll free 800/635-5366; fax 804/253-0986. Exit 242B off I-64. Go ¼ mile on Va 199 W. This new facility in a wooded area is directly across from Water Country USA. **Rooms:** 210 rms and stes. CI 3pm/CO 11am. Express checkout avail. Nonsmoking rms avail. **Amenities:** 🔥 A/C, cable TV w/movies, in-rm safe. Refrigerators and microwaves available on request. **Services:** 🛁 ⌁ **Facilities:** 🔥 🍽 ♿ 1 rst, 1 bar, games rm, washer/dryer. Bar operates during high season only, when motel is popular with construction workers. Pool slated to be enclosed in 1995. Pool table in winter. **Rates:** HS Mem Day–Labor Day $63–$81 S or D; from $63 ste. Extra person $5. Children under 18 stay free. Min stay spec evnts. Lower rates off-season. Higher rates for spec evnts/hols. Pking: Outdoor, free. Maj CC.

≡≡≡ **Econo Lodge Historic Area**, 1402 Richmond Rd, Williamsburg, VA 23185; tel 804/220-2367 or toll free 800/999-ECON; fax 804/220-3527. Exit 238 off I-64. Go ¼ mile on Va 143 E, then south on Va 132, then east on US 60 for 1½ miles. This family-oriented motel is located midway between the Williamsburg Pottery and the historic area. **Rooms:** 163 rms and stes. CI 2pm/CO 11am. Nonsmoking rms avail. All 2-room suites equipped with sleeper sofa. **Amenities:** 🛏 🖭 A/C, cable TV. Some units w/terraces. All 2-room suites have microwave, refrigerator. **Services:** 🖾 🞱 Babysitting. **Facilities:** 🗄 🞱120 🞱 1 rst, 1 bar (w/entertainment), games rm, sauna, whirlpool, playground. Attractive indoor pool in solarium with Jacuzzi and dry sauna. Outdoor pool is shared with adjacent Travelodge. **Rates:** HS June–Sept $69 S; $75 D; from $109 ste. Extra person $6. Children under 18 stay free. Min stay spec evnts. Lower rates off-season. Higher rates for spec evnts/hols. Spec packages avail. Pking: Outdoor, free. Maj CC.

≡≡≡ **The George Washington Inn and Conference Center**, 500 Merrimac Trail, Williamsburg, VA 23185; tel 804/220-1410 or toll free 800/666-8888; fax 804/220-4662. Exit 238 off I-64. Go east on Va 143 to Merrimac Trail. A large, comfortable independent motel midway between Busch Gardens and the historic area. Amenities appeal to commercial guests and tourists alike. **Rooms:** 250 rms and stes. CI 2pm/CO 11am. Nonsmoking rms avail. Renovated in 1993, units feature blue-and-burgundy color scheme. All have 2 vanities, 2 sinks. Many of the tastefully appointed suites have dining table for 4, sleep sofa. **Amenities:** 🛏 A/C, cable TV w/movies. Many suites have refrigerators. Some have microwaves. **Services:** 🖾 🞱 🞱 Babysitting. **Facilities:** 🗄 🖘 🞱900 🞱 1 rst, 1 bar (w/entertainment), games rm, spa, sauna, whirlpool. Olympic-size pool, enclosed in solarium with sliding doors, is largest indoor pool in area. Separate dry saunas for men and women. Meeting facilities are 3rd-largest in Williamsburg. Restaurant, which serves dinner only, is famous for its smorgasbord. **Rates:** HS May–Sept $69–$99 S or D; from $109 ste. Extra person $10. Children under 17 stay free. Lower rates off-season. MAP rates avail. Spec packages avail. Pking: Outdoor, free. Maj CC.

≡≡ **Governor's Inn**, 506 N Henry St, Williamsburg, VA 23187; tel 804/229-1000 or toll free 800/HISTORY; fax 804/220-7019. Exit 238 off I-64. Go ¼ mile east on Va 143, then south on Va 132 for 2 miles. Located just outside the historic

area, this budget-priced, family-oriented motel is part of the Colonial Williamsburg Hotels Group. **Rooms:** 200 rms. CI 3pm/CO noon. Nonsmoking rms avail. Newly renovated, all rooms have attractive blue and beige colors. **Amenities:** 🛏 🞱 A/C, cable TV w/movies. Some units w/terraces. **Services:** 🖾 🞱 🞱 Babysitting. Shuttle to Williamsburg Woodlands for continental breakfast, and to historic area. **Facilities:** 🗄 🞱 Games rm. Williamsburg Woodlands facilities (some for fee) available to guests include 2 pools, tennis, table tennis, shuffleboard, miniature golf, and bikes. Guests also have free use of indoor pool and fitness center discount at Williamsburg Lodge. **Rates (CP):** HS Apr–May/Oct/Nov 23–27/Dec $61–$77 S or D. Extra person $7. Children under 18 stay free. Lower rates off-season. Higher rates for spec evnts/hols. Spec packages avail. Pking: Outdoor, free. Maj CC.

≡≡ **Hampton Inn Williamsburg Center**, 201 Bypass Rd, Williamsburg, VA 23185; tel 804/220-0880 or toll free 800/289-0880; fax 804/229-7175. Exit 238 off I-64. Go ¼ mile east on Va 143 to Va 132; follow Va 132 S to US 60 E (Bypass Rd). A mile from the historic area, this modern, clean motel has many facilities uncommon for this chain. **Rooms:** 122 rms. CI 3pm/CO 11am. Nonsmoking rms avail. **Amenities:** 🛏 A/C, cable TV w/movies. 1 unit w/minibar, some w/Jacuzzis. **Services:** 🖾 🞱 **Facilities:** 🗄 🞱25 🞱 Games rm, sauna, whirlpool. Complimentary continental breakfast served adjacent to lobby. **Rates (CP):** HS May 29–Sept 5 $79–$89 S or D. Children under 18 stay free. Min stay spec evnts. Lower rates off-season. Higher rates for spec evnts/hols. Spec packages avail. Pking: Outdoor, free. Maj CC. Rates cover up to 5 people per room.

≡≡ **Heritage Inn**, 1324 Richmond Rd, Williamsburg, VA 23185; tel 804/229-6220 or toll free 800/782-3800; fax 804/229-2774. Exit 238 off I-64. Go east on Va 143, then south on Va 132, then east on US 60 (Bypass Rd) to Richmond Rd; follow Richmond Rd west for ¼ mile. This small, charming motel is within walking distance of the College of William and Mary, adjacent to shops and cinema. Williamsburg-style Christmas decorations during the season. An Easter egg hunt is held annually. **Rooms:** 54 rms. CI 3pm/CO noon. Nonsmoking rms avail. Traditional furnishings include 4-poster beds and armoires for TVs. Signed historical prints adorn the walls. **Amenities:** 🛏 A/C, cable TV. **Services:** 🞱 🞱 Deluxe continental breakfast ($4 per person) features homemade items daily. **Facilities:** 🗄 Beautiful domed dining room is available for plantation-style dinners on a group basis. Roomy pool area. **Rates:** HS June 15–Labor Day $68 S or D. Extra person $6. Children under 18 stay free. Lower rates off-season. Higher rates for spec evnts/hols. Spec packages avail. Pking: Outdoor, free. Maj CC.

≣≣≣ **Holiday Inn Downtown**, 814 Capitol Landing Rd, Williamsburg, VA 23185; tel 804/229-0200 or toll free 800/368-0200; fax 804/220-1642. Exit 238 off I-64. Take Va 143 E to Capitol Landing Rd (Va 31). Tastefully decorated in the colonial style, this comfortable and modern motel is a mile from the historic area. **Rooms:** 139 rms and stes. CI 3pm/CO noon. Nonsmoking rms avail. Bright and cheerful rooms contain good-quality furnishings. **Amenities:** 🛏 🐲 A/C, cable TV, VCR. **Services:** ✗ ☎ 🛌 🎧 Babysitting. **Facilities:** 🏋 🖳 550 ⅙ 1 rst, 1 bar, games rm, spa, whirlpool, washer/dryer. Large and airy Holidome contains pool, whirlpool, shuffleboard, putting green, and waterfall cascading from restaurant area. Exercise room and sauna are adjacent. **Rates:** HS June–Labor Day $95–$99 S or D; from $180 ste. Extra person $6. Children under 18 stay free. Min stay spec evnts. Lower rates off-season. Spec packages avail. Pking: Outdoor, free. Maj CC.

≣ **Motel 6**, 3030 Richmond Rd, Williamsburg, VA 23185; tel 804/565-3433; fax 804/565-1013. Exit 234 off I-64. Take Va 646 S to US 60 E; go 2½ miles. Set back from the highway in a partially treed area, this budget motel has attractive grounds. Located 3 miles from Williamsburg Pottery and 4 miles from the historic area. **Rooms:** 169 rms. CI 3pm/CO 11am. Express checkout avail. Nonsmoking rms avail. Clean and modern rooms were renovated in 1994. **Amenities:** 🛏 A/C, satel TV. **Services:** 🛌 🎧 🐕 **Facilities:** 🏋 ⅙ Washer/dryer. **Rates:** HS May–Sept $37 S; $41 D. Extra person $4. Children under 18 stay free. Lower rates off-season. Pking: Outdoor, free. Maj CC.

≣≣ **Quality Inn Colony**, 309 Page St, PO Box FF, Williamsburg, VA 23187; tel 804/229-1855 or toll free 800/443-1232; fax 804/229-3470. Exit 238 off I-64. Go east on Va 143 to US 60 E (Page St). This homey, colonial-style motel was recently renovated while keeping its existing charm. Pleasant exterior walkways feature a zig-zag brick pattern, white columns, and mint-colored tongue-in-groove paneling; 1 mile from historic area. **Rooms:** 59 rms. CI 1:30pm/CO 11am. Express checkout avail. Nonsmoking rms avail. Each room has an outer louvered door, which is nice for privacy and fresh air. Tastefully done with white bedspreads; teal-and-tan accents; matted, framed prints on walls. **Amenities:** 🛏 A/C, cable TV. Some units w/Jacuzzis. Outdoor chairs. **Services:** 🛌 🎧 Babysitting. **Facilities:** 🏋 1 rst, 1 bar, washer/dryer. Restaurant is adjacent. **Rates (CP):** HS June–Aug $70–$73 S or D. Extra person $6. Children under 18 stay free. Min stay spec evnts. Lower rates off-season. Higher rates for spec evnts/hols. Spec packages avail. Pking: Outdoor, free. Maj CC.

≣≣≣ **Williamsburg Woodlands**, Va 132 off US 60 (Bypass Rd), PO Box B, Williamsburg, VA 23187; tel 804/229-1000 or toll free 800/HISTORY; fax 804/221-8942. Exit 238 off I-64. Go east on Va 143, then south on Va 132 to motel, at Colonial Williamsburg Visitors Center. A renovated motel operated by Colonial Williamsburg, it has a wonderful woodsy setting especially appealing to families. Genuine, natural feeling. Enough diversions on grounds to make guests forget about other attractions. **Rooms:** 315 rms and stes. CI 3pm/CO noon. Express checkout avail. Nonsmoking rms avail. Updated rooms have authentic Amish-crafted pine poster beds, chests of drawers, armoires. Earth tones. Beautiful forest-green bedspreads, botanical-type prints by local artist featuring the trees found on property. **Amenities:** 🛏 🐲 A/C, cable TV w/movies. Some units w/minibars. **Services:** 🛌 🎧 Social director, children's program, babysitting. Available mid-June to Labor Day, Young Colonials children's program keep kids busy while parents get away for lunch or dinner. **Facilities:** 🏋 🚴 🏌 🍵 2 700 ⅙ 2 rsts (see also "Restaurants" below), 1 bar, lifeguard, games rm, sauna, day-care ctr, playground. A pool for diving, another for swimming. Badminton, miniature golf, shuffleboard, horseshoes, volleyball, table tennis. Nature trail with water cascade. Guests may use facilities at Williamsburg Lodge, including fitness center, golf. **Rates:** HS Apr–May/Oct/Dec $85–$100 S or D; from $91 ste. Children under 18 stay free. Min stay spec evnts. Lower rates off-season. MAP rates avail. Spec packages avail. Pking: Outdoor, free. Maj CC.

Resorts

≣≣≣ **Kingsmill Resort**, 1010 Kingsmill Rd, Williamsburg, VA 23185; tel 804/253-1703 or toll free 800/832-5665; fax 804/253-8246. Exit 242A off I-64. Follow Va 199 W to 1st traffic light, Kingsmill gatehouse is on the left. 2,900 acres. Peaceful and secluded gated community, by the edge of the James River. Only 15–20 minutes from the area's prime attractions. Owned by Anheuser-Busch. **Rooms:** 407 rms and stes; 35 ctges/villas. CI 4pm/CO noon. Express checkout avail. Suites bright and airy, some rooms small and cramped. Pantries in some rooms. Best bets are newer rooms and suites overlooking the river or pond. **Amenities:** 🛏 🐲 A/C, cable TV w/movies, refrig, voice mail, shoe polisher, bathrobes. All units w/terraces, some w/fireplaces. **Services:** ✗ ☎ 🛌 🎧 Twice-daily maid svce, car-rental desk, social director, masseur, children's program, babysitting. Complimentary shuttle around resort; discounted tickets for Busch Gardens and Colonial Williamsburg. Sometimes amateurish staff; lax housekeeping. **Facilities:** 🏋 🚴 ⚠ 🏐 54 🏌 🏐 13 🍵 🖳 700 ⅙ 3 rsts (see also "Restaurants" below), 4 bars (2 w/entertainment), 1 beach (bay), lifeguard, games rm, lawn games, racquetball, spa, sauna, steam rm, whirlpool, day-care ctr, playground, washer/dryer. First-rate golf and tennis facilities, though resort guests vie with several hundred club members for tee times and court time. Complimentary use of par-3 course. Indoor and outdoor pools. **Rates:**

HS Apr–Oct $155–$205 S or D; from $220 ste. Extra person $20. Children under 18 stay free. Lower rates off-season. Spec packages avail. Pking: Outdoor, free. Maj CC. Special packages for families and tennis players are good buys.

≡≡≡≡ **The Williamsburg Inn**, Francis St at S England St, PO Box 1776, Williamsburg, VA 23187 (Historic Area); tel 804/229-1000 or toll free 800/253-2277; fax 804/220-7096. Exit 238 off I-64. Follow Va 143 to Va 132, turn right, then left at 3rd light; go ½ mile. 400 acres. A unique confluence of comfort and refinement, history, and pleasure. Luxury inn features colonial restorations and exquisite gardens and lawns, ponds, and 45 holes of championship golf. **Rooms:** 235 rms and stes; 23 ctges/villas. CI 3pm/CO noon. Express checkout avail. Nonsmoking rms avail. 3 types of accommodations: the spacious, regency-style rooms (with period armoires for TVs) in the inn itself; less expensive rooms in the contemporary garden annex, Providence Hall (ideal for families); and rooms, suites, and cottages (the last of which are particularly good bargains) in authentically restored buildings nearby, in the historic area. **Amenities:** 🛏 ⚲ 🍴 A/C, cable TV w/movies, bathrobes. Some units w/terraces, some w/fireplaces. **Services:** 🍽 🖴 📺 🗄 🛎 🛍 Twice-daily maid svce, social director, children's program, babysitting. Complimentary afternoon tea featuring harp music in the East Lounge. Some sharp service, some sloppy service. Concierge issues tickets for Colonial Williamsburg attractions and makes reservations for the taverns and shows, thus cutting down on lines. Full hotel services, including room service, for guests in Providence Hall and cottages. **Facilities:** 🏊 🚵 ▶₄₅ 🎿 🎱⁸ 🏧²⁰⁰ 💻 ⚓ 2 rsts (*see also "Restaurants" below*), 2 bars (w/entertainment), lifeguard, lawn games, spa, sauna, steam rm, whirlpool, beauty salon, day-care ctr, playground. One of the pools is spring-fed, for adults only. Two 18-hole golf courses and one 9-hole executive course. Tazewell Fitness Center with spa and indoor pool in affiliated hotel, Williamsburg Lodge, across the street. Lounges with woodburning fireplaces. **Rates:** HS mid-Mar–mid-Nov $220–$315 S or D; from $350 ste; from $125 ctge/villa. Children under 18 stay free. Min stay spec evnts. Lower rates off-season. Spec packages avail. Pking: Outdoor, free. Maj CC.

≡≡≡ **Williamsburg Lodge**, 310 S England St, PO Box 1776, Williamsburg, VA 23187; tel 804/229-1000 or toll free 800/HISTORY; fax 804/220-7685. Exit 238 off I-64. Go ¼ mile east on Va 143, then south on Va 132. Turn left on Francis St, then right on S England St. 3 acres. Bordering the historic area and renowned Golden Horseshoe golf course, this lodge offers a casual, relaxed atmosphere enhanced by beautiful grounds, fountain, resident ducks, covered brick walkways lined with wooden rocking chairs. **Rooms:** 315 rms and stes. Exec-level rms avail. CI 3pm/CO noon. Express checkout avail. Nonsmoking rms avail. Early American decor, spacious, thoughtfully

appointed. Tazewell Wing has folk-art motif, with many handmade quilts decorating the hallways. **Amenities:** 🛏 A/C, cable TV w/movies, voice mail. Some units w/terraces, some w/fireplaces, some w/Jacuzzis. Some units have beautifully landscaped patios with rocking chairs. **Services:** ✕ 🖴 📺 🗄 🛎 Social director, masseur, children's program, babysitting. **Facilities:** 🏊 🚵 ▶₄₅ 🎿 🍽 🎱 📻⁹⁵⁰ 💻 ⚓ 2 rsts, 3 bars (1 w/entertainment), lawn games, spa, sauna, steam rm, whirlpool, beauty salon, day-care ctr, washer/dryer. Championship golf course is ranked among best in country. Impressive Tazewell Fitness Center has spa services, aerobic classes, and indoor lap pool equipped with underwater stereo. **Rates:** HS Apr–May/Sept–Oct/Dec $115–$199 S or D; from $425 ste. Extra person $12. Children under 12 stay free. Lower rates off-season. MAP rates avail. Spec packages avail. Pking: Indoor/outdoor, free. Maj CC. Popular Williamsburg Plan includes admission to historic area, meals in a colonial tavern or on premises, and admission to fitness club. Golf Plan includes meals from a variety of restaurants, golf cart for 18 holes a day.

Restaurants 🍴

Aberdeen Barn, 1601 Richmond Rd, Williamsburg; tel 804/229-6661. Exit 238 off I-64. Va 143 E to Va 132 S to US 60 W to Richmond Rd. **Seafood/Steak.** Lots of wood, beamed ceilings with wagon-wheel lights, rich red carpet, and wooden tables make for cozy, intimate air at this steak house. Claim to fame is corn-fed beef: prime rib, barbecued baby-back ribs. Fresh catches too. **FYI:** Reservations recommended. Children's menu. **Open:** Sun–Thurs 5–9:30pm, Fri–Sat 5–10pm. Closed some hols; Jan 1–Jan 15. **Prices:** Main courses $14–$29. Maj CC. 🅿 ⚓

A Good Place to Eat, in Merchants Sq, 410 Duke of Gloucester St, Williamsburg; tel 804/229-1000 ext 2002. Exit 238 off I-64. Va 143 E to Va 132 S; go 2½ miles to shopping center. **Fast food.** Several dining areas (some with tables, others with booths) give a little class to this fast-food restaurant in the historic area. Patio has wire chairs and tables with big umbrellas. Pancakes, biscuits, muffins for breakfast; burgers, sandwiches, salads for lunch and dinner. Yogurt, ice cream sundaes are desserts. **FYI:** Reservations not accepted. Dress code. No liquor license. **Open:** HS June–Aug daily 8am–10pm. Reduced hours off-season. Closed some hols. **Prices:** Main courses $2–$6. Ltd CC. 🍴 ⚓

Berret's Seafood Restaurant, in Merchants Sq, 199 S Boundary St, Williamsburg; tel 804/253-1847. Exit 238 off I-64. Va 143 E to Va 132 S to historic area. **Seafood/Steak.** Transformation from old Esso station to seafood restaurant makes for a unique setting, with many eating spaces of unusual shapes and sizes, large windows, tile or original brick floors, wooden tables and chairs, blue tablecloths. Modern brass fireplace and white canvas ceiling baffles give a contemporary look. Original local artwork displayed. Good sampling of Virginia seafood includes traditional and creative items, such as peanut-crusted soft-shell crab. Outdoor raw bar open 4pm–midnight from April to October. **FYI:** Reservations recommended. Children's menu. **Open:** HS Mar–Dec daily 11:30am–10pm. Reduced hours off-season. Closed some hols. **Prices:** Main courses $13–$18. Maj CC. 🎦 &

The Bray Dining Room, in the Kingsmill Resort, 1010 Kingsmill Rd, Williamsburg; tel 804/253-3900. Exit 242A off I-64. Follow Va 199 W to US 60 E. **Regional American/Continental.** James River view, tasteful furnishings, floral upholstered chairs, large wood columns, and wood trim adorn this resort's fine dining room. Outdoor dining on balcony with river view, weather permitting. Service erratic. Basic cuisine is continental, but summer and winter menus add such regional choices as roast rack of Virginia spring lamb and Virginia fallow deer chops. Friday seafood nights are popular. Buffets at lunch. **FYI:** Reservations recommended. Piano. Dress code. **Open:** HS Apr–Dec breakfast Mon–Fri 6:45am–9:30; lunch Mon–Fri 11:30am–1:30pm; dinner daily 6–9:30pm; brunch–Sun 10:30am–2:30pm. Reduced hours off-season. **Prices:** Main courses $18–$24. Maj CC. 🏔 💟 &

Cascades, in Williamsburg Woodlands, Va 132, off US 60 Bypass, Williamsburg; tel 804/229-1000. Exit 238 off I-64. Va 143 E to Va 132 S to US 60 E. **Regional American.** On the forested grounds of a motel, this restaurant features dark paneled ceilings and a woodsy view. Green wooden chairs and dark-finished butcher-block tables contribute to a relaxed, casual atmosphere attractive to families. Separate dining room has circular tables, cane chairs, domed-motif ceiling. Traditional Virginia favorites highlighted by southern sampler and regional seafood. Virginia wines also featured. **FYI:** Reservations recommended. Children's menu. **Open:** HS Apr–May/Oct/Dec breakfast Mon–Sat 7:30–10am; lunch Mon–Sat 11:30am–2pm; dinner Sun–Mon 5:30–9pm; brunch–Sun 8am–2pm. Reduced hours off-season. Closed 1 week in Jan. **Prices:** Main courses $12–$20. Maj CC. 🍴 🏔 &

Chowning's Tavern, Duke of Gloucester St, Williamsburg; tel 804/229-2141. Exit 238 off I-64. Va 143 E to Va 132 S to historic area. **Regional American.** Part of Colonial Williamsburg, this reconstructed 18th-century tavern is heavy with historic ambience. Rustic wooden tables, eclectic wooden chairs, a heavily traveled plank floor, beamed ceilings, and fireplaces give patrons an idea of what dining was like back then. Traditional meats from the region are offered; Brunswick stew's a favorite. Happy hour, known as Gambols, features period games

and beverages such as grog and julep 10pm–midnight. Lively music. **FYI:** Reservations recommended. Guitar/harp/singer. Children's menu. No smoking. **Open:** HS Mar–Oct/Dec lunch daily 11am–5pm; dinner daily 5–9pm. Reduced hours off-season. Closed Mid-Feb–Mar. **Prices:** Main courses $17–$24. Maj CC. 🍴 🎦

Christina Campbell's Tavern, Waller and Lafayette Sts, Williamsburg; tel 804/229-2141. Exit 238 off I-64. **Regional American/Seafood/Steak.** Another reconstructed 18th-century tavern featuring wooden furniture and floors of that period. Started by a widow, the colonial original was a favorite of George Washington and other notables. Intimate basement room has brick floors and walls, high-backed booths. Seafood offerings include Chesapeake Bay jambalaya with scallops and country ham. **FYI:** Reservations recommended. Guitar/singer. Children's menu. No smoking. **Open:** HS Mar–Oct/Dec Tues–Sat 5–9pm. Reduced hours off-season. Closed Jan–mid-Feb. **Prices:** Main courses $18–$22. Maj CC. 🏰

Dynasty Chinese Restaurant, 1621 Richmond Rd, Williamsburg; tel 804/220-8888. Exit 238 off I-64. Va 143 E to Va 132 S to US 60 W. **American/Chinese/Vegetarian.** Definitely worth a try for both atmosphere and culinary experience. Tasteful, out-of-the-ordinary decor includes goldfish pond with orchids and other plants, large urns, rich blue upholstered chairs, white tablecloths with blue toppers, and wooden arches. Spicy northern Chinese cuisine is good enough to warrant owners teaching cooking classes. **FYI:** Reservations accepted. Children's menu. **Open:** Daily noon–midnight. **Prices:** Main courses $7–$20. Maj CC. 🎦 💟 &

Fireside Steak House and Seafood, 1995 Richmond Rd, Williamsburg; tel 804/229-3310. Exit 238 off I-64. Va 143 E to Va 132 S to US 60 W. **American/Seafood/Steak.** Under same ownership for 2 decades, this unpretentious steak and seafood restaurant dishes up quality and consistency year after year. A warm, rich look is enhanced by stylish, dark-colored wood chairs, red tablecloths, and corner fireplace. Black leather booth seats available. Prime rib is house specialty, but fresh catch, chicken kabobs, and ham steaks with glazed pineapple ring also served daily. **FYI:** Reservations accepted. Children's menu. **Open:** Mon–Sat 4:30–11pm, Sun noon–10pm. **Prices:** Main courses $9–$27. Maj CC. 🎦 💟

The Jefferson Inn, 1453 Richmond Rd, Williamsburg; tel 804/229-2296. Exit 238 off I-64. Va 143 E to Va 132 S to US 60 W. **Regional American/Seafood/Steak.** Melon-colored tablecloths are set off by solid black plates, giving a casual yet dressy look to this restaurant operated by the same family since 1956. Folk-art-motif draperies, nicely framed prints, waitresses in colonial-style uniforms add historic atmosphere. Southern-style specialties include fried chicken, Virginia ham, grain-fed catfish, cornbread stuffing, Surry sausages. Peanut soup is a delight (guests welcome to recipe). **FYI:** Reservations recommended. Children's menu. **Open:** Daily 4–10pm. Closed some hols. **Prices:** Main courses $9–$29. Maj CC. 🍴 ⌖

Kings Arms Tavern, Duke of Gloucester St, Williamsburg; tel 804/229-2141. Exit 238 off I-64. Go east on Va 143, turn right at Capitol Landing Rd, follow to Page St, turn right at Francis St; parking is on left. **American.** Another of Colonial Williamsburg's reconstructed 18th-century taverns, this one has 11 dining rooms, all with rustic wooden floors and furniture from the era. Specialties are from old recipes, including Virginia peanut soup, Smithfield ham with grape sauce, filet mignon stuffed with oysters. **FYI:** Reservations recommended. Guitar/singer. Children's menu. Dress code. No smoking. **Open:** HS Mar–Oct/Dec lunch Wed–Mon 11:30am–2:30pm; dinner Wed–Mon 5–9:30pm. Reduced hours off-season. Closed Jan–mid-Feb. **Prices:** Main courses $19–$25. Maj CC. 🍴

Le Yaca, in Village Shops at Kingsmill, US 60 E, Williamsburg; tel 804/220-3616. Exit 242 off I-64. Va 199 W to US 60 E. **French.** Four separate dining areas, each with different furnishings, range from wicker to cafe-style at this elegant yet homey establishment widely celebrated in the area. Patrons are greeted by rustic, arched fireplace, where legs of lamb roast in cooler months. French country cuisine runs from poached salmon with hollandaise to roast duckling with black-currant sauce. Most dinners are 4 courses. **FYI:** Reservations recommended. **Open:** HS Sept–Dec lunch Mon–Sat 11:30am–2pm; dinner Mon–Sat 6–9:30pm. Reduced hours off-season. Closed some hols; Jan 1–Jan 15. **Prices:** Main courses $17–$39. Maj CC. 💟 🖼 ⌖

Old Chickahominy House, 1211 Jamestown Rd, at jct Va 199/31 S, Williamsburg; tel 804/229-4689. Exit 242A off I-64. Follow Va 199 E. **Regional American.** Ladder-back chairs, semi-rustic wooden tables and flooring, a fireplace, grandfather clock, ornately framed pictures, large table with candelabra give historic flair to this cozy, cottage-like house. Homemade Virginia specialties offered, including ham biscuits, Brunswick stew. Filling plantation-style breakfast is good value. **FYI:** Reservations not accepted. Beer and wine only. No smoking. **Open:** Breakfast daily 8:30–10:15am; lunch daily 11:30am–2:15pm. Closed some hols; 2 weeks in Jan. **Prices:** Lunch main courses $2.50–$6. Ltd CC. 🍴

★ **Pierce's Pitt Bar-B-Que**, 447 Rochambeau Dr, Williamsburg; tel 804/565-2955. Exit 234A off I-64. Go east on Rochambeau Dr (Access Rd) to restaurant. **Barbecue/Fast food.** Bright orange-and-yellow booths and tables accent this regionally famous barbecue and fast-food restaurant. Consistently good pork barbecue is cooked for 8 hours daily in 4 hardwood-fired

grills and served with Pierce's patented sauce. Chicken, ham, and burgers round out the menu. **FYI:** Reservations not accepted. No liquor license. **Open:** HS Mar–Nov Sun–Thurs 7am–9pm, Fri–Sat 7am–10pm. Reduced hours off-season. Closed some hols. **Prices:** Main courses $2.50–$6. Ltd CC. 📷

The Regency Dining Room, in the Williamsburg Inn, Francis St at South England St, Williamsburg (Historic Area); tel 804/229-1000. Exit 238 off I-64. Follow Va 143 to Va 132; turn right, then left at 3rd traffic light. **Continental.** Has a nice old-fashioned gentility, with courteous, attentive service. Elegant regency decor, tall windows overlooking lawns and gardens, crystal chandeliers, and candle-lit tables. Main dining room is spacious enough to offer ballroom dancing on weekends. Specialties include thinly sliced Smithfield ham with local melon and 5-nut relish; noisettes of lamb loin with spicy polenta crust and vegetable-and-bean casserole; and filet of fresh halibut with shiitake mushrooms and saffron risotto. **FYI:** Reservations recommended. Combo/guitar/harp/piano. Children's menu. Jacket required. **Open:** Breakfast daily 7–10am; lunch daily 11:30am–2pm; dinner daily 6–9pm; brunch Sun 10am–1pm. **Prices:** Main courses $21–$26. Maj CC. 💟 🍴 VP ⌖

Shields Tavern, Duke of Gloucester St, Williamsburg; tel 804/229-2141. Exit 238 off I-64. Go east on Va 143, turn right on Capitol Landing Rd, follow to Page St, turn right on Francis St, parking is on left. **New American/Seafood/Steak.** Another of Colonial Williamsburg's reconstructed 18th-century eateries, with 11 dining rooms outfitted in the colonial style. A Chamber Split bed frame pivots and is stored against the wall. The Shields' Sampler appetizer comprises a variety of tastes from the 1700s. For entrees there are traditional favorites, such as Virginia ham, crab cakes, poached seafood, and spoon bread. **FYI:** Reservations recommended. Guitar/singer. Children's menu. Dress code. No smoking. **Open:** HS Mar–Oct/Dec breakfast Mon–Tues 8:30–10am, Thurs–Sat 8:30–10am; lunch Mon–Tues 11:30am–3pm, Thurs–Sat 11:30am–3pm; dinner Thurs–Tues 5–9:15pm; brunch Sun 10am–2:30pm. Reduced hours off-season. Closed Mid-Feb–Mar. **Prices:** Main courses $16–$24. Maj CC. 🍴

★ **Trellis Cafe, Restaurant & Grill**, in Merchants Sq, Duke of Glucester St, Williamsburg; tel 804/229-8610. Exit 238 off I-64. Va 143 E to Va 132 S to N Henry St to Merchants Sq. **Regional American.** A bustling atmosphere reigns during dinner hours at this casual but upscale eatery, whose different dining areas include a recessed cafe and outdoor patio. Menus change seasonally. The hallmark is creativity and freshness, with seafood and produce delivered daily. Hardly any canned or frozen ingredients are used. Even the ice cream is homemade. Legendary for desserts, owner/chef Marcel Desaulniers is author of *Death by Chocolate* (named for 7-layer extravaganza) and hosts nationwide cable TV cooking program. **FYI:** Reservations recommended. Guitar. Children's menu. **Open:** Lunch Mon–Sat 11am–2:30pm; dinner daily 5–9:30pm; brunch Sun 11am–2:30pm. Closed some hols. **Prices:** Main courses $14–$24. Maj CC. 🖴 ⛴ ✅ ♿

Attractions 🖼

COLONIAL WILLIAMSBURG ATTRACTIONS

Colonial Williamsburg. In 1699 the Virginia Colony abandoned the mosquito-infested swamp that was Jamestown for a planned colonial city 6 miles inland. They named it Williamsburg for the reigning English monarch, King William of Orange.

Royal Governor Francis Nicholson laid out the new capital. His plan alotted every house on the main street a half-acre of land and included public greens. The governor's residence was completed in 1720. The town prospered and soon became the major political and cultural center of Virginia. Many of the turbulent events leading up to the Declaration of Independence occurred here.

The Colonial Williamsburg restoration shows the town as it appeared on the eve of the Revolution. There are 88 original structures, 50 major reconstructions, and 40 exhibition buildings; furnishings come from a 100,000-item collection. Researchers, architects, and archeologists have set a high standard of historical authenticity. The operation is overseen by the Colonial Williamsburg Foundation, an educational organization whose activities include an ongoing restoration.

The **Colonial Williamsburg Visitor Center** is located off US 60 Bypass, just east of Va 132 (tel 804/229-1000). This is where block tickets ($$$$) are purchased for the dozens of attractions that make up Colonial Williamsburg. Attractions are open daily 9am–5pm; some exhibits are open to 7pm in summer. In addition, the center offers shopping opportunities, maps, guidebooks, lodging and dining information, and evening activities, as well as 2 reservation services (one for hotel reservations and one for reservations at the 4 colonial taverns run by the Colonial Williamsburg Foundation). A 35-minute orientation film, *Williamsburg—The Story of a Patriot*, is shown continuously throughout the day.

Governor's Palace. A complete reconstruction, this stately Georgian mansion, the residence and official headquarters of royal governors, is today meticulously furnished with authentic colonial pieces. Tours, given continuously throughout the day, wind up in the gardens, where visitors can explore the elaborate geometric parterres, topiary work, bowling green, and a holly maze patterned after the one at Hampton Court.

The Capitol. Virginia legislators met in the H-shaped capitol at the western end of Duke of Gloucester St throughout most of the 18th century. The original capitol burned down in 1747, was rebuilt in 1753, and succumbed to fire again in 1832. The reconstruction is of the 1704 building, complete with Queen Anne's coat-of-arms adorning the tower and the Great Union flag flying overhead. Tours (about 25 minutes) are given throughout the day.

Raleigh Tavern. Reconstructed on its original site in 1932, using data from inventories of past proprietors and information gleaned from archeological excavations, the tavern occupies a central location on the north side of Duke of Gloucester St. After the Governor's Palace, this was the social and political hub of the town. Named for Sir Walter Raleigh, the original tavern, which burned down in 1859, included 2 dining rooms, the famed Apollo Ballroom (scene of elegant entertainments), a club room, a billiards room, and a bar where ale and hot rum punch were the favored drinks. Present-day visitors can still buy such 18th-century confections as gingerbread and Shrewsbury cake, and cider to wash it down.

Wetherburn's Tavern. Though less important than Raleigh's, Wetherburn's also played an important role in colonial Williamsburg. Henry Wetherburn ran a tavern here from 1738 until his death in 1760. It was subsequently used as a school for young ladies, a boardinghouse, and a store. The heart of yellow pine floors are original, so guests can actually walk in the footsteps of George Washington, who was an occasional patron. A detailed inventory from Wetherburn's day listing the contents of the tavern room by room provided an excellent blueprint for furnishings. Guided tours (25 min) are given throughout the day.

George Wythe House. On the west side of the Palace Green is the elegant restored brick home of George Wythe (pronounced "With")—foremost classics scholar in 18th-century Virginia, noted lawyer and teacher (his students included Thomas Jefferson, Henry Clay, and John Marshall), and member of the House of Burgesses. He was the first Virginia signer of the Declaration of Independence. The house served as Washington's headquarters prior to the siege of Yorktown and Rochambeau's after the surrender of Cornwallis.

Domestic crafts typical of the time are demonstrated by artisans in the outbuildings and are sold at stores in the Historic Area. Evening tours of candlelit shops are available; visitors carry lanterns. The 18th-century crafts practiced on the grounds of Wythe House are among numerous similar exhibits throughout the Historic Area; a total of more than 100 master craftspeople are part of an effort to present an accurate picture of colonial society.

Publick Gaol. The jail opened in 1704; debtors' cells were added in 1711 and keeper's quarters were added in 1722. The thick-walled red-brick building served as the Williamsburg city jail through 1910. The building today is restored to its 1720s appearance.

Peyton Randolph House. The Randolph family was one of the most prominent—and wealthy—in colonial Virginia, and Peyton Randolph was one of its most distinguished members. Known as the "great mediator," he was unanimously elected president of the First Continental Congress in Philadelphia in 1774 and, although he was a believer in nonviolence and hoped the colonies could amicably settle their differences with England, was a firm patriot.

The house (actually 2 connected houses) dates to 1715. It is today restored to the period of about 1770, and is open to the public for self-guided tours with period-costumed interpreters in selected rooms. The windmill, in back of the house, is a post mill of a type popular in the 18th century.

Brush–Everard House. One of the oldest buildings in Williamsburg, the Brush–Everard House was occupied without interruption from 1717 through 1946. It was built by armorer and gunsmith John Brush, although its most distinguished owner was Thomas Everard, two-time mayor of Williamsburg. Though not as wealthy as Wythe or Randolph, Everard was a part of their elite circle. He enlarged the house, adding the 2 wings that give it a "U" shape. Today the home is restored and furnished to its appearance during Everard's residence. The smokehouse and kitchen out back are original. After an introductory talk in the library, visitors can tour the house on their own.

James Geddy House & Silversmith Shop. This 2-story, L-shaped 1762 home is an original building. James Geddy, Sr, was an accomplished gunsmith and brass founder. Visitors to this house will see how a comfortably situated middle-class family lived in the 18th century. Unlike the fancier abodes, the Geddy House has no wallpaper or oil paintings; a mirror and spinet from England, however, indicate relative affluence.

The Magazine and Guardhouse. The magazine is a sturdy octagonal brick building constructed in 1715 to house ammunition and arms for the defense of the British colony. It has survived intact to the present day. Today the building is once again stocked with 18th-century equipment—British-made flintlock muskets, cannons and cannonballs, barrels of powder, bayonets, and drums, the latter for communication purposes.

A 20-minute horse-drawn carriage ride around the Historic Area departs from a horse post at the Courthouse of 1770, just across the street.

Carter's Grove. A magnificent plantation home that has been continuously occupied since 1755 (on a site that was settled over 3½ centuries ago) is one of the most intriguing historical attractions in Virginia. The estate is reached via a scenic, one-way, 7-mile wilderness road traversing streams, meadows, woodlands, and ravines. The road (take South England St and follow the signs) is open 8:30am–4pm; you must return to Williamsburg via Va 60.

Robert "King" Carter, Virginia's wealthiest planter, purchased the 1,400-acre property for his daughter, Elizabeth. Today 700 acres remain. Between 1751 and 1754, Elizabeth's son, Carter Burwell, built the beautiful, 2½-story, 200-foot-long mansion, which is considered "the final phase in the evolution of the Georgian mansion." The West Drawing Room is often called the "Refusal Room"; legend has it that southern belle Mary Cary refused George Washington's proposal of marriage in the room, and Rebecca Burwell said "no" there to Thomas Jefferson.

On the grounds of the mansion are a partially reconstructed 1619 village, **Wolstenholme Town,** slave quarters of the 1700s, and the **Winthrop Rockefeller Archeology Museum** (Rockefeller interests acquired the property in 1963, and since 1969 it has been owned and operated by the Colonial Williamsburg Foundation). At the reception center, housed in a red cedar building, visitors can view a 14-minute slide presentation and examine displays of historic photographs and documents. **Open:** Mid-Mar to late Nov and during Christmas season, Tues–Sun 9am–4pm. $$$

Bassett Hall; tel 804/229-1000, ext 4119. Though colonial in origin, Bassett Hall was the mid-1930s residence of Mr and Mrs John D Rockefeller, Jr, and it is restored and furnished to reflect their era. The mansion's name, however, derives from Burwell Bassett, a nephew of Martha Washington. Bassett lived here from 1800 to 1839.

The Rockefellers purchased the 585-acre property in the late 1920s and moved into the restored dwelling in 1936. In spite of the changes they made, much of the interior is original. The furniture is 18th- and 19th-century American in Chippendale, federal, and empire styles. Hundreds of examples of ceramics and china are on display, as are collections of 18th- and 19th-century American and English glass, Canton enamelware, and folk art.

Forty-minute tours of the house are given between 9am and 4:45pm daily by reservation only. Tours conclude in the garden, which can be explored at leisure.

Abby Aldrich Rockefeller Folk Art Center. The works of folk art displayed at Bassett Hall (above) are just a small sampling of enthusiast Abby Aldrich Rockefeller's extensive collection. This museum contains more than 2,600 folk-art paintings, sculptures, and art objects. The collection includes household ornaments and useful wares (hand-stenciled bed covers, butter molds, pottery, utensils, painted furniture), mourning pictures (embroideries honoring departed relatives or national heroes), family and individual portraits, shop signs, carvings, whittled toys, calligraphic drawings, weavings, quilts, and paintings of scenes from everyday life.

Public Hospital. Opened in 1773, the "Public Hospital for Persons of Insane and Disordered Minds" was America's first mental institution. Before its advent, the mentally ill were often thrown in jail or confined to the poorhouse. The self-guided tour includes a 1773 cell, with its filthy staw-filled mattress on the floor, ragged blanket, and manacles; and an 1845 cell, which shows the vast improvement in patient care that resulted from new attitudes toward the mentally ill during what is known as the "Moral Management Period." The Public Hospital is open daily.

DeWitt Wallace Decorative Arts Gallery. Adjoining the Public Hospital is a 62,000-square-foot museum housing some 8,000 17th- to 19th-century English and American decorative art objects. In its galleries are period furnishings, ceramics, textiles, paintings, prints, silver, pewter, clocks, scientific instruments, mechanical devices, and weapons. The Lila Acheson Wallace Garden, on the upper level, centers on a pond with 2 fountains, a trellis-shaded seating area at one end, and a 6-foot gilded bronze statue of Diana by Augustus Saint-Gaudens at the other.

OTHER ATTRACTIONS

Busch Gardens Williamsburg, 1 Busch Gardens Blvd; tel 804/253-3350. This is a 360-acre family amusement park featuring several re-created 17th-century villages serving as theme areas for a variety of shows, rides, and other amusements. More than 30 rides are offered. A monorail line runs to the Anheuser-Busch Hospitality Center, which offers brewery tours. Themed restaurants and shops in each area. **Open:** Apr to mid-May, Sat–Sun; mid-May to Labor Day, daily; Sept–Oct, Fri–Tues. Phone for specific hours. $$$$

Water Country USA, 1 Water Country Pkwy; tel 804/229-9300. Located near the intersection of I-64 and Va 199; follow signs. Virginia's first water theme park, this facility includes Surfer's Bay, a wave pool the size of 5 Olympic swimming pools that produces a perfect 3½-foot wave every 4 seconds; the Jet Stream, a 450-foot water slide that propels riders at up to 25 mph into a splashdown pool; Run-a-Way Rapids, a tandem tubing Amazon River adventure. Polliwog Pond is an area reserved especially for kids under 12. Also high diving and sea lion shows. **Open:** Early May to mid-Sept, daily, hours vary. $$$$

York River State Park, 5526 Riverview Rd; tel 804/566-3036. Located 8 miles northwest of Williamsburg on I-64, at exit 231B; go 1 mile north on Va 607 to Va 606 and go right 1 mile. This

park is known for its rare and delicate estuarine environment, where fresh and salt water meet to create a habitat rich in marine and plant life. One of four estuaries designated as a part of the Chesapeake Bay National Estuarine Research Reserve is located within the park. Visitor center with exhibits focusing on the history, use, and preservation of the York River and its marshes. Activities include hiking, boating, fishing, and picnicking. **Open:** Daily 8am–dusk. $

WINCHESTER
Map page M-3, B5

Hotels 🛏

Hampton Inn, 1655 Apple Blossom Dr, Winchester, VA 22601; tel 703/667-8011 or toll free 800/HAMPTON; fax 703/667-8033. Exit 313 off I-81. Go west on US 50. A sparkling-clean, tasteful facility with inviting lobby area with tables and chairs. **Rooms:** 103 rms and stes. CI 2pm/CO noon. Nonsmoking rms avail. Comfortable, eye-pleasing rooms. Some offer pull-out sofa, reclining chairs; 1 suite has wet bar, fridge, Murphy bed, and queen-size bed; can double as a meeting room. **Amenities:** 🛁 ⚙ ✑ A/C, cable TV w/movies. Computer jacks available, free movies, hair dryers in most bathrooms. Microwave in lobby. **Services:** ⬜ ⇦ Babysitting. Deluxe continental breakfast served in lobby. Local restaurants will deliver to rooms. **Facilities:** ⚄ ⊡ & Within walking distance of chain restaurants. **Rates (CP):** $42–$46 S; $52–$54 D; from $60 ste. Children under 18 stay free. Higher rates for spec evnts/hols. Pking: Outdoor, free. Maj CC.

Travelodge, 160 Front Royal Pike, Winchester, VA 22602; tel 703/665-0685 or toll free 800/578-7878; fax 703/665-0689. Exit 313 off I-81. A delightful facility with friendly, dedicated staff. Lobby has a genteel mood courtesy of mahogany furniture as well as a separate coffee area with TV and tables with soda-fountain chairs. **Rooms:** 152 rms and stes. CI 2pm/CO 11am. Nonsmoking rms avail. Mahogany furnishings and white brick walls give sparkling rooms a distinctive personality. Suites available that have 2 extra-large rooms, oversize baths, kitchenette, and dining area. **Amenities:** 🛁 ⚙ ⊡ A/C, cable TV, voice mail. Some units w/Jacuzzis. **Services:** ✗ 🛒 ⬜ ⇦ ✑ Continental breakfast in lobby. **Facilities:** ⚄ ⊡ 2 rsts, 1 bar, games rm, washer/dryer. Discounts at nearby Nautilus Club. **Rates (CP):** HS July–Oct $48–$53 S or D; from $95 ste. Extra person $5. Children under 17 stay free. Lower rates off-season. Higher rates for spec evnts/hols. Pking: Outdoor, free. Maj CC.

Motels

≣ **Apple Blossom Motor Lodge**, 2951 Valley Ave, Winchester, VA 22601; tel 703/667-1200 or toll free 800/468-8837; fax 703/667-7128. Exit 310 off I-81. Nicely upholstered furnishings and rich burgundy color scheme create attractive lobby sitting area at this pleasant facility in a commercial area outside of town. **Rooms:** 66 rms. CI 11am/CO noon. Nonsmoking rms avail. Rooms have kings, queens, or doubles; an integrated decor; and framed Civil War pictures. Two rooms for guests with disabilities available. **Amenities:** 🛱 👌 A/C, cable TV w/movies. Some rooms have refrigerators and microwaves. **Services:** ✗ 🖃 ⌐ ⌐ Fax machine available. Safe deposit boxes at desk. Room service during dinner hours. **Facilities:** 🖼 [150] 👌 1 rst, 1 bar. Nicely shaped pool surrounded by umbrella tables. **Rates:** HS Mar–Nov $30–$37 S; $44–$49 D. Extra person $6. Children under 16 stay free. Lower rates off-season. Higher rates for spec evnts/hols. Pking: Outdoor, free. Maj CC. Weekly and monthly rates available.

≣ ≣ **Best Western Lee Jackson Motor Inn**, 711 Millwood Ave, Winchester, VA 22601; tel 703/662-4154 or toll free 800/528-1234; fax 703/662-2618. At jct US 50/522, off I-81. Comfortable rooms and friendly staff here, plus some nice touches like flowers blooming in wooden tubs around the parking lot. **Rooms:** 140 rms and stes. CI 2pm/CO noon. Nonsmoking rms avail. Rooms have a king bed or 2 double beds. **Amenities:** 🛱 A/C, cable TV w/movies. Some units w/Jacuzzis. Many rooms have microwaves and refrigerators. Many deluxe suites have large TVs. **Services:** ✗ 🖨 🖃 ⌐ ⌐ Car-rental desk. **Facilities:** 🖼 [600] 👌 2 rsts, 1 bar, washer/dryer. Grassy pool area is pleasant. Special arrangements for guests at nearby Nautilus Club. **Rates:** HS Apr–Oct $45–$50 S or D; from $65 ste. Extra person $5. Children under 12 stay free. Lower rates off-season. Higher rates for spec evnts/hols. Pking: Outdoor, free. Maj CC.

≣ **Days Inn**, 1601 Martinsburg Pike, Winchester, VA 22603; tel 703/667-4400 or toll free 800/329-7466; fax 703/667-2818. Exit 317 off I-81. Conveniently located right at the interstate, but set back from the highway. Lobby includes sitting area for continental breakfast and comfortable sofa and chairs. **Rooms:** 85 rms. CI 2pm/CO noon. Nonsmoking rms avail. Options are 2 double beds, 1 double bed, or king bed. Small patio sitting area. Textured wallpaper adds richness as well as some bright splashes of color, but rooms could be fresher. **Amenities:** 🛱 A/C, cable TV w/movies. All units w/terraces. Microwaves and refrigerators available. **Services:** ⌐ ⌐ Fax available. Safe deposit boxes at desk. **Facilities:** 🖼 [30] 👌 Washer/dryer. Denny's restaurant next door. Picnic tables outside. Fenced-in, carpeted pool area with umbrella tables is inviting. **Rates (CP):** HS May–Oct $43 S;

$54 D. Extra person $3. Children under 18 stay free. Min stay spec evnts. Lower rates off-season. Higher rates for spec evnts/hols. Pking: Outdoor, free. Maj CC. $10 pet fee.

≣ ≣ **Holiday Inn**, I-81 and US 50 E, Winchester, VA 22601; tel 703/667-3300 or toll free 800/HOLIDAY; fax 703/722-2730. Exit 313A off I-81 N, or 313B off I-81 S. Well-maintained facility with nicely appointed lobby containing sitting area, chandeliers, and mahogany furniture. **Rooms:** 175 rms, stes. CI 3pm/CO noon. Express checkout avail. Nonsmoking rms avail. Pleasant, clean rooms in good condition. Some open onto courtyard pool area. **Amenities:** 🛱 👌 A/C, cable TV w/movies. Some units w/terraces. Coffeemakers available in some rooms. VCRs for rent. Refrigerators available free; 4 queen-bed suites have microwaves and refrigerators. **Services:** ✗ 🖃 ⌐ ⌐ Fax available. **Facilities:** 🖼 🍴2 🎱 [150] 👌 1 rst, 1 bar. Nautilus equipment in fitness center. Inviting pool area with deck, umbrella tables. Nearby golf club offers reduced rate to guests. **Rates:** $47–$71 S or D; from $89 ste. Extra person $6. Children under 18 stay free. Spec packages avail. Pking: Outdoor, free. Maj CC. Some packages include continental breakfast. Golf packages available.

Restaurants 🍴

China Gourmet Restaurant, 210 Millwood Ave, Winchester; tel 703/722-3333. Exit 313 off I-81. Near jct US 50/522. **Chinese.** Padded red booths and pink tablecloths, soft music, and Chinese wall decorations are the backdrop at this small, quiet Chinese restaurant. Staff is friendly and eager, and house specialties are Peking duck and seafood. **FYI:** Reservations recommended. **Open:** Mon–Thurs 11am–10pm, Fri–Sat 11am–10:30pm, Sun 11:30am–9:30pm. **Prices:** Main courses $8.95–$18.95. Ltd CC. 🍴

Yams Family Restaurant, 2011 Valley Ave, Winchester; tel 703/722-4777. Exit 310 off I-81. **American/Chinese.** This Chinese restaurant also offers American fare, such as fried chicken and vegetables. Chinese motif throughout the several dining areas, including one with richly upholstered chairs, chandeliers, hearth. All-you-can-eat buffet daily at lunch and Wednesday dinner. Specialties are General Tso's chicken, seafood bird's nest, prime rib. **FYI:** Reservations accepted. Children's menu. **Open:** Mon–Thurs 11am–9:30pm, Fri–Sat 11am–10:30pm. Closed Dec 25. **Prices:** Main courses $7.55–$17.95. Maj CC.

Attractions 📷

Abram's Delight, 1340 S Pleasant Valley Rd; tel 703/662-6519. Adjoining the Winchester Visitors Center is a native limestone residence built in 1754 by Quaker Isaac Hollingsworth. The house is fully restored and furnished with simple 18th-century pieces. Guided tours (40 minutes). **Open:** Apr–Oct, daily 9am–5pm. Closed Nov–Mar. $$

Stonewall Jackson's Headquarters, 415 N Braddock St; tel 703/667-3242. This Victorian cottage, used by Stonewall Jackson during the winter of 1861–62, is filled with maps, photos, and memorabilia. A must for Civil War buffs. **Open:** Apr–Nov 1, daily 9am–5pm; Nov–Dec, Fri–Sun 9am–5pm; mid-Mar to Mar 31, Fri–Sun 9am–5pm. Closed Jan to mid-Mar. $$

Washington's Office Museum, 32 W Cork St; tel 703/662-4412. Washington's office is a very small log cabin museum with relics of the French and Indian War and other conflicts. **Open:** Apr–Nov, daily 9am–5pm. Closed Dec–Mar. $

Handley Library, 100 W Piccadilly St; tel 703/662-9041. Begun in 1907, from an endowment by Judge John Handley, this beaux-arts-style library was opened to the public in 1912. The building, as designed by New York architects Stewart Barney and Otis Chapman, was meant to represent a book—the rotunda being the spine and the 2 wings the open pages. The rotunda is crowned by a copper-covered dome with glass inside.

An addition to the library was completed in 1979 in an appropriate though distinctly modern style. It won an award from the American Institute of Architects. Major improvements that accompanied construction of the new wing were the creation of a children's room, and an archives room, which contains books, newspapers, and manuscripts dealing with local history. **Open:** Mon–Wed 10am–9pm, Thurs–Sat 10am–5pm. Archives, Tues–Wed 1–9pm, Thurs–Sat 10am–5pm. Closed some hols. Free.

WINTERGREEN

Map page M-3, D5 (S of Waynesboro)

Resort 🏨

≣≣≣≣ **Wintergreen Resort**, , PO Box 706, Wintergreen, VA 22958; tel 804/325-2200 or toll free 800/325-2200; fax 804/325-6760. Exit 107 off I-64W. Follow US 250 W to Va 151 S for 14¼ miles to Va 664. 11,000 acres. A high-quality mountaintop resort with well-tended grounds and immaculate facilities. A relaxed, home-like atmosphere prevails. Wide range of activities. **Rooms:** 320 ctges/villas. CI 4pm/CO noon. Express checkout avail. Only condominiums and apartments available, and each is decorated by its owner, so styles vary. **Amenities:** 🛋 ⦿ 🖥 Cable TV w/movies, refrig. All units w/minibars, all w/terraces, some w/fireplaces, some w/Jacuzzis. **Services:** 🚗⦁ Car-rental desk, social director, masseur, children's program,

babysitting. Ski and snow-boarding equipment rental and lessons available. Linens changed when guests depart. **Facilities:** 🏌 🚴 ⛰ 🏐 ▶36 ⛵ 🎿 🎾 ◗25 ⛳ 650 🖥 ⦿ 6 rsts, 2 bars (1 w/entertainment), lifeguard, games rm, spa, sauna, whirlpool, playground, washer/dryer. Bars have seasonal entertainment. **Rates:** HS Dec 20–Mar 20 from $85 ctge/villa. Children under 18 stay free. Min stay. Lower rates off-season. MAP rates avail. Spec packages avail. Pking: Outdoor, free. Maj CC.

WOODSTOCK

Map page M-3, C5

Hotel 🏨

≣≣ **Ramada Inn**, 1130 Motel Dr, Woodstock, VA 22664; tel 703/459-5000 or toll free 800/2-RAMADA; fax 703/459-8219. 1 mi S of downtown. exit 281 off I-81. A comfortable facility set back from highway. A double fireplace in lobby and antique pieces in the hallway that are appropriate for this country setting in the Shenandoah Valley. **Rooms:** 126 rms. CI 3pm/CO 11am. Express checkout avail. Nonsmoking rms avail. Integrated decor in rooms is pleasing to eye. **Amenities:** 🛋 A/C, cable TV w/movies. **Services:** ✗ 🛄 ⦁ **Facilities:** 🏌 250 ⦿ 1 rst, 1 bar. Restaurant offers daily specials, Sunday brunch. **Rates:** HS June–Oct $44–$54 S; $52–$62 D. Extra person $8. Children under 18 stay free. Lower rates off-season. Higher rates for spec evnts/hols. Spec packages avail. Pking: Outdoor, free. Maj CC. Ski packages in season.

Inn 🏨

≣≣≣ **Inn at Narrow Passage**, US 11 S, Woodstock, VA 22664; tel 703/459-8000; fax 703/459-8001. Exit 283 off I-81. 5 acres. This early American log inn was once Stonewall Jackson's headquarters and is impeccably restored with antiques, hand-crafted colonial reproductions, and fireplaces, all in a rustic atmosphere. Rustic log-cabin lobby with comfy sitting area, games, and refrigerator; porches; and chairs under shade trees add to peaceful setting. **Rooms:** 12 rms. CI 2pm/CO 11am. No smoking. Beautifully presented, spotless, and country-fresh, each room is different. A country flavor is created by 4-poster canopy beds and pine furnishings. Nonsmoking rooms only. **Amenities:** 🛋 ⦿ A/C. Some units w/terraces, some w/fireplaces. **Services:** ✗ ⦁ Ice delivered to rooms. Lemonade or hot cider served on the back porch in season. When time permits, an employee will help guests fly-cast in the river. **Facilities:** 25 1 rst. Cozy dining area for guests only. **Rates (BB):** $75–$95 S w/shared bath, $85–$110 S w/private bath. Extra person $8. Pking: Outdoor, free. Ltd CC.

WYTHEVILLE

Map page M-2, E3

Motels 🛏

≣≣ **Best Western Wytheville Inn**, 355 Nye Rd, Wytheville, VA 24382; tel 703/228-7300 or toll free 800/528-1234; fax 703/228-4223. Exit 41 off I-77 or exit 72 off I-81. A homey atmosphere prevails at this motel, whose exceptionally quiet, well-landscaped grounds afford fine views of the Blue Ridge. **Rooms:** 100 rms and stes. CI 2pm/CO noon. Nonsmoking rms avail. **Amenities:** 🛏 A/C, cable TV w/movies. **Services:** 🖵 🖘 **Facilities:** 🖪 20 & **Rates (CP):** $38–$48 S; $45–$54 D; from $85 ste. Extra person $6. Children under 18 stay free. Higher rates for spec evnts/hols. Spec packages avail. Pking: Outdoor, free. Maj CC.

≣≣ **Days Inn**, 150 Malin Dr, Wytheville, VA 24382; tel 703/228-5500 or toll free 800/325-2525; fax 703/228-6301. Exit 73 off I-81 and I-77. Location near 2 major interstates makes this a popular spot. **Rooms:** 118 rms. Exec-level rms avail. CI 3pm/CO noon. Nonsmoking rms avail. Recently renovated, rooms offer views of the surrounding mountains. **Amenities:** 🛏 A/C, cable TV w/movies. **Services:** 🖵 🖘 Complimentary morning coffee and donuts. **Facilities:** & Games rm. Two restaurants, including a local favorite, are just steps away. **Rates:** HS Mar–Nov 15 $42–$48 S; $44–$50 D. Extra person $5. Children under 18 stay free. Lower rates off-season. Higher rates for spec evnts/hols. Spec packages avail. Pking: Outdoor, free. Maj CC.

≣≣ **HoJo Inn**, 120 Lithia Rd, at I-77 and I-81, Wytheville, VA 24382; tel 703/228-3188 or toll free 800/446-4656; fax 703/228-6458. Exit 73 off I-81. Extremely scenic location with excellent views of surrounding mountains is also convenient to 2 major interstates, many restaurants. **Rooms:** 100 rms. CI 2pm/CO noon. Nonsmoking rms avail. **Amenities:** 🛏 A/C, cable TV w/movies. All units w/terraces. Breezy patios with tables and chairs face the mountain panorama. **Services:** 🖵 🖘 **Facilities:** 🖪 **Rates:** HS Apr–Sept $55–$60 S or D. Extra person $6. Children under 18 stay free. Lower rates off-season. Higher rates for spec evnts/hols. Spec packages avail. Pking: Outdoor, free. Maj CC.

≣≣≣ **Ramada Inn**, 955 Pepper's Ferry Rd, Wytheville, VA 24382; tel 703/228-6000 or toll free 800/272-6232 in the US, 800/854-7854 in Canada; fax 703/228-6000 ext 151. Exit 41 off I-77 or exit 72 off I-81. Although just minutes from a highway and a popular outlet mall, this motel enjoys a rural location with refreshing views of pastures and mountains. **Rooms:** 154 rms. CI 2pm/CO noon. Express checkout avail. Nonsmoking rms avail.

Units are exceptionally secure and well soundproofed. **Amenities:** 🛏 🔈 A/C, cable TV w/movies. **Services:** ✕ 🖵 🖘 Babysitting. **Facilities:** 🖪 200 & 1 rst, 1 bar, washer/dryer. Lounge and adjoining bar are quiet and soothing. **Rates:** HS May 15–Nov $52–$65 S; $65 D. Extra person $5. Children under 19 stay free. Min stay spec evnts. Lower rates off-season. Higher rates for spec evnts/hols. Spec packages avail. Pking: Outdoor, free. Maj CC.

Restaurant 🍽

★ **Scrooge's**, in Scrooge's Village, Holston Rd, Wytheville; tel 703/228-6622. Exit 70 off I-81. **American/Continental.** Wood-paneled, English-style interior with soft lighting and brass and burgundy accents. This popular, casual diner has moderate prices and comfortable, understated elegance. Spaciousness adds to relaxed dining. Steaks, seafood, and lighter fare. **FYI:** Reservations recommended. Children's menu. **Open:** Mon–Fri 5–10pm, Sat–Sun 5–11pm. Closed some hols. **Prices:** Main courses $7–$17. Maj CC. &

YORKTOWN

Map page M-3, E7

Motel 🛏

≣≣ **Duke of York Motor Inn**, 508 Water St, PO Box E, Yorktown, VA 23690; tel 804/898-3232; fax 804/898-5922. On the Yorktown waterfront, at Ballard St. This independently owned motel is on the York River waterfront, in historic Yorktown. The view takes in the Coleman Bridge and Coleman Point. Rocky beach is available for sunbathing only, since river is closed to swimmers. **Rooms:** 57 rms. CI 2pm/CO noon. Nonsmoking rms avail. The property slopes, so some units have better views than others. Freshly renovated, rooms have rich teal carpet, dark-finished traditional furniture. **Amenities:** 🛏 A/C, cable TV. Some units w/terraces. Rooms with balconies have outdoor chairs. **Facilities:** 🖪 & 1 rst, 1 beach (cove/inlet). Restaurant open for breakfast and lunch. **Rates:** HS June–Aug $54–$64 S; $64 D. Extra person $6. Min stay spec evnts. Lower rates off-season. Higher rates for spec evnts/hols. Pking: Outdoor, free. Maj CC.

Restaurant 🍽

★ **Nick's Seafood Pavilion**, Water St at Buckner St, Yorktown; tel 804/887-5269. On the Yorktown waterfront. **Greek/Seafood/Steak.** Worth a visit for the eclectic decor at this regionally known Greek seafood restaurant on the Yorktown waterfront.

Pink tablecloths and napkins, bright-aqua domed ceiling, old chandeliers and ornately framed mirrors, wait staff dressed in bolero vests and small round hats all create festive ambience. Floor has large tiles in tan and terra-cotta colors. Statues and plants abound. Seafood kabobs include lobster, shrimp, and scallops. Some seafood is fresh catch. Greek selections too. **FYI:** Reservations not accepted. Children's menu. **Open:** Daily 11am–10pm. Closed Dec 25. **Prices:** Main courses $8–$20. Maj CC. ■ ▦ ♿

Attractions ■

COLONIAL NATIONAL HISTORICAL PARK

Yorktown Battlefield. Located 14 miles NE of Williamsburg on Colonial Pkwy. Yorktown was the setting for the last major battle of the American Revolution. The siege of Yorktown began on September 28, 1781, when American and French troops under Washington occupied a line encircling the town within a mile of the army led by Cornwallis. When Cornwallis evacuated almost all of his forward positions in order to concentrate his forces closer to town, Washington was able to move his men to within 1,000 yards of British lines. Soon, British defeat became inevitable. On October 16, following a last-ditch and fruitless attempt to launch an attack, Cornwallis tried to escape with his troops across the York River to Gloucester Point, but a violent storm scattered his ships. The next day, the British signaled their desire to discuss terms for surrender.

The **Yorktown Battlefield Visitor Center** (tel 804/ 898-3400) screens a 16-minute documentary, *Siege at Yorktown*. Museum displays include Washington's actual headquarters tent, exhibits on Cornwallis's surrender and the events leading up to it, and dioramas detailing the siege. A sound and light show gives an "on-the-scene" account of the battle from the viewpoint of a 13-year-old soldier in the Continental army.

Auto tours following the 7.7-mile Red Route and the 10.2-mile Yellow Route begin at the visitor center. Tourists are given a map, and cassette tapes and players presenting informative narratives and commentary may be rented. See the following entries for highlights of the tour.

Each year on October 19, the anniversary of the British surrender, Yorktown Battlefield is the scene of ceremonies, exercises, and festivities commemorating the final battle of the Revolution. **Open:** Daily 8:30am–sunset; visitor center, daily 9am–5pm. Closed Dec 25. Free.

Grand French Battery. From this area, in the French section of Washington's first siege line, French soliders manning cannons, mortars, and howitzers fired on British and German mercenary troops.

Moore House. When Lord Cornwallis realized the inevitability of his defeat, he sent a message to Gen Washington: "Sir, I propose a cessation of hostilities for 24 hours, and that two officers may be appointed by each side, to meet at Mr Moore's house to settle terms for the surrender of the posts of Yorktown and Gloucester." Washington granted Cornwallis just 2 hours to submit general terms. Representatives from both armies met in this house on the afternoon of October 18, 1781.

The house was pretty much abandoned (even used as a cow barn) until John D Rockefeller, Jr, purchased it in 1931 and the National Park Service restored it to its colonial appearance. It is today furnished with period pieces, some of which are believed to have been in the house during the surrender negotiations. **Open:** June–Oct 19, daily 10am–5pm; fall and spring, daily 1–5pm. Free.

Surrender Field. Here the imagination can evoke the images of the British march out of Yorktown. From here, the Yellow Route leads to the sites of Washington's and Rochambeau's headquarters, a French cemetery and artillery park, and allied encampment sites.

Yorktown Victory Center; tel 804/887-1776. Located 1 mile south via Old Va 238. Set on 21 acres overlooking part of the battlefield of 1781, the center offers an excellent orientation to Yorktown attractions, including a film, a living history program, and museum exhibits. Visitors follow a timeline walkway, "Road to Revolution," to the main building. Exhibits located in pavilions along the way illustrate the relationship between the colonies and Britain beginning in 1750. The timeline ends inside the main building with an exhibit on the first battles of the war and a 12-foot-tall copy of the Declaration of Independence.

In the outdoor **Continental Army Camp,** costumed interpreters re-create the lives of men and women who took part in the siege of Yorktown. Another outdoor exhibit, the **Farmsite,** provides an insight into what life was like for a small planter starting over after the Revolution.

The Road to Yorktown, an evocative 28-minute documentary film produced by David Wolper, follows the movement of Generals Washington and Rochambeau and documents the final grueling days of the Revolution. **Open:** Daily 9am–5pm. Closed some hols. $$

Cornwallis Cave. According to legend, Gen Cornwallis lived here in 2 tiny "rooms" during the final days of the Yorktown siege. The 2 rooms were carved out by various occupants of the cave—which tradition says included the pirate Blackbeard. Confederate soldiers later enlarged the shelter and added a roof. A taped narrative at the entrance tells the story. The cave is at the foot of Great Valley, right on the river.

Dudley Digges House. This restored 18th-century white weatherboard house, located at Main and Smith Sts, is a private residence and may only be viewed from the outside. Its dormer windows set in the roofline and other features, as well as the surrounding outbuildings, are typical of Virginia architecture in the mid-1700s. Owner Dudley Digges was a Revolutionary patriot who served with Patrick Henry, Benjamin Harrison, and Thomas Jefferson on the Committee of Correspondence.

Grace Episcopal Church, Church St; tel 804/898-3261. Located on Church St near the river, Grace Church dates back to 1697 and has been an active house of worship since then. Gunpowder and ammunition were stored here during the siege of Yorktown. During the Civil War, the church served as a hospital. The original communion silver, made in England in 1649, is still in use. Thomas Nelson, Jr, a signer of the Declaration of Independence, is buried in the adjacent graveyard. **Open:** Daily 9am–5pm. Free.

Nelson House, Nelson and Main Sts. Scottish merchant Thomas ("Scotch Tom") Nelson was a prosperous planter, landowner, and owner of the Swan Tavern (see below) by the time he died in 1745. He left a vast estate, which his descendants—including several prominent Revolutionary leaders, one of them a signer of the Declaration of Independence—further enlarged. In 1814, when fire struck the town, church services were temporarily held in the house. During the gala event of Lafayette's visit to Yorktown, the general lodged here.

Though damaged (cannonballs remain embedded in the brickwork), the house survived the Battle of Yorktown and was even seized by Cornwallis, who used it as a command post during part of his occupation. Nelson's descendants continued to occupy the house until 1907. The National Park Service acquired the house in 1968 and restored it to its original appearance. Ranger-guided tours take 30 to 45 minutes. **Open:** Summer, daily 10am–4:30pm; phone ahead for schedule fall–spring. Free.

Sessions House. Just across from the Nelson House, this is the oldest house in Yorktown, built in 1692 by Thomas Sessions. At least 5 US presidents have visited the house. It is a private residence and not open to the public.

Swan Tavern; tel 804/898-3033. For over a century the Swan Tavern, at the corner of Main and Ballard Sts, was Yorktown's leading hostelry. Originally owned by Thomas Nelson, it was in operation 20 years before Williamsburg's famous Raleigh. The Swan was demolished in 1863 by an ammunition explosion at the courthouse across the street, rebuilt, and destroyed again by fire in 1915. Today it is reconstructed as per historical research, and the premises house an antique shop. **Open:** Hours vary; phone ahead.

The Customhouse; tel 804/898-4788. Dating to 1721, this sturdy brick building at the corner of Main and Read was originally the private warehouse of Richard Ambler, collector of ports. It became Gen J B Magruder's headquarters during the Civil War. Today it is maintained by the Daughters of the American Revolution as a museum. **Open:** Weekends only; phone for hours.

Victory Monument, Main St. News of the victory at Yorktown reached Philadelphia on October 24, 1781. On October 29 the Continental Congress resolved "that the United States . . . will cause to be erected at York, in Virginia, a marble column, adorned with emblems of the alliance between the United States and his Most Christian Majesty; and inscribed with a succinct narrative of the surrender of Earl Cornwallis to his excellency General Washington, Commander in Chief of the combined forces of America and France . . . "

The highly symbolic 98-foot marble shaft overlooking the York River was completed in 1884. The podium is adorned with 13 female figures hand in hand in a solemn dance to denote the unity of the 13 colonies; beneath their feet is the inscription ONE COUNTRY, ONE CONSTITUTION, ONE DESTINY. Its stars represent the "constellation" of states in the Union in 1881. Atop the shaft is the figure of Liberty.

WEST VIRGINIA

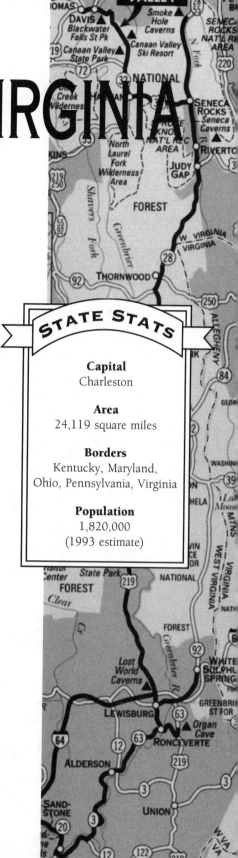

THE MOUNTAIN STATE

In West Virginia it's possible to find some elements of the plantation south, the agricultural midwest, and the industrial northeast. And yet the state is singularly its own. Its most characteristic feature is the mountains that give it its nickname. Part of the ancient Appalachian chain, the mountains roll from one end of the state to the other, covered with forests and sliced through with rivers and streams.

Over the course of its history, people have been drawn to West Virginia because of the natural riches both above and below its surface. Fortunes have been made extracting coal and natural gas from below ground and hauling lumber from the hills. Still, about three-quarters of the state remains forested, with a million or so acres set aside in national and state forests, parks, and recreation areas.

Combine all that natural endowment with a continuing effort to preserve it in its unspoiled state and the result is a scenic grandeur that is not only wonderful to behold, but also a challenge to the sports minded. West Virginia has the best white-water rafting in the eastern United States and the best skiing south of New England. It has a host of trails that hikers, bikers, and horseback riders can follow along rivers, over old covered bridges, and through old railroad tunnels deep into the heart of the wilderness.

The state also has more urbane attractions. If restored towns, historic homes, and period rooms are your cup of tea, there are plenty of relics from the colonial era, Civil War days, and the early 20th century. The state has gracious inns and luxury resort spas as well as ubiquitous campgrounds. It also has a busy calendar of events to keep its rich heritage alive and acquaint visitors with its people and their crafts and customs. You can come back from your trip with a suitcase stuffed with handmade quilts, art glass, and apple butter and a head full of lingering country tunes.

West Virginia remains a mostly rural state, a place where the stunning beauty of nature can be enjoyed for its own sake or put to practical use in a host of outdoor recreation pursuits. It's also a state where you'll find the colorful history of a proud people carefully preserved in ways in which even the jaded traveler can rejoice. You'll see for yourself when you get there.

STATE STATS

Capital
Charleston

Area
24,119 square miles

Borders
Kentucky, Maryland,
Ohio, Pennsylvania, Virginia

Population
1,820,000
(1993 estimate)

A BRIEF HISTORY

ANCIENT TIMES   For Native American hunters who roamed the Ohio and Kanawha Valleys as early as 15,000 years ago, the region's wealth was in its teaming game and fish. Hundreds of Native American burial mounds have survived, dating back to about 100 BC.

Just as West Virginia served as a vast hunting ground for them, it did as well for English explorers in the 1600s. European settlement was delayed until the early 18th century, however, because of the rugged mountains and Native American hostility.

EARLY SETTLERS   In 1731, a man named Morgan Morgan arrived in Berkeley County and became the first European to build a permanent home in the area which was then part of Virginia. The next year, German families from Pennsylvania founded the town of New Mecklenberg, now Shepherdstown. Other colonists soon began settling farther south and west.

PIONEER LIFE   Products from the east could not easily reach this mountainous remote area, so those early settlers were self-reliant. By 1800, however, some small industries had begun, and soon Ohio River steamboats and the opening of the National Pike brought boom times and turned Wheeling into a manufacturing center.

A STATE IS BORN   Settlers in the western part of the state, unhappy with the eastern planters who controlled the far-away state government and paid little heed to their needs out on the frontier, had talked of separating from Virginia as early as 1820.

When Virginia seceded from the Union in 1861, its 26 western counties declared the secession void, adopted a plan to abolish slavery, and applied to Congress for admission to the Union as a separate state. President Abraham Lincoln signed the statehood bill on June 20, 1863. (After the Civil War, Virginia tried to get West Virginia back, but the response of the state whose official motto is *Montani semper liberi*—Mountaineers are always free—was, more or less, "Nothing doing.")

West Virginia was not a major battlefield during the Civil War, but because its border land was prized by both sides, it saw its share of skirmishes. The engagement at Phillippi in June 1861 began campaigns that gave Union forces control of northwestern Virginia, while the Eastern Gateway and Greenbrier Valley continued to be held by the Confederates.

INTO THE PRESENT   Completion of the Baltimore and Ohio Railroad to Wheeling in 1853 had laid the groundwork for West Virginia to prosper after the war. Coal mines were opened and other natural resources were discovered. Towns along the Ohio soon doubled in size. By the 1890s, railroads covered the state, and job-seeking immigrants had arrived to mine the coal upon which both the state and its economy rested. In the 1920s, there were bitter, often violent struggles for workers' right to organize themselves into unions.

The still-thriving chemical industry of the Kanawha Valley began during World War I. During World War II, Charleston was one of the single greatest centers of wartime production in the United States. Although the coal industry declined after the war, other industries—such as glass—grew. Today, mining has again become viable, but tourism—in a state with abundant parkland—is increasing in importance.

◆§ *Fun Facts* §◆

• *West Virginia was conceived when Union loyalists in the western counties of Virginia, angered by Virginia's secession, convened in Wheeling in 1861 and signed a "Declaration of Independence" from Virginia. Statehood was granted on June 20, 1863.*

• *Pearl S Buck, the only American woman to win both the Pulitzer and the Nobel Prizes for Literature, was born in Hillsboro in 1892.*

• *The legendary Greenbrier resort in White Sulphur Springs, one of America's oldest existing grand hotels, has been a vacation spot for 33 US presidents since its establishment in the early 19th century.*

• *West Virginia is home to the largest conical earthen mound in North America. The Adena Indian burial mound, 69 feet high and 900 feet in circumference at its base, was constructed in stages from 250 to 150 BC.*

• *The first Mother's Day service was held at Andrews Methodist Church in Grafton on May 10, 1908.*

A Closer Look

Geography

Vast forests, deep gorges, pristine wildernesses, roiling white water, and wooded trails combine to give the "Mountain State" a wild and free natural beauty, its scenic wonders still largely unspoiled by economic development.

The **Eastern Gateway** sticks out like a panhandle between Maryland and the Potomac River to the north and Virginia and the Shenandoah River to the south, affording easy access to the Appalachian Trail, the Chesapeake and Ohio Canal National Historical Park, warm mineral springs, and white-water rafting.

The town of Harpers Ferry, only 60 miles from Washington, DC, draws an increasing number of urbanites seeking a bit of country on the weekend or a home away from the bustle of the city.

Southwest of this gateway, the **Potomac Highlands,** up in the Allegheny Mountains, is a booming outdoor recreation area year-round. The Monongahela National Forest stretches over most of the area, and the Allegheny Trail and the powerful Cheat River both wind through it. The wild Gauley River begins here, and the Greenbrier, the longest free-flowing river in the East, runs the length of Pocahontas County. Thousands of musicians and dancers come to **Elkins,** the largest town in the highlands, for its celebrated music workshops and festivals.

In the central **Mountain Lakes** region, you'll have more luck shopping for bait and locally made glass than you will finding a neon sign proclaiming a nightspot. What you will find are 7 lakes, 2 state parks, and 5 impressive trout streams.

Mountaineer Country in the north has both old-time coal commerce and agrarian charm, and the state university at Morgantown. **Fairmont** has coal, and the Monongahela River to transport it. Tradition runs deep in the **Clarksburg-Bridgeport** area, with a year-round calendar of living-history programs.

The narrow **Northern Panhandle,** wedged between Pennsylvania and Ohio, is bordered on the west by the Ohio River, whose scenic waterfront ensures that cities like **Wheeling** remain hubs of activity. The West Virginia Border Islands, a series of Ohio River islands, some only a few yards from towns and cities, comprise the state's first national wildlife refuge.

DRIVING DISTANCES:

Charleston

- 56 miles E of Huntington
- 112 miles NW of Bluefield
- 164 miles SW of Wheeling
- 221 miles SW of Pittsburgh, PA
- 331 miles NW of Richmond, VA
- 339 miles NW of Charlotte, NC
- 380 miles SW of Washington, DC

Wheeling

- 60 miles SW of Pittsburgh, PA
- 164 miles NE of Charleston
- 193 miles NE of Huntington
- 229 miles NE of Beckley
- 292 miles NW of Washington, DC
- 347 miles NW of Richmond, VA
- 504 miles N of Charlotte, NC

Bluefield

- 112 miles SE of Charleston
- 197 miles SE of Huntington
- 261 miles NW of Charlotte, NC
- 262 miles SW of Richmond, VA
- 310 miles SW of Washington, DC
- 341 miles SW of Pittsburgh, PA

Huntington

- 56 miles W of Charleston
- 112 miles NW of Beckley
- 193 miles SW of Wheeling
- 197 miles NW of Bluefield
- 277 miles SW of Pittsburgh, PA
- 436 miles SW of Washington, DC

The **Mid-Ohio** region, with its hills rising from the state's western border, the Ohio River, eastward toward the heartland of the state, drew adventurers and pioneers in its early days. Their tradition of self-sufficiency survives in a wealth of crafts shops, centers, and fairs throughout the region's 7 counties. **Parkersburg** is here, a riverfront hub of commercial and cultural activity.

Major cities like the university town of Huntington and the riverfront capital city of **Charleston** dominate the far southwestern **Metro Valley.** The greater Charleston area includes many small towns and communities in the Kanawha Valley. Farther south is "Coal Country" and the town of **Matewan,** site of an infamous anti-union massacre during West Virginia's "Mine Wars" early in the century.

Rivers, mountains, coal, and railroads are the key to the southern **New River–Greenbrier Valley.** The New River takes on the Greenbrier River here before plunging into the famous boulder-strewn New River Gorge, one of the most popular white-water rafting destinations in the eastern United States. And the healing waters of White Sulphur Springs bubble up from the earth here. The coal industry operates along the southernmost border—the view at Bluefield is likely to be of railroad cars carrying black rock.

Climate

The state's climate is generally humid, with hot summers and cool-to-cold winters. Temperatures rarely top 90°F in the mountains, and winters are seldom bitterly cold except at the highest elevations.

Rainfall is moderate throughout the state. Annual snowfall can be 10 feet to 15 feet in some higher areas.

What to Pack

The seasons won't fool you in West Virginia. Bring shorts for summer, mittens for winter, sweaters for fall, and rainwear for spring. In the mountains and forests you'll appreciate long pants and jackets even in summer. It's a casual state that emphasizes outdoor recrea-tion, so pack accordingly. Unless you're heading for a ritzy resort or a metropolitan area, you won't need a dressy outfit. Other handy things to pack are a folding umbrella, travel alarm, good walking shoes or boots, sunglasses, and, in summer, insect repellent.

Tourist Information

Contact the **West Virginia Division of Tourism and Parks,** State Capitol, Charleston, WV 25305 (tel toll free 800-CALL WVA) for the free *West Virginia: It's You* magazine-format travel guide; booklets on state parks, lodging, and activities ranging from golf to white-water rafting; and guides to the larger counties. Each of the state's 8 regions has its own visitors bureau listed in the state guide.

Welcome centers provide information on US 340 at Harpers Ferry and at the Capitol in Charleston. **State information centers** are on I-64 at White Sulphur Springs and Huntington; on I-77 at Mineral Wells; on I-70 at Valley Grove; and on I-79 at Morgantown.

Driving Rules & Regulations

The Interstate speed limit is 65 mph unless otherwise posted. The driver and front-seat passengers must wear seat belts. Children from 3 to 9 years old must wear seat belts whether in the back or front seat; children under 3 must ride in an approved child safety seat. Approved safety helmets for both motorcycle driver and passenger are required.

	Romney	Canaan Valley	Beckley	Charleston
AVERAGE MONTHLY TEMPERATURES (°F) & INCHES OF RAINFALL				
Jan	28/2.2	25/4.1	29/2.9	32/2.9
Feb	32/2.1	28/3.7	32/2.9	35/3.0
Mar	41/2.9	37/4.6	42/3.4	46/3.6
Apr	51/2.0	46/4.3	51/3.4	55/3.3
May	61/3.4	55/4.9	59/3.9	63/3.9
June	69/3.2	62/4.8	66/3.8	71/3.6
July	73/3.7	65/4.9	70/4.7	75/4.9
Aug	72/3.2	64/4.5	69/3.8	74/4.0
Sept	65/3.0	58/3.9	63/3.3	68/3.2
Oct	54/2.8	48/3.7	52/2.8	56/2.9
Nov	44/2.8	39/4.2	43/2.9	47/3.6
Dec	34/2.2	29/4.1	34/3.2	37/3.4

Renting a Car

Major car-rental companies are represented in the larger cities; your travel agent can help you find the best deal. Here are their toll-free numbers:

- **Avis** (tel 800/831-2847)
- **Budget** (tel 800/527-0700)
- **Enterprise** (tel 800/325-8007)
- **Hertz** (tel 800/654-3131)
- **National** (tel 800/227-7368)
- **Thrifty** (tel 800/367-2277)

Essentials

Area Code: The area code for the entire state is **304.**

Emergencies: Call **911** in most counties; for highway questions or emergencies, call 304/558-3028.

Liquor Laws: The drinking age is 21; alcohol is sold at licensed private stores and at some convenience stores.

Taxes: The West Virginia sales tax is 6%. In addition, some municipalities may impose lodging taxes up to 3%.

Time Zone: All of West Virginia is in the Eastern time zone. Daylight saving time (one hour earlier than EST) is in effect from the first Sunday of April until the last Sunday in October.

BEST OF THE STATE
What to See & Do

THE GREAT OUTDOORS Three-fourths of this state is forest, much of it showcased in state parks and forests and the **Monongahela National Forest.** In this land, mountains burst with wildflowers and migratory birds in the spring, and hiking trails wind above swift rivers. Visit the windswept moor of **Dolly Sods Wilderness,** travel the **Greenbrier River Trail**—by bike or foot, and view the 60-foot falls at **Blackwater Falls State Park.** With 2,000 miles of mountain streams alone, West Virginia offers water pleasures in abundance. The beauty of the New River is unmatched, as can be ascertained by standing atop the New River Gorge Bridge, the largest single-arch span bridge in the world.

HISTORIC BUILDINGS & SITES The largest conical Indian burial mound in North America, about 2,000 years old, is at **Grave Creek Mound State Park,** a national historic landmark in the northern panhandle. **Harpers Ferry,** where abolitionist John Brown raided a federal arsenal in 1859 in order to arm a slave rebellion, is now a national historical park. A peaceful town of restored homes and shops, it is the state's most visited attraction.

Numerous towns—**Shepherdstown, Bethany, Wellsburg, Charleston**—have historic districts of more than passing architectural interest. In addition, Charleston has the **State Capitol,** a magnificent structure designed by Cass Gilbert in 1932 and topped by a 293-foot gold dome. The 18th- and 19th-century buildings of **Lewisburg** are a national historic district; nearby, at White Sulphur Springs, is **The Greenbrier Resort,** also a national historic landmark. The springs, discovered in 1778, still provide healing waters. West Virginia also has the nation's first spa, established in 1776 as the town of Bath but now known as **Berkeley Springs.**

Wheeling has a generous supply of Victorian-era residential and commercial buildings, as well as the **Wheeling Suspension Bridge,** the longest suspension bridge in the world when it was built in 1849. The state also has a wealth of old covered bridges, from the 24-foot **Laurel Creek Covered Bridge** (1910) to the 148-foot **Barrackville Covered Bridge** (1853).

FAMILY FAVORITES In addition to family excursions in white-water rafts, children will love cruising on the old sternwheelers that ply the Ohio between Wheeling and Huntington. The **Cass Historic District** is a turn-of-the-century lumber town, and in summer, you can ride from the town up to Bald Knob, the state's 2nd-highest peak, aboard the **Cass Scenic Railroad,** which preserves the steam locomotives and logging cars that used to haul lumber to the mill. Another vintage train, the **Potomac Eagle,** operates on wilderness trips along the South Branch of the Potomac, from Romney to Petersburg; spotting eagles en route is part of the fun. Kids also enjoy Wheeling's 65-acre **Oglebay Park Zoo,** including the planetarium.

MOUNTAIN STATE FOLKLORE The state's folk culture thrives in a multitude of arts and crafts shows and festivals. From mid-July to mid-August in Elkins, you can study quilt-making or old-time fiddling at the **Augusta Heritage Arts Workshops,** week-long classes in traditional Appalachian music, dance, and crafts taught by master musicians and artisans. You can also revel in the state's rich heritage at Charleston's **Vandalia Gathering** over Memorial Day weekend— music, dance, storytelling, a quilt show, even a liar's contest are part of this event. Or sing along with country-music greats at Wheeling's **Capitol Music Hall,** or tune into *Jamboree USA,* America's oldest live country music program, broadcast over WWVA in Wheeling. In July, *Jamboree USA* presents an outdoor **Jamboree in the Hills,** the "Super Bowl" of country music.

Events/Festivals

A month-by-month listing of activities, *West Virginia: It's You,* is available from the Division of Tourism (see "Tourist Information," above).

- **Mountain State 25K Cross-Country Ski Marathon,** Davis. Race through Monongahela National Forest to Blackwater Falls State Park. Late January. Call 304/866-4114.
- **Rendezvous on the River,** Parkersburg. Muzzleloaders and mountain men set up a primitive encampment at Blennerhassett Island. 1st weekend in May. Call 304/428-3000.
- **Greenbrier Trail Bike Trek,** Cass to Ronceverte. Sponsored by the American Lung Association of West Virginia. Mid-May. Call toll free 800/LUNG USA.
- **Webster County Woodchopping Festival,** Webster Springs. Week prior to Memorial Day. Call 304/847-7666.
- **Vandalia Gathering,** Charleston. Music, dancing, craft shows, and other events celebrate the state's multiple heritages. Memorial Day weekend. Call 304/558-0220.
- **National Pike Festival,** Wheeling. Wagons retrace the trek along the National Road from Pennsylvania to the Ohio River. Memorial Day weekend. Call toll free 800/828-3097.
- **Dandelion Festival,** White Sulphur Springs. Dandelion wine, arts and crafts. Memorial Day weekend. Call toll free 800/284-9440.

- **Mountain State Arts and Crafts Fair,** Ripley. Late June–early July. Call 304/372-7866.
- **Jamboree in the Hills,** Wheeling. Country stars from *Jamboree USA* perform outdoors. Mid-July. Call toll free 800/624-5456.
- **Gauley Bridge Anniversary and Civil War Days,** Gauley Bridge. Battle reenactment and pageantry. Early August. Call 304/632-2504.
- **Augusta Heritage Festival,** Elkins. Concerts with folk musicians, jam sessions, crafts exhibits, winding up the Augusta Heritage Arts Workshops. Mid-August. Call 304/636-1903.
- **Appalachian Arts and Crafts Festival,** Beckley. Juried art show, southern West Virginia's largest quilt show. Last full weekend in August. Call 304/252-7328.
- **Sternwheel Regatta Festival,** Charleston. Top entertainment, sternwheel paddleboat races, parades. Late August–early September. Call 304/348-6419.
- **Stonewall Jackson Heritage Arts and Crafts Jubilee,** Weston. Civil War battle reenactments and other events. Labor Day weekend. Call 304/269-1863.
- **Mason-Dixon Festival,** Morgantown. River regatta, events along the Monongahela. September. Call 304/599-1104.
- **Apple Butter Festival,** Berkeley Springs. Crafts, music, home cooking, and apple butter made in the streets. Columbus Day weekend in October. Call 304/258-3738.
- **Bridge Day,** Fayetteville. Jumpers parachute from New River Gorge Bridge. Crafts and music. 3rd Saturday in October. Call 304/465-5617.
- **Old Tyme Christmas,** Harpers Ferry. Period decorations, festivities. First 2 weekends in December. Call 304/725-8019, or toll free 800/848-TOUR.

Spectator Sports

AUTO RACING   Summit Point Raceway, outside Charles Town (tel 304/725-8444), is an important location on the SCC-MARRs circuit, offering Grand Prix–style racing. The **West Virginia Motor Speedway,** south of Parkersburg (tel 304/489-1889), is considered one of the best dirt tracks in the nation.

BASEBALL While there are no big-league professional teams in the state, the Cincinnati Reds Class A farm team, the **Charleston Wheelers** (tel 304/9250-8222), can be seen at Watt-Powell Baseball Park. The **Bluefield Orioles** (tel 304/327-2448), farm team for the Baltimore Orioles, play at Bowen Field in Bluefield.

COLLEGE FOOTBALL In Morgantown, West Virginia University's nationally ranked football team, the **Mountaineers,** plays at Mountaineer Field. Call toll free 800/352-2512 for schedules and tickets.

DOG RACING **Wheeling Downs** (tel 304/232-5050 or toll free 800/445-9475) offers year-round greyhound racing and a clubhouse restaurant at the southern tip of Wheeling Island in the Ohio River. **Tri-State Greyhound Park,** at Cross Lanes near Charleston (tel 304/776-1000 or toll free 800/999-7172), also offers year-round racing.

HORSE RACING The **Charles Town Racetrack** (tel 304/725-7001 or toll free 800/725-7001) is the home of year-round thoroughbred racing and, in September, of the West Virginia Breeder's Classic, the state's richest race. **Mountaineer Racetrack and Resort** (tel 304/387-2400), midway between Weirton and Chester, offers year-round thoroughbred racing as well as the extensive lodging, dining, and sports facilities of a resort.

ICE HOCKEY West Virginia is home to 2 East Coast League teams: the **Huntington Blizzard** (tel 304/697-PUCK), who skate at the Huntington Civic Center, and the **Wheeling Thunderbirds,** who face off at the Wheeling Civic Center. The season runs October through April.

Activities A to Z

BIKING & HIKING West Virginia offers extensive trail systems, including a number of old railroad beds converted to trails for hikers, bikers, and horseback riders. In particular, mountain bikers at all levels can find some of the best terrain in the East here—marked trails, old logging roads, and single tracks. The **Allegheny Trail** is a 220-mile footpath that runs from northern West Virginia south to the Greenbrier Valley, connecting state parks and forests along the way. It includes the 75-mile Greenbrier River Rail Trail, an old Chesapeake and Ohio Railroad grade that follows the

river south from Cass to Caldwell. Another former railroad bed, the North Bend Rail Trail, runs in an east-west direction across the northern part of the state, cutting through tunnels and across bridges from east of Parkersburg to west of Clarksburg. Used by hikers, bikers, and horseback riders, it forms part of the 5,500-mile American Discovery Trail.

For more information call toll free 800/CALL WVA, or contact the West Virginia Scenic Trails Association, PO Box 4042, Charleston, WV 25304; the Rails-to-Trails Council (tel 304/722-6558); or the Monongahela National Forest Supervisor (tel 304/636-1800).

CAMPING Opportunities for camping range from "roughing it" to hooking up the RV; the season usually runs from late April through October. Campgrounds, from primitive to deluxe, are available in state parks, forests, and wildlife management areas; in many, rustic cabins and cottages are a further option. The George Washington National Forest and the Monongahela National Forest also provide campsites. For more information contact the West Virginia Division of Tourism and Parks, State Capitol Complex, 2109 Washington St E, PO Box 50312, Charleston, WV 25305-0312 (tel toll free 800/CALL WVA).

CRUISING Authentic 19th-century sternwheelers cruise the Ohio, Kahawha, and Little Kanawha Rivers, operating from the riverfront in Wheeling, Huntington, Parkersburg, Charleston, and other towns. Excursions range from breakfast, lunch and dinner cruises to day-long sightseeing trips. Cruises to Blennerhasset Island are available out of Parkersburg. For information, call toll free 800/CALL WVA.

FISHING & HUNTING Dense wildlife areas, deep lakes, and churning rivers lure sportsmen. Hunting and fishing licenses are required throughout the state. Licenses for nonresidents, including short-term licenses for state recreational areas, are available from nearly 800 license agents. Regulations are available from the West Virginia Division of Natural Resources in Charleston. Call 304/558-2771. License application forms may be obtained by calling 304/558-2758. For information on wildlife management areas, call 304/558-2754.

GOLF West Virginia has 31 18-hole public golf courses in addition to courses at private resorts. Cacapon State Park boasts a Robert Trent Jones championship course, and at the base of Snowshoe Mountain is a Gary Player–designed golf course featuring canyons and cliffs. Call toll free 800/CALL WVA for more information.

HORSEBACK RIDING   A number of state parks offer horseback riding, and private outfits offer adventures on horseback by the hour, the day, or longer, including tours of Blackwater Falls State Park and overnight pack trips in Canaan Valley. Call toll free 800/CALL WVA.

ROCK CLIMBING   Considered by many to be the best climb in the East, **Seneca Rocks** is for beginners or expert climbers. For information, call 304/567-2827 or 304/257-4488). The New River Gorge offers more than 20 miles of cliffs with 700 completed routes and more being explored. Call toll free 800/CALL WVA.

WHITE-WATER RAFTING & CANOEING   West Virginia is justifiably known as the white-water capital of the East. The New River winds 53 miles through a deep gorge past some of the state's most gorgeous scenery. The **Gauley River,** a 26-mile stretch of white water, is rated the number 2 river in North America, and number 7 in the world.

Whitewater rapids are classed from I to VI for difficulty. Novices can usually run I to II stretches without guides. Segments classed from III to V require paddling skills or qualified leadership, provided by professional outfitters. Class VI water demands the utmost skill.

For information, contact the West Virginia Professional River Outfitters (tel 304/346-4660), or call toll free 800/CALL WVA.

SKIING   West Virginia's Potomac highlands area offers the best skiing in the Mid-Atlantic, both downhill and cross-country, from Thanksgiving weekend to mid-April. **Timberline** is ranked 3rd in the southeast by *Snow Country* report. At the **White Grass Ski Touring,** groomed trails lead nordic skiers to the Dolly Sods Wilderness area. For the booklet *Skiing West Virginia,* call toll free 800/CALL WVA.

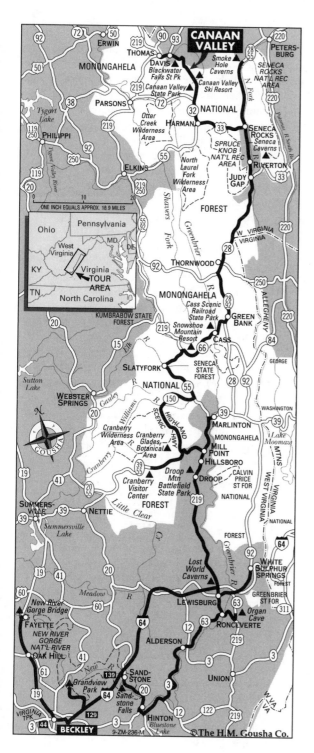

SCENIC DRIVING TOUR

NEW RIVER GORGE TO THE HIGHLANDS

Start: Beckley
Finish: Canaan Valley
Distance: 280 miles
Time: 3–6 days
Highlights: Gorgeous mountain scenery; the awesome New River Gorge; vast national forests and wilderness areas; outdoor theater; visits inside natural caverns and a coal mine; historic towns; a Civil War battlefield; Pearl S Buck's birthplace; a train ride up a steep mountain

Beginning in southern West Virginia at the dramatic, 53-mile-long New River Gorge, this tour takes you northward through the rugged Allegheny Mountains. Much of the drive travels through the Monongahela National Forest, whose nearly 1 million acres contain some of the largest wilderness areas east of the Mississippi. You'll stop at old-fashioned country stores rather than 7-11s, and eat fried chicken instead of filet mignon, for this is a sparsely populated area where deserted roads climb steep mountains and tiny villages are tucked away in lovely valleys. It's a long drive, but West Virginia's great natural beauty will make every mile worth it.

Because the route takes you along very steep and winding mountain roads, be sure your vehicle is in top condition. The mountains get heavy snow during winter, so make this drive only between April and October. The best time for this trip is late September and the first 2 weeks of October, when the mountains are ablaze with autumn colors.

For additional information on accommodations, restaurants, and attractions in the region covered by the tour, look under specific cities in the listings portion of this book.

I-77 and I-64 converge at the first stop:

1. **Beckley,** the coal-mining town that is the transportation and accommodation hub of southern West Virginia. Take exit 44 to Harper Rd east then turn left on Ewart Ave and follow the signs to the **Beckley Exhibition Coal Mine,** located in New River Park (tel 304/256-1747), one of America's

most unusual museums. Veteran miners tell stories and explain how coal is extracted during 45-minute tours via a "man trip" train through 1,500 feet of tunnels under Beckley. Drop in the **visitor center** of the Southern West Virginia Convention & Visitor Bureau, 418 Neville St (tel 304/252-7328), next to the museum's gift shop, where you can get your bearings and obtain maps and information about the region, including white-water rafting on the New River.

The New River Gorge National River runs its 53-mile course north of Beckley, and although we will soon see this awesome canyon, take the time to drive 25 miles north of Beckley on US 19 to the New River Gorge Bridge. The world's longest single-steel-arch bridge, this structure spans the gorge 876 feet above the river. The **Canyon Rim Visitor Center,** WV 19 in Lansing (tel 304/574-2115), has spectacular views of the gorge at its north end and complete information about this national treasure.

From Beckley, follow I-64 east 13 miles to exit 129B, then turn left and drive 5 miles north on WV 9 to:

2. **Grandview Park,** which sits 1,440 feet above the deepest part of the New River Gorge. From mid-June to mid-August, the park is home to **Theater West Virginia,** an outdoor repertory company famous for *Hatfields & McCoys* and *Honey in the Rock,* 2 original plays based on West Virginia lore. The park **visitor center,** exit 129B off I-64 (tel 304/256-6800 or toll free 800/666-9142), is open from Memorial Day to Labor Day.

Backtrack to I-64 and head east for 13 miles down into the New River Gorge. Take exit 139 on the north side of the bridge, turn left on WV 20, and head south up the canyon's side for 3 miles, where an overlook provides a view of Sandstone Falls. From there, descend 7 miles south to:

3. **Hinton,** an old railroad town at the confluence of the New and Greenbrier Rivers. The New River Gorge begins its northwestward journey at Hinton. The **Summers County Visitor Center** on 206 Temple St (turn left at the stoplight) (tel 304/466-5332), shares quarters with a railroad museum and consignment crafts shop; all 3 are worth a visit. The visitors center provides a walking tour

map of the brick streets in Hinton's historic district and directions to **Bluestone Dam,** which harnesses the New River to create lovely **Bluestone Lake,** one of the region's most popular recreation spots. The National Park Service has a summertime **visitor center** on WV 3 (cross the bridge and bear left) (tel 304/466-2805), which is open Memorial Day–Labor Day, Wednesday–Sunday 8am–7:30pm, and Monday–Tuesday 8am–4pm. For refreshment, national chain fast-food outlets are along the river on WV 107 (go straight at the stoplight).

The fast way to the next stop is to backtrack 10 miles north on WV 20 and head east on I-64 for another 31 miles, but you'll want to take the shorter but slower route by driving 39 miles, beginning with WV 3 east along the banks of the gentle Greenbrier River. After 5 miles, you'll climb over Big Bend Tunnel, dug between 1870 and 1872 as a railroad shortcut. At the top sits a statue of John Henry, the legendary digger who died after a race with a new-fangled steel drill. At 10 miles, you'll pass the **Graham House,** built of logs in 1772. At 12 miles look for the **Pence Springs Hotel,** off WV 3 (tel 304/445-2606), a popular 1920s retreat, then a women's prison, and now a country inn. At 21 miles, you'll reach Alderson, a pretty town where you can walk across the old bridge over the Greenbrier.

☕

REFRESHMENT STOP

For inexpensive pizza, sandwiches, burgers, and home-cooked meals, stop at the **Big Wheel Family Restaurant** (tel 304/445-7832), on WV 3 just before Alderson. The same family has operated this small-town eatery since the late 1950s; it's plain and simple with standard American fare.

From Alderson, take WV 12 north, then WV 63 east 12 miles to Ronceverte (French for Greenbrier). Turn left on US 219 and proceed north 2 miles through a commercial strip and the state fairgrounds to:

4. **Lewisburg,** where surveyor Andrew Lewis found a spring in 1751 and, as a general, built **Fort Savannah** during the French and Indian Wars. Part of the fort and a host of other old buildings make this beautiful town worth a walking tour. Turn left on Washington St at the traffic signal, go 2 blocks west and turn left on Church St to the **Lewisburg Visitors Center,** 105 Church St (tel 304/645-1000), opposite the **Old Stone Presbyterian Church,** the oldest place of worship west of the Alleghenies. The center has an excellent walking tour booklet of the town and maps for nearby driving tours (which include covered bridges). Two underground excursions highlighting the natural wonders of stalactites and stalagmites are near Lewisburg: **Lost World Caverns,** 3 miles north of town via Court St (tel 304/645-6677); and **Organ Cave,** east of Ronceverte via WV 63 (tel 304/647-5551). **The Greenbrier Trail,** a hiking and biking path along an old railroad bed, starts at Caldwell (3 miles east of Lewisburg on US 60) and ends 80 miles north at Cass.

Located on I-64, Lewisburg has good chain motels and **The General Lewis Inn,** a charming, antique-filled hostelry built in 1834. The inn also is the best place in Lewisburg to dine. Or you can drive 6 miles east on I-64 or US 60 and stay at the luxurious **Greenbrier** or one of the motels in White Sulphur Springs.

From Lewisburg, take US 219 north for 26 miles across a rolling valley and then up onto flat-top Droop Mountain and:

5. **Droop Mountain Battlefield State Park** (tel 304/653-4254), where Union forces attacked a Confederate stronghold in 1863 and drove the Rebels out of the new state of West Virginia for the last time. A loop road, which goes past a small Civil War museum featuring a contemporary *New York Times* report of the battle, passes an overlook with a fine view before rejoining US 219. The park has picnic facilities and outhouse-style toilets.

From the park, it's 4 miles down the mountain and across the lovely "Lower Levels" valley to:

6. **Hillsboro,** where author Pearl S Buck was born in her mother's ancestral home. Although the only American woman ever to win both the Pulitzer and Nobel Prizes spent only one summer here when she was 9 years old, the **Pearl S Buck Birthplace** (tel 304/653-4430), ¼ mile north of town on US 219, looks very much like it did when she was born on June 26, 1892. Open May–October, Monday–Saturday 9am–5pm; Sunday 1–5pm. Admission is $4 adults, $1 children 18 and under.

🍺

REFRESHMENT STOP

For an ice cream cone, a soft drink out of an old-fashioned Pepsi-Cola vending machine, or some fresh cookies, stop in the **Hillsboro General Store** (tel 304/653-4414), a throwback to the 1890s on US 219 as you drive into town. For something more substantial, try the **Rosewood Cafe** (tel 304/653-4335), in another old store just up the road. The original dry goods shelves, rolling ladders, and pressed-tin ceiling lend an historical ambience to this casual spot serving sandwiches and a mixed menu of Italian and Mexican cuisines. Closed Monday and Tuesday.

From Hillsboro, continue north on US 219 for 2 miles to Mill Point. You can go straight north there for 9 miles to Marlinton for a look at the **Pocahontas County Historical Museum,** at WV 39 (tel 304/799-4973), which has displays on regional history, and rejoin the tour north of town on US 219 atop Lick Mountain. Otherwise, turn left on WV 39 west and climb uphill 6 miles to:

7. **Cranberry Mountain Visitor Center** (tel 304/653-4826 or 846-2695), a key entry to the many recreational activities in the huge Monongahela National Forest. Stop at the center for information about the nearby **Cranberry Glades Botanical Area,** where swampy bogs sit in a bowl at a 3,400-foot altitude; here you can observe rare plants and wildlife usually found in the tundra of Canada. A paved road ½ mile beyond the visitor

center drops into the glades, where boardwalks go through the bogs.

From the visitors center, go straight on WV 150 (part of the Highland Scenic Hwy) for a lovely 23-mile drive along the crest of 4,600-foot-tall Cranberry Mountain. There are overlooks along the way, including one of Cranberry Glades. At the road's end on Lick Mountain, turn left on US 219 north, which drops precipitously into the narrow and extraordinarily beautiful Pleasant Valley. (Have your camera ready, especially if you want photos of an old barn with a Mail Pouch chewing tobacco sign still on its side.) After 10 miles you reach Slatyfork, which consists of the century-old:

8. **Sharp's County Store,** where you can look at stuffed animals, old farming tools, and Civil War relics in its museum-like front windows. You can also fill the tank, use the restrooms, and snack on a deli sandwich and a cold soda. Sharp's is open during the warm months, Monday–Saturday 7am –8pm, Sunday 8am–6pm.

From Sharp's, continue north on US 219 for 4 miles to WV 66. Turn right here and drive 1 mile east to:

9. **Snowshoe Mountain Resort,** on US 219 (tel 304/572-5252), one of the Mid-Atlantic's largest wintertime ski areas. During the summer, activities here include mountain biking, tennis, golf at the Gary Player–designed Hawthorne Valley course, a chili cook-off in July, and the Snowshoe Symphony Weekend in August.

The resort has the only large, up-to-date accommodations between Lewisburg and Canaan Valley, so it's the logical place to spend a night. **The Inn at Snowshoe,** on WV 66 just east of the US 219 intersection, is another modern hotel in the valley below the resort.

From Snowshoe, drive east on WV 66 across Little Mountain to the:

10. **Cass Scenic Railroad State Park** (tel 304/456-4300), where a powerful steam locomotive pulls a train to a lookout atop 4,842-foot-tall Bald Knob, just as it did when this timber line was built in 1911. Excursions run daily from Memorial Day to Labor Day, weekends in September, daily the 1st 2 full weeks in October, and weekends again for the rest of October. Dinner trains operate on Saturday during July and August and on Labor Day weekend. For information on schedules and fares, call 800/CALL WVA.

Train ticket holders can also visit nearby historical and wildlife museums, and the **Cass General Store** is full of souvenirs. The **Last Run Restaurant** is open Sunday–Wednesday 8:30am–6pm, Thursday–Saturday 8:30am–8pm, when the train is running.

At Cass, you'll cross the Greenbrier River for the last time and drive 5 miles east on WV 66, then left onto WV 28. From there, go north 3 miles to:

11. **Green Bank,** where the huge radio telescopes of the **National Radio Astronomy Observatory,** WV 28/92 (tel 304/456-2011), probe the depths of outer space. Free observatory tours providing a wealth of facts about space and radio waves take place daily, mid-June through August, 9am–4pm.

From Green Bank, continue 34 miles north on WV 28, climbing up and over the Allegheny Front, a mighty mountain which is the eastern continental divide (water on the west side flows into the Ohio and Mississippi Rivers; on the east, into the Potomac and Chesapeake Bay). A gravel road at the top of the pass leads to the summit of 4,861-foot Spruce Knob, the highest point in West Virginia. The mountain and its adjacent lake are part of **Spruce Knob-Seneca Rocks National Recreation Area** (tel 304/257-4442).

From the Front, you'll descend on WV 28 along the North Fork River through Judy Gap and Riverton to WV 55. Turn right there and drive a few hundred yards east to the **visitor center** of:

12. **Seneca Rocks,** whose 900-foot, quartzite formation may make you feel like you're in Wyoming, not West Virginia. These Tuscarora sandstone towers are among the most popular rock climbing venues in the eastern states, but you can also fish, hike, picnic, and camp on the site. The visitors center has information about the surrounding national recreation area. Other nearby attractions include **Seneca Caverns** (tel 304/567-2691) at Riverton, the largest commercial cavern in the state, and **Smoke Hole Cavern** (tel 304/257-

4442), which has the nation's 2nd highest underground ceiling, is 13 miles north on WV 28.

REFRESHMENT STOP

South of Seneca Rocks on WV 28 and US 33 stands **Hedrick's 4-U Restaurant** (tel 304/567-2111), a clean, unpretentious establishment serving sandwiches, salads, steaks, country ham, fried chicken, seafood, and home-baked bread.

From the rocks, take US 33 west back up over the Allegheny Front for 12 miles to **Harman.** Turn right there on WV 32 and climb 9 miles north into:

13. **Canaan Valley** (pronounced *Ca-nain,* rhymes with main), a high plateau whose 3,200-foot altitude and surrounding mountains have made it a year-round resort, with skiing from Thanksgiving to April and golf, tennis, hiking, hunting, mountain biking, white-water rafting, and other activities the rest of the year. The valley includes **Canaan Valley State Park** (tel 304/866-4121), **Blackwater Falls State Park** (tel 304/259-5216), and the towns of **Davis** and **Thomas.**

The easiest way out of the mountains is via US 219 north from Thomas to I-64 at Keyers Ridge, Maryland, 51 miles away. Once in Maryland (15 miles from Thomas), you can make good time on US 219, which is wide and well-graded all the way to the Interstate. You will pass through Deep Creek Lake, the end of the driving tour "Western Maryland" (see the Maryland chapter). If you're heading east, you can do that trip in reverse.

ANSTED

Map page M-2, D3

Attraction 💼

Hawks Nest State Park, WV 60; tel 304/658-5212. Located 50 miles east of Charleston on the New River Gorge, this park offers incredible views of the area and access to the New River. A lodge and restaurant are perched on the edge of the gorge, and tramway service provides visitors with a scenic ride to the lake below. Also overlooking the canyon is a small rustic museum displaying artifacts of the Native Americans and the early pioneers who inhabited the area. Recreational opportunities at the park include whitewater rafting on the river, swimming in an outdoor pool, hiking, picnicking, and camping. **Open:** Park, daily 6am–10pm; museum, daily 10:30am–5:30pm. Free.

BARBOURSVILLE

Map page M-2, C2 (E of Huntington)

Motels 🏨

Comfort Inn Barboursville, 3441 US 60 E, Barboursville, WV 25504; tel 304/736-9772 or toll free 800/221-2222; fax 304/736-4386. 12 mi E of Huntington. exit 20 off I-64. E ½ mi on US 60. Good location just off I-64. **Rooms:** 131 rms and effic. Exec-level rms avail. CI 1pm/CO noon. Nonsmoking rms avail. Basic motel rooms are neat and clean. **Amenities:** 🛗 A/C, cable TV. **Services:** 🛎 🍽 **Facilities:** 🛗 🗓 🛗 2 rsts. **Rates (CP):** $48 S or D; from $54 effic. Extra person $4. Children under 18 stay free. Higher rates for spec evnts/hols. Pking: Outdoor, free. Maj CC.

Holiday Inn Gateway, 6007 US 60 E, Barboursville, WV 25504; tel 304/736-8974 or toll free 800/248-2426; fax 304/736-8974. 9 mi E of Huntington. exit 20 off I-64. Nice grounds cover 15 acres, with buildings around a central courtyard. **Rooms:** 208 rms and stes. CI 2pm/CO noon. Express checkout avail. Nonsmoking rms avail. Pleasant rooms recently refurbished. **Amenities:** 🛗 🛁 🖥 A/C, satel TV w/movies. **Services:** ✕ 🚐 🛎 🍽 Babysitting. **Facilities:** 🛗 🏐 🛗 🛗 🛗 1 rst, 2 bars (1 w/entertainment), games rm, lawn games, spa, sauna, beauty salon, playground, washer/dryer. Heated indoor pool, volleyball courts. **Rates:** $66–$70 S; $72–$76 D; from $144 ste. Extra person $6. Children under 19 stay free. Min stay spec evnts. Spec packages avail. Pking: Outdoor, free. Maj CC.

Restaurant 🍴

★ **Gateway Restaurant**, in the Holiday Inn Gateway, 6007 US 60 E, Barboursville; tel 304/736-8974. 9 mi E of Huntington, exit 20 off I-64. W 3 mi on US 60. **American.** Nicer decor than usual for motel restaurants. Specializes in prime rib, country ham, turkey, and ribs. Reasonably priced buffets are a regular feature. Children under 12 eat free when dining with parents who are motel guests. **FYI:** Reservations accepted. Children's menu. **Open:** Daily 6am–10pm. Closed Dec 25. **Prices:** Main courses $7–$16. Maj CC. 🏧 🛗

Attraction 💼

Beech Fork State Park, 5601 Long Branch Rd; tel 304/522-0303. This year-round vacation park is situated on 2,100 acres surrounding Beech Fork Lake. The 760-acre artificial lake offers fishing, swimming, and boating. Other facilities at the park include basketball courts and camping sites. **Open:** Daily sunrise–sunset. Free.

BECKLEY

Map page M-2, D3

Hotel 🏨

Beckley Hotel and Conference Center, 1940 Harper Rd, Beckley, WV 25801; tel 304/252-8661 or toll free 800/274-6010; fax 304/253-4496. Exit 44 off I-77. Highlights are a center court, a giant room with fireplace, and Williamsburg Square, a village-like indoor shopping mall. Near 5 golf courses, skiing, hiking, riding, and other outdoor activities. **Rooms:** 191 rms, stes, and effic. CI 3pm/CO noon. Nonsmoking rms avail. **Amenities:** 🛗 A/C, cable TV w/movies. 1 unit w/Jacuzzi. **Services:** ✕ 🛎 🍽 **Facilities:** 🛗 🛗 🛗 🛗 🛗 2 rsts, 1 bar, games rm, whirlpool, washer/dryer. Driving range has PGA pro instructor. Exceptionally large heated pool has water-polo facilities and ample poolside seating. **Rates:** HS May–Nov $60–$66 S; $65–$71 D; from $90 ste; from $85 effic. Extra person $5. Children under 18 stay free. Min stay spec evnts. Lower rates off-season. AP and MAP rates avail. Spec packages avail. Pking: Outdoor, free. Maj CC.

Restaurant 🍴

The Char, 100 Char Dr, Beckley; tel 304/253-1760. Exit 44 off I-77. Follow WV 3 W, go right at fork. **Italian/Seafood/Steak.** Done up in an upscale country style, this restaurant and bar offer casual dining in a rural setting. Huge picture windows overlook a lily pond. Outdoor benches. Steaks, chops, seafood, and pasta are most popular. **FYI:** Reservations accepted. Dress code. **Open:** Mon–Fri 6–10pm, Sat 6–11pm. Closed some hols; Jan. **Prices:** Main courses $13–$32. Maj CC. 🖼️ 🆅🅿️ ⛄

Attractions 💼

Beckley Exhibition Coal Mine, Ewart Ave, New River Park; tel 304/256-1747. Retired miners lead tours 1,500 feet underground into what was once a working coal mine. The 45-minute trip highlights the process of low-seam coal mining from its earliest manual stages to modern mechanized operation. Mine temperature is a constant 58°F. **Open:** Apr–Nov, daily 10am–5:30pm. $$$

Wildwood House Museum, S Kanawha St; tel 304/252-8614. This historic home (circa 1836) was the residence of Gen Alfred Beckley, founder of Raleigh County and the city of Beckley. Listed on the National Register of Historic Places, the building is furnished with original period pieces. Authentic rooms include a Victorian parlor with handcrafted cherry furniture and a frontier kitchen with a "dry sink." **Open:** May–Oct, Sat 10am–4pm, Sunday 2–4pm. $

Babcock State Park, WV 41; tel 304/438-5662. Start a visit at the administration building at the park entrance. In addition to providing information about the area, the rustic sandstone building houses a restaurant and commissary. Across from the center is the Glad Creek Grist Mill, a fully operable grain mill that is a monument to the over 500 mills that once thrived in West Virginia. Visitors may purchase freshly ground whole-wheat, cornmeal, or buckwheat flour. The park itself is situated on 4,127 acres and features waterfalls, a trout stream, Boley Lake, and 20 miles of hiking trails. Paddleboats and rowboats are available for rent, and swimmers can use an outdoor pool. Camping, stables, tennis courts, playgrounds, picnic areas. **Open:** Daily daylight hours. Free.

BERKELEY SPRINGS

Map page M-3, B5

Hotel 🏨

📧📧📧 **Country Inn**, 207 S Washington St, Berkeley Springs, WV 25411; tel 304/258-2210 or toll free 800/822-6630; fax 304/258-3986. Exit 1B off I-70. This gracious, all-brick colonial country inn has homey touches like old-fashioned porches. Adjoins Berkeley Springs' village green and state-owned spa featuring mineral water baths where George Washington soaked. Sitting-room art gallery for reading, piano playing, or games.

Rooms: 70 rms and stes. CI 3pm/CO noon. Nonsmoking rms avail. Each room individually decorated with charming country fabrics. All have private baths. Honeymoon suite. Computer/fax jack in lobby. **Amenities:** 📺 A/C, cable TV. Suites have refrigerators. **Services:** ✕ ⊘ Masseur, babysitting. **Facilities:** 🍽️ 1 rst, 1 bar, spa, beauty salon. Renaissance Spa has whirlpool baths, plush salon, European facials, body massage. Spacious dining room has Saturday night dancing. **Rates:** $35–$80 S or D; from $85 ste. Extra person $10. Children under 12 stay free. Min stay wknds. MAP rates avail. Spec packages avail. Pking: Outdoor, free. Maj CC.

Lodges

📧📧📧 **Cacapon Lodge**, Cacapon State Park, WV 1, PO Box 304, Berkeley Springs, WV 25411; tel 304/258-1022 or toll free 800/CALL-WVA. On WV 522 S. Set amid mountain woodlands, this 6,000-acre, state-run resort park offers a 50-room lodge as well as 30 cabins and an 11-room inn. Huge, wood-paneled room off lobby, with fireplace, offers view of grounds, and plain but pleasant dining room looks out on Cacapon Mountain. **Rooms:** 60 rms; 30 ctges/villas. CI 3pm/CO noon. Clean and functional. Warm wood paneling in the lodge. Most rooms have queen-size beds. Old inn rooms with hand-hewn log beams have a colonial spirit; they are more rustic than other units, and most share a bath. All cabins set up for light housekeeping. **Amenities:** 📺 A/C, cable TV. Some units w/fireplaces. Neither cabins nor inn rooms have TVs. **Services:** ⊘ Children's program. Naturalist program offered, for adults and children. Weekend activities scheduled. **Facilities:** ⛳ 🏕️ ▶18 🎣 🚣 🏊2 🎱 ⛄ 1 rst, 1 beach (lake shore), lifeguard, games rm, playground. Horseback and hiking trails; 6-acre lake, with beach, for fishing, swimming, and canoeing. Robert Trent Jones, Jr course with golf pro on duty. **Rates:** HS May–Sept $31–$52 S; $33–$58 D; from $85 ctge/villa. Extra person $6. Children under 12 stay free. Min stay wknds. Lower rates off-season. Spec packages avail. Pking: Outdoor, free. Maj CC. Golf package offered, with rate by season. Dinner theater package in winter.

📧📧📧 **Coolfront Resort and Conference Center**, Cold Run Valley Rd, Berkeley Springs, WV 25411; tel 304/258-4500 or toll free 800/888-8768; fax 304/258-5499. Follow WV 9 from Berkeley Springs. Peaceful and rustic resort offers a scenic setting for fun and health on 1,200 wooded acres between Cacapon Mountain and Warm Springs Ridge. Family-owned and -operated with a variety of special programs and activities. Emphasis on relaxation and recreation. **Rooms:** 250 rms, stes, and effic; 45 ctges/villas. CI 3pm/CO 11am. Nonsmoking rms avail. Lodge rooms, chalets, mountaineer homes, log cabins, and hillside hideaways; most have stoves with wood provided. Rooms are individually decorated with country touches like rocking chairs and quilted hangings. **Amenities:** 🛁 ⚗ 🖭 A/C, TV, refrig. Some units w/minibars, some w/terraces, some w/fireplaces, some w/Jacuzzis. Most units have double-size whirlpool tubs. **Services:** ⌒ Social director, masseur, children's program, babysitting. Entertainment on weekends. Recreational, cultural, and health activities offered, ranging from seminar with Pulitzer Prize–winning poet to daily exercise classes. **Facilities:** 🖬 ⛰ 🖂 ⚓ ●³ 🖐 🔟 ⌨ ⚂ 1 rst, 1 bar (w/entertainment), 1 beach (lake shore), lifeguard, games rm, lawn games, spa, sauna, whirlpool, beauty salon, day-care ctr, playground, washer/dryer. Separate 9,000-square-foot swim and fitness center with 60-foot pool, exercise equipment, etc. Spa offers massage, facials. Hiking trails. Lake for boating and fishing. Cooperative arrangement for golf at nearby Cacapon Lodge. Camping. **Rates (MAP):** HS Sept 26–Oct 30 $72–$84 S; $82–$94 D; from $92 ctge/villa. Children under 5 stay free. Min stay spec evnts. Lower rates off-season. AP rates avail. Spec packages avail. Pking: Outdoor, free. Maj CC. Special packages throughout the year include those for skiing, Valentine's Day, Mother's Day.

Attractions 🖼

Berkeley Castle, WV 9 W; tel 304/258-1022. Built in 1885 by Col Samuel Taylor Suite, this Victorian mansion features a stone-walled ballroom, a pine-paneled library, a wide carved staircase, a tower room, and period furnishings. **Open:** Daily 8am–8pm. Free.

Berkeley Springs State Park, 121 S Washington State Park; tel 304/258-2711. Mineral waters flowing from the springs in the park maintain a constant temperature of 74.3°F and have long been thought to possess medicinal powers. Popular with both Native Americans and the colonial elite, the spa was also frequented by George Washington. Among the services offered are mineral baths, massage therapy, and heat treatments. **Open:** Daily 10am–6pm. Free.

Cacapon Resort State Park, WV 1; tel 304/258-1022. This 6,000-acre retreat at the foot of Cacapon Mountain offers swimming, fishing, and boating on Cacapon Lake; golfing on an 18-hole golf course; and hiking and horseback riding on 27 miles of trails. **Open:** Daily sunrise–sunset. Free.

BEVERLY

Map page M-2, C4 (S of Elkins)

Attraction 🖼

Randolph County Historical County Museum, Main St; tel 304/636-0841. Housed in the Blackman-Bosworth general store (1827), the museum presents 200 years of life in Randolph County, including Civil War memorabilia. **Open:** May–Oct, Sat–Sun 1–5pm. Free.

BLUEFIELD

Map page M-2, E3

Motels 🏨

≡≡≡ **Holiday Inn**, US 460, Bluefield, WV 24701; tel 304/325-6170 or toll free 800/465-4329; fax 304/325-6170. Exit 1 off I-77. Well-landscaped property sits on a hill above the highway and has pleasant views of the surrounding mountains. Restaurants and shops nearby. Popular for regional conventions. **Rooms:** 120 rms. Exec-level rms avail. CI 3pm/CO 11am. Nonsmoking rms avail. **Amenities:** 🛁 ⚗ A/C, cable TV w/movies. **Services:** ✕ 🖂 ⌒ **Facilities:** 🖬 🔟 ⚂ 2 rsts, 1 bar (w/entertainment), sauna. **Rates:** $55–$70 S; $62–$80 D. Extra person $7. Children under 18 stay free. Higher rates for spec evnts/hols. Spec packages avail. Pking: Outdoor, free. Maj CC.

≡≡≡ **Ramada East River Mountain**, 3175 E Cumberland Rd, Bluefield, WV 24701; tel 304/325-5421 or toll free 800/272-6232; fax 304/325-6045. Exit 1 off I-77. Follow US 52 N to US 460 W; turn right at 1st light on US 460. Nestled on the side of a mountain, this motel has a great view. **Rooms:** 98 rms and stes. Exec-level rms avail. CI 2pm/CO noon. Nonsmoking rms avail. **Amenities:** 🛁 ⚗ 🖭 A/C, cable TV w/movies. **Services:** ✕ 🖂 ⌒ 🐾 **Facilities:** 🖬 🖐 🔟 ⚂ 1 rst, 1 bar (w/entertainment), games rm, sauna, whirlpool. Large restaurant features stone wall and fireplace. Large indoor area with pool and sports. TV lounge. **Rates:** HS May–Sept $55–$57 S or D; from $100 ste. Extra person $5. Children under 18 stay free. Lower rates off-season. Spec packages avail. Pking: Outdoor, free. Maj CC.

BRIDGEPORT

Map page M-2, B3 (E of Clarksburg)

Motels 🏨

≡≡ **Days Inn**, 112 Tolley St, Bridgeport, WV 26330; tel 304/842-7371 or toll free 800/329-7466; fax 304/842-3904. Exit 119 off I-79. A planned renovation will make over this older motel and add new units and business center. **Rooms:** 62 rms. CI 2pm/CO 11am. Nonsmoking rms avail. **Amenities:** 🛁 A/C, cable TV. Some units w/Jacuzzis. **Services:** ✕ 🖂 ⌒ Babysitting. **Facilities:** 🖬 🔟 ⚂ 1 rst, 1 bar (w/entertainment), games rm, whirlpool. Indoor-outdoor heated pool. Nightclub on premises.

Rates (BB): $50 S; $58 D. Extra person $8. Children under 12 stay free. Higher rates for spec evnts/hols. Pking: Outdoor, free. Maj CC.

▆▆ **Holiday Inn**, 100 Lodgeville Rd, Bridgeport, WV 26330; tel 304/842-5411 or toll free 800/HOLIDAY; fax 304/842-7258. Exit 119 off I-79. Although the front is not particularly pleasing, the recently refurbished interior is appealing. **Rooms:** 160 rms and stes. Exec-level rms avail. CI 2pm/CO noon. Express checkout avail. Nonsmoking rms avail. Average-quality rooms for members of this chain. **Amenities:** ▆ ⚲ ▤ A/C, cable TV w/movies, in-rm safe. **Services:** ✗ ▆▤ ⊿ ⊸ ⟲ Social director, children's program, babysitting. **Facilities:** ⌂ ▦ & 1 rst, 1 bar, washer/dryer. Pool and children's pool are attractive. **Rates:** HS Apr–Oct $62–$75 S; $62–$75 D; from $90 ste. Extra person $5. Children under 19 stay free. Min stay spec evnts. Lower rates off-season. Higher rates for spec evnts/hols. Spec packages avail. Pking: Outdoor, free. Maj CC.

BUCKHANNON

Map page M-2, C3

Attractions 🖼

West Virginia State Wildlife Center, WV 20; tel 304/924-6211. This zoo displays animals in their natural habitats and features wildlife indigenous to West Virginia, such as black bears, river otters, elk, bison, mountain lions, and timber wolves. **Open:** Daily 9am–dusk. $

Audra State Park, Audra Park Rd; tel 304/457-1162. Located along the Middle Fork River, the park offers swimming as well as riverside camping and picnicking. Hikers can choose from a variety of trails that traverse natural rock formations. **Open:** Daily 7am–10pm. Free.

CAIRO

Map page M-2, B3 (SW of Pennsboro)

Attraction 🖼

North Bend State Park, WV 31; tel 304/643-2931. Fishing streams, hiking trails, and abundant wildlife make this park a popular year-round destination. Activities and facilities include horseshoes, basketball, softball, bicycles for the blind, and a paved hiking trail for those with disabilities. Campgrounds, miniature golf, tennis courts. **Open:** Daily sunrise–sunset. Free.

CANAAN VALLEY

See Davis

CASS

Map page M-2, C4 (SE of Linwood)

Attraction 🖼

Cass Scenic Railroad State Park, WV 66; tel 304/456-4300. Operating on the same line bult in 1902 to haul logs to the mill town of Cass, the Cass Scenic Railroad now brings passengers to Bald Knob, the second-highest peak in the state. Original Shay steam locmotives and refurbished logging flatcars transport visitors on the 4½-hour scenic tour past some of the most breathtaking views of mountain scenery in West Virginia. Fall foliage tours, summer dinner trips. **Open:** May–Oct, call for schedule. $$$$

CHARLESTON

Map page M-2, C2

See also **South Charleston**

Hotels 🖼

▆▆▆ **Charleston Marriott Town Center**, 200 Lee St E, Charleston, WV 25301; tel 304/345-6500 or toll free 800/228-9290; fax 304/353-3722. Exit 58C off I-64. Beautiful, tasteful lobby and public areas highlight this resort-like downtown hotel. **Rooms:** 352 rms and stes. Exec-level rms avail. CI 4pm/CO noon. Express checkout avail. Nonsmoking rms avail. Modern rooms with upscale furniture. **Amenities:** ▆ ⚲ A/C, cable TV w/movies, shoe polisher. All units w/terraces. Radios in bedside cabinets. **Services:** ✗ ▆ ⊿ ⊸ Car-rental desk, masseur. Helpful, courteous staff. **Facilities:** ⌂ ●1 ▆ ▣ & 2 rsts (*see also* "Restaurants" below), 1 bar, games rm, spa, sauna, steam rm, whirlpool, washer/dryer. Indoor pool with Jacuzzi opens to rooftop deck. **Rates:** $109–$134 S or D; from $225 ste. Children under 18 stay free. Spec packages avail. Pking: Indoor, $3.50. Maj CC. Rates cover 1 to 5 people per room.

▆ **Knights Inn**, 6401 MacCorkle Ave SE, Charleston, WV 25304; tel 304/925-0451 or toll free 800/843-5644; fax 304/925-4703. Exit 95 off I-64. Follow WV 61 to motel. A basic no-frills motel. **Rooms:** 130 rms. CI 2pm/CO noon. Nonsmoking rms avail. Rooms show their age but are clean. **Amenities:** ▆

A/C, cable TV. **Services:** 🛎️ 🧺 Complimentary coffee all day. **Facilities:** 🅿️ 🔟 ⚿ **Rates:** $37–$38 S; $43–$44 D. Extra person $6. Children under 18 stay free. Pking: Outdoor, free. Maj CC.

Motels

≣≣≣ **Ramada Charleston**, 2nd Ave and B St, Charleston, WV 25303; tel 304/744-4641 or toll free 800/2-RAMADA; fax 304/744-4525. Exit 56 off I-64. Although located in an industrial area of South Charleston, this quite pleasant hotel has large lobby with beautiful antiques. **Rooms:** 256 rms, stes, and effic. CI 2pm/CO noon. Nonsmoking rms avail. Nicely furnished rooms. **Amenities:** 📺 🛁 A/C, cable TV, voice mail, shoe polisher. Some units w/terraces. Phones in bathrooms. **Services:** ✕ 🚗 ☒ 🛎️ 🧺 Car-rental desk, babysitting. **Facilities:** 🅿️ 🍴 🏊 🏋️ 🚗 ⚿ 1 rst, 3 bars (1 w/entertainment), games rm, whirlpool. Large bars feature DJs. **Rates:** $49–$71 S; $54–$76 D; from $125 ste; from $49 effic. Extra person $5. Children under 18 stay free. Spec packages avail. Pking: Outdoor, free. Maj CC.

≣≣ **Red Roof Inn**, 4006 MacCorkle Ave SW, Charleston, WV 25309 (South Charleston); tel 304/744-1500 or toll free 800/ THE-ROOF; fax 304/744-8268. Exit 54 off I-64. In a suburban area yet just minutes away from downtown Charleston. One of the better members of Red Roof chain. **Rooms:** 137 rms. CI noon/CO noon. Nonsmoking rms avail. Rooms are very clean. **Amenities:** 📺 A/C, cable TV. Units for guests with disabilities especially well equipped, including low thermostats. **Services:** 🛎️ 🧺 Complimentary morning coffee in lobby. **Facilities:** 🏋️ ⚿ Spa. Guests have free use of health club across street. **Rates:** HS Apr 30–Nov 1 $38–$42 S; $45–$49 D. Extra person $5. Children under 18 stay free. Lower rates off-season. Pking: Outdoor, free. Maj CC.

Restaurants 🍴

★ **5th Quarter Steak House**, 201 Clendenin St, Charleston; tel 304/345-2726. Exit 58B off I-64. Follow Virginia St to Clendenin St, turn left. **Burgers/Seafood/Steak.** Large brick fireplace reaches to ceiling at one end of this popular local eatery. Old-fashioned mood is enhanced by round globe lights and railroad lanterns. Large burgers, steaks, seafood are augmented by extensive salad bar. **FYI:** Reservations accepted. Blues/country music/jazz. Children's menu. **Open:** Lunch Mon–Fri 11am–2:30pm, Sat–Sun 11am–4pm; dinner Mon–Thurs 5–10pm, Fri 5–11pm, Sat 4–11pm, Sun 4–9pm. Closed Dec 25. **Prices:** Main courses $10–$20. Maj CC. 🍽️ 📷 ⚿

Ⓢ ★ **Harper's**, in Charleston Marriott Town Center, 200 Lee St E, Charleston; tel 304/345-6500. Exit 58C off I-64. **Burgers/**

Seafood/Steak. Pleasantly light, airy atmosphere enhanced by wood tables, cloth-upholstered chairs, many plants. Attractively presented buffets offered for breakfast, lunch, and dinner. Sandwiches and pizza also available. **FYI:** Reservations not accepted. Children's menu. **Open:** Daily 6:30am–10pm. **Prices:** Main courses $5–$16. Maj CC. 🍽️ 🚗 ⚿

♥ **Tarragon**, in Charleston Marriott Town Center, 200 Lee St E, Charleston; tel 304/345-6500. Exit 58C off I-64. **Seafood/ Steak/Veal & Pork.** Not a typical hotel dining room, this upscale restaurant has very sedate surroundings. Visiting chefs prepare special menus during their 10-day stays. Regular menu is well divided between traditional seafood and meat. Incredible wine list includes fine vintages and champagnes, some available by the glass. **FYI:** Reservations recommended. Jacket required. **Open:** Mon–Sat 5:30–10pm. Closed some hols. **Prices:** Main courses $15–$42. Maj CC. ♥ 🚗 ⚿

Attractions 📷

State Capitol, Kanawha Blvd; tel 304/348-3809. Designed by Cass Gilbert, the architect of the US Treasury and the US Supreme Court building, the capitol is constructed of buff limestone over a steel frame and features a 293-foot-high gilded dome. A 2-ton crystal chandelier hangs 180 feet above the rotunda foor. Tours begin at the rotunda information desk.

Within the capitol complex is the **Cultural Center,** featuring a craft shop, reference and archive libraries, and a theater. On the lower level is the **West Virginia State Museum,** tracing the history of the state from Native American migration to the early 20th century, with diplays highlighting a settler's cabin, the Civil War, and a general store. **Open:** Daily 8:30am–4:15pm. Free.

Sunrise Museum and Science Hall, 746 Myrtle Rd; tel 304/ 344-8035. The Sunrise Mansion was once the home of William A MacCorkle, governor of West Virginia from 1893 to 1897. Today it houses a science center that contains over 30 hands-on art and science exhibits as well as a planetarium. A companion mansion, Torquilstone, was built by MacCorkle for his son in 1928 and now houses the Sunrise Museum. Sunrise is situated on 16 acres of wooded grounds and offers a nature trail and gardens. **Open:** Wed–Sat 11am–5pm, Sun noon–5pm. $

Kanawha State Forest, WV 2; tel 304/346-5654. This 9,250-acre forest is noted among naturalists for its diverse wildflower and bird population. There are 25 miles of hiking trails, including the Spotted Salamander Trail designed for blind and wheelchair-bound visitors. Swimming pool, stables, fully equipped campgrounds, playground. **Open:** Daily 6am–10pm. Free.

CHARLES TOWN

Map page M-3, B6

Motel 🛏

≡ **Towne House Motor Lodge**, 549 E Washington St, Charles Town, WV 25414; tel 304/725-8441 or toll free 800/227-2339; fax 304/725-5484. ½ mi E of downtown. Opposite former Charles Town Racetrack on main road into area, although some units are removed from highway. Within walking distance of historic Charles Town. A somewhat ordinary but well-maintained property. Good family place. **Rooms:** 115 rms, stes, and effic. CI 2pm/CO 11am. Nonsmoking rms avail. Tidy, clean rooms; 4 suites have 2 bedrooms, living room with sleep sofa, kitchen. Both room and cottage-style efficiencies available. **Amenities:** 🚭 A/C, satel TV, refrig. 1 unit w/terrace, 1 w/fireplace. 6 efficiencies have stove; all rooms have small refrigerators. **Services:** ⌐ Early check-in available. **Facilities:** 🛄 🐎 🔲 ⅄ 1 rst, lifeguard. Basketball and volleyball courts. **Rates:** HS June–Oct $28–$45 S; $35–$45 D; from $90 ste; from $50 effic. Extra person $4. Children under 12 stay free. Lower rates off-season. Higher rates for spec evnts/hols. Pking: Outdoor, free. Maj CC. On weekends and holidays, doubles rate only.

Attractions 📷

Jefferson County Courthouse, North George St; tel 304/725-9761. This 1836 Greek revival–style building was the site of the famous 1859 treason trial of John Brown. Partially destroyed during the Civil War, it has been extensively renovated, and visitors can tour the building, which is still in use today. **Open:** Mon–Thurs 9am–5pm, Fri 9am–7pm. Free.

Jefferson County Museum, 200 E Washington St; tel 304/725-8628. The small museum documents the history of the county, with special emphasis on the Civil War. Among the items on display are a Confederate flag from Stewart's Horse Artillery and personal items belonging to abolitionist John Brown. **Open:** Apr–Nov, Mon–Sat 10am–4pm. Free.

Site of the John Brown Gallows, S Samuel St. The site where John Brown was hung for treason is marked by a pyramid of stones said to have been taken from his cell in the Charles Town Jail. Present on this spot at the 1859 execution were Gen Stonewall Jackson and John Wilkes Booth. **Open:** Daily sunrise–sunset. Free.

CLARKSBURG

Map page M-2, B3

Motel 🛏

≡≡ **Comfort Inn**, 250 Emily Dr, Clarksburg, WV 26301; tel 304/623-2600 or toll free 800/221-2222; fax 304/622-5240. Exit 119 off I-79. Good location as part of shopping mall. **Rooms:** 112 rms and effic. CI noon/CO noon. Nonsmoking rms avail. Room for guests with disabilities has only wide door, no other special facilities. **Amenities:** 🚭 A/C, satel TV, refrig. **Services:** 🖼 ⌐ **Facilities:** 🔲 ⅄ **Rates (CP):** HS Apr–Oct $42 S or D; from $52 effic. Extra person $5. Children under 18 stay free. Lower rates off-season. Pking: Outdoor, free. Maj CC.

CROSSLANES

Map page M-2, C2 (NE of St Albans)

Motel 🛏

≡≡ **Comfort Inn**, 102 Racer Drive, Crosslanes, WV 25313; tel 304/776-8070 or toll free 800/798-7886; fax 304/776-6460. 10 mi W of Charleston. exit 47 off I-64. Convenient location minutes from Charleston. **Rooms:** 112 rms and stes. CI 2pm/CO noon. Nonsmoking rms avail. Standard motel-style rooms are pleasant. **Amenities:** 🚭 🕭 🖵 A/C, cable TV, refrig, stereo/tape player. **Services:** ✕ ⌐ **Facilities:** 🛄 🔲 ⅄ 1 rst, 1 bar (w/entertainment), whirlpool. **Rates (CP):** HS Apr–Oct $49 S; $56 D; from $66 ste. Extra person $5. Children under 18 stay free. Lower rates off-season. Spec packages avail. Pking: Outdoor, free. Maj CC.

DANIELS

Map page M-2, D3

Resort 🛏

≡≡≡ **Glade Springs Resort**, 3000 Lake Dr at US 19, Daniels, WV 25832; tel 304/763-2000 or toll free 800/634-5233; fax 304/763-3398. Exit 125 off I-64, or exit 28 off I-77. 3,500 acres. Convenient to 2 interstate highways and just 12 minutes from downtown Beckley, this 3,500-acre resort nestled in the mountains offers space, quiet, outdoor and indoor sports, and other activities. **Rooms:** 60 stes; 2 ctges/villas. Exec-level rms avail. CI 3pm/CO noon. Nonsmoking rms avail. **Amenities:** 🚭 🕭 🖵 A/C, cable TV w/movies, refrig, VCR. All units w/minibars, some w/terraces, some w/fireplaces, all w/Jacuzzis. Units have oversize Jacuzzis and 2 TVs. **Services:** 🍴 Social director. Security guards at entrance around the clock plus roving security guards. **Facilities:** 🔟📶▶18🏌🎿🚶🎣🏊8 🎱 🏐400 ⅙ 1 rst, 1 bar (w/entertainment), lifeguard, lawn games, racquetball, squash, playground, washer/dryer. Highly rated golf course, 2 fishing lakes. Heliport. **Rates:** HS Apr–Oct from $78 ste; from $275 ctge/villa. Extra person $10. Children under 12 stay free. Lower rates off-season. Spec packages avail. Pking: Outdoor, free. Maj CC. Golfing packages available.

DAVIS

Map page M-2, B4

Lodge 🖴

≡≡≡ **Blackwater Lodge**, in Blackwater Falls State Park, PO Box 490, Davis, WV 26260; tel 304/259-5216 or toll free 800/225-5982; fax 304/259-5881. Exit I-68 at US 219 S. Situated in a beautiful park with friendly deer. Comfortable lobby has sofas, chairs, piano. **Rooms:** 55 rms and stes; 25 ctges/villas. CI 3pm/CO noon. Nonsmoking rms avail. Units aren't fancy but are clean and neat and have incredible mountain views. Lodge rooms are on 2nd floor, with no elevator access. **Amenities:** 📺 A/C, cable TV. Some units w/terraces, some w/fireplaces. **Services:** ✕ 🔑 🍴 Masseur, children's program, babysitting. A naturalist plans events and gives talks. **Facilities:** 🛆🔟🏌🎿🚶 🎣 🎱2 🏊75 ⅙ 1 rst, 1 beach (lake shore), lifeguard, games rm, lawn games, playground. **Rates:** HS Mem Day–Labor Day/Dec 16–Feb 28 $55 S; $63 D; from $79 ste; from $88 ctge/villa. Extra person $6. Children under 12 stay free. Min stay wknds and spec evnts. Lower rates off-season. Pking: Outdoor, free. Maj CC.

Resorts

≡≡≡ **Black Bear Woods Resort**, Rte 1, Box 55, Davis, WV 26260; tel 304/866-4391 or toll free 800/553-BEAR. 40 mi S of Keyser's Ridge. A well-maintained, remote, wonderfully peaceful and quiet resort with lots of outdoors for children. Convenient to ski lodges, boat rentals, horseback riding. **Rooms:** 10 stes; 50 ctges/villas. CI 4pm/CO 11am. Nonsmoking rms avail. Both suites and pedestal units (small ground floor, larger upstairs) are large, with full kitchens. **Amenities:** 📺 📶 📠 Cable TV, refrig, VCR. No A/C. All units w/terraces, all w/fireplaces, some w/Jacuzzis. Pedestal units have washers and dryers. **Services:** 🛆 🍴 **Facilities:** 🔟🎿🚶🎣🎱1 🏊100 ⅙ 1 rst, 1 bar, games rm, lawn games, playground, washer/dryer. Heated indoor pool with large outdoor deck. **Rates:** HS Dec 15–Mar 15 from $90 ste;

from $140 ctge/villa. Min stay. Lower rates off-season. Spec packages avail. Pking: Outdoor, free. Ltd CC. $2 daily fee for small pets.

≡≡≡ **Canaan Valley Resort and Conference Center**, , PO Box 330, Davis, WV 26260; tel 304/866-4121 or toll free 800/622-4121; fax 304/866-2172. 35 mi NE of Elkins. 6,000 acres. Panoramic view of Allegheny Mountains from all angles of this 2-story multiservice resort in Canaan Valley State Park. **Rooms:** 250 rms and stes; 15 ctges/villas. CI 4pm/CO noon. Nonsmoking rms avail. All rooms similarly decorated with integrated decor of eye-pleasing fabrics. They face out in motor-lodge style. Some cabins have 7-night minimum during high season. **Amenities:** 📺 📠 ⅋ A/C, cable TV w/movies. Shower massage. **Services:** 🍴 Children's program, babysitting. Tennis and golf lessons available. Park naturalist and nature programs. Secretarial service. **Facilities:** 🔟🚴📶▶18🚶🎣🎱6 🏓🏊500 ⅙ 2 rsts, 2 bars (1 w/entertainment), games rm, spa, sauna, whirlpool, playground, washer/dryer. 18 miles of hiking trails. 34 campsites. Scenic chair lift. Miniature golf. Golf pro shop, driving range; ice skating; 33 slopes for downhill skiing, and many trails for cross-country skiing. Kids' "ski 'n' play" nursery. Cafe, coffee shop. **Rates:** HS May 20–Oct 23 $73 S; $79 D; from $108 ste; from $115 ctge/villa. Extra person $6. Children under 12 stay free. Min stay HS. Lower rates off-season. Higher rates for spec evnts/hols. Spec packages avail. Pking: Outdoor, free. Maj CC. Many packages available midweek only.

Attractions 🖼

White Grass Ski Touring Center, Freeland Rd; tel 304/866-4114. Located ½ mile north of Canaan Valley Resort State Park. Specialists in cross-country skiing, White Grass offers backcountry and machine-groomed trails, as well as lessons, guides, and ski schools. A rustic lodge provides specialized equipment sales and a natural foods cafe. **Open:** Dec–Mar, daily 8am–8pm. $$$

Blackwater Falls State Park, WV 32; tel 304/259-5216. This park is most noted for its amber-colored waters, dyed by tannic acids from fallen hemlock and red spruce needles, that converge in a 5-story plunge known as Blackwater Falls. In summer visitors can swim and boat in Pendleton Lake and enjoy the tennis courts, volleyball courts, and riding stables. Some of West Virginia's heaviest snowfalls occur in the Blackwater Falls region in winter, and the park offers cross-country skiing on over 20 miles of trails. The **Blackwater Nordic Center** offers cross-country ski instruction, equipment rentals, and backcountry guides. **Open:** Daily sunrise–sunset. Free.

Canaan Valley Resort State Park, WV 32; tel 304/866-4121. This park, set in a valley 3,200 feet above sea level and surrounded by mountain peaks, is a major winter sports area. The 240-acre ski facility offers downhill skiing, chairlifts, cross-country trails, and ice skating. Also located on the 6,015-acre resort are an 18-hole golf course, an indoor/outdoor pool, hiking trails, and tennis courts. **Open:** Daily 10am–8pm. $

ELKINS
Map page M-2, C4

Attraction 💼

Monongahela National Forest, jct US 219/250/33; tel 304/636-1800. A variety of trees can be found in the 908,000 acres of national forest stretching along the eastern coast of West Virginia, including cherry, maple, oak, yellow poplar, cedar, and even cactus. Rivers and streams support a coldwater fishery that features native and stocked trout. Other popular activities include bird watching, rock climbing, hiking, rafting, canoeing, and both primitive and developed camping. **Open:** Daily sunrise–sunset. Free.

FAIRMONT
Map page M-2, B4

Motels 🏨

Days Inn, 1185 Airport Rd, Fairmont, WV 26554; tel 304/367-1370 or toll free 800/329-7466; fax 304/367-1800. Although just off I-79, this motel is tucked away in an extremely quiet, peaceful area. **Rooms:** 98 rms. CI 2pm/CO noon. Nonsmoking rms avail. Rooms are quite pleasant, with coordinated decor. Fairly upscale for a Days Inn. **Amenities:** 🛁 A/C, cable TV. **Services:** 🔼 🍴 **Facilities:** 🛗 Ᏸ Games rm. **Rates (CP):** $43–$49 S; $48–$54 D. Extra person $5. Children under 18 stay free. Min stay spec evnts. Higher rates for spec evnts/hols. Pking: Outdoor, free. Maj CC.

Holiday Inn, I-79 and Old Grafton Rd, Fairmont, WV 26554; tel 304/366-5500 or toll free 800/HOLIDAY; fax 304/363-3975. Exit 137 off I-79. A chain motel with incredible views of the surrounding countryside. **Rooms:** 106 rms. Exec-level rms avail. CI 1pm/CO noon. Express checkout avail. Nonsmoking rms avail. Pleasant units are kept neat and clean. **Amenities:** 🛁 🍴 📺 A/C, cable TV w/movies, refrig, in-rm safe. Some units have microwaves. VCRs available for fee. **Services:** ✗ 🔼 🍴 🧺 Children's program, babysitting. Special kids program in sum-

mer. **Facilities:** 🛗 🎱 Ᏸ 1 rst, 1 bar. Bar and restaurant are attractive. **Rates:** HS Mar–Oct $50–$70 S or D. Extra person $5. Children under 19 stay free. Lower rates off-season. Higher rates for spec evnts/hols. Spec packages avail. Pking: Outdoor, free. Maj CC.

Red Roof Inn, Rte 1, PO Box 602, Fairmont, WV 26554; tel 304/366-6800 or toll free 800/THE-ROOF; fax 304/366-6812. Exit 132 off I-79. Convenient location near Middletown Mall. **Rooms:** 109 rms. CI noon/CO noon. Nonsmoking rms avail. New owners took over in 1994, were planning to renovate all rooms. **Amenities:** 🛁 A/C, cable TV. **Services:** 🍴 🧺 **Facilities:** 🎱 Ᏸ **Rates:** $32–$35 S; $39–$42 D. Extra person $3. Children under 16 stay free. Higher rates for spec evnts/hols. Pking: Outdoor, free. Maj CC. Senior discounts.

Restaurant 🍽️

$ ★ **Muriale's Restaurant**, 1742 Fairmont Ave Ext, Fairmont; tel 304/363-3190. Exit 132 off I-79. Follow WV 250 N for approximately 1½ miles. **American/Italian/Seafood.** This large, nothing-fancy but pleasant restaurant has wood tables and wood-backed chairs. Walls are lined with copper pots and old pictures. Extensive menu is heavy on Italian and seafood. Freshly baked basil bread is complimentary at each table. Excellent dessert tray. **FYI:** Reservations recommended. Children's menu. **Open:** Sun–Thurs 10am–9pm, Fri–Sat 11am–10pm. Closed some hols. **Prices:** Main courses $8–$16. Maj CC. 🍴 Ᏸ

Attraction 💼

Pricketts Fort State Park, exit 139 off I-79; tel 304/363-3030. Located on the site of an early frontier stronghold, this park features a reconstruction of a 1774 fort. Demonstrations of pioneer crafts are held within the compound, which features 16 cabins, a meeting hall, and a storehouse. The park also offers picnic grounds, an amphitheater, and access to the Monongahela River. An 18th-century Christmas market is held weekends from Thanksgiving through Christmas. **Open:** Apr–Oct, Mon–Sat 10am–5pm, Sun noon–5pm. Free.

FAYETTEVILLE
Map page M-2, D3 (SW of Ansted)

Attraction 💼

Rivers Resort Complex, US 19; tel toll free 800/879-7483. Located on the New River Gorge, Rivers offers white-water trips on the New, Cheat, and Gauley Rivers. Daily white-water excursions include a continental breakfast, equipment, transportation to the river, and a buffet lunch on the riverbank. Facilities at the resort complex include camping grounds, volleyball courts, horseshoe pits, and the Red Dog River Saloon. **Open:** May–Oct, daily 8am–7pm; Nov–Apr, daily 9am–5pm. Closed Dec 25. $$$$

GRAFTON

Map page M-2, B4

Motel ▣

≣ **Crislip Motor Lodge**, 300 Moritz Ave, Grafton, WV 26354; tel 304/265-2100. 20 mi E of Clarksburg. exit 119 off I-79. Follow US 50 E. A nice, well-kept motel from the 1950s in a pretty, peaceful setting away from town. Good place to relax. **Rooms:** 40 rms. CI 3pm/CO 11am. Rooms and baths are spacious. **Amenities:** ▣ ▣ A/C, cable TV. **Services:** ✗ VP ↩ ♨ **Facilities:** ▣ ♿ 1 rst, 1 bar. Breakfast restaurant on premises. **Rates:** $34 S; $43 D. Extra person $4–$5. Children under 12 stay free. Pking: Outdoor, free. Maj CC.

Lodge

≣≣≣ **Tygart Lake State Park Lodge**, Rte 1, PO Box 260, Grafton, WV 26354; tel 304/265-2320 or toll free 800/CALL-WVA. 42 mi S of Morgantown. Take US 119 south into Grafton; follow signs to state park and lodge. A true case of "almost heaven" at this comfortable, state-owned lodge surrounded by gorgeous countryside. View of lake is magnificent. Open only from late April to October. **Rooms:** 20 rms; 10 ctges/villas. CI 4pm/CO noon. Nonsmoking rms avail. Although average, rooms are clean and comfortable. Some face outside, others off indoor corridors. **Amenities:** ▣ A/C, cable TV. **Services:** ↩ Social director, children's program. Park ranger plans nature outings and events. **Facilities:** △ ▣ ▣ ♨ 100 ♿ 1 rst, 1 beach (lake shore), lifeguard, playground. Dining room overlooks lake. Section of lake roped off with concrete beach and adjacent grassy area. **Rates:** HS May 27–Sept 4 $52 S; $58 D. Extra person $6. Children under 12 stay free. Lower rates off-season. Pking: Outdoor, free. Maj CC. Cabins rent by week only (from $385/wk).

Attractions ▣

Grafton National Cemetary, 431 Walnut St; tel 304/265-2044. One of two national cemetaries in the state, this contains the grave of the first Union soldier killed by Confederate forces: T Bailey Brown. **Open:** Daily 24 hours. Free.

Tygart Lake State Park, intersection of US 50 and US 119; tel 304/265-3383. The highlight is the lake created by the US Army Corps of Engineers in the 1930s. Popular activities on its 13 square miles of water include swimming, scuba diving, boating, fishing, and waterskiing. Marina, lodge, camping. **Open:** Daily sunrise–sunset. Free.

GREEN BANK

Map page M-2, C4 (E of Linwood)

Attraction ▣

National Radio Astronomy Observatory, jct WV 28/92; tel 304/456-2011. This is the location of the Green Bank Telescope, which, when completed in 1995, will be the pioneer in radio astronomy for the 21st century. Other large radio telescopes at this location investigate quasars, pulsars, galaxies, stars, planets, and Milky Way gas clouds. **Open:** Mid-June to Labor Day, daily 9am–4pm; day after Labor day through Oct, Sat–Sun 9am–4pm. Free.

HARPERS FERRY

Map page M-3, B6

Motels ▣

≣≣≣ **Cliffside Inn & Conference Center**, US 340, PO Box 786, Harpers Ferry, WV 25425; tel 304/535-6302 or toll free 800/782-9437; fax 304/535-6313. Set atop a hill a mile from Harpers Ferry National Historical Park in the Blue Ridge Mountains, this property affords a commanding view and on-site services and facilities for a pleasurable stay. Large, half-timbered lobby provides a charming welcome. **Rooms:** 102 rms and stes. CI 2pm/CO 11am. Nonsmoking rms avail. Modest but spacious rooms. 1 suite available with queen-size brass bed; 8 poolside rooms. All units have either mountain or valley view. **Amenities:** ▣ A/C, satel TV w/movies. Some units w/terraces. Refrigerators available. Suite has fridge, 25-inch color TV. **Services:** ✗ ▣ ▣ ↩ ♨ **Facilities:** ▣ ▣ ▣2 800 ♿ 1 rst, 1 bar. The bar/lounge also serves food, and the restaurant, which features a buffet, enjoys a nice view. Volleyball and basketball courts. Computer/fax jacks in conference rooms. Gift shop offers local crafts and country wares. **Rates:** HS Apr–Oct $48–$58 S; $54–$58 D; from $95 ste. Extra person $6. Children under 12 stay free. Lower rates off-season. Spec packages avail. Pking: Outdoor, free. Maj CC. Getaway packages include meals and beverages.

Comfort Inn, US 340 and Union St, PO Box 980, Harpers Ferry, WV 25425; tel 304/535-6391 or toll free 800/228-5150; fax 304/535-6395. A small but functional and clean facility. Showing just a bit of wear on carpeting. Within a mile of historic section of Harpers Ferry National Historical Park and the Potomac and Shenandoah rivers. Informal and friendly atmosphere, but efficient service. Small, comfortable sitting area in lobby. **Rooms:** 50 rms. CI 3pm/CO 11am. Nonsmoking rms avail. Neat and tidy look, though some furnishings and blankets appear a bit tired. Bathrooms sparkling clean. **Amenities:** 📺 📠 A/C, cable TV. Rental VCRs and movies. **Services:** 🍴 Free coffee available in lobby. **Facilities:** 🏃 ᕕ Snack machines. **Rates (CP):** HS Apr–Oct $55 S; $61–$63 D. Extra person $6. Children under 18 stay free. Min stay spec evnts. Lower rates off-season. Spec packages avail. Pking: Outdoor, free. Maj CC. Relatively expensive for a modest facility with no frills.

Restaurant 🍴

★ **The Anvil Restaurant**, 1270 Washington St, Harpers Ferry; tel 304/535-2582. Exit US 340 at Harpers Ferry. **Regional American/Seafood.** This restaurant is comfy and convivial, with brick entryway, fireplaces in both bar and dining room, sturdy oak furniture, and some booths in bar area. Seafood is a draw; lighter fare available in bar section. Each evening brings a special: one night a week, it's all-you-can-eat shrimp; another is Mexican night. In a side dining room, mementos from *The Anvil*, a play about John Brown's trial, adorn the walls. **FYI:** Reservations accepted. Children's menu. No smoking. **Open:** Sun 11am–9pm, Tues–Thurs 11am–9pm, Fri–Sat 11am–10pm. Closed some hols. **Prices:** Main courses $9.95–$17.50. Maj CC. ♥ ᕕ

Attractions 📷

Harpers Ferry National Historical Park, US 340; tel 304/535-6298. This beautiful spot at the confluence of the Shenandoah and Potomac rivers—where Maryland, West Virginia, and Virginia meet—was the scene of a violent confrontation between abolitionists led by John Brown and US Marines under the command of Col Robert E Lee.

Today visitors can tour preserved streets, shops, houses, and public buildings that appear much as they did when this town flourished and prospered in the mid-19th century. Begin exploring at the **visitor center,** where there are maps for self-guided tours as well as shuttle buses to Lower Town. Ranger-led tours also initiate here 3 or 4 times a day. Some of the highlights of the area include Lower Town, featuring media presentations, restored buildings, and exhibits about the original town; Bolivar Heights, for the opportunity to walk in the footsteps of Abraham Lincoln and Stonewall Jackson; Camp Hill, the location of

Harper Cemetery; and the Virginius Island area, once home to a thriving 19th-century industrial town along the Shenandoah River. At Loudoun Heights, hikers can ascend the Blue Ridge Mountains via the historic and scenic Appalachian Trail. **Open:** Daily 8am–5pm. Closed Dec 25. Free.

John Brown Wax Museum, High St; tel 304/535-6342. Re-creates the career of the famed abolitionist through life-size exhibits featuring electronic lighting, sound, and animation. **Open:** Apr–Dec, daily 9am–5pm; Feb–Mar, Sat–Sun 10am–5pm. $

HEDGESVILLE
Map page M-3, B5 (N of Martinsburg)

Resort 🏨

The Woods Resort & Conference Center, Mountain Lake Rd, PO Box 5, Hedgesville, WV 25427; tel 304/754-7977 or toll free 800/248-2222; fax 304/754-8146. 12 mi W of Martinsburg. 1,800 acres. A woodsy, country-living resort offering rustic but comfortably sophisticated accommodations and facilities on its mountain acres. Emphasis on relaxation for the harried city-dweller. **Rooms:** 60 rms; 12 ctges/villas. CI 4pm/CO noon. Nonsmoking rms avail. The Walden Lodge rooms, overlooking pond and pool, contain pine furniture, king-size beds. Evergreen Lodge rooms are oversize and have open ceilings. The 2-bedroom cabins have shower-only baths, kitchens. Houses for rent. **Amenities:** 📺 A/C, cable TV w/movies, refrig. Some units w/terraces, some w/fireplaces, all w/Jacuzzis. **Services:** 🍴 Masseur. Business services available in conference room. **Facilities:** 🏐 ⛳ 🏊₂₇ 🎾 🏌₂ 🏐 🏓 💯 ᕕ 2 rsts, 1 bar (w/entertainment), lifeguard, lawn games, racquetball, sauna, steam rm, whirlpool, playground, washer/dryer. Fitness center features weight room and massages. Inside pool is heated. Snack bar on premises. Entertainment in bar/restaurant Saturday evenings. **Rates:** HS Oct $85–$125 S or D. Extra person $10. Children under 6 stay free. Min stay wknds. Lower rates off-season. MAP rates avail. Spec packages avail. Pking: Outdoor, free. Maj CC. Golf packages available. Business travelers' specials offered.

HICO

Map page M-2, D3 (E of Ansted)

Attraction 🧳

Mountain River Tours, Sunday Rd; tel toll free 800/822-1386. These river specialists are in their 20th season of conducting white-water trips on the Gauley and New rivers. All excursions use self-bailing boats. The price of a trip includes a continental breakfast. Campgrounds, hot showers, dining area. **Open:** Apr–Oct, daily 7am–10:15pm. $$$$

HILLSBORO

Map page M-2, D3

Attractions 🧳

Pearl S Buck House, US 219; tel 304/653-4430. This columned white frame house was the home of the only American woman to win both the Pulitzer and the Nobel prizes for literature. Displayed in the home are period furnishings and memorabilia from Buck's literary accomplishments. **Open:** May–Nov, Mon–Sat 9am–5pm, Sun 1–5pm. $$

Watoga State Park, US 219 and WV 39; tel 304/799-4087. Located in the Appalachian highlands on the Virginia border, West Virginia's largest state park encompasses 10,100 acres. Recreational opportunities include swimming and trout fishing in the **Greenbrier River,** rowboat and paddleboat rentals, cross-country skiing and hiking trails, picnicking, and tennis. Restaurant, campgrounds, cabins. **Open:** Daily 6am–10pm. Free.

Droop Mountain Battlefield State Park, US 219; tel 304/653-4254. The oldest state park in West Virginia, this was the site of the Battle of Droop Mountain, fought on November 6, 1863, in which the Union army thwarted serious efforts by the Confederacy to control West Virginia. Hiking trails throughout the park point out highlights of the battle. Picnic area, ski trails, museum. **Open:** Daily 6am–10pm. Free.

HINTON

Map page M-2, D3

For lodging and dining, see Beckley

Attractions 🧳

Hinton Historic District, 206 Temple St; tel 304/466-5420. In 1872, Hinton became the center of a major C&O terminal yard and a building boom swept the area. Today there are over 20 National Historical Sites here, including the Parker Opera House, built in 1885; the colonial revival–style Second Baptist Church, the oldest African-American church in the area; and the C&O passenger depot, still an active train station after 100 years. The visitors center provides self-guided tour maps of the town and its historical buildings. **Open:** Daily 9am–5pm. Free.

New River Scenic Whitewater Tours, Hinton Bypass off WV 20; tel toll free 800/292-0880. The Gauley River has long been a popular spot with white-water enthusiasts for its pristine water and world-class white water. This company specializes in tours down the river geared to all skill levels. The emphasis here is on safety and traditional styles of rafting; due to this, New River uses buckets for water battles instead of self-bailing rafts. Campgrounds. **Open:** Mar–Oct, daily 8am–6pm. $$$$

Bluestone Dam, WV 20; tel 304/466-1234. Closing a 2,048-foot gap between mountains, this concrete gravity dam rises 165 feet above the stream bed. The dam holds back an average 2,040 surface acres of water; the tail waters below offer fishing and canoeing. A visitors center is located at the top of the structure. Tours are offered by the US Army Corps of Engineers June through August on Tues and Wed at 1:30pm and Fri and Sat at 2pm. Free.

Pipestem Resort State Park, WV 20; tel 304/466-1800. Situated near the Bluestone Dam recreation area, this park features an 18-hole golf course, a pool, tennis and basketball courts, miniature golf, a nature center, and stables. Long Branch Lake and Bluestone River afford a variety of fishing and boating opportunities. A unique feature of the park is the Pipestem Aerial Tramway that transports visitors from the Canyon Rim Center to the rugged floor of Bluestone Canyon. **Open:** Daily 6am–10pm. Free.

Bluestone State Park, WV 20; tel 304/466-2805. This heavily wooded park lies adjacent to Bluestone Lake, making it a popular destination in the southern section of the state. Boating, fishing, hiking trails, a pool, boat-launching facilities, and a marina are some of the attractions here. Camping, cabins. **Open:** Daily sunrise–sunset. Free.

HUNTINGTON

Map page M-2, C2

Hotel 🛏

≣≣≣ **Radisson Hotel Huntington**, 1001 3rd Ave, Huntington, WV 25701; tel 304/525-1001 or toll free 800/333-3333; fax 304/525-1001 ext 2041. Exit 11 off I-64. Attractive atrium with trees, sitting areas, tables beside pool makes this hotel seem removed from its downtown location a block from Ohio River. **Rooms:** 200 rms and stes. Exec-level rms avail. CI 3pm/CO noon. Express checkout avail. Nonsmoking rms avail. Warm and comfortable rooms, with upscale furnishings. **Amenities:** 🛏 🖥 A/C, cable TV w/movies, shoe polisher. 1 unit w/Jacuzzi. VCRs and refrigerators can be rented at front desk. **Services:** ✕ 🆅🅿 🚗 ⛷ 🗣 📞 Masseur, babysitting. **Facilities:** 🏋 ⚓ 🌊 800 ⚓ 1 rst, 1 bar, spa, sauna, steam rm. Lively restaurant with bar and entertainment. **Rates:** $78–$88 S; $97–$108 D; from $158 ste. Extra person $10. Children under 16 stay free. Min stay spec evnts. Spec packages avail. Pking: Indoor, free. Maj CC.

Motels

≣≣ **Holiday Inn Downtown/University Area**, 1415 4th Ave, Huntington, WV 25701; tel 304/525-7741 or toll free 800/828-9016; fax 304/525-3508. Exit 11 off I-64. One of only 2 in-town motels convenient to commercial center, Marshall University. **Rooms:** 137 rms and stes. CI 4pm/CO noon. Express checkout avail. Nonsmoking rms avail. Pleasant rooms recently refurbished. 3 economy suites have Murphy beds. **Amenities:** 🛏 🖥 🍽 A/C, satel TV w/movies. **Services:** ✕ 🚗 ⛷ 🗣 🖐 Masseur. Guests who ask are provided breakfast. **Facilities:** 🏋 ⚓ 250 ⚓ 1 rst, 1 bar. **Rates:** $60 S; $65 D; from $90 ste. Extra person $5. Children under 18 stay free. Higher rates for spec evnts/hols. Spec packages avail. Pking: Outdoor, free. Maj CC.

≣≣ **Ramada Inn**, 5600 US 60 E, Huntington, WV 25705; tel 304/736-3451 or toll free 800/228-2828; fax 304/736-3451. Exit 20 off I-64. A 3-story brick motel, convenient to malls, restaurants, downtown. **Rooms:** 120 rms. CI 2pm/CO noon. Nonsmoking rms avail. Comfortable units all recently refurbished. **Amenities:** 🛏 A/C, satel TV, shoe polisher. All units w/terraces. **Services:** 🚗 ⛷ 🗣 🖐 Babysitting. **Facilities:** 🏋 ⚓ 75 ⚓ 1 rst, 1 bar. **Rates:** $54 S; $59 D. Extra person $5. Children under 18 stay free. Pking: Outdoor, free. Maj CC.

Restaurant 🍽

♦ ✦ **Rebels and Redcoats Tavern**, in Colonial Lanes Bowling Alley, 412 7th Ave W, Huntington; tel 304/523-8829. Exit 8 off I-64. Follow US 52 N to 7th Ave, turn left. **American/Seafood/Steak.** Consistently rated one of West Virginia's top restaurants, this place has the aura of a men's club, with dark wood-paneled walls, moldings, candles on walls, leaded-glass windows. Prime rib is the focus, either regular or Cajun-style. Also seafood, rack of lamb, chops. **FYI:** Reservations recommended. Combo. Dress code. **Open:** Lunch Mon–Sat 11:30am–2:30pm; dinner Mon–Thurs 5:30–10pm, Fri–Sat 5:30–11pm. Closed some hols. **Prices:** Main courses $13–$40. Maj CC. ♥ 🏛 🚗

Attractions 💼

Central City Historic District, exit 6 off I-64; tel toll free 800/635-6329. Between 1893 and 1909 this was a flourishing manufacturing town known as St Cloud. The well-preserved Victorian frame houses, brick streets, and cast-iron fences here reflect residential fashions of the times and turn-of-the-century tastes. Visitors can tour the town and view the historic homes, including the Parsons-Abott-Mosser house, a High Victorian frame residence built in 1870 for Captain H Chester Parsons, a leading figure in the settlement of Huntington. **Open:** Daily 9am–4:30pm. Free.

Huntington Museum of Art, 2033 McCoy Rd; tel 304/529-2701. This indoor/outdoor complex features gallery space, nature trails, an observatory with a Celestron-14 telescope, a junior art museum, a sculpture garden, and an amphitheater. Permanent collections include Appalachian folk art, American and European paintings, Georgian Silver, pre-Columbian art, and hand-blown glass. **Open:** Tues–Sat 10am–5pm, Sun noon–5pm. Closed some hols. $

Camden Park, exit 6 off I-64; tel 304/429-4321. A family tradition since 1902, this amusement park features 28 rides including a new looping roller coaster and a log flume. In addition, this is the location of the *C P Huntington* sternwheel excursion boat offering 45-minute narrated rides along the Ohio River. **Open:** Apr and Sept, Sat–Sun 10am–10pm; May–Aug, daily 10am–10pm. $$$

Hamon Glass, 102 Hamon Dr; tel 304/757-9067. Specialists in blown glass and glass sculpture, the design team of Robert and Veronnica Hamon give demonstrations of the glass-sculpting process and present exhibitions of their glasswork. **Open:** Mon–Fri 9am–4pm. Free.

Blenko Glass, exit 28 off I-64; tel 304/743-9081. Located 16 miles east of Huntington in Milton, Blenko is best known as a stained-glass producer. Creations from the factory can be seen in such locations as New York City's St Patrick's Cathedral and Grant's Tomb, and the Rose Window in the Washington Cathedral. In addition to a small museum with examples of blown glass, the Blenko visitors center has a special observation deck where visitors can watch molten glass take its final form. **Open:** Mon–Sat 8am–4pm, Sun noon–4pm. Free.

Pilgrim Glass, exit 1 off I-64; tel 304/453-3553. Pilgrim, located 5 miles west of Huntington in Ceredo, is most noted for its cameo glass, a process where several colors of molten glass are cast in layers and, when cool, carved into designs. Visitors can see this unique process as well as traditional glass blowing at the visitor observation platform. **Open:** Mon–Sat 9am–5pm, Sun noon–5pm. Free.

LANSING
Map page M-2, D3 (N of Beckley)

Attraction 🧳

Wildwater, US 19 and Milroy Grose Rd; tel toll free 800/WVA-RAFT. The oldest white-water outfitter in West Virginia, Wildwater offers 12 different raft trips at all levels on the Gauley, New, and Upper Yough rivers. **Open:** Mar–Nov, daily, hours vary. $$$$

LEWISBURG
Map page M-2, D3

***See also* White Sulphur Springs**

Motels 🛏

▤▤▤ Briar Inn Motel and Convention Center, 540 N Jefferson St, Lewisburg, WV 24986; tel 304/645-7722; fax 304/645-7865. Exit 169 off I-64. Proximity to I-64, center of town, many restaurants, and golfing at the Greenbrier in White Sulphur Springs is a plus for this motel. **Rooms:** 162 rms, stes, and effic. CI 2pm/CO 11am. Nonsmoking rms avail. **Amenities:** 🛢 A/C, cable TV. Some units w/minibars, some w/Jacuzzis. **Services:** 🛆 🖰 🕾 Staff arranges tours of local attractions. **Facilities:** 🖼 🍽 🖵 🕭 1 rst, 1 bar (w/entertainment). **Rates:** $42–$47 S or D; from $70 ste; from $62 effic. Extra person $5. Children under 12 stay free. Higher rates for spec evnts/hols. Pking: Outdoor, free. Maj CC.

▤▤ Budget Host Fort Savannah, 204 N Jefferson St, Lewisburg, WV 24901; tel 304/645-3055 or toll free 800/678-3055. Exit 169 off I-64. Go south on US 219 for 1½ miles. Located next to the remains of a late-18th-century fort and well and across from a park, this is a comfortable place for families. Within walking distance of downtown historic district. **Rooms:** 65 rms. CI 2pm/CO noon. Nonsmoking rms avail. **Amenities:** 🛢 A/C, cable TV, stereo/tape player. **Services:** 🛆 🖰 🕾 **Facilities:** 🖼 🕾 🕭 1 rst, 1 bar (w/entertainment), games rm, whirlpool, washer/dryer. **Rates:** HS Apr–Oct $50–$60 S or D. Extra person $4. Children under 18 stay free. Lower rates off-season. Higher rates for spec evnts/hols. Spec packages avail. Pking: Outdoor, free. Maj CC.

▤▤ Days Inn, 635 N Jefferson St, Lewisburg, WV 24901; tel 304/645-2345 or toll free 800/329-7466. Exit 169 off I-64. Go north on US 219 for ¼ mile. Sitting atop a hill, this motel is close to restaurants, a country club golf course, medical colleges, the Greenbrier, and the West Virginia Fairgrounds. **Rooms:** 26 rms. CI noon/CO 11am. Nonsmoking rms avail. **Amenities:** 🛢 A/C, cable TV. **Services:** 🛆 🖰 🕾 **Facilities:** Washer/dryer. **Rates (CP):** HS June–Oct $40–$45 S; $55–$65 D. Extra person $5. Children under 12 stay free. Min stay spec evnts. Lower rates off-season. Higher rates for spec evnts/hols. Pking: Outdoor, free. Maj CC.

Inn

▤▤▤ The General Lewis Inn, 301 E Washington St, Lewisburg, WV 24901; tel 304/645-2600 or toll free 800/628-4454; fax 304/645-2600. Exit 169 off I-64. Drive south on US 219 to E Washington St, turn left, go 2 blocks. Relaxing in rocking chairs on the veranda or patio and looking out over grounds with a goldfish pond and an old stagecoach evokes memories of days gone by. So to does a plethora of antiques in this comfortable inn, part of which is a circa-1834 home. Conveniently located in historic Lewisburg, near museums and Revolutionary and Civil War sites. **Rooms:** 25 rms and stes. CI 3pm/CO 11am. No smoking. Of varying sizes, rooms are decorated with antiques handed down by the area's early settlers. **Amenities:** 🛢 🕭 A/C, cable TV. **Services:** 🛆 🖰 🕾 Babysitting. Ice placed in rooms each afternoon. **Facilities:** 🕭 1 rst (*see also* "Restaurants" below), guest lounge. **Rates:** $60–$88 D; from $88 ste. Extra person $10. Children under 3 stay free. Higher rates for spec evnts/hols. MAP rates avail. Spec packages avail. Pking: Outdoor, free. Ltd CC.

Restaurant 🍽

The General Lewis Inn Dining Room, in the General Lewis Inn, 301 E Washington St, Lewisburg; tel 304/645-2600. Exit

169 off I-64. Follow US 219 south, turn left at 1st traffic light, go 2 blocks. **Regional American.** Dining room in this original 1834 home is filled with antiques, adding to down-home ambience. Cocktails sipped in living room or on patio. Old-fashioned meals of mountain trout, country ham, and homemade soups, breads, and desserts. **FYI:** Reservations recommended. Children's menu. No smoking. **Open:** Breakfast Mon–Sat 7–11am, Sun 7:30–11am; lunch Mon–Sat 11:30am–3pm; dinner Mon–Sat 5–9pm, Sun noon–9pm. **Prices:** Main courses $10–$18. Maj CC. 💟 🎅 📷

Attraction 🖼

Lewisburg Historic District, 105 Church St; tel 304/645-1000. Set amid the Allegheny Mountains, the area appears much the way it did 200 year ago. A steeple clock tolls the hour, antebellum homes have often been occupied by the same families for generations, gaslamps light the streets, and there are no overhead power lines. Start a walking tour at the visitors center to obtain self-guided tour maps. Special locations include the **Old Stone Presbyterian Church**, 200 Church St; built in 1796, it is the oldest church in continuous use west of the Alleghenies. **North House**, which serves as the museum of the Greenbrier Historical Society, was originally a tavern when it was built in 1820. It is distinguished by its heavily carved ornate woodwork. **Open:** Visitors center, Mon–Sat 9am–5pm, Sun 1–5pm. Free.

LOGAN

Map page M-2, D2

Attractions 🖼

Chief Logan State Park, WV 119; tel 304/792-7125. Set on 3,300 acres in the heart of coal country, this park is a popular camping and hiking location. Pool, physical-fitness trail, tennis courts, miniature golf. **Open:** Daily 6am–10pm. Free.

Watters Smith Memorial State Park, exit 110 off I-79; tel 304/792-7125. This historical park features a late-1700s farm; the original Smith family home (circa 1876); and a museum that houses many early farm artifacts. There's also features swimming, picnicking, and hiking. **Open:** Mem Day–Labor Day, daily 11am–7pm. Free.

MADISON

Map page M-2, D2

Attraction 🖼

Water Ways, WV 119; tel 304/369-1235. A water park featuring water slides, a pool, an 18-hole miniature golf course, and picnic grounds. **Open:** Mem Day–Labor Day, daily 11am–8pm. $$$

MARTINSBURG

Map page M-3, B5

Hotels 🛏

🟰🟰 **Comfort Inn**, 2800 Aikens Center, Martinsburg, WV 25401; tel 304/263-6200 or toll free 800/622-3416; fax 304/263-6200 ext 113. Exit 16E off US 81. Nicely decorated facility, though not fancy. Convenient to interstate and downtown Martinsburg. Impressive for a chain motel. Large lobby features super-size TV, tables, comfy sofa, large easy chairs. **Rooms:** 109 rms and stes. CI 2pm/CO noon. Nonsmoking rms avail. **Amenities:** 🎅 A/C, cable TV w/movies. Some units w/Jacuzzis. **Services:** Social director, babysitting. Very professional staff. **Facilities:** 1 rst, games rm, spa, washer/dryer. 2 restaurants within easy walking distance. **Rates (CP):** $60–$84 S or D; from $84 ste. Extra person $6. Children under 18 stay free. Spec packages avail. Pking: Outdoor, free. Maj CC.

🟰🟰🟰 **Holiday Inn**, 301 Foxcroft Ave, Martinsburg, WV 25401; tel 304/267-5500 or toll free 800/325-3535 in the US, 800/268-9393 in Canada; fax 304/267-3899. Exit 13 off US 81. Set in a shopping plaza just off interstate, but distant enough from other facilities to be quiet, restful. Adjacent to residential neighborhood. Spacious lobby with elegant furnishings, carpeting. **Rooms:** 120 rms and stes. Exec-level rms avail. CI 3pm/CO noon. Express checkout avail. Nonsmoking rms avail. **Amenities:** 🎅 A/C, satel TV w/movies. **Services:** ✗ Twice-daily maid svce. **Facilities:** 1 rst, 1 bar (w/entertainment), lifeguard, spa, sauna, steam rm, whirlpool, washer/dryer. Indoor heated pool and adjoining spa/health club are nicely designed and maintained. **Rates:** HS Mar 15–Oct 31 $70–$110 S; $80–$100 D; from $130 ste. Extra person $10. Children under 18 stay free. Min stay spec evnts. Lower rates off-season. Spec packages avail. Pking: Outdoor, free. Maj CC. Weekend packages available.

Motels

≣≣**Arborgate Inn**, 1599 Edwin Miller Blvd, Martinsburg, WV 25401; tel 304/267-2211 or toll free 800/843-5644; fax 304/267-9606. Exit 16 off US 81. Clean and hospitable. Stone pillars a nice architectural touch, setting this apart from usual chain motel. **Rooms:** 59 rms and effic. CI noon/CO noon. Nonsmoking rms avail. Basic rooms but good color coordination and impressively clean. **Amenities:** 🛏 A/C, cable TV w/movies. Six kitchenettes available with microwave, fridge. VCRs for rent. **Services:** 🔄 🚗 Free coffee in lobby. **Facilities:** 🎱 ⚓ **Rates:** $40 S; $47 D; from $51 effic. Extra person $6. Children under 17 stay free. Pking: Outdoor, free. Maj CC.

≣**Days Inn Shenandoah**, 209 Viking Way, Martinsburg, WV 25401; tel 304/263-1800 or toll free 800/263-1806. Exit 13 off US 81. Conveniently located in a shopping plaza with 8 outlet stores. **Rooms:** 63 rms and stes. CI 4pm/CO noon. Nonsmoking rms avail. **Amenities:** 🛏 A/C, cable TV. **Services:** 🖨 🔄 Coffee in lobby. **Facilities:** ⚓ Washer/dryer. Shopping plaza has chain restaurants. Bar and lounge at Sheraton Martinsburg within walking distance. **Rates (CP):** $51–$56 S or D; from $65 ste. Extra person $6. Children under 18 stay free. Spec packages avail. Pking: Outdoor, free. Maj CC.

Restaurant 🍴

Redfield's Restaurant, 200 W Burke St, Martinsburg; tel 304/263-4997. Exit 13 off I-81. 1 block N of W King St. **Mediterranean/Seafood/Steak.** Four separate dining rooms, all with fireplaces, are found in this 1855 Victorian house sitting on a quiet residential side street. Impressionist paintings hang from the walls, and large windows bring in light. An outdoor patio is open for dining, weather permitting, and 2 small banquet rooms are available upstairs. While some face-lifting on the old house could be done, the ambience is genuine and the food (Mediterranean-accented specialties, seafood, and basic steaks) has a reputation as the best in town. The Louisiana-trained chef likes a Creole touch for many dishes. **FYI:** Reservations accepted. **Open:** Lunch Mon–Sat 11:30am–2:30pm; dinner Mon–Thurs 5–9pm, Fri–Sat 5–10pm, Sun 4–9pm. Closed some hols. **Prices:** Main courses $9.95–$16.95. Maj CC. 💟 🍺 🖼

Attractions 💼

General Adam Stephen House, 309 E John St; tel 304/267-4434. Constructed between 1774 and 1789, this was the home of Gen Adam Stephen, a contemporary of George Washington and Patrick Henry. The house is decorated with period furnishings, and the adjacent Triple Brick Museum contains items of local historical significance. **Open:** Apr–Oct, Sat–Sun 2–5pm. Free.

Boarman Arts Center, 208 S Queen St; tel 304/263-0224. This gallery represents West Virginian artists through year-round juried exhibits that are open to the public. Recent showings have focused on Black History Month; youth art; American etchings in black and white; and a retrospective of Cubert L Smith, a popular local artist. **Open:** Mon–Fri 10am–5pm. Free.

MILL POINT
Map page M-2, D4

Attraction 💼

Cranberry Glades Botanical Area, jct WV 39/150; tel 304/653-4826 or 846-2695. Part of the Monongahela National Forest, the botanical area was created to preserve the natural ecosystem and protect native plant life for future generations. The Cranberry Glades Visitor Center houses interpretive displays that explain the 4 communities of plants and trees on the 750 acres of the preserve. A half-mile boardwalk traverses 2 of the areas, providing visitors with an opportunity to view cranberries on the vine, wild orchids blooming in July, and black bears feasting on skunk cabbage. The first 2 weeks of October the glades are open daily for fall foliage tours. Visitors are restricted to the boardwalk area; however, tours of the area are available if reservations are made in advance. On summer weekends naturalist guides lead 1-hour tours beginning at 2pm. **Open:** Mem Day–Labor Day, daily 9am–5pm; Labor Day–Mem Day, Sat–Sun 9am–5pm. Closed Dec. Free.

MINERAL WELLS
Map page M-2, B2 (S of Parkersburg)

Motel 🛏

≣≣**Comfort Suites**, I-77 and WV 14 S, PO Box 108, Mineral Wells, WV 26150; tel 304/489-9600 or toll free 800/228-5150; fax 304/489-1896. 2 mi S of Parkersburg. exit 170 off I-77. A pleasant drive leads to this all-suites motel with massive stone fireplace in lobby. **Rooms:** 116 stes. CI 4pm/CO noon. Nonsmoking rms avail. Spacious, wonderfully furnished units with large bathrooms. **Amenities:** 🛏 A/C, cable TV, refrig, VCR, voice mail. Some units w/Jacuzzis. Microwaves. **Services:** ✕ 🚐 🖨 🔄 Babysitting. Full complimentary breakfast Tuesday through Friday, continental other mornings. Apple cider served in lobby during winter. Full business services. **Facilities:** [icon] [icon] [icon] [icon] 1 bar (w/entertainment), games rm, spa, sauna, whirlpool, washer/dryer. Attractive indoor-outdoor pool. **Rates (BB):** Extra person $6. Children under 18 stay free. Spec packages avail. Pking: Outdoor, free. Maj CC.

MORGANTOWN

Map page M-2, B4

Hotels [icon]

≣≣≣ Euro-Suites Hotel, 501 Chestnut Ridge Rd, Morgantown, WV 26505; tel 304/598-1000 or toll free 800/678-4837; fax 304/599-2736. Exit 7 off I-68. Wonderful lobby with baby grand piano invites sitting and relaxing in comfortable sofas and chairs. A relatively new hotel with friendly, helpful staff. **Rooms:** 74 rms and stes. Exec-level rms avail. CI 4pm/CO 1pm. Express checkout avail. Nonsmoking rms avail. Spacious rooms tastefully decorated, from wallpaper to artwork. **Amenities:** [icon] [icon] [icon] A/C, cable TV w/movies, refrig, voice mail, shoe polisher. Some units w/Jacuzzis. Suites have microwaves, refrigerators. **Services:** [icon] [icon] [icon] [icon] Babysitting. **Facilities:** [icon] [icon] [icon] 1 bar. Guests can use pool at Lakeview Resort. **Rates (CP):** $69–$69 S; $79–$79 D; from $91 ste. Extra person $10. Children under 18 stay free. Min stay spec evnts. Higher rates for spec evnts/hols. Spec packages avail. Pking: Outdoor, free. Maj CC.

≣≣ Hotel Morgan, 127 High St, Morgantown, WV 26505; tel 304/292-8401; fax 304/292-4601. Take I-68 or I-79 to downtown. Although Morgantown's once-premier hotel has seen better days (it was up for sale at inspection), the high-ceilinged lobby still has the beautiful and charming woodwork and iron railings from bygone days, which would make it ideal for a Raffles-style makeover. Grand ballroom is still grand. Remains a good choice for downtown stays. **Rooms:** 92 rms and stes. CI 2pm/CO 11am. Nonsmoking rms avail. Most rooms are rather small, although some are combined into larger units. Comfortable but dated furniture in older rooms, while renovated units are better equipped. **Amenities:** [icon] A/C, cable TV w/movies. **Services:** [icon] [icon] Validated parking a treat in downtown. **Facilities:** [icon] 1 rst, 3 bars, games rm. Restaurant is popular with locals. Great bakery just off the lobby. **Rates:** $40 S or D; from $50 ste. Children under 18 stay free. Min stay spec evnts. Higher rates for spec evnts/hols. Pking: Outdoor, free. Maj CC.

Motels

≣≣ Comfort Inn, WV 9, PO Box 225, Morgantown, WV 26505; tel 304/296-9364 or toll free 800/221-2222; fax 304/

296-0469. Exit 1 off I-68. Follow US 119 to WV 9. A comfortable, clean, modern motel. **Rooms:** 80 rms, stes, and effic. CI 2pm/CO noon. Nonsmoking rms avail. Comfortable, well-maintained rooms are spacious. **Amenities:** [icon] [icon] A/C, cable TV w/movies, shoe polisher. Some units w/Jacuzzis. **Services:** [icon] [icon] [icon] **Facilities:** [icon] [icon] [icon] [icon] 1 rst, whirlpool. Lovely pool in rear. Restaurant on premises but not in the building. **Rates (CP):** HS May–Oct $50–$80 S; $50–$80 D; from $80 ste; from $50 effic. Extra person $6. Children under 18 stay free. Min stay spec evnts. Lower rates off-season. Higher rates for spec evnts/hols. Spec packages avail. Pking: Outdoor, free. Maj CC.

≣≣ Hampton Inn, 1053 Van Voorhis Rd, Morgantown, WV 26505; tel 304/599-1200 or toll free 800/426-7866; fax 304/599-1200 ext 133. Exit 155 off I-79. A good, basic, clean, and well-maintained motel. **Rooms:** 108 rms and stes. CI 2pm/CO noon. Nonsmoking rms avail. Quite pleasant rooms have 3 large mirrors placed to give full view. **Amenities:** [icon] A/C, cable TV w/movies. **Services:** [icon] [icon] Morning coffee and doughnuts in office. Hospitality suite. **Facilities:** [icon] [icon] **Rates (CP):** $48–$54 S; $53–$59 D; from $75 ste. Children under 18 stay free. Higher rates for spec evnts/hols. Pking: Outdoor, free. Maj CC.

≣≣ Holiday Inn, 1400 Saratoga Ave, Morgantown, WV 26505 (Star City); tel 304/599-1680 or toll free 800/465-4329; fax 304/598-0989. Exit 155 off I-79. A typical Holiday Inn built in the 1970s. **Rooms:** 147 rms. CI 2pm/CO noon. Express checkout avail. Nonsmoking rms avail. Rooms are a bit tired but clean. Each has a sofa. **Amenities:** [icon] [icon] [icon] A/C, cable TV w/movies, in-rm safe. **Services:** [icon] [icon] [icon] [icon] Babysitting. **Facilities:** [icon] [icon] [icon] 1 rst, 1 bar. **Rates:** HS May–Nov $68–$95 S. Children under 18 stay free. Min stay spec evnts. Lower rates off-season. Higher rates for spec evnts/hols. Spec packages avail. Pking: Outdoor, free. Maj CC.

≣≣≣ Ramada Inn, US 119, at jct I-68/I-79, PO Box 1242, Morgantown, WV 26507; tel 304/296-3431 or toll free 800/272-6232, 800/272-6232, 800/834-9766 in WV; fax 304/296-3431 ext 441. This motel enjoys a commanding view of the surrounding mountains. Lobby contains such lovely touches as fountain, planters, flags. **Rooms:** 159 rms and stes. CI 3pm/CO noon. Nonsmoking rms avail. All units recently refurbished. **Amenities:** [icon] [icon] [icon] A/C, satel TV w/movies. Some units w/minibars, 1 w/Jacuzzi. **Services:** [icon] [icon] [icon] [icon] [icon] Babysitting. Boat tours of river for fee. **Facilities:** [icon] [icon] [icon] [icon] [icon] [icon] 1 rst, 1 bar (w/entertainment), lifeguard, games rm. Plans to enclose outdoor heated pool. **Rates:** $55 S; $60 D; from $125 ste. Extra person $5. Children under 18 stay free. Min stay spec evnts. Higher rates for spec evnts/hols. Spec packages avail. Pking: Outdoor, free. Maj CC.

Resort

≣≣ **Lakeview Resort and Conference Center**, WV 6, PO Box 88A, Morgantown, WV 26505; tel 304/594-1111 or toll free 800/624-8300; fax 304/594-9472. Lovely drive through 2 golf courses leads to this resort, whose public areas are quite charming. Lobby invites long sits. **Rooms:** 187 rms and stes; 72 ctges/villas. CI 4pm/CO 2pm. Nonsmoking rms avail. Although clean and neat, rooms don't live up to quality of public areas. **Amenities:** 🛏 🦉 🍴 A/C, cable TV w/movies, refrig, in-rm safe, shoe polisher, bathrobes. Some units w/terraces, some w/fireplaces. **Services:** ✗ 🍽 🚗 🖼 🍽 Car-rental desk, social director, masseur, babysitting. **Facilities:** 🎣 🚲 🛶 ▶36 ▲ 🏖 🛶 🏊 ▶ 🎱 🏊 ⚐ 🚾 ♿ 2 rsts (*see also* "Restaurants" below), 1 bar (w/entertainment), games rm, lawn games, racquetball, spa, sauna, steam rm, whirlpool, day-care ctr, playground, washer/dryer. Beautifully maintained golf courses. Pontoon boats holding up to 15 people available on the lake. **Rates:** HS Apr 15–Nov 15 $129 S; $139 D; from $215 ste; from $280 ctge/villa. Extra person $10. Children under 18 stay free. Min stay wknds. Lower rates off-season. Spec packages avail. Pking: Outdoor, free. Maj CC.

Restaurants 🍴

⑤ ✦ **The Glasshouse Grille**, in Seneca Center, 709 Beechurst Ave, Morgantown; tel 304/296-8460. Exit I-79 at Star City; follow US 119 S. **Continental/Eclectic/Seafood.** Occupying part of an old glass factory, this restaurant exudes historic charm. Leaded windows and beautiful glass chandeliers are everywhere. Famous lump-meat crab cakes headline an eclectic menu, including fettuccine, filet mignon. Excellent preparation includes herbs grown in garden. Desserts are homemade. Outdoor seating on charming patio in good weather. **FYI:** Reservations recommended. Children's menu. **Open:** HS Sept–Nov lunch Mon–Sat 11am–2pm; dinner Mon–Sat 5–9pm; brunch. Reduced hours off-season. Closed some hols. **Prices:** Main courses $5.50–$18. Maj CC. ♥ 🍽 🍽 🚗 ♿

Reflections on the Lake, in Lakeview Resort, WV 6, Box 88A, Morgantown; tel 304/594-1111. Exit 10 off I-68. **New American/Seafood.** A hushed atmosphere prevails in this lovely, club-like restaurant with widely spaced tables. Such well-prepared selections as chicken stir-fry, herbed duck breast, and veal piccata. An evening here will be well spent. **FYI:** Reservations recommended. Children's menu. **Open:** Dinner daily 6–10pm; brunch Sun 11am–2pm. **Prices:** Main courses $15–$23. Maj CC. ♥ 🖼

Attractions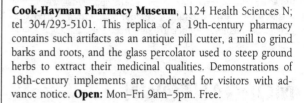

Cook-Hayman Pharmacy Museum, 1124 Health Sciences N; tel 304/293-5101. This replica of a 19th-century pharmacy contains such artifacts as an antique pill cutter, a mill to grind barks and roots, and the glass percolator used to steep ground herbs to extract their medicinal qualities. Demonstrations of 18th-century implements are conducted for visitors with advance notice. **Open:** Mon–Fri 9am–5pm. Free.

Personal Rapid Transit System, 99 8th St; tel 304/293-5011. Connecting West Virginia University's 2 campuses with downtown Morgantown, this is the world's first totally automated transportation system. The entire system is controlled through computers that determine routes and destinations. In addition to providing transportation for the over 26,000 students and employees of WVU, the PRTS serves as a national transportation research laboratory for Boeing Aerospace and the Urban Mass Transit Administration of the US Department of Transportation. **Open:** Sept–May, Mon–Fri 6:30am–10:15pm, Sat 9:30am–5pm; June–Aug, Mon–Fri 6:30am–6pm, Sat 9am–5pm. Closed some hols. $

University Core Arboretum, Monongahela Blvd; tel 304/293-5201. A variety of diverse habitats can be seen from the 8 hiking trails that traverse the 75 acres of this arboretum. The north-flowing river that runs through the grounds makes this an excellent site to observe migratory birds, including a pair of blue herons that have been spotted by the lagoon area. **Open:** Mon–Fri 8am–5pm. Free.

Easton Roller Mill, 536 Harvard Ave; tel 304/599-6496. One of the few remaining 19th-century steam-driven roller mills in the mid-Atlantic area, it demonstrates both ancient and modern milling techniques for visitors. **Open:** By appointment. Free.

NITRO

Map page M-2, C2 (N of St Albans)

Motel 🏨

≣ **Best Western Motor Inn**, 4115 1st Ave, Nitro, WV 25143; tel 304/755-8341 or toll free 800/528-1234; fax 304/755-2933. 20 mi W of Charleston. exit 45 off I-64. Basic but clean motel, convenient to I-64 but far enough away to enjoy quiet location. Plans to add 15–20 rooms in new wing. **Rooms:** 28 rms. CI noon/CO 11am. New furnishings make rooms pleasant. **Amenities:** 🛏 A/C, cable TV. **Services:** 🛎 🦉 **Rates:** $34 S; $39 D. Extra person $5. Children under 12 stay free. Higher rates for spec evnts/hols. Pking: Outdoor, free. Maj CC.

Attraction 💼

Waves of Fun, 1 Valley Park Dr; tel 304/562-0518. West Virginia's largest waterpark features waterslides, a whitewater tube run, and a giant wave pool. Artificial beach, picnic area, changing rooms. **Open:** Mem Day–Labor Day, Mon–Sat 11am–7pm, Sun noon–7pm. $$$

NUTTER FORT

Map page M-2, B3 (S of Clarksburg)

Restaurant 🍽️

♥★ **Jim Reid's Restaurant and Lounge**, 1422 Buckhannon Pike, Nutter Fort; tel 304/623-4909. 1 mi S of Clarksburg, exit 119 off I-79. Drive toward Clarksburg on US 50; head south on Joyce Ave. **American/Seafood/Steak.** Candlelit for dinner and decorated like a club room, this restaurant feels like a comfortable English pub. Fresh seafood ranges from shrimp scampi to swordfish with almonds. Steak and some other meat dishes offered. Large servings. Casual attire acceptable. **FYI:** Reservations recommended. Children's menu. Dress code. **Open:** Lunch Wed–Fri 11am–2pm; dinner Tues–Sat 5–10pm, Sun noon–8pm. Closed some hols. **Prices:** Main courses $9–$26; PF dinner $12–$17. Ltd CC. ♥ 🚗

PARKERSBURG

Map page M-2, B2

Hotel 🏨

🏨🏨🏨 **The Blennerhassett Clarion Hotel**, 320 Market St, Parkersburg, WV 26101 (Downtown); tel 304/422-3131 or toll free 800/262-2536; fax 304/485-0267. Exit 176 off I-77. Follow US 50 W to Market St. A lovely, turreted Victorian-era (1889) brick hotel in downtown Parkersburg. A friendly place to stay. **Rooms:** 104 rms and stes. CI 2pm/CO noon. Express checkout avail. Nonsmoking rms avail. Rooms could use some updating but are comfortable and pleasant and have nice furniture. **Amenities:** 🛁 🔒 🍷 A/C, cable TV w/movies. Some rooms have hair dryers. **Services:** ✕ 🛎️ VP 🚗 🛄 🛎️ Car-rental desk, babysitting. **Facilities:** [300] 🔥 2 rsts, 1 bar. Adorned in antiques, excellent restaurant is worthy of New York or Los Angeles. Guests have free use of pool, sauna, steam room, whirlpool, fitness facilities at local YMCA. **Rates:** HS May–Oct $62–$69 S or D; from $85 ste. Extra person $6. Children under 18 stay free. Min stay spec evnts. Lower rates off-season. Higher rates for spec evnts/hols. Spec packages avail. Pking: Outdoor, free. Maj CC.

Motels

🏨🏨 **Best Western Inn**, I-77 and US 50 E, Parkersburg, WV 26101; tel 304/485-6551 or toll free 800/528-1234; fax 304/485-0679. Exit 176 off I-77. Clean, neat, older motel enjoys choice location. **Rooms:** 67 rms. CI noon/CO 11am. Nonsmoking rms avail. All bedding and furniture recently updated. **Amenities:** 🛁 🔒 🍷 A/C, cable TV. Suites have full-length mirrors and small refrigerators. **Services:** 🛄 🚗 🛎️ **Facilities:** 🔥 [100] 🔥 Attractive heated pool. **Rates:** HS Apr–Nov 1 $32–$36 S; $32–$48 D. Extra person $4. Children under 18 stay free. Lower rates off-season. Higher rates for spec evnts/hols. Spec packages avail. Pking: Outdoor, free. Maj CC.

🏨🏨 **Econo Lodge**, I-77 and US 50, Parkersburg, WV 26101; tel 304/422-5401 or toll free 800/424-4777; fax 304/422-5418. Exit 176 off I-77. With well-maintained grounds, this motel is quite conveniently located. **Rooms:** 102 rms. CI 3pm/CO noon. Nonsmoking rms avail. Average-size rooms have been updated recently. **Amenities:** 🛁 A/C, cable TV. **Services:** 🛄 🚗 🛎️ **Facilities:** 🔥 [18] 1 rst, 1 bar, games rm. Restaurant and bar on 2nd floor. Nice pool with good landscaping in rear. **Rates:** HS Mid-Apr–mid-Nov $32–$35 S; $40–$43 D. Extra person $4. Children under 18 stay free. Lower rates off-season. Pking: Outdoor, free. Maj CC.

🏨🏨 **Red Roof Inn**, 3714 E 7th St, Parkersburg, WV 26101; tel 304/485-1741 or toll free 800/THE-ROOF; fax 304/485-1746. Exit 176 off I-77. Follow US 50 W for ½ mile. One of the better members of the Red Roof chain. **Rooms:** 107 rms. CI 1pm/CO noon. Nonsmoking rms avail. Units have been refurbished recently. **Amenities:** 🛁 A/C, cable TV. **Services:** ✕ 🛄 🚗 🛎️ Shoney's Restaurant, just off the property, provides some room service. **Facilities:** [15] 🔥 **Rates:** HS Apr–Sept $35–$45 S; $45–$52 D. Extra person $3. Children under 18 stay free. Min stay spec evnts. Lower rates off-season. Higher rates for spec evnts/hols. Pking: Outdoor, free. Maj CC.

Restaurants 🍽️

♥★ **Point of View**, Starr Ave and River Hill Rd, Parkersburg; tel 304/863-3366. Exit 176 off I-77. Follow US 50 W to Va 68 S to Starr Ave. **Eclectic/French/Seafood.** Large windows render views of the Ohio River from a perch high on a hill overlooking Blennerhassett Island. Caring staff roasts chicken and ribs over an interior spit. Other options range from shrimp over fettuccine to filet mignon. Coffee bar offers 20 choices of fresh beans. Very popular. Reservations essential on Saturday. **FYI:** Reservations recommended. Children's menu. Dress code. **Open:** Lunch Mon–Sat 11:30am–5pm; dinner Mon–Sat 5:30–9:30pm. Closed some hols. **Prices:** Main courses $9–$33. Maj CC. ♥ 🏞️ 🚗 🔽

★ **Sebastian's**, 3420 Murdoch Ave, Parkersburg; tel 304/485-8800. Exit 176 off I-77. Follow US 50 W to WV 14 N. **American/Burgers/Seafood.** Stained-glass wall panels handmade by a local artist are interesting. Prime rib is the most popular, but other selections include lobster, steaks, and pasta. Good choice for both families and business travelers. **FYI:** Reservations recommended. Children's menu. **Open:** Mon–Thurs 11am–10pm, Fri–Sat 11am–11pm, Sun 11am–9pm. Closed Dec 25. **Prices:** Main courses $7–$16. Maj CC. 🖭 🚗 ⚝

Attractions 🏛

Henry Cooper Log Cabin Museum, City Park; tel 304/422-7841. Considered to be a classic example of American logwork, this cabin combines hand hewing with chinking between the logs to create a gabled roof and rectangle design. The Daughters of the American Pioneers maintain the museum and conduct tours of the grounds. **Open:** Mem Day–Labor Day, Sun 1:30–4:30pm. $

Blennerhassett Historical State Park, Point Park; tel 304/428-3000. The park is actually an island that must be reached by sternwheelers departing from Point Park in downtown Parkersburg. Blennerhassett Island is the location of a mansion built by Harmand Blennerhassett in 1798, destroyed by fire in 1811, and reconstructed in 1973. Bicycle rentals, picnicking, guided mansion tours, horse-drawn wagon rides, and a traditional crafts village with demonstrations are featured on the island. **Open:** May–Oct, Wed–Sun noon–4pm. $$

PETERSBURG

Map page M-3, C5

Hotel 🛏

≣≣ **Hermitage Motor Inn**, 203 Virginia Ave, PO Box 1077, Petersburg, WV 26847; tel 304/257-1711; fax 304/257-4330. Circa 1840 inn on National Register of Historic Places has been used as a hostelry since 1881. Original 3-story main building plus new addition and an adjacent motor lodge. **Rooms:** 39 rms. CI 2pm/CO noon. Nonsmoking rms avail. New rooms are spacious, with integrated decor and framed photos of scenic West Virginia. There are 6 older rooms, not as fresh, in original inn; 3 efficiencies have kitchenettes. **Amenities:** 🛋 A/C, cable TV w/movies, refrig. Some rooms have microwaves and refrigerators. **Services:** ⌂ **Facilities:** 🔒 ⚝ 1 rst (*see also* "Restaurants" below), 1 bar, whirlpool. Attractive pool with wooded sitting

area. Driving range just off premises. **Rates:** $31–$47 S or D. Extra person $5. Children under 12 stay free. Pking: Outdoor, free. Maj CC.

Motel

≣≣ **Homestead Inn and Motel**, Rte 3, PO Box 146, Petersburg, WV 26847; tel 304/257-1049. Rock gardens and plentiful flowers add to country flavor of this sparkling-clean facility with a view of the mountains and large farm adjoining its 6-acre setting. **Rooms:** 12 rms. CI 1pm/CO 11am. Nonsmoking rms avail. All rooms individually decorated with a country-wildlife mural on 1 wall and coordinated knickknacks. Country reproduction furnishings. **Amenities:** 🛋 ⚝ A/C, cable TV w/movies, refrig. All rooms have old wooden icebox-design refrigerators. **Services:** ✕ 🖭 ⌂ **Facilities:** ⚝ Courtesy room for continental breakfast contains microwave, ice machine, tables, coffeepot, toaster. Adjoining gift shop sells local handicrafts. Picnic tables in rear and benches around the property for enjoying the mountain views. **Rates (CP):** HS Apr–Oct $38 S; $45 D. Extra person $5. Children under 6 stay free. Lower rates off-season. Higher rates for spec evnts/hols. Pking: Outdoor, free. Maj CC.

Restaurant 🍽

★ **Highlander Restaurant**, in the Hermitage Motor Inn, 203 Virginia Ave (WV 55), Petersburg; tel 304/257-2355. **Seafood/Steak/Pasta.** Located in a 19th-century hotel listed on the National Register of Historic Places, the multiroom dining area is home to casual dining at oak tables and chairs. Lounge has fireplace, and one dining area sports both old wooden floor and fireplace. The sun room has a wall of lace-paneled windows and Victorian lamps. Buffet and daily specials available. **FYI:** Reservations accepted. **Open:** Mon–Thurs 11am–9pm, Fri 11am–10pm, Sat 8am–10pm, Sun 8am–8pm. Closed Dec 25. **Prices:** Main courses $6.95–$15.95. Maj CC. 🖭

POINT PLEASANT

Map page M-2, C2

Attractions 🏛

West Virginia State Farm Museum, WV 1; tel 304/675-5737. Dedicated to preserving the farm heritage of West Virginia, this museum complex functions as a window to the past. There are over 31 reconstructed buildings, including a 1-room schoolhouse, a Lutheran church, and a country store. A blacksmith and other traditional craftspeople use authentic tools to create their finished wares. Antique farm equipment, such as threshing machines, cultivators, and tractors, are also on display. **Open:** Tues–Sat 9am–5pm, Sun 1–5pm. Free.

Point Pleasant Battle Monument State Park, Main St; tel 304/675-0869. This 85-foot monument commemorates what some consider to be the first battle of the Revolutionary War. It was here that frontiersmen, led by Col Andrew Lewis, fought British-supported Chief Hokolesqua ("Cornstalk") and his Shawnee tribe. The **Mansion House Museum**, operated by the Daughters of the American Revolution, contains artifacts of the early settlers of the area, as well as war memorabilia. **Open:** Park, daily 9am–9pm; museum, May–Nov, daily 9am–4:30pm. Free.

PRINCETON

Map page M-2, D3

Motels 🛏

🏨🏨 **Comfort Inn**, US 460 and Ambrose Lane, Princeton, WV 24740; tel 304/487-6101 or toll free 800/228-5150; fax 304/425-7002. Exit 9 off I-77. An exceptionally well-landscaped property, this motel is near Pipestem State Park, colleges, a shopping mall, and restaurants. **Rooms:** 51 rms and stes. CI 1pm/CO noon. Nonsmoking rms avail. Clean and fresh rooms are decorated in soothing pastel colors. **Amenities:** 🛁 A/C, cable TV w/movies. Some units w/Jacuzzis. **Services:** 🛆 🍴 **Facilities:** 🕭 Whirlpool. Outdoor hot tub. **Rates (CP):** HS May–Oct $60–$65 S or D; from $80 ste. Extra person $6. Children under 18 stay free. Lower rates off-season. Higher rates for spec evnts/hols. Spec packages avail. Pking: Outdoor, free. Maj CC.

🏨🏨 **Days Inn**, I-77 and US 460, PO Box 830, Princeton, WV 24720; tel 304/425-8100 or toll free 800/329-7466; fax 304/425-8100. Exit 9 off I-77. Drive west on US 460 for ½ mile, turn left at light. Close to state parks and 2 ski areas, this older property recently changed hands. New owners have made renovations and expect to make more. **Rooms:** 122 rms and effic. CI 3pm/CO 11am. Nonsmoking rms avail. Rooms are being overhauled, adding new carpeting and air conditioning. **Amenities:** 🛁 A/C, cable TV. **Services:** 🛆 🍴 🔔 **Facilities:** 🖼 📶 🕭 Whirlpool. Pleasant outdoor area with picnic tables, benches, and barbecue grills. Large indoor heated pool. **Rates (CP):** HS May–Sept $54–$57 S or D; from $61 effic. Extra person $5. Children under 16 stay free. Lower rates off-season. Spec packages avail. Pking: Outdoor, free. Maj CC. Pets cost $5 extra.

Restaurant 🍴

Johnston's Inn and Restaurant, Worrell St, Princeton; tel 304/425-7591. Exit 9 off I-77. **American/Italian.** This country-style restaurant attached to a motel near I-77, shopping centers, and services is a popular spot for casual dining. Wooden tables and booths and a local reputation for good food, mostly steaks and Italian cuisine. **FYI:** Reservations accepted. **Open:** Mon–Sat 6:30am–10:30pm, Sun 6:30am–10pm. Closed some hols. **Prices:** Main courses $8–$22. Maj CC. 🍴

RIVERTON

Map page M-2, C4 (N of Judy Gap)

Attraction 🏛

Seneca Caverns, I-33; tel 304/567-2691. Guided tours of the state's largest caverns highlight **Mirror Lake,** an underground waterpool that reflects formations overhead, and the **Grand Ballroom,** 60 feet long, 30 feet wide, and as high as 70 feet, with a natural balcony on its back wall. Stalagmite and stalactite formations in the caves include Niagara Falls Frozen Over, Fairyland, Candy Mountain, and the Upside Down Well. **Open:** Mem Day–Labor Day, daily 8am–7pm. $$$

ROMNEY

Map page M-3, B5

Attraction 🏛

Potomac Eagle, WV 28; tel 304/822-7464. This 3-hour narrated excursion train begins at Wappocomo Station, where passengers board vintage 1920s railroad cars for their trip through the south branch of the Potomac River, known as the Trough. Pristine waters, pastureland, and farms dating from the 1700s are a few of the scenic highlights, but the big draw for wildlife enthusiasts is the frequent sightings of **bald eagles**. This valley is the eastern home of the American bald eagle, and the train often passes both the adult bird and nests of eaglets. Special excursions include Civil War reenactments, dinner trips, and fall foliage tours. **Open:** May–Nov, call for schedule. $$$$

RONCEVERTE

Map page M-2, D3 (S of Lewisburg)

Attraction

Organ Cave, US 219; tel 304/647-5551. During the Civil War, Gen Robert E Lee's troops used this cave as both a safe haven and an important source of saltpeter, an essential ingredient in gunpowder. Today visitors can tour the over 40 miles of mapped passageways in the cave to see limestone and calcite formations, including one that resembles a giant church organ. **Open:** Nov–Mar, daily 9am–5pm; Apr–Oct, daily 9am–7pm. $$$

SALEM

Map page M-2, B3

Attraction

Fort New Salem, US 50; tel 304/782-5245. Located on the campus of Salem College, this collection of relocated log structures re-creates a 19th-century frontier settlement. Mountain artisans practice crafts and trades of the early 1800s in the 20 cabins. There are also seasonal events, such as the Spirit of Christmas in the Mountains held in early December. **Open:** May–Oct, Wed–Fri 10am–5pm, Sat–Sun 1–5pm. Special events. $

SENECA ROCKS

Map page M-2, C4

Attractions

Seneca Rocks, WV 28 and US 33; tel 304/257-4442. A popular hiking and climbing destination, this quartzite formation rises 900 feet above North Fork Valley. At the foot of the rocks is a visitors center with exhibits and displays that explain the area's geology and history. Although the 375 climbing routes are the main draw here, fishing, picnicking, and camping are also available. **Open:** Apr–Oct, daily 9am–5:30pm; Nov–Mar, Sat–Sun 9am–4:30pm. Free.

Smoke Hole Caverns, WV 28 and WV 55; tel 304/257-4442. Unique aspects of this cavern include a crystal-clear coral pool filled with golden and rainbow trout, the world's longest ribbon stalactite, and cave ceilings reaching a towering 274 feet.

Temperatures in the cave remain a constant 56°F. **Open:** Mem Day–Labor Day, daily 8am–7:30pm; day after Labor Day through day before Mem Day, daily 8am–5pm. $$$

SHEPHERDSTOWN

Map page M-3, B6 (N of Harpers Ferry)

Inn

Bavarian Inn and Lodge, WV 480, PO Box 30, Shepherdstown, WV 25433; tel 304/876-2551; fax 304/876-9355. Exit 16E off I-81. 5 acres. Appealing gray-stone mansion with countryside-lodge ambience set on rolling lawn. Separate Bavarian-style chalets overlook the Potomac River. **Rooms:** 42 rms. CI 3pm/CO noon. Individually decorated rooms, many with canopied 4-poster beds, large baths, sitting areas. **Amenities:** A/C, cable TV w/movies. Some units w/terraces, some w/fireplaces, some w/Jacuzzis. **Services:** Gracious, accommodating staff enjoy providing extras to guests. **Facilities:** 2 rsts (*see also* "Restaurants" below), 1 bar (w/entertainment), lifeguard. Restaurant noted for its cuisine. Rathskeller on lower level offers casual dining and weekend entertainment. Outdoor tables for lounging in pool area. Affiliated with adjoining private golf club. **Rates:** $80–$145 D. Extra person $10. Children under 12 stay free. Min stay spec evnts. Higher rates for spec evnts/hols. Spec packages avail. Pking: Outdoor, free. Ltd CC.

Restaurants

Bavarian Inn, WV 480, Shepherdstown; tel 304/876-2551. Exit 16E off I-81. **Continental/German/Seafood.** A touch of elegance in a country setting, this spacious dining room enjoys views of either manicured lawns or the Potomac River. Hand-painted bud vases with a pink carnation; crystal candleholders. With its entryway of dark wood and corridor with framed photos of famous guests, the restaurant feels a bit like a relaxed lodge. Quite reasonably priced for the excellent service, well-presented food, and quiet dining area, intimate despite its size. Specialties are sauerbraten and game in season, including boar, venison, pheasant. The Rathskeller downstairs has full bar, open every evening with entertainment on weekends. **FYI:** Reservations recommended. Guitar/piano/singer. Children's menu. Jacket required. **Open:** Breakfast daily 7:30–10:30am; lunch Mon–Sat 11:30am–2:30pm; dinner Mon–Sat 5–10pm, Sun noon–9pm. **Prices:** Main courses $12.75–$18.50. Maj CC.

★ **Yellow Brick Bank Restaurant**, Princess and W German Sts, Shepherdstown; tel 304/876-2208. **New American/Ital-**

ian. This local favorite, housed in a 1906 bank building on Shepherdstown's main street, also draws patrons from nearby cities. The art-deco style is refreshing and sophisticated in this largely historic area. The food is fresh American and northern Italian: grilled meats, seafood, and unique appetizers, such as grilled portobello mushrooms with lemon butter. Lighter fare is offered in the Wicker Room. **FYI:** Reservations recommended. **Open:** Daily 11:30am–10pm. Closed some hols. **Prices:** Main courses $10–$18. Ltd CC.

Attraction 💼

Historic Shepherdstown Museum, German and Princess Sts; tel 304/876-0910. The oldest town in West Virginia is celebrated in this museum featuring a collection of artifacts, furnishings, and documents that trace the history and commerce of the area. **Open:** Apr–Oct, Sat 11am–5pm, Sun 1–4pm. Free.

SNOWSHOE

Map page M-2, C4 (E of Cass Scenic Railroad)

Hotel 🛏

The Inn at Snowshoe, WV 66 at US 219, PO Box 10, Snowshoe, WV 26209; tel 304/572-5252; fax 304/572-3218. 45 mi S of Elkins. Turn east off US 219 to hotel. Modern, very comfortable hotel situated in a valley 6 miles below Showshoe Mountain Resort, which manages the property. Cass Scenic Railroad is 11 miles away. Unrated. **Rooms:** 150 rms. CI 5pm/CO 11am. Nonsmoking rms avail. **Amenities:** 🛢 🔥 A/C, cable TV. **Services:** ✕ 🗘 **Facilities:** 🚣 🚴 🚵 🐎 🥅 🎣 🚤 & 1 rst, 1 bar, games rm, sauna, whirlpool, washer/dryer. Golf, tennis, skiing, mountain biking, and other sports available nearby. Guests have access to facilities at Showshoe Mountain Resort. **Rates:** HS Mid-Nov to mid-Apr $74–$105 S or D. Children under 18 stay free. Lower rates off-season. Spec packages avail. Pking: Outdoor, free. Maj CC. Off-season rates are approximately half those in winter.

SUMMERSVILLE

Map page M-3, C3

Attractions 💼

Summersville Lake, WV 129; tel 304/872-3412. Created by the Army Corps of Engineers in the 1960s, this scenic lake, the largest in the state, boasts features 60 miles of shoreline. Stocked

with rainbow trout, bass, crappie, bluegill, and catfish, it is a popular destination for anglers. Boating, waterskiing, picnicking, camping. **Open:** Daily 7:15am–4pm. Free.

Carnifex Ferry Battlefield State Park, WV 129; tel 304/872-0825. The site of a major Civil War battle that eventually led to this area's participation in the statehood movement. The **Patterson House,** which was situated between Union and Confederate lines, houses relics of the battle. The park also offers hiking, picnicking, and playgrounds. **Open:** Mem Day–Labor Day, daily 9am–5pm. Free.

TRIADELPHIA

Map page M-2, A3 (S of Wheeling)

Motel 🛏

🏨 **Days Inn**, I-70 and Dallas Pike, Triadelphia, WV 26059; tel 304/547-0610 or toll free 800/329-7466; fax 304/547-9029. 9 mi E of Wheeling. exit 11 off I-70. The highlight of this comfortable motel is the unusual entry to the bar—a converted truck cab. **Rooms:** 106 rms. CI 2pm/CO 11am. Nonsmoking rms avail. **Amenities:** 🛢 🔥 A/C, satel TV w/movies. VCRs and refrigerators available on request. Accessories for guests with disabilities, including close-captioned TV, alarms for door and phone, available upon request. **Services:** ✕ 🚗 🖾 🗘 🖐 Babysitting. **Facilities:** 🚣 🚴 🎱 💯 & 1 rst, 1 bar. **Rates:** $44 S; $47 D. Extra person $6. Children under 19 stay free. Min stay spec evnts. Higher rates for spec evnts/hols. Spec packages avail. Pking: Outdoor, free. Maj CC.

WESTON

Map page M-2, B3

Motel 🛏

🏨 **Comfort Inn**, I-79 and US 33 E, PO Box 666, Weston, WV 26452; tel 304/269-7000 or toll free 800/228-5150; fax 304/269-7000. Exit 99 off I-79. Surrounded by beautiful scenery. **Rooms:** 60 rms. CI 3pm/CO noon. Nonsmoking rms avail. Although of average size, rooms are quite pleasing. **Amenities:** 🛢 A/C, cable TV, shoe polisher. **Services:** 🆅🅿 🗘 **Facilities:** 🚣 & 1 rst, 1 bar. **Rates (CP):** HS Mem Day–Oct $42 S; $48 D. Extra person $6. Children under 18 stay free. Lower rates off-season. Higher rates for spec evnts/hols. Pking: Outdoor, free. Maj CC.

Attractions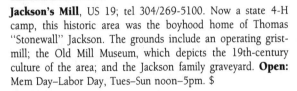

Jackson's Mill, US 19; tel 304/269-5100. Now a state 4-H camp, this historic area was the boyhood home of Thomas "Stonewall" Jackson. The grounds include an operating grist-mill; the Old Mill Museum, which depicts the 19th-century culture of the area; and the Jackson family graveyard. **Open:** Mem Day–Labor Day, Tues–Sun noon–5pm. $

Stonewall Jackson Lake State Park, US 19; tel 304/269-0523. The highlight of this park is the 2,650-acre lake, the result of the damming of the West Fork River in the 1980s. The lake has some of the best fishing in the state, in addition to water sports; however, no swimming is allowed. Hunting, camping, and hiking are other popular activities. **Open:** Daily 6am–10pm. $

WHEELING

Map page M-2, A3

Hotel

Hampton Inn, 795 National Rd, Wheeling, WV 26003; tel 304/233-0440 or toll free 800/HAMPTON; fax 304/233-2198. Exit 2A off I-70. A pleasant hotel that is clean, neat, and orderly. Convenient to restaurants and shops. **Rooms:** 104 rms and stes. CI 3pm/CO noon. Nonsmoking rms avail. Although basic, rooms are clean and well kept. **Amenities:** A/C, cable TV w/movies, voice mail. Some units w/terraces. **Services:** Free local calls. **Facilities:** Day-care ctr. **Rates (CP):** $46–$57 S; $49–$59 D; from $60 ste. Extra person $5. Children under 18 stay free. Min stay spec evnts. Higher rates for spec evnts/hols. Pking: Outdoor, free. Maj CC.

Motel

Best Western Wheeling Inn, 949 Main St, at 10th St, Wheeling, WV 26003; tel 304/233-8500 or toll free 800/528-1234; fax 304/233-8500 ext 345. Exit 1A off I-70. An older, well-maintained motel on the Ohio River in the heart of Wheeling, with great views of surrounding area. **Rooms:** 80 rms, stes. CI 2pm/CO noon. Nonsmoking rms avail. Average older rooms have small baths, large sink area. Housekeeping does good job. **Amenities:** A/C, cable TV. Some units w/Jacuzzis. **Services:** Masseur. Free morning newspapers. Massages by appointment. **Facilities:** 1 rst, 1 bar (w/entertainment), spa, playground. Riverside restaurant has glass-enclosed deck for year-round use. Free use of health spa. **Rates (CP):** $45–$63 S;

$52–$63 D; from $52 ste. Extra person $8. Children under 16 stay free. Min stay spec evnts. Higher rates for spec evnts/hols. Pking: Outdoor, free. Maj CC.

Restaurants

⑤★ Christopher's Cafeteria, 10 Elmgrove Crossing Mall, Wheeling; tel 304/242-4100. Exit 5 off I-70. **American/Cafeteria.** A colonial, Williamsburg-like atmosphere reigns at this very good American-style cafeteria, where waitresses continually clear the tables. Cafeteria line has roast beef, potatoes, and vegetables. Breads and desserts baked on premises. **FYI:** Reservations not accepted. Children's menu. No liquor license. **Open:** Mon–Sat 11:30am–8pm, Sun 11am–8pm. Closed some hols. **Prices:** Main courses $2.25–$5.25; PF dinner $3.95–$4.29. No CC.

♥ Stratford Springs Lodge, 355 Oglebay Dr, Wheeling; tel 304/233-5100. Exit 2A off I-70. Follow WV 88 N. **American.** Pink tablecloths and napkins, pink-and-green drapes, and lovely china make this a beautiful place to dine. Formerly the Wheeling Country Club, established more than 100 years ago. Golf course and gracious grounds surround the building. Primarily meat and chicken dishes with some seafood. **FYI:** Reservations recommended. Children's menu. Jacket required. **Open:** Breakfast Mon–Sat 7–10:30am; lunch Mon–Sat 11:30am–2pm; dinner Mon–Sat 5–10pm; brunch. Closed some hols. **Prices:** Main courses $8–$25. Maj CC.

Attractions

Oglebay Park, exit 2A off I-79; tel toll free 800/624-6988. This 1,500-acre resort began as Waddington Farms, the home of Col Earl W Oglebay, who willed his estate to the city of Wheeling for public use. On the grounds are Schenk Lake, stables, tennis courts, an outdoor pool, jogging trails, and an 18-hole golf course. Among the highlights of Oglebay are the Good Children's Zoo, a 65-acre natural habitat for North American animals; Waddington Gardens, with turn-of-the-century flower gardens; and the Oglebay Institute Museum, featuring the Sweeney Punch Bowl, the largest hand-blown glass piece in existence. **Open:** Daily sunrise–sunset. Free.

The Point, Grandview St; tel 304/639-1093. From the observation deck 465 feet above the Ohio River, visitors can see the entire Victorian cityscape of Wheeling as well as 2 states, 3 counties, 11 churches, and 11 bridges. Inside is a small pictorial museum housing a compilation of photos that re-create the town's history. **Open:** Hours vary, call ahead. $

Capitol Music Hall, 1015 Main St; tel toll free 800/624-5456. The oldest, and one of the largest, theaters in West Virginia, this is the stage for **Jamboree USA**, the second-oldest live country music program in the country after the Grand Ole Opry. Every Saturday night since its 1933 premiere, the stars of country music have performed on its stage. Recent entertainers have included Kathy Mattea, Tammy Wynette, and Little Texas. Every summer Jamboree USA moves outdoors for **Jamboree in the Hills,** an outdoor concert billed as the "Superbowl of Country Music." **Open:** Times vary, call for schedule. $$$$

Centre Market, exit 1A off I-70; tel 304/234-3878. Built in 1853, the Upper Market House is the only cast iron–columned market in the country. Lower Market House, built in 1890, is a Romanesque brick structure. These market houses have been in continuous operation since the mid-19th century and provide many of the same services now as they did then. The interior is a good place to sample homemade food specialties, and there are many small shops with an array of handcrafts and antiques. **Open:** Mon–Sat 10am–6pm. Free.

Grave Creek Mound State Park, WV 2; tel 304/843-1410. This Adena Indian burial site is the largest conical earthen mound of its kind. Adjacent to the burial ground is the Delf Norona Museum and Cultural Center, which houses a collection of artifacts from the Adena period (1000 BC to AD 1), as well as exhibits about the cultural life of this prehistoric people. **Open:** Mon–Sat 10am–4:30pm, Sun 1–5pm. $

WHITE SULPHUR SPRINGS

Map page M-2, D3

See also Lewisburg

Motel 🏨

≣≣ **Old White Motel**, 865 E Main St (US 60 E), PO Box 58, White Sulphur Springs, WV 24986; tel 304/536-2441 or toll free 800/867-2441. Exit 181 off I-64. Go ½ mile west on US 60. An older but well-maintained motel on large lawn with views of the West Virginia highlands. Convenient to the Greenbrier and other golf courses. **Rooms:** 26 rms. CI 11am/CO noon. Nonsmoking rms avail. **Amenities:** 🛏 A/C, cable TV. **Services:** 🛎 🖐 **Facilities:** 🛢 **Rates:** $30–$46 S or D. Extra person $5. Children under 12 stay free. Higher rates for spec evnts/hols. Pking: Outdoor, free. Maj CC.

Resort

🔱 **The Greenbrier**, off I-64, White Sulphur Springs, WV 24986; tel 304/536-1110 or toll free 800/624-6070; fax 304/536-7836. Exit 181 off I-64 W, or exit 175 off I-64 E. 6,500 acres. As grand as they come, this imposing white palace of old-world elegance nestled in the Allegheny Mountains has grounds so vast there are 10 acres for every guest room. A throwback to yesteryears of civility and social norms; a place where gentlemen must still wear a jacket and tie for dinner. Predictably popular for business conferences. **Rooms:** 650 rms and stes; 69 ctges/villas. CI 3pm/CO noon. Express checkout avail. Nonsmoking rms avail. Most rooms are in the main building; others are in 69 hillside cottages. Some are spacious, some snug, and every room is different from its neighbor. Recent hotel-wide renovation has introduced some decor that is almost giddy, with bold greens and flashy reds. **Amenities:** 🛏 🍸 🍴 A/C, cable TV, refrig, shoe polisher, bathrobes. All units w/minibars, some w/terraces, some w/fireplaces. Fireplaces in the lounges, complimentary afternoon tea with classical duo. Historical tours of the hotel, horticultural tours of the grounds. **Services:** 🍽 VP 🚐 🛅 🖐 Twice-daily maid svce, social director, masseur, children's program, babysitting. Enormous breakfasts included. Experienced, dedicated staff. **Facilities:** 🛢 🚴 🏊 ▶₅₄ ▲ 🎿 🏃 ⚓₁₅ 🏌 🎳 🏇₉₀₀ 🛢 5 rsts, 6 bars (3 w/entertainment), lifeguard, games rm, lawn games, spa, sauna, steam rm, whirlpool, beauty salon, playground. 24 shops, 2 putting greens, 2 heated platform tennis courts, indoor tennis, lane bowling, trap and skeet shooting, falconry, horse-drawn carriage rides. Ice skating and horse-drawn sleigh rides in winter. **Rates (MAP):** HS Apr–Oct $226–$441 S; $332–$472 D; from $543 ste; from $546 ctge/villa. Extra person $115. Children under 18 stay free. Min stay spec evnts. Lower rates off-season. Spec packages avail. Pking: Indoor/outdoor, $5. Maj CC. Automatic additions to bills include $14.25 per person per day for maids and waiters. For such an august "Hotel of the Presidents," with so many extras, the resort is not at all overpriced.

Attraction 🏛

Greenbrier State Forest, I-64; tel 304/536-1944. The park comprises 9,302 acres of forest 3 miles south of White Sulphur Springs. Popular activities include trout fishing in Anthony Creek and fishing in the Greenbrier River. A swimming pool is open during the summer. Facilities including restrooms, a gift shop, and a visitors center are open from the 2nd week of April to the last week of October. Hiking and fitness trails, shooting range, playground area, and picnic sites are open year-round. Camping, cabins. **Open:** Daily 6am–10pm. Free.

WILLIAMSTOWN

Map page M-2, B2 (N of Parkersburg)

Attraction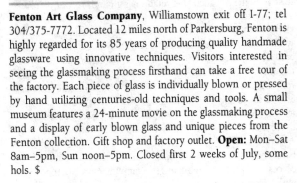

Fenton Art Glass Company, Williamstown exit off I-77; tel 304/375-7772. Located 12 miles north of Parkersburg, Fenton is highly regarded for its 85 years of producing quality handmade glassware using innovative techniques. Visitors interested in seeing the glassmaking process firsthand can take a free tour of the factory. Each piece of glass is individually blown or pressed by hand utilizing centuries-old techniques and tools. A small museum features a 24-minute movie on the glassmaking process and a display of early blown glass and unique pieces from the Fenton collection. Gift shop and factory outlet. **Open:** Mon–Sat 8am–5pm, Sun noon–5pm. Closed first 2 weeks of July, some hols. $

INDEX

SAVE $4 OFF
GENERAL ADMISSION

Present coupon at Front Gate before bill is totalled. Not valid with any other discounts or special offers. Limit 6 guests per coupon. Photocopies not accepted. Operating hours and general admission prices subject to change without notice.

COUPON VALID THRU 12/31/95

PLU# 3175c/23176a An Anheuser-Busch Theme Park

BUSCH GARDENS.
TAMPA BAY, FLORIDA

SAVE $4 OFF
GENERAL ADMISSION

Present coupon at Front Gate before bill is totalled. Not valid with any other discounts or special offers. Limit 6 guests per coupon. Photocopies not accepted. Operating hours and general admission prices subject to change without notice.

COUPON VALID 3/31/95 THRU 10/29/95

PLU# 3175c/23176a An Anheuser-Busch Theme Park

ADVENTURE ISLAND
TAMPA'S WATER PARK

Limit six guests per certificate. Not valid with other discounts or on purchase of multi-park/multi-visit passes or tickets. Present certificate at Front Gate before bill is totaled. Redeemable only at time of ticket purchase. Photocopies not accepted. Certificate has no cash value. Operating hours and general admission price subject to change without notice. Valid through 3/31/95 only.

Sea World®
Orlando, Florida
Anheuser-Busch Theme Parks.

Make Contact With Another World®

©1994 Sea World of Florida, Inc.   PLU# 4556/4555

Discount valid for up to 6 people through 12/31/95.
Coupon has no cash value and is not valid with any other offers.
Offer subject to change without notice. Parking fee not included.
©1994 Universal Studios Florida. All Rights Reserved.

6101944075662

Name _____

Address _____

City _____ State_____ Zip _____

Phone (____)_____

Name _____

Address _____

City _____ State_____ Zip _____

Phone (____)_____

Name _____

Address _____

City _____ State_____ Zip _____

Phone (____)_____

Name _____

Address _____

City _____ State_____ Zip _____

Phone (____)_____

STAY WITH US & SAVE!

10% **10%**

Ramada Limiteds, Inns, Hotels, Resorts and Plaza Hotels offer you the value and accommodations you expect . . . And so much more!

- Over 750 convenient locations
- Children under 18 always stay free
- Non-smoking and handicap rooms available

10% For reservations call 1-800-228-2828 **10%**

1-800-4-CHOICE
(1-800-424-6423)

Advance reservations through 1-800-4-CHOICE required.
Based on availability at participating hotels and cannot be used in conjunction with any other discount.

TERMS AND CONDITIONS

Offer valid on an Intermediate (Group C) through a Full Size 4-Door (Group E) car for a 5-day minimum rental. Coupon must be surrendered at time of rental; one per rental. May not be used in conjunction with any other coupon, promotion or offer. Coupon valid at Avis corporate and participating licensee locations in the continental U.S. Offer not available during holiday and other blackout periods. Offer may not be available on all rates at all times. **An advance reservation is required.** Cars subject to availability. Taxes, local government surcharges and optional items, such as LDW, additional driver fee and refueling, are extra. Renter must meet Avis age, driver and credit requirements. Minimum age is 25 but may vary by location. Offer expires December 31, 1995.

Rental Sales Agent Instructions
At Checkout: • In CPN, enter **MUFA527**. • Complete this information:
RA#_____ Rental Location_____
• Attach to COUPON tape.

AVIS
We try harder.

© 1995 Wizard Co., Inc. 1/95 DTPS/

- **Available at participating properties.**
- **This coupon cannot be combined with any other special discount offer.**
- **Limit one coupon per room, per stay.**
- **Expires December 31, 1996.**

1-800-DAYS INN

Terms and Conditions

Advance reservations are required and blackout periods may apply. Present this certificate at time of rental or, for Gold rentals, at time of return, and receive $10 off Hertz Leisure Weekly rates at participating locations in the U.S. This certificate has no cash value, must be surrendered and may not be used with any other rate, discount or promotion. Standard rental qualifications, rental period and return restrictions must be met or offer is void. Weekly rentals require a minimum rental period of five days, including a Saturday night. Minimum rental age is 25. Taxes and optional items, such as refueling, are not included and are not subject to discount. All cars are subject to availability at time of rental. Certificate expires 12/31/95.

Hertz rents Fords and other fine cars.

HERE ARE SOME OF THE DETAILS YOU SHOULD KNOW:
Just mention promotion code TCB/MCBC087 when you reserve a compact through luxury size car and receive $20 off your weekly rental. Five-day minimum rental necessary to qualify for discount. This offer is valid at participating budget locations through 3/3/96 and is subject to vehicle availability. Car must be returned to renting location, except in some metro areas where inter-area drop-offs are permitted. Local rental and age requirements apply. Discount applies to time and mileage only and is not available in conjunction with any other discount, promotional offer, CorpRate™, government, or tour/wholesale rate. Refueling services, taxes and optional items are extra. Additional driver, under-age driver and other surcharges are extra. Blackout dates may apply.

Terms and Conditions

- Offer includes 10% discount off all time and mileage charges on Cruise America or Cruise Canada vehicles only.
- Offer not available in conjunction with other discount offers or promotional rates.
- Excludes other rental charges, deposits, sales tax, and fuels.
- Normal rental conditions and customer qualification procedures apply.
- Members must reserve vehicles through Central Reservations only, at least one week in advance of pick up and mention **Frommer's America on Wheels** at time of reservation.

For reservations: 1-800-327-7799 - US and Canada

Rental Rates and Conditions

This offer is subject to availability and may not be used in conjunction with any other certificate or promotion. Offers apply only to economy through intermediate size car. Blackout periods may apply. This coupon has no cash value, and must be surrendered at time of rental. Coupon valid at all participating locations in the U.S. Taxes, fuel, LDW/CDW, under age and additional driver fees are extra. Some additional charges may apply.

THE ROAD GUIDE FOR TODAY'S AMERICA
FROM THE FIRST NAME IN TRAVEL

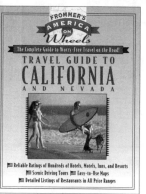

ISBN:0-02-860146-7

ISBN:0-02-860144-0

ISBN:0-02-860145-9

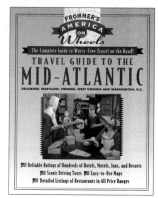

ISBN:0-02-860143-2

New titles coming in 1996

Northeast (includes Maine, Vermont, New Hampshire, Connecticut, Rhode Island, New York, and Massachusetts)

Northwest & North Central (includes Oregon, Washington, Idaho, Montana, Wyoming, North Dakota, South Dakota, Nebraska, Iowa)

Great Lakes (includes Michigan, Wisconsin, Illinois, Indiana, Ohio, Minnesota)

Southeast (includes South Carolina, North Carolina, Kentucky, Tennessee, Mississippi, Georgia, Alabama)

South Central (includes Louisiana, Arkansas, Oklahoma, Texas, Missouri)

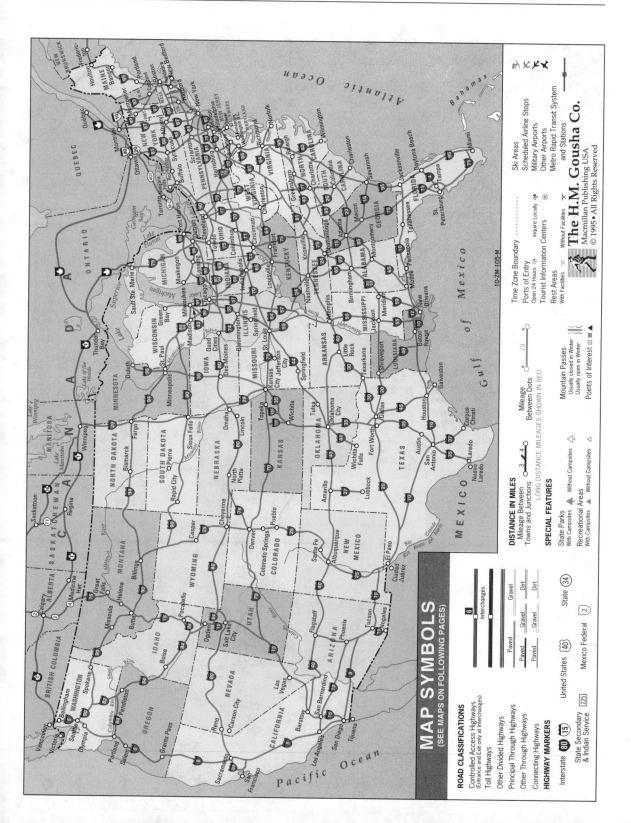

MAP SYMBOLS
(SEE MAPS ON FOLLOWING PAGES)

ROAD CLASSIFICATIONS

Controlled Access Highways
(Entrance and Exit only at interchanges)

Toll Highways

Other Divided Highways

Principal Through Highways

Other Through Highways

Connecting Highways

HIGHWAY MARKERS

Interstate

State Secondary & Indian Service

United States

State

Mexico Federal

Interchanges

Paved   Gravel   Dirt
Paved   Gravel   Dirt
Paved   Gravel   Dirt

DISTANCE IN MILES

Mileage Between Towns and Junctions

Mileage Between Dots

LONG DISTANCE MILEAGES SHOWN IN RED

SPECIAL FEATURES

State Parks
With Campsites   Without Campsites

Recreational Areas
With Campsites   Without Campsites

Mountain Passes
Usually closed in Winter
Usually open in Winter

Points of Interest

Time Zone Boundary

Ports of Entry
Open 24 Hours   Inquire Locally

Tourist Information Centers

Rest Areas
With Facilities   Without Facilities

Ski Areas

Scheduled Airline Stops

Military Airports

Other Airports

Metro Rapid Transit System and Stations

The H.M. Gousha Co.
Macmillan Publishing USA
© 1995 • All Rights Reserved

10-ZM-105-M

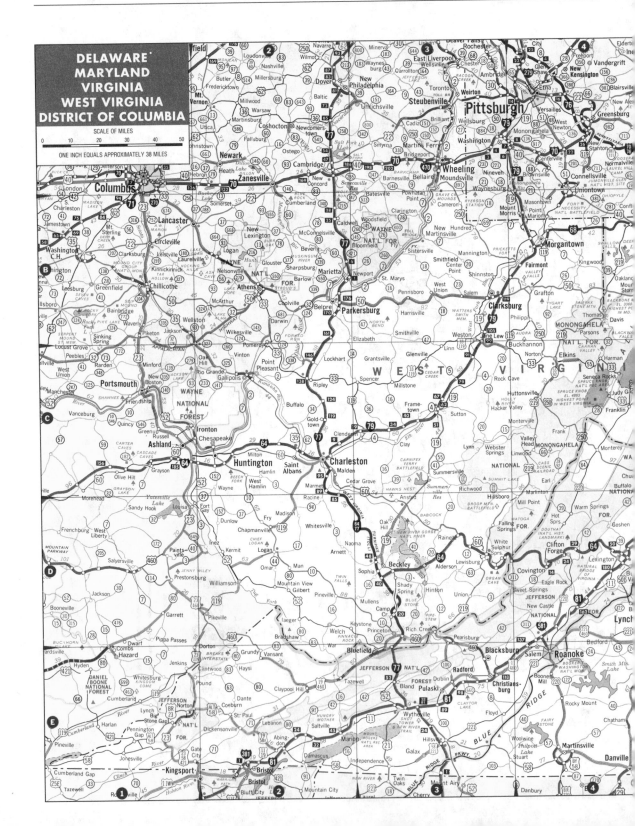

DELAWARE
MARYLAND
VIRGINIA
WEST VIRGINIA
DISTRICT OF COLUMBIA

SCALE OF MILES

0   10   20   30   40   50

ONE INCH EQUALS APPROXIMATELY 38 MILES

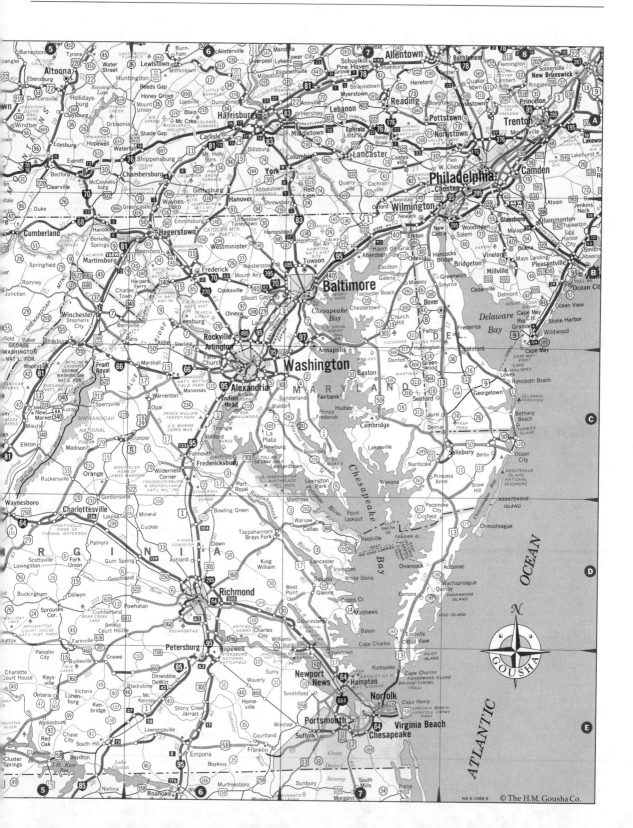

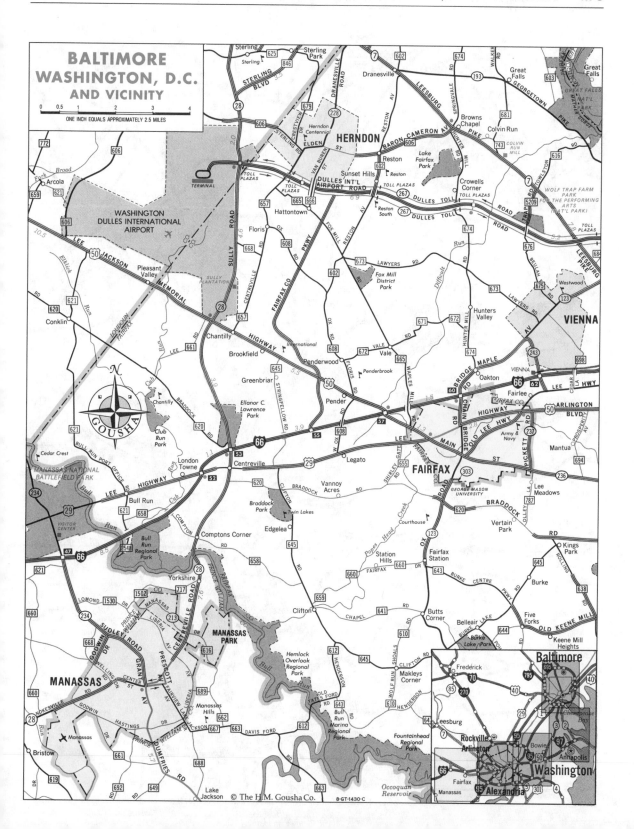

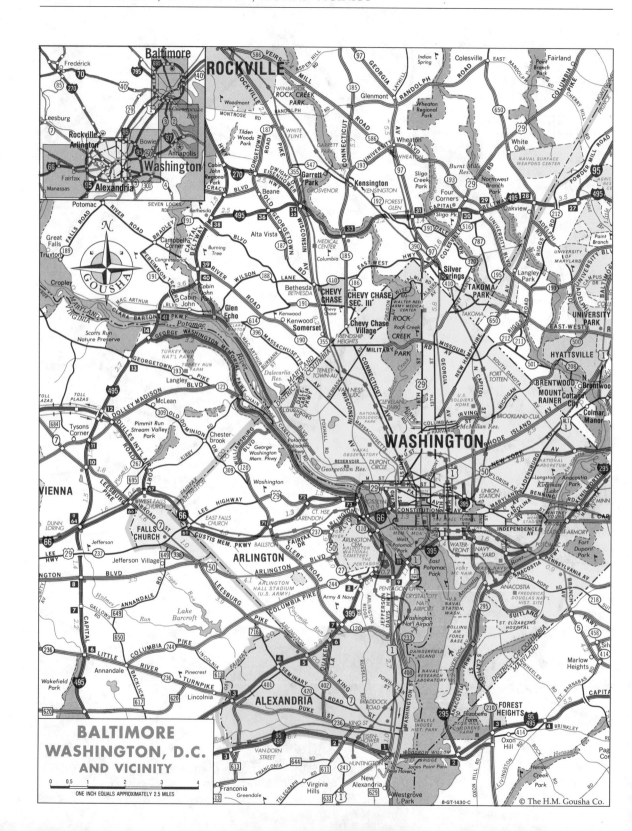

BALTIMORE
WASHINGTON, D.C.
AND VICINITY

0   0.5   1   2   3   4

ONE INCH EQUALS APPROXIMATELY 2.5 MILES

8-GT-1430-C

© The H.M. Gousha Co.

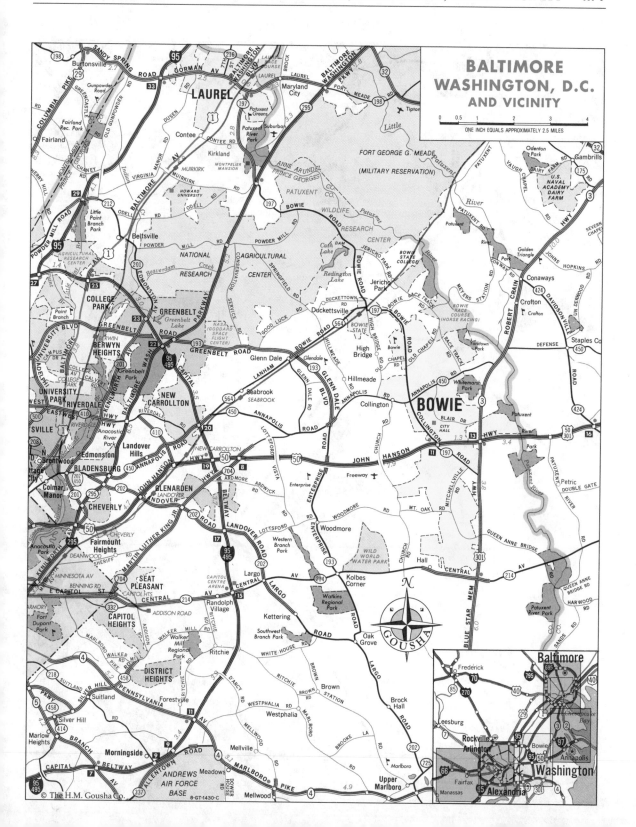

BALTIMORE
WASHINGTON, D.C.
AND VICINITY

ONE INCH EQUALS APPROXIMATELY 2.5 MILES

© The H.M. Gousha Co.

B-GT-1430-C

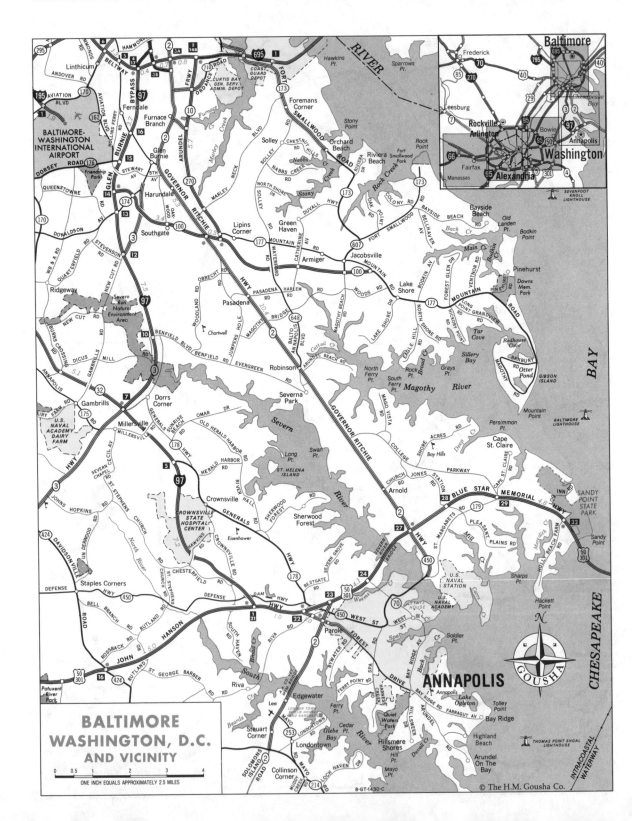

BALTIMORE
WASHINGTON, D.C.
AND VICINITY

0   0.5   1   2   3   4
ONE INCH EQUALS APPROXIMATELY 2.5 MILES

8-GT-1430-C

© The H.M. Gousha Co.

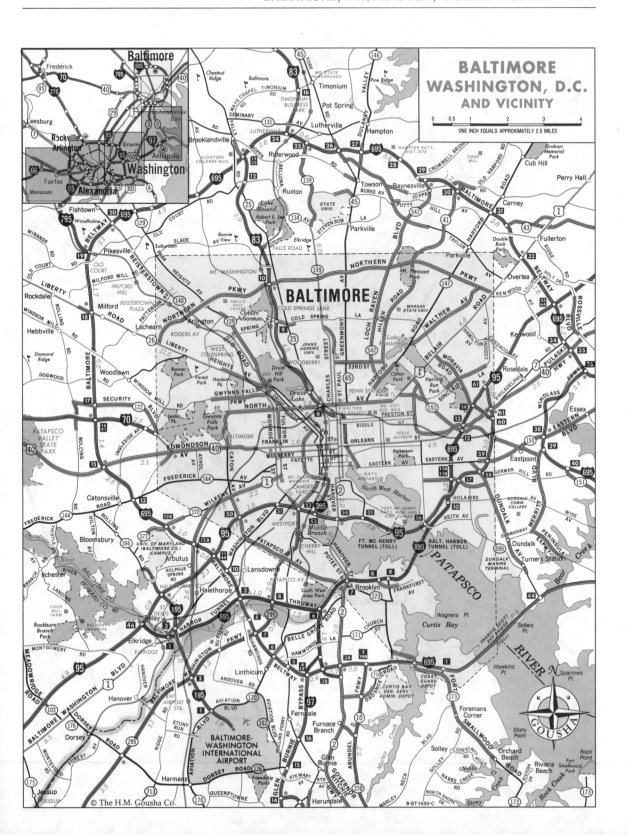

BALTIMORE
WASHINGTON, D.C.
AND VICINITY

ONE INCH EQUALS APPROXIMATELY 2.5 MILES

© The H.M. Gousha Co.

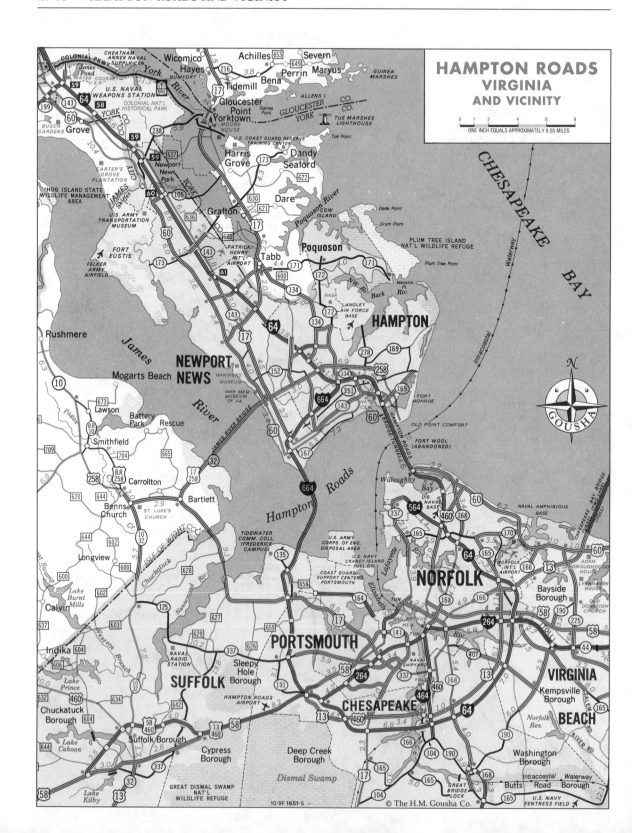

HAMPTON ROADS
VIRGINIA
AND VICINITY

ONE INCH EQUALS APPROXIMATELY 6.55 MILES

CHESAPEAKE BAY

10-SF 1651-S

© The H.M. Gousha Co.

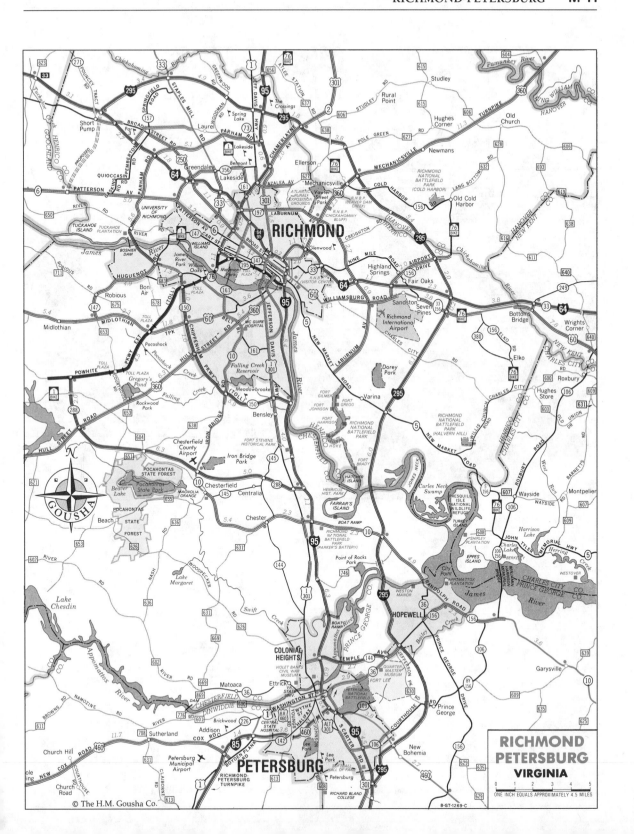

RICHMOND
PETERSBURG
VIRGINIA

0 1 2 3 4 5
ONE INCH EQUALS APPROXIMATELY 4.5 MILES

© The H.M. Gousha Co.

8-GT-1269-C

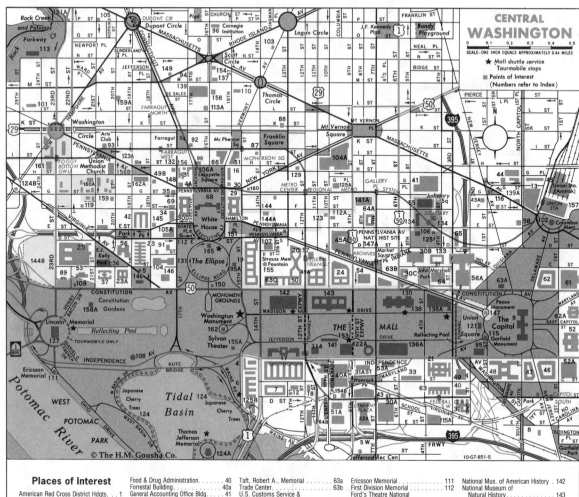

CENTRAL
WASHINGTON

SCALE-ONE INCH EQUALS APPROXIMATELY 0.44 MILES

★ Mall shuttle service
Tourmobile stops
■ Points of Interest
(Numbers refer to Index)

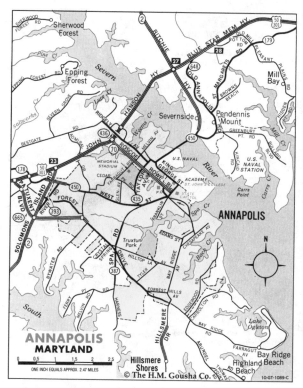

ANNAPOLIS
MARYLAND

ONE INCH EQUALS APPROX. 2.47 MILES

© The H.M. Gousha Co.

10-GT-1089-C

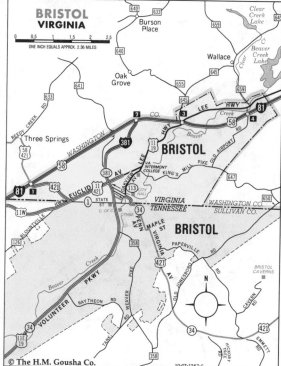

BRISTOL
VIRGINIA

ONE INCH EQUALS APPROX. 2.36 MILES

© The H.M. Gousha Co.

10-GT-1267-C

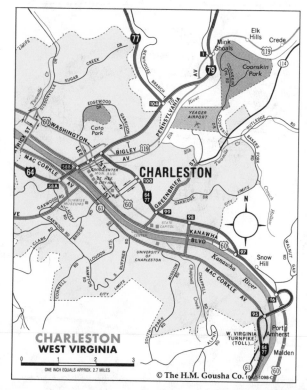

CHARLESTON
WEST VIRGINIA

ONE INCH EQUALS APPROX. 2.7 MILES

© The H.M. Gousha Co.

10-GT-1098-C

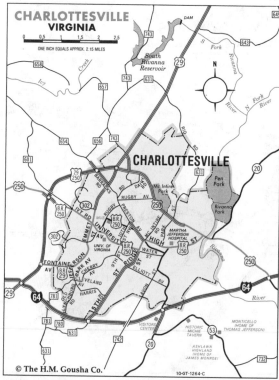

CHARLOTTESVILLE
VIRGINIA

ONE INCH EQUALS APPROX. 2.15 MILES

© The H.M. Gousha Co.

10-GT-1264-C

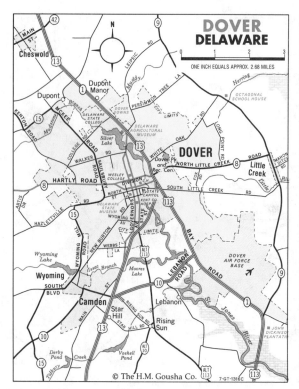

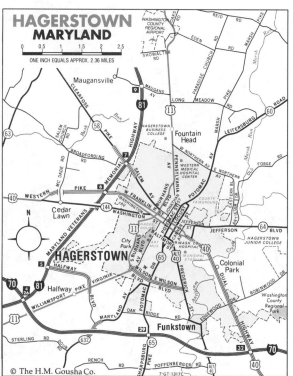

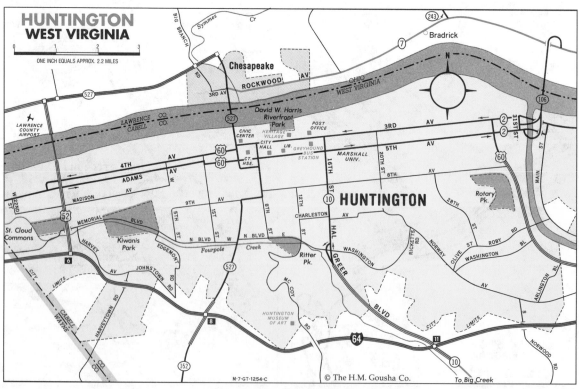

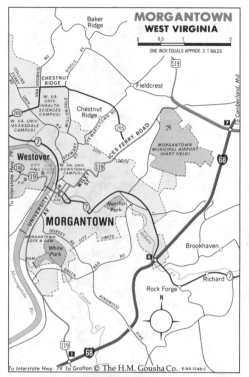

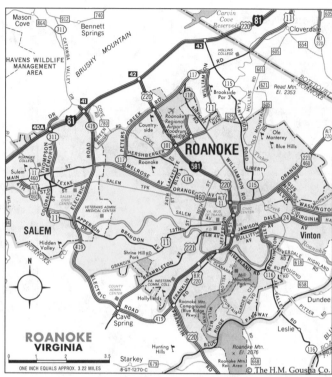

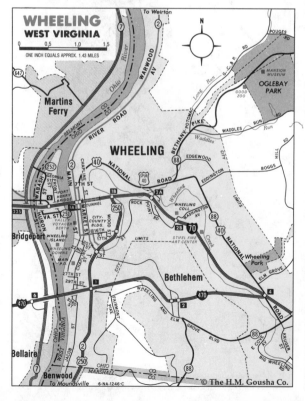

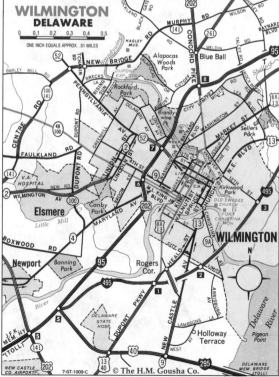

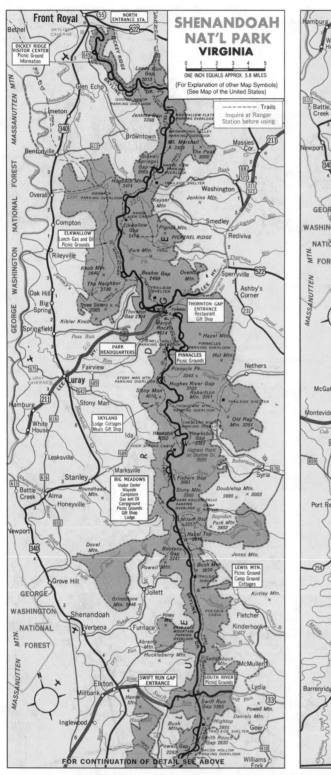

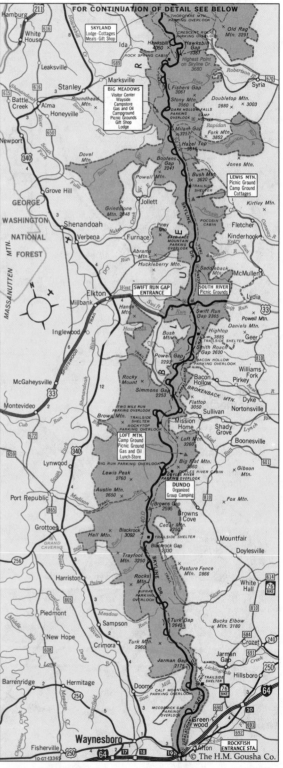

SHENANDOAH NAT'L PARK VIRGINIA

ONE INCH EQUALS APPROX. 5.8 MILES

(For Explanation of other Map Symbols)
(See Map of the United States)

- - - - - Trails
Inquire at Ranger Station before using

FOR CONTINUATION OF DETAIL SEE BELOW

FOR CONTINUATION OF DETAIL SEE ABOVE

© The H.M. Gousha Co.